"What an ambitious, lucid, eye-opening and engaging book! By using the computational theories he developed, Grossberg attempts nothing less than to integrate our knowledge of how our mind works with our knowledge of how the brain works. The topics he covers range from perception to action, from emotion to memory, and from decision making to love, with consciousness and the mind-body problem figuring prominently throughout. The story he weaves, with many incisive, delightful illustrations, is compelling and accessible. The reader is rewarded with a novel appreciation of the human psyche and artificial intelligence, and is left with admiration for Grossberg's achievement."

—Morris Moscovitch, University of Toronto

"This book is first and foremost an account of a personal odyssey of one of the great and most prolific scientific minds of our time trying to understand itself. As a graduate student in the new field of 'neuroscience' in the late 70s I was aware of Grossberg's work, but it was largely inaccessible to me because of my limited mathematical training. I was not alone. What we have here at last is a genuine attempt by the author to make his ideas accessible to most readers as 'a simple story, without mathematics' (or at least with minimal math). The foundation of this story is the concept of 'resonance' in neural systems. Resonance has a certain similarity to Hebb's concept of the cell assembly and its more modern variant, attractor networks. But the resonance concept goes substantially further to capture the idea that when the external input matches the already stored knowledge (expectation and attention) a dynamical structure emerges which can suppress noise and irrelevant details and enable fast and effective responses. When resonance fails, this triggers adaptation. This book is largely a treatise on how the resonance concept can help us understand almost all aspects of sensation, perception, and higher cognition. Even without all the math, this book of 600 plus pages will take considerable dedication to assimilate, but I believe that any student of neuroscience interested in the brain as the basis of mind will find it well worth the effort."

—Bruce McNaughton, University of California at Irvine

"This book is not for the faint of heart. Stephen Grossberg has been a giant in the field of computational neuroscience for 60 years. In this book he presents his carefully developed, integrative neurobiological theory on how the nervous system generates our conscious lives. It is bold yet self-reflective and therein challenging to all students trying to figure out how the brain does its tricks. A must read."

—Michael Gazzaniga, University of California at Santa Barbara

"How a brain makes its mind is one of the most perplexing questions in science. In this book, you will find the most comprehensive account to date by a towering pioneer of brain theory of our time."

—Deliang Wang, Ohio State University

"Don't read Grossberg in the original—unless you are an adept. Start with this exceptional overview of the lifework of a brilliant cognitive neuroscientist; then, organized and inspired, turn to the journals. Grossberg identifies key phenomena that open windows into the functioning of the brain; identifies the key problems that the brain needs to solve relevant to them; constructs elegant modules that might both solve those problems and give rise to the phenomena noted, and finally assembles them into systems and makes new predictions. This is textbook scientific inquiry, executed by a virtuoso. The book would be a fine component of a seminar, with students selecting the problems and modules for a deeper dive, then explicating them to the class."

—Peter Killeen, Arizona State University

"An excellent and wide-ranging view of how the brain perceives the world for us by a pioneering brain theoretician."

—Wolfram Schultz, University of Cambridge

"A tour de force on How the Brain Works ... a masterpiece on brain science and neuro-computing that could only be created by Grossberg."

—Leon Chua, University of California at Berkeley

"After reading many papers by the author, I always wished that he would present them in a coherent whole. And here it is. A magnificent volume of great science from mind to brain and back, a condensed ars poetica of a great scientist."

—György Buzsáki, New York University

"Stephen Grossberg is one of the most original and influential theorists in contemporary cognitive science and computational neuroscience. In *Conscious MIND Resonant BRAIN*, he takes the reader on an eye-opening tour in which he addresses fundamental problems of mind and brain from his unique theoretical perspective. This is an important book that should be of interest to anyone who wonders how a brain can give rise to a mind.

—Daniel L. Schacter, Harvard University

"In this book Stephen Grossberg shares the wisdom and encyclopedic knowledge that he acquired over 50 years of research devoted to unravel the mysteries of the human brain. Stephen pioneered the field of theoretical neuroscience and this approach allowed him to discover general principles that govern functions as diverse as visual perception, learning and memory, attention, emotion, decision making and consciousness. It is the essence of overarching principles to be abstract and to sometimes defy intuition, but Stephen succeeds to convey the essential in a language that is readily accessible to the non-expert. He embeds the discussion of neuronal mechanisms in the rich framework of cognitive psychology and elegantly bridges the gap between scientific evidence and subjective experience. He takes the readers by the hand and lets them discover the often surprising philosophical, ethical and societal implications of neurobiological discoveries. For those who enjoy intellectual adventures and wish to explore the boundaries of the known this scholarly written book is a real treasure."

—Wolf Singer, Max Plank Institute for Brain Research, Frankfurt

"How often do we have the chance to hold a true masterpiece? Grossberg's monumental accomplishments developed over multiple decades now written at an accessible level to a broader audience. What a true privilege!"

—Luis Pessoa, University of Maryland

"Steve Grossberg is one of the most insightful and prolific writers on biological intelligence. This book is a masterful presentation of fundamental methods of modeling minds, brains and their interactions with the world, many of which are due to the author and his collaborators. The models are presented as mathematical systems, including computing and neural networks. The variables, parameters and functions represent biological and environmental concepts; mathematical conclusions are interpreted as predictions of biological behavior. In many cases these have been verified experimentally. There are illuminating and surprising connections to other disciplines, including art, music and economics. Highly recommended to a general audience."

—Morris W. Hirsch, University of California at Berkeley

"This comprehensive overview of Grossberg's contributions to our understanding of the mind and brain shows exactly how prescient he, and his colleagues, have been. Whatever one's specific interest, from visual illusions to mental illness, this book provides a principled treatment of it. The principles flow from Grossberg's early framing of many of the questions that have come to define computational neuroscience—including his early understanding of the centrality of expectations. Kudos to him for pulling it all together here."

—Lynn Nadel, University of Arizona

Conscious MIND Resonant BRAIN

Conscious MIND
Resonant BRAIN

How Each Brain
Makes a Mind

by Stephen Grossberg

OXFORD
UNIVERSITY PRESS

OXFORD
UNIVERSITY PRESS

Oxford University Press is a department of the University of Oxford. It furthers
the University's objective of excellence in research, scholarship, and education
by publishing worldwide. Oxford is a registered trade mark of Oxford University
Press in the UK and certain other countries.

Published in the United States of America by Oxford University Press
198 Madison Avenue, New York, NY 10016, United States of America.

Library of Congress Control Number: 2021931712
ISBN 978–0–19–007055–7

DOI: 10.1093/oso/9780190070557.001.0001

9 8 7 6 5

Printed by LSC Communications, United States of America

Dedicated to

Gail Carpenter

and

Deborah Grossberg Katz

with much love and gratitude

and in loving memory of

Elsie Grossberg

Contents

Preface

Biological intelligence in sickness, health, and technology

How does your mind work? How does your brain give rise to your mind? These are questions that all of us have wondered about at some point in our lives, if only because everything that we know is experienced in our minds. They are also very hard questions to answer. After all, how can a mind understand itself? How can you understand something as complex as the tool that is being used to understand it?

Even knowing how to begin this quest is difficult, because our brains look so different from the mental phenomena that they support. How does one make the link between the small lump of meat that we call a brain and the world of vivid percepts, thoughts, feelings, hopes, plans, and actions that we consciously experience every day? How can a visual percept like a brilliantly colored autumn scene seem so different from the sound of beautiful music, or from an intense experience of pleasure or pain? How do such diverse experiences get combined into unified moments of conscious awareness that all seem to belong to an integrated sense of self? What, after all, is consciousness and how does it work in each brain? What happens in each of our brains when we consciously see, hear, feel, or know something? And *why*, from a deep theoretical perspective, was evolution driven to discover consciousness in the first place?

This book provides an introductory and self-contained description of some of the exciting answers to these questions that modern theories of mind and brain have recently proposed. I am fortunate to be one of the pioneers and research leaders who has contributed to this rapidly growing understanding of how brains make minds, a passion that began unexpectedly when I took introductory psychology as a Dartmouth College freshman in 1957. A summary of how my work began, and some of the discoveries that excited me then, and continue to do so to this day, are described in a lecture on YouTube (https://youtu.be/9n5AnvFur7I) that I gave when I was awarded the 2015 Norman Anderson Lifetime Achievement Award of the Society of Experimental Psychologists (SEP, http://www.sepsych.org/awards.php). These initial insights were followed by a steady stream of discoveries that has continued to the present day.

The book tries to explain the essence of these discoveries as a series of stories that interested readers from all walks of life can enjoy. The book is filled with such stories.

Our brains are not digital computers!

You might immediately wonder: If these discoveries are so simple that they can be turned into stories, then why has it taken so long for them to be made? After all, in one sense, the answer that we are seeking is simple: Our minds emerge from the operations of our brains. Such an answer is, however, profoundly unsatisfying, because our conscious awareness seems so different from the brain's anatomy, physiology, and biochemistry. In particular, the brain contains a very large number of cells, called neurons, that interact with one another in complex circuits. That is why many people in Artificial Intelligence, or AI, thought for a while that the brain is designed like a digital computer. Some of the greatest pioneers of digital computer design, such as John von Neumann, drew inspiration from what people knew about the brain in the 1940s. Very few people today, however, believe that the brain operates like a digital computer. It is quite a different type of system.

Knowing that your brain is not like the computer on your desk, or more recently in your hand, is a comfort. There seems to be more to our mental lives, after all, than just a morass of operating systems and programs. But what we are *not* does not teach us what we *are*. It does not, in particular, help us at all to understand how the brain's networks of neurons give rise to learned behaviors and introspective experience as we know it. How can such different levels of description ever be linked?

A new paradigm for understanding mind and brain: Autonomous adaptive intelligence

I would argue that it has taken so long to begin to understand how a brain gives rise to a mind in a theoretically satisfying way because, to achieve this, one needed to first create a new scientific paradigm. This paradigm concerns how *autonomous adaptive intelligence* is achieved. As I will discuss throughout the book, this is a topic that is just as important for understanding our own minds as it is for the design of intelligent devices in multiple areas of computer science, engineering, and technology, including AI.

The discoveries that contribute to this paradigm have required new design principles that unify multiple disciplines, new mathematical concepts and methods, major computer resources, and multiple experimental techniques. I will write more about what this paradigm is below, when it began, and why it has taken so long to develop. In brief, this paradigm has to do with properties of our lives that we take for granted, like your ability to continue learning at a remarkably fast rate throughout life, without your new learning washing away memories of important information that you learned before. I have called this fundamental property the *stability-plasticity dilemma*. Many gifted colleagues and I have been vigorously developing the theoretical and mathematical foundations of this new paradigm since I began in 1957, as summarized in my YouTube lecture for SEP.

Is the brain just a "bag of tricks"?

The difficulty of solving the *mind-body problem*, which ranks with the greatest problems ever considered by scientists and philosophers, has led many distinguished thinkers to despair of ever being able to explain how a mind emerges from a brain, despite overwhelming experimental evidence that it does. Some distinguished scientists have suggested that the brain is a "bag of tricks" that has been discovered during many cycles of trial and error during millions of years of natural selection (Buckner, 2013; Ramachandran, 1985). Natural selection has indeed been understood to be the dominant force in shaping the evolution of all living things since the epochal work of Charles Darwin (1859) on the origin of species. However, if a brain were *just* a bag of tricks, then it would be difficult, if not impossible, to discover unifying theories of how brains make mind.

The work that my colleagues and I have done contributes to a growing understanding that, in addition to opportunistic evolutionary adaptations in response to changing environments, there is also a deeper level of unifying organizational principles and mechanisms upon which coherent theories of brain and mind can securely build.

Mind-body problem: Brain theories assemble laws and modules into modal architectures

Indeed, one can explain and predict large amounts of psychological and neurobiological data using a small set of mathematical laws, such as the laws for short-term memory (STM), medium-term memory (MTM), and long-term memory (LTM), and a somewhat larger set of characteristic microcircuits, or modules, that embody useful combinations of functional properties, such as properties of learning and memory, decision-making, and prediction. Thus, just as in physics, only a few basic laws, or equations, are used to explain and predict myriad facts about mind and brain, when they are embodied in modules that may be thought of as the "atoms" or "molecules" of intelligence.

Specializations of these laws in variations of these modules are then combined into larger systems that I like to call *modal architectures*, where the word "modal" stands for different modalities of intelligence, such as vision, speech, cognition, emotion, and action. Modal architectures are less general than a general-purpose von Neumann computer, but far more general than a traditional AI algorithm. Modal architectures clarify, for example, why we have the five senses of sight, sound, touch, smell, and taste, and how they work. Continuing with the analogy from physics, modal architectures may be compared with macroscopic objects in the world.

These equations, modules, and modal architectures underlie unifying theoretical principles and mechanisms of all the brain processes that the book will discuss, and that my stories will summarize.

Why so many books about consciousness?

Many scientists are currently working productively on the mind-body problem. An increasing number of popular books has summarized highlights of this exciting progress, often describing interesting facts about mind and brain, including facts about consciousness. Often missing, though, has been a mechanistic theoretical explanation of how a mind emerges from a brain. Without such a mechanistic linkage between mind and brain, however, brain mechanisms have no functional meaning, and behavioral functions have no mechanistic explanation.

This book will describe how, during the past several decades, major progress has been made towards providing such a mechanistic linkage. This incremental progress is embodied in an increasing number of models that *individually* unify the explanation and prediction of psychological, anatomical, neurophysiological, biophysical, and even biochemical data, thereby crossing the divide between mind and brain on multiple organizational levels. These models can often be derived using a particular kind of scientific story that is called a *thought experiment*. I will explain what a thought experiment is as I go along.

I believe that now is a particularly good time to share these discoveries with you. In addition to the fact that a lot is now known, my own sense from talking to friends in many walks of life is that many of them are eager to learn more about how their own minds work. Such a desire may be heightened by the fact that our day-to-day knowledge of the physical world, and its many artifacts in our cities, technology, and weapons, has far outpaced understanding of our internal mental worlds, which cannot be achieved through introspection alone. A book like this can help to better balance how much we understand about our external and internal worlds. I also think that, as we are surrounded by increasingly intelligent machines, we can benefit from a deeper understanding of how we are not "just another machine", while trying to build satisfying and productive lives and societies.

The varieties of brain resonances: All conscious states are resonant states

For example, I will explain that "all conscious states are resonant states". The importance of this assertion motivated the title of this book. I will describe the resonances that seem to underlie our conscious experiences of seeing, hearing, feeling, and knowing. These explanations will include *where* in the brain these resonances take place, *how* they occur there, and *why* evolution may have been driven to discover conscious mental states in the first place. I will also clarify how these resonances interact when we simultaneously see, hear, feel, and know something, all at once, about a person or event in our world. This description is part of a burgeoning classification of resonances. I will also explain why not all resonant states are conscious, and why not all brain dynamics are resonant. These results contribute to solving what has been called the Hard Problem of Consciousness.

From brain science to mental disorders, irrational decisions, and the human condition

Mind-brain insights are as important for understanding the normal mind and brain as they are for understanding various mental disorders. I believe that understanding of "abnormal" mental states requires an understanding of how "normal" or "typical" mental states arise. The book will discuss symptoms of mental disorders from this perspective, including Alzheimer's disease, autism, Fragile X syndrome, schizophrenia, medial temporal amnesia, and visual and auditory agnosia and neglect. These insights typically arose when I noticed, after having derived a sufficient theoretical understanding of an aspect of normal behavior—whether perceptual, cognitive, or affective—that syndromes of clinical symptoms popped out when these normal neural mechanisms became *imbalanced* in particular ways. These imbalances express themselves in behavior as interactive, or emergent, properties of networks of neurons, indeed whole brain systems, interacting together. These *imbalanced emergent properties* illustrate a major reason why mental disorders are so hard to understand: Understanding an "imbalance" first requires that you understand the "balance", and both balance and imbalance are emergent, or interactive, properties of large systems of neurons interacting together. It is not possible to understand such emergent properties without a sufficiently powerful theory to describe and characterize them.

In considering this approach to understanding mental disorders, it is important to realize that there is a vast amount of quantitative psychological and neurobiological data available about normal or typical behaviors. These data provide a secure foundation upon which to derive and test theories of mind and brain. Clinical data tend to be more qualitative and fragmented, if only because of the demands of treating sick people. Although clinical data provide important constraints on theoretical hypotheses, they are typically an insufficient basis upon which to discover them.

An understanding of how brains give rise to minds also leads to practical insights into the "human condition", and how our minds manage to deal with a world that is full of surprises and unexpected events. Such an understanding sheds new light upon how practical wisdom through the ages has divined important truths about how we can try to live our lives in a way that respects how our minds work best, and how we can better adapt to the world's unexpected challenges. In particular, it clarifies various maxims that parents use to try to protect their children from "bad influences".

Along the way, these brain models shed light upon the following challenging questions: If evolution has selected brain mechanisms that can successfully adapt to changing environments, then why are so many behavioral decisions irrational? Why do some people gamble themselves into bankruptcy? More generally, what causes maladaptive decisions in situations that have several outcomes, none of them certain? Our models of cognitive-emotional interactions, or interactions between what we know about the world and how we feel about it, are helpful here. These neural models show how, when several brain processes that are individually essential for our survival are activated together by certain kinds of uncertain or risky environments, they can lead to irrational or even self-destructive behaviors. These adaptive processes thus help to ensure our survival most of the time, but there are situations where they fail. Some of these irrational behavioral properties include preference reversals and self-punitive behaviors. Learning to avoid, or at least to better control, situations where these consequences are most likely to occur is part of practical wisdom.

From brains to autonomously intelligent technologies that include Adaptive Resonance

Understanding how brains give rise to minds is also important for designing revolutionary "smart systems" in computer science, engineering, and technology, including AI and the design of increasingly smart robots. Many companies have applied biologically-inspired algorithms of the kind that this book summarizes in multiple engineering and technological applications, ranging from airplane design and satellite remote sensing to automatic target recognition and robotic control. When neural models are adapted in this way, or arise through less direct kinds of biological inspiration, they are often called *artificial neural networks*.

Companies like Apple and Google have been exploiting the learning and recognition properties of the artificial neural networks that are called Deep Learning networks to make useful contributions to several application areas. Deep Learning networks are based upon the Perceptron learning principles introduced by Frank Rosenblatt (Rosenblatt, 1958, 1962) which led to the back propagation algorithm. I will discuss Rosenblatt's seminal contribution in Chapter 2. I will also discuss more completely in Chapter 2 that back propagation was discovered between the 1970s and early 1980s by people like Shun-ichi Amari, Paul Werbos, and David Parker, reaching its modern form and being successfully simulated in applications by Werbos (1974). The algorithm was then popularized in 1986 in an article by David Rumelhart, Geoffrey Hinton, and Ronald Williams (Rumelhart, Hinton, and Williams, 1986).

Although back propagation was promptly used to classify many different kinds of data, it was also recognized that it has some serious computational limitations. Networks that are based upon back propagation typically require large amounts of data to learn; learn slowly using large numbers of trials; do not solve the stability-plasticity dilemma; and use some nonlocal mathematical operations that are not found in the brain. Huge online databases and ultrafast computers that subsequently came onto the scene helped to compensate for some of these limitations, leading to its recent version as Deep Learning. Geoffrey Hinton has also been a leader of Deep Learning research (Hinton et al., 2012; LeCun, Bengio, and Hinton, 2015).

When using Deep Learning to categorize a huge database, its susceptibility to catastrophic forgetting is an acknowledged problem, since memories of what has already been learned can suddenly and unexpectedly collapse. Perhaps these problems are why Hinton said in an *Axios* interview on September 15, 2017 (LeVine, 2017) that he is "deeply suspicious of back propagation . . . I don't think it's how the brain works. We clearly don't need all the *labeled data* . . . My view is, *throw it all away and start over*" (italics mine). This book argues that we do not need to start over.

The problems of back propagation have been well known since the 1980s. In an article that I published in 1988 (Grossberg, 1988), I listed 17 differences between back propagation and the biologically-inspired Adaptive Resonance Theory, or ART, that I introduced in 1976 and that has been steadily developed by many researchers since then, particularly Gail Carpenter. The third of the 17 differences between back propagation and ART is that ART does not need labeled data to learn.

As the book will explain, notably in Chapter 5, ART exists in two forms: as algorithms that are designed for use in large-scale applications to engineering and technology, and as an incrementally developing biological theory. There is also fertile cross-pollination between these parallel developments. As a biological theory, ART is now the leading cognitive and neural theory about how our brains learn to attend, recognize, and predict objects and events in a changing world that is filled with unexpected events. As of this writing, ART has explained and predicted more psychological and neurobiological data than other available theories. In particular, all of the foundational ART hypotheses have been supported by subsequent psychological and neurobiological data.

Moreover, key ART circuit designs can be derived from thought experiments whose hypotheses are ubiquitous properties of environments that we all experience. ART circuits emerge as computational solutions of multiple environmental constraints to which humans and other terrestrial animals have successfully adapted. This fact suggests that ART designs may, in some form, be embodied in all future autonomous adaptive intelligent devices, whether biological or artificial.

Perhaps this is why ART has done well in benchmark studies where it has been compared with other algorithms, and has been used in many large-scale engineering and technological applications, including engineering design retrieval systems that include millions of parts defined by high-dimensional feature vectors, and that were used to design the Boeing 777 (Caudell et al., 1990, 1991, 1994; Escobedo, Smith, and Caudell, 1993). This same Boeing team created the first dedicated ART optoelectronic hardware implementation (Wunsch et al., 1993). Other applications include classification and prediction of sonar and radar signals, of medical, satellite, face imagery, and social media data, and of musical scores; control of mobile robots and nuclear power plants, air quality monitoring, strength prediction for concrete mixes, signature verification, tool failure monitoring, chemical analysis from ultraviolent and infrared spectra, frequency-selective surface design for electromagnetic system devices, and power transmission line fault diagnosis, among others that will be summarized in Chapter 5.

Based upon 50 years of rapid progress in modeling how our brains become intelligent, and in the context of the current explosion of interest in using neural algorithms in AI, it is exciting to think about how much more may be achieved when deeper insights about brain designs are incorporated into highly funded industrial research and applications.

From Laminar Computing to neuromorphic chips

Government agencies and computer companies are also working to design a new generation of computer chips, the "brains" of our household and industrial computers, that more closely emulate the designs of our biological brains. This development has been inspired by a growing realization that the exponential speed-up of computer chips to which we have grown accustomed, known as Moore's Law, cannot continue for much longer (https://en.wikipedia.org/wiki/Moore%27s_law). The chips in our computers are typically based on classical von Neumann computer designs that have already revolutionized our lives in myriad ways. There are several reasons why this kind of chip may not be able to continue supporting Moore's Law: To achieve greater speed, chips pack their components ever more densely to minimize the time needed to transmit signals around the chip. As chip components get denser, however, they also run hotter, and can burn up if their components get too dense. At very small scales, the laws of physics can also lead to chips with noisy components. Unfortunately, von Neumann architectures cannot work with noisy components.

Overcoming these problems may require novel nanoscale chip designs. One inspiration for such designs is the mammalian neocortex, which is the seat of all higher intelligence, including vision, speech and language, cognition, and action. The neurons in neocortical circuits often interact via discrete signals through time, that are called *spikes*, or action potentials. Communication between a computer chip's components with discrete spikes, rather than continuous signals in time, can reduce the amount of heat that is generated. Neocortical neuronal networks also work well despite experiencing noise levels that would incapacitate a von Neumann chip. Finally, all neocortical circuits share a similar design in which their neurons are organized into characteristic layers, often six layers in the granular neocortex that controls perception and cognition. Chips with layers would provide an extra degree of freedom to densely pack processing units into a fixed area.

Essentially all aspects of higher biological intelligence are supported by variations of this laminar neocortical design. With our brains as prototypes, we can thus expect future laminar chips to embody all types of higher biological intelligence using variations of the same chip design. Moreover, since all laminar chips would share a design, including the same input-output circuits, they could more easily be assembled into modal architectures that can carry out several different modalities of intelligence, leading in the future to increasingly autonomous adaptive systems, including mobile robots. Computers of the future may thus contain a very fast von Neumann chip, or network of chips, that can do many of the things that humans cannot do well, such as adding or multiplying millions of numbers in a flash, as well as a neural coprocessor chip that will embody increasingly sophisticated and diverse types of human intelligence as our understanding of how our brains work advances.

My colleagues and I played a role over the years in proposing laminar cortical designs for such chips in several basic research programs of the Office of Naval Research, or ONR, and the Defense Advanced Research Projects Agency, or DARPA. DARPA, which has also been called ARPA at various periods in its history, has been a leader in advancing many of the technologies on which our lives currently depend, notably the internet, whose precursor was called the ARPANET (https://en.wikipedia.org/wiki/ARPANET).

My earliest encounter with ARPA and the ARPANET occurred in the 1970s as part of an experiment to test how scientific collaborations could be carried out between remote scientific labs. In order to carry out this research, I was handed a modem by a member of the CIA on a street in Technology Square in the shadow of MIT in Cambridge, where I was then a professor. I used this modem to collaborate with the laboratory of Emanuel Donchin at the University of Illinois in Urbana-Champaign, by hooking it up to our home telephone line. Manny, who died in 2018, was a principal founder and innovator in recording electrical potentials from scalp electrodes to understand cognitive processes in humans. He was particularly interested in studying an event-related potential that is called the P300. I sought Manny out because ART predicted a role for the P300 in category learning, as I will explain in Chapter 5. The results of our project, which was published in 1977, concerned how decision-related

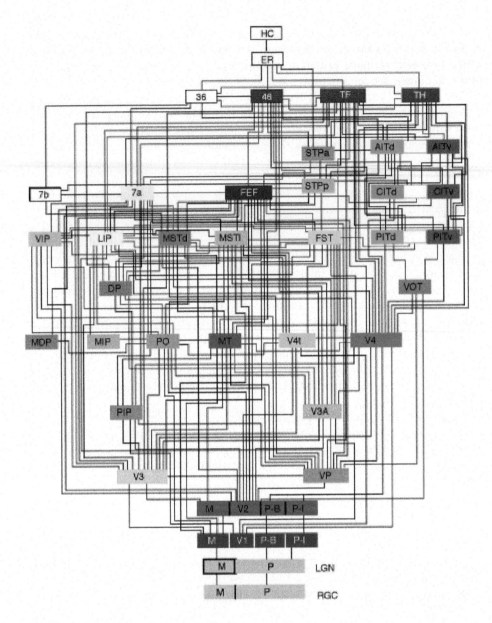

FIGURE 0.1. Macrocircuit of the visual system.

processes could be inferred from task-related P300 changes through time (Squires et al., 1977).

A much more recent DARPA program in which we participated to better understand laminar cortical designs was called the SyNAPSE (Systems of Neuromorphic Adaptive Plastic Scalable Electronics) program: https://en.wikipedia.org/wiki/SyNAPSE. One reason we were included is that I and my colleagues had discovered and developed the most advanced neural models of how laminar neocortical circuits control such varied forms of intelligence as vision, speech, and cognition.

Laminar Computing is the name that I have given to the computational paradigm that models how these laminar neocortical models work. All of the laminar cortical models for vision, speech, and cognition that we have introduced use variations of the same canonical laminar circuit design, and provide functional explanations of how these variations can give rise to such different psychological properties. These models, which go by names like the 3D LAMINART model for vision (see Chapter 11); the conscious

ARTWORD, or cARTWORD, model for speech (see Chapter 12); and the LIST PARSE model for cognitive information processing (again see Chapter 12), have provided an existence proof for the exciting prospect that Laminar Computing can achieve its full potential during this century.

Cognitive impenetrability and a theoretical method for penetrating it

A related factor that makes the mind-body problem so hard to solve is that our conscious experiences do not give us direct introspective access to the architecture of our brains. That is why for centuries it was not even realized that our brains are the source of our minds. We need additional tools to bridge this gap, which is often called the property of *cognitive impenetrability*. Cognitive impenetrability enables us to experience the percepts, thoughts, feelings, memories, and plans that we use to survive in a rapidly changing world, without being needlessly distracted by the intricate brain machinery that underlies these psychological experiences.

Said in a different way, *brain* evolution is shaped by *behavioral* success. No matter how beautiful your ancestors' nerve cells were, they could all too easily have ended up as someone else's meal if they could not work together to generate behavior that was capable of adapting quickly to new environmental challenges. Survival of each species requires that its brains operate quickly and effectively on the *behavioral* level. It is a small price to pay that we cannot then also solve the mind-body problem through introspection alone.

One of the problems faced by classical AI was that it often built its models of how the brain might work using concepts and operations that could be derived from introspection and common sense. Such an approach assumes that you can introspect internal states of the brain with concepts and words that we use to describe objects and actions in our daily lives. It is an appealing approach, but its results were all too often insufficient to build a model of how the biological brain really works, and thus failed to emulate, after decades of trying, the amazing capabilities of our brains. Common-sense concepts tried to imitate the *results* of brain processing on the level of our psychological awareness, rather than probing the *mechanisms* of brain processing that give rise to these results. They fell victim to the problem of cognitive impenetrability.

If introspection is not a reliable guide to understanding how our brains work, then what procedure can we follow to bridge the gap between mind and brain? I will describe a theoretical method in Chapter 2 whereby properties of the brain have been rapidly discovered over the past half century through an analysis of how each of our brains adapts on its own to changing environmental demands. The book hereby illustrates how our behaviors adapt "on the fly", and how they do so even if we do not have a good teacher to help us, other than for the world itself. Along the way, the book analyses how we can learn from novel situations, and how unexpected events are integrated into our corpus of knowledge and expectations about the world. The book also discusses how a good teacher can improve our chances of learning well, even if the teacher knows only *what* the right answer is, Yes or No, but not *why* the answer is right. ART has all of these properties as well, which is why it does not always require labeled data in order to learn.

In order to adapt on the fly to many different situations, our brains have evolved specialized circuits—the microcircuits and modal architectures described above—to adapt to different aspects of the world in which we live. That is one reason why brain architecture is so specialized and complex. Models of how these architectures work have been developed to explain many paradoxical facts about how we see, hear, speak, learn, remember, recognize, plan, feel, and move. I will summarize the most important examples in this book.

New computational paradigms: Laminar Computing and Complementary Computing

As I noted above in the discussion of the mind-body problem, in a rapidly growing number of examples, a *single* model can quantitatively simulate the experimentally recorded dynamics of identified nerve cells interacting with one another in identified circuits *and* the behaviors that these interactions control. One such example concerns how the visual cortex gives rise to conscious visual percepts. It has been known for almost a century that the part of the brain called the cerebral cortex—that convoluted mantle of "little gray cells" which covers much of the surface of our brains and which supports all of our higher intelligence—is typically organized into six characteristic layers of cells. This laminar organization of cells supports neural circuits that interact in prescribed ways. If we want to understand higher intelligence, we therefore need to ask: How does the cerebral cortex work? How does a laminar organization of cells contribute to biological intelligence? As I mentioned above, Laminar Computing is one of the new computational paradigms to which my colleagues and I have made significant contributions. In the special case of how the brain sees, Laminar Computing has helped us to understand: How does the visual cortex develop during childhood, learn during adulthood, group together visual cues into emergent object representations, and pay attention to interesting events in the world? Remarkably, although these seem at first to be separate problems, they all have a single unified solution. Chapter 10 is devoted to a self-contained introduction to Laminar Computing.

Another general brain design clarifies a more global scale of brain organization. This design goes a long way towards explaining the nature of brain specialization. In particular, it has been known for a long time that advanced brains process information into *parallel processing streams*; that is, into multiple pathways that can all respond at the same time to events in the world. Figure 0.1 shows a famous diagram by Edgar DeYoe and David van Essen of the several processing stages, and the streams to which they belong, that form part of the visual system (DeYoe and Van Essen, 1988). Computer scientists and brain theorists have often proposed that such streams function as *independent modules*, with each computing a specific property—such as visual color, form, or motion—independent of the other streams. However, a lot of data about how we see suggests that these processing streams do not, in fact, operate independently from one another. For example, during visual perception, changing the form of an object can change its perceived motion, and conversely; or changing the brightness of an object can change its perceived depth, and conversely.

Rather, these parallel streams often compute *complementary* types of information, much as a key fits into a lock, or pieces of a puzzle fit together. Each processing stream has complementary strengths and weaknesses, and only by interacting together, using multiple processing stages within each stream, can their complementary weaknesses be overcome. I have called this form of computation Complementary Computing. Overcoming complementary deficiencies of individual processing stages when they act alone often requires multiple stages of processing in complementary processing streams. I call this process Hierarchical Resolution of Uncertainty.

Complementary Computing is another revolutionary paradigm for explaining how brains give rise to minds. Accordingly, Complementary Computing helps to explain a lot of data, but more than that, it clarifies how many of the problems of the human condition that we face during life reflect properties of our minds that are deeply built into us. As I noted above in my brief remarks about mental disorders, many problems that we face can be better understood by realizing that they are often problems of *balance*, often because Complementary Computing balances complementary strengths and weaknesses across processing streams before a synthesis can take place through their hierarchical interaction. A scientific understanding of these processes helps to clarify *what* is being balanced, how an *imbalance* can occur, and what can be done to correct it. Later chapters will provide many specific examples of Complementary Computing.

These insights also provide hints about how to live our lives in ways that better respect how our minds actually work. I will outline such implications for daily living throughout the book. These insights make an interpretive leap beyond the science, but they are also supported by it. The first chapter of the book provides an overview of some of the main scientific themes that I will consider throughout the book, before later chapters go into greater detail about the various brain processes that together constitute a mind.

All the chapters strive to be self-contained and mutually independent: Chapter topics

An inspection of the chapter titles shows how the book describes processes that tend to occur at progressively higher levels of brain organization that reflect our perception-cognition-emotion-action cycles with the world. The chapters thus start with topics in perception, and progress towards topics in cognition, emotion, action, cognitive-emotional interactions, adaptively timed behavior, and spatial navigation. These chapters have been written so that they can be read independently of one another. Reading them in the prescribed order builds cumulative insights, but this order can be broken if personal tastes require it.

Taken together, these chapters describe many of the fundamental processes that enable us to be autonomous, adaptive, and intelligent. The first eleven chapters present a lot of information about visual intelligence because vision is such a major source of our knowledge about the world and our ability to find our way through it. Chapter 12 does the same for auditory intelligence and action, while also comparing and contrasting the neural designs that embody these two critical sources of information about the world. Chapter 13 describes how the processes that regulate emotion and motivation interact with perceptual and cognitive processes to help make decisions that can realize valued goals. Chapter 14 goes further by providing a self-contained explanation of how the prefrontal cortex carries out, and integrates, many of the higher cognitive, emotional, and decision-making processes that define human intelligence, while also controlling the release of actions aimed at achieving valued goals. Chapters 15 and 16 describe how we manage to navigate through the world and carry out actions in an adaptively timed way.

Along the way, these explanations include the following topics:

how we experience conscious moments of seeing, hearing, feeling, and knowing;

how these various kinds of awareness can be integrated into unified moments of conscious awareness;

how, where, and why our brains have created conscious states of mind;

how and why we see visual illusions and how many of the visual scenes that we believe to be "real" are built up from illusory percepts;

how we see 2D pictures as representations of 3D scenes, and thus have been able to invent pictorial art, movies, and computer screens with which to represent visual information;

how our ability to see visual motion differs from our ability to see visual form, and how form and motion information interact to help us to track unpredictably moving objects, including prey and predators, through time, even if they are moving at variable speeds behind occluding clutter;

how we learn as children to imitate language from teachers, such as our parents, whose speech sounds occur at different frequencies than our own voices can produce;

how we learn to understand the meaning of language utterances that are spoken by multiple voices at multiple speeds;

how our ability to use tools in space builds upon how we learn to reach objects when we are infants;

how we learn to recognize objects when we see them from multiple viewpoints, distances, and sizes on our retinas, notably how we do this without a teacher as our eyes freely scan complex scenes;

how we learn to pay attention to objects and events that cause valued or threatening consequences, while ignoring those that are predictively irrelevant and can be ignored, again as we freely experience complex situations;

how we learn to adaptively time our responses to occur at the right times in familiar situations, including social situations, where poorly timed responses could cause negative consequences;

how we learn to navigate in space, notably how our minds represent familiar routes to desired goals;

how our ability to navigate in space and our ability to adaptively time our responses exploit similar circuits, and thus why they are computed in the same part of our brains;

how our ability to use numbers, which provides a foundation for all mathematics and thus all technology, arises during evolution from more basic processes of spatial and temporal representation, but ones that are different than those which support spatial navigation and adaptive timing;

how we store sequences of objects, positions, and more general events that we have recently experienced in working memory;

how working memory is designed to enable us to learn plans from this stored information that can be used to acquire valued goals via context-appropriate actions; and

how, when these various processes break down in prescribed ways, symptoms of multiple familiar mental disorders arise.

In order to make the chapters self-contained, I review some model properties each time they occur, even if they appear in more than one chapter. This has a deeper purpose than providing self-contained chapters. It clarifies how a small number of brain mechanisms are used in specialized forms in multiple parts of our brains to realize psychological functions that appear in our daily lives to be quite unrelated.

The unifying perspective of autonomous adaptive intelligence

It is important to realize that the words mind and brain need not be mentioned in the derivations of many of the book's design principles and mechanisms. At bottom, three words characterize the kind of understanding to which this book contributes: *autonomous adaptive intelligence*. The theories in this book are thus just as relevant to the psychological and brain sciences as they are to the design of new intelligent systems in engineering and technology that are capable of autonomously adapting to a changing world that is filled with unexpected events.

Mind and brain become relevant because huge databases support the hypothesis that brains are a natural physical embodiment of these principles and mechanisms. In particular, the hypotheses that I use in gedanken, or thought, experiments to derive brain models of cognition and cognitive-emotional interactions describe familiar properties of environments that we all experience. Coping with these environmental constraints is important for any autonomous adaptively intelligent agent, whether natural or artificial. Indeed, Chapter 16 notes that the processes which the book describes can be unified into an autonomous intelligent controller for a mobile agent.

Building from mind to morals, cellular organisms, and the physical world around us

Because of this universality, Chapter 17 can speculatively discuss more universal concerns of humans in the light of what the earlier chapters have taught. These discussions include biological foundations for such varied topics as morality, religion, creativity, and the human condition.

Chapter 17 also discusses design principles that are shared by brains with all living organisms that are composed of cells, notably mechanisms whereby both neural and non-neural cellular organisms develop. Brains can hereby be understand as part of a "universal developmental code".

Chapter 17 goes on to propose why mental design principles of complementarity, uncertainty, and resonance reflect similar organizational principles of the external physical world. Several examples are provided to illustrate the theme that brains are universal self-organizing measurement devices of, and in, the physical world.

Thank you!

I would like to thank many people and programs for their contributions, both direct and indirect, to my work over the years. First and foremost, I want to thank the love of my life, my wife and best friend, Gail Carpenter, whose love, wise counsel, and adventurous spirit have made my life more fulfilling and happy than I ever dreamed possible. Gail has also been my most important scientific collaborator, and has led many research projects with her own collaborators that have made distinguished contributions to the neural networks literature. It is not possible to briefly capture how essential Gail has been in every part of my life and work during the past 45 years. An article by Barbara Moran that was written when I received the Lifetime Achievement Award of the Society of Experimental Psychologists in 2015 provides more background about our multi-faceted odyssey together (http://www.bu.edu/articles/2015/steve-grossberg-psychologist-brain-research/).

Our daughter, Deborah Grossberg Katz, has made our experiences with parenthood a joy from Day One, and a source of pride as she has gone from success to success, now flourishing as an award-winning architect and co-owner of the architecture firm ISA (http://www.is-architects.com/press). Deb has provided insightful comments about early drafts of this book.

I am thankful to the many colleagues at Boston University and in my extended scientific family around the world who have supported my work in many ways, and participated in harmonious collaborations that have led to a steady stream of scientific discoveries through the years. Along the way, I was lucky to be able to help found new interdisciplinary departments, graduate programs, research institutes, and conferences whereby many scientists and engineers could share their discoveries with a large community of students and scholars. The science and relationships that have emerged from these activities have been precious to me, and have maintained my excitement to try to further understand mind and brain.

I have particularly benefited from fine colleagues and students at the Department of Cognitive and Neural Systems (CNS; http://www.cns.bu.edu), the Center for Adaptive Systems (CAS; http://cns.bu.edu/about/cas.html), and the NSF Center of Excellence for Learning in Education, Science, and Technology (CELEST; https://www.brains-minds-media.org/archive/153/) at Boston University. I founded these and other scientific institutions, including the International Neural Network Society (http://inns.org/) and the journal *Neural Networks* (http://www.journals.elsevier.com/neural-networks), to help create infrastructure for our field. Putting a lot of energy into developing communities for teaching and doing research has been more than repaid by the relationships and collaborations that have been made possible within them.

More information about these infrastructure developments can be found at my *Wikipedia* page https://en.wikipedia.org/wiki/Stephen_Grossberg and in an invited essay that I wrote in *Neural Networks* when I stepped down as its founding Editor-in-Chief in 2010 (http://cns.bu.edu/Profiles/Grossberg/GrossbergNNeditorial2010.pdf). A special issue of *Neural Networks* to honor my 80th birthday on December 31, 2019 also contributes to this narrative, including the introductory essay by the Editor of the special issue, Donald C. Wunsch II (https://arxiv.org/pdf/1910.13351.pdf).

I have been lucky to have support for my work from key academic administrators at several stages of my life. My work may never have gotten off the ground as an undergraduate at Dartmouth College in 1957-1961 were it not for John Kemeny, who was then chairman of the mathematics department, and Albert Hastorf, who was then chairman of the psychology department. They created the academic infrastructure whereby I was able to become the first joint major in mathematics and psychology at Dartmouth. Their continued support enabled me to become a Senior Fellow in my senior year at Dartmouth and to devote that year to doing research in earnest to further develop the discoveries that began in my freshman year. John went on to become president of Dartmouth and managed to co-invent the BASIC programming language as well as one of the world's first time-sharing systems during that time. Al moved to Stanford in 1961 to become a much-loved chairman, dean, vice president, and provost.

At the Rockefeller University where I earned my PhD in 1967, Gian-Carlo Rota was willing to serve as my PhD advisor. He gave me the freedom to do the additional research that led to my PhD thesis, which proved the first global theorems about how neural content addressable memories store information. Mark Kac, who then supervised all mathematical activities at Rockefeller, also supported this work.

Starting in 1975, Boston University's President John Silber and its Dean and Provost Dennis Berkey made it possible for many of our educational and research efforts to success, not least by supporting the creation of CNS, which became a leading department for advanced training and research in how brains make minds, and the transfer of these discoveries to large-scale applications in engineering and technology. I am particularly grateful to the CNS staff for their flawless work and friendship over many years, notably Cindy Bradford, Carol Jefferson, and Brian Bowlby. Administrators at the university's Grant and Accounting Office spent untold hours helping to manage our many grants and to interact with our program managers in Washington, notably Joan Kirkendall, Cynthia Kowal, and Dolores Markey. I can still vividly recall talking to Cynthia over the telephone during a Labor Day weekend working out final details in a major Center grant budget just in time to submit it.

I would particularly like to thank the government agencies that have supported interdisciplinary work such as ours for many years and thereby made it possible. These include the Army Research Office (ARO), Air Force Office of Scientific Research (AFOSR), Defense Advanced Research Projects Agency (DARPA), National Institutes of Health (NIH), National Science Foundation (NSF), and Office of Naval Research (ONR). Every researcher eventually realizes how crucial the vision and support of the program managers at these agencies is to scientific progress. In my case, I would especially like to express my gratitude for the support of program managers like Leila Bram, Genevieve Haddad, Henry Hamburger, Harold Hawkins, Todd Hylton, Soo-Siang Lim, and John

Tangney. They all took a chance on funding our neural network modeling research at a time before it became a hot topic. I very much hope that these agencies will continue to value discoveries at the interdisciplinary cutting edge of science and technology, and will give both young and senior interdisciplinary scientists and engineers in these fields the financial support that they need to help shape the science and technology of the future.

Finally, I would like to thank Martin Baum, Joan Bossert, Phil Vilenov, and Melissa Yanuzzi at Oxford University Press for their support and guidance during the publication of this book, the four anonymous referees who convinced Oxford to accept the book, and the readers Gail Carpenter and Donald Wunsch who have made many useful suggestions for its improvement. Any remaining problems of fact or style will, I hope, not interfere with your pleasure in reading the book.

Overview

From Complementary Computing and Adaptive Resonance to conscious awareness

Expectation, imagination, creativity, and illusion

Just about everything that we know about our minds from daily life is mysterious. For example, when you open your eyes in the morning, you usually see what you *expect* to see. Often it will be your bedroom, with things where you left them before you went to sleep. What if you opened your eyes and unexpectedly found yourself in a steaming tropical jungle? or on top of a mountain during a blizzard? What a shock that would be! Why do we have *expectations* about what is about to happen to us? Why do we get *surprised* when something unexpected happens to us? More generally, why are we Intentional Beings who are always projecting our expectations into the future and predicting what may happen next? How does having such expectations help us to fantasize and plan events that have not yet occurred? Without this ability, all creative thought would be impossible, and we could not imagine different possible futures for ourselves, or our hopes and fears for them.

What is the difference between having a fantasy and experiencing what is really there? What is the difference between illusion and reality? What goes wrong when we lose control over our fantasies and hallucinate objects and events that are not really there? Given that vivid hallucinations are possible, especially in mental disorders like schizophrenia, how can we ever be sure that an experience is really happening and is not just a particularly vivid hallucination? If there is a fundamental difference between reality, fantasy, and illusion, then what is it?

Seeing, recognizing, and consciousness

Once you mention illusion, it is hard not to talk about consciousness. Our consciousness of visual events is particularly vivid to us because we get so much information about the

Conscious MIND Resonant BRAIN. Stephen Grossberg, Oxford University Press. © Oxford University Press 2021.
DOI: 10.1093/oso/9780190070557.003.0001

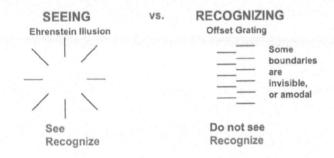

FIGURE 1.1. The difference between seeing and recognizing.

world from our ability to see. But why do we bother to see? One attractive hypothesis is that we see objects in order to recognize them, so that we can then act upon them to test our expectations or fulfill our desires. But do we really need to *see* something in order to *recognize* it? The answer, strange as it may seem, is easily seen to be "no".

For an example of this, look at the image in Figure 1.1 (right column). While looking at this image, we can all *recognize* that there is a vertical line, or boundary, of some sort that is interpolated between the ends of the horizontal blue lines. But we do not *see* this line, because it does not have a different brightness or color from its background. It is invisible. Nor does it separate the image into regions of different brightness or color. Such a percept is often said to be *amodal*. In contrast, a *modal* percept is one which does carry some visible brightness or color difference. Such visible percepts are often called *qualia*. Modal percepts of qualia are the ones that we usually have in mind when we talk about seeing the world.

The example of the offset grating shows that it is not necessary to see something in order to consciously recognize it. Why, then, do we bother to see?! Once you start making observations like this, you realize that things are not what they seem, and that we need a different way of thinking in order to understand how we consciously experience the world.

Illusion and reality

The percept that we get from Figure 1.1 (right column) shows that we can recognize, and be conscious of, events that are invisible. Many people, including distinguished philosophers such as John Searle, have written about visual consciousness as if it only includes consciousness-of-qualia, or of visible sensations. Thus Searle (1998, p. 1938) wrote: "The problem of consciousness is identical with the problem of qualia, because conscious states are qualitative

states right down to the ground. Take away the qualia and there is nothing there". Figure 1.1 (right column) illustrates that this is an incorrect, or at least overly simple, idea.

In Figure 1.1 (left column), in contrast, the circle around the bright disk is visible because the disk that it encloses is brighter than the surrounding background brightness. Both the percept of the invisible vertical boundary and of the visible circular boundary are of interest because they are *visual illusions*—they are not "really there" in the image. Why can we recognize or see illusions? How much of what we see is an illusion? Many Eastern thinkers have spoken about the World-As-Illusion. How correct were they? Did they think we see illusions for the right reasons? Moreover, if our consciousness can include even such bizarre experiences as invisible and visible illusions, then why don't we get hopelessly confused between illusion and reality all the time? Is there some adaptive property of our brains which implies that we can be conscious of visual illusions, without preventing us from experiencing visible "reality" quite well most of the time? If so, what is this adaptive property? I will summarize explanations of various such percepts in subsequent chapters, and will propose how they arise from adaptive properties of our brains that are needed for survival.

Before leaving this set of issues, consider the image in Figure 1.2. This image reminds us that invisible boundaries can sometimes be very useful in helping us to recognize visual objects in the world. Figure 1.2 shows the famous example of a Dalmatian in snow. When we first look at this picture, it may just look like an array of black splotches of different sizes, densities, and orientations across the picture. Gradually, however, we can recognize the Dalmatian in it as new boundaries form in our brain between the black splotches. These emergent boundaries are visual illusions that are not in the image itself. They are created in the visual cortex. Despite being illusory, and invisible!,

FIGURE 1.2. Dalmatian in snow.

these boundary groupings are very useful in enabling us to recognize the dog in the picture. This percept illustrates not only that we can *consciously recognize invisible boundaries*, but that this process of boundary completion and grouping is often very useful as we encounter ambiguous objects in the world. Chapters 3 and 4 will say more about how both invisible and visible boundary groupings help us to group incomplete fragments in scenes and pictures into object boundaries that enable us to recognize the objects of which these fragments form a part.

Art and movies are seen with boundaries and surfaces

For the moment, let me emphasize that the visual arts and the entertainment industry depend greatly upon such visual illusions. Whenever we look at a photograph, painting, movie screen, or computer monitor, we respond to a two-dimensional (2D) picture by constructing from it a representation of a three-dimensional (3D) world—that is, a world that is experienced in depth. The human urge to represent the world using 2D pictures dates back at least to Paleolithic times. Artists from ancient to modern times have sought to understand how a few lines or color patches on a flat surface can induce mental representations of multiple objects in a scene, notably of occluding objects in front of the objects that they partially occlude. I will explain in Chapter 11 how our ability to experience the world through a picture, or a series of pictures in a movie, derives from more basic properties of how we see the world in depth.

Figure 1.3 illustrates what I mean by the claim that percepts derived from pictures are often illusions. Figure 1.3 (left column) shows three rectangular shapes that abut one another. Our percept of this image irresistibly creates a different interpretation, however. We perceive a horizontal bar lying in front of a partially occluded vertical bar that is amodally completed behind it. The alternative percept of two rectangles abutting a horizontal bar is much less frequent, although it provides a more literal description of the image. The percept that is generated by inspecting

Figure 1.3 (left column) is an example of *figure-ground perception*, whereby figures in a scene are separated from one another and their backgrounds, and completed.

Even this simple image raises fundamental questions: Why do the horizontal edges that are shared by two abutting rectangles seem to "belong" to the horizontal bar? This property is often called *border ownership*. When these shared horizontal edges are attributed to the large horizontal bar, the vertical edges of the two small rectangles are somehow detached from these horizontal edges. They can then complete amodal vertical boundaries "behind" the horizontal bar to connect the vertical edges of the two abutting rectangles. These amodal vertical boundaries connect the visible vertical boundaries of the two rectangles to form a percept of a partially occluded vertical bar, as schematized in Figure 1.3 (right column).

How can a 2D picture generate a percept in which something is *behind* something else? How do 2D pictures create a percept in 3D, as they do whenever we see a movie? How do these perceptual properties differ from classical mathematical concepts of geometry? Answers to these questions will be provided in Chapter 11. Whatever its origins, this sort of phenomenon is clearly essential for our ability to recognize the world through pictures, and I will explain how this happens later in the book.

From Helmholtz and Kanizsa to Adaptive Resonance: Unlikely and bistable percepts

Figure 1.4 shows some other examples of how our brains can interpret 2D pictures as events in three dimensions. The images in the top row were described by the great Italian psychologist Gaetano Kanizsa, who was one of the most insightful contributors to visual perception until his death in 1994. They are called *stratification* percepts for the following reasons. As a two-dimensional picture, Figure 1.4 (left column) is just a white region on a black background. This simple picture generates a percept of an occluding object in front of an occluded object. It can be perceived either as a white cross in front of a white outline square, or as a white outline square in front of a white cross. The former percept usually occurs, but the percept can intermittently switch between these two interpretations. When a percept can switch spontaneously through time between two different interpretations, it is said to be a *bistable* percept.

Stratification percepts raise many questions: How does the boundary of the cross get completed across the white regions where it intersects the square? How does the white color within the completed cross boundary get

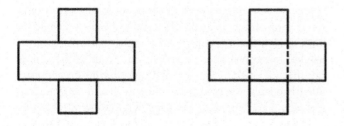

FIGURE 1.3. Amodal completion.

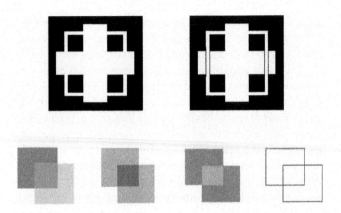

FIGURE 1.4. (top row) Kanizsa stratification; (bottom row) transparency images.

"captured" into a cross-shaped surface that is enclosed by this boundary? How is this cross assigned to a depth that is perceived to be closer than that of the square? How does the rest of the white region get assigned to the square at a more distant depth? How do the incomplete square boundaries get amodally completed "behind" the cross to facilitate recognition of the square? Why do not the completed square boundaries capture the white color within them where they intersect the cross? In particular, why are the square boundaries that are completed behind the cross invisible?

When the percept switches, so that the square appears in front of the cross, why do the completed square boundaries succeed in capturing the white color that previously was attributed to the cross, whereas the completed cross boundaries are then merely amodally completed behind the square, and are invisible?

Why is the percept bistable? And why does the cross percept win over the square percept more often?

One might at first think that such percepts arise because of prior learning about familiar objects in the world, like crosses and squares. Although visual experiences do influence how the brain develops and learns, and then how it perceives, something different is going on when we perceive images such as those in Figure 1.4. Figure 1.4 (right column) illustrates what I mean. In this figure, two pairs of vertical black lines create boundaries that help to capture the intervening white color into two vertical surface regions that belong to the square. These vertical regions are perceived to lie in front of the horizontal bars of the cross all the time. The horizontal boundaries of the cross, where it intersected the square, are now always amodally completed behind the vertical square surface. No bistable percept can any longer occur in this part of the figure.

The effect of these black vertical lines influences the percept only locally, however. When we look to the middle of the picture, we see that the vertical bars of the cross are still completed in front of the square, just as they were in Figure 1.4 (left column). These vertical bars of the

cross appear to lie in front of the square most of the time, even though the horizontal bars of the cross appear to lie behind the square. Kanizsa used this image to argue that knowledge about the world does not determine such percepts because, surely, our many experiences with crosses and squares should place the cross behind the square *everywhere* once it is forced to be behind the vertical bars of the square. This is not, however, what we perceive. We perceive, instead, the highly unlikely situation in which the cross appears to be deformed to lie both in front and in back of the square.

These simple figures contributed to a long-standing controversy about how we see and recognize the world that has continued to the present time. The alternative view, that we see what we expect to see because of prior learning, also has a lot of evidence to support it. Hermann von Helmholtz, one of the greatest scientists of the nineteenth century, proposed that we see using *unconscious inferences*, or learned expectations (Helmholtz, 1866). A modern variant of this viewpoint has been developed by Bayesian modelers. From this Helmholtzian or Bayesian perspective, the percept generated by Figure 1.4 (right column) should be impossible.

In contrast, Kanizsa provided brilliant counterexamples to Helmholtz's hypothesis using images, such as the ones in Figure 1.4 (right column), that violate our learned expectations. Kanizsa emphasized the power of *bottom-up* visual processes, such as filtering and perceptual grouping, that act directly on visual scenes and images at early stages of brain processing, whereas Helmholtz emphasized the impact of *top-down* processes, such as learned expectations, that are activated by processes deeper in the brain and are matched against perceptual representations that are formed by the more peripheral bottom-up processes.

Both Helmholtz and Kanizsa were partly correct. A more comprehensive understanding has arisen from neural models that explain how bottom-up and top-down processes work together to generate an attentive consensus, or *adaptive resonance*, between what is out there in the world and what we expect to see based upon our past experiences. I introduced a theory in 1976, called Adaptive Resonance Theory, or ART, to explain how such a consensus enables us to rapidly learn about a changing world throughout life and become conscious of events as we do so. These results from ART motivated the title of this book. Helmholtz and Kanizsa could not fully make these connections because they did not have some of the critical intuitive concepts and none of the mathematics needed to express them clearly. I am proud to be able to say that all of the main predictions of ART have subsequently been supported by psychological and neurobiological data. Later chapters will use ART, among other neural models, to explain the fascinating facts that have already been mentioned, as well as many others.

Opaque vs. transparent: Geometry vs. contrast

The stratification images in Figure 1.4 (top row) both generate *opaque* percepts. An opaque percept is one in which a viewer cannot see behind an occluding surface, even when a partially occluded object is amodally recognized behind the occluder. Why do these, and indeed most, objects that we see in the world look opaque?

I will explain how this happens in subsequent chapters. For now, we need also to acknowledge from our daily experiences that some percepts are not opaque. For example, when we look through a clear glass window, we can see both the window and objects through the window that are further away. Such percepts are said to be *transparent*. Why are some percepts opaque and others transparent? This is an important distinction for our brains to make, if only because it can greatly influence both how we recognize objects in the world and how we reach and navigate to acquire them.

The images in Figure 1.4 (bottom row) show how easy it is to generate transparent percepts, and how perplexing these percepts can be. Each of the three leftward images in this row has the same geometry, which is outlined within the image in the rightmost column of this row. Each of the three leftward images is defined by different shades of gray in their three visible regions. The middle image exhibits a *bistable transparent* percept. Here, at different times, the lower right square may appear closer than the upper left square, before the percept switches to one in which the lower right square appears further away than the upper left square. Thus, this percept, just as the stratification percept in Figure 1.4 (upper row, left column) is bistable. On the other hand, because one can see one of the squares behind the other one, each of these bistable percepts is also *transparent*. In other words, just as in the case of looking through clear glass, one can consciously see two different surfaces, at different depths, and the same positions, even though the actual image is a picture in two dimensions.

The image in Figure 1.4 (lower row, left image) differs from the bistable transparent percept only in terms of the relative contrasts of the gray shades in its three defining regions. This difference is enough to create a *unimodal transparent* percept in which the lower right square always looks closer than the upper left one. In this case, the positions that the two squares share is always seen transparently behind the lower right square.

Finally, the image in Figure 1.4 (lower row, third-from-left) appears opaque and flat in the 2D pictorial plane. There is no 3D percept here, whether opaque or transparent.

Why do not all occluding objects look transparent? Conscious seeing vs. recognition

These examples illustrate how easily percepts of opacity or transparency can be generated. They hereby raise the following basic question: Given that the boundaries of partially occluding objects can be completed behind their occluders, *why do not all occluding objects look transparent*?! My proposed answer to this question will highlight a profound conflict between the requirements of conscious seeing and of recognition that the brain has solved. I will suggest how this conflict is resolved in different regions of the visual cortex, indeed through parallel and hierarchical interactions between visual cortical areas V2 and V4. Once one understands how the visual cortex resolves this conflict to allow percepts of both opaque and transparent objects to occur, with the outcome depending upon the global configuration of all boundary groupings and surface contrasts, as in response to the various images in Figure 1.4, then one can explain many data about the link between seeing and recognition that would otherwise remain quite mysterious. This explanation is provided in Chapters 4 and 11.

Fast learning, slow forgetting, exploration, and culture

These discussions of visual percepts and illusions raise the question of how much of what we perceive is due to learning. An amazing fact about our lives is how much we can learn, and how fast we can learn it. Just think about your experiences at a crowded party, or an exciting movie. At the party, you can meet a lot of new people, and remember their faces and a great deal of what you discussed with them, especially if they arouse your interest and attention. The same is true when we go to the movies. Movie scenes flash by very quickly, yet you can go home and tell your friends and family a lot about what you experienced in the movie theater. We can continue to learn like this with remarkable rapidity throughout our lives.

A major question is thus: If we can learn so quickly, then why don't we forget just as quickly?

In particular, as I quickly learn new faces at a party, why don't I forget the familiar faces of friends and family members just as quickly? Why doesn't the memory of a new face force out the memory of an old face? If this did happen too easily, then we would be afraid to ever go to a party or even out on the street. Any exploration of the world in all its novelty could have devastating effects on our present knowledge whenever we tried to learn something new. Of course, new experiences can refine and even correct old knowledge. But this is not *catastrophic forgetting*, which could rapidly erase useful knowledge while we are learning about unrelated things.

Balance, Complementary Computing, and the stability-plasticity dilemma

Our ability to learn quickly and stably is one of the most important cornerstones of our ability to learn a unified sense of self and to build the civilized communities in which we live. Our intricate cultures, our knowledge of history, our arts and sciences, and our burgeoning technologies would be impossible without it. I call the problem of how we can learn quickly without catastrophically forgetting our previously learned memories the *stability-plasticity dilemma*. The stability-plasticity dilemma asks: How can our brains be *plastic* and learn quickly about a changing world, without losing the *stability* of our past memories? This is a question of *balance*: Too much plasticity can lead to catastrophic forgetting, while too much stability can lead to a rigid and maladaptive adherence to previous knowledge and beliefs that cannot adjust to a changing world. Maintaining this balance is part of the "art of living".

I will suggest below how many of the brain's designs for adaptive behavior are achieved by balancing between two or more opposing, or *complementary*, processes whose properties are related to each other in the much the same way as a key fits into a lock, or as pieces in a puzzle fit together. The way in which brains balance between stability and plasticity is one example of this kind of Complementary Computing. Due to this balance, our brains can rapidly continue to learn about the world throughout life. We can gradually become "experts" about our own experiences and develop a sense of a self with a coherent personal history, without risking catastrophic forgetting.

Learning, expectation, and attention

How do brains solve the stability-plasticity dilemma? In order to do this, they need to be able to cope with a world that floods us with new experiences. The great nineteenth century American psychologist William James called this the "blooming buzzing confusion" of daily life. Somehow we bring order to this confusion. *Paying attention* to events that interest us is a big help. But what does it mean to pay attention? And what would go wrong if we couldn't pay attention? For example, schizophrenics have a very hard time paying attention, and they do feel flooded by the blooming buzzing confusion of the world. Autistic individuals also have difficulties paying attention, often focusing on specific details but not the overall meaning of an event.

How we pay attention is often driven by our expectations of what is about to happen. For example, if you expect someone to be coming through a door, you may focus your attention on the door to anticipate their arrival, and get ready to see the person whom you are expecting. How does having an expectation control the events to which we pay attention? Why are our brains designed to learn expectations in the first place?

I will propose below how our ability to solve the stability-plasticity dilemma—that is, to learn quickly throughout life without catastrophic forgetting—depends upon our ability to learn expectations about the world—that is, to be Intentional Beings—and to use these expectations to selectively pay attention to a small subset of events in the world—that is, to be Attentional Beings. This perspective emphasizes that most of our expectations are learned from our unique experiences in life. These expectations, in turn, often control the events to which we pay attention, by being matched against the information that we get from the world, and suppressing information that does not conform to these expectations. For example, I might learn to expect where the coat closet is in my house and attend to it selectively to hang up my jacket when I come home, while ignoring the fact that some furniture got moved since I left home.

Taken together, these observations suggest that there is a basic connection between the processes of learning, expectation, and attention in our brains. In Chapter 5, I will suggest what this connection is, why it exists, and how it works, thereby clarifying why it is easier for us to learn about events to which we pay attention. Chapter 5 will show how Adaptive Resonance Theory, or ART, explains what this connection is and how it works. Along the way, I will also clarify why and how we see visual illusions, and will suggest that these illusions derive from adaptive mechanisms whereby we construct representations of reality that help us to solve the stability-plasticity dilemma.

Balancing expected vs. unexpected events: Top-down vs. bottom-up attention

Attention is not controlled only by our expectations. The world is a blooming buzzing confusion in part because surprising, or novel, events can occur. The world is always changing, and we need to try to change with it, or may not survive. In order to keep up with these changes, our attention can also be captured by *unexpected* events. An unexpected attack by a predator in the forest, for example, cannot be ignored without devastating consequences. These unexpected events can automatically attract attention in a bottom-up manner, driven directly by events in the world. They differ from the top-down learned expectations that were earlier mentioned. These bottom-up and top-down bids for attention interact to regulate whether learned plans can persist, or not, against the momentary demands of current events.

How do we balance between the expected and the unexpected? How do we try to satisfy our expectations, yet also stay open and attentive to the demands of novel events? I will also explain in Chapter 5 how our brains maintain a balance between the expected and the unexpected, between the familiar and the novel, and thereby solve the stability-plasticity dilemma. As I noted above, this is just one of the ways in which the brain maintains a balance between a pair of computationally complementary processes. It is a particularly important one because, if we could not adapt to novel experiences and challenges, we could not continue to learn new things throughout life.

Autonomous adaptation in real time to a changing world

This discussion illustrates a more general theme. Our brains are designed to *autonomously adapt to a changing world*. In other words, advanced brains can learn, on the fly, in response to rapidly changing environments, and can do so without any teacher but the world itself. Indeed, brain circuits look the way they do, I claim, because their design embodies a parsimonious solution to how an intelligent system *can* autonomously adapt to a changing world. This assertion implies that any approach to understanding biological intelligence that does *not* tackle the problem of autonomous adaptation to a changing world will not figure out why brains look the way they do, or how they work.

Noise-saturation dilemma: Balancing cooperation and competition

An important implication of the brain's complementary organization is that no single brain process can solve a large-scale problem like vision or speech. Each process has its own strengths and weaknesses. When these processes interact with one another in a balanced way, they can together overcome each other's complementary deficiencies. Our study of these various types of balance will suggest a new way to think about philosophical ideas about balance throughout history, notably Eastern ideas such as Yin vs. Yang. This insight helps to clarify why concepts like this about ourselves and the world have arisen in multiple cultures.

A related question concerns how the complementarity organization of our brains may be related to complementarity properties of the physical world. I will discuss this more in Chapter 17. For the moment, I will note that the Principle of Complementarity was advanced by the great Nobel Prize-winning Danish physicist Niels Bohr in the 1920s during his epochal work that founded quantum mechanics. This Principle explains that objects have complementary properties, such as position and momentum, or wave and particle. To the present, major discoveries about how brains make minds have not required the use of quantum mechanics, if only because the brain seems to work at a macroscopic level. However, the brain is a kind of universal measurement system of many kinds of physical processes, including light, sound, heat, and pressure. This fact raises the question of whether, and if so, how, brains may have assimilated into their own structure basic physical principles during their ceaseless interactions with the physical world throughout evolution.

The brain's complementary processes typically involve different ways in which cells cooperate and compete. Darwin's Theory of Natural Selection describes how cooperative and competitive processes during evolution may determine the survival of species. Cooperation and competition are also built into each of our brain's circuits. There is a basic reason why these processes exist on all levels of biological organization: Cooperation and competition solve a ubiquitous problem that I call the *noise-saturation dilemma*, which all living cells, not only brain cells, need to solve. This problem concerns how brains process *distributed patterns* of inputs across large networks of cells. Such a distributed input pattern may, for example, represent the pixels of a scene or the spectrogram of a voice. These distributed input patterns from the world input to networks of feature-selective neurons. Each such neuron can respond selectively to some features, but not others. Multiple stages of such feature-selective processing exist throughout each brain. The *relative* input sizes typically provide a measure of the importance of that feature in the input pattern (Figure 1.5, top row, left column).

The noise-saturation dilemma arises because each cell can respond using only a finite, indeed very small, range of activity levels, or potentials (Figure 1.5, top row, right column). Without oscilloscopes that greatly amplify cell potentials, their fluctuations would be essentially invisible

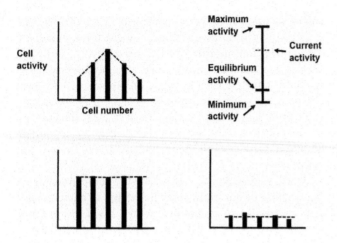

FIGURE 1.5. Noise-saturation dilemma.

to the naked eye. For example, oscilloscopes played a critical role in the work for which H. Keffer Hartline won the Nobel Prize in 1967 for his studies, beginning in the 1930s, of the *Limulus polyphemus*, or horseshoe crab, retina. Without the amplifying power of an oscilloscope, these pioneering studies could not have visualized the responses to light of *Limulus* retinal neurons.

Because of the finite dynamic range of neuronal responses, if an input to a neuron becomes too large, then the activity of this cell could, in principle, saturate at its maximum activity (Figure 1.5, bottom row, left column). When the input to a neuron is too small, then the activity of this cell can, in principle, get lost in internal cellular noise (Figure 1.5, bottom row, right column). Despite this limitation, cells that receive hundreds or even thousands of inputs from other cells—inputs that can individually vary in their amplitude through time between their minimum and maximum sizes—can process distributed patterns of these variable-size inputs without being unduly contaminated by noise or saturation, as in Figure 1.5 (top row, left column). I will explain in Chapter 2 how the noise-saturation dilemma may be solved in all cellular networks, not just neural networks, by using cooperation and competition.

Given that cooperation and competition are ubiquitous in our brains, it is perhaps not surprising that our brains have evolved ingenious ways for networks of neurons to cooperate and compete to carry out many different kinds of functions. This fact raises all sorts of questions about competition and cooperation: Is cooperation better than competition? When is competition a good thing, and when is it bad? As I will illustrate below, both cooperation and competition are necessary for either process to work well, just as wherever there is light, expect also to see a shadow. Properly *balanced* cooperative and competitive processes solve the stability-plasticity dilemma and help us in myriad ways to rapidly adapt to a changing world.

Imbalanced cooperation and competition can cause serious problems, including epileptic seizures, just as other kinds of system imbalances can lead to mental disorders such as autism and schizophrenia.

There is also growing evidence that variants of the same cooperative and competitive mechanisms that the brain has evolved may occur in society, indeed across the entire living world, and that imbalances in these cooperative and competitive processes may also lead to maladaptive outcomes. Chapter 17 summarizes the fact that brain dynamics illustrate a *universal developmental code* that holds for all living cellular tissues, whether neural or not. This result about brains contributes to a mathematical foundation for a general science of cooperation and competition that may become as important for our personal survival as it is for the survival of the societies in which we live. To fix ideas, let me mention the following examples right away:

Short-term memory, working memory, and long-term memory

We all have the capacity for *working memory*. This is the sort of temporary memory whereby if, say, I tell you a friend's telephone number. you can store it temporarily in memory before dialing it on your telephone. Suppose, however, that I distract you before you dial the phone, or you trip and fall before doing so. Then you may have to ask me to tell you the number again, because it has been wiped out, or *reset*, by the distraction. Working memory is thus a type of *short-term memory*. It can easily be reset and forgotten when we are distracted. Working memory is short-term memory for *sequences* of items, or events. Short-term memory differs from *long-term memory*, which is the type of memory whereby you can remember your own name. This latter type of memory is not forgotten due to a momentary distraction.

Whether we learn to understand and speak a language, solve a mathematics problem, cook an elaborate meal, or merely dial a phone number, multiple events in a specific temporal order must somehow be stored temporarily in working memory, after which they can be recalled at variable speeds from this working memory when we want to do so. As event sequences are temporarily stored, they can also be grouped through learning into plans, and can later be performed from these plans, again at variable rates under volitional control. These learned plans are also called *list chunks*. How these processes work remains one of the most important types of problems confronting cognitive scientists and neuroscientists.

Neural models that my colleagues and I have developed propose how sequences of events are temporarily stored in working memories and then coded and rehearsed either directly from working memory, or from learned list chunks. Remarkably, for reasons that will be explained in Chapter 12, similar brain circuit designs are used for linguistic, spatial, and motor working memories. Linguistic working memory may store a telephone number, or other speech, language, or musical utterances. Spatial working memories may store sequences of navigational movements, such as movements that enable us to learn routes to home, school, or work. Finally, motor working memories may store sequences of skilled actions, ranging from the example above of cooking an elaborate meal, to writing or typing, or playing a sport or musical instrument.

In all of these cases, as a sequence of items is seen or heard through time, each item in the sequence activates cells that are selectively responsive to that item. As the sequence is experienced through time, a spatial pattern of activity emerges across these responsive cells. In other words, "time" is recoded by "space". If the items are stored in the correct temporal order, then the first item will have the largest activity, the second item the next largest activity, and so on, thereby generating what is called a *primacy gradient* (Figure 1.6).

In order to maintain its activity in working memory until rehearsal occurs, each activated cell sends itself an excitatory feedback signal. If nothing else happened, these excitatory feedback signals could drive all active cells to their maximal activities, as shown in Figure 1.5 (bottom row, left column), thereby destroying the primacy gradient. This is prevented by inhibitory, or competitive, feedback signals from each active cell to all the other cells in the network. These inhibitory feedback signals are balanced against the excitatory feedback signals. Such a network is called a recurrent (or feedback) on-center (self-excitatory) off-surround (other-inhibitory) network (Figure 1.6). On-center

off-surround networks occur ubiquitously in our brains. In particular, whether such networks are recurrent or non-recurrent (feedforward), they have remarkable properties when they connect cells that obey the laws that are found in neurophysiological experiments. These laws are called the membrane equations of neurophysiology, or *shunting* laws.

In Chapter 2, I will derive neural laws for solving the noise-saturation dilemma using a simple gendanken, or thought, experiment. Along the way, I will also review three of the main historical modeling traditions that preceded this discovery. This explanation clarifies that shunting on-center off-surround networks may also be described in a language that talks about mass action (instead of shunting) cooperative-competitive (instead of on-center off-surround) networks. Such networks are found in all cellular tissues, not only in the brain, in order to solve the noise-saturation dilemma. I will return in Chapter 17 to a more general account of how such laws permeate the bodies of all cellular organisms, not just their brains.

Volition, rehearsal, and inhibition-of-return

Rehearsal of stored activities in a working memory is initiated when we want to recall its stored sequence. This volitional act triggers a rehearsal wave that is sent with equal activity to all the cells in the working memory (Figure 1.6). The rehearsal wave opens gates that enable the various stored activities to be read out of the working memory. The most active cell gets rehearsed first because it exceeds its output threshold first, the next most active cell is rehearsed next, and so on. Each rehearsed item is prevented from being rehearsed over and over again by self-inhibiting its activity in working memory as it is rehearsed (Figure 1.6), thereby enabling the next most active item to be rehearsed, and so on until the entire sequence is performed. This kind of self-inhibition is often called *inhibition of return* since it lasts long enough to enable other items in the list to be rehearsed. In all, if the items are stored in a primacy gradient, and if they receive a rehearsal wave and self-inhibit as they are rehearsed, then the stored sequence can be recalled in the stored temporal order.

Cooperative-competitive dynamics: Stable economic markets and the Invisible Hand

I proved several mathematical theorems in the 1970s about how such recurrent on-center off-surround networks should

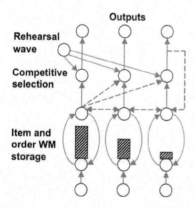

FIGURE 1.6. Primacy gradient of activity stored in working memory within a recurrent shunting on-center off-surround network. Rehearsal is controlled by a nonspecific rehearsal wave and self-inhibitory feedback of the item that is currently being rehearsed. Green = excitatory, red = inhibitory.

be designed in order to exhibit useful properties that I will explain below; e.g., Grossberg (1973). I also proved theorems about more general classes of cooperative-competitive systems that included the recurrent on-center off-surround networks as a special case; e.g., Grossberg (1978d, 1978e).

I called one such class of systems Adaptation Level Systems because each of these systems has a "adaptation level" that is equally experienced by every population in the network. Adaptation Level Systems illustrate how a collectively useful property can emerge from system interactions that permit a considerable amount of local freedom of choice *if* there are communal understandings that constrain the behavior of every actor in the system. This communal understanding in these systems takes the form of a state-dependent *adaptation level* against which individual differences are compared to determine subsequence choices by these individuals. In the case of STM storage in a neuronal network, the adaptation level is the broad recurrent off-surround that inhibits all the competing cell populations. In the case of an economic market where many firms compete to produce the same product, it is the publicly known market price.

Given the adaptation level constraint, I was able to prove that the dynamics of all Adaptation Level Systems are stable in the sense that all of its populations converge through time to one of possibly infinitely many equilibrium states. In the case of a neuronal network, this means that an input pattern is stably stored in STM. I will explain what it means in an economic market in a moment.

Before doing so, I want to note that another name was given to the Adaptation Level System theorem by Morris (or Moe) Hirsch, who liked to call it the ABC Theorem because all of these systems could be defined by terms that I denoted by the letters A, B, and C. Term C is the adaptation level, whereas terms A and B may differ for every population in the network. Moe Hirsch is a famous American mathematician at the University of California at Berkeley who got interested in the theorem and its possible generalizations, and proved some interesting results about them; e.g., Hirsch (1982).

The ABC Theorem let me propose how similar mathematical properties could be used to derive surprising conclusions about other disciplines, such as economics and politics. Why should it be plausible that conclusions about the brain may have possible analogs in economics and politics? The main reason is that recurrent on-center off-surround networks illustrate much more general principles of cooperation and competition that are found at multiple organizational levels in the biological world. The fact that humans share cooperative and competitive design principles that occur throughout the biological world helps to clarify how humans have been able to increasingly well understand this world and our place in it. As Albert Einstein famously noted: "The most incomprehensible thing about the world is that it is comprehensible".

The fact that our design principles are shared across all living things, and even embody physical principles of non-living things, helps to explain why this is true.

As I just briefly noted, one special case of the ABC Theorem provides a novel insight into how to design a stable economic market. This example illustrates how an arbitrary number of firms competing in a market can achieve price stability and balanced books, even if the firms have only their own selfish interests in mind, and even if they have only very indirect information about each other in terms of the publicly reported market price, a price that is influenced by all the firms' different business strategies, which are known only to themselves.

The ABC Theorem hereby provides a rigorous example of the Invisible Hand that Adam Smith described in his classical 1776 book *The Wealth of Nations* (Smith, 1776). Smith wrote:

"By preferring the support of domestic to that of foreign industry, he intends only his own security; and by directing that industry in such as manner as its produce may be of the greatest value, he intends only his own gain, and he is in this, as in many other cases, led by an invisible hand to promote an end which was no part of his intention . . . By pursuing his own interest he frequently promotes that of the society more effectually than when he really intends to promote it".

In particular, the theorem describes an economic market wherein any number of companies make the same product, and producing more of the product by any company tends to drive the market price of the product down. Suppose that each of these companies has totally different operating characteristics, and that the only information that they have about each other is the indirect effect that their strategies have on the aggregate market price, which is publicly known. Suppose in addition, and this is the critical assumption, that each company agrees to make more of the product at any given time only if it will make a net profit at that time by doing so; that is, only if the momentary market price exceeds the total cost per item of the product for their particular company, where the total cost factors in costs of investment, production, saving, etc. that are unique to each company. Under these very weak conditions, the theorem proves that, as time goes on, the market price will become stable and all the companies will balance their books!

Remarkably, the ABC Theorem assures a stable market, even though the companies aim to only make their own profits, and know very little about each other except through the total effect of all the companies' production strategies on the publicly known market price. This kind of result illustrates how cooperative and competitive interactions, whether in a market economy or a brain network, can generate emergent properties that can be both useful and surprising.

Although the theorem assures market stability, it does not predict which companies will become rich and which will go out of business. Further information would be needed to predict that.

Free markets?

The theorem should not be interpreted as arguing for a *free market* wherein competition can take its course without any constraints. Emphatically not! It was mathematically proved by the brilliant American mathematician Stephen Smale in 1976, while he was on the faculty of the University of California at Berkeley, that the class of all competitive systems can generate *any* conceivable dynamics, including generating the worst instabilities that one can imagine (Smale, 1976). Smale hereby showed, 200 years after Adam Smith's famous book, that competition can lead to very different consequences than the Invisible Hand. A truly free economic market can, in fact, lead to catastrophic consequences. Perhaps it is no coincidence that Hirsch and Smale were also close colleagues who wrote a famous textbook about dynamical systems in 1976, which is still in use today, in a later edition, with one of my colleagues at Boston University, Robert Devaney, as a third co-author (Hirsch, Smale, and Devaney, 2012).

The ABC Theorem illustrates that, among the myriad possible dynamical behaviors of cooperative and competitive systems, some of them have useful properties. Nature has discovered such systems during Evolution, and it is our task, as theorists, to figure out what they are. In the particular case of an economic market, the ABC Theorem teaches us that, if all competing companies are willing to play according to self-serving rules, like producing more of a commodity only if it will generate a profit, then important properties for the entire market, such as market stability and balanced books, can still be achieved.

Cooperative and competitive dynamics: Democracy, totalitarianism, and socialism

Another special case of the ABC Theorem has a political interpretation. In this example, changing the shape of the signals that are used to communicate among competing groups, without making any other changes in the network, can alter the activity patterns that the network stores. These stored patterns resemble some key features of "totalitarianism", or "socialism", or "democracy" (Figure 1.7). The quotes are intended to emphasize that these simple examples are little more than amusing caricatures of some key differences between these political systems.

For example, in the totalitarianism example, the signal function is faster-than-linear (Figure 1.7, bottom row). In other words, as the activity of a population increases, the strength of its self-excitatory signal and its inhibitory signals to other populations increase even faster. Here, the population with the largest initial activity competes to win all the network activity ("winner-take-all") and suppresses everyone else's activity. The dictator gets it all!

In the socialism example, the signal function is slower-than-linear (Figure 1.7, middle row). In other words, as the activity of a population increases, the strength of its signals increase more slowly. Here, no matter how big the initial advantages are of some populations, every population ends up with the same activity. Here, it doesn't pay to work harder, because everyone will end up the same.

In the democracy example, the signal function is linear (Figure 1.7, top row). In other words, as the activity of a population increases, the strengths of its signals increase proportionally. Here the relative sizes of the initial population activities continue to be preserved through time, so everyone gets a fair piece of the pie.

One might conclude from these alternatives that (pure) democracy is the way to go. However, I haven't yet told you the entire story: Both the socialism and democracy examples have the disadvantage of *amplifying noise*, or small

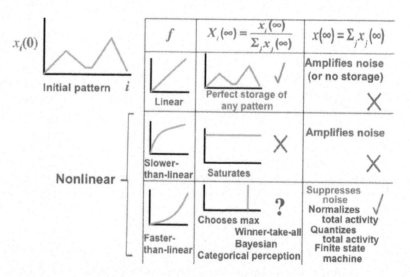

FIGURE 1.7. The choice of signal function *f* determines how an initial activity pattern will be transformed and stored in short-term memory. Among linear, slower-than-linear, and faster-than-linear signal functions, only the last one can suppress noise. It does so as it chooses the population that receives the largest input for storage, while suppressing the activities of all other population, thereby giving rise to a winner-take-all choice.

activities, in the network's cells, individuals, or populations. As a result, large activities can be caused in cells whose only inputs are internal or external sources of small amounts of noise. In the three cases described in Figure 1.7, only totalitarianism does not amplify noise, but totalitarianism is a huge cost to pay for noise suppression!

The above properties hereby raise the following basic question: Is there a way to design the system to suppress noise without leading to a winner-take-all, or "totalitarian", outcome? Fortunately for all of us, the answer is Yes. Here is the simplest way to do this:

Sigmoid signals enable noise suppression without winner-take-all choice

Any signal function that can suppress noise needs to be faster-than-linear at small activities (Figure 1.7). In addition, every biologically realistic signal function needs to have a finite maximal at large activities, because "infinity does not exist in biology". The simplest continuous signal function that combines these properties is a sigmoid, or S-shaped, signal function (Figure 1.8), which is faster-than-linear at small activities, approximately linear at intermediate activities, and slower-than-linear at large activities. Using a sigmoid signal function, which is found ubiquitously in the brain, leads to the following good properties: The network suppresses noise, and consequently enhances the initial differences between population activities (a moment of "totalitarianism"). This latter property is called *contrast enhancement*. Then the approximately linear part of the signal function preserves these enhanced differences through time (a moment of "democracy"), so that winner-take-all "totalitarianism" does not occur. Instead, a subset of the populations with the largest initial activities survives the competition with contrast-enhanced activities.

In summary, a kind of hybrid system works best. It isn't "pure" democracy, but it trades the benefits of noise

suppression against the fact that some individuals or populations will benefit more than others due to contrast enhancement. As illustrated in Figure 1.9, a sigmoid signal function creates a *quenching threshold*: Activities that start out above this threshold are contrast-enhanced and stored in short-term memory. Activities that start out below this threshold are suppressed as noise. A quenching threshold can be dynamically tuned. Increasing the quenching threshold can enable a winner-take-all choice to be made. Decreasing it can enable more features to be stored for further contextual processing, without risking that noise will be amplified.

More sophisticated variations of these networks have also been studied. For example, a "rich get richer" phenomenon is realized by endowing some populations with bigger parameters than others. In such a network, individuals or populations that have structural advantages, such as bigger signals to other populations, or more cells, can suck the activity out of the other populations. This kind of phenomenon occurs in our brains as well. For example, due to our experiences with lots of vertically and horizontally oriented structures in an urban environment, the cells that represent these orientations may have stronger representations in visual cortical maps. As a result, the orientations of lines that are close to vertical or horizontal may be perceived, during sustained viewing, as closer to these "norms". This kind of *line neutralization* effect was reported by James Gibson and Minnie Radner in 1937 (Gibson and Radner, 1937), along with a related effect called the *tilt aftereffect* by which an objectively vertical or horizontal orientation later appears to be tilted in the opposite direction. My PhD student Daniel Levine and I explained and simulated how these effects can occur in an article that we published in 1976 (Grossberg and Levine, 1976). Competitive systems can also oscillate in complicated ways if they are not properly designed, and can even support chaotic dynamics.

Although these examples are too simple to describe realistic economic and political interactions in today's societies, they do begin to identify some of cooperative and competitive principles that need to be incorporated into more realistic models. Of more immediate interest is the fact that we can understand such cooperative and competitive processes on multiple levels of biological and social organization in part because similar processes are built into our brains.

Cooperative-competitive-learning dynamics: ART in the brain and technology

Such mathematical insights about cooperative and competitive dynamics, when combined with analyses of how

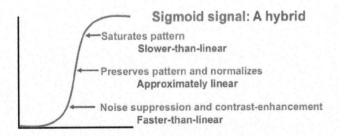

FIGURE 1.8. A sigmoid signal function is a hybrid signal that combines the best properties of faster-than-linear, linear, and slower-than-linear signals. It can suppress noise and store a partially contrast-enhanced activity pattern.

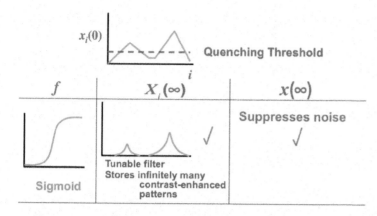

FIGURE 1.9. A sigmoid signal function generates a quenching threshold below which cell activities are treated like noise and suppressed. Activities that are larger than the quenching threshold are contrast enhanced and stored in short-term memory.

biological learning works, have been used extensively both to better understand how brains give rise to minds, and to apply these systems in technology. For example, as I noted above, I introduced Adaptive Resonance Theory, or ART, in 1976 to solve the stability-plasticity dilemma and to thereby explain how humans learn to attend, recognize, and predict objects and events in the world. ART has been progressively developed with many collaborators into the most advanced cognitive and neural theory that currently has the broadest explanatory and predictive range. Chapter 5 will explain how ART works, and will derive it from a thought experiment.

Gail Carpenter has played a key role in developing ART, notably many ART algorithms that have been applied in technology. Many other scientists and engineers have also applied ART in a wide variety of applications, including airplane design, medical database diagnosis and prediction, remote sensing and geospatial mapping and classification, multidimensional data fusion, classification of data from artificial sensors with high noise and dynamic range (synthetic aperture radar, laser radar, multi-spectral infrared, night vision), speaker-normalized speech recognition, automatic rule extraction and hierarchical knowledge discovery, machine vision and image understanding, mobile robot controllers, satellite remote sensing image classification, sonar classification, musical analysis, electrocardiogram wave recognition, prediction of protein secondary structure, strength prediction for concrete mixes, tool failure monitoring, chemical analysis from ultraviolet and infrared spectra, design of electromagnetic systems, face recognition, familiarity discrimination, and power transmission line fault diagnosis. Some of these applications are listed in the techlab.bu.edu web page. This range of applications is possible because ART models embody

general-purpose properties that are needed to solve the stability-plasticity dilemma in many different types of environments. In all these applications, insights about cooperative-competitive dynamics also play a crucial role.

Cognition and emotion: Male or female?

One of the hardest things to understand in our daily lives is how best to balance cognition and emotion. For many years, cultural theorists in the West argued that men are innately endowed with reason and logic, whereas women are dominated by emotions and passions. Such ideas were used to rationalize why men should hold most of the power in Western societies, whereas women should devote themselves to the home, where they were denied such basic rights as the right to a decent education or to vote. The classical book, *Wittgenstein's Vienna*, by Allan Janik and Stephen Toulmin brilliantly summarizes variants of these beliefs in Viennese society before World War I, as well as during other historical epochs (Janik and Toulmin, 1973). Such views of women persist in many societies today.

A more nuanced view is suggested by how our brains are actually designed to use cognitive and emotional processes. Whereas cognitive processes help us to acquire knowledge about the world, emotional processes have a crucial selective role that helps us to learn and use that knowledge to achieve valued goals in the world, notably to seek out rewarding experiences and to avoid punishing ones. Interactions between cognitive and emotional processes, within each individual, enable us to learn how to pay attention to events that have important valued consequences for us, and to decide which events cause these consequences and which are accidental. Cognitive and emotional processes thus need to interact in every brain, whether male or female, in order to help us to attain goals that we value, or indeed to even survive. Chapter 13 is devoted to explaining how this happens.

Social norms that promote a healthy balance between these two kinds of brain processes continue to evolve, with problems continuing to the present day. One has only to note articles like those of Andrew Reiner on April 4, 2016 in the *New York Times* on the topic "Teaching men to be emotionally honest" to realize that this struggle is not over (Reiner, 2016). Perhaps increasing knowledge about how cognition and emotion each contribute to the proper functioning of the brain will make it easier for individuals to find such a balance in themselves.

Causality, superstition, and gambling: Classical conditioning and prediction

Examples of cognitive-emotional interactions are ubiquitous. For example, few of us would say that the wallpaper on a dining room wall *causes* food to appear on the dining room table, even though it is present whenever food is served. On the other hand, if you went into the dining room only when food was served, you might very well associate the distinctive wallpaper in the dining room with eating. In fact, many superstitious societal rituals, such as rain dances, or primitive medical practices that may do more harm than good, may have arisen throughout history due to accidental correlations between events. Even a low probability of reward can, under the proper circumstances, lead some people to indulge in superstitious behaviors, maintain unhealthy relationships, become chronic gamblers, or even pursue fetishistic and self-punitive behaviors.

How our brains manage to do as well as they do in distinguishing between causal and accidental correlations between events has been scientifically studied since at least the great Russian psychologist and physiologist Ivan Pavlov carried out experiments about how dogs learn in response to rewards and punishments (Pavlov, 1927). Because of Pavlov's seminal role, this particular type of learning is often called Pavlovian conditioning, or classical conditioning. The word "conditioning" refers to the type of reinforcement learning that occurs in experiments of this type. Many other scientists subsequently added to Pavlov's insights, notably the American psychologist Leon Kamin in the 1960s. I will use examples from Pavlovian conditioning to make a number of general points about cognition and emotion that are also true in many situations from daily life. The Pavlovian paradigm is a convenient source of examples because it is so simple, and because its lessons generalize so broadly. Chapter 13 will describe these processes and their properties in greater detail.

During a typical Pavlovian conditioning experiment, a dog or other animal is presented with a rewarding or punishing event, such as food or shock, respectively. Such an event causes an array of emotional responses, such as fear reactions in the case of shock. Suppose that a sensory event like a brief buzzer sound precedes the shock on every learning trial. At first, the buzzer may have no emotional consequences. However, after "conditioning" or learning occurs, presentation of the buzzer by itself can evoke fear.

In order to describe this kind of learning in many situations, the shock is called an *unconditioned stimulus*, or US, because it elicits fear without any conditioning. The fearful response is called an *unconditioned response*, or UR, because shock can elicit it without conditioning. The buzzer is called a *conditioned stimulus*, or CS, because

conditioning gives it some properties of the US. The response to the buzzer after conditioning occurs is called a *conditioned response*, or CR. In this case, the CR would include aspects of the fearful response that was originally caused by the shock. The UR and CR are distinguished because the CS may not learn to trigger all the effects of the US.

Classical conditioning is a much more subtle process than this example would suggest. For example, if pairing a CS and US was the only thing that could happen during conditioning, then pairing of the wallpaper in the dining room with food *would* lead us to learn that wallpaper predicts food. However, this is not the only process that regulates classical conditioning, or any other kind of learning. Indeed, the wallpaper is still in the dining room when we pass through it between meals, and are not fed then. Thus, unlike the buzzer, which may always precede shock, the wallpaper can become an irrelevant, or redundant, stimulus that is not reliably associated with food. Models of Pavlovian conditioning, such as the Cognitive-Emotional-Motor, or CogEM, model that I will describe in Chapter 13, clarify how we learn which combinations of events predict valued consequences, and which other events are predictively irrelevant, and thus are not attended or learned about. I introduced CogEM in 1971 (Grossberg, 1971a) and it has been progressively developed with many gifted collaborators up to the present time, including recent contributions that clarify how particular brain dysfunctions may lead to behavioral symptoms of amnesia and autism (Franklin and Grossberg, 2017; Grossberg, 2017a; Grossberg and Kishnan, 2018; Grossberg and Seidman, 2006).

CogEM includes a *cognitive-emotional resonance* that embodies conscious knowledge of what events led to a certain emotional response, the emotional response itself, the motivation to carry out responses that can acquire a valued goal, and the learned action needed to achieve that goal. Such a cognitive-emotional resonance focuses motivated attention upon sensory cues that predict a valued consequence while suppressing those that do not, and thereby enable these cues to control an action that can achieve the goal. This cognitive-emotional resonance was part of the inspiration that led to my first major publication about Adaptive Resonance Theory, or ART, in 1976, for reasons that will now be clarified.

The motivated attention that selects predictive cues and suppresses irrelevant ones during a cognitive-emotional resonance regulates how we learn affective consequences of a particular class of objects or events, without experiencing catastrophic forgetting, while supporting conscious recognition of the attended object and our feelings about it. This was the first kind of resonance that I discovered which solves the stability-plasticity dilemma. Chapter 13 will explain how such a cognitive-emotional resonance works, along with the learning processes that it controls.

During learning to recognize a perceptual object, a *feature-category resonance* enables us to learn a recognition category that selectively responds to critical features of an attended object while suppressing irrelevant features, thereby again preventing catastrophic forgetting, while supporting conscious recognition, or knowing, what the attended object is. I will explain how a feature-category resonance works in Chapter 5. These two types of resonances support conscious feeling and knowing, respectively, as explained in the CogEM and ART models. When these resonances synchronize, we can both recognize and have feelings about objects in the world.

Predicting what happens next in a changing world: Blocking and unblocking

More complex conditioning experiments, called *attentional* blocking, or *overshadowing*, experiments, shed more light on how we learn what events are predictive, or causal, and what events are not. For example, suppose, as in Figure 1.10 (left column), that a buzzer sound (CS_1) is paired with a shock (US) until we are afraid of this sound. On subsequent learning trials, suppose that, before the shock occurs, the buzzer sounds at the same time that a light flashes (CS_2). Under these circumstances, we do not usually become afraid of the flashing light, because it does not predict any consequence that the buzzer sound alone did not already predict. In other words, the flashing light is predictively irrelevant, and is thus *attentionally blocked*, just like the wallpaper in the dining room is.

On the other hand, suppose that whenever the flashing light occurs with the buzzer sound, the intensity of the subsequent shock (US_2) is much greater than when the buzzer sound occurs alone. Then we *do* learn to become afraid of the buzzer sound, because it predicts an increase in shock. If, instead, the intensity of the second shock is much less than when the buzzer sound occurs alone, then a wave of relief may be experienced. The process whereby the CS_2 becomes predictively relevant is called *un*blocking.

Blocking and unblocking experiments show that humans and many other animals behave like *minimal adaptive predictors*. We learn to focus our attention upon events that predict important affective consequences, while ignoring other events, at least until an unexpected consequence occurs.

This fact raises fascinating philosophical issues, because each of us may learn, as a result of our own unique experiences, that a different combination of events causes the same consequence. For example, different people might attend to different combinations of visual features before naming an object a chair. Unless we experience unexpected consequences in our use of chairs, due to erroneous irrelevant features, or events, that influence our behaviors with chairs, we might believe that these irrelevant features predict what chairs are and how to use them. We could, in such a world, learn to worship wallpaper as the source of our food.

It is both interesting, and unsettling, to contemplate that each of us may have learned unique rules whereby to predict similar outcomes, and can live for years—indeed for an entire lifetime!—with a wrong set of rules to determine our behaviors. To protect us against this possibility, at least much of the time, we learn to pay more attention to novel events (like the flashing light) when unexpected consequences (like the increase in shock) occur. Only through experiencing enough unexpected consequences can we narrow the field of possible causes, and learn to pay attention to truly predictive events.

The value of being wrong

Making mistakes is one of the most important ways that we can generate unexpected consequences. Errors test our hypotheses about how the world works, and enable us to learn to discriminate between truly causal events and merely superstitious beliefs. The desire to be "perfect" all the time—to diligently avoid making any mistakes—can thus be a double-edged sword. Although it may provide short-term reassurance and praise, it can also chain us to a narrow world, devoid of adventure, that fixates us at our present level of ignorance, and locks out real personal growth. Taking measured risks is one way to find out what is "really going on" and to broaden the world in which we can learn to thrive. Kathryn Schulz published a stimulating book on *Being Wrong* in 2010 which argues "that error is *the* fundamental human condition and should be celebrated as such" (Schulz, 2010). The current book explains how errors can lead to more knowledge and contextually-appropriate feelings and actions with which to thrive in our uniquely experienced worlds.

The disconfirming moment: On the cusp between past and future

How do our brains learn to benefit from a disconfirming experience? Somehow, such an unexpected consequence needs to be able to alter how we process past events. For example, during the unblocking experiment summarized

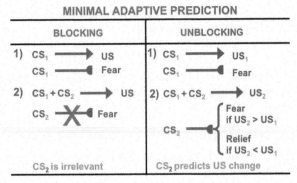

MINIMAL ADAPTIVE PREDICTION

Learn if CS₂ predicts a different (novel) outcome than CS₁
CS₂ is not redundant

FIGURE 1.10. The blocking paradigm shows how sensory cues that are conditioned to predict specific consequences can attentionally block other cues that do not change these predictions. On the other hand, if the total cue context is changed by adding a cue that does change predicted consequences, then the new cues can become conditioned to the direction of that change. They can hereby learn, for example, to predict fear if the shock level unexpectedly increases, or relief if the shock level unexpectedly decreases.

in Figure 1.10 (right column), a more intense shock US_2 may occur only *after* the buzzer sound and the flashing light shut off, yet we can still learn to become afraid of the flashing light. Somehow the sound and the light get stored in our short-term memory for awhile, even after the sensory cues themselves shut off. As a result, the stored representation of the flashing light can be associated with the fear that the increased shock level later causes.

This conclusion draws attention to a paradox. If the shock level had *not* changed, then the flashing light would have been blocked by the buzzer sound, and thus not attended. How does the stored representation of the flashing light survive the blocking effect of the bell in order to become associated with the increased shock level, which only occurs later on?

The moment when the increased shock level occurs has important scientific and philosophical implications. At such a *disconfirming moment*, we do not know what went wrong, only *that* the prediction of the expected shock level has been disconfirmed. At such a disconfirming moment, we are, by definition, focusing our attention on the wrong environmental cues (like the buzzer sound and its predicted shock level), which unexpectedly fail to predict the expected consequence. When such a disconfirmation occurs, we do not know which cues *should* have been attended (like the flashing light) instead of being blocked along with other irrelevant environmental cues.

How does our brain discover the correct combination of cues with which to correctly predict an unexpected consequence?

How does our brain do this without a teacher to tell us the correct answer?

In particular, in response to an unexpected consequence:

How does our brain search its memory to find those particular features or events that should not have been suppressed (like the flashing light), and selectively shift attention to focus upon them?

More generally, how do we ever progress from the unknown to the known without any teacher but for the fact of our predictive failure, which tells us only *that* we have failed, but not *how* to correct our failure?

Predictive mismatch, nonspecific arousal, and memory search

One thing is immediately clear: When an expectation is mismatched by the environment, whatever mechanism drives the search for the correct answer must be able to influence *all* of the cues that have been stored in short-term memory. This is true because, at the disconfirming moment of mismatch, we do not know *which* of these cues are the correct ones. The brain needs to be able to alter the processing of an as-yet-unknown subset of them. A mismatch event that influences all the stored cues is said to have a *nonspecific* effect. This effect is called *nonspecific arousal* because the mismatch turns on, or arouses, a memory search that will lead to amplification of the correct cues to attend (Figure 1.11).

We have often experienced the fact that "novel events are arousing" during our lives without thinking about how

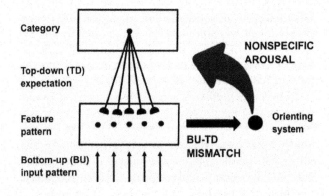

FIGURE 1.11. A sufficiently big mismatch between a bottom-up input pattern and a top-down expectation can activate the orienting system, which triggers a burst of nonspecific arousal that can reset the recognition category that read out the expectation. In this way, unexpected events can reset short-term memory and initiate a search for a category that better represents the current situation.

and why this happens. How an unexpected, or novel, event can trigger a memory search for a better representation of the current situation, notably a new recognition category, will be described in Chapter 5 when I explain how Adaptive Resonance Theory works. First, let me mention some other important implications of what happens when an expectation is disconfirmed.

Unexpected non-occurrences, emotional rebounds, and relaxation responses

If a shock unexpectedly *increases* in an unblocking experiment, then we may learn to respond to the flashing light with fear. But what happens if the shock unexpectedly *decreases*? Then we may learn to respond to the flashing light with a wave of *relief*, as in the unblocking experiment of Figure 1.10 (right column). The amount by which the shock increases or decreases can be calibrated to be equally *novel* in both cases. Thus the novelty, or unexpectedness, of the shock is not the same thing as the affective response that will be learned in response to the light, since the same amount of novelty can predict opposite affective responses. This example emphasizes that cognition (in this case, the learned expectation) and emotion (in this case, the affective response) are distinct processes, albeit distinct processes that may strongly interact.

Relief can be generated even if the shock intensity suddenly decreases without totally shutting off. This situation is harder to understand than the case where shock totally shuts off because, after all, being shocked is a *negative* experience, no matter how intense the shock may be, and feeling relief is a *positive* experience. How can our learned expectations turn a negative experience into a (relatively) positive experience? Where does the positivity come from?

Nor is a negative external event always needed for relief to occur. For example, if you enter a situation where you *expect* to get punished, then you can feel fear before anything negative happens. If you are not punished at around the expected time, then a wave of relief can occur, despite the fact that *still* nothing negative has happened! Thus a wave of relief can occur either if there is a sudden decrease in punishment, or a disconfirmed expectation that punishment will occur. Just *believing* that a punishing event will occur can lead to either negative or positive feelings. The cognitive context can hereby greatly alter the emotions that we will experience in different situations.

The feeling of relief has many implications for understanding, and trying to better organize, our daily lives. For starters, relief is an important source of positive feelings, of "feeling good" about ourselves and our lives. It is also one basis of the Relaxation Response, a term that was popularized by the book of that title in 1975 that was written by Herbert Benson and Miriam Klipper (Benson and Klipper, 1975). This Response is at the root of methods like yoga which are aimed at achieving relaxation through Transcendental Meditation.

A wave of relief in response to an unexpected event illustrates that Transcendental Meditation is only one way to generate a feeling of relaxation. Such a wave of relief is an example of a *positive emotional rebound*; it is a transient positive affect that is triggered by the cessation or reduction of a negative event, or by disconfirmation of a negative expectation. A *negative emotional rebound* can also occur. For example, if a positive reward is suddenly withdrawn, such as an ice cream cone while you are in the midst of eating it, or a sexual partner during sex, then you can feel a wave of *frustration*. Likewise, if you are merely *expecting* something good to eat, or a wonderful night of sex with your lover or spouse, and dinner or your date is unexpectedly cancelled, then that alone can cause a wave of frustration.

Such rebounds are philosophically interesting, if only because the *non*occurrence of an expected punishment or reward—with *nothing really happening*—can cause intense internal feelings of the opposite emotional sign, such as the relief or frustration in the above examples. That is why these events are called antagonistic, or opponent, rebounds. This is one of many examples where the occurrence of "nothing" can trigger strong internal experiences. Philosophers and gurus have long been aware that "nothingness" can itself be a potent experience. I will explain the main properties of how these antagonistic emotional rebounds occur later in this chapter, and more completely using the CogEM model in Chapter 13.

Do we know what we like? Peak shift and behavioral contrast

Before trying to explain the neural mechanism of antagonistic rebounds, let us first acknowledge that, after enough interactions between our beliefs and our feelings go on for a lifetime, it may become difficult for us to predict in advance the experiences that we will like the most when we finally do experience them. For example, when both rewarding and punishing events occur in a given situation, whether due to the direct action of rewards and punishments, or due to antagonistic rebounds, it is possible for us to end up preferring an event that we never experienced more than the events in our lives that have been directly rewarded. This phenomenon is called *peak shift and behavioral contrast*. To the question: "Do we know what we will like?", the answer can thus all too often be "no".

A simple example of peak shift and behavioral contrast occurs when pigeons are trained to respond to one colored light when it flashes on, and to *not* respond to other colored lights when they flash on. These pigeons are not trained by Pavlovian or classical conditioning. Rather, they are trained by Skinnerian or *operant conditioning*. During learning by operant conditioning, animals or humans are rewarded or punished only *after* they emit a certain behavior, or set of behaviors. The probability or reward or punishment can be varied in many ways. Although operant conditioning was first extensively studied by Edward Thorndike (e.g., Thorndike, 1927), B. F. Skinner has often been thought of as the father of operant conditioning since his classical book called *The Behavior of Organisms* was published in 1938 (Skinner, 1938). Skinner and his disciples systematically studied how changing the probabilities of reward and/or punishment in a *reinforcement schedule* could generate different patterns of behavior.

Suppose that a pigeon is trained via a reinforcement schedule to respond to a given colored light cue. After learning occurs, one can test if the pigeon also responds to other colors, and can compare how much it responds to the rewarded color vs. the non-rewarded colors. Such tests generally elicit a *generalization gradient* whereby the pigeon responds progressively less as a function of how different the wavelength of the test light is compared to that of the training light (see Figure 1.12, left column, top row).

Now alter the training of the pigeon in the following way: After training with reward to respond to one colored light, train it with punishment to *not* respond to a different colored light, and do so using a method of shaping the pigeon's behavior called *errorless training* that was published by Herbert Terrace in 1963 (Terrace, 1963). When the pigeon's responses are now tested to other colored lights, the remarkable effect called *peak shift and behavioral contrast* is observed.

Peak shift means that the pigeon now pecks most in response to a color that it has never experienced (Figure 1.12, right column). When the number of pecks is plotted against the wavelength of colors, this preferred color is "repelled" from the wavelength on which the pigeon was earlier punished.

Even more remarkable is the property of *behavioral contrast*: the pigeon responds more to this novel color than it ever did to the rewarded color (compare Figure 1.12, left column, top row, with Figure 1.12, right column). In other words, not only did the pigeon prefer a non-rewarded color, but it preferred it more than it ever preferred the rewarded color!

These response properties show that the cells which selectively respond to different wavelengths of light are organized in orderly cortical maps. Cortical maps of various kinds occur ubiquitously in our brains (see Grossberg (2020b) for a review of cortical map models). When one considers that ordered maps of wavelength-selective cells

may be replaced by a great variety of ordered maps of every conceivable kind of feature, it becomes clear that, after a lifetime of rewards and punishments, we may surprise ourselves by intensely liking options that we never before experienced. In this sense, we may not "know what we like".

The noise-saturation dilemma and short-term memory normalization

Why does the property of behavioral contrast occurs? This may be understood by considering Figure 1.12 (left row, bottom column). This figure shows the *positive* generalization gradient, in green, that ensues after rewarding a particular color, or wavelength. It also shows the *negative* generalization gradient, in red, that would ensue if only one wavelength was punished, and the other wavelength was not rewarded. What happens, then when one color is rewarded *and* another is punished? It makes good intuitive sense to assume that the *net* generalization gradient which would ensue in this case is the *difference* between the positive and negative generalization gradients. This net gradient is shown in purple in Figure 1.12 (left row, bottom column).

This net gradient does exhibit the peak shift in preference. However, it does not exhibit behavioral contrast. The failure of behavioral contrast is due to the fact that a *net* gradient must always be lower than the positive gradient from which it is constructed. However, this is not what happens during behavioral contrast.

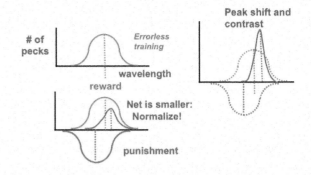

FIGURE 1.12. Peak shift and behavioral contrast. When a negative generalization gradient (in red) is subtracted from a positive generalization gradient (in green), the net gradient (in purple) is shifted away from the negative gradient and has a width that is narrower than that of either of its triggering gradients. Because the total activity of the network tends to be normalized, the renormalized peak of the net gradient is higher than that of the rewarded gradient, thereby illustrating that we can prefer experiences that we have never previously experienced over those for which we have previously been rewarded.

What is missing?

A clue can be found by noting that the width of the net generalization gradient is narrower than the widths of either the positive or the negative generalization gradients. How does the narrower width of the net gradient lead to the greater height that is found during behavioral contrast in Figure 1.12 (right column)?

This property follows directly from the fact that, in many ordered feature maps, not only ones that organize color-sensitive feature detectors, the cells that respond selectively to the features interact via a shunting on-center off-surround network (Figure 1.6). As we noted above, such networks are ubiquitous in cellular tissues, not only brains, in order to solve the noise-saturation dilemma; that is, to be able to process distributed patterns of inputs to a network of feature-selective cells without causing the cells to experience either noise or saturation (Figure 1.5).

I proved in the early 1970s that such networks tend to *normalize their total activity* (Figure 1.7). In other words, they tend to have a maximum activity that is independent of the number of cells in the network. In recurrent shunting on-center off-surround networks—namely, the ones that can store activities in short-term memory (Figure 1.6)—the network tends to maintain a normalized total activity through time as part of the memory storage process. As more cells get activated, then other things being equal, each cell has less activity in order to conserve total activity.

The property of total activity normalization shows itself in many different ways in our lives. In the case of peak shift and behavioral contrast, it causes behavioral contrast: Because the net generalization gradient is narrower, its peak activity is greater in order to (approximately) conserve the total activity under the net generalization gradient. We will see in Chapter 4 how total activity normalization also leads to brightness constancy and contrast during visual perception, and in Chapter 12 to the bowed serial position curve during free recall of items that are stored in short-term memory in a cognitive working memory, among many other properties that follow from the brain's solution of the noise-saturation dilemma.

experience the corresponding cues are disconfirmed when they do not occur. Are these positive and negative rebounds useful for survival? The answer is emphatically "yes".

What is the adaptive value of a positive emotional rebound? As one example, if you enter a fearful situation and are not punished during a sufficient number of these experiences, then the positive relief that you feel can help you to learn not to be afraid of that situation any more, and thus to feel comfortable working or playing in it, and not just to persistently trying to avoid it.

How does the positive relief free you from your learned fears? When the positive relief rebound is balanced against the negative learned fear, we can then learn to cancel the fear with the relief due to competition between them (Figure 1.13, left column). When there is no longer any net fear reaction, we can approach the situation with new hope. This kind of cancellation occurs in brain circuits wherein positive and negative emotional centers interact together. Such circuits are called *opponent processes* because the positive and negative events activate mutually exclusive, or "opponent", pathways that compete with one another. I will explain below how opponent processes are designed to enable antagonistic rebounds to occur.

What is the adaptive value of a negative emotional rebound? As one example, suppose that you are seeking an expected positive reward like food in your refrigerator at home or, if you would prefer a more exotic example, at an oasis in the desert. Suppose that the expected food is not there: In the first case, the refrigerator may be empty, and in the second case, all the coconuts at the oasis may have already been eaten. Frustration may occur in either case when the expectation of food is disconfirmed.

Why is the feeling of frustration when the expected food is gone important to survival? As noted above, part of the story is that frustration can balance and cancel the learned positive motivation to return again and again to the refrigerator, or to the oasis, for food whenever we were hungry (Figure 1.13, middle column). Such perseverative, even obsessive, behavior could lead to death, since we would eventually starve if, whenever we were hungry, we kept going to

Opponent processing, forgetting, obsession, and exploration

As noted above, a positive antagonistic rebound, such as relief, can occur when a negative reinforcer, such as a shock, suddenly turns off (Figure 1.13, left column). A negative antagonistic rebound, such as frustration, can occur when a positive reinforcer, such as food or sex, suddenly shuts off (Figure 1.13, middle column). These rebounds can also occur when expectations to

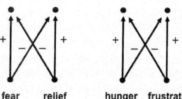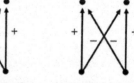

fear   relief   hunger frustration   exploration consummation

FIGURE 1.13. Affective circuits are organized into opponent channels, such as fear vs. relief, and hunger vs. frustration. On a larger scale of affective behaviors, exploration and consummation are also opponent types of behavior. Exploration helps to discover novel sources of reward. Consummation enables expected rewards to be acted upon. Exploration must be inhibited to enable an animal to maintain attention long enough upon a stationary reward in order to consume it.

a place where there was no longer any food. This does not happen to us, in part, because the positive motivation to get our food there is cancelled by negative frustration. The second part of an adaptive response to a disconfirmed expectation is that, when the motivation to seek food in an unproductive place is cancelled, it can no longer inhibit the innate tendency to explore the environment in search of novel sources of reward (Figure 1.13, right column).

The above examples illustrate how a disconnect between the motivation to do something and its affective consequences can enable a wide range of maladaptive behaviors to persist for a long time. Fortunately, when "nothingness" triggers an emotional rebound, it can protect us from obsessively, and self-destructively, seeking rewards where they can no longer be found.

The failure to find food on just one occasion in the refrigerator or oasis does not imply that we will never again seek food in those places. On the other hand, if such a predictive failure happens sufficiently often, then the multiple experiences of negative frustration which it causes can cumulatively cancel the positive approach to the refrigerator or oasis through opponent learning. We then say that the motivation to seek food in that situation is *extinguished*. "Extinction" is the psychological word for emotional "forgetting".

The same sort of conclusion can be drawn from situations where you expect to be punished, but unexpectedly are not punished. Then your learned fear of such a situation can be inhibited by positive relief rebounds. If this happens on enough occasions, the fear can extinguish through opponent learning of the relief rebound. The extinguished fear then no longer inhibits exploratory behavior, so that one can begin anew to explore that situation, or even totally different environments, for sources of positive reward. Cognitively-mediated positive and negative rebounds can hereby help us to flexibly adjust to changing, or poorly understood, environmental contingencies, and thereby permit us to explore the world more fully to find new sources of satisfaction. They are a prime example of how cognition and emotion can work together to learn valuable adaptive skills. Substituting positive for negative affects, by one or another means, is now a standard strategy in what has come to be called Positive Psychiatry (Seligman and Csikszentmihalyi, 2000).

Partial reward: Irrationality, gambling, creativity, and unrequited love

Were life only so simple! These very same mechanisms, which are so important to our survival, can also lead us into maladaptive, irrational, and even bizarre behaviors when they interact with the wrong environments. How

this can happen provides a mechanistic rationale for the commonsense view that you can get into a lot of trouble if you allow yourself to get involved with the wrong people or the wrong situations. This kind of folk wisdom, which is traditionally passed along by parents to their children, often contains a kernel of truth. Our potential weakness in these "bad" situations is a consequence of the very mechanisms that help our species to survive in other, even more life-threatening, situations, and is thus one of the burdens that we have to learn how to cope with as well as we can. As we will see in a moment, our learned expectations can again greatly influence how we behave in these risky situations, so learning the *right* expectations—or more generally, experiencing the right influences on our thinking—can make a huge difference in how well we cope with them.

A striking classical example of what can go wrong is called the *partial reinforcement acquisition effect*, or the partial reward effect, for short. The source of the problem is that a given behavior does not always get rewarded a consistent manner. The world is simply too complicated for that to happen all of the time. To see what I mean, first consider a simple example of consistent reward. Suppose that a rat is rewarded with food pellets every time it runs down an alley to the other end, where food is made available. This is called a *continuous* reward schedule. If a rat is continuously rewarded enough times, then it will learn to run quickly down the alley for food whenever it is hungry. As we briefly noted above, this sort of learning is often called *Skinnerian conditioning* after the famous twentieth century American psychologist, B. F. Skinner, who intensively studied it with his colleagues. Skinnerian conditioning is also called *operant conditioning* because it describes the learned effects of reward or punishment that are given contingent upon the responses, or operants, that an animal or person spontaneously emits. In classical conditioning, responses are, in contrast, elicited by an external stimulus, like a shock or food. Despite this difference, the two types of learning share many properties.

Partial reward is said to occur if the rat is rewarded on only a fraction of the occasions when it runs down the alley. It receives no reward on the other occasions. What happens if the *total* amount of reward is the same under continuous and partial reward schedules? The remarkable fact is that *partially* rewarded animals learn to run down the alley *faster* than continuously rewarded animals, even though they have to work much harder for the same total amount of reward. Moreover, if one gradually decreases the fraction of times that a rat is rewarded for running down the alley, then it will persist in running down the alley to get rewarded on very few trials. Running like a maniac for a very small number of rewards is, on the face of it, not a particularly rational behavior, but once the rat is hooked, it may keep running for a very long time. Does this sound familiar in many lives that we know? The trick is first to get an animal or human "hooked" initially with a sufficient number of rewards, and then to gradually reduce the probability of reward.

Partial reward is not always bad. Because the world is complicated, we cannot always expect to get continuously rewarded, even in situations where reward may very well be forthcoming in the future. One needs to look no further than one's own busy parents for many examples of this basic truth. Partial rewards thus help to keep us trying to get rewards in situations where they are likely to be forthcoming, albeit not on every try. On the other hand, partial reward can also have seriously maladaptive effects on behavior. For example, suppose that a person happens, by chance, to win some money at gambling. Once a person is "hooked", he or she might continue to gamble for a long time, even though a win is very unlikely, and end up losing a lot of money. Or imagine a love affair that begins really wonderfully, with both partners feeling highly rewarded by each other most of the time. Suppose that one partner gets disenchanted, and starts giving the other partner fewer and fewer rewards. The unrequited lover might hang on for a very long time, thrilled by even an occasional phone call that, before the affair got started, may not have had such an intensely rewarding effect.

How do such profound effects on behavior occur? To get started, consider what goes on as a rat runs down an alley on a partial reward schedule. Because it is just *partial* reward, the rat can build up an expectation that it will *not* get rewarded after a given run down the alley. Suppose, however, that the rat *does* get rewarded after that particular run down the alley. The reward will hereby disconfirm the negative expectation of non-reward, and can thereby cause a positive emotional rebound. This positive rebound can add to the direct positive effect of the reward to make that experience feel extremely rewarding—much more rewarding, in fact, than the direct effect of the reward all by itself. The same thing can happen during unrequited love.

A similar thing can happen in many other situations. For example, it may be more thrilling to see a magnificent view at the top of a mountain after climbing it yourself and overcoming lots of dangerous experiences, than it is to just see a video of the view from the top. Partial reward may also help to maintain creative behaviors when they are infrequently rewarded, even over a period of many years. It can thus have both major positive and negative effects on the development of personality, culture, and societies.

Learned helplessness in the lab and society

The mechanisms that operate during partial reward may maintain behavior for a long time. These same mechanisms may also suppress behavior. For example, imagine a situation in which a person or animal tries to escape from one bad situation, only to end up in another one. They then try to escape that situation, and end up where they started. After awhile, the person or animal may just "give up" and develop a *learned helplessness* in which they no longer explore their environment at all, but instead are afflicted with persistent negative feelings. The American psychologist Martin Seligman began to publish studies about learned helplessness in 1967 (Maier and Seligman, 1976; Seligman and Maier, 1967) as a way to better understand depression. The environmental contingencies that lead to learned helplessness are particularly pernicious. Normally, escaping from a negative situation would create a positive relief rebound. But if the escape leads you "from the frying pan into the fire", then the direct negativity of the new situation can cancel the positive rebound from your attempted escape. If you continue to experience such "double-whammies", eventually all net motivation can be cancelled, and a feeling of helplessness can develop.

Learned helplessness has been experimentally studied using rats, dogs, and other animals in a two-way shuttle-box. Suppose that the animal starts out by sitting in one half of the box. Then the floor is electrified. The animal experiences pain and fear from the electric shock, and runs to the other half of the box to escape. This escape behavior would normally elicit a positive relief rebound that, other things being equal, would be associated through learning with sensory cues from the second half of the box. The animal could then later respond to these cues by running to the second half of the box to escape the shock in the first half of the box. Relief can hereby motivate the learning of escape behaviors in many environments.

Unfortunately, in the particular situation of the shuttle-box, other things are not equal, because the experimentalist—or if you view this as a metaphor, the world—does something cruel. Shortly after the animal runs to the second half of the box, the floor in *that* half of the box is also electrified. Now the animal runs to the first half of the box to escape. Again a relief rebound would normally motivate the animal to escape the second half of the box to get back to the first half. But the animal has already learned to associate the cues in the first half of the box with the directly felt pain and fear that it originally experienced, feelings that are strengthened when the experimentalist electrifies the floor of the first half of the box once again. When the animal again experiences shock in the first half of the box, the learned fear response is strengthened and can eventually overwhelm the positive rebound. As a result, the positive relief rebound due to escape from the second half of the box is cancelled by the fear that the animal associates with the first half. The same thing happens in the second half of the box. In time, all positive motivation is cancelled and the animal has no expectation of positive reward. The animal simply sits, shivers, and defecates, totally defeated by his environment.

Humans can also experience learned helplessness, notably in underprivileged ghettos where all opportunities for positive reward may be cancelled by negative contingencies. To help people out of these situations, it is important to create new opportunities whereby positive behaviors and expectations may be learned that will not be inexorably defeated.

Secondary conditioning and advertising

Conditioning often builds upon affective reactions to *primary reinforcers*, such as shock or the taste of food, which are built into our brain circuits from birth. After conditioning occurs, previously meaningless events, like buzzer sounds and flashing lights, can elicit many of the internal emotional reactions of the primary reinforcers with which they are associated. When this happens, these events are said to become *conditioned reinforcers*. Talking about conditioned reinforcers is just another way of saying that classical and operant conditioning are possible.

Conditioned reinforcers do not exist just to amuse psychological experimentalists! They are crucial for survival. For example, the sight of food may not initially elicit any desire to eat in a baby, even if the taste or the smell of the food does. At birth, the baby may not know what food looks like, and different kinds of food have different appearances in different societies. By pairing the sight of food reliably with the taste of food, the sight of food can then elicit appetitive reactions, like approaching the food, salivation, reaching the food, and other preparations to eat. In the negative direction, if you are exposed to a unique situation in which something terrible occurs to you, then that situation, all by itself, can elicit extreme conditioned fear and other emotional reactions, such as learned helplessness, at least until you get a chance to extinguish these fearful reactions if the terrible event stops occurring in that situation. All the examples of learning from antagonistic rebounds are also examples of conditioned reinforcers at work.

More interesting possibilities can occur when conditioned reinforcers are used to condition yet other events that are initially affectively neutral. This process is called *secondary conditioning*. Using secondary conditioning, a whole *chain* of reinforcers can be established through iterated learning experiences. The sensory cues that define the conditioned reinforcers in the chain may be totally different from those of the original primary reinforcer, yet may still generate strong affective reactions. We experience the effects of such secondary reinforcement chains every day, since they are one foundation for the multi-billion dollar field of advertising: Many people associate the visual appearance of a sexually appealing person with primary sexual reinforcement during their lives. Seeing such people, or pictures of them, can generate sexual arousal. Advertising exploits such associations. An ad in which a car, bottle of cologne, or even a bottle of soda, appears with a picture of a sexually enticing person can be used to sell millions of dollars of cars, cologne, or soda based on secondary sexual arousal.

Gated dipole opponent processing: Arousal, habituation, and competition

What *is* sexual arousal, or any other sort of emotional arousal for that matter? We can begin to understand the need for some sort of emotional arousal by thinking more about emotional rebounds. Rebounds are events that can be triggered in our brains when an external event, like a shock or food source, is removed. The *offset* of such an external event triggers the rebound inside our brains. But there is, by definition, no *external* event to trigger the rebound, because the relevant external event has just shut off. There must therefore be an *internal* source of energy, or activation, that triggers the rebound after the external event shuts off. This internal source of activity is one type of arousal. Since we never know *when* an external event will shut off and trigger a rebound, this internal arousal source must be on all the time; that is, it is *tonically* active. But if it is on all the time, then why does it not cause rebounds to occur all the time?

Persistent rebounds are avoided because the arousal activates both of the channels in an opponent processing circuit, such as the one which controls fear and relief, as in Figure 1.14. These channels *compete* with each other before generating a net output, as was partially diagrammed in Figure 1.13. Only if there is more fear than relief, or conversely, do we experience a net emotion. In response to arousal alone, no net output may be generated after competition between the opponent channels takes place.

We are now ready to better understand how emotional rebounds are triggered in the brain. Only a few basic mechanisms, interacting together in the correct order within an opponent processing circuit, are needed to trigger rebounds and to learn from both primary and secondary reinforcers. This circuit is called a *gated dipole* for reasons that will soon become clear (Figure 1.14). I introduced the gated dipole design in 1972 when I was studying how punishment and avoidance work (Grossberg, 1972a, 1972b), but it gradually became clear that variations and

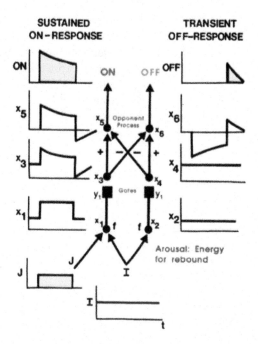

FIGURE 1.14. A gated dipole opponent process can generate a transient antagonistic rebound from its OFF channel in response to offset of an input (J) to its ON channel.

specializations of this circuit design occur all over the brain, in multiple modalities.

When an external event like a shock activates the fear channel (the ON channel in Figure 1.14), then the fear channel gets both a shock-induced input *and* an arousal input. The shock input is *phasic*; it turns on and off through time (see variable J in Figure 1.14). The arousal input is *tonic*; it is on all the time (see variable I in Figure 1.14). For simplicity, arousal is assumed to be constant through time, but in general it can change more slowly than the phasic inputs that it modulates. In contrast, the relief, or OFF, channel receives only the same tonic arousal input as does the ON channel. As a result, when the signals in the ON and OFF channels compete, the ON, or fear, channel wins the competition between the opponent channels, giving rise to a net output of fear. See the yellow output response labeled ON from the ON channel.

When the shock shuts off, both channels receive an equal tonic arousal input I. If both channels now get equal inputs, then why does a relief rebound occur after the shock shuts off?

Here is the main idea: As just described, when the shock input is on, the fear channel gets a larger total input than the relief channel. As a result, the fear channel gets desensitized, fatigued, or *habituated* more than the relief channel does when the shock input is on (see the square synapses labeled y_1 and y_2 in the ON and OFF channels of Figure 1.14). This form of activity-dependent desensitization is called *transmitter habituation*, or *synaptic*

depression. After the shock input shuts off, it takes awhile for the habituated fear channel to recover from the shock. Before it recovers, equal arousal inputs occur in the fear ON channel and the relief OFF channel. However, the fear channel is less sensitive to its arousal input than is the relief channel, due to its lingering greater degree of habituation. The arousal input to the *relief* channel can now generate a larger response than it can in the desensitized fear channel. After the channels compete, a net relief response is generated. This response is the emotional rebound to shock offset in the relief channel. It is the yellow response labeled OFF from the OFF channel.

Why does not the feeling of relief persist forever? Why is the relief rebound transient in time? The rebound lasts until habituation in the fear channel recovers from the previous shock input. When that happens, both channels exhibit the same degree of habituation in response to their equal arousal inputs. As a result, both channels can again respond equally to their arousal inputs and can equally inhibit one another, thereby terminating the relief rebound.

I have called a habituative opponent processing circuit, such as the one summarized in Figure 1.14, a *gated dipole* to emphasize that the habituative transmitters multiply, or *gate*, signals in a pair, or *dipole*, of opponent channels. Chapter 13 uses simple algebra to prove these properties of gated dipole ON and OFF responses. This analysis shows how interactions between the following simple processes, occurring in the correct order, generate these properties, as well as many others: phasic and tonic inputs, habituative transmitters that try to provide unbiased responses to their inputs while habituating to them, opponent competition, and output thresholding. Gated dipoles hereby provide compelling examples of how simple mechanisms, interacting together, can generate surprising emergent properties with profound implications for how our brains work in health and disease.

Short-term memory, medium-term memory, and long-term memory

The habituative process that helps to create an antagonistic rebound in a gated dipole is what I called *medium-term* memory, or MTM, in the book's Preface. MTM variables (variables y_1 and y_2 in Figure 1.14) change more slowly than the short-term memory (STM) traces, or activities, of the gated dipoles (variables x_1 through x_6 in Figure 1.14). The long-term memory (LTM) traces whereby cues become conditioned reinforcers through learning change on an even slower time scale than the MTM traces.

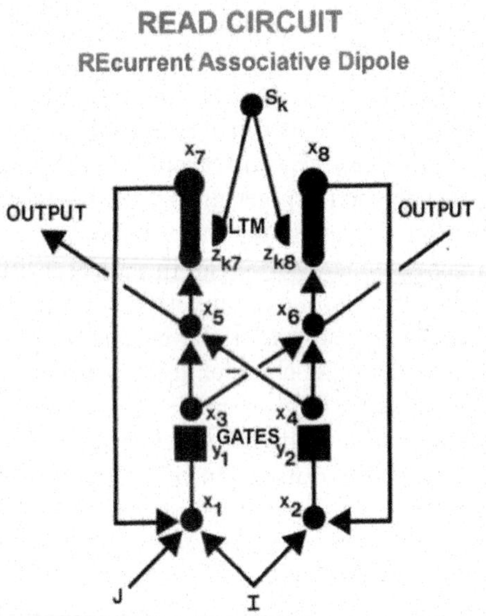

FIGURE 1.15. A recurrent associative dipole, or READ, circuit is a recurrent shunting on-center off-surround network with habituative transmitter gates. Sensory cues sample it with LTM traces and thereby become conditioned reinforcers.

When LTM traces are included in a gated dipole circuit (see Figure 1.15), it can learn positive and negative conditioned reinforcers in response to both phasic cue changes and to disconfirmed expectations. This circuit has recurrent, or feedback, pathways between the ON and OFF dipole channels; notably, the ON channel recurrent pathway from activity x_7 to x_1, and the OFF channel recurrent pathway from activity x_8 to x_2. These recurrent pathways convert the gated dipole into a recurrent on-center off-surround network that can maintain a motivational baseline in STM against momentary distractions, while also normalizing dipole activity across its opponent channels. This recurrent circuit also includes LTM traces (variables z_{k7} and z_{k8}) that can convert sensory CS cues (variables S_k) into secondary positive or negative reinforcers either directly in response to primary reinforcers, or due to antagonistic rebounds across the ON and OFF channels. Because of these new features, the entire circuit was called a REcurrent Associative Dipole, or READ, circuit when my postdoctoral fellow Nestor Schmajuk and I introduced it in 1987 (Grossberg and Schmajuk, 1987). The acronym READ summarizes the ability of the LTM traces to read-in and read-out the results of conditioned reinforcer learning.

The READ circuit illustrates that even simple circuits like opponent processing circuits that are capable of regulating classical and operant conditioning require interactions between STM, MTM, and LTM variables that change on three different time scales. What are the equations that STM, MTM, and LTM obey in the brain? I summarize the simplest versions of these equations and some of their most important functional properties in Chapter 2, where I will

also briefly describe the historical context in which these discoveries were made, including various of the leading scientists who contributed to it. Readers who want to hear me describe these laws, and how I discovered them when I was a Freshman at Dartmouth College in 1957-1958, might want to listen to the lecture that I gave when I received the 2015 Norman Anderson Lifetime Achievement Award by the Society of Experimental Psychologists (see YouTube, https://youtu.be/9n5AnvFur7I).

Drives, satiety, and starving for love

Gated dipole arousal is not the only internal input that energizes emotional behavior. For example, suppose that you got conditioned to the sight of food. Why do we not eat compulsively all day whenever we see any food? In particular, why do we not uncontrollably gorge ourselves every time that we pass a supermarket? Likewise, why do we not try to copulate with every attractive passerby on the street? Additional neural mechanisms are needed to control such inappropriate urges. When these mechanisms fail to work correctly, then uncontrollable eating and sexual exhibitionism *can* be elicited, and are known to occur in certain mental patients.

We all know that emotional behaviors do not occur with equal strength throughout the day. They can wax and wane in response to how changing external cues (like being in a restaurant, or in bed with your lover) interact with changing internal homeostatic cues (like being hungry, or feeling sexually aroused). Internal homeostatic inputs are often called *drive* inputs; see Figure 1.16 (left column). Distinct internal drive inputs energize eating, drinking, and sexual behaviors, among others. These drive inputs are delivered to emotional centers, such as the amygdala, and alter their sensitivity to the external cues that are represented in the sensory cortices, and which also send signals to the amygdala. Different parts of the amygdala, among other midbrain regions, such as the hypothalamus, are sensitive to different drive inputs and different sensory inputs (Figure 1.16, right column) with which to sensitize or desensitize them. For example, if you are hungry, hunger-inducing drive inputs become large, and sensitize eating circuits in the amygdala and hypothalamus to respond to sensory inputs from food and eating-related contexts. Eating can thereby be elicited. After eating a big meal, you can become satiated, and your hunger drive input can become small. These hunger and satiety signals oppose one another, just as fear and relief oppose one another in a gated dipole circuit (Figures 1.14 and 1.15). When the satiety signal gets large, you will ordinarily be less tempted to eat a lot even if food is presented.

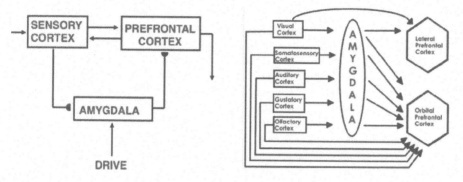

FIGURE 1.16. (left panel) The main processing stages of the Cognitive-Emotional-Motor (CogEM) model have anatomical interpretations in terms of sensory cortex, amygdala, and prefrontal cortex. Chapter 13 will describe in greater detail how CS cues activate invariant object categories in the sensory cortex, value categories in the amygdala, and object-value categories in the prefrontal cortex, notably the orbitofrontal cortex. The amygdala is also modulated by internal drive inputs like hunger and satiety. (right panel) Anatomical data support this circuit, as do many neurophysiological data.

This conclusion needs to be qualified with a lot of caveats, however. For example, the satiety drive input is derived from several factors, ranging from fast-acting signals that indicate how full the stomach currently is, so you do not eat until your stomach bursts, to more slowly-acting signals that reflect the digested metabolic contents of what has been eaten. The fast-acting satiety signal helps to explain why, if you are dieting and do not want to eat too much, drinking a big glass of water before eating food helps to eat less. We can nonetheless often "make room" for a delicious dessert even after eating a big meal. To understand how this happens, I will discuss more carefully below how drives interact with rewarding cues. In particular, we need to ask how a particular motivated behavior gets chosen when several different drives, such as hunger and sex, are simultaneously deprived.

What if you regularly eat a healthy diet, but have no lover or other sexual outlet at the moment? If your sex drive climbs higher than your hunger drive, why does this not prevent you from eating until you can have sex? Why do you not routinely "starve for love"?! One reason is that *both* internal drive inputs *and* external rewarding cues are needed to trigger motivated behaviors like eating. Even if sexual arousal is higher, it is not as effective in the absence of external sexual cues. It is the *combination* of external sensory cues and internal drive cues that control the competition to select a winning behavior, not the drives alone. I have called this sort of circuit a *sensory-drive heterarchy* (Figure 1.17, top row). Such a heterarchy behaves very differently than a *drive hierarchy* (Figure 1.17, bottom row) in which drives compete to determine a winner before the winning drive interacts with compatible external sensory cues.

If our brain circuits were designed to realize a drive hierarchy, then we *could* easily starve for love. In such a circuit, if your sex drive input was higher than your hunger drive input, the sex drive input could totally inhibit the hunger drive input at the competition stage, before sensory cues

could influence the competitive decision. Without any hunger drive input, however, sensory cues of food could not activate the incentive motivation that would be needed to elicit eating behavior (Figure 1.17, bottom row). Moving the competition one step later in the circuit design is sufficient to spare us from this grim fate. In a sensory-drive heterarchy circuit (Figure 1.17, top row), a lower but positive hunger drive input, supplemented by food sensory cues, could generate a larger *total* input to the competitive stage, thereby enabling incentive motivation for eating to win.

This example illustrates that a *specific order* of interacting processes is often needed to assure that our brain circuits work as well as they do. Brain circuits are emphatically not connected together in a random way! The sensory-drive heterarchy circuit also clarifies how we can "make room" for eating a dessert after we have already eaten a big main course. Even if the hunger drive input is then small, a large conditioned reinforcer sensory input from a delicious-looking dessert can again generate a large enough total sensory-plus-drive input to the competition stage to activate incentive motivation for eating.

In order to better understand how this works, we also need to ask: Why have not the conditioned reinforcer pathways for eating already habituated due to eating the main course of the meal? Here we need to acknowledge the genius of concocting a tempting dessert. A tempting

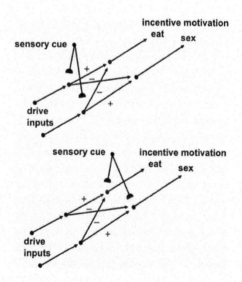

FIGURE 1.17. Sensory-drive heterarchy vs. drive hierarchy. How cues and drives interact to choose the drive and motivation that will control behavioral choices.

dessert often activates conditioned reinforcer pathways that have not yet habituated, say because it will activate a different combination of taste receptors than the main course. Of course, even a delicious-looking dessert can be declined if you feel "totally stuffed" when your drive input is strongly inhibited by fast-acting satiety signals.

The sensory-drive heterarchy protects us from eating so much that our stomachs burst by removing the drive to eat as we become satiated. On the other hand, it does not yet explain why we do not always immediately start eating if we are hungry in a supermarket. This kind of context-sensitive socialized behavior depends upon higher cognitive factors that include plans for preparing and eating dinner at home, and social learning about the contexts in which various kinds of behaviors are appropriate. Such higher factors, which are often controlled by circuits in the prefrontal cortex (Figure 1.16), can "put the brakes on" the purely sensory-drive constraints on behavior. Chapter 14 will explain how the prefrontal cortex learns cognitive plans that are sensitive to environmental context, and how these cognitive plans interact with affective processes that regulate emotion and motivation and to thereby determine whether and when it is appropriate to eat, or indeed to carry out just about any other reactive or learned behavior. For now, we need to focus on other problems that need to be addressed for even the sensory-drive heterarchy to work properly.

Golden Mean, Inverted U, and two types of emotional depression

We saw above that arousal needs to be tonically active in a gated dipole opponent processing circuit (Figure 1.14) so that rebounds can be triggered whenever they are needed. But how is the *level* of arousal chosen? What if it is chosen too small or too large? This is again a question of balance. If there is too little arousal, then there is not enough activation for the system to respond normally to external reinforcing cues. The system becomes *depressed* due to underarousal, and external inputs need to be bigger to compensate for the reduced arousal. In other words, the response *threshold* is elevated. This is not, in itself, surprising. However, a surprising property follows from the habituation process that causes rebounds to occur in the first place: If there is too little arousal, then when the size of external inputs exceeds the elevated response threshold, the system reacts in a *hyper*sensitive way to further increases in external input. Then abnormally large outputs can occur.

What happens if the arousal level is chosen too large? Not surprisingly, the response threshold is then reduced. However, if there is too much arousal, then it can

overwhelm external cues. The system then becomes *hypo*-sensitive to external cues: No matter how large external inputs get, they cannot generate big emotional outputs.

These abnormal hypersensitive and hyposensitive outputs are due to the habituative processes in a gated dipole, which have the effect of *dividing* the net dipole responses. Underarousal causes a small habituated level to occur. Dividing by a smaller number gives rise to a bigger, or hypersensitive, suprathreshold response. Overarousal causes a large habituated level to occur. Dividing by a larger number gives rise to a smaller, or hyposensitive, suprathreshold response.

Only if there is an intermediate amount of arousal, one that is sufficient to energize the system without overwhelming its external inputs, does the network respond optimally. This intermediate level of arousal realizes a kind of *Golden Mean* that balances between the two extremes or underarousal and overarousal. As Figure 1.18 illustrates, this Golden Mean defines an *Inverted-U* of responsiveness as a function of arousal, whereby behavior becomes depressed in both the underaroused and overaroused extremes, albeit in different ways.

This Golden Mean provides some scientific insight into why it is best to do everything in moderation . . . at least most of the time! We also need to keep in mind that the type of balance that helps to moderate our emotions is different from the one that helps us to learn quickly but stably in the manner explained by Adaptive Resonance Theory. Sorting out these different kinds of balanced processes is one of the tasks of this book.

How our brains find and maintain a Golden Mean, and do so every day of our lives, is one of the brain's most impressive accomplishments. Finding and maintaining this balance is a type of *homeostatic plasticity*, whereby the brain adaptively calibrates its most effective operating parameters as conditions change (Chandler and Grossberg, 2012; Turrigiano, 1999). If homeostatic plasticity could

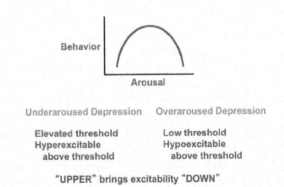

FIGURE 1.18. Inverted U as a function of arousal. A Golden Mean at intermediate levels of arousal generates a combination of behavioral threshold, sensitivity, and activation that can support typical behaviors. Both underarousal and overarousal lead to symptoms that are found in mental disorders.

be incorporated into future computer software and hardware that is designed to emulate biological intelligence, then these computers could continually retune themselves to cope both with short-term variations in daily processing demands, as well as to longer-term variations due to changes in operating parameters as the equipment ages or experiences modest breakdowns due to accidents and other traumas.

Affective neuroscience, mental disorders, and uppers that bring you down

Due to the difficulty of understanding how cognitive and emotional processes work together, practitioners of Artificial Intelligence, or AI, avoided dealing with emotional processes altogether for many years. They focused almost entirely on trying to understand thinking and related cognitive processes. Influential American psychologists like B. F. Skinner, who died in 1990, vigorously urged scientists not to waste their time trying to theorize about mental processes at all, and insisted that his colleagues spend all their time collecting experimental data. Noam Chomsky challenged Skinner's viewpoint in 1959, in response to Skinner's book *Verbal Behavior*, which attempted to provide an analysis of language from the perspective of operant conditioning. Chomsky's critique helped to trigger the Cognitive Revolution, which attracted increasing numbers of psychologists who began in earnest to study cognitive processes. This led to the formation of the Cognitive Science Society in 1979. Now cognitive science is a field in which cognitive modeling is actively practiced, although often without a serious link to underlying brain processes.

More recently, an increasing number of scientists began to study how emotional processes work. This field is now often called Affective Computing, or Affective Neuroscience, depending on whether the emphasis is on technology or on how the brain works. In Affective Neuroscience, experimental neuroscientists, such as the contemporary American neuroscientists, Joseph LeDoux (LeDoux, 1996) and Antonio Damasio (Damasio, 1999), have written interesting books about their laboratory experiments and clinical experiences with emotional processes. The contemporary American engineer, Rosalind Picard (Picard, 1997), has written about progress towards designing wearable sensors and other devices that are sensitive to people's emotional responses. Even more recently, big companies like Google have invested in this kind of technology. Few of these people, however, have modeled how cognition and emotion interact in the brain or, more generally, how to theoretically link brain mechanisms to psychological functions.

My own work began to model how cognition and emotion interact when I realized in the late 1960s that cognition and emotion obey similar laws, albeit in response to different combinations of inputs. This similarity helps the two types of processes to interact seamlessly with one another, thereby enabling our emotions to direct our thoughts and actions towards achieving motivationally valued cognitive goals. I will continue to discuss below how cognitive and emotional processes work together to enable us to quickly learn how to realize valued goals and to escape dangerous situations, and to explain how this may happen in our brains.

I will also illustrate how, when the balance that maintains the Golden Mean gets upset in the brain, then symptoms of mental disorders can arise. In particular, properties of underaroused and overaroused depression, at least in the specific sense that is realized within a gated dipole (Figure 1.18), can clarify symptoms of attention deficit hyperactivity disorder (ADHD), schizophrenia, and autism. This analysis clarifies, for example, why a pharmacological "upper" like amphetamine, which is a speed-like drug, may help children with ADHD by bringing them "down". I propose that many of these children are *under*aroused and thus *hyper*sensitive when their elevated response thresholds are exceeded. The upper drug increases their arousal, bringing them closer to the Golden Mean of their Inverted-U, and thereby desensitizes them.

Such properties clarify why it is so hard to understand various mental disorders. They seem often to be due to problems of *imbalance*, and their symptoms are emergent, or interactive, properties of networks of interacting nerve cells with imbalanced components of various kinds. Before one can understand these imbalances, one first needs to understand how the brain achieves the various types of balance that characterize normal behaviors. I will

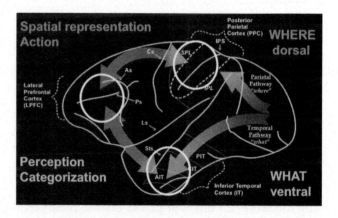

FIGURE 1.19. The ventral What stream is devoted to perception and categorization. The dorsal Where stream is devoted to spatial representation and action. The Where stream is also often called the Where/How stream because of its role in the control of action.

explain how these properties of gated dipoles arise and lead to symptoms of various mental disorders in Chapter 13, including that various individuals with autism may have underaroused emotional dipoles, whereas individuals with schizophrenia may have overaroused ones.

Two types of learning: Perceiving and knowing vs. moving and navigating

The cognitive and emotional processes of thinking and feeling are necessary for our survival, but they become fully effective only if they can lead to appropriate actions in space. Moving an arm under visual guidance to grasp an object, or to defend against an attack, or to carry out a dance gesture, involves figuring out where in space we want our arm to move and how fast we want it to get there. Years of learning are needed in order to flexibly plan and fluently execute such movements. Because our bodies grow so much from the time we are infants until we become adults, the spatial relationships between our eyes and our arms keep changing for many years. Our brains therefore need to keep recalibrating the maps that determine where to move an arm to an object in space that we want to grasp. In addition to recalibrating *where* to move, additional circuits recalibrate *how* to get there by compensating for the changing weight of our arms and the amount of force that they can generate during the execution of motor commands. Very different forces are, for example, needed to successfully move a feather or a boulder to the same position in space. Even working out at the gym can change these "how to do it" parameters by altering the amount of force that our limbs can generate.

Given that our motor systems use learning to work well throughout life, we need to ask: Is the type of learning that goes on during perception and cognition, whereby we learn to understand the world, the same as the spatial and motor learning, whereby we can plan and execute a movement? The answer is No, and for a very basic reason.

Perceptual and cognitive learning need to solve the stability-plasticity dilemma, so that we can continue to learn more and more about the world throughout life, and become expert about increasing numbers of topics, without experiencing catastrophic forgetting. In contrast, we do not want to remember into adulthood the spatial relationships and motor commands that we learned in order to move our infant arms and bodies. These infant commands are totally inappropriate for moving our much larger and stronger adult limbs. Catastrophic forgetting is a *good* property during spatial and motor learning, since it is adaptive to forget old spatial relationships and motor commands, and to remember only the new learning that is suited to moving our limbs in our bodies as they exist today. When these two types of learning work together in the brain, perceptual and cognitive representations can learn more and more about the world in a stable way, even as they control the read-out of learned spatial relationships and motor commands that are continually updated in response to our changing bodies. I sometimes like to think of the difference between a plan to move and how to get there as a modern version of the difference between a Platonic Ideal and the Newtonian forces that are needed to realize the idealized plan.

What and Where cortical processing streams and consciousness

These two types of learning, perceptual/cognitive vs. spatial/motor, typically go on in different brain systems. In the early 1980s, Mortimer Mishkin, Leslie Ungerleider, and their colleagues (e.g., Mishkin, Ungerleider, and Macko, 1983) noted that there are two distinct processing streams, or pathways, in the cerebral cortex of the mammalian brain. The *ventral stream* processes information that enables us to perceive and recognize objects. It is accordingly called the What processing stream. The *dorsal stream* processes information about where objects are in space and how to act upon them. It is accordingly called the Where processing stream, and also the How processing stream after the work of Melvyn Goodale and David Milner in the early 1990s (e.g., Goodale and Milner, 1992) about the role of the dorsal stream in spatial representation and action.

Figure 1.19 illustrates these two streams. I will suggest below how key aspects of learning in the two streams differ, notably that processing in these streams seems to obey *computationally complementary* laws. As noted above, the word "complementary" means that the properties in one stream are related to those in the other stream in much the same way as a key fits into a lock, or as pieces in a puzzle fit together. Complementarity implies the need to *balance* the capabilities of each stream against those of the other.

Only one of these two types of processing is capable of supporting conscious experiences. Although we can be consciously aware of our perceptual and cognitive experiences, we do not have the same sort of conscious representation of a motor command. A motor command does not support conscious sensations like the brightness of an object or the pitch of a sound. We can consciously *will* a motor command to occur by an act of volition. But this is not the same thing as consciously experiencing the internal representation of the command itself. This difference in conscious awareness will be traced below to differences in how we process and learn about these two types of experiences. Indeed, I will suggest that the learning process that solves the stability-plasticity dilemma is controlled by *resonant* brain states that can support conscious mental experiences; hence, the title of this book. Motor learning does not solve the stability-plasticity dilemma, does not utilize resonant dynamics, and hence does not support a conscious experience.

Two revolutionary paradigms: Complementary Computing and Laminar Computing

These comments about computationally complementary properties illustrate one of the revolutionary computational paradigms that are needed to understand how brains give rise to minds, and whose importance cannot be overemphasized. These paradigms embody computational constraints that any general-purpose autonomous intelligent system, not just brains, need in order to self-organize adaptive behaviors in response to a changing world. Students of physics may notice that these paradigms include processes that seem to have analogs in modern physical theories, such as principles of complementarity, uncertainty, and resonance. I will comment about why this may be below, and will offer a more detailed discussion in Chapter 17. If my view is correct, then it points to future progress in the development of physical theory that will enable theories of mind and brain to be better assimilated into a more unified physical theory of the external world.

Complementary processing streams for perception/ cognition and space/action. I have called this paradigm Complementary Computing because it describes how the brain is organized into complementary parallel processing streams whose interactions generate biologically intelligent behaviors. A single cortical processing stream can individually compute some properties well, but cannot, by itself, process other computationally complementary properties. *Pairs* of complementary cortical processing streams interact, using multiple processing stages, to generate emergent properties that overcome their complementary deficiencies to compute complete information with which to represent or control some faculty of intelligent behavior. Table 1.1 lists some of these pairs of complementary streams.

For example, as noted in the previous section, processes of object attention, category learning, recognition,

TABLE 1.1. Some pairs of complementary cortical processing streams.

SOME COMPLEMENTARY PROCESSES	
Visual Boundary	Visual Surface
Interblob Stream V1-V2-V4	Blob Stream V1-V2-V4
Visual Boundary	Visual Motion
Interblob Stream V1-V2-V4	Magno Stream V1-MT-MST
WHAT Steam	WHERE Stream
Perception & Recognition	Space & Action
Inferotemporal and Prefrontal areas	Parietal and Prefrontal areas
Object Tracking	Optic Flow Navigation
MT⁻ Interbands and MSTv	MT⁺ Bands and MSTd
Motor Target Position	Volitional Speed
Motor and Parietal Cortex	Basal Ganglia

and prediction are part of the ventral, or What, cortical processing stream for perception and cognition. The ventral stream exhibits properties that are often computationally complementary to those of the dorsal, or Where and How, cortical processing steam for spatial representation and action. One reason for this What-Where complementarity is that the What stream learns object recognition categories that are substantially invariant under changes in an object's view, size, and position. These invariant object categories enable our brains to recognize a valued object quickly, and without experiencing the combinatorial explosion that could occur if we needed to search individual exemplars of the object in order to recognize it. However, because they are invariant, these categories cannot locate and act upon a desired object in space. Where stream spatial and motor representations can locate objects and trigger actions towards them, but cannot recognize them. By interacting together, the What and Where streams can recognize valued objects *and* direct appropriate goal-oriented actions towards them. How this happens will be explained in Chapter 6.

Table 1.2 summarizes basic complementary properties of the What and Where cortical streams. As will be discussed in Chapter 5, perceptual/cognitive processes in the What stream often use ART-like *excitatory matching* and *match-based learning* to create self-stabilizing categorical representations of objects and events that solve the stability-plasticity dilemma. They thereby enable increasing expertise, and an ever-expanding sense of self, to emerge throughout life.

Table 1.2 also shows that complementary spatial/motor processes in the Where stream often use *inhibitory matching*

TABLE 1.2. The What and Where cortical processing streams obey computationally complementary laws. These laws enable the What stream to rapidly and stably learn invariant object categories without experiencing catastrophic forgetting, while the Where stream learns labile spatial and action representations to control actions that are aimed towards these objects.

WHAT	WHERE
Spatially-invariant object learning and recognition	Spatially-variant reaching and movement
Fast learning without catastrophic forgetting	Continually update sensory-motor maps and gains
IT	PPC

	WHAT	WHERE
MATCHING	EXCITATORY	INHIBITORY
LEARNING	MATCH	MISMATCH

and *mismatch-based learning* to continually update spatial maps and motor controllers that can effectively control our changing bodies throughout life. As explained in Chapter 12, inhibitory matching can take place by subtracting from a representation of where we want to move one that computes where we are now. When we arrive at where we want to be, these two representations code for the same position in space, so the match equals zero. This kind of inhibitory matching cannot solve the stability-plasticity dilemma, and thus spatial and motor learning does experience catastrophic forgetting. This is a good property when it occurs during spatial and motor learning, because we need to forget the spatial maps and motor control parameters that were used to move our bodies when we were younger, so that they can continue to learn how to accurately move our changing bodies throughout life. Likewise, because excitatory matching is needed to generate resonances that support conscious internal representations, spatial and motor memories, which are often called *procedural memories* (Cohen and Squire, 1980; Scoville and Milner, 1957; Squire and Cohen, 1984), cannot generate conscious internal representations.

Together these complementary processes create a self-stabilizing perceptual/cognitive front end in the What stream for learning about the world and becoming conscious of it, while it intelligently commands more labile spatial/motor processes in the Where stream that control our changing bodies. Thus, if only due to the complementary organization of the brain, ART is not "a theory of everything".

Our bilateral brains use cerebral dominance to do complementary computing: Split brains. The fact that cognitive and motor processes use computationally complementary laws occurs within a body that exhibits bilateral symmetry, with two (approximately) symmetrically placed eyes, arms, and legs, and a brain that is divided into two communicating halves to control it. If both halves of the brain equally well controlled cognitive and motor processes, that would be both redundant and a possible source of confusion in determining which half would have its say.

This bilateral symmetry is, however, known not to be perfect. For example, some people are right handed and some left handed. This broken symmetry is sometimes referred to as *cerebral dominance*, with the right half of the brain controlling the left half of the body, and conversely. John Hughlings Jackson was perhaps the first neurologist to comment on cerebral dominance in 1874 (Jackson, 1874).

It has also been known for a long time that the left half of the brain is more involved in the control of more analytic *temporal* processes such as speech and language, calculating, reading, and writing, whereas the right half of the brain is more involved in the control of more holistic *spatial* processes such as navigating a maze, judging visual distance or direction, and recognizing visual scenes and auditory tones. Chapters 3-5, 9, and 11 will, among others, discuss basic spatial processes that are involved in seeing, recognizing, and navigating, and Chapter 12, among others, will discuss basic processes that are involved in speech, language, and other sequentially controlled behaviors.

These biases do not imply that the non-dominant hemisphere has no role to play in carrying out the processes of the dominant hemisphere. Rather, I have found it helpful to think of cerebral dominance as a kind of *symmetry-breaking* whereby higher cortical areas in one of the hemispheres may be more devoted to spatial or temporal processing, respectively. Indeed, one can perfectly well see through either eye, but higher-order spatial processing may be elaborated in the right hemisphere of a right-handed person.

The subsequent chapters will explain that the mechanisms which *reset* spatial and temporal representations are different. Indeed, both spatial inputs such as visual images, and temporal inputs such as lists of items that are experienced one at a time, are transformed by our brains into *spatial patterns of activation* at higher processing stages. The distinct spatial and temporal reset mechanisms convert these spatial activity patterns into either spatial or temporal rehearsals. This kind of mechanistic specialization casts additional light on why cerebral dominance has evolved.

Fascinating data about cerebral dominance have been collected since the pioneering studies of Roger Sperry and his student Michael Gazzaniga (Gazzaniga, 1967; Sperry, 1964) from *split brain* patients. In these patients, the corpus callosum that connects their two hemispheres is severed, so that communication between the two hemispheres is greatly reduced. As a result, Sperry could write in his 1964 famous review that "if the connections are cut, the organism functions quite well but behaves much as though it had two brains". For example, a typical split brain patient who is exposed to flashing lights in the left visual field, which projects to the right hemisphere, cannot report that experience using language because speech processing is dominant in the left hemisphere. Sperry was awarded the Nobel Prize in Physiology or Medicine in 1981 for this discovery, and Gazzaniga went on to become a key founder of the field of cognitive neuroscience. Mike Gazzaniga and I actually graduated from Dartmouth College in the same 1961 class, and have reminisced about how we used to sit near each other in large exam rooms where student seats were assigned in alphabetical order.

Laminar neocortical circuits to represent higher-order biological intelligence. A second revolutionary computational paradigm is called Laminar Computing. Laminar Computing describes how the entire cerebral cortex is organized into layered circuits whose specializations support all higher-order biological intelligence (Figure 1.20). The laminar circuits realize a revolutionary computational synthesis that has been shown, in a series of my articles since 1999, to combine properties of feedforward and feedback processing, digital and analog processing, and data-driven bottom-up processing and hypothesis-driven top-down processing (Grossberg, 2007b, 2013a, 2017a, 2017b). ART mechanisms have, to the present, been naturally embodied in laminar cortical models of vision, speech, and cognition, specifically in the 3D LAMINART model of 3D vision and figure-ground separation (see Chapter 11), the cARTWORD model of speech perception (see Chapter 12), and the LIST PARSE model of cognitive working memory and planning (see Chapter 12). Each model uses variations of the same canonical laminar cortical circuitry, thereby providing additional insights into how specialized resonances use similar types of circuits to support different conscious experiences. By showing how different kinds of intelligence can be realized using variations of the same laminar circuit design, these models also clarify how different kinds

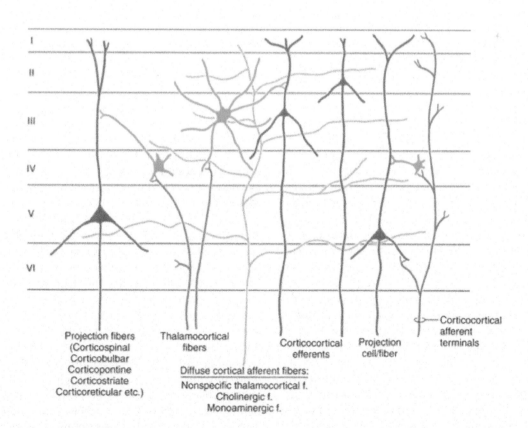

FIGURE 1.20. A schematic cross-section of a slice of laminar neocortex whose cells are organized in a characteristic way in six layers, which themselves may be organized into distinct sublaminae. The computational paradigm of Laminar Computing attempts to show how different parts of neocortex can represent and control very different kinds of behavior —including vision, speech, and cognition—using specializations of the same canonical laminar cortical design.

of intelligent computation can be joined together into a larger autonomous adaptive system, whether that system is the brain or a VLSI chip that controls an intelligent agent in technology.

Complementary Computing vs. Independent Modules

Before properties of complementary computing were discovered, many scientists believed that our brains possess different kinds of information using *independent modules*, as in a digital computer. An independent module may be thought of as a little piece of computing machinery that is very good at processing one type of information. Such modules are "specialists" or "experts" at doing a limited task, and intelligent behavior was proposed to arise from the collective action of many such specialists. For example, it was proposed that we see by separately processing perceptual qualities such as luminance, motion, binocular disparity, color, and texture, using independent brain modules, and then somehow put all of these qualities together to derive a unified visual percept.

The brain does have many regions that carry out specialized functions, but this does not imply that they are independent modules. As illustrated in Figure 0.1, the brain is organized in parallel processing streams. This is true at all levels of brain organization, including vision. The simplified circuit diagram in Figure 1.21, which was published by Edgar DeYoe and David van Essen in 1988 (DeYoe and van Essen, 1988), shows that the processing of visual stimuli uses at least three processing streams, one through the V1 blobs, another through the V1 interblobs, and the third through V1 layer 4B. These streams, in turn, influence higher-level What and Where cortical regions such as inferotemporal cortex (IT) and posterior parietal cortex (PPC) in multiple ways (Figure 1.19).

Proponents of "independent modules" have looked to such processing streams to support their proposal. The existence of processing streams certainly supports the idea that brain processing is *specialized*, but it does not imply that these streams contain independent modules. Independent modules should be able to fully compute their particular processes on their own. As I noted in the Preface, much perceptual data over the last century argue against such independence, because strong interactions are known to occur between perceptual qualities. In particular, changes in perceived form or color can cause changes in perceived motion, and conversely. Changes in perceived brightness can cause changes in perceived depth, and conversely. Just making an object in a picture brighter can make it look closer, relative to other objects in the scene, a property that was called *proximity-luminance*

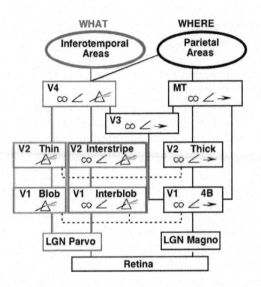

FIGURE 1.21. At least three parallel visual cortical streams respond to visual inputs that reach the retina. Two parvocellular streams process visual surfaces (blob stream) and visual boundaries (interblob stream). The magnocellular stream processes visual motion.

covariance by Barry Schwartz and George Sperling in 1983, and by Barbara Dosher, Sperling, and Stephen Wurst in 1986 (Dosher, Sperling, and Wurst, 1986; Schwartz and Sperling, 1983). How and why do these qualities interact? An answer to this question is needed to determine the functional and computational units that govern behavior as we know it.

I have proposed that the brain's organization is much more interesting than a collection of independent modules, and that these processing streams compute computationally *complementary* properties. Table 1.1 lists some of the pairs of brain processes (in each row) that our neural models assert to be computationally complementary, along with where they occur in the brain.

Each of these pairs of processes exhibits complementary strengths and weaknesses. For example, Table 1.1 (top row) asserts that visual boundaries and surfaces are complementary. These are the processing streams that are marked in red and green, respectively in Figure 1.21. How do their complementary properties get synthesized into a unified behavioral experience? Our neural models have shown how appropriately designed *interactions* between these processes overcome their complementary deficiencies and generate psychological properties that realize the unity of conscious experiences. These interactions occur between many thousands of nerve cells, in multiple processing stages, through time. That is one reason why efforts to link brain to mind have been so difficult: The functional units that control emergent behaviors are not easy to localize in the brain. Instead, *pairs of complementary processing streams* are the brain's functional units, because only through their interactions can key psychological properties be competently computed.

Analogies like a key fitting its lock, or puzzle pieces fitting together, albeit suggestive, do not fully capture the dynamism of what complementarity means in the brain. Chapter 3 will begin to clarify what complementarity means by explaining why and how visual boundaries and surfaces obey complementary laws, and how they interact to overcome their computationally complementary deficiencies.

Hierarchical resolution of uncertainty and complementary consistency

Figures 0.1 and 1.21 illustrate that the brain often needs several processing stages to form a processing stream. Why is this necessary? Accumulating evidence supports my prediction that these stages realize a process of *hierarchical resolution of uncertainty*. "Uncertainty" is often due to the fact that computing one set of properties at a given stage can suppress information about a complementary set of properties at that stage. These uncertainties are overcome by using more than one processing stage to recover these lost properties. These several processing stages together form a processing stream. Overcoming informational uncertainty thus utilizes both hierarchical interactions within each stream and parallel interactions between streams to overcome their complementary deficiencies. When these uncertainties are overcome, the brain has achieved a consistent solution of an environmental problem. I like to summarize this state of affairs by saying that the brain has then achieved *complementary consistency*.

Given this background, if a friend asks you why there are so many processing stages in the brain, one pithy answer is: to achieve Complementary Consistency!

Complementarity and uncertainty principles also arise in physics, notably in quantum mechanics. Since brains form part of the physical world, and interact ceaselessly with it to adapt to environmental challenges, it is perhaps not surprising that brains also obey principles of complementarity and uncertainty. Indeed, each brain is a measurement device for recording and analyzing events in the physical world. In fact, the human brain can detect even small numbers of the photons that give rise to percepts of light, and is tuned just above the noise level of phonons that give rise to percepts of sound.

Experimental and theoretical evidence will be summarized in several chapters in support of the hypothesis that principles of complementarity and uncertainty that are realized within processing streams, such as those summarized in Table 1.1, better explain the brain's functional organization than concepts about independent modules. Given this conclusion, we need to ask: If the brain and the physical world are both organized according to such principles, then in what way is the brain *different* from the types of physical theories that are already well-known? Why haven't good theoretical physicists already "solved" the brain using known physical theories?

Differences between physical and brain measurements: Self-organization

The progress of physical theory during the past few centuries has led to a progressively deeper understanding of how we know the world through physical measurements. In Newton's mechanics, events were measured within *absolute* spatial and temporal coordinates, and instantaneous action at a distance was permitted. In Einstein's Special Relativity Theory, the finite velocity of light was shown to have important effects on physical measurements (Einstein, 1905). Measurements of one system by another system were shown as a result to depend on their *relative* motion. Quantum Mechanics carried the theory of measurement even further by showing that the particles used to carry out measurements could influence the results of such measurements, thereby creating unavoidable measurement uncertainties that were summarized in the Uncertainty Principle of Werner Heisenberg (Heisenberg, 1927). The Uncertainty Principle identified complementary variables, such as the position and momentum of a particle, that could not both be measured with perfect precision. In all of these theories, however, the measurer who was initiating and recording measurements remained outside the measurement process.

When we try to understand the brain, this is no longer possible. The brain *is* the measurement device, and the process of understanding mind and brain is the study of how brains measure the world. The measurement process is hereby brought into physical theory to an unprecedented degree. As a result of their measurement processes, brains can alter their structure, through development and learning, in response to the signals that they are measuring, and do so at a remarkably rapid rate. Brains can also unify into coherent moments of conscious experience within a unified self measurements taken from multiple physical sources—light, sound, pressure, temperature, bodily biochemical processes, and the like. The brain is thus a *universal self-organizing measurement system* of the world, and in the world.

As such, advanced brains play a role in biology that is reminiscent of the role played in physics by the law of black-body radiation that was described in 1900 by the great German physicist and Nobel Laureate Max Planck (http://en.wikipedia.org/wiki/Black-body_radiation). This law describes a radiation spectrum that is universal across all matter, and ushered in the revolution of Quantum Theory that rapidly developed into Quantum Mechanics. Since brains are also universal measurement devices, how do they differ from these more classical physical ideas? I believe that it is the brain's ability to rapidly *self-organize*, through development and life-long learning, that sets it apart from previous physical theories. The brain thus represents a new frontier in measurement theory for the physical sciences, no less than the biological sciences. It remains to be seen how physical theories will develop to increasingly incorporate concepts about the self-organization of matter, and how these theories will be related to the special case of brain self-organization.

Universal designs for self-organizing measurement and prediction systems

Implicit in these conclusions is the fact that the principles, mechanisms, and architectures that are derived, explained, and applied in this book are about fundamental problems of measurement, and about how a self-organizing measurement system can successfully represent and predict outcomes in a changing world. Mind and brain data are successfully explained and predicted by these theories because brains are a natural computational embodiment of these principles, mechanisms, and architectures. These ingredients can also equally be applied to the design and implementation of future autonomous adaptive intelligent agents of multiple kinds.

Is the conscious present in the physical past?

Measurements of the world occur in both space and time. When we have a conscious experience of the world, it is often so vivid that it seems to define the here-and-now. After all, if conscious experiences do not define what is happening to us now, then what does? In reality, however, many events that we are conscious of now often actually occurred a tenth, or even a fifth, of a second ago. This may

not sound like a very long time at first, but when you think about the fact that the neurons of the brain operate ten to one hundred times faster than that, it becomes quite a paradox. It is also a little strange to realize that the words that you are saying in a conversation now will not be consciously heard by the listener until 50 to 150 milliseconds later, and that the same is true about the words that they are saying to you. This fact alone suggests that we do not "directly" hear the acoustic signals that are in the world. How, and why, do our conscious percepts of sound differ from these acoustic signals? In particular, to what extent are our conscious percepts of speech and language auditory illusions?

Phonemic restoration and stable learning about a changing world

A famous example of such a delay in conscious awareness during the perception of speech and language was described by the American psychologist Richard Warren and his colleagues starting in 1970. It is called *phonemic restoration*. In the study of Richard and Roslyn Warren in that year (Warren and Warren, 1970), the spectrogram of the word "legislatures" (Figure 1.22, top row) is manipulated. In one manipulation, a phoneme such as the first /s/ in the word "legislatures" is excised, and replaced by broad-band noise. Broad-band noise includes all sound frequencies within the audible range (Figure 1.22, bottom row). Then the excised phoneme is perceived by listeners as being present and intact in the stimulus. When the phoneme is removed and simply replaced by silence (Figure 1.22, middle row), then the silent gap is perceived and no such restoration occurs. The exact cues that determined these percepts were not fully controlled in cases where "legislatures" was presented as part of a sentence such as "The state governors met with their respective *legislatures* convening in the capital city".

Additional experiments showed that the phoneme that is restored, and consciously heard, depends only on acoustic signals that arrive *after* the broad-band noise is presented, thereby strikingly illustrating how conscious percepts can depend upon events that occur later in time. For example, Richard Warren and Gary Sherman showed this in 1974 (Warren and Sherman, 1974). Their study considers two words, 'delivery' and 'deliberation', that are contextually neutral until the /v/ or /b/. Before presentation of /v/ or /b/, the initial portions of the two words, 'deli' are virtually indistinguishable and do not contain sufficient coarticulatory information to predict whether /v/ or /b/ will follow. After presentation of 'deli', /v/ and /b/ are both deleted and

Normal presentation

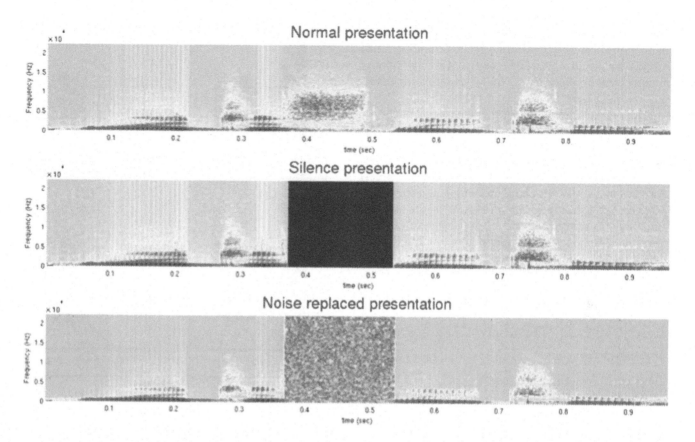

Silence presentation

Noise replaced presentation

FIGURE 1.22. A classical example of phonemic restoration. The spectrogram of the word "legislatures" is either excised, leaving a silent interval, or filled with broad-band noise. A percept of the restored phoneme is heard when it is replaced by noise, but not by silence.

replaced by broad-band noise. The 'deli#' speech segment is then followed by either 'ery' or 'eration'. Presentation of 'ery' results in the perceptual restoration of the phoneme /v/, whereas presentation of 'eration' results in the restoration of the phoneme /b/. This does not, however, happen if the deleted segments are not replaced by noise.

How does a future disambiguating cue ('y' or 'ation' in 'delivery' and 'deliberation', respectively) influence the earlier ambiguous stimulus 'deli#' in such a way that a different restored word, 'delivery' or 'deliberation', respectively, can be consciously heard in the correct temporal order, and without interfering with the conscious perception of the intervening word segment 'er'? Why does this not happen if there is no noise?

This type of auditory illusion is a percept that we consciously *hear*—it is a *phonemic* restoration effect—and is not just due to a symbolic hypothesis about the meaning of the sentence. The evidence for this conclusion was strengthened by the American psychologist Arthur Samuel during the 1980s; e.g., Samuel (1981a, 1981b). Samuel showed that, if the noise does not contain all the frequencies of the expected sound, then the restored sound will be distorted to include only the frequencies in the noise that are part of the expected sound. Thus, our brains can *select* the

expected sound from a noise that contains it, but cannot *create* a new sound out of silence. That is why, when silence replaces noise—as when only 'deli ery' or 'deli eration' is presented—only silence is heard in the position of the missing phoneme /v/ or /b/, since silence contains no frequencies that can be selected, so no phonemic restoration is possible.

Warren and Sherman (1974) also demonstrated a role for sentence context in phonemic restoration. During a typical experiment of this kind, a listener may hear a broad-band noise /#/ followed immediately by the rapidly uttered words "eel was on the . . . ". If the next word after "the" is "wagon", and all the words are uttered quickly enough, then the listener hears "wheel" instead of "#eel" in the sentence "wheel was on the wagon". Likewise, if the last word is "shoe", the listener hears the sentence "heel was on the shoe". If the last word is "orange", the listener hears "peel was on the orange". And so on. Thus, although the noise is received by the brain several words before the last word of the sentence was received, the listener may not consciously hear the noise. Rather, the listener may consciously hear the sound that is *expected* based on his or her past learning experiences with the English language. This example again shows that future sounds can influence the past sounds that we consciously hear, and that the meaning of an entire sentence can disambiguate, or restore, heard sounds that would otherwise be lost in noise. This is clearly an important benefit when we try to hear anything in this noisy world of ours.

This example provides further evidence that phonemic restoration is a *phonemic* restoration effect, and is not just due to a symbolic hypothesis about the meaning of the sentence. In particular, if the noise is replaced by an interval of silence in sentences like "eel is on the table" or "eel is on the shoe", then the entire meaning of the sentence is changed. We do not infer the word "meal" in the first case and "heel" in the second. In fact, the sentence "eel is on the shoe" is heard just as it is said, and we understand it to have a rather disgusting meaning that is totally different from the meaning of "heel is on the shoe".

Learned expectations again! Resonance between item chunks and list chunks

Phonemic restoration shows that we are often not consciously aware of the raw signals that enter our brains. These signals initially activate cells at multiple processing stages of the brain in a bottom-up way; that is, in a way that proceeds from the outside world ever deeper into the brain. Figure 1.23 schematizes in a simplified way how two of these stages might react as a sequence of items x, y, and z is stored in a working memory through time. At first, the items are stored through time in working memory as an evolving *spatial pattern* of activity (cf. Figure 1.6) across *item categories*, or *item chunks*, that respond selectively to each (Figure 1.23a, lower processing level). As these item categories are activated through time, they generate bottom-up signals to the next processing level, where *list categories*, or *list chunks*, are activated that respond selectively to particular sequences of item chunks in working memory. Bottom-up interactions are also said to be *feedforward* interactions. Figure 1.23a schematizes in a simple way the case where item chunks 'x' and 'y' are stored and activate list chunk 'xy' strongly while only weakly activating, or priming, the list chunk 'xyz'. The list chunk 'xyz' is at most weakly activated because item chunk 'z' is not yet stored in working memory. There is thus insufficient evidence to strongly activate chunk 'xyz'.

After list chunk 'xy' is activated, it sends learned top-down expectation signals back to the working memory (Figure 1.23b) where they select and amplify the activities of the item chunks 'x' and 'y'. Such a top-down expectation is also called a *feedback* signal to the working memory.

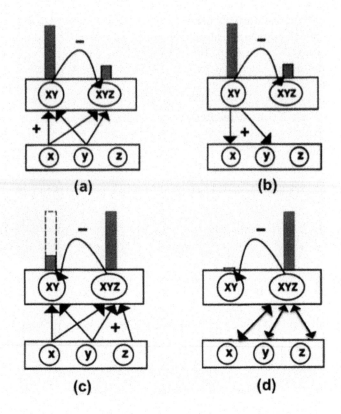

FIGURE 1.23. As more items are stored in working memory through time, they can select larger chunks with which to represent the longer list of stored items.

As these events unfold through time, additional items may be stored in working memory, such as item 'z', thereby enabling all the item chunks 'x', 'y', and 'z' to send bottom-up signals to the corresponding list chunks (Figure 1.23c). Now the list chunk 'xyz' does have enough inputs to fire vigorously and to thereby quickly begin to inhibit list chunk 'xy', as well as list chunks for all other subsets of the list, while it also sends top-down expectation signals to the working memory (Figure 1.23d). Now the working memory item chunks 'x', 'y', and 'z' can send bottom-up excitatory signals to the list chunk 'xyz', while they also receive top-down excitatory signals from 'xyz'. This mutual exchange of excitatory feedback signals persists long enough to reinforce the activities of all the affected chunks, thereby leading to a state of *resonance*.

This simplified circuit shows how, in response to an evolving sequence of inputs through time, list chunks are selected to provide the most predictive representation of the items that are currently stored in working memory. Figure 1.23 illustrates only the simple case of two levels of processing, and one in which list items are not repeated, as they are in many behaviors, whether in words like 'mama' or sentences like "Maybe I may be a mayor" and "Dog eats dog", or sequences of skilled actions that repeat a gesture, or navigational movements that repeat a right turn at different street corners in an urban environment. Three level circuits can easily overcome both limitations, as illustrated in Figure 1.24. This kind of circuit will be explained more completely in Chapter 12. For the present, it suffices to make the following comments:

Each of the three levels has a similar circuit design, which is called an Item-Order-Rank, or IOR, working memory that can store arbitrary sequences of item chunks in working memory, including item chunks that are repeated at different positions in a sequence, such as ABACBD. Such repeats are said to have different "ranks", hence the name Item-Order-Rank.

The upper two IOR working memories are also called Masking Fields because they are IOR working memories that can stored *sequences* of item chunks, as in the second level of Figure 1.23. However, the list chunks in a Masking Field IOR can selectively respond to sequences of variable lengths, and can also store sequences with repeated chunks. Their different processing capabilities are determined by their different positions in the hierarchy of processing stages, even though each processing level is built from a similar circuit design.

In particular, each of the three levels is activated by a bottom-up adaptive filter and generates top-down expectation signals that focus attention at the preceding level upon compatible combinations of item or list chunks.

The third level can already represent sentences with repeated words, such as 'Dog eats dog', because a list category at level three can represent a sequence of list categories, including repeated list categories, at level two. Thus, just a few properly designed network levels, all sharing the same design, can represent complex sequential information, including full sentences with repeated words.

What makes these levels special? As I will explain in Chapter 12, this particular design allows the brain to quickly learn to categorize sequences of events *without experiencing catastrophic forgetting*. It clarifies, in particular, how we can learn language, motor skills, and navigational routines quickly and can remember them for a long time. This example is just a case of Adaptive Resonance Theory acting through time, or *ART In Time*, for short. The resonant state that binds together multiple levels in such a processing hierarchy drives fast learning of the attended sequential information.

Phonemic restoration illustrates that feedforward activations do not, in themselves, lead to conscious experiences. In order to have a conscious experience, learned top-down expectations also need to be activated by the list categories that respond to a particular list in working memory, much as we learn to expect the first word to sound like "heel" in response to the sequence '#eel was on the' when the next word is "shoe". The list chunks that read-out these top-down expectations are sensitive to more than one word in the sentence in order to unambiguously

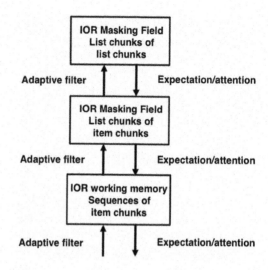

FIGURE 1.24. Only three processing stages are needed to learn how to store and categorize sentences with repeated words in working memory. See the text for more discussion.

compute that "heel" goes with "shoe" but "wheel" goes with "wagon". Such expectations are sensitive to whole *sequences* of word sounds, as in the Masking Field of level three in Figure 1.24. As an expectation gets activated by a particular sequence of word sounds, it sends a top-down, or *feedback*, signal to the working memory where the sequences of individual words (level two) and word sounds (level one) are being stored. There, at cells that have already been activated by the many frequencies of the broad-band noise, the expectation selects and amplifies the activities of cells whose frequencies are consistent with it, while the activities of other cells are suppressed.

These are the spectral components to which we will "pay attention", much as list chunk 'xy' attentively supports item chunks 'x' and 'y' in Figure 1.23b only to be supplanted by list chunk 'xyz' which, in turn, attentively supports item chunks 'x', 'y', and 'z' in Figure 1.23d. As the cells that comprise this emerging attentional focus start to get amplified by sufficiently sustained top-down expectations, they reactivate the bottom-up pathways that activated the expectation in the first place, until the whole bottom-up and top-down feedback process equilibrates. The activation of these top-down expectations, the focusing of attention, and the equilibration between the bottom-up and top-down interactions take awhile to occur. This lag enables future contextual events, such as the words "shoe" or "wagon", to influence which expectations can influence the processing of earlier words. During phonemic restoration, we consciously hear the restored sound only after the expectations that are activated by the entire sentential context get a chance to act upon it. That is why our conscious experiences lag behind their inducing sensory events.

How does object attention work? ART Matching Rule

The process by which object attention focuses upon compatible item or list chunks obeys what is called the ART Matching Rule. Gail Carpenter and I mathematically proved in the 1980s that this Rule is needed to dynamically stabilize the learning of new recognition categories (Figures 1.23 and 1.24), and thereby solve the stability-plasticity dilemma; e.g., Carpenter and Grossberg (1987a). Figure 1.25 summarizes the kind of brain circuit that embodies the ART Matching Rule, in all the brain regions where this Rule occurs in the brain: a top-down, modulatory on-center, off-surround circuit that reads out the learned expectations to be matched against bottom-up input patterns. This is the circuit that carries out the excitatory matching process that is summarized in Table 1.2. This matching process has the following properties:

When a bottom-up input pattern (upward facing green pathways) is received at a processing stage of feature detectors, it can activate its target cells, if nothing else is happening. When an active category reads-out a top-down expectation (downward facing green pathways), it can provide excitatory modulatory, or priming, signals to cells in its on-center, and driving inhibitory signals to cells in its off-surround, if nothing else is happening. The on-center can only modulate the activities of its targeted feature detectors because the off-surround (red pathways) also inhibits the on-center cells (Figure 1.25), and these excitatory and inhibitory inputs are approximately balanced ("one-against-one"). As a result, a top-down expectation cannot, by itself, fully activate its target cells. When a bottom-up input pattern *and* a top-down expectation are both active, cells that receive both bottom-up excitatory inputs and top-down excitatory priming signals can fire ("two-against-one"), while other cells are inhibited ("one-against-one"). In this way, only cells can fire whose features are "expected" by the top-down expectation, and an attentional focus starts to form at these cells.

As I will explain in Chapter 5, the properties of the ART Matching Rule, naturally explain the properties of phonemic restoration, notably how future context can influence past conscious percepts, why restoration occurs when noise replaces phonetic information, and why restoration does not occur without noise. With this explanation in hand, phonemic restoration no longer seems to be a charming, but unimportant, phenomenon. Rather, it uses the processes whereby the brain can solve the stability-plasticity dilemma and thereby learn quickly without also catastrophically forgetting useful memories. Phonemic restoration hereby supports the prediction that the ART Matching Rule enables speech and language to be learned quickly, without risking catastrophic forgetting.

All conscious states are resonant states

These interacting bottom-up and top-down processes give rise to a *resonant* state in the brain. As explained in greater detail in subsequent chapters, a *resonance* is a dynamical state during which neuronal firings across a brain network are amplified and synchronized when they interact via reciprocal excitatory feedback signals during a matching process that occurs between bottom-up and top-down pathways, as illustrated by Figures 1.23 and 1.24. Often the activities of these synchronized cells oscillate in phase with one another. Resonating cell activities also focus attention upon a subset of cells, thereby clarifying how the brain can become conscious of attended events.

I predicted in the 1970s that "all conscious states are resonant states", and that resonant states can trigger rapid learning about a changing world without causing catastrophic forgetting, thereby solving the stability-plasticity dilemma. A resonance represents a kind of system-wide consensus that the attended information is worthy of being learned. Because resonances can trigger fast learning, they are called *adaptive* resonances, which is why I called the theory Adaptive Resonance Theory, or ART. ART's proposed solution of the stability-plasticity dilemma mechanistically links the process of stable learning with the mechanisms of expectation, attention, resonance, and synchrony that enable it, while also clarifying why our conscious experiences can lag behind their initiating sensory events. Because of these mechanistic relationships, I like to group together the processes of Consciousness, Learning,

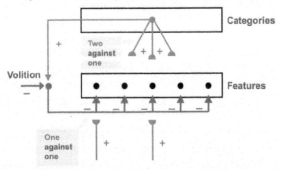

ART MATCHING RULE
Stabilizes Learning
Top-down, modulatory on-center, off-surround network

FIGURE 1.25. The ART Matching Rule stabilizes real time learning using a top-down, modulatory on-center, off-surround network. Object attention is realized by such a network. See text for additional discussion.

Expectation, Attention, Resonance, and Synchrony, and often abbreviate them as the CLEARS processes.

ART hereby predicts that all brain representations that solve the stability-plasticity dilemma use variations of CLEARS mechanisms. The CLEARS mechanisms clarify why many animals are *intentional* and *attentional* beings who use learned expectations to pay attention to salient objects and events, why "all conscious states are resonant states", and how brains can learn both *many-to-one maps* (representations whereby many object views, positions, and sizes all activate the same invariant object category) and *one-to-many maps* (representations that enable us to expertly know many things about individual objects and events). I explain these and many other properties of ART in Chapter 5.

The emergence of self, the longing for unity, and the appeal of monotheism

Resonances enable data from all of our external senses, including sight, sound, and touch, as well as internal senses that give rise to our emotions and conscious feelings, to be bound together into coherent moments of unified conscious experience, rather than being just a jumble of disjoint sense impressions, and enable us to consciously know what these experiences are. We hereby overcome the "blooming buzzing confusion" that the world presents us with every day.

This book will focus upon resonances that support conscious seeing, hearing, feeling, and knowing (Table 1.3). With resonance as a mediating event that binds together attended representations in widely separated brain areas while we stably accumulate knowledge about the world, a unified sense of self can emerge, as well as a longing for a unified view of the world. The system-wide unity and coherence of resonances may be one of the wellsprings of religious as well as scientific thought. It is through the binding of multiple types of information through adaptive resonances that brains act like universal self-organizing measurement systems which overcome the limitations of computationally complementary cortical processing streams.

TABLE 1.3. The link between consciousness and movement.
VISUAL seeing, knowing, and reaching
AUDITORY hearing, knowing, and speaking
EMOTIONAL feeling, knowing, and acting

Invariant learning, expectation, and cognitive-emotional resonance in early religious beliefs

A few more remarks about how ART dynamics in our brains may influence religious and scientific thought will be briefly mentioned here in order to illustrate the scope of the insights that ART enables. Chapter 17 will provide additional discussion.

As noted in the discussion of attentional blocking and unblocking (Figure 1.10), our brains generate hypotheses about the world using learned expectations that may be confirmed or disconfirmed by subsequent events (Figure 1.11). Using the ART Matching Rule (Figure 1.25), an active top-down expectation that is disconfirmed by a current situation can suppress the disconfirmed features in the expectation, while shifting attention to focus upon feature combinations that will subsequently lead to confirmed expectations in that situation.

Although these mechanisms usually work amazingly well, they also have shortcomings. One shortcoming is that different people may use different feature and event combinations to predict the same outcomes. If an environment does not require precise testing of expectations, then some expectations, and the beliefs that arise from them, may include irrelevant information, or may at best correlate with outcomes without causing them. When humans in primitive societies were confronted with the many aspects of their environments that they could not control, it become possible to learn expectations that embodied accidental correlations between cues and their outcomes, leading to unfounded beliefs about the causes of health or sickness, good or bad weather, crop fecundity or failure, and other vitally important life experiences.

Powerlessness in the face of changing and demanding environments can lead to a strong tendency towards belief synthesis, or unification, when it is combined with another fundamental type of brain process. This is the process whereby our brains learn *invariant* representations of objects and events that will be described in greater detail in Chapter 6, where I will discuss learning of invariant visual recognition categories, and in Chapter 12, where I will do the same for invariant speech recognition categories. An invariant representation is one that is activated by many different feature and event combinations, much as we can visually recognize our parents' faces from multiple viewpoints, distances, and positions; or we can auditorily recognize language that is spoken by men, women, and children in different acoustic frequency ranges and at different rates. As these examples illustrate, by grouping together many situational variations, invariant learning can be incredibly useful. However, lumping together situational variations can also cause serious predictive errors to occur. Indeed, as invariant categories of objects, persons, or events are being learned, they also control learning of expectations about outcomes which may, in fact, be accidental, but may not be disconfirmed if we are powerless to control them, such as floods, volcano eruptions, disease outbreaks, and the like. Unless and until they are disconfirmed, the cues that activate invariant categories may continue to be recognized as being immanent in, and predictors of, accidentally correlated outcomes.

Invariant categories may also learn to trigger the strong feelings that we experience during these outcomes, via cognitive-emotional learning (e.g., see Figures 1.10 and 1.16). These feelings can include learned fear, say when a the health of a loved one is expected to get worse, or an emotional rebound of relief that is learned when this fearful outcome is disconfirmed by an unexpected recovery (see Figures 1.14 and 1.15). Learned invariance, expectation, and cognitive-emotional interactions may hereby combine to create strong synchronized cognitive and cognitive-emotional resonances between sensory and prefrontal cortices and the amygdala (Figure 1.16) that support the beliefs that are consistent with the expectations, and that can attentionally block disconfirming evidence, at least if this evidence is sufficiently rare.

This sketch of some factors that may support strongly held beliefs for which there is little evidence, including religious beliefs, does not support or deny any particular set of these beliefs. It does, however, clarify how religious beliefs may persist in the lives of many people around the world because of the way these beliefs engage fundamental cognitive and emotional processes whereby humans try to make sense of the world.

Scientific discovery is limited by the same combinations of cognitive and cognitive-emotional factors. However, the scientific method is designed to carefully test our expectations about the world, and to hereby efficiently eliminate accidental correlations that are disconfirmed, as it incrementally approaches an understanding of the true causes of things.

Conscious seeing, hearing, feeling, and knowing: Linking consciousness to action

As I will further document later in this chapter, many philosophers have asked what kind of "event" occurs in the brain during a conscious experience that is anything more than just a "whir of information-processing"? They have additionally asked: What happens when conscious mental states "light up" and directly appear to the subject? This book proposes that, over and above "just" information processing, our brains sometimes go into a context-sensitive *resonant state* that can involve multiple brain regions. Because not all brain dynamics are resonant, consciousness is not just a "whir of information-processing".

It is fair to ask: *When* does a resonant state embody a conscious experience? *Why* is it conscious? And *how* do different resonant states support different kinds of conscious experiences? The other side of the coin is equally important: When does a resonant state fail to embody a conscious experience?

In order to provide partial answers to these questions, I will explain how various evolutionary challenges that advanced brains face in order to adapt to changing environments have been overcome with particular conscious states, and how these conscious states form part of larger adaptive behavioral capabilities. In this regard, Adaptive Resonance Theory argues that humans are not conscious just to Platonically contemplate the beauty of the world. Humans are conscious in order to enable them to better adapt to the world's changing demands. To illustrate these claims, in addition to proposing how the brain generates resonances that support particular conscious experiences of seeing, hearing, feeling, and knowing, the book will also explain how resonances for conscious seeing help to ensure effective looking and reaching, resonances for conscious hearing help to ensure effective auditory communication and speaking, and resonances for conscious feeling help to ensure effective actions towards valued goal objects (Table 1.3). ART also proposes why different resonances are triggered at the brain processing stages that they are, and suggests how several functionally different kinds of resonances can interact with one another, so that when we consciously see a familiar valued object, we can also know some things about it, and have appropriate feelings that are directed towards it.

Why did consciousness evolve?

In particular, the book will show how and why *multiple* processing stages are needed before the brain can construct a complete and stable enough representation of the information in the world with which to control effective behaviors. This happens because the sensory signals that our brains process are often noisy and ambiguous, as are the representations that our brains form in response to them at the earliest processing stages. Complementary computing and hierarchical resolution of uncertainty overcome these problems until perceptual representations that are sufficiently complete, context-sensitive, and stable can be formed. The brain regions where these representations are completed are different for seeing, hearing, feeling, and knowing. But then how do our brains select these representations? My proposed answer is: A resonant state is generated that selectively "lights up" these representations and thereby renders them conscious. These conscious representations can then be used to trigger effective behaviors.

Consciousness hereby enables our brains to prevent the noisy and ambiguous information that is computed at earlier processing stages from triggering actions that could lead to disastrous consequences. Conscious states thus provide an *extra degree of freedom* whereby the brain ensures that its interactions with the environment, whether external or internal, are as effective as possible, given the information at hand. These conclusions will be supported by theoretical analyses throughout the book that enable explanations of many psychological and neurobiological data about normal and clinical behaviors that have no other mechanistic explanations at the present time.

Self-stabilizing memories and the challenge of learning without bias through life

An emerging self can stabilize its learning by filtering experiences through resonant bottom-up and top-down matching processes (Figures 1.23 and 1.24), much as we perceive "heel" rather than "noise-eel" when restoring the sentence "heel is on the shoe" during phonemic restoration. These matching processes dynamically buffer our current knowledge against being catastrophically overwritten by novel experiences. They also extract a cost that may become increasingly burdensome as we become older.

As we learn more and more about the world, it becomes harder for new events to be experienced with a fresh eye. Our difficulties in learning a new foreign language after a certain age illustrate this problem. New languages need to be filtered by the language representations that we already know. In contrast, if two or more languages are learned simultaneously at an early enough age, they can, from the start, organize bottom-up filters to accommodate them both. Novelty may thus become harder to experience as an increasing number of experiences get matched against, and possibly confused with, an ever richer repertoire of previously learned expectations. Apart from the inevitable decline of memory with age, the increased dynamic buffering and novelty-reducing effects of resonant matching as we learn more about our world can make it harder to learn new things as we get older.

These difficulties are part of the price we pay to stabilize the memories that enable us to enrich our sense of self and to gain some wisdom with age. They are part of the human condition. If we could just turn on a second or third self with its own fresh filters and expectations, then we might not face this problem. But that would be tantamount to being someone else. And where is the satisfaction and wisdom in that?

One approach to successfully pursuing an interesting life is to figure out how to develop an ever-expanding sense of self by seeking constructive new challenges which previous knowledge can enhance, while still being novel enough to escape the trap of rigid stability. Achieving a balance between the satisfactions of a unified self and its established view of the world, and an adventurousness that can keep our minds engaged in novel pursuits, is hard to do, if only because we each develop our own personalized definitions of novelty as our lives unfold on their unique trajectories. We typically need to discover a productive road on our own. Despite these difficulties, it is a comfort to realize that the nature of the problem derives from basic qualities of our minds that we hold most dear, such as being able to learn about an ever-changing world, develop a self, and have stable social relationships. It is something to be embraced, and worked with to the best of our abilities.

The road to ART: Helmholtz, James, and Gregory

The road towards the discovery of ART has a long history. The great German psychologist, physiologist, and physicist Hermann von Helmholtz realized during the nineteenth century that expectations can greatly influence what we see (Helmholtz, 1866). His concept is known as the doctrine of *unconscious inference*. This doctrine held that a raw sensory experience, or *perzeption*, is modified by previous experiences via a learned imaginal increment, or *vorstellung*, before it becomes a true perception, or *anschauung*. Thus Helmholtz realized that we perceive, in part, what we expect to perceive based upon past learning. His realization of this was one of the factors that led him to leave psychology towards the end of his life and to focus even more on physics, since sufficient information, both empirical and mathematical, about how top-down expectations are learned and how they interact with bottom-up sensory data were not available at that time. Chapter 2 provides more discussion of Helmholtz's struggle.

Many other scientists since Helmholtz have had related ideas. These include some of the core concepts in the doctrine of *pragmatism* that was espoused by the great American psychologist William James during the last half of the nineteenth century (James, 1907). More recent thinkers, such as the influential British psychologist Richard Gregory, who died in 2010, have discussed how top-down *cognitive contours* might influence what we see (Gregory, 1972). None of these thinkers seems to have realized, however, the critical role of the stability-plasticity dilemma in guiding the brain's design of these top-down processes. It was only with the introduction of ART that a quantitative synthesis of the CLEARS processes of Consciousness, Learning, Expectation, Attention, Resonance, and Synchrony became possible. The subsequent chapters will survey some of the fascinating phenomena about mind and brain, and their implications for daily living, that can be given a unified explanation from this perspective.

TABLE 1.4. The six main kinds of resonances which support different kinds of conscious awareness that will be explained and discussed in this book.

TYPE OF RESONANCE	TYPE OF CONSCIOUSNESS
surface-shroud	see visual object or scene
feature-category	recognize visual object or scene
stream-shroud	hear auditory object or stream
spectral-pitch-and-timbre	recognize auditory object or stream
item-list	recognize speech and language
cognitive-emotional	feel emotion and know its source

The varieties of resonant experiences during seeing, hearing, feeling, and knowing

As I remarked above, I have been able, as part of the development of ART, to begin classifying resonances that support different types of conscious experiences, such as the conscious experiences of seeing, hearing, feeling, and knowing. Table 1.4 lists six of these different types of resonances, and the kind of conscious experiences that they support. To fix ideas, let me list these resonances here; cf. Grossberg (2017b). Later chapters will explain how they work, where they occur in the brain and why, and some of the fascinating psychological and neurobiological data that they have enabled me to explain and predict.

Surface-shroud resonances are predicted to support conscious percepts of visual qualia (see Chapter 6). *Feature-category resonances* are predicted to support conscious recognition of visual objects and scenes (see Chapter 5). Both kinds of resonances may synchronize during conscious seeing and recognition. *Stream-shroud resonances* are predicted to support conscious percepts of auditory qualia (see Chapter 12). *Spectral-pitch-and-timbre resonances* are predicted to support conscious recognition of sources in auditory streams (see Chapter 12). Spectral-shroud and spectral-pitch-and-timbre resonances may synchronize during conscious hearing and recognition of auditory streams. *Item-list resonances* are predicted to support recognition of speech and language (see Chapter 12). They may synchronize with stream-shroud and spectral-pitch-and-timbre resonances during conscious hearing of speech and language, and build upon the selection of auditory sources by spectral-pitch-and-timbre resonances in order to recognize the acoustical signals that are grouped

together within these streams. *Cognitive-emotional resonances* are predicted to support conscious percepts of feelings, as well as recognition of the source of these feelings (see Chapter 13). Cognitive-emotional resonances can also synchronize with resonances that support conscious qualia and knowledge about them.

All of these resonances have distinct anatomical substrates. Not all cells that sustain an adaptive resonance may represent conscious contents of an experience. Subsequent chapters explain why only cells that are sensitive to the kinds of psychological discriminations (e.g., color, fear) that are embodied within the conscious experience can do this, and why these discriminations can occur only at prescribed stages of brain processing. Neurophysiological data about perceptual experiences like binocular rivalry (see Chapter 11) illustrate this fact, and my neural models about how the brain sees have explained, and indeed predicted, key properties of these data.

It cannot be overemphasized that these resonances are not just correlates of consciousness. Rather, they embody the subjective properties of individual conscious experiences, while also enabling effective behaviors to be elicited (Table 1.3).

All conscious states are resonant states, but some resonant states are not conscious

The ART prediction that "all conscious states are resonant states" provides a linking hypothesis between brain mechanisms and psychological functions that enables our explanations of consciousness to be experimentally tested.

It is the dynamical state that "lights up" to enable a conscious experience to occur, and is not just a "whir of information processing". It is not, however, predicted that "all resonant states are conscious states". If, in fact, the concept of resonance is more general than that of consciousness, then the theory needs to explain why that is so, and how conscious states arise from that more general function. The resonances that are unconscious typically do not have readily available names from day-to-day language. That is because they do not include feature detectors that are activated by external senses, such as those that support vision or audition, or internal senses, such as those that support emotion, despite the fact that they are functionally important for survival.

For example, Chapter 12 will discuss *parietal-prefrontal resonances* that are predicted to trigger the selective opening of basal ganglia gates to enable the read out of context-appropriate thoughts and actions. These gating actions subserve what we often intuitively think of as volitional control. When they break down, life-threatening problems like Parkinson's disease may result. Chapter 16 describes *entorhinal-hippocampal resonances* that are predicted to dynamically stabilize the learning of entorhinal grid cells and hippocampal place cells, which play an important role in spatial navigation. Indeed, John O'Keefe at University College London, and Edvard and May-Britt Moser at the Norwegian University of Science and Technology in Trondheim, Norway, won the 2014 Nobel Prize in Physiology or Medicine for their great experimental work in discovering hippocampal place cells and entorhinal grid cells, respectively, and demonstrating many of their most important psychological and neurobiological properties, many of which have been explained by neural models.

All of these resonances, both the conscious ones and the unconscious ones, help to solve the stability-plasticity dilemma in their respective domains. As will be explained in Chapter 12, brain dynamics can also occur that do not include any possibility of resonance, notably during the activation of spatial and motor representations (Table 1.2), and thus may not support any conscious experiences for that reason.

Towards solving the Hard Problem of Consciousness: A philosophical third rail?

My preceding remarks make the claim that, in effect, this book is proposing major progress towards solving what is called the Hard Problem of Consciousness; namely, it is summarizing an emerging theory of the events that occur in our brains when we have specific conscious experiences.

Before turning to the scientific results themselves, it may be helpful to summarize what the Hard Problem of Consciousness is, and the limits to what such a theory can achieve.

First, what is the "hard problem of consciousness"? Wikipedia (https://en.wikipedia.org/wiki/Hard_problem_of_consciousness) says: "The **hard problem of consciousness** is the problem of explaining how and why we have qualia or phenomenal experiences—how sensations acquire characteristics, such as colors and tastes". David Chalmers, who introduced the term 'hard problem' of consciousness, contrasts this with the 'easy problems' of explaining the ability to discriminate, integrate information, report mental states, focus attention, etc. As Chalmers (1995) has noted: "The really hard problem of consciousness is the problem of *experience*. When we think and perceive, there is a whir of information-processing, but there is also a subjective aspect. As Nagel (1974) has put it, there is *something it is like* to be a conscious organism. This subjective aspect is experience. When we see, for example, we *experience* visual sensations: the felt quality of redness, the experience of dark and light, the quality of depth in a visual field. Other experiences go along with perception in different modalities: the sound of a clarinet, the smell of mothballs. Then there are bodily sensations, from pains to orgasms; mental images that are conjured up internally; the felt quality of emotion, and the experience of a stream of conscious thought. What unites all of these states is that there is something it is like to be in them. All of them are states of experience".

The Internet Encyclopedia of Philosophy (http://www.iep.utm.edu/hard-con/) goes on to say: "The hard problem of consciousness is the problem of explaining why any physical state is conscious rather than nonconscious. It is the problem of explaining why there is 'something it is like' for a subject in conscious experience, why conscious mental states 'light up' and directly appear to the subject. The usual methods of science involve explanation of functional, dynamical, and structural properties—explanation of what a thing does, how it changes over time, and how it is put together. But even after we have explained the functional, dynamical, and structural properties of the conscious mind, we can still meaningfully ask the question, *Why is it conscious?* This suggests that an explanation of consciousness will have to go beyond the usual methods of science. Consciousness therefore presents a hard problem for science, or perhaps it marks the limits of what science can explain. Explaining why consciousness occurs at all can be contrasted with so-called 'easy problems' of consciousness: the problems of explaining the function, dynamics, and structure of consciousness. These features *can* be explained using the usual methods of science. But that leaves the question of why there is something it is like for the subject when these functions, dynamics, and structures are present. This is the hard problem . . . There seems to be an unbridgeable *explanatory gap* between the physical world and consciousness. All these factors make the hard problem hard".

Philosophical opinions about the Hard Problem are so diverse and strongly felt by their supporters, that even attempting a possible scientific approach to solving the Hard Problem may sometimes feel like stepping on a philosophical "third rail". This is because philosophers vary passionately in their views between the claim that no Hard Problem remains once it is explained how the brain generates experience, as in the writings of Daniel Dennett, to the claim that it cannot in principle be solved by the scientific method, as in the writings of David Chalmers. See the above reference for a good summary of these opinions.

To what extent can any scientific theory clarify the Hard Problem?

This book will argue that Adaptive Resonance Theory proposes answers, however incomplete, that respond to various of these philosophical concerns by showing how ART scientifically clarifies various of the distinctions that philosophers have discussed. To link to the above philosophical concerns, let me immediately note the following:

First, it is fair to ask, as Chalmers does above, what kind of "event" occurs in the brain during a conscious experience that is anything more than just a "whir of information-processing"? What happens when conscious mental states "light up" and directly appear to the subject? As I indicated above, I will show that that, over and above "just" information processing, our brains sometimes go into a context-sensitive *resonant state* that can involve multiple brain regions. This discussion will explain some of the abundant experimental evidence that "all conscious states are resonant states", just as phonemic restoration has already illustrated (see Figures 1.22-1.24). Not all brain dynamics are "resonant", and thus consciousness is not just a "whir of information-processing".

Second, it is fair to ask: When does a resonant state embody a conscious experience? "Why is it conscious"? And how do different resonant states support different kinds of conscious qualia? The other side of the coin is equally important: When does a resonant state fail to embody a conscious experience? As I have already noted above, advanced brains have evolved in response to various evolutionary challenges in order to adapt to changing environments in real time. ART explains how consciousness enables such brains to better adapt to the world's changing demands, as summarized in Table 1.3, and how the several functionally different kinds of resonances in Table 1.4 can interact with one another.

A linking hypothesis between resonant brain dynamics and the conscious mind

Before presenting more facts about ART, it is important to also ask: How far can any scientific theory go towards solving the Hard Problem? Let us suppose that a theory exists whose neural mechanisms interact to generate dynamical states with properties that mimic the parametric properties of the individual qualia that we consciously experience, notably the spatio-temporal patterning and dynamics of the resonant neural representations that represent these qualia. Suppose that these resonant dynamical states, in addition to mirroring properties of subjective reports of these qualia, predict properties of these experiences that are confirmed by psychological and non-invasive neurobiological experiments on humans, and are consistent with psychological, multiple-electrode neurophysiological data, and other types of neurobiological data that are collected from monkeys who experience the same stimulus conditions.

Given such detailed correspondences with experienced qualia and multiple types of data, it can be argued that these dynamical resonant states are not just "neural correlates of consciousness" that various authors have also discussed, notably David Chalmers and Christof Koch and their colleagues. Rather, they are mechanistic representations of the qualia that embody individual conscious experiences on the psychological level. If such a correspondence between detailed brain representations and detailed properties of conscious qualia occurs for a sufficiently large body of psychological data, then it would provide strong evidence that these brain representations create and support these conscious experiences. A theory of this kind would have provided a *linking hypothesis* between brain dynamics and the conscious mind. Such a linking hypothesis between brain and mind must be demonstrated before one can claim to have a "theory of consciousness".

If, despite such a linking hypothesis, a philosopher or scientist claims that, unless one can "see red" or "feel fear" in a theory of the Hard Problem, then it does not contribute to solving that problem, then no scientific theory can ever hope to solve the Hard Problem. This is true because science as we know it cannot do more than to provide a mechanistic theoretical description of the dynamical events that occur when individual conscious qualia are experienced. However, as such a principled, albeit incrementally developing, theory of consciousness becomes available, including increasingly detailed psychological, neurobiological, and even biochemical processes in its explanations, it can dramatically shift the focus of discussions about consciousness, just as relativity theory transformed discussions of space and time, and quantum theory of how matter works. As in quantum theory, there are measurement limitations in understanding our brains. We can no more personally ride an electron than we can enter a neuron that is participating in a conscious experience. Such an empathic limitation has not deterred physicists from believing that they have acquired an effective understanding of the physical world, based on their ability to explain and predict enough facts about it. This book subscribes to the view that it will not deter psychologists and neurobiologists from believing that they have acquired an effective understanding of the Hard Problem, based on our own explanatory and predictive successes.

Before explaining in subsequent chapters how ART can clarify the brain substrates of conscious experiences, it is useful to emphasize that ART was not developed to explain consciousness. Rather, it was developed to explain and predict large psychological and neurobiological databases about learning, perception, cognition, and emotion that clarify how our brains solve the stability-plasticity dilemma. These explanations led ART to specify mechanistic links between brain processes of learning, expectation, attention, resonance, and synchrony to explain psychological data about seeing, hearing, feeling, and knowing. As these discoveries were made, it became clear that the resonances hereby discovered also exhibit parametrical properties of individual conscious experiences, as embodied within the spatio-temporal patterning of cell activities across networks of feature detectors. Indeed, my early mathematical results from the 1960s and 1970s about the brain's functional units of short-term memory (STM) and long-term memory (LTM) proved that the functional units of both STM and LTM are *distributed patterns* across networks of feature-selective cells. See Chapter 2 for these laws. Later results showed how these distributed patterns form part of synchronous resonant states that focus attention upon the critical features that represent predictive neural information, including those feature patterns that embody the parametric properties of individual conscious experiences. Such discoveries, repeated multiple times over a period of decades, led to a growing understanding of how *Consciousness* interacts with processes of Learning, Expectation, Attention, Resonance, and Synchrony. ART was hereby led to predict that all brain representations that solve the stability-plasticity dilemma use variations of CLEARS mechanisms.

These discoveries were often made in multiple separate modeling projects. Synthesizing all of these projects is needed to explain the current understanding of how ART can help to solve the Hard Problem. This synthesis is called the *conscious ART*, or cART, model when focusing on explaining data about consciousness. Even if one's personal definition of the Hard Problem excludes any scientific theory, or if one is not interested in the Hard Problem, one can benefit from how the current cART theory explains the functional meaning of many different kinds of psychological and neurobiological data, both normal and clinical, that no other theory has yet explained, and makes predictions to further test these explanations.

Some facts that support CLEARS predictions

The processes that are summarized by the CLEARS mnemonic are related to one another in specific ways that subsequent psychological and neurobiological data have supported. For example, attention must often be focused on the cues to be learned during visual perceptual learning, as scientists like Merav Ahissar and Shaul Hochstein (Ahissar and Hochstein, 1998), Minami Ito, Gerald Westheimer, and Charles Gilbert (Ito, Westheimer, and Gilbert, 1998), and Zhong-Lin Lu and Barbara Dosher (Lu and Dosher, 2004) have shown. The same is true during auditory learning, as Enquan Gao and Nobuo Suga (Gao and Suga, 1998) have shown, and during somatosensory learning, as David Krupa, Asif Ghazanfar, and Miguel Nicolelis (Krupa, Ghazanfar, and Nicolelis, 1999) and Jayson Parker and Jonathan Dostrovsky (Parker and Dostrovsky, 1999) have shown.

However, there are also situations where perceptual learning can occur without focused attention or conscious awareness, as Takeo Watanabe, José Náñez, and Yuka Sasaki have shown in a series of remarkable experiments (e.g., Watanabe, Náñez, and Sasaki, 2001). I explain the Watanabe et al. data in Chapter 10 after describing a laminar cortical extension of ART that I have called LAMINART.

ART's predicted links between attention and synchronous oscillations have been experimentally supported by experiments reported by Timothy Buschman and Earl Miller (Buschman and Miller, 2007), Andreas Engel, Pascal Fries, and Wolf Singer (Engel, Fries, and Singer, 2001), Georgia Gregoriou, Stephen Gotts, Huihui Zhou, and Robert Desimone (Gregorious, Gotts, Zhou, and Desimone, 2009), Gregoriou and Desimone with Andrew Rossi and Leslie Ungerleider (Gregoriou, Rossi,

Ungerleider, and Desimone, 2014), and Daniel Pollen (Pollen, 1999).

Of particular interest are data supporting ART's predicted link between synchronous oscillations and consciousness that neuroscientists such as Victor Lamme (Lamme, 2006), Rudolfo Llinas (Llinas, Ribary, Contreras, and Pedroarena, 1998), and Wolf Singer (Singer, 1998) and their colleagues have reported.

In my discussions throughout the book, links between attention and consciousness will play an important role, and include several functionally different kinds of attention, such as *prototype attention* during recognition learning, and *boundary attention* and *surface attention* during visual perception. Some authors have nonetheless argued that visual attention and consciousness can be dissociated. For example, in 2007, Christof Koch and Naotsugu Tsuchiya (Koch and Tsuchiya, 2007) noted that "subjects can attend to a location for many seconds and yet fail to see one or more attributes of an object at that location . . . In lateral masking (*visual crowding*), the orientation of a peripherally-presented grating is hidden from conscious sight but remains sufficiently potent to induce an orientation-dependent aftereffect . . . " In fact, the data that Koch and Tsuchiya describe can be explained by how ART links attention and consciousness, notably by using properties of a *surface-shroud resonance* (Table 1.4). Properties of conscious visual crowding experiences follow immediately from properties of the surface-shroud resonances that are formed in response to visual crowding stimuli, for reasons that I will explain in Chapter 6.

Since I introduced ART in 1976, it has undergone continual development to explain and predict increasingly large psychological and neurobiological databases. Let me list some of them now so that you can realize that I am not talking about a future promissory note. Rather, I would argue that we are in the midst of an ongoing scientific revolution. ART has helped to explain data ranging from normal and abnormal aspects of human and animal perception and cognition, to the spiking and oscillatory dynamics of hierarchically-organized laminar thalamo-cortical and cortico-cortical networks in multiple modalities.

Indeed, some ART models individually explain, simulate, and predict psychological, anatomical, neurophysiological, biophysical, and even biochemical data. ART currently provides functional and mechanistic explanations of data concerning such diverse topics as laminar cortical circuitry; invariant object and scenic gist learning and recognition; prototype, surface, and boundary attention; gamma and beta oscillations; learning of entorhinal grid cells and hippocampal place cells; computation of homologous spatial and temporal mechanisms in the entorhinal-hippocampal system; vigilance breakdowns during autism, medial temporal amnesia, and Alzheimer's disease; cognitive-emotional interactions that focus attention

on valued objects in an adaptively timed way; Item-Order-Rank working memories and learned list chunks for the planning and control of sequences of linguistic, spatial, and motor information; conscious speech percepts that are influenced by future context; auditory streaming in noise during source segregation; and speaker normalization. Brain regions whose functions are clarified by ART include visual and auditory neocortex; specific and nonspecific thalamic nuclei; inferotemporal, parietal, prefrontal, entorhinal, hippocampal, parahippocampal, perirhinal, and motor cortices; frontal eye fields; supplementary eye fields; amygdala; basal ganglia: cerebellum; and superior colliculus. These unified explanations of many different types of data increased confidence in the emerging classification of resonances.

The book first describes resonances (Table 1.3) that support visual seeing, knowing, and reaching (Chapters 5-11); then auditory hearing, knowing, and speaking (Chapter 12); and finally emotional feeling, knowing, and acting (Chapter 13), while also proposing how these various kinds of resonances may interact together.

Equations, modules, and modal architectures

Before describing how these resonances work, it is helpful to review the kind of mind-brain theory that enables links between brain mechanisms and psychological functions to be established, and how similar organizational principles and mechanisms, suitably specialized, can support conscious qualia across modalities. This discussion highlights from the viewpoint of consciousness some of the concepts that have been introduced earlier in this chapter.

One reason for this inter-modality unity is that a *small number of equations* suffice to model all modalities, whether visual, auditory, emotional, or cognitive. These include equations for short-term memory, or STM; medium-term memory, or MTM; and long-term memory, or LTM, that I first published in 1967-8.

These equations are used to define a *somewhat larger number of modules*, or microcircuits, that can carry out different functions within each modality. These modules include shunting on-center off-surround networks, gated dipole opponent processing networks, associative learning networks, spectral adaptively timed learning networks, and the like. Each of these types of modules exhibits a rich, but not universal, set of useful computational properties that I will describe as we go along. For example, shunting on-center off-surround networks can carry out properties like contrast normalization, including discounting the illuminant; contrast enhancement, noise suppression, and winner-take-all choice; short-term memory and working memory storage; attentive matching of bottom-up input patterns and top-down learned expectations; and synchronous oscillations and traveling waves.

These equations and modules are specialized and assembled into *modal architectures*, where "modal" stands for different modalities of biological intelligence, including architectures for vision, audition, cognition, cognitive-emotional interactions, and sensory-motor control. An integrated self is possible because it builds, across all modalities, on a shared set of equations and modules within modal architectures that can interact seamlessly together. In particular, modal architectures are *general-purpose*, in that they can process any kind of inputs to that modality, whether from the external world or from other modal architectures. They are also *self-organizing*, in that they can autonomously develop and learn in response to these inputs. Modal architectures are thus less general than the von Neumann architecture that provides the mathematical foundation of modern computers, but much more general than a traditional AI algorithm. ART networks form part of several different modal architectures, including modal architectures that enable seeing, hearing, feeling, and knowing. Without these unifying mechanistic ingredients, evolution could not have progressed to give us the wonders of our daily conscious experiences.

Some other approaches to understanding consciousness. Before moving on to more thoroughly explain how ART, and various other neural models, explains data about our conscious and unconscious experiences, it is useful to put these explanations into the context of other approaches to understanding consciousness.

The field of consciousness studies has exploded since the seminal article of Francis Crick and Christof Koch was published in 1990 (Crick and Koch, 1990), and boasts its own journals and conferences. Crick was already world famous for receiving the Nobel Prize with James Watson in 1953 for their contributions to understanding the double helix shape of the DNA molecule. He then became interested in how brains work, as did several other Nobel Laureates, notably Gerald Edelman, after they won their Nobel Prizes for work in other fields. Edelman won his Prize, which was shared with Rodney Porter, for their discoveries concerning the chemical structure of antibodies. They all realized that understanding mind and brain was the next great frontier in science.

In their 1990 article, Crick and Koch, described two forms of consciousness "a very fast form, linked to iconic memory . . . ; and a slower one [wherein] an attentional mechanism transiently binds together all those neurons whose activity relates to the relevant features of a single visual object". This conclusion was consistent with available results about ART at that time, but did not offer a linking hypothesis between brain dynamics and the perceptual, cognitive, and cognitive-emotional representations whose

resonances support different conscious qualia. A great deal of additional experimental evidence for neural correlates of consciousness has been reported since 1990, but has typically led to theoretical conclusions that fail to make the crucial linking hypothesis between specific dynamical brain representations and specific conscious psychological qualia (e.g., Baars, 2005; Dehaene, 2014; Dennett, 1991; Edelman and Tononi, 2000; Koch et al., 2016; Tononi, 2004, 2015).

For example, the *neural global workspace* model that was published in 2014 by Stanislas Dehaene (Dehaene, 2014) builds upon the *global workspace* of Bernard Baars (Baars, 2005) and claims that "consciousness is global information broadcasting within the cortex [to achieve] massive sharing of pertinent information throughout the brain" (p. 13). Dehaene also makes a number of other useful observations, including that "the time that our conscious vision spends entertaining an interpretation is directly related to its likelihood, given the sensory evidence received" (p. 97) and that "the conditioning paradigm suggests that consciousness has a specific evolutionary role: learning over time, rather than simply living in the instant. The system formed by the prefrontal cortex and its interconnected areas, including the hippocampus, may serve the essential role of bridging temporal gaps" (p. 103). Such claims are consistent with the analyses in this book, but they do not describe the underlying organizational principles, neural mechanisms, or brain representations that embody subjective conscious aspects of experience.

In particular, the claim about "global information broadcasting" is consistent with analyses of how adaptive resonances—such as surface-shroud resonances for consciously seeing objects and events, and feature-category resonances for recognizing them—may synchronize the dynamics of multiple brain regions, but does not provide insights into the contents of conscious experiences, or the different kinds of resonances that support them, as summarized by Table 1.4. The observation that links conscious vision to likelihood is clarified by properties of the shunting competitive networks (Chapter 2) wherein winning conscious resonances are chosen, whether at the level of surface-shroud or stream-shroud resonances for representing individual percepts (Chapters 6 and 12) or of higher-order decisions about the most predictive list categories in a Masking Field (Chapter 12) for representing the most likely interpretation of a recent sequences of events, and the best prediction for what will happen next. Moreover, the comment about the role of hippocampal-prefrontal interactions during conditioning does not provide insight into how or why adaptively timed learning occurs, notably the distinction between expected and unexpected disconfirmations during terrestrial exploration and learning, or the functional role, or neural mechanisms, that cause the famous Weber law property that is evident in data about adaptively timed learning (Chapter 14).

Gerald Edelman also got interested in consciousness and published a book in 2008 with Giulio Tononi with the arresting title *A Universe of Consciousness: How Matter Becomes Imagination* (Edelman and Tononi, 2000). Continuing in the spirit of this work, Tononi published an article in 2004 entitled "An Information Integration Theory of Consciousness" (Tononi, 2004). In this article, he defined a scalar function Φ, "the quantity of consciousness available to a system . . . as the value of a complex of elements. Φ is the amount of causally effective information that can be integrated across the informational weakest link of a subset of elements . . . " In 2012 and 2015, Tononi further develop postulates for his Integrated Information Theory (IIT) for physical systems that include consciousness (Tononi, 2012, 2015). These postulates are *intrinsic existence, compositionality, information, integration,* and *exclusion.* These postulates summarize some basic facts about consciousness, but do not explain them.

For example, the *integration* postulate claims that each experience is unified and cannot be reduced to independent components, much as an adaptive resonance is a bound state that develops when resonance emerges due to reciprocal bottom-up and top-down signals (Chapter 5). The *exclusion* postulate claims that every experience is limited to particular things and not others, and has its own spatio-temporal grain, much as a resonance develops through time, focuses attention on some feature combinations while inhibiting others (Chapter 5), and may be adaptively timed by what I call spectral timing circuits (Chapter 14). The *information* postulate claims that selective past causes and selective future effects are represented, much as a cognitive-emotional resonance can discover which combinations of features are predictive and which are accidental and attentionally blocked (Chapter 13). And so on. Although these postulates tangentially touch upon some of the themes that the current book discusses, they have not demonstrated an ability to explain or predict significant psychological or neurobiological databases. The current book provides ample evidence that no scalar-valued function can explain the brain principles, neural mechanisms, and dynamical events that give rise to specific conscious experiences.

Both Dehaene and Tononi used the word "information" as a critical component of their hypotheses. But what is "information"? The scientific concept of "information" in the mathematical sense of Information Theory was defined and mathematically characterized in 1948 by the great American mathematician, electrical engineer, and cryptographer, Claude Shannon (Shannon, 1948). Shannon's remarkable contributions also include his founding of the field of digital circuit design theory in 1937 as part of his Master's Degree at MIT when he was just 21 years old!

In order to even discuss what "information" is requires that a set of *states* exist whose "information" can be computed, and that fixed probabilities exist for transitions between these states. In contrast, the brain is a self-organizing system that continually *creates new states* through development and learning, and whose probability structure is continually changing along with them. Without a theory that explains how these states arise, and how their transition probabilities may change through time in response to changing environmental statistics, the classical concept of information is useless. How such states arise is a key explanatory target of ART, and is one reason why ART can offer a classification of the resonances that are proposed to embody specific conscious experiences.

The influential philosopher of mind, Daniel Dennett, wrote a highly cited book in 1991 with the arresting title *Consciousness Explained* (Dennett, 1991). In this book, Dennett argued against a Cartesian Theater model; that is, a place in the brain where "it all comes together" and generates subjective judgments. Instead, Dennett advocated a Multiple Drafts model where discriminations are distributed in space and time across the brain, a concept that, without further elaboration, is too vague to have explanatory power.

To the extent that Dennett supported his claim with a discussion of visual percepts, he made some mistakes. For example, when discussing surface filling-in, he claimed: "The fundamental flaw in the idea of 'filling-in' is that it suggests that the brain is providing something when in fact the brain is ignoring something" (p. 356). "The brain doesn't have to 'fill in' for the blind spot . . . We don't notice these gaps, but they don't have to be filled in *because* we're designed not to notice them" (p. 355). In other words, Dennett argued that a physical process of filling-in does not occur. Given that Dennett put an example of neon color spreading on the back cover of his book, he clearly viewed this claim as an important part of his proposals about consciousness. I will summarize in Chapter 4, after describing neon color spreading and how it works, why Dennett's remarks are not supported by the data.

Various other authors have made interesting comments about consciousness based upon properties of perceptual and neurobiological data. Notable among them are the excellent Dutch experimental neuroscientist, Victor Lamme, and his colleagues (e.g., Keizer, Hommel, and Lamme, 2015; Tsuchiya, Wilke, Frassle, and Lamme, 2016). However, these contributions have not proposed organizational principles or brain mechanisms whereby to understand the brain dynamics of individual conscious experiences, including how they may share similar principles of resonant dynamics, yet also occur in different brain regions where they embody solutions to environmental constraints that differentiate seeing, hearing, feeling, and knowing.

Perhaps the theory of the highly influential Portuguese-American neuroscientist and author, Antonio Damasio comes closest to theoretically linking brain to mind in his beautifully written 1999 book with the title *The Feeling of What Happens: Body and Emotion in the Making of Consciousness* (Damasio, 1999). As I will explain in Chapter 13, Damasio used the clinical data that he elegantly summarized in his book to guide him to what is, in effect, a heuristic derivation of the Cognitive-Emotional-Motor, or CogEM, model that I had first published in 1971. I further developed CogEM with several PhD students and postdoctoral fellows over the years to explain and predict a huge amount of interdisciplinary data about cognitive-emotional interactions. Unlike CogEM and its refinements, Damasio's theory provides no mechanistic account, and could therefore provide no data simulations or predictions based upon the model's emergent properties. Nor could he situate his heuristic concepts within a larger theory of how brain resonances and consciousness may be linked.

These various alternative efforts to explaining consciousness dramatize that, without a principled theory that can mechanistically link brain mechanisms to mental functions, even the most ingenious heuristic insights ultimately hit a brick wall and cannot be further developed into a truly predictive theory of how our brains work.

How a Brain Makes a Mind

Physics and psychology split as brain theories were born

A historical watershed: When physicists were also neuroscientists

Several of the greatest physicists during the nineteenth century were also great psychologists or neuroscientists. Surprisingly, this was no longer true at the beginning of the twentieth century. Why not? An answer to this question clarifies the kind of problem that linking mind to brain is, and the nature of recent progress in doing so. I will briefly frame this answer in terms of the issues that confronted these great scientists at the end of the nineteenth century.

In addition to carrying out great work in physics, scientists such as Hermann von Helmholtz in Germany, Clerk Maxwell in England, and Ernst Mach in Austria also made seminal contributions to psychology and neuroscience. Their interests in the structure of physical space and time were enhanced by a fascination with psychological space and time. Their contributions to understanding the observed world developed side-by-side their analysis of the observer.

For example, every physicist knows about the *Mach numbers* which help to understand supersonic flight, and about the influence of Mach's critique of classical physical concepts about space and time upon Albert Einstein's thinking during his development of General Relativity Theory. Mach is also famous, however, for his investigation of the *Mach bands* in vision. Mach bands are perceived bright and dark bands that do not match the measured physical luminances in these visual displays, as illustrated in Figure 2.1. Surprisingly few scientists have studied both Mach numbers and Mach bands in school. Indeed, in 1914 Mach expressed "the profound conviction that the foundations of science as a whole, and of physics in particular, await their next great elucidations from the side of biology, and especially from the analysis of the sensations . . . Psychological observation on the one side and physical observation on the other may make such progress that they will ultimately come into contact, and that in this way new facts may be brought to light. The result of this investigation will not be a dualism but rather a science which, embracing both the organic and the inorganic, shall

Conscious MIND Resonant BRAIN. Stephen Grossberg, Oxford University Press. © Oxford University Press 2021.
DOI: 10.1093/oso/9780190070557.003.0002

FIGURE 2.1. Along the boundaries between adjacent shades of gray, lateral inhibition makes the darker area appear even darker, and the lighter area appear even lighter.

interpret the facts that are common to the two departments" (Mach, 1914).

In a similar vein, every physicist knows about Maxwell's fundamental contributions to electromagnetic theory, notably the famous Maxwell's equations, upon which so many modern inventions—electric lights, computers, electric household appliances of all kinds, telephones, radio, TV, cell phones, etc.—are based. Maxwell also made famous contributions to the molecular theory of gases. Maxwell is often considered one of the top three theoretical physicists to have ever lived, along with Isaac Newton and Albert Einstein (Harman, 1990). In addition to these great contributions to physics, Maxwell was an influential psychologist. He developed a "trichromatic color theory" which anticipated the discovery that there are three distinct classes of color-sensitive photoreceptors, or cones, in the normal human retina.

Helmholtz's life in many ways epitomizes an interdisciplinary scientific career that crossed seamlessly between biology and physics. Trained as a medical doctor, his experiments on the velocity of electrical signals in nerve pathways and how they caused movements led him to help discover the Principle of Conservation of Energy, which is one of the cornerstones of nineteenth-century physics. He also made fundamental contributions to optics, which served as a foundation for his classical contributions to visual perception (Helmholtz, 1866). His work in physical acoustics likewise supported his major contributions to understanding auditory perception and music (Helmholtz, 1875). Thus, during the last half of the nineteenth century, a number of great scientists functioned successfully in an interdisciplinary research mode and made lasting contributions to both the physical sciences, and the psychological and brain sciences.

It is often accepted as a truism that success breeds success, just as money makes money. The great interdisciplinary successes of Helmholtz, Maxwell, and Mach might have been expected to breed droves of dedicated interdisciplinary disciples. This did not, however, occur. In the next generation of physicists, Albert Einstein himself, in a letter

to his friend Queen Elizabeth of Belgium in 1933, wrote: "Most of us prefer to look outside rather than inside ourselves; for in the latter case we see but a dark hole, which means: nothing at all." We see a "dark hole, which means nothing at all" because the neural computations that regulate our daily experiences are inaccessible to us due to the property of *cognitive impenetrability*. Because of this impenetrability, we can behave in a world of interacting percepts, feelings, and ideas without having to worry about, or to be distracted by, our individual nerve cells, electrical potentials, and chemical transmitters. We experience the apparent *simplicity* of our behavioral *mastery* rather than the actual *complexity* of its generative neural machinery.

Once we acknowledge that neural computations are not intuitively obvious, we should not be surprised that they may seem strange or even bizarre when we finally discover them, albeit also conceptually simple once you learn to think in a new way about how brains self-organize. Once we acknowledge that neural computations generate behaviors in an interactive fashion across large networks of neurons, we should not be surprised if the boundary between external reality and internal illusion cannot be sharply drawn. These themes will be dramatically illustrated when I explain how our brains see, starting in Chapter 3.

These considerations do not, however, explain why even Einstein was uninterested in trying to cast scientific light on the "dark hole" of the mind. Why did not Einstein try to build upon the insights of his predecessors Maxwell and Mach in psychology and neuroscience, in the way that he did in physics through his great work on the kinetic theory of gases and relativity theory?

Einstein's comment reflects a major schism that occurred between the physical and brain sciences towards the end of the nineteenth century. Scientists whose work was previously greatly energized by interdisciplinary investigations of physics and psychology were rapidly replaced by scientists who rarely had even a rudimentary knowledge of the other field. Although the explosion of scientific knowledge during the twentieth century, with its attendant specialization, surely contributed to this schism, deeper intellectual factors were, I believe, the immediate trigger. An understanding of these factors is useful for appreciating the scientific climate in which modeling how the brain works has been carried out during most of the twentieth century, and the nature of the major scientific revolution that we are now experiencing, and which has been accelerating during the last half-century.

Basic causes of this schism emerged from the scientific discoveries of the very pioneers, such as Helmholtz, Maxwell, and Mach, who built such successful interdisciplinary careers. Two examples from Helmholtz's work on visual perception are illustrative.

The Three N's: Nonlinear, Nonlocal, and Nonstationary

Color Theory. Isaac Newton reported in 1704 his great discovery that white light is composed of equal intensities of all the visible wavelengths of light (Newton, 1704). Newton showed this by using a prism to refract the different colored components of white light into a rainbow. The Newtonian definition of white light is based on measuring the light at individual positions in space. In contrast, Helmholtz realized that the *average* color of a scene is perceived to be desaturated; that is, it tends to look more white than it really is. Thus, if the scene is illuminated with a certain hue—say reddish at sunset or bluish if you are under water—then that color tends to be neutralized so that we can better see the "real" colors of objects in the scene.

As Helmholtz began to realize, conscious percepts of colors, including white, depend upon the relationships between multiple lit positions of a scene or picture. Thus, instead of being reducible to measurements at each position, the analysis of how humans perceive white light at each position necessitates an investigation of long-range (or *nonlocal*) interactions across the positions of a network. These network interactions help to compensate for variable illumination conditions, or to "discount the illuminant," so that humans and other species can better see the actual colors of visible surfaces under a wide variety of illumination conditions.

The neural process whereby an illuminant is discounted is still the subject of intensive experimental and theoretical investigation. Discounting the illuminant somehow "divides out" the illuminant so that the real colors of a scene can be perceived. Any process, like division, that involves operations other than addition and subtraction is said to be *nonlinear*. How the brain discounts the illuminant using nonlocal and nonlinear interactions will be discussed in Chapter 3.

Learning, expectation, and matching. Helmholtz faced another barrier when he attempted to conceptualize the process of visual perception. As I noted in Chapter 1, he developed the doctrine of *unconscious inference* to express the idea that we often perceive what we *expect* to perceive based on past *learning*. Helmholtz's doctrine is recast in the more modern terminology of Adaptive Resonance Theory in Figure 2.2. This figure illustrates how environmentally activated inputs can drive a bottom-up learning process, via *adaptive weights* or *long-term memory* (LTM) traces, that determines which cells will selectively respond to these inputs in the future. These selective cells are called *recognition categories*. When recognition categories are activated, they can trigger the read-out of *learned top-down*

expectations via their own LTM traces. Such expectations are matched against the bottom-up inputs across a network of feature-selective cells. These top-down expectations play the role of an unconscious inference. In order to simplify the figure, arrays of connections between processing stages are represented by a single connection. This simplified notation is used throughout the book, where appropriate.

The bottom-up and top-down signals cooperate and compete through the matching process. The effect of this matching process is to generate a consensus that leads to the final percept by using excitatory (or cooperative) bottom-up and top-down signals to select and focus attention upon expected combinations of features, and inhibitory (or competitive) interactions within each processing level to suppress irrelevant features and categories. Cooperative and competitive matching also requires nonlinear and nonlocal interactions. In addition, the bottom-up and top-down learning processes are *nonstationary*; that is, they are processes that change their LTM traces through time in order to adapt to a changing world.

In summary, Helmholtz's experimental discoveries led him to at least instinctively realize that a theoretical understanding of visual perception would require the discovery of new nonlinear, nonlocal, and nonstationary intuitive concepts and mathematical equations. In contrast, much physical theorizing during the nineteenth century used linear, local, and stationary mathematics. Since theoretical scientists rely upon appropriate mathematical concepts and methods with which to express and develop

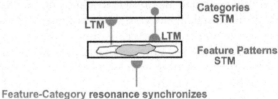

ADAPTIVE RESONANCE

Attended **feature clusters reactivate bottom-up pathways**

Activated categories reactivate their top-down pathways

Feature-Category resonance synchronizes
amplifies
prolongs system response

Resonance triggers learning in bottom-up and top-down adaptive weights: *adaptive* **resonance!**

FIGURE 2.2. Feature-category resonances enable us to rapidly learn how to recognize objects without experiencing catastrophic forgetting. Attentive matching between bottom-up feature pattern inputs and top-down expectations prevent catastrophic forgetting by focusing object attention upon expected patterns of features, while suppressing outlier features that might otherwise have caused catastrophic forgetting if they were learned also.

their deepest intuitive ideas, the inability of nineteenth-century physical concepts and mathematics to explain psychological and neurobiological data created an intellectual crisis for all theorists who might have wished to study mind and brain.

This schism was exacerbated by the fact that the major revolutions of twentieth-century physics *could* be supported by nineteenth-century mathematics. For example, Einstein's Special Theory of Relativity needed only elementary algebra to carry out its computations (Einstein, 1905). The genius in this theory was in knowing what was fundamental and how to think about it. When Einstein realized that he needed a more advanced type of mathematics to express the intuitions that led to the theory of General Relativity (Einstein, 1915), his burden was significantly lightened by the help he received from his friend, Marcel Grossmann, who introduced him to nineteenth-century Riemannian geometry, which provided a perfect tool. As the early developers of quantum mechanics, such as Werner Heisenberg and Max Born, struggled to express their intuitive insights, they too were greatly aided by nineteenth-century mathematics, notably the theory of matrices. Quantum mechanics also benefited from the existence of linear operator theory that had been significantly developed by one of the greatest nineteenth- and early twentieth-century mathematicians, David Hilbert.

A century of controversy as a major scientific revolution is born

A major approach-avoidance hereby arose in the practice of theoretical science at the end of the nineteenth century: Theoretical physicists abandoned psychology and neuroscience to rapidly fashion physical theories about the external world that could be quantitatively supported by available mathematical concepts and methods. Psychologists and neuroscientists returned the favor by abandoning physical concepts and mathematics that seemed irrelevant to their data and, over time, by also eschewing and even denigrating theoretical and mathematical training in general. This bifurcation was already apparent during the unfolding of Helmholtz's scientific life. Beginning his career as a medical doctor, and progressing to his interdisciplinary studies that crossed between mind, brain, and the external physical world, he ended his career as the first President and Director of the new Physico-Technical Institute in Berlin after leaving psychology and physiology behind.

Left without an appropriate framework of concepts and mathematical techniques for interpreting and unifying their experiments, psychologists and neuroscientists nonetheless went about accumulating one of the largest and most sophisticated sets of databases in the history of science. Remarkably, they accomplished this feat during a century of controversy that was spawned by the unavailability of a unifying theoretical and mathematical framework for explaining their data. Even as recently as 1975, Ernest Hilgard and Gordon Bower noted on page 2 of their classic textbook *Theories of Learning* that "Psychology seems to be constantly in a state of ferment and change, if not of turmoil and revolution" (Hilgard and Bower, 1975).

While most mind and brain experimentalists ignored theory, and most theorists looked for more hospitable frontiers, there arose the widespread tendency to fill this theoretical vacuum by interpreting brain function in terms of whatever technology happened to be current. The ever-expanding list of technological metaphors to which the brain has been compared includes telegraph circuits, hydraulic systems, information processing channels, digital computers, linear control systems, catastrophes (in the mathematical sense of René Thom (Thom, 1977), holograms, spin glasses, Bayesian networks, and Deep Learning. All of these metaphors have been unable to explain substantial databases that link mind and brain, since none of them arose from a sustained analysis of mind and brain data.

The schism between physics and neuroscience encouraged many physicists to believe that no theories of mind and brain exist. An inquiry about available theories by an interested physicist more often than not would confirm this impression, because the schism prevented most experimental psychologists and neuroscientists from getting the training needed to understand and value the theories that were already explaining, and in a principled way, difficult nonlinear, nonlocal, and nonstationary data about mind and brain. Indeed, experimentalists who might otherwise have understood the significance of these new insights from properties of their own data typically had no theoretical or mathematical training at all. This gap in training created serious literacy and communication problems over and beyond the very real intellectual challenges inherent in understanding the phenomena themselves.

I hope that this brief summary helps to put into historical perspective why it has taken so long to begin to theoretically understand how a brain can give rise to a mind. Such progress required the introduction of a new scientific paradigm that simultaneously discovered new conceptual intuitions *and* new mathematics with which to understand the nonlinear, nonlocal, and nonstationary laws that link brain to mind. In many scientific revolutions, such as relativity theory and quantum mechanics, once the new physical intuitions were discovered, relevant mathematics was available with which to convert them into rigorous theoretical science. In the mind and brain sciences, we have not been so lucky, since both new intuitions *and* new mathematics needed to be developed. The Newtonian revolution was also of this kind, since Newton had to both derive the laws of celestial mechanics *and* to discover calculus with which to mathematically analyze them. My own scientific work since 1957, when I was a Freshman in Dartmouth College, has been devoted to introducing and developing foundational intuitions, mathematics, and the behavioral and neural models built upon them into the mind-brain sciences. I could never have imagined then how much I would be able to discover and understand with the help of many gifted PhD student, postdoctoral fellow, and faculty collaborators.

As in the case of the Newtonian revolution, the mind-brain revolution is a difficult one to understand. Without new interdisciplinary intuitions about the functional meaning of the data, there is no possibility of understanding. But without new mathematics, there is no way to realize these intuitions in rigorous neural models that can be communicated to other scientists in a compelling way. It needs also to be said that, once one realizes how to think intuitively about various of these processes, many of their key ideas can be described simply in story form. This book is devoted to telling you some of these stories.

What cannot be achieved in this way is a sense of the *inevitability* of these ideas. That can best be seen, first, by understanding how elegantly key psychological facts arise as emergent, or interactive, properties of neural networks and, second, by seeing how the most basic properties of brain designs and mechanisms can be proved with simple mathematics, often with little more than elementary algebra and simple properties of differential equations. I will include some of this mathematics in the book to show you what I mean, but the book can be enjoyed and understood without it.

Fortunately for the field as a whole, during the past thirty years, a number of new academic departments, research centers, societies, and journals have been established with which to expedite the discovery and transmission of this new interdisciplinary knowledge. I have been fortunate to have had the opportunity to found and lead several of these institutions. My 2010 essay Towards Building a Neural Networks Community (Grossberg, 2010) provides a personal account of how this happened to me. This essay can also be downloaded from sites.bu.edu/steveg/files/2016/06/GrossbergNNeditorial2010.pdf.

The Astonishing Hypothesis

Today, as during the time of great pioneering scientists like Helmholtz, Maxwell, and Mach, we are confronted with the same fundamental questions: How are our experiences of the world represented by the brain? How can we find a method and a language to connect two such apparently different types of descriptions? Finding the link between mind and brain is particularly important if we ever want to understand consciousness: A theory of consciousness

that cannot explain psychological experiences and data fails to deal with the *contents* of consciousness.

Francis Crick, who is most famous for his classical Nobel Prize–winning work on understanding DNA, published a book in 1994, with the arresting title *The Astonishing Hypothesis*, in which he discussed some aspects of consciousness (Frick, 1994). The *astonishing* hypothesis refers to the fact that all of our mental phenomena arise from activities of the nerve cells, or neurons, of our brains. Crick claimed that "this hypothesis is so alien to the ideas of most people alive today that it can truly be called astonishing" (p. 3). Why is that? For centuries, due to the problem of cognitive impenetrability, people did not even realize that the brain is the seat of the mind. We are immediately aware of our own personal behavioral experiences, but have to be taught about neurons in school. Even after being taught, the activities of individual nerve cells do not look at all like our daily experiences.

Brains are designed to control behavioral success

A species could have the most beautiful neurons imaginable, but if these *individual neurons* were not properly designed to be able to interact together in correctly designed *neural networks* to cause *adaptive behaviors*, then that species could not survive evolution's challenges. Thus, any theory that hopes to link brain to mind, using design principles that have been shaped by evolution, needs to describe the computational level on which *brain mechanisms* interact to control *behavioral success*. Such interactive properties are often called *emergent* properties, because they are not properties of the individual neurons taken in isolation.

Measuring emergent brain properties directly is not something that even the most advanced experimental techniques can do easily, although recent methods using electrode arrays to simultaneously record from multiple neurons in multiple brain areas are approaching this goal, as in many experiments of MIT neuroscientist Earl Miller and his colleagues; e.g., Wutz et al. (2018). Even the very existence of neurons was a controversial issue at the beginning of the twentieth century. At that time, even this most basic fact about the brain was vigorously debated by two of the greatest names in neuroscience—Ramon y Cajal of Spain and Camillo Golgi of Italy. It was such a hot issue that a strange thing happened on the day in 1906 that Cajal and Golgi shared the Nobel Prize in Physiology or Medicine for their experimental work in neuroscience.

Golgi had discovered a revolutionary staining method whereby brain tissue could be visualized. Using his method, he thought that nerve fibers were part of a continuous electrical network, or reticulum, and thus proposed his Reticular Theory. Cajal modified the Golgi method to discover that individual neurons exist. Cajal's Neuron Doctrine is now taken for granted as gospel. However, on the day that Cajal and Golgi shared the Nobel Prize, Golgi used his own Nobel lecture to deny that individual neurons exist, even as Cajal asserted that they do (e.g., Warmflash, 2016)! Controversy existed then in psychology and neuroscience, and it continues to exist today. How could it be otherwise, given the complexity of the subject matter, and its importance to human identity and society?

Keeping the forest, trees, and leaves all in view

How can such different levels of description—behavior, neural networks, and individual neurons in all their complexity—be kept in mind all at once? This is a little like trying to keep in mind everything that is known about a whole forest, its individual trees, and all the leaves on all the trees. Such a feat requires the use of a scientific language that is powerful enough to simultaneously express all three levels in a natural way, including the emergent properties of very large numbers of interacting neurons that map onto properties of behavior. As is often the case in science, this is best done using a *mathematical* language, since only mathematics has the precision to express such complexity in direct and unambiguous terms.

Despite the widespread prejudice that "math is hard," in reality mathematics can make difficult concepts and mechanisms much simpler to understand. That is why scientists have always turned to mathematics to express their most profound insights. *Differential equations* are the universally accepted mathematical formalism in many scientific disciplines, including physics, because they describe how events evolve in time. They are called "differential" equations because they describe the rates, or "differentials," with which processes evolve in time. By summing up, or integrating, all of these changes through time, one can predict how the processes evolve as time goes on. It turns out that just a few different types of differential equations, indexed properly to keep track of which neurons they are describing, can conveniently describe the dynamics of huge numbers of individual neurons, how they interact in neural networks, and the behavioral properties that emerge from these interactions. Such a language has been getting developed within the field of neural networks for the last sixty years, with steadily accelerating progress since the 1960s.

As I remarked above, I began my own odyssey to discover intuitive concepts and mathematical equations that link brain to mind in 1957 when I was a Freshman undergraduate student at Dartmouth College. I then had the thrilling experience, triggered when I took the Introductory Psychology course, of discovering laws for short-term memory (STM), medium-term memory (MTM), and long-term memory (LTM) whose variants are still used by most computational neuroscientists. By showing how these interacting laws could explain data about human learning, I introduced, by example, the paradigm of using systems of nonlinear differential equations to describe neural networks whose emergent properties match observable behaviors.

Despite these successes, given the anti-theoretical paradigm that governed the mind and brain sciences then, it took ten years, until 1967 (Grossberg, 1967, 1968d) before I could get these results published in archival journals. After that, it took many more years before they began to have a large scientific impact. The central intellectual project of my life continues to be one of contributing to the exciting paradigm of explaining how our brains make our minds, how these insights help to explain what goes wrong in our brains when we are afflicted with mental disorders, and how these discoveries can be used to develop biologically-inspired solutions to large-scale problems in engineering and technology.

Given this rocky start, I am particularly grateful that this combination of biological discovery and technological innovation has been acknowledged by awards from several scientific societies, including most recently the 2015 Norman Anderson Lifetime Achievement Award of the Society of Experimental Psychologists (http://www.sepsych.org/awards.php), the 2017 Frank Rosenblatt Award in computational neuroscience of the Institute of Electrical and Electronics Engineers (http://sites.ieee.org/r1/2016/08/24/r1-fellow-stephen-grossberg-receive-ieee-frank-rosenblatt-award/), and the 2019 Donald O. Hebb award of the International Neural Network Society (https://www.inns.org).

Why differential equations? The case of phonemic restoration

Let me give you a concrete example, right away, of why differential equations are so important in linking brain to mind. In Chapter 1, I mentioned the phenomenon of *phonemic restoration* (Figure 1.22). I pointed out that, when listening to words like "delivery" and "deliberation", replacing the "v" and "b" with broad-band noise still enables the complete words to be heard, but replacing the letters with silence does not support restoration. Likewise, given a rapidly presented sentence with broad-band noise immediately occurring before "eel is on the . . . ," if the last word after "the" is "table," then "noise-eel" can sound like "meal," whereas if the last word is "wagon," then "noise-eel" can sound like "wheel," and so on. I suggested that, as words, or other sequences of auditory items, enter your brain, they are stored in a *working memory*, as in Figures 1.6 and 1.23. As sequences of items enter the working memory, they are categorized at a higher processing level. Each of these categories responds selectively to a list of items that is stored in working memory, and is thus called a *list chunk*. List chunks continue to compete for dominance as more items are stored in working memory (Figure 1.23a), in order to choose the list chunk that best represents, or predicts, the currently stored sequence of items. As this competition for list chunk dominance unfolds through time, the winning list chunks start to activate top-down learned expectations that get matched against the stored working memory items (Figure 1.23b). The matching process selects those items that match the sounds which are expected in the sentence, and suppresses those that are not. As the selected bottom-up and top-down signals cyclically reinforce each other through feedback exchanges, the selected neuronal activities start to "resonate," or to mutually reinforce one another (Figures 1.23c and 1.23d), until we become conscious of the resonating activities, but not necessarily all of the sounds, including noise, that were initially stored in the working memory.

Given that a resonant event may lag behind the environmental inputs that cause it, we need to distinguish perceived psychological time from the times at which inputs are presented. In particular, we need to explain how "future" inputs—like "wagon"—can influence the conscious perception of "past" inputs—as when "noise-eel" sounds like "wheel". The "formal" time variable that is used to define the "differentials" in the underlying differential equations also labels the times at which the inputs turn on and off. The times at which we consciously hear sounds like "wheel" are emergent properties of these differential equations.

These emergent properties explain how sounds may be consciously perceived to flow from past to future, in the order that they were received in "formal time", despite the fact that future contextual information can alter what we consciously perceive in the past. I suggest that this is accomplished by a *resonant wave* that develops from past to future, even while it incorporates future contextual constraints into its top-down matching process, until each event in the resonance equilibrates. Only the resonant wave enters consciousness. It is driven by external inputs in the order that they are received, but it can incorporate future constraints into the resonance until the time that the resonance becomes suprathreshold and conscious. This resonant wave is called an Item-List resonance (Table 1.4) because winning list chunks select and bind together compatible sequences of items that are stored in working memory to determine what we consciously hear.

The hypothesis that "conscious speech is a resonant wave" represents a revolutionary break from previous concepts about how speech and language work, and from current approaches to speech technology, such as the ones that we experience every day when we use Siri on our iPhones. In order to represent such a resonant process, we need to distinguish the external input rate from the internal rate at which resonance evolves. Because external events may occur at variable rates, the internal processing rate must have a finer time scale than any detectable external rate. The internal rate must also be faster than the resonance time scale that emerges as a result of bottom-up and top-down interactions. Differential equations provide a natural language for describing such a resonance because their variables are parameterized by a fast enough "formal time" scale to evolve moment-by-moment in response to external and internal inputs that may arrive at arbitrary times. Hopefully, when such resonant dynamics are incorporated into our iPhones, Siri's descendants will be able to rapidly and stably learn in more challenging acoustic contexts.

From behavior to brain: Autonomous adaptation to a changing world

As part of my discovery of laws for STM, MTM, and LTM, I also introduced a theoretical method model of discovery and development that has led to more theoretical breakthroughs over the years than I could ever have imagined. This method clarifies the proper level of description for linking brain to mind, and operationalizes a sense in which one cannot "derive the whole brain" in one step. Just as *biological evolution* operated in stages over millennia, this method embodies a theoretical cycle that carries out a kind of *conceptual evolution*, leading to the discovery of neural models that are capable of ever finer levels of description of brain architecture and dynamics, along with correspondingly deeper and broader explanatory and predictive ranges.

For me, it has been critical to begin with psychological data, typically scores or even hundreds of behavioral experiments in a particular problem domain, such as vision, audition, cognitive information processing, cognitive-emotional interactions, or sensory-motor control. One begins with behavioral data because **brain evolution needs to achieve behavioral success**. One works with large amounts of data because otherwise too many seemingly plausible, but incorrect, hypotheses about how the brain works cannot be ruled out. The great thing about starting with behavioral data is that, in many fields of psychology, tons of such data have been reported and replicated during the past century. The full corpus of psychological data represents one of the largest databases of any science. Although any good theorist can probably suggest multiple explanations of a few facts, trying to find even one principled explanation of the data from hundreds of experiments is a very challenging task, and one that has led me to make many surprising discoveries.

One also needs to incorporate the key fact that our minds can adapt on their own to changing environmental conditions, even if they are not told that or how these conditions have changed. One thus needs to frontally attack the problem of *how an individual autonomously adapts in real time to a changing world that is filled with unexpected events*. Knowing how to do this is currently an art form. There are no algorithms at present that can assure success in this endeavor. It requires that one be able to translate piles of static data curves into hypotheses about an underlying mental process that is evolving continuously in time within each individual mind. Doing this well requires that one develops intuition into the functional meaning that is hidden in these piles of static data curves, and have enough modeling training to express one's intuitions with appropriate mathematical concepts and equations. How to do this is one of the most important things that I tried to teach to my PhD students and postdoctoral fellows. I will describe this theoretical method in more detail later in this chapter.

Why does the brain use neural networks?

Whenever I have carried out an analysis of how an individual's behavior autonomously adapts to a changing world, no matter what faculty of intelligence was being analyzed, I have always been led to a model that looks like part of a brain or, more exactly, like a *neural network*, or network of interacting neurons. When this first happened to me in 1957, I knew no neuroscience. My first neural network naturally grew out of an analysis of psychological data about how humans do verbal learning, notably how individuals learn lists of words or other lexical items by practicing them multiple times, and then recall them one item at a time later on. This is a kind of data that forces you to think about what is happening through time.

It was only when I talked to some premedical student friends of mine, who were studying neuroscience, that I began to realize that my psychological analysis of learning dynamics had managed to derive basic properties of the brain. Processes that my friends were learning about in their neuroscience studies—including nerve cell bodies, the axons along which signals travel between neurons, the synaptic knobs at the ends of the axons, the chemical transmitters that are produced in the synaptic knobs and released by them in response to axonal signals, the synapses into which the chemical transmitters are released before

they activate the next nerve cell body, and the cell body potentials whereby neurons get activated or inhibited by their inputs from these synapses (Figure 2.3)—were already represented in my behaviorally-derived neural network! I had used psychological data to derive the basic facts about the Neuron Doctrine, without having known anything about this Doctrine. This realization was incredibly exciting to me, and illustrated the power of this theoretical method. Having linked mind to brain, I began to voraciously read everything that I could get my hands on about neuroscience. The experience of deriving new insights about the brain by studying the mind has repeated itself scores of times over the years. I like to say that, whereas I am known as one of the fathers of the field of neural networks, I have never tried to derive a neural network!

Although these behaviorally-derived neural networks have always included known brain mechanisms, the functional meaning of these brain mechanisms has often been surprising, because the psychological analyses whereby they were derived included new insights about their emergent properties. Behaviorally-derived neural networks have also often predicted the existence of unknown psychological and neural data, and scores of these predictions have been supported by subsequent psychological, neurophysiological, anatomical, and even biochemical experiments from five to thirty years after the predictions were made. This theoretical method is thus emphatically not just a way to fit known data.

In summary, there is a succinct answer to the basic question: Why does a brain look the way that it does? The answer seems to be this:

Brains look the way they do to be able to achieve *autonomous adaptation in real time of individual behavior to a changing world that is filled with unexpected events*.

In other words, brain networks define a natural computational embodiment of design principles whereby individuals can adapt on their own to a changing world, and this is why brain anatomies look the way that they do. Models of such brain networks naturally incorporate the types of nonlinear, nonlocal, and nonstationary processes that scientists like Helmholtz, Maxwell, and Mach had already begun to realize are essential.

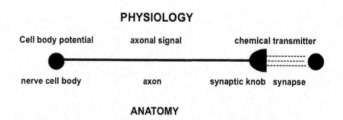

FIGURE 2.3. Some basic anatomical and physiological properties of individual neurons. See the text for additional discussion.

First love: Serial learning, events that go "backwards in time", and the middle is a muddle

When I took Introductory Psychology in 1957, I studied data about human verbal learning and animal discrimination learning, among other topics. To me, these data were filled with philosophical paradoxes that I found very exciting.

For example, data about serial verbal learning in humans (Figure 2.4) seemed to suggest that events can go "backwards in time". I was therefore forced to ask: What is time? Why does it always seem to proceed from the past to the future. Or does it? These data also directed me to confront basic questions about what sort of spaces our minds create in order to represent events that can go backwards in time. Questions about space and time are also among the most fundamental ones that great physicists have pondered over the centuries, notably Newton and Einstein. They also arise ubiquitously in psychological data.

A serial learning experiment is often run by presenting subjects with a list of items. The subjects' task is, in response to a currently seen item, to guess the next item in a list, before showing that item, and then asking the subject what item follows that item, and so on until the entire list is presented. This is called the *serial anticipation method*. Then the list is repeated and practiced again until a criterion for learning the entire list is reached, such as being able to correctly guess all the next items twice throughout the list. The serial anticipation method is thus just a way to analyze how Practice Makes Perfect.

The rate with which the items are presented within the list is called the *intra-trial interval*, and the rest interval between successive list presentations is called the *inter-trial interval* (Figure 2.4). Varying each of these rates can cause major changes in the speed of learning and in the distribution of errors that are made while learning.

The simplest case occurs when learning a short list AB. Remarkably, one then also learns to perform the reverse list BA with higher probability. This property is called "backward learning" and it is sometimes said to illustrate "symmetry of associations". However, this is far from the whole story, since we all know that if C later occurs, the longer list ABC can easily be learned. To understand this simple fact of life actually confronts us with both a scientific and a philosophical problem. In particular, suppose that the intra-trial interval between A and B, and between B and C, is duration *w*. To further fix ideas, suppose that *w* is chosen between 1 to 4 seconds in duration. After B occurs, but before C occurs, the subject experiences just the list AB for a duration of *w* seconds before C occurs, so backward associations should start to form from B to A during that time interval.

Despite this initial learning, somehow, after C is also presented, the learned "forward" association from B to C becomes stronger than the "backward" association from B to A, so that the list ABC can be learned. Symmetry of associations clearly no longer holds when we learn longer lists! Rather, it seems that forward associations are stronger than backward associations so that the "global arrow in time" of the list ABC can be learned from past to future. Why is this? What sort of spatial and temporal interactions can make this happen? Remarkably, this is just the kind of thing that naturally happens if the events A, B, and C activate their own item categories within a neural network!

Before going further, let us immediately acknowledge that such results demand an explanation using differential equations in which events that occur at different moments through time, such as A, then B, and then C, can dramatically change learning outcomes.

Further evidence that a neural network is behind this "asymmetry between the future and the past" is a classical piece of data that is called the *bowed serial position curve*. The bowed serial position curve obtains when a longer list is presented again and again on multiple learning trials until a learning criterion for the entire list is reached. One then plots the cumulative number of errors, summed across all the learning trials, against list position, and finds the kind of error curves that are qualitatively summarized in Figure 2.5. Figure 2.5 redraws data curves from a series of classical experiments that the great American psychologist Carl Hovland published in 1938 (Hovland, 1938a, 1938b, 1938c). Here the short intra-trial interval is two seconds long and the longer intra-trial interval is four seconds long, whereas the short inter-trial interval *W* is six

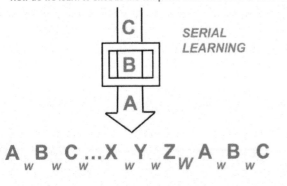

LEARNING A GLOBAL ARROW IN TIME
How do we learn to encode the temporal order of events in LTM?

SERIAL LEARNING

A B C ... X Y Z A B C
w w w w w W w w

w = intratrial interval   W = intertrial interval

FIGURE 2.4. Serial learning paradigm: Learning the temporal order of events by practicing them in the order that they occur in time.

EFFECTS OF INTERTRIAL AND INTRATRIAL INTERVALS

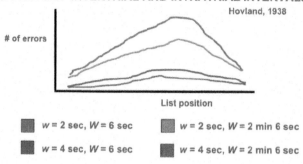

Hovland, 1938

# of errors

List position

■ w = 2 sec, W = 6 sec   ■ w = 2 sec, W = 2 min 6 sec

■ w = 4 sec, W = 6 sec   ■ w = 4 sec, W = 2 min 6 sec

NONoccurrence of future items reduces the number of errors
in response to past items

*These data require a real-time theory for their explanation!
that is, DIFFERENTIAL EQUATIONS*

FIGURE 2.5. Bowed serial position curve. This kind of data emphasizes the importance of modeling how our brains give rise to our minds using nonlinear systems of differential equations.

seconds long and the long inter-trial interval *W* equals two minutes and six seconds long. Intuitively, the list is presented either quickly or slowly, followed by a little rest or a lot of rest before it is presented again. Hovland used these different intra-trial and inter-trial intervals in list learning experiments with different groups of subjects.

The error curves in Figure 2.5 are said to be "bowed" because the beginning and the end of a list are learned and remembered more easily than the middle. This property is characteristic of many life experiences that unfold as sequences of events through time. It is often the case that we can better remember how they began and ended than what happened in between. The middle is a muddle! I like to give the example of a torrential love affair whose beginning and end are vividly remembered, but a lot of details in between can seem to be a blur. The bowed serial position curve is, moreover, asymmetric, with the most errors occurring at list positions nearer to the end than the beginning of the list. When I first studied these data in 1957, I wondered if the asymmetric bowed error curve could also arise from the asymmetry between the strength of future and past associations, such as BC vs BA.

Asymmetry between past and future: How the occurrence of "nothing" influences learning

It is important to realize that these bows imply that the *non*-occurrence of future items influences the difficulty of

learning all past items in the list. This is thus a massive "backward effect in time". To better understand why this is so, imagine a situation where the entire list is presented with an intra-trial interval of *w* and an inter-trial interval of *W = w*. For example, if the list is the alphabet A, B, C, ..., X, Y, Z, turn on a masking stimulus *w* time units after Z is presented. Design the masking stimulus to interfere with further processing of the alphabet. Repeat this procedure on multiple learning trials, and then test how many errors occur at each list position.

If the mask succeeds in interfering with further processing of the alphabet on each learning trial, then there should be an increasing number of errors at later list positions, as illustrated in the top curve of 2.6. The increase of errors with list position can be attributed to associative interference from the list items that occurred before each tested list position. More errors would occur at the latest positions in the list because the occurrence of more earlier items could cause more associative interference. In particular, the most errors should occur at the end of the list. Another way of saying this is that a monotonically increasing error curve is what we would expect if only the past influenced the future.

However, if *W* is larger than *w*, and no masking stimulus is presented between learning trials, then a bowed error curve will obtain, as illustrated by the bottom curve of Figure 2.6, and as it does in all the data curves in Figure 2.5. In effect, letting *W* become larger than *w defines* Z as the last item in the list due to the *non*-occurrence of any letter after Z between the time that the intra-trial interval is exceeded and the next learning trial begins. This fact again argues for differential equations to represent the passage of time so that, after the non-occurrence of a letter after Z, the brain's internal dynamics can continue

BOW DUE TO BACKWARD EFFECT IN TIME

If the past influenced the future, but not conversely:

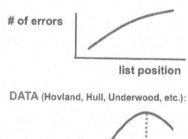

# of errors

list position

DATA (Hovland, Hull, Underwood, etc.):

# of errors

list position

FIGURE 2.6. The bowed serial position curve illustrates the sense in which "events can go backwards in time" during serial learning.

to influence the ease of learning at earlier positions in the list.

The importance of associative interference between items can be highlighted by contrasting learning with short vs. long intra-trial intervals *w*, and short vs. long inter-trial intervals *W*, as Hovland did. If the list is presented quickly (*w* = two seconds), then a lot of associative interference can occur because the activations, or STM traces, that are caused by many previously occurring items can simultaneously remain active. If there is also a short rest period (*W* = six seconds), as in the red curve in Figure 2.5, then there is not enough time for this interference to subside between successive list presentations, so there are more errors at all list positions than in any other condition, but many more errors near the list middle.

If the list is presented quickly (*w* = two seconds) but with a long rest period (*W* = two minutes and six seconds), as in the green curve, then there is enough time between successive list presentations for interference to subside. As a result, errors in the list middle collapse the most, and errors are fewer at all list positions.

If the list is presented more slowly (*w* = four seconds), then fewer STM traces of previously presented items are simultaneously active, so there are fewer errors at all list positions, as the blue and purple curves illustrate. Thus, if the items are presented slowly enough, increasing the inter-trial interval has a smaller effect on reducing errors at all list positions.

Position-specific error gradients in performance also illustrate "backwards in time" dynamics (Figure 2.7). Testing an item at the list beginning tends to cause recall errors of items later in the list, with fewer errors made for items further from the list beginning. Such errors, taken together, are called an *anticipatory error gradient*. In contrast, testing an item near the list end tends to cause recall errors of items earlier in the list, again with fewer errors made for items much earlier in the list. Such errors, taken together, are called a *perseverative error gradient*. Presenting items near the list middle combines both types of gradients, with more anticipatory errors than perseverative errors, thereby creating a *bowed error gradient*. The error gradients near the middle of the list thus, once again, reflect the "asymmetry between past and future".

How do both forward and backward learning occur? How can the *non*-occurrence of future items influence the past? Serial learning data hereby raise a number of basic problems that need to be solved to better understand all phenomena about serial order in behavior, whether we are thinking about language, motor skills, or spatial navigation in a complex environment. I gradually realized that a solution required a real-time theory using differential equations that could describe how learning changes LTM values through time as the number and distribution of STM traces change in response to different list presentation conditions.

What is the functional stimulus: Items or sequence chunks?

Before moving forward, I hasten to note that backward effects in time are just one of many intellectual challenges that serial learning data force upon us. Indeed, one of the main issues in serial learning is: What is the *functional stimulus*? This issue is illustrated by the fact that *transfer of learning* from serial learning to paired associate learning is much worse than from paired associate to serial learning. Unlike serial learning, where the same item order is repeated over and over again on successive learning trials, during paired associate learning, individual stimulus-response pairs can be presented in any order on successive learning trials. For example, on a given trial, the item pairs AB, CD, EF, . . . may be presented in that temporal order, but on the next trial the same pairs may be presented again, but in a different temporal order EF, CD, AB, . . . , with the recall task being to predict the second item in each pair after seeing the first one (e.g., B given A), and doing so before the second item is also presented. The asymmetric transfer occurs when the paired associate pairs are also successive items in the serial list. Asymmetric transfer means that some prior paired associate learning improves the learning of a compatible serial list much more than the converse.

Many scientists from the 1930s through the 1960s struggled with these transfer data, which imply that the functional stimulus in serial learning is not the individual items of the list. But then, what *is* the functional stimulus?!

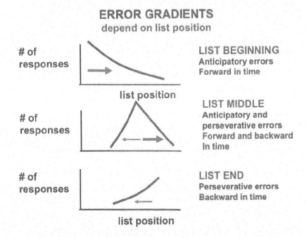

FIGURE 2.7. Position-specific forward and backward error gradients illustrate how associations can form in both the forward and backward directions in time before the list is completely learned.

I gradually realized how sequences of items that are stored in a working memory can be unitized into learned *list chunks* during serial learning (Figures 1.23 and 1.24). This can happen *because* the same list order is repeated over and over. These list chunks are the functional units that predict the next item in a serially learned list, not the individual items that are presented by the experimentalist. In order to make this hypothesis precise, I had to jump into cognitive studies to discover how working memories are designed, and how list chunks are learned from them. My neural models eventually showed how to design cognitive Item-Order-Rank working memories and the Masking Field list chunk learning networks with which they interact, as the discussion in Chapter 1 has illustrated. Chapter 12 will explain how these working memories are designed and list chunks are learned from them, as well as how these core ingredients help to explain and predict a breathtaking amount of data about audition, speech, language, cognition, and sensory-motor control. My first article about neural models of working memory and list chunks was published in 1978, However, in 1957 I was worried about much simpler problems.

From serial learning to neural networks: Discovering the dynamics of STM and LTM

These data about forward and backward learning, the bowed serial position curve, and position-dependent error gradients forced me into a neural network formalism (Figure 2.8), In such a network, activities of cells code for recently occurring events. In the case of learning the list AB, cells coding A and then B would be activated. In particular, when list items like A and B are presented, inputs to the corresponding cells turn on their activities, or STM traces. That is why these cells are said to be *content-addressable*. A major challenge for me, and other cognitive scientists, was to explain how such content-addressable item categories are learned. I will explain this in Chapters 5 and 9, starting with discoveries that I began to publish in 1976. In 1957, however, I could only assume that these item categories exist, and hope to explain how they are learned sometime in the future.

After receiving an input, an item category's activity would persist for awhile, even after its input shut off, before

HOW THESE RESULTS LED TO NEURAL NETWORKS
NETWORKS CAN LEARN FORWARD AND BACKWARD ASSOCIATIONS!

Because learning AB is not the same as learning BA, you need STM traces, or activations, x_i, at the nodes, or cells, and LTM traces, or adaptive weights, z_{ij}, for learning at the synapses

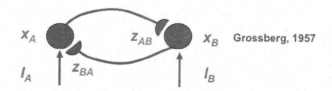

FIGURE 2.8. The existence of forward and backward associations, such as from A to B and from B to A is naturally explained by a network of neurons with their own activities or STM traces, and bidirectional connections between them with their own adaptive weights or LTM traces.

decaying back to zero. Because of this persistence, the activities were also called short-term memory (STM) traces. I could then see how the simultaneous persistence of STM traces across multiple item categories could cause the associative learning and interference that leads to the bowed serial error curve.

The STM variables are different from more slowly varying learning variables, which are also called long-term memory (LTM) traces, or adaptive weights. Due to the network connections, there can be different LTM traces to code for the lists AB and BA. These are the variables z_{AB} and z_{BA}, respectively, in Figure 2.8. Thus, a network geometry with distinct, and directed, connections from A to B, and from B to A, with different LTM traces at the synapse of each connection, made backward learning easy to understand, at least qualitatively, because these associations can both be learned when the item categories of A and B are simultaneously active. More generally, the dynamically changing *spatial pattern* of all the STM trace activities through time drove the learning of the LTM traces, and was, in turn, altered by the read-out of these LTM traces through time, in response to different sequences of inputs to the network. Although I could intuitively see how these interacting STM and LTM traces could explain the list learning data, the trick was to find the correct STM and LTM laws to actually do it! I was able to do this in 1957-58, and variants of these laws are still used ubiquitously today to explain many different kinds of psychological and neurobiological data about human and animal learning.

Dissociating STM and LTM: Bilateral hippocampectomy in HM

The distinction between STM and LTM should not be taken for granted. Due to the strong interactions between these distinct processes, they can be confused or lumped together. This kind of uncertainty was especially true when I derived my laws for these processes in 1957. To remind us of how very long ago this was, in the same year, 1957, William Scoville and Brenda Milner published their landmark paper about the effects on learning and memory of bilaterally removing the hippocampus, and adjacent structures (Scoville and Milner, 1957). The effects of this ablation illustrated that properties of STM and LTM could be dissociated.

This surgery was carried out in an effort to control intractable epilepsy in the patient who was called HM to protect his privacy. HM was revealed to be Henry Molaison after his death in 2008 at the age of 82. His surgery was done in 1952, when Henry was 27 years old. Henry retained many cognitive functions after his surgery, but had severe deficits in committing to LTM new explicit and conscious memories of experienced events, memories that are often lumped together as *declarative memory*. Although Henry could store recent events in STM, if he was distracted, all trace of these events could be abolished. For example, one could be introduced to Henry, and receive his warm welcome, leave the room, and come in to be introduced again with Henry none the wiser.

Despite Henry's profound declarative memory deficits, his *procedural memory* for learning and remembering motor skills remained intact, even though he had no conscious recollection of having practiced the skill. Many scientists interviewed and tested Henry over the years to better understand how the hippocampus contributes to learning and memory. The Scoville and Milner article also triggered thousands of additional clinical and experimental studies on multiple humans and animals to better understand how learning and memory work, and many of the resulting deficits can currently be mechanistically explained by the cognitive and cognitive-emotional interactions in Adaptive Resonance Theory. In particular, the different properties of declarative and procedural memories illustrate the brain's organization into computationally complementary cortical processing streams (Table 1.1). Several subsequent chapters will be devoted to explaining how these different processes work, and how they break down in amnesic individuals like HM.

On the shoulders of giants: The functional units of STM and LTM are spatial patterns

Learning at the model's synapses was part of a time-honored tradition of *associative learning* by many great psychologists, including Ivan Pavlov (Pavlov, 1927), Donald Hebb (Hebb, 1949), Clark Hull (Hull, 1943), Edward Thorndike (Thorndike, 1927), B. F. Skinner (Skinner, 1938), Edward Tolman (Tolman, 1948), and William Estes (Estes, 1950). However, how learning works in my STM-LTM model went beyond the concepts of these great scientists.

That is true because my conceptual and mathematical analyses of these networks in the 1960s showed that the functional units of learning are *distributed patterns*, or *vectors*, of LTM traces across a *network*, not individual traces between a particular pair of *cells*; e.g., Grossberg (1968c). Indeed, analysis of such patterns in the case of serial learning enabled me to understand data like the bowed serial position curve; e.g., Grossberg (1969c). In order for a *pattern* of LTM traces to *match*, through learning, a *pattern* of STM traces, some of the LTM traces may need to *increase*, while others need to *decrease*. Thus, my LTM laws combined what some scientists would later call Hebbian (increasing LTM strength) *and* anti-Hebbian (decreasing LTM strength) properties. In other words, an LTM trace increases (Hebbian) as it learns to match a large STM activity, or decreases (anti-Hebbian) as it learns to match a small STM activity.

This conclusion contradicts the famous Hebb Postulate that practice always strengthens associations. Hebb wrote in 1949 that "when the axon of cell A is near enough to excite a cell B . . . A's efficacy, as one of the cells firing B is increased" (Hebb, 1949). Despite its great constructive effects on the research of many scientists, the Hebb Postulate is wrong, and it is wrong for a fundamental reason: Hebb chose the wrong computational unit. The unit is not a single pathway. Instead, the unit of LTM is a pattern of LTM traces that is distributed across a network. When one needs to match an LTM pattern to an STM pattern, then both increases *and* decreases of LTM strength are needed.

The Hebb postulate fails for a basic reason that does not depend upon this insight: If in fact an LTM trace could only increase, and if all LTM traces have a finite upper bound, then there could come a time when an LTM trace reached its maximum value. After that time, further learning with that LTM trace would be impossible, even if the world changed.

This problem does not occur with the LTM laws that I introduced, because my LTM traces can increase or decrease as changing environmental demands require.

I was first led to this conclusion by analyzing how learning occurs at different list positions to explain serial learning data. I called the learning law that could explain these data *gated steepest descent learning*. During gated steepest descent learning, an LTM trace (e.g., z_{AB} in Figure 2.8) tracks and approaches the value of a post-synaptic STM signal (e.g., x_B in Figure 2.8) through time (steepest descent). Learning only occurs when a pre-synaptic STM "sampling" signal (e.g., x_A in Figure 2.8 is active enough, and thereby opens a learning "gate" that enables steepest descent to occur. Gated steepest descent learning also proved to be invaluable to explain many other kinds of learning as well, including the bottom-up learning that tunes the adaptive filters that choose recognition categories and the top-down learning of expectations that select the critical feature patterns upon which attention is focused (Figures 1.25 and 2.2). These processes are explained in Chapter 5 as part of the competitive learning, self-organizing map, and ART models. The fact that LTM traces in the brain exhibit gated steepest descent properties started to be confirmed experimentally by neurophysiologists like Wolf Singer and William ("Chip") Levy 20 years later (Levy, Brassel, and Moore, 1983; Levy and Desmond, 1985; Rauschecker and Singer, 1979; Singer, 1983).

Despite the fact that the Hebb postulate cannot possibly be the whole truth, and that learning laws like gated steepest descent fit behavioral and neurobiological data better, many psychologists and neuroscientists continue to invoke the term "Hebbian learning" to describe any example of associative learning. Some may wish to do this to honor Hebb's many contributions to memory research, despite the fact that his hypothesis about how learning works was wrong. On the other hand, Hebb was not the first, or even the greatest, pioneer of memory research. There were other greats before him or as his contemporaries. We should not overlook the seminal contributions of memory researchers such as Pavlov, Hull, Thorndike, Skinner, Tolman, and Estes, among others. My own preference is to be clear about the specific hypotheses in different learning laws and their historical origins, and to give them functional names, like gated steepest descent, that reflect how they work. Only in this way can one avoid confusion about different learning properties and build upon previous discoveries in an efficient and rational way.

My mathematical analyses in the mid-1960s to early 1970s proved that the LTM traces learn a time average of the spatial patterns of STM traces that are active when the sampling signal is on. As Chapter 5 will explain, these LTM traces encode the *relative* activities of the STM traces that characterize the spatial patterns. Said in another way, the LTM traces learn the *synchronous* part of these STM patterns, since the relative activities

of a spatial pattern stay constant through time, even if their total activities oscillate together. This result led me to predictions about synchronous dynamics in the mid-1970s that influenced the experimental work of neurophysiologists like Charles Gray and Wolf Singer (Gray and Singer, 1989) and Reinhard Eckhorn and his colleagues (Eckhorn et al., 1988) in the 1980s.

In this way, I derived, during my Freshman year at Dartmouth in 1957-58, the *paradigm* of using systems of nonlinear differential equations to describe neural networks whose STM and LTM interactions explain and predict quite a bit of psychological and neurobiological data. I called the simplest versions of this model the *Additive Model* and the *Shunting Model*.

The Additive Model got its name from the fact that each cell's activity is the result of influences that add their effects on its rate of change. Figure 2.9 describes the Additive Model equation and defines its various terms, including the decay rate of the activity x_i, the sum of all positive and negative feedback signals from other cells, and any external inputs from the world. Understanding of the book does not, however, depend upon knowing this or other equations that I will occasionally mention.

Additive responses to arbitrarily large inputs can lead to activities that have no upper or lower bounds, since every increment in an input can cause a proportional increment in the resulting activity. But all cells have fixed, indeed small, bounds on their activities. This is a basic property of all cells, whether they are in your brain or your kidney: Infinity does not exist in biology! I therefore also introduced the Shunting Model, of which the Additive Model is a special case. The Shunting Model keeps cell activities within fixed upper and lower bounds (Figure 2.10) using what are called *automatic gain control* terms (red

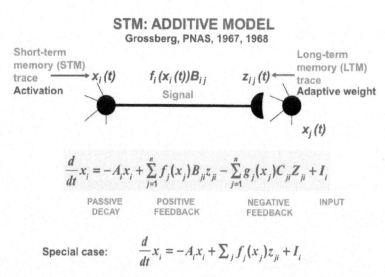

STM: ADDITIVE MODEL
Grossberg, PNAS, 1967, 1968

Short-term memory (STM) trace — $x_i(t)$ $f_i(x_i(t))B_{ij}$ $z_{ij}(t)$ ← Long-term memory (LTM) trace

Activation   Signal   Adaptive weight

$x_j(t)$

$$\frac{d}{dt}x_i = -A_i x_i + \sum_{j=1}^{n} f_j(x_j)B_{ji}z_{ji} - \sum_{j=1}^{n} g_j(x_j)C_{ji}Z_{ji} + I_i$$

PASSIVE DECAY   POSITIVE FEEDBACK   NEGATIVE FEEDBACK   INPUT

Special case: $\dfrac{d}{dt}x_i = -A_i x_i + \sum_j f_j(x_j)z_{ji} + I_i$

FIGURE 2.9. The Additive Model describes how multiple effects add up influence the activities, or STM, traces of neurons.

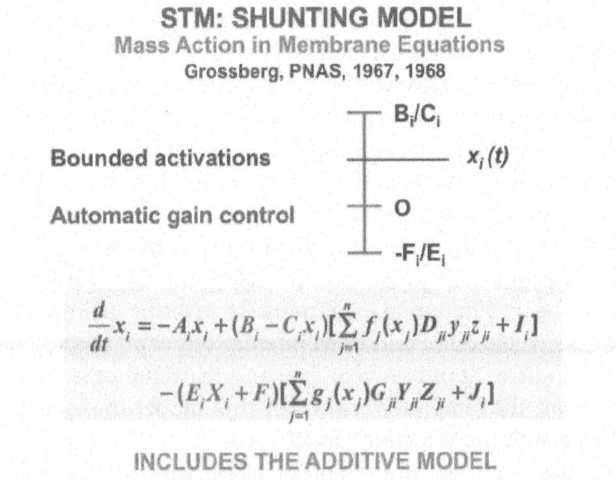

STM: SHUNTING MODEL
Mass Action in Membrane Equations
Grossberg, PNAS, 1967, 1968

Bounded activations

Automatic gain control

B_i/C_i

$x_i(t)$

O

$-F_i/E_i$

$$\frac{d}{dt}x_i = -A_i x_i + (B_i - C_i x_i)[\sum_{j=1}^{n} f_j(x_j)D_{ji}y_{ji}z_{ji} + I_i]$$

$$- (E_i X_i + F_i)[\sum_{j=1}^{n} g_j(x_j)G_{ji}Y_{ji}Z_{ji} + J_i]$$

INCLUDES THE ADDITIVE MODEL

FIGURE 2.10. The Shunting Model includes upper and lower bounds on neuronal activities. These bounds have the effect of multiplying additive terms by excitatory and inhibitory automatic gain terms that enable such models to preserve their sensitivity to inputs whose size may vary greatly in size through time, while also approximately normalizing their total activities.

terms in Figure 2.10) that play many useful roles in brain dynamics. The Shunting Model embodies the membrane equations of neurophysiology, which describe how cell potentials respond to their inputs (Hodgkin and Huxley, 1952). At the time in 1957 that I derived it from psychological considerations, I did not yet know any neurophysiology. Variants of the Additive and Shunting models are used today by essentially all biological modelers in computational neuroscience.

With the Additive and Shunting STM equations before us, it is now easy to also write down the simplest versions of the medium-term memory, or MTM, law which is realized by a habituative transmitter gate; and the long-term memory, or LTM law which is realized by gated steepest descent learning (Figure 2.11). MTM changes more slowly than STM, and LTM changes even more slowly than MTM. The MTM law in Figure 2.11 is called a transmitter *gate* because it multiplies signals that are activated by STM traces, as illustrated by term $D_{ji}y_{ji}z_{ji}$ in Figure 2.10. It is called *habituative* because the release or inactivation of transmitter by these signals, as in term $-Lf_k(x_k)y_{ki}$ in Figure 2.11, reduces the efficacy of the signal pathway.

The LTM law in Figure 2.11 is called gated steepest descent because learning turns on when the learning *gate*, or sampling signal, $f_k(x_k)$ is positive, thereby enabling the adaptive weight, or LTM trace, z_{ki} to approach the sampled signal $h_i(x_i)$ by *steepest descent* via term $(h_i(x_i) - z_{ki})$. When the learning gate shuts off, learning stops, and the adaptive weight can remember what it has learned until it turns on again, which might not happen for a long time. LTM also gates the readout of signals, as term $D_{ji}y_{ji}z_{ji}$ in Figure 2.10 again illustrates.

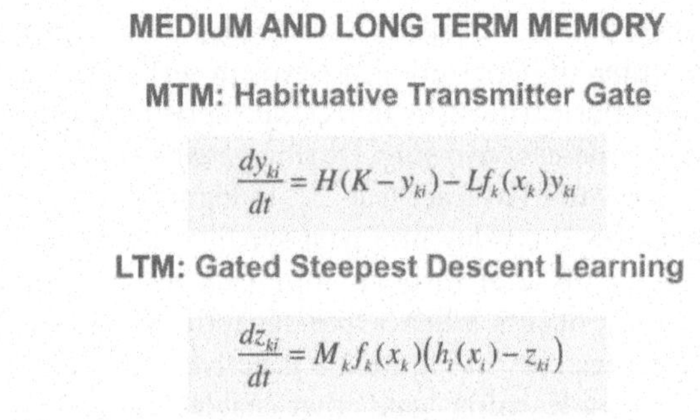

MEDIUM AND LONG TERM MEMORY

MTM: Habituative Transmitter Gate

$$\frac{dy_{ki}}{dt} = H(K - y_{ki}) - Lf_k(x_k)y_{ki}$$

LTM: Gated Steepest Descent Learning

$$\frac{dz_{ki}}{dt} = M_k f_k(x_k)\big(h_i(x_i) - z_{ki}\big)$$

FIGURE 2.11. Medium-term memory (MTM) and long-term memory (LTM) equations complement the Additive and Shunting Models of STM. MTM is typically defined by a chemical transmitter that is released from the synaptic knobs of a neuron (Figure 2.3). Its release or inactivation in an activity-dependent way is also called habituation. LTM defines how associative learning occurs between a pair of neurons whose activities are appropriately correlated through time. See the text for details.

All of these equations were needed, for example, to define the gated dipole opponent processing circuits in Figures 2.8 and 2.9, and their variations and specializations have enabled the explanation and prediction of a vast number and variety of psychological and neurobiological data. One reason, therefore, for summarizing these equations here, even without a mathematical analysis of them, is to illustrate that in the psychological and brain sciences, no less than the physical sciences, a small number of fundamental equations can explain and predict many important and interesting data.

Three sources of neural network research: Binary, linear, and continuous-nonlinear

My own work pioneered biological neural network models capable of linking brains to minds, but this was certainly not the only historical source of models that have been used to explain aspects of how brains work. At least three such sources should be noted (Figure 2.12):

Binary models

McCulloch-Pitts model and the digital computer. Binary systems were inspired in part by neurophysiological observations showing that signals between many neurons are carried by all-or-none spikes. When the activity,

THREE SOURCES OF NEURAL NETWORK RESEARCH

BINARY	LINEAR
NEURAL NETWORK SIGNAL PROCESSING	SYSTEM THEORY
McCullogh-Pitts, 1943	Widrow, 1962
$X_i(t+1) = \text{sgn}\left[\sum_j A_{ij} X_j(t) - B_i\right]$	Anderson, 1968
	Kohonen, 1971
Von Neumann, 1945	Y=AX
Caianiello, 1961	CROSS-CORRELATE
Rosenblatt, 1962	STEEPEST DESCENT
DIGITAL COMPUTER	

CONTINUOUS and NONLINEAR
NEUROPHYSIOLOGY and PSYCHOLOGY
Hodgkin and Huxley, 1952
Hartline and Ratliff, 1957
Grossberg, 1957
Von der Malsburg, 1973

FIGURE 2.12. Three sources of neural network research: Binary, linear, and continuous and nonlinear. My own work has contributed primarily to the third.

or potential, of a neuron exceeds a firing threshold, then a spike can be generated and can travel, without decrement, down the axon of the neuron for long distances (Figure 2.3). Spikes may be triggered more frequently as the cell activity increases, so that increasingly active cells can emit spikes with an ever higher frequency that can have an increasingly large impact on neurons that receive its signals.

The binary stream was initiated by a classical article that was published in 1943 by Warren McCulloch and Walter Pitts when they were working at MIT (McCulloch and Pitts, 1943). Their model describes a threshold logic system. The activities, or STM traces, x_i of the ith node in such a network interact in discrete time according to the equation in the upper left panel of Figure 2.12. In this equation, the signum function, denoted by sgn, can take on the values +1 if $w > 0$, 0 if $w = 0$, and −1 if $w < 0$. In particular, a cell generates a binary signal, or spike, with amplitude +1 if the activity is positive. The negative signal −1 when the activity is negative has no analog in neuronal signaling, however. Its role in the McCulloch-Pitts model was to enable the computation of useful logical operations, as indicated by the arresting title of their article: "A Logical Calculus of the Ideas Immanent in Nervous Activity". The model's goal was thus to demonstrate how complex logical operations could be computed just by using suitable combinations of +1, 0, and −1 signals between multiple elements in a computing network.

The McCulloch-Pitts model had an influence far beyond the field of neural networks. One of its most enduring influences was upon John Von Neumann, one of the greatest mathematicians of the twentieth century, when he was at the Institute for Advanced Study in Princeton, developing the digital computer that has totally revolutionized our lives. This influence is illustrated by a famous series of Silliman Lectures that Von Neumann gave at Yale University in 1956, which he called *The Computer and the Brain* (von Neumann, 1958).

The McCulloch-Pitts model was not the only contribution to the binary model literature. Eduardo Caianiello (Caianiello, 1961), working in Naples, Italy, used a binary STM equation that also operated at discrete time steps and whose activity was influenced by activities at multiple times in the past. The signals emitted by a Caianiello neuron could be +1 if the activity was positive, or 0 if it was not, so it eliminated the biologically implausible negative signals of the McCulloch-Pitts model.

Perceptron. In 1958, Frank Rosenblatt, who worked at the Cornell Aeronautical Laboratory before he became a professor at Cornell University, introduced a STM equation that evolves in continuous time, whose activities can spontaneously decay, and which can generate binary signals above a non-zero threshold. Rosenblatt's equation was used in his classical Perceptron model (Rosenblatt, 1958), which is a linear classifier that can learn to separate input vectors, and thereby classify them as being in different categories (e.g., cat vs. dog), if they are linearly separable.

Both Caianiello and Rosenblatt were interested in learning, and both introduced equations to change the adaptive weights, or LTM traces, in their equations through learning. However, in both models, interactions between STM and LTM were uncoupled in order to simplify the analysis: First there would be a change in STM, then the algorithm would allow LTM to adjust to it, and then the cycle would repeat. This meant that these models did not operate autonomously in real time, where both STM and LTM would adjust to changing contingencies as they occurred. These LTM equations also had a digital aspect. The Caianiello LTM equations increased or decreased at constant rates until they hit finite upper or lower bounds.

From Perceptrons to Back Propagation and Deep Learning. I had the pleasure of knowing both Caianiello and Rosenblatt. Frank Rosenblatt died tragically in a boating accident when he was only 43 years old. His pioneering work is having a major impact even today. His ambitious goals are illustrated by the fact that he followed his 1958 article about the Perceptron model with a classical 1962 book called *Principles of Neurodynamics* (Rosenblatt, 1962). Although the original Perceptron model had only an input layer and output layer of neurons with which to classify linearly separable patterns into two categories, Frank realized that classifiers with more layers were needed, and introduced the name "back propagation" to describe how the adaptive weights in such an expanded network would be trained. He did not, however, translate this heuristic insight into a computationally competent back propagation algorithm.

Variants of the back propagation model were introduced independently by several authors, including

Shun-Ichi Amari in 1972 in Japan (Amari, 1972), Paul Werbos in 1974 as part of his PhD thesis at Harvard University (Werbos, 1974, 1994), and David Parker in 1982 in California (Parker, 1982, 1985, 1986, 1987). Paul Werbos seems to be the first person to have published the algorithm in its modern form and use it successfully in applications. Back propagation finally became popular in response to an oft-cited article by David Rumelhart, Geoffrey Hinton, and Ronald Williams that was published in 1986 (Rumelhart, Hinton, and Williams, 1986). Their 1986 article has often been incorrectly cited as the source of the algorithm by people who are unaware of its history.

Technically, back propagation uses an old idea in mathematics, steepest or gradient descent, that goes back at least to Carl Friedrich Gauss (Gauss, 1814), who lived in Germany between 1777-1855 and was one of the greatest mathematicians who ever lived. Steepest descent works by attracting adaptive weights to target values during learning trials. In back propagation, the learned weights, or LTM traces, need to be transported from where they are learned to where they are needed to filter incoming data. That is, the LTM traces are computed at one location in the algorithm and their learned values are then moved algorithmically to another location. One can think of this as a physical, not just a functional, separation of learning and recall. Such a non-local transport of weights has no analog in our brains.

Back propagation became very popular for awhile, and helped to develop some useful applications. However, its conceptual and practical limitations were soon realized by practitioners. As I earlier remarked in the Preface, my 1988 article in the inaugural issue of the journal *Neural Networks* (Grossberg, 1988) listed 17 major limitations of learning by back propagation that were not problems for Adaptive Resonance Theory. After this period of cooling down, during the past decade, Hinton and his colleagues vigorously applied and developed the variant of back propagation that is called Deep Learning (e.g., Hinton et al., 2012; LeCun, Bengio, and Hinton, 2015). They were able to achieve useful results in multiple applications by exploiting the huge databases that have emerged with the World Wide Web (e.g., millions of pictures of cats on the World Wide Web), and the incredibly fast computer networks that have evolved at the same time. Deep Learning has typically derived these results by carrying out slow learning (meaning that adaptive weights change very little on each learning trial) using many supervised learning trials of large numbers of exemplars from huge databases. Many scientists have become excited by the promise of Deep Learning, even while acknowledging problems such as catastrophic forgetting and poor generalization (Bengio and LeCun, 2007).

Even if Deep Learning generalizes well in response to a subset of data, it cannot easily be determined whether the knowledge that has been embodied in its adaptive weights reflect an understanding of the environment that it is predicting. This problem is called the Explainable AI problem, and is a subject of current intense interest in the AI community (https://en.wikipedia.org/wiki/Explainable_artificial_intelligence). Also see Grossberg (2020a).

Variants of Deep Learning have been developed to at least partially overcome these problems, including using unsupervised pre-training before supervised fine-tuning (Erhan et al., 2010). These and other applications of Deep Learning have driven a renaissance in AI that has brought improved products into our everyday lives, especially applications that classify huge databases of images and sounds.

Despite these successes, Deep Learning, being a variant of back propagation, is emphatically not how our brains work. Its architecture is not supported by brain data, and it does not realize the kinds of general-purpose and flexible capabilities that we associate with animal intelligence, including our own. As the Preface has already noted, Hinton himself acknowledged this in a 2017 article in the September 15, 2017 issue of *Axios* where he said that he is "deeply suspicious" of back-propagation", that "I suspect that means getting rid of back-propagation . . . I don't think it's how the brain works. We clearly don't need all the labeled data . . .", and that "my view is, throw it all away and start over" (LeVine, 2017).

Actually, we do not need to "start over". One just needs to read the mainstream published literature in which, over the past 50 years, many fundamental properties of human intelligence have been steadily explained and rigorously modeled that Deep Learning cannot explain, including how to quickly learn to classify and predict huge non-stationary databases without experiencing catastrophic forgetting. For example, variants of ART models can, in fast learning mode, learn to classify a complete database on a single learning trial, can do so without experiencing catastrophic forgetting, and its learning can after every learning trial be interpreted in terms of fuzzy IF-THEN rules.

Linear

ADELINE and MADELINE. Bernard Widrow at Stanford University also drew inspiration from the brain to introduce the gradient descent ADELINE adaptive pattern recognition algorithm (Widrow, 1962). This algorithm uses a linear filter with adaptive weights, or LTM traces, that slowly converge to values which reduce the least mean square of the error between a desired output and the current output. Widrow's models have been used in many signal processing applications, including adaptive noise canceling in a wide variety of devices, including earphones, communication lines, and modems. These algorithms also find echoes in back propagation, which also learns by gradient descent using a least mean square criterion.

Brain-State-in-a-Box. James Anderson at Brown University described his intuitions about neural pattern recognition by also adapting concepts from linear system theory to represent some aspects of neural dynamics. The activities in his model obey a linear equation. However, each neuron's output combines continuous and binary properties: Although the outputs increase linearly with cell activity within a given range of intermediate values, they saturate at negative and positive constant values in response to sufficiently small and large activities. This output function is charmingly summarized by the name of Anderson's model, Brain-State-in-a-Box, or BSB (Anderson, Silverstein, Ritz, and Jones, 1977). The BSB model has been used in various pattern classification applications. However, it has several conceptual problems, a major one being that its activities can amplify, rather than suppress, noise. I had, in fact, mathematically proved how to solve this noise suppression problem in my 1973 article about "Contour Enhancement, Short-Term Memory, and Constancies in Reverberating Neural Networks" (Grossberg, 1973). I summarize in Figure 1.7 how signal functions may be chosen to avoid noise amplification.

From Moore-Penrose pseudo-inverse to Self-Organizing Maps. Teuvo Kohonen at Helsinki University also made a transition from linear algebra concepts, such as the Moore-Penrose pseudoinverse (e.g., Albert, 1972), to more biologically motivated models that include nonlinear interactions. In the latter category, Kohonen used a simplified version of a Self-Organizing Map, or SOM, model in various applications (e.g., Kohonen, 1984). The SOM model feeds the outputs of an adaptive filter into a competition that chooses a winning category, or small set of categories, from the cells that receive the largest total inputs through the adaptive filter. These winning categories are used to classify incoming data.

The SOM had earlier been introduced and developed in the early 1970s by myself working in Cambridge and Boston, and Christoph von der Malsburg, who was then working at the Max-Planck Institute for Biophysical Chemistry in Göttingen (Grossberg, 1972c, 1976a, 1976b; Malsburg, 1973). I had even earlier introduced and mathematically analyzed the learning laws and competitive networks that go into the SOM model, starting in the 1960s (e.g., Grossberg, 1968c, 1969c, 1971b, 1973, 1974).

I will explain how biological SOMs work in Chapter 5, including how they can undergo catastrophic forgetting, and how they solve the *stability-plasticity dilemma*, and thus do not catastrophically forget, when they are suitably

embedded within larger Adaptive Resonance Theory, or ART, neural architectures. Biological versions of SOMs include essential properties, such as Medium Term Memory, or MTM, that the simplified version of Kohonen does not. These enhanced SOMs, and the larger ART architectures in which they live, are used in a remarkably wide range of brain processes, ranging from vision and speech to cognitive-emotional interactions and spatial navigation.

Continuous-Nonlinear

Hartline-Ratliff equation for the horseshoe crab retina. Continuous-nonlinear network laws typically arose from an analysis of behavioral or brain data. Neurophysiological experiments on the lateral eye of the *Limulus*, or horseshoe crab, led to the award of a Nobel Prize in Physiology or Medicine in 1967 to H. Keffer Hartline, who had done his work at The Rockefeller Institute for Medical Research in Manhattan. Hartline used to collect the crabs on Long Island.

In addition to doing these important experiments, Hartline also worked with Floyd Ratliff to model their data (Hartline and Ratliff, 1957). This interdisciplinary research provided an inspiring prototype for how cutting-edge neurophysiological experimentation and theoretical modeling could be mutually reinforcing. The original Hartline-Ratliff model describes network activities at steady-state in response to constant inputs. This model shows how recurrent inhibition across cells can reduce the net activities in the retina; cf. Figures 1.6 and 1.7. An inhibitory feedback signal is generated in the model when the cell's activity exceeds a firing threshold.

The Hartline-Ratliff equation was generalized with their collaborator William Miller to the Hartline-Ratliff-Miller model, which models the dynamics of recurrent inhibition through time (Ratliff, Hartline, and Miller, 1963). Figure 2.13 describes how the model's cell activities e_i are transformed into smaller net activities h_i by the sum $-\sum_{j=1}^{n} [\int_{0}^{t} e^{-A(t-v)} h_j(v) dv - \Gamma_j]^+ B_{ji}$ of all the inhibitory feedback signals. Each inhibitory feedback signal is itself a difference of two terms. The first term is a time-average, from the start time $v = 0$ to the present time $v = t$, of the net activity $h_j(v)$ of the jth inhibitory cell as it exponentially decays through time at rate A. The second term subtracts the firing threshold Γ_j from the average activity to determine the inhibitory feedback signal. The Hartline-Ratliff-Miller model is thus a kind of continuous threshold-logic system. This model is a precursor of the Additive Model that that I had independently discovered in 1957-58 (Figure 2.9).

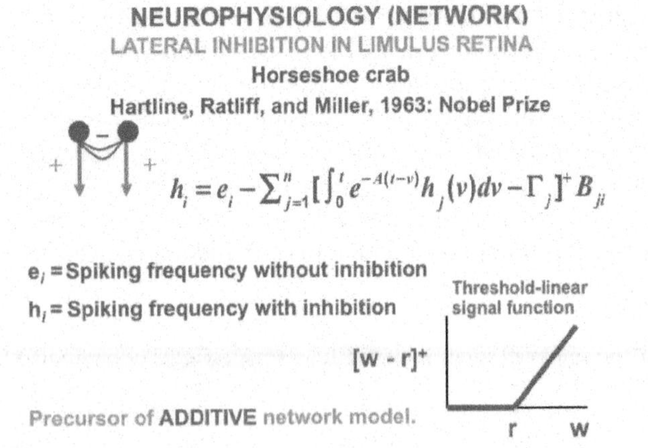

NEUROPHYSIOLOGY (NETWORK)
LATERAL INHIBITION IN LIMULUS RETINA
Horseshoe crab
Hartline, Ratliff, and Miller, 1963: Nobel Prize

$$h_i = e_i - \sum_{j=1}^{n} [\int_0^t e^{-A(t-v)} h_j(v)dv - \Gamma_j]^+ B_{ji}$$

e_i = Spiking frequency without inhibition

h_i = Spiking frequency with inhibition

$[w - r]^+$

Threshold-linear signal function

Precursor of **ADDITIVE** network model.

FIGURE 2.13. Hartline's lab developed a model to describe signal processing by the retina of the horseshoe crab.

NEUROPHYSIOLOGY (SINGLE CELL)
SPIKE POTENTIALS IN SQUID GIANT AXON
Hodgkin and Huxley, 1952: Nobel Prize

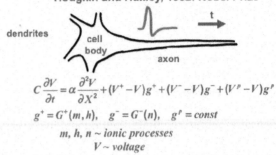

dendrites — cell body — axon — t

$$C\frac{\partial V}{\partial t} = \alpha \frac{\partial^2 V}{\partial X^2} + (V^+ - V)g^+ + (V^- - V)g^- + (V^p - V)g^p$$

$$g^+ = G^+(m, h), \quad g^- = G^-(n), \quad g^p = const$$

$$m, h, n \sim ionic\ processes$$
$$V \sim voltage$$

PRECURSOR OF **SHUNTING** NETWORK MODEL
Rall, 1962

FIGURE 2.14. Hodgkin and Huxley developed a model to explain how spikes travel down the squid giant axon.

Coincidentally, the year 1967 when Hartline won the Nobel Prize was also the year that I earned my PhD in mathematics from Rockefeller for a thesis that proved global limit and oscillation theorems for the neural networks that I had discovered in 1957–58 (see below). My neural networks included as a special case the Hartline-Ratliff-Miller model. I was able to prove these global limit and oscillation theorems for networks with an arbitrarily large number of neurons, which was an unusual kind of theorem in applied mathematics. The theorems characterized all the trajectories of the STM and LTM traces of the networks as they learned through time, and thus showed how the networks function as content-addressable memories for storing learned patterns.

Hodgkin-Huxley equations for the squid giant axon. Another classical contribution arose from the analysis of how the excitable membrane of a single neuron can generate electrical spikes (the red curve in Figure 2.14) that are capable of rapidly and non-decrementally traversing the axon, or pathway, from one neuron's cell body to a neuron to which it is sending signals. This experimental work was done on the squid giant axon because it was big enough to allow the electrode to be placed inside it. Sir Alan Hodgkin and Sir Andrew Huxley did these epochal experiments both at the Physiological Laboratory in Cambridge, England, and at the Laboratory of the Marine Biological Association in Plymouth, Massachusetts (Hodgkin and Huxley, 1952). I call the work epochal because it remains one of the most important foundational neurophysiological studies that has ever been done. Hodgkin and Huxley also introduced the Hodgkin-Huxley model of nerve impulse propagation to explain their data about how spikes are generated and travel down an axon (Figure 2.14). Theirs was thus another inspiring example of a highly successful interdisciplinary experimental and modeling enterprise. Their work earned them the Nobel Prize in Physiology or Medicine in 1963.

Despite its great importance and usefulness, the Hodgkin-Huxley model was basically a curve fit to their data from a single kind of cell. Later models and mathematical analyses, notably in a classical series of articles by Gail Carpenter between 1976 and 1981, provided a more robust mathematical definition of a generalized Hodgkin-Huxley model that included many biophysical variations which could occur in different kinds of neurons, as well as a mathematical analysis of how individual spikes are generated in a wide variety of cells. Carpenter also proved when and how periodic sequences and bursts of spikes could occur under both normal and abnormal conditions (Carpenter, 1976, 1977a, 1977b, 1979, 1981). These results provided a deep geometrical insight into how and when different spiking patterns are caused in large classes of model neurons.

Since the Hodgkin-Huxley equation focuses on individual neurons rather than neural networks, it will not be further discussed herein except to note that it provides a historical context for the neural network Shunting Model that I discovered in 1957-58 and finally got published in 1967 in the *Proceedings of the National Academy of Sciences* (Grossberg, 1967; Figure 2.10).

Linking brain to mind: The units that govern behavioral success are distributed patterns. I hope that these historical comments give the reader a better idea of the state-of-the-art around the time that I introduced the paradigm of using nonlinear neural networks to link brain mechanisms to psychological functions in 1957-1958. Despite the fact that these laws are foundational and classical today, it took a decade to get them published because they represented a major paradigm shift in how the psychological and brain sciences were then being studied. This paradigm shift is still ongoing today.

As I have noted above, these discoveries were derived from an analysis of how an individual learner adapts autonomously in real time. Because of the psychological origins of this discovery, and the fact that I was so young, I did not at the time know anything about how brains work, or about the contemporary work of Hodgkin and Huxley.

Once I realized, however, that my psychologically derived laws explained basic facts about brain dynamics and learning, I leaped into the neurobiological literature with an enthusiasm that has never abated. The ensuing models aimed at explaining interdisciplinary experimental literatures highlighted profound differences between what I was doing and the classical results on single neurons, as in the work of Hodgkin and Huxley, or small networks of neurons, as in the work of Hartline and Ratliff. Instead, modeling of how an individual's behavior adapts in real time to a changing environment led to new functional insights about how our brains look and function, including the basic fact that the functional units that govern behavioral success are *distributed patterns* on the network and system levels, not single spikes, or sequences or bursts of spikes, in individual neurons.

Why does the brain use nonlinear multiple-scale feedback networks?

With these STM, MTM, and LTM equations in hand, I can tell you more about what *kind* of differential equations are needed to explain how a brain gives rise to a mind. Essentially all of the known self-adapting behavioral and brain systems are *nonlinear feedback systems* with large numbers of components operating over *multiple spatial and temporal scales*. What do these words mean? As I noted in my discussion of Helmholtz's insights about how we "discount the illuminant," a *linear* system is one in which the "whole is the sum of its parts." In a linear system, the effects of the parts on the whole are just added or subtracted. A *nonlinear* system is one in which this is not true. In particular, lots of the effects that occur in the brain use multiplication or division. The class of all nonlinear systems is huge, and there are a very large number of nonlinear systems that do not describe a brain. The task of selecting appropriate nonlinear systems requires a sustained analysis of behavioral and brain data.

A *feedforward* system is one in which information flows in only one direction: from the outside of the system progressively inward. As noted in my discussion in Chapter 1 of Helmholtz's theory of *unconscious inference*, the brain also needs to include *feedback*. In a feedback system, interactions occur in both directions, both to and from a given neuron (Figure 2.2). In the case of phonemic restoration, feedback enables an adaptive resonance to occur between a working memory that stores a sequence of individual events, and list categories that code whole sequences of events (Figure 1.23). As noted earlier, this kind of feedback is said to be *top-down*, from deeper in the brain towards more peripheral processing stages.

Another kind of feedback can occur within a given neural region, often among cells of a similar type. Such networks are often said to be *recurrent* (Figure 1.6). Feedback can also occur between the brain and its environment, as when we use an arm to move an object, while watching the object move. The fact that *multiple temporal scales* are needed is evident from the definitions of STM, MTM, and LTM, with STM variables changing on a time scale of milliseconds, MTM variables changing on a time scale of tens or hundreds of milliseconds, and LTM variables changing on a time scale of from seconds to a lifetime. For example, the process whereby we hear a new word using STM operates more quickly than the learning process whereby we remember the word on a future occasion using LTM.

Multiple spatial scales are needed because the brain needs to process object parts as well as wholes. For example, when we look at a face, we can see it as a whole, as well as its various distinctive parts, such as the eyes, nose, mouth, hair, and even small skin blemishes. Multiple scales are also needed to categorize words of different length. And so on. Multiple spatial scales can be defined using the summation signs $\sum$ that combine all the signals from other cells to a given cell. Each modal architecture allows different numbers of cells to influence each other, ranging from only nearby cells to widespread connections. Masking Fields (Figures 1.23 and 1.24) show that a single network level can contain multiple scales, in this instance to be able to selectively categorize, or chunk, list sequences of multiple lengths. Subsequent chapters, notably Chapters 8 on motion perception, Chapter 11 on form perception, and Chapter 12 on speech perception, will illustrate how multiple scales work with specific examples.

What about nonlinear *feedback*? The sums of excitatory and inhibitory signals are feedback signals because, just as the kth cell activity x_k can influence the ith cell activity x_i with such a signal, the ith cell activity can often reciprocally influence the kth cell activity in return. This happens all the time, whether as schematized in the anatomical diagram of visual system connections in Figure 0.1, in backward learning in Figure 2.8, or in adaptive resonance in Figures 1.23, 1.24, and 2.2.

The STM, MTM, and LTM equations in Figures 2.9–2.11 enable a more precise description of the kind of nonlinear feedback, and multiple spatial and temporal scales, that our brains use. For example, wherever you see the variables x (STM), y (MTM), or z (LTM) multiplied in Figures 2.9–2.11, that is a *nonlinear* term. Consider the shunting STM equation in Figure 2.10 for definiteness. All the product terms f(x)yz and g(x)YZ are nonlinear. As

I noted earlier in this chapter, these terms say that MTM and LTM *multiplicatively gate* an STM signal f(x) between cells before this net signal can influence the recipient cell. The equations that these variables obey are the *least* non-linear equations that can accomplish their various functional requirements.

These nonlinear feedback and multiple-scale properties are all easy to describe intuitively, but translating them into workable systems, within the tough honesty of mathematics, has always been a big challenge. The hardest thing is often to figure out *what* problem the brain is trying to solve and *how* it is going about it. For example, realizing that the CLEARS mechanisms of Adaptive Resonance Theory are related took many years of thought. This book can now be written because, after intuition and mathematics successfully combine to discover new organizational principles and mechanisms, the resulting insights can often be stated as a simple story, without the mathematics. However, as I noted above, a full understanding of *why* a result has the properties that it does, along with a sense of its *inevitability*, does require that one study the underlying mathematical equations and derivations that reveal their implications. Fortunately, many basic conclusions can be proved by using just high school mathematics. Deeper properties sometimes require additional mathematics for their proof, but one can go a long way with simple methods. In all cases, mathematics provides the springboard from which we can cross the bridge from individual neurons to the emergent properties of large networks of interacting neurons that map directly onto observable behaviors.

A gedanken experiment for solving the noise-saturation dilemma in cellular tissues

Cooperation and competition are universal in biology, including in brain networks. I will now explain how the brain solves the *noise-saturation dilemma* in order to illustrate how simple mathematics can rapidly lead to profound conclusions that would otherwise be very difficult to understand. I will use a gedanken, or thought, experiment to derive the simplest laws that realize this solution. Such a gedanken experiment celebrates the triumph of pure reason in science by showing how obvious hypotheses, with which no one would disagree, together imply conclusions about deep properties of brain organization that required ingenious experiments to discover. One can think of such a gedanken experiment as exposing some of the evolutionary pressures that led to these properties of brain organization.

The general theme that will be clarified by this particular gedanken experiment is why neurons cooperate and compete. Cooperation and competition are well known to occur in biology, one of whose classical cornerstones is the transformative work of Charles Darwin, *On the Origin of Species by Means of Natural Selection* in 1859 (Darwin, 1859), which explained how evolution may be shaped by the competitive interactions that drive natural selection. Darwin's work focused on how competition can shape the evolution of species. But why is competition ubiquitous on the level of cells? The gedanken experiment provides an answer that is just as important for non-neural cellular tissues as for brains.

What is a cell: Computing with cellular patterns. In order to proceed, we first need to ask: What is a cell? A sufficient answer to such a challenging question will not be attempted in this book, and indeed is still a work in progress throughout biology. However, I can immediately state a necessary condition that holds for all cells, whatever else they may be: *A cell has only finitely many excitable sites that can be turned on or off by external or internal inputs.* This is just a special case of the claim that infinity does not exist in biology. This fact alone leads to enormous conceptual pressure whereby to understand how competition must work in cells, indeed how to solve the noise-saturation dilemma that I summarized in Figure 1.5, if one thinks about the problem in the right way. This solution, in turn, provides a framework for discussing profound theoretical issues in a unified way, notably the many-faceted question: How do we reconcile the probabilistic nature of the world with the fact that our behaviors can be carried out with deterministic precision?

I will combine this simple constraint on the definition of a cell with the fact that, in order to bridge between brain mechanisms and mental functions, one must study *distributed patterns of activation across a network of cells*, rather than the activity of an individual cell. This can easily be seen by considering some of the facts about vision and audition that I described in Chapter 1. One cannot understand how we see and recognize pictures such as those in Figures 1.1-1.4, or the sounds such as those in Figure 1.22, without analyzing how the networks of cells that are activated by these pictures or sounds respond to them. Responses of individual visual or auditory cells, taken in isolation, are usually too ambiguous to control any behavior. The distributed pattern of activity to which these cells contribute provides a *context* in which their individual activities take on functional meaning.

Noise-saturation dilemma: Pattern processing by cell networks without noise or saturation. With this in mind, I can immediately ask how activity patterns across networks of noisy cells with finitely many sites maintain their sensitivity to inputs patterns whose overall size may change wildly through time. In particular, multiple input sources may converge on individual cells, and do so at different times and with different amplitudes. How do the cells manage to respond without being contaminated by either internal cellular noise—when the sizes of their inputs are all small—or by saturating their activities at their maximal value—when the sizes of all their inputs are large? I have called this basic problem the *noise-saturation dilemma* (Figures 1.5 and 2.15).

Figure 2.15 emphasizes that all of the cell activities x_i fluctuate within a finite range of values, indeed such a small range of values that oscilloscopes were needed to amplify them enough so that they would be visible to experimentalists. H. Keffer Hartline, whose Hartline-Ratliff-Miller equation is summarized in Figure 2.13, was an early user of oscilloscopes to amplify the signals that he was recording from in optic nerve fibers and, later, from networks of cells in the retina of the *Limulus*, or horseshoe crab.

Despite being restricted to such small activity values, cells can respond to input patterns without them being unduly contaminated by noise or saturation. Figure 1.5 already depicted the problem that is avoided in this way by illustrating the desired cell activities in response to an input pattern, as contrasted with a saturated activity pattern in response to large inputs in the lower left, and a noisy response in response to small inputs in the lower right. To achieve further clarity, Figure 2.16 shows both the input patterns, in the left column, and the activity patterns that they could have caused, in the right column, if the noise-saturation dilemma were not solved. Showing both is needed to understand how this problem can be solved.

The upper left image in Figure 2.16 shows an input pattern I_i across a network of feature-selective cells. Although there are only finitely many cells, the green curve that depicts input size at each cell is interpolated between cells for simplicity. This input pattern has two peaks, corresponding to the fact that the inputs to the corresponding

NOISE-SATURATION DILEMMA
Grossberg (1968-1973)

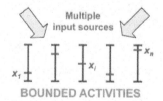

If activities x_i are sensitive to SMALL inputs, then why don't they SATURATE to large inputs?

If x_i are sensitive to LARGE inputs, then why don't small inputs get lost in system NOISE?

THE FUNCTIONAL UNIT IS A SPATIAL ACTIVITY PATTERN

FIGURE 2.15. The noise-saturation dilemma: How do neurons retain their sensitivity to the relative sizes of input patterns whose total sizes can change greatly through time?

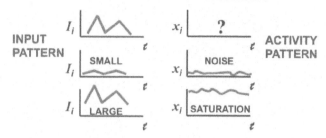

PROBLEM: remain sensitive to input RATIOS $\theta_i = \dfrac{I_i}{\sum_j I_j}$

as total input $I = \sum_j I_j \rightarrow \infty$

Many kinds of data exhibit sensitivity to ratios of inputs

FIGURE 2.16. To solve the noise-saturation dilemma, individual neurons in a network that is receiving a distributed spatial patterns of inputs need to remain sensitive to the ratio of the input to them divided by all the inputs in that spatial pattern. Although the inputs are delivered to a finite number of neurons, the input and activity patterns are drawn continuously across the cells for simplicity.

feature-selective cells are the most important. The input pattern below this one reduces all the input sizes proportionally, thereby preserving the relative important of inputs to the cells, until all the inputs are small. Because all of these inputs are sufficiently small, the activity pattern x_i that they cause is contaminated by noise, as shown in the figure to the right of the input pattern. The lowest input pattern increases all the input sizes proportionally, again preserving the relative importance of the inputs, until even the smallest input is large. Here, even the smallest input is sufficiently large that it can turn on all the sites at its target cell, as can all the other inputs as well. The result is a saturated activity pattern, as illustrated to the right of this input pattern.

Computing ratios: Brightness constancy and contrast as two sides of a coin. In order to solve the noise-saturation problem, somehow the cells in the network need to remain sensitive to the relative sizes, or ratios $\theta_i = I_i / \sum_j I_j$, of the inputs, as the total input becomes arbitrarily large. In fact, many kinds of data show that neurons can preserve their sensitivity to input ratios as total inputs increase without changing their relative size. A famous example of this property is called *brightness constancy*. Brightness constancy illustrates the far more general process of *discounting the illuminant*, which enables us to perceive the real colors of scenes as we see them under very different illumination conditions, a process that I will explain in greater detail in Chapter 4. In Figure 2.17, a light gray disk is surrounded by a darker gray annulus. A light shines on this entire

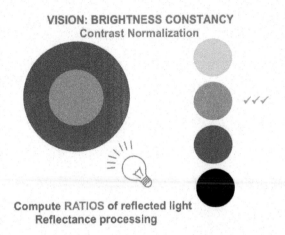

FIGURE 2.17. Brightness constancy.

FIGURE 2.18. Brightness contrast.

image. The illumination level is chosen to have a series of different intensities. No matter what intensity is chosen, within a wide range, an observer who is asked to match the perceived brightness of the gray disk will always chose the same disk from the array of possible matches in the right column of the figure. In other words, the perceived brightness of the gray disk is constant despite changes in overall illumination. On the other hand, if only the gray disk were illuminated at increasing intensities, with the annulus illuminated at a constant intensity, then the gray disk would look progressively brighter.

When any part of an image is illuminated at higher intensities, the *relative* amount of light that is reflected to our eyes remains the same, even while the *total* amount of light increases with the intensity of the incident illumination. Each shade of gray reflects a different fraction of the light that it receives. This fraction is called its *reflectance*, with a lighter gray reflecting a larger fraction of light than a darker gray. Thus, when the entire image is illuminated by the same light intensity, the relative amounts of light that are reflected from every position of the image remain the same, even while that intensity varies a lot. Our brains compute these constant ratios to solve the noise-saturation dilemma. However, if only the gray disk receives increasing illumination, then the relative amounts of light that are reflected by the disk and the annulus are no longer constant, so brightness constancy is not perceived in this case.

One implication of the fact that our brains compute relative amounts of light is that ratios add up to a constant, namely 1. This fact implies another famous visual property that is called *brightness contrast*, which may be understood as the other side of the coin to brightness constancy. As illustrated by Figure 2.18, consider two images with the same gray disk in the middle, but surround one by a darker gray annulus than the other one. Then the disk that is surrounded by the darker gray annulus looks brighter than the disk that is surrounded by the lighter gray annulus. This contrast effect occurs because, if all the ratios sum

to a constant value, then smaller ratios from the annulus will lead to the perception of larger ratios, and thus greater brightness, from the disk.

A thought experiment for solving the noise-saturation dilemma in cellular networks. I will now use a simple gedanken, or thought, experiment to explain how our brains compute the ratios of input sizes. Despite the simplicity of the ideas that I will now describe, they have far reaching implications that influence how all kinds of input patterns are computed by networks of cells, both throughout our brains and in essentially all cellular organs of multicellular living creatures.

All that I need to proceed with the thought experiment is a property that I mentioned above which all cells share: They only have finitely many excitable sites. Infinity does not exist in biology! Accordingly, Figure 2.19 shows a network of cells each of which has the same finite number B of excitable sites, with the ith cell V_i receiving an input I_i that may have any finite intensity, including zero. Also depicted are the cell activities x_i that are proportional to the number of *excited* sites. For simplicity, assume that this proportionality constant is equal to 1. We can then conclude that there are $B - x_i$ *unexcited* sites in each cell.

How can inputs I_i saturate all the excitable sites B of their cell? Figure 2.20 shows how this can happen using the simplest equation whereby an input I_i can excite its cell. There are no interactions between the cells in this network, as illustrated by the image in the upper right of Figure 2.20. The term $\frac{d}{dt}x_i$ in this equation just describes the *rate* with which activity x_i gets turned on or off through time. That is why it is called the *time derivative* of x_i. The first term $-Ax_i$ on the right hand side of this equation just says that activity x_i decays spontaneously (note the minus sign that tends to make $\frac{d}{dt}x_i$ negative) at the finite rate A

COMPUTING IN A BOUNDED ACTIVITY DOMAIN
GEDANKEN EXPERIMENT
Grossberg (1970)

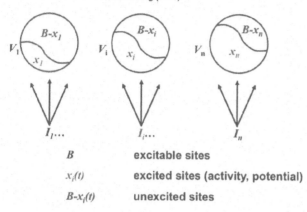

B	**excitable sites**
$x_i(t)$	**excited sites (activity, potential)**
$B-x_i(t)$	**unexcited sites**

FIGURE 2.19. Computing with cells: Infinity does not exist in biology!

SHUNTING SATURATION

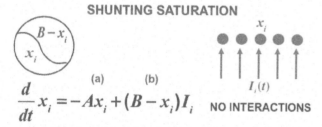

(a) (b)

$$\frac{d}{dt}x_i = -Ax_i + (B-x_i)I_i$$ **NO INTERACTIONS**

(a) Spontanous decay of activity x_i to equilibrium

(b) Turn on unexcited sites $B - x_i$ by inputs I_i (mass action)

Inadequate response to a SPATIAL PATTERN of inputs:

$$I_i(t) = \theta_i I(t)$$

θ_i relative intensity (cf., reflectance)

$I(t)$ total intensity (cf., luminance)

FIGURE 2.20. Shunting saturation occurs when inputs get larger to non-interacting cells.

through time until it reaches an equilibrium value of zero. The main action takes place as a result of the second term of this equation, namely $+(B - x_i)I_i$. This term says that the unexcited sites, which number $(B - x_i)$ can get excited (note the plus sign that tends to make $\frac{d}{dt}x_i$ positive) at a rate that increases with the intensity of the input I_i. The multiplicative interaction between these two terms can also be described as *mass action* between unexcited sites and input intensity.

You can see how saturation occurs by writing each input I_i as its relative intensity θ_i times its total intensity $I = \sum_j I_j$. Thus $I_i = \theta_i I$.

Figure 2.21 shows what happens when each input stays constant long enough for all the activities x_i to converge to zero. To solve for the equilibrium value of each activity x_i, just set its rate of change $\frac{d}{dt}x_i$ equal to zero and rearrange terms in the resulting equation to compute its equilibrium value. Then substitute $I_i = \theta_i I$ into this equation. And increase the total intensity I. As I increases to sufficiently large values, each x_i approaches B. In other words, each activity across the network *saturates* at its maximal value.

The reason for saturation is clear: There is nothing to stop unexcited sites from getting excited more and more as the total input increases. How, then, must the network be modified to compute the pattern-sensitive ratios $\theta_i = I_i / \sum_j I_j$? As Figure 2.22 notes, in order for the ith

SHUNTING SATURATION

At equilibrium: $0 = \frac{d}{dt}x_i = -Ax_i + (B-x_i)I_i$

$$x_i = \frac{BI_i}{A+I_i} = \frac{B\theta_i I}{A+\theta_i I} \rightarrow B \quad as \quad I \rightarrow \infty$$

$$I_i = \theta_i I, \ I = \sum_j I_j$$

I small: lost in noise   *I* large: saturates

Sensitivity loss to relative intensity as total intensity increases

FIGURE 2.21. How shunting saturation turns on all of a cell's excitable sites as input intensity increases.

COMPUTING WITH PATTERNS
How to compute the pattern-sensitive variable:

$$\theta_i = \frac{I_i}{\sum_{k=1}^n I_k} \ ?$$

Need interactions! What type?

$$\theta_i = \frac{I_i}{I_i + \sum_{k \neq i} I_k}$$

$I_i \uparrow \Rightarrow \theta_i \uparrow$ excitation

$I_k \uparrow \Rightarrow \theta_i \downarrow, k \neq i$ inhibition

On-center off-surround network:

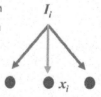

FIGURE 2.22. An on-center off-surround network is capable of computing input ratios.

cell V_i to compute the ratio of all the inputs, interactions between the cells are needed so that each cell knows what the inputs from the other cells are, which occur in the denominator of the ratio that defines θ_i. Figure 2.22 points to what kind of interaction between cells can compute input ratios at each cell.

On-center off-surround anatomies can compute input ratios. Figure 2.22 distinguishes the input I_i that tries to turn on unexcited sites at cell V_i from the other inputs that are needed to compute θ_i. In particular, input I_i occurs in both the numerator and the denominator of θ_i, so increasing I_i also increases θ_i. In other words, I_i *excites* the cell. In contrast, all of the inputs I_k from the other cells occur only in the denominator of θ_i. Increasing any of these inputs causes θ_i to decrease. In other words, all the other inputs *inhibit* the cell.

Said in another way, each input I_i excites its own cell and inhibits all the other cells. Figure 2.22 draws this kind of interaction in the lower right. It describes an on-center off-surround anatomy! Thus, one reason why on-center off-surround anatomies are ubiquitous in brains and other cellular tissues is that they define interactions that can solve the noise-saturation dilemma, and thereby enable cellular networks to process distributed input patterns without noise or saturation even if these input patterns arrive with very different intensities through time.

Shunting on-center off-surround networks solve the noise-saturation dilemma. Figure 2.22 describes the kind of anatomical interactions that can solve the noise-saturation dilemma, but not the dynamics, or neurophysiological laws, that can do so in these anatomies. Figure 2.23 summarizes the kinds of dynamics that interact in these anatomies to accomplish that goal.

The top equation in Figure 2.23 provides the solution. The first two terms on the right hand side of this equation are just the ones that, left to themselves, would cause saturation, as shown in Figure 2.21. The first term allows passive decay of activity. The second term $+(B - x_i)I_i$ allows *unexcited* sites $(B - x_i)$ to be turned *on* by input I_i. The third term $-x_i \sum_{k \neq i} I_k$ on the right hand side of the equation in Figure 2.23 says that *excited* sites x_i are turned *off* (note the minus sign) at a rate proportional to the number of excited sites x_i times the total input $\sum_{k \neq i} I_k$ from the off-surround of the network.

When the inputs stay constant for awhile, the activities again converge to constant values, so the time derivatives $\frac{d}{dt}x_i$ can be set equal to zero to compute equilibrium activities. When this is done, the following

SHUNTING ON-CENTER OFF-SURROUND NETWORK

Mass action: $\dfrac{d}{dt}x_i = -Ax_i + (B - x_i)I_i - x_i\sum_{k \neq i} I_k$

$\qquad\qquad\qquad\quad$ Turn on $\qquad$ Turn off
$\qquad\qquad\qquad$ unexcited sites $\quad$ excited sites

At equilibrium:

$$0 = \frac{d}{dt}x_i = -\left(A + I_i + \sum_{k \neq i} I_k\right)x_i + BI_i = -(A + I)x_i + BI_i$$

$$x_i = \frac{BI_i}{A + I} = \frac{B\theta_i I}{A + I} = \theta_i \frac{BI}{A + I}$$

No saturation!
Infinite dynamical range
Automatic gain control
Compute ratio scale
Weber law

$$x = \sum_{k=1}^{n} x_k = \frac{BI}{A + I} \leq B$$

Conserve total activity
NORMALIZATION
Limited capacity
Real-time probability

FIGURE 2.23. The equations for a shunting on-center off-surround network. Shunting terms lead to many beautiful and important properties of these networks, which are found ubiquitously, in one form or another, in all cellular tissues.

Minor Mathematical Miracle occurs: Bringing together all the input terms that have the common multiple of x_i yields the term $-(A + I_i + \sum_{k \neq i} I_k)x_i$. Note that the on-center input I_i and the off-surround input $\sum_{k \neq i} I_k$ sum to the total input I! As a result, the equilibrium activity $x_i = I_i /(A + I)$ has the total input I, not the ith input I_i, in its denominator, as it did in Figure 2.21. If we now substitute $I_i = \theta_i I$ into this equation and rearrange terms, we find the equilibrium activity $x_i = \theta_i[BI/(A + I)]$.

Remarkably, this equilibrium activity x_i remains proportional to the ratio θ_i no matter how large the total input I is chosen. The noise-saturation dilemma has been solved! It has been solved by using mass action dynamics in an on-center off-surround anatomy.

The ability of each equilibrium activity to remain proportional to its ratio is the main property that is needed to explain how brightness constancy occurs (Figure 2.17). What about brightness contrast (Figure 2.18)? Is the total activity conserved? The bottom equation in Figure 2.23 shows that the answer is Yes. One can see this just by adding all the activities and showing that the total activity $x = \sum_{k=1}^{n} x_k$ is bounded by B, no matter how large the total activity I may be chosen, thereby proving total activity normalization.

Infinite dynamic range, automatic gain control, limited capacity, and real-time probabilities. The properties of this shunting on-center off-surround network can be described in several ways that are all worth thinking about. For one, the fact that cell activities remain proportional to the relative input sizes, no matter how large the total input becomes, can be called an *infinite dynamic range.* This crucial property arises because the inputs *multiply* the activities, in both the on-center and off-surround of the network. This multiplicative property is also called *automatic gain control* because it enables the circuit to work well in response to a wide range of input sizes. The terms where inputs multiply activities control the equilibrium activities and also the rates with which activities converge to equilibrium, with larger inputs causing faster reaction rates.

As I noted in Figure 1.8, the property of total activity normalization also occurs in recurrent, or feedback, shunting on-center off-surround networks (Figure 1.6) that are used to store input patterns in short term memory. Total activity normalization implies a *limited capacity* of the network (Posner, 1980). Because of limited capacity, when more cells compete, each one will tend to be less active. Said in another way, increasing the activity of one cell comes at the cost of decreasing the activities of other cells. When too many inputs occur, some of their cells may thus not be activated enough to overcome their quenching threshold, and will not be stored in short term memory (Figure 1.9).

The sum of all of the activities is bounded by a constant in a non-recurrent on-center off-surround network (Figure 2.23). This sum converges through time to a constant in a recurrent network (Figure 1.7). Activities in such a recurrent network thus behave like probabilities that are dynamically changing through time. A larger activity may be interpreted to mean that the features coded by its cell population are more probable. Various of the neural architectures that this book describes may likewise be interpreted as carrying out one or another kind of probabilistic decision making, planning, or the like.

Deriving the membrane equations of neurophysiological from a thought experiment. The mass action, or shunting, dynamics that we have been led to by the thought experiment are the dynamics used by neurons. They are also called the membrane equations of neurophysiology. The equation at the top of Figure 2.24 shows this familiar equation for the variable voltage V of a cell in terms of its capacitance C; three constant saturation voltages: an excitatory saturation voltage V^+, an inhibitory saturation voltage V^-, and a passive saturation voltage V^p; and three conductances that may or may not vary through time: an excitatory conductance g^+, an inhibitory conductance g^-, and a passive conductance g^p. When these variables are set equal to the values in the lower right of Figure 2.24, the result is the equation at the top of Figure 2.23. We have hereby been led to derive the membrane equations of neurophysiology from our thought experiment.

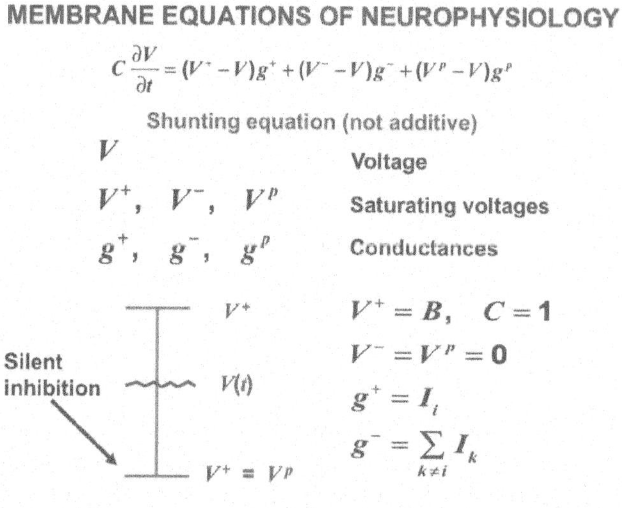

MEMBRANE EQUATIONS OF NEUROPHYSIOLOGY

$$C\frac{\partial V}{\partial t} = (V^+ - V)g^+ + (V^- - V)g^- + (V^p - V)g^p$$

Shunting equation (not additive)

V	Voltage
$V^+, \quad V^-, \quad V^p$	Saturating voltages
$g^+, \quad g^-, \quad g^p$	Conductances

V^+

Silent inhibition — $V(t)$

$V^+ = V^p$

$$V^+ = B, \quad C = 1$$
$$V^- = V^p = 0$$
$$g^+ = I_i$$
$$g^- = \sum_{k \neq i} I_k$$

FIGURE 2.24. The membrane equations of neurophysiology describe how cell voltages change in response to excitatory, inhibitory, and passive input channels. Each channel is described by a potential difference multiplied by a conductance. With the special choices shown in the lower right hand corner, this equation defines a feedforward shunting on-center off-surround network.

Towards a universal developmental code using mass action cooperative-competitive dynamics

We have actually done a lot more than that, because this kind of shunting dynamics solves the noise-saturation dilemma *only* if it is carried out an on-center off-surround anatomy. This basic fact raises the question: Did the membrane equations and on-center off-surround anatomies *co-evolve* during the evolutionary process, so that cell networks could process distributed feature patterns without noise or saturation from the earliest stages of the evolution of cellular organisms?

Two languages can equally well describe this result, and one of them generalizes to all cellular tissues: On the one hand, there are the shunting on-center off-surround anatomies that are found in our brains. On the other hand, there are the mass action cooperative-competitive systems that can be found in all cellular tissues. It is this latter language that generalizes throughout the world of living cellular organisms and that clarifies an important reason why competition occurs, not only to guide natural selection on the level of species, but also to support processing of distributed patterns at every organizational level in all cellular organisms. This latter language is part of a universal developmental code that I will further discuss in Chapter 17.

Weber law, adaptation, and shift property. So far, I have mostly discussed the simplest feedforward, or non-recurrent, shunting on-center off-surround network. Even this network has important properties that are also found in the brain. After describing one of these properties, I will show you how the simplest equation can be altered in easy incremental steps to realize a wide range of additional useful properties. These examples illustrate a kind of conceptual evolution of competitive systems that describes and mechanistically organizes the useful properties of ever-more-complex non-recurrent shunting on-center off-surround networks. I already showed you in Chapter 1 how different feedback signal functions of a feedback, or recurrent, shunting on-center off-surround network (Figure 1.6) can support very different transformations of input patterns into stored short-term memories (Figures 1.7-1.9).

The new property of the simplest non-recurrent network is a manifestation of how solving the noise-saturation dilemma enables it to maintain its sensitivity to inputs even when the off-surround may vary greatly in strength. This *shift property* is most easily seen by plotting each equilibrium activity x_i against the logarithm $K = \ln(I_i)$ of the input I_i to its on-center. The subscript i is not included in the notation K for simplicity. When this is done, $x_i(K, J)$ can be plotted as a function of K for different fixed values $J = \sum_{k \neq i} I_k$ of the total off-surround input. The resulting plots at the top of Figure 2.25 show how each activity x_i increases with increases in K when the total off-surround input J is fixed at successively larger values $J_1, J_2, \ldots$. As J is chosen at successively larger values, the curves of the corresponding activity functions x_i shift to the right; hence the name *shift property*. The main point is that each x_i begins to increase at larger values of K in response to a larger choice of J, but the same maximum activity is eventually approached. This property is also called a Weber law because it shows how the sensitivity of each cell to excitatory on-center inputs is *divided* by the size J of the total inhibitory input to it.

The shift property can be proved with simple high school algebra. The main idea is shown in the bottom equation in Figure 2.25. Here two of the curves in the figure, with different off-surround inputs J_1 and J_2, are equated, one a shift S of the other. Then one solves for S. The resulting shift S is shown at the lower right of Figure 2.25.

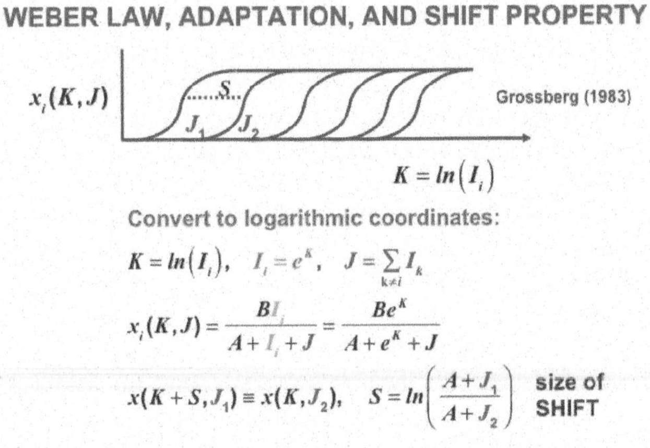

Shift property and shunting on-center off-surround network in the mudpuppy retina. In 1971, Frank Werblin published neurophysiological data from the retina of an aquatic salamander called the mudpuppy, or *Necturus maculosus* (Werblin, 1971). His data also describe a shift property when the on-center input is plotted in logarithmic coordinates (Figure 2.26). The main point to emphasize is what did *not* happen: The dynamic range of the

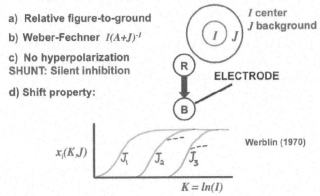

WEBER LAW, ADAPTATION, AND SHIFT PROPERTY

Grossberg (1983)

$$K = \ln(I_i)$$

Convert to logarithmic coordinates:

$$K = \ln(I_i), \quad I_i = e^K, \quad J = \sum_{k \neq i} I_k$$

$$x_i(K, J) = \frac{BI_i}{A + I_i + J} = \frac{Be^K}{A + e^K + J}$$

$$x(K + S, J_1) \equiv x(K, J_2), \quad S = \ln\left(\frac{A + J_1}{A + J_2}\right) \quad \text{size of} \; \text{SHIFT}$$

FIGURE 2.25. An on-center off-surround network can respond to increasing on-center excitatory inputs without a loss of sensitivity. Instead, as the off-surround input increases, the region of a cell's maximal sensitivity to an increasing on-center input shifts to a range of larger inputs. This is because the off-surround divides the effect of the on-center input, an effect that is often called a Weber law.

MUDPUPPY RETINA NEUROPHYSIOLOGY

a) **Relative figure-to-ground**

b) **Weber-Fechner** $I(A+J)^{-1}$

c) **No hyperpolarization**
SHUNT: Silent inhibition

d) **Shift property:**

I center
J background

ELECTRODE

$$x_i(K, J)$$

Werblin (1970)

$$K = \ln(I)$$

ADAPTATION: sensitivity *SHIFTS* for different backgrounds
NO COMPRESSION

FIGURE 2.26. The mudpuppy retina exhibits the shift property that occurs in the feedforward shunting on-center off-surround network in Figure 2.25. As a result, its sensitivity also shifts in response to different background off-surrounds, and therefore exhibits no compression (dashed purple lines).

cell responses did not get smaller as the off-surround was chosen at larger values, as illustrated by the dashed purple curves in Figure 2.26. Thus, the mudpuppy retina solves the noise-saturation dilemma, leading one to wonder if it does so using a shunting on-center off-surround network. Earlier studies showed that, in fact, an on-center off-surround network does exist in the mudpuppy retina. As illustrated at the bottom of Figure 2.27, retinal photoreceptors (R) excite their target bipolar cells (B) as well as horizontal cells (H) that carry inhibitory off-surround signals to other photoreceptors. Thus, by the time the second

MECHANISM: COOPERATIVE-COMPETITIVE DYNAMICS

ON-CENTER OFF-SURROUND

Kuffler (1953) cat retina

SUBTRACTIVE LATERAL INHIBITION

Hartline and Ratcliff (1956/7+) limulus retina

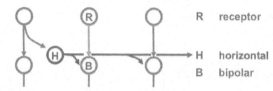

R	receptor
H	horizontal
B	bipolar

Werblin, Dowling, et al. (1969+) mudpuppy retina

FIGURE 2.27. A schematic of the on-center off-surround network that occurs in the mudpuppy retina, including the three main cell types: Receptors, horizontal cells, and bipolar cells.

WEBER LAW AND ADAPTATION LEVEL

Hyperpolarization vs Silent Inhibition

$$\frac{d}{dt}x_i = -Ax_i + (B - x_i)I_i - (x_i + C)\sum_{k \neq i}I_k$$

At equilibrium:
$$0 = \frac{d}{dt}x_i = -\left(A + I_i + \sum_{k \neq i}I_k\right)x_i + BI_i - C\sum_{k \neq i}I_k$$

$$= -(A + I)x_i + (B + C)I_i - CI$$

$$= -(A + I)x_i + (B + C)I\left[\theta_i - \frac{C}{B + C}\right]$$

$$x_i = \frac{(B + C)I}{A + I}\left[\theta_i - \frac{C}{B + C}\right]$$

Weber Law   Reflectance   Adaptation Level

FIGURE 2.28. Silent inhibition is replaced by hyperpolarization when the inhibitory saturating potential is smaller than the passive saturating potential. Then an adaptation level is created that determines how big input ratios need to be to activate their cells.

layer of cells in the retina, the bipolar cells, are activated by light inputs, the noise-saturation dilemma has already been solved.

Intracellular adaptation within photoreceptors creates a Weber law acting in time. The noise-saturation dilemma must actually already be solved in the photoreceptors, even before they activate the bipolar-horizontal cell network. This has to happen because, otherwise, individual photoreceptors could saturate in response to intense inputs even before they could generate outputs to the bipolar cells and horizontal cells. Indeed, we are capable of seeing in bright sunlight as well as in dimly lit rooms, at least after undergoing a suitable interval of adaptation to the new ambient illumination level. Photoreceptor adaptation is, however, *intracellular*, not *intercellular* like an on-center off-surround network. Its intracellular process adapts *through time*, rather than *across space* as in the case of an on-center off-surround network, by using a habituative transmitter gate, or medium-term memory (Figures 2.3 and 2.11), to divide current inputs by a time average of previous inputs. In this way, intense ambient illumination causes division of the large current light intensity by a time average of recent large light intensities, thereby normalizing the response via an intracellular Weber law, thereby keeping the cell's responses within its sensitive dynamic range. Thus, both intracellular adaptation within photoreceptors and intercellular adaptation by the on-center off-surround networks that photoreceptors activate both give rise to Weber laws that normalize and maintain cell sensitivity in response to inputs that may vary greatly through time. Interested readers can find a lot of classical neurophysiological data about photoreceptor adaptation and a model that explains them in a 1981 article by Gail

Carpenter and myself about light adaptation in turtle cones (Carpenter and Grossberg, 1981).

From silent inhibition to hyperpolarization and adaptation levels. The shift property describes an important property of the simplest shunting on-center off-surround network by using logarithmic coordinates. Additional properties may be realized by refining this network in simple stages. One such refinement replaces the property of *silent inhibition* (Figures 2.23 and 2.24). This property says that the inhibitory saturation voltage V^- and the passive saturation voltage V^p are the same. As a result, no matter how strong off-surround inhibition may become, the activity or potential of a cell can only be driven towards the equilibrium potential that is defined by the passive saturation voltage, but not below it.

Figure 2.28 replaces silent inhibition by choosing the inhibitory saturation voltage V^- to be smaller than the passive saturation voltage V^p, so that activities, or voltages, can be driven by large enough off-surround inhibitory inputs to be smaller than the equilibrium voltage. In the notation of the top equation in Figure 2.28, the choice of the inhibitory saturation voltage C that is greater than zero accomplishes this because activity x_i may then be driven to the negative voltage $-C$ before the term $(x_i + C)$ equals zero, and thus prevents the off-surround from further inhibiting the activity. When activity x_i is less than zero, it is said to be *hyperpolarized*, or less than the equilibrium voltage.

The other equations in Figure 2.28 use the usual method to compute the equilibrium activity that is caused by constant inputs. This is described by the last equation in Figure 2.28. As in the simplest shunting competitive network, a Weber law term $(B + C)I / (A + I)$ multiplies the relative activity, or ratio, θ_i of inputs. In addition, there is a new term $C/(B+C)$ that is called the *adaptation level*. The activity x_i is positive if θ_i is bigger than the adaptation level, and negative, or hyperpolarized, if it is smaller than the adaptation level.

Adaptation levels require a broken symmetry between excitation and inhibition. This fact immediately raises the question: How does the brain ensure that enough ratios are bigger than the adaptation level? This is necessary to make their activities positive, and some of them large enough both to represent important features and to trigger output signals to other processing levels.

All the ratios are, by definition, less than one. So too is the adaptation level $C/(B+C)$, because both the excitatory saturation voltage B and the inhibitory saturation voltage C are positive. However, if there are n cells in the network, and all the ratios sum to one, then quite a few ratios will have to be less than 1/n for enough of them to be bigger than 1/n.

These considerations imply that the adaptation level $C/(B+C)$ needs to be chosen considerably smaller than one in order for sufficiently many ratios to be positive. As Figure 2.29 summarizes, this implies that B must be much larger than C. In other words, the difference between the smallest possible activity $-C$ and the equilibrium activity 0 is much smaller than the difference between the largest possible activity B and 0, as illustrated in the upper left corner of Figure 2.29. If we consider that an equal distance between these parameters and 0 would be a symmetric solution to how to choose these parameters, then what actually occurs represents a *broken symmetry* between excitatory and inhibition, with excitation favored. Consequences of this broken symmetry between excitation and inhibition are ubiquitous throughout our brains.

Informational noise suppression and the selection of potentially informative activity patterns. One property of great importance can immediately be derived from this broken symmetry. It is one of the properties which ensure that noise will be suppressed before it can contaminate useful information processing. I have already mentioned one kind of noise suppression that is carried out by recurrent shunting on-center off-surround networks. This kind of noise is the familiar kind: random or quasi-random small endogenous activations of neurons that could otherwise interfere with information processing. Figures 1.7-1.9 show how signals that are faster-than-linear at small activity levels can suppress this kind of noise.

There is also another potentially catastrophic kind of noise that can occur even when endogenous or external inputs may be large. I call this kind of noise *informational noise*. Consider the following example of informational noise in order to fix ideas. Suppose that there are multiple inputs converging on individual cells through time. Suppose moreover that, during a given time interval, the total inputs to each of the cells in the network are equal, even though the individual inputs that contribute to these total inputs may differ across cells. This state of affairs is illustrated in the top left graph of Figure 2.30. Such an input pattern is uniform, or has a zero spatial frequency.

A uniform input pattern is uninformative. It does not provide more evidence for some features over others. It would be catastrophic if uniform input patterns could drive new learning across a network, since all featurally-selective LTM traces could be wiped out.

The broken symmetry provides a simple solution to this problem. It can quickly transform a uniform input pattern, no matter how large its shared input size may be, into a zero activity pattern, as illustrated by the figure on the top right of Figure 2.30. Such an activity pattern could not,

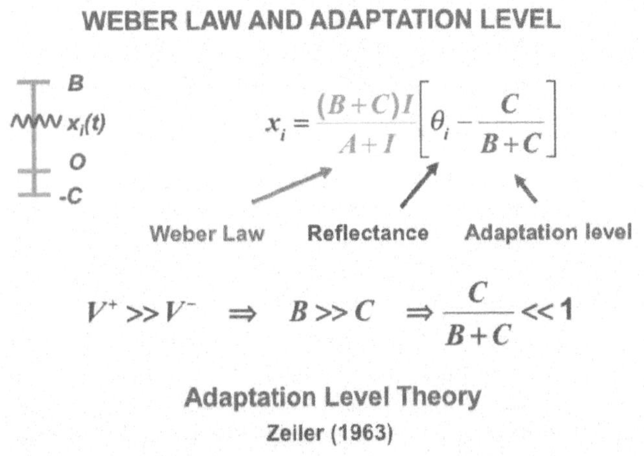

WEBER LAW AND ADAPTATION LEVEL

$$x_i = \frac{(B+C)I}{A+I}\left[\theta_i - \frac{C}{B+C}\right]$$

Weber Law   Reflectance   Adaptation level

$$V^+ \gg V^- \quad \Rightarrow \quad B \gg C \quad \Rightarrow \quad \frac{C}{B+C} \ll 1$$

Adaptation Level Theory

Zeiler (1963)

FIGURE 2.29. How the adaptation level is chosen to enable sufficiently distinct inputs to activate their cells.

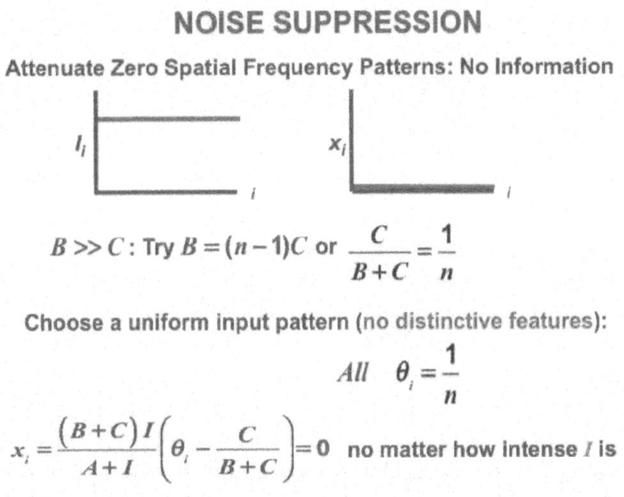

NOISE SUPPRESSION

Attenuate Zero Spatial Frequency Patterns: No Information

$$B \gg C : \text{Try } B = (n-1)C \text{ or } \frac{C}{B+C} = \frac{1}{n}$$

Choose a uniform input pattern (no distinctive features):

$$\text{All} \quad \theta_i = \frac{1}{n}$$

$$x_i = \frac{(B+C)I}{A+I}\left(\theta_i - \frac{C}{B+C}\right) = 0 \quad \text{no matter how intense } I \text{ is}$$

FIGURE 2.30. Choosing the adaptation level to achieve informational noise suppression.

for example, drive any learning via gated steepest descent (Figure 2.11) because all learning gates would be closed. As Chapter 5 will explain, informational noise suppression helps to prevent our brains from spuriously using noise to learn new recognition categories via the instar learning laws that obey the gated steepest descent learning law.

How does the broken symmetry cause informational noise suppression? If the total input to every cell is the same for awhile, then each activity will also become the same, so that all the cell activity ratios will equal 1/n if there are n cells in the network. Noise suppression immediately follows by choosing the adaptation level to also equal 1/n (Figure 2.30). Then all activities will equal zero no matter how intense the total input to each cell may be. The choice 1/n for the adaptation level will also, in response to a non-uniform input pattern, allow quite a few cell activities to be positive if enough other cells are hyperpolarized.

Informational noise suppression and bottom-up/top-down pattern matching. Informational noise suppression has many useful properties, as well. For example, it suggests how bottom-up and top-down input patterns to a network should be matched. Figure 1.11 called attention to this situation by summarizing some of the dynamics that occur when a learned top-down expectation is sufficiently badly mismatched with a bottom-up input pattern. Chapter 5 will discuss how and why this occurs by introducing and explaining how Adaptive Resonance Theory, or ART, works.

But how should patterns be matched in the first place? The property of informational noise suppression provided an early clue that then evolved into a more precise understanding when ART came on the scene a decade later. Figure 2.31 summarizes the main idea. The top image shows two input patterns that are out of phase with each other, with the most important features of one input pattern occurring where the least important features occur in the other input pattern, and conversely. When these input patterns add at their target cells, the result is a uniform input pattern that is suppressed as informational noise. In other words, input patterns that are out of phase with each other are mismatched and suppressed.

In contrast, if both input patterns are in phase with each other, as in the bottom image of Figure 2.31, then they are added and, in fact, amplified by the automatic gain control that occur during shunting dynamics (Figure 2.32).

These properties were eventually incorporated into the ART Matching Rule that describes how such matching occurs (Figure 1.25). ART went beyond these heuristics by also showing how a top-down expectation, when it acts alone, can modulate, sensitize, or prime target cells, but not fully activate them. Chapter 5 will explain this and much more about how object attention works.

How does informational noise suppression arise during development? Opposites attract! The above examples illustrate how useful the property of information noise suppression is in many brain processes. But how does it arise during development? A big clue, indeed a prediction that goes beyond current data, can be seen by rewriting this property in a different way using the equation in Figure 2.33. This equation is easily derived by setting the adaptation level $C/(B+C)$ equal to 1/n and then rearranging terms.

Rearranging terms is very simple to do, but the implications of the result are potentially profound. This is because the excitatory and inhibitory saturation voltages C and B, respectively, on the left hand side of the equation are *intra*cellular parameters, whereas the numbers 1 and $(n-1)$ on the right hand side of the equation are *inter*cellular parameters, indeed the number of on-center (1) and off-surround ($n-1$) connections of each input I_i to the network, as illustrated by the figure below the equation.

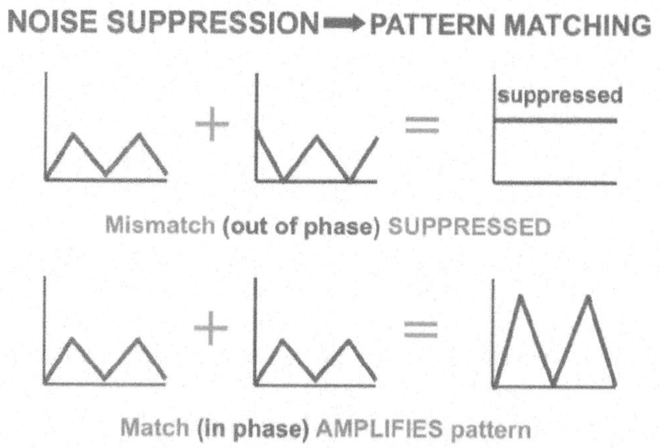

NOISE SUPPRESSION ➡ PATTERN MATCHING

Mismatch **(out of phase)** SUPPRESSED

Match **(in phase)** AMPLIFIES pattern

FIGURE 2.31. How noise suppression enables matching of bottom-up and top-down input patterns.

SUBSTRATE OF RESONANCE
Match **(in phase)** of BU and TD input patterns
AMPLIFIES matched pattern due to
automatic gain control by shunting terms

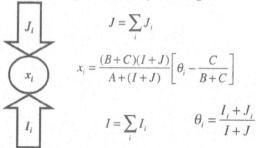

$$J = \sum_i J_i$$

$$x_i = \frac{(B+C)(I+J)}{A+(I+J)}\left[\theta_i - \frac{C}{B+C}\right]$$

$$I = \sum_i I_i \qquad \theta_i = \frac{I_i + J_i}{I + J}$$

Need top-down expectations to be MODULATORY

FIGURE 2.32. Matching amplifies the matched pattern due to automatic gain control. See terms *I* and *J* in the equation.

HOW DO NOISE SUPPRESSION PARAMETERS ARISE?

Symmetry-breaking during morphogenesis?

Opposites Attract Rule

$$\text{Intracellular parameters} \quad \frac{C}{B} = \frac{1}{n-1} \quad \text{Intercellular parameters}$$

Predicts that
intracellular excitatory and inhibitory saturation points can control the growth during development of intercellular excitatory and inhibitory connections

FIGURE 2.33. An opposite-attracts rule during the development of intercellular connections can lead to a mature network that realizes informational noise suppression.

SYMMETRY-BREAKING: DYNAMICS AND ANATOMY

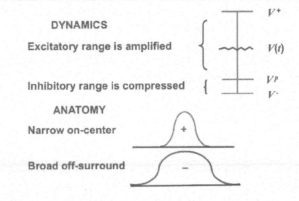

Noise Suppression: Attenuates uniform patterns
Contour detection: Enhances pattern gradients

FIGURE 2.34. How to achieve informational noise suppression in a network with multiple parallel processing channels.

How can such an equality emerge as a result of development? The obvious answer is: Use an Opposite Attracts Rule in which the broken *intra*cellular asymmetry between inhibitory and excitatory saturation voltages attracts the growth of excitatory and inhibitory connections until they create and match a broken *inter*cellular asymmetry. Then informational noise suppression will follow automatically.

This way of thinking suggests that varying the degree of asymmetry of depolarization to hyperpolarization in Figure 2.29 can alter how on-center and off-surround connections will grow during development. I do not know any experiments that have tried to explain how these intracellular biophysical parameters and the ensuing network intercellular connectivity are coordinated to achieve informational noise suppression. They would not be easy experiments to do, but the answer should be interesting, especially if deviations from informational noise suppression covary with predicted properties of a cell's adaptation level.

From a global off-surround to a distance-dependent one that preserves noise suppression. The on-center of the network in Figure 2.23 consists of only one cell, or cell population, and the off-surround inhibits all other cells equally. This is a limiting case of the on-center and off-surround connections that are typically found in vivo. A more typical situation is depicted in Figure 2.34. Here, the on-center may be narrow, but nonetheless may include several cells. An input to the ith cell will often excite nearby cells with a connection strength that decreases in a Gaussian manner with distance from the ith cell, as illustrated by the green on-center profile in Figure 2.34. The off-surround is broader than the on-center, but instead of inhibiting all other cells equally, may inhibit all cells around the ith cell, including the ith cell, with a strength that also decreases in a Gaussian manner with distance,

but more slowly than the on-center kernel, as illustrated by the red off-surround profile in Figure 2.34.

The connections in Figure 2.34 replace the "single channel" network of Figure 2.23 with a "multiple channel" network in which neighboring cells influence one another, but may be hardly influenced, if at all, by cells that are not within the span of their off-surround. Because the multiple channel anatomy preserves the broken symmetry of narrower on-center than off-surround network connections, it can still interact with the intracellular broken symmetry to achieve informational noise suppression.

The top equation in Figure 2.35 describes such a multiple scale network. Instead of the very narrow on-center and global off-surround that is depicted in the upper left image, there is a Gaussian on-center and a broader Gaussian off-surround in the multiple scale network, as depicted in the upper right image. These excitatory and inhibitory interactions are defined by the Gaussian kernels C_{ki} and E_{ki}, respectively. The equilibrium activity x_i is shown in the lower left of Figure 2.35. In this equation, the total activity I again defined a Weber law effect. Instead of a single ratio θ_i on the right hand side of this equation, as in Figure 2.23, all the ratios θ_k of all the cells V_k, ranging from 1 through n, appear in the numerator of this equation. The ratios θ_k in the numerator are multiplied by kernels F_{ki} that are defined by a weighted *difference* of the on-center and off-surround kernels, which is why it is called a weighted Difference Of Gaussians, or DOG (Figure 2.35). The ratios θ_k in the denominator are multiplied by kernels G_{ki} that are defined by a weighted sum of the on-center and off-surround kernels, which is why it is called a Sum Of Gaussians, or SOG. The SOG normalizes the effect of the DOG. This equation hereby shows how both ratio processing and total activity normalization are realized in a multiple scale network.

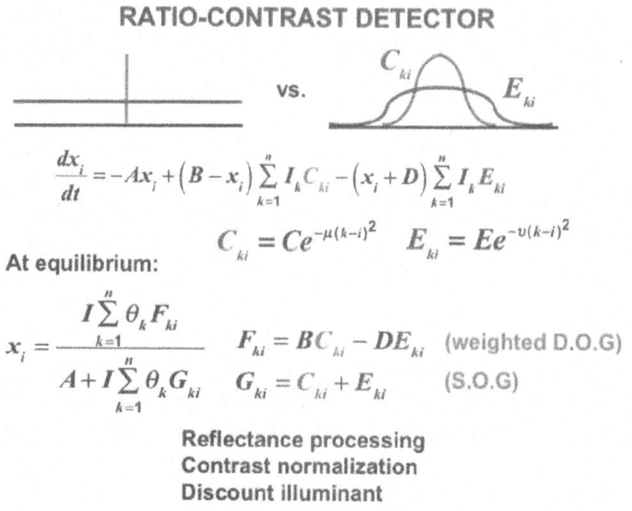

RATIO-CONTRAST DETECTOR

$$\frac{dx_i}{dt} = -Ax_i + (B - x_i)\sum_{k=1}^{n} I_k C_{ki} - (x_i + D)\sum_{k=1}^{n} I_k E_{ki}$$

$$C_{ki} = Ce^{-\mu(k-i)^2} \qquad E_{ki} = Ee^{-\upsilon(k-i)^2}$$

At equilibrium:

$$x_i = \frac{I\sum\limits_{k=1}^{n}\theta_k F_{ki}}{A + I\sum\limits_{k=1}^{n}\theta_k G_{ki}} \qquad F_{ki} = BC_{ki} - DE_{ki} \quad \text{(weighted D.O.G)}$$
$$G_{ki} = C_{ki} + E_{ki} \quad \text{(S.O.G)}$$

Reflectance processing
Contrast normalization
Discount illuminant

FIGURE 2.35. The equilibrium activities of a shunting network with Gaussian on-center off-surround kernels are sensitive to the ratio-contrasts of the input patterns that they process. The terms in the denominator of the equilibrium activities accomplish this using the shunting on-center and off-surround terms.

Informational noise suppression implies contour detection in a multiple scale network. Dividing a DOG by a SOG computes the *contrast* of the inputs to each position. In particular, when the network is calibrated to also suppress informational noise, cells selectively respond at positions in the network where input contrasts change sufficiently rapidly across the network. In response to a visual image, for example, such a network responds selectively to positions where there are sufficiently intense luminance edges, textures, or shading. This property will be essential for understanding all of my explanations of how vision works in Chapter 3 and beyond.

Informational noise suppression can easily be realized in a multiple scale network. Simply choose all ratios θ_k to equal 1/n and require that all the resulting equilibrium activities x_i be less than or equal to zero. When this is done, the sums can be carried out separately for the on-center and off-surround kernels in the numerator of the equation for equilibrium activity in Figure 2.35, leading to the inequality $B\sum_{k=1}^{n} C_{ki} \le D\sum_{k=1}^{n} E_{ki}$ at the top left of Figure 2.36. This inequality again shows how intracellular saturation voltages and intercellular connections work together to accomplish informational noise suppression.

When this is done, it is easy to see how this network responds selectively at positions where the input size changes sufficiently rapidly across space, whether due to an edge, texture, or shading gradient. The rectangular input I_i in Figure 2.36 illustrates why this is true. Due to informational noise suppression, cells are not activated at positions either where the input equals zero *or* where the input is large but constant across space. Cells are only activated where the input changes rapidly, as illustrated by the response profile for x_i across position in Figure 2.36.

NOISE SUPPRESSION AND CONTOUR DETECTION

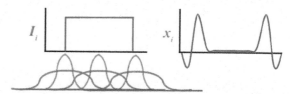

If $\quad B\sum\limits_{k=1}^{n} C_{ki} \le D\sum\limits_{k=1}^{n} E_{ki}\quad$ then

uniform patterns are suppressed
contrasts are selectively enhanced
contours are detected

Responses are selective to REFLECTANCE
SPATIAL SCALE
e.g., color (feature, surface) contours

FIGURE 2.36. Informational noise suppression in network with Gaussian on-center and off-surround function as contour detectors that are sensitive to ratio-contrast.

By including multiple scales, informational noise suppression thus provides us with a contour detector that is sensitive to the relative size of input changes across space. In applications to vision, such a *ratio contrast detector* is sensitive to the reflectances of objects that reflect light to the eyes. This property helps to explain how our brains compensate for variable illumination levels, or "discount the illuminant". I will explain more completely how our brains accomplish this feat in Chapter 4, where I will also show you computer simulations of this and other visual properties that we use every day to accomplish multiple tasks.

How does one evolve a computational brain? My theoretical method

The above discussion illustrates that no single step of theoretical derivation can derive a whole brain. One needs a method for deriving a brain in stages, or cycles, much as evolution has incrementally discovered ever more complex brains over many thousands of years. The following theoretical method has been successfully applied many times since I first used it in 1957. It embodies a kind of conceptual evolutionary process for deriving a brain.

Because "brain evolution needs to achieve behavioral success", we need to start with data that embody indices of behavioral success. That is why, as, as illustrated in Figure 2.37, one starts with Behavioral Data from scores or hundreds of psychological experiments. These data are analyzed as the result of an individual adapting

MODELING METHOD AND CYCLE

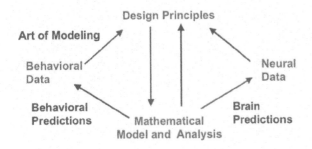

Operationalizes "proper level of abstraction"

Operationalizes that you cannot "derive a brain"
in one step

FIGURE 2.37. My models begin with behavioral data, since brains are designed to achieve behavioral success. The text explains how the models evolve in stages, through a process of successive refinements, or unlumpings. These unlumpings together carry out a kind of conceptual evolution, leading to models that can explain and predict ever larger psychological and neurobiological databases.

autonomously in real time to a changing world. This is the Art of Modeling. It requires that one be able to infer from static data curves the dynamical processes that control individual behaviors occurring in real time. One of the hardest things that I teach to my students to do is "how to think in real time" to be able to carry out this speculative leap.

Properly carried out, this analysis leads to the discovery of new Design Principles that are embodied by these behavioral processes. These Design Principles highlight the functional meaning of the data, and clarify how individual behaviors occurring in real time give rise to these static data curves.

These principles are then converted into the simplest Mathematical Model using a *method of minimal anatomies*, which is a form of Occam's Razor, or principle of parsimony. Such a mathematical model embodies the psychological principles using the *simplest* possible differential equations. By "simplest" I mean that, if any part of the derived model is removed, then a significant fraction of the targeted data could no longer be explained. One then analyzes the model mathematically and simulates it on the computer, showing along the way how variations on the minimal anatomy can realize the design principles in different individuals or species.

This analysis has always provided functional explanations and Behavioral Predictions for much larger behavioral data bases than those used to discover the Design Principles. The most remarkable fact is, however, that the behaviorally derived model always looks like part of a brain, thereby explaining a body of challenging Neural Data and making novel Brain Predictions.

The derivation hereby links mind to brain via psychological organizational principles and their mechanistic realization as a mathematically defined neural network. This startling fact is what I first experienced as a college Freshman taking Introductory Psychology, and it changed my life forever.

I conclude from having had this experience scores of times since 1957 that brains look the way that they do because they embody a natural computational realization for controlling autonomous adaptation in real-time to a changing world. Moreover, the Behavior→Principles→Model→Neural derivation predicts new functional roles for both known and unknown brain mechanisms by linking the brain data to how it helps to ensure behavioral success. As I noted above, the power of this method is illustrated by the fact that scores of these predictions about brain and behavior have been supported by experimental data 5-30 years after they were first published.

Having made the link from behavior to brain, one can then "burn the candle from both ends" by pressing both top-down from Behavioral Data and bottom-up from Brain Data to clarify what the model can and cannot explain at its current stage of derivation. No model can explain everything. At each stage of development, the model can cope with certain environmental challenges but not others. An important part of the mathematical and computational analyses is to characterize the *boundary between the known and the unknown*; that is, *which* challenges the model can cope with and which it cannot. The *shape* of this boundary between the known and the unknown helps to direct the theorist's attention to new design principles that have been omitted from the previous analyses.

The next step is to show how these new design principles can be incorporated into the evolving model in a self-consistent way, without undermining its previous mechanisms, thereby leading to a progressively more realistic model, one that can explain and predict ever more behavioral and neural data. In this way, the model undergoes a type of evolutionary development, as it becomes able to cope behaviorally with environmental constraints of ever increasing subtlety and complexity. The Method of Minimal Anatomies may hereby be viewed as way to functionally understand how increasingly demanding combinations of environmental pressures were incorporated into brains during the evolutionary process.

If such an Embedding Principle cannot be carried out—that is, if the model cannot be unlumped or refined in a self-consistent way—then the previous model was, put simply, wrong, and one needs to figure out which parts must be discarded. Such a model is, as it were, an evolutionary dead end. Fortunately, this has not happened to me since I began my work in 1957 because the theoretical method is so conservative. No theoretical addition is made unless it is supported by multiple experiments that cannot be explained in its absence. Where multiple mechanistic instantiations of some Design Principles were possible, they were all developed in models to better understand their explanatory implications. Not all of these instantiations could survive the pressure of the evolutionary method, but some always could. As a happy result, all earlier models have been capable of incremental refinement and expansion.

The cycle of model evolution has been carried out many times since 1957, leading today to increasing numbers of models that *individually* can explain and predict psychological, neurophysiological, anatomical, biophysical, and even biochemical data. In this specific sense, the classical mind-body problem is now being incrementally solved.

Embedding, unlumping, and correspondence principles

There are several equivalent ways to describe such a refinement procedure: It embodies an *embedding, unlumping,* or *correspondence principle* constraint: One needs to be able to consistently *embed* the previous model into the new expanded model; the previous model needs to be *unlumpable* into an increasingly complex model; a *correspondence principle* characterizes how the variables of a lumped version of the model can be unlumped into the finer variables of a more realistic model.

Correspondence principles are also well known in physics: https://en.wikipedia.org/wiki/Correspondence_principle. One famous one is the correspondence principle that the great Danish physicist, Niels Bohr, used in the early 1900s to link principles of classical mechanics to principles of quantum theory, and then subsequently to quantum mechanics. Another is how Albert Einstein linked principles of classical mechanics to Special Relativity Theory. When a correspondence principle is applied to mind and brain, it places a surprisingly severe test on the adequacy of previously discovered theoretical hypotheses. Many concepts and mechanisms that have been proposed by scientists over the years fail to satisfy the embedding constraint. They seem plausible within a restricted explanatory context, but fall to pieces when they are confronted with more severe environmental challenges. That is why many models come and go with surprising rapidity, and do not get integrated into principled theories of ever greater predictive power. In the past, the main organizational principles I have discovered have survived multiple model unlumping cycles, even while their mathematical realizations in neural circuits may have become increasingly sophisticated and subtle.

I realized when I began my scientific work in 1957 that one would have to derive mind and brain models in successive approximations by using such an embedding constraint. That is why I called my earliest models *Embedding Fields.* The word "embedding" summarized the unlumping constraint. The word "fields" was a short-hand for the fact that interactions within a neural network generate the emergent properties that map onto behavior. These ideas were considered radical in those days, and they took twenty-five years to start to become popular. I wrote a monograph about Embedding Fields during my first year as a graduate student at the Rockefeller Institute in 1964, to which I transferred after studying a lot of graduate mathematics and other scientific topics at Stanford University from 1961-1964 (Grossberg, 1964). This monograph summarized the research that I had done since I was a college Freshman in 1957. It was mailed to 125 of the world's top psychologists and neuroscientists. At that time, the scientific community, by and large, had no idea what to do with it. It can be found at the website http://sites.bu.edu/steveg/files/2016/06/Gro1964EmbeddingFields.pdf.

Many cycles of model evolution have occurred since 1957, with many more colleagues joining this activity starting in the 1980s. All of these evolutionary stages have successfully built a foundation for their progeny. I did not dream when this work began that, in my own lifetime, we could achieve the kind of quantitative understanding of both psychological and neurobiological data that we are experiencing today, including as one example explanatory linkages between fine details of the anatomy and neurophysiology of identified neurons and brain circuits in the cerebral cortex with the psychological functions that they control. Nor did I dream—although I dearly hoped—that this type of work would become so mainstream in the scientific community. The present book will necessarily omit many of these modeling cycles and sociological transformations. I would like you to realize, however, that this process of successive approximations is an essential tool for linking mind to brain, and it still continues today. The remainder of the book will survey some of the results that have been derived with this method, starting with visual perception, since so much of our brain is specialized for seeing. A reader who wants to get a larger sample of the archival technical research articles on which this book is based can scan or download them from my personal web page, sites.bu.edu/steveg.

A never-ending controversy?

I have spent so much time discussing a particular approach to understanding how brains give rise to minds for several reasons. The most direct reason is for the reader to realize that there exists a systematic method for linking brains to minds that has been incrementally developing ever more powerful explanatory and predictive theories of different aspects of biological intelligence for over a half century. I hope readers of this book will therefore become skeptical about, and challenge, claims that "we know nothing about how the brain works". A no less important reason for discussing this approach is that the question of how to understand mind and brain is still controversial. Productive psychologists and neuroscientists may hold very different opinions about the state of the art and how to advance it. I believe that there are at least two related reasons for this enduring controversy:

First, linking brain to mind is one of the most intellectually challenging endeavors in the history of science. It will take a long time before even simple, and redundantly supported, theoretical explanations of subtle data will be universally appreciated, if only because they are based upon new ways of thinking and neural networks that typically exhibit nonlinear, nonlocal, and nonstationary properties.

Second, despite enormous progress during the last thirty years in building scientific infrastructure to transmit knowledge about our field, including the creation of interdisciplinary educational departments and programs, scientific societies, conferences, and journals, our field still faces a major literacy problem. Part of the reason for this is that theoretical progress has been so fast that it has been difficult to incorporate it into these institutions. A more serious problem is that the deepest theoretical discoveries have been highly interdisciplinary and have unified knowledge about multiple levels of biological intelligence using model neural architectures and their emergent psychological properties. The emergent properties of these modal architectures follow from the dynamics of carefully chosen nonlinear systems of differential equations. Unfortunately, most universities and scientific conferences still do not, by and large, teach the range of interdisciplinary knowledge that is needed to link brain to mind on an advanced level. Even today, although much less than in the past, great experimental neuroscientists may be naïve or dismissive about psychology, and conversely, since that was not part of their own training. And most psychological and neurobiological experimentalists have little or no training in mathematics or how to model. They are simply unqualified to understand, or even to hold an informed opinion about, the state of the art in mind-brain theory. Since a lot of political power in psychology and neuroscience is held by experimentalists, this tends to warp how the field evolves in a way that does not adequately exploit important theoretical discoveries.

These limitations have led people who believe in Big Data to suggest that nothing can be understood theoretically unless we first collect huge amounts of data about every aspect of brain organization. Some neuroscientists also believe that a model is not "realistic" unless it includes every fact from their own laboratories, irrespective of whether these facts are rate-limiting in the explanation and quantitative simulation of important databases about

mental functions. These beliefs are contradicted by the cyclic and incremental nature of the modeling Method of Minimal Anatomies depicted in Figure 2.37, and by the huge amount of explanatory and predictive theoretical success of the ensuing models over the past half century.

To overcome these unfounded beliefs, sustained tutorials about theoretical breakthroughs, as is often practiced in theoretical physics, need to be scheduled into major experimental conferences, workshops, and educational programs, and adequately funded to enable theorists, experimentalists, and students of all persuasions to get an opportunity to keep abreast of theoretical advances in our most exciting field as its progress accelerates even more in the years ahead.

From brain theories to technological applications

There is one additional, and very important, feature of the modeling cycle that needs to be described; namely, at *every* stage of the modeling cycle, applications are spun off to be used by engineers and technologists who are interested in developing systems that are capable of increasingly autonomous intelligence and control (Figure 2.38). Why are these mind-brain theories useful to technologists? Every technological application needs both to identify a *function* in the real world that an new application should handle, as well as a *mechanism* with which to realize it. Neural networks that link brain to mind provide both mechanism and function, respectively. Function is derived from the psychological analyses that lead to the discovery of new design principles, whereas mechanism is specified within the neural networks that are derived from these design principles. Moreover, these neural networks are designed to achieve autonomous adaptation in a changing world, and increasing numbers of technological applications require such a competence.

I would argue, moreover, that the development of increasingly autonomous adaptive intelligent agents will become the most important technological revolution of our age, and that insights from biological intelligence will play an increasingly vital role in these developments during the next generation. Finally, unlike many psychological and neurobiological experimentalists, engineers and technologists often have the mathematical and computational training needed to be able to fluently read and understand the mathematical equations that define these neural networks, even if they may not know much about the psychological and neurobiological data that they explain.

Even in technology, however, there are conservative tendencies, as indeed there should be. Engineers usually want to use tried and true methods to solve their problems,

MODELING METHOD AND CYCLE

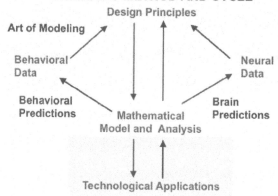

At every stage, spin off new model designs and mechanisms to technologists who need autonomous intelligent applications

FIGURE 2.38. Our models have been used in many large-scale applications to engineering and technology. Linking brain to behavior explains how brain mechanisms give rise to psychological functions, and do so autonomously. The combination of mechanism, function, and autonomy helps to explain their value in helping to solve outstanding problems in technology.

if only to ensure the reliability of their solutions. They do not want their bridges or airplanes to fall down! However, as increasing numbers of problems arise that are best solved using autonomously intelligent systems that can learn on the fly from huge databases that exhibit rapidly changing statistics and unexpected events, the number of tried and true methods to solve these problems becomes vanishingly small. So new approaches need to be tried and developed. Models that embody the brain's superb autonomously intelligent capabilities are consequently becoming increasingly used. Indeed, most of the government grants that supported my research for over thirty years were interested in discovering new brain designs for autonomous intelligence that could be applied to outstanding technological problems. A lot of scientists, engineers, and companies have used models that Gail Carpenter and I, separately and together, developed with other colleagues with this grant support for both scientific and large-scale applications in technology. A partial list of applications can be found on the CNS Technology website: http://techlab.bu.edu/resources/articles/C5.

It is particularly exciting that some of the biggest technology companies in the world, including Apple and Google, are currently investing heavily in neural networks. Much of that investment is going into trying to solve various Big Data problems by applying Deep Learning. As I noted above, Deep Learning uses the learning algorithm of the earlier back propagation model, which in turn uses a variant of the methods of steepest descent that have been developed by mathematicians since at least the time of Gauss. Thus, the mechanisms that are used in back propagation and Deep Learning are based on classical mathematical ideas. I therefore often call them "neo-classical" models. It should therefore not be a surprise that these models are not consistent with mechanisms that are found in the brain, and that they can experience catastrophic forgetting if they try to learn too quickly, or in a too dense environment, or an environment whose statistics change rapidly and unpredictably. Unfortunately, these properties are often found in real-world Big Data databases. When technology companies fully face the challenges of realizing adaptive autonomous intelligence in rapidly changing environments, my belief is that they will then increasingly turn away from Deep Learning to models like Adaptive Resonance Theory to try to solve their Big Data problems.

How a Brain Sees: Constructing Reality

Visual reality as illusions that explain how we see art

Why do we bother to see?

Seeing provides us with one of our most vital sources of information about the external world. A large fraction of our brains—often half or more of the entire brain in some primates—is devoted to processing visual information. In addition to its crucial role in our daily lives, our visual intelligence permeates all of our mathematics, science, and technology. As just one example, vision, along with the eye, arm, and limb movements that we make when we manipulate and navigate the world, provides the intuitive foundation for inventing the geometrical concepts and axioms with which we describe the world. Every field of quantitative science is founded on geometrical ideas, partly because they provide tools for scientific measurement, and partly because they provide a language with which to describe scientific concepts. Indeed, one of the greatest revolutions in physics in the 20th century required a revision of our concepts about the correct type of geometry with which to describe the Universe. At that time, Einstein expressed the equations of his General Relativity Theory using a Riemannian, or curved, geometrical representation of space-time.

Understanding of the processes whereby vision governs geometrical thinking has lagged far behind our use of this faculty. This lag has been due to the sheer difficulty of the problem, not to any lack of data. A major breakthrough in this problem area should have implications wherever the human use of geometrical ideas has influenced mathematical, scientific, and technological thinking.

Progress during the past thirty years concerning the brain processes that govern visual perception has led to a host of new ideas. These ideas have clarified that the classical axioms of geometry do not accurately describe the brain processes whereby we see and act upon the world, even though these brain processes enable us to make the physical measurements in the world that mathematical and computational concepts have codified. It remains to fully explain how these brain processes generate and represent these mathematical and computational concepts, a step that would go a long way

Conscious MIND Resonant BRAIN. Stephen Grossberg, Oxford University Press. © Oxford University Press 2021.
DOI: 10.1093/oso/9780190070557.003.0003

towards explaining away Einstein's observation that "the most incomprehensible thing about the universe is that it is comprehensible". The emerging theory that I review in this book provides a foundation for beginning this task.

In order to explain and predict psychological and neurobiological data about vision, this theory has introduced new types of nonlinear dynamical systems, new concepts in geometry, new ideas about statistical decision theory, new examples of phase transitions, new uncertainty principles for physical measurements, and new parallel architectures for computer vision machines. Despite this progress, a great deal more work remains to be done to fill in the gaps in current theoretical and experimental knowledge.

Figure 0.1 summarizes the anatomical stages of visual processing and their main connections. Figure 3.1 summarizes various visual functions that are embodied within these stages, based upon several decades of modeling and over one hundred years of experiments.

To start my discussion of vision, let me first consider the classical distinction between *seeing* and *knowing*, which

many authors have heatedly debated throughout the last century, including Helmholtz and Kanizsa. I would first like to describe some of the reasons why this issue has been so hotly debated, and how this debate may be resolved.

The distinction between seeing and knowing can be restated as one between *seeing* and *recognizing*. The images in Figure 1.1 illustrate what I mean. The image in the left panel consists of a series of concentric blue lines that face the same central point on the paper. Our percept of the figure is one in which we both see *and* recognize a circle that abuts the ends of the blue lines. We *see* this circle because it separates the brighter white disk within the circle from the darker background that lies outside it. This circle is a visual illusion, since neither the circle nor the bright disk within it are part of the picture itself. It is called the Ehrenstein illusion in honor of the German perceptual scientist, Walter Ehrenstein, who described it. Images such as these raise the following types of questions:

- Why are there so many visual illusions?

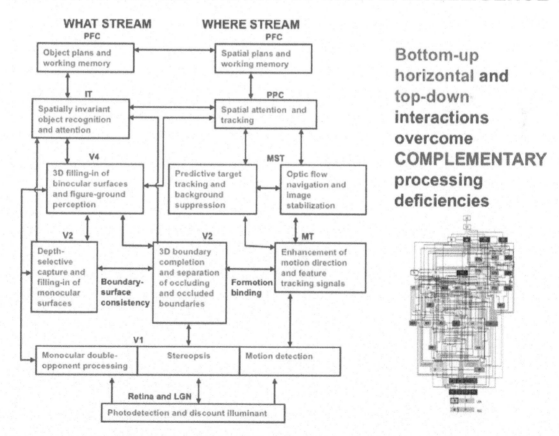

FIGURE 3.1. A macrocircuit of key visual processes (in green) and the cortical areas in which they primarily occur (in red), from the retina to the prefrontal cortex (PFC), including both the What and Where cortical streams. The bottom-up, horizontal, and top-down interactions help each of these processes to overcome computationally complementary processing deficiencies that they would experience without them, and also to read-out top-down expectations that help to stabilize learning while they focus attention on salient objects and positions.

- How does illusion differ from reality?
- Why do not illusory percepts undermine successful adaptation to the "real" world?

I will show how illusions provide vital clues about how the brain successfully adapts to the real world, and that many percepts and other experiences that we believe to be real are, in actuality, mentally constructed illusions that just happen to match the structure of the world very well. How this happens clarifies why the debate about the difference between illusion and reality has gone on for so long, why many cultures have emphasized mystical states of mind that exploit the constructive properties of the mind, and why the classical proposal of Artificial Intelligence that the brain can be modeled by a non-Neumann computer is wrong.

Consciousness without qualia: Why do we bother to see?

The offset grating image in the right panel of Figure 1.1 provides a simple example of a percept that can be recognized but not seen. When you look at this image, you recognize a vertical boundary that abuts the ends of the horizontal blue lines in the grating. You can easily *recognize* that such a vertical boundary is there, but you cannot easily *see* it. By this I mean that the salience of the vertical boundary is far greater than any small differences in brightness or color that you may manage to perceive due to momentary shifts in your focus of attention. The vertical boundary is thus a percept that you can *recognize* but cannot *see*. You *know* that it is there, and you are *conscious* of knowing this, but it is *invisible*.

Such percepts are said to be "amodal" in the perceptual literature, to distinguish them from "modal" percepts that do carry visible signs of brightness, color, or other "qualia". This use of the term amodal generalizes the more traditional use by authors such as Albert Michotte, Gabio Metelli, and Gaetano Kanizsa (e.g., Kanizsa, 1976) because the mechanistic analysis of how boundaries and surfaces interact, that will be summarized below, supports a more general terminology in which perceptual boundaries are formed without any corresponding visible surface qualia.

Before going further, it's important to clearly understand what the word "qualia" means, or at least the sense that I will use it in this book. The following summary from the Stanford Encyclopedia of Philosophy nicely summarizes this meaning:

"Feelings and experiences vary widely. For example, I run my fingers over sandpaper, smell a skunk, feel a sharp pain in my finger, seem to see bright purple, become extremely angry. In each of these cases, I am the subject of a mental state with a very distinctive subjective character. There is something it is *like* for me to undergo each state, some phenomenology that it has. Philosophers often use the term 'qualia' (singular 'quale') to refer to the introspectively accessible, phenomenal aspects of our mental lives." (https://plato.stanford.edu/entries/qualia/)

The fact that we can consciously recognize percepts that have no qualia does not support opinions of distinguished philosophers like John Searle who wrote an article in 1998 about "How to Study Consciousness Scientifically" asserting that *"The problem of consciousness is identical with the problem of qualia . . . That is why I seldom use the word 'qualia', except in sneer quotes, because it suggests that there is something else to consciousness besides qualia, and there is not"* (Searle, 1998). One way out of this problem is to define qualia to be essentially equivalent with every conscious experience. The rest of the book avoids such a convention when using words like seeing, hearing, feeling, and knowing, by writing clearly about the phenomena that are included in these descriptions.

Our percepts of simple images like the offset grating challenge familiar views about the function of seeing. For example, one intuitively appealing answer to the question: "Why do we see?" is that "We see things in order to recognize them." But we can recognize the vertical boundary of an offset grating without seeing it. This example contradicts the idea that seeing is *necessary* for recognizing. But if we do not always need to see things in order to recognize them, then why do we bother to see at all?

As I noted in the discussion of Table 1.3, conscious experiences like seeing, hearing, and feeling embody brain representations that can control effective actions of one sort or the other, whether they are reaching, speaking, or acting in other ways. I will further develop the evidence for this perspective in Chapters 3, 4, 6, and 11. You might at this point want to complain that the offset grating is pretty flimsy evidence on which to base such grand conclusions. Even the fact that the offset grating is "just" a visual illusion may give you pause. The next section suggests that the offset grating is actually illustrative of a large number of experiences whereby we perceive the "real" world.

All boundaries are invisible: From Kanizsa squares to figure-ground separation

The vertical percept in the offset grating shows us that "some boundaries are invisible". Now I would like to show you a sense in which "*all* boundaries are invisible", at least within the brain system that forms such boundaries. Along the way, I will need to tell you what perceptual boundaries are, how the brain computes them, and why this is not just a crazy idea.

To get started, consider Figure 3.2. This type of image was yet another example that Kanizsa introduced to argue against Helmholtz's position that all seeing is based on a type of knowledge-based hypothesis testing. I earlier discussed how the stratification images in Figure 1.4 were also used for this purpose. In Figure 3.2, Kanizsa noted that our experiences with a regular black-and-white checkerboard should lead us to expect that a white square is occluded by the gray disk in the lower left of the image, and a black square is occluded by the gray disk in the upper right of the image. Instead, there is a strong percept of an amodally completed black cross behind the gray disk in the lower left, and of a white cross behind the gray disk in the upper right.

I will use Figure 3.2 to call your attention to a different issue. Let your eye wander along the circular boundary of the lower-left gray disk. At successive moments, the boundary may abut a white square, then a black one, then another white one, and so on. Where the square is white, the *contrast* between the white background and the gray disk goes from white to gray; that is, from a lighter to a darker shade of gray. Where the square is black, the contrast goes from black to gray, or from a darker to a lighter shade of gray. As your eye traverses the entire circular boundary, the contrast keeps flipping between light-to-dark and dark-to-light. Despite these contrast reversals, we perceive a single continuous boundary surrounding the gray disk. It is not broken into two sets of four boundary

fragments, depending whether the direction-of-contrast goes from light-to-dark or from dark-to-light.

These fragmented boundaries would have been created if all that happened in perceiving the circular boundary was for cells that are sensitive to a light-to-dark contrast, or to a dark-to-light contrast, but not both, responded along the circle. Instead, the fact that we perceive a single continuous circular boundary that includes both contrast polarities illustrates that the brain pools, or adds, signals from cells that are sensitive to both of these contrast polarities, at every position, in order to detect the entire boundaries of objects, irrespective of the direction-of-contrast at different boundary positions. The same thing may be said about the checkerboard background of the image: We can recognize long vertical boundaries from the top to the bottom of the image, even though these boundaries are formed from alternating contrast polarities. The long horizontal boundaries of the checkerboard are also recognized in the same way.

The punch line is: If the brain adds together signals from opposite contrast polarities in order to build boundaries around objects, then these boundaries cannot tell the difference between light and dark, and thus cannot carry a visible signal of lightness or darkness. In other words, *all boundaries are invisible!* And they are invisible for a basic reason: The brain needs to build boundaries around objects that lie in front of textured backgrounds whose relative contrast with respect to the object can reverse as the boundary is traversed.

Perhaps the simplest example of this boundary-pooling property of the brain can be perceived by viewing the images in Figure 3.3. The image in Figure 3.3a is another famous image due to Kanizsa. This image consists of four black pac-man, or pie-shaped, figures on white paper. The percept of the square that abuts the pac-men is a visual illusion that is called the Kanizsa square. The enhanced brightness of the square is also an illusion. The percept derived from Figure 3.3c shows that these boundaries can be induced by either collinear edges or perpendicular line ends, and that both kinds of inducers cooperate to generate an even stronger boundary. These inducers need to lie along the positions of the illusory contour in order to cooperate. Figure 3.3d shows that, if the perpendicular lines cross the positions of the illusory contours, then they can inhibit the strength of these contours.

Now consider the image in Figure 3.3b. The percept that it elicits is called a "reverse-contrast Kanizsa square". Again a square boundary can be *recognized*. However, if the contrast of the gray background relative to the white and black pac-men is chosen correctly, then you will *not see* a gray square that is brighter or darker than its gray background. Both the interior of the square and the background around the square will often both appear to have the same shade of gray.

FIGURE 3.2. What do you think lies under the two gray disks?

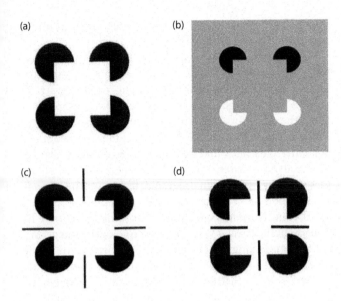

(a) (b) (c) (d)

FIGURE 3.3. Kanizsa square and reverse-contrast Kanizsa square percepts. The spatial arrangement of pac-men, lines, and relative contrasts determines the perceived brightnesses of the squares, and even if they exhibit no brightness difference from their backgrounds, as in (b). These factors also determine whether pac-men will appear to be amodally completed behind the squares, and how far behind them.

In this percept, the two vertical boundaries of the square are formed between pac-man edges of opposite contrast polarity: white-to-gray (light-to-dark) below, and black-to-white (dark-to-light) above. To form these vertical boundaries, the brain pools signals from opposite directions-of-contrast to complete an object boundary, albeit the boundary of an illusory object that receives no bottom-up contrastive signals between the aligned pac-men. In addition, the two horizontal boundaries of the square are formed between like directions-of-contrast. Significantly, both sets of boundaries can join together to form the square. Thus both like-contrast and opposite-contrast polarities are pooled together to form an object's boundary, thereby illustrating once again why all boundaries are invisible. Another way to say this property is that boundaries are *insensitive to contrast polarity*, in the sense that they pool signals from cells that are sensitive to opposite contrast polarities.

The Kanizsa square images in Figure 3.3 generate percepts that illustrate other important visual processes as well. Each figure generates a percept of an emergent square that occludes part of four circular disks, whose unoccluded portions are the visible pac-men. In particular, each of these 2D images creates a 3D percept of a square figure separated in depth from its background. These figure-ground percepts confront us with the same fundamental questions that were also raised by the Kanizsa stratification images in Figure 1.4: How are the disks completed behind the squares? And why are the occluded pie-shaped regions invisible?

Brighter objects look closer: Proximity-contrast covariance

An even more remarkable combination of properties can be seen by comparing the percepts generated by the two figures in the left column of Figure 3.3. When viewed under controlled conditions, the Kanizsa square percept that is induced by Figure 3.3c looks brighter than the Kanizsa square percept that is induced by Figure 3.3a. This enhanced brightness is due to the extra four lines in Figure 3.3c that cooperate with the pac-men to induce the Kanizsa square percept. The brighter Kanizsa square also looks even closer than its background does in Figure 3.3a. Why do brighter objects often look closer?

Variants of this kind of observation has been made by many vision scientists, going back at least to a paper of M. L. Ashley in 1898 (Ashley, 1898), and also include Kanizsa (Kanizsa, 1974, 1976), Hiroyuki Egusa (Egusa, 1983), Drake Bradley and Susan Dumais (Bradley and Dumais, 1984), Barbara Dosher, George Sperling, and Stephen Wurst (Dosher, Sperling, and Wurst, 1986), and Franco Purghé and Stanley Coren (Purghé and Coren, 1992), over the years. This interaction between brightness and depth is yet another example of the fact that visual properties are not processed by independent modules, but rather as complementary boundary and surface streams many of whose visual qualities interact, as in Figures 3.1 and 1.21. Why brighter Kanizsa squares look closer will be explained in Chapter 4. See particularly Figure 4.53.

The phrase *proximity-luminance covariance* is sometimes used for examples where increasing the luminance of one part of an image makes it look closer. In particular, Dosher, Sperling, and Wurst used this phrase in an excellent article about this topic in 1986 (Dosher, Sperling, and Wurst, 1986). I like to call the Kanizsa square percept an example of *proximity-contrast covariance* instead, because the white luminance in the Kanizsa square image is the same across the image. The brightness that makes the Kanizsa square look closer is a property of the *contrast* of the emergent square relative to its background.

Finally, in the percept generated by Figure 3.3d, although the four lines block the square boundaries *in their depth plane*, the Kanizsa square sides can be completed *behind them*, even while the inner ends of the lines cooperate to induce a percept of a circular Ehrenstein disk (Figure 1.1) *in front of* them. This figure hereby generates a percept with three depth planes! How all these percepts arise will be explained later in the next chapter.

You may by now be wondering, if all boundaries are really invisible, then how do we see the Kanizsa squares in Figure 3.3a? How, indeed, do we see anything?! Something else must also be going on that lets us see the visible world of surface brightnesses and colors. In 1984, in addition to predicting that "all boundaries are invisible", I also predicted that "all conscious visual qualia are surface percepts" (Grossberg, 1984a). What is this additional surface perception process and how is it related to the process whereby the brain forms boundaries? I will now build up an answer to these basic questions in several simple stages.

Living with your blind spot

To get started, let me first point out that perceptual boundaries and surfaces are not just high-level constructs that have to do with sophisticated processes like object recognition and cognition. Boundaries and surfaces play a role in processing signals from the very earliest stage of visual processing, the eye itself.

The image in the top row of Figure 3.4 shows a cross-sectional view through an eye. Light streams in from the left, passes through the lens and vitreous humor, and finally hits the photosensitive retina. The most sensitive region of the retina is called the *fovea*. The fovea is the region of the retina with the highest acuity and the highest concentration of color-sensitive photoreceptors. The fovea processes a region of visual space that is approximately one degree wide. Retinal acuity gradually decreases with distance from the fovea. Our eyes move in our heads to direct our sensitive fovea to focus on new points of interest.

Although the retina is a miracle of biological design, it is also a very *noisy* detector. Without the help of additional processing by the brain, retinal noise could easily defeat our ability to see. The image at the bottom of Figure 3.4 illustrates two sources of noise on the surface of the retina. To the left of the figure, you can see the fovea. To the right, you can see the *blind spot*. The blind spot is a region of the retina that is totally blind; it has no light-sensitive photodetectors. The blind spot exists because of the way in which the photodetectors in other parts of the retina send light-activated signals to the brain along nerve pathways, called axons, that are brought together in the optic nerve (see again the upper image in Figure 3.4) which sends light-activated electrical signals to the brain. The blind spot lies right

in front of the retinal positions where all the axons come together to be bundled into the optic nerve.

The blind spot is large! It is at least as large as the fovea. Despite this fact, many of us manage to go through life without ever realizing that we have a large blind hole in our retinas. We certainly do not see a roving hole in the world as our eyes scan a scene. Why not? In addition to the blind spot, Figure 3.4 shows that a lot of veins lie between the source of light and the retina. These veins nourish the eye. Why do we not see the veins either?

Figure 3.5 illustrates yet another sense in which retinal processing is noisy. It shows a cross-sectional view through the retina, which is a complex organ in its own right. Light is processed by several layers of retinal cells before the processed signals are collected in the optic nerve and sent to the brain. If you look closely, however, you will see that there is something strange about how the light goes through the retinal layers. Indeed, light passes through

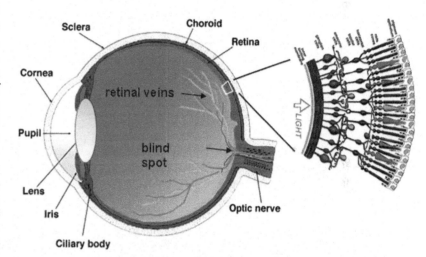

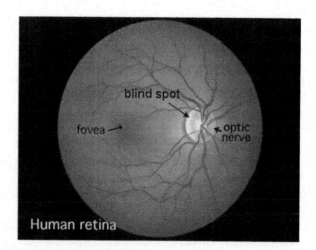

FIGURE 3.4. A cross-section of the eye, and top-down view of the retina, show how the blind spot and retinal veins can occlude the registration of light signals at their positions on the retina.

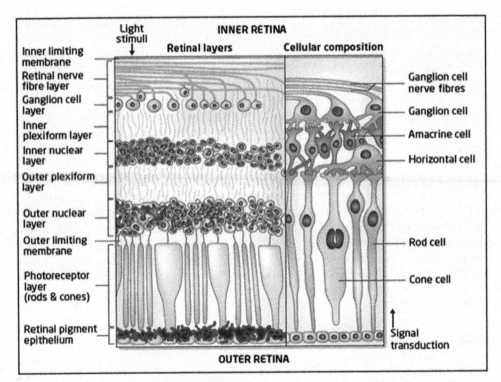

FIGURE 3.5. A cross-section of the retinal layers. Note that light stimuli need to go through all the retinal layers before they reach the photoreceptor layer at which the light signals are registered.

all the retinal layers before it ever hits the photodetectors and activates them! All these layers of cells can absorb and scatter the light before it ever reaches the photodetectors.

This inversion of the retinal layers may make sense from the viewpoint of how the retina develops, but it seems very peculiar from the viewpoint of how the brain sees. Richard Feynman, one of the most brilliant physicists of the twentieth century, got very interested in how the brain sees until he became aware of these facts. Feynman was a famously honest man who realized that he could not think of a sensible explanation for how the brain sees so well despite the retina's peculiarities of having a blind spot as well as retinal veins and retinal layers in front of the photoreceptors. Every scientist needs heuristics, or intuitive design principles, on which to base a principled scientific theory. These heuristics need to make sense, and in the best cases are even parsimonious and beautiful, for a top theorist to be comfortable with them. Feynman realized that he could not find intuitively plausible principles for how the brain copes with its noisy retinas, so he got out of vision. Of course, a man with Feynman's abundant intellectual and personal resources could not be long deterred by this disappointment. He rapidly moved on to successfully pioneer the fields of quantum computing and nanotechnology.

In the next few sections, I will suggest how seemingly strange ideas such as "all boundaries are invisible" help to explain how the brain compensates for the noisy design of the retina. From a more general viewpoint, this discussion will illustrate how deficiencies of image processing at one stage of brain organization—in this case, due to physical and developmental constraints on how the retina and optic nerve grow, and how the retina gets nourished by blood—are compensated by processing at higher stages of brain organization. As I noted in Chapter 1, I call this design principle *hierarchical resolution of uncertainty*. This principle helps us to understand how the noisy and rapidly metabolizing meat that makes up our eyes and brain cells gives rise to the Platonic world of visual forms of which we are consciously aware as we go through our lives.

Jiggling eyes and occluded objects: Beware moving dinosaurs!

How does the brain avoid seeing the retinal veins and the blind spot? One contributing factor is that, even when we think our eyes are fixated on a stationary object in the world, they are rapidly jiggling in their orbits, back and forth, by such a small amount that we are not consciously aware of these tiny movements. This jiggle acts like a "refresh" operation that maintains the sensitivity of visual nerve cells to the stationary object. It does so by creating small relative motions between the object and the retina. Many visual cells are sensitive to these motion *transients* and fire in response to them. Images that do not move relative to the jiggling retina are said to be *stabilized*. Percepts of stabilized images fade away. They cannot be seen after a little while because they are not refreshed. The retinal veins and blind spot are stabilized images because they are attached to the retina. They therefore are not visible, at least not under ordinary viewing conditions.

Those of you who saw the vastly entertaining movie *Jurassic Park* will recall the frantic request that the humans stop moving as the ravenous Tyrannosaurus Rex dinosaur approached. This request was made because, presumably, T Rex could not see stationary objects. Unfortunately, this did not stop T Rex from moving, and it is *relative* motion of its eyes relative to the world that would presumably have stimulated its visually sensitive cells . . . ooops!

One way to check that you really do have retinal veins is to hold a small flashlight to the side of your head, and jiggle the light from the flashlight on your retina, preferably when you are in a dimly lit room. You will suddenly see the moving shadows cast by the veins on your retina. These shadows are quite large. Be glad, therefore, that the veins are stabilized on your retinas!

The retinal jiggle helps to discount the veins and blind spot, but more is needed to see the world of continuous objects that we take for granted every day. To get a feel for what is missing, imagine that a simple image, like one of a thick straight edge, is registered by the retina in a region that includes the blind spot and some retinal veins. Parts of the edge cannot effectively activate retinal photoreceptors, because their visual signals are received where there are veins or the blind spot. Because the veins and blind spot are stabilized images on the retina, they fade. What remains is not a representation of the entire edge, however, but rather discontinuous fragments of the edge's unoccluded regions (Figure 3.6, top image). How does the brain transform these discontinuous fragments into a percept of a continuous edge?

How illusions may represent reality

We can now begin to better understand how the brain can use the discontinuous fragments of an edge to complete a continuous edge percept. In Figure 3.6 (top image), the occluded fragments of the edge are surrounded by unoccluded fragments that are approximately collinear, or aligned. The brain uses these collinear fragments to

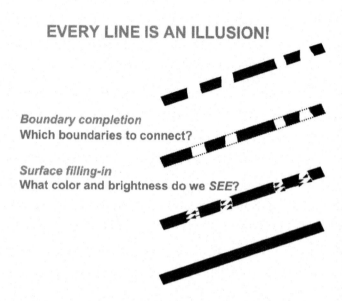

EVERY LINE IS AN ILLUSION!

Boundary completion
Which boundaries to connect?

Surface filling-in
What color and brightness do we *SEE*?

FIGURE 3.6. Every line is an illusion because regions of the line that are occluded by the blind spot or retinal veins are completed at higher levels of brain processing by boundary completion and surface filling-in.

complete edge boundaries wherever they are missing. In particular, the brain has cells that can form boundaries *inwardly* between pairs, or greater numbers, of collinear (or nearly collinear) contrasts (Figure 3.6, second image from top). In other words, a boundary can form in a region that receives no visual inputs of its own if it has collinear inducers on both sides of the region. Then all the boundaries that were occluded can be completed.

Using these ideas, we can begin to understand how Kanizsa square percepts form in response to the images in Figure 3.3. In particular, the brain does not known if there is a retinal vein or blind spot between the pac-men in Figure 3.3a. It will therefore complete boundaries between pairs of such collinear contrasts whenever they are long enough and not too far apart. If these boundary-forming cells can also pool collinear signals from opposite contrast polarities, as in the case of the reverse-contrast Kanizsa square of Figure 3.3b, then they can complete the edge even if the unoccluded edge fragments have opposite contrasts with respect to a textured background. The existence of these variants of the Kanizsa square illusion is a small price to pay for having percepts of the world that are not occluded by the blind spot and retinal veins!

These examples illustrate why boundaries form *inwardly* between *pairs*, or greater numbers, of inducing contrasts. It is fortunate that boundaries cannot form *outwardly* from a single inducer. Imagine that they could. Then any speck of contrast in an image or scene could induce an expanding web of boundaries that could fill our field of view. Such boundaries would do more to drive us mad than to accurately represent objects in the world. It is also clear from these examples that boundaries form in an *oriented* way between collinear, or nearly collinear, inducers, as in the case of the Kanizsa squares in Figure 3.3. Finally, we know from the example of the reverse-contrast Kanizsa square in Figure 3.3b, and the Kanizsa disk-on-texture display in Figure 3.2, that boundaries are *insensitive* to contrast polarity. These three properties of boundary completion are summarized in Figure 3.7 (bottom left).

While emphasizing the *inward* completion of boundaries, I also want to mention that the process that forms visible surfaces can propagates *outward* from individual sources of brightness or color. For example, in Figure 3.6 (third image from top), the brightness and color of the unoccluded parts of an edge—after the stabilized blind spot and veins fade—flow outwards into the occluded parts of the edge, thereby restoring brightness and color to the edge percept at positions that were occluded by the blind spot or retinal veins (Figure 3.6, bottom image). This flow of brightness and color behaves much like a fluid that diffuses away from a source. It is called *surface filling-in*.

Boundaries contain filling-in of feature contours within surfaces

Boundaries act like a dam that contains the flow of brightness and color, and keeps it from flowing outside the contours of the boundary. By acting like barriers, or obstructions, to the flow of brightness and color, boundaries can make themselves visible, by causing a different brightness or color to occur on opposite sides of the boundary. In the case of the Kanizsa square of Figure 3.3a, for example, the four black pac-men induce local regions of enhanced brightness, called *feature contours*, just inside the boundary. A computer simulation that I published with my PhD student Alan Gove and Ennio Mingolla in 1995 illustrates the percept that we see in response to the Kanizsa square, and how it arises (Gove, Grossberg, and Mingolla, 1995). Figure 3.8B shows the feature contours that are induced just inside the pac-man boundaries. These feature contours fill-in within the square boundary (Figure 3.8C) to create a percept of enhanced brightness throughout the square surface, as shown in Figure 3.8D.

A simulation of the percept that we see in response to the reverse-contrast Kanizsa square was also published in that article (Figure 3.9). In this simulation, whereas bright feature contours are induced just inside the boundaries of the two black pac-men at the bottom of the figure, dark feature contours are induced just inside the boundaries of the two white pac-men at the top of the figure (Figure 3.9B). Because these dark and bright feature contours are approximately balanced, the filled-in surface color inside the square is indistinguishable from the filled-in surface color outside of the square (Figure 3.9D), so that the square boundary is recognized, via the boundary representation in Figure 3.9C, but not seen.

The model mechanisms that simulate the Kanizsa square percepts in Figures 3.8 and 3.9 do not include the neural mechanisms of 3D vision that lead to depthful figure-ground percepts, such as those induced by the images in Figure 3.3. Rather, these mechanisms show how the emergent boundaries and perceived brightnesses of the square surfaces are created. How figure-ground percepts of Kanizsa squares and many other images arise will be explained in Chapter 4, as I use the Method of Minimal Anatomies between here and there to incrementally expand and deepen the explanatory and predictive range of our theoretical concepts.

To briefly summarize the lessons summarized in Figures 3.6, 3.8, and 3.9, with the occluded line in Figure 3.6 as a primary example: A combination of inward boundary completion and outward filling-in of surface brightness and color help to complete the representation of a line that is occluded by retinal veins or the blind spot. A remarkable implication of this discussion is that: "*Every line percept is an illusion*".

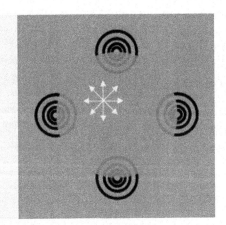

Complementary Properties of Boundaries and Surfaces

Boundary Completion	Surface Filling-in
Inward	Outward
Oriented	Unoriented
Insensitive to direction-of-contrast	Sensitive to direction-of-contrast

FIGURE 3.7. The processes of boundary completion and surface filling-in are computationally complementary.

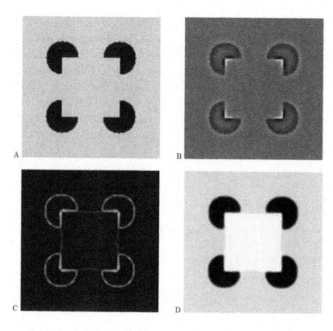

FIGURE 3.8. Computer simulation of a Kanizsa square percept. See the text for details.

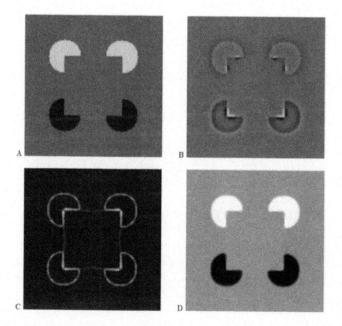

FIGURE 3.9. Simulation of a reverse-contrast Kanizsa square percept. See the text for details.

How do we distinguish the "real" from the "illusory"?

What I mean by this is that our conscious percepts of those parts of the edge that are occluded by retinal veins or the blind spot are actively constructed by the brain, just as are the more obviously illusory percepts like the Kanizsa square. The unoccluded parts of the edge are more "real" than the occluded parts, because they generate their own visual signals at the retina. But we do not know which parts are which! Both types of parts look just as "real" to us. Moreover, as our eyes move along a line, these "real" and "illusory" regions may be interchanged, with no one the wiser, as different parts of the line are occluded. In summary, even the percept of such a simple image as a "real" line will often include a series of "illusory" percepts that just happen to look "real".

If even "real" percepts can be "illusory", then how do we decide that a percept like the Kanizsa square is a visual illusion? We can begin to understand how this happens by using the concepts of boundary completion and surface filling-in, especially the fact that "all boundaries are invisible." Here is a possible tentative definition of percepts that we tend to call visual illusions, notwithstanding that many percepts that we believe to be real have boundaries and surface colors that are not directly received from retinal images:

Definition of a Visual Illusion: A visual illusion is a percept whose combination of boundaries and surfaces looks unfamiliar.

For example, in the percept of the offset grating of Figure 1.1, there is a vertical boundary that has no brightness or color. We call this unfamiliar combination of boundary and surface color an illusion. On the other hand, the part of an edge that is perceived at the locations over the blind spot is believed to be a "real" percept, even though it is not due to direct visual input from the retina, because it combines boundary and surface properties in a familiar way.

Neon color spreading

A famous example of color filling-in, called *neon color spreading*, is shown in Figure 3.10. Neon color spreading nicely illustrates three key properties of color filling-in. The image in the right panel of Figure 3.10 consists of circular annuli, part of which are black and part blue, just like the ones in the left panel image. When we view this figure, we can see an illusory square filled with a vivid, but illusory, blue color, even though the only blue in the image is in the blue circular arcs.

Neon color spreading was reported in 1971 by the Italian psychologist D. Varin (Varin, 1971), who studied a "chromatic spreading" effect that was induced when viewing an image similar to the one in Figure 3.10. In 1975, the Dutch psychologist Harrie F. J. M. van Tuijl (van Tuijl, 1975), and again with Charles M. M. de Weert in 1979 (van Tuijl and de Weert, 1979), independently introduced a lattice of horizontal and vertical lines, such as the one discussed in Figure 3.11, and called it "neon-like

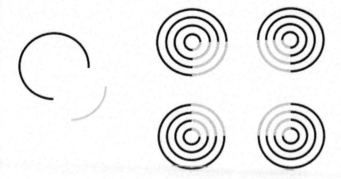

FIGURE 3.10. The visual illusion of neon color spreading. Neither the square nor the blue color that are perceived within it are in the image that defines a neon color display. The display consists only of black and blue arcs.

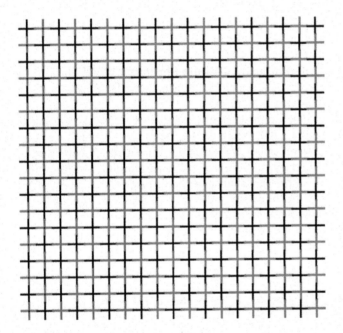

FIGURE 3.11. Another example of neon color spreading. The image is composed of black and red crosses. See the text for details.

color spreading". I will explain more fully below how such illusory percepts arise from an interaction between boundary and surface system properties that are useful for survival.

For now, let me just assert that the black arcs and the blue arcs in Figure 3.10 both create boundaries in our brains. At the positions where the boundaries join, the boundaries caused by the black arcs cause small breaks to occur in the boundaries caused by the blue arcs. I call these breaks *end gaps*. The blue color within the arcs can spread through the end gaps into the illusory square. Color can then spread *outwardly* from all these end gaps in all

directions. Its spread is thus *unoriented*. The blue color continues to spread outwardly in all directions until it fills the illusory square boundary, beyond which it cannot spread any further. In addition to the two filling-in properties of unoriented and outward spread, we can also add the obvious property that filling-in is *sensitive* to contrast polarity, because we can see its effects. These three properties of surface filling-in are summarized in Figure 3.7 (bottom right).

Complementary computation of boundaries and surfaces

In Chapter 1, I proposed that the brain is organized into parallel processing streams that often exhibit computationally complementary properties. Visual boundary completion and surface filling-in provide an excellent example of processes with complementary properties. Figure 3.7 summarizes that boundaries are completed *inwardly* between pairs or greater numbers of inducers, in an *oriented* fashion, and are *insensitive* to contrast polarity. On the other hand, surface filling-in proceeds *outwardly* in an *unoriented* fashion, and is *sensitive* to contrast polarity. These properties are manifestly complementary: inward vs. outward, oriented vs. unoriented, insensitive vs. sensitive. They fit together like a key and lock, like yin and yang.

Complementarity of boundary and surface processing is important for the success of each process. For example, filling-in needs to be unoriented so that it can cover an entire surface. On the other hand, the unoriented flow of brightness can only be efficiently contained by an oriented boundary. Likewise, a seeing process cannot efficiently build boundaries around objects in front of textured backgrounds. Both types of process are needed for either process to work well. Moreover, both types of process need to interact to overcome each other's complementary deficiencies.

The ability of boundaries to serve as barriers to surface filling-in provides an important example of how interactions between the boundary and surface systems help them to achieve a better result than either one could attain by itself. One of the challenges facing our visual system is to combine these complementary properties into a higher synthesis, which we experience as unified visual percepts. Said in another way, the challenge is to reconcile the *complementarity* of boundary and surface properties with the *consistency* of conscious percepts. I call this resolution the property of *complementary consistency*.

Complementary processing streams in visual cortex

How are these complementary processes represented in the brain? Much evidence suggests that they are carried out by parallel processing streams within the visual cortex. Figure 1.21 notes that visual signals activate the light-sensitive retinas within our eyes. The retinas, in turn, send signals to the lateral geniculate nucleus, or LGN. The LGN has a beautiful laminar organization that may, in first approximation, be broken up into a *parvocellular* part and a *magnocellular* part, so named after their parvocellular and magnocellular cell types. Output signals from the LGN branch out and activate several parallel subsystems of the visual cortex. Figure 1.21 summarizes a simplified description of these parallel processing streams.

Three streams are easy to track in Figure 1.21. Two of these streams proceed from the parvocellular LGN to regions of the first cortical stage, called the striate cortex. This cortical stage is also called area V1 in monkeys and area 17 in cats. One of these streams goes through structures that are called the *blobs* of V1. Blobs were discovered by Margaret Wong-Riley in 1979 (Wong-Riley, 1979). The blobs are small regions that are distributed in regular arrays throughout V1. They are highly active metabolically and therefore light up when probed by a chemical marker called cytochrome oxidase. The blobs project, in turn, to a region that is called the *thin stripes* of the prestriate cortex. Thin stripes occur within an area that is called V2 in monkeys and area 18 in cats. The thin stripes then project to prestriate area V4. I predicted in 1984 that the LGN→blob→thin stripe→V4 processing stream generates visual *surface* representations (green stream in Figure 1.21), and that the parallel LGN→interblob→interstripe→V4 processing stream generates visual *boundary* representations (red stream in Figure 1.21). I will, for short, call these streams the blob and interblob streams.

Other investigators, notably Margaret Livingstone and David Hubel (Livingstone and Hubel, 1988), have made related but distinct proposals. They suggested that the blob stream computes "color" and the interblob stream computes "orientation." Their proposal and mine lead to different sets of predictions. In particular, a boundary system can complete boundaries—both "real" and "illusory"— over positions in space that receive no inputs, let alone oriented inputs, as I have illustrated with many examples, including the offset grating and Ehrenstein illusion (Figure 1.1), Kanizsa squares (Figure 3.3), and neon color spreading (Figures 3.10 and 3.11). Likewise, a surface system can generate filled-in representations of figure-ground relationships that do not directly represent the local brightnesses and colors of a scene, as I have illustrated with examples of the Ehrenstein illusion (Figure 1.1), Kanizsa stratification and transparency (Figure 1.4), and neon color spreading (Figures 3.10 and 3.11). Many vision scientists now routinely use the boundary/surface distinction to interpret their experiments.

Multiple-scale symmetry-breaking generates complementary streams during development

How do the complementary properties of these parallel streams arise? I have predicted that they arise when the brain develops as part of a process of *symmetry-breaking*. This concept envisages that pairs of streams may arise from an earlier shared set of cells that bifurcates into complementary streams as developmental specialization occurs. This hypothesis helps to account for the related, but complementary, computational properties of each stream, as well as the often topographic connections between them. Symmetry-breaking is a widespread phenomenon in many parts of physics and biology. In the case of the brain, current models suggest that, during brain development, there is a *cascade of symmetry-breaking operations on multiple spatial scales*, with some complementary processes arising as sub-streams of larger streams that also exhibit complementary relationships.

Table 1.1 and Figure 3.1 illustrate these properties. Here I will just summarize some of these complementary relationships. In later chapters, I will explain how they arise and work. As we have already seen, visual boundaries and surfaces are proposed to be computed in the parallel interblob and blob cortical streams (Figure 1.21). Both of these streams occur within the more inclusive ventral What cortical processing stream (Figure 1.19). There are also complementary streams between the ventral What and dorsal Where visual cortical streams (Figure 1.19), and complementary streams within the Where cortical processing stream. For example, the medial temporal (MT) cortical area carries out *motion* processing within the Where cortical stream. Cortical areas MT$^+$ and MT$^-$ carry out different aspects of motion processing, as part of computationally complementary streams within MT. MT$^-$ and MT$^+$ project, respectively, to ventral medial superior temporal (MSTv) cortex, and to dorsal medial superior temporal (MSTd) cortex, thereby forming substreams of the Where cortical stream from MT to MST. MT$^-$ helps to track objects moving relative to the observer, whereas MT$^+$ helps to control visually-based (also called *optic flow*) navigation of the observer with respect to the world. Thus object tracking and optic flow navigation are computationally complementary streams within cortical area MT of the Where cortical stream. I will explain how these motion processes work in Chapters 8 and 9.

Area MT is, in turn, complementary to the pale stripe, also called the interstripe, region in prestriate cortical area V2. Recall from Figure 1.21 that V2 interstripes receive inputs from V1 interblobs, and that this entire boundary stream is part of the ventral What cortical stream. As noted above, V2 interstripes carry out boundary grouping of static percepts of object *form*. In other words, form and motion processing, which are carried out between V2 and MT, are complementary, as are visual tracking and navigation, which are carried out within MT. The former complementary relationship exists between different cortical streams, one in the What stream and the other in the Where stream, whereas the latter relationship is carried out within complementary sub-streams of the Where stream. These *inter*stream and *intra*stream complementary relationships illustrate what I mean by saying that there are *multiple scales* of symmetry-breaking during the development of complementary streams within the visual cortex. The genetic and developmental mechanisms whereby the brain may unfold a cascade of complementary streams operating on different spatial scales are not yet well understood. Even without this additional understanding, it should now be clear how different Complementary Computing is from the assertion that the brain computes using independent modules.

Special-purpose modules or general-purpose modal systems?

In Chapter 1, I noted that classical vision models have often espoused the view that different vision processes are represented as *independent modules* which carry out their own specialized tasks. Many Artificial Intelligence models have traditionally been of this type, as have the models of various visual neuroscientists. In this conception, one module might detect edges in a scene, another texture, another shading, and so on.

There are several problems with this idea. One problem is that many natural scenes usually contain several, if not all, of these scenic qualities in the same position. An example of this is the famous picture of Einstein's face that is seen in Figure 3.12, where many edges are part of texture and shading gradients. Another problem is that the lighting of the scene may vary with time, position, or the observer's viewpoint. Even in cases where scenic edges, texture, and shading are spatially separated from one another in different parts of the scene, in order for the specialized modules to be able to do their work, one would first need a smart, general-purpose preprocessor, or front

FIGURE 3.12. In this picture of Einstein's face, edges, texture, and shading are overlaid.

end, that could identify what type of features were in each particular region in order to use the correct module there. This preprocessor would need to be so smart that it could identify whether, say, there was a texture throughout a given region, and would need to do this for all the types of textures that would need to be identified. But if the general-purpose preprocessor is that smart, then why do we need specialized modules?

There are two possible ways to try to escape this critique. One is to restrict the visual environment so that it contains *only* edges, *or* texture, *or* shading. This is how many specialized vision algorithms have been used in applications. For example, they may be used to process scenes which have been carefully selected so that, given properly controlled lighting, only object edges that are of high enough contrast need to be detected. Clearly such an approach can only work with a limited collection of relatively simple scenes that are under the vigilant control of an external operator. Humans and animals do not, however, live in such simple visual environments. Our visual worlds are filled with unexpected combinations of visual features. These features are, moreover, lit differently with every passing moment.

The other possible answer is that the brain has a *general-purpose* vision system that can process many different combinations of visual features, even unfamiliar ones, and can do so under variable lighting conditions. Boundaries are, for example, not just representations of an object's edges. Boundaries can also represent form-sensitive combinations of edges, texture, shading, and depth information. Likewise, surfaces represent combinations of brightness, color, depth, form, and figure-ground information. Processes whose computational units can represent so many types of information are said to *multiplex* this information. Multiplexing combines multiple types of information at individual nerve cells. The complementary properties of boundaries and surfaces in Figure 3.7 illustrate one type of multiplexing. The *patterning* of information, or its *spatial context*, across many such cells disambiguates its meaning in a context-sensitive way. Indeed, if you view the picture of Einstein's face through a small aperture, then you just see a jumble of edges, textures, and shading which, taken alone, mean nothing.

The architecture is the algorithm

More examples of complementarity, such as those summarized in Table 1.1, Figure 3.1, and briefly discussed above, will be described in greater detail throughout the book. In every case, they help to achieve a general-purpose competence within a prescribed *modality* of intelligence, such as vision, audition, cognition, emotion, or sensory-motor control. It is in this sense that the brain is designed to realize *general-purpose solutions of modal problems.* Such solutions are far more general than the special-purpose algorithms of Artificial Intelligence. But they are far less general than the computations of a modern von Neumann computer. By being general-purpose in each modality of intelligence—hence the name *modal* problem—the brain can handle many types of inputs and tasks in that particular modality. But no single system of the brain can do everything. Brain systems that carry out different modal behaviors have different anatomical designs, and may cooperate and compete in specific ways that enable the entire brain to achieve goals that individual modal systems could not achieve on their own. This insight is often summarized by the phrase: "The architecture is the algorithm"; namely, the emergent properties that can solve a given modal problem, or several modal problems interacting, depend upon how the anatomy and neurobiology of that brain system have been specialized through development and learning to solve its tasks.

A new geometry: Cooperation and competition across space and orientation

The concepts of boundary completion and surface filling-in also represent a radical break with classical geometrical

concepts that mathematical scientists have developed over the centuries with which to describe the "real" world. In school, we learn geometrical concepts about lines and curves that have been known since at least the work of the great mathematician Euclid in ancient Greece. We learn, for example, that a line or curve is made up of a series of points. We also learn how to define surfaces using concepts like surface elements and the normals, or perpendicular lines, to each surface element. These concepts were developed by the great nineteenth century German mathematicians Karl Friedrich Gauss and Bernhard Riemann, among others, and have been used with great success to mathematically characterize surfaces for over a century.

When we ask, however, "What are the units of visual perception? Are they the familiar units of classical geometry that we have learned in school?", we need to answer "Emphatically not!" A line or curve, at least as it is defined by classical geometry, is just a set of individual points that are organized in a prescribed way. Such a set of points has no internal coherence; each point can be chosen independently of the others. To understand how we *see* lines and curves, we need to replace these classical concepts with that of a boundary, or perceptual grouping. A boundary is an *emergent property*, with a *coherent structure* that arises from several types of interactions among the many cells that respond to the line stimulus.

For example, in Figure 3.3c, lines are drawn perpendicular to the orientations of the Kanizsa square with each line ending at one of the illusory square boundaries. As a result, the square boundaries are strengthened along their entire length. Said in another way: The lines whose ends are *perpendicular* to the emerging square boundary *cooperate* with the *parallel* edges of the pac-men that induce them to generate the boundary. In contrast, in Figure 3.3d, lines are drawn that intersect where the square boundaries would usually be. These lines interfere with the formation of the square boundaries by a process of *orientational competition.* This boundary suppression occurs despite the fact that there is no change in the pac-man inducers that would otherwise generate them. These examples illustrate that cooperation and competition, across both space and orientation, determine the final outcome of the boundary completion process. How these processes work will be discussed in greater detail below.

Here is another famous example: Start with the left image of Figure 3.13, that defines a vivid Ehrenstein circle enclosing a bright disk. Now tilt the orientations of the lines without changing the positions of the line endpoints. Then, as the right image shows, the percepts of the circle and disk are greatly weakened, even though none of the endpoints of the lines is changed. If the Ehrenstein circle were "just" a series of points going through the endpoints of these lines, then nothing would have changed.

Taken together, the Kanizsa square (Figure 3.3) and Ehrenstein circle (Figure 3.13) show that boundaries form

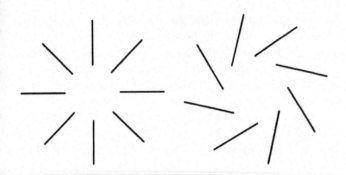

FIGURE 3.13. The Ehrenstein percept in the left panel is significantly weakened as the orientations of the lines that induce it deviate from being perpendicular to the illusory circle.

best when they are either (almost) parallel to lines, as in Kanizsa squares, or (almost) perpendicular to line ends, as in Ehrenstein circles. It is also clear from Figure 3.13 that orientations that are too far from being perpendicular to a line end cannot support an emergent boundary. On the other hand, perfect perpendicularity is not required, either. The emergent circle and square percepts that are induced by the two images in the top row of Figure 3.14 show that locally preferred perpendicular line ends may induce either a circular or square boundary. In the square boundary percept, the boundary changes its orientation abruptly to match the orientation of its nearest inducers. In both cases, the locally preferred perpendicular orientations can group together to form the globally preferred boundary shape.

In contrast, the bottom image in Figure 3.14 induces a boundary whose orientations are not perpendicular to their respective line ends. This figure shows that there

is a range of orientations at each line end that can cooperate in a grouping, and that the best combination of these grouping inducers is chosen to form a possible global grouping, while inhibiting other boundaries that have less support from nearby inducers. In this case, locally unpreferred orientations that are not perpendicular to their line ends are selected because they can cooperate to form a globally preferred boundary shape.

From fuzzy to sharp groupings: Hierarchical resolution of uncertainty

Why are there multiple possible orientations at line ends that can support a global boundary grouping? If perfect alignment of a single possible orientation at each line end were required before grouping could start, then there would be a vanishingly small probability that boundary completion could begin. However, our brains are made out of meat, not silicon! They cannot be expected to operate with the precision of a computer chip. Instead, the receptive fields of the cells that create the groupings—that is, the spatial distribution of inputs that can drive the cell— must be coarse enough to enable multiple nearly collinear and nearly orientationally aligned inducers to start the grouping process. As a result, when a boundary grouping first starts to form, multiple orientations can start to group, leading to a web of possible groupings that are initially fuzzy across space (Figure 3.15, left column). This fuzziness can be understood as the embodiment within these receptive fields of perceptual experiences with nearly collinear and aligned visual stimuli during cortical development. However, if all perceptual groupings remained fuzzy, visual perception would be significantly degraded.

In fact, most consciously recognized groupings are spatially sharp (Figure 3.15, right column), as we have seen in multiple examples above. Given that groupings start out fuzzy in order to enable grouping to begin, why are

Locally preferred and globally preferred

Locally unpreferred and globally preferred

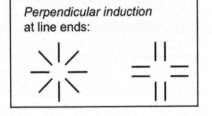

FIGURE 3.14. Boundaries are completed with the orientations that receive the largest total amount of evidence, or support. Some can form in the locally preferred orientations that are perpendicular to the inducing lines, while others can form through orientations that are not locally preferred, thus showing that there is initially a fuzzy band of almost perpendicular initial grouping orientations at the end of each line.

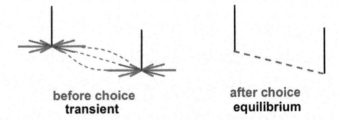

before choice
transient

after choice
equilibrium

FIGURE 3.15. A fuzzy band of possible initial grouping orientations allows grouping to get started. Cooperative-competitive feedback via a hierarchical resolution of uncertainty chooses a sharp final grouping that has the most evidence to support it.

so many completed boundaries sharp? We will see below how *feedback* within the boundary system can rapidly choose a final grouping that is maximally consistent with the spatial organization of the positional and orientational evidence in all of its inducers. This feedback uses a combination of cooperation and competition to choose the strongest grouping that has accommodate all of its inducers. This feedback process provides another example of hierarchical resolution of uncertainty. A number of such hierarchical resolutions are needed to generate sufficiently complete, context-sensitive, and stable perceptual representations upon which effective actions can be based. I will offer explanations of them all before using them to explain how they can help us to understand where, how, and why in our brains our visual percepts become conscious.

Not all boundaries are as spatially separated as they are in the examples of Kanizsa squares, Ehrenstein disks, and Kanizsa stratification percepts. In response to shaded and textured objects, for example, the boundaries that form typically create a form-sensitive *boundary web* that fits itself to the statistics of the shading and texture in the object. When we see a shaded or textured object in depth, that percept is typically supported by multiple boundary webs, each one created by cells with different receptive field sizes, or scales. I will explain why and how this happens in this chapter, Chapter 4, and especially Chapter 11. Classical geometrical concepts about surfaces, such as surface elements and normals, are hereby replaced by concepts of *surface filling-in within a multiple-scale boundary web*. How boundary webs form, and how surfaces fill-in within them, will also provide us with additional examples of complementary computing and hierarchical resolution of uncertainty.

Grouping of shading and texture, breaking camouflage, and 3D percepts of 2D pictures

Recognition is facilitated by invisible boundary groupings. We can now better understand how visual illusions help to understand how the visual brain works. First, by their very unfamiliarity, they vividly draw our attention to important perceptual processes that we might otherwise take for granted. Second, many of them are crucial for our survival, as is illustrated by the fact that the percept even of an object's edge may be illusory due to occlusions caused by the blind spot and retinal veins, as illustrated in Figure 3.6, or may be constructed to better recognize textured images such as the Dalmatian in snow (Figure

1.2). Boundaries will only be seen if they fill-in the surface representation of a bounded object with a different brightness, color, or depth than its background, as in the case of the Kanizsa square percept that is generated by the image in Figure 3.3a and simulated in Figure 3.8.

Much neurophysiological evidence suggest that critical stages of visual object recognition occurs in the inferotemporal, or IT, cortex, whereas perceptual boundaries and surfaces are formed in the earlier interblob and blob processing streams of the visual cortex, as illustrated in Figure 1.21. We can recognize boundaries that we cannot see in part because recognition and seeing are carried out by different parts of the brain.

The Dalmatian in snow example is important because it illustrates a problem that our ancestors confronted in the wild. Imagine that the image is not of a Dalmatian, but rather of a deadly predator, such as a snow leopard, that is stealthily tracking you in the snow. All that you can see are the predator's spots, because its white coat blends into the snow. By using your emergent invisible boundaries, you can hopefully recognize the predator in time to initiate evasive or other survival techniques. Emergent boundaries, whether invisible or not, hereby help us to break through camouflage in the many situations where local properties of an object—such as its curves and surface elements—would be insufficient for its recognition. In fact, one way to disable our ability to break through camouflage is to generate images whose orientations create emergent boundary groupings that compete with those of the target.

Emergent boundary orientations obey Gestalt rules: Diagonals from horizontals and verticals. Figures 3.16-3.18 provide some other examples of how invisible boundary groupings can segregate textured regions from one another, or separate figures from their backgrounds. Figure 3.16 is a famous image due to the distinguished American psychologist, Jacob Beck (Beck, 1966), who died in 2003. It is a texture composed of the letters L and T. Although the regions with vertical and diagonal T's are contiguous, the vertical T's group together with the vertical L's, rather than with the diagonal T's. One reason for this is that the vertical T's and L's both have vertical and horizontal lines, whereas the diagonal T's do not. Invisible vertical and horizontal emergent boundaries can connect, and thereby group together, the vertical T's and L's, but cannot link the diagonal T's with the vertical T's. The boundary grouping process is thus sensitive to the relative orientations of image contrasts. As in the boundary which completes the Kanizsa square, inducer orientations that are *collinear*—that is, have the same orientation and are aligned across space—are strongly favored in the grouping process. Because the properties of boundary grouping can occur automatically at an earlier processing stage than the one that recognizes T's and L's, this percept is consistent

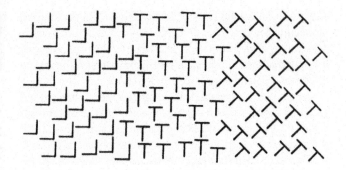

FIGURE 3.16. T's and L's group together based on shared orientations, not identities.

with the hypothesis that collinear grouping occurs in prestriate visual cortex, notably in cortical area V2, before the emergent boundary and surface representations that are formed there are passed to the inferotemporal cortex for object recognition, as indicated in Figure 1.21.

The texture in Figure 3.17, which was studied by Jacob Beck, Anne Sutter, and Richard Ivry (Beck, Sutter, and Ivry, 1987), illustrates that boundary grouping is sensitive to the distance between the inducing elements. It is easier for boundaries to form between elements that are closer together, other things being equal. Such Gestalt rules for visual perception were proposed by German psychologists like Wolfgang Köhler (Henle, 1971) and Max Wertheimer (Wertheimer, 1961) during the first half of the twentieth century.

Figure 3.17 is called a tripartite texture because, although the entire picture is constructed from black squares on a white background, our brains group it into three distinct regions. Each of the black squares in the left and right regions is closer to one another in the horizontal than vertical direction. As a result, our brains form horizontal boundaries between the collinear tops of the squares, as well as the between the collinear bottoms of the squares, thereby grouping the squares into perceived rows. The boundaries between the squares are invisible. In the middle region, emergent diagonal boundaries are perceived, even though there are no diagonal orientations in any of the individual squares, but only horizontal and vertical orientations. The global arrangement of the square inducers is thus sensitive to both relative position and orientation in determining which grouping will win.

Figure 3.18 is a computer simulation of these grouping properties that Ennio Mingolla and I published in 1987 (Grossberg and Mingolla, 1987). Although each of the four input images in parts (a), (c), (e), and (g) of Figure 3.18 is composed of three columns of three objects each composed of six vertical line segments, their spatial arrangement can generate strikingly different percepts. The grouping induced in Figure 3.18b by the image in Figure 3.18a is of emergent vertical boundaries. The grouping induced in Figure 3.18d by the image in Figure 3.18c is

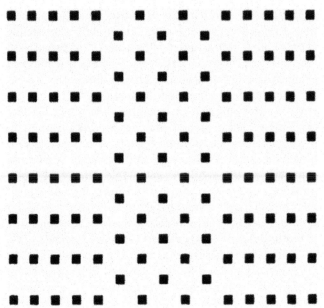

FIGURE 3.17. The relative positions of the squares give rise to a percept of three regions. In the middle region, emergent diagonal groupings form, despite the fact that all the orientations in the image are verticals and horizontals.

one of both emergent vertical and horizontal boundaries. The grouping induced in Figure 3.18f by the image in Figure 3.18e is of horizontal emergent boundaries. Finally, the grouping induced in Figure 3.18h by the image in Figure 3.18g is of both emergent horizontal and diagonal boundaries. Percepts of horizontal or diagonal boundaries emerge in response to the images in Figures 3.18c, 3.18e, and 3.18g even though there are only vertical line segments in the inducing images. The global arrangement of the line elements determines which grouping will win. These boundary properties simulate the kinds of grouping possibilities that are illustrated by the image in Figure 3.17. They also use the same grouping mechanisms that give rise to the percepts of neon color spreading in response to Figure 3.10 and 3.11, and that I will explain below.

Perceiving the forest before the trees: Typography portraits. One implication of this result can immediately be illustrated in Figure 3.19, where the boundaries of the letters E, S, A, and H are generated as emergent properties of groupings of the letters A, H, E, and S, respectively. This sort of global "forest before trees" structuring of a percept was particularly emphasized by David Navon (Navon, 1977). In the vertical parts of the global letter S, parallel, or collinear, grouping of local orientations is used, whereas in the horizontal parts of the S, groupings perpendicular to the local orientations form the emergent boundary. The top, left, and right sides of the global letter E, in contrast, complete groupings that are diagonal to the orientations

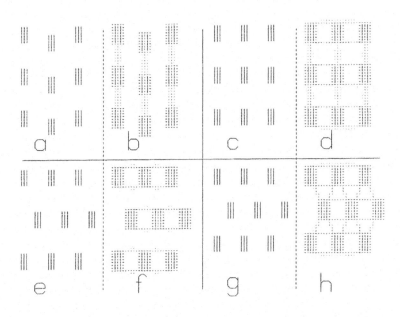

FIGURE 3.18. Computer simulations in b, c, f, and h of groupings in response to different spatial arrangements in a, c, e, and g of inducers that are composed of short vertical boundaries. Note the emergent horizontal groupings in d, f, and h, and the diagonal groupings in h, despite the fact that all its inducers have vertical orientations.

of the constituent letters A, yet only horizontal and vertical orientations occur in the emergent global boundary contour of the E. Figure 3.19 hereby vividly illustrates how multiple orientations can cooperation to induce boundary completion of an object.

These grouping properties have also inspired many artists. Figure 3.20 shows a Typography Portrait by the artist Sean Williams that is entirely composed of letters whose various orientations generate a vivid global grouping of a face, while also spelling out multiple embedded phrases; see https://www.pinterest.it/pin/408349891190092040/.

Many percepts that we observe in real life are illusions of this type. We are continually separating figures from their backgrounds based on boundary groupings that form between regions with different textures and colors. As we will discuss below, many visual artists, notably the Impressionists and Fauvists, exploited this property of visual perception to create some of the most beautiful paintings ever made. They were masters at showing how to arrange small patches of color on a canvas in such a way that the invisible groupings that were thereby induced in the brain, and the surfaces that

they organized from these color patches, can be recognized as objects in a scene.

Many perceptual skills that we take for granted in real life build upon these properties of emergent boundaries. For example, Figure 3.21a shows a texture of short line segments with different orientations. Some of the lines are approximately collinear. As in the Kanizsa square, they can get grouped together collinearly by amodal boundaries and the entire emergent boundary can "pop out" for fast recognition. In response to Figure 3.21b, an emergent boundary can separate the figure of the zebra from the background. This is an example of figure-ground separation. As in Figures 3.18 and 3.19, this emergent boundary is in some positions perpendicular to the inducing contrasts and in other positions diagonal with respect to them. Why does the zebra look like it is in front of the background, even though both the zebra and background lie in the same picture plane? One factor is the existence of T-junctions in the image; namely, positions where boundaries intersect in approximately the shape of a T. How T-junctions can cause this figure-ground percept will be explained below.

The zebra percept illustrates the fact that a 2D image can give rise to a 3D percept. As I noted in Chapter 1, all movies and pictorial art exploit this basic fact. Figure 3.21c provides a particularly vivid example

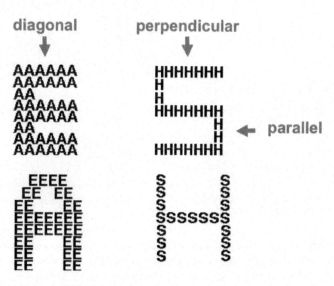

FIGURE 3.19. As in Figure 3.18, emergent groupings can form whose orientations differ from those of the inducing stimuli.

FIGURE 3.20. This typography portrait by Sean Williams exploits how boundaries can form through non-preferred orientations of their inducers.

of this fact. Percepts that are induced by images like this were studied by James Todd and Robin Akerstrom in an important paper that they published in 1987 (Todd and

Akerstrom, 1987). This image is built up from spatially separated black shapes, as was the Dalmatian in snow in Figure 1.2. However, due to the different sizes, orientations, and spatial arrangement of the discrete black shapes, a percept is generated of a continuously curved 3D surface. Note that the spatial scale of the shapes is smaller near the bounding contour of the figure. This kind of perspective effect enables boundary cells of different sizes, or scales, to form emergent boundary groupings in response to different parts of the image, with the smallest boundary cells responding most near the bounding contour.

Each spatial scale of boundary cells hereby generates a boundary web that tends to be aligned with the dominant orientations of the inducing image contrasts. One can think of these boundary webs as a continuously varying version across space of the boundaries that form in response to the simpler figures in Figure 3.18. These depth-selective boundary webs project to depth-selective surface representations where filling-in of surface brightness and color occur (Figure 3.22). The boundary web inputs to these surface Filling-In Domains, or FIDOs, are called Boundary Contour, or BC, signals. These BC signals capture surface brightness and color signals, called Feature Contour, or FC, signals in the FIDOs. When these captured signals fill in within their depth-selective domains, the total filled-in surface representation, across all the filling-in domains, generates the percept of a continuously curved 3D surface.

More will be said about how boundary webs form in the next chapter, and especially in Chapter 11, which is devoted to explaining in greater detail how we see the world in depth. Even now, however, several properties of this percept illustrate how radically different visual boundaries and surfaces are from classical mathematical concepts of curves and surfaces. For one, a 2D image can generate a 3D percept. This, in itself, challenges classical concepts of the *dimension* of a space. For another, the spatially discrete black shapes generate a continuously curved surface percept. We do not see the emergent boundary webs that support this continuous percept because "all boundaries are invisible". What we see are the filled-in surface brightnesses and colors that result when their FC inputs fill-in within depth-selective boundary webs.

3D curved shapes from filling-in within multiple-scale invisible boundary webs. The picture of a shaded ellipse in Figure 3.21d illustrates these and other important points even more vividly. This 2D picture of a shaded ellipse generates a 3D percept of an ellipsoid. How does this happen? The first thing to notice is that this percept could not be explained if we used only

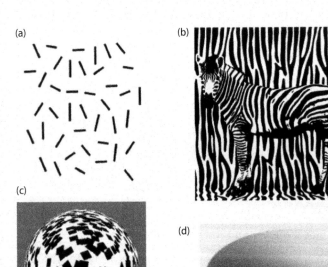

(a) (b) (c) (d)

FIGURE 3.21. Four examples of how emergent boundaries can form in response to different kinds of images. These examples illustrate how boundary webs can shape themselves to textures, as in (c), and shading, as in (d), in addition to lines, as in (a). In all these cases, the boundaries are invisible, but reveal themselves by supporting filling-in of surface brightness and color within their form-sensitive webs.

the classical concept of an edge. There is only one edge in this image, the bounding edge that surrounds the ellipse. If one thought that boundaries were only edges, then there would be nothing to prevent the gray shading inside the ellipse from spreading throughout its interior via surface filling-in, as it does to generate the percept of neon color spreading in Figures 3.10 and 3.11 until it reaches the bounding edge, yielding a percept of a uniformly gray 2D ellipse. This is, however, emphatically *not* what we see!

What happens instead is that multiple scales of boundary cells group together in form-sensitive boundary webs. As in the case of the textured disk image, the smallest cells preferentially group near the bounding contour of the ellipse. When all the boundary webs project to their respective depth-selective surface filling-in domains (Figure 3.22), they trap the gray that occurs within their own boundary web. The total filled-in surface representation, across all the filling-in domains, generates the percept of a 3D ellipsoid.

You might still object: "If these boundary webs are so important, then why don't we see them?" The answer is: "We do see them, but only indirectly through their effects on surface filling-in." You might then ask: "But why is that?" to which the answer is "Because all boundaries are invisible!"

Boundary webs support percepts of Impressionist paintings. The French Impressionists exploited this property of visual perception to create some of the most beautiful paintings ever made. Pointillists like Georges Seurat and Paul Signac were masters at arranging small patches, or "points", of color on a canvas in such a way that the groupings and filled-in surface regions that were thereby induced in the brain could be recognized as objects in the

world. The famous painting by Seurat called *A Sunday on La Grande Jatte* illustrates this kind of mastery (Figure 3.23). The Impressionists understood implicitly how to "break camouflage" for aesthetic purposes, and to thereby induce emergent forms that are not explicitly represented within the brush strokes of their paintings. Of course, the Impressionists and other visual artists did not use only boundaries to generate our percepts of their paintings. They also sensitively probed how to compose surfaces suffused with brightness and color, and how these qualities mutually influence one another in a context-sensitive manner.

From Seurat to SAR. The same principles that help to explain how we understand a pointillist painting can also be used to generate effective representations of radar images whose pixels may differ in luminance by five orders of magnitude of power in the radar return. In 1989, my PhD student William Ross, and I, together with Ennio Mingolla, and in cooperation with colleagues at MIT Lincoln Laboratories, processed Synthetic Aperture Radar, or SAR, images to generate boundary and surface representations that can easily be interpreted by human observers (Mingolla, Ross, and Grossberg, 1999). SAR is the kind of radar that can see through the weather. It is used in applications for remote sensing and mapping of the surfaces of the Earth and other planets. Figure 3.24 summarizes the processing of a SAR image showing a road crossing over a highway in a wooded area of New York State. The image in the lower right corner is the reconstruction of the original image in the upper left corner. The original image (Figure 3.24 (left column, top row) looks so dark on the limited dynamic range of the printed page because a small number of very high luminance pixels drives most of the image luminances towards zero values. After the image is

3D VISION AND FIGURE-GROUND SEPARATION
Multiple-scale, depth-selective boundary webs

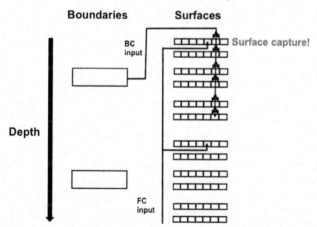

FIGURE 3.22. Depth-selective boundary representations capture brightnesses and colors in surface filling-in domains. See the text for details.

FIGURE 3.23. The pointillist painting *A Sunday on La Grande Jatte* by Georges Seurat illustrates how we group together both large-scale coherence among the pixels of the painting, as well as forming small groupings around the individual dabs of color.

normalized to a more manageable range, as in Figure 3.24 (right column, top row), one can clearly see its "pointillist" structure. This normalized image is then used to control both boundary completion and surface filling-in. Figure 3.24 (left column, bottom row) shows how the boundaries form in response to the most statistically regular combinations of normalized activities. The surface reconstruction of the image in Figure 3.24 (right column, bottom row) is created by filling-in the upper right normalized image within the boundaries within the lower left image. This filled-in surface representation exhibits the tiny posts along the sides of the road just as vividly as the large-scale structure of the trees and their shadows in the top half of the scene.

From the Optical Society of America to working with MIT Lincoln Laboratories. Our work on processing images that were created with artificial sensors, such as SAR, began unexpectedly in 1985 after I gave a lecture at the annual Optical Society of America conference about our work on understanding vision. A few group leaders at MIT Lincoln Laboratories heard my talk. Lincoln Labs is in Lexington, Massachusetts. It is a United States Department of Defense research and development center that is chartered to apply advanced technology to problems of national security (https://www.ll.mit.edu/about).

Among its many projects, it was perhaps the leading research laboratory in the country at that time for developing and applying artificial sensors of various kinds to large-scale civilian and military applications, including SAR, laser radar, multispectral infrared, night vision, and so on. These program managers thought that the ability of our models to deal with the kinds of discontinuities, noise, and large dynamic range of the images that their artificial sensors created would be natural tools for processing them, unlike more traditional algorithms.

Their intuition turned out to be correct. I was invited to give a year-long lecture series on my neural network research at the Labs. These lectures were videotaped and passed around the Labs. The Lincoln Labs Director watched them, and concluded from them that the time was ripe to carry out a national study of neural networks. This led to the DARPA Neural Network Study from October, 1987 to February, 1988, which issued an influential report that energized funding for the entire neural networks field. Also, within the Labs, our models were used to successfully process all the kinds of image data that I just listed. This kind of symbiosis between rigorous biological modeling and technological application continued for many years. Many of the students and postdoctoral fellows who came to study with me were interested in both, often with an emphasis on one or the other. Several of them became lab members or even group leaders at Lincoln Labs.

DO THESE IDEAS WORK ON HARD PROBLEMS? SAR!

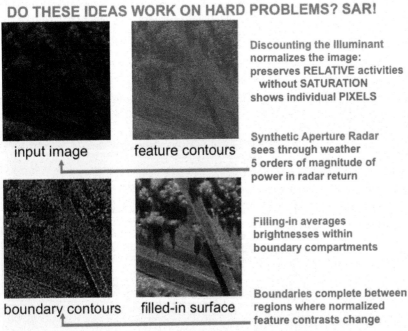

input image   feature contours

Discounting the Illuminant normalizes the image: preserves RELATIVE activities without SATURATION shows individual PIXELS

Synthetic Aperture Radar sees through weather 5 orders of magnitude of power in radar return

Filling-in averages brightnesses within boundary compartments

boundary contours   filled-in surface

Boundaries complete between regions where normalized feature contrasts change

FIGURE 3.24. In response to the Synthetic Aperture Image (upper left corner), a shunting on-center off-surround network "discounts the illuminant" and thereby normalizes cell activities to compute feature contours, without causing saturation (upper right corner). Multiple-scale boundaries form in response to spatially coherent activities in the feature contours (lower left corner) and create the webs, or containers, into which the feature contours fill-in the final surface representations (lower right corner).

Did Matisse know that "all boundaries are invisible"?

The great French artist Henri Matisse, who lived from 1869 until 1854, was a particularly insightful observer and innovator in exploiting interactions between the brain's boundary and surface processes for aesthetic purposes. For example, Matisse wrote about "the eternal conflict between drawing and color . . . Instead of drawing an outline and filling in the color . . . I am drawing directly in color" (Matisse, 1947/1992). We can interpret his aesthetic intuitions about drawing and color in terms of the distinct properties of boundaries and surfaces. In particular, I believe that Matisse intuitively understood that "all boundaries are invisible." By this I mean the following.

The Fauvists, or les Fauves (French for "the wild beasts"), emphasized the use of vivid colors and painterly qualities in creating their pictures. Matisse, who was one of the leading practitioners of Fauvism, developed a painterly technique whereby he could "draw directly with color" and could do so without surrounding these colors with explicit, differently colored, outlines. One purpose of such outlines in more traditional paintings and drawings was to group together several colored regions into representations of object surfaces.

How does "drawing directly in color" change how a painting looks? If instead of drawing directly in color, Matisse drew visible outlines around his surfaces, and did so in a dark color, then these contours could darken the surface colors of the entire scene, via *color assimilation*. Color assimilation occurs due to mechanisms whereby boundaries control the filling-in of surface color. Figure 4.10 below will provide a simulation of color assimilation. Matisse, however, wanted to create bright, glowing surface colors, which were a goal of the entire Fauve movement to which he belonged. He therefore figured out how to prevent the darkening and other distorting effects of visibly drawn contours, without preventing a viewer from perceiving the surface representations of the objects that are needed to fully appreciate his paintings.

Matisse was already "drawing directly in color" in his paintings from the Fauve period, as illustrated in his painting from 1905 called *The Roofs of Collioure* (Figure 3.25). He showed how patches of pure color, when laid down properly on a canvas, could be grouped by the brain into emergent boundaries, without the intervention of visible outlines. These emergent boundaries, in turn, could trigger filling-in of the colors into perceived surface representations of objects (Figure 3.26). The trick was that these emergent boundaries, being invisible, or amodal, did not

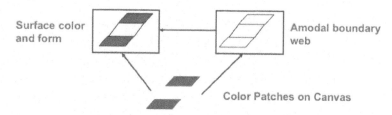

FIGURE 3.26. How "drawing directly in color" leads to colored surface representations. Amodal boundary webs control the filling-in of color within these surface representations. See the text for details.

darken the colors in the surface representations. In this sense, Matisse intuitively realized that "all boundaries are invisible" through the masterful way in which he arranged his colors on canvas to generate boundaries that could support compelling surface representations.

Several of his famous paintings of 1905, including *The Roofs of Collioure* and *The Open Window* (Figure 3.27), went a step further. They combined discrete color patches and continuous regions of surface color to generate harmonious surface representations in which both types of strokes are unified. By thinking about these paintings from the perspective of brain processes, I find them to be brilliantly insightful, even brazenly so, because of how boldly Matisse interspersed discrete and continuous brush strokes that combined together into a beautiful harmonious scene.

Matisse had a life-long interest in these issues. It was in his book *Jazz*, which he published in 1947 towards the end of his life, that he wrote the above quote about the exquisite paper cutout maquettes that he created during this period, when he could no longer manage the rigors of painting: "Instead of drawing an outline and filling in the color . . . I am drawing directly in color." He struggled for a long time during his life to figure out how to do this in a masterful way, I think, because "all boundaries are invisible." How this actually happens is not an easy thing to understand without scientific concepts and methods.

Matisse also illustrated through his art one of the most perplexing subtleties about boundaries and surfaces; namely, *both* boundaries and surfaces can be activated by the same visual features in the world, or by the same strokes of color in a picture (Figure 3.26), as illustrated by how the retina, through the LGN, activates both the interblob and blob streams of the visual cortex (Figure 1.21). Boundaries and surfaces are activated in parallel, but they respond in different ways to the same external stimuli because boundary and surface properties are computationally complementary (Figure 3.7), as neon color spreading vividly illustrates (Figure 3.10 and 3.11). Because boundaries and surfaces may be coactivated by the same visual features, there is often such a close correlation between them that it is often hard to separate an invisible boundary from the surface filling-in properties that may render it visible.

FIGURE 3.25. *The Roofs of Collioure* by Matisse. See the text for details.

Continuously
induced
surface

Matisse,
Open
Window,
Collioure
1905

Sparsely
induced
surfaces

FIGURE 3.27. Matisse's painting *Open Window, Collioure* combines continuously colored surfaces with color patches that created surface representations using amodal boundaries, as in Figure 3.26. Both kinds of surfaces cooperate to form the final painterly percept.

Boundary contrast, assimilation, chiaroscuro, and the watercolor illusion

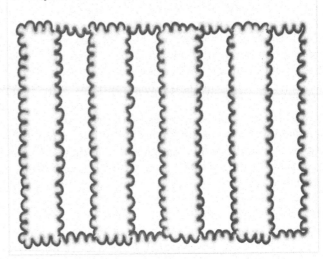

FIGURE 3.28. The watercolor illusion of Baingio Pinna can be explained using spatial competition between like-oriented boundary signals. This occurs at what I have called the First Competitive Stage. This is one stage in the brain's computation of hypercomplex cells, which are also called endstopped complex cells. Why the blue regions seem to bulge in depth may be explained using multiple-scale, depth-selective boundary webs. See the text for details.

Color assimilation due to filling-in across weakened boundaries in the watercolor illusion. A striking example of color assimilation due to visible contours is the watercolor illusion of Baingio Pinna (Pinna, 1987; Figure 3.28), a contemporary Italian vision scientist whom many colleagues think is a worthy successor to Kanizsa. Although Kanizsa holds a unique place in the history of Italian visual science, I share this high opinion of Pinna. In Figure 3.28, dark blue wavy lines surround light blue wavy lines. The resulting percept shows whole regions filled with the light blue color. In other words, these regions "assimilate" the color of the light blue wavy lines. I have explained this variant of color assimilation using neural mechanisms that are summarized below (Pinna and Grossberg, 2005). In particular, for reasons that I will soon explain, competition occurs between nearby boundaries. The image in Figure 3.28 generates boundaries wherever contrasts change rapidly enough across space, such as where a dark blue contour abuts the white background, or a dark blue contour abuts a light blue contour, or a light blue contour abuts the white background. The strongest of these boundaries occurs where a dark blue contour abuts the white background, since these are the positions in the image with the largest contrast. My explanation proposes that a stronger

boundary can inhibit a nearby weaker boundary more than conversely. When the light blue boundaries are weakened in this way, the light blue color that they would otherwise contain can spread across the weakened boundary, and be assimilated, into the contiguous white surface via surface filling-in.

The filled-in watercolor regions also seem to bulge in 3D, a property that can be traced to how boundary webs respond to the spatial gradient of boundary contrasts. In particular, the boundaries formed in response to the watercolor image proceed from stronger to weaker across space. The strongest are the white-to-(dark blue) boundaries, then the (dark blue)-to-(light blue) boundaries, and finally the (light blue)-to-white boundaries. This discrete boundary gradient is a spatially discrete analog of the continuous boundary web that is caused by the shaded ellipse of Figure 3.21d. In both examples, the 3D percept may be explained by how boundary cells with different size receptive fields, or spatial scales, react differently to the discrete or continuous change in contrasts. This multiple-scale boundary response creates multiple-depth boundary webs that capture surface color at different depths and fill-in a 3D surface percept. I will describe how this works in greater detail in Chapter 11.

Multiple-scale boundary webs and the depthful percepts of chiaroscuro and trompe l'oeil. This bulging effect can also be found as a result of the painterly technique of *chiaroscuro*, whereby light and dark paints are organized in gradients that cause a percept of a bulging 3D figure instead of the actual 2D painted surface. Leonardo da Vinci was one of the first painters to master the chiaroscuro technique. The self-portrait by the young Rembrandt in Figure 3.29 (left panel), painted in 1629 when he was 23 years old, and now hanging in the Mauritshuis, The Hague, illustrates how chiaroscuro can generate a vivid percept of depth. So too do the trompe l'oeil paintings of the contemporary British painter, Graham Rust (Rust, 1988; Figure 3.29, right panel).

The watercolor illusion already appeared in paintings of the minimalist American artist, Jo Baer, in the 1960s. Her entry in Wikipedia notes: "In many works that Baer created between 1964 and 1966, the peripheries and edges of the canvas continued to be marked by two square or rectangular bands of color. The outer, thicker border was black; inside it, a thinner band was painted in another color, such as red, green, lavender, or blue" (https://en.wikipedia.org/wiki/Jo_Baer). Figure 3.30 shows her triptych called *Primary Light Group: Red, Green, Blue* that was painted in 1964–65 and is now part of the Museum of Modern Art collection in New York. Scientists like Baingio Pinna have done many variations of the watercolor illusion to better understand its perceptual properties, but it is of historical

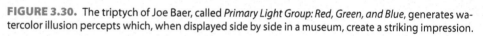

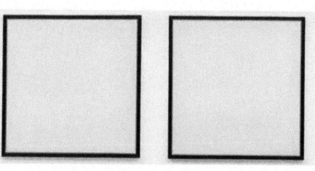

FIGURE 3.30. The triptych of Joe Baer, called *Primary Light Group: Red, Green, and Blue*, generates watercolor illusion percepts which, when displayed side by side in a museum, create a striking impression.

interest that Baer was earlier drawn to how percepts of surface color could spread beyond the positions in a painting where it is applied, just as Matisse was drawn to drawing directly in color without outlines.

Cape Cod School of Art: Hawthorne and Hensche and *plein air* painting

Many other artists have also struggled with how to represent object surfaces without drawing explicit boundaries around them, including the leading members of the Cape Cod school of art, notably Charles Hawthorne, its founder, and his most famous student, Henry Hensche. The Cape Cod school championed painting *en plein air* and was thus especially interested in representing the vivid colors of natural scenes seen in full sunlight or the lighting of other times of day. Their statements below, which were aimed at teaching the art of seeing and painting, reflect some of the same themes that concerned Matisse.

Hawthorne (Hawthorne, 1938/1960) wrote: "Beauty in art is the delicious notes of color one against the other . . . all we have to do is to get the color notes in their proper relation" (p. 18). ". . . put down spots of color . . . the outline and size of each spot of color against every other spot of color it touches, is the only kind of drawing you need bother about . . . Let color make form—do not make form and color it. Forget about drawing . . ." (pp. 25–26). "You don't hear me say much about drawing. It is because I think drawing the form, and painting, are better separated. The first thing is to learn to see color" (pp. 41–42).

Hensche further developed these concepts and put them into a historical context in which Monet played a

CHIAROSCURO
Rembrandt self-portrait

TROMPE L'OEIL
Graham Rust

FIGURE 3.29. The 3D percepts that are generated by chiaroscuro and trompe l'oeil both exploit the same kind of multiple-scale, depth-selective boundary webs that create the impression of a 3D bulge of the blue regions in the watercolor percept in Figure 3.28.

FIGURE 3.31. Henry Hensche's painting of *The Bather* is suffused with light.

FIGURE 3.32. Claude Monet's painting of *Poppies Near Argenteuil*. See the text for details.

pivotal role (Hensche, 1988): "When Monet came along . . . he revolutionized the 'art of seeing.' . . . it was the method of expressing light in color, and not value, to allow the key of nature to show clearly . . . The landscape helped Monet determine how color expressing the light key was the first ingredient in a painting, not drawing" (Robichaux, 1997, p. 27). "The untrained eye is fooled to think he sees forms by the model edges, not with color...Fool the eye into seeing form without edges" (Robichaux, 1997, p. 31). "Every form change must be a color change" (Robichaux, 1997, p. 33). Figure 3.31 illustrates how Hensche applied these ideas to suffuse with light his still life of *The Bather*.

Claude Monet and Impressionist painting: Seeing the forest and the leaves

Weak boundaries, as in the watercolor effect, have also been used to good effect by many artists other than Jo Baer, including Claude Monet. For example, in the famous painting *The Poppy Field Near Argenteuil* (Figure 3.32) that Monet

painted in 1873, now in the collection of Musée d'Orsay in Paris, the red poppies and the green field around them are painted to have almost the same luminance; that is, they are almost *equiluminant*. As a result, the boundaries between the red and green regions are weak and positionally unstable, thereby facilitating an occasional impression of the poppies moving in a gentle breeze, especially as one's attention wanders over the scene. Various reproductions of the painting, by distorting these equiluminant colors, do not lead to an equally vivid experience of this motion.

Monet, who lived from 1840 to 1926, was one of the founders of the French Impressionist movement, which derived its name from his painting called *Impression, Soleil Levant (Impression, Sunrise)*. This painting was exhibited in 1874 in an exhibition that was organized by Monet and his associates as an alternative to the Salon de Paris. Monet's use of color significantly departed from the established Academic painting style that dominated the Salon de Paris at that time. The surfaces of his paintings of natural scenes are built up from small brushstrokes, as in the *The Poppy Field Near Argenteuil* in Figure 3.32 that Monet painted at around this time. Using these discrete, but juxtaposed, color elements, Monet created complex surfaces that induced boundary webs which defined the structures of object forms. These emergent forms can be seen even though the individual compartments from which they are composed are also visible when spatial attention is focused upon them.

Without a certain degree of orientational uncertainty embedded in the boundary completion system (e.g., Figures 3.14, 3.15, and 3.17-3.21), long-range boundary completion and emergent segmentation would be nearly impossible in response to Monet's paintings. His paintings exemplify the paradoxical prediction that orientationally "fuzzy" computations often lead to sharp segmentations despite the fact that there are hardly any sharp edges in them. Continuous boundaries, smooth surface forms, and light are perceived in these paintings despite the fact that they consist of irregular color patches of varying densities of luminance and color. Observers can appreciate both the microstructure and the macrostructure (brushstrokes and scene, respectively) of his paintings as a result of the existence of multiple scales of oriented local contrast detectors, and the boundary groupings and filled-in surfaces that they induce (Figure 3.22) in order for us to effectively see and interact with the 3D world. Similar to how we can perceive both the boundaries in the watercolor illusion and the color spread across the weaker boundaries (Figure 3.28), we are able to perceive many of the individual strokes of paint within Monet's paintings as well as the color assimilation among these strokes within the emergent forms in his paintings.

How humans see paintings and paintings illuminate how humans see

The above examples of paintings by artists like Jo Baer, Charles Hawthorne, Henry Hensche, Henri Matisse, Claude Monet, and Georges Seurat illustrate the general theme that, whenever an artist manipulates a canvas, and experiences conscious percepts of an emerging painting, the artist is performing an experiment that probes different combinations of the brain processes whereby we see. Artists typically succeed in doing so without having explicit knowledge about the brain processes that mediate between painterly manipulation and percept. The particular interests and aesthetic sensibilities of different artists have led each of them to instinctively emphasize different combinations of these brain processes. These different combinations may be one hallmark of different artists' styles, and indeed of entire artistic movements.

Below the work of several other artists will be interspersed with scientific descriptions and explanations of how our brains see. Paintings by Banksy, Ross Bleckner, Leonardo da Vinci, Gene Davis, Claude Monet, Jules Olitski, and Frank Stella will be discussed. I began this analysis in my 2008 article (Grossberg, 2008), whose title "The Art of Seeing and Painting" is the same as that of Hensche's book to emphasize its focus on similar artistic themes. This analysis was further developed with my PhD student Lauren Zajac in our 2017 article in the *Art & Perception* journal (Grossberg and Zajac, 2017). These examples continue to illustrate how different artists have intuitively understood how multiple brain processes contribute to the conscious perception of a painting, and used this understanding to achieve their own unique aesthetic goals. In this way, the paintings of different artists clarify how our brains consciously see paintings, while also shedding light on how paintings illuminate how our brains see.

Boundary webs, self-luminosity, glare, double brilliant illusion, and gloss

An astonishing variety of surprising percepts can occur when boundary webs form in response to images or scenes. By creating boundary webs with particular properties, the spatial context in which a luminance occurs within a scene can even create a percept of *self-luminosity*, whereby different parts of a scene seem to glow or to emit an inner light. This can be seen in examples such as the *glare effect* that has been studied by Daniele Zavagno (Zavagno, 1999), the *double brilliant illusion* that has been studied by Paola Bressan (Bressan, 2001), and percepts of gloss that have been studied by Jacob Beck and Slava Prazdny (Beck and Prazdny, 1981).

In the glare effect (Figure 3.33, left column, top row), the interior white region of all four figures is the same, but an increasingly strong luminance gradient surrounds this region as one proceeds from the left figure in the first row to the right figure in the second row. The percept in response to the strongest gradient in the lower right image is one of a glowing self-luminosity, with lesser effects occurring in response to the weaker luminance gradients. This effect may be explained as the result of the boundary webs that are generated in response to the luminance gradients and how they control the filling-in of lightness within themselves and abutting regions. In particular, such a boundary web is like a continuous version of the boundary web that enables color spreading to occur out of the weakest boundary in the watercolor illusion (Figure 3.28). Due to the mutually inhibitory interactions across the boundaries that comprise these boundary webs, more lightness can spread into the central square as the steepness of the boundary gradients increases.

A similar way of thinking helps to explain the double brilliant illusion that is illustrated in Figure 3.33 (right column, top row). A computer simulation of this percept is summarized in Figure 3.33 (right column, bottom two rows) using the *anchored Filling-In Lightness Model*, or aFILM, that I published in 2006 with my PhD student Simon Hong (Grossberg and Hong, 2006). aFILM explains and simulates this percept using mathematically rigorous embodiments of the concepts that will be described more fully below and in the next chapter. The upper right panel of this simulation, labeled Anchored Lightness, shows the model's output of the double brilliant illusion.

Finally, there is the no less remarkable gloss effect that is perceived in response to Figure 3.33 (left column, bottom row). Here two almost identical vases are shown. The right vase is a matte vase, or vase with a dull and flat color, without any shine or highlights. In the left vase, a highlight has been added to a local region of the vase surface. Remarkably, this local change makes the entire vase look glossy compared

BOUNDARY WEB GRADIENT CAN CAUSE SELF-LUMINOSITY
Similar to WATERCOLOR ILLUSION

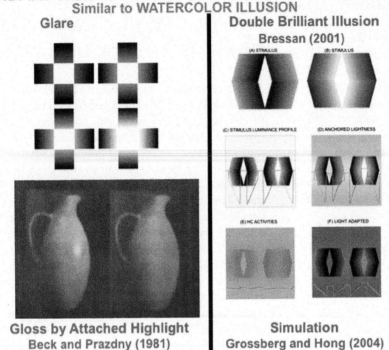

FIGURE 3.33. Various ways that spatial gradients in boundary webs can cause self-luminous percepts. See the text for details.

with the matte vase from which it was constructed. This glossy percept can be explained by the way in which the boundary web that is induced by the highlight consistently joins the boundary web that is generated by the rest of the vase's form. The lightness within the highlight can hereby spread to abutting areas of the vase, rendering its appearance glossy. As with the case of the shaded ellipse (Figure 3.21d), this boundary web is invisible and is seen only through the gradients of surface lightnesses that it traps within its compartments. In support of this explanation, Beck and Prazdny showed in 1981 (Beck and Prazdny, 1981) that changing the gradual luminance gradient of the highlight to a spatially abrupt one, or changing its relative orientation with respect to the rest of the vase, eliminate the glossy percept.

Lightness anchoring and Ross Bleckner's self-luminous paintings

Self-luminosity in paintings. Examples of self-luminous percepts can be found in paintings as well, notably in the work of the American painter Ross Bleckner. Bleckner has described his paintings as attempts to "eke out of a formal code a maximum amount of light" (Rankin, 1987). Bleckner does this, not by painting large surface areas with high reflectances or bright colors, but rather by creating compositions of small, star-like, circular regions that are perceived as self-luminous, as in Figure 3.34. At least three interacting properties of the paintings in Figure 3.34 contribute to their self-luminosity: high luminance areas relative to a dark background; a smooth luminance gradient that surrounds many of them; and their small size. The large luminance difference enhances the effects of brightness contrast. The luminance gradient can enhance self-luminosity using boundary webs, much as in percepts like the glare and double-brilliant percepts that are induced by Figure 3.33. Finally, the small size can also enhance self-luminosity via a neural mechanism that is explained in the aFILM model, and that is called the BHLAW rule.

FIGURE 3.34. Examples of Ross Bleckner's self-luminous paintings.

Blurred Highest Luminance As White and lightness anchoring. The letters BHLAW stand for *Blurred Highest Luminance As White,* which is a neural mechanism within the aFILM model that helps to determine when lightnesses in a picture or scene will appear self-luminous. This mechanism contributes to the larger issue that is called *lightness anchoring,* whereby brain networks determine what parts of a scene will appear to be white. There is a rich and often paradoxical experimental literature about how the brain does this, and along the way sometimes generates percepts of self-luminosity. Other famous effects for which Simon Hong and I offered mechanistic explanations include: the Gelb effect, whereby a black surface can look white when it is intensely illuminated; and the Area effect that is often demonstrated by placing a subject's head within a dome that is divided into two regions. When the higher luminance area in the dome occupies more than half of the visual field, it appears white, while the darker region looks gray. When the darker luminance area occupies more than half of the visual field, it tends to look increasingly white, while the lighter area appears to be self-luminous.

The American vision scientist Alan Gilchrist and his colleagues have been leaders in demonstrating such anchoring effects (Gilchrist et al., 1999). Great predecessors in the study of how anchoring may work include Helmholtz (Helmholtz, 1866) and Hans Wallach (Wallach, 1976), a great American vision scientist who died in 1998. Wallach proposed his famous *Highest Luminance As White* (HLAW) rule whereby the perceptual quality "white" is assigned to the highest luminance in a scene, and gray values of less luminous surface regions are assigned relative to the white standard. Although this rule works in many situations (Figure 3.35, top row), there are many other situations in which it leads to the wrong answer (Figure 3.35, bottom row). The BHLAW rule that Hong and I proposed overcomes many of these problems and enabled us to simulate the key data reported by Gilchrist and his colleagues (Figure 3.36). In particular, it explains how, when the highest luminance of a scene occupies a smaller area than the size of a receptive field that defines the "blurring" kernel that defines the rule (Figure 3.37, right panel), then it will appear self-luminous, other things being equal. When the highest luminance of a scene occupies a region as large as, or larger than, the blurring kernel, it will be renormalized to look white (Figure 3.37, left panel).

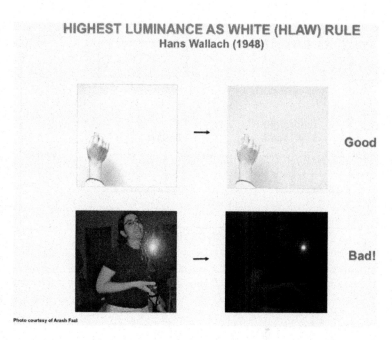

HIGHEST LUMINANCE AS WHITE (HLAW) RULE
Hans Wallach (1948)

Good

Bad!

Photo courtesy of Arash Fazl

FIGURE 3.35. The Highest Luminance As White rule of Hans Wallach works in some cases (top row) but not others (bottom row).

When the points of light surrounded by a boundary web are magnified, as in the center of Figure 3.34, they can still appear self-luminous, despite their larger size. Such examples illustrate the independence of the BHLAW rule and the self-luminosity effects that arise from boundary webs, since a boundary web with a steep gradient may still be present even when the figure is too large for the BHLAW rule to cause self-luminosity.

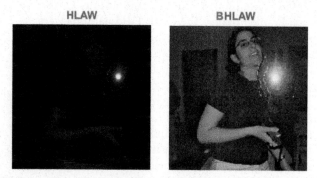

BLURRED HIGHEST LUMINANCE AS WHITE (BHLAW) RULE
Grossberg and Hong (2004, 2006)

HLAW   BHLAW

Spatial integration (blurring) adds spatial context to lightness perception

FIGURE 3.36. The Blurred Highest Luminance As White rule that I developed with my PhD student, Simon Hong, works in cases where the rule of Hans Wallach fails, as can be seen by comparing the simulation in Figure 3.35 with the one in this figure.

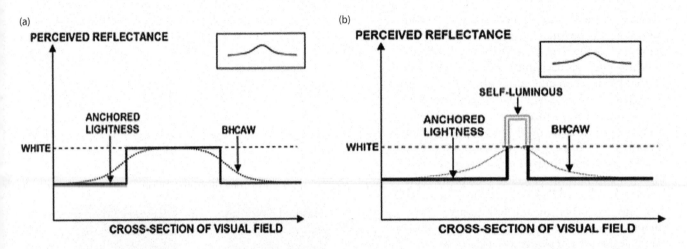

FIGURE 3.37. How the Blurred Highest Luminance As White rule sometimes normalizes the highest luminance to white (left panel) but at other times normalizes it to be self-luminous (right panel). See the text for details.

Boundary webs and color field paintings: Jules Olitski's paintings that "hang like a cloud"

Boundary webs do not necessarily lead to percepts with a definite 3D shape, as in Figure 3.29, or a self-luminous percept, as in Figures 3.33 and 3.34. They can support much more ambiguous painterly percepts. Indeed, nearly a century after the Impressionists formed their movement, the abstract painting movement called Color Field painting began to flourish in the United States. This term is generally used to describe the canonical Color Field painters, such as Mark Rothko and Barnett Newman. These painters were, in turn, part of the larger Abstract Expressionist movement and their successors, who painted in the 1960s and 1970s, such as Jules Olitski and Helen Frankenthaler. The Color Field painters were primarily concerned with exploring the pure emotional power of color. Thus, color—particularly contained within large, ambiguously structured surfaces—is a dominant element in these paintings. Jules Olitski created several such paintings when he lived and worked in New York City. By 1965, Olitski developed a technique in which he used spray bottles and guns to spray paint onto unprimed canvases and created some of his most famous paintings, which are known as the "spray paintings" (Figure 3.38).

Spraying paint onto a canvas in fine mists gave Olitski control over the color density on the canvas. In contrast to many of Monet's paintings, in which the viewer can discern a multitude of individual brushstrokes contained within a coarse boundary web (e.g., Figure 3.32),

it is impossible to visually perceive discrete colored units within the boundary webs in Olitski's spray paintings. Unlike the boundary webs for the shaded ellipse (Figure 3.21d), the boundary webs that spread over the surface of Olitski's spray paintings create a sense of ambiguous depth in the viewer, similar to staring into a space filled with colored fog, or into the sky during a sunset free of discrete clouds. Olitski intentionally created this effect, writing that: "When the conception of internal form is governed by edge, color . . . appears to remain on or above the surface. I think . . . of color as being seen in and throughout, not solely on, the surface" (Riggs, 1997). Occasional sharp

COLOR FIELD PAINTING
Jules Olitski, Spray paintings

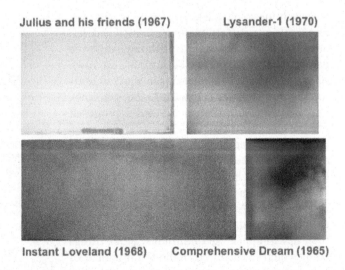

FIGURE 3.38. Four color-field spray paintings of Jules Olitski. The text explains why they generate surfaces percepts with such ambiguous depth.

spatial discontinuities along the bounding contours in some of these paintings awaken in the viewer an acknowledgment that drawing plays little or no role in creating the surface percept that is induced by most of the painting.

The vision models that I will describe in the next chapter and Chapter 11 clarify why the structure of Olitski's spray paintings create the sense that one is looking into a mist of color within a 3D space. These models highlight the importance of closed boundary contours to create percepts of surfaces that are restricted to specific depth planes (cf. Figure 3.22). Within the mists of color in Olitski's paintings, sharp, closed boundary contours are not perceptible. Instead, gradual chromatic and luminance spatial gradients coexist, thereby enabling multiple scales to form boundary webs, and to thereby capture smooth color transitions on multiple depth-selective surfaces whose gradients often coexist at similar positions. Unlike the example of the shaded ellipse, these gradients and their boundary webs do not vary in either orientation or scale in a systematic way across space, as is also needed to create the percept of glossiness in the vase in Figure 3.33 (left column, bottom row). Thus, we do not perceive the shaded surfaces of these paintings to be clearly contained within one depth plane. In this way, Olitski was able to achieve color that is "seen in and throughout".

Gene Davis's lines: From color assimilation to depth and surface-shroud resonances

The paintings of Gene Davis provide additional examples of how boundary groupings and surface filling-in can influence painterly percepts of depth and size. Although Gene Davis was a journalist, he began to paint seriously in Washington, D.C. in 1950. His paintings in Figure 3.39 are built up from vertical stripes. They do not contain size differences, shading, or recognizable objects. Despite this uniformity of each painting's compositional units, they nonetheless create percepts of variable depths and sizes in different parts of the painting. In response to the painting in Figure 3.39 (left column, top row), which is called *Black Popcorn*, the "brightest" stripes—namely, the four intermingled yellow and pale blue stripes located approximately one-third of the length of the canvas from the left—appear

to be in the nearest depth plane. In contrast, in the painting *Flamingo* (Figure 3.39, right column, top row), both individual stripes and stripe groupings can be perceived as nearer or further in depth, with brighter stripes appearing closer. How do these percepts arise?

For starters, color similarities and/or almost equal luminances between stripes can influence whether the viewer's eyes are drawn to individual stripes or groups of stripes. The achromatic versions of the two paintings more clearly show regions where color assimilation is facilitated. Note, for example, the much smaller differences in luminance of the stripes within *Black Popcorn* (Figure 3.39, left column, bottom row) than of *Flamingo* (Figure 3.39, right column, bottom row). The boundaries between stripes that have low luminance contrast are weak, thereby facilitating increased surface filling-in across several stripes. Such color assimilation calls to mind the watercolor illusion (Figure 3.28) and the paintings of Jo Baer (Figure 3.30). As a result of weak boundaries and color assimilation, spatial attention can cover a region that is larger than one stripe during viewing of *Black Popcorn*, thereby enabling viewers to perceive multiple stripes as one object. Such form-sensitive spatial attention is called an *attentional shroud*. An attentional shroud, in turn, is created by a dynamical state in the brain that I call a *surface-shroud resonance*. The multiple roles of attentional shrouds in conscious seeing (Table 1.4), recognition, and search will be explained in Chapter 6.

Assimilation between stripes can influence scene stratification and apparent depth within these paintings because it can group individual stripes into larger bands. In

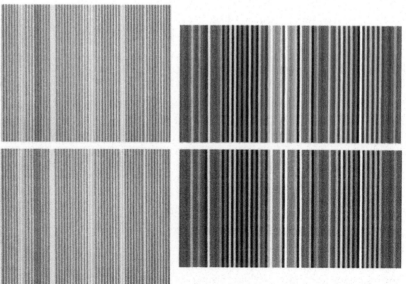

FIGURE 3.39. Two of Gene Davis's paintings in full color (top row) and in the monochromatic versions (bottom row). The text explains how they achieve their different percepts of grouping and relative depth.

Black Popcorn, bright and dim stripes tend to be grouped into larger stripes composed of four or more individual stripes. In *Flamingo*, individual bright stripes tend to be isolated between individual or groups of dimmer stripes, and the luminance and color of adjacent stripes vary more across space compared to those in *Black Popcorn*. I have already noted how multiple-scale boundary webs can support percepts of depth in response to the textured disk and shaded ellipse in Figures 3.21c and 3.21d. Size differences also play a role in depth perception in these paintings as well.

Larger objects often—but not always!—tend to appear closer to the viewer because they more strongly activate larger receptive fields, or spatial scales, in the visual system. How this works in enabling depth perception will be discussed in Chapters 4 and 11. In the paintings of Gene Davis, the grouping of bright stripes into larger units results in larger spatial scales being sensitive to them, which can cause them to appear closer to the viewer. This property helps to explain why the four stripe unit in the left part of *Black Popcorn* appears to be nearer than the individual bright white stripes in *Flamingo*, despite the fact that the latter stripes appear to be brighter than any individual stripe in *Black Popcorn*.

Flamingo contains brighter stripes and a wide range of luminance variation, but the lack of assimilation between the brightest stripes within the painting and their neighbors results in a less stable stratification of the stripes into different depth planes. Grouping into larger, bright stripe units helps one stably perceive them in a near depth plane. The grouping and depth effects when viewing paintings of Gene Davis are thus not just a simple example of the proximity-contrast covariance property that can make a brighter Kanizsa square look closer in Figure 3.3c, if only because, in these paintings, brightness and spatial scale do not always covary.

Perspective, T-junctions, end gaps, and the *Mona Lisa*

Artists since the Renaissance have exploited many other properties of how the brain sees for aesthetic purposes. I will summarize a few more of these properties to illustrate the wealth of possibilities that unifying concepts like the surface filling-in of multiple-scale boundary

webs can explain, before turning to an analysis of these neural mechanisms and how they generate conscious visual percepts.

Many Renaissance artists learned how to use *perspective* cues, as illustrated in Figure 3.40 (left column, top row). Perspective cues can generate a percept of depth in response to a 2D picture by activating cells with oriented receptive fields of different sizes to different degrees, in much the same way as a 3D scene does. A cell with an oriented receptive field is sensitive to a narrow range of favored orientations of image contrasts at its position. As in the percepts generated by the multiple-scale texture and the shaded ellipse of Figures 3.21c and 3.21d, and by the paintings of Gene Davis (Figure 3.39), receptive fields of different sizes can contribute to percepts of different depths.

Renaissance artists also understood how to use T-junctions, like the ones that occur where the vertical and horizontal edges intersect in Figure 3.40 (left column, bottom row), or in the Kanizsa square percepts in Figure 3.3, or in the zebra image in Figure 3.21b. They realized that putting T-junctions between a figure and its background in a picture can help to make the figure appear in front of the background, and thereby lead to a percept of figure-ground separation.

Chapter 4 will explain how the same boundary grouping process that helps us to see and recognize the Dalmatian in snow (Figure 1.2), and all the percepts generated by the images of Figure 3.21, is also sensitive

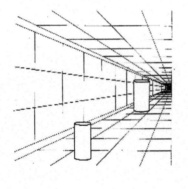
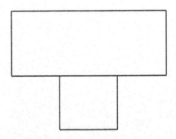

FIGURE 3.40. A combination of T-junctions and perspective cues can create a strong percept of depth in response to 2D images, with a famous example being Leonardo da Vinci's painting of the Mona Lisa.

to T-junctions, and can use them to trigger the initial steps of figure-ground separation that lead to depthful percepts. Consider, for example, the two T-junctions in Figure 3.40 (left column, bottom row). The horizontal boundary that forms at the top of each T can cause a small break in the vertical boundary that forms where the stem of the T touches the top. This hole in the boundary is called an *end gap*. How and why end gaps form, and how they contribute to figure-ground separation, will be explained in Chapter 4. For now, let me make the following observation to highlight the existence of end gaps: End gaps enable neon color to spread in response to the images in Figures 3.10 and 3.11 at positions near the ends of the blue or red lines, where they abut the black lines (Figure 3.41). The stronger black line boundaries inhibit the weaker color boundaries, thereby enabling colored feature contour activities to flow out of these boundaries, just as it does where boundaries are weakened during the watercolor illusion of Figure 3.28.

Perspective, T-junctions, and chiaroscuro are all employed in the *Mona Lisa* of Leonardo da Vinci (Figure 3.40, right column) that hangs in the Louvre Museum in Paris. Each of these processes affects the perceptual grouping process in its own way to create the 3D appearance of the *Mona Lisa* and to project her in front of the landscape background.

Frank Stella: Occlusions, amodal completions, kineticism, and spatial attention shifts

The luminance and color structure within a painting affects how it groups and stratifies the figures within it.

These processes, in turn, affect the formation of attentional shrouds that organize how spatial attention is allocated as we view them. The larger stripe groupings within *Black Popcorn* illustrate how a larger-scale attentional shroud can help to induce a percept of nearer depth. Paintings like the *Mona Lisa* illustrate how T-junctions can influence percepts of depth. Frank Stella's *Protractor* paintings exploit the perceptual consequences of both kinds of perceptual cues, among others.

These Stella paintings are abstract, brightly colored, and contain a number of interwoven and/or overlapping figures. The series is called the Protractor series because the paintings in this series are based on the semicircular form of a protractor. Figure 3.42 (top row) shows *Firuzabad* and Figure 4.42 (bottom row) shows *Khurasan Gate (Variation) I*. In describing Firuzabad and other similarly-structured paintings, Stella wrote: "I was looking for a really symmetrical base and the protractor image provided that for me. *Firuzabad* is a good example of looking for stability and trying to create as much instability as possible. 'Cause those things are like bicycle wheels spinning around'" (Frank Stella and the art of the protractor, *Anonymous*, 2000).

Stella also describes being inspired by decorative art in Iran in which patterns "doubled back on themselves" ("Collection: MOCA's first thirty years", 2010). Others have described these paintings as having an "engaging kineticism" ("Collection: MOCA's first thirty years", 2010) because the paintings contain interwoven patterns that create a sense of movement in the viewer.

The brain processes that lead to these percepts will be explained more completely below, but here I can immediately make the following qualitative observations. In

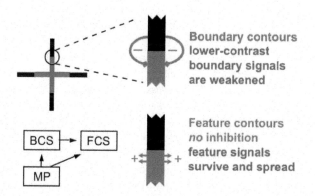

FIGURE 3.41. End gaps, or small breaks or weakenings of boundaries, can form where a stronger boundary abuts a weaker, like-oriented, boundary, as occurs where black boundaries touch red boundaries in the neon color spreading image of Figure 3.11.

FIGURE 3.42. Two paintings of Frank Stella. See the text for details.

Firuzabad, the circular form of the outer protractor shapes mirrors the shapes of the interlocking rings within the painting. The T-junctions where the surfaces of differently-colored segments meet, signal which segments weave in front of other segments. As in many other percepts, end gaps support boundary completion of the nearer figure and a discontinuity in the boundary of the figure that is "behind" the nearer figure. Only the non-occluded part of each figure is consciously seen, but whole protractor figures may nonetheless be amodally recognized, much as in response to the partially occluded shapes in Figures 1.3 and 1.4.

The center region of *Firuzabad* contains a number of interwoven segments, some of which are recognized as whole protractors due to amodal completion, and others as smaller segments that are nested in the overall circular shape of the canvas and/or within other protractors. Importantly, no one segment in this center portion of *Firuzabad* is "on top" of all the others; each segment weaves under and over other segments.

Similarly, in *Khurasan Gate (Variation) I*, no one segment, or protractor, in the entire painting lies completely on top of all the others, even though each distinctly colored protractor segment has exposed visible regions that are sufficient to allow the viewer to understand the whole shape of the protractor. As a result, these structures are perceived as overlapping segments in different, but similar, depth planes. Importantly, amodal boundary completion and surface filling-in of distinct segment colors help us divide the painting into separate, interlocking protractor forms that are tightly linked in a larger structure. In particular, amodal boundary completion allows perceptual completion of protractor boundaries that lay behind other forms. At the same time, consistent segment colors that surround amodally-completed protractor surfaces allow disconnected segments to emerge as unified protractor surfaces. These boundary and surface completion processes enable an attentional shroud to spread across a whole protractor form, whether or not the entire form is consciously visible. Once an attentional shroud can form on a given protractor, a surface-shroud resonance regulates eye movement sequences to different regions of this particular protractor, and guides these movements in and out of different depth planes, because no one protractor lies on top of all the others. How a surface-shroud resonance directs eye movements to search a surface will be explained in Chapter 6.

An attentional shroud that adheres to one protractor surface inevitably collapses. Collapse can be due either to *inhibition of return* or to *activity-dependent habituation* of the surface-shroud resonance itself. Said in another way, we have a tendency not to perseverate at looking at the same position in space over and over again (inhibition of return) and we tend to get bored looking at the same object for too long (activity-dependent habituation). When a shroud collapses, spatial attention is *disengaged* from that object surface, thereby freeing it to become *engaged* by a new surface of interest, as many cognitive neuroscientists have noted since Michael Posner discussed this property in 1980 (Posner, 1980).

Because multiple boundary groupings are possible within the Stella paintings due to the clever nesting of protractor figures between each another, and within the shape of the canvas as a whole, attentional shrouds can span individual segments or multiple segments at a time. For example, in *Firuzabad*, one can perceive two full circles, multiple nested protractor structures, and each individual segment within the painting. The multiple groupings and segmentations within these paintings, along with the attendant formation and collapse of their surface-shroud resonances as the eyes explore the painting, contributes to their perceived dynamism. The attentional shifts and eye movements through different depth planes and across different segmentations of these static interleaved patterns create the sense of visual movement that are a hallmark of Stella's paintings.

Back to Monet: Gist, multiple-scale attentional shrouds, and scene recognition

As discussed in the context of the paintings of Gene Davis and Frank Stella, artists can direct viewers' attention across a painting through the composition and grouping of its features. Many artists do this with a conceptual or aesthetic goal in mind. In the case of Impressionist painters like Monet (Figure 3.32) and Seurat (Figure 3.23), viewers can perceive individual visible brushstrokes as well as the emergent forms that these brushstrokes induce through boundary cooperation and competition among them. In addition, Monet's painting technique supported his desire to preserve a fresh "first glance" at a painting, and how he achieved this illustrates an important general theme about how we understand all scenes.

Monet's painting process started with distributed patches of local contrast and slowly added to these patches until long-range cooperation between his brushstrokes could more easily and unambiguously occur. In 1927, a year after Monet died, Lilla Cabot Perry described a canvas that Monet had painted only once (Perry, 1927): "It was covered with strokes about an inch apart and a quarter of an inch thick, out to the very edge of the canvas". She also described a canvas that was painted twice: "The strokes were nearer together and the subject began to emerge more clearly". Monet directly painted the visible colors in a scene as he viewed it, rather than constructing a scene by drawing its boundaries and then filling them in. Support for this idea lies within Monet's advice: "When you go out to paint, try to forget what objects you have before you, a tree, a house, a field, or whatever. Merely think, here is a little square of blue, here an oblong of pink . . . paint it just as it looks to you, the exact color and shape, until it gives your own naïve impression of the scene before you". This approach to painting was vigorously pursued by many subsequent painters, notably *plein air* painters such as other Impressionists, Charles Hawthorne, and Henry Hensche (Figure 3.31).

Monet's painting process reflects how humans may initially, and very rapidly, perceive coarse global information about a scene. This process is often called "getting the gist" of the scene. *Gist* can include being able to recognize what kind of scene it is, whether of a city street, a mountain range, or a body of water. After gist is computed, spatial attention and the eye movements that it controls can zoom into finer details of the scene. Chapter 14 explains how gist may be rapidly computed as a large-scale, or spatially coarse, texture category. Then shifts of spatial attention may form finer attentional shrouds to enable finer scenic textures to be classified. When the gist category and a few finer texture categories vote on the best interpretation of a scene, very high classification accuracy can be achieved.

The principle that scene gist is the first available information in a scene is mirrored by Monet's aesthetic goal to preserve the first glance, or first impression, of a scene and allow it to determine the course of the painting. As Perry wrote in 1927 (Perry, 1927): "[Monet] held that the first real look at the *motif* was likely to be the truest and most unprejudiced one, and said that the first painting should cover as much of the canvas as possible, no matter how roughly, so as to determine at the outset the tonality of the whole".

Monet instinctively carried out the kind of global-to-local process of painting a natural scene that humans use to understand scenes, gradually building detail with more and more brushstrokes, but never explicitly drawing fine scenic structures. For example, in the paintings of the Rouen cathedral shown in Figures 3.43 and 3.44, the viewer can infer that there are sculptural elements on the facade of the cathedral, but the fine structure of these elements is not explicitly present in the paintings. Monet recognized that the coarse, global information in a scene is what one sees during the "first real look" and preserved the freshness of this first look at a scene by eliminating distracting details. Monet hereby enabled the larger-scale attentional shrouds to dominate viewers' perception and understanding of the scenes that are depicted in his paintings.

Impressionist painting relies on the ability of the visual system to form amodal boundaries and emergent segmentations from the statistics of visual stimuli. In some of his mature work, Monet uses nearby colors that are nearly equiluminant, and sharp, high-contrast, luminance-defined edges are sparse. He hereby creates weaker boundary signals within and between the parts of many forms, and stronger boundary signals between forms. This combination facilitates color spreading within forms and better separation of brightness and color differences between forms. Figure 3.43 (top row) shows four paintings from Monet's Rouen Cathedral series and their grayscale counterparts (Figure 3.43, bottom row). This famous series, created in the 1890s, includes over 30 paintings of similar views of the Rouen Cathedral at different times of day. The grayscale versions of these paintings demonstrate the near equiluminance of the brushstrokes within forms, and places in which brightness and color differences significantly influence the groupings that differentiate between forms, including the differentiation between the cathedral and the sky.

Monet took advantage of the statistical uncertainty that our visual system overcomes to create work in which both color and luminance play a role in creating form, rather than luminance alone, as in the first and fourth images from left to right. It is instructive to compare and contrast these paintings with those of Gene Davis (Figure 3.39), even though their subject matter is totally different. Taking the color out of Monet's paintings removes some of the critical closed boundaries that allow us to segregate forms within it. The boundary system pools color and brightness signals, as also occurs to create boundaries in response to the gray disks on the black-and-white checkerboard in Figure 3.2, and the reverse-contrast Kanizsa square in Figure 3.3b. As a result, boundaries can form that may be due almost entirely to a color difference, without a corresponding achromatic brightness difference, as in the fourth image to the right in the upper row of Figure 3.43.

Figures 3.44-3.46 further discuss two paintings from Monet's Rouen cathedral series that illustrate how different lighting of the same object can lead to dramatically different percepts. The painting in Figure 3.44 captures the lighting on the cathedral facade while the sun is setting, whereas the painting in Figures 3.45 and 3.46 does so in full sunlight. The painting in full sunlight generates a more depthful percept than does the one at sunset. This is due to multiple factors interacting together. One factor is that the colors in the painting at sunset are more equiluminant, and the ensuing boundary webs coarser and more uniform. The strong gradients of light that are evident in the painting in full sunlight, including effects of sharp architectural features and shadows, are not seen at sunset. The greater range of contrasts in the right painting also enable many more nearly horizontal boundaries to be clearly seen as occluded by vertical boundaries. Such T-junction boundary occlusions

FIGURE 3.43. Four paintings by Monet of the Rouen cathedral under different lighting conditions (top row) and their monochromatic versions (bottom row). See the text for details.

ROUEN CATHEDRAL
Monet, 1892-1894
At sunset

Lighting almost equiluminant across most of the painting

Most boundaries are thus caused by color differences, not luminance differences

Fine architectural details are obscured, leading to...

Coarser and more uniform boundary webs, so...

Less depth in the painting

FIGURE 3.44. The Rouen cathedral at sunset generates very different boundary webs than it does in full sunlight, as illustrated by Figure 3.45.

ROUEN CATHEDRAL
Monet, 1892-1894
Full sunlight

Lighting is strongly non-uniform across most of the painting

Strong boundaries due to both luminance and color differences

Fine architectural details are much clearer, leading to...

Finer and more non-uniform boundary webs, so...

Much more detail and depth

FIGURE 3.45. The Rouen cathedral in full sunlight.

ROUEN CATHEDRAL
Monet, 1892-1894
Full sunlight

There are also more T-junctions where vertical boundaries occlude horizontal boundaries, or conversely...

Leading to even more depth

FIGURE 3.46. The Rouen cathedral in full sunlight contains T-junctions that are not salient in the painting of it at simset. These are among the painting's features that give it a much more depthful appearance.

(Figure 3.46) can generate percepts of depth in the absence of any other visual cues.

The next chapter begins to explain in greater detail how the rich variety of perceptual properties of boundary grouping and surface filling-in processes are generated in our brains, whether during the most mundane activities of our daily lives, or during our appreciation of great visual art.

How a Brain Sees: Neural Mechanisms

From boundary completion and surface filling-in to figure-ground perception

Boundaries are barriers to surface filling-in

In the 1960s, a number of psychologists, notably John Krauskopf in the United States (Krauskopf, 1963) and A. L. Yarbus in the Soviet Union (Yarbus, 1967), studied filling-in in the laboratory by exploiting the fact that stabilized images fade, just as the blind spot and retinal veins fade because they are stabilized on a jiggling retina (Figure 3.6). Figure 4.1 (left panel) illustrates a variant of one of the images that Yarbus used. This figure contains two red disks, with each disk surrounded by a white or a black rectangle. The two rectangles, in turn, are surrounded by a red background. Imagine that the rectangular boundaries are stabilized with respect to the jiggle of the eyes, as illustrated by the rectangular outline at the bottom of the figure. There are at least two ways to do this. Only the heroic way was available in the 1960s, and Yarbus used it. He attached a suction cup to the eyeball with part of the scene painted on its otherwise transparent viewing glass. In this way, the regions near the selected boundaries were stabilized with respect to the retina. The rest of the scene was visible on a display through the glass, and thus moved with respect to the retina as the eye jiggled in its orbit. A more modern, and less daunting, way to achieve the same effect is to monitor the jiggle of the eye with a sensor, and to use the signal from the sensor to jiggle part of a computer-generated image along with the eye, thereby stabilizing it on the retina.

Using either method, the net effect is that the stabilized boundaries fade. When they do, a remarkable thing happens. The red color outside the stabilized rectangular boundaries spreads over the black and white areas. The red color cannot, however, cross the circular boundaries that surround the small red disks, because these boundaries, not being stabilized, are still strong. The net effect of this filling-in process is to create a percept wherein the left disk looks light red, the right disk looks dark red, and the entire background, including where the black and white hemifields were previously visible, looks like a uniform but intermediate shade of red, as in Figure 4.1 (right panel).

Conscious MIND Resonant BRAIN. Stephen Grossberg, Oxford University Press. © Oxford University Press 2021.
DOI: 10.1093/oso/9780190070557.003.0004

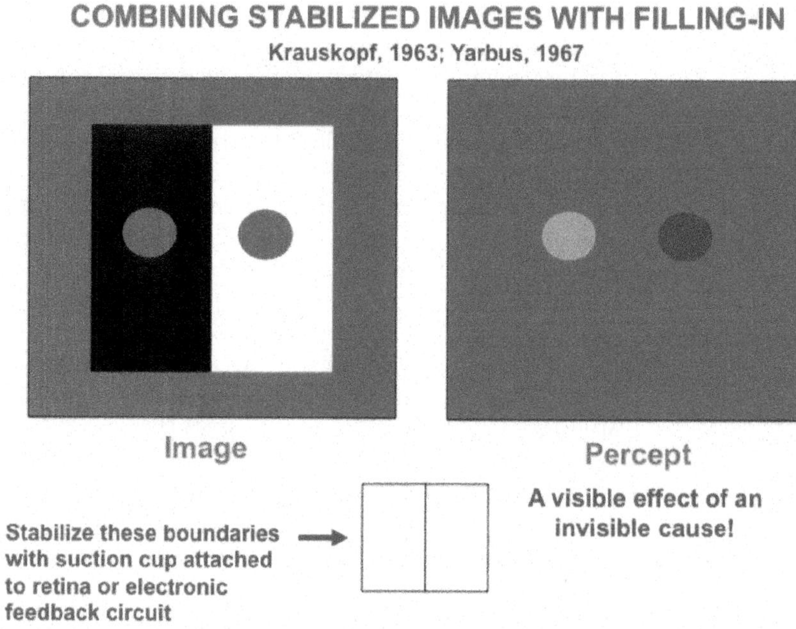

COMBINING STABILIZED IMAGES WITH FILLING-IN
Krauskopf, 1963; Yarbus, 1967

Image

Percept

Stabilize these boundaries with suction cup attached to retina or electronic feedback circuit

A visible effect of an invisible cause!

FIGURE 4.1. A classical example of how boundaries are barriers to filling-in.

Visible effect of an invisible cause: Boundaries are also filling-in generators

This example of filling-in illustrates several key points. For one, it shows in a striking way that boundaries contain the flow of filled-in brightness or color. Boundaries are *barriers* to filling-in, just as in the percepts of neon color spreading in Figures 3.10 and 3.11. Where there is no boundary, filling-in can spread across space without impediment until it is attenuated by spreading too far. Note also the remarkable fact that the perceived red disks are darker (on the right) or lighter (on the left) than the red background, even though they are physically identical in the image. The darker red disk lies on a white background in the original image, whereas the lighter red disk lies on a black background. This difference in backgrounds is what causes the *brightness contrast* to occur that makes the disks look different. The contrast effect persists in the percept even though the white and black regions in the image are covered by filled-in red. The percept that is summarized by Figure 4.1 (right panel) thus suggests that the computation of brightness and color contrast occurs at a processing stage prior to the stage where filling-in occurs, just as the stage of boundary formation occurs prior to the stage where object recognition occurs. This percept is an interesting example of "a visible effect of an invisible cause"; that is, we can see the *effect* of the background white and black, but not the background white and black themselves, in the final conscious percept.

You can try to implement another striking example of filling-in on your home computer. Color two halves of your computer screen red and green, respectively. Suppose that the red and green regions meet in a vertical edge in the middle of the screen. Try to adjust the luminant energy of the colors until they are balanced, or equiluminant. We already discussed how boundaries are weakened by using almost equiluminant red and green in our discussion of Monet's painting *Poppies Near Argenteuil* in Figure 3.32. When this is done just right, the boundary between the red and green regions can become so weak that it can no longer contain the colors. At the moment that this happens, the red and green colors can suddenly flow over one another so that red and green simultaneously cover the entire screen. These superimposed colors generate the percept of a mixed color, typically yellow, that is seen uniformly over the entire surface.

Figure 4.1 illustrates another basic property of how boundaries and surfaces interact. The percept clearly illustrates that boundaries are *barriers* to filling-in. Boundaries are also *generators* of filling-in. In other words, when the rectangular boundaries fade, they can no longer support the filling-in of the white and black feature contours with which they are aligned (cf. Figure 3.22). The circular boundaries continue to be able to generate filling-in of color, whether it is of the red feature contours inside them, or the black or white feature contours outside them. Likewise, the boundary of the computer screen can support the red and green colors that flow over one another after the vertical boundary between them becomes too weak to contain them.

Another striking example of how boundaries generate filling-in is the phenomenon of *binocular rivalry*. During rivalry, different images are presented to the two eyes. The boundaries that are induced by these images compete for dominance. Only the winning boundaries can support a conscious percept of visible surface brightnesses or colors. Even though the visual input of the suppressed eye continues to be processed, it cannot reach consciousness because the boundaries that would be needed to support filling-in of its brightnesses and colors are suppressed. The feature contours of the dominant eye that are aligned with the winning boundaries can, however, fill in the conscious surface percept of what the dominant eye sees. Chapter 11 will discuss the mechanisms that cause binocular rivalry in greater detail. It should be immediately realized, however, that all of these examples provide further evidence for the claims that "all boundaries are invisible" and "consciously visible qualia are surface percepts," properties that follow naturally from the fundamental fact that boundaries and surfaces are computationally complementary (Figure 3.7).

Craik-O'Brien-Cornsweet Effect: Now you see it, now you don't

The Craik-O'Brien-Cornsweet Effect, or COCE, provides another classical example of how powerful the effects of filling-in are. You can see this illusion by looking at Figure 4.2 (left column). The figure appears to have a uniformly dark gray rectangle to the left of a uniformly light gray rectangle, with both rectangles surrounded by a black border. The uniform gray in the two rectangles is a visual illusion that is due to filling-in.

This can be vividly seen by removing the black border and replacing it with a uniform gray border, thereby creating Figure 4.2 (right column). Look at the part of the image inside where the black border used to be. You can now see luminance cusps; namely, there is a cusp of increased luminant energy, or luminance, to the right of the vertical edge that divides the figure in the middle, and a cusp of decreased luminance to the left of the edge. Apart from these cusps, most of the figure has the same luminance, including positions that looked either dark gray or light gray inside the black border. These cusps are not clearly visible in Figure 4.2 (left column), even though the cusps are identical to the cusp in Figure 4.2 (right column). Why not?

The COCE figure is designed so that the boundaries are created by it in our brains at the vertical edge that separates the two cusps, and at the edges of the black region that bounds the central figure. As a result, the extra luminance from the right cusp can fill-in the entire right-hand rectangle, while the lower luminance from the left cusp fills-in the entire left-hand rectangle, giving rise to a percept of two uniformly gray rectangles. The two levels of luminance cannot mix because they are contained by the closed boundaries induced by the black background, together with the vertical boundary between the two luminance cusps.

When the cusp is no longer surrounded by a black background, there are no boundaries around the cusp that can contain the filling-in process within the rectangles. Instead, the larger and smaller luminance levels can flow around the cusps in both directions, and can thereby equalize in the background, just as in the case of the offset grating in Figure 1.1. This version of the COCE was developed by the Serbian perceptual psychologist, Dejan Todorovic (Todorovic, 1987), with whom I had the pleasure of working as my postdoctoral fellow at Boston University in the 1980s.

It remains to ask: Why are the cusps themselves visible in Figure 4.2 (right column), if there are no other boundaries than the vertical boundary between the cusps to prevent filling-in? Actually, boundary webs are caused by the luminance gradients that form the cusps, and these boundaries can capture some of the gray gradients that create them, just as they can in the glare percept of Figure 3.33, and in the percept of a shaded ellipse in Figure 3.21d. The shading of the cusps is, however, overwhelmed by the spread of the remaining gray from the cusp regions throughout the rectangular regions formed by the COCE stimulus.

Brightness perception

Figures 4.1 and 4.2 illustrate how different the luminance levels in an image can be from the conscious percepts of brightness and color that they induce. In the luminance profile of the COCE image in Figure 4.2, for example, the background levels of luminance in both rectangles of the image are the same. However, their perceived levels of brightness are different. Is there an adaptive reason why the brain produces such dramatic perceptual distortions of the signals that are received by the retina? Is there an explanation of why these distortions usually seem to cause no more trouble in our lives than some amusing illusions?

Discounting the illuminant

We can find an explanation of why this happens by considering how a brain *discounts the illuminant*. An analysis of how we discount the illuminant also provides another reason why boundaries are barriers to filling-in. Discounting the illuminant is the process whereby we compensate for the effects of ever-changing illumination on our percepts of object brightness, color, and form. As I

FIGURE 4.2. The vertical cusp of lesser and greater luminance is the same in both images, but the one on the left prevents brightness from flowing around it by creating closed boundaries that tightly surround the cusp.

noted in Chapter 2, the critical role in visual perception of discounting the illuminant has been known at least since the time of Helmholtz. Helmholtz realized that the average color of a scene tends to become desaturated; that is, it tends to look more white than it really is. Thus, if the scene is illuminated with a certain hue—say reddish at sunset or bluish if you are under water—then that color tends to be neutralized so that we can better see the "real" colors of objects in the scene. Seeing correct color relations despite illuminant variations is often important for survival. For example, the color of food often provides important cues about its identity, palatability, and freshness. Just think about how differently you feel about eating yellow or green bananas, or red or gray meat, or distinguishing a large orange from a small grapefruit based on their orange or yellow colors.

The process of discounting the illuminant illustrates in a vivid way the difference between a physicist's and a biologist's accounts of color perception. As I noted in Chapter 2, Newton showed that white light is composed of equal amounts of all the visible wavelengths of light. The Newtonian definition of white light is based on measuring the intensity of light of different wavelengths at individual positions in space. Helmholtz realized, however, that our conscious *perception* of colors, including white, depends upon the relationships between multiple sources of light across many positions of a scene or picture. Painters have also known this for hundreds of years, and great colorists like Matisse, Monet, and van Gogh intuitively exploited these relationships to achieve striking aesthetic effects in their paintings.

For a long time, however, it was not clear to scientists how to replace this intuition about how we see colors by a quantitative theory of the kind that Newton and other physicists could appreciate. As I mentioned in Chapter 2, Helmholtz's realization that complex brain interactions across a whole scene determine even such apparently simple percepts as the color at a single position gradually led him to do less psychology and more physics as he got older.

How different are the Newtonian and Helmholtzian views of color? We will see in the next section how the process of discounting the illuminate *suppresses* many color signals in order to selectively process the "real" colors of objects. In fact, left to its own devices, the discounting process would make it very hard for us to see continuous object surfaces at all. We would, instead, tend to perceive a world that looked like a series of colored cartoons, with colored outlines but no continuous surfaces between these outlines. These colored outlines are the *feature contours* that have been discussed intermittently in preceding chapters; e.g., Figure 3.22. The brain compensates for this loss of surface information by using the surviving feature contour color signals to fill in missing surface information at a later processing stage, as we saw vividly in percepts of neon

color spreading (Figures 3.10 and 3.11) and the Craik-O'Brien-Cornsweet Effect, or COCE (Figure 4.2). The perceived colors in these filled-in surfaces have the advantage that they are not unduly contaminated by fluctuations in the illuminant. This surface reconstruction process is a good example of how the brain achieves "hierarchical resolution of uncertainty" because, through it, the surface information that is lost through discounting the illuminant is restored at a later processing stage by surface filling-in.

Filling-in cannot allow an object's brightness and color signals to spread beyond the object's borders. Boundaries prevent this spread by being barriers to filling-in. Boundaries hereby control the filled-in recovery of surface color after the illuminant has been discounted. That is why the boundaries around the red disks in the Yarbus display of Figure 4.1 can prevent the red that spreads over the black and white backgrounds from also spreading into the red disks. That is also why the Craik-O'Brien-Cornsweet Effect occurs in response to the image in Figure 4.2 (left column), but not the one in Figure 4.2 (right column). This argument predicts that a boundary process evolves in each species no later than the evolutionary period when the brain can compensate for variable illumination to create surface percepts from illuminant-discounted feature contours.

Many surface percepts that are derived from filling-in are visual illusions, in the sense that they are not explicitly represented within the visual signals that activate our retinas but, rather, are actively constructed by our brains. This observation was already made during the discussion of the blind spot (Figure 3.4), leading to the conclusion that "every line percept is an illusion" (Figure 3.6). We also think that most of the surfaces that we perceive every day are "real" partly because they look so familiar, despite the fact that the signals that reach our retinas from the world are contaminated by illuminants. These surfaces can become so familiar because, by discounting the illuminant, the brain eliminates the variability of illumination at an early stage in the internal representations of object form. These discounted surface representations are then stable enough, over many encounters with them under variable illumination conditions, to enable us to learn to recognize them until they become familiar. In brief, familiar surface "illusions" underlie our ability to learn to recognize "real" objects.

Brightness constancy

Edwin Land, the founder of the Polaroid Corporation, is famous as a prolific inventor in the field of instant photography. He was also an avid investigator of how the brain sees color. Land and his colleagues developed a number of experiments that provide useful information about how discounting the illuminant and filling-in work. They also developed a model of these processes, called the Retinex model, which the theory that I will describe substantially extends (Land, 1977, 1983).

Land got a lot of mileage out of images that are called McCann Mondrians in honor of his collaborator John McCann and the Dutch painter Piet Mondrian, some of whose paintings resemble these images. Figure 4.3 illustrates a typical McCann Mondrian (Land and McCann, 1971). It is a patchwork quilt of overlapping regions with different colors. The number of regions and the number of different colors that abut each region are carefully selected.

In order to understand the significance of Land's results, we first need to know a little about how a colored surface reflects colored light. A basic concept concerns the *reflectances* of a surface. These numbers describe the *fraction* of light of a given wavelength that is reflected from each position on a surface. Let us ignore for the moment all the subtleties of how different positions interact to determine perceived colors. Then we can say, in first approximation, that a surface patch of a prescribed wavelength tends to have the color associated with that wavelength when we look at it in white light. For example, an object with the same reflectance across its entire surface might look green if it reflects a lot of white light at wavelength 500 nm and red if it reflects a lot of white light at wavelength 640 nm.

Due to discounting of the illuminant, the colors of a surface like a McCann Mondrian look about the same if you view them using light sources of very different colors and intensities. This is a remarkable finding because, as the intensity of incident light increases, the amount of light that is reflected from each position increases proportionally. If the incident light is colored, then the total amount

of reflected light having the wavelength of the illuminating color increases with the intensity of the illuminant. For example, as one increases the intensity of an illuminating red light, the amount of reflected red light increases from every location. When this happens, why does not the scene look increasingly red? How does the brain discount the "extra" red light due to the illuminant and figure out the real colors of the scene, as Helmholtz already realized must occur?

To better understand how the brain does this, let us start off by considering a simpler example than the McCann Mondrian. Figure 2.17 shows a central gray disk that is surrounded by a darker gray annulus. White light uniformly illuminates both the disk and the annulus. The intensity of this light is varied between wide limits. On the right hand side of Figure 2.17 is a series of gray disks of varying shade; that is, of different reflectance. These disks are illuminated by a separate source of illumination whose intensity is held constant through time. The observer's task is to choose the reference disk on the right whose perceived brightness best matches the perceived brightness of the test disk on the left, as the intensity of illumination of the test disk and annulus are varied.

Remarkably, as the intensity of incident light is increased by a factor of one hundred or more, the observer continues to choose the same reference disk, even when the test disk reflects very different intensities of light. This property is called *brightness constancy*. It is called a "constancy" because, although the actual signals hitting our eyes are increasing in intensity, the test patch continues to look equally bright. Brightness constancy is an analog in the brightness domain of the *color constancy* that is perceived using a McCann Mondrian that is composed of different colored patches, when it is illuminated by lights of different colors. How are either of these constancy properties achieved?

How this happens can be better understood by letting the test light intensity increase only where it hits the central gray circular test disk. Light intensity is held constant over the annulus in this variation of the experiment. Then, as the incident light intensity increases, the test patch looks increasingly bright and is matched by the subject against increasingly reflectant reference disks.

How do these two experimental conditions differ? In the first condition, the *relative* amounts of light that are reflected by the test disk and the annulus are constant, even though the *absolute* amounts of light that are reflected increase with the intensity of the illuminant. In the second condition, both the relative and the absolute amounts of light that are reflected by the test disk increase with the intensity of the illuminant.

This comparison suggests that the brain computes the *relative* amounts of light that are reflected by different locations of an image and thereby discounts the total illumination level. In particular, the brain estimates

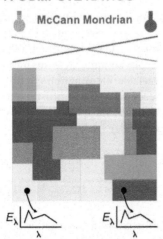

FIGURE 4.3. A McCann Mondrian is an excellent display with which to illustrate how our brains discount the illuminant to compute the "real" colors of objects. See the text for details.

the reflectances of individual patches by comparing the amounts of light that are reflected by different, but abutting, patches. As the total illumination increases, this ratio remains the same because it estimates the constant relative reflectance of the two patches. This example illustrates in a simple setting what Helmholtz already realized about discounting the illuminant; namely, that it involves comparisons across many locations of a scene.

When competition is good: Making analog computation possible

How does the brain do this? How can such a clever strategy have evolved through blind evolution? How did nerve cells, which are individually totally unaware of the physics of light and of the very existence of reflectances, ever manage to participate in such a clever scheme? Brain cells manage to do this by *competing* with each other. Moreover, their competition to discount the illuminant is just one of innumerable examples wherein a similar type of competition occurs in biology, even in non-neural tissues.

Why is the world so competitive? One reason is that we live in an *analog* world—a world whose signals can take on a continuum of values, ranging from very small to very large, just like the amount of light that illuminates a room. The photodetectors of the retina, for example, can experience differences in photon intensity that can vary by a factor of a million when we go from a lit room into a dark room. But whereas nerve cells may be activated by such widely varying input sizes, their activities and output signals can vary only over a very small range. That is why we need oscilloscopes and other sensitive electronic instruments to detect neural signals. The total input size to a cell deep in the brain can also vary greatly even if the individual inputs to the cell do not. This can happen when many different cells have connections to a single cell, what we call a *many-to-one* interaction. If a few of these cells are on, then the total input can be small, but when a large number of them are on, then the total input can be much larger. How do brain cells, which individually can vary so little in their activities, manage to sensitively register and respond to inputs that vary so greatly?

This problem is the *noise-saturation dilemma* that I mentioned in Chapter 1 (Figure 1.5) and Chapter 2 (Figures 2.15 and 2.16). The brain's solution to this dilemma enables cells to process *distributed patterns* of inputs across a network of cells, without suffering noise or saturation, as the inputs get too small or too large, respectively. The pattern of inputs in Figure 2.17 is the light intensities across all the positions in the central disk and its surrounding annulus. Maintaining sensitivity to the relative sizes of these inputs,

as the total light intensity increases, enables the true reflectances of the image to be computed, leading to brightness constancy.

Hierarchical resolution: Discounting the illuminant, feature contours, and surface filling-in

Competition across cells is one general method for achieving this goal, as illustrated by the network of excitatory (green) and inhibitory (red) interactions in the lower right corner of Figure 2.22. As this figure reminds us, an appropriately designed competitive network quite naturally computes the *relative* strength $\theta_i = \dfrac{I_i}{\sum_{k=1}^{n} I_k}$ of input signals I_i to the ith cell in the network. These relative strengths are registered in the cells' activities across the network. In the case of networks that discount the illuminant, these ratios estimate the reflectances of object surfaces, so that cell activities estimate the reflectances of objects, independently of the illuminant that is used to observe them. In other neural circuits, they provide a measure of which inputs, and the features that these inputs represent, are the most intense, and thus potentially the most important for making decisions of one kind or another. All of these processes work because they are "computing with patterns" that solve the noise-saturation dilemma (Figure 2.22).

To better understand how competition helps, let us think some more about McCann Mondrians (Figure 4.3). How does the brain know whether it is computing a ratio between positions on different color patches or on the same patch? This distinction must be made to avoid confusing the illuminant with an object's reflectance. To see why, suppose that a Mondrian is illuminated by a gradient of light where the light is more intense at one side of the picture and becomes gradually less intense as the picture is traversed to its other side. This will tend to happen whenever a single light source illuminates a large object from one side. Figure 4.3 illustrates this situation with blue and red lights at the two opposite ends of the McCann Mondrian, and gradients of decreasing light intensity as the figure is traversed. If all the brain did was to compute ratios between *arbitrary* pairs of image positions, say within a single patch, then it would compute the relative *illuminant* intensities, not the relative *reflectances*, which is just the opposite result from the one that is needed. To show you why this is true, let me use some simple mathematical notation to say what I mean precisely. The main points can be understood by using just a little multiplication and division. You can skip them if you want without missing the main conclusions.

Suppose that the reflectance R within a patch is constant, but the illuminant changes as the patch is traversed. Suppose that the illuminant intensity is I at one position and J at another. Then the total amount of light reflected by this reflectance at the two positions is the product of reflectance and light intensity; namely, RI and RJ, respectively. The ratio of these numbers is I divided by J, because the common reflectance factor R cancels out. This result is, unfortunately, the opposite of the one that we want. We want to discount (or cancel) the illuminant, not the reflectances!

What has gone wrong? How can the brain detect reflectance changes *across* patches, uncontaminated by illumination differences, but still compute zero change *within* patches where the reflectance is constant, even if the illumination level changes across positions within the patch? In a McCann Mondrian, when a boundary between patches is crossed, the reflectances change suddenly. The total amount of reflected light changes suddenly too if the gradient of illuminant intensity across the patch boundary changes more slowly with position than the reflectances. This state of affairs is illustrated in Figure 4.4, which shows a cross section of two patches with different reflectances that are illuminated by a gradient of light. Suppose that the light intensity at a patch boundary is I. Just to the left of the boundary, the light intensity is a little bigger, say $I + \varepsilon$, where ε is a small positive number. Just to the right of the boundary, it is a little smaller, say $I - \varepsilon$. The reflectances jump from, say, A, in the region just to the left of the boundary, to B in the region across the boundary. The total reflected light therefore jumps from $A(I + \varepsilon)$ to $B(I - \varepsilon)$ when crossing the patch boundary. Near the boundary, the number ε is much smaller than I, so the ratio of $I + \varepsilon$ to

$I - \varepsilon$ approximately equals one. Thus the ratio of $A(I + \varepsilon)$ to $B(I - \varepsilon)$ thus approximately equals the ratio of A to B. This latter ratio is independent of I, so the illuminant has been discounted. What remains is a measure of the relative reflectances of the two contiguous patches, as desired.

The above example shows that if the brain restricts its comparisons to nearby positions where the total reflected light changes suddenly—like at the boundaries of two color patches—then it can discount the illuminant there. Comparisons between nearby positions within a patch need to be suppressed, or else the brain could compute illumination differences within each patch, as noted above. How can ratios be computed *across* a patch boundary while gradual changes in the illumination level across nearby positions *within* a patch are suppressed?

To illustrate how this can happen, suppose that the brain could compute the *difference* of the reflected light at two nearby positions, divided by its sum, as in

$$\frac{A(I + \varepsilon) - B(I - \varepsilon)}{A(I + \varepsilon) + B(I - \varepsilon)}$$

Both the difference in the numerator, and its division by the sum in the denominator, are due to the *competition* between nearby cells that I earlier showed more mathematically in Figure 2.35. Just as before, the terms $I + \varepsilon$ and $I - \varepsilon$ approximately cancel in the numerator and denominator, leaving the result

$$\frac{A - B}{A + B}.$$

Within a patch, the reflectances are everywhere the same. Thus $A = B$ and the result is zero. *Between* patches, $A \neq B$, so the brain can compute a normalized measure of the reflectance change. The ratio of $A - B$ to $A + B$ is called the *contrast* at the patch boundary. If the brain can compute contrasts across positions, then it can also discount the illuminant and recover a measure of the scene's reflectances. This contrast measure is non-zero only near positions at which the reflectance changes more quickly across space than the illumination gradient (Figure 4.5). Such a contrast measure is either a "color contour" or a "brightness contour", depending upon whether the image contains chromatic or achromatic contrasts. Color differences often coexist at the same positions with achromatic contrast differences, as in the Monet Rouen Cathedral paintings during full sunlight (Figure 3.45).

More generally, these illuminant-discounted activities are called "feature contours" to have a term that includes both chromatic and achromatic information. The word "feature" suggests that these are the signals that eventually give rise to the visible features, or qualia, that we consciously see in surface percepts. The main conclusion is that feature contours greatly distort the original luminance profile in response to the images in Figures 2.17, 4.2,

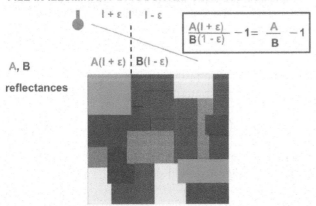

COMPUTE REFLECTANCE CHANGES AT CONTOURS
FILL-IN ILLUMINANT-DISCOUNTED SURFACE COLORS

FIGURE 4.4. When a gradient of light illuminates a McCann Mondrian, there is a jump in the total light that is reflected at nearby positions where the reflectances of the patches change.

COMPUTE REFLECTANCE CHANGES AT CONTOURS
FILL-IN ILLUMINANT-DISCOUNTED SURFACE COLORS

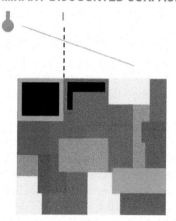

Discount
Illuminant:
Compute
color
contours

FIGURE 4.5. Multiple-scale balanced competition chooses color contours where the reflectances of the patches change. These color contours discount the illuminant.

and 4.4 in order to discount the illumination within the different regions of these figures.

This is just the sort of property that Edwin Land found during his experiments with McCann Mondrians. Land ingeniously set up gradients of light from two or more colored light sources. He adjusted the lights so that the amounts of reflected light from visible wavelengths were the same at positions within two different patches, as indicated in Figure 4.3 for the yellow and purple patches at the lower left and right, respectively, of the McCann Mondrian. According to a Newtonian definition of color, both patches should have had the same color. This is not what subjects reported. They reported seeing approximately the same colors that they would have seen if the Mondrian was illuminated uniformly by white light. This result means that the brain was able to greatly attenuate the color signals from the interiors of the test patches. Otherwise, the patches would have looked the same, because the spectrum of light that they reflected to the eyes was the same. The colors at the patch boundaries were not suppressed, however, notably their feature contour contrasts.

If the only thing that happened during discounting the illuminant was suppression of color signals except near boundaries, then we would see a world of colored outlines, as illustrated in the upper left of Figure 4.5. Our daily experience insists that something more occurs, because we can see colors that fill entire surfaces, not just their color contours. In fact, the brain uses the color contours that survive the discounting process to fill-in the color of the patch interiors with better estimates of the true colors of the patches, as illustrated in Figure 4.6. The brain carries out this filling-in process at a processing stage that occurs subsequent to the one that discounts the illuminant. For example, the illuminant starts to get discounted even in

the retina, and measures of contrast are computed at essentially all subsequent processing stages in the visual cortex. It is not until cortical areas V2 and V4 in the blob stream (Figure 1.21) that filled-in surfaces get fully computed.

There are several implications of this analysis that are worth thinking about for a long time. Although discounting the illuminant aims at computing the real colors of a scene, it greatly distorts the pattern of retinal color signals across space in order to do so. The discounting process can convert the continuous pattern of surface color that the retina receives (Figure 4.4) into a discrete skeleton of color contours (Figure 4.5). The brain does this to prevent gradual illumination changes across space from being confused with real reflectance changes. This distortion is corrected by the filling-in process, which restores a representation of continuous surface color (Figure 4.6). Thus, it is not the case that every stage of brain processing yields increasingly accurate representations of the external world. Computing color contours with greater "certainty" implies that the colors of the regions within the patches are suppressed, and thus become more "uncertain", at that processing stage. This is an example of an uncertainty principle at work. This uncertainty is resolved hierarchically by a later stage of surface filling-in, and is thus an example of "hierarchical resolution of uncertainty".

A second implication of the analysis is that the distortion process is sensitive to image contrast. We need to ask how the brain computes these contrasts without requiring too much intelligence from individual nerve cells. In particular, what type of competition between cells can manage such a neat trick? It turns out to be a ubiquitous type of competition that helps cells throughout the brain maintain sensitive responses to inputs whose amplitudes can change greatly through time. Indeed, the so-called membrane equations of neurophysiology embody

COMPUTE REFLECTANCE CHANGES AT CONTOURS
FILL-IN ILLUMINANT-DISCOUNTED SURFACE COLORS

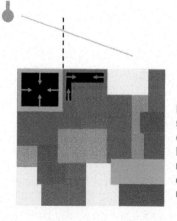

Fill-in
surface
color:
Hierarchical
resolution
of
uncertainty

FIGURE 4.6. Filling-in of color contours restores a surface percept with colors that substantially discount the illuminant.

shunting, or automatic gain control, properties that naturally compute the contrasts of input and activity patterns. These cell equations, interacting in on-center off-surround networks, solve the stability-plasticity dilemma. Chapter 2 described a simple gedanken experiment to derive these equations.

Brightness constancy, contrast, and assimilation

Discounting the illuminant often, but not always, helps to achieve a more accurate representation of the real reflectances of objects in the world. It also distorts reflectances under certain circumstances, thereby giving rise to percepts that we call visual illusions. Such examples illustrate yet again how processes which help us to better experience "reality" can also lead to "illusion". Some of these illusions are useful, others not. Figures 4.7 and 4.8 illustrate how this can happen.

The following text summarizes some of the explanations and computer simulations that I published with Dejan Todorovic when he was my postdoctoral fellow (Grossberg and Todorovic, 1988). The bottom panel of Figure 4.7, labeled Stimulus, shows a horizontal cross-section of a uniformly illuminated image with two vertical bars of an equal luminance that is greater than the luminance of the background. The panel labeled Feature illustrates how the competition discounts the illuminant except near the edges of the bars. The peak activities here are the feature contours that are extracted by

the competition. The panel labeled Boundary shows the boundary contours that are derived from the Feature pattern. Boundaries are created by the peaks in the Feature pattern because the boundary formation process is sensitive to contrast. The panel labeled Output shows the pattern of brightness that is caused when the Feature pattern fills-in within the Boundary pattern that is projected to the surface stream. The filling-in process tends to average all of the Feature inputs which it receives between each pair of boundaries. This average filled-in activity is higher within the bars than in the background. The brightness pattern hereby faithfully represents the original luminance pattern. From this figure alone, one might conclude that the brain has gone through an awful lot of trouble just to reproduce the pattern in the Stimulus!

The real payoff by these processes is seen when they discount the illuminant. This is illustrated in Figure 4.8. Here the Stimulus from Figure 4.7 is distorted by being viewed in a gradient of light, whose light source is to the right of the figure. The *relative* luminances, or reflectances, on both sides of each edge in the Feature pattern in Figure 4.8 are the same as in the Stimulus pattern, but the Stimulus pattern luminances are drastically distorted in the Feature pattern in order to discount the illuminant. Remarkably, the Feature pattern in Figure 4.8 is the same as the Feature pattern in Figure 4.7. The reason for this is, as noted above, that the discounting process estimates the *contrast* at nearby positions, not absolute luminances. Because the *relative* luminances, or contrasts, at each edge are not changed by a gradient of light, the Boundary and Output patterns in Figure 4.8 are the same as those in Figure 4.7. The brightness pattern here provides a good representation of the actual reflectances in the image. This is an example of *brightness constancy*.

Figure 4.9 shows that the discounting process can also cause perceptual distortions, and therefore visual illusions. The distortion caused in this case is called *brightness contrast*. Here, as can be seen in the Stimulus luminance pattern, the two bars again have equal luminance, but they are placed on a background whose luminance gradually decreases from left to right. As a result, the *contrast* of the right bar relative to its background is greater than the contrast of the left bar relative to its background, even though both bars have the same *luminance*. As a result, the Feature pattern creates more activity in response to the right bar than the left bar, because the discounting process is sensitive to contrast. When this Feature pattern fills-in the Boundaries, the brightness profile in the Output shows that the right bar is brighter than the left bar, even though both bars have the same luminance. Brightness contrast can hereby help to make more contrastive objects stand out better in a scene. Also note

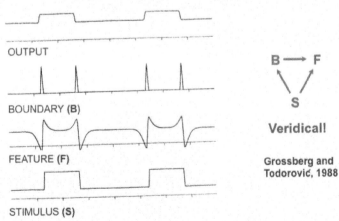

SIMULATION OF BRIGHTNESS CONSTANCY
Uniform illumination

OUTPUT

BOUNDARY (B)

FEATURE (F)

STIMULUS (S)

B ⟶ F

S

Veridical!

Grossberg and
Todorović, 1988

Boundary peaks are spatially *narrower* than Feature peaks

FIGURE 4.7. Simulation of brightness reconstancy under uniform illumination.

SIMULATION OF BRIGHTNESS CONSTANCY
Discount the Illuminant

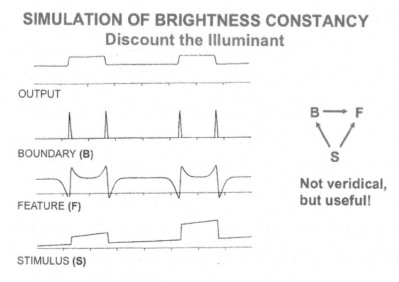

Ratio-sensitive feature contours (F)

FIGURE 4.8. Simulation of brightness constancy under an illumination gradient. Note that the feature contour pattern (F) is the same in both cases, so too is the boundary contour (B) pattern that is derived from it, and the final filled-in surface.

that the gradient of luminance in the Stimulus is not visible in the brightness profile, because no boundaries prevent its Feature pattern from spreading into a uniform pattern of brightness in the Output. This is thus another example of "a visible effect of an invisible cause," much as the Yarbus display in Figure 4.1. In the present case, the invisible cause is the gradient of luminance in the background, which spreads into a uniform background brightness level in the percept.

A classical example of brightness contrast is seen when viewing Figure 2.18, which is the brightness contrast variant of the brightness constancy percept that is seen when viewing Figure 2.17. The inner gray disks in the left and right images are identical in Figure 2.18. However, the less luminous annulus to the left makes its inner disk look lighter, whereas the more luminous annulus to the right makes its inner disk look darker. Brightness constancy showed us that the brain tends to *normalize* the total amount of reflected light to our eyes from across an image in order to discount the illuminant. Such total activity normalization enables computation of the reflectances, or *ratios*, of reflected light to be computed, even as the illuminant varies in intensity. Brightness contrast shows us the other side of this coin; namely, that by tending to normalize the total activity that is reflected from an image, reducing activity in one part of the image, as in the darker annulus, tends to increase it from

another part of the image, as in the lighter appearing inner disk, and conversely for the case of the lighter annulus and the darker appearing inner disk.

Brightness contrast enhances differences between the luminances of adjacent regions. The discounting and filling-in processes can also have the opposite effect. They can also cause *brightness assimilation* to occur. Here luminance differences between adjacent regions can be *decreased*, rather than increased. The necessary process of discounting the illuminant can hereby cause quite a variety of illusory percepts to occur, but we manage to survive quite well despite them.

Figure 4.10 shows an example of brightness assimilation. On the left half of this image, a more luminous step is surrounded by a less luminous step on a still less luminous background. On the right half of the image, the *same* luminous steps are surrounded by a more luminous background. The effect of this on perception is that the step to the left looks brighter than the one to the right. This is a case of "assimilation" because the darkening effect of the more luminous background on the right upon its contiguous region gets incorporated into the brightness of the step in the middle. The Feature and Boundary patterns show how this happens. When the Feature pattern spreads within the boundaries, the perceived assimilation results.

SIMULATION OF BRIGHTNESS CONTRAST

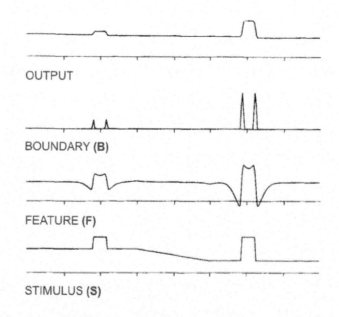

FIGURE 4.9. Simulation of brightness contrast.

SIMULATION OF BRIGHTNESS ASSIMILATION

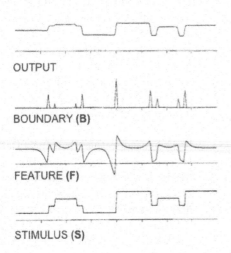

FIGURE 4.10. Simulation of brightness assimilation. Note how the equal steps on the left and right sides of the luminance profile are transformed into different brightness levels.

Figure 4.11 shows another important example of how the brain's efforts to accurately represent the world can lead to illusory percepts. In the left panel of Figure 4.11 two adjacent vertical bars of differing luminance, with the more luminous bar to the left, are processed by the discounting (Feature) and filling-in (Output) mechanisms. The Output is a brightness profile that mirrors the luminance profile in the Stimulus. This example is shown for comparison with the right panel of Figure 4.11 which shows how the Craik-O'Brien-Cornsweet Effect may be caused, as in Figure 4.2. The Craik-O'Brien-Cornsweet stimulus leads to the same brightness profile as the double step stimulus, because both images have similar contrasts at their edges. As a result, the Feature pattern that is created by the discounting process is essentially the same in both cases.

The percepts caused by the images of Figure 4.11 have caused quite a bit of controversy in the vision community. Some authors, such as Floyd Ratliff and Larry Sirovich in 1978 (Ratliff and Sirovich, 1978), argued that the similarity of activity patterns at the Feature level is sufficient to explain why the double step and Craik-O'Brien-Cornsweet Effect images look the same. These authors promoted such a view because the Feature patterns could be explained by classical ideas about visual filters, such as filters based on Fourier Analysis. According to this view, the brain processes an image using multiple filters that are sensitive

to different spatial scales, or wavelengths, in the image. Although such multiple-scale filters are well-known to exist in the brain, such an account faces an obvious difficulty: It does not explain why some positions that have the same activity in the Feature pattern may have different brightnesses in the percept, or why other positions that have different activities in the Feature pattern may have the same brightness in the percept.

Any explanation based on the Feature pattern alone must thus abandon any hope of relating its activity levels to consciously perceived brightnesses. All visual percepts and experiments would have no relevance to underlying neural mechanisms because same/different judgments on the perceptual level would imply nothing about same/different measurements of the underlying neural code. This problem evaporates as soon as one realizes that the brain does not just filter the image. Rather, it filters the image to discount the illuminant before using the filtered Feature signals to recover a surface representation using filling-in. The simplified examples in Figure 4.11 make this point using a Feature filter with a fixed size, or spatial scale. In the brain, as well as in more advanced models of visual perception, filters with multiple spatial scales are needed.

Figure 4.12 shows simulations that I published in 1988 with Dejan Todorovic of the 2D Craik-O'Brien-Cornsweet Effect percepts that are generated by the stimulus in the left panel of Figure 4.2 (Grossberg and Todorovic, 1988). In this figure, the size of a circle is proportional to the activity

SIMULATION OF DOUBLE STEP AND COCE

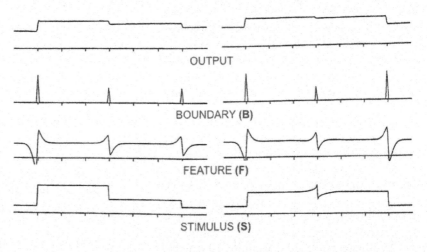

FIGURE 4.11. Simulations of a double step (left panel) and the Craik-O'Brien-Cornsweet (COCE) illusion. Note that discounting the illuminant creates similar feature contour patterns, from which the fact that the COCE looks like the double step follows immediately.

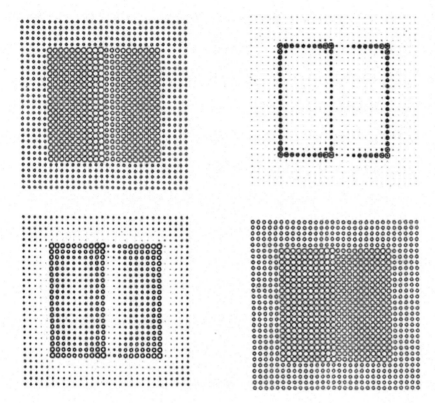

FIGURE 4.12. Simulation of the 2D COCE.

enclosed in the upper left red square have lower activities than the cells in the lower right red square, due to the gradient of illumination. After the illuminant is discounted (left column, bottom row), and the boundaries computed (right column, top row), the perceived surface representation is created by filling-in the illuminant-discounted pattern within the boundaries (right column, bottom row). In this percept, the cell activities in the upper left red square are *more* active than those in the lower right red square, which is the opposite of what happens in the upper left image due to the gradient of illumination. This result accurately describes the true contrasts in the image after the illuminant is discounted. I therefore call it an example of *contrast constancy*.

Figures 4.7 to 4.13 show how the discounting mechanism can often yield veridical percepts with the illuminant discounted, but can sometimes create visual illusions. From a mechanistic point of view, even a brightness constancy percept like that in Figure 4.8 is a visual illusion because the Output does not accurately represent the luminance pattern in the Stimulus. It just happens that this particular "illusion" accurately represents the reflectances of objects in the world, so that we can learn to recognize these objects from multiple experiences with them under variable illumination conditions.

of the cell at the corresponding position. The upper left image represents the stimulus. The black background is represented by small circles. The equal luminance backgrounds within the rectangles, away from the cusps, are represented by somewhat larger circles. The more luminous cusp to the left of the vertical line is represented by even larger circles, whereas the less luminous cusp to the right of the vertical line is represented by smaller circles. The lower left image represents cell activities at the processing stage that discounts the illuminant. The upper right image represents the boundary that is extracted from these activities, and the lower right image represents the COCE percept after surface filling-in occurs.

Contrast constancy

Figure 4.13 illustrates how the contrasts of a more complex image can be preserved when they are seen in a gradient of illumination. The image chosen is shown in the upper left corner of the figure. It is a McCann Mondrian that is illuminated by a light source at the lower right corner of the image. The illuminant intensity decreases gradually as it crosses the image from its lower right corner to its top left corner. Two regions of the image have been enclosed by red squares to make the main point. The cells

Catching filling-in "on the fly"

Given that some scientists may still have not accepted the existence of filling-in, it is important to marshall as much evidence as possible that this process really exists. There are many more data that support this hypothesis than I can review here. However, one experiment is particularly informative. The article that I published with Dejan Todorovic in 1988 developed a neural model of brightness perception that simulated the above brightness percepts, and many more. Michael Paradiso and Ken Nakayama responded to this article by doing experiments aimed at trying to catch this filling-in process "on the fly". Their experiments were published in 1991 (Paradiso and Nakayama, 1991). They briefly flashed a white disk on a screen and then a masking stimulus a little while later. They reasoned that the inner contour of the white disk should generate a brightness contour that would propagate inwards toward the masking

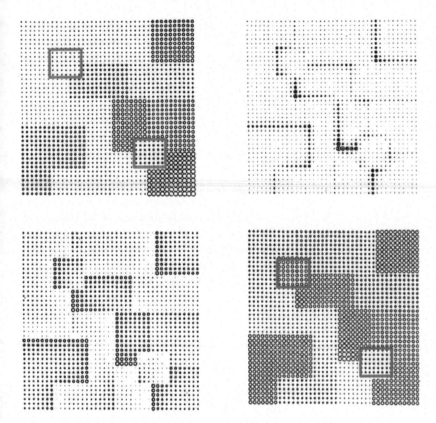

and Spekreijse, 1999) and Michael Paradiso and his colleagues in Providence (Paradiso and Hahn, 1996), have since directly recorded properties of filling-in within the visual cortex.

Why is neon color spreading an important probe of how we consciously see?

I will now show you that neon color spreading is the effect of three hierarchical resolutions of uncertainty acting together. Each of them is essential for us to be able to consciously see. The first of these hierarchical resolutions of uncertainty enables us to discount the illuminant. The other two enable us to build effective boundary groupings of objects in the world. These latter two resolutions will now be discussed.

FIGURE 4.13. Contrast constancy shows how the relative luminances when a picture is viewed in an illumination gradient can even be reversed to restore the correct reflectances due to discounting the illuminant.

shape. The masking shape should, in turn, block the progress of filling-in. The observed brightness profile should reflect these spreading and blocking processes. Paradiso and Nakayama asked their subjects to report the brightness profiles that they saw. Their results are summarized in Figure 4.14.

Paradiso and Nakayama could hereby report that a physical filling-in process was supported by their results, but expressed reservations about whether this process behaved like the Grossberg-Todorovic model. Todorovic and I had used the model to explain only steady-state brightness data, not the dynamics of filling-in. Our model did, however, represent filling-in dynamics too, because it was described using differential equations that we just happened to simulate at steady state in order to simulate available brightness data. To test this issue quantitatively, my PhD student Karl Arrington used the experimental stimuli of Paradiso and Nakayama as inputs to the Grossberg-Todorovic model. Karl showed that the model simulated the brightness profiles of Paradiso and Nakayama so well that his simulation was printed on the cover of the issue of *Vision Research* in which his results were published in 1994 (Arrington, 1994). Neurophysiological experiments, notably by investigators like Victor Lamme and his colleagues in Amsterdam (Lamme, Rodriguez-Rodriguez,

EXPERIMENTS ON FILLING-IN

Paradiso and Nakayama 1991
Catching filling-in "in the act"

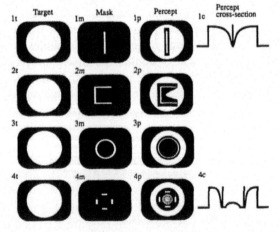

Arrington, 1994, *Vision Research*, 34, 3371-3387 simulated these data using the model of Grossberg and Todorovic, 1988

FIGURE 4.14. The kinds of displays that Michael Paradiso and Ken Nakayama used to catch filling-in "in the act" and which Karl Arrington then simulated using the Grossberg and Todorovic model.

It is only after all of these uncertainties are resolved that the brain can generate complete and stable enough visual surface representations of the world with which to control adaptive behaviors. My exposition will explain how and why such surface representations are proposed to get completed by prestriate visual cortical area V4 (Figure 1.21). This fact clarifies why a surface-shroud resonance that can mark these representations with conscious awareness (Table 1.4) seems to be triggered between V4 and the posterior parietal cortex, or PPC (Figure 1.21) before this resonance propagates to, and synchronizes, the dynamics of, lower cortical areas such as V2 and V1, and higher cortical areas such as the prefrontal cortex, or PFC.

Why resonance?

The three pairs of complementary computational properties of boundaries and surfaces (Figure 3.7), along with the three hierarchical resolutions of uncertainty, illustrate that there is a great deal of uncertainty in the early stages of visual processing by the brain. Only after all three hierarchical resolutions of uncertainty are complete, and after boundaries are completed and surfaces filled-in, has the brain constructed a contextually informative and temporally stable enough representation of scenic objects on which to base adaptive behaviors.

If this is indeed the case, then why do not the earlier stages undermine behavior? What prevents the brain from accidentally using noisy and incomplete data from these early processing stages to generate responses that might lead to disastrous results? My proposed answer is that *brain resonance, and with it conscious awareness, is triggered at the processing stages that represent boundary and surface representations, after they are complete and stable enough to control visually-based behaviors like attentive looking and reaching* (Table 1.3). The facts that invisible boundaries can be recognized (e.g., Figures 1.1, 1.3, 1.4, and 3.3) and that all conscious qualia are surface percepts (e.g., Figures 3.2, 3.24, and 3.25) suggest, moreover, that both boundaries and surfaces contribute to resonances that support recognition and seeing. In particular, visual resonances focus attention upon these predictive boundary and surface representations while gain-amplifying and synchronizing them, without destroying their representational patterns, as I will explain in Chapter 6.

Can philosophers help us out?

An inescapable implication of filling-in data, and of our theory's attempts to explain them, is that filling-in, in general, and neon color spreading, in particular, are realized by actual physical processes that go on in the brain. Various philosophers, notably the talented and prolific Daniel Dennett, have argued otherwise. I was gratified when Dennett attended lectures of mine about neon color spreading in the 1980s, since I believed then, as I do now, that theoretical discoveries about how each brain makes a mind offer a treasure trove of new ideas for philosophical discussion and analysis. I was therefore surprised when he later wrote in his 1991 book *Consciousness Explained* (Dennett, 1991): "The fundamental flaw in the idea of 'filling-in' is that it suggests that the brain is providing something when in fact the brain is ignoring something" (p. 356). "The brain doesn't have to 'fill in' for the blind spot . . . We don't notice these gaps, but they don't have to be filled in *because* we're designed not to notice them" (p. 355). In other words, Dennett argued that a physical process of filling-in does not occur. Given that Dennett put an example of neon color spreading on the back cover of his book, he clearly viewed this claim as an important part of his proposals about consciousness.

There were problems with Dennett's viewpoint even when he first published it. First and foremost, it explained no data about how filling-in works and what its properties are. Although Dennett heard me give a lecture in which I offered a detailed neural explanation of a lot of data about neon color spreading, in his book, he did not attempt to explain any of these data. He offered a personal opinion, not a scientific theory. Any viable scientific proposal about experimental data, however, must explain these data at least as well as competing theories. A reader of Dennett's book might come away thinking that there were no theories available to explain how filling-in happens, and Dennett's proposal was at least a step in that direction. This was not, unfortunately, the case.

In fact, the lecture that Dennett heard provided a unified explanation of neon color spreading and many other data that we could only explain by invoking filling-in. This model was published in 1985 in two visible journals in psychology, *Psychological Review* and *Perception and Psychophysics* with Ennio Mingolla when he was my postdoctoral fellow (Grossberg and Mingolla, 1985a, 1985b). The article that discussed neon color spreading was published in *Psychological Review*, which was then the most visible journal in psychology. Our model was further developed in the 1980s with my colleagues Michael Cohen and Dejan Todorovic to show how the interaction between boundary formation and surface filling-in can simulate many challenging brightness percepts, including those that I just summarized above (Cohen and Grossberg, 1984; Grossberg and Todorovic, 1988). Many articles have since been published to qualitatively explain, quantitatively simulate, and successfully predict even more data in which filling-in plays an essential role, and for which no alternative explanations are available.

Unfortunately, Dennett ignored this evidence, and did not try to provide an alternative explanation of the phenomena. Instead, he offered sarcasm: "This idea of filling in is common in the thinking of even sophisticated theorists, and it is a dead giveaway to vestigial Cartesian materialism. What is amusing is that those who use the term often know better, but since they find the term irresistible, they cover themselves by putting in scare-quotes" (p. 344). Philosophers may yet play an important role in elucidating discoveries about mind and brain, but not if they ignore the critical data and theoretical advances within the fields about which they write.

I will now show you how a sustained analysis of neon color spreading clarifies how boundaries and surfaces form, and how these insights also enable many other explanations and predictions to be made about how the brain sees.

How are boundaries formed? Evidence from filling-in

How are perceptual boundaries formed? One thing is immediately clear: They arise as a result of some form of *cooperation* that occurs between multiple boundary inducers, such as the multiple line ends in the offset grating and Ehrenstein images in Figure 1.1, and the pac-man edges and line ends in the Kanizsa square images in Figure 3.3. This cooperation can, moreover, span long distances—even a few degrees of visual angle. Boundary formation thus uses a spatially *long-range cooperation*. Cooperation is not, however, the only process used to form perceptual boundaries. This can be seen particularly well by considering the percept of neon color spreading that is generated by the image in Figure 3.11, which was described in 1981 by Christoph Redies and Lothar Spillmann (Redies and Spillmann, 1981). I explained this percept in my 1985 *Psychological Review* article with Ennio Mingolla. This image seems innocent enough, consisting as it does of alternating red and black crosses on white paper. Despite this simple arrangement, many people see a shimmering red color that extends beyond the boundaries of each red cross. Two types of percept are frequently observed: diamonds or circles filled with neon red color around each red cross, or diagonal bands of red color that intersect several aligned red crosses.

One reason why neon color spreading is of such great interest scientifically—and the reason why I was so drawn to it—is because it provides visible evidence of the rules whereby boundaries are formed. We can *see* where color spreads in response to such an image. If it spreads to places where it has no right to be, then we can ask: Why could not the boundaries hold the color within the regions where there are edges in the image? How can holes be created in continuous boundaries that allow color to spread through them? Every image that generates an illusory contour also helps to discover boundary formation rules, including the Ehrenstein image in Figure 1.1, where a sufficient number of radial lines induce a circular illusory contour that forms perpendicular to the line ends. The same thing happens in response to the offset grating image of Figure 1.1. When only four black lines are used as inducers, as in the center of Figure 3.3d, the percept may be more ambiguous. An illusory circle, square, or even a diamond may be perceived, depending upon factors such as line length, thickness, and mutual distance. For present purposes, note that the four black lines at the ends of each red cross in Figure 3.11 form an Ehrenstein image. If you focus your attention on only one red cross in Figure 3.11, you can see that red color flows out of the red cross until it hits the illusory contour generated by the bounding four black lines.

This property confirms several conclusions that we noted before; namely: Boundaries act as barriers to filling-in; and all boundaries, whether "real" or "illusory", are equally good at blocking the flow of filled-in color. These conclusions do not, however, capture the main property that makes neon color spreading so striking.

Balancing cooperation with competition during boundary formation

What is especially interesting about neon color spreading is that the red color somehow escapes from the boundaries that surround each red cross. How and why does this happen? The obvious answer is that there are gaps in the boundaries that are big enough for some of the color to flow out, much like small breaks in a dam allow some water to escape. These *end gaps* occur at the ends of each red cross, where they touch the black cross edges, as I have already noted in Figure 3.41. How do these gaps arise?

In order for neon color spreading to occur, the contrast of the black crosses with respect to the white background must be larger than that of the red cross with respect to the white background. As a result, the vertical boundaries surrounding the black cross are stronger than the vertical boundaries that surround the red cross. These boundaries *compete* with each other across space, as shown in Figure 3.41, much as colors do in order to discount the illuminant. The weaker boundaries at the ends of the red cross are weakened, or even broken, by competition from the stronger boundaries at the ends of the black crosses. Some red color can consequently spill out from the ensuing boundary gaps. This competition occurs across a smaller region of space than does the long-range cooperation that helps to form boundaries; it is a *short-range spatial competition*. Neon color spreading thus arises due to interactions of long-range cooperation *and* short-range competition within the boundary system, combined with color filling-in within these boundaries in the surface system.

These assertions may be raising in your mind as many questions as they are answering. For starters, why should the brain bother to use long-range cooperation and short-range competition to build boundaries? Surely not just to generate amusing percepts like neon color spreading, which represents a *failure* of boundaries to contain their color! Indeed, we have all survived perfectly well despite these broken boundaries that enable neon color to spread!

Whereas these boundary mechanisms sometimes fail to contain their colors, I will now show why there would be much more catastrophic perceptual failures if boundaries did not cooperate and compete with one another as they do. Without these mechanisms, color could flow out of every line end and object corner, which would be maddening and terribly destructive of effective vision. Most of the time, the interaction of long-range cooperation and short-range competition helps to select those boundaries that best represent the objects in the world.

In fact, neon color spreading, which seems so anomalous when it is first experienced, may be understood, as I remarked above, as the combined effect of three instances of hierarchical resolution of uncertainty, each one of which is needed to see the world well. From this perspective, neon color spreading is yet another example of how interactions among several adaptive brain mechanisms can lead to maladaptive consequences in response to certain environments. One of these hierarchical resolutions is already familiar: It is the process whereby a later stage of filling-in compensates for the distortions caused by discounting the illuminant. This hierarchical resolution of uncertainty occurs within the surface system. The other two hierarchical resolutions are realized by basic processes within the boundary system that we have yet to consider. Neon color spreading will then be explained as a harmless by-product of three essential brain processes when they interact in response to unlikely images such as the neon color spreading images in Figures 3.10 and 3.11.

How does the boundary system work? From brains to the chips of future devices

In the next few sections, I will introduce you to some of the organizational principles and mechanisms that our brains use to build boundary groupings of visual scenes

and pictures. I will do this in simple stages until we have an entire model circuit at our disposal. My exposition will follow the path of historical discovery. At the moment, we know quite a bit about how boundary interactions seem to be carried out in known laminar circuits of the visual cortex. Such a laminar model provides a detailed link between brain anatomy, neurophysiology, perception, and even development. Before describing these laminar circuits, I will first introduce key perceptual issues and data that clarify the relevant mechanisms. Only then, when you have a good idea about why such mechanisms exist at all, will I give you a self-contained summary of these laminar circuits in Chapter 10.

The laminar circuits are worth knowing about for several reasons. First, they embody an ingenious, parsimonious, and beautiful design. Second, similar laminar circuits seem to exist in *all* parts of the sensory and cognitive neocortex of the What cortical stream. Thus we can anticipate that variants of these circuits are used for such diverse processes as visual perception and object recognition; auditory, speech, and language perception; and cognitive information processing . . . indeed *all* of the processes of higher intelligence that make us human. In fact, variations on the *same* canonical model circuit have been used to explain and simulate data about vision, speech, and cognition. More will be said about these models in Chapter 10. Finally, these laminar cortical designs can provide a blueprint for designing a new generation of computer chips that can better emulate human intelligence in the computers and robots of the future. If all the chips that control different aspects of intelligence use specializations of a shared canonical laminar circuit, then they can be self-consistently joined together in increasingly general-purpose autonomous adaptive algorithms and robots.

To compute a boundary, the brain needs to determine the *orientation* of the contrasts in a scene or picture. Recall from images like the Kanizsa squares in Figure 3.3 that boundaries often tend to form between contrasts with approximately the same orientation that are approximately aligned, or collinear, across space. Only if you first compute the orientations of the contrasts can you then preferentially link similar contrasts together into collinear boundaries. These contrasts may be due to edges, textures, or shading in the image, as in Figure 4.15. It has been known at least since the Nobel Prize–winning research of David Hubel and Thorstein Wiesel in the 1960s and 1970s (Hubel and Wiesel, 1962, 1968, 1977) that the striate cortex—namely, cortical area V1 in Figure 1.21—contains cells with *oriented receptive fields*, a concept that I will explain in a moment. These are the oriented filters that Ratliff and Sirovich used to discuss the Craik-O'Brien-Cornsweet Effect in Figure 4.2. It was only realized in the 1980s, after Margaret Wong-Riley's discovery of the blobs (Wong-Riley, 1979), that these oriented cells are concentrated in the interblobs of V1, and are not by

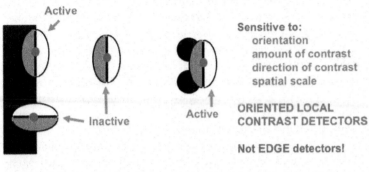

**FROM ORIENTED FILTERING
TO GROUPING AND BOUNDARY COMPLETION**
Oriented Receptive Fields: SIMPLE CELLS
Hubel and Wiesel, 1968

Active

Sensitive to:
orientation
amount of contrast
direction of contrast
spatial scale

← Inactive   Active

ORIENTED LOCAL
CONTRAST DETECTORS

Not EDGE detectors!

FIGURE 4.15. Simple cells are oriented local contrast detectors, not edge detectors.

and large found in the blobs, which are more devoted to color-sensitive cells.

My theory of how boundaries and surfaces form was introduced at just around the time that neurophysiologists were beginning to realize that the blobs contain cells whose receptive field properties differ from those in the interblob areas. Because this theory was, at that time, derived by analyzing psychological data about visual perception, it was a great relief to realize that a brain substrate of boundaries and surfaces exists in the interblob and blob streams, respectively. It should be noted that the neurophysiologists themselves did not make this claim. Rather, their data showed only that there were oriented cells in the interblobs and unoriented color-selective cells in the blobs. Margaret Livingstone and David Hubel, two of the most distinguished neurophysiologists in making this discovery, suggested that interblobs code *orientation* whereas blobs code *color* (Livingstone and Hubel, 1988). It was also known that the interblobs receive inputs from color-selective cells of the lateral geniculate nucleus (LGN). Why the blobs and interblobs both received LGN inputs that they segregated in different ways was not well understood.

These experiments did not test the idea that many cortical oriented cells can complete boundaries from multiple types of image contrasts over positions that receive no external oriented inputs, as illustrated by the Kanizsa square (Figure 3.3). Nor did they test the hypothesis that these boundaries carry no visible perceptual quality of their own but, rather, organize the process of surface filling-in, which does support visibility, and can be directly recognized by higher cortical stages. The concept of surface filling-in is also not captured by the claim that the blob stream is a "color" system. The proposed role of the surface system is far more general; namely, to generate representations of continuous surface *form* which may be imbued with visible perceptual properties like brightness,

color, and depth. In addition, there can also be amodal, or invisible, filling-in of surface form, as occurs whenever we "know" what the color of an occluded surface should be without being able to see it; e.g., Figures 1.3 and 3.2. Despite the ability of boundary and surface concepts and mechanisms to explain a large amount of perceptual and neural data that have not been explained by alternative accounts, there still seem to be no definitive neurophysiological tests of the hypothesis that all boundaries are invisible in the interblob stream and that the blob stream supports a surface filling-in system that can represent properties of visible surface brightness, color, and depth of unoccluded opaque surface regions, as well as of similar qualia of occluded transparent surface regions.

I called the boundary model the Boundary Contour System, or BCS, because it clarified how boundaries are generated at contrasts, or contours, in a scene, much as in the Boundary patterns in Figures 4.7– 4.14. The neutral word "boundary" was used because the same system was proposed to respond in a form-sensitive way to edges, textures, and shading, thereby giving rise to boundary webs on multiple scales. The BCS is thus emphatically not just an "edge" detector model, as was often proposed in traditional computer vision algorithms. The previous discussions of how boundary webs help us to see 3D form-from-texture (Figure 3.21c) and 3D form-from-shading (Figure 3.21d) illustrate this point. I called the surface model the Feature Contour System, or FCS, because it clarified how visible surface properties—the visible "features" in a scene—may be constructed through surface filling-in from the "feature contours" that are generated at contrasts of a scene, just like the "color contours" that were used to discuss the McCann Mondrian is Figures 4.4-4.6, and the Feature patterns that were used to discuss brightness constancy, contrast, assimilation, and the Craik O'Brien Cornsweet Effect in Figures 4.8–4.13.

FACADE Theory vs. Naïve Realism

I call the entire vision theory of which the BCS and FCS form a part FACADE theory. The acronym FACADE stands for Form-And-Color-And-DEpth. This name was chosen for two reasons.

First, it emphasizes that individual brain cells that code visible representations combine, or *multiplex*, properties of Form-And-Color-and-DEpth. These properties are not separately represented by independent modules.

Rather, I predict that such multiplexed FACADE representations are computed via computationally complementary cortical streams and completed in prestriate visual area V4 (Figure 1.21).

Second, the name FACADE reminds us that, although the visual world looks "real," the brain's internal representations of the world are not isomorphic to it. We can experience a "real" world without falling into the philosophical trap of Naïve Realism, which asserts that the world looks so real because our senses provide us with direct awareness of objects as they really are. Our visual representations are no more isomorphic to the "real world" than are the facades that form the sets in an old fashioned Western film.

Receptive fields detect oriented local contrasts: Avoiding edge detectors implies uncertainty

What is an *oriented receptive field* and why is it useful to begin the process of boundary formation? Figure 4.15 illustrates key properties of interblob oriented cells. Cell populations that are sensitive to different orientations occur at each position across space. As a result, multiple orientations in an image or scene can be detected at each position by a population of similarly oriented cells. Each cell can respond to only a narrow range of favored orientations of image contrasts at its position. That is why the cell with a vertically oriented receptive field in Figure 4.15 can respond to a vertical edge, but the horizontally oriented cell does not. As the orientation of the edge in the image progressively diverges from the preferred orientation of the cell, the cell is activated less and less. As the contrast of the edge gets smaller, so too does the cell's output response, no matter how luminous the scene may otherwise be.

Talking about contrast, Figure 4.15 illustrates that these oriented cells respond to contrast differences across space, such as a texture or shading difference, as well as to edges. Such a contrast difference is illustrated by the two vertical oriented black dots in Figure 4.15, to which a vertically-oriented cell can respond if it overlaps this net contrast. These oriented cells do not, however, respond just to input activity *per se*. No matter how intensely a cell it activated, it will not fire if this activity is the same at every position of its receptive field. Oriented cells also come in different sizes, and thus respond differently to image features of variable size, or spatial scale.

In summary, these cells are *oriented local contrast detectors* that can respond to many different sources of image contrast. They are emphatically not just edge detectors.

The brain hereby avoids a proliferation of specialized edge, texture, and shading detectors. If it did use a large number of different types of specialized detectors, then it would need a smart preprocessor to sort out how to merge all of their outputs together in the final percept.

Avoiding a proliferation of overly specialized detectors implies that the brain's oriented contrast detectors exhibit a certain amount of *uncertainty* about the identity of the features that can activate them: they can respond to a range of orientations and sizes of edges, textures, and shading. How is this uncertainty overcome? I will suggest below how it is overcome by the types of context-sensitive cooperative and competitive interactions that we have already seen in many of the above examples. Uncertainty reduction is thus an emergent property of the boundary system, including the two other "hierarchical resolutions of uncertainty" that will be explained in this chapter.

Simple cells and half-wave rectification

How are cells that behave like oriented local contrast detectors constructed? Let me simplify to make the main point. Imagine that each cell has an oriented *receptive field* that is broken up into two halves, as in Figure 4.16. The receptive field describes the set of all positions at which light inputs can influence the cell's activity. The shape of the receptive field determines the range of orientations to which the cell responds. If light is received at positions corresponding to the "light" half of the receptive field, it excites the cell. Light inputs to positions corresponding to

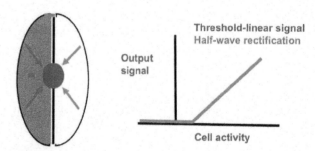

"SIMPLEST" SIMPLE CELL MODEL
need more complexity for processing natural scenes

FIGURE 4.16. The simplest way to realize an odd simple cell receptive field and firing threshold.

the "dark" half of the field inhibit the cell. The cell adds all of its inputs to determine the cell's net activity (excitatory minus inhibitory). An output signal is elicited if the net activity exceeds a *threshold*, as illustrated by the *threshold-linear signal* function in Figure 4.19. Below this threshold, there is no output. As the cell's net activity increases above the threshold, it generates an increasingly large output signal. This sort of one-sided analog thresholding is often called *half-wave rectification* in the engineering literature. Cells with oriented receptive fields and half-wave rectified outputs exist within the interblob stream. They are called *simple cells.*

The simple cell receptive field that is depicted in Figure 4.16 is called an *odd* receptive field. Simple cells may also have receptive fields with three oriented lobes, such that the middle lobe is excited by light and the flanking lobes are inhibited by light, or conversely, before the net activity is half-wave rectified to generate an output. Simple cells of this type are said to have *even* receptive fields. Hubel and Wiesel reported both types of simple cells in the classical neurophysiological experiments that won them the Nobel Prize in Physiology or Medicine in 1981. Both types of cells can respond to oriented contrasts, but an odd cell can respond better to one-sided luminance changes like edges, whereas an even cell can respond better to two-sided luminance changes like lines.

Complex cells pool opposite contrast polarities: Amodal boundary detectors

Simple cells begin to determine the orientation of boundaries. Their sensitivity to a particular contrast polarity helps them to respond at positions where similar oriented contrasts exist in a picture or scene. We already know, however, from our discussion of Figure 3.2 that the perceptual boundaries that support our percepts pool signals from opposite contrast polarities at each position in order to build boundaries around objects seen against textured backgrounds. How does the brain go from a simple cell, whose response is sensitive to one or another contrast polarity, but not to both, to a cell that combines inputs from both contrast polarities at each position?

The cells that do this in the striate cortex are called *complex cells*. These cells were also discovered by Hubel and Wiesel. A simple way to think about them is to assume that each complex cell of a given preferred orientation sums the outputs from a pair of like-oriented but oppositely-polarized simple cells at each position, as illustrated in Figure 4.17. Complex cells hereby become sensitive to the position, orientation, size, and amount of contrast that impinges upon their receptive fields, but not to its contrast

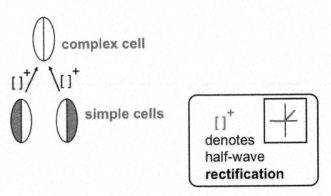

COMPLEX CELLS
pool signals from like-oriented simple cells
of opposite contrast polarity
at the same position

They are "insensitive to contrast polarity"

complex cell

simple cells

$[\ ]^+$ denotes half-wave **rectification**

FIGURE 4.17. Complex cells pool inputs from simple cells that are sensitive to opposite contrast polarities. Complex cells hereby become contrast invariant, and can respond to contrasts of either polarity.

polarity. Complex cells are thus *insensitive* to the spatial phase of the contrast within their receptive fields. This insensitivity to contrast polarity, or direction-of-contrast, is one of their defining characteristics, as well as one of the properties of the boundary completion system that is complementary to a corresponding property of the surface filling-in system (Figure 3.7).

Complex cells have three other properties that are worth mentioning. Because they receive half-wave rectified signals from pairs of oppositely polarized simple cells, complex cells perform a *full-wave* rectification of their inputs. This property means that complex cells respond to the absolute size of a contrast, independent of its polarity. When this property is relayed to higher levels of boundary completion, it enables a brain to build boundaries around objects in front of textured backgrounds, as it does in response to viewing the image in Figure 3.2.

The second property is that complex cells combine inputs from both the left eye and the right eye. When both eyes fixate on a particular part of an object, light signals from the other parts of the object hit the two eyes at different positions relative to their foveas, as illustrated in Figure 4.18. By combining signals from these different positions, the brain can begin to estimate the depth of the object relative to the observer. The size of this positional difference is called *binocular disparity*. These positionally-shifted, disparate signals activate simple cells at different, but nearby, positions in the visual cortex. The outputs from these simple cells are pooled at complex cells after some further processing that requires cells in at least three different layers in cortical area V1,

Binocular Disparity

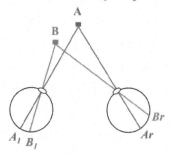

Binocular disparities are used in the brain to reconstruct depth from 2D retinal inputs, for relatively near objects

FIGURE 4.18. The images formed on the two retinas in response to a single object in the world are displaced by different amounts with respect to their foveas. This binocular disparity is a powerful cue for determining the depth of the object from an observer.

namely layers 4, 3B, and 2/3A (Figure 4.19). Different complex cells hereby become sensitive to different ranges of binocular disparity, and thus to different depths of objects from the observer. I will explain this microcircuit and incorporate it into a larger laminar cortical architecture in Chapters 10 and 11.

The third property concerns the kind of pooling of inputs that goes on at complex cells. Simple cells respond with narrow selectivity to specific color contrasts, or to brightness contrast, in a scene. Complex cells pool inputs from multiple simple cells—whether red, green, blue, yellow, black, or white—and therefore respond to a broad range of chromatic and achromatic contrasts.

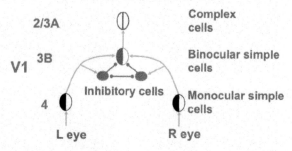

Inhibitory cells (red) ensure that binocular fusion occurs only when contrasts in left and right eye are almost equal

FIGURE 4.19. A laminar cortical circuit for computing binocular disparities in layer 3B of V1 at binocular simple cells. These cells add positionally disparate inputs from like polarized monocular simple cells. Binocular simple cells at each position that are sensitive to opposite polarities then add their outputs at complex cells in layer 2/3. Chapter 10 will explain how these laminar circuits work in greater detail.

FACADE theory predicts that this kind of pooling from all the sources of chromatic or achromatic oriented contrast builds the most reliable possible boundaries from scenic data. However, such pooling across all these brightness and color contrasts makes it impossible for complex cells to detect particular qualia, leading to the paradoxical conclusion that "all boundaries are invisible" and to the need for a complementary surface brightness and color system for conscious perception of visible qualia.

The conclusion that complex cells are part of an amodal boundary system was not well understood by the neurophysiologists who collected complex cell data. For example, the distinguished American neuroscientist, Russell DeValois, and his colleagues Lisa Thorell and Duane Albrecht, published an important paper about the neurophysiology of complex cells in 1984 (Thorell, DeValois, and Albrecht, 1984). This paper showed that "simple cells . . . are distinguished by relatively narrow color specificity". They also noted that "complex color cells . . . responded uniformly to many (or, in the extreme, all) equiluminant wavelength changes. . . . The RFs of many of these cells (15/31, 48%) were composed of overlapping color-regions . . . these cells always responded with the same polarity to all colors tested. This was in keeping with one of the criterial features of complex cell behavior: their lack of phase specificity." Finally, they concluded that complex cells "must surely be considered color cells in the broadest sense . . . "

If complex cells were "color" cells in any traditional sense, they would encode distinctions that could lead to a color percept. However, the very fact that they pool signals from multiple colors and all polarities shows that this could not be true. DeValois and his colleagues did not realize that, as a result of this pooling process, they were providing evidence for the existence of amodal boundary detectors, or said more provocatively that "all boundaries are invisible". Understanding how amodal boundaries interact with filled-in surfaces to generate visible surface percepts was a major conceptual step forward in understanding how the brain sees, and one that took me many years to be able to state clearly and simply.

In summary, complex cells are *amodal boundary detectors* that pool inputs from multiple color and luminance sources, opposite contrast polarities, and both eyes in order to create the most informative boundary signals at each position. Complex cells can hereby respond selectively to—that is, *multiplex*—information about object position, orientation, size, depth, and *amount* of contrast, but are insensitive to *polarity* and *wavelength* of contrast. Complex cells can then activate boundary completion cells that represent objects in front of textured backgrounds at different depths from the observer. I will now explain how this boundary completion process works.

Glass patterns differentiate short-range cooperation from long-range cooperation

The phase-insensitivity of complex cells does not deny that the simple cells that input to them *are* sensitive to contrast polarity, as they must be to detect contrast at all. This distinction is illustrated by the two columns of images in Figure 4.20. Figure 4.20a (left column) shows a *Glass pattern*, named after the Canadian scientist Leon Glass, who introduced this type of image in 1969 (Glass, 1969). A Glass pattern can be made by, say, placing black dots randomly on a page with a uniformly gray background. Then rotate the entire picture a little, and replicate the black dots at their new positions. Now both sets of black dots are in the picture, but they are rotated a little with respect to each other. This can easily be done by Xeroxing a single picture of black dots onto two transparencies, and then rotating one transparency with respect to the other one. When viewing this composite picture, one under the other, you can recognize emergent invisible, or amodal, boundaries with a generally circular shape. Figure 4.20a shows, instead, white dots on a black background.

Figure 4.20a (right column) is created in the same way, except that the first set of dots is white and the second set of dots is black, both on a gray background, so that they have opposite contrast polarities with respect to the gray background. This image is called is a *reverse-contrast Glass pattern*. Now, you can no longer recognize the circular boundaries, even though the positions of the dots are identical in the two pictures.

These two percepts can be explained by the way in which simple cells respond to oriented contrast polarities before they input to complex cells, which in turn trigger an oriented boundary completion process at the bipole grouping cells that I will describe soon. In response to the Glass pattern in Figure 4.20a (left column), individual simple cells can be activated by pairs of dots that are positionally shifted with respect to one another, just as occurs in Figure 4.15. At each position, the simple cell whose orientational preference best matches the orientation of the dot pair will be most strongly activated. Because the dot pairs are rotated a little with respect to each other, the spatial distribution of the active simple cells will tend to follow a circular arrangement. These simple cells, in turn, activate the corresponding complex cells. The simulated responses of complex cells are shown in Figure 4.20b (left column). The complex cells can then activate the collinear boundary completion process, just as in the case of the Kanizsa squares in Figures 3.3 and 3.8, thereby leading to the percept of circular boundaries. The simulated circular responses of bipole cells are shown in Figure 4.20c (left column).

In Figure 4.20a (right column), however, the pairs of dots have opposite contrast polarity. Because a simple cell can be activated by only one contrast polarity, no simple cell can be activated by such a pair of dots. Simple cells can be activated by dots of one or the other contrast polarity, but the circular arrangement of the dot pairs will not be detected by them. As a result, the boundary completion process does not receive a circularly organized distribution of activity on which it can build, but uses its long-range boundary completion process to form groupings between the dots, irrespective of their relative contrast, just as in the case of the reverse-contrast Kanizsa square in Figure 3.3b. Figure 4.20b (right column) shows the simulated responses of model complex cells, and Figure 4.20c (right column) shows the simulated responses of model bipole cells. Note that, in this case, the boundary pattern is more radial than circular.

The Glass pattern and reverse-contrast Glass pattern illustrate that (at least) two types of cooperation are used to build perceptual boundaries. One is spatially short-range and the other is spatially long-range. The short-range process is just the simple cell receptive field, which pools signals from the *same* contrast polarity in a given orientation.

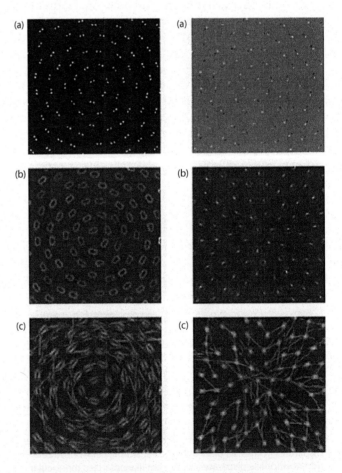

FIGURE 4.20. A Glass pattern and a reverse-contrast Glass pattern give rise to different boundary groupings because simple cells can only pool signals from like-polarity visual features. See the text for details.

The long-range process is the boundary completion process, which can pool signals from *both* contrast polarities to form object boundaries around textured backgrounds. The next few sections will build up the foundations needed to understand how this long-range cooperative boundary completion process by bipole cells works.

Orientational certainty implies positional uncertainty

Given that the response of an individual complex cell can signal so many different visual attributes, how does the brain determine what combinations of attributes should be bound together to form the boundary representation of an object? In order to answer this question, we need to ask: How do whole *networks* of oriented cells interact together to resolve local ambiguities of cell responses by using global contextual information? Otherwise expressed, we need to think *statistically* about the behavior of whole networks of neurons.

To begin this task, let us look at how networks of oriented cells respond to simple images. Since we are interested in oriented boundaries, let us look at simple images where there is a *change* in orientation to see how the brain copes with such a change. For example, at a line end, oriented information abruptly terminates. At a corner, there is an abrupt change in orientation. As soon as we investigate this situation carefully, we realize that the useful property of orientational tuning comes at a cost. Because of oriented tuning, there will be positions, such as the positions near line ends and corners, where an oriented cell cannot detect anything.

This realization led me in the early 1980s to articulate a new Uncertainty Principle. An Uncertainty Principle says that a process that attempts to compute a given property cannot, as a consequence, compute another, complementary, property. I will first state this principle in words and then illustrate what it means in pictures, before showing how it can help to explain a lot of paradoxical data, including data about neon color spreading and illusory contour formation.

Position-Orientation Uncertainty Principle: Orientational certainty implies positional uncertainty at line ends and corners.

Figure 4.21 illustrates what I mean by this. The figure draws in solid gray the end of a vertically-oriented bar. It also draws to the right of the bar a line end. Both of these figures are drawn relative to the scale of a simple cell receptive field size. The figure also schematizes in red how a network of oriented simple cells will respond to the ends of the bar and line.

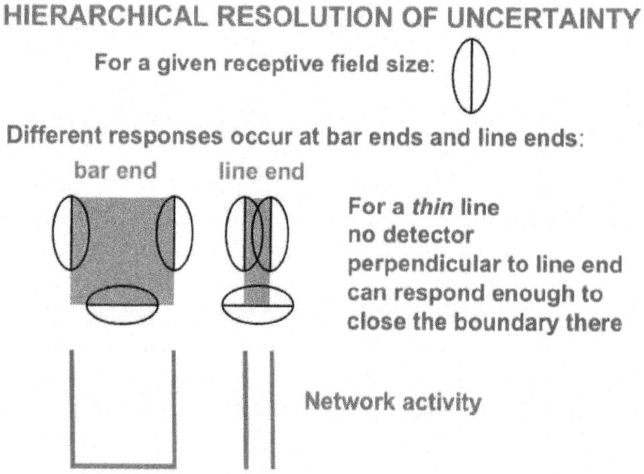

HIERARCHICAL RESOLUTION OF UNCERTAINTY

For a given receptive field size:

FIGURE 4.21. Oriented simple cells can respond at the ends of thick enough bar ends, but not at the ends of thin enough lines. See the text for an explanation of why this is true, and its implications for visual system design.

The bar is sufficiently thick that it has a nice thick horizontal edge at its end. In response to this image, vertical simple cells respond vigorously to the left and right vertical edges of the bar, and horizontal simple cells respond to the bottom horizontal edge of the bar. No simple cells respond within the central portion of the bar because they detect no contrast there. This outcome is illustrated in red by the U-shaped distribution of oriented cell activities below the bar.

The vertical line end is depicted with a width that is smaller than the simple cell receptive fields. Such an input illustrates the type of uncertainty that the Position-Orientation Uncertainty Principle summarizes. The oriented simple cells respond well to the two vertical sides of the edge, but do not respond at the bottom of the edge, because there is not enough oriented input there for the cells to exceed their firing thresholds. As a result, there is a gap in the simple cell responses at the bottom of the line. This outcome is illustrated by the two parallel vertical bands of cell activity shown below the line. Without further processing, there would be a gap at the bottom of the boundary. This boundary gap would, in turn, be relayed to the next level of complex cells. This is one kind of *end gap*. I will call it a *Type 1 end gap* to distinguish it from the *Type 2 end gaps* that allow color to flow in the examples of neon color spreading in Figures 3.10 and 3.11. The subsequent discussion will clarify that these two types of end gaps are generated by different network interactions, hence their different names. Type 1 end gaps show that even lines with perfectly clear contrasts may not generate a boundary that completely surrounds them.

If the line is drawn even thinner, it could generate vertically-oriented simple cell responses that fill the space within the line. Such a very thin line would not generate a Type 1 end gap.

I should emphasize that, when we consider simple cells that have oriented receptive fields of different sizes—as we must to understand how we see the world in depth—then we can always find a bar or line of the right widths to cause the boundaries depicted in Figure 4.21.

Figure 4.22 summarizes a computer simulation of an end gap that Ennio Mingolla and I published in 1985 (Grossberg and Mingolla, 1985a). The left figure represents the response of a network of simple cells to the end of a vertically oriented black line on white paper. The black line is rendered in gray to enable the spatial distribution of simple cell responses to be visible. The size of a typical simple cell receptive field size is indicated by the dark dashed lines, with one half of the receptive field turned on by light, and the other hand turned off by light. Each short line segment that is superimposed over the line and its surrounding white background represents the response of an oriented simple cell in this computer simulation. The *orientation* of the line segment represents the preferred orientation of the simple cell receptive field. Eight different simple cells, each with a slightly different orientational preference, are represented at each position in the network. The *length* of each line segment is proportional to the half-wave rectified output of the corresponding simple cell. The total pattern of simple cell responses across the figure is called an *orientation field*.

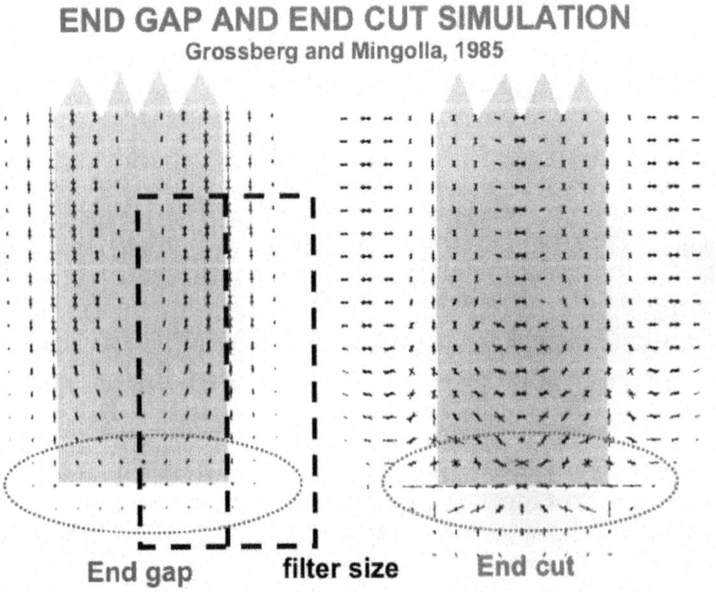

Note that responses are largest at vertical simple cells along the vertical sides of the line. This is because simple cell receptive fields are oriented and contrast-sensitive. For the same reason, simple cells whose orientations are almost vertical respond too, but not as vigorously as cells with a vertical orientational preference. Simple cells respond less as their distance increases from the two vertical sides of the line, because they experience a less contrastive input there. Finally, note that there are *no responses at the end of the line*! This is the Type 1 end gap. End gaps occur in this figure despite the fact that the output threshold of the simple cells was chosen low enough to allow a band of almost-vertically oriented cells to respond at the two sides of the line.

End gaps are caused by the fact that the receptive fields of the simple cells are oriented. The very process that makes a given cell sensitive to some orientations more than others makes that cell insensitive to contrast at line ends, corners, or other positions where orientation changes rapidly relative to receptive field size. Just as in the case of discounting the illuminant, one useful property comes at the cost of losing information about another, equally useful, property. I will show below that, just as in the case of discounting the illuminant, this loss of information can be recovered by a hierarchical resolution of uncertainty.

Your response to this claim might at first be: Why bother? Who cares?! What, after all, is so terrible if there is a small gap in the boundary that is formed at a line end or corner? This is an understandable response if you believe that boundaries and color are processed in independent modules. If, on the other hand, they are processed by mutually complementary and interacting processing streams, as I have proposed above, then the state of affairs depicted by the end gap could easily lead to

END GAP AND END CUT SIMULATION
Grossberg and Mingolla, 1985

End gap   **filter size**   **End cut**

FIGURE 4.22. Computer simulation of how simple and complex cells respond to the end of a line (gray region) that is thin enough relative to the receptive field size (thick dashed region in the left panel). These cells cannot detect the line end, as indicated by the lack of responses there in the left panel (oriented short lines denote the cells' preferred positions and orientations, and their lengths denote relative cell activations). Such an end gap is corrected in the responses of hypercomplex cells that create a boundary at the line end which is called an end cut (right panel). See the text for details.

A perceptual disaster: Uncontrolled filling-in

Figure 4.23 shows what could go wrong. When the line end activates the Boundary Contour System, or BCS, the ensuing boundary would have a hole in its bottom. Within the Feature Contour System, or FCS, the line end has its illuminant discounted before the Feature Contour signals that survive the discounting process spread via the filling-in process. They continue to spread until they hit the nearest boundaries, or are attenuated by spreading across space. If there is no boundary at the bottom of the line, then their color or brightness will spill out of the line end.

End gaps can be generated by simple cells of every possible size. There is always a range of

**A PERCEPTUAL DISASTER
IN THE FEATURE CONTOUR SYSTEM**

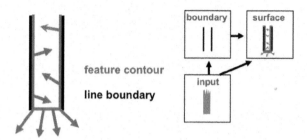

**Color would flow from EVERY line end!
as it does during neon color spreading**

FIGURE 4.23. If end gaps were not closed by end cuts, then color could flow out of every line end!

line widths that leads to simple cell responses with a gap at the end of the line. Unless the visual system can compensate for these gaps, our visual percepts could become hopelessly smudged, with brightnesses and colors spreading from multiple line ends and corners within every scene.

Every line end is an illusion! A second hierarchical resolution of uncertainty

It is clear from the preceding discussion what the visual system needs to do to prevent this calamity from happening: It must synthesize a line end to close the end gap at a subsequent processing stage of the BCS. Only after this happens can the BCS project the *completed* boundary representation into the FCS to contain the flow of brightness and color there.

Figure 4.24 depicts what this additional stage of BCS processing must be able to accomplish. The left column of this figure depicts the thin line. To the right of that is the boundary representation that is directly computed by simple cells and then transferred to complex cells. This boundary representation shows the undesired boundary gap at the line end. To the right of that is the boundary that is desired after the end gap is removed. Such a completed boundary could prevent the flow of brightness and color out of the line end and into the scene, by creating a boundary at the end of the line. The operation whereby the boundary is completed in this way is called an *end cut*. End cuts are visual illusions because they are constructed by brain cells at positions where they receive no bottom-up inputs.

In summary, the very existence of oriented receptive fields, which every neurophysiologist has known about since the seminal work of Hubel and Wiesel in the 1960s,

**HIERARCHICAL RESOLUTION OF UNCERTAINTY
END CUTS**

The boundary system must CREATE a line end at next processing stage:

EVERY LINE END IS ILLUSORY!

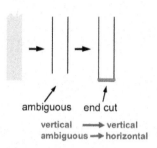

ambiguous   end cut

vertical ⟶ vertical
ambiguous ⟶ horizontal

A pattern-to-pattern map
Not a pixel-to-pixel map

FIGURE 4.24. A brain's task in creating an end cut to replace an ambiguous end gap requires that it be sensitive to the pattern of signals across the network, not just the activities of individual neurons.

carries implicit within it the prediction that end gaps will exist in the simple cell responses to a wide range of line ends. These end gaps need to be closed by end cuts at a higher processing stage. Thus, end cuts compensate for end gaps, much as filling-in compensates for discounting the illuminant. Both are examples of hierarchical resolution of uncertainty, and both generate visual illusions, albeit visual illusions that are critical for survival in the real world.

Roman typeface letter fonts supply their own end cuts using serifs

The difficulties which oriented receptive fields have in representing line ends, and their solution using end cuts, help to explain many data about visual perception. They also help to explain how printed letter fonts are designed, such as Times and Times New Roman fonts. For example, look at the letter fonts that have been used to print this book. Note that the font typically adds little line segments to line ends; for example, at the bottom of a small letter *p* or the bottom and top of a small letter *l*. Designers of letter fonts often attach such a small line, or *serif*, to the end of a stroke in a letter.

There are many possible historical explanations of serifs, or "Roman" typefaces, but one psychological benefit of them is to strengthen the boundary at a line end. As the *Wikipedia* article about serifs notes: "Serifed fonts are widely used for body text because they are considered easier to read than sans-serif fonts in print". Thus, although our brains try to make their own serifs using end cuts, font designers have helped our brains to better see the full extent of letters by obviating the need for end cuts to do all the work.

Computing with patterns, not pixels

The end cut operation needs to do two things, as illustrated in Figure 4.24: It transforms vertical responses of complex cells into vertical responses at the same positions of the next processing stage. It also converts the gap where complex cells cannot detect the line end into strong horizontal end cut responses at the next processing stage. How does the brain figure out that it should convert "nothing into something"—namely, a non-response into a strong horizontal response—at the end of the line?

Clearly, this could never happen if the brain operated on individual pixels in a picture without any regard for what was going on around them. What would stop it, then, from activating *all* locations that were previously inactive? Figure 4.24 shows that end cuts must be caused by a *pattern-to-pattern* map, not a *pixel-to-pixel* map. Such a pattern-to-pattern map is sensitive to the *global context* of vertical responses separated by a gap. This *pattern of activity* is the input to the end cut transformation. The brain thus computes with *context-sensitive patterns*, not individual pixels.

What is the nature of this pattern-to-pattern map? If all it had to do was to generate end cuts, then there might be several different ways to accomplish it. To rule out a lot of irrelevant possibilities, I sought a mechanism that could also explain a lot of other data. I will now tell you what I originally proposed in 1984 (Cohen and Grossberg, 1984; Grossberg, 1984a), which is perhaps the simplest way to generate an end cut. Subsequent work, especially in the laminar cortical models, has refined the original proposal without undermining the main idea. All of these proposals have been realized as neural networks, because this sort of network representation provides a natural computational framework for realizing the desired pattern-to-pattern transformation.

Short-range competition across space and orientation

Figure 4.25 describes the original neural network for generating end cuts in response to Type 1 end

gaps. This figure shows the outputs of complex cells inputting to another type of cell that is called a *hypercomplex* cell, or an *endstopped complex* cell. This type of cell was also discovered by Hubel and Wiesel. Such cells are sensitive to the length of their inputs. They respond less as the length of an input extends beyond the cell's receptive field. This response reduction is due to inhibition around the receptive field. Endstopped cells respond best near the ends of oriented lines whose orientation matches that of their receptive fields.

I have proposed that model simple, complex, and hypercomplex cells form part of a circuit one of whose functional roles is to generate end cuts through a process of hierarchical resolution of uncertainty. This proposal castes the classical neurophysiological discoveries of these cells in a new perceptual light which has been partially tested by a combination of psychophysical and neurophysiological experiments, as I will summarize shortly.

The circuit in Figure 4.25 suggests how two stages of short-range competition can convert end gaps into end cuts. The first competitive stage is a *spatial competition* within orientation and across position. The second competitive stage is an *orientational competition* across orientation and within position. This summary can be stated in greater detail as follows:

In the first competitive stage, a complex cell of fixed orientation at a given position excites a like-oriented hypercomplex cell at the same position. Each complex cell also inhibits like-oriented and other similarly oriented hypercomplex cells at nearby positions; hence

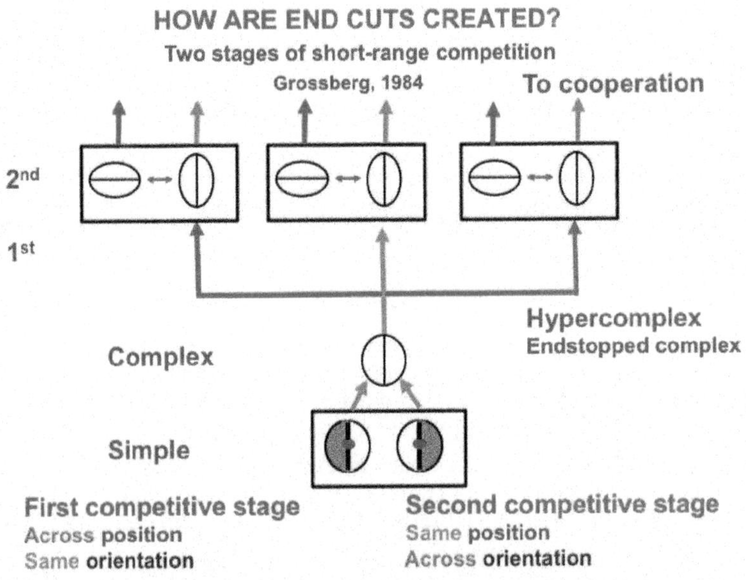

HOW ARE END CUTS CREATED?
Two stages of short-range competition

FIGURE 4.25. Networks of simple, complex, and hypercomplex cells can create end cuts as an example of hierarchical resolution of uncertainty. See the text for details.

the name *spatial* competition. Said in yet another way: Complex cells activate an *on-center off-surround* network of interactions within orientation and across position at hypercomplex cells. The inhibitory off-surround realizes the *endstopping* property that makes hypercomplex cells length-sensitive. This happens when hypercomplex cells inhibit lines that become so long that they activate off-surround cells. Recall from Figure 2.22 that a different on-center off-surround network helps to discount the illuminant. These two examples illustrate the many uses of such competitive interactions throughout the brain.

Yet another type of competition is needed to complete an end cut. In addition to the short-range *spatial* competition that carries out the endstopping operation, there is also a second type of competition that works with it to generate end cuts. As illustrated in Figure 4.25, this later competition is an *orientational* competition. By its action, hypercomplex cells of different orientational tunings, but at the *same* position, compete across orientation, with competition maximal between cells that are tuned to *perpendicular* orientations. This orientational competition is also a *push-pull* competition: It is assumed that hypercomplex cells are always active. When cells are endogenously active in this way, one often says that they are *tonically* active, just as in the gated dipole opponent processing circuits in Figures 1.14 and 1.15. Because the cells compete with each other across orientation, the tonic activity is held in check by balanced competition when no inputs are active. When a cell of a given orientation is inhibited, however, its perpendicular competitor is freed from inhibition. The tonic activity of the perpendicularly oriented cell can then activate it. Its activity is an example of *disinhibition,* or release from inhibition.

Making an end cut by hierarchical resolution of simple cell uncertainty

The combination of short-range spatial and orientational competition can generate an end cut. First, vertically oriented complex cells that are at or near the line end respond to either the left or right side of the line. Consider complex cells near the right side of the line, for definiteness. These cells inhibit nearby vertically oriented hypercomplex cells via the spatial endstopping competition. Vertically oriented hypercomplex cells that lie beyond the line end have not, however, received any input from the line. Thus they are strongly inhibited by the spatial competition. These inhibited cells compete via orientational competition with

horizontally oriented hypercomplex cells at the same position. When the vertically oriented cells are shut down by spatial competition, the horizontally oriented cells become activated via disinhibition. The activity of these horizontally oriented hypercomplex cells forms the end cut. Thus, an end cut occurs due to the three stages of hierarchical resolution of uncertainty whereby interacting simple, complex, and hypercomplex cells eliminate the Type 1 end gaps that are formed by using simple cells with oriented receptive fields.

The right image in Figure 4.22 shows a computer simulation of the end cut that is formed in response to the simple cell outputs that were generated in the left image of Figure 4.22. The end cut has two properties that are immediately worthy of note: The first is that the end cut is *positionally hyperacute*. Otherwise expressed, the end cut exhibits subpixel positional accuracy. This means, speaking intuitively, that the end cut occurs at the correct location of the actual line end in the image, despite the fact that the simple cell receptive fields from which it is generated are so large that they respond at locations that lie well beyond the two sides of the line.

The second property is that the end cut is *orientationally fuzzy*. This property means that cells whose receptive fields prefer several different orientations respond at each position of the end cut. The responding orientations tend either to be perpendicular to the line, or almost perpendicular to it. These bands of almost perpendicular orientations are derived from the bands of simple cell orientations that are activated at the two sides of the line in Figure 4.22 (left panel). Both the positional hyperacuity and the orientational fuzziness have important perceptual roles to play, the first in determining an accurate positional estimate for the location of each line end or corner, and the second in making it possible for line ends to even begin to group across space, as Figure 3.15 schematizes and the Ehrenstein and offset grating percepts in response to the images in Figure 1.1 demonstrate.

Neurophysiological data support end cut predictions

I published these end cut predictions in 1984 based upon a theoretical analysis of a large body of psychophysical experiments; that is, perceptual experiments in which quantitative response measures of subjects' percepts are carefully made. At that time, there was no direct evidence for the type of hierarchical resolution of uncertainty that I envisaged. As luck would have it, compatible neurophysiological evidence was almost immediately forthcoming. Rudiger von der Heydt, Esther Peterhans, and Günter Baumgartner, working in Zurich, published a famous paper in 1984 in which they reported neurophysiological data which exhibited just the properties that our theory required (von der Heydt, Peterhans, and Baumgartner, 1984); namely, although cells in area V1 of the visual cortex of monkeys, such as simple cells or complex cells, did not respond at line ends, cells in the higher area V2 did respond at line ends. A paper of von der Heydt and Peterhans in 1989 reported that these end cut responses exhibited orientational fuzziness (Peterhans and von der Heydt, 1989; von der Heydt and Peterhans, 1989). Although positional hyperacuity was not investigated through neurophysiological experiments, it was investigated in psychophysical experiments by the American vision scientists David Badcock and Gerald Westheimer in 1985 (Badcock and Westheimer, 1985a, 1985b). The results of these experiments also strikingly supported theoretical expectations in other ways, as I will show you shortly.

In summary, although this theory of how our brains see was just getting off the ground in 1984, within a surprisingly short time, new psychophysical and neurophysiological data provided support for key theoretical predictions. These successes showed that, despite its incompleteness and possible errors, the theory was not merely a *metaphorical* brain theory that was based on analogies with other kinds of systems, unlike many earlier theoretical efforts. It was a theory in which identified nerve cells have clearly defined perceptual roles that can be directly tested.

End cuts during neon color spreading?

End cuts play a role in explaining many perceptual phenomena. For example, they help us to explain how neon color spreading occurs. Once one understands this explanation, then it is easy to apply the same ideas to explain many other interesting percepts. My main point in outlining this particular explanation is to show that, whereas neon color spreading seems to be a pretty weird percept, it can be explained as the combined effect of three hierarchical resolutions of uncertainty, each one of which facilitates proper functioning of our visual systems. In fact, all the visual illusions that I have analyzed so far can be explained as consequences of adaptive brain processes. As such, they help us to probe normal visual functioning by calling our attention to the properties of adaptive brain mechanisms.

Figure 4.26 summarizes the first part of the explanation. Consider the edge where a vertical black line of the black Ehrenstein pattern touches a vertical red line of the red cross in a Redies-Spillman neon color spreading display (Figure 3.11). The contrast of the black line against the white background is greater than that of the red line against

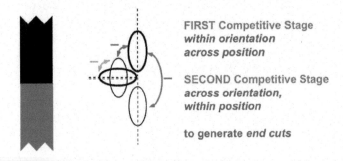

END CUT DURING NEON COLOR SPREADING

FIRST Competitive Stage
*within orientation
across position*

SECOND Competitive Stage
*across orientation,
within position*

to generate *end cuts*

FIGURE 4.26. End cuts are formed during neon color spreading in the same way that they are formed at line ends.

the white background. As a result, vertical simple cells respond more to the black line than to the red line. Near the black-red edge interface, the black vertical complex cells can therefore inhibit the red vertical hypercomplex cells more than conversely, using the spatial endstopping competition. End gaps hereby form where the red lines touch the black lines. I call them Type 2 end gaps to distinguish them from the Type 1 end gaps that occur at simple and complex cell responses to line ends. Inhibiting the red vertical hypercomplex cells disinhibits the horizontal hypercomplex cells with which they interact via orientational inhibition. An end cut is hereby generated at the black-red edge, just as it is at a line end. The line end is, after all, just a special case of a higher contrast competing across space with a lower contrast—in particular, the zero contrast of empty space. The same argument holds at the end of each black line in the Ehrenstein figure.

Figure 4.27 illustrates how, once all the end cuts are formed, they use long-range cooperation to form an illusory contour between them. For reasons that I describe below, this cooperative process also further weakens the boundaries at the end gaps and helps to break them totally. After the illuminant is discounted, some of the red color within the red cross can flow through the end gaps and fill-in the region bounded by the circular illusory contour, thereby generating a percept of red neon color. Red color can flow, despite the existence of end cuts that bound the black lines, because the source of red color lies at positions *beyond* the end cuts, where boundaries of the red cross are weakened by end gaps.

I should emphasize right away that this explanation of neon color spreading is incomplete, since it does not take into account a number of factors. These factors include how color signals are pre-processed before they reach the stages where filling-in occurs, and how neon percepts can be influenced by properties of figure-ground perception and depth perception. However, we have already gone far enough to clarify two of the three hierarchical resolutions of uncertainty:

BIPOLE CELLS: BOUNDARY COMPLETION

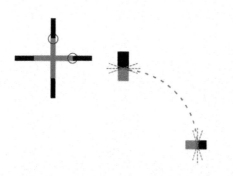

**long-range cooperation and short-range inhibition
complete winning boundary groupings
and suppress weaker boundaries**

FIGURE 4.27. Bipole cells can form boundaries that interpolate end cuts, and use their cooperative-competitive interactions to choose the boundary groupings that have the most support from them.

The first one is that oriented receptive fields create end gaps, which are hierarchically resolved within the boundary cortical stream by spatial and orientational competition at hypercomplex cells to create end cuts.

The second one is that discounting the illuminant inhibits regions of uniform brightness and color, which are hierarchically restored within the surface cortical stream by filling-in of surface color and lightness.

The third one is about the process of long-range cooperation whereby boundaries are completed. I now turn to a description of what this last uncertainty principle is, and how boundary completion overcomes it.

How does long-range cooperative grouping occur?

The spatial and orientational competition that we have considered above are spatially short-range. In order to complete and sharpen boundaries, whether over the blind spot or the retinal veins (Figure 3.4), a longer-range type of interaction is needed. This interaction needs to be able to bridge the gap between spatially separated collinear (or almost collinear) inducing signals, whether these signals are derived from an edge that is partially occluded by retinal veins, or from collinear pac-man edges in a Kanizsa square, or from the perpendicular end cuts that are generated in response to an Ehrenstein figure, as in Figure 4.27. This interaction enables these inducers to *cooperate* across space in order to form an intervening boundary.

Let us go back to Figure 3.14 to discuss some of the requirements of this long-range cooperative grouping process in greater detail. Figure 3.14 (right column, top row) depicts a variant of the Ehrenstein display in which pairs of inducing lines are parallel, and all of the pairs are either mutually parallel or perpendicular to one another. In response to this image, most people tend to see and recognize a figure that approximates an illusory square which encloses a region of enhanced brightness. The boundary of the illusory square is perpendicular to all of the inducing edges. It thus passes through the favored perpendicular orientation of each of the end cuts that are formed at each line end. This percept illustrates a case where the *locally* preferred orientations of the inducing line ends, namely the perpendicular orientations, agree with the *globally* preferred orientation of the emergent illusory boundary.

Figure 3.14 (bottom row) depicts an example in which the locally preferred and globally preferred orientations disagree. Here, once again, the locally preferred orientations are perpendicular to the line ends, but it is not possible to interpolate a simply shaped boundary through all of these preferred orientations. The illusory contour that does emerge again often appears with a square shape, but the orientations of this emergent square no longer go through the locally favored perpendicular orientations of the end cuts that induce it. This figure hereby illustrates several important points. For one, an emergent boundary can form using orientations other than those that are perpendicular to their inducing line ends. This shows that a *fuzzy band* of end cuts exists at every line end. Such a fuzzy band was illustrated in the computer simulation of Figure 4.22. Every line end can, in principle, induce boundaries whose orientations fall within the span of these fuzzy orientations.

This conclusion raises the main problem that we need to solve: If fuzzy bands of orientations exist at the end of every line, then why is the final percept perceptually sharp? Why cannot *all* of the orientations in the fuzzy bands be used to form emergent boundary groupings that are just as fuzzy? Were this the case, then our percepts would suffer from a considerable loss of acuity.

One might at first wonder if it is wrong to claim that fuzzy bands of orientations form at the ends of lines. Would not the solution be much simpler if the brain computed sharp end cuts that form only in the orientation perpendicular to each line end? Then there would be no problem with fuzzy groupings, because there would be no fuzzy bands of orientations from which they could emerge.

A moment's further thought shows, however, that this solution could not possibly work. Just ask yourself this: What is the probability that parallel edges or perpendicular end cuts are perfectly aligned across space during a typical perceptual experience? What is the probability of perfect alignment in a brain that is made out of metabolizing cells . . . out of meat? This probability is almost zero. In other words, if there were no fuzzy bands of possible orientations to compensate for small misalignments of inducers, then the process of cooperative grouping could never get started. These fuzzy bands represent the possible grouping orientations, or the initial probabilities of grouping in a given orientation. The brain hereby allows a certain amount of uncertainty in order to get an important process started, much as it does in the design of simple cells to prevent a proliferation of specialized detectors. As in the case of simple cells, the resulting uncertainty needs to be overcome through an appropriate type of hierarchical resolution of uncertainty.

Figure 3.15 schematizes my prediction about how this particular kind of hierarchical resolution of uncertainty works. Initially, multiple long-range groupings do begin to form along several orientations between the fuzzy bands of inducers at cooperating line ends, as in Figure 3.15 (left panel). This is the price that the brain pays in order to be able to initiate the grouping process with some degree of reliability. By the time (on the order of ten to a hundred milliseconds) these groupings reach equilibrium, however, a winning grouping has been chosen from the fuzzy band of possibilities, and all the weaker groupings are inhibited, as in Figure 3.15 (right panel). In summary, the existence of fuzzy bands ensures a high grouping probability, but also risks a substantial loss of acuity. Hierarchical resolution of uncertainty selects a winning grouping and thereby restores high acuity.

A great additional benefit is also derived from this process. Because fuzzy bands of orientations exist, the brain can group individual inducers in a variety of orientations. Which orientations will be chosen depends upon the global context that is defined by all the inducers, as illustrated in Figures 3.14, 3.17, 3.19, and 3.20. Thus, by not eliminating fuzziness too soon, the brain has at its disposal a powerful tool for grouping inducers into multiple emergent orientations. The computer simulation summarized in Figure 3.18 shows how arrays of vertical lines can generate collinear (vertical), perpendicular (horizontal), or oblique boundary grouping using the boundary completion process that I will describe below. The final grouping thus depends upon the spatial distribution of the inducers.

What are other desired properties of this cooperative grouping process? Our perceptual experience shows us that it should be able to complete sharp boundaries quickly in the statistically most favored orientations, suppress less favored orientations, and manage to do this in a self-scaling fashion over variable distances. What sort of cells and neural networks can achieve these properties in response to *arbitrary* combinations of inducers?

Bipole cells initiate boundary completion

I predicted in 1984 that a heretofore unknown type of cell, that I called a *bipole cell*, would be needed to realize these functional properties (Cohen and Grossberg, 1984; Grossberg, 1984a). Figure 4.28 indicates that bipole cells have receptive fields which are broken into two oriented branches, or poles, that are labeled A and B in the figure. In many cases, the two branches of the receptive field are collinear with respect to one another. A bipole cell can be made to fire in either of two ways: The cell body can receive a bottom-up input directly from hypercomplex cells, as when it represents a "real" edge. It can also be made to fire even if the cell body does not receive a bottom-up input. It is in these latter cases that bipole cells help to build illusory boundaries, whether to complete over the blind spot and retinal veins, or to group textures or shading. For a bipole cell to fire under these conditions, *both* branches of its receptive field need to receive properly oriented inputs from hypercomplex cells—hence the name *bi*pole cell. This property realizes the idea that boundaries form *inwardly* between pairs, or greater numbers, of inducers. This property is one of the complementary properties of boundaries and surfaces in Figure 3.7.

Although bipole cells had many properties that I needed to explain perceptual data about boundary completion, there was at first no neurophysiological evidence that such cells actually exist in the brain. Such evidence was not long in coming, however. The same 1984 article of von der Heydt, Peterhans, and Baumgartner that reported cells in area V2 which exhibited end cuts, also reported cells that exhibited a bipole property. In their experiments (Figure 4.29), they moved one or two oriented stimuli to various positions in space, and thereby demonstrated that both receptive fields, or poles, of the bipole cell must be

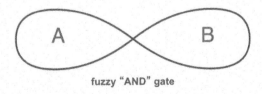

BIPOLE PROPERTY

Boundary completion via long-range cooperation

Completing boundaries inwardly between pairs or great numbers of inducers in an oriented way

fuzzy "AND" gate

FIGURE 4.28. Bipole cells have two branches (A and B), or poles, in their receptive fields. They help to carry out long-range boundary completion.

BIPOLES: FIRST NEUROPHYSIOLOGICAL EVIDENCE (V2)

Stimulus:		Cells in V2	Grossberg, 1984, prediction
Probe location:	●	Response?	
		YES	von der Heydt, Peterhans, and Baumgartner, 1984
		NO	
		NO	Peterhans and von der Heydt, 1988
		YES	
(more contrast)	●	NO	
		YES	

Evidence for receptive field:

FIGURE 4.29. Experimental evidence of bipole cells in cortical area V2 was reported by Von der Heydt, Peterhans, and Baumgarter (1984).

activated in order to fire the cell body, unless the cell body itself directly receives a sufficiently strong input. von der Heydt et al. also showed that more inducer evidence can lead to the formation of sharper boundaries.

Since that time, a number of other perceptual, anatomical, and neurophysiological experiments have reported evidence supporting this prediction. In fact, cells with similar long-range horizontal connections have been reported not only in several parts of visual cortex, but also in other sensory and cognitive neocortices. For example, Figure 4.30 summarizes anatomical data showing long-range connections with two receptive fields, or poles, in cells within cortical area V1, from the laboratory of David Fitzpatrick (Bosking, Zhang, Schofield, and Fitzpatrick, 1997). Many of these cells occur in layer 2/3 of the cortex. The laboratory of Charles Gilbert reported psychophysical and neurophysiological data which support the hypothesis that long-range horizontal connections occur in V1 (Kapadia, Westheimer, and Gilbert, 1995). I will discuss more evidence for bipole cells and their variations as we go along. One type of evidence is reviewed immediately in order to avoid possible misunderstanding. It concerns the shape of the bipole cell receptive field.

A bipole cell with a preferred orientation and collinear direction does not receive inputs *only* from hypercomplex cells which code the same orientation. Were this true, then bipole cells could build boundaries only from perfectly aligned inducers, and they could not be used to build curved boundaries. To avoid these calamities, each branch of a bipole cell receptive field was predicted to receive inputs from spatially distributed cells whose positions and preferred orientations are close enough to the cell body,

and almost collinear with the preferred orientation of the cell. A horizontal bipole cell can be excited, for example, by hypercomplex cells that code *nearly* horizontal orientations, but not by hypercomplex cells that code nearly vertical orientations. These hypercomplex cell inputs can be located at sufficiently nearby positions that are nearly collinear with respect to the preferred orientation of the bipole cell. As a result, bipole cells can fire even if their inducers are not perfectly aligned, and they can interpolate certain types of curves. Our proposed receptive field in 1984–1985 is shown in Figure 4.31 (left column, top row).

After line ends induce fuzzy bands of end cuts at hypercomplex cells, fuzzy bipole receptive fields enable these end cuts to trigger boundary completion within a range of positions and orientations. Both types of fuzziness realize a kind of "real-time probability theory" in which the fuzzy receptive fields represent the *possible* grouping directions.

Psychophysical evidence for these predicted receptive field properties was published in 1993 by David Field, Anthony Hayes, and Robert Hess (Field, Hayes, and Hess, 1993), who described an "association field" with properties like those of a bipole cell receptive field, as shown in Figure 4.31 (right column, top row). The bottom half of this figure shows that several different authors have converged on variants of the bipole cell hypothesis. Notably, Philip Kellman and Thomas Shipley described "relatability conditions" to characterize what types of curved boundary interpolation could occur in response to contour fragments (Kellman and Shipley, 1991). These

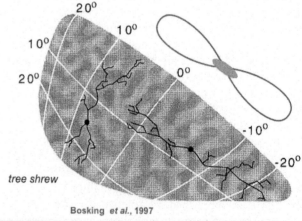

ANATOMY: HORIZONTAL CONNECTIONS (V1)

tree shrew

Bosking *et al.*, 1997

FIGURE 4.30. Anatomical evidence for long-range horizontal connections has also been reported, as illustrated by the example above from Bosking et al. (1997).

BIPOLES THROUGH THE AGES

Grossberg, 1984
Grossberg and Mingolla, 1985

Field, Hayes, and Hess, 1993

"association field"

Heitger and von der Heydt, 1993

Williams and Jacobs, 1997

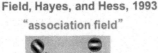

Cf. "relatability" geometric constraints on which contours
    get to group **Kellman and Shipley, 1991**
    Also "tensor voting" **Ullman, Zucker, Mumford, Guy, Medioni,...**

FIGURE 4.31. The predicted bipole cell receptive field (upper left corner) has been supported by both neurophysiological data and psychophysical data, and used in various forms by many modelers. See the text for details.

grouping laws follow readily from bipole cell grouping properties.

Cooperative-competitive feedback selects the final grouping

In response to a sufficiently simple visual scene or image, whose features generate unambiguous and widely separated groupings, bipole cells may be sufficient to generate pretty good boundaries, because their inputs are already preprocessed by competitive interactions that can "clean up" various types of image noise. More complex scenes, however, often contain features that may be grouped in multiple possible ways. The fuzzy receptive fields of bipole cells in Figure 4.31 (left column, top row) can then generate too many possible groupings.

Further processing is needed to choose the strongest grouping—that is, the grouping which is most strongly supported by the total configuration of all inducing inputs—while suppressing weaker groupings. I predicted that this is accomplished by a network in which long-range cooperation interacts with short-range competition via a feedback process to choose the boundaries with the most statistical support. The main idea is that active bipole cells use a feedback pathway to excite hypercomplex cells that are tuned to the same orientation and position. The

activity of these hypercomplex cells is amplified by this positive feedback. This shifts the balance of activity across the hypercomplex cells which, you will recall from Figure 4.25, compete with one another over space and orientation. The cells that get the greatest amount of positive feedback can, other things being equal, win the competition and help to select a winning grouping. This cooperative-competitive feedback process, or loop, is called the *CC Loop* for short.

This description suggests that that the competition among hypercomplex cells does double duty by helping to resolve two different types of uncertainty. For one, it helps to generate end cuts to complete the boundaries at line ends whose end gaps are due to the fact that simple cells have oriented receptive fields. For another, it helps to resolve the uncertainty that is caused by fuzzy bands of activation at end cuts and at bipole cells, by helping to choose a winning boundary among the many possible boundaries that could otherwise form using the initial fuzzy bands. This is the third of the hierarchical resolutions of uncertainty that I promised to explain to you.

We can now better understand properties of neon color spreading in terms of the coordinated action of these three hierarchical resolutions of uncertainty. Each of these processes plays an important adaptive role in vision, yet their conjoint action in response to a neon display leads to a strange visual illusion. I will show as we go along how quite a few strange behaviors may be elicited by combinations of adaptive processes that are activated together by unusual environmental conditions.

Consciousness again!

To summarize what has already been described from the perspective of visual consciousness: The first hierarchical resolution of uncertainty uses spatial and orientational competition to overcome boundary uncertainties caused by simple cells. The second hierarchical resolution of uncertainty uses bipole grouping feedback to generate sharp groupings that overcome uncertainties in initial fuzzy groupings. The third hierarchical resolution of uncertainty uses surface filling-in to compensate for uncertainties caused by discounting the illuminant. It is only after all of these uncertainties are resolved, and boundaries are completed and surfaces filling-in, that the brain can generate complete, context-sensitive, and stable enough visual representations of the world with which to control adaptive behaviors, and to mark these representations with resonances that trigger conscious awareness. My exposition will continue to explain how and why such representations are proposed to occur in cortical area V4, and thus why the generators of surface-shroud resonances that trigger conscious percepts of seeing are predicted to occur between V4 and PPC.

I will now summarize for you several more examples from the large body of experimental and theoretical evidence that supports the theory to further illustrate its explanatory power. I believe that any alternative theory must be able to explain and predict at least as much data as FACADE theory and the 3D LAMINART model have already explained.

All roads lead to a double filter and grouping network

We have reached a good place to review the type of BCS circuit to which our discussions of uncertainty principles have led us. In Figure 4.32, oppositely polarized simple cells send their half-wave rectified output signals to complex cells, which thereby perform a full-wave rectification of the scene. Complex cells activate short-range spatial and orientational competition at hypercomplex cells. The hypercomplex cells whose activity survives the competition attempt to activate bipole cells which, in turn, send feedback to the hypercomplex cells. The bipole-hypercomplex feedback network chooses the final boundary groupings.

This entire circuit can be broken into two basic building blocks: a *double filter* and a *grouping network*. I use the term *double* filter because the simple cells filter the input scene via their oriented receptive fields, before the spatial competition—which operates on a larger spatial scale than the simple cell filter—performs a second stage of filtering. The double filter and the grouping network, working together, help to explain a lot of data, and have found their way into a number of models by other authors, notably the *complex channels* texture segregation model that was published by Anne Sutter, Jacob Beck, and Norma Graham starting in 1989 (Sutter, Beck, and Graham, 1989). I will review some of these data below for three related reasons.

One reason is to reinforce your confidence that these mechanisms exist. Each mechanism is supported by multiple types of data. Three types of data will first be discussed: data about texture segregation, hyperacuity, and illusory contour strength. Another reason is to show you how, once you understand a few basic concepts, you can explain lots of other facts about vision on your own. The final reason is so you can begin to see how the brain can do "general-purpose vision," and in so doing, clarify mechanistic relationships among perceptual and brain data that on the surface seem to be quite different.

These examples are not meant to imply that the model in this form is complete. Indeed, the subsequently discovered laminar cortical embodiments of the model enabled many additional perceptual and neurobiological data to be explained and predicted. The examples do suggest, however, that mechanisms of this type need to form part of any subsequent, and more complete, theory. I will show you in Chapter 11 how these mechanisms fit naturally into the FACADE theory of 3D vision and figure-ground perception, and the even more advanced 3D LAMINART model that goes beyond FACADE and provides detailed functional explanations of identified cell types in the laminar circuits of the visual cortex. These extensions will clarify how an already successful model can be consistently unlumped in stages to achieve an increasingly realistic theory with an ever-widening explanatory and predictive range.

DOUBLE FILTER AND GROUPING NETWORK

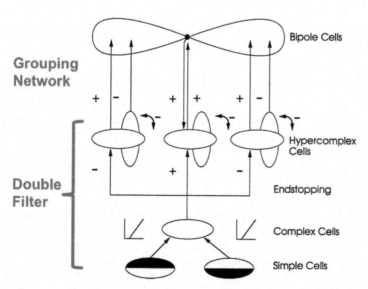

FIGURE 4.32. The double filter network embodies simple, complex, and hypercomplex (or endstopped complex) cells. It feeds into a network of bipole cells that can complete boundaries when it properly interacts with the double filter.

Living with uncertainty until there is enough information to make a choice

The above examples illustrate a general theme that comes up in many explanations of brain data, and that is worth summarizing from a more general perspective. The brain's computational unit is often a pattern of activation across a spatially distributed network of cells (cf. Figure 1.5). Such a pattern of activation provides a context-sensitive representation of external inputs or internal signals that are currently being processed. This point was illustrated by the facts that individual pixels of Einstein's face (Figure 3.12) have no meaning out of context, and that creating an end cut at a line end at positions where there were previously no cell activations cannot be accomplished if only individual pixels or cells are the functionally meaningful computational units (Figure 4.24).

At early processing stages, such a pattern of activation represents the range of possibilities that the network is capable of processing. The multiple possibilities, or uncertainty, in these patterns is useful because it enables the brain to select from among those possibilities the one, or small number, that have the most contextual evidence. That is why this uncertainty is often only resolved at later processing stages after enough evidence has been utilized to choose a final perceptual, cognitive, or emotional representation, or motor action.

This early uncertainty is well illustrated by the way in which oriented simple cells may exhibit orientational and positional uncertainty even when they respond to a straight line (Figures 4.21 and 4.22). End cuts, in turn, exhibit orientational uncertainty as a result of the simple cell uncertainty (Figure 4.22). Simple cell and end cut uncertainty are reflected by activation patterns that embody the positional and orientational possibilities that are capable of supporting a potentially large number of perceptual groupings. Bipole grouping kernels (Figures 4.28–4.31) also incorporate uncertainty, namely the multiple grouping possibilities that can go through a given position with a given preferred orientation, and that may develop in response to the statistics of the visual world that are experienced early in life. By interacting together, these uncertainty-laden properties enable groupings to be chosen at positions and orientations that are likely to represent important scenic information.

Effective choice requires that the cells which form these distributed patterns undergo competitive interactions, particularly via shunting on-center off-surround networks at multiple levels of cortical processing (e.g., Figures 1.6 and 2.22). These cooperative-competitive networks tend to *normalize* their total activities in order to preserve the network's sensitivity to relative input sizes. Brightness constancy (Figure 2.17) and brightness contrast (Figure 2.18) provide classical examples of normalization. In other words, the activities in the patterns represent a kind of *real-time probability distribution*. Probability theory represents event probabilities by a set of non-negative numbers that add up to one. The total probability is normalized, just as is the total activity in a shunting on-center off-surround network. Because of normalization, larger positive activities

can be interpreted as more probable possibilities. Adding these outcomes to a total probability of one says that the probabilities represent all the possibilities in a given situation. Neural activation patterns embody their possibilities in a spatially formatted representation that is capable of being coherently bound together into emergent representations, such as perceptual groupings. Many of the operations that convert initial activation patterns into coherent and selective outcomes, such as the perceptual groupings that enter conscious perception, can be thought of as a kind of real-time probabilistic decision-making, or inference. However, these decision-making properties go beyond the formalism and properties of classical probability theory.

A brain without Bayes

I am pausing here to emphasize this comparison of normalized brain activity patterns with probability theory because various cognitive scientists and neuroscientists have recently popularized classical ideas from probability theory, notably Bayesian concepts about optimal prediction and decision making, to discuss various behavioral and brain data. They have suggested that the variability in neuronal responses, and the fact that prior knowledge or information influences what we see, imply explicit Bayesian inference in the brain. Bayesian statistical concepts are one way to formalize aspects of the hypothesis of Helmholtz that I mentioned in Chapter 1 that the visual system works by making an *unconscious inference* about the world based upon probable interpretations of incomplete or ambiguous data. Kanizsa and his disciples have, in contrast, described many visual percepts that cannot be explained by unconscious inference. The Helmholtz vs. Kanizsa perspectives exemplify top-down vs. bottom-up approaches to visual perception, as two extremes in a continuum. The neural models proposed herein characterize and join together both bottom-up and top-down processes to explain challenging mind and brain data (e.g., Figures 2.2 and 3.1). They also do so using dynamical interactions that work well in rapidly changing environments, and that cannot be explained by classical probabilistic formalisms.

For example, it is well known that brain development and learning are sensitive to statistical properties of the environment. This basic fact, however, does not in itself support classical statistical models. For example, classical Bayesian ideas typically depend on having stationary probabilities, or unchanging statistical properties, through time. The brain, in contrast, is designed to self-organize new representations in response to an ever-changing, or nonstationary, world. Rapid language learning by children is a classical example of this brain competence.

Classical statistical ideas work best when there are large sample sizes in order to define *a priori* probabilities for events. The brain, in contrast, is designed to respond adaptively to rare but important experiences for which there are no large samples, and there may be no prior examples of a particular event. Identification of a rare disease before it becomes an epidemic is an example of such a rare but important event, and one which classical probabilistic methods could easily lump together with other more familiar diseases while computing their stationary probabilities.

Part of the appeal of classical statistical approaches like Bayesian statistics is their simplicity and generality. This simplicity and generality are, however, a double-edged sword. The Bayes rule is so general that it may be applied, as a statistical method for analyzing data, to problems in any science. This is true because the Bayes rule follows from writing the probability p(A, B) of any two events A and B in two different ways and then dividing both sides of this identity by a term on one side of the resulting equation. In particular, one way to rewrite p(A, B) is as the probability p(A/B) times p(B); that is, as the probability of event A, given that event B occurs, times the probability of event B. The other way to rewrite p(A, B) is as the probability p(B/A) times p(A); that is, as the probability of event B, given that event A occurs, times the probability of event A. These two expressions are equal. After setting them equal, divide both sides of the equation by p(A) and find the Bayes Rule; namely, that p(B/A) = p(A/B)p(B)/p(A). What could be simpler and more general than that?

Although this simplicity and generality is part of the appeal of Bayesian methods, it is also its weakness because it does not provide constraints to discover appropriate design principles or mechanisms whereby to model any particular science. In particular, the Bayes Rule does not explain the distinct physical processes that give rise to a tornado, flower, or electron. Nor does the Bayes Rule clarify the similarities and differences of the processes whereby we see, hear, feel, or know, nor how and when we become conscious of these events.

A key question is thus whether Bayesian statistical methods, by themselves, can suggest specific hypotheses that can differentiate different parts of the world. This has not proved to be the case in other sciences, such as physics, chemistry, and biology, so why should we expect it to be true for psychology and neuroscience? Classical statistical approaches are appealing because the brain does carry out information processing using inherently uncertain representations. But the way in which the brain does so transcends classical metaphors by embodying a way to *compute with self-organizing patterns to achieve adaptive responses to an ever-changing world.*

When I review more detailed properties of how the laminar circuits of the cerebral cortex work in Chapter 10, it will become even clearer that the brain has discovered a different way to compute than any traditional scientific or engineering method. Laminar Computing holds great promise both for understanding how brains work, and for developing new types of self-organizing intelligent algorithms, machines, and chips that can more harmoniously interact with human operators while they both adapt and co-adapt to a changing world.

Emergent features in texture segregation

Let's now continue with a review of how the above ideas about perceptual grouping can explain several additional, and seemingly quite different, types of data. Data about texture segregation provide support for both the double filter and the grouping network of the model. Many of these data come from the laboratory of Jacob Beck who, along with his colleagues, has contributed many of the most revealing experiments in this discipline. Jacob came to our department in 1994 as a Research Professor after he retired from the University of Oregon. He was a highly esteemed and much loved colleague with us until he tragically died of pancreatic cancer in 2003. I very much enjoyed talking about many topics in visual perception with this wonderfully warm, wise, and scholarly man.

Beck was a master of showing how textures that are built up from simple but completely controllable features can illuminate a surprisingly rich and challenging set of phenomena. A 1983 article by Beck, Kvetoslav ("Slava") Prazdny, and Azriel Rosenfeld included the images in Figure 4.33, which shows three textures (Beck, Prazdny, and Rosenfeld, 1983). The texture in the top row is *tripartite*—that is, it consists of three abutting regions each containing a different arrangement of features. The textures in the bottom row are *bipartite*—here each texture consists of two abutting regions each containing a different arrangement of features. The beauty of these textures as controllable experimental stimuli is that each one is constructed from the same set of elements, but in different spatial arrangements. In particular, the top texture is composed of vertical and diagonal lines, whereas the bottom two textures are composed of U and inverted-U shapes. The subjects' task was to rank the discriminability of the different parts of each texture. Explaining the discriminability rankings of many such textures is a challenging task for any theory of vision.

These textures illustrate the relevance of long-range cooperation in making such a judgment. For example, in Figure 4.33 (top row), the top and bottom regions of the texture have vertical line segments that are collinearly arranged. These line segments can be collinearly grouped into vertical *emergent features* that enhance the

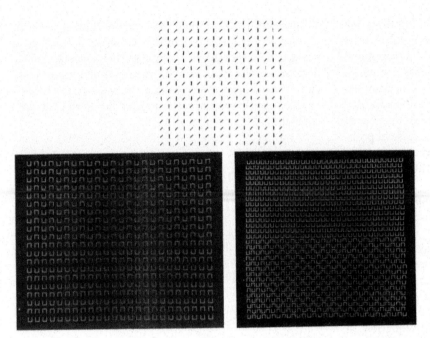

FIGURE 4.33. A tripartite texture (top row) and two bipartite textures (bottom row) that illustrate how emergent boundary groupings can segregate textured regions from one another.

discriminability of the top and bottom of the texture from its middle. This texture provides yet another example wherein an emergent feature can be *recognized* even though it is not *seen*, since only the short line segments are seen, not the emergent boundaries that group them together. This texture also illustrates how *collinear* grouping can influence texture segregation.

Figure 4.33 (bottom row, left panel) is a texture in which horizontal illusory contours form *perpendicular* to the ends of the U and inverted-U shapes in the bottom half of the texture, thereby enhancing its discriminability. Finally, in Figure 4.33 (bottom row, right panel), one can recognize *diagonal* groupings in the bottom half of the texture even though all of the line segments in the figure are vertical and horizontal. These three examples thus illustrate how collinear, perpendicular, and diagonal grouping can all influence texture segregation. Which grouping emerges depends upon the global spatial and orientational organization of the texture elements.

The CC Loop can generate all of these types of groupings. The computer simulation in Figure 3.18 has already illustrated these possibilities. Panels (a), (c), (e), and (g) represent idealized activity patterns across the complex cells that input to the CC Loop. Each pattern is composed of activities at cells whose preferred orientation is vertical, which is why the patterns consist of small vertical lines, using the same notation as in the end gap and end cut simulations of Figure 4.22. As usual, the length of these lines is chosen proportional to the activity of the corresponding cell. Panels (b), (d), (f), and (h) depict the

emergent groupings after the CC Loop grouping forms in response to these complex cell inputs. These groupings include cells with collinear, perpendicular, and diagonal orientation preferences.

The CC Loop creates these different kinds of boundary groupings by automatically responding differently to different input *patterns*. These input patterns define different *contexts* to which the grouping process is sensitive. Such an autonomous response to the data, without any external monitoring, is called in the engineering literature a *nonparametric* process because there are no *a priori* settings of system parameters in order to make this happen. Moreover, when the inputs are left on, the CC Loop spontaneously approaches and maintains these groupings on its own. In other words, it converges to *equilibrium* groupings. There is no external operator who manipulates parameters in order to control the approach to equilibrium. In fact, just one or two cycles of feedback through the CC Loop are often sufficient for it to reach equilibrium. Thus the CC Loop is both a nonparametric process and a *real-time autonomous* process.

Many alternative approaches to image processing and machine learning, notably approaches that are based upon ideas from statistical mechanics, such as the *Boltzmann Machine* algorithm that David Ackley, Geoffrey Hinton, and Terrence Sejnowski published in 1985 (Ackley, Hinton, and Sejnowski, 1985), do depend upon an *a priori* setting of parameters that bias the system to form previously selected groupings. They also require that an external parameter, such as a formal temperature variable, be slowly adjusted to control the approach to equilibrium. Such approaches are neither nonparametric, autonomous, nor real-time. They tend to work best in carefully restricted environments wherein the grouping process can be run off-line under external control at a slow rate. They are not designed to deal on their own in real time with a world that may be filled with unfamiliar events. Such machine learning algorithms therefore provide little insight into how our brains work.

Explaining texture data with the double filter

Many authors have applied variants of the BCS double filter to explain texture segregation data, or to design image processing models of texture segregation for technology. It has acquired the status of a standard concept in this literature. The *complex channels* model that was published by Anne Sutter, Jacob Beck, and Norma Graham in 1989 is a particularly successful example. This model can profitably be compared with the BCS circuit in Figure 4.32. The first stage of the complex channels model is an oriented receptive field, which plays the role of simple cells in the BCS. The next stage performs a full-wave rectification, which plays the role of complex cells in the BCS. Then there is a second filter, which operates on a larger spatial scale than the first one. This plays the role of the endstopping spatial competition in the BCS. All of these stages are duplicated in multiple copies with different receptive field sizes. The complex channels model is completed by a stage of spatial pooling, which is used to derive a measure of texture discriminability that is then compared with ratings from human subjects of how well the textures at the bottom and top of each bipartite texture can be discriminated. Here the complex channels model differs from the BCS. In the BCS, a long-range boundary grouping network using bipole cells comes after the double filter, instead of just a pooling together of filter outputs.

In 1992, Graham, Beck, and Sutter (Graham, Beck, and Sutter, 1992) went on to obtain good fits of most of the texture data in that article to the complex channels model, but noted that some of their data, notably the effects of element-to-background contrast, required an additional nonlinear processing stage. Figure 4.34 summarizes one of texture arrays whose discriminability ratings were collected in their psychophysical experiments with human observers. They suggested that this nonlinearity might occur either before or after the stages of oriented filtering in the complex channel, and concluded that the latter approach fitted their data better. This compressive nonlinearity was achieved by a cross-orientation inhibition analogous to the second competitive stage in the BCS circuits in Figures 4.25 and 4.32. These authors also remarked that "higher level processes may turn out to play a substantial role in region segregation but such processes should not be invoked until they are needed". Such "higher level" processes include the cooperative linking, or binding, of features by bipole cells into "emergent features". Dan Cruthirds, Ennio Mingolla, and I showed in 1993 (Cruthirds, Grossberg, and Mingolla, 1993) that problems with the fits of the complex channel model to their texture

data were naturally overcome by the BCS due to the fact that it also includes cooperative bipole cells.

The two halves of texture (g) in Figure 4.34 are much less discriminable by human observers than the complex channels model predicts, and texture (i) is much more discriminable by humans than the model predicts. Inspection of texture (g) suggests that one factor in causing poor discriminability is the existence of vertical long-range emergent boundaries that join the top and bottom halves of the texture, thereby making them less discriminable. Texture (i), in contrast, generates the same sort of long-range horizontal boundaries in the bottom half of the texture as were discussed in Figure 4.33 (bottom row, left panel). These groupings enhance the discriminability of the two halves of the texture. Our article reported simulations showing that both the double filter and the grouping network were needed to accurately simulate these data. In particular, whereas the complex channels model predicts that texture (g) is much more discriminable than texture (i), the BCS model computes the correct reverse ordering of these textures.

In summary, although the double filter and the grouping network of the BCS were not derived to explain texture segregation data, this model is competent to

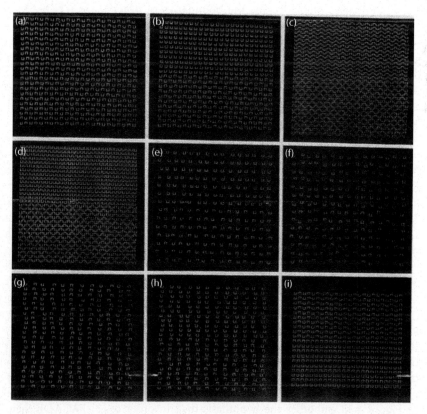

FIGURE 4.34. Some textures that were simulated with mixed success by the complex channels model. In particular, the model gets the wrong answer for the textures in (g) and (i). The Boundary Contour System model of Figure 4.32, which includes both a double filter and a bipole grouping network, simulates the observed results.

simulate key properties of this challenging data base, and subsequent modelers have used variants of the double filter as a front end for their own simulation studies.

The BCS simulations of the texture data in Figure 4.34 remind us, as Einstein's version of Occam's razor noted: "Everything should be made as simple as possible, but not simpler".

Spatial impenetrability of occluding objects

The simulations in Figure 3.18, panels (d), (f), and (h), exhibit an important property that is worthy of additional discussion. Note that horizontal end cuts form all around the vertical line inputs, even along their sides. Yet horizontal groupings emerge from these end cuts only at line ends. Why do not *all* the collinear horizontal end cuts group together? In particular, what prevents the horizontal end cuts at the sides of the lines from forming *across* the vertical lines, and thereby *penetrating* them?

These extraneous groupings do not form because the brain realizes the property of *spatial impenetrability*. The need for this property is illustrated by the fact that an object's boundaries often occlude the boundaries of other objects in a scene. This occurs, for example, in Figure 3.40, where the face and body of Mona Lisa are occlude other objects in the scenic background. Likewise, the cylinders in the upper left column of Figure 3.40 occlude diagonal lines that converge in the distance. What prevents the occluded contours from completing boundary groupings across the Mona Lisa or the cylinders? More generally, what prevents *all* collinear line segments in a scene, whether part of the same object or not, from penetrating all intervening forms in the scene with emergent groupings? Were this to happen, these extra boundaries would seriously degrade our ability to perceive and recognize objects. Figure 3.3b (right panel) illustrates the same idea with Kanizsa squares. Putting lines in the picture that are perpendicular to the orientations of the square's illusory contours prevents these contours from forming *in the same depth plane*, but not in a farther depth plane that represents a partially occluded object, like the horizon.

How does the brain realize this property of *spatial impenetrability*? The BCS model proposes the following solution of this problem: Until the present, we have assumed that output from a horizontal hypercomplex cell excites a horizontal bipole cell, and that output from a vertical hypercomplex cell excites a vertical bipole cell. The model in Figure 4.32 embodies the hypothesis that, in order to achieve spatial impenetrability, output from a *vertical* hypercomplex cell also *inhibits* a *horizontal* bipole cell at its position, and output from a *horizontal* hypercomplex cell

inhibits a *vertical* bipole cell at its position, and so on for all the represented orientations. Then, the horizontal bipole cells that attempt to complete horizontally across the scene in Figure 3.40 will be inhibited by the vertical hypercomplex cells that are activated by the contours of the Mona Lisa's body. Likewise, if you consider Figure 3.18, you will see that the vertical cell responses along the sides of each line segment inhibit the horizontal bipole cells at these locations. In contrast, the horizontal bipole cells at the line ends receive many horizontal hypercomplex cell inputs but much fewer vertical inputs, and thus can complete long-range horizontal groupings between line *ends* that are (almost) collinear, as in Figures 1.1, 3.18d and 3.18f, or even perpendicular if they are sufficiently far away, as in Figure 3.13, 3.14, and 4.27. For the same reason, collinear inducers can also generate bipole groupings between them because there are so many collinear cells active near a line end, as in Figures 1.4 (top row), 3.3, 3.18b, and 3.18d.

Spatial impenetrability enables T-junctions to trigger figure-ground separation

A relationship between spatial impenetrability and how the brain processes T-junctions in an image can now be noted. In fact, spatial impenetrability enables T-junctions to successfully trigger figure-ground separation. In Figure 3.40, the cylinders and Mona Lisa create T-junctions where they touch the horizon. End gaps can be created here which push the horizon to a further depth plane, for reasons that I will explain later in this chapter.

Another excellent example of spatial impenetrability at work can be seen by looking at Figure 4.35 where the pacmen of two Kanizsa squares are superimposed on a background of alternating black and white squares. In the image shown in the left panel, the horizontal boundaries of the background squares interfere with vertical boundary completion by vertically-oriented bipole cells, again by spatial impenetrability. In the image shown in the right panel, in contrast, the vertical boundaries of the background squares are collinear with the vertical pac-man inducers, thereby supporting formation of the square boundaries. Finer aspects of these percepts, such as why the square in Figure 4.35 (right panel) appears to lie in front of four partially occluded circular disks, as regularly occurs when the Kanizsa square can form (e.g., Figure 3.3), can be understood using FACADE theory mechanisms that will be shown below to explain many figure-ground percepts using natural extensions to the three dimensional world of boundary and surface mechanisms that we have already discussed.

FIGURE 4.35. Spatial impenetrability prevents grouping between the pac-men figures in the left figure, but not in the figure on the right.

In summary, as with so many things in life, it is the balance between cooperative and competitive effects that determines these varied outcomes.

Graffiti artists and Mooney faces

Properties of spatial impenetrability have also influenced the techniques that are used by artists. In particular, when a painting is not rendered on a smooth surface such as a canvas, additional constraints may influence an artist's technique. This occurs, for example, in the work of graffiti artists whose paintings were often made on the walls of buildings, such as those illustrated in Banksy's 2005 book *Wall and Piece* (Banksy, 2005). As I noted in my 2017 article with my PhD student, Lauren Zajac (Grossberg and Zajac, 2017), the perceptual psychologist, Nava Rubin, has written in 2015 about Banksy's paintings that "analysis of a large corpus of work by the graffiti artist Banksy suggests that the type and condition of the background wall significantly affected his artistic choices. To minimize on-site production time, Banksy renders his famous subjects (e.g., the rat) by applying single-color paint over pre-fabricated stencils. When the wall is smooth, Banksy leaves the regions previously covered by the stencil unpainted, relying on observers' perception to segregate figural regions from the (identically colored) background. But when the wall is patterned with large-scale luminance edges—e.g., due to bricks—Banksy takes the extra time to fill in unpainted figural regions with another color" (Rubin, 2015).

An example of a rat wall painting by Banksy is shown in Figure 4.36 (left panel). Rubin has compared such paintings with "two-tone images obtained by binarizing the luminance levels of pictures of real-world objects or scenes," as illustrated by the *Mooney faces* that Craig Mooney introduced in 1957. Mooney faces, just like many paintings by graffiti artists, depict their subjects in black and white, as they would appear in strongly lighted photographs (Figure 4.36, middle panel). Mooney used such stimuli to study the development of "closure" in schoolchildren; namely "the perception of an object or event which is not completely or immediately represented" (Mooney, 1957, p. 219). To illustrate what a Mooney face might look like if it was painted on a brick wall, Rubin modified Mooney faces with a lattice much like the bricks on a wall (Figure 4.36, right panel). Such a lattice substantially degrades the percept of the face.

How does this happen? To understand how, let us first consider some of the processes that lead to a percept of the Mooney face in Figure 4.36 (middle panel), before considering how the brickwork degrades this percept. Recognition of this face is facilitated when an illusory contour forms, using bipole cell cooperation, between the chin of the face at the picture's bottom right and the cheek of the face at the picture's middle right. This illusory contour proceeds obliquely upwards and to the right from the chin to the cheek. Once formed, the illusory contour helps us to recognize the face by organizing the surface filling-in process, notably to separate the white of the face, to the left of the illusory contour, from the white of the background, to its right, just as illusory contours separate the white body of a Dalmatian from its snowy background in response to the Dalmatian in snow picture (Figure 1.2).

How does the brickwork pattern in Figure 4.36 (right panel) interfere with the Mooney face percept? This interference is due to the way in which at least two neural mechanisms react to the bricks:

The first mechanism activates the property of spatial impenetrability (Figure 4.32). In the present example, horizontally-oriented hypercomplex cells that

FIGURE 4.36. Graffiti art by Banksy exploits properties of amodal boundary completion and spatial impenetrability.

are activated by the brick horizontal edges inhibit the (almost)-vertically-oriented bipole cells that would otherwise create the illusory contour between the chin and the cheek of the face. Because this illusory contour cannot form, it cannot separate the face from its background during the surface filling-in of white in the right half of the percept.

The second mechanism causes the amodal completion of the horizontal boundaries of the bricks "behind" the black shapes in the image, in the same way that the vertical boundaries in response to the image in Figure 1.3 are completed behind the horizontal rectangle there. All the white parts of the face are thereby captured by the background bricks of the percept, instead of helping to form a percept of the face. This process is again triggered by the boundary system, with consequences for the course of subsequent surface filling-in.

Hyperacuity and spatial localization

Another type of data that are clarified by the BCS model concern how the brain achieves *hyperacute* positional estimates, or estimates that are finer than the spatial resolution that one might expect from the sizes of cell receptive fields. Recall from Figure 4.22 (right panel) that end cuts are positionally hyperacute. The data that I will summarize here suggest that the BCS can explain other properties of hyperacuity as well.

A useful paradigm for probing hyperacuity measures the influence of a flanking line on the perceived position of a test line. David Badcock and Gerald Westheimer published seminal data about this property of hyperacuity in their 1985 articles (Babcock and Westheimer, 1985a, 1985b). In their experiments, a test line is aligned above a reference line. Then a flanking line is placed adjacent to the test line. The influence of the nearby flanking line can change the apparent position of the test line relative to the reference line. Badcock and Westheimer investigated what manipulations would make the perceived position of the test line be *attracted* towards the position of the flanking line or *repelled* away from it. They found that an important factor was the relative contrast of the flanking line and the test line with respect to the background. In one of their manipulations, both the flanking line and the test line had the same contrast polarity with respect to the background. For example, they may both have a higher luminance than the background. In another manipulation, the flanking and test lines had opposite contrast polarities with respect to the background. In this case, one line had higher luminance and the other a lower luminance than the background.

Using these manipulations, Badcock and Westheimer were led to conclude that there are "two separate underlying mechanisms, one concerned with the luminance distribution within a restricted region and the other reflecting interactions between features." Within the restricted "central zone," they found that, if the flanking line has the same contrast polarity as the test line, then it attracts the test line to its position. If, however, the two lines have opposite contrast within the central region, then the flanking line repels the test line. This is what one would expect if the flanking and test lines fell within the receptive field of a simple cell, due to the way in which simple cells pool signals within their oriented receptive fields, as in Figure 4.16. One mechanism that is implicated by these experiments is thus just the oriented receptive field of a simple cell.

What is the second mechanism? The main property of the second mechanism is that "outside this central zone, repulsion effects are obtained independent of the contrast polarity of the flank." This is what happens when complex cells pool inputs from opposite-polarity simple cells before outputting to a spatial competition network. The simple, complex, and hypercomplex cell network in Figure 4.25 explains this result in the following way: Suppose that the flanking line and a test line are farther apart than the span of a simple cell receptive field. Because each complex cells pools inputs from pairs of opposite-polarity simple cells, the flanking line will activate such a complex cell, whether it has a higher or a lower luminance than the background. The complex cell then feeds its output signal through the spatial competition of the first competitive stage, which has a broader spatial extent than the receptive field of a simple cell. Because of its inhibitory nature, the spatial competition has a repulsive effect on the perceived position of the test line, whatever its contrast polarity may be with respect to the background. This spatial competition, you will recall, is also the mechanism that gives rise to the positional hyperacuity of end cuts (Figure 4.22).

These data of Badcock and Westheimer on spatial localization and hyperacuity provide additional evidence for the hypothesis that opposite polarity simple cells pool their half-wave rectified outputs at complex cells, which thereupon activate a longer-range spatial competition. Their experiments hereby provide support from the hyperacuity literature for the double filter idea that has already proved so valuable for explaining texture segregation data.

Further evidence that this interpretation of the hyperacuity data is correct comes from the following striking facts: Badcock and Westheimer noted earlier data of Wolfgang Köhler and Hans Wallach in 1944 (Köhler and Wallach, 1944), and of Leo Ganz and Ross Day in 1965 (Ganz and Day, 1965), that the repulsive effect of a flanking line on a test line occurs even if the two lines are presented *dichoptically*; that is, if the flanking line and the test line are presented to different eyes. However, Ganz and Day failed to find an attractive effect with dichoptic presentation. These manipulations further support the BCS model because complex cells pool signals from opposite contrast polarities *and* from both eyes. Such cells are said to be *binocular*, and are an early stage in processing perceptual representations of objects seen in depth. The dichoptic presentation probes the stage at which boundaries become binocular, and shows that it occurs prior to the "repulsive" spatial competition, and after the simple cells, which are monocular, as predicted by the BCS.

Inverted-U in illusory contour strength: Cooperation and competition

Texture segregation data and hyperacuity data both supply evidence for the existence of a double filter. The texture segregation data also provides evidence for a grouping network like the CC Loop. The next set of data provide additional evidence for grouping mechanisms. They were collected by Gregory Lesher, then a PhD student in our department, and Ennio Mingolla to test a prediction of the BCS with which alternative models of perceptual grouping were incompatible. The texture segregation and hyperacuity data also successfully tested predictions of the BCS, because the model was published before these data were collected. In fact, Jacob Beck had studied the BCS model before his complex channels adaptation of it was formulated, since he was already a close colleague of ours and, as I noted above, retired to our department in 1994.

The 1993 article of Lesher and Mingolla (Lesher and Mingolla, 1993) summarized experiments which exploited the fact that Kanizsa squares can be induced perpendicular to line ends as well as parallel to edges, as illustrated in Figure 4.37 (right panel). The left panel shows the usual Kanizsa square stimuli. The other Kanizsa square stimuli use line ends to generate emergent Kanizsa squares. Lesher and Mingolla tested how the density of the line inducers, their widths, and the inducer sizes influenced the perceived contour strength of the emergent square boundaries. As predicted by the BCS, they found an Inverted-U in contour strength as a function of line density. This means that the perceived strength of the contour first increased and then decreased as the

density of the inducers was increased. In 1996, Manuel Soriano, Lothar Spillman, and Michael Bach reported a similar Inverted-U effect using offset gratings, such as the one in Figure 1.1, with an ever-increasing density of lines (Soriano, Spillman, and Bach, 1996).

Why does the BCS predict an Inverted-U in boundary strength as the density of inducers increases? Why does not boundary strength just continue to increase as more and more inducers are used? This effect may be explained by the action of the short-range competition that occurs *before* the stage of long-range cooperative grouping by bipole cells (Figure 4.32). It is thus yet another example of the balance between cooperative and competitive mechanisms.

To understand how this works, first consider what the BCS predicts if only bipole cells influenced the strength of the emergent boundary. Then, as more and more inputs are used with higher and higher density, a larger total input would activate each branch of the bipole receptive field, so that the output of the bipole cell would progressively increase (Figure 4.38, top row). In the BCS, however, these inputs are first processed by the spatial competition circuit before they can activate a bipole cell, as in Figure 4.32. When the inputs are sufficiently far apart to lie outside the inhibitory influence of the other lines, then increasing the number of lines does increase boundary strength. However, as the inputs get closer and closer together, they eventually get so close that spatial inhibition from each line reduces the excitatory effect of nearby lines (Figure 4.38, middle row). This inhibitory effect gets progressively stronger as the lines get closer together, both since inhibition is often bigger from a nearer cell's off-surround, and also because

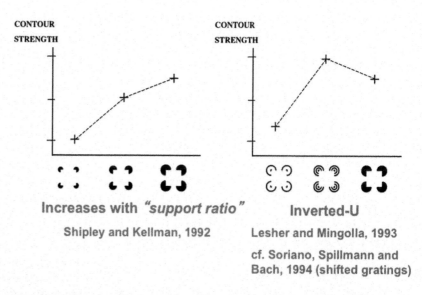

ANALOG-SENSITIVE BOUNDARY COMPLETION

CONTOUR STRENGTH

CONTOUR STRENGTH

Increases with *"support ratio"*

Shipley and Kellman, 1992

Inverted-U

Lesher and Mingolla, 1993

cf. Soriano, Spillmann and Bach, 1994 (shifted gratings)

FIGURE 4.37. Kanizsa squares that form either collinearly to their inducers (left panel) or perpendicular to them (right panel) confirm predictions of the BCS boundary completion model.

COOPERATION AND COMPETITION DURING GROUPING

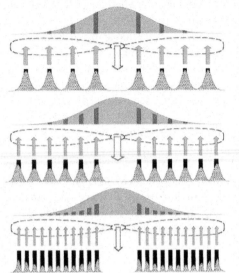

few lines,
wide spacing,
inputs outside spatial
range of competition,
more inputs cause
higher bipole activity

more lines,
narrower spacing,
slightly weakens
net input to bipoles
from each inducer

increasing line density
causes inhibition
to reduce net total
input to bipoles

FIGURE 4.38. How long-range cooperation among bipole cells and short-range competition at hypercomplex cells work together to generate the Inverted-U in boundary strength that is found in the data of Figure 4.37 (right panel).

the inhibitory effects of more complex cells can then converge at each hypercomplex cell. As a result, although there are more inputs when higher line densities are used, each of the inputs contributes an ever smaller net signal to the bipole cell receptive field after spatial competition acts (Figure 4.38, bottom row). The net effect is an Inverted-U in the total output from bipole cells as input density increases, as shown in the simulation in Figure 4.37 (right column).

Figure 4.37 (left column) shows a simulation wherein Kanizsa squares are induced by pac-man figures with continuous edges. Here changes in boundary strength are determined when the Kanizsa squares have an increasing *support ratio*; that is, a large proportion of inducer length to boundary completion length. Then BCS boundary strength increases monotonically, consistent with psychophysical data that Thomas Shipley and Philip Kellman published in 1992 (Shipley and Kellman, 1992). An inverted-U does not occur here because continuous pac-man edges are the inducers at every support ratio. There is no decreasing spacing between inducers as in the case of perpendicular line inducers.

Analog coherence and the laminar cortical architecture of visual cortex

In summary, the ability of the BCS to explain the Inverted-U in boundary strength provided additional support for

the proposal that the double filter, notably spatial competition, processes visual inputs before they reach the bipole cells, and that bipole cells then group the filtered inputs before generating outputs. In 2000, my PhD student, Bill Ross, Ennio Mingolla, and I published a BCS computer simulation of the inverted-U, along with various other boundary grouping processes (Ross, Grossberg, and Mingolla, 2000). Although the model produced the desired effect, this simulation project sensitized us to how difficult it was becoming to reconcile two key properties of grouping using a single set of parameters: On the one hand, choosing a winning grouping seems to be an *all-or-none* property of the grouping process. Weaker groupings are suppressed, while the winning grouping is selected and bound together by recurrent interactions. When this happens, I say that the grouping is *coherent*. On the other hand, the *strength* of the winning grouping needs to covary with the *evidence* for it. In particular, the chosen grouping should be sensitive to the number, positions, orientations, and relative contrasts of all its inducers, or else the correct grouping may not be selected in many situations. In other words, the grouping needs to retain its sensitivity to *analog* values. I introduced the name *analog coherence* to describe situations in which both of these properties are realized.

By simulating the Inverted-U, we could see that the model was capable of exhibiting analog coherence, but it also became clear that analog coherence was too difficult to achieve in the model, given how fundamental a property it is. We realized that something important was still missing from the BCS model.

This analysis and several others guided the next steps that I took with Bill Ross to better understand how BCS mechanisms may be realized by identified cells and cell connections within the visual cortex. A major fact about visual cortex, and indeed all neocortex, is that it has a *laminar* organization: its cells are organized into layers, with characteristic interactions within and between these layers. Neocortex is the seat of all the "little grey cells" of Agatha Christie's redoubtable detective, Hercule Poirot. Different parts of the neocortex subserve all the higher forms of biological intelligence, including vision, audition, language, and cognition. The systematic study of how perceptual grouping works hereby led Bill and me towards a major discovery; namely, how the laminar circuits of visual cortex, and by extension all neocortex, are marvelously designed to robustly achieve analog coherence, among other important properties.

We were able to make this discovery because the BCS already included important brain mechanisms taking place *in a certain order*, indeed the order of operations within the double filter and bipole grouping network. This

BCS model enabled us to provide unified explanations of many different kinds of perceptual data, as well as to explain and predict important properties of simple, complex, hypercomplex, and bipole cell neurophysiological data. With these linking hypotheses in mind, we were able to recast all the mechanisms of the non-laminar BCS model, and their ordering, in terms of identified cell types within the laminar circuits of visual cortical areas V1 and V2. This laminar interpretation was, moreover, more parsimonious, and represented an elegant, indeed beautiful, way to realize these mechanistic requirements.

Thus, the Embedding Principle that I discussed in Chapter 2 was satisfied. The laminar realization provided much more, however, than a prettier rendering of known mechanisms and their explanations. For starters, it enabled me to propose an elegant solution to a major conceptual mystery about the relationship of perception to recognition that had been bothering me for many years, and to explain a huge amount of additional, hitherto mysterious, psychological and neurobiological data about how our brains see.

Laminar models of vision, speech, and cognition: A universal design for intelligence?

The first article about laminar computing, in 1997 with William Ross and Ennio Mingolla, proposed how the laminar cortical model could process 2D pictures using bottom-up filtering and horizontal bipole grouping interactions (Grossberg, Mingolla, and Ross, 1997). In 1999, I was able to extend the model to also include top-down circuits for expectation and attention (Grossberg, 1999; Figure 4.39, right panel). Such a synthesis of laminar bottom-up, horizontal, and top-down circuits is characteristic of the cerebral cortex (e.g., Figure 4.39, left panel). I called it the LAMINART model because it began to show how properties of Adaptive Resonance Theory, or ART, notably the ART prediction about how top-down expectations and attention work, are realized by identified cortical cells and circuits. You can immediately see from the schematic laminar circuit diagram in Figure 4.39 (right panel) that circuits in V2 seem to repeat circuits in V1, albeit

with a larger spatial scale, despite the fact that V1 and V2 carry out different functions. How this anatomical similarity can coexist with functional diversity will be clarified in subsequent sections and chapters. It enables different kinds of biological intelligence to communicate seamlessly while carrying out their different psychological functions.

I had also been working between 1987-1997 to show how the BCS/FCS model could be extended from processing 2D pictures to processing 3D scenes. This extension led to a number of exciting new discoveries about how we see the world in depth that I unified within the FACADE (Form-And-Color-And-DEpth) model (Grossberg, 1994, 1997). One could not take for granted that the 2D BCS/FCS mechanisms could be extended to 3D vision. However, this worked beautifully, thereby providing another important example of the Embedding Principle. One could also not take for granted that the non-laminar FACADE model could be extended to a laminar model of 3D vision and figure-ground perception by visual cortex. This also worked beautifully! Every cell and process in these circuits was exactly where I needed it to be. These various successful embeddings provided strong meta-theoretical support for the truth of the design principles and mechanisms that were embodied in the models. I called this 3D extension of the LAMINART model the 3D LAMINART model. 3D LAMINART has been getting incrementally developed since the 1990s, notably in collaborations with many gifted PhD students, postdoctoral fellows, and other faculty, right up to the present time. 3D LAMINART is currently the most advanced theory of how the visual cortex sees, in the precise sense that it is a principled neural theory with

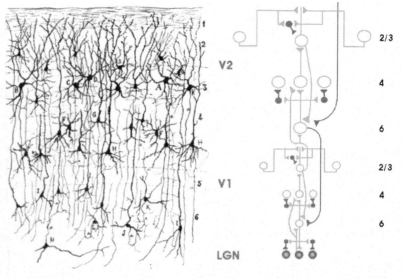

rg. S. (1999). How does
ention and grouping by t

FIGURE 4.39. A schematic of the LAMINART model that explains key aspects of laminar visual cortical anatomy and dynamics.

the largest explanatory and predictive range of perceptual and neurobiological data.

Given the circuit homologs between V1 and V2 in Figure 4.39, one might also wonder: Why are these results restricted only to visual perception? In fact, I had been working since the 1970s by myself and with PhD students and other colleagues on non-laminar theories of speech perception and cognition. With the LAMINART and 3D LAMINART models as a foundation, I continued this work with other collaborators to develop laminar cortical theories of speech perception, notably the conscious ARTWORD, or cARTWORD, model with Sohrob Kazerounian from 2011 to 2016 (Grossberg and Kazerounian, 2011, 2016; Kazerounian and Grossberg, 2014); and of cognition, notably the LIST PARSE model of working memory and list chunking with Lance Pearson in 2008 (Grossberg and Pearson, 2008), and its further development within the lisTELOS model with Matthew Silver, Daniel Bullock, Mark Histed, and Earl Miller in 2011 (Silver et al., 2011).

In all of these cases, variations of the *same* laminar cortical circuits could be used to explain and predict data about visual perception, speech perception, and cognition. And in every case, these laminar theories could explain and predict much more data than their non-laminar forebears. Taken together, these laminar models of vision, speech, and cognition provide the foundations for a general theory of how and why laminar neocortex can support all higher biological intelligence, as well as a blueprint for designing computer chips that can become the controllers in future autonomous adaptive agents, including adaptive mobile robots. Before we are ready to directly study laminar cortical dynamics in Chapter 10, I will first highlight other important properties of how vision works by using the non-laminar model to explain them, again with the view of establishing high confidence that the BCS/FCS and FACADE models embody correct design principles and neural mechanisms with which to understand how the brain sees. Chapter 11 will summarize key properties of 3D vision and figure-ground separation and explain them using the FACADE and 3D LAMINART models.

Filling-in and the Koffka-Benussi ring

The explanations of data about texture segregation, hyperacuity, and the Inverted-U in illusory contour strength provide accumulating evidence in support of the BCS model of boundary formation and perceptual grouping. A different kind of evidence for the BCS will be described in Chapter 7, which discusses how boundaries are dynamically formed and reset to represent objects moving in the

world. These discussions will set the stage for explaining how we see moving objects in Chapter 8. Before doing that, I would like to provide more evidence for how the Feature Contour System, or FCS, explains data about surface filling-in and brightness perception. I have chosen the Koffka-Benussi ring (Koffka, 1935; Berman and Leibowitz, 1965) and the Kanizsa-Minguzzi ring (Kanizsa and Minguzzi, 1986) because they illustrate perceptual properties that are hard to explain without invoking filling-in, and which BCS/FCS interactions can naturally explain.

The Koffka-Benussi ring is illustrated by the two images of Figure 4.40. The left image is constructed from three regions of uniform luminance: two background regions and a ring-shaped region that intersects both of them. The luminance of the ring is intermediate between the luminances of the two background regions. Its perceived brightness is also between the brightnesses of the two background regions, and appears to be uniform throughout. The right image differs from the left only in that a vertical line divides the two halves of the ring where it intersects the two halves of the background. Although the luminance of the ring is still uniform throughout, the two halves of the ring now have noticeably different brightnesses, with the left half of the ring looking darker than the right half. How can drawing a line have such a profound effect on the brightnesses of surface positions that are so far away from the line?

Filling-in plays a central role in the explanation. The line creates a boundary that the filling-in process cannot cross. Given this fact, why does the left half of the ring appear darker than the right half? This can be explained as an example of *brightness contrast*, much as in Figures 2.18 and 4.9. The background on the left is more luminous than the left half of the ring. It inhibits the abutting half-ring's feature contour activities that abut this background *more* than conversely, using the on-center off-surround network that discounts the illuminant (see Figures 2.22

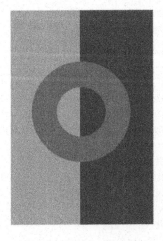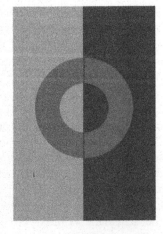

FIGURE 4.40. The Koffka-Benussi ring. See the text for details.

and 4.8). The background on the right is less luminous than its contiguous half-ring. It inhibits the abutting half-ring's feature contour activities *less* than conversely. The resulting feature contour activities that abut the inside of the left half of the ring are thus smaller than those abutting the inside of the right half of the ring. After these activities get filled-in uniformly across their respective half-ring, the resulting percept is one of a darker half-ring on the left and a brighter half-ring on the right. When the line is removed, these activities can fill-in, and therefore average, throughout the entire ring, and make it look uniformly bright with an intermediate level of brightness, much as occurs during the COCE percept (see Figures 4.2 and 4.12).

The Kanizsa-Minguzzi ring

The Kanizsa-Minguzzi ring induces a percept that is called *anomalous brightness differentiation*. This percept illustrates more subtle aspects of how boundaries interact with surface filling-in. The inducing image consists of a central black disk and a surrounding black annulus between which is sandwiched an annulus region of uniformly higher luminance. In Figure 4.41 (left panel), the annulus is divided by two line segments into annular sectors of unequal area. Careful viewing shows that the smaller sector looks a little brighter than the larger one. Kanizsa and Minguzzi (1986) noted that "this unexpected effect is not easily explained. In fact, it cannot be accounted for by any simple physiological mechanism such as lateral inhibition or frequency filtering. Furthermore, it does not seem obvious to invoke organizational factors, like figural belongingness or figure-ground articulation". Kanizsa had a genius for discovering simple images with profound implications for perceptual psychology. This one is no exception.

Why is the percept so hard to explain? To see this, imagine that the figure is divided into little pie-shaped regions of equal size, as in Figure 4.41 (right panel). Each

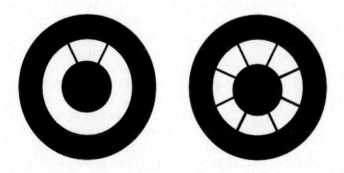

FIGURE 4.41. The Kanizsa-Minguzzi ring. See the text for details.

pie-shaped region has inner and outer black regions of approximately the same size, that are cut from the disk and annulus, respectively. Their effect on the perceived brightness of the intervening white annulus is the same within each pie-shaped region all around the ring, due to the figure's symmetry. That is why most classical explanations fall on their face. The only asymmetric thing in the image in the Kanizsa-Minguzzi ring is the placement of the two black radial lines so that they form annular white sectors of very unequal size. Why should the relative placement of two *lines* have *any* effect on the brightness of the two much larger regions that they bound?

The unified explanation that my postdoctoral fellow, Dejan Todorovic, and I gave of this brightness percept, and many others, in 1988 provides additional support for the model's conception of how surface percepts are formed, at the same time that it clarifies why this display represents such a brilliant intuitive insight by Kanizsa and Minguzzi (Grossberg and Todorovic, 1988). Our main claim is that the two radial lines play two roles, one in the formation of boundaries with which to contain the filling-in process, and the other as a source of feature contour signals that are filled-in within the annular regions to create a surface brightness percept. In more neurobiological terms, Figure 1.21 summarizes how the LGN inputs to both the interblob boundary stream and the blob surface stream. The line inputs to the interblob stream lead to the formation of boundary contours. The line inputs to the blob stream lead to the formation of feature contours. The boundaries send topographic signals from the boundary stream to the surface stream (Figure 3.22) that act both as filling-in generators which enable the feature contours to spread, as well as filling-in barriers that bound the extent of their spread.

In the Kanizsa-Minguzzi ring, each radial line plays the role of a "darker background" that enhances the brightness of both white sectors, just as in other brightness contrast percepts; cf., Figures 2.18 and 4.9. Because each of these black lines is thin, its effects as a brightness inducer are rather weak. In addition, the *local* brightening effect of the feature contours that each line induces is the same in each sector, because both sides of the black line abut white regions with the same luminance.

Given that all of these factors have an equal local effect, why does the smaller region look brighter? This is because the equal feature contour brightening effects are averaged over regions of different size during surface filling-in. The larger sector dilutes the brightness-enhancing effect more than the smaller sector, hence appears slightly darker.

This argument explains the main effect, but it still remains to explain why thin lines, which have such a small contrast-enhancing effect, can lead to a noticeable, albeit small, brightness difference in the first place. Here one can really appreciate the brilliance of the display design: All of the other brightness-inducing features are symmetrically organized in the display, so that the small, but asymmetric, effects of the lines can create a noticeable difference. In the Koffka-Benussi display, by contrast, the feature contour signals are equally strong on both sides of the line, and the hemi-disks on both sides of the line have the same area. These effects are overwhelmed by the much larger, and opposite, feature contours that are induced in the hemi-disks by the backgrounds. Due to the globally asymmetric organization of the Koffka-Benussi display, the line can activate a boundary that serves as a barrier to filling-in, but does not noticeably influence the relative filled-in brightness levels. The symmetric organization of the Kanizsa-Minguzzi display, except for the two lines, enables the lines to play a measurable role as inputs to the boundary *and* the surface streams.

Figure 4.42 shows a computer simulation of the Koffka-Benussi percept that Todorovic and I published. In our simulation we used rectangular regions instead of circular ones, for simplicity. In the first stimulus, a square annular test region with a uniform gray color was surrounded by two rectangular gray backgrounds, one more luminous

and the other less luminous than the test region (Figure 4.42a). The result was a model percept in which the test region appears uniformly gray (Figure 4.42b), as it does to human observers. In the stimulus shown in Figure 4.42c, there is a dark gray vertical line separating two halves of the test annulus. As a result, the model's filled-in cell activities (Figure 4.42d) are larger (larger circles) in the annular region that is surrounded by a less luminous background (in the right half of the display) than they are in the annular region that is surrounded by a more luminous background (in the left half of the display), again as in the human percept. Todorovic and I also simulated the Kanizsa-Minguzzi ring illusion, but this effect can most easily be seen in our original 1988 publication due to the fact that the brightness increment is small in the smaller sector of the display.

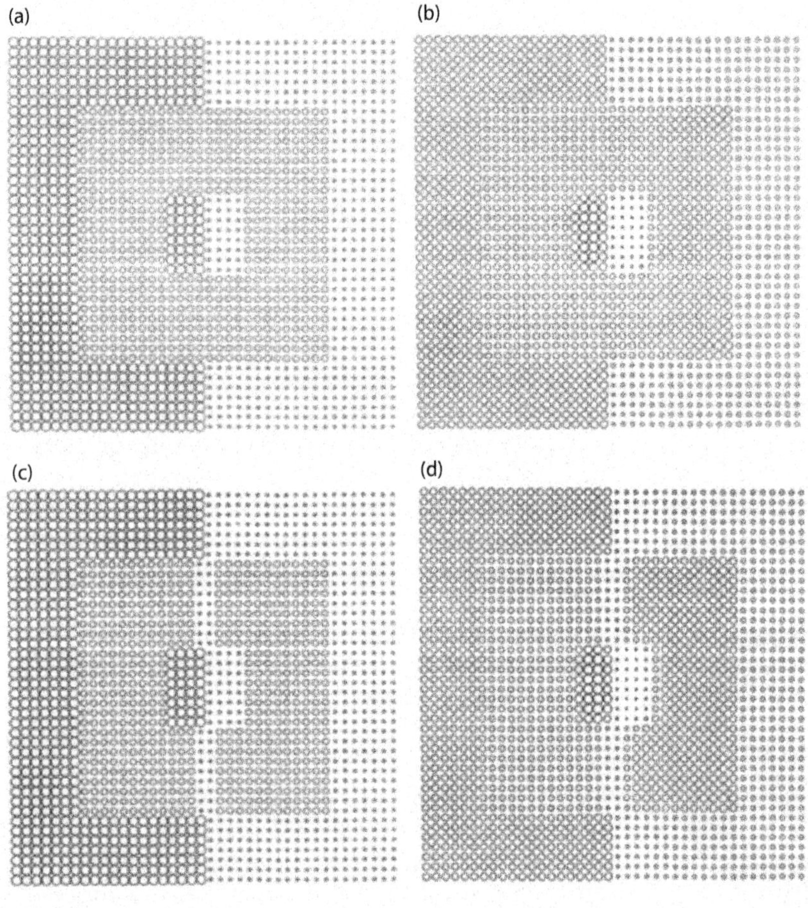

Properties such as brightness constancy, contrast, and assimilation; the Craik-O'Brien-Cornsweet effect; neon color spreading; the Koffka-Benussi ring; and the Kanizsa-Minguzzi ring illustrate that the brightnesses and colors that we see do not always conform to the luminances, or even the reflectances, of their inducing images. My discussions above illustrate how many such percepts can be explained using simple interactions between the computationally complementary boundary and surface cortical streams. Indeed, more recently discovered phenomena, such as the watercolor illusion that was reported by Baingio Pinna (Figure 3.28), were inspired by these boundary/surface concepts. The key properties of this delightful illusion, that visual artists like Jo Baer had even earlier noticed (Figure 3.30), have since been explained in a joint article by Pinna and me in 2005 using the spatial competition of the first competitive stage (Figure 4.25), combined with properties of surface filling-in, that have also explained many other percepts (Pinna and Grossberg, 2005).

In summary, two basic processes that enable these explanations are: (1) discounting the illuminant and filling-in surface brightnesses and colors using the illuminant-discounted signals; and (2) completing boundaries with which to control and contain the filling-in of surface brightnesses and colors. The natural explanations of these and many other data suggest that these processes have captured some, if not yet all, of the key brain design constraints that govern boundary grouping and surface filling-in.

(a)   (b)   (c)   (d)

FIGURE 4.42. Computer simulation of Kanizsa-Minguzzi ring percept. See the text for details.

Seeing the world in depth: From 2D picture to 3D percept

The previous discussions in this chapter have focused on how boundary and surface interactions help to explain how we see percepts in two-dimensions (2D). However, our brains are designed to experience the world in three-dimensions (3D). Chapter 11 will discuss more completely how boundary and surface concepts about 2D perception naturally generalize to a neural theory of how we see the world in depth. This is the FACADE, or Form-And-Color-And-DEpth, theory that I mentioned earlier, and its laminar cortical embodiment and generalization in the 3D LAMINART model. The reverse implication is also true: FACADE theory explains how the processes whereby humans see a 3D world also enable us to also interpret the 2D images of the natural world that we see in photographs, movies, and computer screens as representations of the world in depth.

To make the transition from 2D to 3D perception, the remainder of this chapter will consider some percepts that look 3D in response to a 2D picture. These percepts point to some of the mechanisms that enable us to see the natural world in depth, and to separate figures from each other and their backgrounds along the way.

Let us start with the left image in Figure 1.3. In fact, the figure-ground percept that is generated when viewing this figure follows directly from basic properties of boundary grouping that we have already discussed earlier in this chapter. Said in a more enticing way: You already know enough to explain this figure-ground percept, but you just don't realize it yet! That is one of the great things about a theory that correctly probes how brains work: Such a theory can explain many facts using just a few basic design principles and mechanisms. This fact helps to answer the question: How might such a seemingly sophisticated process like figure-ground perception have arisen during evolution? FACADE theory and the 3D LAMINART model explain how the key properties of figure-ground perception arise from basic properties of perceptual grouping and complementary consistency, notably how the computationally complementary properties of boundary completion and surface filling-in (Figure 3.7) interact to give rise to consistent percepts of the world.

To get started, consider one of the T-junctions in Figure 1.3 (left column); that is, a place where a horizontal boundary (the top of the T) is intersected by a vertical boundary (its stem), as in

the top left image of Figure 4.43a. The top middle image of Figure 4.43a depicted the long-range oriented cooperation that activates bipole grouping cells, and the shorter-range competition that inhibits nearby bipole cells as part of the grouping process (Figures 4.27-4.34). Consider how such bipole cells respond when they are centered where the top and stem of the T join.

Let us first consider bipole cells that have the horizontal orientational preference of the top of the T, and then bipole cells that have the vertical orientational preference of the stem of the T. As in the discussions of Kanizsa squares (Figures 3.3, 3.8, and 3.9), neon color spreading (Figure 3.10), and Gestalt grouping laws (Figures 3.17 and 3.18), a bipole cell that has the same horizontal orientation as the top receives excitatory inputs to both sides of its receptive field, and can thus strongly inhibit nearby bipole cells that respond preferentially to different orientations. A bipole cell that has the same vertical orientation as the stem gets excitatory inputs from only one side of its receptive field, so can either not respond at all, or can respond at best relatively weakly. As a result, just as in the example of neon color spreading (Figure 4.26), a Type 2 end gap is created in the stem boundary near where it intersects the top boundary, as in Figure 4.43a (right panel). Color can then spread across the end gap to both sides of this boundary, as it does during neon color spreading. This process enables figure-ground perception to begin when it interacts

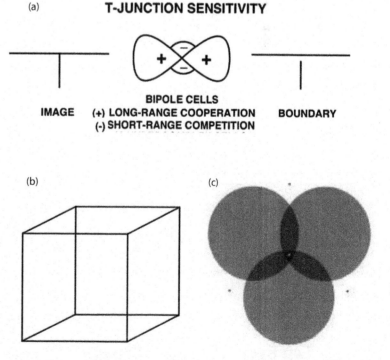

FIGURE 4.43. (a) How bipole cells cause end cuts. (b) The Necker cube generates a bistable percept of two 3D parallelopipeds. (c) Focusing spatial attention on one of the disks makes it look both nearer and darker, as Tse (1995) noted and Grossberg and Yazdanbakhsh (1995) explained.

with processes leading to complementary consistency in a manner that is now explained.

Boundaries are filling-in generators and filling-in barriers: Double opponent competition

As noted above, cells with multiple receptive field sizes, or spatial scales, are needed to generate boundary and surface representations that are capable of representing a 3D scene during normal vision. Each of these boundary and surface representations can selectively respond to a different range of depths from an observer (Figure 3.22). The form- and depth-sensitive filling-in of all these surface representations, or Filling-In-DOmains (FIDOs), gives rise to the 3D percept. In particular, FACADE theory predicts how binocular boundary signals are topographically projected, from where they form in layer 2/3 of the

interstripes of cortical area V2 (Figure 4.39), to the monocular surface FIDOs within the thin stripes of cortical area V2. In Figure 4.44, these boundary and surface regions are labeled V2 Layer 2/3 Binocular Boundary and V2 Monocular Surface, respectively. These boundaries act as *filling-in generators* that initiate filling-in of surface brightness and color at positions where the boundary contour and feature contour signals are positionally aligned. After filling-in is initiated, boundaries also act as *filling-in barriers* that prevent the filling-in of brightness and color from crossing object boundaries, as they do to generate all the percepts that have already been described.

How do boundary contours act as *filling-in generators* of positionally aligned feature contours? Figures 4.45 and 4.46 illustrate the main idea. The top of Figure 4.45 shows a step of scenic contrast change, say at the edge of a figure. Figure 4.45a shows that feature contours (FC) are activated by this edge at ON cells. In addition, there is an inverse FC response at the corresponding OFF cells. As their names suggest, an ON cell turns *on* when it receives an input, whereas an OFF cell turns *off* when that input is delivered to its ON cell. ON cells and OFF cells are often organized into opponent processing FIDOs, in much the same way as the ON and OFF channels of the gated dipole circuits shown in Figures 1.14 and 1.15. The ON and OFF cells may respond to achromatic light and dark inputs, or chromatic red and green inputs or blue and yellow inputs, just as in the opponent organization of the three pairs of FIDOs at each depth in Figure 3.22.

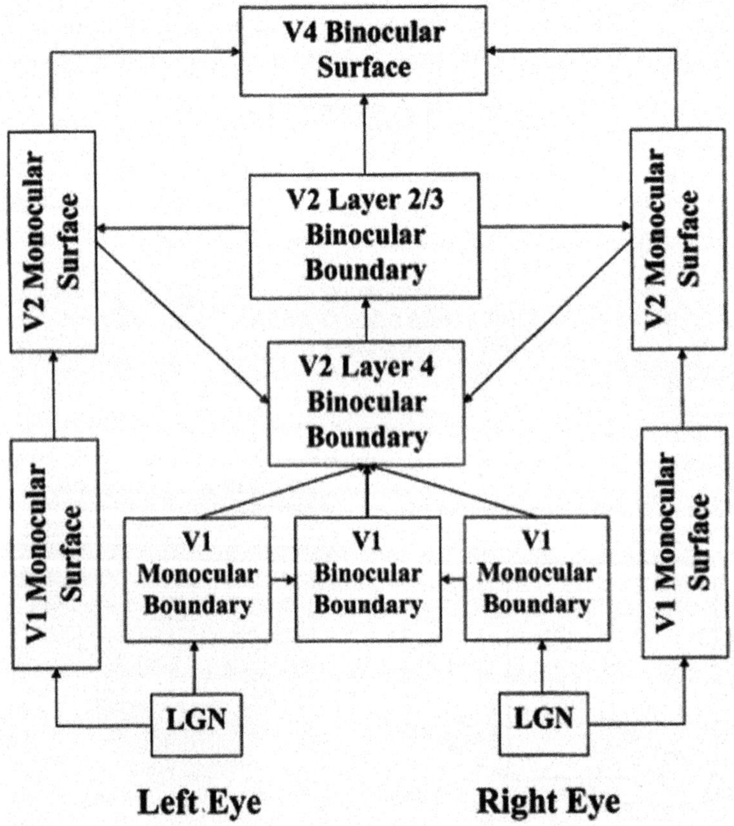

Returning to the discussion of filling-in generators: Suppose that pairs of ON and OFF cells input to opponent FIDO surface representations, as shown in Figure 3.22. Suppose that a boundary is aligned between these ON and OFF cell responses. This is shown in Figure 4.45b in a one-dimensional cross-section, and in Figure 4.46b in two dimensions, where the positions of ON cell inputs are marked by "+" signs, and OFF cell inputs are marked by "–" signs. When the boundary separates the ON and OFF feature contours, then filling-in of activity can occur in the corresponding ON and OFF FIDOs at either side of this boundary. As shown in Figure 4.45b (left column), ON cell activity can fill-in on one side of the boundary while OFF cell activity can fill-in on the other side of the boundary. A contrast-sensitive on-center off-surround network can respond to this filled-in activity to generate output signals from the ON and OFF FIDOs, as shown in Figure 4.45b (right column). This on-center off-surround output network is diagrammed in Figure 4.47 in a one-dimensional cross-section. It is a kind of first competitive stage that operates across the positions within each FIDO.

FIGURE 4.44. Macrocircuit of the main boundary and surface formation stages that take place from the lateral geniculate nucleus, or LGN, through cortical areas V1, V2, and V4. See the text for details.

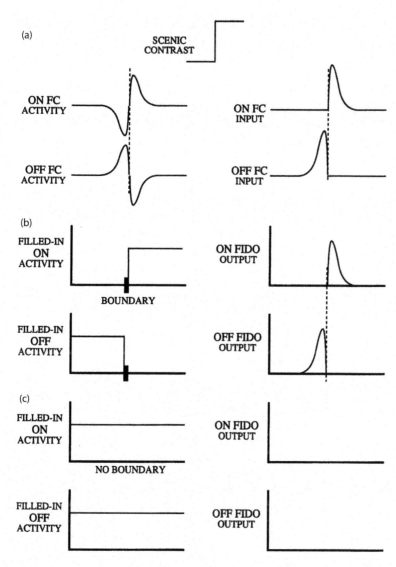

FIGURE 4.45. How ON and OFF feature contour (FC) activities give rise to filled-in surface regions when they are adjacent to a like oriented boundary, but not otherwise.

stage inhibit each other at each position using the second competitive stage. All outputs are hereby inhibited from the FIDOs whose feature contours are not positionally aligned with the winning boundary contours by the *double opponent* network that consists of these two competitive stages.

It is in this way that boundary contours that are positionally-aligned with feature contours act as *filling-in generators*, while those that are not aligned are inhibited by spatial competition across position, and opponent color competition at each position. Boundaries also act as *filling-in barriers* by inhibiting the ability of surface signals to spread across their positions.

Tissue contrast and double-opponent color processing: Lines are thick!

In summary, the two stages of competition in Figure 4.47—on-center off-surround networks across each of the opponent ON and OFF FIDOs, followed by opponent color competition across the ON and OFF FIDOs at each position—is called a *double opponent* network. This type of network helps to explain a remarkable example, that was described by Helmholtz (Helmholtz, 1866, 1962) of how the placement of a single line or curve can dramatically change a percept. Suppose that a gray disk is surrounded by a red annulus. In the old days, a piece of translucent tissue paper might be put in front of this picture to ensure that the picture was entirely uniform within each of these two regions, and that the boundary between them was very thin. Under these conditions, the gray disk can look green, and the percept is called *tissue contrast*.

An explanation of this percept is readily given: Colors are processed by the brain in opponent pairs of ON and OFF FIDOs, such as red-green and blue-yellow. As illustrated in Figure 4.45a, if red abuts gray in its ON FIDO, a red feature contour is generated by its on-center off-surround output network (Figure 4.47). This network acts within its FIDO and across position via spatial competition. An opponent green feature contour can be generated just past the boundary in the corresponding OFF FIDO output network. This happens because, at each position, red cells and green cells compete with each other at each position across their respective FIDOs (Figure 4.47). These

Suppose, however, that the boundary contour and the feature contour are *not* positionally aligned, but instead cross each other, as illustrated in Figure 4.46b. Then the ON and OFF cell activities can both fill-in uniformly on each side of the boundary. No output signal arises from the interior of these FIDO regions because there is no contrast difference that each on-center off-surround network can detect there. However, this is not the case where the filled-in regions abut a boundary because, as I will explain in greater detail in the next section, "all lines are thick". As a result, there will be a ridge of contrast abutting each boundary that is created by the first competitive stage in both the ON and the OFF FIDOs. Here is where the second competitive stage comes in, the one that occurs across FIDOs and within each position (Figure 4.47). The opponent contrasts that are generated by the first competitive

(a)

(b)

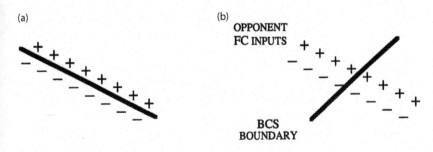

OPPONENT
FC INPUTS

BCS
BOUNDARY

FIGURE 4.46. Surface regions can fill-in using feature contour inputs (+ and – signs) if they are adjacent to and collinear with boundary contour inputs (solid) line, as in (a), but not otherwise, as in (b).

opponent cells are tonically active, but their mutual inhibition keeps each other's activity down in the absence of external inputs. When the red cells are inhibited just across the boundary by its FIDO's first competitive stage (Figure 4.45a), the corresponding green cells are disinhibited there, thereby creating a green feature contour. Then the green feature contour can fill in the disk within the boundary that separates the two images. When the filled-in green adds to the achromatic gray color that fills-in its own achromatic FIDO, the net effect is a green contrast effect in the gray region.

A remarkable thing happens if a black line is drawn on the tissue to separate the red and gray regions. Then the gray region looks gray again. This is because "all lines are thick". By this I mean that, a line that is drawn by a typical pencil or pen may have boundaries on both of its

sides, as illustrated in Figures 4.21 and 4.22 that motivated the need for end cuts. The spatial competition that computes the green feature contour now lies within the boundaries that surround the black line. The filling-in of green color is thus restricted to the region of the black line. As a result, the green color is overwhelmed by the black. The spatial competition that determines the color of the gray disk in this case occurs between the feature contours of the black line and the gray disk. As a result, the gray disk continues to look gray, but may be lightened a little due to brightness contrast from the black line.

Only closed boundaries can lead to visible surface percepts

The above conclusions hold if the filling-in process is contained within a closed boundary. We already saw the importance of a closed boundary in containing the filling-in process when we considered the two variants of the Craik-O'Brien-Cornsweet Effect, or COCE, in Figure 4.2. Recall that, in response to the image in Figure 4.2 (right panel), filling-in could flow around the cusp in the center of the figure, thereby enabling the background brightnesses to become equal, because the background luminances are equal. In response to the image in Figure 4.2 (left column), filling-in was trapped by both the boundary of the vertical cusp and the inner closed boundary of the surrounding black region, thereby creating two closed rectangular boundaries. Filling-in was contained within each of these rectangular boundaries, thereby causing the COCE illusion to occur.

Figure 4.48 illustrates this property in a way that will generalize to 3D vision. Figure 4.48 (top row) illustrates a closed boundary contour (shown in black) that surrounds the feature contour signals that are created by a red rectangular region. Figure 4.48 (bottom row, left panel) illustrates how the closed boundary contour contains the filling-in of red color. In contrast, if the boundary contour has a sufficiently big gap in it, as in Figure 4.48 (bottom row, right panel), then color can spread through the gap and surround the boundary on both sides, thereby equalizing the contrasts on both sides of the boundary. When this happens, the contrast-sensitive on-center off-surround network that generates outputs from filled-in FIDO's (Figure 4.47) will respond only to the filled-in color that is surrounded by the closed boundary. As we will soon see, as a result of this property, only closed boundaries can contribute to visible 3D surface percepts.

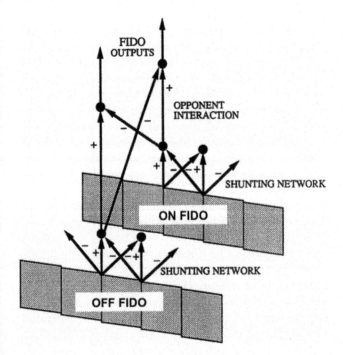

FIDO
OUTPUTS

OPPONENT
INTERACTION

SHUNTING NETWORK

ON FIDO

SHUNTING NETWORK

OFF FIDO

FIGURE 4.47. A double-opponent network processes output signals from opponent ON and OFF Filling-In DOmains, or FIDOs.

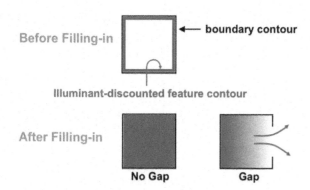

FIGURE 4.48. How closed boundaries contain filling-in of feature contour signals, whereas open boundaries allow color to spread to both sides of the boundary.

These properties of filling-in within closed boundaries will also be used to explain how end gaps, such as those that occur during neon color spreading in Figure 3.41, and in response to the abutting rectangles in Figures 1.3 and 3.40, can give rise to figure-ground percepts. But first we need to understand how, when we view a 3D scene or 2D picture that induces a figure-ground percept, closed boundaries can form at a given depth, while open boundaries—at the same positions!—form at different depths. As a result, only the depth at which the closed boundary occurs can contribute to a visible 3D surface percept.

How are DaVinci stereopsis surfaces that are monocularly viewed seen in depth?

How do closed boundaries help to form a visible 3D percept? I will now describe how this process helps to achieve complementary consistency, and to thereby, as a surprising consequence, enable figure-ground separation and the completion of partially occluded objects, such as in the figure-ground percepts that we see when viewing images like Figures 1.3, 1.4, 3.40, 3.42, 4.35, and 4.36.

This discussion may be motivated by the following type of percept, which we experience many times each day. When we look at a farther surface that is partly occluded by a nearer surface, one eye typically registers more of the farther surface than the other eye does. For example, Figure 4.49 shows a scene in which one wall, between the edges C and D, is closer to the observer than the other wall. Because of where the viewer is standing, her left eye sees more of the wall on which the red picture hangs. In particular, only the Left eye can see the wall in the region between positions B and C. In the Right eye

view, part of the picture is occluded by the nearer wall, which is why the positions B and C are identified in the Right eye view. We typically do not give this kind of ubiquitous situation a second thought because our conscious percept of the farther surface is derived from the view of the eye that registers more of this surface, in this case the Left eye.

This type of ubiquitous perceptual condition has been known since the time of Leonardo da Vinci, who lived between 1452 and 1519, and is thus often called DaVinci stereopsis. Some of the fascinating perceptual properties that give rise to this apparently innocuous percept will now be briefly discussed to make my main points. More discussion will be deferred until Chapter 11.

One crucial property is that, although the region BC is seen only by the Left eye, it appears to have the same depth as the region AB that is seen by both eyes.

From sparse binocular boundaries to continuous surfaces in depth: Allelotropia. This property raises basic questions about how we see, notably: How is a percept of relative depth of the two room walls AB and CD derived at all? And how does the depth estimate of AB get inherited by the monocularly viewed region BC of the Left eye?

These questions are hard to answer if only because only a few places in the Left and Right eye images carry information about the relative depths of the walls, notably the vertical edges A, C, and D. These are positions where the Left eye and Right eye views can be unambiguously matched. This matching process brings the property of *binocular disparity* back into the story.

Recall from Figure 4.18 that, because each eye views the world from a different position in the head, the same material point on an object is registered at a different positions on the two retinas, except for the object region that is foveally fixated by both eyes (Figure 3.4). In particular, when the Left and Right eye views of the vertical edge A are binocularly fused in the visual cortex at binocular simple cells, before their activation is relayed to complex cells (Figure 4.19), their binocular disparity carries

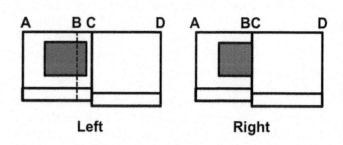

Left   **Right**

FIGURE 4.49. An example of DaVinci stereopsis in which the left eye sees more of the wall between A and C then the right eye does. The region between B and C is seen only by the left eye because the nearer wall between C and D occludes it from the right eye view.

information about the relative depth of A from the observer. The same is true for the left vertical edge of the red picture on the farther wall, and of the vertical edges C and D of the nearer wall.

In order to binocularly fuse such disparate pairs of monocular edges, the two monocular edges, which are positionally displaced when they are first registered on the cortical map, must be deformed into one binocular edge. This process is called displacement, or *allelotropia*, which has been studied by several vision scientists, including Heinz Werner in 1937 (Werner, 1937), Armin von Tschermak-Seysenegg in 1952 (von Tschermak-Seysenegg, 1952), and Lloyd Kaufman in 1974 (Kaufman, 1974), after Helmholtz wrote about it in his classic *Treatise on Physiological Optics* (Helmholtz, 1866, 1962).

An example of displacement can be seen when a pattern EF G is viewed through one eye, with a space between F and G, and a pattern E FG is viewed through the other eye, with a space between E and F. Here, E and G have no binocular disparity between their Left and Right eye views, but F does. If this is done properly, then the letter F can be seen *in depth* at a position halfway between E and G. Thus, the process of binocular fusion deforms the two monocular appearances of F into one binocular percept of F whose spatial position differs from either monocular position of F with respect to E and G. This displacement of F's relative position is necessitated by the disparity of the two monocular F positions when E and G are binocularly fused. During inspection of a 3D scene, the amount of displacement that is needed to achieve binocular fusion depends upon how far away each object is with respect to an observer's retinas. For example, during crossed-disparity viewing of images in 3D (Figure 4.18), closer objects are more disparate than images of farther objects. Thus, different parts of the Left eye and Right eye images are displaced by different amounts to generate a single binocular percept of the world. During Da Vinci stereopsis, the vertical boundaries that bound region CD, and that bound and are within region AC in the Left and Right eye images of Figure 4.49 are deformed by different amounts in order to be binocularly fused.

Given that *only* these boundaries carry depth information, because the rest of the images have uniform contrast, how do the surface walls inherit the relative depth that is computed by these boundaries? How does such a small part of the image control the depth percepts of all the surfaces in the image?!

Just as important: How does the *monocularly* viewed region BC of the Left eye view, which contains no disparity information, inherit the depth that is computed from the *binocularly* viewed boundaries in region BC?

Remarkably, both answers follow from the properties whereby boundaries act as filling-in generators, and whereby only surfaces that fill-in within closed boundaries may contribute to 3D percepts. In particular, we need to describe how

these depth-selective boundaries capture surface brightness and color at the corresponding depth-selective surface FIDOs (Figure 3.22), which thereby fill-in the depths that they inherit from their generative boundaries.

These challenges are vividly on display in the DaVinci stereopsis example of Figure 4.49. There, only the left vertical boundary of the red picture is binocularly viewed. The right vertical boundary of the red picture is only monocularly viewed, because it falls within region BC. In addition, the two horizontal boundaries at the top and bottom of the red picture do not generate strong binocular disparities because they contain no distinctive features that can unambiguously be binocularly fused across the Left and Right eye views. In summary, only the left vertical boundary contains information about the depth of the red picture. We can now put together the properties that are summarized in Figures 4.45–4.49 to understand how figure-ground separation is initiated, once one more crucial fact is added. This is now done below.

How are closed and open boundaries created in depth-selective boundary representations?

Suppose for definiteness that the binocular disparity of the left vertical boundary of the red picture in Figure 4.49 assigns it to boundaries that are selective for Depth 1. This then creates a binocular boundary at the complex cells of V1. This is the blue boundary in Figure 4.50. However, none of the other boundaries of the red picture in Figure 4.49 generate strong disparity signals, because they are either horizontal boundaries or a monocularly viewed vertical boundary. These are the inverted-C shaped black boundaries in Figure 4.50. Given that only one of the boundaries of the figure carries depth information, *how is a closed boundary generated at any depth*? In particular, how does the brain decide to what depth, or depths, the other boundaries should be assigned?

I predicted in 1994 that these boundaries are assigned to *all* depths along their lines of sight in the V2 thin stripes where boundaries are computed. Figure 4.50 shows how the inverted-C-shaped black boundaries are projected to both Depth 1 and Depth 2. For simplicity of illustration, Figure 4.50 shows only one other depth, Depth 2, but the argument holds for an arbitrary finite number of depth planes. The projection along the lines of sight of the black boundaries creates a closed boundary only at Depth 1, which combines the binocular blue boundary with the monocular black boundaries. Open boundaries occur at all other depths. My colleagues Arash Yazdanbakhsh and

HOW ARE CLOSED 3D BOUNDARIES FORMED?

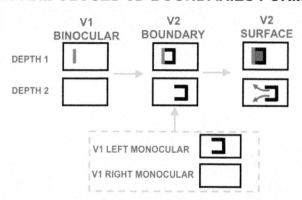

Prediction: Monocular and horizontal boundaries are added to ALL binocular boundaries along the line of sight

Regions that are surrounded by a CLOSED boundary can *depth-selectively* contain filling-in of lightness and color signals

FIGURE 4.50. This figure illustrates how a closed boundary can be formed in a prescribed depth due to addition of binocular and monocular boundaries, but not at other depths.

Takeo Watanabe published psychophysical experiments in 2004 that support this prediction (Yazdanbakhsh and Watanabe, 2004).

The mechanisms described in Figures 4.45-4.49 now enable output signals to be created only at the borders of the filled-in closed rectangular surface representation at Depth 1 of V2, which is shown in red in Figure 4.50, since the red color can spill out of the open boundaries at all other depths in V2, notably Depth 2, where the contrast-sensitive network in Figure 4.47 cannot respond to it.

Surface contours realize complementary consistency and begin figure-ground separation

These depth-selective output signals from filled-in V2 surfaces that are surrounded by closed boundaries hold the key to understanding how complementary consistency and figure-ground separation are achieved. This is because, in addition to the *boundary-to-surface* interactions whereby boundaries act as filling-in generators and barriers (Figure 3.22), there are also *surface-to-boundary* feedback interactions from the filled-in surfaces that are surrounded by closed boundaries in the V2 thin stripes to the depth-selective boundaries in the V2 interstripes (Figure 4.51). They are called *surface contour* signals because they are generated at the bounding contours of

filled-in surface regions. Surface contours are generated by the contrast-sensitive on-center off-surround network shown in Figure 4.47, which generates output signals only in response to filled-in surfaces that are surrounded by a closed boundary, as shown in Figure 4.48.

It cannot be overemphasized that surface contours form at these positions because the outputs from the filled-in surface regions are generated by a *contrast-sensitive* on-center off-surround network (Figure 4.47). The inhibitory connections of this network's off-surround act *across position* and *within depth*—and thus within a FIDO—to generate output signals only at positions where the filled-in contrasts change rapidly across space. These are precisely the positions where boundaries, acting as filling-in barriers, block the spread of the filling-in process (Figure 4.48, bottom row, left panel). As a result, the positions of surface contours and of the closed boundaries that surround the filled-in surface regions to which they react are the same.

Surface contour signals are not, however, generated at boundary positions near a big enough boundary gap, such as an end gap, because brightnesses and colors can then spread across the gap and equalize on both sides of the boundary, thereby causing zero contrast across the boundary, which generates no output from the contrast-sensitive network (Figure 4.48, bottom row, right panel).

Surface contour output signals generate feedback signals to the boundary representations that induced them. In Figure 4.51, the positions that activate surface contour signals are depicted by the blue rectangle that surrounds the filled-in red rectangular region. The surface contour signals deliver feedback to their generative boundary representations via another on-center off-surround network: The on-center signals, which are marked in green, strengthen the boundaries that generated the successfully filled-in surfaces. The off-surround signals, which are marked in red, inhibit redundant boundaries at the same positions but farther depths. This inhibitory process is called *boundary pruning*. In other words, the inhibitory surface-to-boundary connections of this network act *within position* and *across depth*. By inhibiting boundaries from near to far, this off-surround provides an example of an organizational principle that is called the *asymmetry between near and far*, whose general significance for generates percepts of occluding and occluded objects in depth will be further discussed in Chapters 8 and 11.

Surface contour signals achieve complementary consistency by strengthening consistent boundaries and pruning redundant boundaries at the same positions. Only "good" boundaries—the ones that can contain the filling-in process by being closed—are strengthened. The

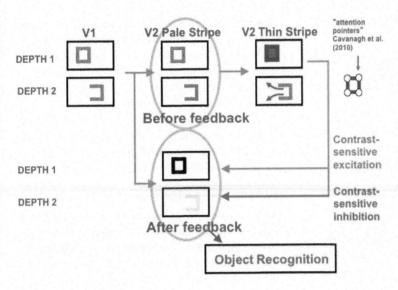

FIGURE 4.51. The same feedback circuit that ensures complementary consistency between boundaries and surfaces also, automatically, initiates figure-ground separation! See the text for details.

inhibited incomplete boundaries can then contribute to neither seeing nor recognition in the final percept. Eliminating these incomplete boundaries enables the brain to generate 3D percepts that are uncluttered with irrelevant boundary fragments.

This benefit is illustrated by the computer simulation shown in Figure 4.52 of how the 3D LAMINART model can extract a 3D percept from a random dot stereogram. Random dot stereograms were popularized through the influential 1971 book on *Foundations of Cyclopean Perception* by Bela Julesz (Julesz, 1971). They show how binocular disparity contributes to depth perception when all other cues to depth are eliminated.

In a typical random dot stereogram, two images are created, each composed of random dots (Figure 4.52, top row). One image is shown to each eye. The second image is constructed from the first by shifting a region of dots in the first image within the second image, removing the random dots that are covered in this way, and adding more random dots in the space created by the shift. One typically shifts a region of dots that has the shape of a familiar object. The shift creates a binocular disparity between the shape in the two images, but this cannot be seen in either image alone because it is composed of random dots. However, when each eye looks at one of the random dot images, the

brain can binocularly fuse them, and can vividly see the hidden shape in depth. This property is illustrated by the computer simulation shown in Figure 4.52 (bottom row) that was published with my PhD student Liang Fang in 2009 using the 3D LAMINART model (Fang and Grossberg, 2009). The hidden image consists of a letter L in the fixation plane and an upside-down L in the near plane. The rest of the random dots are relegated to the background in the far plane.

Boundary pruning at farther depths enables figure-ground separation

We can now see how ensuring complementary consistency *automatically* initiates figure-ground separation! Figure-ground separation is ensured by eliminating redundant boundaries at farther depths via boundary pruning. For example, the image of three rectangles in Figure 1.3 (left column) contains four T-junctions where end gaps will form in the brain of an observer. After end gaps form, only the horizontal rectangle

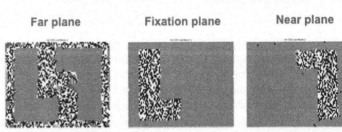

FIGURE 4.52. An example of how the 3D LAMINART model can transform the two monocular images of the random dot stereogram in the top row into the three depth-separated surfaces representations in the bottom row.

is surrounded by a closed boundary at its depth, so only the bounding contours of the horizontal rectangle will generate surface contour feedback signals that strengthen these boundaries. These surface contours use the near-to-far inhibition shown in Figure 4.51 to eliminate redundant copies of the boundaries of the horizontal rectangle at farther depths. The two pairs of collinear vertical boundaries due to the T stems then have no obstructing horizontal boundaries between them at these farther depths. Each pair of vertical boundaries at a farther depth can therefore use bipole grouping cells (Figures 4.33-4.40) to complete a vertical boundary between them (Figure 1.3, right column), hereby forming two complete vertical boundaries that are part of a closed vertically oriented rectangle at that depth. Because this boundary completion occurs at a farther depth, the completed vertical rectangle is recognized to lie "behind" the horizontal rectangle.

Why are the occluded parts of the vertical rectangle's boundary invisible? These are the dashed vertical lines in Figure 1.3 (right column). This is easy to explain, because *all* boundaries are invisible! The harder part is to explain why only the *unoccluded* surface regions of opaque objects are visible, such as the surfaces in Figure 1.3 (left column). These visible surface percepts are predicted to occur in cortical area V4, whereas cortical area V2 is proposed to generate amodal recognition of the occluded parts of the scene. An explanation of how, and from a functional perspective *why*, this distinction between amodal recognition by V2 and modal, or visible, seeing and recognition by V4 will be explained in greater detail later in this chapter. The bottom line is to answer a basic question that takes awhile to realize is even an issue worth considering; namely, why do not *all* occluding objects look transparent? If they did, that property could strongly influence where we look and reach. Preventing all occluders from looking transparent requires a hierarchical resolution of uncertainty that enables V4, but not V2, to support conscious visual qualia that can be used to direct looking and reaching behaviors.

We can now begin to understand how basic mechanisms of perceptual grouping using bipole cells, and of complementary consistency using surface contours, can give rise to properties of figure-ground perception, notably 3D percepts of partially occluded objects in response to 2D pictures. Many other challenging percepts can also be explained using this foundation. In particular, it can be used to explain temporally bistable percepts, or percepts that switch intermittently through time, between pairs of 3D percepts that are seen in response to the same 2D image. A classical example of this is the 3D Necker cube percepts that oscillate in response to the 2D picture in Figure 4.43b, and that were reported by L. A. Necker in 1832 (Necker, 1832). Focusing spatial attention upon one or another edge of the image can encourage the 3D percept in which this edge looks closer. My PhD student Guru Swaminathan and I explained and simulated bistable 3D percepts of the Necker cube in 2004 (Grossberg and Swaminathan, 2004). A related percept can be seen by looking at the 2D picture of three overlapping disks in Figure 4.43c. Here, paying attention to one disk makes that disk look nearer and brighter, as Peter Tse reported in 2005 (Tse, 2005). This is also an example of bistable transparency, because one can "see through" the closer disk to the overlapping disks behind it. It was a delightful coincidence that an explanation and computer simulation of such bistable transparency percepts, including the correlation between looking nearer and brighter, was given with my PhD student Arash Yazdanbakhsh in 2005 in an article that was in press in the same journal, *Vision Research*, as the one in which Peter Tse's article was also simultaneously in press (Grossberg and Yazdanbakhsh, 2005). I will discuss how these percepts arise in greater detail later in this chapter.

Proximity-luminance covariance: Why do brighter Kanizsa squares look closer?

Many other paradoxical percepts can be explained by the neural circuits that we have already discussed. For example, the boundary pruning mechanisms that are summarized in Figure 4.51 also help to explain properties of *proximity-luminance covariance* as part of the figure-ground separation process. Proximity-luminance covariance is the property that brighter objects often look closer. As I noted in Chapter 1, the phrase "proximity-luminance covariance" was used in insightful psychophysical studies of Barry Schwartz and George Sperling in 1983 (Schwartz and Sperling, 1983), and again by Barbara Dosher, Sperling, and Stephen Wurst in 1986 (Dosher, Sperling, and Wurst, 1986), but phenomena of this type were known quite a bit before then.

Indeed, this correlation between brightness and depth percepts is an excellent example of the fact that visual properties are not computed in independent modules, but rather in parallel cortical streams (Figure 1.21) that obey computationally complementary properties (Figure 3.7). For example, a Kanizsa square can be made to look brighter by adding more inducers of the emergent illusory square. This can be done, for example, by increasing the length of the pac-man inducers, as in Figure 4.37 (left panel), or by adding some extra lines perpendicular to the illusory square between pairs of pac-men, as when one compares Figure 3.3a with Figure 3.3c. Remarkably, when this is done carefully under laboratory conditions, as the Kanizsa square looks brighter, it also looks closer. This property was reported by the great Gaetano Kanizsa in 1955 and 1974 (Kanizsa, 1955, 1974), by Drake Bradley and Susan Dumais in 1984 (Bradley and Dumais, 1984), and by Franco Purghé and Stanley Coren in 1992 (Purghé and Coren, 1992). That is, a brighter square appears to be even closer to the observer than its inducing pac-men, which are perceived to be partially occluded circular disks that lie behind the square. Why do brighter Kanizsa squares look closer?

One might at first be unimpressed by the value of explaining such an odd fact. However, just as in physics, where Einstein's Generality Relativity Theory was able to quantitatively explain the precession of the perihelion of the planet Mercury in a way that Newton's otherwise epochal theory of planetary orbits could not, the ability to naturally explain such "anomalies" provides the kind of evidence that argues for one theory above another.

As it turns out, I have already told you enough to qualitatively understand how this example of proximity-luminance covariance works. It follows directly from the boundary pruning by surface contour feedback signals (Figure 4.51) that achieves complementary consistency and initiates figure-ground perception. As I noted above, boundary pruning signals are delivered to the boundary representations by an on-center off-surround network whose inhibitory surface-to-boundary connections act *within position* and *across depth*. Said in another way, these inhibitory signals are part of an off-surround network whose strength decreases with the distance from the source cell, where this "distance" is a difference in depth (Figure 4.53). The strength of the inhibitory surface contour signal thus *decreases* as the depth difference *increases* between the surface that generates the signal and its recipient boundaries.

How do these inhibitory signals cause a brighter Kanizsa square to look even closer? We first must note that a Kanizsa square's perceived brightness is an emergent property that is determined after *all* brightness and darkness inducers fill-in within the square, as illustrated by the computer simulations in Figures 3.8 and 3.9. The emergent brightness of the square as a whole can only then influence the square's perceived depth. In particular, the computation that leads the square surface to appear closer can only occur *after* filling-in occurs within the surface Filling-In DOmains, or FIDOs. Within FACADE theory, the perceived depth of a surface is controlled by the boundaries that act as its filling-in generators and barriers (Figure 3.22), since these boundaries select the depth-selective FIDOs within which filling-in can occur, and thereby achieve surface capture. These boundaries, in turn, are themselves strengthened after surface-to-boundary surface contour feedback eliminates redundant boundaries that cannot support successful filling-in (Figure 4.51). These surface contour feedback signals have precisely the properties that are needed to explain why brighter Kanizsa squares look closer!

In particular, the brightness of a Kanizsa square increases with the amplitude of the filled-in activity within

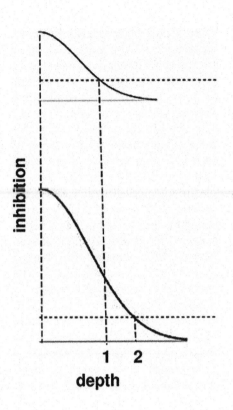

FIGURE 4.53. The on-center off-surround network within position and across depth helps to explain why brighter Kanizsa squares look closer.

the square. Because of this basic fact, *any* explanation of why brighter Kanizsa squares look closer must begin with properties of filled-in surface representations. In the current explanation, a brighter surface generates a larger surface contour signal. A larger surface contour signals creates larger inhibitory boundary pruning signals at each position (Figures 4.51 and 4.53). These signals are multiplied by the strengths of the inhibitory connections from the signal source to the recipient boundary at the same position but a different depth. Due to the decrease in size of the inhibitory connections across depth, these net signals also get smaller as the depth difference increases. The top curve in Figure 4.53 represents the total strength of these inhibitory signals across depth at a lower level of brightness, and the bottom curve represents the total inhibitory signals across depth at a higher level of brightness. The numbers 1 and 2 illustrate that the same level of inhibition is achieved at a larger depth difference in response to a brighter Kanizsa square. In other words, a larger number of boundary depths are inhibited by a brighter square than a dimmer one, so that the depths of the boundaries that survive well enough to represent the background are further away in depth than those that survive in response to a dimmer square. In short, brighter Kanizsa squares look closer, relative to their backgrounds, than dimmer ones.

The importance of the fact that brighter Kanizsa squares look closer is revealed by the nature of its explanation, which uses basic brain mechanisms that ensure complementary consistency and thereby lead to figure-ground separation.

V2 and V4: Recognizing occluded objects, seeing unoccluded surfaces, and DaVinci again

Amodal completed boundaries and filled-in surface representations in V2. Although some of the above figure-ground mechanisms act in cortical area V2, cortical area V4 is also needed to complete the process of generating a 3D surface representation. Then a surface-shroud resonance can be triggered between V4 and PPC in order to render this surface conscious. Why are both V2 and V4 needed?

The FACADE and 3D LAMINART models propose that cortical areas V2 and V4 resolve a basic design tension between recognition and seeing. This resolution prevents all occluding objects from looking transparent during 3D vision and figure-ground separation. Since I made this prediction in two articles in 1994 and 1997 (Grossberg, 1994, 1999), subsequent articles with multiple PhD students and postdoctoral fellows have succeeded in using these model neural mechanisms to successfully explain, simulate, and predict many interdisciplinary data about the visual percepts that occur during 3D vision and figure-ground perception (e.g., Cao and Grossberg, 2005, 2012; Fang and Grossberg, 2009; Grossberg, 1994, 1997; Grossberg, Kuhlmann, and Mingolla, 2007; Grossberg and McLoughlin, 1997; Grossberg and Swaminathan, 2004; Grossberg and Yazdanbakhsh, 2005; Kelly and Grossberg, 2000; and Leveille, Versace, and Grossberg, 2010).

In particular, V4 is predicted to be the cortical region where figure-ground-separated 3D surface representations of the *unoccluded* regions of *opaque* object regions are completed, and thereupon support both seeing *and* recognition of these regions. These unoccluded object surface regions are the parts of a scene that are typically seen as we explore the world. The same neural mechanisms also explain how V4 also supports seeing of 3D *transparent* surfaces, as will be shown below. Cortical area V2, in contrast, is proposed to complete object boundaries and surfaces of *occluded* object regions that may be amodally recognized, but not seen.

The percept that is generated by Figure 1.3 (left panel) illustrates this issue. As I have already noted, although this image is composed of three abutting rectangles, it generates a compelling percept of a vertical bar that is partially occluded by a horizontal bar. The partially occluded portion of the vertical bar (Figure 1.3, right panel, dashed line) is amodally recognized, but it is not consciously seen. As I have explained above (e.g., Figure 4.51), the model proposes how this horizontal rectangle is separated from the partially-occluded vertical rectangle, which can then be completed "behind" the horizontal rectangle in cortical area V2, and then used to control filling-in of a surface representation within its boundaries. Then direct pathways from V2 to category representations in cortical areas such as inferotemporal (IT) cortex (e.g., Figure 3.1), and back, are used to *recognize* these completed boundary and surface representations as part of a *feature-category resonance* (Table 1.4), despite the fact that the occluded part of this rectangle is not consciously *seen*.

Of course, each reader must weigh whether or not to believe this explanation based on available experimental evidence. Let me therefore note before continuing with this analysis that, in addition to explaining many perceptual data about 3D vision and figure-ground perception, the FACADE and 3D LAMINART models have explained and anticipated many neurophysiological data about figure-ground properties of V2 cells. For example, in my article (Grossberg, 2016a), the theory was able to explain *all* the key data properties about border ownership, stereoscopic cues, and gestalt grouping rules that were reported in a remarkable series of neurophysiological experiments on V2 cells from the laboratory of Rudiger von der Heydt at Johns Hopkins University (O'Herron and von der Heydt, 2009; Qiu, Sugihara, and von der Heydt, 2007; Qiu and von der Heydt, 2005; von der Heydt, Zhou, and Friedman, 2000; Zhang and von der Heydt, 2010; Zhou, Friedman, and von der Heydt, 2000).

Why are not all occluders transparent? If the completed boundary and surface behind the horizontal rectangle could also be seen, then the horizontal rectangle would look transparent, because both the horizontal and vertical rectangles could be seen at the same spatial positions, albeit at different depths. V2 and V4 are predicted to work together to ensure that not all objects look transparent. As a result of this teamwork between V2 and V4, partially occluded objects can be recognized without forcing all occluders to look transparent. The hypothesis that V4 represents 3D surfaces whose objects have been separated from one another in depth is consistent with several different types of neurobiological experiments (e.g., Chelazzi et al., 2001; Desimone and Schein, 1987; Lueck et al., 1989; Ogawa and Komatsu, 2004; Reynolds, Pasternak, and Desimone, 2000; Schiller and Lee, 1991; Zeki, 1983). Thus the model hypothesis that V2 and V4 carry out different roles in recognition and seeing are supported by both psychological and neurobiological data.

Modal surface representations in V4 and surface-shroud resonances between V4 and PPC. A surface-shroud resonance is assumed to be triggered between V4 and PPC because V4 is predicted to be the earliest cortical stage that generates a sufficiently complete, context-sensitive, and stable surface representation after the three hierarchical resolutions of uncertainty have taken place, and all boundaries have been completed and surfaces filled in. These processes generate a figure-ground-separated 3D surface representation of unoccluded object regions. With this V4 surface representation as a trigger, a surface-shroud resonance between V4 and PPC initiates the process whereby these surface representations may become consciously visible.

Given the critical importance of these model V2 and V4 processes to understanding why V2 and V4 are both needed to enable opaque occluders to exist, and why a surface-shroud resonance is triggered between V4 and PPC, I include the following figures and surrounding discussion to explain them more completely. Figure 4.54 (top row, left column) repeats the image in Figure 1.3 (left panel). Figure 4.54 (top row, right column) shows again the long-range cooperation and short-range competition that are controlled by the bipole grouping process; cf. Figure 4.43a (middle panel). Figure 4.54 (bottom row, left column) shows the end gaps that are caused by these bipole grouping mechanisms, and Figure 4.54 (bottom row, right column) shows how surface filling-in is contained within the closed horizontal rectangular boundary, but spills out of the end gaps formed in the other two rectangles.

After surface contour inhibitory signals act (Figures 4.51 and 4.53), the redundant horizontal boundaries in the farther depth planes are eliminated. Then bipole cells can complete the partially occluded rectangular boundaries in V2, after which surface filling-in can occur in V2 within both of the closed rectangular boundaries (Figure 4.55). The model proposes that these boundary and surface

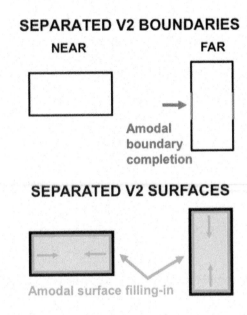

FIGURE 4.55. Amodal completion of boundaries and surfaces in V2.

representations are amodal, or invisible, even though they can be consciously recognized using direct output signals between V2 and IT (Figure 3.1). Finer points, such as how the boundaries in the near depth plane of the broken vertical rectangle with end gaps (Figure 4.54, bottom row, left column) are eliminated, can be explained as well, but this detail will not be considered here. Instead, let us focus on the main point: Given that the V2 representations are amodal to prevent all occluders from looking transparent, how does the brain consciously see the unoccluded regions of opaque surfaces?

The critical importance of boundary enrichment in allowing opaque occluders to be seen. Figure 4.56 summarizes how this is proposed to happen using interactions between V2 and V4. This figure represents boundaries and surfaces at just two depths, near and far, for simplicity. Not surprisingly, each depth-selective boundary representation in V2 projects topographically to V4. These are the vertical arrows in the upper half of the figure. In this way, the horizontal and vertical boundaries in V2 are also created in V4. In addition, it is assumed that the V2 boundaries that represent nearer depths also add to the V4 boundaries that represent farther depths. This process is called *boundary enrichment*. Such an enriched boundary is illustrated by the diagonal arrow in the upper half of the figure. This arrow represents the pathway whereby the horizontal rectangular boundary in V2 at the near depth is added to the vertical boundary in the far depth boundary representation in V4.

The need for boundary enrichment was already implicit in our explanation of DaVinci stereopsis using the stereogram formed by the two images in Figure 4.49. Here,

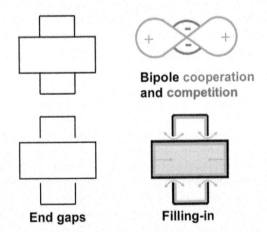

FIGURE 4.54. Initial steps in figure-ground separation. See the text for details.

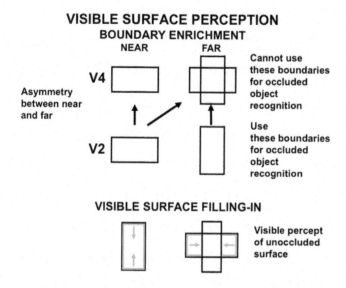

FIGURE 4.56. Final steps in generating a visible, figure-ground separated, 3D surface representation in V4 of the unoccluded parts of opaque surfaces.

the monocularly viewed surface BC inherits the depth of the binocularly viewed surface AB. We are now ready to understand how this happens. First, the depth-selective boundaries in region AB capture the feature contours that they abut in the corresponding depth-selective FIDO (Figure 4.48). To fix ideas, consider how the white color of the farther wall between A and C fills in. When the white color fills-in the surface region AB, it captures this surface at that depth. Then filling-in can progress beyond region AB to include region BC, again at the same surface depth, despite the fact that BC is viewed only monocularly. So far, so good.

What prevents the white color from continuing to flow beyond BC and behind the nearer surface CD? If this could happen, then in every scene that contains abutting surfaces at different depths, *every near surface would look transparent relative to every farther surface*! This is the problem that boundary enrichment solves. The near boundary C in Figure 4.49 projects to the FIDO at its own depth as well as to FIDOs that represent farther depths, thereby blocking the flow of white color past C, and ensuring that surface CD continues to look opaque.

Boundary enrichment has the same effect on the percept that is generated by the image in Figure 4.54 (top row, left column). As shown at the bottom of Figure 4.56, filling-in of the vertical rectangular surface at the near depth proceeds as expected. Due to boundary enrichment, filling-in of the horizontal rectangular surface at the far depth is prevented from flowing behind the vertical rectangular surface (cf. the diagonal arrow in the top half of Figure 4.56), so that the latter can appear opaque.

The reader might also wonder: What happened to the feature contours in the middle of the horizontal rectangle at

the far depth? These are inhibited by V2-to-V4 signals that carry out a process that I call *surface pruning* about which I will not say more here. In all, the combined effects of boundary pruning and enrichment, together with surface pruning, enable us to see and recognize the unoccluded parts of opaque 3D surfaces in V4 (see the filled-in regions in the bottom figure of Figure 4.56), while also amodally recognizing the completed representations of partially occluded objects that are created in V2 (Figure 4.55).

There are many other examples of how V2 and V4 work together to enable us to see and recognize objects in the world. The reader might try, for example, to use these concepts to explain the percepts that we see and recognize when we view the Kanizsa stratification images in Figure 1.4 (top row). There is no reason to stop there, however. There are many examples that you now have the tools to explain everywhere in the visual world around you!

An evolutionary design tension between requirements of recognition and reaching

If occluding and partially occluded objects can be recognized using boundary and surface representations that are completed in V2, then what functions are enabled by conscious 3D percepts of the unoccluded parts of opaque surfaces that are proposed to occur in V4? The FACADE and ARTSCAN models propose that a surface-shroud resonance with V4 provides an *extra degree of freedom*, namely conscious visibility, with which to distinguish directly reachable surfaces from non-reachable ones.

The need for such an extra degree of freedom seems to have arisen because of the urgent need during evolution for more powerful object recognition capabilities, notably the ability to complete the boundaries and surfaces of partially occluded objects behind their occluders so that they can be recognized. Animals in the wild who could not recognize such partially occluded objects—including lurking predators—would be at a severe survival disadvantage compared to those who could. Fortunately, basic properties of bipole cells for perceptual grouping, and simple feedback interactions between the boundary and surface streams, go a long way to accomplish figure-ground separation.

If the completed parts of these partially occluded object parts could also be seen, then great confusion could occur in the planning of looking and reaching behaviors, let alone navigational movements, since *all occluders would look transparent*, and it would seem natural to look, reach, and move directly through occluding objec* to the occluded objects behind them. In brief, then, there is a *design tension during evolution between the requirements of recognition and reaching*. Conscious visibility enables the unoccluded parts of many surfaces to appear opaque, and thus good targets for reaching, without eliminating the ability of the visual cortex to amodally recognize partially occluded objects, or to correctly represent surfaces that are transparent.

Thus, triggering a surface-shroud resonance between V4 and PPC not only selects surface representations that are sufficiently complete, context-sensitive, and stable to support adaptive behaviors, but also provides a surface visibility signal to mark the opaque surface regions, as opposed to the completed regions of occluded surfaces right behind them, to which orienting eye movements and reaching arm movements can be successfully directed.

In 1995, Francis Crick and Christof Koch (Crick and Koch, 1995) also proposed that visual awareness may be related to planning of voluntary movements, but without any analysis of how 3D vision occurs. They also made the strong claim that "What does enter awareness, we believe, is some form of the neural activity in certain higher visual areas, because they project directly to prefrontal areas" that help to plan movements. This claim captures part of the current claim, but also ignores the main issue of where the brain completes 3D surface representations that separate unoccluded surface regions from one another in depth. Only after this stage can these representations be brought into consciousness by a surface-shroud resonance, also not specified by Crick and Koch in 1995 or in their subsequent writings.

It needs also to be acknowledged that reaching behind occluders is possible, and does not require conscious seeing of occluded object features. However, this skill builds upon a great deal of experience with the circular reactions that support direct reaching behaviors during development (see Chapter 12). Further evidence for a role of consciously visible 3D surface representations in movement planning is discussed as part of the explanations of clinical data about visual neglect in Chapter 6.

V2 and V4: Explaining when surfaces look opaque and transparent

The images in Figure 1.4 (bottom row) raise the opposite concern. Do the processes that I have discussed above explain percepts of opaque surfaces so well that the theory cannot explain when we see transparent surfaces, such those in Figure 1.4? If this were true, then the theory be wrong, or at best fundamentally incomplete. Any theory of 3D vision must be able to explain when

surfaces look opaque *and* when they look transparent. As I will now show, the *same* mechanisms explain when we see unimodal transparency, bistable transparency, or no transparency at all. All three pictures in in this figure have the same boundary geometry, which consists of two intersecting squares (Figure 1.4, bottom row, right panel). The pictures differ only in having different luminances within the three shapes that are surrounded by these boundaries. These seemingly innocuous luminance differences make a huge difference in the percepts that we see, thereby showing that relative contrasts in a scene can strongly interact with the scene geometry to determine what we consciously see.

The leftmost image provides an example of unique, or unimodal, transparency. Here, the lower right square seems always to lie "in front of" the upper left square, which can be seen "behind" it. This percept raises deep issues about our understanding of space. In addition to having to understand how anything can appear to lie "behind" something else in a 2D picture, we also need to understand here how we can "see through" part of a 2D picture to also see an object that lies "behind" it?

The figure that is second from the left is an example of bistable transparency. At some times, the lower right square appears to lie in front of the upper left square, but at other times, the reverse percept can be seen. In both cases, the viewer can see the square that appears to lie behind the square that appears to lie in front. In addition, paying attention to one of the squares can "pull it forward" so that the other square is then seen behind it. How can a single picture generate two different percepts of the objects in it? Why do these different percepts flip through time? How can attention change which figure appears to be in front? If some figures can flip their interpretations through time, then why cannot all pictures do so?

The figure that is third from the left is seen as an opaque 2D picture with three gray regions that all lie in the picture plane. There is no depth percept.

Taken together, these three images raise the question: Why can just changing luminance differences in images with the same geometry have such dramatic effects on the percepts that we consciously see?

A careful inspection of the contrast relationships between the different parts of the images reveals factors that may underlie these dramatically different percepts. Figure 4.57 focuses on contrast relationships at the X-junction that joins the vertical right boundary of the upper left square and the horizontal top boundary of the lower right square in each figure. In Figure 4.57 (left column, top row), contrast polarity is preserved along the vertical edge near the X-junction where the squares intersect. Said in another way, the contrasts of the vertical edges both above and below the X-junction are dark-to-light, reading from left-to-right. This is not true for the contrast polarities of the horizontal edges to the left and right of the X-junction.

Here, contrast polarity reverses along the horizontal branch as the X-junction is crossed: To the left of the X-junction, the contrast is dark-to-light reading from top-to-bottom. However, to the right of the X-junction, the contrast is light-to-dark reading from top-to-bottom. In other words, the percept of the lower right square appearing in front of the upper left square correlates with the property that the contrast polarity of the horizontal edge of the lower right square reverses at the X-junction, but the contrast polarity of vertical edge of the upper left square does not. We will soon see that this happens because the polarity-reversing horizontal boundary is stronger than the polarity-preserving vertical boundary where they meet at the X-junction. As a result, the stronger horizontal boundary can cause end gaps in the weaker horizontal boundary at both sides of the X-junction.

In Figure 4.57 (right column, top row), contrast polarity is preserved along both the vertical and the horizontal edges where they intersect at the X-junction. In this case, both boundaries are weaker, but neither boundary is significantly weaker than the other. Spatial attention that is focused on one of these boundaries can therefore make it significantly stronger than the other boundary. The stronger boundary can then cause end gaps on both sides of the X-junction where it intersects the weaker boundary, thereby creating a transparent percept with the square of the stronger boundary perceived in front. As spatial attention wanders between boundaries, the percept can flip bistably through time, with the stronger boundary always belonging to the nearer square.

Finally, Figure 4.57 (left column, bottom row) does not induce a percept of transparency. Here contrast polarity reverses along both edges where they cross the X-junction. Both boundaries are therefore strong, but neither boundary is significantly stronger than the other. Because these boundaries are already strong, attention shifts

cannot make one significantly stronger than the other. No depth stratification occurs in this case. Instead, the image generates a percept of an opaque surface in which a bright small square in the middle is surrounded by two dark L-shaped figures in the same picture plane.

These and other related transparency percepts were explained and simulated using the 3D LAMINART model in a 2005 article with my postdoctoral fellow Arash Yazdanbakhsh (Grossberg and Yazdanbakhsh, 2005). As I mentioned above, I had introduced the 3D LAMINART model in 1999 and used it with several colleagues to explain many data about 3D vision and figure-ground perception before 2005, but not all the key data about transparency. Explanations of all the main transparency data properties from multiple labs became clear when I finally realized how known bipole grouping and surface filling-in processes of the model interact with one other key process, which explains *why* polarity-preserving and polarity-reversing contrasts at X-junctions have the effects that they do on boundary strength. This process is a spatial competition that is *orientationally-selective*, *monocular*, and *polarity-specific*. An orientationally-selective competition occurs between cells that are tuned to a similar orientation. A monocular competition occurs between cells that receive inputs from the same eye, and only that eye. A polarity-specific competition occurs between cells that are sensitive to either dark-light or light-dark contrasts, but not to both.

In order to be monocular, the spatial competition has to occur before layer 3B of cortical area V1, as illustrated in Figures 4.19 and 4.58 (see the circuit between layers 6 and 4 in V1 that is surrounded by the dashed rectangle). Figure 4.58 includes only boundary interactions of the model. Interactions between boundaries and surfaces follow the format in Figure 4.44. It was natural to seek the monocular spatial competition before layer 3B because

> my PhD student Piers Howe and I had shown in 2003 how to explain many psychophysical and visual cortical data using the known anatomical fact that various simple cells become binocular in layer 3B (Grossberg and Howe, 2003; Figure 4.19). Then pairs of these binocular simple cells that are sensitive to opposite contrast polarities input to binocular complex cells in layer 2/3 of V1, before the binocular complex cells activate bipole cells in layer 2/3 of V2 (also surrounded by a dashed rectangle in Figure 4.58). In order for the spatial competition to be monocular, we therefore needed to find it in layer 4 of cortical area V1.

This realization was a relief in one way, because it pointed to how to explain lots of transparency data. It was also a possible source of considerable anxiety if it was just an *ad hoc* kludge that was thrown into the model to fit these data.

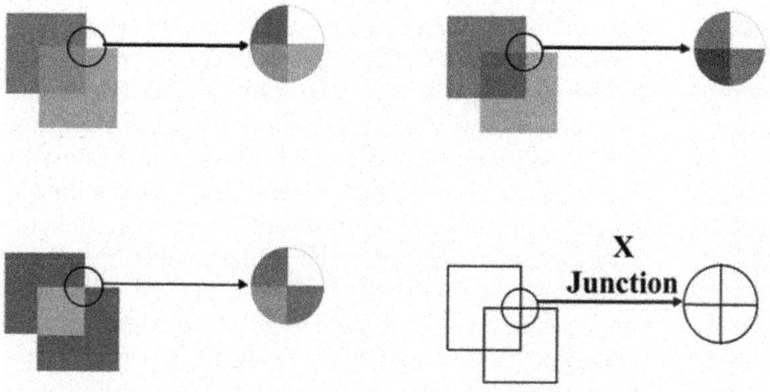

FIGURE 4.57. Percepts of unimodal and bistable transparency (top row) as well as of a flat 2D surface (bottom row, left column) can be induced just by changing the relative contrasts in an image with a fixed geometry.

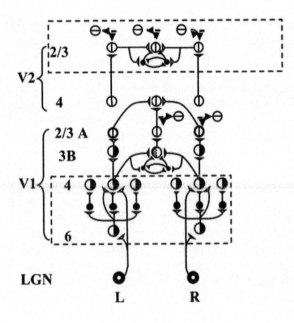

V2 { 2/3   4

V1 { 2/3 A   3B   4   6

LGN

L   R

◖ **Monocular Simple Cells**   ◖◗ **Monocular Complex Cells**

◉ **Binocular Simple Cells**   ◑◗ **Binocular Complex Cells**

⊤ **Excitatory connections**   ⊤ **Inhibitory connections**

● **Inhibitory Cells**

FIGURE 4.58. LAMINART model processing stage that are sufficient to explain many percepts of transparency, including those summarized in Figure 4.57.

However, I immediately realized, to my delight and relief, that such a spatial competition was already part of the 3D LAMINART model! In fact, it had already been simulated as part of a 3D LAMINART study of cortical development with my PhD student James Williamson in a 2001 article (Grossberg and Williamson, 2001). However, Jim and I did not realize the significance of this property for explaining transparency data. That required the sustained data analysis that Arash and I carried out. From it, we realized that the monocular, oriented, spatial competition causes boundaries that preserve their contrast polarity on both sides of an X-junction to be weaker than boundaries that reverse their contrast polarity as the X-junction is crossed. This is true because the spatial competition is *orientationally-selective* and *polarity-specific*, so only acts on like-oriented boundaries across the X-junction if both of their inducing edges have the same contrast polarity. This implies that, at the X-junction, a stronger opposite-polarity boundary can create an end gap in a weaker like-polarity perpendicular boundary. Other experiments, notably of Hiroshige Takeichi, Shinsuke Shimojo, and Takeo Watanabe in 1992 (Takeichi, Shimojo, and Watanabe, 1992) showed that the spatial competition is monocular by demonstrating that key properties disappeared if the displays were broken up between the two eyes and had to be

fused binocularly to recover the entire input display. Their data also followed easily from the property that the spatial competition in layer 4 of V1 is also monocular.

Is there any visible evidence that end gaps contribute to the formation of transparency percepts? I noted above the amusing historical accident that, just as my article with Arash Yazdanbakhsh was in press in the journal *Vision Research*, another vision researcher, Peter Tse, had a paper about bistable transparency that was also in press at the same journal. Peter's paper demonstrated how a shift of spatial attention to one of the three disks in Figure 4.43c could have two correlated effects: First, it could pull the attended disk forward in depth, and create a percept of transparency behind it. Second, it could make the attended disk look darker. It was a delightful coincidence that the explanation of bistable transparency that Arash and I already had in press explained both of these properties!

In our explanation, why does the attended disk look closer *and* darker? This is because of end gaps! Recall that, during neon color spreading (Figure 4.26), brightness or color can flow through an end gap that is caused when a stronger boundary inhibits an abutting weaker boundary. The same thing can occur during a unique or bistable transparency percept in response to the images in Figure 1.4 (bottom row). In Peter Tse's display in Figure 4.43c, when spatial attention is focused upon one disk, it can strengthen its boundaries relative to those of the other disks. Given this property, the boundary of the attended disk can cause end gaps in the boundary of an abutting disk with which it shares an X-junction. As a result, some of the darker color from within the disk with an end gap can flow into the attended disk, thereby darkening its color relative to that of an unattended disk. In addition, the attended disk looks closer than the one whose boundary has an end gap, and the other disks can be seen behind it for the same reason that explains bistable transparency in the analysis of Figure 4.57 (right column, top row). The example of bistable transparency hereby illustrates the close relationship that exists between the mechanisms that cause neon color spreading and those that cause transparency.

Before leaving this topic, it is interesting to ask: Why is the spatial competition in layer 4 of V1 polarity-specific? The model of how V1 cortex develops that I had published with Jim Williamson suggests that this is true because the objects in our early visual experiences typically do not change their polarity too often across space, so the correlations that are learned as the spatial competition develops are also polarity-specific. What if, instead, an animal was raised in an environment all of whose edges reversed polarity regularly across space, say by using scenes whose objects are filled with small-scale black-and-white checkerboards (cf. Figures 3.2 and 4.35)? If the spatial competition developed so that it could act between opposite contrast polarities, then the properties of transparency in response to the images in Figure 1.4 (bottom row) might be eliminated. This is an interesting thought experiment, if not perhaps one that could easily be run in the laboratory.

Principled incremental theorizing using the Method of Minimal Anatomies

A useful metatheoretical conclusion may be drawn from these examples. Had we used the full 3D LAMINART circuit from the start to simulate the transparency percepts, the importance of the polarity-specific competition would have become clear. However, simulating large-scale neural models can take a long time on a computer. As computers become faster, this time cost decreases. When Jim Williamson and I did these simulations, we always tried to simulate the *minimal* version of the model that was competent to explain a targeted data set. This parsimony not only made the simulations possible in a reasonable amount of time, but also called attention to the combinations of mechanisms that were essential to explain the targeted data, in keeping with the Method of Minimal Anatomies. Thus, when Arash and I began our study of transparency, the 3D LAMINART model could already explain key properties of transparency data, but we did not yet realize this because the monocular, oriented, polarity-specific spatial competition had often been omitted from its simulations in order to speed them up. This circuit was, however, an important component of the developmental simulations that I carried out with Jim.

I had believed for 20 years before this work was done that there is a close relationship between my explanation of neon color spreading and what an explanation of transparency should look like. I also knew that something was missing from the transparency explanation, but could not yet put my finger on what it was. It was only through carefully analyzing parametric properties of transparency data that the importance of the polarity-specific competition came into view. And this was only possible because I could see how other 3D LAMINART model properties explained key properties of the transparency data, including how end gaps influence figure-ground percepts. Without these other model properties, it would have been much more difficult to isolate the property that was still missing from the explanation.

Thus, no single kind of data is sufficient to explain how the brain sees. The accumulation of multiple data constraints, whether through data about transparency, hyperacuity, neon color spreading, Craik-O'Brien-Cornsweet effect, texture segregation, or Inverted-U in illusory contour strength, can guide us to incrementally refine our models and expand their explanatory and predictive range. This state of affairs dramatizes the advantage of painstakingly, and in multiple incremental stages, using the Method of Minimal Anatomies to develop a principled theory that can explain many different kinds of data. I like to say that, as I get older, my models get smarter as I get stupider. Because of that, together we can still do useful theoretical work! Principled models have, throughout my life, thrust me into understanding all sorts of phenomena that I would not have a clue about without them.

What's next?

We are now at a watershed moment in this exposition. Most of our explanations in the last two chapters have dealt with how the brain processes data that do not change significantly through time while we are processing them, such as static 2D pictures and 3D scenes. Much of this processing goes on in the What, or ventral, cortical stream (Figure 1.19). The exposition could now proceed directly to describe how the brain processes signals that change dynamically through time, notably how moving objects are processed. That would involve analyses at similar levels of processing, but would involve processes in the Where, or dorsal, cortical stream.

Instead, I will first describe and explain processes that go on at higher levels of brain processing, but primarily process data in the What cortical stream. These processes include object and event learning, recognition, prediction, attention, working memory, and planning. Along the way, I will also, necessarily, begin to describe the strong interactions that occur between the computationally complementary processes in the What and Where cortical streams (Table 1.2). One particularly important interaction occurs during *invariant* object learning, recognition, and search. It enables us to learn to recognize objects that are seen from multiple viewpoints and at variable sizes and positions on our retinas. The main challenge is to understand how we do this autonomously, and without any external teacher; that is, while we carry out *unsupervised* learning. After analyzing these interactions, we will be better prepared to dive directly into an explanation of many Where stream processes, starting in Chapters 7 and 8.

Learning to Attend, Recognize, and Predict the World

From vigilant conscious awareness to autism, amnesia, and Alzheimer's disease

This chapter will discuss how we

- rapidly learn to categorize and recognize so many objects in the world
- remember this information as well as we do over a period of years
- learn to expect and anticipate events that may occur in familiar situations
- pay attention to events that are of particular interest to us
- become conscious of these events
- balance between expected and unexpected events, and orient to unexpected events
- engage in fantasy activities such as visual imagery, internalized speech, and planning
- learn language quickly and consciously hear completed speech sounds in noise
- hallucinate during mental disorders.

I claim that a common set of brain mechanisms controls all of these processes. Adaptive Resonance Theory, or ART, has been incrementally developed to explain what these mechanisms are, and how they work and interact, since I introduced it in 1976 (Grossberg, 1976a, 1976b) and it was incrementally developed in many articles to the present, notably with the help and leadership of Gail Carpenter, as I will elaborate upon below. There are many aspects of these processes that are worth considering. For example, we need to understand the difference between

Conscious MIND Resonant BRAIN. Stephen Grossberg, Oxford University Press. © Oxford University Press 2021.
DOI: 10.1093/oso/9780190070557.003.0005

Perceiving vs. recognizing

The existence of *amodal* percepts, such as the offset grating in Figure 1.1 (right panel) that started off the book, shows that we can recognize and be conscious of events that we cannot see. Said in another way: the perception of qualia is not *necessary* for conscious recognition, and thus perception and recognition are distinct processes. Given that perception and recognition are not the same process, as we discussed in Chapter 1 with regard to the work of Helmholtz and Kanizsa, why do they seem to be so closely linked? How can we characterize the differences between these processes?

Another way to understand why perception and recognition are different is the following: When we open our eyes in a reasonably lit place, we can see what is in it, whether or not we know what we are looking at. In this sense, perception is general-purpose since it can process both familiar and unfamiliar objects and events in the world. On the other hand, we can only recognize objects and events that we have previously experienced and learned about. Although the ART laws that I will begin to explain in this chapter are general-purpose for learning to attend, recognize, and predict objects and events in a changing world, recognition is clearly "less general-purpose" than perception by only applying to what we already know.

A second important theme concerns

Patterns vs. symbols

Sensory processes like seeing and hearing typically deal with continuously varying *patterns* of activation, such as the varying colors and luminances across a scene, or the auditory frequencies and amplitudes in a piece of music. In contrast, much of our thinking has a more *symbolic* quality. For example, the concept of a "chair" is more general than the particular sizes, shapes, and colors of particular chairs that we may have previously experienced. We can hereby use language to represent abstract concepts that are far removed from individual sensory experiences. How does our mind transform the continuous perceptual patterns that we perceive into abstract cognitive symbols? How do we extract symbolic rules from the continuous ebb and flow of experience? In the other direction, how do we use symbols and rules to reorganize and interpret the world of continuously patterned sensory information?

A thought experiment about category learning

To set the stage for my analysis, I will first describe several phenomena and issues to focus our thoughts on what

needs to be explained. Then I will summarize a unified explanation of these phenomena. Finally, I will use a thought experiment to derive these mechanisms from first principles. Thought experiments can reveal in a clear and compelling way the underlying logic behind the development of a theory, and thus are a powerful tool for understanding the basic concepts on which a theory is built. Perhaps the most famous thought experiments in science are the ones that Einstein used to derive key concepts of Relativity Theory.

Thought experiments have also played a useful role in helping me to understand how and why the cognitive and cognitive-emotional mechanisms of our brains are organized as they are. These thought experiments require no advanced knowledge of psychology or neuroscience to carry out. They require only some facts that we all know about from daily life, and questions that every person could ask about those facts with no prior technical knowledge. Remarkably, when we put together the right facts and ask the right questions about them, then the answers to these questions leads us straight to brain mechanisms that we typically learn about in specialized college and graduate school courses about psychology and neuroscience, or that go beyond current knowledge.

Talking about the potential benefits of thought experiments is easy. However, the most likely outcome of the effort to carry out a thought experiment is . . . nothing at all. Thought experiments work out only when you have correctly identified the right combination of facts and the right questions about them. These facts are familiar to us all because they exemplify environmental constraints that we experience all the time during our daily lives. The conclusions that a thought experiment derives illuminate how evolution has adapted to the combination of environmental constraints that the facts impose. A thought experiment hereby celebrates the role of pure reason in the world by showing how complex scientific processes can be logically derived from simple principles in story form.

In addition to explaining a lot of psychological and neurobiological data, the thought experiment that leads to ART also led to predictions that have subsequently been confirmed by psychological and neurobiological experiments. Before describing this thought experiment, let me introduce a little background.

Stability-plasticity dilemma: Fast learning and stable memory of recognition categories

A unifying theme in this analysis concerns how we learn to *categorize* specific instances of an object, or set of objects,

LEARN MANY-TO-ONE and ONE-TO-MANY MAPS

Many-to-One	One-to-Many
Compression, Naming	Expert Knowledge
(a_1, b)	(a, b_1)
(a_2, b)	(a, b_2)
(a_3, b)	(a, b_3)
(a_4, b)	(a, b_4)

Fruit

Animal
Mammal
Pet
Dog
Dalmatian
Fireman's
Mascot
"Rover"

FIGURE 5.1. Humans and other autonomous adaptive intelligent agents need to be able to learn both many-to-one and one-to-many maps.

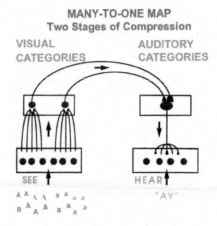

MANY-TO-ONE MAP
Two Stages of Compression

VISUAL CATEGORIES   AUDITORY CATEGORIES

SEE   HEAR   "AY"

FIGURE 5.2. Learning a many-to-one map from multiple visual fonts of a letter to the letter's name requires a stage of category learning followed by one of associatively learned mapping.

into a more general concept. There are at least two versions of this problem: the learning of *many-to-one* maps, and the learning of *one-to-many* maps (Figure 5.1).

Many-to-one and one-to-many maps. In a many-to-one map, many different objects can all predict the same category label, much as all the images of different fruits in Figure 5.1 (left panel) can be called a "fruit". In a one-to-many map, we know many things about individual objects. Otherwise expressed, we have expert knowledge about that object. As in Figure 5.1 (right panel), we can know lots of things about a single dog, ranging from it being an animal to knowing that this particular dog is our dog Rover.

Many-to-one maps can be learned about radically different aspects of our experience. For example, we can learn that many different printed or script letter fonts all represent the letter A, as illustrated in Figure 5.2. There are two stages of learning in this process. First, variations on the shape of a single letter's font are categorized into a single visual category. Different letters, or letters that are created in a different font, are categorized into different visual categories. In Figure 5.2, different categories are learned to visually recognize variations of capital letter "A" fonts, and small letter "a" fonts. Then all of these visual categories are mapped, through an associative learning process (the pathways with the rightward-facing arrow), into an auditory category whereby we can reply to seeing a letter "A" or "a" with the verbal report "ay". There are thus two successive stages of many-to-one learning in this process, a category learning stage within the visual system, and an associative learning stage between the visual and auditory systems.

Figure 5.3 illustrates the diverse kinds of information that such a many-to-one process can learn to recognize

and predict. Here, different combinations of patient symptoms, tests, and treatments are mapped into the predicted length of stay in a hospital, again through two stages of many-to-one learning, the first via learned categorization, and the second via associative mapping.

Learning concrete and abstract knowledge: The need for fast stable learning on the fly. During the category learning process, we can effortlessly control how general our categories will become. For some purposes, like recognizing a particular view of one person's face, we need to learn specific, or concrete, visual categories, before learning to associate that category with the person's name. For other purposes, like recognizing that every person has a face, the learned visual categories are more general, or abstract, and are associatively mapped into corresponding abstract descriptive labels.

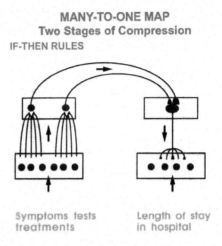

MANY-TO-ONE MAP
Two Stages of Compression
IF-THEN RULES

Symptoms tests treatments   Length of stay in hospital

FIGURE 5.3. Many-to-one maps can learn a huge variety of kinds of predictive information.

Our ability to regulate how concrete or general a learned category will be enables us to learn about rare but important events, even if they may be experienced among frequent and familiar events. This ability confronts our brains with challenging problems that most learning algorithms have not yet solved. For example, how do we manage to detect, learn, and remember the first cases of a new medical epidemic among the vast amounts of medical information that floods our hospitals through time? Why is not this small amount of data treated like noise, and obliterated by the flood of more frequent events? Or, almost as bad, why is it not erroneously recognized as an already familiar disease, thereby preventing its correct diagnosis and treatment?

Clearly, for us to learn about rare events, we must be capable of *fast learning* that can encode the rare event when it occurs, even if it occurs just once. Many learning algorithms utilize a form of slow learning that requires an event to occur multiple times before it can be adequately registered. In contrast, humans and other animals often learn quickly and on the fly. Our very survival often requires this. In many situations, you will not get a second chance to learn how to avoid a dangerous outcome, such as a ferocious predator. Fast learning can also greatly enhance the enjoyment in our lives. For example, we can attend an exciting movie and go home to describe to our friends and family many details about the film, even though we experienced them only once, and only fleetingly as the scenes flash by.

Given that we are capable of learning quickly, why do we not also forget just as quickly? How can we learn quickly, yet retain memories of important experiences for a long time, often for many years? In particular, how can we learn from new situations without unlearning what we have already learned in old situations. For example, when I live in Boston and take trips to Los Angeles, why can I quickly learn to get around Los Angeles without just as quickly forgetting how to get around Boston? This is an example of the *stability-plasticity dilemma* that I mentioned in Chapter 1. We need to be plastic in order to learn from new experiences, but also have stable enough memories to avoid catastrophic forgetting of familiar, but still useful, information.

Unsupervised and supervised learning of many-to-one and one-to-many maps

Figure 5.2 illustrated that category learning often involves the learning of a *many-to-one map*; that is, we can learn that *many* examples, or exemplars, of an event can all be recognized using *one* recognition category. I want to describe this kind of learning in a little more detail than I did above to be sure that you fully understand what it accomplishes. During many-to-one map learning, a single category can represent different exemplars of a single, visually perceived, letter font that may vary in size, position, and even shape to some extent, but ultimately depends upon similarities between the features of the different exemplars to learn each category. With suitable preprocessing of visually presented letters, such similarity learning can go on spontaneously, without an external teacher. This type of learning is often called *unsupervised learning*. Multiple visual categories may be learned in response to distinct letter fonts that may have no visual features in common, but that all represent the same letter, such as lower case and capital letter fonts for the letter "ay" (Figure 5.2) Each of these categories *compresses* information about its font into a more symbolic representation of that font.

Given that multiple categories are learned in order to compress information about different fonts, how do we learn to respond to all of these categories with the same verbal response "ay?" As Figure 5.2 illustrates, this transformation often occurs between different modalities, namely vision and audition. The fact that dissimilar visual letter fonts may all evoke the same verbal name is determined by our culture, and not by the similarity of their visual features. We must be taught that they all symbolize the same letter. Learning that uses such an external supervisor is called *supervised learning*. When an external teacher tells us the name of a visually presented letter, both the letter and its sound are categorized in our brains within their own modalities. Associative learning between the categories in these different modalities can then occur. Learning a many-to-one map between individual letters and their verbal name hereby uses at least two stages of generalization, or compression (Figure 5.2): The first stage compresses information that is derived from many similar exemplars into individual categories. This category may be learned using a combination of unsupervised and supervised learning. The second stage uses supervised learning to associate multiple categories with a single name category.

If the letter exemplars that activate a single visual category share similar visual features, then why might supervised learning sometimes be needed to decide which letters activate which visual categories? Why is not unsupervised learning, which is sensitive to feature similarity, already sufficient? A comparison between the letters "E" and "F" clarifies this issue. The letter "F" shares many features of the letter "E". How does the brain determine that these images, albeit similar, should represent different sounds in the alphabet? This must, in principle, be determined by cultural factors, which need to be communicated between individuals who share the same language. In fact, if an "E" is written carelessly, with a shorter bottom horizontal stroke than usual, or if an "F" is printed with a larger than usual horizontal stroke at its bottom, then these letters may easily be confused with each other. Supervised learning can define the culturally-determined boundary conditions that control which combinations of similar exemplars go together, and which represent a different category altogether.

One-to-many map learning and catastrophic forgetting. In addition to learning many-to-one maps, we also need to be able to learn *one-to-many maps*. A one-to-many map enables us to learn *many* properties or predictions in response to *one* object or event. One-to-many maps hereby help us to become experts about the world. Figure 5.1 illustrates this property with an example in which seeing *one* picture of a dog can trigger *many* different learned responses, such as animal, mammal, dog, Dalmatian, and my dog Rover. Similarly, if I see my mom, I can think a lot of different things about her as a human, woman, devoted teacher, excellent cook, kind person, cheerful personality, loving mom, and my mom Elsie, in addition to what activities she may be planning to do that day, and so on. Learning one-to-many maps takes full advantage of solving the stability-plasticity dilemma, since while you are learning additional concepts or responses in response to seeing one person or event, you do not want to overwrite, and thereby catastrophically forget, the knowledge and responses that were previously learned.

Such catastrophic forgetting can easily occur if a learning algorithm just associates an input pattern, such as a picture of a dog, with an output pattern, such as the name "animal" or "Rover". If the dog picture was previously associated with "animal", then associating the dog with "Rover" can erase the learned adaptive weights that previously predicted "animal" unless there is some additional mechanism to prevent this from happening.

Many popular learning models that are used in Artificial Intelligence, such as the popular Deep Learning algorithms, do experience catastrophic forgetting. This can be a huge problem if they are used to learn a large and complex database, since unpredictable combinations of previously learned categories can suddenly be wiped out from memory without warning.

The above considerations focus on properties of learning in normal, or typical, brains. We also need to understand how our learning and memory may break down when something goes wrong in our brains. For example, it is known that lesions to a part of the brain called the hippocampal system can cause a form of amnesia, called medial temporal amnesia, whereby, among other

properties, and at the risk of oversimplifying a complex and subtle literature, patients find it hard to learn and remember new information, but previously learned information about which their memory has "consolidated" can readily be retrieved. Thus, an amnesic patient can typically carry out an intelligent conversation about experiences that happened a significant time before the lesion occurred.

HM, hippocampus, and amnesia

The patient HM is perhaps the most famous example of what can go wrong in a human when their hippocampus is not functioning normally (e.g., Corkin, 2002; Scoville and Milner, 1957). HM's name, Henry Molaison, was revealed after he died in 2012 at the age of 82. He had a bilateral hippocampectomy when he was 27 years old to relieve intractable epilepsy. During this procedure, the hippocampus on both sides of his brain was removed along with nearby brain regions (Figure 5.4). If HM was distracted after meeting someone, he would not recognize that he had just met that person a moment later. Once his short-term memory was reset, repeating the same verbal information to him had to be processed, by and large, as if it were totally new. HM had no immediate past, so could not adequately plan his future, at least when it came to what is called *declarative memories*. These are memories of facts and events that can be consciously recalled, or "declared". Henry Molaison was thus condemned to live in the eternal present, bolstered by memories of events experienced long ago. Perhaps the closest popular account of what this means for one's daily life was dramatized in Christopher Nolan's film *Memento* (https://en.wikipedia.org/wiki/Memento_(film)).

In contrast, HM's ability to learn new *procedural memories*, such as motor skills, was intact, but even when he performed such a skill competently, he could not remember having learned it. It is a great challenge for all theories of learning and cognition to understand how particular breakdowns in the brain's normal learning machinery can lead to such a constellation of clinical symptoms. Indeed, early vs. late ablations of brain regions like the hippocampus, amygdala, and orbitofrontal cortex after learning something new can have dramatically different effects on whether memories will consolidate properly for later recall. How Adaptive Resonance Theory can naturally explain and simulate this complex pattern of symptoms will be described later in the book after some of its basic mechanisms are reviewed.

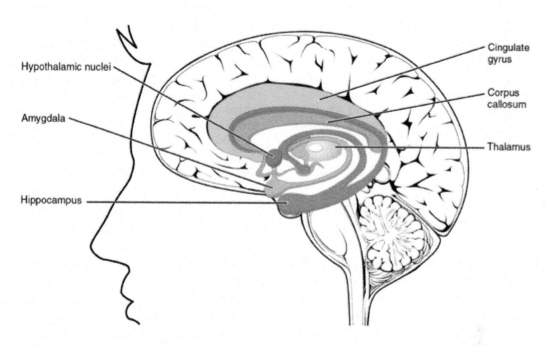

FIGURE 5.4. The hippocampus is one of several brain regions that are important in learning and remembering about objects and events that we experience throughout life. The book will describe several hippocampal processes that contribute to this achievement in different ways.

The Predictive brain: Intention, attention, and consciousness

We can now return to an overview of Adaptive Resonance Theory, or ART. ART claims that, in order to solve the stability-plasticity dilemma, only resonant states typically drive learning. That is why the theory is called *adaptive resonance theory*. Because solving the stability-plasticity dilemma has been so important for the survival and success of humanity, I will start by discussing the stabilizing role of top-down learned expectations from several different perspectives.

From the perspective of philosophy, these top-down expectations suggest a mechanistic answer to why humans are "intentional" beings who are always anticipating, predicting, or planning their next behaviors and their expected consequences. ART suggests that "stability implies intentionality". That is, our ability to learn rapidly about the world, without experiencing catastrophic forgetting, requires that we also learn top-down expectations about the world that are continually matched against world data.

Without stable memories of our past experiences, we could learn very little about the world, since our present learning would tend to wash away our previous memories unless we continually rehearsed them. But if we had to continuously rehearse everything that we learned, then we could learn very little, because there is just so much time in a day to rehearse! Having an active top-down matching mechanism greatly amplifies the amount of information

that we can quickly learn and stably remember about the world. This capability, in turn, sets the stage for developing a sense of self, which requires that we can learn and remember a record of many experiences that are uniquely ours over a period of years.

I am using the word "intentionality" in two different senses. One sense concerns how expectations can anticipate events that may or may not occur. The second sense concerns the ability of expectations to control the read-out of planned sequences of behaviors aimed at achieving prescribed behavioral goals. The former sense will be emphasized first; the latter in my subsequent discussions, especially after I explain in Chapter 12 how sequences of events are stored in working memory and used to help predict our future behaviors. My main point in lumping these two senses together is that ART uses the same kinds of mechanisms to understand both kinds of intentional processes.

The second implication of ART ideas is that "intention implies attention and consciousness". That is, expectations start to focus attention on data worthy of learning and recognizing, and these attentional foci are confirmed when the system as a whole incorporates them into resonant states that can become conscious (Table 1.4).

Implicit in the concept of intentionality is the idea that we can *get ready* to experience an expected event so that, when it finally occurs, we can react to it more quickly and vigorously, and until it occurs, we are able to ignore other, less desired, events. This property is often called attentional *priming*. Because of this priming property, when a top-down expectation is read-out in the absence of a bottom-up input, it can *modulate*, or subliminally sensitize, the cells that would ordinarily respond to the bottom-up input. The priming input does not usually fire these cells, but it gets them ready for a bottom-up input that may soon activate them. The priming input can also vigorously suppress the activity of cells that are not included within the expected event, and thereby facilitates search for expected information. These properties occur because the ART Matching Rule that realizes object attention is defined by a top-down, modulatory on-center, off-surround network.

Computational Properties of the ART Matching Rule

This is a good place to summarize the main properties of the ART Matching Rule in greater detail (Figure 1.25):

Bottom-Up Automatic Activation: A cell (or cell population) can become active enough to generate output signals if it receives a large enough bottom-up input. This property means that events in the world can, by themselves, drive information processing by the brain, other things being equal.

Top-Down Priming: If a cell receives only a top-down expectation, or priming, signal, from an active recognition category, it can become modulated, sensitized, or subliminally active, but it cannot be activated enough to generate large output signals, because the excitatory effect of the expectation, or learned prototype (downward facing green pathways with plus signs in Figure 1.25), is balanced against the inhibitory effect of an off-surround network that is also activated by the category (lateral red pathways with minus signs in Figure 1.25). Such a top-down priming signal prepares some cells to react more quickly and vigorously to subsequent bottom-up inputs that match the top-down prime, while suppressing cells that are not expected and that are inhibited by the off-surround.

Match: A cell can become active if it receives large convergent bottom-up and top-down expectation inputs ("two-against-one" in Figure 1.25). Such a matching process can synchronize and amplify the firing of cells across the matched population of cells as a resonance takes hold. The resonating cells encode the "critical features" to which the network pays attention.

Mismatch: A cell's activity is suppressed when a top-down expectation is active, even if it receives a large bottom-up input, if it receives a zero, or sufficiently small, top-down expectation input ("one-against-one" in Figure 1.25 in the off-surround).

When all of these properties act, partial matches can amplify and synchronize the activities of matched cells, while suppressing those of mismatched cells.

I claim that this ART Matching Rule operates in all the brain systems that solve the stability-plasticity dilemma, notably systems devoted to perception and cognition. In all these systems, we can continue to rapidly learn and stably remember new experiences throughout life by matching bottom-up signal patterns from more peripheral to more central brain processing stages against top-down signal patterns from more central to more peripheral processing stages. These top-down signals represent the brain's learned expectations of what the bottom-up signal patterns should be based upon past experience. The matching process is designed to amplify those combinations of critical features in the bottom-up pattern that are consistent with the top-down expectations, and to suppress those features that are inconsistent. Top-down matching initiates the process whereby the brain selectively pays attention to experiences that it expects, binds them into coherent internal representations through resonant states, incorporates them through learning into its knowledge about the world, and becomes conscious of them.

ART matching: Expectation and attention during brightness perception

Examples abound of how the ART Matching Rule operates at multiple levels of visual and auditory processing. Auditory processing will be discussed in Chapter 12. In order to illustrate that the ART Matching Rule operates at early levels of the visual system, I will first summarize how to explain a familiar visual percept that may at first seem to be totally unrelated to it. This explanation also clarifies the functional meaning of neuroanatomical and neurophysiological data that operate as early in the visual system as the Lateral Geniculate Nucleus, or LGN (Figure 1.21).

This percept is the enhanced brightness of the illusory disk that humans see when they look at the Ehrenstein display in Figure 1.1 (left panel). This apparently simple percept has attracted a great deal of attention from vision scientists because one could imagine many reasons why no brightness difference, or even the reverse brightness difference, might have been seen instead. The Canadian vision scientist John Kennedy (Kennedy, 1979, 1988) attempted in the 1970s and 1980s to explain this percept by positing that *brightness buttons* occur at the ends of black lines, like the black lines that form the Ehrenstein display. A brightness button is a small area at the end of the line whose brightness is enhanced relative to that of the surrounding region. A brightness button is just a particular type of feature contour (Figure 3.22). I earlier discussed the role of brightness buttons in explaining how we see the enhanced brightness of the Kanizsa square; see Figures 3.3a and 3.8. Brightness buttons also played a key role in explaining other examples of brightness contrast, such as in Figure 4.9.

One might imagine that no additional processes are needed to explain the bright disk in the Ehrenstein illusion, but this would be an incorrect conclusion. This can be understood by noting that the textbook mechanism for explaining brightness contrast uses the on-center, off-surround receptive fields of early visual processing. A cell that possesses such a receptive field is excited by inputs near the cell's position (the on-center) but inhibited by inputs to more distant positions (the off-surround), as in Figure 2.22. Such a cell is called an ON cell. ON cells are not, however, the only cells that may respond to a visual input. OFF cells, or cells with an off-center on-surround, are also found in the LGN. Whereas ON cells are turned on by a visual input, OFF cells at the same positions may be turned off by the same input. An analysis of how such cells respond to dark lines, such as those that occur in the Ehrenstein stimulus, shows that they cannot, by themselves, explain the enhanced brightness of the Ehrenstein disk. In fact, if only the responses of ON and OFF cells to dark lines were involved, then the Ehrenstein disk should look *darker*, not brighter, than its background. The explanation of why the Ehrenstein disk looks brighter involves the ART Matching Rule in an unexpected way, and one that constitutes a conceptually important and testable neurophysiological prediction.

Before studying how ON and OFF cells respond to a black line on white paper, let me set the stage by first commenting about why brightness buttons are not typically seen in response to an isolated line segment. Clues were provided by John Kennedy, who analyzed a number of illusory contour stimuli. One good example is the offset grating in Figure 1.1. Here the brightening effect can spread via filling-in throughout the region around the line segments, except where the vertical amodal boundary is formed at their line ends. Another good example where brightness buttons may have no visible effect is the reverse-contrast Kanizsa square in Figure 3.3 (top row, right column) and Figure 3.9, where the brightness and darkness buttons can cancel out as they spread due to filling-in.

Given this background, I will show you in a moment that the Ehrenstein disk would look darker, not brighter, if the only factor influencing the strength of the brightness buttons were the responses of ON and OFF cells to bottom-up inputs from the retina. When confronted with such a disconfirmation of a model's predictions, one can either discard the model or ask what principled mechanisms are not yet included in it that lead to the correct answer. If the model is merely incomplete, rather than wrong, then discarding it would amount to throwing out the baby with the bathwater: If one discards part of the correct answer, then one can never complete that answer. This is a problem that all theorists must face, and one that recommends a cautious approach to model rejection.

Given that so many brightness data had already been correctly predicted by the model, including data collected after its publication, the question arose of whether and how the model's description was incomplete. At the time when I asked this question in the late 1980s, my colleagues and I already knew that an important mechanism had been omitted from our brightness simulations, indeed a mechanism that other colleagues and I had used to explain different types of data. In fact, adding an anatomically known top-down feedback pathway from visual cortical area V1 to the LGN is sufficient to explain the correct brightness of the Ehrenstein disk without disturbing the model's previous explanations of other brightness data. Moreover, in order for this top-down pathway to explain the Ehrenstein illusion, it needs to obey the ART Matching Rule!

If indeed the ART Matching Rule is at work, then it should be stabilizing the learning of some circuit between LGN and V1. This is another reason why I believe the circuit is there, as I will explain below.

First, though, we need to understand why ON and OFF cell responses to bottom-up inputs from the Ehrenstein stimulus cannot, by themselves, explain the Ehrenstein illusion. This is true because ON and OFF cells respond to positions at the end of a line with less activation than along its sides. These cell responses could lead to the Ehrenstein disk looking darker, rather than brighter, than its background. To see why this is so, first consider how OFF cells respond to a black line on a white background, as illustrated in Figure 5.5b. Since OFF cells respond best to low luminance in their receptive field center and high luminance in their surround, OFF cells whose centers lie inside the line will be activated. Furthermore, OFF cells near the line end (but still inside the line) will be more strongly activated than OFF cells in the middle of the line, because their on-surround is more activated there. A similar analysis can be applied to the ON cells, as summarized in Figure 5.5c. An ON cell is excited by high luminance in the center of its receptive field and low luminance in its surround. The ON cells that are active, then, are those centered outside the bar, where their on-centers can get activated. An ON cell whose center is just outside the side of the line will respond more strongly than an ON cell centered just outside the end of the line, because the off-surround is more strongly activated at the end of the line, and thus inhibits the cell there more than at the side of the line. In summary, if the only mechanisms at work were ON and OFF cells, then Ehrenstein disks could look darker than their surrounds, rather than brighter. Given that LGN ON and OFF cells alone cannot explain the perceived brightness of the Ehrenstein disk, we were led to ask: What is missing?

Brightness buttons are, by definition, a brightness contrast effect that is due to an *oriented* structure such as a line or, more generally, a corner or sharp bend in a contour. Within the explanation given so far, the computations leading to brightness perception are unoriented, in the sense that they are caused by ON and OFF cells with circularly symmetric receptive fields. How can an oriented filter enhance the brightness contrast at line ends, beyond

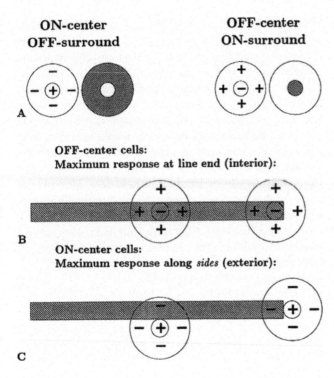

ON-center OFF-surround

OFF-center ON-surround

A

OFF-center cells:
Maximum response at line end (interior):

B

ON-center cells:
Maximum response along *sides* (exterior):

C

FIGURE 5.5. ON and OFF cells in the LGN respond differently to the sides and ends of lines.

feedback can, among other things, stabilize the learning of the oriented receptive fields of cortical simple cells and complex cells (Figure 4.25). In so doing, the learned corticogeniculate feedback should enhance the activity of those LGN cells that support the activity of presently active cortical cells in V1, and suppress the activity of LGN cells that do not (Grossberg, 1976a, 1976b, 1980). In the case where the LGN and cortex respond to a line, the active LGN cells form a spatial array that is oriented to match the line's orientation. This spatial array of active LGN cells, in turn, activates V1 cells with the corresponding orientational tuning.

Because this feedback was predicted to obey the ART Matching Rule, in the absence of input from the retina, the corticogeniculate feedback that is activated by these V1 cells was predicted to have a modulatory, or priming, effect on its target array of LGN cells. However, this corticogeniculate feedback was also predicted to synchronize and amplify consistent bottom-up retinal inputs to the LGN while suppressing unmatched, and therefore inconsistent, bottom-up signals. Figure 5.6 depicts the two variants of the corticogeniculate feedback circuit that I modeled in a 1995 article with my PhD student Alan Gove, with Ennio Mingolla also as a collaborator (Gove, Grossberg, and Mingolla, 1995). In one

what can be achieved using only an unoriented on-center off-surround filter? For such an oriented filter to work well, it must be able to have its effects at the ends of the lines, at which the brightness buttons occur. Oriented cells that are sensitive to the ends of lines are well known to exist, but they are not found in the brain until cortical area V1. A natural candidate for such cells are the *endstopped* complex, or hypercomplex, cells that I discussed while explaining end gaps and end cuts (Figure 4.25). These oriented cells are selectively activated at and near the ends of lines.

How can hypercomplex cells in the visual cortex influence the outputs of the ON and OFF cells in the LGN? Having come this far, we are now led to propose that the cortex influences LGN cells via top-down feedback from V1, which it is well known to do. It is not plausible, however, that this massive feedback pathway exists just to make Ehrenstein disks appear bright! I had, however, already predicted in 1976, and again in 1980, that corticogeniculate feedback exists for an important functional reason; namely, to realize the ART Matching Rule in order to stabilize learned changes in LGN-to-cortical LTM traces in response to the flood of visual inputs from the LGN. In particular, this

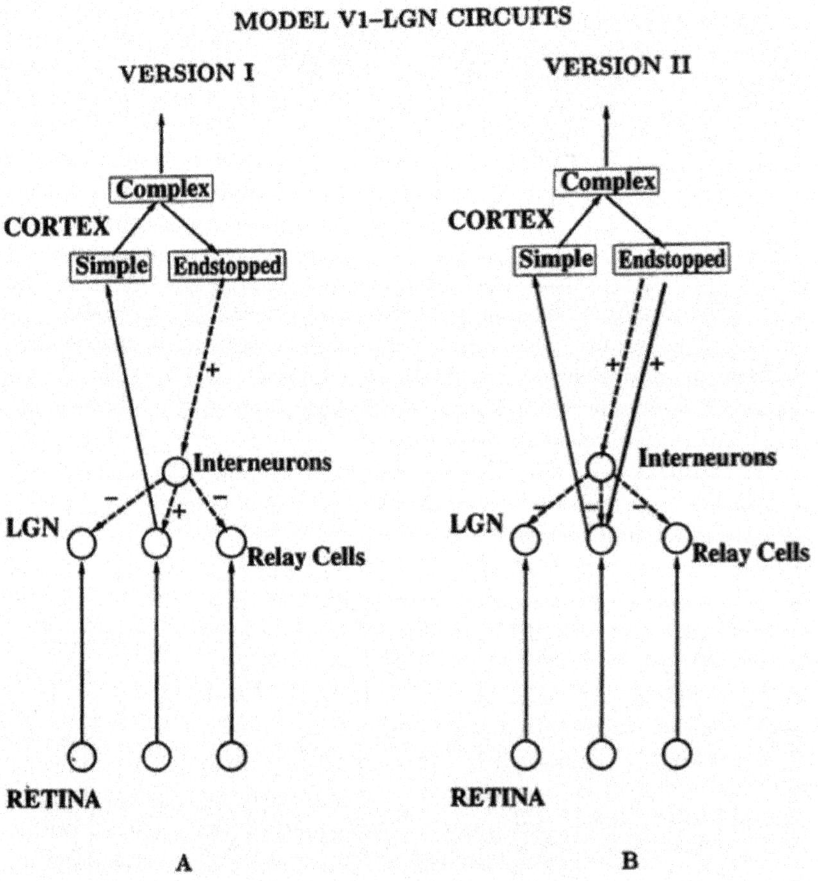

MODEL V1–LGN CIRCUITS

VERSION I

VERSION II

CORTEX

Complex

Simple Endstopped

+

Interneurons

LGN

Relay Cells

RETINA

A

CORTEX

Complex

Simple Endstopped

+/+

Interneurons

LGN

Relay Cells

RETINA

B

FIGURE 5.6. Bottom-up and top-down circuits between the LGN and cortical area V1. The top-down circuits obey the ART Matching Rule for matching with bottom-up input patterns and focusing attention on expected critical features.

version (A), a single pathway creates the top-down, modulatory on-center, off-surround network that realizes the ART Matching Rule. In the second version (B), a separate pathway controls the inhibitory interneurons. The known top-down V1-to-LGN pathways are depicted in Figure 5.7, which shows that the separate pathway scheme in (B) occurs in the brain (Weber et al., 1989).

Figure 5.8 summarizes how this type of corticogeniculate feedback can produce brightness buttons. Figure 5.8A shows the brightness buttons (open circles) and darkness buttons (filled circles) that are produced in ON cells and OFF cells, respectively, by bottom-up Ehrenstein signals without the benefit of top-down signals. As I explained above, there is less excitation outside the ends of the line than its sides. Figure 5.8B shows the excitatory (+) and inhibitory (–) top-down feedback signals from V1 to the LGN. Note the excitatory signals at both line ends. Figure 5.8C shows the final result, with both bottom-up and top-down inputs, on LGN activity, showing enhanced brightness buttons at the line ends. In brief, the top-down oriented and endstopped feedback from V1 enhances the LGN responses at line ends and supplements whatever contrast is caused by the bottom-up signals.

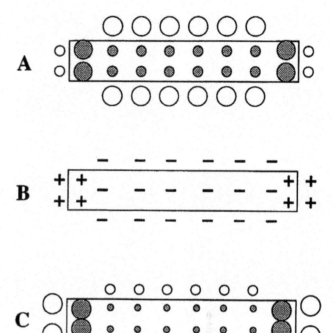

FIGURE 5.8. The patterns of LGN activation and inhibition on the sides and ends of a line without top-down feedback (A) and with it (C). The top-down distribution of excitation (+) and inhibition (-) are shown in (B).

Figure 5.9 shows a computer simulation of the Ehrenstein percept. Figure 5.9B shows how the model computes brightness buttons at the line ends in response to the Ehrenstein display of Figure 5.9A. Figure 5.9C shows the circular illusory contour that is formed within the model's boundary completion network. Finally, Figure 5.9D shows the final brightness levels after the pattern of brightness buttons in Figure 5.9B fills-in within the filling-in domain that is surrounded by the circular illusory contour in Figure 5.9C. The result is an Ehrenstein disk with uniformly enhanced brightness relative to its surround, as in the consciously perceived percept.

Neurobiological data for ART matching by corticogeniculate feedback

Is there direct neurophysiological evidence that supports my 1976 prediction that corticogeniculate feedback can alter LGN cell properties in the manner predicted by ART? I was delighted to read such evidence from the laboratory of Adam Sillito in London. In 1987, Penelope Murphy and Sillito (Murphy and Sillito, 1987) showed that cell responses in the LGN of cats are influenced by the length of

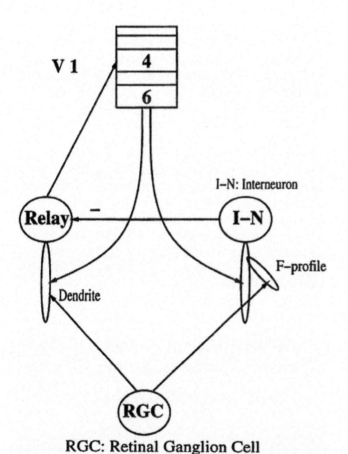

FIGURE 5.7. A more detailed description of the connections between retinal ganglion cells, the LGN, and V1.

FIGURE 5.9. A computer simulation of the percept (D) that is generated by feature contours (B) and boundary contours (C) in response to an Ehrenstein disk stimulus (A).

visually viewed lines. The LGN response to a line grows rapidly as a function of line length and then abruptly declines for longer lines, which is similar to the response observed at endstopped cortical cells. In addition Christoph Redies, John Crook, and Otto Creutzfeldt reported in 1986 that LGN cells and strongly endstopped cortical complex cells in cats both responded best at line ends (Redies, Crook, and Creutzfeldt, 1986). In other words, the response of the LGN cells to line ends was enhanced relative to the response to line sides, again consistent with the ART prediction.

Experimental evidence has also been reported for the prediction that corticogeniculate feedback carries out ART matching and resonance. In a remarkable 1994 article that appeared in *Nature*, Sillito, Jones, George Gerstein, and David West (Sillito et al., 1994) published neurophysiological data that strikingly support this prediction. They wrote that "cortically induced correlation of relay cell activity produces coherent firing in those groups of relay cells with receptive field alignments appropriate to signal the particular orientation of the moving contour to the cortex . . . this increases the gain of the input for feature-linked events detected by the cortex . . . the cortico-thalamic input is only strong enough to exert an effect on those dLGN cells that are additionally polarized by their retinal input . . . the feedback circuit searches for correlations that support the 'hypothesis' represented by a particular pattern of cortical activity . . . cortically induced correlation of relay cell activity produces coherent firing in those groups of relay cells with receptive-field alignments appropriate to signal

the particular orientation of the moving contour to the cortex . . . this increases the gain of the input for feature-linked events detected by the cortex". In a follow-up 1999 experimental study that was published in *Science*, Murphy, Simon Duckett, and Sillito (Murphy, Duckett, and Sillito, 1999) showed that corticogeniculate feedback selectively activates an array of LGN cells at positions that match the orientation of the cortical cells that caused the feedback. During normal vision, an oriented stimulus in the world would activate such an oriented array of LGN cells, which in turn would activate cortical simple, complex, and hypercomplex cells whose orientational tuning matches the LGN activation pattern. Since orientational selectivity develops with experience, the Murphy et al. data support the ART hypothesis that geniculocortical and corticogeniculate feedback interactions help to control the bidirectional development and learning of connections between the visual cortex and the LGN.

In short, Sillito and his colleagues verified all the properties of the ART Matching Rule, including the property that the effect of the on-center feedback is, by itself, modulatory: Top-down priming, by itself, cannot fully activate LGN cells; it needs matched bottom-up retinal inputs to do so; and those LGN cells whose bottom-up signals support cortical activity get amplified and synchronized by this feedback. In addition, anatomical studies by multiple authors have shown that the V1-to-LGN pathway realizes a top-down on-center off-surround network (Dubin and Cleland, 1977; Sillito et al., 1994; Weber, Kalil, and Behan, 1989).

One final comment is worth considering: The bottom-up signals from LGN to V1 form an *adaptive filter* that learns to activate perceptual *categories* in V1, and the top-down signals from V1 to LGN play the role of learned *expectations*. Category learning and intentional feedback are hereby illustrated to occur at very early levels of the visual system, even though the learned receptive fields of simple cells are much more concrete than the receptive fields of categories in inferotemporal cortex that can learn to recognize faces and other objects. At all of these levels, the stability-plasticity dilemma must be solved, and the ART Matching Rule is used to solve it.

Neurobiological data for ART matching in visual, auditory, and somatosensory cortex

Data supporting the existence of ART Matching Rule circuits in other parts of the visual cortex have also been reported by many scientists. An early report was published in *Nature* in 1988 by Semir Zeki and Stewart Shipp (Zeki and Shipp, 1988, p. 316) who reported that "backward connections seem not to excite cells in lower areas, but instead influence the way they respond to stimuli"; that is, they are modulatory. These early data preceded a veritable flood of later psychological and neurobiological data about how attention works at multiple levels of brain organization. including data about modulatory on-center, off-surround interactions; excitatory priming of features in the on-center; suppression of features in the off-surround; and gain amplification of matched data (e.g., Bullier, Hupé, James, and Girard, 1996; Caputo and Guerra, 1998; Downing, 1988; Hupé et al., 1997; Mounts, 2000; Reynolds, Chelazzi, and Desimone, 1999; Sillito, Jones, Gerstein, and West, 1994; Somers, Dale, Seiffert, and Tootell, 1999; Steinman, Steinman, and Lehmkuhle, 1995; Vanduffel, Tootell, and Orban, 2000). The ART Matching Rule was later popularized in the neuroscience community using the descriptor "biased competition" for object attention by experimental neurophysiologists such as Robert Desimone and Leslie Ungerleider in the late 1990s and beyond (Desimone, 1998; Kastner and Ungerleider, 2001).

Properties of the ART Matching Rule have also been reported in brain regions that process other sensory modalities, as would be expected from the prediction that this kind of circuit is needed wherever the stability-plasticity dilemma is solved. Here are a few examples that involve the thalamus in other modalities, thereby showing that not only the visual thalamic LGN receives ART Matching Rule feedback: In a series of articles, Nobuo Suga and colleagues reported in 1990s and early 2000s that feedback from auditory cortex to the medial geniculate nucleus (MGN) and the inferior colliculus (IC) has an on-center off-surround form that gain-amplifies matched thalamic responses and is needed for plastic changes in this circuit (Zhang, Suga, and Yan, 1997). In a series of articles between 2001 and 2008 about the rodent barrel system of the somatosensory cortex, Simona Temereanca and Daniel Simons produced evidence for an on-center off-surround organization that can amplify and synchronize responses in this system (e.g., Temereanca and Simons, 2001), and an additional 2008 article with Emory Brown further demonstrated "millisecond by millisecond changes in thalamic near-synchronous firing . . . that may ensure transmission of preferred sensory information in local thalamocortical circuits during whisking and active touch" (Temereanca, Brown, and Simons, 2008).

Excitatory matching vs. suppressive matching

The property of the ART Matching Rule that bottom-up sensory activity may be enhanced when matched by top-down signals is in accord with an extensive neurophysiological literature showing the facilitatory effect of attentional feedback (e.g., Luck et al., 1997; Roelfsema, Lamme, and Spekreijse, 1998; Sillito et al., 1994). This property cannot be taken for granted, if only because it contradicts popular models that have been published during the 1990s, such as Bayesian "explaining away" models of productive scientists like David Mumford, Rajesh Rao, and Dana Ballard, in which matches with top-down feedback cause only suppression (Mumford, 1992; Rao and Ballard, 1999). Such models became popular in part because they emphasize "predictive coding" in the visual cortex. ART also explains how such "predictive coding" may occur. But whereas ART predictions have been supported by experimental evidence such as that summarized above, Bayesian models of predictive coding have not. One of many serious problems of the Bayesian models is that fully suppressive matching circuits cannot solve the stability-plasticity dilemma.

Mathematical form of the ART Matching Rule

Data can clarify qualitative properties of brain processes, but one needs rigorous mathematical models to characterize their quantitative properties. ART is one such rigorous model. In addition to ART, there has recently been a convergence across models concerning how to mathematically instantiate the ART Matching Rule attentional circuit. For example, in 2009, John Reynolds and David Heeger published their "normalization model of attention" and used the model to simulate several types of experiments on attention (Reynolds and Heeger, 2009). These simulations used the same equation for attention as did a 2007 variant of ART, called the distributed ARTEXture, or the dARTEX, model that Gail Carpenter and our PhD student Rushi Bhatt described (Bhatt, Carpenter, and Grossberg, 2007, equation (A5)). Our article used this equation to simulate human psychophysical data that were published in 2004 by Ohad Ben-Shahar and Steven Zucker about orientation-based texture segmentation (Ben-Shahar and Zucker, 2004). These textures contribute to the texture discrimination literature that is illustrated by the textures used by Jacob Beck and his colleagues in Figures 4.33 and 4.34. dARTEX shows how ART can learn texture categories that enable the model to quantitatively simulate the texture judgments of human subjects.

It is a source of considerable pride to me that John Reynolds did his PhD thesis about ART with Gail Carpenter as his advisor and me as a collaborator (e.g., Carpenter et al., 1992; Carpenter, Grossberg, and Reynolds, 1991) before moving on to a distinguished career as a neuroscientist. However, whereas the normalization model provided only a steady-state equation with which to fit attentional data, dARTEX describes the neuronal dynamics that are activated by psychophysical texture stimuli. The dARTEX dynamical equations reduce to the same kind of steady-state equation as in the normalization model when they are at equilibrium. In this sense, dARTEX "explains" where the steady-state form factor comes from in a way that the normalization model does not.

From automatic to task-selective attentional control

If we take the above results about LGN-V1 interactions at face value, then it would appear that corticogeniculate feedback helps to "focus attention" upon expected patterns of LGN activity. Until data such as these started to appear, it was often argued that visual attention first acts at higher levels of cortical organization, starting with extrastriate visual cortical areas like V2, V4, and MT. Is there a contradiction here?

The answer depends upon how you define attention. If attention refers only to processes that can be controlled voluntarily, then corticogeniculate feedback, being automatic, may not qualify. On the other hand, corticogeniculate feedback does appear to have the selective properties of an "automatic" attention process. ART explains why such attentional processes may exist at all levels of sensory and cognitive neocortex in terms of the need to stabilize learning thalamic and cortical receptive field properties. In Chapter 10, I will propose how such an automatic attentional process seems to be realized within the laminar circuits of visual cortex and, by extension, in all sensory and cognitive neocortex. This proposal identifies which identified cortical cell types and which cortical layers seem to realize the top-down, modulatory on-center, off-surround network that was predicted by the ART Matching Rule. This work has greatly clarified how the laminar organization of neocortex is used for purposes of perceptual grouping, attention, development, and learning.

Bottom-up automatic attention? I should also mention that bottom-up signals, all by themselves, embody a kind of automatic attention. Bottom-up signals are indeed selective because they do not activate all the cells in a given part of the brain. They can also actively suppress unactivated cells via the on-center off-surround networks that help to solve the noise-saturation dilemma; cf. Chapters 1 and 4. Chapter 8 will add another factor to the discussion of bottom-up attention by describing cells in the Where cortical stream that are sensitive to input transients. Activating these cells can attract automatic attention to changes in bottom-up input patterns. Automatic attention using the ART Matching Rule provides additional selectivity by using the ART Matching Rule to amplify and synchronize attended cells while suppressing unattended one.

Top-down task-selective attention and memory search for new categories. Given that the top-down attentional circuits are ubiquitous in the visual cortex, and by extension in other types of cortex, it is important to ask: What additional mechanisms does the brain need in order to generate a more flexible, *task-selective* type of attentional control and switching? This question leads us to our next example, that of visual object category learning and recognition. I will suggest how novel events that mismatch currently active top-down expectations can trigger a task-selective memory search, or hypothesis testing, that helps to regulate the learning of new recognition categories with which to recognize these events in the future. This memory search mechanism (cf. Figure 1.11), together with top-down matching using the ART Matching Rule, is part of the brain's solution of the stability-plasticity dilemma. By working together, these mechanisms have greatly expanded the amount of knowledge that human and other sufficiently advanced brains can learn, and the speed with which they can learn it. As I explain how this works, I will also explain how, when this novelty system breaks down, serious learning and memory deficits occur which resemble, among other difficulties, the symptoms of human patients who are afflicted with medial temporal amnesia.

We learn, therefore we can imagine, think, plan, and hallucinate

Before discussing visual object category learning and recognition, a related question can quickly be answered: How is visual imagery possible if top-down expectations are modulatory in their on-center, as the ART Matching Rule proposes (Figure 1.25)? Would not conscious visual imagery require supra-threshold, indeed resonant, cell activation to occur? How does a modulatory top-down expectation cause a resonant activation? Figure 1.25 includes an answer to this question. Volitional signals can alter the balance between excitation and inhibition in the on-center of the top-down expectation by weakening inhibition relative to excitation. Then read-out of a top-down expectation from a recognition category *can* fire cells to suprathreshold activities in the on-center prototype, leading to a bottom-up and top-down cycling of signals, and resonance. These volitional signals are controlled by the basal ganglia, a part of the brain whose psychological and neurobiological properties will be discussed in Chapter 15. This effect of the basal ganglia on whether cortical feedback is modulatory or driving is just one of many examples of basal ganglia volitional control that neural models have mechanistically clarified.

The fact that a top-down expectation is not always modulatory has had profound effects on the development of civilization. In addition to enabling us to activate visual imagery, these volitional signals can also support the ability to think and plan ahead without requiring external cues or actions. These imaginative capacities represent a crucial type of predictive competence in humans.

There is also a down-side to this scheme: When it does not work well, we can lose our minds! It works well if the volitional signals are under our voluntary control, so we can fantasize and plan at will. However, if the basal ganglia cells that control these volitional signals become tonically—that is, persistently—hyperactive, then top-down expectations can fire without us wanting them to do so. Then we can experience sights and sounds that we are not receiving from the outside world, and that are not under our control. I proposed in a 2000 article that this is one way that schizophrenic hallucinations may arise (Grossberg, 2000a). The ability to imagine and think thus carries the risk that some of us will experience hallucinations and "go crazy".

Let me summarize this line of causation because it clarifies how some of our most prized human endowments can be a double-edged sword: The ability to imagine, think, and plan arises from the solution of the stability-plasticity dilemma; namely, the ability to learn quickly throughout life without experiencing catastrophic forgetting. First and foremost, the ART Matching Rule, and its top-down modulatory on-center, dynamically stabilizes learned memories. The discovery during evolution that this modulatory signal can be volitionally controlled brought with it huge evolutionary advantages of being able to imagine visual imagery, and to quietly think and plan. But these precious consequences of our ability to learn rapidly and stably about our changing world, which is a prerequisite for developing a sense of self and civilized societies, also carry with them the risk of going crazy when volitional control goes awry. This risk is just part of the human condition. It is a risk that evolution has maintained because of its very powerful positive consequences for most of us most of the time.

Why are auditory hallucinations more prevalent than visual ones? Auditory hallucinations are most frequently experienced during schizophrenia, including hearing one's own thoughts being spoken aloud, or hearing voices speaking to or about oneself. Visual, tactile, and olfactory hallucinations have also been reported. These include seeing frightening faces, the feeling of being strangled, and experiencing food as repulsive. In 1998, Christopher Frith (Frith, 1998) summarized three properties of these experiences: They occur in the absence of sensation; self-generated activity is perceived to come from an external source; and the voice (in the case of an auditory hallucination) is perceived to come from an agent who is attempting to influence the patient. Frith hypothesized that these effects are due to disruption of the interactions between prefrontal cortex and posterior brain regions. ART shows how learned top-down expectations acting from prefrontal cortex to posterior sensory cortices, among other top-down pathways, help to ensure the stability of normal learning and memory, but can cause hallucinations when they are converted from modulatory expectations to experienced percepts and thoughts due to tonically-active volitional signals (Grossberg, 2000a).

Properties of the ART Matching Rule also clarify more detailed properties of hallucinations. For example, ART clarifies why unstructured auditory inputs, such as white noise, can increase the severity of hallucinations, while listening to speech or music helps to reduce them, as A. Margo, David Hemsley, and Peter Slade reported in 1981 (Margo, Hemsley, and Slade, 1981). Both types of data are consistent with the ART Matching Rule, which selects those auditory signals that are consistent with the top-down expectation, while suppressing those that are not. In the case of white noise, the broad-band nature of the noise enables it to supply more bottom-up activity to the active components of the top-down expectation, and thereby to generate an even stronger hallucination. The top-down expectation can by itself activate target cells during a hallucination, but can do so even more effectively when it is energized by noise.

In this situation, hallucinations would use the same systems that are usually used when listening to external speech or to generate inner speech. In addition, the fact that external "voices" in schizophrenics tend to match the content of whispers or subvocal speech, as Louis Gould noted in 1949 (Gould, 1949), is clarified by ART, because both exploit the top-down expectations of the individual.

How does the ART Matching Rule explain how speech or music helps to reduce auditory hallucinations? In brief, a bottom-up input that does *not* match an internally generated top-down expectation can *reset* it and impose the representation mandated by the bottom-up input. This reset operation is proposed below to be part of the machinery whereby the brain responds to novel inputs by resetting mismatched categories and searching for new, or better matching, categories with which to recognize novel information, as part of the ART memory search and learning cycle that I will soon explain (see Figure 5.19).

This explanation also clarifies why auditory hallucinations may be more frequent than visual hallucinations. We actively receive bottom-up visual inputs whenever our eyes are open in a room that is not totally dark. Thus, there is a continual stream of visual inputs to reset top-down visual expectations that might otherwise cause hallucinations in a schizophrenic. In contrast, we can often find ourselves in a quiet place, even if our ears are "open" to surrounding sounds. This asymmetry between vision and audition can be reduced when an individual is in a continually noisy space, with corresponding reductions in auditory hallucinations. Of course, many caveats must be added to this simple observation, including that: seeing familiar people, objects, or scenes can cause a cross-modality activation of their auditorily coded names, thereby creating an intermodal "bottom-up" visual input; or a visual scene may be boring or so familiar that it does not engage many attentional resources; and so on. However, the asymmetry between the frequency of visual and auditory bottom-up inputs provides useful food for additional thought.

The contents of a conscious percept can also be modified by task-sensitive signals that control our *vigilance* (parameter ρ in Figure 5.19 below). When vigilance is high, specific categories are learned, and when vigilance is low, abstract categories are learned. ART predicts that when specific prototypes are learned, then specific hallucinations will be read-out by these prototypes, and when abstract prototypes are learned, then they will lead to similarly abstract hallucinations. This prediction adds a new twist to the idea that hallucinations are formed within the same systems that are usually used to experience conscious percepts. It suggests, not only that learned top-down expectations control the perceptual contents of hallucinations, but also that these contents may be dynamically refined or generalized based on the task-selective constraints that were operative during individual learning experiences.

Thus, other things being equal, if a schizophrenic patient is also amnesic and is able to learn coarse categories in the amnesic state, then the patient's hallucinations about these experiences might also be predicted to involve coarsely categorized information.

Volitional signals that convert primes to driving activities across multiple modalities

One of the recurrent themes of this book is that evolution is opportunistic in using the same mechanism, suitably specialized, for multiple tasks. Above I noted the role of volitional signals in converting a modulatory top-down expectation into a driving one, and how visual imagery, thinking, and planning depend upon this property. A similar role for volition, again modulated by the basal ganglia, is predicted to control when sequences of objects or events (e.g., telephone numbers) are temporarily stored in short-term working memory in the prefrontal cortex, and how such storage will be reset, as I will explain in Chapters 12 and 14 (Grossberg, 2018; Grossberg and Pearson, 2008). In addition, the span of spatial attention—a property called *useful-field-of-view*—in the parietal and prefrontal cortices can be volitionally expanded or contracted to deal strategically with different kinds of scenes and visual tasks (Foley, Grossberg, and Mingolla, 2012). A striking example of an increase in spatial attentional span is known to occur as video game players practice to become more expert. I will describe the basal ganglia mechanisms that control this effect in Chapter 12 (Green and Bavelier, 2003). All of these properties can be viewed as variations on the fundamental ability to learn quickly throughout life without catastrophic forgetting by using top-down expectations to stabilize learned memories.

Category learning transforms distributed features into category choices

Let us now return to explaining how visual object categories may be learned and consciously recognized. In order to transform distributed and analog feature representations into more symbolic and abstract category representations, their processing levels need to interact. This interaction occurs via pathways that branch out (or fan-out, or diverge) from individual feature cells, so that they can influence the learning of multiple categories, and are combined (or fan-in, or converge) at their target category cells (Figure 5.10), which occur at the *category level*, or F_2. As a result, a given category cell may receive signals from many feature representations. It can hereby become sensitive to the patterning

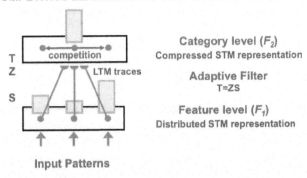

FIGURE 5.10. A competitive learning circuit learns to transform distributed feature patterns into selective responses of recognition categories.

of activity across these feature representations, which occur at the *feature level*, or F_1.

The feature level F_1 in Figure 5.10 contains a network of cells, or cell populations, each of which is activated by a particular combination of sensory features via inputs from an earlier processing stage. I will sometimes call such a cell unit a "node" because it may represent either an individual feature-selective cell, or a population of cells with similar featural preferences. The category level F_2 contains a network of nodes that represent recognition categories. Each category node is selectively activated by activation patterns across F_1 that represents similar objects or events. Different category nodes are activated by sufficiently different sets of activation patterns at the feature level. As illustrated in Figure 5.10, each F_1 node sends output signals via pathways, called *axons*, to a subset of F_2 nodes (Figure 2.3). Each F_2 node may thus receive signals from many F_1 nodes. Learning takes place at the ends of the axons. This is a location where two types of information are spatially contiguous: signals from an F_1 cell that travel down the axon, and activities of a contiguous F_2 cell. Axons end in a specialized structure that is called a *synapse*, which is depicted by a hemispherical disk in Figures 2.3 and 5.10. Synapses, and the postsynaptic cell bodies that they contact, are well placed to be sites of learning because, at these locations, the learning process can correlate information about active features in F_1 with active categories in F_2.

Instar bottom-up category learning and outstar top-down expectation learning

Learning in these bottom-up pathways enables F_2 category nodes to become selectively tuned to particular combinations of activation patterns across F_1 feature detectors. This tuning process changes the adaptive weights, or long-term memory (LTM) traces, that occur within the synapses and/or at the postsynaptic cell. I published a widely-used learning rule for this process in 1967 and 1968 in the *Proceedings of the National Academy of Sciences* (Grossberg, 1967, 1968c, 1968d). Norman Levinson, who was then an Institute Professor at MIT and its most famous mathematician, as well as a member of the National Academy of Sciences, submitted these articles for me to PNAS. I mention this because the learning law was discovered 10 years earlier when I was a college Freshman, but there was no recognized field then for publishing models that link brain to mind. It was both kind and generous of Levinson to put his reputation on the line by submitting work to PNAS in a field where he was not personally an expert. Variants of this law have subsequently been used by me (e.g., Grossberg, 1975b, 1976a, 1976b, 1978a, 1980, 1982, 1984c,

1984d), and later, starting in the 1980s, with my colleagues and many other authors, notably by Teuvo Kohonen in his version of the Self-Organizing Map model (Kohonen, 1984), and by Robert Hecht-Nielsen in his version of the Counterpropagation model (Hecht-Nielsen, 1987).

A key property of this learning law is that adaptive weights can change through learning at a synapse only if the abutting category node is active. When a category node is active for a long enough time, the adaptive weights in all synapses that abut this category node can change. These weights learn by tracking the sizes of the signals that they receive along their pathway through time. More exactly, they compute an average of the bottom-up signals that are received by the category code at times when it is active. The bottom-up signals are emitted when the corresponding feature node is active. An adaptive weight can thus change in response to the correlated activities in both the feature node and the category node that are linked by its pathway.

Category learning by instars. This is a type of *correlation learning law* which is so-called because it correlates activities in the feature and category nodes. I called one version of this learning law the *instar* learning law because activity in a category node triggers learning in all the pathways that face the category node (Grossberg, 1976a; Figure 5.11). These pathways hereby form an inward-facing "star" at the category node (Figure 5.12, right panel). In brief: Instar learning can train category nodes to respond selectively to the bottom-up signals that they receive from their feature-selective inputs. The name "instar learning" summarizes the anatomy that supports category learning.

INSTAR LEARNING

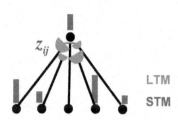

Need both increases and decreases in strength for the LTM pattern to learn the STM pattern

$$\frac{d}{dt} z_{ij} = -M z_{ij} + f_i(x_i) h_j(x_j)$$

$$\frac{d}{dt} z_{ij} = f_j(x_j) \left[h_i(x_i) - z_{ij} \right]$$

FIGURE 5.11. Instar learning enables a bottom-up adaptive filter to become selectively tuned to particular feature patterns. Such pattern learning needs adaptive weights that can either increase or decrease to match the featural activations that they filter.

DUALITY OF OUTSTAR AND INSTAR

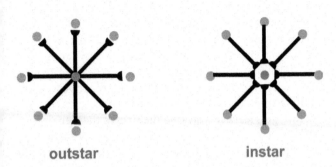

outstar   instar

FIGURE 5.12. The duality of the outstar and instar networks is evident when they are drawn as above.

Another name for this type of learning highlights its dynamical, or neurophysiological, properties; namely, *gated steepest descent* learning. These dynamical properties will be summarized below, where I will also start to explain how instar learning opened a huge and diverse world of phenomena to me.

Learning in the pathways from distributed feature nodes to compressed category nodes is a form of *bottom-up* learning, because it proceeds from a more peripheral to a more central processing stage in the brain. Adaptive Resonance Theory explains, however, why bottom-up instar learning is not sufficient to solve the stability-plasticity dilemma, and that *top-down* learning of expectations is also needed (Figure 5.13, top panel).

Spatial and spatiotemporal pattern learning by outstars. A related learning law, and one that is complementary to instar learning, is used to learn these top-down expectations. This is the *outstar* learning law that I introduced in 1967. This breakthrough supported a burst of productivity during which I was able to mathematically prove how this kind of learning works in increasingly complicated networks, and to show how it can help to explain widely different kinds of data, ranging from data about the production and release of chemical transmitters, through data about human serial learning of lists, to data about animal reinforcement learning and about mental disorders like schizophrenia. To give a sense of how a single discovery like the characterization of a fundamental learning law can trigger rapid progress, I list some of the first wave of these articles here so that interested readers can get a better sense of this diversity by reading the article titles; e.g., Grossberg, 1967, 1968a, 1968b, 1968c, 1969a, 1969b, 1969c, 1970, 1971a, 1971b, 1972a, 1972b, 1974, 1975a, 1975b, 1976a, 1976b; Grossberg and Pepe, 1970, 1971. Because most of my journal articles can be downloaded from my personal web page sites.bu.edu/steveg, readers who have a particular interest in going deeper into any topic can download the corresponding articles for further study.

During outstar learning, a single category node sends multiple diverging pathways to a network of feature nodes (Figures 5.12, 5.14 and 5.15). Such a category node is a *sampling node* that controls learning within the outstar's pathways (Figures 5.14 and 5.15). It is called a sampling node because learning happens only when the category node sends a *sampling signal* along all the pathways to the *sampled nodes*. The sampling signal "opens a learning gate" when it is active. This gate is defined by term $f_i(x_i)$

EXPECTATIONS FOCUS ATTENTION

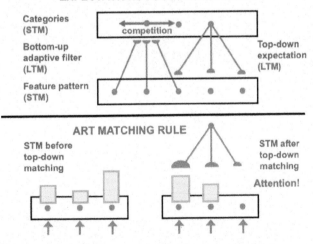

Categories (STM)
competition
Bottom-up adaptive filter (LTM)
Top-down expectation (LTM)
Feature pattern (STM)

ART MATCHING RULE

STM before top-down matching
STM after top-down matching
Attention!

FIGURE 5.13. Instar and outstar learning are often used to learn the adaptive weights in the bottom-up filters and top-down expectations that occur in ART. The ART Matching Rule for object attention enables top-down expectations to select, amplify, and synchronize expected patterns of critical features, while suppressing unexpected features.

OUTSTAR LEARNING

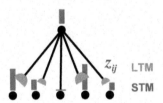

z_{ij} LTM

STM

Need both increases and decreases in strength for the LTM pattern to learn the STM pattern

$$\frac{d}{dt}z_{ij} = -Mz_{ij} + f_i(x_i)h_j(x_j) \qquad \text{Passive Decay}$$

$$\frac{d}{dt}z_{ij} = Mf_i(x_i)\left[h_j(x_j) - z_{ij}\right] \qquad \text{Gated Steepest Descent}$$

FIGURE 5.14 Outstar learning enables individual sampling cells to learn distributed spatial patterns of activation at the network of cells that they sample. Again, both increases and decreases in LTM traces must be possible to enable them to match the activity pattern at the sampled cells.

in the *gated steepest descent* learning law in Figure 5.14. In particular, when the gate is closed—that is, $f_i(x_i)$ equals zero—the time rate of change $\dfrac{dz_{ij}}{dt}$ of the adaptive weight, or long-term memory (LTM) trace, z_{ij} in each outstar pathway equals zero, so that no z_{ij} learns at that time. The adaptive weights in all the outstar pathways learn the *average pattern* of activity across the feature level nodes throughout the time interval when the sampling signal $f_i(x_i)$ is positive. When the outstar is part of the network that sends top-down signals to a network of feature nodes in an ART network (Figure 5.13), these adaptive weights learn to encode the pattern that the category node "expects" to find there, based on its past experience.

Given that bottom-up instar learning can learn to tune category nodes, why is top-down outstar learning also needed? To explain why this is so, I first need to tell you more about how bottom-up instar learning works in the typical situation where multiple category nodes exist at the category level.

Joining competitive choice to instar learning: Competitive learning. In this situation, category learning needs to be combined with competition, or lateral inhibition, among the category nodes (Figure 5.13, top panel). This is because each feature node can activate many category nodes. Without competition to suppress category nodes that receive relatively small inputs, each category node could learn about too many different feature patterns. Competition selects the category node, or small number of nodes, that best represent the distributed feature pattern that is active at any time. These are the categories that receive the largest signals from the feature level, and are thus most active. While the competition is choosing the most active category nodes, it also suppresses the activities of all the less active category nodes.

The instar learning rule activates learning at a synapse only if the abutting category node is active; that is only if the sampling signal $f_j(x_j)$ is positive, where x_j is the activity of the jth category in the second equation in Figure 5.11. As a result, learning can occur only within LTM traces z_{ij} at synapses that contact *winning* category nodes.

With this background, I can now describe how such a model learns in more precise language. To fix ideas, I will describe only the simplest version of these concepts and equations. Many useful variations have also been developed over the years. The reader who is content with the heuristic discussion so far can skip the subsequent discussion and move on to the next section.

As shown in Figure 5.11, an input pattern registers itself as a pattern of activity, or STM, across the feature detectors of level F_1, with the red vertical bars denoting different activity levels across the cells, or nodes, of the network. If the ith F_1 node is sufficiently active, then its activity x_i generates a signal $h_i(x_i)$ within the pathways that it sends to the category level F_2. Each signal is multiplied, or *gated*, by the adaptive weight, or LTM trace, z_{ij} in its respective pathway.

Learning enables a winning category node in F_2 to change the adaptive weights z_{ij} in the pathways that face it. This learning makes the adaptive weights more similar to the signals that are then traveling from F_1 to F_2 in these pathways. This learned change "tunes the bottom-up adaptive filter" and thereby enables the activity pattern at F_1 to generate bigger inputs to the winning category in the future, thus making it easier for this category to win the competition.

For readers who want to get a more precise idea about how the adaptive weights use the instar learning law to select a category node, I will introduce some mathematical notation. For readers who feel comfortable reading this notation, it makes the learning process simpler to understand. These details can, however, also be skipped without losing the main idea.

For definiteness, let S_i be the signal that is generated by activity in the ith feature node in F_1. As above, call z_{ij} the adaptive weight, or LTM trace, from this i^{th} feature node to the jth category node in F_2. This weight multiplies, or gates, the signal in its pathway. The net input to the jth category node is thus the product of S_i and z_{ij}, which is $S_i z_{ij}$. All of these LTM-gated signals are added up at their target F_2 category nodes, so the total input to the jth F_2 node is $T_j = \Sigma_k S_k z_{kj}$. Such a sum of products is called the *dot product*, or *inner product*, of the *signal vector* $S = (S_1, \ldots, S_n)$ consisting of all the signals across the network,

SPATIAL PATTERN LEARNING
Outstar learning

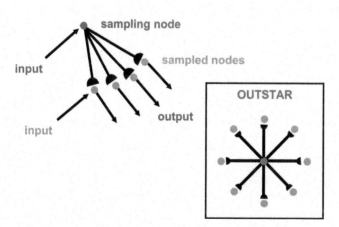

FIGURE 5.15. An outstar can learn an arbitrary spatial pattern of activation at its sampled nodes, or cells. The net pattern that is learned is a time average of all the patterns that are active at the sampled nodes when the sampling node is active.

and the *adaptive weight vector* $z_j = (z_{1j}, \ldots, z_{nj})$ consisting of all the adaptive weights from feature nodes to the jth category node, where n is the number of cells in level F_1. Such a dot product is often denoted in vector notation by $T = S \cdot z$, for simplicity.

Another way to say this is that the dot product acts to *filter* the signals S_i using the adaptive weights z_{ij}. Such a filter generates larger total inputs I_{2j} to those F_2 category nodes whose weight vectors z_j are most similar to the input vector $S = \theta$. This state of affairs is illustrated in Figure 5.16 for the special case in which there are just three cells in F_2 whose total inputs from F_1 equal $I_{2j} = S \cdot z_j$. As can be seen from the graph of I_{2j} sizes, the node numbered 1 in F_2 gets the biggest input. That is because LTM vector z_1 is "closest" to the input vector θ, as can be seen from the lower panel of Figure 5.16. As a result, node 1 wins the competition across F_2, as shown by the graph of winning x_{2j} activities in Figure 5.16 (top row, right panel).

Figure 5.17 shows how learning changes the LTM vectors: It makes the LTM vector z_1 of the winning category node, and *only* this vector, become more parallel to the input vector θ. As this happens, the total input I_{21} to the winning category node increases. In fact, I_{21} equals the length of the vectors z_1 and θ multiplied by the cosine of the angle between them. As the vectors become more parallel, the cosine approaches its maximum value of 1, so the weight vectors that are most similar to their input vector θ generate the biggest inputs to their category nodes. If node $j = 1$ in F_2 receives the biggest total input, then competition will choose it over all other nodes $j = 2, 3, \ldots, n$. Then instar learning will make the weight vector z_1 become even more parallel to θ, and thus will further increase the size of the input I_{21}. This is how category $j = 1$ gets incrementally tuned by learning to respond more vigorously to some signal patterns than others.

Competitive decisions: Contrast enhancement and normalization during category learning

Given that many category cells in F_2 can be activated to different degrees by an input pattern S, how does competition across F_2 choose the node, or small number of nodes, that gets the largest input, and thus best represents S? Before discussing how competition works, let me clarify a related point that may cause confusion. You might ask: Why is learning needed if some nodes in F_2 already "best represent" S before any learning occurs?

Before learning occurs, the initial values of the bottom-up adaptive weights may be randomly chosen and very *small*. Some nodes will get bigger inputs simply due to random fluctuations in the small initial weights, not due to any special tuning of these weights. Due to the small initial weights, inputs to the category nodes may also be small. As noted in Figure 5.17, learning helps to tune subsets of these weights to better match the inputs that the network experiences—thereby making them more parallel to combinations of the input patterns that are experienced—while also causing the weights to grow and thereby to more vigorously activate the corresponding category nodes.

This explanation does not, however, deal with with a potentially devastating problem: If the *initial* signals from the feature cells in F_1 to category cells in F_2 are small, then how do they manage to activate their target nodes

GEOMETRY OF CHOICE AND LEARNING

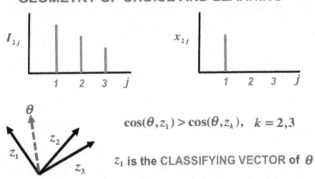

$$\cos(\theta, z_1) > \cos(\theta, z_k), \quad k = 2, 3$$

z_1 is the CLASSIFYING VECTOR of θ

FIGURE 5.16. In the simplest example of category learning, the category that receives the largest total input from the feature level is chosen, and drives learning in the adaptive weights that abut it. Learning in this "classifying vector", denoted by z_1, makes this vector more parallel to the input vector from the feature level that is driving the learning (dashed red arrow).

GEOMETRY OF CHOICE AND LEARNING

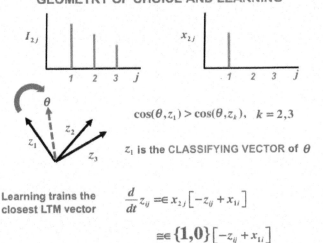

$$\cos(\theta, z_1) > \cos(\theta, z_k), \quad k = 2, 3$$

z_1 is the CLASSIFYING VECTOR of θ

Learning trains the closest LTM vector

$$\frac{d}{dt} z_{ij} = \in x_{2j} \left[-z_{ij} + x_{1i} \right]$$

$$\cong \in \{1, 0\} \left[-z_{ij} + x_{1i} \right]$$

FIGURE 5.17. This figure summarizes the simplest equations whereby the adaptive weights of a winning category learn the input pattern that drove it to win, or more generally a time-average of all the input patterns that succeeded in doing so.

strongly enough to drive learning? How does learning get *started*? This is a general problem that always occurs in self-organizing systems: How does a self-organizing process get started on its own, with no external teacher except the input environment? Here is where properties of competition that I described in Chapters 1 and 4 come to the rescue during category learning.

Category learning can start because the competition among the category nodes amplifies the largest signals while it chooses them. As I noted in Chapter 1, this choice-and-amplification process is called *contrast enhancement*. Although the initial inputs to the category nodes may have been too small to drive learning, the amplified signals are large enough to support reasonably fast learning rates. For this to work, a *recurrent* (or feedback) *on-center off-surround* feedback network is needed in which the competitive, or lateral inhibitory, interactions among the category nodes are supplemented by self-excitatory feedback signals from each category node to itself (Figures 1.6 and 1.15). I earlier discussed such a network when considering how an input pattern is stored in short-term memory, or STM (Figures 1.6–1.9). In all my examples of such an on-center off-surround network, the cells obey the membrane equations of neurophysiology, which enable *shunting*, or automatic gain control, properties to obtain. Shunting properties were earlier used in Chapter 4 to explain discounting the illuminant, and the properties of brightness constancy, contrast, and assimilation that follow from it in response to different images and scenes.

In addition to contrast enhancement, such a network can also conserve, or *normalize*, its total activity across all active cells. This property implies that strengthening the activity of one cell weakens the activities of other cells. This happens in both feedforward and feedback shunting on-center off-surround networks. The normalization properties in feedforward networks were, for example, used in Chapter 4 to explain how end gaps and end cuts of visual boundaries form (Figures 4.24 and 4.25).

Feedback, or recurrent, networks, unlike feedforward networks, can contrast enhance and thereby amplify their choices, even in response to small inputs, all the while normalizing the total activity pattern. Both the contrast enhancement and normalization properties in feedback networks were used, for example, in Chapter 4 during my discussion of how the "fuzzy" receptive fields of bipole cells (Figure 4.31) embody a kind of "real-time probability theory" of the possible grouping directions at a given position in space. The best combination of grouping positions and directions across space is then chosen using contrast enhancement and STM by a recurrent shunting on-center off-surround network to form a final boundary grouping.

These properties of recurrent shunting on-center off-surround networks can be applied with confidence because

they are supported by rigorous mathematical theorems (Figures 1.6–1.9) that I began to prove in 1973 (Grossberg, 1973; reviewed in Grossberg, 1980). The contrast normalization property has gotten an increasing amount of play since work that I did with colleagues like Gail Carpenter, Michael Cohen, Jonathan Marshall, Ennio Mingolla, and Dejan Todorovic in the 1980s established its utility in explaining many facts about the cortical dynamics of visual perception and attention (e.g., Carpenter and Grossberg, 1987a, 1987b; Cohen and Grossberg, 1984; Grossberg, 1987a, 1987b; Grossberg and Marshall, 1989; Grossberg and Mingolla, 1985a, 1985b, 1987; Grossberg and Todorovic, 1988).

Subsequent studies of contrast normalization and attention in recurrent neocortical networks include David Heeger's 1992 article about "Normalization of Cell Responses in Cat Striate Cortex" (Heeger, 1992); the 1995 article of Rodney Douglas, Christof Koch, Misha Mahowald, Kevan Martin, and Humbert Suarez about "Recurrent Excitation in Neocortical Circuits" (Douglas et al., 1995); the 2009 article of John Reynolds and Heeger about "The Normalization Model of Attention"; and the 2012 article of Matteo Carandini and Heeger about "Normalization as a Canonical Neural Computation" (Carandini and Heeger, 2012). These articles illustrate that properties of contrast enhancement and normalization in recurrent shunting on-center off-surround networks are now well established.

My theorems about competition had just the properties that I needed to explain how category learning works. A particularly relevant discovery was how a *sigmoid*, or S-shaped, signal function (Figure 1.8) can contrast-enhance cell activity patterns, while simultaneously suppressing noise (Figure 1.7, bottom row) in such a recurrent shunting network. As I noted in Chapter 1, a sigmoid signal function can suppress initial activities that are smaller than a *quenching threshold* (Figure 1.9), and thus treated like noise, while suprathreshold activities are contrast-enhanced and stored in STM.

This mathematical analysis also demonstrated that sigmoid signal functions are the simplest ones that avoid one or another problem (Figure 1.7). For example, although a linear signal function can store *any* pattern in short-term memory, or STM, without changing its relative activities, it also amplifies noise. A slower-than-linear signal function also amplifies noise, while it also eliminates differences in initial activities. A faster-than-linear signal function suppresses noise, but it does so with such vigor that only the node with the initially largest activity is stored in STM. Such a winner-take-all network is often useful for making choices, but in general a less severe kind of contrast-enhancement is desirable.

A sigmoid signal function is a "hybrid" signal that combines the best properties of the simpler faster-than-linear, linear, and slower-than-linear signal functions, as summarized in Figure 1.8. Because a sigmoid signal function gives rise to a quenching threshold (Figure 1.9), it is a *tunable* filter which, when the quenching threshold is chosen high enough, can make a winner-take-all choice, whereas, when the quenching threshold is chosen low enough, can store all previously active features to enable a new category to be chosen in response to a predictive failure.

A review of the mathematical equations whereby sigmoid signals combine the properties of faster-than-linear, linear, and slower-than-linear signals is found in my 2013 article about "Recurrent Neural Networks" in *Scholarpedia* (Grossberg, 2013b). This article also compactly summarizes quite a few concepts and mechanisms about the foundations of neurodynamics.

Additional computational analyses have shown how sigmoid signal functions arise in networks of shunting neurons whose neurons communicate using discrete spikes through time. In these networks, increasing cell body potentials increase the spiking frequencies in the axons that communicate with other cells in the network (Figure 2.3). In a spiking neuron, the sigmoid signal function is not explicitly defined. Rather, it is an emergent property of cell dynamics. Two articles with my PhD student Jesse Palma and my postdoctoral fellow Maximiliano Versace show how the shape of the sigmoid signal function may be determined by interactions of three afterhyperpolarization currents with the neurotransmitter acetylcholine. This is quite a technical, albeit fascinating and important, topic that is worthy of further study. Readers who might want to take the plunge into understanding sigmoids better can find this analysis in the two articles by Palma, Grossberg, and Versace (2012) and Palma, Versace, and Grossberg (2012) on my web page.

Gated steepest descent combines Hebbian and anti-Hebbian learning

During both instar and outstar learning, an LTM trace can either increase or decrease to track the signals in its pathway. When an LTM trace increases, it is sometimes said to undergo Hebbian learning, after the famous law of Donald Hebb (Hebb, 1949) which said that LTM traces always increase during learning. When an LTM trace decreases, it is said to undergo anti-Hebbian learning.

As I noted in Chapter 2, Hebbian learning is not a sufficient description of learning for several reasons, one being that all LTM traces could eventually saturate at their maximum values. This problem arose from the even more serious problem of choosing the wrong computational unit of learning. The correct unit is a pattern, or vector, of LTM traces that learns a distributed pattern of STM activities across a network, not a single LTM trace that samples the

activity of only one postsynaptic cell. Gated steepest descent incorporates both Hebbian and anti-Hebbian properties in a single synapse, so that the pattern of LTM traces can track and match the distributed STM activity pattern that is being learned across the network. See Figure 2.11.

Competitive learning and self-organizing maps: On the road to adaptive resonance

Models that combine instar learning and competition are often called competitive learning or self-organizing map models Such models were introduced and computationally characterized by Christoph von der Malsburg and myself between 1972–1978 (Grossberg, 1972c, 1976a, 1978a; von der Malsburg, 1973; Willshaw and Malsburg, 1976). They were subsequently applied and further developed by many authors, notably Teuvo Kohonen, whose 1984 book on the subject, and its subsequent editions, helped to popularize them (Kohonen, 1984).

Nice properties of competitive learning in sparse environments. Models like competitive learning and self-organizing maps that combine associative learning and competition exhibit many useful properties, especially if there are not too many input patterns, or clusters of input patterns, activating the feature level F_1 relative to the number of categories in level F_2 that are there to classify them. I published a mathematical proof in 1976 that, under these "sparse" environmental conditions, category learning has nice properties, at least if network competition selects for storage in STM only the category that receives the largest input, while suppressing less activated category cells.

First and foremost, category learning is *stable* in the sense that its LTM traces learn to activate an unchanging set of categories after a sufficient number of learning trials occur. In addition, the LTM traces track the statistics of the distribution of inputs through time, are self-normalizing, oscillate a minimum number of times while learning proceeds and, finally, the adaptive filter whereby categories are chosen in response to bottom-up input patterns tends to minimize error, like a Bayesian classifier (Grossberg, 1976a).

If this sort of learning has such nice properties, then why is not bottom-up learning sufficient? This is because these nice properties can only be guaranteed to occur under *sparse* learning conditions. Under arbitrary environmental conditions, during which there can be many more inputs patterns than the number of category nodes, and during which statistically irregular drifts or repetitions of input patterns can occur, I also proved that learning can become unstable, indeed can undergo catastrophic forgetting (Grossberg, 1976b). Figure 5.18 provides one example of how this can happen. In such a situation, the learning that occurs in response to a given input pattern can be erased by the learning that occurs in response to later input patterns. When the same input pattern is presented later on, it may activate a different category than it did due to previous learning.

Figure 5.18 shows, in particular, how the nice learning property that is illustrated in Figure 5.17 can cause catastrophic forgetting when a series of similar input patterns is presented that exhibits a statistical "drift". For example, in Figure 5.18, adaptive weight z_1 is first attracted to the input pattern $\theta^{(1)}$. This initial learning brings it close enough to the next input pattern $\theta^{(2)}$ for it to also train z_1, after which the next input pattern in the series of inputs can also recode it, and so on. Such a model could forget your parents' faces when it learns a new face. Kohonen and others (e.g., Kohonen, 1984) suggested that a gradual switching off of plasticity can partially overcome this problem in a self-organizing map. I had earlier noted, however, that such a mechanism cannot work in a learning system whose plasticity needs to maintained throughout adulthood, which is how humans learn. In a self-organizing map, learning could be shut down before new information is presented that the system may need to learn, or may stay on long enough to suffer a massive erasure of previous memories due to catastrophic forgetting.

As Figure 5.18 shows, this memory instability is due to basic properties of associative learning and competition when they interact. Each of these processes is needed, however, to carry out even the most basic neural functions, such as being able to register information in STM, and being able to learn and remember it in LTM. Thus the instability cannot be solved by getting rid of either of these basic processes. Instead, additional processes need to be sought that can exploit the good properties of associative learning and competition, while protecting against the instability that their interaction can cause. In brief, these models are incomplete, not "wrong". A mathematical analysis of this instability, together with data about human and animal categorization, conditioning, and attention, led me to introduce Adaptive Resonance Theory, or ART, models in 1976 to dynamically stabilize the memory of self-organizing feature maps in response to an arbitrary stream of input patterns (Grossberg, 1976b).

How does ART stabilize learning?

Hypothesis testing using top-down learned expectations. How does an ART model prevent such memory instabilities from developing? As I noted above, in an ART model, learning does not occur just because some F_2 category nodes win the competition and their activities are stored in STM. Instead, activation of F_2 nodes may be interpreted as "making a hypothesis" about the object or event that is represented by the activity pattern at F_1. When a category or hypothesis at F_2 is activated, it quickly generates an output pattern that is transmitted along the top-down adaptive pathways from F_2 to F_1, as illustrated by Figure 5.13 (top panel). These top-down signals are multiplied in their respective pathways by LTM traces at the semicircular synaptic knobs. The LTM-gated signals from all the active F_2 category nodes are added to generate the total top-down feedback pattern from F_2 to F_1. It is this pattern, which may be a mixture of signals that are read out simultaneously from several categories or hypotheses, that plays the role of a learned expectation.

Activation of this expectation may be interpreted as "testing the hypothesis", or "reading out the prototype", of the active F_2 categories. This prototype sends learned signals to those features across F_1 with which the active F_2 categories have been associated in the past. As shown in Figure 5.13 (bottom panel), ART networks are designed to *match* the "expected prototype" of the category that is read out by this expectation against the bottom-up input pattern, or exemplar, that is received by F_1. The ART Matching Rule (Figure 1.25) controls this matching process. Feature nodes at F_1 that are activated by this exemplar are suppressed if they do not correspond to large enough LTM traces in the top-down prototype pattern. The F_1 activity pattern is reorganized by this matching process between a bottom-up input pattern and a learned top-down expectation to select a set of *critical features* from the exemplar that is consistent with the currently active expectation and to which the network will "pay attention".

LEARNING FROM PATTERN SEQUENCES

Practicing a sequence of spatial patterns can recode all of them!

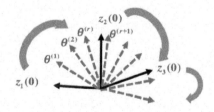

When is learning STABLE?

Input patterns cannot be too DENSE relative to the number of categories

Either: Not too many DISTRIBUTED INPUTS relative to
the number of categories, or
Not too many INPUT CLUSTERS

FIGURE 5.18. How catastrophic forgetting can occur in a competitive learning or self-organizing map model due to basic properties of competition and associative learning.

When a good enough match occurs between a bottom-up input pattern and a learned top-down expectation, the initially attended features can reactivate the category via the bottom-up adaptive filter, and the activated category can reactivate the attended features via its top-down expectation (Figure 2.2). This self-reinforcing excitatory feedback cycle leads to a sustained *feature-category resonance* (Table 1.4), which can support attentional focusing and conscious recognition. Resonance can trigger fast learning of the attended, or matched, feature pattern within the LTM traces of the bottom-up adaptive filter and the top-down expectation, hence the name *adaptive* resonance. One psychophysiological marker of such a resonant match is the Processing Negativity, or PN, event-related potential (see below Figures 5.20 and 5.25; Banquet and Grossberg, 1987; Grossberg, 1978, 1984b; Näätänen, 1982).

How do initial expectations match every possible learned pattern? For a top-down expectation of a *new* recognition category to match the feature pattern that activates it, *all* of its top-down adaptive weights initially have large values, so that it can match *any* feature pattern. These adaptive weights are *pruned* as learning proceeds—that is, LTM traces abutting small featural activities learn to become small while LTM traces abutting large featural activities remain large, and may even grow. This pruning process leads to learning of the *critical feature pattern* (Figure 2.2), or prototype, that defines the focus of attention when its category is active. Gail Carpenter and I proved mathematically in 1987 that this sort of *match learning* can solve the stability-plasticity dilemma by creating stable categories in response to arbitrary sequences of events presented in any order (Carpenter and Grossberg, 1987a, 1991). Category learning goes on within the *attentional system* of ART which, for visual categories, includes brain regions such as prestriate visual cortex, inferotemporal cortex, and prefrontal cortex (Table 1.1).

How do we learn anything new? Match learning requires mismatch reset and search

Given that a resonant matching process occurs in the brain, how does the brain react when there is a big mismatch between bottom-up feature patterns and the currently active top-down expectation? The ART Matching Rule implies that a big enough mismatch will cause massive inhibition at the matching level. Such a collapse of activation raises an urgent question: If a mismatch causes activity to collapse, then why does not all processing just stop? How does the brain manage to usefully process the unexpected event that caused the mismatch?

There is another way to state this problem, which is the other side of the coin: Why does not the brain get stuck refining the learning of what it already knows? How does it ever learn anything that is really new? How does it break out of the cycle of match or crash?

This cycle is broken because the collapse of bottom-up activation due to a top-down mismatch initiates a rapid *reset* of activity at both the matching level and at the subsequent levels that it feeds. This reset event, in turn, initiates a *memory search*, or hypothesis testing, for a better matching recognition category that it already knows—if the reset is caused by inputting a different, but familiar, pattern than the one currently being processed—or by creating a new category with which to recognize novel information about the world.

This search process is carried out by interactions of the ART *attentional system*, where the category learning takes place, and its *orienting system*, which regulates reset and search of the attentional system (Figure 5.19). The ART orienting system includes the nonspecific thalamus and the hippocampal system, among other brain regions. Carpenter and Grossberg (1993) and Grossberg and Versace (2008) summarize supportive data. ART hereby proposes that memory search and hypothesis testing are part of the process whereby we learn to categorize and recognize events in the world.

ART cycle of hypothesis testing and category learning

A self-organizing production system with creative properties. This category learning process is thus part of a dynamical cycle wherein states of *resonance* and *reset* alternate as an ART system searches for cells in the category layer that can be used to learn about new objects and events in the world. Aspects of this cycle have already been illustrated by Figures 1.11, 1.23, 1.24, 2.2, and 5.13. Here these fragments are unified within the full cycle of resonance and reset. In particular, the resets that occur during this cycle may be thought of as a kind of *hypothesis testing*, or memory search, that discovers the best recognition category with which to represent the current input pattern. The cycle of hypothesis testing and category learning is depicted in Figure 5.19 with some mathematical symbols to describe the different processes that are engaged during this cycle.

For readers who are familiar with other kinds of search methods in engineering or artificial intelligence, it may be helpful for me to remark that the ART search and learning cycle realizes a *self-organizing production system*, or a *self-organizing expert system*. Said in yet another way, ART can discover new *knowledge from information* that it learns about one experience at a time, via what is called *incremental learning* in real time. ART's discoveries of new categories represent a kind of simple creativity whereby the system autonomously learns to understand its world by creating novel hypotheses about it that it then tests through experience, while continually revising and refining its understanding in a controlled way that avoids catastrophic forgetting. The "creativity" of the ART search and learning cycle groups novel combinations of features into the critical feature patterns that it discovers using newly learned categories, thereby building an expanding knowledge representation of what combinations of features are predictive in different situations.

This search and learning cycle begins when, as shown in Figure 5.19a, an input pattern I is stored across feature detectors at level F_1 as an activity pattern X, which is designated in gray. Activity pattern X codes the features that are in the input pattern I. In order to simplify the figure, arrays of connections between processing stages are represented by a single connection, as they were in Figure 2.2. The bottom-up pathways that instate input pattern I as activity pattern X also send parallel branches to the orienting system A. At the same time that activity pattern X is getting instated in F_1, the input pattern I generates excitatory signals via these parallel pathways to the orienting system A (Figure 5.19a). These signals to A are multiplied by a gain parameter ρ that is called the *vigilance* parameter. We will soon see how vigilance determines whether the knowledge we learn is concrete or abstract.

As activity pattern X is instated in F_1, it activates two kinds of output signals (Figure 5.19a): The first kind of output signals generate inhibitory inputs to the orienting system A. The second kind of output signals generate a bottom-up excitatory input pattern S to the category level F_2. At this moment, there are as many excitatory inputs from I to A as there are inhibitory inputs from X to A, because it is the positive inputs I that also activate pattern X. A dynamic balance is thus created within A between the excitatory inputs from I and the inhibitory inputs from X (one-against-one again!). The orienting system A thus remains quiet, even though it is being excited by I, while the bottom-up inputs from F_1 are activating a category in F_2.

In order to activate a category in F_2, the bottom-up signals S are multiplied by learned adaptive weights (in the hemispherical synapses in Figure 5.19a) to form the input pattern T to the category level F_2. As I have noted above, the inputs T are contrast-enhanced and normalized within F_2 by a recurrent shunting on-center off-surround network. This competition leads to selection and activation of a small number of cells within F_2 that

receive the largest inputs. The chosen cells represent the category Y that codes for the feature pattern at F_1. In Figure 5.19, a winner-take-all category is shown (narrow gray bar in F_2).

After a category Y is chosen in F_2, it generates top-down signals U that are multiplied by adaptive weights to form a prototype, or critical feature pattern, V that encodes the expectation that the active F_2 category has learned for what feature pattern to expect at F_1 (Figure 5.19b). This top-down expectation input V delivers an excitatory modulatory signal at F_1 cells in its on-center, at the same time that it inhibits F_1 cells in its off-surround, via the connections that embody the ART Matching Rule (Figure 1.25). This top-down expectation can be interpreted as *testing the hypothesis Y*, and the expectation V can be thought of as a *query* that tests this hypothesis.

If V mismatches I at F_1 (Figure 5.19b), then the ART Matching Rule creates a new STM activity pattern X^* (the hatched pattern) at cells where the bottom-up and top-down patterns match. In other words, X^* is active at I features that are *confirmed by the query V*. Mismatched features (white area) are inhibited.

If the pattern X^* of attended features across F_1 supports a good enough match between the bottom-up input pattern I and the top-down expectation V, then it reactivates the pattern Y at F_2 which, in turn, reactivates X^* at F_1. The network hereby locks into a resonant state through a positive

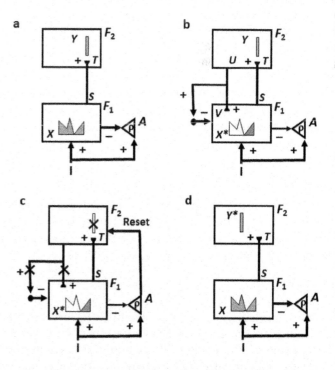

FIGURE 5.19. The ART hypothesis testing and learning cycle. See the text for details about how the attentional system and orienting system interact in order to incorporate learning of novel categories into the corpus of already learned categories without causing catastrophic forgetting.

feedback loop that dynamically links, or binds, X^* with Y. Such a resonance binds the spatially distributed features at F_1 and the active category at F_2 into either a stable equilibrium or a synchronous oscillation, depending upon the choice of network parameters, notably the relative sizes of excitatory and inhibitory cell response rates.

Most available mathematical results about ART properties consider this winner-take-all case. Gail Carpenter initiated the development and analysis of distributed ART algorithms; e.g., Carpenter (1997) and Carpenter, Milenova, and Noeske (1998). This is an important area for further research; e.g., Da Silva, Elnabarawy, and Wunsch (2020).

ART links synchronous oscillations to attention and learning. Choosing a sufficiently slow response rate of inhibitory interactions relative to excitatory interactions is one way to cause oscillatory dynamics within ART and other recurrent neural networks (e.g., Ellias and Grossberg, 1975; Engel, Fries, and Singer, 2001; Fries, 2009; Fries et al., 2001; Gregorious et al., 2014; Grossberg and Grunewald, 1997; Grossberg and Versace, 2008; Yazdanbakhsh and Grossberg, 2004). During an oscillatory resonance, all resonating feature cells across F_1 maintain their relative sizes through time, so that features that are important at a given time remain important at other times during the oscillation. I called this kind of oscillation an *order-preserving limit cycle* in Grossberg (1976b). These days, this kind of oscillation is often called a *synchronous oscillation*.

I believe that this term is too general because it could also include an order-reversing limit cycle in which features that are most active in one phase of the cycle could become least active in the next phase of the cycle (Ellias and Grossberg, 1975), which occurs during useful dynamics such as the gaits that control interlimb oscillations (Pribe, Grossberg, and Cohen, 1997), as well as both adaptive and maladaptive traveling waves, such as the theta oscillations that support many aspects of normal hippocampal dynamics (Lubenov and Siapas, 2009), and the traveling waves that occur during hippocampal seizures (Lenck-Santini, 2017; Neumann et al., 2017).

In ART, the resonant state, rather than bottom-up activation, is predicted to drive the learning process; hence the name *adaptive* resonance. The resonant state persists for a long enough time, and at high enough and synchronous activity levels, to significantly alter the learned values of the LTM traces. The fact that resonance drives learning helps to explain how LTM traces can regulate the brain's fast information processing without necessarily learning about all the signals that they process. Not every signal that is gated by an adaptive weight and that activates a postsynaptic cell, whether in a pathway from F_1 to F_2 or from F_2 to F_1, will necessarily cause a large change in that adaptive weight. If activations continue to change quickly over time, say due to repeated reset events, without benefit of the amplification and duration of a resonance, then the weights will not get a chance to learn from them.

The need to reach a network-wide consensus via resonance before learning occurs buffers previously learned memories against catastrophic forgetting. In particular, outlier features that are not in the attentional focus in Figure 2.2 will not be learned. Said in another way, the resonance provides enough context-sensitive evidence for a brain network to risk rapidly changing its understanding of the world, without incurring the risk of catastrophic forgetting. Such context-sensitive gating of learning is thus one of the ways that the brain solves the stability-plasticity dilemma.

In summary, by using resonance as a mediating event, the combination of top-down matching and attentional focusing helps to trigger fast learning and self-stabilizing memory in response to an arbitrary input environment. The stabilizing properties of resonance-driven learning may be one reason for the ubiquitous occurrence of reciprocal bottom-up and top-down cortico-cortical and corticothalamic interactions in the brain.

Complementary attentional and orienting systems

It cannot be overemphasized that the attentional and orienting systems in an ART network experience computationally *complementary* informational deficiencies. At the moment when a predictive error occurs, the system does not know why the currently active category was insufficient to predict the correct outcome. In particular, when the orienting system gets activated by a mismatch in the attentional system, the orienting system has no way of knowing what went wrong in the attentional system. The attentional system has information about how inputs are categorized, but not whether the categorization is correct, whereas the orienting system has information about whether the categorization is correct, but not about what is being categorized. These complementary uncertainties are what raises the basic question: How does the orienting system cope with the daunting challenge of resetting and driving a memory search within the attentional system in a way that leads to a better outcome after the search ends?

Sufficient Reason and novelty-sensitive nonspecific arousal: Novel events are arousing!

Because the orienting system does not know what cells in the attentional system caused the predictive error, its activation needs to influence *all* potential sources of the error equally. Thus, mismatch triggers a burst of *nonspecific arousal* that activates all cells in the attentional system equally. In other words, novel events are arousing! Said in a more philosophical way, a novelty-sensitive burst of nonspecific arousal implements the Principle of Sufficient Reason. As illustrated in Figures 5.19c and 5.19d, the current state of activation of the attentional system interacts with such an arousal burst to selectively reset cells that caused the mismatch, and to thereby drive a search leading to a better predictive outcome.

Mismatch-activated nonspecific arousal is triggered in the following way: When X changes to X^* in Figures 5.19b and 5.19c, total inhibition decreases from F_1 to A. If inhibition decreases sufficiently, then inhibition is insufficient to prevent A from getting activated by bottom-up excitation from I. Intuitively, when this happens, the new input is too "novel" to be incorporated by learning into the prototype of the currently active category at F_2. Instead, the excess excitation of A triggers a nonspecific arousal burst from A to F_2. This is the brain event that embodies the familiar fact that "novel events are arousing". "Nonspecific" means that *every* cell in F_2 gets the same arousal signal because, at A, it is not known *which* active category in F_2 caused the mismatch, but only that a mismatch was caused by one of the categories in F_2.

The interaction between the arousal signal and the current activity of category cells in F_2 is sufficient to reset F_2 and begin a memory search for a category that can better match the feature pattern at F_1. The arousal burst triggers a memory search for a better-matching category, as follows: Arousal resets F_2 by inhibiting Y (Figure 5.19c). After Y is inhibited, its top-down prototype also shuts off, so X is reinstated. In addition, Y stays inhibited throughout the ensuing search, notably in the next moments when X activates a different category that is denoted by Y^* at F_2 (Figure 5.19d).

Medium-term memory: Habituative transmitter gates in nonstationary hypothesis testing

Search can proceed only if Y stays inhibited so that a new category Y^* can be activated. How are these two properties achieved? The enduring inhibition of Y can be caused by habituative, or depressing, transmitters that multiply, or *gate*, signals traveling along the pathways that activate the categories. That is why I like to call them *habituative transmitter gates*. These habituative transmitter gates may also usefully be thought of as a type of *medium-term* memory, or MTM, acting at category cells (Figure 2.11). The name medium-term memory emphasizes that the transmitters recover at a slower rate than the rate of activity-dependent search, which helps to keep Y inhibited during the search.

I first described laws for habituative transmitter gates in 1968 in the *Proceedings of the National Academy of Sciences* (Grossberg, 1968d). Recall that they were used in Chapter 1 to explain properties of the gated dipole opponent processing circuits that I introduced in 1972 to explain data about punishment and avoidance behaviors that are regulated by reinforcement learning (Grossberg, 1972a, 1972b; Figures 1.14 and 1.15). Such habituative transmitter gates are sometimes also called *depressing synapses*, a term that Larry Abbott, Juan Varela, Kamal Sen, and Sacha Nelson introduced in a 1997 article that experimentally confirmed predicted properties of habituative transmitter gates in the visual cortex (Abbott et al., 1997). Habituative transmitter gates have also been used to help explain a wide range of data about processes other than category learning, including reset and afterimage dynamics of visual perception, cognitive-emotional interactions, adaptive sensory-motor control, and mental disorders (Francis and Grossberg, 1996; Francis, Grossberg, and Mingolla, 1994; Gaudiano and Grossberg, 1991, 1992; Grossberg, 1972b, 1980, 1984b, 1984c).

Due to habituative gating, recently active category cells are more habituated than inactive cells, just as in a gated dipole. Think of each category cell as an ON cell in a gated dipole (Figures 1.14 and 1.15). Then, just as in any gated dipole—or, in this case, network of gated dipoles—when a nonspecific arousal burst is caused by a novel event, it will cause antagonistic rebounds that reset the previously active categories. In other words, *nonspecific arousal can specifically, or selectively, reset previously active category cells*. The categories that caused the incorrect prediction are hereby inhibited, or "disconfirmed". Because habituation changes on a slower time scale than the search, once an active category is inhibited, it stays off until the transmitters can recover from habituation, and allows the search to discover better-matching categories.

The prediction that habituative transmitter gates help to reset ongoing dynamics and trigger a memory search is worthy of additional experimental study. It gains its credence from the fact that these transmitter gates also help to explain many other data using the same properties in the same circuits. As in all the predictions in this book, it is the weight of accumulating interdisciplinary data that breathes credibility into the models that explain them.

How self-normalizing total activity enables search

Antagonistic rebounds due to habituative transmitters in gated dipole category cells is not, however, sufficient to explain how bottom-up inputs can activate a new F_2 category Y^* after the old category Y is shut off. Rebounds are insufficient because the cells Y^* must be receiving smaller bottom-up inputs than the original category Y did, or else they would have been the first cells that were chosen to categorize the input. Why are not the inputs to these less favored cells too small to activate them vigorously after the favored cells are inhibited?

A second property clarifies how this happens. As I earlier noted, the category cells interact among themselves via a recurrent shunting on-center off-surround network that tends to normalize the total activity across all the network cells, while contrast-enhancing the activity of the most active cells at the expense of less active cells, and storing the activities of these winning cells in STM (Figures 1.7–1.9). When the cells that previously got the biggest inputs are reset and inhibited, and their inhibition is maintained by MTM, the normalization property reallocates the total network activity to the category cells that can still become activated by inputs. As a result, even if these eligible cells get smaller bottom-up inputs, the normalizing recurrent interactions within F_2 will amplify their activities. They, in effect, "inherit" some of the normalized activity of the inhibited category Y. Thus, when habituation and normalization act together, a different category Y^* can be vigorously activated after a previously active category Y is inhibited, or an uncommitted population is selected and new category learning initiated.

Search continues until a better matching, or novel, category is selected. When search ends, an attentive resonance triggers learning of the attended data in adaptive weights within both the bottom-up and top-down pathways. As learning stabilizes, inputs I can activate their globally best-matching categories directly through the adaptive filter, without activating the orienting system. This *direct access* property was first mathematically proved in the ART 1 article that Gail Carpenter and I published in 1987 (Carpenter and Grossberg, 1987a). It clarifies how, for example, we can rapidly recognize familiar family members as we grow older, even though we have learned a huge amount of additional information about the world since we first learned to recognize them. There is no need to search through all the more recent memories, or even a subset of them, to recognize and say "Hi mom!" only after an embarrassing delay.

In considering how matching controls learning, one also needs to keep in mind how learning works during partial mismatches that are not bad enough to trigger an orienting search. During such a partial mismatch, there may simultaneously be cells at which matching and learning occurs, as well as other cells at which mismatch, inhibition,

and suppression of learning occurs. Thus, in describing match vs. mismatch states, one needs to keep in mind that there may be cells at which bottom-up and top-down signals mismatch, even though there is a good enough partial match for a synchronous resonant state to persist long enough to support learning at the matched features.

Category networks are gated dipole fields: Probabilistic hypothesis testing and prediction

In summary, hypothesis testing in an ART network utilizes a category network F_2 that embeds gated dipoles into a recurrent on-center off-surround shunting network. I call such a network a *gated dipole field*. Variants of gated dipole fields occur in many parts of the brain. Figure 4.47 illustrates one such variant, which helps to understand how conscious 3D visual surface percepts are chosen.

The ability of a gated dipole field to normalize its total activity enables the activities of its cells to be interpreted as a kind of real-time probability distribution. I already mentioned in Chapter 4, during my explanation of brightness constancy (Figure 4.4) and brightness contrast (Figure 2.18), how shunting on-center off-surround networks may generally be interpreted as computing a real-time probability distribution. ART adds a process for active reorganization of such a distribution to achieve better predictive success. The selective reorganization of this probability distribution in response to novelty-triggered arousal bursts enables an ART search cycle to be interpreted as a probabilistic hypothesis testing and decision making process that optimizes its predictions in response to a changing world. Reset of gated dipole fields during a search also prevents accumulation of coding errors during the iterative operations of the brain. They do this by rebalancing the activities of ON and OFF cells in the gated dipoles using antagonistic rebounds. Additional examples of how this occurs will be given in Chapter 8 when I explain how the brain perceives and tracks moving objects.

Feature-category resonances and complementary PN and N200 event-related potentials

How much data support is there for the operations that occur during the ART cycles of hypothesis testing and category learning? One such data marker will be summarized immediately, others further along in the exposition.

A top-down expectation is a *top-down, conditionable,* and *specific* event that activates its target cells during a *match* (Figures 2.2, 5.13, and 5.19b-c). "Conditionable" means that the top-down pathways contain adaptive weights, or LTM traces, that can learn, or be conditioned, to encode a prototype of the recognition category that activates it. "Specific" means that each top-down expectation reads out its own learned prototype pattern. Target cells are activated that "match" the prototype due to properties of the ART Matching Rule (Figure 1.25).

When a good enough match occurs between a bottom-up input pattern and a learned top-down expectation, the initially attended features can reactivate the category via the bottom-up adaptive filter, and the activated category can reactivate the attended features via its top-down expectation (Figure 2.2). This self-reinforcing excitatory feedback cycle leads to a sustained *feature-category resonance* (Table 1.4), which can support attentional focusing and conscious recognition of visual objects and scenes. One psychophysiological marker of such a resonant match is the processing negativity, or PN, event-related potential (Figure 5.20) that I predicted in 1978 and noted above that Risto Näätänen reported experimentally in 1982 (Näätänen, 1982).

In contrast to the *top-down, conditionable, specific,* and *match* properties that occur during an attentive match, an orienting system mismatch is a *bottom-up, unconditionable, nonspecific,* and *mismatch* event (Figures 1.11 and 5.19c): A mismatch occurs when *bottom-up* activation of the orienting system cannot be adequately inhibited by the bottom-up inhibition from the matched pattern. These signals to the orienting system are *unconditionable,* or not subject to learning. Mismatch-activated output from the orienting system *nonspecifically* arouses all the category cells because the orienting system cannot determine which categories read out the expectation that led to mismatch. Any category may be responsible, and may thus need to be reset by arousal. Finally, the orienting system is activated by a sufficiently big *mismatch.*

These are properties of the N200 event-related potential, or ERP (Figure 5.20; Näätänen, Simpson, and Loveless, 1982, Sams et al., 1985). More generally, during an ART memory search, sequences of mismatch (Figure 5.19b), arousal (Figure 5.19c), and reset (Figure 5.19d), events occur that exhibit properties of P120, N200, and P300 ERPs, respectively, as Jean-Paul Banquet and I showed in 1987 (Figure 5.21; Banquet and Grossberg, 1987).

As Figure 5.20 summarizes, four sets of properties of the attentional system are complementary to those of the

orienting system (top-down vs. bottom-up, conditionable vs. unconditionable, specific vs. nonspecific, match vs. mismatch), with the PN and N200 ERPs illustrating these complementary properties. The orienting system can detect that an error has occurred, but does know what category prediction caused it. The attentional system knows what categories are active, but not if these categories adequately represent current inputs. By interacting, these systems can determine what the error is and discover a new category to correct it.

PN AND N200 ARE COMPLEMENTARY WAVES

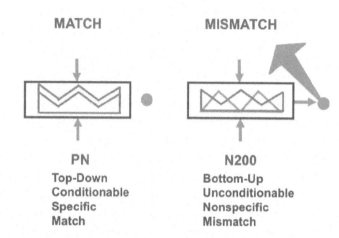

FIGURE 5.20. The PN and N200 event-related potentials are computationally complementary events that are computed within the attentional and orienting systems.

ERP SUPPORT FOR MISMATCH-MEDIATED RESET
Event-Related Potentials: Human Scalp Potentials

ART predicted correlated sequences of P120-N200-P300
Event Related Potentials during oddball learning
P120 - mismatch; N200 - arousal/novelty; P300 - STM reset
Confirmed in: Banquet and Grossberg (1987)

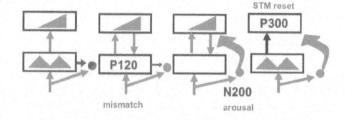

FIGURE 5.21. Sequences of P120, N200, and P300 event-related potentials occur during oddball learning EEG experiments under conditions that ART predicted should occur during sequences of mismatch, arousal, and STM reset events, respectively.

A thought experiment that leads to ART

The computationally complementary relationship between PN and N200 points to the existence of informational uncertainties at individual processing stages that can only be resolved by appropriate interactions between these stages. How could the evolving brain have been smart enough to create these interactions? I will now use a gedanken, or thought, experiment to illuminate this basic fact and thereby derive the basic ART concepts and mechanisms that have been described above. This thought experiment shows how ART solves fundamental problems about how predictive errors can be corrected in response to a changing world. It requires no psychological or neurobiological knowledge to be understood. As such, one can expect similar kinds of mechanisms and architectures to be useful in *any* system that can autonomously learn to recognize objects and events in a changing world. The main tool of the thought experiment is the Principle of Sufficient Reason. The thought experiment is thus a good way to teach ART to people who have very little factual or theoretical background, but who are interested in how we learn things on our own. I published this thought experiment in my 1980 *Psychological Review* article that was appropriately entitled "How Does a Brain Build a Cognitive Code?" (Grossberg, 1980).

How can a coding error be corrected if no individual cell knows that one has occurred? The central theoretical question of the thought experiment is: *How can a coding error be corrected if no individual cell knows that one has occurred?* The importance of this issue becomes clear when we realize that irrelevant features can accidentally be incorporated into a recognition code when our interactions with our environment are limited, and will only become clearer when they lead to errors as we interact more frequently with our environment. As I noted in my discussion of causality, superstition, and gambling in Chapter 1, you might erroneously conclude that wallpaper in the dining room *causes* us to receive food if you only go into that room when food is being served. Even if our recognition codes perfectly predict a given environment, we could easily make errors as the environment itself changes, much as we might not recognize a male friend's face if he grows a bushy mustache and beard and we do not see him for several years. Furthermore, it may be hard to tell whether our understanding of a fixed environment is faulty, or the environment that we thought we understood is no longer the same. In real life, there is often no one there to tell us the difference. The problem of error correction is fundamental whenever either we continue to learn ever-deepening interpretations of an environment using stricter criteria of behavioral success, or the environment itself changes.

I begin the thought experiment by reviewing the basic functional elements on which my analysis will build. In this sense, every thought experiment begins in the middle, if only to avoid an infinite regress. These functional elements are the processes of learning and competition that are ubiquitous throughout our brains, and that come together in learning models like competitive learning.

To start, consider a network of feature-selective cells, or cell populations, in which each cell responds to a prescribed combination of environmental features. Suppose that the jth cell has an activity, or potential, $x_j(t)$ at every time t. This activity is due to inputs $I_j(t)$ that are activated by environmental features that activate the brain at an earlier processing stage. At each time, all of these activities, taken together, form an *activity pattern* $X(t)=(x_1(t), x_2(t), \ldots, x_n(t))$. The notation $X(t)$ is just shorthand for representing all of the features which are processed at time *t*.

As in Figure 5.19, let F_1 denote the processing level at which these feature-selective cells occur. Also suppose that signal-carrying pathways occur between F_1 and the next processing level F_2. These pathways are adaptive, much as in the dot product $T = S \bullet z$ that was used to explain how learning of adaptive weights z occurs in competitive learning and self-organizing map models (Figures 5.16-5.17). These details about learning are not important, however, to carry out the thought experiment. All that we need to assume is that prior learning enables activity pattern X across F_1 to activate, *by whatever means*, a *compressed representation Y* of this pattern at F_2. This compressed representation can, as before, be called a category, symbol, or code. Knowing the detailed structure of this code is unnecessary to complete the thought experiment.

Suppose, after the system learns to code feature pattern X by category Y, that a different feature pattern is activated across F_1, by a different input pattern, and that this new feature pattern is erroneously coded at F_2 by the same code Y. By "the same code," I mean a code that has the same functional effects throughout the system, not necessarily the identical activation pattern Y.

In order to discuss this situation without ambiguity, let me denote by $X^{(1)}$ and $X^{(2)}$ the two different activity patterns that each activate symbol Y, where $X^{(1)}$ has previously learned to activate Y and $X^{(2)}$ now does so erroneously (Figure 5.22). The main problem to be solved can then be stated as: How can the erroneous coding of $X^{(2)}$ by Y be corrected if no individual cell knows that an error has occurred?

Symbols cannot detect errors. Our first robust conclusion can now be made: Whatever the mechanism is that corrects this error, it cannot exist within F_2 because, by definition, both of the activity patterns $X^{(1)}$ and $X^{(2)}$ activate the same symbol Y at F_2. Thus F_2 does not have the ability to distinguish the fact that the incorrect pattern

By prior learning, $X^{(1)}$ at F_1 is coded at F_2

Suppose that $X^{(2)}$ incorrectly activates the same F_2 code

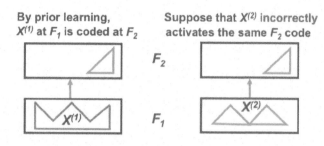

How to correct the error?

The problem occurs no matter how you define an "error"

FIGURE 5.22. Suppose that a very different exemplar activates a category than the one that originally learned how to do this.

COMPRESSION VS. ERROR CORRECTION

Past   Present

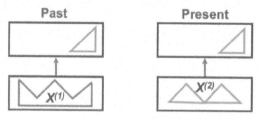

Where is the knowledge that error was made?

Not at F_2! The compressed code cannot tell the difference!

$X^{(2)}$ is at F_1 when ◿ is at F_2 defines the error

There is a MISMATCH between $X^{(1)}$ and $X^{(2)}$ at F_1

How does the system know this?

FIGURE 5.23. A category, symbol, or other highly compressed representation cannot determine whether an error has occurred.

$X^{(2)}$, and not the correct pattern $X^{(1)}$, is now presently active in F_1 and activating the symbol Y. So far as F_2 knows, the correct pattern $X^{(1)}$ *is* active at F_1, in which case there is no error to correct. Thus, by the very nature of being a compressed representation, the symbol or category Y that is active at F_2 cannot tell an error has occurred that needs to be corrected. The error must be computed somewhere else.

This is our first use of the Principle of Sufficient Reason. This conclusion is, moreover, independent of how an error is defined. It could be an error caused by an internal inconsistency in the representation of different feature patterns. It could also be an error that is detected when a punishment or external correction is given. It does not matter how an error is defined for the argument to go through, since no matter how an error is defined, the information for correcting it does not exist at the compressed, categorical, or symbolic representations in F_2 (Figure 5.23).

It is important to realize that this argument is independent of coding details. It is based only on the type of information that a symbolic representation cannot, in principle, possess, by the very nature of being a symbol. In particular, symbols do not represent the contents of the feature patterns that they code. They merely "symbolize" these patterns. The robustness of this and subsequent arguments suggests why the ART design that overcomes these limitations seems to occur ubiquitously, in one form or another, in so many sensory and cognitive processes. In effect, our brains have discovered through evolution how to correct category errors despite this limitation.

Why learning of top-down expectations is necessary. If the error cannot, in principle, be detected in F_2, then where in the network *can* the error be detected? In order to correct the error, the network somehow has to know that, when it is coding $X^{(2)}$ with symbol Y, that this is an error *because* $X^{(2)}$ is too different from the pattern $X^{(1)}$ which has previously been associated with symbol Y. However, at the time when the incorrect pattern $X^{(2)}$ is activated by

bottom-up inputs at F_1, the correct pattern $X^{(1)}$ is not activated by bottom-up inputs there!

This observation leads to the key question: When *was* $X^{(1)}$ active in the network at a time when Y was also active there? This only happens on the learning trials when $X^{(1)}$ was learning to activate symbol Y by training the bottom-up adaptive pathways from F_1 to F_2. Since $X^{(1)}$ is not activated by bottom-up inputs when $X^{(2)}$ is erroneously activating Y, then somehow Y itself must be able to read out $X^{(1)}$ at F_1 using a top-down pathway, so that $X^{(1)}$ can be compared with $X^{(2)}$ there, and the difference between $X^{(1)}$ and $X^{(2)}$ used to compute that an error has occurred.

In order for this to be possible, top-down learning from Y to $X^{(1)}$ also had to occur when $X^{(1)}$ was learning to activate symbol Y via bottom-up learning (Figure 5.24). As a result of this top-down learning in pathways from F_2 to F_1, activating Y can lead to the read-out of the correct pattern $X^{(1)}$ across F_1 (Figure 5.25). When this happens, the two patterns $X^{(1)}$ and $X^{(2)}$ will be simultaneously active across F_1, and they can be compared, or matched, to test whether or not the correct pattern has activated F_1. In summary, because of the nature of symbolic compression, error correction requires that there must exist top-down learning of the pattern that the network *expects* to find at the feature level, based upon its past experience.

Complementary information is computed at distributed and symbolic levels. A second design problem can now be stated: Somehow the mismatch between the patterns $X^{(1)}$ and $X^{(2)}$ at F_1 must rapidly inhibit $X^{(2)}$ at F_1. Otherwise, $X^{(2)}$ could learn to be coded by Y in the same way as $X^{(1)}$ learned to code Y on preceding learning trials. Pattern Y must also be rapidly shut off to prevent it from activating later network stages and causing behavioral errors to occur. Moreover, Y must be shut off in such a fashion that

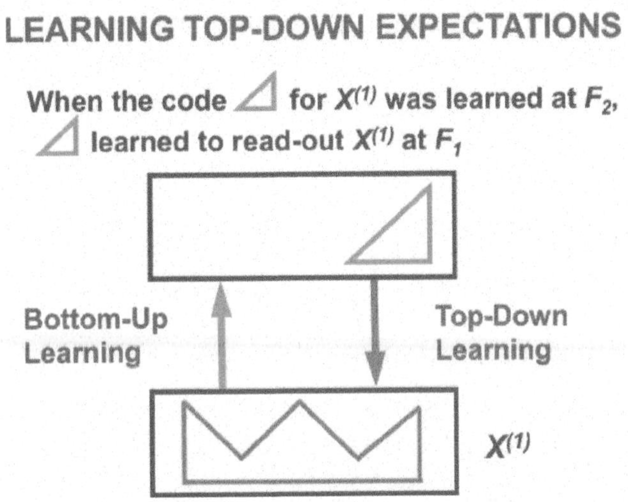

LEARNING TOP-DOWN EXPECTATIONS

When the code ◿ for $X^{(1)}$ was learned at F_2, ◿ learned to read-out $X^{(1)}$ at F_1

Bottom-Up Learning   **Top-Down Learning**

$X^{(1)}$

FIGURE 5.24. Learning of a top-down expectation must occur during bottom-up learning in the adaptive filter in order to be able to match the previously associated feature pattern with the one that is currently active.

$X^{(2)}$ can thereupon be coded by a more suitable symbol at F_2. How does this happen?

Given that $X^{(2)}$ is suppressed at F_1 due to mismatch with the top-down expectation read-out by F_2, this suppression must be used to inhibit Y at F_2, since the mismatch at F_1 is the only mechanism in the network that can, in principle, distinguish whether or not an error has occurred at F_2. Moreover, until Y is inhibited, it will continue to read out its expectation to F_1, which will prevent F_1 from activating a new, and more correct, symbol at Y.

We previously noted that the symbols at level F_2 cannot compute *that* an error has occurred. Now we can see that F_1 also has limited information. Level F_1 can detect that an

error has occurred by matching the distributed patterns $X^{(1)}$ and $X^{(2)}$, but such a mismatch cannot tell *which* symbol at F_2 caused the mismatch at F_1. It could have been any symbol whatsoever. All that F_1 knows is that a mismatch has occurred. *Whatever* pattern Y at F_2 caused the mismatch must be inhibited.

The levels F_1 and F_2 thus experience *complementary* information. By themselves, they are incapable of correcting the error. Only by working together can they overcome their complementary forms of ignorance to correct the error. We therefore ask: How does the mismatch of distributed patterns across F_1 inhibit the activity of symbols across F_2?

Nonspecific arousal as an error-correcting reset event. Given that F_1 does not know which symbol at F_2 needs to be inhibited, the mismatch at F_1 must have a *nonspecific*, or uniform, effect on all the cells of F_2, since any of these cells in F_2 might be the cells that must be inhibited. This is another use of the Principle of Sufficient Reason. We are hereby led to ask: How does mismatch across F_1 elicit a nonspecific, or uniform, signal to F_2?

I identify this nonspecific signal with a type of *arousal* because it computationally instantiates the intuition that *mismatched, or novel, events are arousing*. In fact, such an arousal event maps nicely onto subsequently reported data from humans about the novelty-sensitive N200 event-related potential, or ERP (Figure 5.26). We can now see, just using Sufficient Reason, that the match (Figure 5.25) and mismatch (Figure 5.26) processes have computationally complementary properties, that are proposed to be

MISMATCH TRIGGERS NONSPECIFIC AROUSAL

Mismatch at F_1 elicits a nonspecific event at F_2
Call this event nonspecific arousal

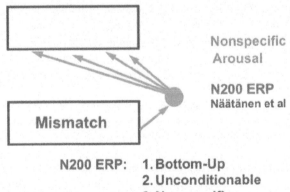

Nonspecific Arousal

N200 ERP
Näätänen et al

Mismatch

HOW IS AN ERROR CORRECTED

During bottom-up learning, top-down learning must also occur so that the pattern that is read-out top-down can be compared with the pattern that is activated by bottom-up inputs

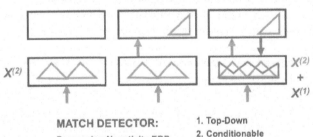

$X^{(2)}$

$X^{(2)}$ + $X^{(1)}$

MATCH DETECTOR:
Processing Negativity ERP

1. Top-Down
2. Conditionable
3. Specific
4. Match

N200 ERP:

1. Bottom-Up
2. Unconditionable
3. Nonspecific
4. Mismatch

FIGURE 5.25. The sequence of events whereby a novel input pattern can activate a category which, in turn, reads out its learned top-down expectation to be matched against the input pattern. Error correction thus requires the use of a Match Detector that has properties of the Processing Negativity ERP.

FIGURE 5.26. When a big enough mismatch occurs, the orienting system is activated and sends a burst of nonspecific arousal to the category level. This Mismatch Detector has properties of the N200 ERP.

reflected by the PN and N200 Event-Related Potentials (Figure 5.20). More generally, as I have already noted above, the sequence of events that Sufficient Reason implies from mismatch to arousal to category reset maps well onto human data about sequences of P120, N200, and P300 ERPs that Jean-Paul Banquet and I reported in 1987 during oddball experiments whose effects were measured by ERPs (Figure 5.21; Banquet and Grossberg, 1987).

Parallel processing of expected and unexpected events in attentional and orienting systems. The need to convert a mismatch into a nonspecific arousal signal leads directly to the hypothesis that an *orienting system* works in parallel with the *attentional system* where top-down expectations are matched. This conclusion can be derived from the answer to the next gedanken experiment question:

Where does the activity that drives the arousal come from, and why is it released when a mismatch occurs at F_1. There are two possible answers to the first part of the question, but only one of them survives closer inspection. The arousal is either *endogenous*—that is, internally and persistently generated—or the arousal is *exogenous*—that is, activated by the sensory input. If the activity were endogenous, then arousal would occur whenever F_1 was inactive, whether this inactivity was due to active inhibition by mismatched feedback at F_1 or to the absence of any bottom-up inputs to F_1. An endogenous source of arousal could not tell the difference. Endogenous arousal would lead to the untenable conclusion that F_2 would be persistently flooded with arousal whenever nothing was happening at F_1.

The second alternative must therefore be true; namely, the arousal is activated by the sensory input. For this to happen, sensory input pathways to F_1 bifurcate before they reach F_1 (Figure 5.27). One pathway is *specific*: It is the input pathway that we already knew about, the one that delivers featural information about the sensory events to be represented at F_1. The other pathway is *nonspecific*: It activates the arousal mechanism that is capable of nonspecifically resetting the incorrect category at F_2. The idea that sensory events have both informative (specific) and arousal (nonspecific) functions has been empirically known at least since the 1949 article of Giuseppe Moruzzi and Horace Magoun on the reticular formation, and the proposal in 1955 by Donald Hebb, based on this earlier work, that every event has a cue and arousal function (Figure 5.27; Hebb, 1955; Moruzzi and Magoun, 1949). The gedanken experiment, and its realization in ART, give these data a clear functional meaning.

Mismatch in the attentional system activates nonspecific arousal from the orienting system. We are now ready to ask the next thought experiment questions:

Given that the sensory inputs to F_1 also activate the nonspecific arousal pathway, what prevents arousal from flooding F_2 whenever these inputs are active? How is

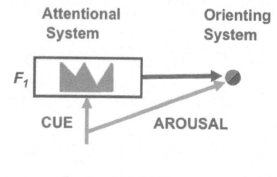

ATTENTIONAL AND ORIENTING SYSTEMS

Every event has a CUE (specific) and an AROUSAL (nonspecific) function

FIGURE 5.27. Every event activates both the attentional system and the orienting system. The text explains why.

arousal prevented except when activity at F_1 is being actively mismatched? The answer is now clear: Activity at F_1 inhibits the arousal pathway (Figure 5.27), and inhibition of F_1 activity by mismatch with a top-down expectation removes the source of this inhibition, and thereby disinhibits the arousal pathway (Figure 5.28). There must therefore be a network population, or node, where the arousal signal can be inhibited by F_1 before it can activate F_2. This node is called the orienting system A (Figures 1.11 and 5.28). We have hereby been led by the gedanken experiment to the main properties of the ART memory search, or hypothesis testing, cycle that is summarized in Figure 5.19.

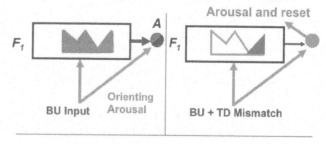

MISMATCH ⇨ INHIBITION ⇨ AROUSAL ⇨ RESET

ART MATCHING RULE:
TD mismatch can suppress a part of F_1 STM pattern
F_2 is reset if degree of match < vigilance

FIGURE 5.28. How a mismatch between bottom-up and top-down input patterns can trigger activation of the orienting system A and, with it, a burst of nonspecific arousal to the category level.

The remaining questions that need to be answered for the search cycle to actually work are now also clear:

How does a nonspecific arousal burst selectively inhibit active category cells in F_2 but nonetheless allow inactive F_2 cells to correct the error by categorizing the previously mismatched input pattern in the next moments? How does arousal, which is an excitatory event, get translated into selective inhibition? What is the source of this selective inhibition at each active category cell? Why are not previously inactive category cells also inhibited?

How does this inhibition last throughout a memory search cycle so that the system does not perseverate on an error? Arousal and selective inhibition must act on a fast time scale to enable the memory search to proceed. What is the slower time scale that enables the selective inhibition to last for awhile?

How is activation across F_2 reallocated so that categories, or symbols, that are selected later in the cycle can be sufficiently activated, even though they receive smaller bottom-up inputs from F_1? The categories that are selected later lost the competition earlier because they received smaller inputs. They still receive smaller inputs during the search. How are these smaller inhibits converted into sufficiently large activations to win during the search cycle?

At the time that I first confronted these issues in 1974, I fortunately had already discovered and mathematically characterized network mechanisms that could provide a unified and principled answer to all of these questions.

Recurrent double-opponent networks help to discover the most predictive categories. How, then, does a nonspecific arousal burst selectively inhibit active category cells in F_2 but allow inactive F_2 cells to correct the error in the next moments? Suppose that F_2 categories are realized as ON cells in (ON cell)-(OFF cell) opponent processing circuits. As noted in Chapters 1 and 4, and earlier in this chapter, opponent circuits may be modeled by *gated dipoles* (Figures 1.14 and 1.15). Gated dipoles were themselves derived from a thought experiment in 1972 about how previously learned cognitive-emotional associations can be extinguished, or selectively forgotten, in response to environmental changes, including unexpected non-occurrences of rewards (Grossberg, 1972a, 1972b). This thought experiment will be described in Chapter 13.

Gated dipole antagonistic rebound properties also facilitate the search for predictive categories in the following way: As earlier depicted in Figure 5.19c, a burst of nonspecific arousal can be triggered when a top-down expectation from F_2 causes a big enough mismatch with a bottom-up input at F_1. A sufficiently large burst of nonspecific arousal to a gated dipole field selectively inhibits its active ON cells while it disinhibits the corresponding OFF cells via antagonistic rebounds. Because the inhibition between a pair of inactive ON and OFF cells is balanced, and will remain

so when arousal inputs to both of them, the next bottom-up specific input to an inactive F_2 cell can activate it, and thereby continue the search.

How does this inhibition last throughout a memory search cycle? Recall that antagonistic rebounds within a gated dipole are caused by an imbalance of habituative transmitter gates, or medium-term memories, in the dipole's ON-cells and OFF-cells (Figures 1.14 and 1.15). Habituation recovers more slowly than cell activation. In addition, the category cells interact via recurrent shunting on-center off-surround networks (Figures 1.6-1.9 and 5.13) that carry out the contrast-enhancement and short-term memory storage of the winning categories. The enduring habituation of the dipoles, when combined with the persistence of short-term memory storage, can keep the inhibited categories quiet during a search cycle.

Finally, how is activation across F_2 reallocated so that categories that are selected later in the cycle can be sufficiently activated, even though they receive smaller bottom-up inputs from F_1? This is also accomplished by the recurrent shunting on-center off-surround network. Because such a network tends to normalize the total stored activity across F_2 (Figure 1.7), it reallocates activity that previously was devoted to the inhibited ON cells to categories that get smaller bottom-up inputs. This renormalization process lets the network behave like a type of deterministic real-time "probabilistic hypothesis testing" machine that chooses categories that are most predictive, conditional on previous disconfirmations.

In summary, *all three* of the requirements that are needed to search for new categories in response to disconfirmed expectations are parsimoniously realized by designing the category level F_2 as a *recurrent shunting double-opponent network*, or gated dipole field. In such a network, ON cells are linked by recurrent on-center off-surround interactions, OFF cells are linked by their own recurrent on-center off-surround interactions, and ON cells and OFF cells compete via habituative gated dipole interactions, just as in the Figure 4.47 circuit that selects 3D surfaces that are supported by consistent boundaries. We can now see that this visual circuit is a special case of a more general design that is used to support search for perceptual and cognitive categories throughout the brain.

Resonance of distributed features and compressed categories solves symbol grounding

Another kind of complementary ignorance than that between attentional focusing via PN and orienting search via N200 (Figure 5.20) is overcome through resonance within the attentional system. Understanding how ART overcomes it offers a solution of what has been called the *symbol grounding problem* by Stevan Harnad in 1990 (Harnad, 1990). Harnad described the problem as follows: "How can the semantic interpretation of a formal symbol system be made intrinsic to the system, rather than just parasitic on the meanings in our heads? How can the meanings of the meaningless symbol tokens, manipulated solely on the basis of their (arbitrary) shapes, be grounded in anything but other meaningless symbols?"

I prefer to recast the problem as follows: No single pixel in a picture has meaning. Pixels acquire meaning by being processed as part of a picture. The same is true for other kinds of features. Individual features implicitly acquire meaning by being embedded in the context of a distributed pattern of features. This meaning remains implicit because no individual feature in such a spatial pattern may have any knowledge about the other features in that pattern. It is the category, or symbol, level that renders this contextual meaning explicit by responding selectively to the entire distributed pattern of features.

These considerations may be restated as follows within ART: When a feature pattern is activated at level F_1 in an ART system (Figure 5.19), its individual features have no meaning. They become meaningful only as part of the spatial pattern of features to which they belong. A recognition category at level F_2 can selectively respond to this feature pattern, but does not know what these features are. For example, if a "grandmother cell" fires, then this category cell has no idea whether it represents a grandmother or a house.

In other words, the category level does not represent the *contents* of a featurally-based experience. The features embody the contents of the experience, but they are individually meaningless. The categories can represent the *meaning* of the experience, but not its contents. These are complementary forms of information. The resonant state that develops when the feature pattern and its category are synchronously activated by reciprocal bottom-up and top-down signals overcomes these complementary informational deficiencies by coherently binding distributed pattern and symbolic context together into a unified *bound state*. It is this bound state that is the functional unit of the network. It is this bound state that makes it possible for us to be conscious of the featural contents of an experience *and* its meaning, all in the same moment of resonant awareness. The informational complementarity between distributed features and compressed categories, and how it is resolved by resonance, shines additional light on my prediction that "all conscious states are resonant states".

In particular, when levels F_1 and F_2 in Figure 2.2 interact via mutual positive feedback during a resonant state, then the attended features at F_1 are coherently bound together by the top-down expectation that is read out by the active category at F_2. The attended pattern of features at F_1, in turn, maintains activation of the recognition category at F_2 via the bottom-up adaptive filter. The resulting *feature-category resonance* is a classical example of a *synchronous bound state* that carries information about both what category is active and what features are represented by it, and thus embodies sufficient information to support conscious recognition of a visual object or scene (Table 1.4). These system-wide bound states, not individual processing stages, can overcome symbol grounding ignorance.

How is the generality of knowledge controlled? Exemplars vs. prototypes

Given that resonant bound states represent the content and meaning of an experience, we now need to analyze what contents of an experience are learned. In particular: How does a brain learn both concrete and general knowledge about the world? This is a challenging problem because we learn from specific experiences, yet can come away from these experiences with both specific and abstract knowledge about the world. Cognitive modelers have tried to answer this question by breaking into two camps. Some modelers have proposed that humans learn the individual inputs, or *exemplars*, that they experience (Medin, Dewey, and Murphy, 1983; Medin and Schaffer, 1978; Medin and Smith, 1981). Such a proposal clarifies how individual events, such as a particular view of a familiar face, can be recognized. But it also raises a number of serious problems: How can such a huge collection of stored exemplars be efficiently searched, recognized, and recalled? Would such storage not lead to a combinatorial explosion of memory, as well as to unmanageable problems of memory retrieval? How are novel variations on exemplars recognized and recalled?

It must also be explained: How can abstract information that is an emergent property of many individual experiences be derived from individual exemplars? To answer this question, other modelers have proposed that humans learn *prototypes* that abstract information from many exemplars (Posner and Keele, 1970; Smith and Minda, 1998, 2000; Smith, Murray, and Minda, 1997). For example, we can recognize that everyone has a face. This approach clarifies how abstract information may be stored, and much less memory is needed to store prototypes than exemplars.

However, this proposal also raises serious problems: How can individual exemplars be learned and recognized? How is the level of abstraction controlled so that the advantages of both concrete exemplars and abstract proto-types can be achieved? Yet other modelers, notably Robert Nosofsky of Indiana University and his colleagues, have attempted to reconcile these views by proposing a hybrid approach that is sometimes called a Rule-and-Exceptions approach (Nosofsky, 1984, 1987; Nosofsky, Krushke, and McKinley, 1992; Palmeri and Nosofsky, 1995). Here, the rule plays the role of an abstract prototype, and the excep-tions play the role of concrete exemplars that do not obey the rule. These cognitive models have been able to provide reasonably good fits to human categorization data, but none of them has explained how the various exemplars, prototypes, or rule-and-exceptions are learned through time, or how their recognition and recall may be realized in a brain.

ART provides a different answer to this question that overcomes problems faced by the cognitive models. In par-ticular, ART systems learn prototypes, rather than indi-vidual inputs or exemplars. Why, then, does not ART face the same problems as other prototype models? One reason is that ART proposes a new definition of prototype than is used in standard prototype models. In the cognitive pro-totype models, the *experimentalist* defines the prototypes and then constructs particular exemplars that are sup-posed to partially match these prototypes. These exem-plars are then used in human categorization experiments to test how well humans actually learn these prototypes when they are exposed to the exemplars.

In contrast, ART prototypes are not defined *a priori*. Rather, they are discovered on-line through a learning process during which individual events are experienced as they occur in real time. As a result of such incremental learning, ART learns *critical feature patterns*. Critical feature patterns are the matched patterns X^* in Figure 5.19, at least those that represent a good enough match to trigger a resonance, by which they are incorporated through learning into the category's prototype. Critical feature patterns are learned in both the bottom-up and top-down LTM traces between F_1 and F_2. The bottom-up LTM traces control how the adaptive filters choose win-ning categories at F_2. The top-down LTM traces deter-mine what features the expectations that are activated by winning categories focus attention upon at F_1. As illus-trated in Figure 5.19b, this top-down matching process inhibits features that mismatch the learned top-down prototype V and amplify features that match V. An ART category hereby incrementally learns a prototype whose features are derived from all the exemplars that can res-onate with it.

Given that ART systems learn prototypes, how can they also learn to recognize unique experiences, such as a particular view of a friend's face? Remarkably, the pro-totypes learned by ART systems can also learn individual exemplars. Each ART model can learn general prototypes that embody abstract properties that are shared by many exemplars, as well as concrete prototypes that represent individual events. Moreover, as will be explained below, whether learning is concrete or abstract can be controlled in a task-selective way.

The general prototypes are a simple example of "sym-bols." Various practitioners of Artificial Intelligence have claimed that neural network models cannot learn symbols, and that symbols are a uniquely appropriate topic for AI symbolic methods to explain. However, AI does not do a good job of explaining where symbols come from, particularly how they arise from our on-going learning experiences with the world's exemplars. ART provides an answer to the question of where sym-bols come from by showing how ART prototypes can achieve a task-appropriate balance between abstraction and concreteness.

Both concrete and abstract categories emerge from minimax learning

ART suggests how both concrete and abstract information can be learned by conjointly *maximizing* category gener-alization while *minimizing* predictive error (Bradski and Grossberg, 1995; Carpenter and Grossberg, 1987a, 1987b; Carpenter, Grossberg and Reynolds, 1991; Carpenter et al., 1992). This type of learning is said to obey a *min-imax learning* principle. The utility of such a principle can be motivated as follows: It is obviously useful to use as few precious memory resources as possible—that is, to maximize generalization—in order to remember any ex-perience. If we took this goal to an extreme, then we could achieve maximal generalization, or memory compression, if a single cell population could categorize all of our expe-riences. If this were possible, then our brains could then be significantly smaller!

Such a "world category" is not sufficient, however, be-cause we need to discriminate among qualitatively different experiences. We need to distinguish faces from words and automobiles. We also need to distinguish between the in-dividual faces of people we know, and the different letters of the alphabet. We could not do any of these things if the degree of generalization was so great that all of these distinct experiences were all lumped together through learning. More than a single world category is thus needed to discriminate between multiple experiences. That is why balancing the goals of maximizing generalization and of minimizing error makes sense: We want to have the max-imal generalization possible, but too much generalization can lead to too much error. More memory resources need to be expended as we try to discriminate and understand the many facets of a complex world. ART models control how general their prototypes can become in any situation by using the top-down attentive matching process. Said in another way: ART links issues about intention and attention to issues about abstraction and symbolic representation. How the matching process achieves this is discussed below.

Mismatch-mediated memory search and resonance together stabilize learned memories

In order to explain how minimax learning is achieved, we first need to consider what happens if the mismatch between bottom-up and top-down information is too great at the feature level F_1 for a resonance to develop. Then, as described in the ART thought experiment, the currently active F_2 category is quickly reset and a memory search, or hypothesis testing, for a better category is initiated, as illustrated by Figure 5.19. A combination of top-down matching, attention focusing, and memory search is what stabilizes ART learning and memory in response to an arbitrary input environment. The attentional focusing by top-down matching prevents inputs that represent irrelevant features at F_1 from eroding the memory of previously learned LTM prototypes. The memory search resets F_2 categories so quickly when their prototype V mismatches an input vector I that the more slowly varying LTM traces do not have an opportunity to correlate the corresponding F_1 activity vector X^* with them. Conversely, the resonant event, when it does occur, maintains, amplifies, and synchronizes the matched STM activities for long enough and at high enough amplitudes for new learning to occur at the LTM traces.

Novelty, vigilance control, and task-selective learning of concrete and abstract categories

Whether or not a resonance occurs depends upon the level of mismatch, or novelty, that the network is able to tolerate without triggering a memory search for a new category. Novelty is measured by how many features in a bottom-up input exemplar I mismatch the top-down prototype V that its presentation evokes, as in Figures 5.19b and 5.19c. Gail Carpenter and I predicted that the criterion of an

acceptable match is defined by process called *vigilance control* (Carpenter and Grossberg, 1987a). A vigilance parameter ρ is computed within the *orienting system A* of the network, as illustrated in Figure 5.19. If vigilance is set high, then only exemplars that are very similar to the active prototype can cause resonance. In this vigilance range, a *concrete prototype* is learned. In the limit of very high vigilance, the prototypes that are learned resemble individual exemplars, leading to learning of an *exemplar prototype*. If vigilance is set low, then many different exemplars can all match an active prototype well enough to cause resonance. Low vigilance enables the network to learn an *abstract prototype*. By dynamically varying the vigilance level in response to situational demands, an ART system can autonomously learn concrete or abstract prototypes, and mixtures thereof, in response to a sequence of input patterns.

Vigilance is computed in the orienting system

The vigilance parameter ρ determines how bad a match will be tolerated before a burst of nonspecific arousal is triggered. A simple mathematical inequality is sufficient to understand how vigilance works, and to explain why vigilance is computed in the orienting system. Readers who would prefer to skip the explanation of how the balance between bottom-up excitation and feature-activated inhibition varies through time can still understand the main purpose of vigilance control. Here is the simple math needed to clearly understand this balance:

Vigilance is computed within the orienting system of an ART model (Figures 5.19b-d) because it is here that bottom-up excitation from all the active inputs in an input pattern I are compared with inhibition from all the active features in a distributed feature representation across F_1. This comparison is achieved by letting the vigilance parameter ρ multiply the bottom-up inputs I to the orienting system A; that is, ρ is the *gain*, or sensitivity, of the excitatory signals that the inputs I deliver to the orienting system A. The total strength $\rho|I|$ of the active excitatory input to A is inhibited by the total strength $|X^*|$ of the current activity at F_1.

Memory search is prevented, and resonance allowed to develop, if the net input $\rho|I|-|X^*|$ to the orienting system from the attentional system is less than or equal to zero. This inequality says that the total output $|X^*|$ from active cells in the attentional focus X^* inhibits the orienting system A (note the minus sign) in $\rho|I|-|X^*|$ more than the total input $\rho|I|$ at that time *excites* it.

This state of affairs is illustrated by Figure 5.19a. Here, the net input $\rho|I|-|X^*|$ is negative in the "bottom-up

VIGILANCE CONTROL

$$\rho|I| - |X^*| \leq 0 \quad \text{resonate and learn}$$
$$\rho|I| - |X^*| > 0 \quad \text{reset and search}$$

ρ **is a** sensitivity or gain **parameter**

FIGURE 5.29. Vigilance is a gain parameter on inputs to the orienting system that regulates whether net excitation from bottom-up inputs or inhibition from activated categories will dominate the orienting system. If excitation wins, then a memory search for a better matching category will occur. If inhibition wins, then the orienting system will remain quiet, thereby enabling resonance and learning to occur.

mode" after the inputs I have activated the features across F_1 but before any top-down feedback from F_2 is able to reach F_1 (Figure 5.29). This is true because X^* equals I then, and ρ is always less than or equal to 1. While the orienting subsystem remains quiet, the input pattern I can cause selection of a category at F_2 (Figure 5.19a) and this category can activate a top-down expectation to test if its prototype matches I adequately (Figure 5.19b). When such a top-down prototype is delivered to F_1 from an active F_2 category, an attentional focus X^* forms at F_1. By the ART Matching Rule, cells remain active in X^* if they are activated by the bottom-up input I *and* receive a sufficiently large top-down input from the prototype. If the prototype does not perfectly match the input I, then the number of active features in the attentional focus X^* may be smaller than the number of active features in the input I itself (Figure 5.19b).

If $|X^*|$ is so small that $\rho|I| - |X^*|$ becomes positive, then the orienting system A is activated, as in Figure 5.19c. The inequality $\rho|I| - |X^*| > 0$ can be rewritten as $\rho > |X^*||I|^{-1}$ to show that the orienting system is activated whenever ρ is chosen higher than the ratio of the number of active matched features in X^* to the total number of features in I. In other words, the vigilance parameter controls how bad a match can be before search for a new category is initiated. If the vigilance parameter is low, then many exemplars can all influence the learning of a shared prototype, by chipping away at the features that are not shared with all the exemplars. If the vigilance parameter is high, then even a small difference between a new exemplar and a known prototype (e.g., F vs. E) can drive the search for a new category with which to represent F.

Either a larger value of the vigilance ρ, or a smaller match ratio $|X^*||I|^{-1}$ makes it harder to achieve resonance. This is true because, when ρ is larger, it is easier to make $\rho|I| - |X^*|$ positive, thereby activating the orienting system and leading to memory search. In other words,

a large vigilance makes the network more intolerant of differences between the input and the learned prototype. Alternatively, for fixed vigilance, if the input is chosen to be increasingly different from the learned prototype, then X^* becomes smaller and the match ratio $\rho|I| - |X^*|$ becomes larger until $\rho|I| - |X^*|$ becomes positive, and a memory search is triggered by a burst of arousal.

Balancing between the remembered past and the anticipated future

Prototype refinement does not occur only when different events may be classified by the same category. It can also occur when exemplars of a single individual or event vary through time. For example, prototype refinement can occur when we meet our friends intermittently over a period of years. We can recognize our friends because they look similar enough to the prototypes that we have learned from our previous experiences with them. But even as we recognize them, our criteria for recognizing them in the future can be refined as they age, change their hair style, become ill or healthy, and the like. We are balanced between the remembered past and the anticipated future during every moment of recognition. Stability does not imply rigidity to change. Rather, our adaptive intelligence is built upon a dynamic and controlled form of stability that continually adjusts its learned criteria for resonance and recognition as we go on with our lives. That is why I have called this issue the stability-plasticity *dilemma*. It concerns a question of *balance*. Maintaining such a balance flawlessly throughout life is often too much to ask.

Vigilance can vary across learning experiences in a task-sensitive manner. As a result, recognition categories capable of encoding widely differing degrees of generalization or abstraction can be learned by a single ART system. Low vigilance leads to broad generalization and abstract prototypes. High vigilance leads to narrow generalization and to prototypes that represent fewer input exemplars, even a single exemplar. Thus, a single ART system with a variable vigilance level may be used, say, to learn "abstract prototypes" with which to recognize general categories of faces and dogs, as well as "exemplar prototypes" with which to recognize individual faces and dogs.

Vigilance control hereby allows ART to overcome fundamental difficulties that have been faced by classical exemplar and prototype theories of learning and recognition. Classical exemplar models face a serious combinatorial explosion, since they need to suppose that all experienced exemplars are somehow stored in memory and searched during performance. Classical prototype theories face the problem that they find it hard to explain how individual exemplars are learned, such as a particular view of a familiar face. Vigilance control enables ART to achieve the best of both types of model, by learning the most general category that is consistent with environmental feedback.

Minimax learning via match tracking: Learning the most general predictive categories

One way to achieve this balance between the abstract and the concrete is by a patented process called *match tracking* that was introduced by Gail Carpenter and myself in articles published in 1991 and 1992 with several PhD students (Carpenter, Grossberg, and Reynolds, 1991; Carpenter et al., 1992). Match tracking is one way in which minimax learning can be achieved, so that we use the minimum amount of memory that is required to adequately predict the outcome in any given situation. Match tracking works as follows. After any mismatch between the network's predicted answer and feedback from the world, the mismatch triggers a signal that is sent to the orienting system *A*. This mismatch signal causes the vigilance value to increase until it just exceeds the level of match between the current bottom-up input exemplar and the current top-down prototype.

In order for a prediction to be made at all, the analog match must be higher than the current vigilance parameter (Figure 5.30a). Keep in mind that maintaining the

lowest possible vigilance allows the learning of the most general recognition categories and, along with it, conserves memory resources. When match tracking is operative, in response to a predictive error (e.g., E is predicted in response to F), the vigilance parameter ρ increases just enough to trigger reset and search for a better-matching category (Figure 5.30b). In other words, vigilance "tracks" the degree of match between input exemplar and matched prototype.

Each increase in vigilance spells a decrease in generalization, and thus uses more memory resources. By increasing vigilance just enough to trigger a memory search, the minimum amount of generalization is sacrificed to correct a predictive error. Match tracking hereby realizes a Minimax Learning Rule that *maximizes* category generality while it conjointly *minimizes* predictive error. Through this simple mechanism, the minimax learning rule can be realized on every learning trial, even in a rapidly changing world, using only locally computed quantities in the network.

Because the baseline level of vigilance is initially set at the lowest level that has led to predictive success in the past, ART models try to learn the most general category that is consistent with the data. This tendency can, for example, lead to the type of overgeneralization that is seen in young children until further learning leads to category refinement (Chapman et al., 1986; Clark, 1973; Smith et al., 1985; Smith and Kemler, 1978; Ward, 1983).

Figure 5.31 more explicitly illustrates how match tracking can be realized. In Figure 5.31, two ART networks are connected by a map field. Suppose that the first ART system, call it ARTa, learns how to recognize visually

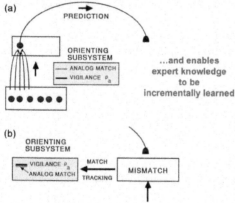

MATCH TRACKING realizes MINIMAX LEARNING PRINCIPLE
Given a predictive error, vigilance increases just enough to trigger search and thus sacrifices the minimum generalization to correct the error

FIGURE 5.30. When a predictive disconfirmation occurs, vigilance increases enough to drive a search for a more predictive category. If vigilance increases just enough to exceed the analog match between features that survive top-down matching and the entire bottom-up input pattern, then minimax learning occurs. In this case, the minimum amount of category generalization is given up to correct the predictive error.

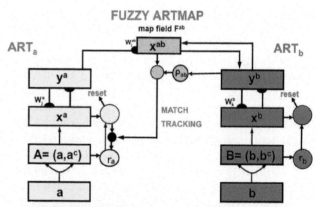

MATCH TRACKING realizes Minimax Learning Principle:
Vigilance increases to just above the match ratio of prototype / exemplar, thereby triggering search

FIGURE 5.31. A system like Fuzzy ARTMAP can learn to associate learned categories in one ART network with learned categories in a second ART network. Because both bottom-up and top-down interactions occur in both networks, a bottom-up input pattern to the first ART network can learn to generate a top-down output pattern from the second ART network.

presented letters, and that the second ART system, call it ARTb, learns to hear and say the letter names. These visual and auditory categorizations are linked by associative learning at the map field.

Match tracking describes one way by which the network can automatically respond to predictive errors. It is not, however, the only way that vigilance can be controlled. We all know that our "vigilance" can increase rapidly if something unpleasant occurs, such as a physical punishment or verbal insult. Within an ART network, *any* consequence that increases vigilance can cause a refinement in the discriminations that we are capable of learning. Vigilance control illustrates how the generality of what we attend and learn, and thus our conscious percepts, can be modified by several types of environmental feedback.

Vigilance control depends upon complementary computing. Vigilance control is easy to define within an ART system because it contains complementary attentional and orienting systems that process expected and familiar events vs. unexpected and unfamiliar events, respectively. The attentional system learns bottom-up categories and top-down expectations of familiar events, whereas the orienting system enables the attentional system to learn about novel experiences without causing catastrophic forgetting of what it already knows. Without these complementary systems, a vigilance concept could not easily be computationally realized, let alone conceived. Thus, ART's proposed solution of the stability-plasticity dilemma through the use of these complementary systems contains implicit within it the ability to also solve the problem of automatically learning the right level of abstractness or concreteness with which to understand the world.

Another property worth mentioning is that so much of what goes on in this network is not in any way preprogrammed, or even explicitly represented. When a mismatch occurs in the "auditory" ARTb, ARTb can compute *that* a "visual" category in ARTa has predicted an erroneous response, but it does not know *which* category made the erroneous prediction. When the mismatch causes an increase in vigilance, the network's sensitivity goes up within the orienting system and leads to memory search within ARTa, but the actual categories that are searched within ARTa are unknown to both the orienting system and to ARTb. The new categories that the network learns in this way are thus a complex emergent property of interactions between the entire neural system and the world, with no one part of this cyclic brain/environmental system knowing what the other parts are doing.

Given that there is no single observer providing an all-intelligent analysis of these system-wide interactions, it remains to ask: Do they work? Can they learn anything interesting? Do humans actually use ART-like processes in their brains. A positive answer can now be given to all these questions. I will intersperse additional examples about ART's learning capabilities and its explanations of psychological and neurobiological data throughout the remainder of this chapter.

Multiple applications of ART to large-scale problems in engineering and technology. Let's first consider what sorts of things ART can learn, beyond its psychological and neurobiological learning properties. Many benchmark studies have demonstrated that ART learns well when exposed to a wide variety of challenging pattern recognition and prediction problems in science and technology. These include the classification of airplane parts; of sonar and radar signals; of medical, satellite, and face imagery; and of musical scores. Other applications have been made to the control of mobile robots and nuclear power plants, cancer diagnosis, air quality monitoring, strength prediction for concrete mixes, solar hot water system monitoring, chemical process monitoring, signature verification, electric load forecasting, tool failure monitoring, fault diagnosis of pneumatic systems, chemical analysis from ultraviolet and infrared spectra, decision support for situation awareness, vision-based driver assistance, user profiles for personalized information dissemination, frequency-selective surface design for electromagnetic system devices, Chinese text categorization, semiconductor manufacturing, gene expression analysis, sleep apnea and narcolepsy detection, stock association discovery, viability of recommender systems, power transmission line fault diagnosis, million city traveling salesman problem, identification of long-range aerosol transport patterns, product redesign based on customer requirements, photometric clustering of regenerated plants of gladiolus, manufacturing cell formation with production data, and discovery of hierarchical thematic structure in text collections, among others.

There are now hundreds of ART researchers applying and developing ART to a wide range of large-scale applications in engineering and technology, and thousands of citations to these articles. A standard ART algorithm for applications is called Default ARTMAP (Amis and Carpenter, 2007; Carpenter, 2003). Early important ART algorithms for applications include ART 1, ART 2, and fuzzy ART for unsupervised learning and classification (Carpenter and Grossberg, 1987a, 1987b; Carpenter, Grossberg, and Rosen, 1991), and ARTMAP and fuzzy ARTMAP for both unsupervised and supervised learning and classification (Carpenter et al., 1992; Carpenter, Grossberg, and Reynolds, 1991). More recent algorithms from Gail Carpenter and her students include distributed ARTMAP, which combines distributed coding with fast, stable, incremental learning (Carpenter, 1997; Carpenter, Milenova, and Noeske, 1998); ARTMAP Information Fusion, which can incrementally learn a cognitive hierarchy of rules in response to probabilistic, incomplete, and even contradictory data that are collected by multiple observers (Carpenter, Martens, and Ogas, 2005; Carpenter and Ravindran, 2008; Parsons and

Carpenter, 2003); Self-supervised ART, which shows how some supervised learning "in school" can lead to effective knowledge acquisition later on by unsupervised learning "in the real world" (Amis and Carpenter, 2010); and Biased ART, which shows how attention can be selectively diverted from features that cause predictive errors (Carpenter and Gaddam, 2010). Computer code for running various ART algorithms and related neural models that were discovered and developed at Boston University can be found at http://techlab.bu.edu/resources/software/C51.

Many variants of ART have been developed and applied by authors around the world. These contributions include the following sample of articles published between 1991 and 2012: Akhbardeh et al., 2007; Anagnostopoulos and Georgiopoulos, 2000; Anton-Rodriguez et al., 2009; Brannon et al., 2009; Cai et al., 2011; Cano-Izquierdo et al., 2009; Caudell, 1992; Caudell et al., 1991; Chao et al., 2011; Cherng et al., 2009; Demetgul, Tansel, and Taskin, 2009; Dunbar, 2012; He et al., 2012; He, Tan, and Tan, 2000; Healy, Caudell, and Smith, 1993; Ho et al., 1994; Hsieh, 2008; Hsieh and Yang, 2008; Hsu and Chien, 2007; Kawamura, Takahashi, and Honda, 2008; Kaylani et al., 2009; Keskin and Ozkan, 2009; Liu et al., 2009; Liu, Pang, and Lloyd, 2008; Lopes, Minussi, and Lotufo, 2005; Marchiori et al., 2011; Martin-Guerrero et al., 2007; Massey, 2009; Mulder and Wunsch, 2003; Owega et al., 2006; Prasad and Gupta, 2008; Shieh, Yan, and Chen, 2008; Sudhakara Pandian and Mahapatra, 2009; Takahashi et al., 2007; Tan, 1997; Tan et al., 2008; Tan and Teo, 1998; Wienke and Buydens, 1995; Wunsch et al, 1993; Xu et al., 2009; and Zhang and Kezunovic, 2007.

Donald C. Wunsch II and his colleagues have been particularly active in developing and applying ART algorithms. Three notable recent contributions from them occur in the December, 2019 special issue of the journal *Neural Networks* with Wunsch as its Editor. The title of his lead article summarizes the purpose of the special issue: "Admiring the Great Mountain: A Celebration Special Issue in Honor of Stephen Grossberg's 80th Birthday" (Wunsch, 2019). The following comprehensive review article in the special issue by Don and his colleagues may be a useful resource for scientists and engineers who are interested in ART applications. Its title is: "A Survey of Adaptive Resonance Theory Neural Network Models for Engineering Applications" (da Silva, Elnabarawy, and Wunsch, 2019). The research of this team on ART is actively continuing, as illustrated by their recent article about what seems to be the most powerful ART-based clustering algorithm for retrieving arbitrary-shaped clusters (da Silva, Elnabarawy, and Wunsch, 2020).

The above articles illustrate that ART has become one of the standard neural network models to which practitioners turn to solve their applications. See the web site http://techlab.bu.edu/resources/articles/C5 of the CNS Tech Lab for a partial list of illustrative benchmark studies and technology transfers.

Learning resonant hierarchies of grandmother cohorts

Categories that vary in generality have been reported in neurophysiological experiments on monkeys. Some cells in the inferotemporal cortex of monkeys may respond selectively to particular views of the familiar faces of laboratory personnel, whereas others may respond to much more general aspects of the environment. Cells that seem to respond very selectively have led to the concept of a "grandmother cell", or cell that would respond only to the face of your grandmother. *Wikipedia* defines a grandmother cell as follows: "The grandmother cell is a hypothetical neuron that represents a complex but specific concept or object. It activates when a person 'sees, hears, or otherwise sensibly discriminates' a specific entity, such as his or her grandmother."

The possibility that grandmother cells might be learned as a result of vigilance control raises the following general question, to which ART provides at least partial answers: How distributed does a recognition category have to be in order to successfully predict future outcomes? In particular, can a single winner-take-all category code all the critical features that may be needed to control and predict all aspects of an object's recognition during goal-oriented behaviors with it?

In general the answer is No. Gail Carpenter and her PhD students introduced and developed the distributed ARTMAP model (Carpenter, 1997; Carpenter, Milenova, and Noeske, 1998) to show how, during supervised learning—which is sensitive to the predictive success of a recognition category in generating a desired outcome—the ART learning cycle tries to discover the optimal degree of compression that is needed to categorize the predictively successful critical feature patterns that are hidden within the database that is currently being learned. In support of such an idea, a number of neurophysiologists, including Charles Gross at Princeton and his colleagues (Desimone et al., 1992), have published data which suggest that recognition of a complex object, such as a face, may be distributed over a population of cells. Michael Hasselmo at Boston University and his colleagues noted in 1989 that, during face recognition, cells selective for facial expression tend to be located within the superior temporal sulcus, whereas cells selective for identity tend to be located on the inferior temporal gyrus (Hasselmo et al., 1989).

I have proposed that such examples are all special cases of what I have called a *grandmother cohort*, which is a distributed network of compressed categories with which to represent an object or event. I have further suggested that such grandmother cohorts are a part of bound states in resonant hierarchies that can involve multiple cortical re-gions. Further research on how to design and mathematically analyze grandmother cohorts can keep a lot of talented investigators profitably engaged for a long time.

Vigilance control by match tracking during learning of the alphabet

As noted above, minimax learning is realized if, in response to a predictive error, vigilance is raised just enough to trigger a new memory search for a better matching category. Every increase in vigilance leads to new learning that reduces the generality of the learned category that triggered the search.

Figure 5.32 illustrates how different vigilance levels in a single ART model can lead to learning of both concrete and general prototypes. This figure summarizes the results of computer simulations that Gail Carpenter and I published in 1987 to show how the ART 1 model, which illustrates key ART properties in a mathematically provable setting, can learn to classify the letters of the alphabet (Carpenter and Grossberg, 1987a). When presented to a real human learner, the raw letters would not be directly input into the brain's recognition categories, which exist in the inferotemporal cortex, among other places (Figure 1.21). They would first be preprocessed into boundary and surface representations in the visual cortex, before these boundary and surface representations input to the inferotemporal cortex. To make my main point about vigilance control in the simplest way, this example does input letters directly to the ART classifier.

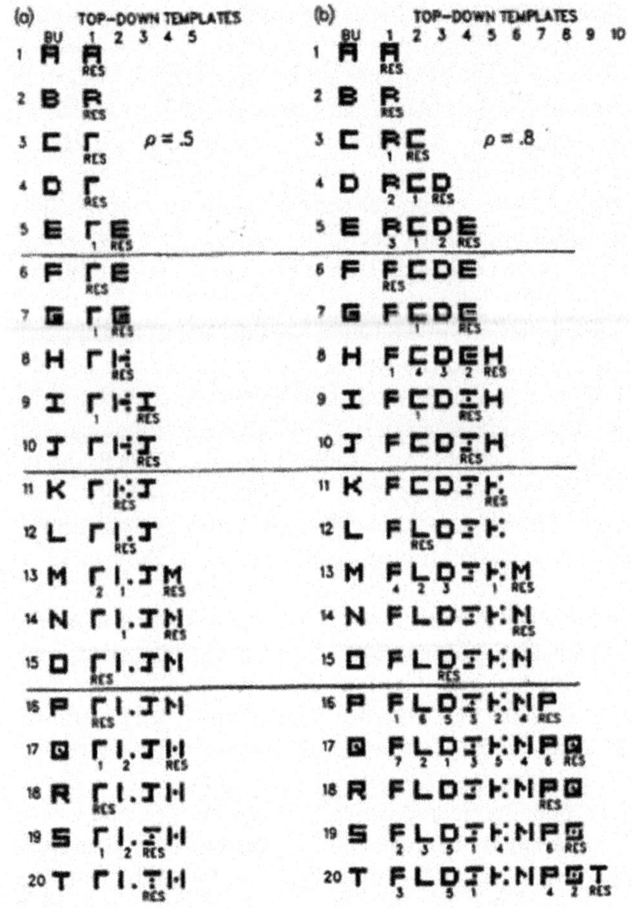

If the vigilance is set to its maximum value of 1, then no variability in a letter is tolerated, and every letter is classified into its own category. This is the limit of exemplar prototypes. Figure 5.32 shows how the letters are classified if vigilance is set at a smaller value 0.5 (Figure 5.32a), and a larger value 0.8 (Figure 5.32b). In both cases, the network's learning rate is chosen to be high. Going down the column in Figure 5.32a shows how the network learns in response to the first 20 letters of the alphabet. Each row describes what categories and prototypes are learned through time. Black pixels represent prototype values equal to 1 at the corresponding positions. White pixels represent prototype values equal to 0 at their positions. Note that each prototype gets to be more abstract as learning goes on. By the time the 20th letter T has been learned, only 4 categories have been learned with which to classify all 20 letters. The symbol RES, for resonance, under one of the prototypes on each learning trial shows which category classifies the letter that was presented on that trial. In particular, category 1

FIGURE 5.32. Learning the alphabet with two different levels of vigilance. The learning in column (b) is higher than in column (a), leading to more concrete categories with less abstract prototypes. See the text for details.

classifies letter A, B, C, and D, among others, when they are presented, whereas category 2 classifies the letters E, G, and H, among others, when they are presented.

In contrast, when the vigilance is increased to 0.8, as illustrated in Figure 5.32b, 9 categories are learned in response to the first 20 letters, instead of just 4. Moreover, letter C is no longer lumped into category 1 with A and B. Now it forms a new category 2 because it cannot satisfy the vigilance constraint when it is matched against the prototype of category 1. Thus, just by changing the sensitivity of the network, it can either learn more abstract or more concrete categories and prototypes with which to classify and recognize the world.

During search, arousal bursts from the orienting system interact with the attentional system to rapidly reset mismatched categories, as in Figure 5.19c, and to thereby allow selection of better F_2 representations with which to categorize novel inputs at F_1, as in Figure 5.19d. Search may end with a familiar category, if its prototype

EARLY ARTMAP BENCHMARK STUDIES

Database benchmark:
MACHINE LEARNING (90-95% correct)
ARTMAP (100% correct on a training set an order of magnitude smaller)
Medical database:
STATISTICAL METHOD (60% correct)
ARTMAP (96% correct)
Letter recognition database:
GENETIC ALGORITHM (82% correct)
ARTMAP (96% correct)
Database benchmarks:
BACKPROPAGATION (10,000 – 20,000 training epochs)
ARTMAP (1-5 epochs)

Used in applications where other algorithms fail
e.g. Boeing CAD Group Technology
Airplane part design reuse and inventory compression
Need fast stable learning and search of a huge airplane part inventory, each of 16 million parts defined by a 1 million dimensional vector
This inventory can also continue growing unpredictably

FIGURE 5.33. Some early ARTMAP benchmark studies. These successes led to the use of ARTMAP, and the many variants that we and other groups have developed, in many large-scale applications in engineering and technology that has not abated even today.

is similar enough to the input exemplar to satisfy the resonance criterion. This prototype may then be refined by attentional focusing to incorporate the new information that is embodied in the exemplar. Figure 5.32 illustrates several examples of such prototype refinement. For example, in Figure 5.32a, the prototype of category 1 is refined when B and C are classified by it. Likewise, the prototype of category 2 is refined when G, H, and K are classified by it. If, however, the input is too different from any previously learned prototype, then an uncommitted population of F_2 nodes is selected and learning of a totally new category is initiated. This is illustrated in Figure 5.32a when E is classified by category 2 and when I is classified by category 3. Search hereby uses vigilance control to determine how much a category prototype can change and, within these limits, protects previously learned categories from experiencing catastrophic forgetting.

It should, however, be noted that the simulations in Figure 5.32 were carried out using unsupervised learning, without any match tracking in response to erroneous predictions. Figures 5.33 and 5.34 show some ARTMAP benchmarks against competing technologies in which match tracking did occur in response to predictive disconfirmations during learning. The benchmarks speak for themselves. Readers who want more details can study some of the original archival articles (Carpenter, Grossberg, and Reynolds, 1991; Carpenter et al., 1992, 1996, 1997). More

application benchmarks by Gail Carpenter and her colleagues can be found at http://techlab.bu.edu/members/gail/pubs_articles.html#pubs92_94.

Catastrophic forgetting without the top-down ART Matching Rule

In our 1987 article, Gail Carpenter and I also described infinitely many sequences of inputs that would experience catastrophic forgetting if top-down expectations that obey the ART Matching Rule are eliminated. Remarkably, sequences of just four input patterns, suitably ordered, could lead to catastrophic forgetting. Figure 5.35 summarizes the mathematical rules that generate such sequences, and Figure 5.36 summarizes a computer simulation that demonstrates catastrophic forgetting. As Figure 5.36 illustrates, unstable coding can occur if a subset prototype gets recoded as a superset prototype when a superset input pattern is categorized by that category.

This kind of recoding happens every time the sequence of four input patterns is presented in the order *ABCAD*, where the inputs in this sequence obey the relationships that are defined in Figure 5.35. Note that the same superset input pattern *A* is presented as the first and the fourth input in the sequence. When it is presented as the first input, it is categorized by category node 1, but when it is presented as

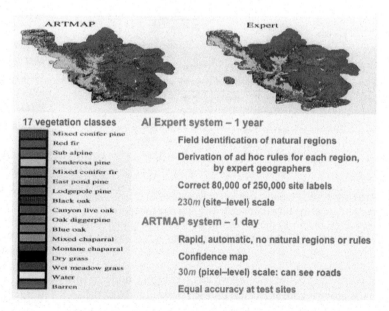

17 vegetation classes

AI Expert system – 1 year

Field identification of natural regions

Derivation of ad hoc rules for each region, by expert geographers

Correct 80,000 of 250,000 site labels

230*m* (site–level) scale

ARTMAP system – 1 day

Rapid, automatic, no natural regions or rules

Confidence map

30*m* (pixel–level) scale: can see roads

Equal accuracy at test sites

Mixed conifer pine
Red fir
Sub alpine
Ponderosa pine
Mixed conifer fir
East pond pine
Lodgepole pine
Black oak
Canyon live oak
Oak diggerpine
Blue oak
Mixed chaparral
Montane chaparral
Dry grass
Wet meadow grass
Water
Barren

FIGURE 5.34. ARTMAP was successfully used to learn maps of natural terrains with many advantages over those of mapping projects that used AI expert systems. The advantages are so great that many mapping projects started to use this technology.

CODE INSTABILITY INPUT SEQUENCES

$$D \subset C \subset A$$

$$B \subset A$$

$$B \cap C = \varnothing$$

$$|D| < |B| < |C|$$

where $|E|$ is the number of features in the set E

Any set of input vectors that satisfy the above conditions will lead to unstable coding if they are periodically presented in the order

ABCAD

and the top-down ART Matching Rule is shut off

FIGURE 5.35. I had shown in 1976 how a competitive learning or self-organizing map model could undergo catastrophic forgetting if the input environment was sufficiently dense and nonstationary, as illustrated by Figure 5.18. Later work with Gail Carpenter showed how, if the ART Matching Rule was shut off, repeating just four input patterns in the correct order could also cause catastrophic forgetting by causing superset recoding, as illustrated in Figure 5.36.

STABLE AND UNSTABLE LEARNING

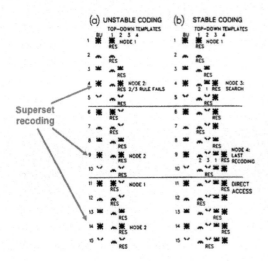

FIGURE 5.36. Column (a) shows catastrophic forgetting when the ART Matching Rule is not operative. It is due to superset recoding. Column (b) shows how category learning quickly stabilizes when the ART Matching Rule is restored.

the fourth input, it is categorized by category node 2. This oscillatory recoding occurs on each presentation of the sequence, thereby illustrating catastrophic forgetting of this input pattern. The ART Matching Rule prevents this kind of "superset recoding".

Statistical hypothesis testing and decision making in a nonstationary world

The importance of fast learning under both unsupervised and supervised conditions. I briefly noted above that the ART cycle of hypothesis testing and category learning can be described using a different language, notably concepts that are familiar from probability theory and statistics. It is useful to emphasize this interpretation to highlight the broad applicability of ART design principles to many problems of hypothesis testing and prediction in a changing, or nonstationary, world.

As I mentioned above, the network's self-normalization property is like the familiar postulate from probability theory that the probabilities of all possible events sum up to 1. The reallocation of activity to new categories after old categories have been reset is like selecting a new hypothesis conditioned on the rejection of a previous hypothesis. The read-out of the top-down expectation based on the current hypothesis is analogous to testing a hypothesis against available data. Learning is like updating statistical priors. Indeed, the mechanism whereby categories are chosen via a bottom-up adaptive filter is like a decision rule in Bayesian statistics.

Given these similarities, what is the difference between ART and classical statistical ideas? Many statistical concepts work best in a stationary world whose rules are unchanging through time. Where learning is allowed, it must often proceed slowly, and with an external supervisor. ART is designed to succeed in a world that is filled with unexpected events, and whose rules may change in unpredictable and nonstationary ways. Learning in ART can be fast or slow, and can proceed with an external teacher (supervised) or without one (unsupervised), with supervision supplied on an arbitrary subset of learning trials. During supervised learning, a teacher provides an explicit correct answer. During unsupervised learning, the world itself is the only source of information about possible correct answers. Much learning by humans is unsupervised, such as how we learn to recognize many visual objects and scenes as we autonomously navigate and search our unique environments. Learning in many statistical prediction models is always supervised, with the back propagation model being perhaps the most famous classical example (Rumelhart, Hinton, and Williams, 1986; Werbos, 1974, 1994).

Fast learning means that the adaptive weights that are being learned approach their new equilibrium points on each learning trial. This is the kind of learning that enables one to quickly learn about a unique new situation, like the first case of a disease outbreak. Remarkably, such one-trial learning in ART can occur without also forcing catastrophic forgetting. In contrast, when many statistical learning rules are driven to do fast learning, they do experience catastrophic forgetting. And if they learn slowly, they may erroneously mix a unique event with statistically more probable but similar events.

Given this comparison between ART and statistical learning, I find it particularly interesting that ART can be expressed using deterministic, not probabilistic, laws for the average, or mean, activities of cells in a neural network. This observation does not deny that the cells which occur in ART and other brain networks may experience cellular noise. Then the corresponding neural laws are defined by stochastic, or probabilistic, systems of differential equations, rather than deterministic ones. However, the mean potentials, firing frequencies, transmitter production rates, and other network quantities obey deterministic laws that have the desired learning, recognition, and prediction properties that I have been summarizing.

Why can deterministic laws describe noisy interacting neurons? Why can deterministic laws adequately describe neural networks whose individual cells may be subject to cellular noise from one cause or another? One reason for this is that the mean values of the various quantities that define the networks are typically larger than their statistical variances, so that *mean field equations* can successfully predict network dynamics. From the perspective of the Method of Minimal Anatomies, all of the model networks that are summarized in this book can be unlumped to describe cells in which these noise sources are explicitly modeled, without undermining conclusions of the deterministic analysis of the lumped networks.

This was a core idea in my early work, which led me to call my earliest theory about the brain dynamics that can control behavior *The Theory of Embedding Fields* in my 1964 monograph about this subject that I completed when I was a PhD student at The Rockefeller Institute for Medical Research, now the Rockefeller University, in New York (Grossberg, 1964). This essential insight enabled me to choose and analyze a computational and functional level of neuronal interaction that could link brain mechanisms to psychological functions, while simultaneously having a clear pathway in mind to unlump finer representations as the pressure of data demanded, and without the fear that the lumped model conclusions would not continue to hold. As I mentioned in Chapter 2, this monograph was distributed to 125 of the world's leading psychologists and neuroscientists. Its foundational insights have held to the present day, through greatly expanded and refined by a series of new discoveries that has continued unabated.

The current book explains how such deterministic laws are sufficient to mechanistically explain many behaviors

of a performing individual as they evolve in time. I believe that at least some of the axioms of probability theory that have been discovered by mathematicians may have been enabled by their brains' ability to carry out the type of non-stationary hypothesis testing, learning, and decision-making that ART describes. From this perspective, current probability theories can be viewed as approximate descriptions of our cognitive endowment that may be extended by systems like ART to deal with incremental fast learning in response to huge nonstationary environments. There is currently enormous interest across science and technology in this kind of problem under the label of Big Data. Because ART is a *self-stabilizing* hypothesis testing and prediction tool, I believe that it will increasingly be profitably be applied to solving Big Data problems.

ART direct access solves the local minimum problem. As sequences of inputs are practiced over learning trials, the search process eventually converges upon stable categories. I noted above that Gail Carpenter and I published theorems in 1987 showing that familiar inputs directly activate the category whose prototype provides the globally best match to the input pattern, without undergoing any search, while unfamiliar inputs can continue to engage the orienting subsystem to trigger memory searches for better categories until they too become familiar. This process of search and category learning continues until the memory capacity, which can be chosen arbitrarily large, is fully utilized.

Because ART chooses the globally best matching category, it provides a solution of the *local minimum problem*—or, roughly speaking, getting trapped in the wrong solution—that various other popular artificial neural network algorithms, such as back propagation and its variant Deep Learning, do not solve, although these algorithms are sometimes modified in various ways in order to partially cope with it.

Memory consolidation, amnesia, and lesions of amygdala, hippocampus, and neocortex

The process whereby search is automatically disengaged is a form of *memory consolidation* that emerges from network interactions. The first example of memory consolidation that was described by ART concerns interactions between the thalamus and neocortex with the hippocampus or, for short, corticohippocampal interactions. For example, in Figure 5.19, F_1 may represent a cortical region, say prestriate cortical area V4, F_2 a higher cortical region, say inferotemporal cortex, and the orienting system A a part of the hippocampus. With this kind of interpretation, Gail Carpenter and I proposed in 1993 how a hippocampal ablation may cause symptoms of medial temporal amnesia (Carpenter and Grossberg, 1993). How this is proposed to occur is explained later in this chapter.

However, this explanation includes only perceptual and cognitive processes. A mechanistically distinct kind of memory consolidation also involves cognitive-emotional and adaptively timed learning processes. In particular, after some learning occurs, early vs. late lesions of the hippocampus, as well as of the thalamus, amygdala, or orbitofrontal cortex, can have different effects on whether or not memory consolidation occurs. My PhD student Daniel Franklin and I published in 2017 the *neurotrophic Spectrally Timed ART* model, or nSTART, model (Figure 5.37) to explain and simulate this complex experimental literature (Franklin and Grossberg, 2017), which was greatly energized by the example of the amnesia of HM that I mentioned earlier in this chapter. These data, and the issues that they illustrate, will be discussed in Chapters 13 and 14.

Learning of fuzzy IF-THEN rules by a self-organizing ART production system

ART provides autonomous solutions for Explainable AI. One problem that is faced by many learning systems, including neural networks, is that, even after such a system can learn to predict outcomes correctly in response to a data set, it is often impossible to determine what kind of "intelligence" or "knowledge" is embodied in its learned LTM traces. For many applications, high predictive accuracy alone on previous benchmarks is not enough, especially if there is no reason to believe that it will continue to succeed in response to novel environments. Many kinds of practitioners, such as medical doctors who may be considering using an algorithm to help predict the best disease diagnosis in response to a particular set of medical symptoms, want a way to evaluate if the model is "working for the right reasons".

ART overcomes this problem. It has been shown, for example, that the

adaptive weights that are learned by the fuzzy ARTMAP model (Carpenter et al., 1992)—which is an ART model that incorporates some of the operations of fuzzy logic—can, at any stage of learning, be translated into fuzzy IF-THEN rules that allow practitioners to understand the nature of the knowledge that the model has learned, as well as the amount of variability in the data that each of the learned rules can tolerate. Thus the ART model is a self-organizing production and *rule discovery* system, as well as a neural network that can learn symbols with which to predict changing environments. Said more simply, these IF-THEN rules "explain" why the learned predictions work. They show that the claims of some cognitive scientists and AI practitioners that neural network models cannot learn rule-based behaviors are as incorrect as the claims that neural models cannot learn symbols.

This problem has not yet been solved in traditional AI, as illustrated by the current DARPA Explainable AI, or XAI, program. The DARPA website for this current research program states the following (https://www.darpa.mil/program/explainable-artificial-intelligence):

"Dramatic success in machine learning has led to a torrent of Artificial Intelligence (AI) applications. Continued advances promise to produce autonomous systems that will perceive, learn, decide, and act on their own. However, the effectiveness of these systems is limited by the machine's current inability to explain their decisions and actions to human users. The Department of Defense (DoD) is facing challenges that demand more intelligent, autonomous, and symbiotic systems. Explainable AI—especially

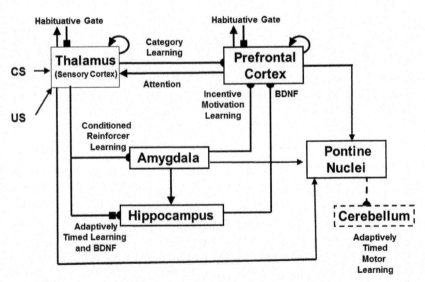

FIGURE 5.37. A macrocircuit of the neurotrophic Spectrally Timed ART, or nSTART, model. I developed nSTART with my PhD student Daniel Franklin. It proposes how adaptively timed learning in the hippocampus, bolstered by Brain Derived Neurotrophic Factor, or BDNF, helps to ensure normal memory consolidation.

explainable machine learning—will be essential if future warfighters are to understand, appropriately trust, and effectively manage an emerging generation of artificially intelligent machine partners".

As I have been illustrating above and throughout the book, ART already has already provided computationally rigorous and effective solutions of these problems for multiple kinds of applications. Moreover, all of our biological models of perception, cognition, emotion, and action are explainable, as I detail in Grossberg (2020a). One important reason for this is that key processing stages in these models compute distributed STM representations of one kind or another. In contrast, the Deep Learning model includes only LTM representations.

Additional brain data about attentive category learning and orienting search

In 2015, Scott Brincat and Earl Miller (Brincat and Miller, 2015) reported neurophysiological data that support the ART distinction between category learning within the attentional system, that includes prefrontal cortex (PFC), and the orienting system, that includes the hippocampus (HPC). They collected data from PFC and HPC in monkeys learning object-pair associations, and wrote (p. 576): "PFC spiking activity reflected learning in parallel with behavioral performance, while HPC neurons reflected feedback about whether trial-and-error guesses were correct or incorrect . . . Rapid object associative learning may occur in PFC, while HPC may guide neocortical plasticity by signaling success or failure via oscillatory synchrony in different frequency bands".

These results contribute to a long history of neurobiological experiments that have implicated the hippocampus in mismatch processing, notably the processing of novel events, including experiments and theoretical concepts about habituation of novelty in the hippocampus as learning proceeds. This experimental tradition goes back at least to the 1960s with the work of the Russian psychophysiologists Evgenii Sokolov in 1968 and Olga Vinogradova in 1975, follows by experiments in 1979 of Deadwyler, West, and Lynch, of Deadwyler, West, and Robinson in 1981, and of Otto and Eichenbaum in 1992 (Deadwyler, West, and Lynch, 1979; Deadwyler, West, and Robinson, 1981; Otto and Eichenbaum, 1992; Sokolov, 1968; Vinogradova, 1975). The ART hypothesis testing and category learning cycle hereby clarifies and unifies an important series of psychophysiological experiments that go back at least 50 years.

Gamma and beta oscillations during attentive resonance and mismatch reset

SMART: A laminar cortical hierarchy of spiking neurons. Several other kinds of data that clarify how attentive recognition and mismatch reset work may be understood in terms of the following discovery that was published in 2008 with my PhD student Massimiliano Versace (Grossberg and Versace, 2008). As can be seen in Figure 5.38, this Synchronous Matching Adaptive Resonance Theory, or SMART, model proposes a detailed account of how identified neurons in specific cortical layers interact within a hierarchy of cortical and thalamic processing stages. Moreover, the neurons in the model are spiking neurons that communicate with each other using non-decremental spikes that travel down their axons to activate target neurons. The SMART model built on earlier laminar cortical models that I developed with other students, and which I generically call LAMINART models. An analysis of why neocortex utilizes cells organized in layers in provided in Chapter 10.

How SMART carries out an ART hypothesis testing and category learning cycle is depicted in Figure 5.39. The name SMART is supported by the following model properties. SMART computer simulations demonstrate that a good enough *match* of a top-down expectation with a bottom-up feature pattern generates an attentive resonance during which the spikes of active cells synchronize in the gamma frequency range of 20–70 Hz (Figure 5.40). Many labs have reported a link between attention and gamma oscillations in the brain, including two articles published in 2001, one from the laboratory of Robert Desimone when he was at the National Institute of Mental Health in Bethesda (Fries, Reynolds, Rorie, and Desimone, 2001), and the other from the laboratory of Wolf Singer in Frankfurt (Engel, Fries, and Singer, 2001). You'll notice that Pascal Fries participated in both studies, and is an acknowledged leader in neurobiological studies of gamma oscillations; e.g., Fries (2009).

As I noted above, the articles that introduced ART predicted such match-mediated oscillations, called *order-preserving limit cycles* (Grossberg, 1976a, 1976b, 1978a). Such an oscillation frequency is fast enough to support the kind of synaptic learning that is called *spike-timing-dependent plasticity*, or STDP (Levy and Steward, 1983; Markram et al., 1997; Bi and Poo, 2001), since STDP is maximal when presynaptic and postsynaptic cells (Figure 2.3) fire within 10-20 milliseconds of each other (Traub et al., 1998; Wespatat et al., 2004).

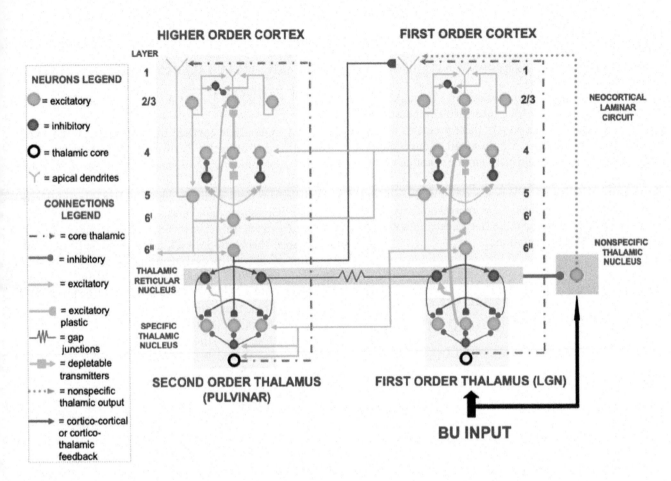

FIGURE 5.38. The Synchronous Matching ART, or SMART, model includes spiking neurons in a laminar cortical hierarchy. I developed SMART with my PhD student Massimiliano Versace. By unlumping LAMINART to include spiking neurons, finer details of neurodynamics, such as the existence of faster gamma oscillations during good enough matches, and slower beta oscillations during bad enough mismatches, could be shown as emergent properties of network interactions.

Our second discovery about oscillations concerns what happens when there is a big enough *mismatch* between a top-down expectation and a bottom-up feature pattern, This discovery was unexpected to us. In particular, when there is a big enough mismatch, then the altered balance between excitation and inhibition during the mismatch event causes a slower oscillation within the beta frequency range of 4–20 Hz (Figure 5.40). STDP is disabled at this lower frequency.

Both types of oscillations are emergent properties of network dynamics. The SMART model hereby proposes how attentive matching, synchronous oscillations, and STDP learning may be coordinated, notably how match-sensitive differences in oscillation frequency can enable or disable learning, The model hereby discloses another mechanism that helps to solve the stability-plasticity dilemma by showing how big enough mismatches prevent STDP learning, over and beyond the mismatch/reset that initiates a memory search cycle and thereby also prevents new learning until the search cycles leads to another resonant state.

This predicted match-mismatch gamma-beta dichotomy has subsequently been reported in neurophysiological experiments that were carried out in several parts of the brain, in keeping with the expectation that the ART Matching Rule is embodied in top-down circuits across all brain systems that solve the stability-plasticity dilemma. Three examples of such data are the following:

Beta oscillations in the deeper layers of visual cortex

One kind of data supports another SMART prediction about the sequence of brain events that occur during a mismatch/reset across the cortical layers. Figure 5.41 summarizes the predicted sequence of events. First, in response to a big enough mismatch in the visual cortex, the nonspecific thalamus is activated and triggers a burst

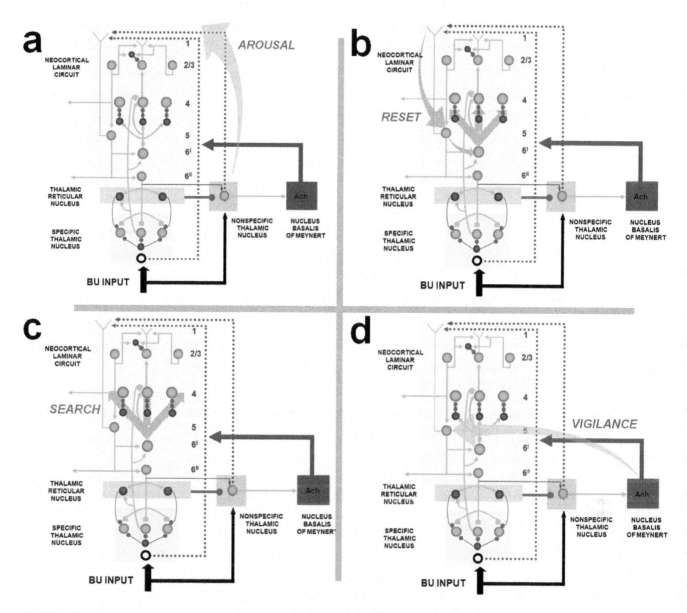

FIGURE 5.39. The SMART hypothesis testing and learning cycle predicts that vigilance increases when a mismatch in subcortical regions like the nonspecific thalamus activates the nucleus basalis of Meynert which, in turn, broadcasts a burst of the neurotransmitter acetylcholine, or ACh, to deeper cortical layers. Due to the way in which LAMINART proposes that cortical matching and mismatching occurs, this ACh burst can increase vigilance and thereby trigger a memory search. See the text for details.

of nonspecific arousal to layer 1 of multiple cortical areas (Figure 5.41a). Figures 5.41a-5.41c show how arousal sends a signal from layer 1 to layer 5 cells, which in turn activate layer 6 cells. Layer 6 cells, in turn, relay this excitatory burst to layer 4 cells. Because these layer 6-to-4 signals are multiplied, or gated, by habituative transmitters, or medium-term memory traces, the arousal burst causes the layer 4 cells to be reset, thereby initiating a hypothesis testing, or memory search, cycle for a different category. The main point is that reset was predicted by SMART to be initiated within the deeper layers of the visual cortex.

Because of the importance of this predicted refinement of the ART hypothesis testing and category learning cycle, I will describe it in greater detail with comparisons to the processing stages in Figure 5.19. When there is a big enough mismatch, say, between a bottom-up feature pattern from the retina to a specific thalamic nucleus (e.g., the lateral geniculate nucleus, or LGN) and a top-down expectation from a neocortical laminar circuit (e.g., cortical areas V1, V2, or V4) to the thalamic nucleus (e.g., LGN), then the balance between bottom-up excitation and inhibition from the specific thalamic nucleus to the

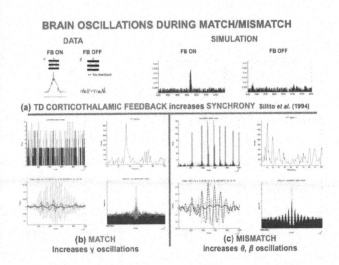

BRAIN OSCILLATIONS DURING MATCH/MISMATCH

(a) TD CORTICOTHALAMIC FEEDBACK increases SYNCHRONY Sillito *et al.* (1994)

(b) MATCH
Increases γ oscillations

(c) MISMATCH
increases θ, β oscillations

FIGURE 5.40. Computer simulation of how the SMART model generates (a) gamma oscillations if a good enough match occurs, or (c) beta oscillations if a bad enough match occurs. See the text for details.

nonspecific thalamic nucleus enables the nonspecific thalamic nucleus to be activated (Figure 5.39a, just as the orienting system *A* is activated in Figure 5.19c. Nonspecific thalamic activation is then broadcast as an arousal signal (Figure 5.39a), again just as it happens in Figure 5.19c. In the detailed laminar circuit of the SMART model, this arousal signal is delivered from the nonspecific thalamic nucleus across cortical layer 1 to many cortical areas via diffuse anatomical connections. Apical dendrites in layer 1 of layer 5 cells receive this arousal input. If some of these layer 5 cells are active when the arousal burst occurs, then their firing rate is enhanced in response to the arousal input. This enhancement of layer 5 cell firing triggers a selective reset of cortical and thalamic cells in the following way:

Layer 5 cells project to cells in layer 4 via cells in layer 6 (Figure 5.39b). The signals from layer 6 to 4 are multiplied, or gated, by habituative transmitters (also see Figure 7.1 below). When the arousal burst occurs,

these previously active cells are disadvantaged relative to cells that were not active, so that an antagonistic rebound can occur within the gated dipole circuits that are part of ART circuits (Figure 1.14). A reset event that is caused by the arousal burst inhibits the previously active cells as it selects new cells with which to better code the novel input, just as it does in the ART memory search cycle of Figure 5.19.

Experimental support for this prediction was reported in 2011 by Elizabeth Buffalo, Pascal Fries, Rogier Landman, Timothy Buschman, and Robert Desimone (Buffalo et al., 2011). who found more gamma oscillations in the superficial layers of the visual cortical areas V1, V2, and V4 and more beta oscillations in deeper layers of these cortices (Figure 5.42). These authors described the slower frequencies as occurring in the alpha range, which occurs between 6–16 Hz, and which is included in the beta range that Versace and I described. This is just the predicted laminar difference in oscillation frequencies that SMART predicted in Figures 5.40 and 5.41.

What kinds of additional experiments can be done to test this explanation? At least two issues could be further probed by additional experiments:

Does varying the amount of novelty change the amount of beta? One possible test would be to carry out a series of experiments on the same animal in which the animal

MISMATCH CAUSES LAYER 5 DENDRITIC SPIKES THAT TRIGGER RESET

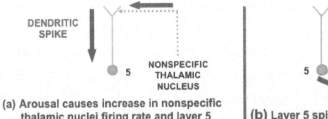

DENDRITIC SPIKE

NONSPECIFIC THALAMIC NUCLEUS

(a) Arousal causes increase in nonspecific thalamic nuclei firing rate and layer 5 dendritic and later somatic spikes
Larkum and Zhu (2002), Williams and Stuart (1999)

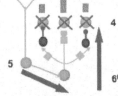

(b) Layer 5 spikes reach layer 4 via layer 6ᴵ and inhibitory interneurons
Lund and Boothe (1975), Gilbert and Wiesel (1979)

(c) Habituative neurotransmitters in layer 6ᴵ shift the balance of active cells in layer 4
Grossberg (1972, 1976)

Dendritic stimulation fires layer 5

Larkum and Zhu (2002)

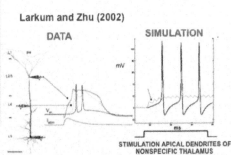

DATA   SIMULATION

STIMULATION APICAL DENDRITES OF NONSPECIFIC THALAMUS

FIGURE 5.41. (a)–(c). The sequence of interlaminar events that SMART predicts during a mismatch reset. (d) Some of the compatible neurophysiological data.

IS THERE EVIDENCE FOR THE GAMMA/BETA PREDICTION?
Yes, in at least three parts of the brain

Buffalo, E.A., Fries, P., Landman, R., Buschman, T.J., and Desimone, R. (2011). PNAS, 108, 11262-11267.

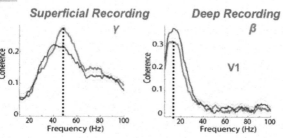

Does this difference in average oscillation frequencies in the superficial and deep layers reflect layer 4 reset?

Berke et al., 2008, hippocampus; Buschman and Miller, 2009, FEF

FIGURE 5.42. Mismatch-induced beta oscillations have been reported in at least three parts of the brain: V1, V4, and hippocampus. Although there may be other reasons for beta oscillations in the brain, those that are caused by a mismatch should be studied in concert with the gamma oscillations that occur during a good enough match. See the text for details.

is exposed to environments with progressively more novel events. More novel events should cause more cortical resets. Do more cortical resets per unit time cause more beta oscillations in the lower cortical layers and thereby decrease the ratio of gamma to beta power per unit time?

Do superficial and deeper layers synchronize and desynchronize during resonance and reset? The second test proceeds from the observation that the differences between the experimentally reported oscillation frequencies in the deeper and more superficial cortical layers are averages over time. This fact is relevant to a modeling study that I published in 2004 with my PhD student Arash Yazdanbakhsh (Yazdanbakhsh and Grossberg, 2004). Our computer simulations with a laminar cortical model led us to predict that *inter*laminar, but *intra*cortical, feedback loops—that is, feedback signals between the cortical layers within one cortical region— synchronize all the cortical layers during a match event. Indeed, these are the intracortical feedback loops that I proposed in 1999 (Grossberg, 1999) enable neocortex to develop its circuits, without a loss of stability, even before intercortical attentional circuits can develop, as I will explain in Chapter 10. Taken together, these considerations lead to the experimentally testable question: Do the cortical layers desynchronize into superficial-layer gamma oscillations and deeper-layer beta oscillations during a reset, and then resynchronize into gamma oscillations during an attentive resonance?

Beta oscillations during spatial attention shifts in the frontal eye fields

The predicted match/mismatch gamma/beta dichotomy was subsequently reported in at least two other parts of the brain. In 2009, Timothy Buschman and Earl Miller reported beta oscillations during spatial attention shifts in the frontal eye fields of monkeys (Buschman and Miller, 2007). Earl learned about the SMART prediction as a member of the NSF Center of Excellence for Learning in Education, Science, and Technology (CELEST) that I founded and directed at that time. He and Tim then reanalyzed their spatial attention data, aligning them in time with respect to the attention shifts, reasoning that a reset would accompany every spatial attention shift, and thereby found the underlying beta oscillations.

Beta oscillations during the learning of hippocampal place fields in novel environments

In 2008, Joshua Berke, Vaughn Hetrick, Jason Breck, and Robert Greene reported beta oscillations during the learning of place cell selectivity while rats navigated a novel environment (Berke et al., 2008). These results illustrate how beta oscillations may be related to ART category learning for the following reasons.

I will explain mechanistically in Chapter 16 how place cells in the hippocampus learn to fire when an animal or human is in a particular location, or "place", in a spatial environment. Place cells hereby play a critical role in spatial navigation. It has been known at least since the 1990s that place cell receptive field selectivity can develop within seconds to minutes as an animal navigates, and can remain stable for months (Frank et al., 2004; Muller, 1996; Thompson and Best, 1990; Wilson and McNaughton, 1993). Place cell learning thus seems to solve the stability-plasticity dilemma. This fact raises two kinds of questions: Are these beta oscillations part of the match-mismatch gamma-beta story? And what does top-down attention and the ART Matching Rule have to do with place cell learning? I will suggest answers to both of these questions in turn.

Inverted-U in beta power through time during hippocampal place cell learning. Are place cells learned using ART dynamics? The Berke et al. data are consistent with this hypothesis. They showed that, paradoxically, beta power was low as a mouse traversed a lap for the first time in a novel environment, grew to full strength on the second and third laps, became low again after two minutes of exploration, and remained low on subsequent days. Beta oscillation power also correlated with the rate at which place cells became spatially selective, and did not correlate with other kinds of oscillations, notably the theta oscillations that are well known to occur during spatial navigation. Given the rapidity with which place cell learning occurred, and the sharp increase in beta activity during the second exposure to the environment, it would seem that a highly selective learning mechanism was at work.

I explained these data in a 2009 article in the following way (Grossberg, 2009a): In any ART system, the top-down adaptive weights that represent learned expectations need to be broadly distributed and large before learning occurs, so that they can match whatever input pattern first initiates learning of a new category. Indeed, when a new category is first activated, it is not known at the category level what pattern of features caused the category to be activated. *Whatever* feature pattern was active needs to be matched by the top-down expectation on the first learning trial, so that resonance and weight learning can begin. Hence the need for the initial values of top-down weights to be broadly distributed and sufficiently large to match *any* feature pattern. The low beta power on the first lap of exploration can be explained by the initial top-down match.

Given that top-down weights are initially broadly distributed, the learning of top-down expectations is, as usual in any ART learning system, a process of *pruning* weights on subsequent learning trials, and uses mismatch-based reset events to discover categories capable of representing the environment. Beta power on subsequent laps can be explained by mismatch reset events that correlate with the rate at which place cells become spatially selective. After learning stabilizes, there are no more mismatches, so beta power subsides. Such an inverted-U in beta power through time is thus a signature of ART category learning in any environment.

I first heard about the Berke et al. data when I gave a lecture about my new results with Versace to his department at the University of Michigan. I then had the opportunity to chat with Josh after the lecture as I met various other faculty and students who heard my talk. That is when Josh told me that he had new data about beta oscillations during the learning of new hippocampal place cells. I then did something that I rarely venture to do, given the number of different factors that may influence experimental outcomes. I usually like to study data carefully before proposing explanations of them. But in this case, because of the basic issues that his data may have probed, I said that, if his data have anything to do with basic properties of ART matching, then he found an inverted-U in beta power. Josh then told me, to my delight, that this was the main finding of their study.

The gamma-beta dichotomy described in terms of encoding and default states

Four additional implications of the gamma-beta dichotomy during match-mismatch dynamics are: they should occur in bursts; these bursts should occur inversely through time; the gamma bursts should be the ones that encode "information"; and the gamma bursts should exhibit higher spiking rates because they embody a resonant match state. All of these properties have been reported in 2016 by Mikael Lundqvist, Jonas Rose, Pawel Herman, Scott Brincat, Timothy Buschman, and Earl Miller in experiments on working memory whose recordings were taken from lateral prefrontal cortex and the frontal eye fields (Lundqvist et al., 2016). These authors interpret their results in terms of working memory, and discuss the gamma oscillations in terms of "encoding/decoding events" and "re-activation of sensory information", whereas beta oscillations are viewed as a "default state interrupted by encoding and decoding" (p. 152). This "default" interpretation does not explain why beta bursts are "interrupted by encoding and decoding" or why the gamma oscillations embody "encoding/decoding events". The ART hypothesis in terms of dichotomous states of attentive match and mismatch reset does explain these findings.

The Lundqvist et al. article went on to propose modeling ideas in which there is no temporal order represented in working memory, although temporal order information is essential for proper functioning of a working memory, as I will show in Chapter 12. It may be useful to test if and how these neurophysiological data fit into an alternative scheme of how sequences of item chunks are learned through adaptive resonance before they are encoded in a working memory that includes both item and temporal order information.

Gamma and beta oscillations regulate working memory dynamics

Still more recent data have also been reported by the laboratory of Earl Miller showing distinct roles for gamma oscillations in the superficial layers and beta oscillations in the deeper layers of frontal and prefrontal working memory circuits. These results are consistent with the LIST PARSE model of laminar working memory dynamics that I published with my PhD student Lance Pearson in 2008 (Grossberg and Pearson, 2008), and that will be explained in Chapter 12.

In particular, as Bastos et al. (2018, p. 117) report: "Spiking and gamma-band activity (50–150 Hz) in the superficial layers reflected active maintenance of working memories. Alpha/beta frequencies (4–22 Hz) in the deep layers modulated the gamma activity in the superficial layers. This might serve a control function, allowing information to enter or exit active storage in superficial layers".

Lundqvist et al. (2018, p. 152) additionally write: "There are brief bursts of gamma (~50–120 Hz) and beta (~20–35 Hz) oscillations, the former linked to stimulus information in spiking. We examined these dynamics in relation to readout and control mechanisms of WM. Monkeys held sequences of two objects in WM to match to subsequent sequences. Changes in beta and gamma bursting suggested their distinct roles. In anticipation of having to use an object for the match decision, there was an increase in gamma and spiking information about that object and reduced beta bursting. This readout signal was only seen before relevant test objects, and was related to premotor activity. When the objects were no longer needed, beta increased and gamma decreased together with object spiking information. Deviations from these dynamics predicted behavioral errors. Thus, beta could regulate gamma and the information in WM".

These results were further described in https://picower. mit.edu/new-study-reveals-how-brain-waves-control-working-memory:

"In a memory task requiring information to be held in working memory for short periods of time, the MIT team found that the brain uses beta waves to consciously switch between different pieces of information. The findings support the researchers' hypothesis that beta rhythms act as a gate that determines when information held in working memory is either read out or cleared out so we can think about something else.

"The beta rhythm acts like a brake, controlling when to express information held in working memory and allow it to influence behavior", says Mikael Lundqvist, a postdoc at MIT's Picower Institute for Learning and Memory and the lead author of the study".

In summary, there are now direct neurophysiological data that support the predicted gamma-beta dichotomy in V1, V4, hippocampus, and prefrontal cortex.

Cholinergic modulation of category learning via nucleus basalis vigilance control

Given the importance of vigilance control to regulating the concreteness or abstractness of the knowledge that

an ART system can learn, it is essential to understand how it is realized by identified neurons in laminar cortical circuits. The SMART model fortunately provides this kind of detailed information. In brief, SMART predicts how vigilance may be altered by acetylcholine release when the nucleus basalis of Meynert is activated via the nonspecific thalamus (Kraus et al., 1994; van Der Werf et al., 2002), which is itself activated by corticothalamic mismatches with one or more specific thalamic nuclei (5.39d and 5.43).

Here is some background with which to better understand the above summary: In general, it is known that the neurotransmitter acetylcholine, or ACh, is an essential ingredient in cortical plasticity (e.g., Kilgard and Merzenich, 1998), in addition to its role in enabling neurotransmission at synapses (Figure 2.3). It has also been shown (Saar et al. (2001) that the release of ACh can increase the excitability of cells in cortical layer 5 (Figure 5.39b). It does this by reducing a kind of cellular current that is called an after-hyperpolarization, or AHP, current that down-regulates a cell's excitability. ACh "disinhibits" cell excitability by inhibiting the AHP.

In the SMART model, increased layer 5 excitability due to a predictive mismatch may cause reset of a currently active category via the layer 5-to-6^I-to-4 circuit that realizes part of the model's ART Matching Rule (Figure 5.39b). Such an ACh-modulated reset can occur even in cases where top-down feedback may have, just moments before, sufficiently matched a bottom-up input to prevent reset. This enhanced sensitivity to a mismatch is a key property of vigilance control. The increase of ACh hereby promotes search for finer recognition categories in response to environmental feedback, even when bottom-up and top-down signals have a pretty good match based on similarity alone.

There are many more experimental data that summarize properties of vigilance control. As I noted earlier in this chapter, in 2012, my PhD student Jesse Palma worked with me and Versace to explain various of these data by simulating how ACh may modulate the transformation and STM storage of input patterns in recurrent shunting on-center off-surround networks (Figure 1.6) that are composed of spiking neurons (Palma, Grossberg, and Versace, 2012; Palma, Versace, and Grossberg, 2012). In particular, these simulations show how the quenching threshold (Figure 1.9) may be regulated by acetylcholine in realistic cortical networks of spiking neurons.

In summary, recent variants of ART show how spiking neurons in laminar cortical circuits with identified neurons may learn concrete or general recognition categories via a cycle of attentional matching and orienting search that is regulated by cholinergically-modulated vigilance control. All of these categories are learned using localist representations that may, in the limit of strong contrast enhancement by a category-selecting recurrent on-center

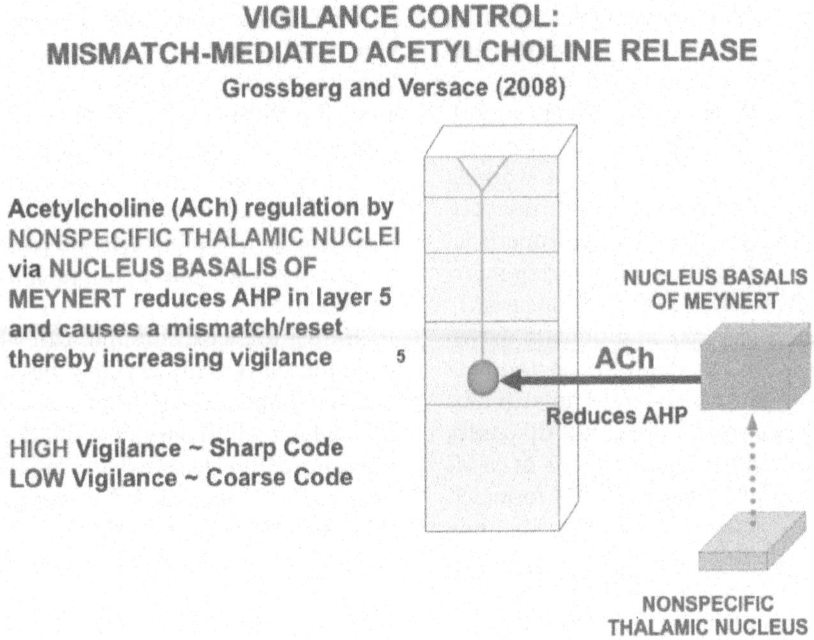

VIGILANCE CONTROL: MISMATCH-MEDIATED ACETYLCHOLINE RELEASE
Grossberg and Versace (2008)

Acetylcholine (ACh) regulation by NONSPECIFIC THALAMIC NUCLEI via NUCLEUS BASALIS OF MEYNERT reduces AHP in layer 5 and causes a mismatch/reset thereby increasing vigilance

HIGH Vigilance ~ Sharp Code
LOW Vigilance ~ Coarse Code

NUCLEUS BASALIS OF MEYNERT

ACh

Reduces AHP

NONSPECIFIC THALAMIC NUCLEUS

FIGURE 5.43. The activation of the nucleus basalis of Meynert, and its subsequent release of ACh into deeper layers of neocortex, notably layer 5, is assumed to increase vigilance by reducing afterhyperpolarization (AHP) currents.

off-surround network, encode their critical feature patterns using winner-take-all grandmother cells (Figures 1.7 and 5.19) or, more generally, resonant hierarchies of grandmother cohorts.

Tonic vs. phasic vigilance control: How vigilance may vary with the task at hand

Match tracking (Figure 5.30) illustrates how vigilance can rapidly change in response to a predictive disconfirmation. This can happen no matter how the baseline vigilance is chosen. I call the difference between these two processes *tonic* vs. *phasic* vigilance control, with the choice of baseline vigilance being the tonic process, and changes due to predictive disconfirmation being the phasic process. Both tonic and phasic vigilance control can be traced to how acetylcholine is regulated by the nucleus basalis of Meynert and at its target neocortical neurons. One might speculate that the baseline vigilance may slowly increase with the rate of predictive disconfirmation in a given environment until the disconfirmation rate is reduced to an acceptable threshold value because higher vigilance enables finer discriminations to be made. Further experiments are needed to characterize how such gradual mismatch-mediated changes may occur.

Vigilance varies with the difficulty of a visual discrimination. In 1988, Hedva Spitzer, Robert Desimone, and Jeffrey Moran (Spitzer, Desimone, and Moran, 1988) published neurophysiological data from cortical area V4 of rhesus monkeys that are relevant to vigilance control. These monkeys were trained on a visual discrimination task with two levels of difficulty. Their behavioral data showed that the discriminative abilities of the monkeys improved when the task was made more difficult. In particular, they report "in the difficult condition, the animals adopted a stricter internal criterion for discriminating matching from non-matching stimuli . . . The animal's internal representations of the stimuli were better separated . . . increased effort appeared to cause enhancement of the responses and sharpened selectivity for attended stimuli . . . ". These are all properties of ART vigilance control, where higher vigilance is needed to make more difficult discriminations.

Combining several of the above paradigms can lead to additional experimental tests of the corticohippocampal interactions that regulate vigilance while discrimination difficulty is varied. In particular, more difficult discriminations, at least under proper circumstances, should lead to higher vigilance, more mismatch events, and thus more of the hippocampal novelty responses that were reported in 2015 by Brincat and Miller (Brincat and Miller, 2015), as well as in 1992 by Tim Otto and Howard Eichenbaum (Otto and Eichenbaum, 1992). During these mismatch events, ERPs should progress in the temporal order that I described in 1987 with Jean-Paul Banquet from P120 to N200 to P300 (Banquet and Grossberg, 1987). If additional measures could also be taken of ACh release as a result of activation of the nucleus basalis of Meynert, then a much more complete picture of vigilance control would be achieved.

Vigilance diseases: Autism, medial temporal amnesia, and Alzheimer's disease.

When vigilance control is working well, it can ensure that our recognition categories and attentional foci fit themselves to the statistics of changing environments and their task demands. However, vigilance control, just like any other bodily function, can sometimes break down. When it does, our recognition categories and attentional foci may not adjust well enough to ensure successful adaptations to all the kinds of social environments that humans typically experience in advanced societies. ART has been used to explain how symptoms of some mental disorders may be due to vigilance being stuck at either too high or too low values. Mental disorders that include problems with vigilance control can usefully be grouped together as "vigilance diseases". I should add the caveat right away that a problem with vigilance control is typically only one of a constellation of other problems which, taken together, distinguish one mental disorder from another.

Below I will review how individuals with autism, medial temporal amnesia, and Alzheimer's disease may all be suffering from a failure of vigilance control, albeit due to different causes and with different degrees of severity. Alzheimer's disease, in particular, is often preceded by, and coincides with, problems with sleep that will also be discussed. All of the clinical symptoms that I will discuss in these examples can be viewed as primarily problems with *tonic* vigilance control.

High vigilance and hyperspecific category learning in autism. Vigilance that is stuck at high values was predicted, in a 2006 article that I published with the clinician Don Seidman (Grossberg and Seidman, 2006), to cause symptoms that are familiar in various individuals with autism, including the learning of hyperspecific recognition categories, with an attendant narrow attentional focus. In a network whose vigilance is fixed through time at an abnormally high level, the system would be literally "hypervigilant," and environmental events would be classified with extreme concreteness and hyperspecificity, with learned categories coding highly specific, exemplar-like information, as well as controlling a narrow focus of attention. This can render autistic individuals unable to learn and attend general properties of objects and events,

leading to the hyperspecificity that is observed in many autistic individuals. Seidman and I made this prediction as part of the *imbalanced Spectrally Timed Adaptive Resonance Theory*, or iSTART, model. This model shows how imbalances in cognitive, emotional, and adaptive timing processes combine to create various of the most salient behavioral symptoms of autism. High vigilance is part of the model's cognitive imbalance.

Psychophysical experiments have been done in at least two laboratories to successfully test this prediction in high-functioning autistic individuals, one with my postdoctoral fellow Tony Vladusich in 2010, with additional collaboration from Helen Tager-Flusberg, Femi Lafe, Dae-Shik Kim, and myself (Vladusich et al., 2010). The other was done in the laboratory of Eduardo Mercado, also in 2010, with his collaborators Barbara Church, Maria Krauss, Christopher Lopata, Jennifer Toomey, Marcus Thomeer, Mariana Coutinho, and Martin Volker (Church et al., 2010). It is also known, for example from experiments in 2001 of Elaine Perry with 10 collaborators (Perry et al., 2001), that there is abnormal cholinergic activity in the parietal and frontal cortices of autistic individuals that is correlated with abnormalities in the nucleus basalis of Meynert, consistent with the predicted role of the nucleus basalis and ACh in regulating vigilance.

In addition to the direct effects on behavior of the narrow focus of attention and the concreteness of categorical recognition, hypervigilance can also contribute to emotionally aversive reactions to novel events when it interacts with emotional mechanisms; see Chapter 13. Given hypervigilance, even small variations of concretely categorized information can cause mismatches with top-down expectations, thereby leading to a large number of novelty-activated arousal bursts. When these frequent arousal bursts interact with imbalanced emotional mechanisms, aversive emotional responses can be generated. The need to avoid these mismatch-activated aversive responses can encourage the "need for sameness" as a coping strategy that many autistic individuals pursue.

A 2018 article with my graduate student Devika Kishnan (Grossberg and Kishnan, 2018) added to this theoretical analysis by proposing what kind of imbalance can cause motoric symptoms in autistics such as perseverative behaviors. These results will be discussed in Chapter 14.

Low vigilance in corticohippampal dynamics during medial temporal amnesia. Low vigilance has been predicted in 1992 and 1993 by Gail Carpenter, John Merrill, and myself to occur in individuals with medial temporal amnesia (Carpenter and Grossberg, 1993; Grossberg and Merrill, 1992). This kind of amnesia can be caused by a hippocampal lesion. Its consequences were illustrated in Chapter 2 by a discussion of the amnesia of Henry Molaison who experienced a bilateral hippocampectomy at 27 years of age. Henry's surgery also removed nearby structures as well. Let us assume for the sake of clarity that we are considering a lesion of the orienting system of ART during corticohippocampal interactions (Figure 5.19). An ART system with a lesioned orienting system shares quite a few symptoms of humans and animals who exhibit this kind of medial temporal amnesia.

This link of ART to amnesia data depends on an important emergent property of the ART learning process. As sequences of inputs are practiced over learning trials, the search process in an ART model eventually converges upon stable categories. Gail Carpenter and I proved mathematically in 1987 (Carpenter and Grossberg, 1987a) that familiar input exemplars directly access the category whose prototype best matches the exemplar without causing a memory search. Indeed, one can *define* an exemplar to be familiar when it is close enough to previously experienced exemplars for it to satisfy the vigilance criterion, and thus not lead to a memory search. In contrast, unfamiliar inputs cause the orienting system to trigger memory searches for better categories until they, too, become familiar.

The process whereby search is automatically disengaged as events become familiar is a form of *memory consolidation*. This type of memory consolidation is not built into the model. It is an emergent property of model interactions between the attentional and orienting system during memory searches (Figure 5.19). Emergent consolidation does not preclude the existence of structural or biochemical changes at individual cells, since the amplified, synchronized, and prolonged activities that define a resonance may be a trigger for learning-dependent cellular processes, such as protein synthesis, cell growth, and transmitter production.

The attentional system of ART has been used to model aspects of inferotemporal (IT) cortex, and the orienting system models part of the hippocampal system. In particular, a number of different labs have shown that cells in monkey IT cortex can respond selectively to particular objects in the environment, such as a particular view of a familiar person's face, or to broader categories of environmental objects. This fact raises the question of whether monkeys might use vigilance control to determine how general their learned categories will become. I have already summarized supportive evidence for this hypothesis from the 1988 experiments of Hedva Spitzer, Robert Desimone, and Jeffrey Moran (Spitzer, Desimone, and Moran, 1988) on monkeys who had to make easy or difficult discriminations. Experiments of Earl Miller, Lin Li, and Robert Desimone in 1991 (Miller, Li, and Desimone, 1991) successfully tested another prediction of ART when they showed that cells in monkey IT cortex undergo an "active matching process that was reset between trials" in a working memory task, and that "the neuronal response to novel stimuli declined as the stimuli became familiar to the animal. IT neurons appear to function as adaptive mnemonic 'filters' that preferentially pass information about new, unexpected, or not recently seen stimuli".

The ART prediction that the orienting system is represented, at least in part, within the hippocampal system implies that aspects of mismatch/novelty detection are represented within the hippocampal system. In fact, the hippocampal system has long been known to be involved in mismatch processing, including the processing of novel events. I noted above data of Brincat and Miller, Sokolov, and Vinogradova, among others, that have supported this hypothesis. Normal memory searches occur in an ART system as a result of interactions between its attentional and orienting systems, as in Figure 5.19. If we interpret these systems in terms of IT cortex and the hippocampal system, respectively, then we can now see how a lesion of the ART model's orienting system creates a formal memory disorder with symptoms much like the medial temporal amnesia that is caused in animals and human patients after hippocampal system lesions (Carpenter and Grossberg, 1993; Grossberg and Merrill, 1996).

In particular, removing the orienting system prevents memory search (Figures 5.19b-d). Such a lesion, in effect, keeps vigilance equal to zero, and any learning that can occur without mismatch-mediated reset and memory search can form only very general categories. Consistent with this property, a suitable hippocampal lesion *in vivo* causes symptoms called unlimited anterograde amnesia; limited retrograde amnesia; failure of consolidation; tendency to learn the first event in a series; abnormal reactions to novelty, including perseverative reactions; normal priming; and normal information processing of familiar events (Cohen, 1984; Graf, Squire, and Mandler, 1984; Lynch, McGaugh, and Weinberger, 1984; Squire and Butters, 1984; Squire and Cohen, 1984; Warrington and Weiskrantz, 1974; Zola-Morgan and Squire, 1990).

Unlimited anterograde amnesia means that all future learning and memory are impaired. This occurs in a lesioned ART model because it cannot carry out a memory search to discover and learn a new recognition category. Limited retrograde amnesia means that more recently learned memories are impaired, but very old memories are reasonably intact. This occurs in an ART model because already familiar events can directly access correct recognition categories without activating the orienting system. Before events become familiar, memory consolidation occurs which does make use of the orienting system. This failure of consolidation does not necessarily prevent all learning from occurring. Instead, learning would tend to influence the first recognition category that was activated by bottom-up processing, much as amnesics are particularly strongly wedded to the first response they learn. Perseverative, or repetitive, reactions can occur because the orienting system cannot reset sensory representations or top-down expectations that may be persistently mismatched by bottom-up cues. The inability to search memory prevents ART from discovering more appropriate stimulus combinations to attend. Normal priming occurs because it is mediated by residual activity of previously activated categories within the attentional system, and does not need to involve the orienting system.

Similar behavioral problems have been identified in hippocampectomized monkeys. In 1985, David Gaffan noted that transection of the fornix, which is a major source of inputs and outputs to the hippocampus, "impairs ability to change an established habit . . . in a different set of circumstances that is similar to the first and therefore liable to be confused with it" (Gaffan, 1985). In ART, a defective orienting system prevents the memory search whereby different representations could be learned for similar events. In 1986, Karl Pribram called such a process a "competence for recombinant context-sensitive processing" (Pribram, 1986).

These ART mechanisms illustrate how, as Stuart Zola-Morgan and Larry Squire reported in 1990, memory consolidation and novelty detection may be mediated by the same neural structures (Zola-Morgan and Squire, 1990), since the orienting system, which registers the novelty of events, also controls the memory searches that lead to memory consolidation. A similar interaction clarifies why hippocampectomized rats have difficulty orienting to novel cues and why there is a progressive reduction in novelty-related hippocampal potentials as learning proceeds in normal rats (Deadwyler, West, and Lynch, 1979; Deadwyler, West, and Robinson, 1981). In particular, the orienting system is automatically disengaged as events become familiar during the memory consolidation process.

When the cognitive ART search cycle in Figure 5.19 is joined to the cognitive-emotional interactions via the amygdala and hippocampus, as represented within the nSTART model of Figure 5.37, then properties of adaptively timed learning that depend upon an intact hippocampus enable a much larger set of data may be explained about amnesia and, more generally, normal and abnormal memory consolidation, as I will explain in Chapter 15.

ART shows how the hippocampal orienting system can modulate learning within the neocortical attentional system, even if the hippocampus does not itself learn the categories that are learned by the neocortex. If this is true, then experimental manipulations that make the novelty-related potentials of the hippocampus more sensitive to input changes should trigger the formation of more selective inferotemporal recognition categories. Can such a correlation between discrimination by the inferotemporal cortex and hippocampal novelty potentials be recorded, say, in a variant of the Spitzer, Desimone, and Moran experiments in which monkeys are made to learn easy and difficult discriminations? Conversely, operations that progressively block the expression of hippocampal novelty potentials are predicted to cause learning

of coarser recognition categories, with amnesic symptoms as a limiting case wherein the orienting system is totally inoperative.

This latter prediction is consistent with data of Barbara Knowlton and Larry Squire, who reported in 1993 that amnesics can classify items as members of a large category even if they are impaired on remembering the individual items (Knowlton and Squire, 1993). To account for these results, Knowlton and Squire proposed that item (read: exemplar) memories and category (read: prototype) memories are formed by different brain systems. This hypothesis does not, however, explain what these systems are, how they interact, or how some large categories may form in amnesics even though item memories do not. The ART hypothesis is consistent with their data, but does not require two different systems, and indeed clarifies how both specific and general knowledge may be learned by normals.

Modeling work published in 2003 of Safa Zaki, Robert Nosofsky, Nenette Jessup, and Frederick Unverzagt (Zaki et al., 2003) were able to quantitatively fit the Knowlton and Squire data with a single exemplar-based model whose sensitivity parameter was chosen lower for amnesic individuals than for normal subjects. An exemplar model explains and fits data about categorization by assuming that each individual stimulus, or exemplar, is stored in memory. As noted in *Wikipedia*, an exemplar "model proposes that people create the 'bird' category by maintaining in their memory a collection of all the birds they have experienced: sparrows, robins, ostriches, penguins, etc. If a new stimulus is similar enough to some of these stored bird examples, the person categorizes the stimulus in the 'bird category'".

This particular exemplar model, which is called the Generalized Context Model, was developed by Robert Nosofsky and his colleagues at Indiana University and has been able to successfully fit quite a bit of cognitive data about categorization. The model is defined using formal algebraic equations. I have, however, been able to recast it as a real-time dynamical process during which their formal algebraic equations arise as a result of locally defined network interactions; that is, interactions that carry information around the network to where it is needed to compute the model's algebraic equations. When this is done, the algebraic exemplar model becomes a dynamical prototype model that computes prototypes and top-down expectations akin to those that are found in ART. Moreover, a low sensitivity parameter c in the exemplar model (see their equation (4)) plays a role similar to that played by a low vigilance parameter ρ in an ART model (Amis et al., 2009). The Zaki et al. simulations thus provide additional quantitative support for the ART prediction that a lesion of the hippocampal orienting system, and with it a collapse of the vigilance parameter, can lead to symptoms of medial temporal amnesia.

Converting algebraic exemplar models into dynamical ART prototype models

How can an algebraic exemplar model be recast as an ART prototype model? This can be accomplished by providing a dynamical interpretation of the key algebraic equation of the exemplar model:

$$P_{iA} = \frac{\sum_{j \in A} S_{ij}}{\sum_{j \in A} S_{ij} + \sum_{j \in B} S_{ij}}.$$

This equation says that the probability P_{iA} of a category A response to the ith exemplar equals the sum $\sum_{j \in A} S_{ij}$ of the similarities S_{ij} between the test item i and the stored exemplars of A, divided by the sum $\sum_{j \in A} S_{ij} + \sum_{j \in B} S_{ij}$ of the similarities between the test item i and all the stored exemplars of both category A and category B. This is a reasonable probabilistic description of the evidence that is needed to make a decision between categories A and B. However, this equation does not explain how this evidence is brought together in one place within the brain so that the decision can be made.

In particular, how does any test exemplar i know what other exemplars are in category A, as it would need to do to compute the sum $\sum_{j \in A} S_{ij}$? It must know this in order to compare *only* these exemplars with the test item in order to compute their similarity. For this to happen, there must be some internal representation with which *every* exemplar in A can be associated during the category learning process. This associative process is a kind of bottom-up learning (Figure 5.44). Let us call this internal representation the category A. Moreover, category A must be able to activate all the other exemplars of category A when it is activated by any test item i that is categorized by A. This ability implies that a type of top-down learning also occurs from category A to the currently active exemplar i when the bottom-up association of i to A is occurring (Figure 5.44). Only then, when activated by a test item after learning has occurred, can the category activate all the exemplars of A via top-down signalling, as would be necessary to bring all the information in $\sum_{j \in A} S_{ij}$ into an active state for further decision-making. The top-down feedback that selectively

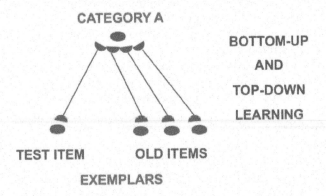

HOW DOES THE MODEL KNOW WHICH EXEMPLARS ARE IN CATEGORY A?

CATEGORY A

BOTTOM-UP AND TOP-DOWN LEARNING

TEST ITEM   OLD ITEMS

EXEMPLARS

How does a NOVEL test item access category A?

FIGURE 5.44. When an algebraic exemplar model is realized using only local computations, it starts looks like an ART prototype model.

activates all the exemplars in A is a learned top-down expectation whose prototype includes all the exemplars of A, and only these exemplars.

The same argument holds for the learning of a category B that can activate all of its exemplars via a learned top-down expectation in response to a test item that is capable of activating it via learned bottom-up adaptive filtering. We hereby find ourselves in an ART framework in order to bring together, using only local signals, all the information that is needed to compute the probability P_{iA}.

When a novel exemplar is presented, it will activate both category A and category B with a strength that depends on its similarity to the prototype of those categories. When those categories compete with each other via the recurrent on-center off-surround network that exists at a category level (Figures 5.13 and 5.19), the normalization by the network's shunting dynamics of category activities naturally generates the ratio of the two category similarities that defines P_{iA}.

There are only two more questions that still need to be answered. Remarkably, they both have the same answer. The first question is this: We know from ART that the top-down expectation signals are only modulatory in the absence of other currently active exemplars. How, then, do the other exemplars in categories A and B make themselves felt when just one test exemplar is presented? This question has the same answer as an even more basic question: How does a *novel* exemplar, one that has never been experienced before, activate these categories in the first place? The answer to both questions is that the bottom-up adaptive filter to a category *normalizes* its adaptive weights, or LTM traces, in response to *all* the exemplars that ever succeeded in activating this category. A single exemplar, whether familiar or novel, thus generates category responses that reflect how similar it is to all the other exemplars that ever activated the category. This is a basic property of competitive learning and self-organizing maps (Figures 5.16–5.18) as well as of the ART systems that dynamically stabilize their learning using attentional matching. Thus, the combination of adaptive filtering and competitive normalization are sufficient to compute the equation for P_{iA}, when they are combined with the top-down attentive matching that is needed to select the learned critical feature patterns in the bottom-up and top-down pathways with which to predictively code the represented exemplars.

Explaining human categorization data with ART: Learning rules-plus-exceptions

Given that algebraic exemplar models can be recast as dynamical ART models, we need to ask: Can ART dynamics help to explain the kinds of cognitive data about human learning that the algebraic exemplar models were developed to explain? Here, I will briefly review results from a study which shows how ART can quantitatively simulate cognitive data about normal human category learning. Gail Carpenter and I did this in a study that I have already mentioned with our PhD students Gregory Amis and Bilgin Ersoy in 2009 (Amis et al., 2009).

Many exemplar, prototype, and rule-plus-exceptions approaches to modeling human category learning data have attempted to explain, among others, some subset of 30 experiments that all exhibit the same underlying category structure, called a "4/5 category structure" (Figure 5.45), that David Smith and John Paul Minda reviewed in 2000 (Smith and Minda, 2000). These experiments used a variety of stimulus materials, including geometric shapes, Brunswick faces, yearbook photos, verbal descriptions, and rocket ship drawings. Each exemplar is defined by selecting one of two possible values (designated by 0 and 1) of 4 category features. Each row in Figure 5.45 describes one such exemplar. Five exemplars are selected by the experimentalist to belong to category A, and four exemplars are selected to belong to category B.

The exemplars in category A are selected to be closer to the experimenter-defined prototype (1,1,1,1), labelled T12 in Figure 5.45. The exemplars in category B are selected to be closer to the experimenter-defined prototype (0,0,0,0). Exemplar B4 equals the prototype (0,0,0,0) of category B. It should immediately be noted that these prototypes are not the ones that are discovered by the brain through learning. They are imposed by the experimentalist based on a simple concept of exemplar-to-prototype similarity.

The difficulty of the task can be assessed by defining the within-category similarity (namely, the average number of features that exemplars within a category share), the between-category similarity (namely, the average number of features that exemplars across categories share), and the *structural ratio* (namely, the ratio of within-category similarity to between-category similarity). Clearly, a high structural ratio makes it easier to learn two distinct categories, other things being equal. In the 4/5 category structure, the within-category similarity is 2.4 and the between-category similarity is 1.6, so the structural ratio is 1.5. A structural ratio of 1.0 allows no category differentiation, and one greater than 3 permits easy differentiation, so the 4/5 category structure is a challenging categorization problem.

The various exemplar, prototype, and rule-plus-exception algebraic exemplar models can all simulate these data to one degree or another. However, none of these models learns any categories. Instead, they fit the data to pre-defined algebraic formulas. These models also do not clarify how these formulas carry out a real-time process of memory search and recognition. Finally, the prototype models assume that humans use the (0,0,0,0) and (1,1,1,1)

5-4 CATEGORY STRUCTURE

Type and Stimulus	Dimension (D)			
	D1	D2	D3	D4
Category A				
A1	1	1	1	0
A2	1	0	1	0
A3	1	0	1	1
A4	1	1	0	1
A5	0	1	1	1
Category B				
B1	1	1	0	0
B2	0	1	1	0
B3	0	0	0	1
B4	0	0	0	0
Transfer (T)				
T10	1	0	0	1
T11	1	0	0	0
T12	1	1	1	1
T13	0	0	1	0
T14	0	1	0	1
T15	0	0	1	1
T16	0	1	0	0

(TRAINING (OLD) ITEMS — rows Category A through B4; NEW TEST ITEMS — Transfer (T) rows)

A1-A5: **closer to the (1 1 1 1) prototype**   B1-B4: **closer to (0 0 0 0) prototype**

FIGURE 5.45. The 5-4 category structure is one example of how an ART network learns the same kinds of categories as human learners. See the text for details.

prototypes, but there is no independent evidence that this is the case.

Figure 5.46 shows how two variants of the distributed ARTMAP model incrementally learn categories through time in response to the presentation of the individual exemplars in the 4/5 category structure. Both variants can quantitatively fit all 30 experiments in this data base. A key property of these data that can be seen in Figure 5.46 is that, after subjects are trained on a subset of exemplars, they are tested on both these *old* exemplars and a subset of *new* exemplars that they never before experienced. Recognition proceeds without receiving any feedback about whether categorization answers are right or wrong. In this situation, the percent recognition of the old exemplars does not form a horizontal straight line through 1. Instead, it forms a curve that is significantly below 1. This means that the process of recognizing old exemplars mixed with new exemplars causes some forgetting of the old exemplars. ART explains this kind of forgetting by assuming that, when an exemplar is recognized, the recognition event also triggers a form of slow self-supervised learning that can shift the category boundaries and thereby cause some active forgetting in the system. This example illustrates how a system that can solve the stability-plasticity dilemma can nonetheless undergo a controlled form of selective forgetting under certain circumstances. The categories that are learned in this way may be interpreted as learning rules-plus-exceptions; that is, learning a combination of both big and small category boxes.

Self-supervised ARTMAP: Learning on our own after leaving school. Gregory Amis and Gail Carpenter further developed distributed ARTMAP to create Self-supervised ARTMAP. In their 2010 article about this subject (Amis and Carpenter, 2010), they showed how such

a model, after being trained using supervised learning in which explicit answers are given, can go out into the world to continue learning on its own in an unsupervised way *without undermining its previous supervised learning*. This competence is like learning some things from teachers in school before continuing to learn a lot more on one's own from new environments that we later experience throughout life. Self-supervised ARTMAP can, in particular, learn about novel features from unlabeled patterns without destroying partial knowledge previously acquired from labeled patterns. The model was shown to improve test accuracy significantly on illustrative low-dimensional problems and on high-dimensional benchmarks as a result of its unsupervised real-world experiences.

Is there a collapse of tonic and phasic vigilance control during Alzheimer's disease?

The final group of topics of this chapter illustrates how fundamental research on neural modeling of normal, or typical, behaviors can lead to surprising, and potentially important, insights about mental disorders that afflict millions of people. This group of topics includes Alzheimer's disease and related sleep disorders.

For more than 30 years, Alzheimer's disease has been one of the most common causes of mental deterioration in the elderly. Alzheimer's disease includes significant structural abnormalities that may be caused by complex interacting factors in many brain regions, leading to the formation of neuritic plaques and neurofibrillary tangles

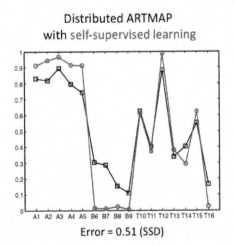

Distributed ARTMAP
with self-supervised learning

Error = 0.51 (SSD)

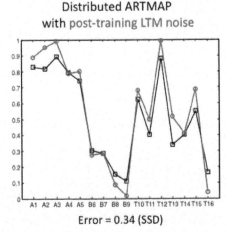

Distributed ARTMAP
with post-training LTM noise

Error = 0.34 (SSD)

FIGURE 5.46. Computer simulations of how two variants of Distributed ARTMAP incrementally learn the 5-4 category structure. See the text for details.

(Arnold et al., 1991; Tomlinson et al., 1968, 1970). A huge amount of important research continues to be done on how these structural changes can lead to neuronal degeneration. However, these studies typically do not explain how these structural changes cause the particular behavior symptoms that afflict individuals with Alzheimer's. The following discussion adds one more link to this chain of causation.

From our current perspective, it is particularly significant that major structural degeneration in the brains of Alzheimer's patients often occurs in cortical layers 3 and 5, which are also layers where vigilance control is mediated by acetylcholine, or ACh (Figures 5.39 and 5.43). These are also cortical layers where key properties of slow wave sleep seem to be generated, as I will discuss below. As I began to study this literature, I needed to confront the question: Are facts that link plaques and tangles with ACh just accidental correlations, or clues to the possibility that many Alzheimer's patients experience a collapse of both tonic and phasic vigilance control?

I will now review some of the clinical and experimental evidence that support this vigilance control hypothesis. I will hereby propose that the process of vigilance control clarifies key dynamical consequences of causal structural events such as the plaque and tangle formation. Indeed, a failure of both tonic and phasic vigilance control could cause a generalized collapse of the cognitive processing that involves learning, memory, recognition, and even consciousness, way beyond anything that would be caused by the imbalances in the dynamical processing of vigilance that may contribute to behavioral symptoms of autism and medial temporal amnesia.

Consistent with the vigilance control hypothesis is the classical fact that, during Alzheimer's disease, ACh-releasing neurons, whose cell bodies lie in the basal forebrain, selectively degenerate and thereby influence widespread areas of the cerebral cortex and related structures that play an important role in cognitive functions, notably learning and memory (Coyle, Price, and DeLong, 1983). Postmortem studies of patients with Alzheimer's disease have demonstrated profound reduction in the presynaptic markers for cholinergic neurons in their cortical tissue (Whitehouse et al., 1982). In particular, neurons of the nucleus basalis of Meynert undergo a greater than 75 percent selective degeneration in these patients.

In addition to these clinical observations, experimental studies using Alzheimer's disease animal models show that anticholinergic drugs and lesions of the nucleus basalis of Meynert disrupt learning or memory in a number of reinforcement learning paradigms, including passive avoidance learning and Morris water maze tests (Francis et al., 1999; Friedman, Lerer, and Kuster, 1983; Iqbal and Grundke-Iqbal, 2008; Lo Conte et al., 1982; Pimplikar, 2009). In a passive avoidance learning test, subjects learn to avoid an environment in which an aversive stimulus, such as a shock, was previously delivered. The Morris water maze, which was introduced by Richard Morris in 1981 (Morris, 1981), consists of a large circular pool of water with a hidden platform submerged just below the water surface. During a Morris water maze test, the subject learns to escape from the water by locating the hidden platform with the help of distal visual cues.

Can these clinical and experimental facts lead to treatments that may possibly ameliorate or delay Alzheimer's symptoms? One approach is based on the fact that acetylcholinesterase (AChE) is the main enzyme that can break down acetylcholine in the brain. Inhibition of AChE is one of the treatment strategies to ameliorate symptoms of Alzheimer's disease (e.g., Mukherjee et al., 2007; Orhan et al., 2004). Indeed, in 2017, Monica Janeczek with eight collaborators (Janeczek et al., 2017) described an extensive network of cortical pyramidal neurons in the human brain with abundant AChE activity. They quantified the density and staining intensity of these neurons using histochemical procedures. Their methods enabled them to show that brains of adults above age 80 with unusually preserved memory performance (so-called SuperAgers) showed significantly lower staining intensity and density of AChE neurons when compared with same-age peers, leading them to speculate that low levels of AChE activity could enhance the impact of acetylcholine on pyramidal neurons to counterbalance factors that mediate the decline of memory capacity during normal aging.

Another possible approach to enhancing ACh function has been reported by Zahra Rabiei and four collaborators (Rabiei et al., 2014, p. 353). They note that *Ziziphus jujuba* (ZJ) activates choline acetyltransferase (ChAT), a transferase enzyme that is responsible for the synthesis of ACh. Their study investigates the effect of ZJ extract in intact rats and in a rat model of Alzheimer's disease with lesions of the nucleus basalis of Meynert. Learning and memory performance were again assessed using a passive avoidance paradigm, and spatial learning and memory were evaluated by again using the Morris water maze. These results suggest that ZJ has repairing effects on memory and behavioral disorders produced by lesions of the nucleus basalis of Meynert, and therefore suggest that ZJ may also have beneficial effects treating Alzheimer's patients.

Many studies (e.g., Wang et al., 2000a, 2000b) have clarified how the structural degeneration that may cause ACh deficits in Alzheimer's patients can be traced to the role of the 42-amino acid β-amyloid peptide ($A\beta_{1-42}$) in the formation of neuritic plaques. These authors noted that the α7 nicotinic ACh receptor (α7nAChR) is highly expressed in the basal forebrain cholinergic neurons that project to the hippocampus and cortex of normal and Alzheimer brains (e.g., Perry et al., 1992) and correlates well with brain areas that exhibit neuritic plaques in Alzheimer's disease. In 2002, R. G. Nagele and colleagues (Nagele et al., 2002) showed how $A\beta_{1-42}$ binds with exceptionally high affinity to α7nAChR and accumulates intracellularly in neurons of Alzheimer's disease brains. These amyloid peptides can inhibit the release of ACh (Kar et al., 1996).

How do cortical layers 3 and 5 come into this story? As I noted above, several studies have documented that plaques and neurofibrillary tangles occur more frequently in cortical layers 3 and 5 (e.g., Arnold et al., 1991; Tomlinson et al., 1968, 1970). Neurofibrillary tangles are aggregates of hyperphosphorylated tau protein that exist in an insoluble form and are known as a primary marker of Alzheimer's disease. In summary, all of these studies are consistent with the kinds of structural degeneration in layers 3 and 5 that would be consistent with the massive collapse of ACh function and how it supports learning, memory, and cognition through tonic and phasic vigilance control.

Relating sleep and Alzheimer disease pathology

Sleep is a very complex phenomenon that I will make no attempt to explain completely. Even a moment's thought about all the things that need to happen in the right order for you to progress safely from a fully awake vertical body to one that is passively relaxed in a horizontal position illustrate this complexity. I review relevant data properties of sleep in my 2017 article about ACh modulation during normal and abnormal learning and memory (Grossberg, 2017a). Here I just want to note the relevance of ACh-mediated vigilance control to links that are known to exist between abnormalities in slow wave sleep that occur before Alzheimer's develops, and continue throughout its course. The most striking fact is that the laminar cortical circuits that I have already mentioned help to clarify data about properties of slow wave sleep that are called Up and Down states by many scientists. These results also shed light on how sleep disruptions may contribute to a vicious cycle of plaque formation in cortical layers 3 and 5.

Beginning with the seminal work of Mircea Steriade several decades ago, many investigators have studied the several phases of sleep, including REM sleep, during which rapid eye movements and dreaming may occur, and the deeper non-REM, or slow wave sleep, so named because it exhibits a slow rhythm, with a frequency that is less than one cycle per second, in the electroencephalogram, or EEG. Slow wave sleep was just one of Steriade's many important discoveries (e.g., Steriade, 2006; Steriade et al., 1993). This slow rhythm has been proposed to carry out multiple functions, ranging from metabolic clearance from the brain (Xie et al., 2013) to memory consolidation (Marshall et al., 2006; Steriade and Timofeev, 2003). Lesions of the basal forebrain cholinergic nuclei, or pharmacological block of ACh receptors, lead to slow waves throughout the neocortex (Buzsáki et al., 1988; Vanderwolf, 1988). In the reverse direction, during wakefulness, there is an increased release of ACh in the thalamus and cerebral cortex (e.g., Steriade, 2004).

How do layers 3 and 5 get involved in slow wave sleep? Slow wave generation in cortical layer 5 (Ball et al., 1977; Calvet et al., 1973; Rappelsberger et al., 1982) is supported by bursting pyramidal cells in layer 5 that synchronize activity across the neocortex (e.g., Chagnac-Amitai and Connors, 1989; Connors, 1984; Silva et al., 1991; Wang and McCormick, 1993). Bursting cells have also been reported in layer 3 (Steriade, Nunez, and Amzica, 1993a, 1993b).

The Up and Down states during slow wave sleep are called Active and Silent states by Steriade. He noted that, when cortical neurons go from Active to Silent states, they excite reticular thalamic neurons, which inhibit thalamocortical neurons. Thus, active inhibition dominates thalamocortical neurons during the Active network state so, in Steriade's view, this state cannot be called an Up state. Since many other authors have accepted the Up-Down terminology, I will also use it here, but it is important to keep Steriade's valid concern in mind when considering how these states influence other parts of the brain.

What are the properties of these Up and Down states? Remarkably, as Maxim Volgushev, Sylvain Chauvette, Mikhail Mukovski, and Igor Timofeev observed in 2006 (Volgushev et al., 2006, p. 5671): "all cells, excitatory as well as inhibitory, were involved in the same slow rhythm, and we never observed a cell to be systematically active while other neurons were silent . . . high synchrony of the silent state onsets implies the existence of a network mechanism that switches activity to silence . . . This would lead to termination of activity of both excitatory and inhibitory cells, including those cells that have generated the silencing discharge". These authors went on to review evidence that bursting neurons in layer 5 large pyramidal cells initiate this activity cycle, and that fast-spiking inhibitory interneurons have an early onset during the subsequent Up and Down states. These dynamics are, moreover, due to intracortical interactions that occur even when thalamic gates do not permit the intrusion of signals from the outside world during slow wave sleep (e.g., Steriade and Timofeev, 2003). An intracortical origin for these slow waves is also supported by their survival after extensive thalamic lesions (Steriade, Nuñez, and Amzica, 1993b) and by the absence of slow waves in the thalamus of decorticated cats (Timofeev and Steriade, 1996). In their mean field model of the Up-Down cycle, Maria Sanchez-Vives and Maurizio Mattia (Sanchez-Vives and Mattia, 2014) have also observed a role for "activity-dependent fatigue" in regulating the relative duration of the Down state.

In order to more fully understand properties of slow wave sleep, I will show how they may arise from basic properties of the LAMINART (Figure 4.58) and SMART (Figures 5.38 and 5.39) laminar neocortical models. These models have already been used to explain many psychological and neurobiological properties of the awake state. This explanation thus clarifies, not only data about slow wave sleep, but also how the same cortical circuits can then transition to conscious waking behaviors. This explanation also sheds some light on the following questions: Why do not the bursts that occur during slow wave sleep cause movement, let alone consciousness, especially given that layer 5 cells project to movement causing areas of the brain such as the superior colliculus and spinal cord, as well as subcortical targets such as the pontine nuclei (Wang and McCormick, 1993)? Multiple mechanisms may contribute to this result, but I will show now how a prescribed intracortical circuit within the LAMINART model also plays a role.

Self-normalizing laminar cortical circuits balance excitation and inhibition. Although my discussion will focus on the laminar cortical circuits in the visual cortex that are modeled by the LAMINART model, and its 3D LAMINART and SMART model extensions, similar laminar circuits, with suitable specializations, have been used to simulate speech perception data using the cARTWORD model (see Figure 12.30 and surrounding discussion), and data about cognitive working memory and list chunking using the LIST PARSE model (see Figure 12.42 and surrounding discussion). These mechanisms thus seem to be conserved, albeit with suitable specializations to carry out different psychological functions, across at least the granular neocortex (Figure 1.20), whose six layers of cells occur in many perceptual and cognitive circuits (Brodmann, 1909; Martin, 1989).

Two kinds of interactions within layers 2/3 and 5/6 are of special interest in my current explanation: Long-range excitatory horizontal connections, and shorter-range self-normalizing networks that balance excitatory and inhibitory interactions. As we have already seen, the long-range horizontal connections within cortical layers 2/3 in LAMINART (Figures 4.28-4.32 and 4.58) carry out the process of boundary completion, also called perceptual grouping, while shorter-range excitatory horizontal connections in layers 2/3 and 5/6 carry out processes such as binocular fusion (e.g., Figure 4.19). These cell properties in cortical layers 2/3 and 5/6 take on new significance in the context of sleep research for at least two reasons: (1) As noted above, layers 3 and 5 contain intrinsically bursting neurons that may be influenced by ACh modulation, and (2) long-range excitatory connections may help to synchronize the ACh-modulated slow waves within local cortical networks. Long-range connections may also help to propagate these synchronous activations in traveling waves across the cortex (Massimini et al., 2004; Volgushev et al., 2006), which they are known to support in the waking state when spatial attention flows along a perceptual boundary (see Figure 6.5 below and surrounding discussion).

The networks with self-normalizing, balanced excitatory and recurrent inhibitory interneurons are at least as important from the present perspective. They occur, with a similar design, in both layers 2/3 and 5/6. In layers 2/3, they are part of a larger LAMINART circuit that also includes the long-range excitatory horizontal connections (Figure 4.58). Together with the long-range horizontal connections, the shorter-range recurrent inhibitory network realize the *bipole property* for boundary completion and perceptual grouping (e.g., Figure 4.28) that I predicted in 1984 (Grossberg, 1984a) at around the same time as these properties were experimentally reported in neurophysiological experiments on cortical area V2 by Rudiger von der Heydt, Esther Peterhans, and Günter Baumgarner (Figures 4.28 and 4.29 von der Heydt et al., 1984). How bipole cell properties are explained by the LAMINART model is summarized in Figure 5.47.

Self-normalizing inhibition during boundary completion. In Figure 5.47a, a single pac-man figure (in black) initiates the formation of a boundary using simple and complex cells in cortical area V1 (Figures 4.17 and 4.19) whose orientation preferences are the same as, or similar to, those of the pac-man's bounding contour. This boundary representation activates long-range excitatory

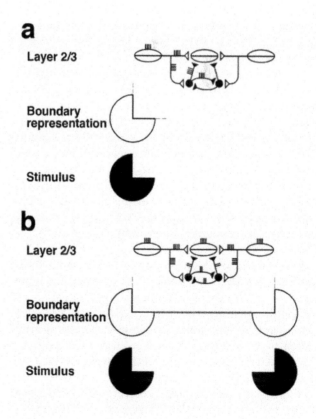

FIGURE 5.47. How long-range excitatory connections and short-range disynaptic inhibitory connections realize the bipole grouping law.

horizontal connections in layer 2/3 of cortical area V2 (Figure 4.58). Excitatory signals in these horizontal connections also excite inhibitory interneurons on their way to target cells in layer 2/3. The inhibition from the disynaptic inhibitory interneurons balances the excitation from the long-range horizontal connection, thereby preventing the target cell from firing. It is a case of *one-against-one*. By this mechanism, a single contrast in an image is prevented from creating outwardly spreading boundaries across the entire image.

In Figure 5.47b, two like-oriented pac-man figures are aligned across space, and are sufficiently near one another to complete a boundary between them. In this case, the excitatory signals from their long-range horizontal connections summate at the target cell. The disynaptic inhibitory signals from the inhibitory interneurons also summate there. Why, then, does not the total inhibition again cancel the total excitation? As I explained in Chapter 4, this is because the inhibitory interneurons also inhibit each other to form a recurrent lateral inhibitory network. I mathematically proved in 1973 (Grossberg, 1973; see also the review in Grossberg, 1980) that, if the inhibitory cells in such a recurrent network obey the membrane equations of neurophysiology—also called the shunting dynamics that I have already mentioned in Chapter 1—then the inhibitory network's *total activity tends to be normalized*, and independent of the number of active inhibitory cells. Thus, although the total excitation increases, the total inhibition does not. It is a case of *two-against-one*, so excitation wins and the boundary can form.

Layers 5/6 also include the same kind of recurrent self-normalizing circuit, as does the circuit in layer 3B that computes binocular disparity (Figure 4.19). This kind of circuit, in fact, seems to occur in many parts of the neocortex, where it helps to ensure properties in the waking state like contrast normalization, attentional modulation, decision-making, activity-dependent habituation, and mismatch-mediated reset (e.g., Cao and Grossberg, 2005, 2012; Francis and Grossberg, 1996; Francis, Grossberg, and Mingolla, 1994; Grossberg, 2003, 2016a; Grossberg and Pilly, 2008; Grossberg and Yazdanbakhsh, 2005).

Self-normalizing inhibition during attentional priming and the ART Matching Rule. A self-normalizing inhibitory circuit also controls top-down object attention and the ART Matching Rule (Figure 1.25). These properties can be understood within the laminar circuits of visual cortex by considering Figure 5.48, which describes the LAMINART circuit that I published with my PhD student Rajeev Raizada in a series of articles between 2000 and 2003; e.g., Raizada and Grossberg (2001). In Figure 5.48a, the network from layer 6-to-4 creates a *modulatory on-center* as part of the bottom-up on-center off-surround network that inputs to layer 4 from the lateral geniculate nucleus, or LGN. Such a modulatory on-center requires

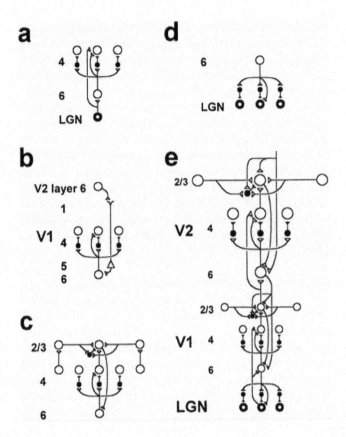

FIGURE 5.48. Microcircuits of the LAMINART model that I developed with Rajeev Raizada. See the text for details of how they integrate bottom-up adaptive filtering, horizontal bipole grouping, and top-down attentional matching that satisfied the ART Matching Rule.

that excitatory and inhibitory inputs are approximately equal, or balanced, to the on-center cells. The LGN is able to fire target cells in layer 4 by also activating a *direct* LGN-to-4 excitatory pathway. The indirect LGN-to-6-to-4 is not useless, however, because the direct LGN-to-4 pathway, when combined with the LGN-to-6-to-4 network, can both activate and *contrast normalize* the inputs to layer 4 cells in response to input patterns from the LGN. In other words, this network can compute the contrasts, or relative sizes, of inputs from the LGN, while normalizing cell responses, even when the input varies between wide limits.

Why is the combination of a direct LGN-to-4 network *and* a modulatory on-center off-surround network from LGN-to-6-to-4 needed? Why could not the LGN-to-6-to-4 network be designed so that its excitatory on-center could, all by itself, fire target layer 4 cells, thereby eliminating the need for a separate LGN-to-4 pathway? Why, in other words, is the brain's anatomy not "wasting a lot of wire," as a computer chip designer might ask?

This can be understood by considering how the modulatory on-center in the 6-to-4 network does double duty by helping to realize top-down attention via the ART Matching Rule in Figure 5.48b. As noted in Figure 1.25, the ART Matching Rule asserts that top-down object attention is achieved using a top-down, *modulatory* on-center, off-surround network in order to achieve stable learning and memory. The excitation and inhibition in the on-center of the layer 6-to-4 network thus need to be approximately *balanced*. This constraint clarifies the need for a direct LGN-to-4 pathway that is sufficient on its own to fire target layer 4 cells.

When the ART Matching Rule is realized in laminar neocortical circuits, the top-down signals from layer 6 of a higher cortical area find their way to layer 6 of a lower cortical area before being "folded" back to layer 4 via an on-center off-surround network. Thus, the entire top-down attentional circuit is said to be realized by *folded feedback* from layer 6 of a higher cortical area to layer 4 of a lower cortical area.

The "double duty" of the layer 6-to-4 network has major consequences for cortical processing, since the modulatory on-center off-surround network between layers 6 and 4 helps to process both data-driven bottom-up inputs and task-selective top-down attentional constraints. These "deep" cortical layers thus serve as a *decision interface* where the most salient combination of data and task constraints can cooperate and compete to choose the best compromise in the current situation. Even more remarkably, preattentive grouping circuits also use the same decision interface, so that bottom-up inputs, horizontal grouping, and top-down attention all cooperate or compete in these deeper layers to generate the best consensus of all these constraints acting together. Chapter 10 will explain these and other important properties of laminar neocortical circuits in greater detail; see Figures 10.3 and 10.13.

Recurrent off-surround normalizes cell responses to converging sources. The above considerations explain why the layer 6-to-4 on-center is modulatory, but not why the off-surround needs to be a *recurrent* inhibitory network. The main design constraint that forces recurrence is that the modulatory requirement must be maintained when *multiple* input sources contribute simultaneously to the total top-down attentional priming signal, or to the total bottom-up feature pattern. Under these "variable load" conditions, the modulatory requirement would fail if the inhibitory network was feedforward. In particular, if the total activity of off-surround cells grew proportionally with the number of cells inputting to it, then the excitatory inputs to the on-center would be overwhelmed. Self-normalization of total inhibition by the recurrent inhibitory network, no matter how many input sources are active, solves this problem. I emphasize this property here because this recurrent inhibitory network will also be critical in my proposed explanation of Up and Down states during slow wave sleep.

Balancing excitation and inhibition in these circuits achieves several other useful functional roles. For starters,

it helps to avoid seizures that could result if excitation was too much stronger than inhibition, or depression if inhibition was too much stronger than excitation. This balance also maintains the cortex at a "cusp of excitability" wherein enough intermittent endogenous activation occurs to prevent atrophy during rest intervals when a cortical area is not actively processing inputs ("use it or lose it"), while also enabling the cortex to respond efficiently and vigorously, indeed synchronously, to external inputs when they do occur.

Given that balanced excitation and inhibition are useful, how do they develop in an infant's brain? The laminar cortical model that I published in 2001 with my PhD student James Williamson (Grossberg and Williamson, 2001) showed how the desired balance of excitation and inhibition could autonomously develop from simple developmental rules, leading to circuits capable of bipole grouping in layer 2/3, and contrast-normalizing attentional modulation in layers 6-to-4. These developed circuits, with the same parameters that were discovered during the developmental process, were used in that article and subsequent ones with Rajeev Raizada (e.g., Grossberg and Raizada, 2000; Raizada and Grossberg, 2001) to simulate a wide range of psychophysical and neurophysiological data about adult visual perception and attention. I discuss these data and how they may be explained more fully in Chapter 10. They show how LAMINART can provide a unified explanation of data about both cortical development in the infant, and adult attention and visual perception in the adult.

It is also worth noting that a recurrent inhibitory network is probably easier to grow during development than a feedforward network, since inhibitory connections can then grow to *all* nearby cells, both excitatory and inhibitory, not just to excitatory cells.

From grouping and attention during waking to Up and Down states during slow wave sleep. These recurrent inhibitory circuits naturally lead to properties of Up and Down states during slow wave sleep (Steriade, Nuñez, and Amzica, 1993b; Steriade and Timofeev, 2003; Timofeev and Steriade, 1996; Volgushev et al., 2006), including the fast reaction of inhibitory interneurons, and the silencing of both excitatory and inhibitory neurons during the Down state. The simplest version of such a recurrent inhibitory circuit between layers 6 and 4 also includes ACh-modulated inputs from layer 5 cells (cf. Figures 5.43) that intermittently burst during slow wave sleep.

The analysis herein does not mathematically model how layer 5 cells generate intermittent bursts during slow wave sleep as a result of ACh down-regulation. Other modeling articles make proposals about how this may happen; e.g., Bazhenov et al. (2002) and Esser, Hill, and Tononi (2009). *Given* such a excitatory burst emanating from the layer 5 cell to the recurrent inhibitory network in Figure 5.49, the burst inputs to both the on-center and the off-surround of the layer 6-to-4 network, just as it does in the LAMINART model. If the inhibitory interneurons obey dynamics of fast spiking cells, they may thus begin to be activated a little before the excitatory on-center cells. Despite such a brief advantage, the on-center cells can nonetheless begin to fire before signals from the inhibitory interneurons can take effect at the on-center, due to the extra stage of axonal delay due to the inhibitory interneurons in the off-surround anatomy. This period of on-center activation is an Up state.

This Up state is transient due to the transient nature of the layer 5 excitatory input burst, combined with the balanced total excitatory and inhibitory inputs to the on-center. When the inhibitory interneuronal signals take effect at the on-center cells, the on-center cells will be completely inhibited due to this balance. As the on-center cells are inhibited, so too will the inhibitory interneurons by the recurrent inhibitory feedback that they deliver to each other. When both on-center and off-surround cells are silenced, a Down state is created.

Another relevant factor is that the layer 6-to-4 connections in the LAMINART model are gated by activity-dependent habituative transmitters. These habituating gates help to explain many data, ranging from data about visual persistence (see Chapter 7) to mismatch-mediated reset during an ART search (Figure 5.19). In the case of slow wave sleep, such habituation may influence the duration of the Down state (Sanchez-Vives and Mattia, 2014).

Slow wave sleep can disrupt and be disrupted by Alzheimer's disease: A vicious circle. In 2014, Yo-El Ju, Brendan Lucey, and David Holtman (Ju, Lucey, and Holtzman, 2014, p. 115) reviewed evidence that "the sleep-wake cycle directly influences levels of Aβ [amyloid-β peptide] in the brain. In experimental models, sleep

deprivation increases the concentration of soluble Aβ and results in chronic accumulation of Aβ, whereas sleep extension has the opposite effect." The authors go on to note that changes in sleep precede the onset of cognitive symptoms in Alzheimer's patients, and that disrupted sleep patterns occur in patients with Alzheimer's disease. Moreover, there is a diurnal variation in the level of soluble Aβ in the interstitial fluid. During the Down state of slow wave sleep, less Aβ is released than during wakefulness or REM sleep. A disruption of slow wave sleep can hereby lead to higher sustained extracellular concentrations of Aβ. These higher sustained Aβ concentrations are, in turn, associated with early amyloid plaque formation.

As noted above, plaques are found more frequently in cortical layers 3 and 5, where they can disrupt the ACh-mediated Up and Down oscillations in slow wave sleep that are diagrammed in Figure 5.49. By disrupting slow wave sleep in this way, and thereby indirectly causing higher Aβ extracellular concentrations, a vicious cycle can be perpetuated.

Can novelty-seeking behaviors lower the chance of developing Alzheimer's? My focus on vigilance control, together with the experimental evidence suggesting how the normal ACh dynamics that support vigilance dynamics may be devastated in Alzheimer's patients, raises the following question: Can non-invasive behavioral activities that promote normal ACh dynamics, in addition to all appropriate drug and other medical interventions, help to delay, or lower the chances of developing, Alzheimer's disease? In other words, can some types of behavior better support the brain's design to solve the stability-plasticity dilemma (cf. Chapter 1), and thereby allow learning to continue throughout life without a loss of memory stability?

Since unexpected events phasically raise vigilance by releasing ACh (Figures 5.39 and 5.43), it is natural to ask whether novelty-seeking activities can help? Some data suggest that this may be the case (e.g., Fritsch, Smyth, and Debanne, 2005), while other studies report diminished novelty-seeking behavior in patients with probable Alzheimer's disease, that is distinct from general cognitive decline (Daffner et al., 1999). It may thus be of use to consider whether and how novelty-rich experiences can be designed to help slow the onset of Alzheimer's, while keeping in mind the larger mechanistic theme that ACh release and vigilance control are triggered by the mismatch events that occur in response to novel experiences.

Sleep disturbances in autism and schizophrenia: Due to vigilance abnormalities? Alzheimer's disease is not the only vigilance disease that includes sleep disturbances among its symptoms. Recall my hypotheses that vigilance is abnormally high in many autistic individuals and abnormally low in many schizophrenics. As in the case of Alzheimer's disease, these tonic vigilance

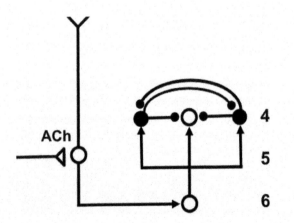

FIGURE 5.49. This circuit of the LAMINART model helps to explain properties of Up and Down states during slow wave sleep, and how disturbances in ACh dynamics can disrupt them.

abnormalities may be assumed to be due to problems in how the nucleus basalis of Meynert regulates neocortical and other brain ACh levels. Given this shared link to sleep problems in Alzheimer's patients, it is perhaps not surprising that autistic individuals and schizophrenics also experience sleep disorders (e.g., Chouinard, Poulin, Stip, and Godbout, 2004; Mannion and Leader, 2014). A great deal more research needs to be done to clarify the similarities and differences in the ways in which vigilance problems may influence sleep in these various types of individuals. To the extent that vigilance problems are indeed part of the story, it will be necessary to broaden the description of pharmacological substrates of autistic and schizophrenic symptoms to include ACh, as well as dopamine.

Many kinds of psychological and neurobiological data have been explained by ART

The ART category learning and search cycle that is summarized in Figure 5.19 has been applied and refined in a series of modeling studies over the past 40 years to explain many different kinds of data. In addition to those already reviewed above, these studies explain data about such varied topics as texture segregation (Bhatt, Carpenter, and Grossberg, 2007); visual scene recognition (Grossberg and Huang, 2009); and fast visual attention switching during the recognition of letter or number targets during rapid serial visual presentations (Grossberg and Stone, 1986a).

As will be seen in Chapter 12, similar model mechanisms, specialized for learning about *sequences* of events,

support explanations of data about contextually-cued search of visual scenes (Huang and Grossberg, 2010), recognition and recall of visually presented words (Grossberg and Stone, 1986b), and recognition and recall of auditorily presented words (Boardman et al., 1999; Grossberg, Boardman, and Cohen, 1997; Grossberg and Kazerounian, 2011, 2016; Grossberg and Myers, 2000; Kazerounian and Grossberg, 2014). The empirical and theoretical support for the foundational concepts and mechanisms of ART is thus strong enough for us to build upon them with confidence in the rest of this book.

We have now reached another crossroads in the exposition. I could proceed in any of several directions, and invite readers to read the chapters first that are of most interest to them. I could have, for example, jumped right into explaining more about how we see the world in depth than I covered in Chapter 4. This clarifies how we see objects and scenes in the world, and I will return to this important topic in Chapter 11. However, during our daily experiences, we see sequences of objects and scenes, not just individual ones. I will describe in Chapter 7 how we experience such sequences without previous ones interfering with our ability to see and recognize current ones. Right after that, I will explain how we see and track moving objects in Chapter 8. I could also have explained more about why the cerebral cortex is organized into characteristic layers of cells, and begun to explain how this kind of Laminar Computing supports important properties of intelligence in all modalities. I will come back to this subject in Chapter 10. Each of these topics, is better understood after we know more about how our brains use vision to attend, learn, recognize, and search for objects as our eyes freely scan a scene. I will accordingly discuss how this happens in the next chapter. This analysis will begin to explain how humans and other terrestrial animals autonomously learn about their worlds as they move around in them.

6

Conscious Seeing and Invariant Recognition

Complementary cortical streams coordinate attention for seeing and recognition

From learning specific categories to learning invariant categories

Autonomous learning during free scanning of a scene with eye movements. The ART search and learning cycle that is summarized in Figure 5.19 clarifies how we learn view-*specific* and position-*specific* categories of objects that we see. In other words, these categories respond best when we see similar views of the objects that trained them in similar positions to those they were in relative to us when training occurred. This process provides a foundation for understanding the processes that I will discuss in this chapter, notably how view-, position-, and size-*invariant* object categories are learned and recognized. Such invariant object categories respond selectively to objects that are seen from multiple views, positions, and distances from an observer. In our brains, both specific and invariant object categories are found in the inferotemporal cortex (Figure 1.21; Desimone, 1998; Gochin, Miller, Gross, and Gerstein, 1991; Harries and Perrett, 1991; Mishkin, 1982; Mishkin, Ungerleider, and Macko, 1983; Seger and Miller, 2010; Ungerleider and Mishkin, 1982). Invariant object recognition is as important for our survival as it is for engineering and AI algorithms and machines that are designed to recognize visual images and scenes.

In order to autonomously learn an invariant object category, the eyes or cameras of a person or machine freely scan a scene in which the objects to be learned occur, so that the objects can be seen at different views, positions, and distances. As I will explain below, this is a challenging problem that I have been able to solve with my colleagues just within the last 10 years.

As I noted in Chapter 1, the ventral What cortical stream (Figure 1.19) learns invariant object categories to enable our brains to recognize valued objects without experiencing the combinatorial explosion that would occur if they needed to store every individual experience, or exemplar, of every object that we ever encountered. However, because they are invariant, these categories cannot locate and act upon a desired object

Conscious MIND Resonant BRAIN. Stephen Grossberg, Oxford University Press. © Oxford University Press 2021.
DOI: 10.1093/oso/9780190070557.003.0006

in space. Dorsal Where stream spatial and motor representations (Figure 1.19) can locate objects and trigger actions towards them, but cannot recognize them. By interacting together to overcome their computationally complementary deficiencies (Table 1.2), the What and Where streams can recognize valued objects *and* direct appropriate goal-oriented actions towards them. How this happens will also be explained in this chapter.

Do cortical streams even exist? How interacting streams can obscure this basic fact. Before delving into particulars, however, let me emphasize one consequence of the fact that so many pairs of cortical processing streams compute computationally complementary properties (e.g., Table 1.1). Overcoming their complementary processing deficiencies requires these streams to strongly interact together. Properties of cells that are computed in one stream will hereby be projected through these interactions to the complementary stream, where they will mingle with the properties that cells in that stream compute on their own. These overlapping properties can obscure the fact that the streams compute complementary properties, and may even challenge the very idea that distinct cortical streams exist.

This issue has been recognized as a problem for a long time, albeit without the insight that it is largely due to a fundamental design constraint like complementary computing. For example, David van Essen and Edgar DeYoe wrote about it in their seminal 1995 article that summarized their classical macrocircuit of the visual system (Figure 0.1; Van Essen and DeYoe, 1995): "although there is widespread support for this hypothesis in general terms, it has proved difficult to decipher what exactly constitutes a visual processing stream and to ascertain the key functional difference between streams" (p. 383). I would argue that the concept of complementary computing helps to do this, when it is applied with mathematical precision to characterize the properties of each stream and how their interactions overcome their complementary deficiencies.

This analysis of invariant object category learning and recognition will lead directly to the concept of *surface-shroud resonance* (Table 1.4) and will clarify how this kind of resonance supports conscious percepts of seeing qualia. It will also clarify how *surface-shroud resonances* interact with the *feature-category resonances* whereby we visually recognize objects, so that we can consciously see *and* know about familiar objects at the same time. This enriched foundation of concepts and mechanisms will be used to explain many additional psychological and neurobiological facts about how we visually see and understand the world.

Coordinated category learning between the posterior and anterior inferotemporal cortex. These view-specific and position-specific ART object categories are proposed to occur in the posterior part of the inferotemporal cortex,

variously abbreviated as ITp, or PIT in Figure 1.19. This chapter will show how learning can link several such ART categories in ITp to an invariant object recognition category in the anterior part of inferotemporal cortex, abbreviated as ITa, or AIT in Figure 1.19. Crucially, this learning of invariant object categories occurs while eye movements freely scan a scene. That is why the extensions of ART that explain how this happens are called the ARTSCAN family of models, which I have progressively developed in a series of articles starting in 2007 with my PhD students Hung-Cheng Chang, Arash Fazl, Nicholas Foley, Jeffrey Markowitz, and Karthik Srinivasan, in collaboration with my colleagues Yongqiang Cao, Ennio Mingolla, and Arash Yazdanbakhsh. (Cao, Grossberg, and Markowitz, 2011; Chang, Grossberg, and Cao, 2014; Fazl, Grossberg, and Mingolla, 2009; Foley, Grossberg, and Mingolla, 2012; Grossberg, 2007a, 2009b; Grossberg, Srinivasan, and Yazdanbakhsh, 2014)

The ART dynamics in Figure 5.19 also consider only one form of attention, which in 1980 Michael Posner called object attention (Posner, 1980). Because there are at least three mechanistically different kinds of attention that are devoted to representing objects, I will call this kind of attention *prototype attention* to avoid confusion. Prototype attention within the What cortical stream focuses attention using the ART Matching Rule (Figure 1.25) upon the critical feature pattern of a view- and position-specific category prototype (Figure 2.2). In order to explain how invariant category learning occurs with the help of surface-shroud resonances, ARTSCAN proposes how prototype attention interacts with another kind of attention that in 1984 John Duncan called *spatial attention* (Duncan, 1984). Spatial attention is computed within the Where/How cortical stream where it can highlight the positions of attended objects in space. I will call this kind of spatial attention *surface attention* to mechanistically distinguish it from *boundary attention*, which is another kind of spatial attention. Each type of attention supports conscious perception or recognition of different aspects of our experiences.

Surface-shroud resonances are generated between V4 and PPC

The previous descriptions of visual boundaries and surfaces in Chapters 3 and 4 set the stage for understanding surface-shroud resonances and their role in both invariant object category learning and in supporting the conscious awareness of visual experiences. Several perceptual and cognitive scientists have reported that spatial attention can fit itself to the shape of an attended object, including scientists like Patrick Cavanagh and his colleagues who use the term *sprite* (Cavanagh, Labianca, and Thornton, 2001) and Zenon Pylyshyn who uses the term *finst* (Pylyshyn, 1989). The term *attentional shroud* for such a form-fitting distribution of spatial attention was introduced in 1995 by Christopher Tyler and Leonid Kontsevich (Tyler and Kontsevich, 1995). Their concern was not about object category learning, recognition, or search. Rather, it was about how attention is allocated during transparent percepts wherein several depth planes are perceived (cf. Figure 1.4). I personally think that their term "attentional shroud" is most evocative of the concept that it represents. Using it, I predicted how attentional shrouds help to regulate object category learning, recognition, and search and then developed it within the ARTSCAN family of models into rigorous data explanations and simulations with my colleagues.

An attentional shroud can form when one or more objects send bottom-up topographic excitatory signals from their surface representations in prestriate cortical area V4 to cells in the posterior parietal cortex, or PPC, in the Where/How cortical stream (Figure 1.19). Figure 6.1 illustrates this process by depicting the cross-section of a simple image in which two bars of slightly different luminance send their bottom-up signals to the spatial attention region in PPC. These surface representations then compete for spatial attention while also sending top-down topographic excitatory signals back to V4 (Figure 6.2). Taken together, these signals form a *recurrent* on-center off-surround network that is capable of contrast-enhancing and normalizing its activities in the manner that I discussed in Chapter 1; see Figures 1.6-1.9.

This recurrent exchange of excitatory signals between V4 and PPC, combined with competitive inhibitory signals within PPC, helps to choose a winning focus of spatial attention in PPC that fits itself to the shape of the attended object surface in V4. The resulting *surface-shroud resonance* between a surface representation in V4 and spatial attention in PPC corresponds to *paying sustained spatial attention to consciously visible surface qualia*. Once triggered, a surface-shroud resonance can propagate top-down to earlier cortical areas such as V2 and V1, where it can attentively amplify and select consistent cell activations while inhibiting inconsistent ones, and bottom-up to higher cortical areas such as prefrontal cortex, or PFC.

V2 and V4: Recognizing occluded objects, seeing unoccluded surfaces, and transparency

Why is a surface-shroud resonance assumed to be triggered between V4 and PPC? As I discussed in Chapter 4, the FACADE and 3D LAMINART models propose that cortical areas V2 and V4 resolve a basic design tension between recognition and seeing whose resolution prevents all occluding objects from looking transparent during 3D vision and figure-ground separation (Grossberg, 1994, 1997). In particular, V4 is predicted to be the cortical region where figure-ground-separated 3D surface representations of the *unoccluded* regions of *opaque* object regions are completed. This surface representation can then support both seeing *and* recognition of these regions. These unoccluded object surface regions can then control orienting eye movements and reaching arm movements. The same neural mechanisms also explain how V4 also supports seeing of 3D *transparent* surfaces (Grossberg and Yazdanbakhsh, 2005). Cortical area V2, in contrast, is predicted to complete object boundaries and surfaces of partially *occluded* object regions that may be amodally recognized, but not seen, as in Figure 1.3.

It has been known for a long time that parietal cortex is a site of spatial attention, and that attentionally amplified positional representations there can command the intention to make eye and arm movements (e.g., Bushnell, Goldberg, and Robinson, 1981; Colby and Goldberg, 1999; Gnadt and Andersen, 1988; Snyder, Batista, and Andersen, 1997, 1998). These important studies did not, however, explain why it is at the parietal cortex in the cortical hierarchy that this happens,

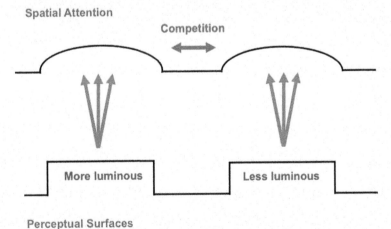

BOTTOM-UP SPATIAL ATTENTIONAL COMPETITION

Spatial Attention

Competition

More luminous

Less luminous

Perceptual Surfaces

FIGURE 6.1. A surface-shroud resonance begins to form when the surface representations of objects bid for spatial attention. In addition to these topographic excitatory inputs, there is long-range inhibition of the spatial attention cells that determines which inputs with attract spatial attention.

SURFACE-SHROUD RESONANCE

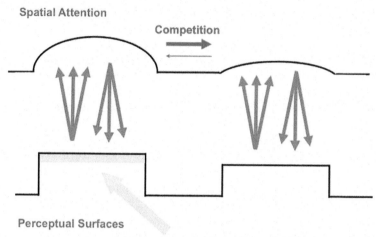

Carrasco, Penpeci-Talgar, and Eckstein (2000)
Reynolds and Desimone (2003)

FIGURE 6.2. After bottom-up surface inputs activate spatial attentional cells, they send top-down topographic excitatory signals back to the surface representations. This *recurrent* shunting on-center off-surround network contrast-enhances larger attentional activities while approximately normalizing the total spatial attentional activity. A surface-shroud resonance hereby forms that selects an attentional shroud, enhances the perceived contrast of the attended surface (light blue region), and maintains spatial attention on it.

nor the role of surface-shroud resonances and conscious seeing in supporting these attentional and movement functions, nor indeed why—from a deeper computational perspective—a focus of spatial attention is used to control looking and reaching. These newer insights are the focus of the current chapter.

Some of the discussion in Chapter 4 will be briefly summarized again here to avoid having to jump back and forth between text in two chapters. The image in Figure 1.3 (left panel) generates a compelling percept of a vertical bar that is partially occluded by a horizontal bar. The partially occluded portion of the vertical bar (Figure 1.3, right panel, dashed line) is amodally recognized, but it is not consciously seen. The model proposes how the horizontal rectangle is separated from the partially occluded vertical rectangle, which can then be completed "behind" the horizontal rectangle in V2. Then direct pathways from V2 to higher cortical areas such as IT cortex, and back, are used to *recognize* this completed perceptual representation as part of a feature-category resonance (Table 1.4), despite the fact that the occluded part of this rectangle is not consciously *seen*. Such recognition without seeing is said to be *amodal*.

If the completed boundary and surface behind the horizontal rectangle could also be seen, then the horizontal rectangle would look transparent, because both the horizontal and vertical rectangles could be seen at the same spatial positions, albeit at different depths. V2 and V4 are

predicted to work together to ensure that not all objects look transparent. As a result of this teamwork between V2 and V4, partially occluded objects can be recognized without forcing all occluders to look transparent. Chapter 4 mentioned some of the neurobiological data that support this hypothesis.

As also noted in Chapter 4: A surface-shroud resonance is assumed to be triggered between V4 and PPC because V4 is predicted to be the earliest cortical stage that generates a sufficiently complete, context-sensitive, and stable surface representation after the three hierarchical resolutions of uncertainty have taken place, and boundaries have been completed and surfaces filled in. These processes generate figure-ground-separated 3D surface representations of unoccluded object regions. With such a V4 surface representation as a trigger, surface-shroud resonances between V4 and PPC initiate the process whereby these surface representations may become consciously visible. Conscious visibility is proposed to provide an "extra degree of freedom" which the brain "lights up" so that it can selectively use the V4 surface representation to help guide orienting eye movements and reaching arm movements.

The ambiguous, noisy, and incomplete earlier visual representations are hereby prevented from generating maladaptive movements, and the top-down attentional feedback to these regions that is triggered by the surface-shroud resonance, in concert with any feature-category resonance with which it may synchronize (Table 1.4), selects from these representations those signals that are compatible with the V4 representation.

Solving the view-to-object binding problem during free scanning of a scene

The route to my prediction that a surface-shroud resonance supports conscious seeing and reaching was quite indirect, because I discovered the concept of a surface-shroud resonance while I was modeling invariant object recognition. It only then became clear to me that this was the resonance that I had been seeking for many years in response to my predictions that "all conscious states are resonant states" (e.g., Grossberg, 1980) and "all consciously visible qualia are surface percepts" (e.g., Grossberg, 1994). Putting these two assertions together led to the urgent question: What kind of resonance supports conscious percepts of visible qualia? As progress on modeling invariant category learning progressed, I could begin to see that surface-shroud resonances had the requisite properties. I could then also begin to more deeply understand how feature-category resonances for recognition interact with surface-shroud resonances for seeing, and how surface-shroud resonances for seeing select surface representations that could be used to direct looking and reaching.

I write about a *family* of ARTSCAN models because the road to understanding invariant object recognition has developed in stages using the Method of Minimal Anatomies that I defined in Chapter 2 (Figure 2.37). The simplest ARTSCAN model focused on learning view-invariant object categories in a 2D image (Fazl, Grossberg, and Mingolla, 2009). The currently most advanced ARTSCAN model can learn invariant object categories and search for these objects in a 3D scene. It is thus called the 3D ARTSCAN Search model, in which Figure 6.3 illustrates Where-to-What stream processes that regulate invariant

category learning, and Figure 6.4 illustrates What-to-Where stream processes that can drive a search from a name category to the position of a valued object during a Where's Waldo search (Chang, Grossberg, and Cao, 2014; Grossberg, Srinivasan, and Yazdanbakhsh, 2014).

Because all of the ARTSCAN models explain how invariant object categories are learned as our eyes scan a scene, they all contribute to the area that is called "active vision" in the computer vision community; e.g., Aloimonos, Weiss, and Bandyopadhyay (1988). The models propose solutions to basic problems that confront humans and many other animals as they learn to recognize objects in a 2D image or 3D scene while scanning the scene with eye movements. One such problem is called the *view-to-object binding problem*. This problem arises because, as our eyes scan a scene, two successive eye movements may focus on different parts of the same object or

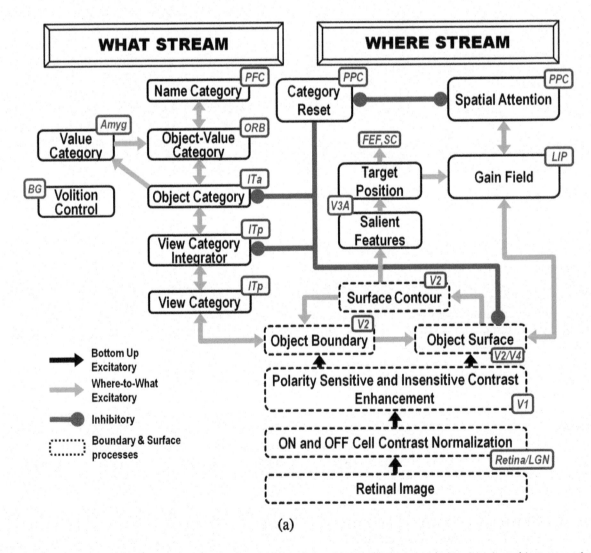

(a)

FIGURE 6.3. These interactions of the ARTSCAN Search model enable it to learn to recognize and name invariant object categories. Interactions between spatial attention in the Where cortical stream, via surface-shroud resonances, and object attention in the What cortical stream, that obeys the ART Matching Rule, coordinate these learning, recognition, and naming processes.

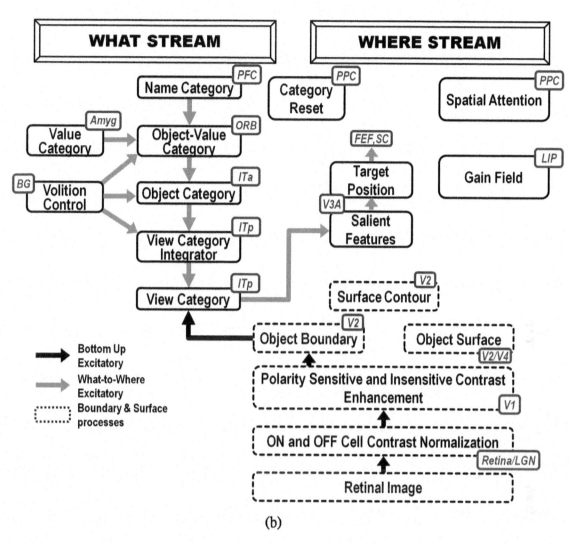

(b)

FIGURE 6.4. The ARTSCAN Search model can also search for a desired target object in a scene, thereby clarifying how our brains solve the Where's Waldo problem.

on different objects. How does the brain avoid learning to erroneously classify views of different objects together, without an external teacher? For example, suppose that the eyes sequentially scan a bird, cloud, and face in the scene. Why does not the brain learn to associate them all with the same invariant object category? Or, if the scan path included three distinct faces in a scene, why would not all of them be linked together? If this did happen, we could not learn to recognize *any* individual object because everything that we saw could be jumbled together by promiscuous learning. One cannot say that the brain avoids this problem by knowing that some views belong together in a single object, whereas others do not, because this can happen even before the brain has a concept of what the object is. Indeed, such scanning eye movements are used to learn the object concept in the first place.

In order to better appreciate how dynamic this process of scanning is, it is instructive to watch videos of where infants look through time. Videos were made, for example, by Yoshida and Smith (2008) using a camera that was placed on the heads of 18 to 24 month old infants in the context of toy play with a parent. This work included evidence of the coupling of head and eye movements during these experiments. Smith et al. (2015) provide a more recent overview of this method. In addition, Franchak et al. (2011) using head-mounted eye trackers that recorded the gaze of 14 month old infants during free play with their mothers. Both kinds of studies emphasize how remarkable is our ability to extract invariant object category information from the highly dynamic experiences of infants while they freely scan their environments during play and other activities.

Invariant object category learning is regulated by a surface-shroud resonance

The ARTSCAN models propose how the view-to-object binding problem may be solved by coordinating spatial attention and eye movements in the Where cortical processing stream with object attention and invariant object category learning in the What cortical stream (Mishkin, Ungerleider, and Macko, 1983). This coordination is only possible because a surface-shroud resonance can sustain spatial attention upon an object surface while its invariant object category is being learned. And one cannot understand what an object surface is without the kind of overview that was given in Chapters 3 and 4 of how such a surface forms.

As I noted above, the Where stream is also called the How stream because of its important role in controlling actions in space (Goodale and Milner, 1992). This proposed linkage of space to action gains new significance in terms of my proposal of how the conscious qualia of unoccluded surface regions help to determine reachable target positions in space. The ARTSCAN models hereby link consciousness to action. To emphasize this link, the Where stream will henceforth be called the Where/How stream.

Explaining data about visual neglect: Coordinates, competition, grouping, and action

The hypothesis that a surface-shroud resonance has its generators between V4 and PPC helps to explain various data about visual consciousness, such as data about visual neglect (e.g., Bellmann, Meuli, and Clarke, 2001; Driver and Mattingley, 1998; Marshall, 2001; Mesulam, 1999), perceptual crowding (e.g., Bouma, 1970, 1973; Foley et al., 2012; Green and Bavelier, 2007; He, Cavanagh, and Intriligator, 1996; Intriligator and Cavanagh, 2001; Levi, 2008), change blindness (e.g., Pashler, 1988; Phillips, 1974; Rensink, O'Regan, and Clark, 1997; Simons and Rensink, 2005), and motion-induced blindness (e.g., Grindley and Townsend, 1965; Ramachandran and Gregory, 1991), all of which will now be discussed. After providing these explanations of clinical and perceptual data, the text will return in subsequent sections to answer the question of how a surface-shroud resonance maintains spatial attention on an object of interest as it controls the eye movements that

scan the object surface in order to learn an invariant object category. As this process takes place, the brain can consciously *see* the object at the same time that it *knows* how to search for and recognize it in a cluttered scene. In particular, this summary will explain how we consciously see the object in *retinotopic* coordinates, or coordinates that move around with the eyes, even while the perceptual stability that is maintained during scanning eye movements is achieved by computing the attentional shroud in head-centered, or *spatial* coordinates, that are invariant under eye movements.

Visual neglect. Visual neglect is often called hemispatial neglect because it is may arise after damage to one hemisphere of the brain, notably of the parietal cortex, due to a stroke or other accident. A deficit in attention to, and awareness of, one side of space is then often observed. Famous examples include patients who draw only half of the visual world, or who only eat food on one half of their plate, even if, by doing so, they may remain hungry.

The clinical literature on visual neglect is extensive, complex, and subtle, with uncertainties and debates still ongoing (e.g., Behrmann, Geng, and Shomstein, 2004; Husain and Nachev, 2007; Karnath and Rorden, 2012; Nachev and Husain, 2006). Despite these uncertainties, there is convergent evidence that a particular region of PPC, the inferior parietal lobule (IPL; Figure 1.21), plays an important role in visual neglect. In 2001, Hans-Otto Karnath, Susanne Ferber, and Marc Himmelbach had concluded that a different part of the brain, the superior temporal cortex (STC), not the IPL, is important in neglect (Karnath, Ferber, and Himmelbach, 2001), but other investigators raised doubts about this strong claim. For example, in 2007, Masud Husain and Parashkev Nachev wrote that "the disparity between this new proposal and the results of other studies has attracted considerable debate and has been attributed to differences in clinical selection criteria, quality of imaging and the methods of ensuring comparisons between homologous structures across subjects . . . " (Husain and Nachev, 2007, p. 34). Other studies (e.g., Mort et al., 2003) provided compelling evidence that the IPL "is the crucial anatomical correlate of neglect" (Behrmann, Geng, and Shomstein (2004, p. 215), leading Karnath and Christopher Rorden to describe in 2012 a perisylvian network for spatial neglect that includes IPL and STC (Karnath and Rorden, 2012).

One reason for the subtlety of data about visual neglect is, as we shall see in this section, that properties of surface-shroud resonances, including the competitive attentional mechanisms that allow shrouds to be selected (Figure 6.2) and the coordinates in which they are computed, interact with all the visual processes that go into creating visible surface representations, including properties of boundary completion and figure-ground separation, as well as with category learning and recognition processes, and the motor planning and execution processes that attended surfaces feed.

Despite these complexities, a main fact about visual neglect is immediately clear from the most basic properties of a surface-shroud resonance: The very fact that visual neglect occurs at all when an appropriate region of parietal cortex such as IPL is lesioned is immediately clarified by the proposed role of a surface-shroud resonance in visual consciousness: Assuming that IPL is part of the PPC anatomy that supports surface-shroud resonances, a lesion of IPL will prevent a surface-shroud resonance from occurring that involves this part of PPC, so the corresponding visual surface representations in V4 cannot reaching consciousness, even if the visual cortex is itself fully intact. Despite the apparent simplicity of this assertion, this hypothesis can also explain subtle clinical properties of visual neglect. A classical 1989 article of Jon Driver and Jason Mattingley (Driver and Mattingley, 1998) reviews visual neglect properties in individuals who have experienced IPL lesions, particularly in the right hemisphere of their cerebral cortex. The text below takes as explanatory targets properties emphasized in that article, which include the following:

Head-centered shroud coexists with retinotopic surface qualia. A neglect patient who appeared to be blind in the left visual field when fixating straight ahead, or to her left, could detect events in her left visual field when she fixated to the right (Kooistra and Heilman, 1989). This shows that neglect is not computed entirely in retinotopic coordinates. Rather, these and related data can be explained by the fact that the attentional shroud is computed in head-centered coordinates that are invariant under eye movements, even though consciously seen surface qualia are computed in retinotopic coordinates that move with the eyes. These properties will be explained later in this chapter.

Competition for spatial attention across parietal cortex. Some visual neglect patients show a deficit in response to an isolated stimulus on the affected side, but others do not. In the latter patients, whose lesions are presumed to be less severe, a deficit in awareness only emerges when stimuli are presented simultaneously on both sides; e.g., Posner et al. (1984). This type of effect can be explained by the spatial competition across the parietal cortex that leads to the choice of a surface-shroud resonance (see Figure 6.2).

Preserved figure-ground segmentation during neglect. Several kinds of stimuli illustrate that perceptual groupings of the kind that I described in previous chapters (e.g., Figures 1.1-1.4 and throughout Chapters 3 and 4) can restore awareness in a hemifield that would otherwise be

neglected. In particular, as noted in the previous paragraph, when two visual stimuli are briefly presented, the more contralesional stimulus (one in the half of the brain away from the lesion site) can be extinguished from awareness while the ipsilesional stimulus (one on the same side as the lesion) captures attention entirely. However, such extinction can be eliminated if the two events get grouped as a single object, even if the link between the two stimuli is amodally completed behind an occluder (Figures 1.3, 1.4, 3.2, and 3.3; Mattingley, Davis, and Driver, 1997). This effect can be explained by how boundaries can get amodally completed and by how boundary and surface attention can flow behind an occluder. For example, bipole grouping mechanisms can generate amodal boundary completions of occluded object parts in response to the images in Figures 1.3 and 1.4.

It is also important to realize that spatial attention can flow along such a boundary grouping, whether real or illusory. This property clarifies how, when spatial attention is focused on one part of an object boundary, it can "light up" the entire boundary, thereby directing attention to the entire object. The ability of spatial attention to flow along a boundary grouping was reported in neurophysiological experiments for real boundary contours in 1998 by Pieter Roelfsema, Victor Lamme, and Henk Spekreijse (Figure 6.5; Roelfsema, Lamme, and Spekreijse, 1998), and for illusory contours in 2011 by Roelfsema with his collaborators Aurel Wannig and Liviu Stanisor (Wanning, Stanisor, and Roelfsema, 2011). These properties were explained and

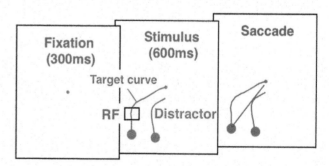

ATTENTION FLOWS ALONG CURVES: ROELFSEMA ET AL. (1998): MACAQUE V1

Crossed-curve condition: Attention flows across junction between smoothly connected curve segments Gestalt good continuation

FIGURE 6.5. A curve tracing task with monkeys was used by Roelfsema, Lamme, and Spekreijse in 1998 to demonstrate how spatial attention can flow along object boundaries. See the text for details.

SIMULATION OF ROELFSEMA ET AL. (1998)

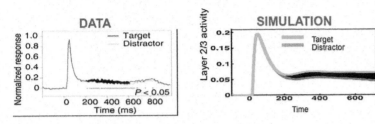

Attention directed only to far end of curve

Propagates along active layer 2/3 grouping to distal neurons

FIGURE 6.6. Neurophysiological data and simulation of how attention can flow along a curve. See the text for details.

simulated on the computer using the interactions between cortical layers in the LAMINART model in 2000 by my PhD student Rajeev Raizada and myself (Grossberg and Raizada, 2000). These explanations showed how attention can interact across cortical layers with the bipole grouping process that occurs in layer 2/3 of the model. The data and simulation thereof for a real contour are shown in Figure 6.6. Note the enhanced activity in the attended curve relative to that in the unattended curve when spatial attention reaches the position where the electrode was placed. Raizada and I also simulated, and thereby predicted, how such a boundary flow can occur along an illusory contour before the Roelfsema lab verified this property in 2011. How spatial attention flows along a boundary grouping will be explained in Chapter 10.

In addition, surface attention can flow from one part of a surface to another via filling-in. This is illustrated by how a top-down *attentional spotlight* (Figure 6.7), or spatially localized focus of attention, can enhance the contrast of the attended part of a surface, thereby triggering filling-in of that entire surface region. As filling-in is occurring, the resulting form-fitting enhanced filled-in surface activity sends bottom-up topographic excitatory signals from the surface to the PPC, thereby closing the feedback loop between V4 and PPC (Figure 6.2). Again, a surface-shroud resonance results, this time via a top-down, rather than a bottom-up, route.

When these boundary and surface properties act, a shroud that forms in response to the ipsilesional stimulus can flow between the ipsilesional and contralesional stimulus, thereby rendering the latter stimulus visible as well. I will also explain in Chapter 15 how this kind

of spatial attentional flow also helps to explain properties of social cognition, such as the *joint attention* that is shared between a teacher and a student who is watching and learning about the teacher's actions in space, albeit from a different viewpoint than that of the teacher (Grossberg and Vladusich, 2010), and how joint attention may break down during autism, with major effects on how these autistic individuals interact with others in educational and social situations (Grossberg and Seidman, 2006).

Unconscious processing of neglected object identity. Unconscious processing of neglected stimuli can occur in parietal patients to a much larger degree than in patients who have visual cortical lesions yet still exhibit what is called *blindsight*. Blindsight can occur in people who have lesions to cortical area V1 and thus cannot see, yet who can respond to these unseen visual stimuli. How this happens depends upon the lesion. For example, the brain region called the superior colliculus, or SC, contains a map of visual space that can control eye movements. Lesions of V1 may spare the pathways to the SC. The implicit, or unconscious, knowledge of parietal patients includes object attributes of neglected stimuli such as their color, shape, identity, and meaning (Mattingley, Bradshaw, and Bradshaw, 1995; McGlinchey-Berroth et al., 1993). These properties can be explained by the fact that feature-category resonances in the What cortical stream (Table 1.4 and Figures 1.19 and 2.2) can be triggered by visual cortical representations in order to control object learning, recognition, and prediction, and these resonances are

RECONCILING SPOTLIGHTS AND SHROUDS: TOP-DOWN ATTENTIONAL SPOTLIGHT BECOMES A SHROUD

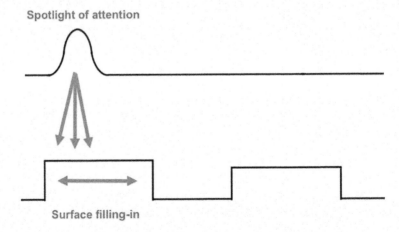

FIGURE 6.7. A top-down spotlight of attention can also be converted into a shroud. This process begins when the spotlight triggers surface filling-in within a region. Figure 6.8 shows how it is completed.

not eliminated by a parietal lesion in the Where cortical stream. In other words, there are distinct resonances for conscious seeing and knowing. It is easy to overlook this fact because these resonances are often triggered together, so that we know what familiar objects are when we see them, as I will further discuss later in this chapter. When the surface-shroud resonance for seeing is eliminated by a parietal lesion, the feature-category resonance for knowing can still be activated by visual stimuli.

A link between visual neglect and motor planning deficits: Seeing to reach. Patients who experience inferior parietal lobe lesions that lead to visual neglect often also experience abnormal motor biases. These include a reluctance to respond to the left, even with the ipsilesional right hand (Heilman et al., 1985), and slowness in initiating leftward movements of the right hand towards visual targets in the left hemispace (Mattingley et al., 1998). These data support the hypothesis that surface-shroud resonances between V4 and PPC create visibility properties whereby PPC can contribute to guiding actions to reachable surfaces.

Visual agnosia. The converse problem of visual agnosia can also occur when there is a lesion in inferotemporal cortex that spares prestriate cortex and parietal cortex. As Melvyn Goodale and his colleagues have shown, patients who exhibit visual agnosias and cannot therefore recognize basic properties of object shape can, as in the case of patient DF, nonetheless carry out accurate reaches to these objects (Goodale and Milner, 1992; Goodale et al., 1991).

IPL lesions lead to deficits in sustained visual attention. Lesions of the right IPL that cause visual neglect also impair the ability to maintain visual attention over sustained temporal intervals (Rueckert and Grafman, 1998). This is true both for visual and auditory attention (Robertson et al., 1997). This impairment can be explained by the fact that a surface-shroud resonance sustains spatial attention on an object surface (Figure 6.2), so that when a suitable parietal lesion occurs, this resonance collapses, and along with it the ability to sustain spatial attention.

Explaining data about visual crowding and situational awareness

An explanation of data about crowding requires more background about how ART, notably ARTSCAN, supports learning of recognition

categories. An outline of this explanation is immediately given to set the stage for further clarification in the subsequent paragraphs. As in the case of visual neglect, explaining the full range of crowding data also requires understanding of visual processes such as boundary completion, surface filling-in, and figure-ground separation.

An explanation and computer simulation of a main property of crowding data was presented in 2012 as part of a research project with my PhD student Nicholas Foley along with Ennio Mingolla using a variant of the ARTSCAN model that is called the *distributed ARTSCAN*, or dARTSCAN, model (Foley, Grossberg, and Mingolla, 2012) whose macrocircuit is shown in Figure 6.8. The model explained the 2007 crowding data of Christof Koch and Naotsugu Tsuchiya that I mentioned in Chapter 1; namely, that "subjects can attend to a location for many seconds and yet fail to see one or more attributes of an object at that location". Koch and Tsuchiya (2007) used this fact about crowding to claim that "top-down attention and consciousness . . . need not occur together". My explanation of crowding data follows from an analysis of how a surface-shroud resonance regulates both seeing and recognition of objects. In particular, unless a shroud can form around an individual object that occurs near other objects in a scene, then that object may be impaired in driving a feature-category resonance whereby it can be recognized (Table 1.4). Thus, although attention and consciousness are different processes, *how* spatial attention

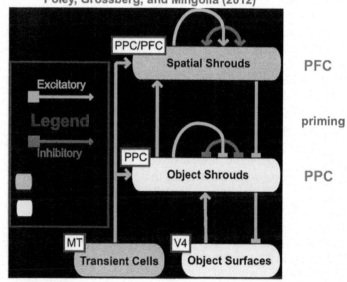

dARTSCAN SPATIAL ATTENTIONAL HIERARCHY
Foley, Grossberg, and Mingolla (2012)

FIGURE 6.8. The distributed ARTSCAN, or dARTSCAN, model includes spatial attention in both PPC and PFC, and both fast-acting attention, triggered by transient cells in Where cortical areas such as MT, and slower-acting surface-shroud resonances in What cortical areas such as V4 and PPC. See the text for details.

CROWDING:
VISIBLE OBJECTS AND CONFUSED RECOGNITION

Accurate target recognition requires increased flanker spacing at higher eccentricity

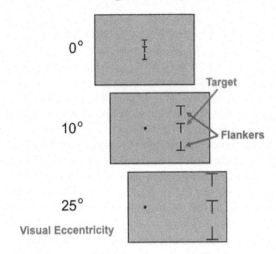

FIGURE 6.9. Crowding in the periphery of the eye can be avoided by expanding the size and spacing of the letters to match the cortical magnification factor.

influences conscious seeing and recognition can help to explain crowding data.

In the simplest crowding experiment, an object, such as a letter, is visible and recognizable when presented by itself, but it is not recognizable when the letter is presented concurrently with similar flanking letters (Levi, 2008; Toet and Levi, 1992). The distance between the target letter and the flanking letters at which the target letter becomes unrecognizable is a function of the eccentricity, and relative positions, of the target and the flankers on the retina. Larger letter sizes and spacing between the letters are needed to see and recognize a target letter as the eccentricity of the letters from the fovea increases (Figure 6.9; Bouma, 1970, 1973; Levi, 2008).

Given the proposed link within ARTSCAN between conscious perception and recognition, the most basic property of crowding has a simple explanation; namely, if several objects share a single surface-shroud resonance—that is, they are all covered by a single spatially-extended shroud—then they cannot be individually recognized.

Under what conditions can multiple objects all be covered by a single shroud? Cortical area V1 embodies a *cortical magnification factor* whereby spatial representations of retinal inputs (Figure 6.10a) get coarser as they are moved from the foveal region to the periphery (Figure 6.10b; Daniel and Whitteridge, 1961; Fischer, 1973; Polimeni, Balasubramanian, and Schwartz, 2006; Schwartz, 1984; Tootell et al., 1982). A

group of spatially close objects that have their own shrouds when viewed on the fovea may thus share a single shroud when they are viewed in the periphery if their mutual distances do not change. Since surface-shroud resonances create a link between conscious perception and recognition, objects that share a single shroud cannot be individually seen or recognized.

Figure 6.11 shows a simulation from my article with Nico Foley wherein target and flanker objects are moved together to larger retinal eccentricities without increasing their size or spacing. If they are sufficiently close together, the individual shrouds that covered them at the fovea merge into a single shroud at larger retinal eccentricities due to the larger receptive fields there. When this happens, recognition of individual objects breaks down. In contrast, if the objects and their spacing are magnified by the cortical magnification factor as they are moved to the periphery, as in Figure 6.11, then they can retain their own shrouds and can thus still be individually seen and recognized.

Confidence in dARTMAP model explanations was increased by using it to simulate other challenging psychophysical data that involve manipulations of spatial attention. These data include the following properties, that are explained and simulated in Foley, Grossberg, and Mingolla (2012): the smaller reaction times that are caused by intra-object attention shifts than inter-object attention shifts, or by shifts between visible objects and covertly cued locations (Brown and Denney, 2007; Egly, Driver, and Rafal, 1994); individual differences in reaction times for invalid cues in the two-object cueing paradigm (Roggeveen et al., 2009); and individual differences in detection rate of peripheral targets in useful-field-of-view tasks, which vary the span of spatial attention during

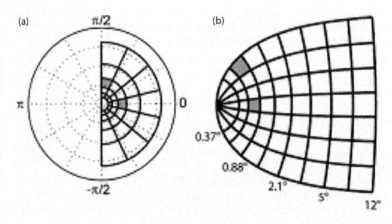

FIGURE 6.10. The cortical magnification factor transforms (A) artesian coordinates in the retina into (B) log polar coordinates in visual cortical area V1.

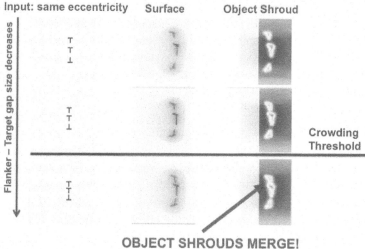

CROWDING:
VISIBLE OBJECTS AND CONFUSED RECOGNITION
Log compression and center-surround processing cause...

Input: same eccentricity   Surface   Object Shroud

Crowding Threshold

OBJECT SHROUDS MERGE!

FIGURE 6.11. If the sizes and distances between the letters stays the same as they are received by more peripheral parts of the retina, then all three letters may be covered by a single shroud, thereby preventing their individual perception and recognition.

detection tasks. Useful-field-of-view simulations include data from video game vs. non video game players (Green and Bavelier, 2003, 2007). The example of video game players is particularly interesting because modest experience in playing video games helps to rapidly increase an observer's useful-field-of-view, or situational awareness. This makes playing video games a potentially useful tool for visual rehabilitation, and also for training soldiers who need to take in a broad field of view to make potentially life-saving choices on the battlefield (Achtman, Green, and Bavelier, 2008).

Crowding percepts can be influenced by processes of perceptual grouping and figure-ground separation, just as they can influence the visual neglect properties that I discussed above. For example, in 2015, Michael Herzog, Bilge Sayim, Bitaly Chicherov, and Mauro Manassi (Herzog et al., 2015) asserted "that the spatial configuration across the entire visual field determines crowding. Only when one understands how all elements of a visual scene group with each other, can one determine crowding strength. We put forward the hypothesis that appearance (i.e., how stimuli look) is a good predictor for crowding, because both crowding and appearance reflect the output of recurrent processing . . . " Implicit in this assertion is that processes like boundary grouping and surface filling-in properties can influence, and be influenced by, the allocation of spatial attention, which in turn can influence conscious visual "appearance" and thus recognition, again through interactions of spatial attention in the Where cortical stream and recognition within the What cortical stream.

In 2016, Manassi and Herzog, along with Sophie Lonchampt and Aaron Clarke, described psychophysical experiments wherein adding additional flankers can lead to a release from, or reduction of, crowding (Manassi et al., 2016). Such results emphasize that surface-shroud resonances are only part of the story. Once psychophysical manipulations influence boundary grouping and surface filling-in properties that can cause more or less crowding, the utility of even using the word crowding begins to weaken. What one is then studying are how boundary completion, surface filling-in, spatial attention, and object attention processes interact to regulate seeing and recognizing. This is a huge issue that goes way beyond classical concerns of crowding experiments.

Towards a unified explanation of data about crowding, visual search, and neglect. Crowding data are not the only kind of data that require such an analysis. The same is true, as one of many examples, of data about visual search. Being able to rapidly and accurately search a visual scene is a crucial competence in real life. Many psychophysical experiments have been carried out to better understand how we do this. Often these experiments quantify how humans can find target objects amid distractors. For example, in Figure 6.12, how long does it take to detect the letter L among the distracting letters T in the left panel of the figure? How does this reaction time depend upon the relative positions of L amid the T's, as well as the number and spatial density of the T's? During this search, only shape differences between the L and T shapes are relevant. This is no longer the case we we try to detect the unique red vertical bar target in the right panel of Figure 6.12. This type of search is harder. It requires that a *conjunction* of the target's orientation *and* its color be used to identify it, because distractors can be vertical-and-blue or horizontal-and-red. In visual search, no less than

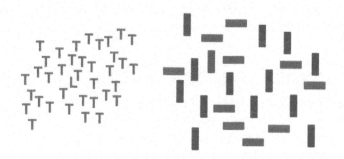

FIGURE 6.12. Pop-out of the L among T's can easily occur when inspecting the picture to the left. In the picture to the right, a more serial search is needed to detect the vertical red bar due to overlapping conjunctions of features.

crowding and neglect experiences, our brains use interactions between boundary, surface, spatial attention, and object attention processes to regulate seeing and recognizing. That is the main point of the article that I published with my PhD student William Ross with collaboration of Ennio Mingolla in 1994 (Grossberg, Mingolla, and Ross, 1994). The title of the article reflected this emphasis: "A Neural Theory of Attentive Visual Search: Interactions of Boundary, Surface, Spatial, and Object Representations". This article developed the Spatial Object Search, or SOS, model to explain and simulate many classical and recent visual search data whose properties are clarified by interactions of these four basic types of processes.

In summary, visual neglect, crowding (or the lack thereof), and visual search data probe different aspects of a similar set of interacting processes. Further experimental and modeling studies that combine crowding and visual search are much to be desired and, as illustrated by the modeling simulations with Arash Fazl and Nicholas Foley, need to include surface-shroud resonances as one part of a unifying theory.

Before leaving the discussion of the dARTMAP model in Figure 6.8, it is useful to note some of the processes that it describes which go beyond those simulated in the ARTSCAN model of Figure 6.3. These processes clarify why scenic features outside an object that is attended by a surface-shroud resonance do not just go dark, and how rapid changes in a scene outside this attentional focus can automatically attract attention. The former property is traced in dARTSCAN to the fact that spatial attention is represented in prefrontal cortex, or PFC, as well as the posterior parietal cortex, or PPC, and that PFC can read-out top-down spatial attentional priming signals to PPC. The latter property is traced to inputs from cortical area MT whose transient cells react quickly to changes in a scene. Thus Figure 6.8 includes influences on spatial attention of both rapidly reacting transient motion signals from MT in the Where stream, and more slowly changing sustained surface signals from V4 in the What stream. Chapter 12 will explain why both kinds of motion signals are important during imitation learning. Chapter 8 will explain how the transient signals from MT are generated in response to moving targets.

Explaining data about change blindness and motion-induced blindness: No map?

For a long time it was thought that the brain somehow builds up a global representation, or map, of the visual world from the momentary glimpses that it gets between eye movements. This view has been abandoned after being disconfirmed by many experiments. These experiments have led to a diametrically opposed view, that is well illustrated by remarkable phenomena called *change blindness* and *inattentional blindness*, which have been particularly well explored by contemporary American scientists like John Grimes, George McConkie, Hal Pashler, Ronald Rensink, Irwin Rock, and Daniel Simons, among others.

Inattentional blindness refers to the failure to notice an unexpected stimulus that is in your field of vision when other tasks are being performed that require your attention. Daniel Simons and his colleagues have developed some striking examples of this phenomena. One famous example is the Invisible Gorilla Study (Simons and Chabris, 1999). Here, subjects look at a video in which a group of people, some wearing white T-shirts and the others wearing black T-shirts, are passing a ball between them. The subject's task is to count how many times the players wearing white T-shirts pass the ball. As this is going on, a black gorilla walks across the scene. Most subjects do not notice the gorilla! As you can easily imagine, inattentional blindness phenomena have important implications for the reliability of eye witness testimony during jury trials, and shed light on how easy it is to have false memories.

Change blindness refers to fact that humans can be surprisingly insensitive to even massive changes in scenes. For example, in the Door Study, which was again conducted by the Simons lab, a pedestrian provides directions to a person on the street as a door is moved between him and the person (Simons and Levin, 1998). A different person, who was walking along behind the door is then substituted for the first person, and the pedestrian continues giving directions to the new person without noticing that he is talking to a different person! You can see these videos by going to the Simons web site www.simonslab.com/videos.html .

It can be argued that the Door Study is actually probing inattentional blindness, but in an example where there is just one big change. Indeed, there are many overlaps in mechanistic explanations of inattentional blindness and change blindness. In a purer set of examples of change blindness, a pair of pictures is flashed onto a screen in rapid alternation, with each picture separated by a blank screen for a moment. In one striking classical example that was described in 1997 by Ronald Rensink, Kevin O'Regan, and James Clark, alternating displays of an original and a modified scene are separated in time by brief blank fields (Rensink, O'Regan, and Clark, 1997). Even large changes that are persistently repeated between the alternating scenes—such as the removal and replacement of an airplane wing, or the change in color of a pair of trousers—may not be noticed for a long time, or ever. Look at the following video on YouTube and get ready to be astonished: https://www.youtube.com/watch?v=bh_9XFzbWV8 . The same thing will happen with essentially *any* natural scene in which you make big changes of some scenic part while alternating appearances of the altered scene with the original scene: https://www.youtube.com/watch?v=GOF-saZ1XSQ. In striking contrast, these changes are readily seen when spatial attention is directly focused at the scenic positions where the changes occur.

One mechanism that contributes to an explanation of change blindness is the competition for spatial attention that occurs across the parietal cortex, and that helps to select winning shrouds (Figure 6.2). The same property also played a role in explaining the deficit in awareness of visual neglect patients when stimuli are presented simultaneously on both sides of a display. This competition uses a network of cells that obey the membrane, or shunting, equations of neurophysiology. As I have explained in previous examples, when such cells compete in an on-center off-surround network, they tend to normalize the total activity across the network (Figure 1.7), so that activating more cells may make each cell less active, other things being equal. This property of *contrast normalization* (Grossberg, 1973, 1980; Heeger, 1992) implies that, when attention focuses upon one position, activity decreases at other positions.

A second important factor is that the alternating scenes are separated by blank intervals. Thus, each time a scene turns on or off, it activates cells across the entire scene that are sensitive to transient changes in each scenic input. I mentioned in Chapter 1 the importance of cells that are sensitive to transients in a scene when I discussed how our eyes jiggle back and forth through time to help discount retinal veins and the blind spot. There are both transient ON cells and OFF cells that respond to onsets and offsets of the alternating scenes, respectively. During the change blindness manipulation, these transient signals flood each just presented or withdrawn scene. These properties will be further explained in Chapters 7 and 8 when I discuss how we see, recognize, and track changing and moving objects.

The third important factor is that transient scenic changes automatically attract spatial attention (e.g., Corbetta and Shulman, 2002; Yantis and Jonides, 1990), a property that will also be further discussed in Chapter 8. When these three properties (contrast normalization, transient cell activation, attention automatically drawn to transients), work together in response to change blindness stimuli, spatial attention is spread thinly across the entire scene, so that only the most persistent scenic properties—the ones that occur in both scenes—may have enough activity to resonate sufficiently to be consciously seen. As soon as spatial attention is volitionally focused on the region of change, however, a strong surface-shroud resonance can form around that region and trigger conscious awareness.

Motion-induced blindness has been discussed at least since the 1965 article of Gwilym Grindley and Valerie Townsend (Grindley and Townsend, 1965; Ramachandran and Gregory, 1991). It is another intriguing phenomenon

that is closely related to change blindness. During motion-induced blindness, salient objects may fluctuate into and out of conscious awareness when superimposed on certain global motion patterns. For example, peripherally-viewed yellow dots may intermittently fluctuate in and out of consciousness when a blue-and-black rectangular grid that intersects and extends beyond them rotates around a flashing central fixation point. Look at the following YouTube video to experience this for yourself: https://www.youtube.com/watch?v=Hfrb94mKCJw. Many scientists have commented about factors that may influence this striking percept. For example, in 2001, Yoram Bonneh, Alexander Cooperman, and Dov Sagi (Bonneh, Cooperman, and Sagi, 2001, p. 798) wrote that motion-induced blindness may be influenced by "perceptual grouping effects, object rivalry, and visual field anisotropy . . . Disappearance might reflect a disruption of attentional processing . . . uncovering the dynamics of competition between object representations within the human visual system".

Many motion-induced blindness percepts may be explained by the same processes that have already been used to explain data about visual neglect and crowding. For example, boundary grouping helps to determine whether individual objects fluctuate into and out of awareness independently, or together when they are parts of a single object. Stephen Mitroff and Brian Scholl showed in 2005 how the latter kind of situation can occur, for example, when two discs are connected into a dumbbell by a single-pixel line (Mitroff and Scholl, 2005) These authors also wrote "that object representations can be formed and updated without awareness" by making changes in displays when they were out of awareness (e.g., connecting or disconnecting the discs with a line) and demonstrating how these changes could influence whether the objects reappeared simultaneously or separately. A boundary grouping can occur automatically and pre-attentively (e.g., Figure 4.32) and, once formed, enable spatial attention to flow along the entire grouping (Figures 6.5 and 6.6) as a conscious percept emerges through a surface-shroud resonance (e.g., Figure 6.2), in particular between the surface representation of the connected disks.

Motion-induced blindness also illustrates the role of transient detectors that continually refresh the moving grid and thereby support its visibility, whereas the peripheral stationary dots do not activate their transient detectors to the same degree when the observer fixates on a central flashing fixation point. This difference can strengthen the boundaries of the moving grid relative to those of the stationary dots, and therefore better enables grid boundaries to inhibit dot boundaries during boundary completion and competition (e.g., Figure 4.32).

In 2009, Thomas Wallis and Derek Arnold (Wallis and Arnold, 2009) presented data to support the idea that motion-induced blindness is influenced by *motion streak suppression*, which prevents moving objects from causing aftereffects that would leave a "comet's tail" of residual activation at positions that they have recently crossed. I will explain how such "comet's tails" are avoided in Chapter 7 when I explain how our visual systems suppress prolonged persistence of object boundaries in the wake of moving objects. There I will explain how, in response to any moving target, the visual boundary system triggers an antagonistic rebound after a boundary moves by in order to prevent uncontrolled boundary persistence, and consequent perceptual smearing, or streaking, in its wake. In 1994, my PhD student Gregory Francis and I, along with Ennio Mingolla (Francis, Grossberg, and Mingolla, 1994) quantitatively simulated many psychophysical data about visual persistence in which such an inhibitory rebound mechanism plays an important role. Significantly, activity-dependent transient responses help to cause these rebounds, since the circuits that rebound include gated dipoles (Figures 1.14 and 1.15).

When this transiently acting inhibition occurs as a grid boundary moves across a peripheral dot boundary, it can momentarily inhibit the dot boundary, and thus the filling-in of surface color and brightness within it. The inhibited surface cannot then compete for spatial attention and visibility. In the case where the stationary dots and the moving grid are yellow and blue, respectively, opponent color competition may additionally occur when they intersect in space because they are part of a gated dipole field (Figure 4.47), thereby directly suppressing the surface color of the stationary dot.

Explaining many data with the same model mechanisms

The prediction that surface-shroud resonances support conscious percepts of visual qualia is consistent with many additional FACADE and 3D LAMINART model simulations of the quantitative properties of consciously seen surfaces during 3D vision and figure-ground perception, including percepts of random dot stereograms (e.g., Figure 4.52; Fang and Grossberg, 2009); Necker cubes (e.g., Figure 4.43b; Grossberg and Swaminathan, 2004); unique and bistable transparency (Figure 1.4; Grossberg and Yazdanbakhsh, 2005); Panum's limiting case, dichoptic masking, the Venetian blind illusion, and DaVinci stereopsis (e.g., Figure 4.49; Cao and Grossberg, 2005; Grossberg and Howe, 2003; Grossberg and McLoughlin, 1997); texture segregation (e.g., Figures 3.17, 3.18, 4.33, and 4.34; Bhatt, Carpenter, and Grossberg, 2007; Grossberg and Pessoa, 1998); 3D shape-from-texture (Figure 3.21 and Chapter 11; Grossberg, Kuhlmann, and Mingolla, 2007); visual persistence (see Chapter 7; Francis and Grossberg,

1996; Francis, Grossberg, and Mingolla, 1994); Bregman-Kanizsa figure-ground separation, Kanizsa stratification, and the Munker-White, Benary cross, and checkerboard percepts (e.g., Figures 1.3 and 1.4; Kelly and Grossberg, 2000); the McCullough effect (Grossberg, Hwang, and Mingolla, 2002); neon color spreading and the watercolor illusion (e.g., Figures 3.10, 3.11, and 3.28; Grossberg and Mingolla, 1985a; Grossberg and Yazdanbakhsh, 2005; Pinna and Grossberg, 2005); and illumination-discounted and anchored brightness and color percepts (e.g., Figures 2.17, 2.18, 2.22, 3.35-3.37, 4.1-4.14; Grossberg and Hong, 2006; Grossberg and Todorovic, 1988; Hong and Grossberg, 2004). These unified explanations and simulations of many different kinds of surface percepts, and their quantitative properties in psychophysical data, provide accumulating evidence for the correctness of the prediction that surface-shroud resonances, interacting with boundary and surface perceptual processes, support percepts of conscious visual qualia.

Shrouds have complex internal structure that influences properties of visual search

These modeling results clarify that 3D surface representations are typically distributed over multiple depth-selective and color-selective Filling-In-Domains (Figure 3.22). The shrouds with which they resonate reflect these structural distinctions, which influence how easily different combinations of surface features can found during visual search (e.g., Figure 6.12; e.g., Grossberg, Mingolla, and Ross, 1994; He and Nakayama, 1992; Humphreys, Quinlan, and Riddoch, 1989; Nakayama and Silverman, 1986; Treisman and Gelade, 1980; Treisman and Gormican, 1988; Wolfe, 1994; Wolfe, Cave, and Franzel, 1989). These complexities of internal shroud structure in the parietal cortex (e.g., Silver and Kastner, 2009; Swisher et al., 2007) will not be further discussed in this book.

From View- and Position-Specific Categories to View- and Position-Invariant Categories

Conscious visual qualia are computed in retinotopic coordinates. I will now discuss how we learn invariant object recognition categories that can individually respond to multiple views, positions, and sizes of an object in a 2D image as we freely scan the scene with eye movements (Cao, Grossberg, and Markowitz, 2011; Fazl, Grossberg, and Mingolla, 2009; Foley, Grossberg, and Mingolla, 2012; Grossberg, 2009b; Grossberg, Markowitz, and Cao, 2011). Having learned such invariant object categories, I will then discuss how we can efficiently search for a valued object in in a 3D scene, even though, by learning an object category that is significantly invariant under position, we cannot use the category itself to localize the object in space (Chang, Grossberg, and Cao, 2014; Grossberg, Srinivasan, and Yazdanbakhsh, 2014). Along the way, I will offer explanations of data that seem to have no other explanations at the present time, including fascinating properties of our conscious visual experiences.

Let's begin with the observation that the visual qualia of an object that we consciously see in a scene shift in a direction opposite to each eye movement that moves our eyes to look at a different part of the scene. In other words, *conscious visual qualia are computed in retinotopic coordinates*, where retinotopic coordinates are the positions on the retina that the object activates with light signals. Understanding how this happens sheds light on data showing that percepts of visual qualia may be influenced by how objects activate cortical areas V1 and V2. For example, there is a lot of interest in understanding whether the same parts of the visual cortex are used when we imagine seeing an object or scene using visual imagery, and when we actually see the same object or scene. One way to compare brain responses to visual perception and visual imagery in humans is to use various brain imaging methods, such as positron emission tomography, or PET, and repetitive transcranial magnetic stimulation, or rTMS. Both of these imaging methods show activation of V1 during both kinds of percepts, and interference of both by applying rTMS to V1 (Kosslyn et al., 1999). How can these facts be reconciled with the hypothesis that a surface-shroud resonance is triggered between V4 and PPC? The simplest explanation is that V4 cannot operate if it does not receive inputs from V1. This fact does not, however, fully explain how V1 and V2 contribute to conscious percepts when they are both intact. My analysis below leads to additional insights.

Visual imagery: Basal ganglia volition converts top-down modulation to driving inputs. Before turning to this analysis, a related question can quickly be answered: How is visual imagery possible if top-down expectations are modulatory in their excitatory on-center, as the

ART Matching Rule proposes (Figure 1.25)? Would not conscious visual imagery require supra-threshold, indeed resonant, cell activation to occur? How does a modulatory top-down expectation cause a resonant activation? Figure 1.25 includes an answer to this question. Volitional signals can alter the balance between excitation and inhibition in the on-center of the top-down expectation by weakening inhibition relative to excitation. The on-center of the expectation can then fire targeted cells to suprathreshold values and lead to resonance. These volitional signals are controlled by the basal ganglia of the brain, which open and close gates that enable or prevent cognitive or motor circuits from completing their computations. Figure 6.13, which comes from a 2009 review article by Jessica Grahn, John Parkinson, and Adrian Owen, diagrams the basic property that different parts of the basal ganglia can gate the dynamics of different parts of the brain (Grahn, Parkinson, and Owen, 2009). This effect of the basal ganglia on whether cortical feedback is modulatory or driving is just one of many examples of basal ganglia volitional control that neural models have explained (Grossberg, 2016b).

From complementary consistency to figure-ground separation: Surface contours

Let us now consider how an invariant object category is learned during free scanning of a scene with eye movements, and how that analysis clarifies data about conscious seeing and recognition. In order to be able to focus spatial attention upon one object rather than another, the brain

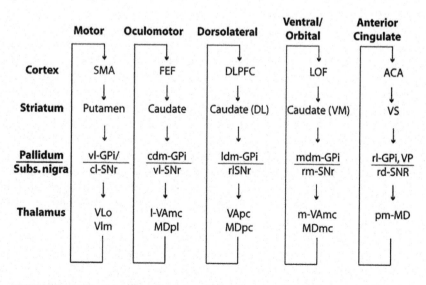

	Motor	Oculomotor	Dorsolateral	Ventral/Orbital	Anterior Cingulate
Cortex	SMA	FEF	DLPFC	LOF	ACA
Striatum	Putamen	Caudate	Caudate (DL)	Caudate (VM)	VS
Pallidum Subs. nigra	vl-GPi/ cl-SNr	cdm-GPi vl-SNr	ldm-GPi rlSNr	mdm-GPi rm-SNr	rl-GPi, VP rd-SNR
Thalamus	VLo Vlm	l-VAmc MDpl	VApc MDpc	m-VAmc MDmc	pm-MD

FIGURE 6.13. The basal ganglia gate perceptual, cognitive, emotional, and motor processes through parallel loops.

must first separate the surface representations of different objects from each other and from the visual background via figure-ground separation. Figure 4.51 summarizes one step in this process, which is closely linked to the way in which visual boundaries and surfaces are computed.

As noted in Chapters 3 and 4, visual boundaries and surfaces are computed using computationally complementary laws (Figure 3.7). How, then, is a consistent percept generated from these complementary processes? I call the process whereby the brain converts complementary boundary and surface computations into a consistent percept *complementary consistency*. I predicted how this is proposed to occur in a pair of articles in 1994 and 1997 (Grossberg, 1994, 1997). These articles, which were devoted to understanding how we see the world in depth, made the surprising prediction that the process that assures complementary consistency also initiates figure-ground separation. Because, as we will see in a moment, complementary consistency follows from simple feedback interactions between the boundary and surface cortical streams, it also follows that figure-ground separation is initiated in a simple way. This explanation helps to assuage the otherwise serious concern: How could evolution be smart enough to figure out a process that is as seemingly subtle as figure-ground separation?

The process that achieves complementary consistency is proposed to occur using feedback signals between boundary representations in the V2 interstripes and surface representations in the V2 thin stripes (Figure 1.21). As noted in numerous previous figures, object boundaries act as barriers to the filling-in of object surfaces. In addition, successfully filled-in surfaces generate topographic feedback signals to the boundaries that generated them. These feedback signals, which I call *surface contours* (Figure 4.51), are generated by contrast-sensitive on-center off-surround networks that act across space and within each depth. Because of their contrast-sensitivity, these networks generate output signals only at positions where they detect a rapid change in contrast across space. Such rapid contrast changes occur only at the contours of successfully filled-in surfaces, which are the surfaces that are surrounded by closed boundaries (Figure 4.48, bottom row, left column). Surface contours are not generated at positions where open boundaries occur (Figure 4.48, bottom row, right column) because the surface filling-in that is caused by feature contours within regions with open boundaries can spread to both sides of their boundaries, and thus do not generate large contrasts at boundary positions.

The example shown in Figures 4.50 and 4.51 illustrates the simple case where a rectangular boundary is viewed in depth, but only its left vertical boundary can be seen by both eyes, as often happens in examples of DaVinci stereopsis (Figure 4.49) when distant surfaces are partially occluded by nearer surfaces to different extents in the two eyes (Cao and Grossberg, 2005, 2012; Nakayama and Shimojo, 1990). As I discussed in Chapter 4, the surface contour signals that are generated at Depth 1 send excitatory signals to boundaries at their own depth and positions, and inhibitory signals to further depths at the corresponding positions (Figure 4.51). As a result, the *closed* boundary is strengthened, whereas open boundaries at the same positions and further depths are inhibited. This feedback assures complementary consistency by selecting and strengthening only the "correct" boundaries that generate surfaces which are worthy of further processing, and can project to object recognition regions in inferotemporal cortex and beyond.

Inhibition of spurious boundaries at further depths enables amodal completion to occur at Depth 2 behind the occluding rectangle between any collinear uninhibited boundaries that are generated by the image or scene, as it does in response to images in Figures 1.3 and 1.4. Figure-ground separation is hereby initiated by the surface contour feedback signals in cortical area V2 that achieve complementary consistency (Figure 6.14).

The main problem: Why inhibiting view categories does not inhibit invariant categories

The process that enables the brain to focus spatial attention on different surfaces must occur *after* their figure-ground separation occurs in V2, so that spatial attention *can* selectively focus on individual objects. With this constraint in mind, we can now turn to how the brain learns view-invariant categories as the eyes scan a scene.

Suppose that the first view of a novel object leads to rapid learning of a view-specific category in posterior inferotemporal cortex (ITp). Suppose that this view category also activates some cells in anterior inferotemporal cortex (ITa) that will become a view-invariant object category via associative learning with multiple view-specific categories (Figure 6.3). Each view-specific category is reset to enable the next view-specific category to be learned when the object view changes sufficiently. When the first view-specific category is reset, the input is removed that it generated from ITp to ITa, and that initially activated the emerging view-invariant category.

We can now ask the main design question: How does the brain prevent the invariant object category in ITa from also being reset when its input from ITp shuts off? How does the brain maintain activity of these ITa cells while they are associated with multiple view-specific categories

PERCEPTUAL CONSISTENCY AND FIGURE-GROUND SEPARATION

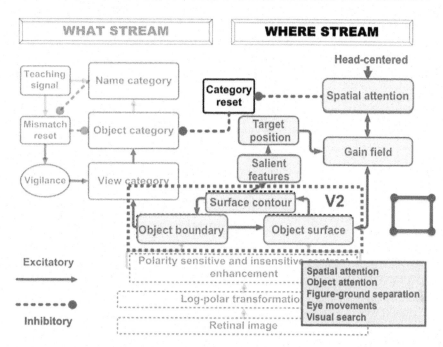

FIGURE 6.14. Feedback from object surfaces to object boundaries uses surface contours. This feedback assures complementary consistency and enables figure-ground separation. A corollary discharge of the surface contours can be used to compute salient object feature positions.

of a single object—categories that *are* shut off as the eyes move to focus on other views of the object—and thereby become a view-invariant category with which to represent this object?

Attentional shroud inhibits reset of invariant object category during object search. ARTSCAN predicts that an object's *preattentively* formed surface representation in V4 activates an attentional shroud, even before the brain learns to recognize the surface as representing a particular object (Figures 6.2 and 6.14). This shroud persists via a surface-shroud resonance during active scanning of an object (Figure 6.15). The shroud protects the view-invariant category from getting reset, even while view-specific categories are reset, as the eyes explore an object. The shroud does this by *inhibiting the reset mechanism* while spatial attention is focused on the object. This inhibition is carried by the inhibitory connections from the Spatial Attention to Category Reset processing stages in Figures 6.3 and 6.14 (red pathway from Spatial Attention to Category Reset). The reset mechanism is found in the parietal cortex, as is the attentional shroud.

When spatial attention shifts from an object, its shroud collapses, thereby disinhibiting the Category Reset stage in PPC (see Figure 6.14, red pathway from Category Reset to Object Category stage). A transient burst of inhibition is then released that resets the active invariant object

category in ITa. The collapse of the shroud hereby enables the eyes to move to and attend another surface *and* allows new view-specific and view-invariant object categories to be learned because the previously active invariant category has been inhibited. The cycle can then repeat itself.

Human and monkey data support shroud reset properties: Explanations and predictions

Is there experimental evidence to support this predicted series of events? Happily, just as my 2009 article with Arash Fazl was being published, Yu-Chin Chiu and Steven Yantis were publishing a 2009 article in *The Journal of Neuroscience* about experiments using rapid event-related MRI in humans to document how a surface-shroud resonance in the Where/How stream may protect an emerging view-invariant category from being prematurely reset in the What stream (Chiu and Yantis, 2009). These authors found that a shift of spatial attention evokes a transient domain-independent signal in the medial superior parietal lobule that corresponds to a shift in categorization

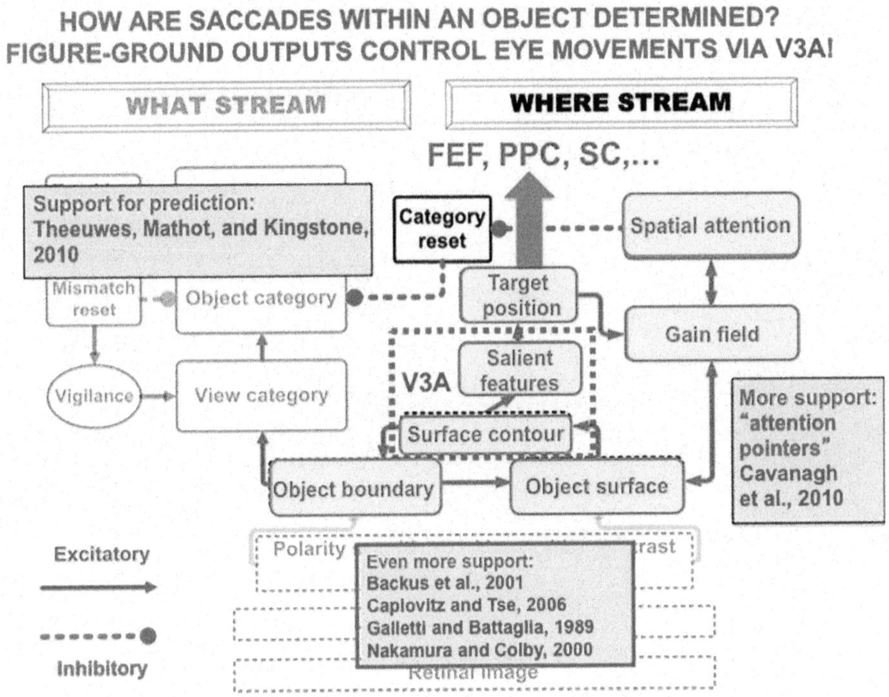

FIGURE 6.15. The largest salient feature signal is chosen to determine the next target position of a saccadic eye movement. This target position signal self-inhibits to enable the next most salient position to be foveated. In this way, multiple feature combinations of the object can be foveated and categorized. This process clarifies how the eyes can explore even novel objects before moving to other objects. These eye movements enable invariant categories to be learned. Each newly chosen target position is, moreover, an "attention pointer" whereby attention shifts to the newly foveated object position.

rules. In ARTSCAN (Figure 6.14), collapse of an attentional shroud (spatial attention shift) disinhibits the parietal reset mechanism (transient signal) that leads to inhibition of the active invariant object category and instatement of a new one (shift in categorization rules). The transient signal is "domain-independent" because the parietal reset mechanism can be inhibited by spatial attention in PPC that focuses upon *any* object surface, and can reset *any* active invariant category in ITa when it is disinhibited. In other words, the category reset population of cells should receive converging inhibitory signals from many parts of PPC and emit diverging inhibitory signals to many parts of ITa. This experiment provides a useful marker for experimentally testing additional properties of the ARTSCAN model and its variants.

A surface-shroud resonance enables the eyes to explore multiple object views

Exploring the same object for awhile using attentional pointers to the next saccadic target. In order for a view-invariant object category to be learned, the eyes need to look at several views of the object before saccading to attend a

different object. Indeed, if saccadic eye movements were made randomly, jumping erratically from one part of a scene to another, then invariant object category learning would be impossible. The neural circuits in Figure 6.14 and 6.15 automatically enable the eyes to explore several salient features of one object before jumping to a different object, thereby enabling invariant object category learning to occur.

Using the circuit in Figure 6.14, I can now explain how eye movements can scan salient features of a single object before leaving that object to inspect another object. In particular, surface contour signals can generate target position commands whereby eye movements can foveate salient features of an object surface while a surface-shroud resonance maintains spatial attention upon that surface (Figures 6.14 and 6.15). This happens because surface contours are computed using a contrast-sensitive on-center off-surround network whose activities are largest at high curvature positions along the object boundary (see the rectangular red surface contour with higher activity positions in purple at its corners in Figure 6.14; also note the white open circles in Figure 4.51). These high curvature positions mark the locations of salient features. They can therefore be chosen, one at a time, by a second competitive network that chooses the most active position along the surface contour as a target position for the next eye movement. This is accomplished in the Figure 6.14 circuit by a competitive choice at the Target Position stage of the largest surface contour signal from the Salient Features stage. As each choice generates output signals, it inhibits itself by a recurrent inhibitory interneuron, as in Figure 1.6. In this way, the eyes can explore salient features while the object is attended, and different view-specific categories can be learned during this exploratory process.

This model property clarifies psychophysical data which have demonstrated that the eyes prefer to explore the same object for awhile before jumping to look at a different object, This property was reported in 2010 in psychophysical experiments by Jan Theeuwes, Sebastiaan Mathot, and Alan Kingstone (Theeuwes, Mathot, and Kingstone, 2010). We can now understand these data from the perspective of learning view-invariant object categories. The target positions to which the eyes move occur as a result of shifts of spatial attention across the attended object surface, and have properties that were called *attention pointers* in a 2010 article by Patrick Cavanagh, Amelia Hunt, Arash Afraz, and Martin Rolfs (Cavanagh et al., 2010); see Figure 4.51. Both the Theeuwes and Cavanagh experiments were published in 2010, after our first ARTSCAN papers were published. Their data may thus be viewed as experimental support for model predictions.

Transforming between vision and action occurs after figure-ground separation: V3A! Where does this transformation from visual computations to motor commands occur in the brain? Wherever it occurs in the brain, it must occur *after* the processing stage where objects are separated from one another by figure-ground separation. Otherwise, objects could not be individually attended in space. As I noted above, the FACADE theory of 3D vision and figure-ground perception (see Chapter 11) proposes that a key stage of figure-ground separation occurs in cortical area V2 (Figure 6.14). Thus the transformation from surface attention to the control of eye movement target positions must occur after V2. ARTSCAN proposes that it occurs in cortical area V3A (Figure 6.15). Supportive data were reported in a 2007 article by Gideon Caplovitz and Peter Tse (2007, p. 1179) who noted that: "neurons within V3A . . . process continuously moving contour curvature as a trackable feature . . . not to solve the 'ventral problem' of determining object shape but in order to solve the 'dorsal problem' of what is going where". ARTSCAN explains how this may happen.

Predictive remapping: Gain fields maintain shroud stability

Data about *predictive remapping* are particularly relevant to understanding how we consciously see visual qualia that are computed in *retinotopic coordinates* (Figure 6.16). In other words, we see whatever the eyes currently foveate

in the center of our view, with previously foveated parts of a scene shifted to positions that lie in a direction opposite to that of the last eye movement. When a large eye movement occurs on an object surface, why does not the newly foveated position sometimes lie off positions of the shroud, thereby causing a collapse of the shroud as it the eye moves? Such a collapse would disinhibit category reset cells, which can then inhibit the emerging invariant category, thereby preventing invariant object category learning from proceeding. Somehow the currently active shroud must remain stable as the eyes explore the surface of one object.

ARTSCAN proposes that this is accomplished by computing shrouds in *head-centered coordinates* that do not move when the eyes move. This transformation of a retinotopic surface representation into a head-centered shroud is proposed to occur by using *gain fields* (Figure 6.16). Gain fields are populations of cells that are activated by outflow eye movement target position signals. They are used to transform the retinotopic coordinates of the attended object surface into the head-centered coordinates of the attentional shroud. The (target position)-to-(gain field) signals that are used to update a head-centered shroud are assumed to occur very quickly, before an eye movement is complete, to preserve the shroud's head-centered representation.

The process that controls this kind of rapid coordinate change is often called *predictive remapping*. Predictive remapping has been used to interpret neurophysiological data about how parietal representations are updated by intended eye movements (Duhamel et al., 1992; Gottlieb et al., 1998; Mathot and Theeuwes, 2010a; Melcher, 2007, 2008, 2009; Saygin and Sereno, 2008; Sommer and Wurtz, 2006; Tolias et al., 2001; Umeno and Goldberg, 1997) by using gain fields (Andersen, Essick, and Siegel, 1985, 1987; Andersen and Mountcastle, 1983; Deneve and Pouget, 2003; Fazl, Grossberg, and Mingolla, 2009; Gancarz and Grossberg, 1999; Grossberg and Kuperstein, 1986; Pouget, Dayan, and Zemel, 2003; see the parietal area LIP that is labeled Gain Field in Figure 6.3. The ARTSCAN model explains how the process of predictive mapping may support several closely coordinated processes in a unified neural architecture, including how spatial attention is maintained upon an object surface during conscious seeing of that object, how eye movements to salient features within the object are controlled, and how view-invariant object categories are learned (Figures 6.14-6.16). Data explanations by the model provide multiple experimental markers in several brain regions that are proposed to interact as a coordinated system. Further tests of the predicted interactions between spatial and object attention, figure-ground separation, predictive mapping, eye movements, and visual search with psychophysical, multiple microelectrode, and functional neuroimaging methods should disclose a wealth of important new information about these fundamental processes, and how they interact.

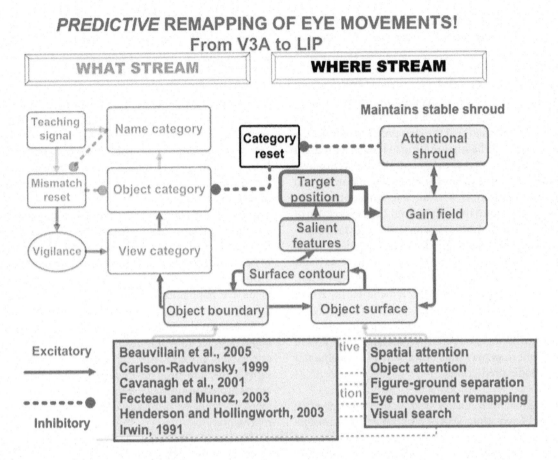

FIGURE 6.16. The same target position signal that can command the next saccade also updates a gain field that predictively maintains the attentional shroud in head-centered coordinates, even before the eye movement is complete. This process keeps the shroud invariant under eye movements, so that it can continue to inhibit reset of an emerging invariant category as it is associated with multiple object views, even while the conscious surface representation shifts with each eye movement in retinotopic coordinates. This updating process is often called *predictive remapping*.

Both retinotopic and spatial coordinates are needed during active vision

Explaining how the visual world appears to remain stable as our eyes actively scan a scene requires an analysis of how interacting combinations of retinotopic and head-centered, or spatial, representations work together in the neocortex. As I noted above, conscious visual percepts shift with the positions that are foveated by the eyes, and are thus computed in retinotopic coordinates. Attentional shrouds, in contrast, are computed in spatial coordinates to maintain sustained spatial attention upon an object surface, while enabling an invariant object category to be learned. Functional neuroimaging (fMRI) data that were published in 2011 by David Burr and Maria Morrone (Burr and Morrone, 2011, p. 504) illustrate this subtlety. These authors write: "We firstly report recent evidence from imaging studies in humans showing that many brain regions are tuned in spatiotopic [head-centered] coordinates, but only for items that are actively attended." The current theory provides a clear mechanistic explanation of this otherwise potentially confusing assertion, since it is "attention pointers" that rapidly update gain fields via predictive remapping to maintain spatiotopic shroud stability during eye movements that scan an attended object, even while the conscious visual representation of the object surface moves around with the eyes.

Learning view-, position-, and size-invariant object categories: Persistent IT cells

Additional experimental tests can be derived from an ARTSCAN extension that proposes how view-, position-, and size-invariant object categories are learned, not just view-invariant ones. This particular discovery may be useful in many important applications in technology that have not yet been fully exploited, since it offers a self-organizing way to solve pattern recognition problems using unsupervised learning without a priori constraints on the objects to be recognized.

In particular, my PhD student Jeffrey Markowitz, colleague Yongqiang Cao, and I published in 2011 an article that developed the *positional ARTSCAN*, or pARTSCAN, extension of the ARTSCAN model to explain how these additional object category invariances can be learned (Cao, Grossberg, and Markowitz, 2011). Remarkably, this extension required only that the model incorporate known properties of IT cells that exhibit persistent activity after their triggering inputs shut off (Figure 6.17; Brunel, 2003; Fuster and Jervey, 1981; Miyashita and Chang, 1988; Tomita et al., 1999). These IT cells with persistent activity were modeled in pARTSCAN as *view category integrator cells* (Figure 6.18) The view category integrator stage in pARTSCAN occurs between the view category and object category stages (Figure 6.3). A view category integrator cell, unlike a view category cell, is not reset when the eyes explore new views of the same object. It gets reset along with the invariant object category stage when its attentional shroud collapses due to a shift of spatial attention to a different object. This small addition enables learning of size- and positional-invariance as well as view-invariance.

The next two paragraphs explain how view category integrators lead to full invariance. These paragraphs can be skipped if the reader would prefer to immediately read about the interesting data that this invariance helps to explain, data which strongly support the hypothesis that a reset signal inhibits an active invariant category in ITa when a shroud collapses in PPC during a spatial attention shift to another object.

Without the view category integrator, the following problem can occur, that is summarized in Figures 6.19a-6.19c: Suppose that, as in Figure 6.19a, an object P is foveated and triggers learning of view-specific category V and view-invariant object category O. If the same object P appears in the periphery of the retina, as in Figure 6.19b, the model learns a new view-specific category V1 which in turns activates object category O1. Once a saccadic eye movement foveates object P (Figure 6.19c), it activates the previously learned view-specific category V and object category O. Without the view category integrator, view category V1 is shut off during the saccade and it cannot learn to be associated with the object category O. This reset event is depicted with the open circles and Xed dashed line connection. As a result, object P learns to activate two object categories O and O1 corresponding to foveal and peripheral positions, respectively, and the same object at different positions can create different object categories.

Figures 6.19d-6.19f show how a view category integrator keeps its object from proliferating multiple invariant object categories. In Figures 6.19d and 6.19e, the view category integrators T and T1 preserve the activities of view categories V and V1 and learn connections to object categories O and O1. In Figure 6.19f, after the object P is foveated again, T1 is still active due to persistent activity, even though V1 is shut off by a saccade. Therefore, view category integrator T1 can be associated with the originally learned invariant object category O, so invariant category proliferation is prevented.

Target swapping data: Why catastrophic forgetting of invariant categories does not happen. Given its new ability to categorize objects that are viewed at non-foveated positions, the model was able to explain and simulate neurophysiological data from articles published in 2008 and 2010 by Nuo Li and James DiCarlo (Li and DiCarlo, 2008, 2010). The 2008 article showed, in particular, that features from different objects can be merged through learning within a single invariant IT category when monkeys are presented with an object that is swapped with another object during an eye movement to foveate the original object (Figure 6.20).

PERSISTENT ACTIVITY IN IT

Physiological data show that persistent activity exists in IT
Fuster and Jervey (1981); Miyashita and Chang (1988); Tomita et al. (1999)

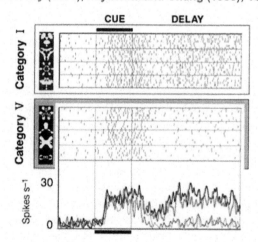

Adapted from Tomita et al. (1999, Nature)

FIGURE 6.17. Persistent activity in IT cells is just what is needed to enable view-invariant object category learning by ARTSCAN to be generalized to view-, position-, and size-invariant category learning by positional ARTSCAN, or pARTSCAN. See the text for details.

pARTSCAN: POSITIONALLY-INVARIANT OBJECT LEARNING
Cao, Grossberg, and Markowitz (2011)

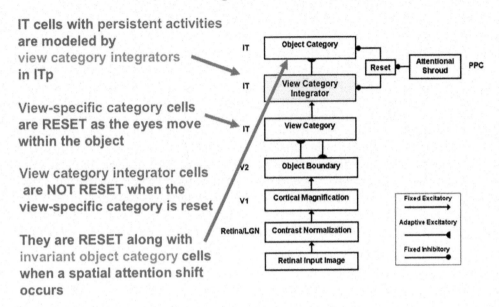

IT cells with persistent activities
are modeled by
view category integrators
in ITp

View-specific category cells
are RESET as the eyes move
within the object

View category integrator cells
are NOT RESET when the
view-specific category is reset

They are RESET along with
invariant object category cells
when a spatial attention shift
occurs

FIGURE 6.18. The pARTSCAN model can learn view-, position-, and size-invariant categories by adding view category integrator cells that have the properties of persistent neurons in IT. These integrator cells get reset with the invariant object category, not the view category.

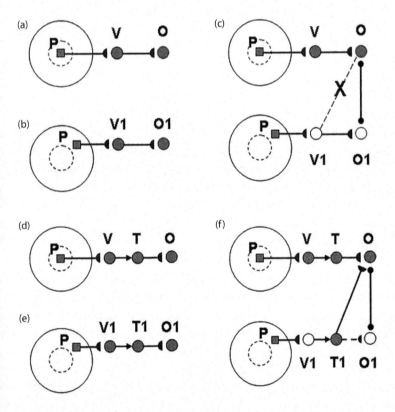

FIGURE 6.19. The various parts of this figure explain why persistent activity is needed in order to learn positionally-invariant object categories, and how this fails when persistent activity is not available. See the text for details.

Why does not such a learned merging of features across objects lead to catastrophic forgetting of *all* learned invariant recognition categories? pARTSCAN simulates the swapping data by showing how, because the swap occurs during an eye movement, the swap occurs before the animal can shift its spatial attention, so it does not activate the reset mechanism. Thus the brain has no way to prevent the views of different objects from being associated with a single invariant category. The swapping procedure hereby defeats the brain's solution of the view-to-object binding problem.

Prediction: Vary the ISI in a combined shroud and swapping experiment. The Li and DiCarlo (2008, 2010) target swapping paradigm may be combined with the Chiu and Yantis (2009) attention shift paradigm to further test the model prediction of how spatial attention may modulate learning of invariant object categories. The prediction is that there should not be a transient parietal burst under the usual target swapping conditions, hence the invariant object category in ITa is not reset, so features from the two different objects could be associated with it. As the delay between the initial target and the swap is increased, a reset should occur at a sufficiently

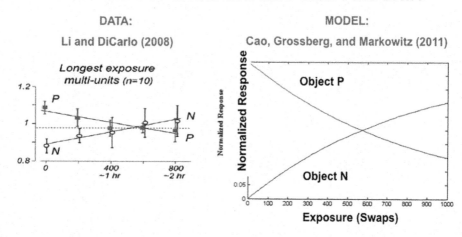

SIMULATION OF LI AND DICARLO SWAPPING DATA

FIGURE 6.20. pARTSCAN can simulate the IT cell recoding that Li and DiCarlo reported in their swapping experiments because the swapping procedure happens without causing a parietal reset burst to occur. Thus the originally activated invariant category remains activated and can get associated with the swapped object features.

long inter-stimulus interval. When that happens, the learning of merged categories should either be prevented or significantly attenuated.

Explaining the tradeoff between object selectivity and tolerance. Many additional paradoxical data have been explained by these concepts. Each explanation constitutes a detailed mechanistic prediction that can inspire and benefit from additional experimental tests.

Many of the explanations above concern how spatial attention coordinates eye movements and invariant category learning. Yet another kind of data about spatial attention is that it can increase the perceived brightness of an attended surface, as illustrated by how a surface-shroud resonance delivers positive feedback to the attended surface in Figure 6.2. This property was reported in 2000 in psychophysical experiments of Marisa Carrasco, Cigdem Penpeci-Talgar, and Miguel Eckstein, and in 2003 in neurophysiological experiments of John Reynolds and Robert Desimone (Carrasco et al, 2000; Reynolds and Desimone, 2003), among other studies.

Yet another kind of data that the current theory explains concerns the type of positional category invariance that can be learned. Perfect positional invariance cannot be learned if only because of limitations that are imposed by the cortical magnification factor (Figure 6.19). Because receptive field sizes get bigger in the periphery of the retina, one would expect different degrees of position invariance and response selectivity when objects are processed at different positions on the retina. In 2007, Davide Zoccolan, Minjoon Kouh, Tomaso Poggio, and James DiCarlo sharpened our understanding of how this happens through their report of a trade-off between object selectivity and tolerance during neurophysiological recordings of cell firing patterns

of monkey IT cells (Zoccolan et al., 2007). These data were simulated in another 2011 article with my colleagues Cao and Markowitz (Grossberg, Markowitz, and Cao, 2011). Figure 6.21 shows the data and one of our computer simulations. The tradeoff shows, perhaps not surprisingly, that IT cells with greater position invariance, or tolerance, respond less selectively to natural objects, whereas cells with less tolerance exhibited higher selectivity. In order to represent the effect of the cortical magnification factor, we simulated these data using the ART model with multiple spatial scales, with scale size increasing further from the foveal region to mirror the cortical magnification factor. The inputs to the model were the same kind of natural images that were used to train the monkeys.

Another important property of this computer simulation was, as in any ART explanation, that a level of vigilance had to be chosen (Figure 5.29). Because the task required only passive viewing by the monkeys, the vigilance was chosen low. A direct estimate of vigilance was not made during the experiment, but future variations on it might want to consider such a measure in the light of the book's explanations of how vigilance is controlled; e.g., Figure 5.43.

Such an additional measure of vigilance would also be valuable in enhancements of other experiments where vigilance has not traditionally been measured, since it could shed valuable light on performance. In this regard, we also did a simulation of neurophysiological data from IT about invariant recognition, but here the task was performed at high vigilance. This experiment was published in 2009 by Athena Akrami, Yan Liu, Alessandro Treves, and Bharathi Jagadeesh (Akrami et al., 2009) to measure IT cell firing as images were morphed from one into another, such as from an image of a dinosaur into one of a Buddha (Figure 6.22). An image was presented for 320 milliseconds before

TRADE-OFF IN IT CELL RESPONSE PROPERTIES
Inferotemporal cortex cells with greater
position invariance **respond less selectively to**
natural objects

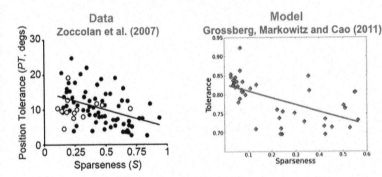

Invariance~tolerance
Selectivity~sparseness

FIGURE 6.21. pARTSCAN can also simulate the trade-off in IT cell responses between position invariance and selectivity that was reported by Zoccolan et al. (2007). This trade-off limits the amount of position invariance that can be learned by a cortical area like V1 that is constrained by the cortical magnification factor.

a delay of from 700–1100 milliseconds, followed by a choice between two images, one of which was a morph of the original image and the other was not. High vigilance was used to simulate these data because this task required monkeys to make active discriminations of image morphs, and between targets and non-targets. Figure 6.23 shows the data in the left column and the model simulation in the right column. Thus, in addition to simulating very different kinds of data about IT cell firing properties,

AKRAMI ET AL. SIMULATION:
A CASE OF HIGH VIGILANCE

Tested on morphs between image pairs

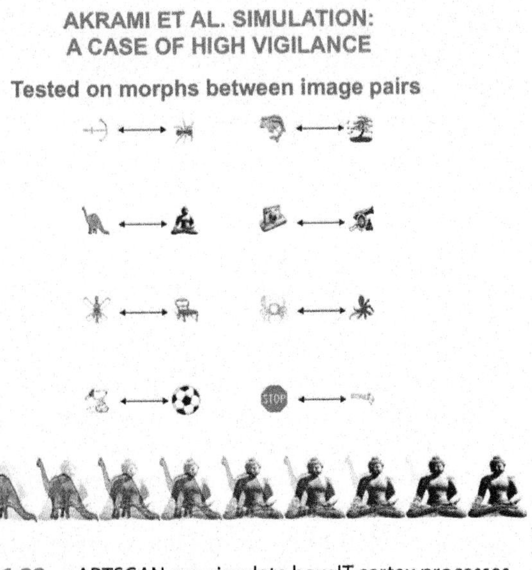

FIGURE 6.22. pARTSCAN can simulate how IT cortex processes image morphs, when it learns with high vigilance. See the text for details.

these simulations also showed the importance once again of task-selective setting of the vigilance level.

Perceptual stability: Binocular fusion during eye movements

Predictive remapping with gain fields is not only used to maintain shroud stability, as it is in Figure 6.16. It also directly impacts how a 3D scene is consciously seen in retinotopic coordinates as it is scanned with eye movements, even while the scene appears to remain stable as our eyes scan in. In particular, it seems obvious that our brains seamlessly maintain binocular fusion as eye movements occur, thereby supporting stable percepts through time of the world in depth.

This apparent simplicity disguises complex underlying machinery, as can be realized by noting that each eye movement causes each of our foveas to process a different set of scenic features on each retina. Each eye looks at the world from a slightly different position. When both eyes look at a particular position (position A in Figure 4.18), that position is processed by the photosensitive fovea (Figure 3.4). All features that are processed by the eyes at non-foveal positions (e.g., position B in Figure 4.18) are registered at different positions on their respective retinas (e.g., positions B_l and B_r on the left and right retinas are activated by B). These different positions relative to those on the fovea of the same eye (e.g., positions A_l and A_r in Figure 4.18) define a *binocular disparity*. Binocular disparities change in a systematic way when objects are viewed at different distances from the eyes, with the disparities of objects at longer distances being smaller than those of objects at shorter distances, other things being equal. The brain uses these binocular disparities, along with other information, to generate estimates of how far different parts of objects are from the eyes.

With this information in mind, now consider what happens when an observer views different parts of an object that is seen in depth. Each eye movement foveates the eyes on a different set of object features. As a result, new combinations of features have to be binocularly fused. If all representations of binocularly fused features were computed only in retinotopic coordinates, then there would be temporal breaks in binocular fusion after each eye movement. Such breaks would undermine the perceived stability of the scene and are not consciously perceived. How does the brain convert these intermittent fusions into a stable 3D percept that persists across eye movements to create the impression of a stable visual world?

IT RESPONSES TO IMAGE MORPHS

Akrami et al. (2009)

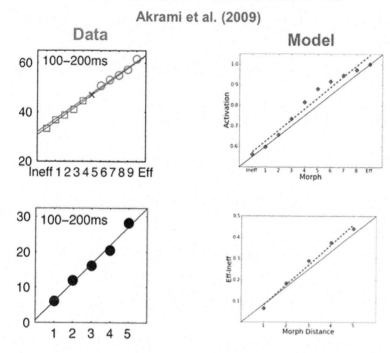

FIGURE 6.23. Data from Akrami et al. (2009) and our simulation of it. See the text for details.

Although the apparent stability of the visual world during eye movements is so familiar that it does not initially seem to require explanation, this is no longer the case when we binocularly fuse a random dot stereogram or a Magic Eye autostereogram, in which the number of salient fusable features is less than in a typical natural scene. A random dot stereogram consists of a pair of images, each composed of a random array of dots (Figure 6.24, top row). The second image is constructed from the first one by imagining one or more objects in that image, and shifting those objects in the second image to create a binocular disparity between the shifted parts of the image. Where the shifted image covers old dots, they are removed. Where the shifted image leaves some empty spaces, they are filled with more random dots. Thus, both images still contain random dots, but they contain within them hidden pairs of objects that can be seen only by correlating their disparate dot features.

It may take tens or hundreds of milliseconds to *initially* binocularly fuse the left and right eye images in these stereograms. Figure 6.24 (bottom row) shows the 3D surface percept that is generated by the 3D LAMINART model in response to the binocular stereogram in Figure

6.24 (top row). This simulation was published in 2009 with my PhD student Liang Fang (Fang and Grossberg, 2009), along with simulations of the conscious 3D surface percepts that are generated in response to sparse stereograms (that is, stereograms where very few dots can generate continuous surface percepts in depth), and to stereograms with partially occluded objects (notably a stereogram of the image in Figure 1.3 that is composed entirely of random dots).

After fusion occurs, if you scan the fused image with eye movements, fusion is maintained even though all the retinotopic matches are different after each eye movement. Why does not each eye movement require tens or hundreds of milliseconds to binocularly fuse each new set of retinotopic matches?

The 3D ARTSCAN model that I published in 2014 extends ARTSCAN to model how we see and learn to recognize the world in depth. I developed this extension with my PhD student Karthik Srinivasan and my colleague Arash Yazdanbakhsh (Grossberg, Srinivasan, and Yazdanbakhsh, 2014). 3D ARTSCAN predicts how this extension can be accomplished by augmenting the ARTSCAN machinery in Figures 6.14-6.16 with additional processes of predictive remapping. In addition to the predictive remapping that enables a head-centered attentional

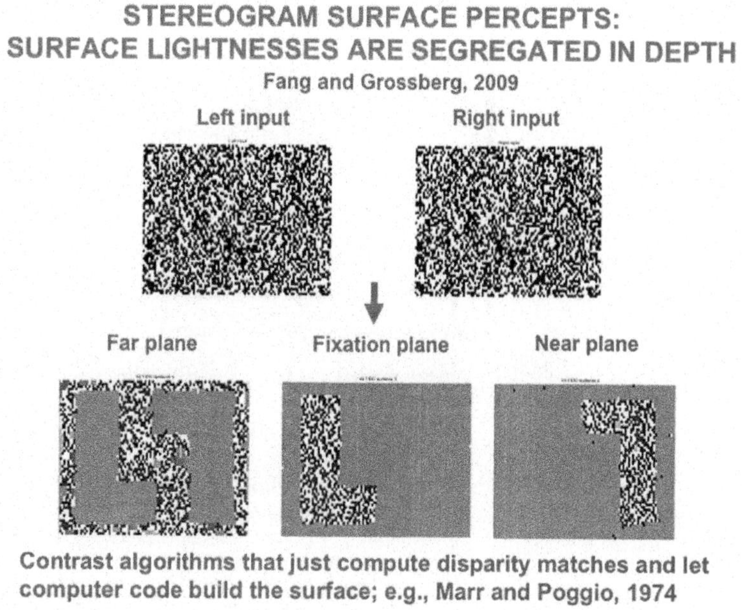

STEREOGRAM SURFACE PERCEPTS:
SURFACE LIGHTNESSES ARE SEGREGATED IN DEPTH

Fang and Grossberg, 2009

FIGURE 6.24. Left and Right eye stereogram inputs are constructed to generate percepts of objects in depth. These percepts include the features of the objects, not only their relative depths, a property that is not realized in some other models of stereopsis. See the text for details.

shroud to maintain its stability during eye movements and thereby modulate learning of invariant object categories, predictive remapping circuitry with additional gain fields enables head-centered binocular boundary representations to maintain their stability during eye movements, and thereby to stabilize their surface filling-in of conscious qualia in retinotopic binocular surface representations (Figure 6.25). The 3D ARTSCAN model simulates why and how breaks in binocular fusion are not seen in retinotopic binocular surface percepts because their head-centered binocular boundary representations are predictively updated before each eye movement is complete.

Figure 6.25 summarizes three of the gain fields, encircled in red, at different stages of processing, that support such seamless percepts. The gain field that maintains the stability of the shroud is highlighted in the purple box that surrounded the processing stages which generate a surface-shroud resonance. The gain field to the lower right transforms a surface contour that is computed in retinotopic coordinates into one that is computed in head-centered coordinates. It can then continue to support the stability of a binocular invariant boundary, also computed in head-centered coordinates, during the eye movement.

The gain field that is activated by this invariant binocular boundary converts it back into retinotopic coordinates so that it can control the filling-in of monocular and binocular surface percepts that are also computed in retinotopic coordinates. Additional gain fields, shown in Figure 6.26, regulate the formation of monocular and binocular boundaries in retinotopic and head-centered coordinates. This proposal has been supported by simulations of predictive updating of 3D percepts in response to natural images from the CalTech 101 dataset (https://en.wikipedia.org/wiki/Caltech_101; http://www.vision.caltech.edu/Image_Datasets/Caltech101/), and by simulations of human reaction time data during spatial attention shifts under different perceptual conditions.

Two types of perceptual stability cooperate during active conscious vision

We can now reconcile the claim that a surface-shroud resonance has its generators in V4 and PPC with the fact

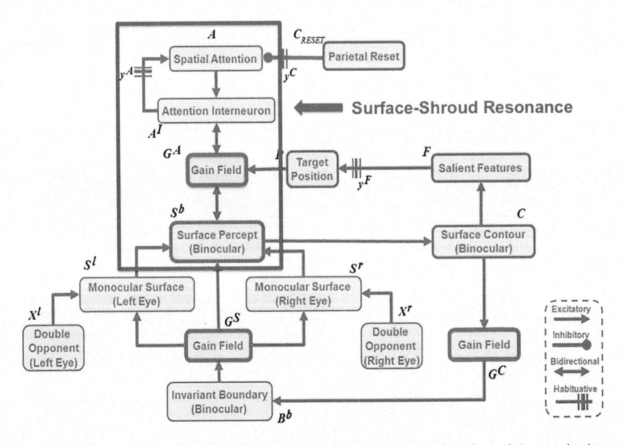

FIGURE 6.25. In addition to the gain field that predictively maintains a shroud in head-centered coordinates during saccades, there are gain fields that predictively maintain binocular boundaries in head-centered coordinates so that they can maintain binocular fusion during saccades and control the filling-in of surfaces in retinotopic coordinates.

that various critical perceptual processes occur in V2 and V1. A surface-shroud resonance is triggered when the filled-in 3D surface representations in V4 are complete, context-sensitive, and stable enough to support the resonance's excitatory surface-shroud feedback interactions with PPC. These resonant signals can then also propagate down to V2 and V1, where they can select and focus attention upon signals at these levels that support the ongoing resonances.

The main new fact is that binocular boundary signals in V2 also contribute to perceptual stability: They are transformed from retinotopic into head-centered coordinates, using gain fields, in order to retain the stability of their binocularly-fused boundaries during eye movements (Figure 6.26), and then are converted back from head-centered to retinotopic coordinates, again using gain fields, in order to maintain the stability of consciously seen binocular surface representations that are computed in retinotopic coordinates (Figure 6.25). These retinotopic surface representations include feature-selective cells that can support percepts of conscious qualia, whether in response to bottom-up inputs

from the world, or top-down signals that cause percepts of visual imagery.

In summary, the simulated interactions that are summarized in Figures 6.25 and 6.26 include the minimal number of processing stages and gain-field-mediated coordinate transformations that are needed to maintain perceptual stability of consciously seen surface qualia as our eyes scan a scene. Let us interpret in these figures the monocular left and right eye surface representations as occurring in V1 and V2, the binocular surface representation that drives a surface-shroud resonance as occurring in V4, the shroud itself as occurring in PPC, and the invariant binocular boundaries as occurring in V2. Then these figures illustrate how the requirements of perceptual stability include V4 and PPC, as well as lower cortical levels such as V1 and V2, all connected via resonant feedback loops. This predicted circuitry can guide many new experiments about how predictive remapping maintains the stability of 3D percepts as the eyes scan a scene, while coordinating the various visual representations that link conscious visual perception and invariant object recognition.

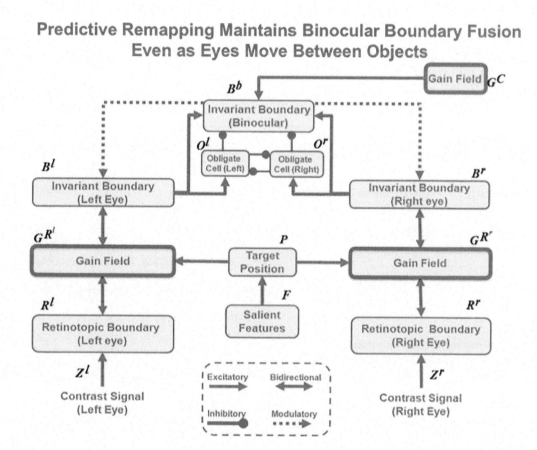

Predictive Remapping Maintains Binocular Boundary Fusion Even as Eyes Move Between Objects

FIGURE 6.26. Gain fields also enable predictive remapping that maintain binocular boundary fusion as the eyes move between objects. See the text for details.

Seeing and Knowing: Synchronous Surface-Shroud and Feature-Category Resonances

Now is a good time to summarize some of the things that we have learned about the difference between seeing and knowing, because we are ready to more deeply understand how we search for familiar objects in unfamiliar scenes. This understanding will follow from an analysis of how Where-to-What and What-to-Where stream interactions are coordinated to regulate both invariant object learning and search for those objects after they are learned.

First, here are some things that we already know: Often when we consciously *see* a familiar object, we also *know* what it is. ART proposes that these two kinds of awareness are due to different kinds of resonances (Figure 6.27), with knowing what is seen supported by feature-category resonances that include What stream regions such as IT, while conscious seeing is supported by surface-shroud resonances that include Where/How stream regions such as PPC. How, then, do we know what a familiar object is when we see it? ART proposes that this happens because these resonances interact with shared visual cortical areas, including V2 and V4, and can thus synchronize with each other, often with gamma oscillations (Fries, 2009; Grossberg and Versace, 2008).

Agnosia: Parietal attention and intention control seeing and reaching without knowing

Symptoms of visual neglect were explained earlier in the chapter as a result of lesions of parietal cortex and related Where cortical stream regions, leading to subsequent problems in forming the surface-shroud resonances that support conscious seeing. I also remarked that symptoms of visual agnosia, or reaching without knowing, can occur as a result of lesions of inferotemporal cortex and related What cortical stream regions, leading to subsequent problems in forming the feature-category resonances that can support conscious recognition. Patients who exhibit visual agnosias cannot recognize basic properties of object shape, yet can nonetheless carry out accurate reaches to these objects, as in the case of the famous patient DF (Goodale and Milner, 1992; Goodale et al., 1991).

The black X in Figure 6.28 depicts such a What stream lesion. This figure also emphasizes that a surface-shroud resonance can still support seeing of objects after such a lesion, as well as the important processes that I earlier discussed of parietal attention and intention. Top-down parietal signals sustain spatial *attention* upon a object during

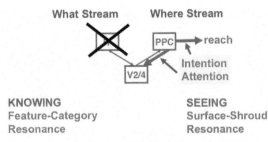

WHAT KINDS OF RESONANCES SUPPORT KNOWING VS. SEEING?

KNOWING
Feature-Category
Resonance

SEEING
Surface-Shroud
Resonance

VISUAL AGNOSIA: reaching without knowing
Patient DF Goodale et al, 1991

Attention and Intention both parietal cortical functions
Andersen, Essick, and Siegel, 1985; Gnadt and Andersen, 1988; Snyder, Batista, and Andersen, 1997, 1998

FIGURE 6.28. If the feature-category resonances cannot form, say due to a lesion in IT, then a surface-shroud resonance can still support conscious seeing of an attended object, and looking at or reaching for it, even if the individual doing so knows nothing about the object, as occurs during visual agnosia. The surface-shroud resonance supports both spatial attention and releases commands that embody the intention to move towards the attended object.

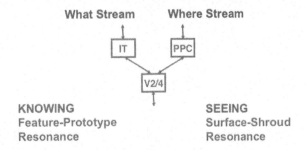

WHAT KINDS OF RESONANCES SUPPORT KNOWING VS. SEEING?

KNOWING
Feature-Prototype
Resonance

SEEING
Surface-Shroud
Resonance

Synchronous linkage between resonances enables us to consciously KNOW what the object is as we SEE it

FIGURE 6.27. A surface-shroud resonance through the Where stream enables us to consciously see an object while a feature-category resonance into the What stream enables us to recognize it. Both kinds of resonances can synchronize via visual cortex so that we can know what an object is when we see it.

a surface-shroud resonance. The active shroud also supports the *intention* to look and reach, in the manner that I explained using Figures 6.14-6.16 as part of my analysis of how we learn invariant object categories.

Where's Waldo search: From Where-to-What to What-to-Where interactions

The ARTSCAN model hereby shows how the brain can learn view-, size-, and position-invariant visual object categories using Where-to-What cortical stream interactions. These categories can then be amplified by motivational attention, as I will explain in Chapter 13, to enable valued objects to be selectively attended. We must then ask: How do our brains use an attended invariant object category to find a valued object in a cluttered scene? This is sometimes called the Where's Waldo problem. When a person can orient to the object in space with eye, arm, or bodily movements, then the Where's Waldo problem is solved.

The main subtlety here is that an *invariant* representation of an object does not represent *where* the object is. Positional information is stripped away in an invariant category to prevent the need for a multiplicity of object representations—indeed, a combinatorial explosion of them—to recognize the object when it is seen in different positions, sizes, and orientations on our retinas. How, then, does an invariant category, that is itself insensitive to object position, activate the object's position? Surely it must be able to do this because we do not just Platonically contemplate people and objects of interest. We also interact with them in space so that we can live our lives.

In order to solve the Where's Waldo problem, What-to-Where stream interactions are needed to convert the desire to find Waldo into the movements that enable us to engage him. To accomplish this, an invariant object category in the What stream must be able to activate representations of the object that are also positionally-selective, so that Waldo's position can be computed. The ARTSCAN Search model in Figures 6.3 and 6.4 describes a minimal neural architecture that can both learn invariant object categories *and* move to acquire them in space.

This minimal model does not, however, include various properties that enable humans and other advanced primates to solve the Where's Waldo problem more efficiently. For example, the ARTSCAN Search circuit does not *accumulate contextual evidence* from sequences of previously experienced objects and their positions to determine what and where to look at next. Storage of sequences is a competence of *working memory*. Chapter 12 will describe how working memories are designed to store sequences of experienced objects and their positions. ARTSCAN Search does include *value categories* that can guide a search to find a valued goal object. An explanation of how we search for a valued goal object requires an understanding of the brain mechanisms for reinforcement learning in response to rewards, punishments, and disconfirmed expectations, and the motivated attention that these mechanisms control. Chapter 13 will explain how such affective circuits work. Finally, Chapter 14 will expand this analysis by explaining how the prefrontal cortex can *selectively* store only a subset of desired goals in working memory, before searching among these goals for the currently most valued objects using evidence that was accumulated from sequences of previously experienced objects and their positions. This most comprehensive solution of the Where's Waldo problem will also summarize how the minimal ARTSCAN Search architecture works before augmenting it.

7

How Do We See a Changing World?

How vision regulates object and scene persistence

From perception of static to changing visual forms

Let us now begin to study the basic facts and explanations of how we see things move. Objects in the world are continually moving around us, and we ourselves often move relative to the world. Our own motions are not restricted to walking or running. Our eyes move restlessly in our heads, and our heads in our bodies, to look at new objects of interest. How do our visual percepts keep up with all this change? How do we synthesize these momentary glimpses of different views of the world into the impression that the world around us is stable?

The phenomena of change blindness, inattentional blindness, and motion-induced blindness that I discussed in Chapter 6 dramatize the fact that many aspects of a scene are not stored in memory after we look at them. This chapter further explains one key process that occurs in response to changing scenes; namely, how boundary representations are formed and reset in response to a change in a visual scene. By studying this issue, we more deeply understand how these various kinds of "blindness" occur than I was able to explain in Chapter 6. In fact, if we did not rapidly reset our visual representations when the world changes, then much worse consequences than overlooking an intermittently vanishing airplane wing could occur. With this foundation in place, Chapter 8 can discuss how we perceive moving objects, and why the brain has invested an enormous amount of processing machinery to evolve separate cortical processing streams for representing static and moving forms; namely, the stream from V1 to V2 to V4 for representing static forms, and the stream from V1 to MT to MST for representing moving forms (Figure 3.1).

Conscious MIND Resonant BRAIN. Stephen Grossberg, Oxford University Press. © Oxford University Press 2021.
DOI: 10.1093/oso/9780190070557.003.0007

Visual persistence and boundary reset

How do boundary representations keep up with rapid changes in visual scenes? All of our discussions of boundary formation so far have considered boundaries that represent a stationary object while a stationary observer inspects it. We take for granted that the boundaries of objects that are stationary with respect to an observer retain their stability and coherence when these objects move through time. During the discussion of Jiggling Eyes in Chapter 3, however, I noted that, even when an object does not change its position relative to a stationary observer, the observer's eyes are jiggling in their orbits to create small motions relative to the object to refresh the sensitivity of brain cells to it. These jiggling motions generate responses in retinal cells that are sensitive to transient changes in a scene, the same kinds of cells that are also activated during the onsets and offsets of the alternating scenes that can cause change blindness.

In the real world, objects of different sizes and shapes are continually moving with variable speeds in front of scenic backgrounds that themselves may be stationary or moving. For simplicity, consider the motion of a single object in front of a stationary background. As the object moves across a scene, its boundaries need to be rapidly reset, and thereby inhibited, in a form-sensitive way. Otherwise, boundaries that formed when the object was at a given position could persist long after the object moved past that position. There would then be massive *smearing* or *streaking* of boundaries as objects moved through time, much as a comet leaves a tail behind itself. Such a tail of persisting boundaries could seriously interfere with our ability to perceive new objects at those positions. How does a brain automatically reset its boundaries when the corresponding objects move or vanish from view in a scene, and do so *selectively*, without undermining the persistence of boundaries that continue to represent stationary objects? Explaining how this sort of selective boundary reset occurs when some scenic inputs change goes a long way towards explaining why we experience change blindness.

Positive feedback helps to choose and store the strongest boundaries in a scene, whether in the non-laminar circuits of the Boundary Contour System, or BCS, in Figure 4.32, or the more complete laminar circuits of the LAMINART model in Figure 4.39 and the SMART model in Figure 5.38. Positive feedback can maintain these boundaries while we gaze steadily at the stationary objects from which they arise. These benefits of positive feedback come at a price, however. Positive feedback tends to preserve the activities that already exist in the circuit even after their inputs change or shut off entirely. Said using more technical language: Positive feedback can causes

hysteresis to occur in the circuit. How do boundaries overcome the hysteretic tendency to maintain the persistence of boundaries, even after an object moves to a different location, or totally vanishes from view? Why does not the positive feedback cause old boundaries to be smeared into massive boundary "comet" tails as their inducing objects move across a scene?

Remarkably, adding habituative transmitter gates (Figure 2.11), as in the gated dipole circuit of Figure 1.14, to some of pathways of the BCS, LAMINART, SMART, or other boundary formation circuits prevents this from happening, and quantitatively explains many psychological data about boundary persistence. Such habituative pathways occur in many parts of the brain, as I have already discussed in Chapter 1. Without these habituative gates, boundaries could not cope with moving imagery, and thus would have failed to satisfy the Embedding Constraint that I discussed in Chapter 2. The fact that the BCS, and its incremental extensions to LAMINART and SMART, can handle moving imagery provides additional evidence, from data about a totally different type of experiment, that its double-filter-and-grouping circuit in Figure 4.32 embodies a significant grain of truth.

Before describing how the model may be easily extended, or unlumped, with habituative gates, I will summarize some important facts that such a model should be able to explain about how human observers react to changing images. Such data concern the phenomenon of *visual persistence*. Persistence measures how long it takes after a visual image shuts off for its percept to disappear. Intuitively, very long persistence could create large boundary tails.

How one measures offset of a percept raises a number of methodological issues, including the relationship of percept offset to any *afterimages* or *residual traces* of the percept to which it may give rise. Afterimages include phenomena like the following: Suppose that you look for awhile at an image composed of radial lines that intersect at a single point, before shifting your attention to look at a blank piece of white paper. Often you will see superimposed on the blank paper a percept of ghostly circular forms that are perpendicular to the radial lines. This is an example of an orientational afterimage. This afterimage is called the MacKay illusion after the British psychologist, Donald MacKay. I will say more about the MacKay illusion in Chapter 8 when I discuss how we perceive object motion (Figure 8.3). For now, I want to focus on explaining data about visual persistence, so that you get a better sense of how the brain prevents boundaries from smearing too much when objects move. Remarkably, we already know how to explain persistence data, even though we do not yet know that we know this! Our models are already smart enough to do this, just as they were in the case of explaining data about transparency.

In fact, when my PhD student Gregory Francis and I tried to understand persistence data, we found to our delight that such data provide support for *each* of the BCS mechanisms that I had already used with various colleagues to explain how stationary images are grouped. Our results, which were published in 1994 and 1996, thus predicted that the same mechanisms that are involved in *forming* a boundary are also involved in *resetting* it (Francis and Grossberg, 1996; Francis, Grossberg, and Mingolla, 1994). Greg and I proposed that persistence covaries with the amount of time it takes to reset a boundary after its inducing stimulus shuts off. Once the boundary starts to break up, its filled-in brightnesses and colors will also rapidly dissipate, thereby ending the visible percept.

The flip side of reset is *resonance*: In regions where inputs are maintained, as in percepts of a stationary scene, positive feedback within the boundary grouping circuit helps to store the boundary until the input changes or shuts off. Thus the study of persistence data helps us to understand the *tradeoff between boundary resonance and reset* that gives our percepts their coherence without condemning us to perceive massive tails of smeared boundaries.

Because persistence data are quite paradoxical, they present a serious challenge to all models of perceptual grouping. Moreover, persistence data are *parametric*. In other words, persistence varies in a numerically predictable way in response to multiple types of stimulus variations. For example, visual persistence:

decreases with stimulus duration of real contours

decreases with stimulus luminance of real contours

decreases to a test stimulus after adaptation to a stimulus of similar orientation

increases to a test stimulus after adaptation to a stimulus of perpendicular orientation

increases with the distance between a test stimulus and a subsequent masking stimulus

increases with the interstimulus interval between a test stimulus and a subsequent masking stimulus

is *longer* for illusory contours than for real contours

increases before decreasing with stimulus duration in response to illusory contours.

The last two persistence properties involve illusory contours, and thus demonstrate that key persistence properties are computed within the visual cortex where illusory contours are formed, notably in cortical area V2, rather than at earlier processing sites. In fact, I will now show that *all* of these properties follow in a natural way from the cortical double-filter-and-grouping mechanisms that we have already derived.

I first need to explain how a mechanism of reset can be incorporated into this model without damaging any of the explanations that the model has already provided. The additional mechanism that I will propose is not, in itself, a reset mechanism. The network *as a whole* behaves like a reset mechanism, while also supporting boundary completion, choice, and resonant storage. Reset is thus an emergent property that is due to several model mechanisms interacting together. In fact, *all* of the double-filter-and-grouping mechanisms are needed to explain the full range of persistence data. Were not the entire circuit already available when we approached these data, it is doubtful that we could have ever understood how boundary reset works, let alone how it could explain all the persistence data. Said in another way, the BCS mechanistically links persistence data to other, seemingly unrelated, data about texture segregation (Figures 4.33 and 4.34), hyperacuity (Figure 4.22), inverted-U in illusory contour strength (Figures 4.37 and 4.38), neon color spreading (Figures 3.10, 3.11, 4.26, and 4.27), and the like. Conversely, persistence data provide additional support for all the BCS mechanisms. These examples again illustrate how a good model can unify the understanding of many data that previously were studied as separate scientific specialties, and can thereby suggest novel experiments that combine concepts from all of these specialties.

Gated dipoles and boundary reset

As I noted above, the main new idea is that some of the BCS pathways can *habituate*, or weaken, due to use. In other words, activating the pathways that support a boundary representation can cause the signals in these pathways to weaken in an activity-dependent way. Such a weakening effect can prevent boundary hysteresis from going on forever. Figure 7.1 shows a simple extension of the BCS in which the *spatial competition* pathways habituate. When I mentioned habituative transmitter gates in Chapter 1, it was in the context of cognitive-emotional interactions, notably as part of opponent processing circuits called *gated dipoles* (Figures 1.14 and 1.15). Remarkably, adding habituative transmitters to the BCS automatically embeds gated dipole opponent processes in this circuit as well, but now to support effective visual perception. All the other gated dipole processes are already there! Gated dipoles are thus a basic design module, or microcircuit, that is used in many different kinds of brain representations. As I noted in Chapter 1, all current biological models build upon a small number of basic equations (e.g., Figures 2.9-2.11) and a somewhat larger number of modules, or microcircuits, whose variations and specialization are assembled

BOUNDARY PROCESSING WITH HABITUATIVE GATES

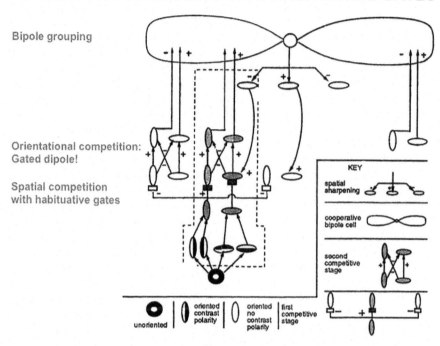

FIGURE 7.1. The usual boundary processing stages of simple, complex, hypercomplex, and bipole cells enable our brains to correct uncontrolled persistence of previously excited cells just by adding habituative transmitter gates, or MTM traces, at appropriate places in the network.

together into modal architectures. Gated dipoles are one of the modules that are used throughout the brain to carry out processes like adaptation and reset via antagonistic rebounds.

To see how gated dipoles get into the story of boundary reset, assume that the spatial competition pathways in the BCS become progressively less effective when these pathways remain active through time. This happens because active pathways release chemical transmitters in order to excite or inhibit their target cells, and these transmitters become progressively inactivated, or depressed, when their pathways continue to carry persistent signals. These transmitters are proposed to occur at synaptic knobs that exist at the ends of the spatial competition pathways. The relevant synaptic knobs are represented by rectangles in Figure 7.1. This model refinement does not influence any of our previous explanations, because they did not depend on how the transmitters habituate through time. The previous explanations all go through if we use the steady-state habituated values of these transmitters.

Figure 7.1 shows how, when habituative transmitters are added to the BCS circuit, the circuit *as a whole* contains networks of gated dipoles embedded within it. Recall from Chapter 1 that a gated dipole opponent processing circuit has the following crucial property: It reacts to offset

of a sustained input to its ON-channel with a transient *antagonistic rebound* of activity in its OFF-channel (Figure 1.14). This rebound is an emergent property of the entire dipole circuit. It arises from an interaction between four of the key dipole mechanisms, which are all mechanisms within the habituative BCS circuit: (1) tonic arousal, (2) habituative transmitters, (3) opponent interactions, and (4) half-wave rectified output signals.

Where in the BCS model do all of these ingredients come together? The answer can be seen in Figure 7.1. Here we see that orientational competition at each position occurs subsequent to the spatial competition stage at which the habituative transmitters act. The orientational competition is particularly strong between hypercomplex cells that code mutually perpendicular orientations. This property provides the opponent interaction that we need, and at a location subsequent to the action of habituative transmitters.

What about the property of tonic arousal? The hypercomplex cells that process output signals from the spatial competition are tonically active, so that they can generate end cuts (Figure 4.26). With this in mind, consider what happens when the spatial competition inhibits one population of these hypercomplex cells. The inhibitory signals from these hypercomplex cells are then removed from the hypercomplex cells that code for the perpendicular orientation at that position. These perpendicularly tuned cells can then become excited through disinhibition of their tonic arousal. The tonic arousal that is used to generate *end cuts* can hereby also cause *boundary reset*, as will become clear in a moment.

The gated dipole property of half-wave rectification is a basic property of all cell output signals, including the output signals from hypercomplex cells. It just says that the cell potential needs to get larger than a threshold value before it can emit output signals, and that the frequency of output signals then grows with the suprathreshold potential of the cells.

We are now ready to understand how these gated dipoles in the BCS reset an active boundary grouping when their inputs change through time. Remarkably, boundary *reset* is accomplished by the same mechanism that was used to implement the property of *spatial impenetrability* (Figures 4.32 and 4.35), which is a property of boundary

PERSISTENCE DATA AND SIMULATIONS
Francis, Grossberg, and Mingolla, 1994, *Vision Research, 34,* 1089-1104

Persistence decreases with flash luminance and duration

Bowen, Pola, and Matin, 1974;
Breitmeyer, 1984; Coltheart, 1980

Higher luminance or longer duration habituates the gated dipole ON channel more

Causes larger and faster rebound in the OFF channel to shut persisting ON activity off

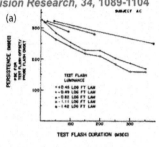

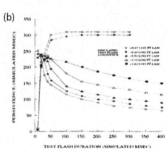

FIGURE 7.2. Psychophysical data (top row) and simulation (bottom row) of how persistence decreases with flash luminance and duration.

formation. This connection further elaborates my hypothesis that boundary formation and reset use the same BCS cortical circuits.

To fix ideas, suppose, as in Figure 7.1, that a horizontal edge in an image activates a horizontal boundary via horizontally tuned complex, hypercomplex, and bipole cells. This activation causes the chemical transmitters in the corresponding pathways to habituate. Now suppose that the horizontal edge moves or shuts off. Because of the positive feedback loop that exists between these cells, horizontally tuned bipole cells could, other things being equal, continue to activate horizontally tuned hypercomplex cells and thereby maintain the horizontal grouping even in the absence of external inputs.

This is prevented from happening as follows. Offset of input to a horizontal hypercomplex cell causes an antagonistic rebound of activity in the corresponding vertical hypercomplex cell. This vertical hypercomplex cell can now inhibit the horizontal bipole cell using the spatial impenetrability mechanism, thereby forcing the horizontal boundary to collapse. In summary, once the spatial competition is made habituative, the BCS circuit as a whole responds to offset of an object by injecting inhibition in a form-sensitive way into those bipole cells that were previously supporting the object's boundary representation. This simple reset mechanism can be used to explain all of the parametric data about persistence that were summarized above, as I will now explain, along with illustrative figures of the relevant data and computer simulations of them.

Persistence of real contours

Figure 7.2 reprints psychophysical data from 1974 of Richard Bowen, Jordan Pola, and Leonard Matin, who published experiments in 1974 (Bowen et al., 1974) showing that persistence is a *decreasing* function of the duration that a real contour remains on, before being switched off. Persistence is also a *decreasing* function of the luminance of the input when it remains on for a fixed time. These inverse relationships between persistence and stimulus duration and luminance imply that persistence cannot be understood as a simple decay of activity of some neural stimulus representation. Indeed, the initial strength of a stimulus representation at the moment of stimulus offset would presumably increase with stimulus duration or luminance, yielding a higher starting point from which decay would begin, and thus longer persistence, which is the opposite of what happens.

Each curve in Figure 7.2a represents the effects on boundary persistence of a flash of fixed luminance. The abscissa of the graph (the horizontal axis) plots the duration of each flash. The ordinate (the vertical axis) plots the measured persistence in milliseconds. Each curve decreases at higher values of flash duration; that is, persistence decreases with flash duration. Curves corresponding to higher luminances lie beneath one another; that is, persistence decreases with flash luminance.

Figure 7.2b shows the computer simulation of these data that was generated by the BCS model. The simulation shows that the time to reset the boundary representation induced by a flash decreases with flash duration and with flash luminance, as in the data. The simulation captures these data properties qualitatively, rather than quantitatively, because the model greatly simplifies the brain processes that take place from initial reception of the flash by the retina to a conscious cognitive judgment of flash offset.

What is the intuitive explanation of why a boundary resets *faster* in response to a *longer* flash? Figure 7.3 provides a pictorial summary of the explanation. If the input to the ON-channel of the dipole stays on longer, then its chemical transmitter habituates more. When the input shuts off, the ON-channel can inhibit the opponent OFF-channel less as the duration of a flash to the ON-channel increases because its transmitter level is lower. A larger antagonistic rebound therefore occurs in the OFF-channel in response to the equal arousal inputs to both channels.

PERSISTENCE DATA AND SIMULATIONS
Francis, Grossberg, and Mingolla, 1994, *Vision Research, 34*, 1089-1104

Persistence decreases with flash luminance and duration

Horizontal input excites a horizontal bipole cell, which supports persistence

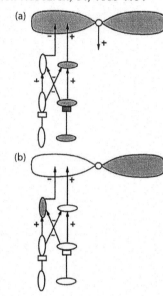

Offset of the horizontal input causes a rebound of activity in the vertical pathway, which inhibits the horizontal bipole cell, thereby terminating persistence

FIGURE 7.3. Persistence decreases with flash luminance and duration due to the way in which habituative transmitters regulate the strength of the rebound in response to offset of a stimulating input, and how this rebound inhibits previously activated bipole cells.

This larger OFF response injects more inhibition into the bipole cell, thereby shutting it off faster. A similar argument shows why a boundary resets faster in response to a more luminous flash. A more luminous flash generates a larger input to the ON-channel of the dipole. This larger input causes its chemical transmitter to habituate more. The rest of the argument now proceeds as before.

These data about persistence provide support for several BCS mechanisms: Rebound size is calibrated by how habituative chemical transmitters interact with tonically active cells whose output signals compete across perpendicular orientations. Boundary reset occurs when bipole cells receive big enough inhibitory signals from a perpendicular antagonistic rebound.

Persistence of illusory contours

Glenn Meyer and Chow Yu Ming published experiments in 1988 (Meyer and Ming, 1988) using Kanizsa squares to show how the persistence of an illusory contour depends upon the duration of its inducing stimulus. The upper two curves of Figure 7.4a graph persistence in response to two types of Kanizsa square inducers: edges and line ends. A pair of parallel edges can induce an collinear illusory contour between them by directly activating like-oriented

bipole cells, as in Figure 7.3. Aligned line ends can induce perpendicular end cuts which can also induce an illusory contour between them, as in Figures 3.18 and 4.27. The other three curves replicate the data of Bowen et al. which showed a decrease of persistence with flash duration when no illusory contours are involved.

Two facts are notable in the upper two curves. First, illusory contours persist longer than real contours. Second, the persistence of illusory contours first increases and then decreases as a function of flash duration, unlike the persistence of real contours, which always decreases with flash duration. Figure 7.4b summarizes model simulations of these data. In these simulations, the upper curves represent how long it took to reset the illusory contour after its inducing stimulus shuts off.

Why do illusory contours persist longer than real contours? According to the BCS model, a reset signal is generated only at positions where an input shuts off. In the case of the Kanizsa square, inputs are derived from the four pac-men that induce the square illusory contour. The illusory contour itself generates no reset signals. In contrast, when a real contour that is as long as the illusory contour shuts off, reset signals are generated along the full length of the contour. Thus, there are more reset signals that shut off a real contour than an illusory contour of equal length. The source of *persistence,* in contrast, comes from every position of a contour, whether it is real or illusory, because positive feedback with bipole cells is activated along a contour's entire length. Thus real contours persist less than illusory contours because they have more reset signals with which to shut off an equal length of persisting boundary.

Why does illusory contour persistence increase before it decreases as a function of flash duration? The model suggests that the increasing part of the curve reflects the amount of time that it takes for the illusory contour to form. Recall that boundary formation with bipole cells proceeds *inwardly* from pairs (or great numbers) of boundary inducers. Much evidence suggests that this can take quite a while. Just think of the Dalmatian in snow scene (Figure 1.2) to recall how long this can take. Real contours, in contrast, can be directly activated at all positions by their image-activated bottom-up inputs. The increasing part of the curves reflects the increasing strength of the illusory contours if their inducers stay on longer. The decreasing part of the curves reflects how habituation influences reset times, as in the case of real contours.

Both the longer formation time and the longer reset time for illusory contours than real contours can be

PERSISTENCE DATA AND SIMULATIONS

Illusory contours persist
longer than real contours

Meyer and Ming, 1988;
Reynolds, 1981

Increasing portion of curve is
due to formation time of the
illusory contour

Longer persistence is due to fewer
bottom-up inducers of an illusory
contour that has the same length
as a real contour: Only luminance-
derived edges generate reset signals

When bottom-up inducers are
inhibited by OFF cell rebounds,
their offset gradually propagates
to the center of the illusory contour

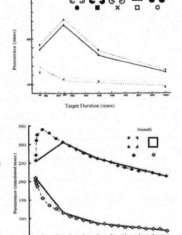

(a)

(b)

FIGURE 7.4. Illusory contours persist longer than real contours because real contours have more inducers whose rebound at contour offset can cause faster boundary reset. Illusory contours also take longer to form than real contours, which explains the increasing portion of the curve.

explained by the following BCS mechanisms: Habituative chemical transmitters in bottom-up pathways lead to activation of bipole cells, bipole cells form illusory contours inwardly between pairs (or greater numbers) of boundary inducers, positive feedback maintains an illusory contour, and reset signals at positions that receive bottom-up inputs cause the inward collapse of this contour.

The bipole property implies that illusory contours are reset inwardly from their inducers towards their middle. Figure 7.5 summarizes a computer simulation of this inward erosion property that was published as Figure 8 in Francis, Grossberg, and Mingolla (1994). In 1996, Dario Ringach and Robert Shapley published data from psychophysical experiments that supported our 1994 prediction for such an inward decay of illusory contours (Ringach and Shapley, 1996).

Persistence after oriented adapting stimuli

Other persistence data provide more direct evidence that gated dipole dynamics are at work, notably of the competition between perpendicular orientations in their opponent processing channels. In the previous examples, the persistence of a test stimulus was measured when the subject was in an unbiased state. In experiments of Glenn Meyer, Robert Lawson, and Walter Cohen that were published in 1975, persistence in response to a test stimulus was measured after a prior adapting stimulus was presented, and compared with persistence in the absence of the adapting stimulus (Meyer, Lawson, and Cohen, 1975). For example, suppose that a vertical bar is the adapting stimulus that is presented to an observer. If the subsequent test stimulus is also a vertical bar, then its persistence is *briefer* than it would have been in the absence of the adapting stimulus. On the other hand, if the test stimulus is a horizontal bar, then its persistence is *longer* than it would have been in the absence of the adapting stimulus. Figure 7.6 shows their data along with our simulations of it. The horizontal line in the figure measures the baseline amount of persistence that is caused without an adapting stimulus. The abscissa indicates whether the test stimulus has the same orientation or the perpendicular orientation of the adapting stimulus. The ordinate measures change in persistence, with positive values indicating more persistence and negative values less persistence than in the no-adapting case.

These data provide strong evidence that persistence is controlled by gated dipoles whose competing ON-channels and OFF-channels code perpendicular orientations. For example, when the adapting and test stimuli both have the same (say) vertical orientation, then these stimuli both habituate the same chemical transmitter. It is just like keeping the same stimulus on with a longer duration. Persistence is hereby decreased, because the antagonistic rebound of the perpendicular horizontal orientation

PERSISTENCE DATA AND SIMULATIONS

Illusory contours persist
longer than real contours

Meyer and Ming, 1988;
Reynolds, 1981

When bottom-up inducers are
inhibited by OFF cell rebounds,
their offset gradually propagates
to the center of the illusory contour

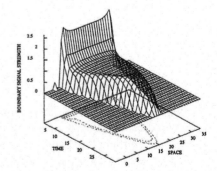

FIGURE 7.5. This figure shows the propagation through time of illusory contour offset from the rebounded cells that got direct inputs to the center of the contour.

PERSISTENCE DATA AND SIMULATIONS

Change in persistence
depends on whether
adaptation stimulus
has same or orthogonal
orientation as test grating

Meyer, Lawson, and Cohen, 1975

If adaptation stimulus and test
stimulus have the same
orientation, they cause
cumulative habituation, which
causes a stronger reset signal,
hence less persistence

When they are orthogonal, the competition on
the ON channel is less, hence more persistence

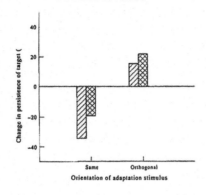

FIGURE 7.6. The relative durations of persistence that occur due to an adaptation stimulus of the same or orthogonal orientation follow from the properties of the habituative gated dipoles that are embedded in the boundary completion system.

is stronger. The case where the adapting and test stimuli have perpendicular orientations is more interesting, because here the adapting stimulus habituates (say) the vertical transmitter of the dipole, whereas the test stimulus habituates (say) the horizontal transmitter of the dipole. Offset of the test stimulus now generates a weak antagonistic rebound in the opponent channel, because the transmitter in the opponent channel is still habituated due to the adapting stimulus. As a result of this more balanced habituation across the ON-channel and OFF-channel, the net inhibitory input to the bipole cells is weak, so that the boundary can persist longer. These data hereby support the following model mechanisms: Habituative transmitters exist in both opponent channels, opponent channels compete across perpendicular orientations, and antagonistic rebound size determines the speed of bipole reset.

Persistence and spatial competition

The previous experiments on persistence have been explained using the interaction between *orientational* competition and bipole cells after pathways of the previous stage of *spatial* competition habituate. Other persistence data may be explained by the spatial competition itself. Joyce Farrell, Misha Pavel, and George Sperling

reported such evidence in 1990 (Farrell, Pavel, and Sperling, 1990). Their experiment was aimed at better understanding a paradox that previous investigators had noted; namely, the visible persistence of a continuously moving stimulus is relatively short when it is compared to the persistence of a stimulus that is stroboscopically flashed at successive positions. Figure 7.7a summarizes their data. Their experiment used vertical lines moving stroboscopically in opposite directions. They showed that the persistence of the test line depends on its spatial distance from trailing flanking lines. Closer flanking lines decreased the persistence of the test line. Other studies have found similar effects using different experimental methods, and have suggested that perceived motion was not an important factor. The lower panel of Figure 7.7b summarizes our computer simulation of these data. An explanation of these data follows from the model's spatial competition mechanism (Figure 7.1), since a flanking stimulus inhibits the effects of a test stimulus more as the two stimuli come closer together, just as in the explanation of the Inverted-U in illusory contour strength as a function of the number of inducers (Figures 4.37 and 4.38). The dashed line in Figure 7.7b shows what happens in the model if the spatial competition is turned off, Then the effect goes away.

PERSISTENCE DATA AND SIMULATIONS

Persistence increases
with distance between
a target and a masking
stimulus

Farrell, Pavel, and Sperling, 1990

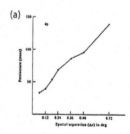

There is less spatial competition
from the masker to the
target when they are
more distance, hence the
target is more persistent

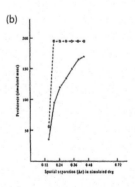

FIGURE 7.7. Persistence increases with distance between a target and a masking stimulus due to weakening of the spatial competition in the first competitive stage of hypercomplex cells.

The same mechanisms have been used to explain and simulate additional data about spatial interactions that influence persistence. For example, Gregory Francis also showed in 1996 that the BCS can simulate paradoxical data of such authors as Eric Castet, Vincent DiLollo, and John Hogben showing that the persistence of a test stimulus *decreases* as the inter-stimulus interval between it and a spatially displaced flanking stimulus *increases* (Francis, 1996). Without the BCS model in hand, one might have expected the influence of the flanking stimulus to become less, not greater, as it was delayed more. These data can be explained by combining spatial competition between the test and flanking stimuli with the way in which orientational competition normally resets the boundary grouping that represents the test stimulus. In particular, when the flanking stimulus occurs soon after the test stimulus, its effects are less because the positive feedback that is supporting the test stimulus grouping is still strong. After the boundary has had a chance to be reset more, however, the same flanking stimulus can more powerfully and quickly reset the residual boundary signals. These data thus support the model's conception of how both spatial competition and orientational competition interact with bipole cooperation.

It is worth mentioning parenthetically that a similar paradoxical effect due to reset occurs during speech perception, as I will explain in Chapter 12. Here, increasing the silence interval between a pair of words like *gray* and *chip* increases the probability that *gray* will sound like *great*. This is paradoxical because increasing the silence interval between a pair of words might have been expected to facilitate their independent processing. Instead, the longer silence interval somehow makes it easier for the /ch/ sound in the word *chip* to cooperate with the sounds that had been supporting the *gray* category and thereby together activate the category for *great*. This happens because the *great* category can more easily inhibit the *gray* category after a longer silence interval occurs between *gray* and *chip*, because the *gray* category representation is weaker then due to the greater extent of habituation in the pathways that activate it.

Taken together, the above experiments on persistence can be explained by, and provide strong additional experimental support for, all of the boundary completion, choice, resonance, and reset mechanisms of the BCS model, and the order in which they are proposed to interact.

I have dwelled on persistence data in such detail because they provide a particularly clear example of how parametric properties of a large data base can be used to support or defeat any of the mechanisms of a model, as well as the order in which these mechanisms are applied. The fact that the BCS model has survived this and other tests so well provides accumulating evidence that its mechanisms, and their order, are realized in some form in the visual cortex. Persistence data also provide a good example of how a simpler model can be embedded, or unlumped, into a more complex model in a natural and principled way. Now is a good time for the reader to think back over all of the data that we have discussed, and to recall how each model mechanism, and the principles from which it was derived, can be used to provide a unifying conceptual bridge between many different types of data. Such a principled unification of large data bases is a fundamental goal of any successful scientific theory.

How We See and Recognize Object Motion

Visual form and motion perception obey complementary laws

Why does the brain need separate form and motion streams?

The discussion of boundary reset in Chapter 7 is part of an analysis of static form perception. It clarifies how the boundary representation of an object is *reset* when the object disappears or begins to move. These reset events alter how perceptual boundaries are completed and surfaces are filled-in within the interblob and blob cortical processing streams that are devoted to perceiving object form (Figures 1.21 and 3.1). These processing streams are specialized to perceive *static* views of object form, albeit static forms that are jiggling with respect to our retinas, as I discussed in Chapter 3, in order to maintain their visibility by activating transient cells. Static form processing begins in visual cortical area V1, which activates prestriate visual cortical areas like V2 and V4, then temporal cortical areas such as the inferotemporal (IT) cortex, and finally the prefrontal cortex (PFC). There are also connections that bypass some of these way stations.

This chapter begins to discuss how our brains perceive objects as they move across a scene. When an object moves across a scene, its boundary and surface representations are recreated time and time again, leading to a succession of individual object views. An immediate question therefore arises: Is object motion just a temporal succession of static form representations that are incrementally shifted across space? The answer is: No! Much experimental evidence has shown that object motion is not just a temporal succession of shifting static form representations. In fact, the brain devotes an enormous number of nerve cells and several processing regions to process object motion. These motion-processing areas also branch out from cortical area V1 and go on to activate cortical areas like MT and MST, then the parietal cortex, and finally the prefrontal cortex; see Figure 3.1.

These anatomical facts raise a basic question: *Why* has evolution evolved parallel cortical streams from V1 through V2 *and* from V1 through MT for the processing of static form and moving form, respectively? Simple cells of cortical area V1 are already sensitive to form-related properties, such as an object's orientation, and to motion-related properties, such as an object's direction-of-motion. If simple cells in V1 can already compute properties of both form and motion, then why did the brain need to evolve two separate processing streams to compute form and motion properties? Why is this not a huge waste of processing resources? Why could not one stream do both?

Chapter 1 noted that the brain utilizes different processing streams for representing What an object is and for representing Where it is in space and How to reach it. The cortical form stream that passes through area V2 is part of the What processing stream, which makes sense because this stream processes properties of visual form that are used to recognize objects. The cortical motion stream through MT feeds into the Where processing stream, which also makes sense, since an object's motion can be used to track it through time and to predict its spatial position. Although the distinction between the What and Where/How streams is one of the most important facts of cognitive neuroscience, it does not explain from a computational viewpoint why a single stream could not have accomplished both of these types of computations.

I have proposed that the two streams compute visual properties that are computationally *complementary*, and that computing one set of these properties precludes computation of the complementary set of properties by the same cells (Table 1.2). From this computational perspective, the parallel processing of static form and moving form by the What and Where streams is no more redundant than the parallel processing of the complementary properties of object boundaries and surfaces by the Interblob and Blob streams. As in the case of static boundaries and surfaces, the form and motion streams also need to interact to overcome their complementary deficiencies. These interactions between the form and motion streams clarify how the brain tracks objects moving in depth.

I will now briefly summarize some of these complementary properties, before using them to explain some of the paradoxical experimental data showing how our brains compute object motion.

Complementary computing of orientation and direction: Long-range directional filter

Chapter 3 showed that the form system is sensitive to the *orientation* of an object's contrasts with respect to its surround, and uses these oriented contrast estimates to complete object boundaries, often with the help of illusory contours. Such oriented contrast estimates are also needed to represent objects in depth: Because the two eyes look out on the world from slightly different positions in the head, they typically register object features

at different positions on their respective retinas, as summarized in Figures 4.18, 4.19, and 6.24. This binocular disparity is one of the cues used by the brain to help determine how far objects are from the observer, at least for objects that are not too far away. The binocular matching process, which is called *stereopsis*, begins in area V1 of the visual cortex. Binocular matching is highly sensitive to the orientation of the matched features, thereby helping to ensure that only features that come from the same object are matched. Thus the form system depends on its ability to make precise estimates of feature orientation during both the earliest stages of stereopsis and the later stages of boundary completion.

In contrast, the motion system generates an estimate of an object's *direction* of motion. Because a single object can contain features with many different orientations that are all moving in the same direction, the motion system pools directional information that is derived from features with multiple orientations. For example, consider a rectangular object moving diagonally upwards and to the right, in the direction of the red arrows in Figure 8.1. At the lower right corner of the rectangle, a dark-to-light vertical edge and a light-to-dark horizontal edge both move diagonally upwards. The brain pools the directional information in which these two orientations are moving using directionally-selective receptive fields (the green elliptical area in Figure 8.1), despite the fact that they have opposite contrast polarities, to estimate the direction in which the object as a whole is moving.

This type of directional pooling over opposite contrast polarities in the motion stream is analogous to the process

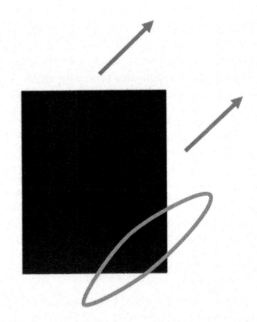

FIGURE 8.1. Motion in a given direction pools all possible contrast-sensitive sources of information that are moving in that direction.

whereby complex cells of the form system pool outputs from like-oriented simple cells that are sensitive to opposite contrast polarities, as in Figures 4.17 and 4.19. The motion pooling process uses a filter that is big enough to accumulate directional evidence from multiple positions as an object moves in a given direction. By pooling signals from features with different orientations but the same motion direction, the brain can compute much better estimates of an object's true direction-of-motion. Such a filter, which operates between cortical areas V1 and MT in the motion system of the Where cortical stream, is called a *long-range directional filter*. More will be said about this filter later in this chapter.

Directional pooling exacts a cost, however: It prevents the type of orientation-specific binocular matching that is needed to generate precise estimates of object depth (Figure 4.19). Thus the motion system, on its own, can generate precise estimates of an object's direction-of-motion, but at best coarse estimates of object depth. Properties of the motion system that are consistent with this prediction were reported in 1981 by Joseph Malpeli, Peter Schiller, and Carol Colby (Malpeli, Schiller, and Colby, 1981) in neurophysiological recordings under conditions where the inputs to the form system from the lateral geniculate nucleus, or LGN (Figures 1.21 and 3.1), were pharmacologically inhibited.

In contrast, the form system, on its own, can generate precise estimates of an object's depth, but only coarse estimates of its direction-of-motion. Supportive neurophysiological recordings published by Kent Foster, James Gaska, Miriam Nagler, and Daniel Pollen in 1985 (Foster et al., 1985) showed that many complex cells in V1, which have precise orientational tuning, respond to objects moving in opposite directions-of-motion, as illustrated in Figure 8.2. These kinds of neurophysiological data supported my

modeling efforts to explain psychophysical data about form and motion perception that led me to predict that the properties of the orientationally-based form system and the directionally-based motion system may be computationally *complementary* (Table 1.1), where the form stream, on its own, can compute precise estimates of object depth but coarse estimates of object direction, whereas the motion stream, on its own, can compute coarse estimates of object depth but precise estimates of object direction.

In particular, I could see that the orientationally-selective binocular matching mechanisms that lead to depth-selective binocular boundaries also forced the corresponding cells to have at best coarse directional selectivity, as Foster et al. (1985) reported. In contrast, the mechanisms for pooling over multiple orientationally-tuned cells to generate direction-selective cells for tracking moving objects forced these cells to exhibit only coarse depth selectivity, as Malpeli et al. (1981) reported. The article that I published in 1991 in *Perception & Psychophysics* entitled "Why Do Parallel Cortical Systems Exist for the Perception of Static Form and Moving Form?" summarized these models and predicted that these orientational and directional properties are computationally complementary (Grossberg, 1991).

This analysis of the complementary strengths and weaknesses of the form and motion streams, acting on their own, led to the following question: How does the brain use interactions between the form stream and the motion stream, which I have called *formotion* interactions, to overcome the complementary deficiencies of either stream acting alone? I predicted that such formotion signals arise in area V2 of the What stream of visual cortex after boundaries are completed there, and generate cross-stream inputs to cells in area MT of the Where stream of visual cortex. This prediction proposed that the depth-selective boundary groupings that are computed in V2 use these cross-stream V2-to-MT interactions to select motion signals in MT that are consistent with them. These selected motion directional signals could then effectively represent an object's motion-direction-in-depth, with which the later stages of the Where cortical stream (see Chapter 9) could track the object as it moves through space.

Distinguished neuroscientists such as Margaret Livingstone and David Hubel in 1988, and Gregory DeAngelis, Bruce Cumming, and William Newsome, also in 1998 (DeAngelis, Cumming, and Newsome, 1998; Livingstone and Hubel, 1987, 1988), had drawn a different conclusion from their neurophysiological data. They proposed that object depth is computed directly in MT. This proposal raised perplexing questions about why depth is computed in MT of the motion stream, given that binocular disparity is already computed by complex cells in cortical area V1 of the form stream (Figures 4.18 and 4.19) and that depth-selective form boundaries seem to be completed in area V2 of the form stream, consistent with the 1984 report

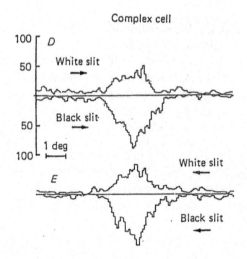

FIGURE 8.2. Complex cells can respond to motion in opposite directions and from features with opposite contrast polarities.

of Rudiger von der Heydt, Esther Peterhans, and Günter Baumgartner, noted in Figure 4.29, that V2 contains orientationally tuned cells that respond to illusory contours (von der Heydt, Peterhans, and Baumgartner, 1984).

My prediction that the form and motion streams compute computationally complementary properties provided an explanation that reconciled all these data: It proposed that the fine depth-selective properties recorded in MT are synthesized via V2-to-MT interactions from fine depth-selective boundary properties in V2. Support for my V2-to-MT prediction was published in 2008 by Carlos Ponce, Stephen Lomber, and Richard Born, who did an ingenious experiment in which they reversibly cooled cells in V2 and recorded from cells in MT (Ponce, Lomber, and Born, 2008). They found that, under these conditions, MT cells preserved their directional selectivity but could only code coarse depth estimates. When the cooling was reversed, MT cells coded both good directional selectivity and fine depth estimates, as I had predicted in 1991.

Negative aftereffects of orientation and direction

Negative aftereffects provide a vivid example of how the form and motion systems use complementary computations to process orientation and direction, respectively. For example, suppose that you look at the radial pattern of straight lines in the left upper image of Figure 8.3 for awhile, and then look at a blank white wall or piece of paper. If you looked at the original image for long enough, you will see a negative afterimage of nested concentric circles on the blank surface, as in the left lower image of Figure

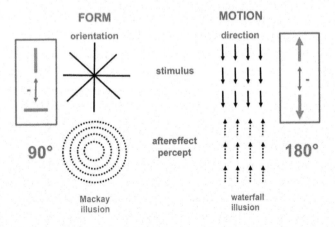

FORM AND MOTION AFTEREFFECTS
different inhibitory symmetries govern orientation and direction

FIGURE 8.3. The MacKay and waterfall illusion aftereffects dramatically illustrate the different symmetries that occur in the orientational form stream and the directional motion stream.

8.3. As I mentioned earlier, this is called the MacKay illusion. The *orientations* of the afterimage are perpendicular to those of the inducing image. On the other hand, if you look at water flowing vertically downwards for awhile, as in the right upper image of Figure 8.3, and then at a blank white wall or piece of paper, you will see a negative afterimage that seems to move vertically upwards on the blank surface, as in the right lower image of Figure 8.3. The afterimage is in the opposite *direction*. This is called the Waterfall illusion.

The afterimage of the static form in the MacKay illusion differs by 90 degrees from its inducing image, whereas the afterimage of the moving form in the Waterfall illusion differs by 180 degrees from its inducing image. The different symmetries of these afterimages illustrate in a striking way that the brain uses different rules, and in fact different processing streams, to process object form and motion. These afterimages illustrate that perpendicular orientations strongly inhibit each other, whereas opposite directions strongly inhibit each other. These mutually inhibitory interactions occur in gated dipole circuits, including the ones that control perpendicular interactions during the reset of static boundaries that control visual persistence (Figures 7.1, 7.3, and 7.6). During form or motion aftereffects, offset of the inducing stimulus causes antagonistic rebounds in the gated dipole cells that are tuned to perpendicular orientations or opposite directions, respectively.

Motion perception in the forest primeval

With this background in mind, I will now discuss some striking accomplishments of the motion system before returning to describe more properties of formotion interactions with this new information in mind. Imagine a predator or prey darting intermittently behind protective cover in a forest or jungle. As the animal moves, patterns of light and shade play upon its body through the overhanging foliage. These moving patterns of light and shade mingle with the movements caused on the animal's body as its limbs and muscles deform the textured patterns on its coat. The luminance and color contours of these regions may move in a variety of directions that do not necessarily point in the direction of the animal's physical movement. Rather, a scintillating mosaic of moving contours may be generated that could easily prevent the animal's detection, as in Figure 8.4.

Being able to detect an animal under these rather typical conditions in the wild is obviously of great value to predators and prey alike. Doing so, however, requires that their visual systems be able to solve several difficult perceptual problems: How does the observer separate the forest cover from the moving animal, so that cover and animal can be independently recognized? In particular, how does the forest cover pop-out in front of the animal so that the contours of the animal are not confused with those of the cover? How is the scintillating mosaic of moving object contours reorganized into a coherent object percept whose perceived motion direction accurately represents the direction in which the animal is actually moving? How are the intermittent appearances of the prey or predator through the forest cover integrated into a percept of continuous motion that is amodally completed behind the cover, thereby enabling the animal's trajectory to more easily be tracked? How does this amodally completed motion trajectory adapt itself to the animal's variable speed of locomotion? How does attention track the animal's moving trajectory as appropriate actions are planned?

The problem of separating a prey or predator from its cover is a special case of the more general problem of *3D figure-ground separation*, which enables us to distinguish occluded objects from their occluders. For example, when we look at a friend sitting on a chair, our friend's body is an occluder of the chair, because the part of the chair that is behind our friend's body cannot be seen. We already saw a variety of percepts that include figure-ground perception, and I have offered at least partial explanations of them, in images including Figures 1.3, 1.4, 3.3, 3.21, 3.23, 3.31, 3.40, 4.35, 4.36, 4.43, 4.54-4.57, and 6.24. Without the process of figure-ground separation, it would be hard for us to separate our friend from the chair, which could make it very difficult to recognize either our friend or the chair. I will say more about solving the problem of figure-ground separation in Chapter 11 when I propose how we see the visual world in depth, notably how 3D boundaries and surfaces are formed, which leads directly to explanations of figure-ground perception. This FACADE model, and its extension to the laminar cortical 3D LAMINART model, provide a unified description of key processes from the retina through cortical area V4 and beyond, including those proposed in Figures 4.54-4.56 that enable amodal recognition of partially occluded objects in V2, and modal, or visible, seeing and recognition of the unoccluded surface regions of figure-ground separated objects in cortical area V4.

Feature tracking and the short-range directional filter

With these questions in mind, let us consider in greater detail the problem that the visual system faces when a predator, such as a leopard, is approaching you in the

MOST MOTION SIGNALS MAY NOT NOT POINT IN AN OBJECT'S DIRECTION OF MOTION
Aperture Problem

EVERY neuron's receptive field experiences an aperture problem

How does the brain use
the small number of correct, unambiguous motion signals
to compute an object's motion direction?

FIGURE 8.4. Most local motion signals on a moving natural object (red arrows) may not point in the direction of the object's real motion (green arrows). This problem besets every neuron due to the fact that it receives signals only in a space-limited aperture.

jungle, as in Figure 8.4. Due to the shadows from moving foliage on the predator's coat, and the motions of the predator's muscles as they deform the spots on its coat, many locations of the predator's body move in directions other than its overall direction of motion towards you. The red arrows in Figure 8.4 illustrate some of these other directions. Often the bounding contour of the predator, where its body occludes the background, provides the only reliable signals for computing the direction in which it is actually moving. The green arrows in Figure 8.4 illustrate two of these motion direction signals. Somehow your brain can use this very small set of motion signals to transform the motions computed across the predator's entire body into a coherent representation of the animal's true direction-of-motion. These unambiguous *feature tracking* signals at the predator's bounding contour propagate inwardly to select, or *capture*, consistent motion direction signals from within the coat, while inhibiting direction signals that are not. Together, all of the selected motion direction signals compute the true motion direction.

The emergent percept of the predator's true direction-of-motion helps a potential prey to detect the predator before it is too late to initiate evasive action. This perceived motion direction is a visual illusion—in particular, a form of *apparent motion*—because it transforms the diverse local motion directions on the predator's coat into a more accurate global percept of the predator's motion direction as a whole. Motion capture accomplishes this transformation by accumulating and reorganizing motion signals over a large spatial region. As noted in Figure 8.1, a *long-range directional filter* helps to do this by pooling similar motion directional signals from object contours with multiple orientations and contrast polarities into a better estimate of object motion direction.

The long-range filter is a processing stage that occurs after a *short-range directional filter* that pools motion signals through time over a smaller spatial range. What does the short-range directional filter accomplish that the long-range filter does not? Recall that a small set of feature tracking signals are generated by the leaping leopard of Figure 8.4. These are the signals that are moving in the real motion direction of the leopard. There are many more motion signals that move in other directions. How can the perceived motion of the leopard be determined by such a small number of feature tracking signals?

The brain compensates for the relatively small number feature tracking signals by amplifying their activities, and weakening the activities of spurious motion signals. Activity trumps number in this case. In particular, the short-range directional filter accumulates directional evidence that strengthens feature tracking signals much more than it can do for locally ambiguous motion signals. This happens because the feature tracking signals move in the real motion direction of the leopard, so that the corresponding short-range directional filter cells get activated at multiple successive positions and times while the leopard moves. In contrast, most ambiguous motion signals do not accumulate directional evidence through time because the leopard is not moving in the directions of their directional preferences. As the short-range directional filter accumulates directional evidence in the true motion direction, it amplifies the activities of the feature tracking cells. Because other directions do not accumulate directional evidence over time, their cells become relatively inactive. In addition, as I will explain more completely in a moment, there is also competition among directional cells, just as there is competition among differently oriented cells in the form stream (Figure 4.32). The stronger feature tracking signals can win this competition. After feature tracking signals become stronger than spurious motion signals, motion capture by processes that include the long-range directional filter can begin to estimate the object's true motion direction over a larger spatial scale.

Computing an object's direction-of-motion often makes use of boundaries that are completed in the form system. Such boundaries can group an animal's textures into a well-defined boundary representation, as in the case of the Dalmatian in snow in Figure 1.2. When you track the motion direction of a Dalmatian in snow by using such a formotion interaction, you are really perceiving a "double illusion." The first illusion is the Dalmatian's bounding illusory contours as it moves through the snow. The second illusion is the coherent direction of object motion that is achieved by motion capture using the feature tracking signals that are computed along these illusory contours. Such examples illustrate that visual illusions are just as important in percepts of motion as they are in percepts of form.

The Aperture Problem, barberpole illusion, and global motion capture

Given this background, I can now summarize, in several simple steps, a unified explanation of how the motion stream computes an object's direction and speed of motion, even under many of the challenging lighting conditions that occur in the wild. I call the simplest model for doing this the Motion BCS model, because there are strong homologs in the motion stream of the processes that are used to explain how static boundaries are generated in the form stream. The BCS model for static boundary formation will henceforth be called the Static BCS model to avoid confusion. Just as the Static BCS model will get generalized to the FACADE and 3D LAMINART models as the underlying design principles and mechanisms of static form perception are more thoroughly articulated in Chapter 11, the Motion BCS will get generalized into the FORMOTION and 3D FORMOTION models. The Motion BCS model and its generalizations will also clarify how attention can be focused on moving objects, and how they may become consciously visible.

The example of a leaping leopard in Figure 8.4 illustrated the fact that, when an object moves under real world conditions, only a small subset of its image features, such as the object's bounding contours, may generate motion direction cues that accurately describe the object's direction-of-motion. The ambiguity of most local motion signals is, in fact, faced by all motion detectors with a finite receptive field. In 1935, Hans Wallach (translated by Wuerger, Shapley, & Rubin, 1996), following the lead of observations by J.P. Guilford in 1929 (Guilford, 1929), showed that the motion direction of a line seen within a circular aperture is perceptually ambiguous: No matter what the line's real direction of motion may be, its perceived direction is perpendicular to its orientation. It is hereby perceived to move in the object's *normal component* of motion, which is only one of the possible directions of motion that could be computed within the circular aperture, or receptive field, on the right side of Figure 8.4. This phenomenon was called the *aperture problem* by David Marr and Shimon Ullman in 1981 (Marr and Ullman, 1981). The aperture problem is faced by any localized neural motion sensor, such as a neuron in the early visual pathway, that responds to a moving local contour through an aperture-like receptive field.

Only when a contour within an aperture contains unambiguous features—such as line terminators, object corners, or high contrast blobs or dots—can a local motion detector accurately measure the direction and speed of motion, as illustrated in Figure 8.5. As I began to explain above, our brains are capable of using these feature

APERTURE PROBLEM

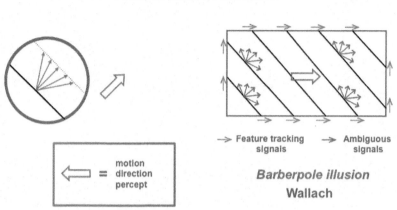

→ Feature tracking signals   → Ambiguous signals

Barberpole illusion
Wallach

How do sparse feature tracking signals **capture so many ambiguous** motion signals **to determine the perceived motion direction?**

FIGURE 8.5. The perceived direction of an object is derived either from a small subset of feature tracking signals, or by voting among ambiguous signals when feature tracking signals are not available.

tracking signals to impose their directions on other parts of an object that are computing only ambiguous motion signals. How the brain may do this is illustrated by the percept generated by the classical barberpole display shown in the right image of Figure 8.5. In this display, diagonal lines are seen moving within an invisible rectangular aperture; that is, within an aperture that is the same color as the paper. The figure draws the rectangle explicitly, but imagine that it is not there. Only the moving diagonal lines are there.

In this situation, all the motion directions within the interior of the display are ambiguous. However, unambiguous feature tracking signals are computed at the line ends that bound this "barberpole". These feature tracking signals can propagate through time to positions within the object's interior to select, or capture, motion signals that code the same direction, while suppressing signals that code different directions. I will explain how this happens later in the chapter. For now, it suffices to note that the feature tracking signals that are computed at the barberpole's long axis dominate the motion percept. A video of the the aperture problem percept and the barberpole illusion can be seen at https://www.liverpool.ac.uk/~marcob/Trieste/aperture.html. A number of investigators have presented supportive data for this explanation of how the illusion occurs (e.g. Hildreth, 1984; Nakayama and Silverman, 1988a, 1988b), and it will enable me to explain a number of interesting facts about motion perception below.

From motion capture to long-range apparent motion

Remarkably, the process of motion capture also clarifies how we can track a predator or prey animal through time when it moves at variable speeds behind intermittent occluders, such as bushes and trees, that lie between the observer and the animal who is being tracked.

How are the intermittent glimpses, or "flashes," of an animal interpolated as it moves at variable speeds behind and between occluding objects? In particular, how are these "flashes" used to compute a continuous motion trajectory between them that can help to track and predict the animal's position through time? Such an interpolation process between intermittent views of a target object is a type of *long-range apparent motion*. After the form system separates the forest cover from the unoccluded "flashes" of the animal, the long-range apparent motion process can amodally complete these intermittent flashes behind the occluding cover to form a continuous motion trajectory that smoothly interpolates the flashes through time.

Thus, at least three types of visual illusion may influence our percepts of "real" objects moving in the world: the illusory contours that may be needed to create a complete boundary contour of the object; the motion capture process whereby spurious motion signals—which are often the most probable signals throughout the object's interior—are suppressed while informative feature tracking signals are amplified; and the long-range apparent motion process whereby intermittent views of a moving object are continuously interpolated for purposes of object tracking.

I will begin my discussion of how we see these illusions with a review of some facts about long-range apparent motion. Although these facts may be fascinating in their own right, they may also seem to be functionally quite pointless, and even bizarre, when studied in isolation in the laboratory. Their great functional importance to our survival can be understood when we consider them from the perspective of tracking a target that is moving with variable speeds behind occluding objects like bushes and trees in the real world.

Introduction to apparent motion

In 1875, Sigmund Exner provided the first empirical evidence that the visual perception of motion is a distinct perceptual quality, rather than being merely a series of spatially displaced static percepts of a moving object (Exner, 1875). Exner did this by placing two sources of electrical sparks close together in space (Figure 8.6). When the sparks were flashed with an appropriate time interval between them, observers reported a compelling percept of a single flash moving continuously from one location to another, even though neither flash actually moved. This demonstration provided compelling evidence that perceived motion is not just a succession of moving forms, because no formed moved in the Exner displays.

The interstimulus interval, or ISI, is the time duration between the offset of one flash and the onset of the next flash. At very short ISIs, flashes look simultaneous and stationary. At sufficiently long ISIs, they look like successive stationary flashes, with no intervening motion percept. At some intermediate ISIs, a "figureless" or "objectless" motion called *phi motion* is perceived, which is a sense of motion without a clearly defined percept of moving form. A smooth and continuous motion of a perceptually well-defined form, called *beta motion*, can be seen at larger ISIs (Figure 8.7).

How apparent motion speed varies with flash ISI, distance, and luminance

This classical demonstration of apparent motion was followed by a series of remarkable discoveries by Gestalt

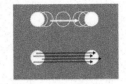

BETA AND PHI MOTION PERCEPTS

Beta Motion
Percepts of continuous motion of a well-defined object across empty intervening space

Phi Motion
Sense of "pure" motion without a concurrent percept of moving object

Exner (1875)

http://www.yorku.ca/eye/balls.htm

FIGURE 8.7. When two flashes turn on and off out of phase with the correct range of interstimulus intervals, and not too far from one another, then either beta motion or phi motion are perceived.

psychologists concerning the properties of motion perception. These properties raise philosophical as well as scientific questions. Many of these discoveries are summarized in the classical 1972 book of Paul Kolers (Kolers, 1972) on *Aspects of Motion Perception*. For example, it was noticed that a decrease in the ISI between successive flashes causes the speed of the apparent motion between them to increase just enough to smoothly interpolate the reduced delay between the inducing flashes. A motion percept can also smoothly interpolate flashes separated by different distances, speeding up if the ISI between the flashes is fixed as the distance between them is increased. As Kolers noted: "large variations in distance are accommodated within a near-constant amount of time" (p. 25). Motion properties also depend on the intensity of the flashes, as well as their position and timing. All of the following properties, among others, have been simulated by our motion model. I will include illustrative simulation figures for some of these percepts before explaining the simple model mechanisms that imply all of these results, and many more.

For example, if a more intense flash follows a less intense flash, then the perceived motion can travel backwards from the second flash to the first flash (Figure 8.8). This percept, called *delta motion*, was discovered by A. Korte, then a student of Koffka (Korte, 1915). *Gamma motion* is the apparent expansion of the area of a flash at its onset, or its contraction at its offset. It was described in 1941 by S. Howard Bartley (Bartley, 1941). A similar expansion-then-contraction may be perceived when a region is suddenly darkened relative to its background, and then restored to the background luminance. *Split motion*, which was reported in 1926 by Harry DeSilva (DeSilva, 1926), can be observed when a single flash is followed by a pair of flashes on opposite sides of the first flash. Then one can often perceive motion radiating simultaneously in opposite directions from the first flash (Figure 8.9). Split motion provides particularly compelling evidence

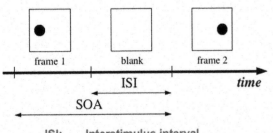

SIMPLEST LONG-RANGE MOTION PARADIGM

| frame 1 | blank | frame 2 |

ISI

time

SOA

ISI: Interstimulus interval
SOA: Stimulus onset synchrony

FIGURE 8.6. In the simplest example of apparent motion, two dots turning on and off out of phase in time generate a compelling percept of continuous motion between them.

DELTA MOTION:
MOTION FROM THE SECOND TO THE FIRST FLASH
Data: Kolers (1972) and Korte (1915); Simulation: Grossberg and Rudd (1992)
This occurs when the luminance or contrast of the
second flash is large compared to that of the first flash

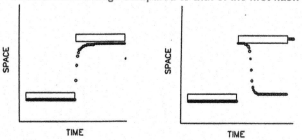

Sustained and transient cells obey shunting dynamics
whose averaging rates speed up with input intensity

The first flash to wane is the one that will be the source of the G-wave

FIGURE 8.8. When a second flash is more intense than the first flash, then apparent motion may occur from the second to the first flash.

that motion is not due just to the changing positions of an object, since how can an object move in opposite directions at the same time? Other curious properties include the fact that "the less you see it, the faster it moves" that was reported in 1989 by Deborah Giaschi and Stuart Anstis (Giaschi and Anstis, 1989; Figure 8.10). In this percept, shorter flash durations may be associated with higher judged motion speeds.

SPLIT MOTION

Data: H. R. Silva (1926); Simulation: Grossberg and Rudd (1992)

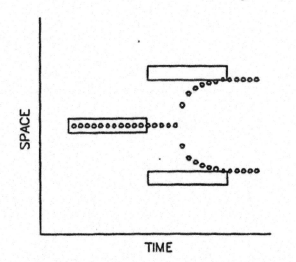

FIGURE 8.9. Simulation of motion in opposite directions that is perceived when two later flashes occur on either side of the first flash.

The Motion ESP Problem: Tracking a variable-speed target behind occluding clutter

These discoveries raise perplexing issues concerning the nature of the brain mechanisms that generate a continuous motion percept between two stationary flashes and, thus, more generally about how the brain perceives motion in the first place. For example, if a continuous motion seems to grow out of the first flash when the second flash occurs, then there must be some sort of long-range interaction that can link the two flashes across space. But then why is this long-range interaction not perceived when only a single light is flashed? In particular, why are not outward waves of motion signals induced by a single flash?

A motion signal is often generated from the position of the first flash only after the first flash has already terminated, indeed only after the second flash turns on some time later. How does the brain "know" that a second flash will be occurring after the first flash shuts off, so that it can create a continuous motion from the first flash to the second flash? I like to call this the Motion ESP Problem, since it would seem that the brain needs to know in advance whether a second flash will occur, when it will occur, and in what direction and distance it will occur, in order to create a continuous motion signal from the first flash to the second flash. Delta motion illustrates this problem in a particularly dramatic way, since it shows how motion can be perceived from the second flash to the first flash under some conditions.

In addition to explaining how long-range motion takes place only after the second flash occurs, we also need to understand: How does the motion signal adapt itself to the variable distances and ISIs of the second flash? In particular, if you place the flashes farther apart in space but keep the ISI constant, then the motion moves faster. If you keep the flashes at the same spatial separation but decrease the ISI, then the motion again moves faster. How can the motion signal adapt its speed to the ISI and the distance between two flashes even though such adaptation can only occur after the second flash begins?

Although these properties may appear strange in the laboratory, as I mentioned above, in the real world the "flashes" may be intermittent appearances between occluding bushes and trees of a predator or prey who is moving with

"THE LESS YOU SEE IT, THE FASTER IT MOVES"
Data: Giaschi and Anstis (1989); Simulation: Grossberg and Rudd (1992)

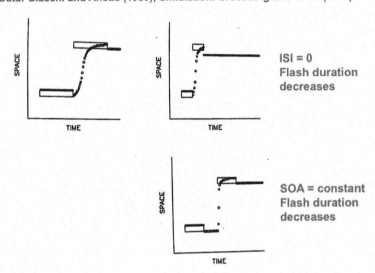

ISI = 0
Flash duration decreases

SOA = constant
Flash duration decreases

FIGURE 8.10. Simulation of the motion speed-up that is perceived when flash duration decreases.

variable speed. The ability of apparent motion to bridge these variable durations and distances enables the brain to form a continuous trajectory of an intermittently seen target as it moves with variable speeds behind occluders of variable sizes.

One can imagine all sorts of hypotheses to explain at least some of these properties. Some authors have even speculated that such evidence implies that the brain does not operate according to classical physical laws. In fact, a surprisingly simple mechanism, that I will summarize below, can be used to explain all of these properties in a natural way. Indeed, this mechanism is known to exist in several parts of the brain. The fact that it can generate properties of apparent motion is not obvious, however. Indeed, if one does not notice this simple mechanism, then one could, in desperation, be led to all sorts of wild ideas, and still not explain all the relevant data.

Other properties of apparent motion also challenge our common-sense ideas about how we see things move, and many of them can now be explained. For example, if a white spot on a gray background is followed by a nearby black spot on a gray background, then a continuous motion between the spots can occur while the percept changes abruptly from white to black at an intermediate position. Likewise, a red spot followed by a green spot on a white background leads to a continuous motion percept combined with a binary switch from perceiving red to green along the motion pathway (Kolers and von Grünau, 1975; Squires, 1931; van der Waals and Roelofs, 1930, 1931; Wertheimer, 1912/1961). These results are interesting because they show how the brain can combine *continuous motion* with *binary color switching*. How can the color red

spread continuously with the motion signal from the red spot to intermediate positions, before switching to green at an intermediate position before the green spot is reached?

Apparent motion of illusory contours and formotion complementarity

I propose that all of these percepts can be explained by a formotion interaction, in which boundary formation and color filling-in take place in the What processing stream, whereas the motion trajectory is computed in the Where cortical processing stream. A "double illusion" due to such What-Where interactions is illustrated by the percept of apparent motion of illusory contours (Figure 8.11), which is a temporally discrete version of the percept of seeing a Dalmatian moving in snow (Figure 1.2). Apparent motion of illusory contours strikingly illustrates how a boundary that is completed in cortical area V2 of the form stream can induce apparent motion in cortical area MT of the motion stream. This example also nicely illustrates the complementary properties of the form and motion cortical streams, and

FORM-MOTION INTERACTIONS
Apparent Motion of Illusory Contours
Ramachandran (1985)

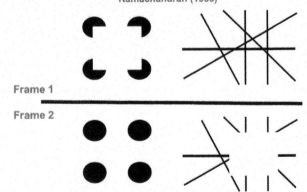

Frame 1

Frame 2

Double illusion!
Illusory contour is created in form stream V1-V2
Apparent motion of illusory contours occurs in motion stream due to a V2-MT interaction

FIGURE 8.11. This formotion percept is a double illusion due to boundary completion in the form stream followed by long-range apparent motion using the completed boundaries in in the motion stream.

how they overcome their complementary deficiencies by interacting together via a V2-to-MT interaction.

This type of percept was described by V. S. Ramachandran and his colleagues in 1973 and 1985 (Ramachandran, Rao, and Vidyasagar, 1973; Ramachandran, 1985). Figure 8.11 summarizes how the percept was generated. The left image in Frame 1 of this display generates the percept of an illusory square using a Kanizsa figure. The right image in Frame 2 generates the percept of an illusory square using a different combination of lines. The main thing to note is that one cannot match the features that induce the two illusory squares. Only the squares themselves have features that can be matched.

Frame 2 is flashed on after Frame 1 shuts off at ISIs that are capable of generating apparent motion. Then the illusory square is seen to move continuously from its position in Frame 1 to its position in Frame 2. Because matching the image elements between the two frames is impossible, this experiment demonstrates that the illusory squares, not the image elements that generate them, are undergoing apparent motion. The illusory square in response to Frame 1 is generated in the form stream using collinear completion by bipole cells (Figure 4.32). The illusory square in response to Frame 2 is generated, also in the form stream, by a combination of end cutting and bipole collinear completion, at angles that are oriented perpendicular or oblique to the inducing lines (e.g., Figures 3.13, 3.14, and 3.17-3.20). The completed boundaries are injected into the motion stream via V2-to-MT formotion interactions. In the motion stream, the square boundaries undergo apparent motion. Many other illusory motion percepts have also been explained using these formotion mechanisms, including the line motion illusion, motion induction, transformational apparent motion, and Korte's laws. I published these explanations with my PhD students Aijaz Baloch and Gregory Francis (Baloch and Grossberg, 1997; Francis and Grossberg, 1996), and will explain what they are and how they arise later in this chapter.

In summary, from the viewpoint of complementary computing, apparent motion of illusory contours is not just a laboratory curiosity. Rather, it provides a visually compelling example of how moving-form-in-depth, or formotion-in-depth, is accomplished by cortical interstream interactions to enable tracking of a moving object in depth. Once formotion-in-depth is computed, it can, in turn, activate mechanisms of object tracking via interactions from cortical area MT to MST, and then to the posterior parietal cortex, or PPC; cf., Figure 3.1. Apparent motion of illusory contours illustrates this tracking property, albeit in response to such a reduced visual stimulus that the percept seems more like a laboratory curiosity than an illustration of a fundamental competence that is needed for survival. Chapter 9 will explain some of the main processes that the brain uses to track moving visual objects.

Explaining variable-speed apparent motion and continuous tracking

Many apparent motion data can be explained, without invoking ESP (!), by combining three simple mechanisms that are individually well-known to psychologists and neuroscientists. When these mechanisms work together, they generate apparent motion data as emergent properties of their interaction. The mechanisms are:

(1) inputs activate receptive fields that have a Gaussian shape across space (Figure 8.12);

(2) responses are sharpened across space by a mechanism of spatial competition, or lateral inhibition (Figure 8.12); and

(3) responses to inputs decay gradually, indeed exponentially, through time after the inputs shut off (Figure 8.13).

The third property, of temporal decay, has been shown through experiments to take quite a long time to occur, as illustrated by data published in 1987 by Stuart Anstis and V. S. Ramachandran (Anstis and Ramachandran, 1987). Figure 8.14 plots what these authors call "visual inertia". Visual inertia can take up to a half second to fully decay.

G-waves of apparent motion and shifting spatial attention

How do the three simple properties (1)-(3) work together to generate apparent motion? Remarkably, when two input flashes occur in succession at different positions in space, these mechanisms can together generate a *traveling wave* of activation whose peak activity can move continuously through time between the two flashes with the same properties as the data. I have called such a wave a Gaussian-wave, or *G-wave*, because it can occur in any part of the brain that uses overlapping Gaussian receptive fields that are activated one after the other through time. In fact, shifts in spatial attention through time often have the same properties as apparent motion, as I will note below. Indeed, they may be caused by the same wave of apparent motion that enables target tracking to occur, since spatial attention can then shift with the wave as it triggers commands to the eyes and head to track the target accordingly.

How is a traveling wave generated by these mechanisms? Figure 8.12 illustrates how a spatially localized flash (Figure 8.12a) leads to a Gaussian activation across space (Figure 8.12b). This broad Gaussian activation is

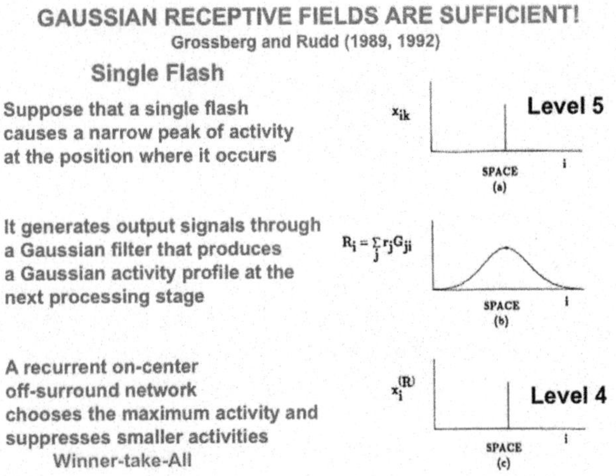

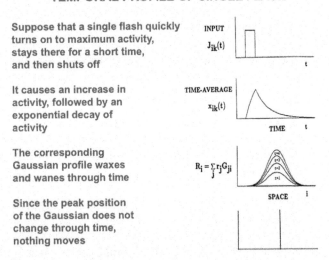

GAUSSIAN RECEPTIVE FIELDS ARE SUFFICIENT!
Grossberg and Rudd (1989, 1992)

Single Flash

Suppose that a single flash causes a narrow peak of activity at the position where it occurs

x_{ik} **Level 5**

SPACE (a)

It generates output signals through a Gaussian filter that produces a Gaussian activity profile at the next processing stage

$R_i = \sum_j r_j G_{ji}$

SPACE (b)

A recurrent on-center off-surround network chooses the maximum activity and suppresses smaller activities
Winner-take-All

$x_i^{(R)}$ **Level 4**

SPACE (c)

FIGURE 8.12. A single flash activates a Gaussian receptive field across space whose maximum is chosen by a winner-take-all recurrent on-center off-surround network.

sharpened by spatial competition into a focal activation at the position that is most active across these cells (Figure 8.12c). Figure 8.13 illustrates how such an input activation looks through time. For simplicity, it is assumed that the input turns on to a fixed intensity which it maintains until shutting off, as in Figure 8.13a. Such an input generates a gradually increasing cell activation followed, after the input shuts off, by a slowly decaying activity through time, as in Figure 8.13b. This decaying trace looks very much like the visual inertia shown in Figure 8.14. When this temporal profile activates the Gaussian filter across space, it generates a spatially distributed input at the next level of

TEMPORAL PROFILE OF SINGLE FLASH

Suppose that a single flash quickly turns on to maximum activity, stays there for a short time, and then shuts off

INPUT
$J_{ik}(t)$

t

It causes an increase in activity, followed by an exponential decay of activity

TIME-AVERAGE
$x_{ik}(t)$

TIME   t

The corresponding Gaussian profile waxes and wanes through time

$R_i = \sum_j r_j G_{ji}$

SPACE   i

Since the peak position of the Gaussian does not change through time, nothing moves

FIGURE 8.13. As a flash waxes and wanes through time, so too do the activities of the cells in its Gaussian receptive field. Because the maximum of each Gaussian occurs at the same position, nothing is perceived to move.

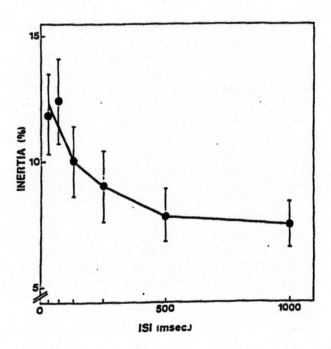

FIGURE 8.14. Visual inertia depicts how the effects of a flash decay after the flash shuts off.

cells. This Gaussian profile of activation waxes and wanes through time, without spreading across space. Its waxing phase is shown in Figure 8.13c. The position of the maximum value of this Gaussian activity profile does not move through time. Figure 8.13d shows how this broad Gaussian activation is sharpened into a focal activation by spatial competition across these cells. If we suppose that the percept of motion covaries with this maximum value, then we can understand why a single flash does not cause a movement across space, despite the fact that it causes distributed activation across space.

Suppose, however, that two successive flashes occur at nearby positions (Figure 8.15). Imagine that the activation in response to the flash at the first position is decaying while activation is growing in response to a flash at the second position. Under these circumstances, the *total* input from both flashes is the sum of a temporally waning Gaussian plus a temporally waxing Gaussian, as in Figure 8.16 (left column). Competition selects the position of the sum's maximum activity at each time. Under appropriate spatial and temporal conditions, the maximum activity moves on the peak of a traveling wave through time from the position of the first flash to the position of the second flash, as in Figure 8.16 (right column).

In summary, the space-averaged and time-averaged cell responses to individual flashes do not change their positions of maximal activation through time. In this sense, nothing moves in response to a single flash. When a series of properly timed and spaced flashes is presented, however, the sum of their responses can produce a continuously

TEMPORAL PROFILE OF TWO FLASHES

If two flashes occur in rapid succession, the waning of the activity due to the first flash may overlap in time with the waxing of the activity due to the second flash

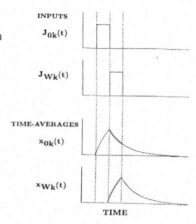

FIGURE 8.15. If two flashes occur in succession, then the cell activation that is caused by the first one can be waning while the activation due to the second one is waxing.

moving peak of activity between the positions of the flashes. This is an emergent property of network interactions across multiple cells through time, rather than a property of any cell acting alone.

The Motion ESP problem may thus be solved using the fact that the Gaussian response to the first flash is still waning—without causing a percept of motion—when the second flash occurs. It is this residual effect of the first flash as it combines with the waxing effect of the second flash that enables the travelling wave to continuously

TRAVELING WAVE (G-WAVE): LONG-RANGE MOTION

If the Gaussian activity profiles of two flashes overlap sufficiently in space and time, then the sum of Gaussians produced by the waning of the first flash added to the Gaussian produced by the waxing of the second flash, can produce a single-peaked traveling wave from the position of the first flash to that of the second flash

The wave is then processed through a WTA choice network.

The resulting continuous motion percept is both long-range and sharp

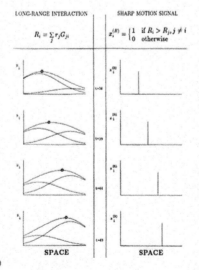

FIGURE 8.16. The sum of the waning Gaussian activity profile due to the first flash and the waxing Gaussian activity profile due to the second flash has a maximum that moves like a traveling wave from the first to the second flash.

interpolate variable ISIs and distances between the two flashes, as well as various other paradoxical properties of long-range apparent motion and attention shifts.

Motion ESP: Variable speed and multi-scale synchrony of apparent motion trajectories

I was inspired to discover G-waves in the early 1970s when I first read Kolers's classical 1972 book on motion perception (Kolers, 1972). It was deeply satisfying to me that mathematical properties of G-waves could explain so many of the classical paradoxes about apparent motion data. I did not try to publish these exciting results right away, though, because it was not clear to me at that time where the long-range Gaussian filter that generates G-waves fit into a larger theory of motion perception. In particular, it was unclear how motion signals were processed before they reached the stage of G-wave propagation. It took another twelve years, until 1989, to develop and publish a more complete model, called the Motion BCS, in a pair of articles in 1989 and 1992 with my postdoctoral fellow Michael Rudd (Grossberg and Rudd, 1989, 1992).

One of the most interesting mathematical properties of G-waves concerns the ESP properties whereby they speed up or slow down to fit changing ISIs and distances between flashes. The equation that proves this property also proves another property of these waves that is no less important. This latter property concerns the fact that motion percepts, just like percepts of form, are derived from interactions between multiple receptive field sizes, or scales. Several scales can be simultaneously activated by the same inputs, with larger scales often, but not always (see Figure 11.26), representing objects at nearer distances. This state of affairs raises the question: If multiple scales get activated by the same sequence of flashes, or other moving features, then how do the G-waves in all the scales stay aligned in space? Remarkably, the same equation that describes how motion can speed up with decreasing ISI also shows that the maximum values of the waves carried by different receptive field sizes stay spatially superimposed through time.

MOTION SPEED-UP WITH INCREASING DISTANCE

For a fixed ISI, how does perceived velocity increase with distance between the flashes?

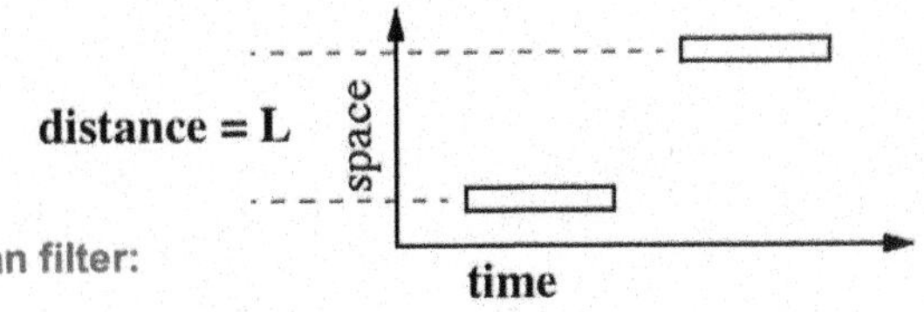

distance = L

Gaussian filter:

$$G_{ji} = \exp\left\{\frac{-(j-i)^2}{2K^2}\right\}$$

The largest separation, L_{crit}, for which sufficient spatial overlap between two Gaussians centered at locations i and j will exist to support a traveling wave of summed peak activity is:

$$L_{crit} = 2K$$

FIGURE 8.17. An important constraint on whether long-range apparent motion occurs is whether the Gaussian kernel is broad enough to span the distance between successive flashes.

These results are summarized in Figures 8.17-8.21. Figure 8.17 represents the duration through time (open rectangles) and the spacing L between the two flashes, and defines the Gaussian receptive field of cells that each input flash activates. As parameter K in the definition of the Gaussian increases, the Gaussian gets narrower in space. The last line of this figure asserts that the maximum spacing L_{max} between flashes that can support a G-wave is $2K$. This makes sense intuitively because, if the Gaussian is narrower, then the two flashes need to be closer in space in order to interact. I summarize the relevant equations below because they vividly demonstrate these properties.

Figure 8.18 defines the activities x_0 and x_L at the positions 0 and L that are activated by these flashes. The function $G(w,t)$ is the G-wave equation that multiples each activity through time with its Gaussian kernel and sums the two Gaussian activations. Theorem 1 says that the peak of the G-wave moves like a traveling wave from position 0 to L if and only if L is less than $2K$. In the computer simulations that are summarized in Figure 8.19, all the combinations of L and $2K$ that are under the dashed red line satisfy this inequality, and one can see their apparent motion trajectories. There is no apparent motion above the dashed red line.

Finally, Figure 8.20 shows the equation for the time at which the motion signal reaches the position L/2 that lies half way between positions 0 and L of the two flashes. Remarkably, this time depends neither upon the distance L between

the flashes, nor upon the spatial scale K of the Gaussian! That means that the traveling wave exhibits the ESP property of speeding up or slowing down to smoothly interpolate the onset times of the two flashes, no matter how far away from each other they are, and that this will happen no matter how big or small K is, just so long as K and L are chosen to support a G-wave at all. In other words, all spatial scales support motions that are aligned across space!

Figure 8.21 summarizes a computer simulation showing the apparent motion trajectories that are generated with variable spatial scales K. Note that they all intersect when they reach the half-way mark of the motion trajectory. G-waves can thus continuously interpolate the motions of intermittently viewed targets across multiple spatial scales. When one experiences enough such useful properties emerging from simple neural mechanisms that explain many data, one begins to believe that they really exist in the brain.

Korte's Laws and Ternus motion as examples of formotion complementarity

As I have noted in my discussions above, one of the nice things about studying vision, apart from the intrinsic satisfactions of understanding how we see and explaining so

G-WAVE PROPERTIES
Grossberg (1977)

Let flashes occur at positions $i = 0$ and $i = L$.
Suppose that:

$$\frac{dx_0}{dt} = -Ax_0 + J_0$$

$$\frac{dx_L}{dt} = -Ax_L + J_L$$

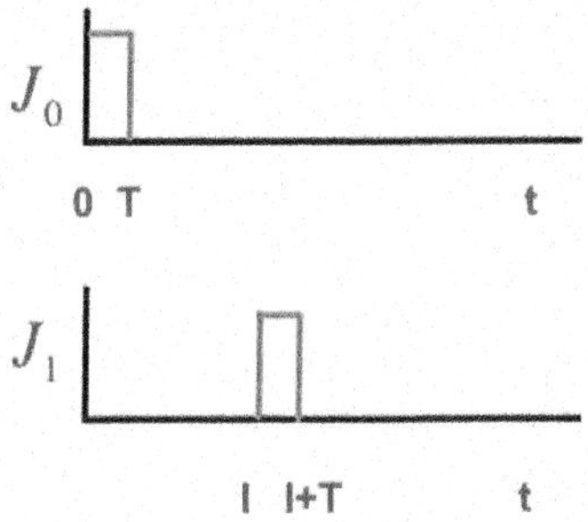

Define $G(w,t) = x_0(t)\exp[-\frac{w^2}{2K^2}] + x_L(t)\exp[-(w-L)^2/2K^2]$

Theorem 1. $\max_w G(w,t)$ **moves continuously through time from** $w = 0$ **to** $w = L$ **if and only if** $L < 2K$.

FIGURE 8.18. This theorem shows how far away (L), given a fixed Gaussian width, two flashes can be to generate a wave of apparent motion between them.

NO MOTION VS. MOTION AT MULTIPLE SCALES

Interactions between
flash spatial separation (*L*)
and filter scale (*K*)

Multiple spatial scales!

Above dashed red line:
NO MOTION (*L* ≥ 2*K*)

Why?

The waxing and waning
Gaussian profiles do not
add up to create a
single peaked traveling wave

Below dashed red line:
MOTION (*L* < 2*K*)

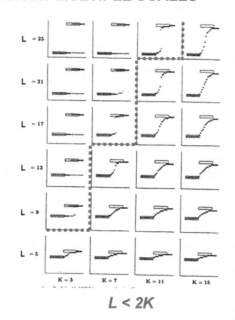

$$L < 2K$$

FIGURE 8.19. The dashed red line divides combinations of flash distance L and Gaussian width K into two regions of no apparent motion (above the line) and apparent motion (below the line).

many interesting visual properties along the way, is that there are lots of experiments available that can guide one's thinking, while also ruling out lots of otherwise initially appealing, but wrong, ideas about how vision works. Visual psychophysicists often vary every conceivable property of stimuli to explore how they may alter perceived percepts.

One such class of studies asks: What is the largest inter-stimulus interval, or ISI, between two stimuli that enables a percept of apparent motion to occur? This property is

G-WAVE PROPERTIES
Grossberg (1977)

Theorem 2 (Equal Half-Time Property). The time at which the motion signal reaches position w = L/2 is

$$t_{1/2} = t + \frac{1}{A}\ln[\exp(AI) + (1 - \exp(-AT))].$$

Apparent motion speed-up with distance:
This time is independent of the distance *L* between the two flashes

Consistent motion across scales:
This time is independent of the scale size *K*

Method of proof: Elementary algebra and calculus
See Grossberg and Rudd (1989, Appendix) for proof

FIGURE 8.20. The G-wave speeds up with the distance between flashes at a fixed delay, and has a consistent motion across multiple spatial scales.

important because it influences how well a target can be continuously tracked behind occluding clutter. Korte's Laws (Figure 8.22a) provide an answer to this question by showing how factors like target luminance, duration, and distance can influence the maximal ISI for which motion is perceived (Boring, 1950; Kolers, 1972; Korte, 1915). In particular, the maximum ISI for perceiving motion decreases as the spatial separation of the flashes increases, with the maximum ISI equal to around half a second for small spatial separations. It makes intuitive sense that smaller separations may be easier to track. But this still leaves open the question of what brain process stores the effects of the first flash for half a second after it terminates, as illustrated by visual inertia (Figure 8.14), since this duration is two orders of magnitude longer than the passive decay rate of individual neurons. What brain process enables the effects of individual flashes to persist for such a long time?

Here is where interactions between form and motion, or formotion, interactions come to the rescue. Chapter 7 reviewed some of my results with Gregory Francis about the persistence of boundaries in the What stream. During my work with Greg, I also proposed that we could explain Korte's Laws as a result of how boundary persistence in the What stream influences the persistence of apparent motion in the Where stream via a formotion interaction from V2 to MT. Our computer simulation (Figure 8.22b) of this formotion interaction nicely captures the main properties of Korte's Laws, including the striking fact that apparent motion can occur with an ISI of over 350 milliseconds in response to brief flashes. Thus, Korte's Laws, no less than the apparent motion of illusory contours (Figure 8.11) illustrate the fact that the form and motion cortical streams overcome their complementary deficiencies through V2-to-MT formotion interactions.

Another kind of display, called a Ternus display, after the Gestalt psychologist Joseph Ternus who first reported it in 1926 (Ternus, 1926/1950, 1938), generates remarkable motion percepts that illustrate how seemingly minor changes in the spatial layout, relative contrast, or ISI of stimuli can cause dramatic perceptual changes. You can see Ternus motion at https://en.wikipedia.org/wiki/Ternus_illusion. For example, in Frame 1 of the simplest type of Ternus display, three white disks, or other regular shapes, are placed in a horizontal row on a black background. After

EQUAL HALF-TIME PROPERTY
How multiple scales cooperate to generate motion percept

Traveling waves from Gaussian filters of different sizes bridge the same distance in comparable times

The time needed to bridge half the distance between flashes is the same:

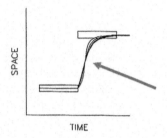

FIGURE 8.21. A computer simulation of the equal half-time property whereby the apparent motions within different scales that respond to the same flashes all reach the halfway point in the motion trajectory at the same time.

KORTE'S LAWS
Data: Korte (1915); Simulation: Francis and Grossberg (1996)

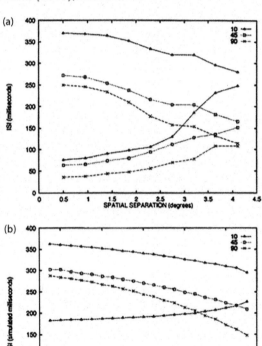

FIGURE 8.22. Data (top image) and simulation (bottom image) of Korte's laws. These laws raise the question of how ISIs in the hundreds of milliseconds can cause apparent motion.

an ISI, in Frame 2 all three elements are shifted to the right so that the two rightward elements in Frame 1 are in the same positions as the two leftward elements in Frame 2; see Figure 8.23. Depending on the ISI, the observer perceives one of four percepts. At very short ISIs, all four elements appear to occur simultaneously. At slightly longer ISIs, the leftmost element in Frame 1 appears to jump to the position of the rightmost element in Frame 2. This percept is called *element motion*. At longer ISIs, all three flashes seem to move together rigidly between Frame 1 to end at the positions of the elements in Frame 2. This is called *group motion*. At even longer ISIs, observers do not perceive motion at all. They just perceive the temporal succession of two static spatial arrays.

The percept of group motion might suggest that Ternus percepts are due to a cognitive process that groups the flashes into attended objects, and that motion perception occurs only after object perception is complete. Such an explanation is not, however, consistent with the percept of element motion. To explain a percept like element motion, it has been argued that, at short ISIs, the visual persistence of the brain's response to the two rightmost flashes of Frame 1 continues until the two leftmost flashes of Frame 2 occur (Braddick, 1980; Braddick and Adlard, 1978; Breitmeyer and Ritter, 1986a, 1986b; Pantle and Petersik, 1980). As a result, nothing changes at the two shared flash locations when Frame 2 occurs, so they do not seem to move. This type of explanation suggests that at least part of the apparent motion percept is determined at early processing stages. It does not, however, explain *how* we see element motion. In particular, why does not the element motion percept of the extreme flashes collide with the two intervening stationary flash percepts? What kind of perceptual space can carry element motion across, or over, the stationary flashes?

Another variant of Ternus motion, called *reverse-contrast Ternus motion*, also suggests that these motion properties may be determined at early processing stages. In this paradigm, that was reported by Allan Pantle and Lucinda Picciano in 1976 (Pantle and Picciano, 1976), three white spots on a gray background in Frame 1 are followed by three black spots on the gray background in Frame 2 (Figure 8.24). Because of this change, the dots in Frames 1 and 2 have opposite contrasts relative to the background. Just this change in relative contrasts, other things being equal, eliminates the percept of element

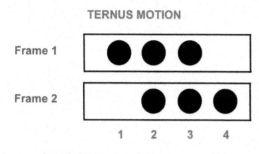

TERNUS MOTION

Frame 1

Frame 2

1   2   3   4

Small ISI: Stationarity
Intermediate ISI: Element motion
Larger ISI: Group motion

http://en.wikipedia.org/wiki/Ternus_illusion

FIGURE 8.23. Despite its simplicity, the Ternus display can induce one of four possible percepts, depending on the ISI.

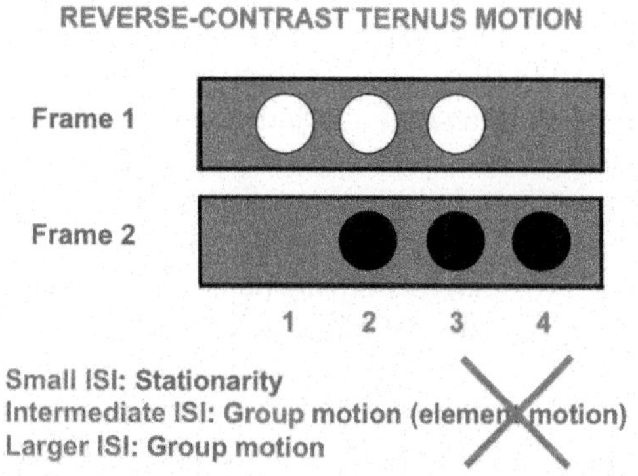

REVERSE-CONTRAST TERNUS MOTION

Frame 1

Frame 2

1   2   3   4

Small ISI: Stationarity
Intermediate ISI: Group motion (element motion)
Larger ISI: Group motion

FIGURE 8.24. When each stimulus has an opposite contrast relative to the background, element motion is eliminated and replaced by group motion at intermediate values of the ISI.

motion! At the ISIs where element motion previously occurred, group motion now occurs. How does a change just of contrast between Frame 1 and Frame 2 obliterate element motion? Such a change, whatever its cause, also seems to rule out higher cognitive factors.

Motion direction filter and the Motion BCS model

These kinds of paradoxical data, among others, guided me to develop, in collaboration with several PhD students, the Motion BCS, model (Figure 8.25) (Baloch and Grossberg, 1997; Berzhanskaya, Grossberg, and Mingolla, 2007; Chey, Grossberg, and Mingolla, 1997; Grossberg, 1991, 1998; Francis and Grossberg, 1996; Grossberg, Mingolla, and Viswanathan, 2001). As I noted above, the Motion BCS model was so named because its mechanisms are in many ways homologous to those of the BCS model (see Chapter

4) that was developed to explain boundary formation within the static form processing stream. Accordingly, the original BCS model is sometimes called the Form BCS, or Static BCS, model to distinguish it from the Motion BCS model. As in the Form BCS, the Motion BCS consists of a filter followed by a grouping network, but these networks in the Motion BCS are *directionally*-selective, rather than being *orientationally*-selective, as they are in the Form BCS. These similarities suggest that the brain parsimoniously uses homologous orientationally-selective and directionally-selective mechanisms to carry out the complementary requirements of form and motion processing.

The Motion BCS filter possesses the minimal number of processing stages that are capable of tracking an object's direction-of-motion independent of whether the object's individual parts are darker or lighter than the background upon which they are moving. The earliest version of the model was published in 1989 and 1992 with my postdoctoral fellow Michael Rudd to show that each of the model's processing stages was needed to explain the full range of known data about long-range apparent motion (Grossberg and Rudd, 1989, 1992).

A key insight of the Motion BCS model is that oriented cells that respond in a sustained way to inputs, such as the simple cells in V1 (Level 2 in Figure 8.25), interact with unoriented cells that respond in a transient way to onsets (upward facing arrow) or offsets (downward facing arrow) of the same inputs (Level 3). Output signals from these sustained and transient cells at each position are then multiplied to generate cells that are sensitive to the direction-of-motion that they experience (Level 4).

For example, if a vertical dark-light edge moves to the left, with lightness occupying larger regions of the visual field as the motion proceeds, then the Level 2 dark-light vertically-oriented simple cells that are arrayed side-by-side at nearby positions (leftmost image) get successively activated. They pool their outputs topographically at short-range filter cells, which time-average them. Because the visual field is getting lighter, the Level 3 ON-transient cells also get activated (upward facing arrow). When these sustained and transient signals are multiplied at Level 4, they signal unambiguously that a dark-light vertical edge is moving to the left. All other combinations of orientational preference, polarity, and lightening or darkening are multiplied at Level 4 cells to selectively signal dark-light or light-dark edges moving in any direction.

Because each Level 4 cell is derived from polarity-sensitive simple cells, it is also sensitive to polarity, or direction-of-contrast. True directional cells are formed by using a long-range directional filter to combine inputs from all Level 4 cells that have the same directional preference (Figure 8.1). This pooling process occurs across multiple orientations, opposite directions-of-contrast, and both eyes. The resulting cells at Level 5 in Figure 8.25 are these "true" directional cells, and due to their pooling

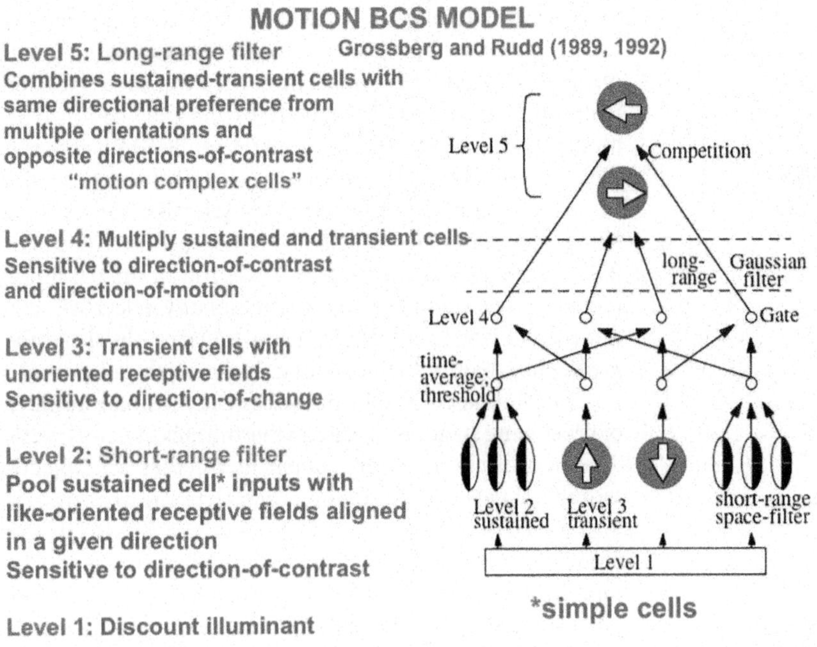

MOTION BCS MODEL

Grossberg and Rudd (1989, 1992)

Level 5: Long-range filter
Combines sustained-transient cells with same directional preference from multiple orientations and opposite directions-of-contrast
"motion complex cells"

Level 4: Multiply sustained and transient cells
Sensitive to direction-of-contrast and direction-of-motion

Level 3: Transient cells with unoriented receptive fields
Sensitive to direction-of-change

Level 2: Short-range filter
Pool sustained cell* inputs with like-oriented receptive fields aligned in a given direction
Sensitive to direction-of-contrast

Level 1: Discount illuminant

FIGURE 8.25. The Motion BCS model can explain and simulate all the long-range apparent motion percepts that this chapter describes.

properties across polarities and both eyes, they are a kind of complex cell, albeit a complex cell that is sensitive to a motion's direction rather than to a form's orientation. As I have already noted, the pooling across orientation is one

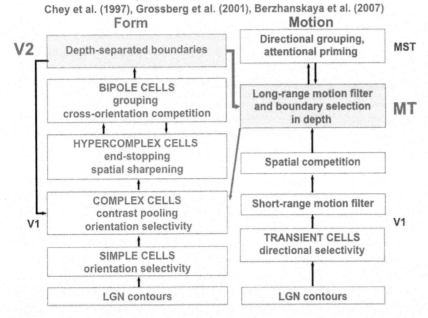

3D FORMOTION MODEL

Chey et al. (1997), Grossberg et al. (2001), Berzhanskaya et al. (2007)

FIGURE 8.26. The 3D FORMOTION model combines mechanisms for determining the relative depth of a visual form with mechanisms for both short-range and long-range motion filtering and grouping. A formotion interaction from V2 to MT is predicted to enable the motion stream to track objects moving in depth.

reason that these motion complex cells cannot be used to compute sharp estimates of object depth.

The shape of the long-range directional filter is typically an elongated Gaussian (Figure 8.1). The Motion BCS hereby leads to the remarkable conclusion that the same operation that creates directional complex cells can also create G-waves, and can thereby initiate the computation of continuous motion trajectories that can track targets moving at variable speeds behind occluding clutter.

Because the Motion BCS only models up to the stage of "motion complex cells" and its long-range directional filter, it does not include a directionally-tuned grouping process that is akin to orientationally-tuned grouping by bipole cells in the form stream (Figure 4.32). A series of additional modeling studies did include such processes in order to explain a large body of additional data, including the article Baloch and Grossberg (1997) that I mentioned above. These additional explanations of motion percepts will be summarized later in this chapter.

These studies led to the steady development of a laminar cortical 3D FORMOTION model (Figure 8.26), with a still greater explanatory and predictive range. Here again, combinations of sustained and transient inputs are essential in order to achieve good directional estimates, but they derive their orientationally-tuned sustained signals from the 3D boundaries that are generated in V2 before being used to select depth-consistent motion signals in MT. The 3D FORMOTION motion model can hereby track objects whose boundaries get completed in V2, as in the example of apparent motion of illusory contours (Figure 8.11). In addition, as I will explain below, the 3D FORMOTION model can also solve the global aperture problem.

Ternus motion: Transient cells and G-waves

Using just the Motion BCS processing stages, it is easy to explain how Ternus and reverse-contrast Ternus motion properties arise. A key property of the motion-sensitive cells in Layers 4 and 5 of Figure 8.25 is that they are activated by *transient cells.* As their name suggests, transient cells are activated by *changes* in inputs, and respond transiently to onsets and offsets of inputs. Given that motion perception is a perception of change, or transiency, it is perhaps not surprising that the brain has developed specialized detectors for sensing such events. Recall the importance of motion transients in discussing percepts like change blindness (Chapter 7).

Transient cells play an important role in explaining how element motion (Figure 8.23) is perceived at a short ISI. As in the discussion of change blindness, there are two types of transient cells to consider: ON-transient cells that are activated by the onset of an input, and OFF-transient cells that are activated by the offset of an input. Recall from the explanation of the traveling wave in Figure 8.16 that the waning activation due to the first flash sums with the waxing activation due to the second flash in the long-range Gaussian filter to cause the G-wave. The model proposes that the waning of activation due to first flash turns on OFF-transient cells, and the waxing of activation due to the second flash turns on ON-transient cells. The model further predicts that a G-wave can occur when the OFF-transient cell activation adds to the ON-transient cell activation through the Gaussian filter.

With this background, consider how the transient cells behave when the Ternus display is presented with a short ISI. In response to the first frame of the Ternus display (Figure 8.23), the ON-transient cells respond at the locations of all three flashes. Now consider how the transient cells respond to the three flashes in the second frame of the display. Recall that two of the three positions are the same in the two sets of flashes. If the ISI is sufficiently short, then the waning activation to the first flash and the waxing activation to the second flash tend to cancel out at these positions. As a result, neither the OFF-transient cells nor the ON-transient cells can be activated at the shared positions when the second frame occurs, as illustrated by the computer simulation summaried in Figure 8.27 (left column). Only the leftmost flash in the first frame and the rightmost flash in the second frame can substantially activate transient cells at this time. The leftmost flash activates OFF-transient cells, and the rightmost flash activates ON-transient cells. These transients combine in a G-wave that travels from the leftmost flash to the rightmost flash, yielding a percept of element motion. This traveling wave does not "bump into" the shared flash

locations because it is caused by summed signals in the long-range directional filter, which activates a processing stage beyond the one where the transient cell responses are computed.

How about group motion? When the ISI is longer, then OFF-transient cells can be activated at all flash positions in Frame 1, and ON-transient cells can be activated at all flash positions in Frame 2 (Figure 8.27, right column). The three flash activations in each frame can then add across space via the Gaussian filter to produce a summed gradient with its maximum in the middle of its three flashes (Figure 8.28, left column). When spatial competition acts on this sum, it selects a single peak of activation that occurs at the middle of the three flashes. This happens to the sum of the OFF-transient cells in response to the first frame, and to the sum of the ON-transient cells in response to the second frame. The group motion percept arises from the traveling wave that occurs between these peaks, as in Figure 8.28 (right column). In summary, the group motion percept can be explained by the same Gaussian long-range directional filter that enables directional responses *and* long-range apparent motion to occur at all, and the element motion percept calls attention to the importance of transient cells at an earlier motion processing stage.

Why is element motion eliminated when the flashes of the first and second frames have different relative contrasts relative to the background, as in Figure 8.24? To fix ideas, suppose that the three stimulus dots in Frame 1 are more luminous than their background, whereas the three dots in Frame 2 are less luminous than their background. The explanation is intuitively simple, once one realizes the key

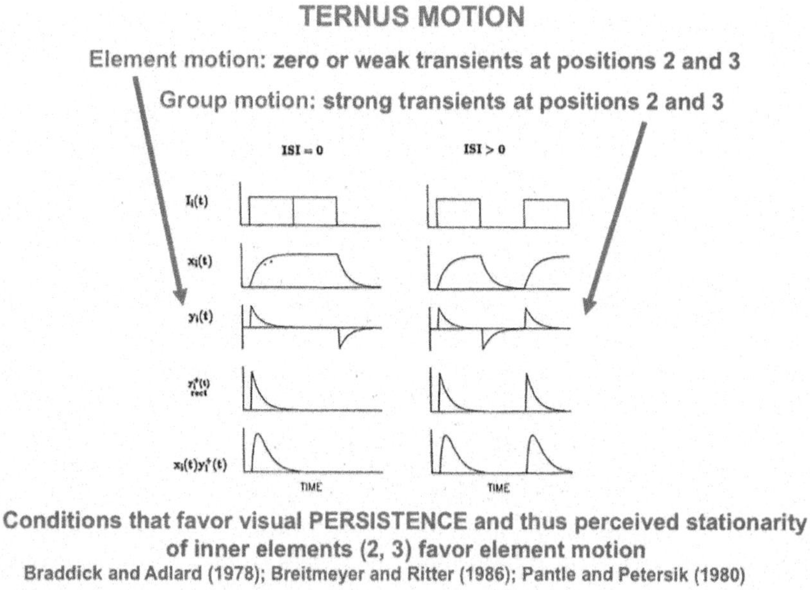

TERNUS MOTION

Element motion: zero or weak transients at positions 2 and 3

Group motion: strong transients at positions 2 and 3

Conditions that favor visual PERSISTENCE and thus perceived stationarity of inner elements (2, 3) favor element motion
Braddick and Adlard (1978); Breitmeyer and Ritter (1986); Pantle and Petersik (1980)

FIGURE 8.27. The distribution of transients through time at onsets and offsets of Ternus display flashes helps to determine whether element motion or group motion will be perceived.

TERNUS GROUP MOTION SIMULATION

If *L* < *2K*, Gaussian filter of three flashes forms one global maximum

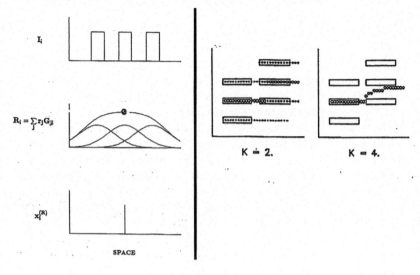

FIGURE 8.28. The Gaussian distributions of activity that arise from the three simultaneous flashes in a Ternus display add to generate a maximum value at their midpoint. The motion of this group gives rise to group motion.

role of ON- and OFF-transient cells in the motion filtering process. Onset of Frame 1 activates ON-transient cells, as before. However, onset of Frame 2 activates OFF-transient cells, no matter how small the ISI is chosen, due to the reversal of contrast between Frames 1 and 2. The offset of Frame 1 can therefore activate OFF-transient cells at all dot positions, just as in the case of a large ISI without contrast-reversed frames. All three locations in both frames can therefore influence the formation of a unimodal motion signal, centered at the middle of each grouping of dots, thereby leading to a percept of group motion at ISIs which, in the same-contrast case, led to element motion.

It should also be noted that, when complete boundary groupings from V2 interact with motion cells in MT and MST due to formotion interactions, as in Figure 8.26, then the illusory contours that are formed between the dots also undergo apparent motion, just as in the percept caused by the apparent motion of illusory contours (Figure 8.11). This kind of formotion interaction will also play an important role below in my explanation of how we see objects that are moving while some of their parts may also be moving relative to them, as in the Duncker illusion.

After reading an explanation like this, one might still think: That is all well and good. But how do I *know* that this explanation, albeit simple and based on elementary mechanisms that are known to occur, is correct? Nothing is certain in science but, as I remarked above, if the same small combination of mechanisms can explain lots of different data properties in a principled and unified way, then one's confidence in them increases accordingly. It would also help to further test these explanations, and to guide

future theoretical developments, if neurophysiological experiments would be done to directly look for parametric properties of G-waves in the motion stream using long-range apparent motion stimuli. Particularly informative data would look for evidence of G-waves of variable speed in response to different inter-flash distances and ISIs, split motion, apparent motion between illusory contours, and Ternus and reverse-contrast Ternus displays, among others.

Spatial attention shifts and tracking by the Where cortical stream

Is there evidence to support the hypothesis that spatial attention shifts may sometimes also be controlled by a G-wave? If this were the case, then spatial attention, just like long-range apparent motion, should be able to adapt its speed to the distance between two successive events. The experiments of several investigators, including Roger Remington and Leslie Pierce in 1984, and Ho-Wan Kwak, Dale Dagenbach, and Howard Egeth in 1991, have, in fact, shown that spatial attention can speed up to cover variable distances in equal time (Kwak, Dagenbach, and Egeth, 1991; Remington and Pierce, 1984).

The hypothesis that G-waves may give rise to both apparent motion and spatial attention shifts is also consistent with anatomical evidence. For example, G-waves for apparent motion are predicted to occur within cortical area MT, or at least no later than MST, which is part of the motion cortical processing stream that is labeled *magnocellular* in Figure 1.21; also see Figure 3.1. The motion stream is, in turn, part of the larger Where cortical processing stream that includes cortical regions MT, MST, and posterior parietal cortex (PPC), as well as their projections to the prefrontal cortex (PFC) (Figure 3.1). Higher processing stages in the Where stream, including the parietal cortex, compute the positions of targets with respect to an observer and direct spatial attention and action towards them (Goodale and Milner, 1992; Mishkin, Ungerlieder, and Macko, 1983; Ungerlieder and Mishkin, 1982).

Data consistent with the prediction that an interpolative process, such as a G-wave, occurs in the Where stream have been reported from the PPC of monkeys (Albright, 1995; Assad and Maunsell, 1995). In particular, in 1995, John Assad and John Maunsell reported that there are motion-sensitive cells in PPC that respond to motion in image regions where no physical motion occurred, but where motion was implied by the temporary disappearance of the stimulus, as occurs when a moving object is temporarily occluded. This is just what would be expected if these cells were influenced by G-waves that arise either in the parietal cortex itself, or in the MT cortex whose outputs can influence parietal activation in the same processing stream. In 1986, William Newsome, Akichika Mikami, and Robert Wurtz described neurophysiological evidence for apparent motion selectivity in MT for higher speed stimuli in macaque monkeys (Newsome, Mikami, and Wurtz, 1996). In 1998, Rainer Goebel, Darius Khorram-Sefat, Lars Muckli, Hans Hacker, and Wolf Singer (Goebel et al., 1998) provided evidence from echoplanar functional magnetic resonance imaging in humans that MT and MST were the first areas of visual cortex to respond with an increase in signal intensity as compared with flickering control conditions.

In evaluating the hypothesis that long-range apparent motion inputs to spatial attention mechanisms, it needs to be kept in mind that a spatially continuous motion signal is generated only under certain spatiotemporal conditions, that the speed of the motion signal is nonuniform in time (e.g., Figure 8.21), and that spatially discrete jumps in activation may occur in cases where continuous motion is not observed; for example, if the distance between "flashes", or intermittent appearances of a target, is too great to be spanned by the spatial scales that subserve the waves (e.g., Figure 8.19). These considerations may help to clarify some of the variability in data about how quickly attention may shift under different conditions, and whether it does so continuously or discretely.

Solving the Aperture Problem: Global capture of object direction and speed

Given this background, we can now outline the Motion BCS explanation of how the motion stream computes an object's direction and speed of motion, even under many of the challenging lighting conditions that occur in the wild. The model also clarifies how attention can be focused on moving objects, and how they may become consciously visible.

The example of a leaping leopard in Figure 8.4 illustrates the fact that, when an object moves under real-world conditions, only a small subset of its image features, such as the object's bounding contours, may generate motion direction cues that accurately describe the object's direction of motion. Despite this fact, object percepts often seem to pop-out with a well-defined motion direction

and speed. As I noted above, the ambiguity of most local motion signals is, in fact, faced by all motion detectors with a finite receptive field due to the aperture problem. Only when a contour within an aperture contains unambiguous features—such as line terminators, object corners, or high contrast blobs or dots—can a local motion detector accurately measure the direction and speed of motion. The brain is capable of using these *feature tracking* signals to impose their directions on other parts of an object which are receiving ambiguous motion signals.

How a brain may do this is illustrated by the percept generated by the classical barberpole display shown in Figure 8.5. As I noted above, in this display, lines are seen moving within an invisible rectangular aperture; that is, within an aperture that is the same color as the paper. In this situation, all the motion directions within the interior of the display are ambiguous, as illustrated by the "fan" of possible motion directions within the interior of each line in Figure 8.5, but the unambiguous feature tracking signals that are computed at the line ends that bound the barberpole can propagate to its interior to select, or capture, motion signals that code the same direction, while suppressing signals that code different directions. In particular, the feature tracking signals that are computed at the barberpole's long axis dominate the motion percept. A number of investigators have presented supportive psychophysical data for this viewpoint, including Ellen Hildreth in 1984, and Ken Nakayama and Gerald Silverman in 1988 (Hildreth, 1984; Nakayama and Silverman, 1988a, 1988b).

From ambiguous local motion to correct object motion: Integration and segmentation

The barberpole illusion illustrates how the brain can generate an unambiguous percept of an object's direction and speed of motion even if most of its local motion signals do not code this direction and speed. This illusion illustrates a brain process that is often called *motion integration*, by which the brain joins spatially separated motion signals into a single object motion percept. Motion integration is complemented by a process of *motion segmentation* that determines when spatially separate motion signals belong to different objects. To accomplish either process, the visual system uses the relatively few feature tracking signals to capture the same motion direction signal at positions where aperture ambiguity holds, while suppressing other directions. As I will explain below, this motion capture process involves cooperative and competitive interactions across space, and the balance between cooperation and competition can determine whether motion integration or segmentation will occur. In addition, when an object is partially occluded, it may not have any strong feature tracking signals, for reasons noted below. Then the visual system uses the same cooperative-competitive interactions among the available ambiguous motion signals to select the statistically most dominant ambiguous motion direction as its best estimate of object direction and speed.

In order to more deeply understand how the global aperture problem is solved, let me first summarize how the design of the 3D FORMOTION model is motivated by five facts about motion perception. I will then show how a model that can explain all these facts can also solve the aperture problem:

The first fact is that, as noted in Figures 8.4 and 8.5, unambiguous feature tracking signals, where they exist, can capture ambiguous motion signals to generate a coherent representation of an object's direction of motion.

A second fact is that a moving object's direction *and* speed are computed by the same set of neural mechanisms. Perceived speed, no less than direction, is an emergent property of the neural interactions that capture and transform ambiguous motion signals into unambiguous ones. A good example of this fact are the percepts that occur when viewing the motion of *plaid stimuli*. To construct such a stimulus, two arrays of parallel lines with different orientations simultaneously move perpendicular to their orientations, as in Figure 8.29. Two distinct percepts can be caused by such motion: one can see either a pair of independently moving, or incoherent, components moving in different directions, or a single coherently moving plaid. When coherent plaid motion is perceived, the plaid seems to move with a direction and speed different from either of its components when they move incoherently. The percepts can switch from one to the other through time. When such a switch occurs, both the direction *and* the speed of the percept change together.

Simultaneous estimation of an object's motion direction and speed

These considerations lead to the model's central design problem: What type of feature tracking process can simultaneously select unambiguous direction *and* accurate speed signals from ambiguous motion signals? To better understand this issue, consider the horizontal motion of a vertical line and of a tilted line that are both moving at the same speed. Suppose that the unambiguous feature tracking signals at the line ends are used to capture the ambiguous motion signals near the line middle. The preferred ambiguous motion direction and speed within the line interior are normal to the line's orientation in both cases. Consequently, the speed of the feature tracking signals at the ends of a vertical line equals the preferred ambiguous speed near the line's middle. For the tilted line, however, the preferred ambiguous speed is less than that of the feature tracking speed, since only the cosine of the preferred ambiguous directional vector is moving in the direction of the line. If the speed of the line is judged using some weighted average of feature tracking signals and ambiguous signals, then a briefly viewed tilted line will be perceived to move slower than a vertical line.

Figure 8.30 (left panel) summarizes data reported in 1993 by Eric Castet, Jean Lorenceau, Maggie Shiffrar, and Claude Bonnet (Castet et al. 1993) that demonstrate this effect. These data also show that the ambiguous speeds, which code slower speeds at larger tilts, have a greater effect as line length increases. Since capture takes longer to complete when lines are longer and have more ambiguous signals, the ambiguous motion signals have a larger effect on longer lines, and lead to percepts of slower speeds of the longer lines. Figure 8.30 (right panel) shows computer simulations of these data that I published in 1997 with my PhD student Jonathan Chey and my colleague Ennio Mingolla (Chey, Grossberg, and Mingolla, 1997) using only the motion processing stages of the 3D FORMOTION model (Figure 8.26, right column). These stages augmented the original Motion BCS model (Figure 8.25) by adding a directional grouping stage in the model's cortical area MST. MST interacts with MT via positive feedback (Figure 8.26). This augmented model can solve the aperture problem, as I will explain shortly.

In addition to simulating data of Castet et al. on how the perceived speeds of moving lines are affected by their length and angle, the model also simulates data about how the barberpole illusion and its variants are produced (Wallach, 1976), and how plaid patterns move both coherently and incoherently (Adelson

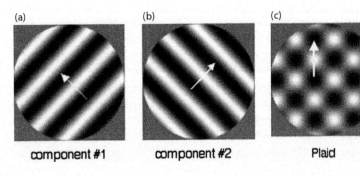

(a) component #1   (b) component #2   (c) Plaid

FIGURE 8.29. When the individual component motions in (A) and (B) combine into a plaid motion (C), both their perceived direction and speed changes.

SOLVING THE APERTURE PROBLEM

A KEY DESIGN PROBLEM:

How do amplified feature tracking signals propagate within depth to select the correct motion directions at ambiguous positions?

This propagation from feature tracking signals to the line interior determines perceived speed in Castet et al. data, which is why speed depends on line tilt and length

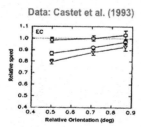 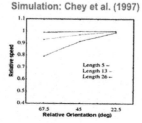

FIGURE 8.30. The data of Castet et al. (1993) in the left image was simulated in the right image by the 3D FORMOTION model that I developed with my PhD student Jonathan Chey. These data provide insight into how feature tracking signals propagate from the ends of a line to its interior, where they capture consistent motion directional signals and inhibit inconsistent ones.

and Movshon, 1982; Ferrera and Wilson, 1990, 1991; Kim and Wilson, 1993; Lindsey and Todd, 1996; Stone, Watson and Mulligan, 1990; Yo and Wilson, 1992).

A third fact is that perceived motion direction and speed result from the collective action of multiple populations of cells with different receptive field sizes, or scales. Recall from the discussion of apparent motion that the G-waves of multiple scales can remain spatially aligned through time (Figures 8.20 and 8.21). The importance of this fact can be better appreciated now, because multiple scales are needed to estimate object direction and speed, which is proposed to occur in the following way.

Experiments that Oliver Braddick published in 1974 disclosed what is often called the *short-range motion process.* This process typically operates over distances under 15 minutes of visual angle and at inter-stimulus intervals under 100 milliseconds (Braddick, 1974, 1980). The limits on short-range apparent motion are due to the spatial and temporal integration properties of early motion detectors. In contrast, long-range apparent motion, which includes examples like beta motion and Ternus motion, operates over distances up to several degrees, and over inter-stimulus intervals up to half a

second, as I observed during the discussion of Korte's laws (Figure 8.22; Kolers, 1972).

There are short-range directional filters with multiple spatial scales, as in Figure 8.32. Each scale in this short-range filter processes outputs from transient cells, which respond to changes in input stimuli. Recall how transient cells helped to explain Ternus element and group motion, as in Figure 8.27. The short-range filter cells accumulate evidence from the transient cells for motion in their preferred directions by using receptive fields that are elongated in that direction.

Speed selectivity from interactions among multiple scales of directional cells

Cells in the directional short-range filter (Figure 8.31) pool directional transient signals from object features that have the same contrast polarity. The polarity-selectivity of these cells is analogous to that of the simple cells of the form perception system (Figures 4.15-4.17). Larger scales, or receptive fields, within the short-range filter preferentially respond to higher speeds. The intuitive rationale for this property is simple: When objects move faster, they can cover a fixed amount of distance in less time. Larger receptive fields have a better chance of accumulating evidence for faster motions, since

WHY ARE SO MANY MOTION PROCESSING STAGES NEEDED?

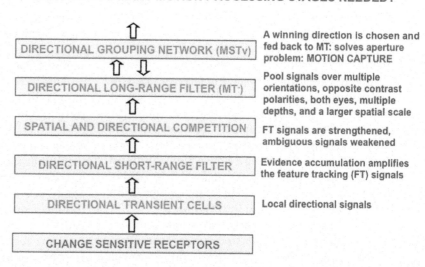

FIGURE 8.31. Processing stages of the Motion BCS convert locally ambiguous motion signals from transient cells into a globally coherent percept of object motion, thereby solving the aperture problem.

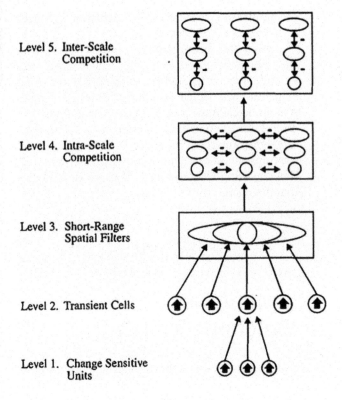

Level 5. Inter-Scale Competition

Level 4. Intra-Scale Competition

Level 3. Short-Range Spatial Filters

Level 2. Transient Cells

Level 1. Change Sensitive Units

FIGURE 8.32. Schematic of motion filtering circuits.

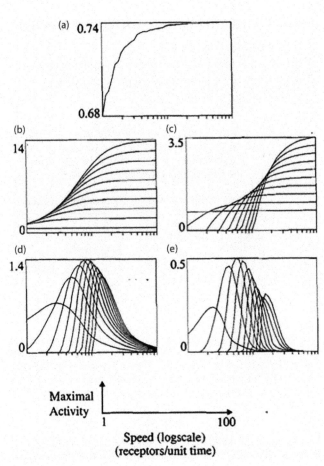

FIGURE 8.33. Processing motion signals by a population of speed-tuned neurons.

faster motions remain within larger receptive fields for a longer amount of time than they will within smaller receptive fields.

Given this advantage of larger receptive fields in accumulating activity through time, a key problem in designing a multiple-scale filter is to prevent the largest scale from winning the competition at *all* motion speeds, simply because it has a larger receptive field with which to attain a higher level of activation. Figure 8.33 illustrates this problem. Figure 8.33a simulates the total response of transient cells at higher speeds, and the series of curves in Figure 8.33b shows that the largest scale cells (top curve; smaller scale cells, lower curves) are always more activated at every speed. Given this advantage of larger scales, how do smaller scales selectively produce larger output signals at lower speeds, while larger scales continue to produce larger output signals at higher speeds? Jonathan Chey and I showed in 1998 (Chey, Grossberg, and Mingolla, 1998) how this could be done by using a simple mechanism that is found in many parts of the brain, and which had earlier been used to model several different brain functions. This mechanism can be realized in at least two ways.

One way to realize this property is to assume that every receptive field, independent of its size, receives connections to its cell body that are *normalized*; that is, the connection strengths to each of the cells have the same *total* connection strength. As a result, individual inputs to a larger receptive field have a smaller effect on cell firing, but there are more of

them. This is a property that occurs quite generally in many different kinds of adaptive filters in the brain, notably the ones that control category learning and choice in an ART network (Figure 5.19a). Such normalized receptive fields develop naturally in laminar models of the visual cortex, as I showed with my PhD students James Williamson and Aaron Seitz in two papers published in *Cerebral Cortex* (Grossberg and Seitz, 2003; Grossberg and Williamson, 2001).

Due to receptive field normalization, all scales of the motion filter accumulate evidence in their prescribed direction, but the larger scales need to accumulate more evidence than the smaller scales in order to generate an equivalent output signal. This hypothesis begins to make the output signals selective to receptive field size, as illustrated in Figure 8.33c, where different scales are maximally activated in different speed ranges. When these thresholded output signals activate the two kinds of competitive interactions in Levels 4 and 5 of the model circuit in Figure 8.32, then each cell scale generates a unimodal response profile for its maximal responses as a function of speed, with each scale having its peak maximal activity at a different preferred speed (Figure 8.33d and 8.33e). The *population* of *all* these speed-selective cells, with their overlapping responses at each speed, determines the perceived speed of an object after it is further processed by the circuits in Figure 8.31. This speed estimate enabled Jon Chey and me to accurately simulate how visual speed perception and discrimination in humans are affected by stimulus contrast, duration, density, and spatial frequency of the moving stimuli.

The fourth design principle concerns how nearby object contours of different contrast polarity and orientation that are moving in the same direction can all pool their signals via the directional long-range filter (Figure 8.31) to generate a pooled motion direction signal, as in Figure 8.1. Recall that this pooling process differentiates the *direction-sensitive* motion cortical stream from the *orientation-sensitive* form cortical stream, and is a key difference in their complementary computations. As I have already noted, these long-range directional filter cells are the first true direction-selective cells in the model. They are analogous to the complex cells of the form perception system, as in Figures 4.17 and 4.19. This is the same long-range directional Gaussian filter that generates the G-wave which simulates data about long-range apparent motion, as in Figure 8.16, including beta, gamma, delta, reverse, split, Ternus, and reverse-contrast Ternus motion, and Korte's laws.

Explaining properties of cells in cortical area MT

The Motion BCS model hereby explains how long-range apparent motion and target tracking properties may arise from more basic constraints on generating direction-selective "complex cells" in the motion system. This analysis suggests that the earliest anatomical stage at which the long-range directional filter can occur is cortical area MT in the Where cortical processing stream (Figures 1.21 and 3.1). One important experimental fact about MT cells that is also exhibited by the long-range directional filter is that they each combine inputs from both eyes, as shown in experiments in 1983 by John Maunsell and David van Essen, and in 1995 by David Bradley, Ning Qian, and Richard Andersen (Bradley, Qian, and Andersen, 1995; Maunsell and van Essen, 1983). The model hypothesis that the long-range directional filter carries the G-wave, and also receives inputs from both eyes, is consistent with data showing that long-range apparent motion occurs with dichoptically presented stimuli. Thus, if Flash 1 is presented to one eye and Flash 2 to the other eye, then long-range apparent motion may still be perceived, as was reported in 1948 by J. A. Gengerelli and in 1968 by Irwin Spigel (Gengerelli, 1948; Spigel, 1968).

This last property is one of the reasons that the original ideas of Gestalt psychologists about apparent motion being

due to a "field theory" were rejected. It was not clear what sort of continuous field could react to different stimuli to the two eyes. A binocular long-range directional filter has no problem with these data, since it can generate a G-wave from dichoptically presented stimuli because inputs from both eyes activate the directional long-range filter (Figure 8.31).

Other data about the properties of MT cells are also consistent with this model prediction. For example, Akichika Mikami published neurophysiological data in 1991 that was recorded from macaque monkeys whose MT cells responded to long-range apparent motion (Mikami, 1991). Using a multi-channel biomagnetometer, the human homolog of MT was also shown to respond to long-range apparent motion in 1997 by Yoshiki Kaneoke, Masahiko Bundou, Sachiko Koyama, Hiroyuki Suzuki, and Ryusuke Kakigi (Kaneoke et al., 1997). Thomas Albright and Hillary Rodman published neurophysiological data in 1985 and 1987 showing that most MT cells are directionally selective for a wide variety of stimulus forms (Albright, 1984; Rodman and Albright, 1987), consistent with the model hypothesis that the long-range filter pools over multiple orientations moving in the same direction (Figure 8.31).

In a similar vein, the orientational selectivity of MT neurons appears to be weaker than their directional selectivity, in the sense that movement in the preferred direction will usually evoke a response even from a bar aligned in a non-preferred orientation (Albright, 1984). In addition, John Maunsell and David Van Essen showed in 1983 that responses to oriented bars are transient even for preferred orientations (Maunsell and Van Essen, 1983), consistent with the idea that MT cells are fed by transient cells from lower processing stages (Figure 8.31). These various authors also reported that MT cells exhibit well-defined speed tuning curves (Maunsell and Van Essen, 1983; Rodman and Albright, 1987), consistent with the hypothesis that they come after the multi-scale short-range filter (Figure 8.31). Thus, all the model stages of processing by transient cells, a speed-tuned directional short-range filter, and a long-range directional filter are consistent with neurophysiological data about MT cells.

Solving the Aperture Problem: Cycling bottom-up motion grouping and top-down priming

The fifth design principle concerns how motion capture occurs. The processing stages up to the long-range directional filter creates direction-selective cells that can interpolate continuous motion trajectories through spatially discrete appearances, or "flashes", of motion cues.

But these stages cannot solve the aperture problem. They can amplify the strengths of feature tracking signals relative to ambiguous motion signals using the directional short-range filter and the spatial and directional competition (Figure 8.31), but they cannot remove the ambiguous motion signals. The key remaining problem is to explain how feature tracking signals can select, or capture, the correct *object motion direction* from among the large array of ambiguous motion directional signals (see Figure 8.4), while suppressing incorrect motion directions, without distorting or destroying the *speed* estimate of the selected direction. Thus, motion capture is a process of capturing motion-direction-and-speed. This hypothesis is supported by many psychophysical data showing that direction and speed are selected together, as is vividly illustrated during switches between percepts of incoherent and coherent plaid motion (Figure 8.29), which can be seen in the video https://www.youtube.com/watch?v=WhbZesV2GRk.

A single feedback loop controls motion capture and attentional priming of motion direction. My proposed solution to the global aperture problem leads to a surprising prediction that is consistent with neurophysiological and functional neuroimaging experiments, but has not yet been directly tested. The prediction is that motion capture and attentional priming can both be achieved by the same process; namely, a single long-range grouping and priming network, as in Figure 8.31. *Attentional priming* is the process whereby recent exposures to a stimulus or to other stimuli that are similar to, or associated with, that stimulus can decrease the time it takes to find the stimulus when it is presented among distracting stimuli. Thus, if I say: "Look for your brother John," you may detect John more quickly in a crowd than if you did not activate the prime. The prediction that motion capture and attentional priming may use the same process is surprising because motion capture is an automatic and *preattentive* process. Why should this preattentive process also be used by volition to focus, or prime, attention to selectively look for motions in a desired direction, and to amplify any such motions that may occur? In this regard, several authors have shown that attention *can* focus selectively on a desired motion direction (Groner, Hofer, and Groner, 1986; Sekuler and Ball, 1977; Stelmach and Herdman, 1991; Stelmach, Herdman, and McNeil, 1994).

How can a preattentive process, which typically uses *bottom-up* circuits that relay signals from peripheral processing stages to ones deeper in the brain, share the same mechanisms as an attentive process, which typically uses *top-down* circuits that relay signals from deeper in the brain towards the periphery? The Motion BCS model predicts that preattentive motion capture and attentive motion priming process are achieved by bottom-up and top-down pathways, respectively, that define a *feedback* circuit between the same pair of processing stages (Figure 8.31). These processing stages are proposed to be cortical areas MT and MST. More specifically, they occur in a particular substream of MT, called *MT minus* (MT⁻), and of MST, called *ventral MST* (MSTv). This prediction is consistent with the fact that MSTv has large directionally-tuned receptive fields that are specialized for detecting moving objects, as was reported in 1993 by K. Tanaka, Y. Sugita, M. Moriya, and H. Saito (Tanaka, Sugita, Moriya, and Saito, 1993).

Complementary motion streams for motion capture and visually-based navigation. Just as MT⁻ and MSTv are specialized to detect and track moving objects, a parallel cortical stream through regions MT⁺ and dorsal MST, or MSTd, is specialized to carry out visually-based navigation based on optic flow signals (Figure 8.34). Optic flow is the pattern of motion that is generated in an observer's brain when objects in a visual scene move relative to the observer. How optic flow can be used to guide

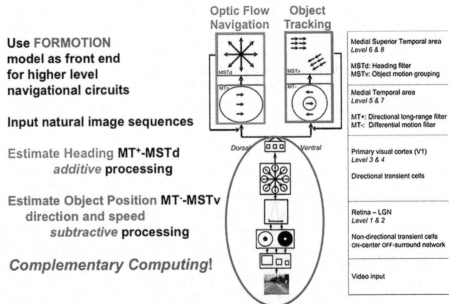

FIGURE 8.34. The ViSTARS model for visually-based spatial navigation. It uses the Motion BCS as a front end and feeds its output signals into two computationally complementary cortical processing streams for computing optic flow and target tracking information.

navigation using the MT⁻-to-MSTv and MT⁺-to-MSTd cortical streams will be discussed in Chapter 9. For now, let me just note that these two parallel processing streams use computationally complementary processes. These complementary computations are illustrated in Figure 8.34 by the assertion that *additive* processing enables the brain to determine the direction of *heading*, or a navigator's self-motion direction, whereas *subtractive* processing is used to determine the position, direction, and speed of a moving object. These complementary types of processing enable the computation of an observer's heading while moving relative to a scene, and of an object's movements relative to the observer. This latter information, in turn, can be used to avoid collisions with objects in a scene while moving through it.

Chapter 9 will discuss how navigation based on optic flow signals work. Then Chapter 16 will discuss how navigation based on path integration signals works. Whereas optic flow navigation computations occur in cortical areas MT and MST, among others, path integration navigation computations occur in the entorhinal and hippocampal cortices. Chapter 16 will propose why path integration computations occur there, as part of an analysis which suggests that time and space—or, more specifically, adaptively-timed learning and spatial navigation—both occur in the entorhinal-hippocampal system because they both exploit variations of the same circuit designs. Chapter 16 will also discuss work that remains to be done to unify our understanding of how vision and path integration work together to control navigation under multiple conditions, including in the dark.

ART again: Choosing an object's motion direction and speed. Let us now return to how our brains solve the aperture problem, MSTv cells in the model combine bottom-up directional signals from the long-range filter stage of MT⁻ (Figures 8.26 and 8.34). A competitive circuit within MSTv then chooses the most active MSTv cells; in other words, chooses the direction that has the most evidence within their receptive fields (Figure 8.35). The active MSTv cells then send top-down attentional feedback signals that obey the ART Matching Rule (Figure 1.25) back to MT⁻ (Figure 8.35). Due to the modulatory on-center, off-surround interactions of these feedback signals, they select MT⁻ cells with the same, or similar, directional preferences, and suppress cells that code different directions. Importantly, this selection process does not distort the speed estimates of the selected MT⁻ cells because the on-center is modulatory.

Why does the ART Matching Rule control the attentional feedback signals from MSTv to MT⁻? This is true for the same reason that it always

controls object attention: This kind of circuit dynamically stabilizes the memory of learned receptive fields. In this case, the receptive fields that are learned are directional grouping cells in MSTv. Directional grouping cells are thus a kind of directional recognition category within an ART feedback circuit.

ART again: Dynamically stabilizing learned directional cells also solves the aperture problem. By dynamically stabilizing the learning of directional grouping cells in MSTv, the ART Matching Rule also automatically solves the global aperture problem! In other words, evolution did not have to design a specialized solution of the aperture problem. All it had to do was to implement the usual ART feedback dynamics to dynamically stabilize the memory of learned categories, in this case learned directional categories. I will return to this issue below, right after using the MT⁻-MSTv feedback network to solve the global aperture problem.

The Castet et al. (1993) data in Figure 8.30 about the perceived speeds of moving tilted lines provide a vivid example of how the global aperture problem is solved by this feedback circuit. Recall that the feature tracking signals at the ends of the tilted moving lines are amplified by the directional short-range filter and the competitive stages in Figure 8.31. As a result, these feature tracking signals are the ones that typically win the directional competition in MSTv and feed back their winning directional signals to MT⁻. Due to the ART Matching Rule, the feature tracking

HOW TO SELECT CORRECT DIRECTION AND PRESERVE SPEED ESTIMATES?

Prediction:
Feedback from MSTv to MT⁻ obeys *ART Matching Rule*
Top-down, modulatory on-center, off-surround network
Grossberg, 1976, 1980; Carpenter and Grossberg, 1987, 1991
Explains how directional grouping network can stably develop
and how top-down directional attention can work
Cavanagh, 1992; Goner et al., 1986; Sekuler and Ball, 1977; Stelmach et al, 1994

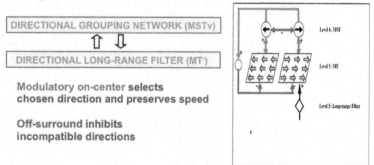

FIGURE 8.35. The output signals from the directional grouping network obey the ART Matching Rule. They thereby select consist motion directional signals while suppressing inconsistent ones, and do not distort the velocities that the spared cells code. The aperture problem is hereby solved by the same mechanism that dynamically stabilizes the learning of directional grouping cells.

directions in MT⁻ are selected by these feedback signals, while the other ambiguous motion signals are suppressed (Figure 8.36). Thus, after MT-MSTv feedback acts in a given region of space, the only cells that remain active at positions that previously computed ambiguous motion directions are those that code the feature tracking direction.

All the active MT⁻ cells in this region now code for the feature tracking direction, and cells that had ambiguous signals in that region will no longer be active (Figure 8.36). During the next cycle, the bottom-up signals from MT⁻ near the border of this region can enhance the activities of MSTv cells that are outside the original region, but near it. Then these MSTv cells can win the directional competition at their position, and feed back to MT⁻ the winning direction to again suppress different directional signals. The cycle can iterate in this way and propagate the feature tracking direction across the entire object by selecting directionally-compatible ambiguous motion signals and suppressing cells that code for different directions.

What is remarkable about the propagation across space of the feature tracking direction is that it arises through a feedback cycle that just activates the same cells between MT⁻ and MSTv over and over again. There is no explicit lateral motion mechanism, just the cyclic action of bottom-up and top-down feedback exchanges. The effect, though, is one of a laterally propagating wave of directional selection, as occurs in the percepts and simulations of tilted moving lines (Figures 8.30 and 8.36) that were reported by Castet et al. (1993).

Figure 8.37 summarizes a computer simulation showing how motion capture occurs as a diagonally oriented line moves to the right. The left column shows responses of the directionally-selective transient cells and short-range filter cells. The top row of the right column shows how enhanced rightward-pointing feature tracking signals at the line ends initially coexist with ambiguous aperture signals within the line interior at the directional long-range filter cells. The second and third rows of this column show how the rightward feature tracking direction propagates towards the middle of the line through time, selecting consistent directional signals, while suppressing inconsistent ones, as it does so.

Stable learning unifies preattentive motion capture and attentive directional priming

Such a feedback circuit also helps to understand how motions in the world that automatically attract attention via a bottom-up route interact with volitional top-down attentive motion priming. The bottom-up route activates transient signals, such as those that occur during change blindness (see Chapter 7), and during long-range apparent motion. The ART feedback circuit creates an interface wherein bottom-up automatic attention and top-down volitional attention can cooperate and compete until they reach a consensus. Processes of learning, expectation, and attention are hereby parsimoniously unified within a single circuit. As Chapter 5 noted, these three processes are a subset of the CLEARS design whereby processes of Consciousness, Learning, Expectation, Attention, Resonance, and Synchrony work together.

Data supporting the MT⁻-MSTv prediction

Psychophysical, functional imaging, and neurophysiological data in humans and animals support the prediction that preattentive motion capture and attentional motion priming share the same feedback circuit between cortical areas MT⁻ and

MOTION CAPTURE BY DIRECTIONAL GROUPING FEEDBACK

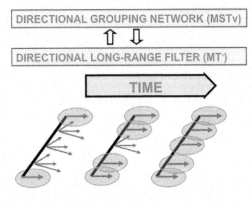

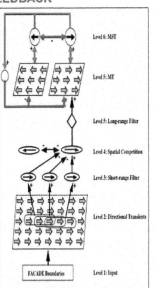

It takes longer to capture ambiguous motion signals in the line interior as the length of the line increases
cf. Castet et al., 1993)

FIGURE 8.36. How the directional grouping network, notably properties of the ART Matching Rule, enables a small set of amplified feature tracking signals at the ends of a line to select consistent directions in the line interior, while suppressing inconsistent directions.

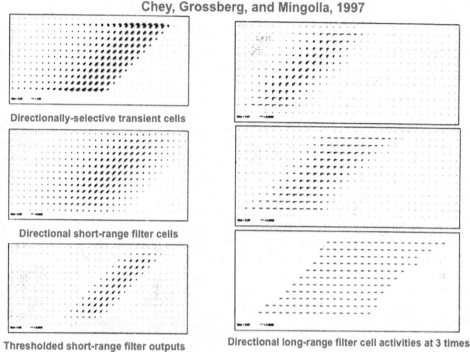

MOTION CAPTURE BY DIRECTIONAL GROUPING FEEDBACK
Chey, Grossberg, and Mingolla, 1997

Directionally-selective transient cells

Directional short-range filter cells

Thresholded short-range filter outputs

Directional long-range filter cell activities at 3 times

FIGURE 8.37. Processing stages that transform the transient cell inputs in response to a tilted moving line into a global percept of the object's direction of motion. The orientations of the lines denote the directional preferences of the corresponding cells, whereas line lengths are proportional to cell activities.

MSTv. For example, in 1992, Patrick Cavanagh (Cavanagh, 1992) described psychophysical data about what he called an attention-based motion process that he proposed exists in addition to low-level or automatic motion processes. He showed that this attention-based process enables human subjects to make accurate velocity judgments. The Motion BCS model explains these data by showing how the attentive process solves the aperture problem while it selects the correct speeds for the captured motion directions. In 1996, Stefan Treue and John Maunsell (Treue and Maunsell, 1996) published neurophysiological data showing that attention can modulate motion processing in cortical areas MT and MST of macaque monkeys. In 1997, Kathleen O'Craven, Bruce Rosen, Kenneth Kwong, Anne Treisman, and Robert Savoy (O'Craven et al., 1997) showed by using magnetic resonance imaging that attention can modulate the MT/MST complex in humans.

In addition, there is growing evidence that the ART Matching Rule regulates attention during form and motion perception, visual object recognition, auditory streaming, speech perception, and cognitive working memory and list chunking, among other processes, as I have reviewed in several articles (Grossberg, 1999, 2013a, 2017b, 2018). Even within the context of motion processing *per se*, this hypothesis, when suitably modeled, enabled

me in 1997 to publish an article with my PhD student Aijaz Baloch (Baloch and Grossberg, 1997) in which we simulated many data that were collected in psychophysical experiments with humans, including percepts that are called the line motion illusion (Hikosaka, Miyauchi, and Shimojo, 1993a, 1993b), motion induction (Faubert and von Grünau, 1992, 1995; von Grünau and Faubert, 1994; von Grünau, Racette, and Kwas, 1996), and transformational apparent motion (Tse and Cavanagh, 1995; Tse, Cavanagh, and Nakayama, 1996). I will now explain these percepts to add additional experimental evidence for the role of the ART Matching Rule, as well as to articulate various perceptual issues that are of interest in their own right.

Line motion illusion: Attentive or preattentive?

The *line motion illusion* illustrates how attention can influence the perception of preattentive motion signals. In this percept, which was described in 1993 by Okihide Hikosaka, Satoru Miyauchi, and Shinsuke Shimojo (Hikosaka et al., 1993a, 1993b), a line or bar is presented so that its end touches the position where a previously presented dot appeared just a moment before. Under these conditions, the line seems to smoothly grow out of that position through time. This compelling motion illusion was attributed to an attentional gradient, such that regions of the line closest to the attended spot are processed faster and thereby activate higher-level motion detectors earlier. One can think of this attentional gradient as having a Gaussian distribution across space, so that locations nearest to the attentional focus get more total activation from attention-plus-line than locations further away get from line alone, so that cells at the most active positions can fire first.

Such a Gaussian distribution, or "attentional spotlight", would not, however, be expected to extend across the entire length of the line. What other processes are activated by the attentional spotlight that enable such a long-range effect to be seen? Other studies clarify how such a long-range effect may be caused by showing that preattentive factors often play a critical role in generating such motion percepts, and that the balance between attentive and preattentive factors can be altered by rather small changes in the visual stimuli. For example, Jocelyn Fauert and Michael von Grünau showed in a series of articles between 1992 and 1995 (Faubert and von Grünau, 1992, 1995; von Grünau and Faubert, 1994) a number of striking motion percepts, including the following ones: When the line that causes the line motion illusion is shut off, motion appears to reverse, and the line seems to be sucked back into the spot. In split priming experiments, when a line is presented between two spatially separated priming spots, motion emerges from both spots and collides in the middle of the line. When the spots are not turned on simultaneously, the collision point occurs closer to the first spot. Faubert and von Grünau have generically called these percepts "motion induction".

Why does a process like attention cause split priming or reverse motion at line offset? In 1997, Aijaz Baloch and I offered a unified explanation, supported by computer simulations, of all these percepts using the Motion BCS model (Baloch and Grossberg, 1997). A big hint about how to explain these data can be seen in Figures 6.5 and 6.6 which show neurophysiological data and a model computer simulation of how spatial attention can flow along a boundary grouping. Recall that boundary groupings can form automatically and pre-attentively. This kind of data will be explained with greater mechanistic insight in Chapter 10 after I explain how and why the circuits of the visual cortex, and more generally the circuits within all granular neocortex, are organized into layers of cells, as Figures 4.58 and 5.38 have already illustrated. Top-down attention and preattentively formed groupings come together in these laminar circuits to choose the final percept.

Psychophysical and neurophysiological data supporting feedback during motion capture

One possible concern about the hypothesis that feedback is involved is that iterating feedback through multiple cycles would require quite a bit to time to propagate the feature tracking direction across space, indeed much more time than would a purely feedforward system. In fact, this is exactly what happens in many experiments. Indeed, the influence of feature tracking signals requires far more time to take effect than does the initial detection of object motion. For example, the psychophysical data of Castet et al. (1993) that were summarized in Figure 8.30 show that varying the length of a tilted line can alter the perceived speed of the line when it is briefly presented. This effect of line length on perceived speed operates much more slowly than the operation of a single feedforward pathway would take. In fact, each line was displayed for 167 milliseconds. The data are consistent with the hypothesis that feature tracking information has not yet fully propagated along the line within 167 milliseconds, and that speed biases are due to residual ambiguous motion signals that are present along the line length even after that amount of time has elapsed.

Likewise, in 1990, Vincent Ferrera and Hugh Wilson (Ferrera and Wilson, 1990) reported that the perceived directions of certain plaid patterns (the so-called Type II plaids) moved towards the feature tracking directions over a time period between 60 and 150 milliseconds, which is much longer than a purely feedforward process would take. In 1992, Wilson, Ferrera, and Christopher Yo (Wilson, Ferrera, and Yo, 1992) interpreted this effect as being due to a longer integration time in a separate pathway that is specialized for processing feature tracking signals. Additional data that Linda Bowns published in 1996 (Bowns, 1996) are inconsistent with this interpretation, but support the current feature tracking proposal that this amount of time naturally arises within a *single* processing stream as a result of feedback between bottom-up directional grouping and top-down directional priming, attention, and selection, as in Figure 8.31.

Perhaps the most compelling direct evidence for the feedback process was collected by my PhD student Christopher Pack when he was working as a postdoctoral fellow with Richard Born at Harvard Medical School. Chris had learned about my 1997 article with Jonathan Chey that simulated a solution to the aperture problem while he was doing his PhD with me in our department. In 2001, Pack and Born published a neurophysiological experiment done with alert macaque monkeys that tested the prediction about how long it takes for the brain to solve the aperture problem (Pack and Born, 2001). They reported that MT neurons initially respond primarily to the component of motion perpendicular to a contour's orientation, which is the expected ambiguous direction response due to the aperture problem. Over a period of approximately 170 milliseconds, the responses of MT cells gradually shifted to code the true feature tracking direction, regardless of orientation, again a much longer time than a feedforward process could explain. Their experiment also tested whether these MT cells controlled the direction of eye movements. Their behavioral data showed that the initial velocity of pursuit eye movements also deviated in a direction perpendicular to local contour orientation.

The Pack and Born data from 2001 are plotted in Figure 8.38 alongside the 1997 simulation that I did with Jonathan Chey about this transition (Chey, Grossberg, and Mingolla, 1997). This simulation also fit the Castet et al. (1993) data on the apparent speed of a tilted line moving to the right (Figure 8.30). As I noted above, Castet et al. displayed each line for 167 milliseconds. The time scale that led to our good fits to those data in Figure 8.30 also led to the perceived direction simulation in Figure 8.38 (right column). In this simulation, the perceived direction gradually shifts from the tilted aperture-ambiguous initial direction towards the correct object motion direction of zero degrees. The time scale in the simulation is shown in arbitrary units. When converted to the time scale of the Castet et al. speed data, this arbitrary time scale is converted to approximately the 170 millisecond time scale that was reported in the neurophysiological recordings of Pack and Born (2001) that are summarized in Figure 8.38 (left column). The fact that these two time scales so closely agree, especially given that the 1997 simulations of psychophysical data anticipated the 2001 recordings from MT cells, provides additional support for the model hypothesis

of how the aperture problem is solved using feedback interactions between MT and MSTv.

ART Matching Rule explains induced motion

The same modulatory property whereby the ART Matching Rule chooses the feature tracking direction without distorting the speed estimates of the surviving MT cells also clarifies why motion signals do not appear to propagate throughout regions of empty space. *Induced motion*, which was described by Hans Wallach in 1976 (Wallach, 1976), illustrates this property. During induced motion, when a square outline moves to the right, this motion can make an enclosed stationary dot appear to move to the left. However, the intervening space does not appear to move. Likewise, during motion capture, randomly scintillating dots may be captured by unambiguous motion signals, but empty space is not, as was shown in 1985 by V. S. Ramachandran and V. Inada (Ramachandran and Inada, 1985).

These data properties are consistent with the the model prediction that top-down excitatory feedback from MSTv to MT is directional and *modulatory*: Top-down, modulatory on-center signals can help to *select* a motion direction that has already been activated by the bottom-up long-range filter, but cannot, by itself, *activate* a cell.

Although the top-down, modulatory feedback cannot create a suprathreshold motion signal in empty space, it can do so at the position of the stationary dot, which receives a bottom-up input, thereby generating the percept of induced motion.

An exception to this rule may seem to occur during long-range apparent motion, where motion is perceived at positions between the offset of one flash and the onset of another flash. However, this can be explained by a G-wave of *bottom-up* activation that travels between the flashes as it propagates across the long-range filter in MT *before* this wave can activate the circuits that trigger top-down ART Matching Rule feedback from MSTv.

In summary, the feedback exchange of signals between MT and MSTv can support the multiple tasks of stable learning of directionally-tuned motion-selective cells, preattentive motion capture, directional attentional priming, and conscious perception of moving

SOLVING THE APERTURE PROBLEM TAKES TIME

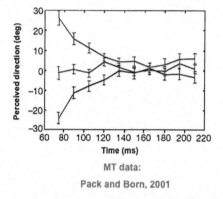

MT data:

Pack and Born, 2001

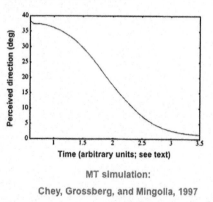

MT simulation:

Chey, Grossberg, and Mingolla, 1997

FIGURE 8.38. The neurophysiological data from MT (left image) confirms the prediction embodied in the simulation of MT (right image) concerning the fact that it takes a long time for MT to compute an object's real direction of motion.

objects. The original modeling articles with my students Aijaz Baloch, Julia Berzhanskaya, Jonathan Chey, Praveen Pilly, and Lavanya Viswanathan provide explanations and computer simulations of many more motion percepts (Baloch and Grossberg, 1997; Baloch et al., 1999; Berzhanskaya, Grossberg, and Mingolla, 2007; Chey, Grossberg, and Mingolla, 1997, 1998; Grossberg, Mingolla, and Viswanathan. 2001; Grossberg and Pilly, 2008). Here I will select a few more percepts for explanation that further demonstrate how key design principles of motion perception work.

Barberpole motion

The next level of complexity in simulating the motion of simple forms arises when one or more moving oriented contours are viewed through an aperture. We already know that the motion of a contour is ambiguous when it moves within a circular aperture, due to the aperture problem (Figure 8.5, left image). The barberpole display has a long and a short axis that break the symmetry of the circular aperture (Figure 8.5, right image). If a single diagonal line moves in this rectangular aperture at any time, then it is perceived to move diagonally in the corner regions and horizontally in the long central region. The presence of multiple moving lines tends to lock the percept into a single direction of motion along the length of the aperture. A computer simulation of these effects is summarized in Figure 8.39 (right column), with the top row showing the diagonal direction that is perceived when the line first enters the rectangular aperture from the left, and the bottom row showing the horizontal direction that is perceived when the line is moving in the middle of the rectangular aperture.

There are at least two possible explanations for the perceived diagonal motion in the corner of the barberpole display: It could be that the diagonal motion is the result of a compromise, or average, between the horizontal and vertical feature tracking signals that are present at each end of the line at the corner positions. Alternatively, it could be that the competing feature tracking signals may cancel each other out, leaving the ambiguous motion signals with their propensity to favor the direction normal to the orientation of the line.

A simple way to distinguish between these two explanations is to alter the orientation of the line. According to the first explanation, this should result in, at most, a small shift towards the direction normal to the new orientation. According to the second explanation, such a change in orientation should also have little effect until the orientation becomes sufficient to favor one of the feature tracking directions, at which time the motion of the line may be entirely captured by that direction. Informal observations of barberpole displays suggest that the second of these explanations is correct: In barberpole displays containing lines whose orientation is not exactly intermediate between the two aperture edges, the percept in the corner region seems to move in the direction equal to that of the aperture edge whose orientation is most nearly perpendicular to the line.

This result suggests that the diagonal motion seen in the corner of barberpole displays is a result of inconclusive competition between different feature tracking signals, in the sense that no one feature tracking signal is able to gain dominance and propagate to the rest of the moving line. Interference between multiple feature tracking signals is attributed in the model to the grouping filter that occurs from cortical areas MT⁻ to MSTv. The receptive fields of this filter are sufficiently large to overlap several feature tracking signals.

The difficulty of integrating feature tracking signals that code different directions of motion was also demonstrated in psychophysical experiments by Jean Lorenceau and Maggie Shiffrar in 1992 (Lorenceau and Shiffrar, 1992) and again later in 2001 in an article by Lorenceau with David Alais (Lorenceau and Alais, 2001). Lorenceau and Shiffrar studied the integration of motion information between multiple apertures, each of which revealed a portion of a translating diamond shape. One can think of apertures as the result of occlusion of the moving object via a surface with holes of an irregular shape. Under some conditions, observers could perceive the diamond's rigid motion, but under other conditions,

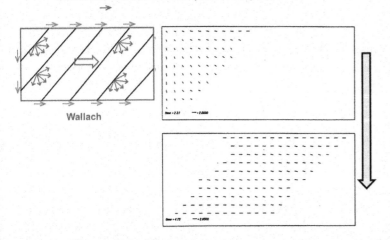

BARBERPOLE ILLUSION (ONE LINE) SIMULATION

Wallach

FIGURE 8.39. Simulation of the barberpole illusion direction field at two times. Note that the initial multiple directions due to the feature tracking signals at the contiguous vertical and horizontal sides of the barberpole (upper image) get supplanted by the horizontal direction of the two horizontal sides (lower image).

MOTION GROUPING ACROSS OCCLUDERS

J. Lorenceau and D. Alais, 2001

Rotating contours observed through apertures

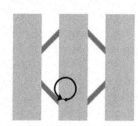

Determine direction of a circular motion

Visible occluders

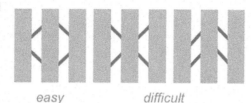

easy   *difficult*

Invisible occluders

difficult

http://persci.mit.edu/demos/square/square.html

FIGURE 8.40. Visible occluders capture the boundaries that they share with moving edges. Invisible occluders do not. Consequently, the two types of motions are influenced by different combinations of feature tracking signals.

observers instead perceived different directions of motion in each aperture. These percepts dramatically illustrate circumstances under which feature information cannot be integrated across apertures. In some displays, the apertures are visible (e.g., Figure 8.40, right column, top row), in others invisible (that is, have the same luminance as the surrounding background; e.g., Figure 8.40, right column, bottom row). In addition, in some displays, distinctive features like object corners are visible inside the apertures, in others they are not (e.g., all the red lines in Figure 8.40). These seemingly innocuous variations can greatly change whether a percept of a rotating partially-occluded object is perceived or not. The Motion BCS model has successfully simulated the percepts that are seen by observers in all of these cases, using the same combination of processes that I have already described (Berzhanskaya, Grossberg, and Mingolla, 2007; Grossberg, Mingolla, and Viswanathan, 2001).

Motion transparency, opponent directions, rebounds, and asymmetry between near and far

Sometimes more than one motion direction can be perceived at each position. The phenomenon of *motion transparency* is illustrative. A typical motion transparency display consists of two fields of superimposed dots moving across a computer screen. When the direction of motion of the two fields of dots is different (Figure 8.41, top half, left image), the visual system may perceive one field of dots to be closer than the other (Figure 8.41, top half, right image), despite the fact that they coexist in the same depth plane on the screen. The motion dissimilarity between the two fields is alone responsible for their depth segregation. Such percepts of motion transparency, no less than those of form transparency (see Figures 1.4 (bottom row) and 4.43c), challenge traditional concepts of how we perceive the world in depth.

We saw in Chapters 3 and 4 that the form system uses multiple scales, or receptive field sizes, to perceive the depths of static objects. The motion system also uses multiple scales to estimate the depths at which objects are moving, in addition to estimating their speeds (Figures 8.32 and 8.33). How do the cells within and between these scales interact? One important factor was discussed earlier in this chapter when I reviewed the fact that form aftereffects, or rebounds, are often rotated 90 degrees from their inducers, as in the MacKay illusion, whereas motion aftereffects are often rotated 180 degrees from their inducers, as in the waterfall illusion (Figure 8.3).

These 180 degree aftereffects arise from mutual inhibition between tonically active cells whose directional preferences differ by 180 degrees in cortical areas like MT, as illustrated in Figure 8.3, and reported in 1984 by Thomas Albright (Albright, 1984). In the Motion BCS, when neither direction is activated by an external input, the mutual inhibition between cells that code opposite directions can keep them quiet. When one direction gets activated by an input, the other gets more inhibited due to their mutual inhibition. Because the output signals of these opponent motion pathways are gated by habituative transmitters, the transmitter in the active channel habituates more than that in the inactive channel while the input is on. When the motion input shuts off, the equal tonic inputs to the opponent motion channels can then generate a larger net input through the channel that did not habituate. The previously inactive direction can hereby get activated. This is the typical situation in any gated dipole opponent processing circuit (Figures 1.14 and 1.15), where rebounds in the OFF channel can occur when inputs to the ON channel terminate. A similar type of gated dipole circuit, albeit between perpendicular orientations (Figures 7.1 and 7.3), was used to explain data about the visual persistence of static visual inputs (Figures 7.2 and 7.4-7.6). In the case of motion

MOTION TRANSPARENCY

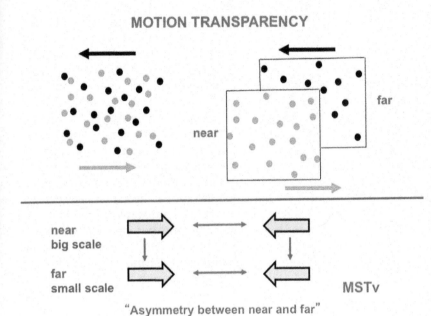

"Asymmetry between near and far"
Inhibition from near (large scales) to far (small scales) at each position

FIGURE 8.41. A percept of motion transparency can be achieved by using motion grouping feedback that embodies the "asymmetry between near and far" along with the usual opponent competition between opposite motion directions.

perception, rebounds between opponent directions can also help to explain the multi-stability of transparent motion, whereby one direction moves in front at some times, while the opposite direction moves in front at other times.

Although opponent direction inhibition has been found in MT, in partial support of the model, it has also been shown capable of suppressing transparent motion. Why does this fact not contradict the model? A closer inspection of these data suggests how they actually support the model. For example, in 1991, Robert Snowden, Stefan Treue, Roger Erickson, and Richard Andersen (Snowden et al., 1991) reported that the response of an MT cell to the motion of random dots in the cell's preferred direction is strongly reduced when a second, transparent dot pattern moves in the opposite direction. In 1997, Gregg Recanzone, Robert Wurtz, and U. Schwarz demonstrated that this result extended to cells in MST and can also be observed when discrete objects are substituted for whole-field motions (Recanzone, Wurtz, and Schwarz, 1997). However, in 1994 and 1995, Richard Andersen and his colleagues (Bradley, Qian, and Andersen, 1995; Qian and Andersen, 1994; Qian, Anderson, and Adelson, 1994) showed that opponent direction inhibition occurs mainly between motion signals whose cells code *similar binocular disparities*, whereas transparent motions occur at different depths that are represented independently in MT, and do not inhibit each other.

The Motion BCS shows how motion transparency can be explained with multiple spatial scales, such that each scale is sensitive to a particular range of depths. Such a

correlation between size and depth is often called the *size-disparity correlation,* both in the form and the motion systems. This is a basic property that the visual system uses to distinguish objects in depth even under conditions where no transparent percept is seen. Such a correlation needs to be computed if only because the image of an object grows on the retina as the object gets closer to it. As a result, an object's retinal image could be large even it is a small object that is very near to the observer. Similarly, an object's retinal image could be small even if it is a large object that is far from the observer. Computing a size-disparity correlation enables the brain to use binocular disparity information, along with retinal size information, to disambiguate these possibilities.

However, during a percept of motion transparency, when both fields of dots are perceived on the same computer screen, there is no difference in binocular disparity between them. How do multiple spatial scales create a 3D percept of transparency from such a 2D display? More generally, how do our adaptations to a 3D world enable us to interpret 2D pictorial representations of the world? This issue was discussed for the case of perceiving figure-ground percepts from static pictures in Chapter 4 (see Figure 4.54-4.56). As I noted there, knowing how the brain accomplishes this feat is needed to understand how a wide range of human activities have evolved, including visual arts such as painting and drawing, and entertainments such as movies. Implicit in the explanation that I gave in Chapter 4 of how an occluder looks closer than the object it occludes is the fact that different combinations of scales are activated in the final depthful percept.

This fact will be explained more fully when I discuss 3D form perception in Chapter 11. Both in the case of depthful form and motion perception, one of the design principles that is needed to process 3D scenes is called the *asymmetry between near and far.* This asymmetry arises because an object's image gets bigger on the retina as the object gets closer to an observer. As a result of this statistically powerful effect, bigger scales often code for a nearer perceived distance. This is not always the case, as is illustrated by my comments above about the retinal image sizes of small nearby objects and large distant objects. The asymmetry between near and far nonetheless asserts that cortical circuits develop with this asymmetry reflected in the interactions between scales, with inhibition stronger from scales that represent nearer depths to scales that represent farther depths, than conversely. Thus, in addition to the competition between opponent directions within each scale, there is also asymmetric competition within direction from larger to smaller scales, as illustrated by Figure 8.41 (bottom half). Such an asymmetry between near and far was also used to explain how percepts of occluded objects can get completed behind their occluders, as summarized in Figure 4.51.

How does the asymmetry between near and far abet transparency if two fields of dots are otherwise symmetrically processed by the visual system, as in Figure 8.41 (top half, left image)? Fluctuations within the visual system, whether due to small asymmetries in activation, or to momentary attentional biases, can break the symmetry of activation of opponent directional cells by the two arrays of dots moving in opposite directions. Such an asymmetry can render one direction of motion momentarily more active than another. This asymmetry may be implemented computationally by randomly selecting one of the two active directions of motion, say rightward motion within a given scale, say the big scale in Figure 8.41 (bottom), and does so inside the foveal region. Then the rightward direction would tend to be enhanced in the near depth. Because the big scale inhibits the rightward directional cells of small scale at the corresponding position in MSTv, the leftward directional cells would be disinhibited at the further depth. This would begin the process of perceiving two coherently moving sheets of dots moving in opposite directions at different depths.

In order to achieve such a coherent percept, interactions between MT⁻ and MSTv must propagate across space, as they always do to solve the aperture problem; cf. Figure 8.36. In particular, the chosen directions, at the chosen depths, in MSTv would select the corresponding directions and depths due to MSTv-to-MT⁻ attentional signals. Such an operation is consistent with data showing attentional enhancement in MT/MST in both monkeys and humans (O'Craven et al., 1997; Treue and Martinez Trujillo, 1999; Treue and Maunsell, 1996, 1999). As this feedback cycle continues between MT⁻ and MSTv, two sheets of coherently moving dots at different depths will emerge. In the computer simulations of this motion capture process that I published in 2001 with Lavanya Viswanathan, the attentional change was applied only within the selected direction and scale and inside an attentional locus that is 6.25% of the total display area, and propagated outwards from there to envelop the entire display.

Chopsticks illusion and feedback between V1, MT, and MST

The final example that I will discuss illustrates how feedback may propagate between multiple levels of the visual system, notably cortical areas V1, V2, MT, and MST

(Figure 8.26), in order to process visual signals that are ambiguous in both their form and motion properties. In other words, formotion interactions between the form and motion cortical processing streams are often needed to generate an unambiguous percept of objects moving in depth. The apparent motion of illusory contours that is described in Figure 8.11 illustrates such a formotion interaction. I will now explain another example that emphasizes new properties of how formotion processes interact with figure-ground processes: namely, the chopsticks illusion that Stuart Anstis reported in 1990 (Anstis, 1990). Here, as with all of the examples that I discuss, my conclusions are not restricted to stimuli as simple as chopsticks. These simpler stimuli illustrate general perceptual problems and the mechanisms that can solve them in response to far more complex form and motion stimuli.

In the displays that generate the chopsticks illusion (Figure 8.42), two overlapping diagonal bars of the same luminance (the "chopsticks") move in opposite directions, to the left or to the right. The display contains two kinds of features: the terminators of each line and the intersection of the two lines. The two line terminators of one bar move leftward while the two lines terminators of the other bar move rightward. The intersection of the two lines moves upward.

When the lines are viewed behind visible occluders, as in Figure 8.42 (left column, top row), they appear to move together as a welded unit in the upward direction, as in Figure 8.42 (left column, bottom row). When the occluders are made invisible, as in Figure 8.42 (right column, top row), the lines no longer cohere. Instead, they appear to slide one on top of the other in opposite directions, as in

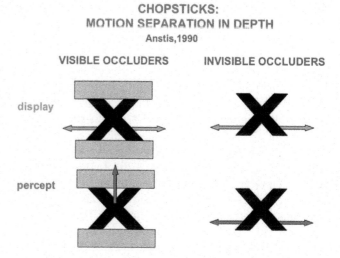

FIGURE 8.42. The chopsticks illusion not only depends upon how feature tracking signals are altered by visible and invisible occluders, but also upon how the form system disambiguates the ambiguous region where the two chopsticks intersect and uses figure-ground mechanisms to separate them in depth.

Figure 8.42 (right column, bottom row). The chopsticks illusion forces us to consider how visible occluders give rise to a percept of one rigid object moving upward within a single depth plane, whereas invisible occluders lead us to perceive one chopstick moving incoherently in the opposite direction, and at a different depth, than the other chopstick.

A major factor governing this perceptual difference is this: When the occluder is visible, the ends of the chopstick appear to belong to the occluder, and are no longer perceived to be part of the chopstick itself. Such an occluder was called an *extrinsic terminator* in a 1989 article by Shinsuke Shimojo, Gerald Silverman, and Ken Nakayama (Shimojo, Silverman, and Nakayama, 1989). When the occluder is invisible, the ends of the chopstick appear to belong to the chopstick. Such an occluder is called an *intrinsic terminator*. These distinctions were also important in explanations of static figure-ground percepts, such as the explanation that is summarized in Figures 4.54-4.56 and explained using mechanisms such as the asymmetry-between-near-and-far interactions that are summarized in Figure 4.51.

To explain the chopsticks illusion, I will first consider the case where line terminators are extrinsic because the occluding bars are visible, as in Figure 8.42 (left column, top row). Then the feature tracking signals at the intersection of the two lines are stronger than those at the line terminators because the line ends get attached to the horizontal gray occluder, not the moving bars, much as they get attached to the occluding horizontal rectangle in Figure 1.3. The upward moving feature tracking signals at the intersection of the two lines can therefore win the competition in the MT⁻-MSTv feedback loop and propagate along both lines, much as they do along the moving tilted line in Figure 8.36. Both lines then appear to move upward as a single coherent unit.

When the occluders are invisible, as in Figure 8.42 (right column, top row). the percept of the two bars moving horizontally, one in front of the other, requires a deeper analysis. Here a formotion interaction plays an important role. This chopsticks percept emerges from *feedforward* interactions from V1 to V2, a *cross-stream* interaction from V2 to MT⁻, and a *feedback* interaction between MT⁻ and MSTv that is part of a larger feedback interaction from MSTv-to-MT⁻-to-V1 (Figure 8.26). To start, note that the X-shaped boundary of the overlapping chopsticks can be processed within V1 and V2 and can influence MT via a formation interaction from V2 to MT⁻. The main new problem is: How does the ambiguous diamond-shaped region at the center of the X, where the two chopsticks cross, get assigned to the motion of one or the other chopstick, but not to both? This is very much like the problem of Kanizsa stratification in the form stream (Figure 1.4, left column, top row), where the ambiguous white regions are assigned to the cross or the square, but not to both.

In the chopsticks illusion, there is no difference of figural width with which to provide a competitive advantage, as there was between the cross and the square in the stratification example. Because the two chopsticks have an identical shape, and move at the same speed, albeit in opposite directions, factors like spatial attention and noise fluctuations within the brain can play an important role in determining which chopstick will be seen in front, as I will now explain.

The motion system responds to the moving images in Figure 8.42 (right column, top row) by computing strong feature tracking signals at both the line terminators of the chopsticks and their intersection. If both chopsticks were processed equally, the directional grouping and attentional priming MT⁻-MSTv loop, could send conflicting motion signals from the line terminators down towards their intersection, just as can happen when a line first appears during the barberpole illusion (Figure 8.39, top column). However, such perfectly balanced processing represents an unstable situation. Either a reactive or volitional focus of attention on one bar end, attracted by the motion of that end of the bar, or some internal noise fluctuation, will with high probability differentially enhance the activation of one of the two chopsticks at some position along its length, say the bar end, for definiteness (Figure 8.43, left image). Just as in my discussion of motion transparency (Figure 8.41), even a small asymmetry in activation is sufficient to break the deadlock where the chopsticks overlap.

For definiteness, let us assume that an attentional fluctuation is the cause. Then attentional enhancement of the motion signals in one chopstick can propagate along the form boundaries of that chopstick, just like feature tracking signals do in general, and can amplify these propagating feature tracking signals (Figure 8.43, right image). This

THE AMBIGUOUS X-JUNCTION
Motion system

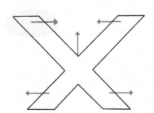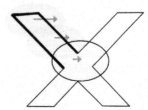

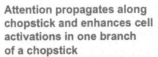

Attention propagates along chopstick and enhances cell activations in one branch of a chopstick

MT⁻-MST directional motion grouping helps to bridge the ambiguous junction

FIGURE 8.43. Attention can flow along the boundaries of one chopstick and enable it to win the orientational competition where the two chopsticks cross, thereby enabling bipole grouping and figure-ground mechanisms to separate them in depth within the form cortical stream.

THE ROLE OF MT-V1 FEEDBACK

Motion-form feedback

MT⁻-to-V2 feedback strengthens boundaries of one bar

Bipole boundary completion

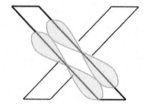

Bipole grouping **helps to complete bar boundary even if motion grouping does not cross the gap**

FIGURE 8.44. Attentional feedback from MST-to-MT-to-V2 can strengthen one branch of a chopstick (left image). Then bipole cell activations that are strengthened by this feedback can complete that chopstick's boundaries across the ambiguous X region (right image).

top-down attentional priming effect from MSTv to MT⁻ can then propagate to V1 via top-down MT⁻-to-V1 signals, and then bottom-up via V1-to-V2 connections (Figure 8.26). In this MT⁻-to-V1-to-V2 circuit, these properties of attention amplify the boundaries that are formed at the attended chopstick (Figure 8.44, left image), in much the same way that increasing the contrast of one of the chopsticks would do (cf. Figure 6.6). Then attentional enhancement of the motion signals in one chopstick can propagate along the form boundaries of that chopstick in V2 until it reaches the ambiguous X-junction, whereupon the advantage to bipole grouping that is realized by attentional enhancement enables the corresponding boundary grouping to be completed across the ambiguous X-junction (Figure 8.44, right image).

Let me pause to affirm that these properties are consistent with the neuroanatomical data that enable us to draw a figure like Figure 8.26. But are they also consistent with neurophysiological data about the dynamics and functional role of these circuits? Indeed they are. For example, in 1998, Jean-Michel Hupé, Andrew James, Bertram Payne, Stephen Lomber, Pascal Girard, and Jean Bullier showed that feedback connections from MT-to-V1 are important in the differentiation of figure from ground (Hupé et al., 1998), and that these feedback connections facilitate responses to moving objects in the center and inhibit responses in the surround of V1 cells. This is the same sort of attentional circuit that was needed to explain motion capture by feedback from MSTv to MT⁻ using the ART Matching Rule (Figure 8.35).

As one bar's boundary grouping is enhanced, it causes end gaps in the boundary of the other bar where that bar's boundaries intersect the bar of the completed boundary, thereby triggering figure-ground separation and resulting

CLOSING FORMOTION FEEDBACK LOOP

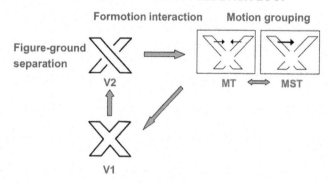

FIGURE 8.45. The feedback loop between MT/MST-to-V1-to-V2-to-MT/MST enables a percept of two chopsticks sliding one in front of the other while moving in opposite directions.

in the percept of the enhanced bar occluding the other bar, just as in Figure 4.54-4.56. Once these boundaries are separated in depth and completed within V1 and V2, they can inject their depth-separated and boundary-completed representations into the motion system via a V2-to-MT⁻ formotion interaction. The attentional bias hereby propagates cyclically throughout the MSTv-to-MT⁻-to-V1-to-V2-to-MT⁻ feedback loop (Figure 8.45). Once figure-ground separation is accomplished via this loop, the continuing cycle through the model's MT⁻-MSTv interactions, using the separated chopsticks and their motion signals as inputs, can complete the motion capture process and determine the perceived motion directions throughout the entire length of each bar at its corresponding depth, notably the direction of the occluding chopstick in the ambiguous zone where the two chopsticks intersect. A percept of incoherent motion by two chopsticks moving in opposite directions on different depth planes is hereby realized. Computer simulations of this percept and many other motion capture percepts is found in the 2001 article with my PhD student Lavanya Viswanathan (Grossberg, Mingolla, and Viswanathan, 2001).

How do these results help to explain conscious perception?

The proposed explanations of motion phenomena in the above sections use cortical feedback for several purposes. The MT⁻-MSTv feedback loop is predicted to solve the global aperture problem by carrying out motion capture. The same circuit is also predicted to carry out attentional priming of motion direction. Feedback from MT⁻ to V1, and then back up to V2, uses a similar type of attentional priming circuit to carry out figure-ground separation of two objects that are moving in different directions onto different depth planes. These proposals show the functional utility of these feedback pathways, but they do not disclose the deeper functional reasons why feedback pathways with similar properties occur throughout the brain, and why they seem to share a number of important computational properties.

In Chapter 1 and intermittently throughout the book, I have noted that there is a deep functional relationship between how we continue to learn throughout our lives, how we pay attention, and how we become conscious of the world. The feedback loops between V1 and MT, and between MT⁻ and MSTv, that we have just discussed are all predicted to obey the ART Matching Rule. To the extent that this is true, resonance among these circuits will also support conscious motion percepts. Neurophysiological evidence in support this ART prediction include the 2001 article by Alvaro Pascual-Leone and Vincent Walsh showing that fast backprojections from the motion to the primary visual area are necessary for visual awareness of motion (Pascual-Leone and Walsh, 2001).

Being necessary does not imply, however, that it is sufficient. The example of induced motion shows that motion becomes visible when it is bound to boundary groupings from the form stream via formotion interactions (Figure 8.26). These V2 boundary groupings can, in turn, support visible surface percepts of a moving object when they interact with the surface cortical stream to trigger a surface-shroud resonance (Figure 6.2; Table 1.4) between cortical areas V4 and PPC (Figure 6.3). Even this is not enough, however, to be able to *recognize* the motion direction of the moving object. Just as a feature-category resonance is needed to recognize the attended critical feature patterns of a static object while it is consciously seen using a surface-shroud resonance (Figure 6.27), I would argue that a feature-category resonance is also needed to recognize the attended critical feature patterns of a moving object as well. The feature-category resonance in the form stream is predicted to be triggered between prestriate and inferotemporal cortex, whereas the feature-category resonance in the motion stream may occur between prestriate cortex and regions like the superior temporal sulcus (Grossman and Blake, 2002; Zeki, 1974). In both case, top-down ART Matching Rule signals are predicted to select feature patterns that are consistent with the resonating data, while suppressing those that are not.

From moving dots and bars to moving people

The aperture problem forced us to confront the fact that, as an object moves, its various parts may move in different directions relative to it, as in the example of the leaping

leopard (Figure 8.4). I can now explain how we can accurately perceive the directions of these moving parts, relative to the object motion that is computed by the solution of the aperture problem. This analysis will show how the V1-V2-MT-MSTv feedback loop helps to automatically accomplish this remarkable feat as yet another emergent property of the dynamics of object motion direction and top-down directional priming that we have already discussed.

Object reference frames and motion vector decomposition via a directional peak shift

The object motion direction and speed that are computed to solve the aperture problem define a *reference frame* against which the motion of its various parts can be compared. What this means can be seen from the example in Figure 8.46. Suppose, as in the upper figure of Figure 8.46, we keep our eyes fixated straight ahead (red star) as a car moves to the right with a child waving at us in the car window. In this case, our reference frame is stationary and the car moves relative to it. The child's up-and-down arm movements then generate a rightward-moving oscillatory trajectory (dashed wiggly red curve) as the car moves to the right. In contrast, suppose that our eyes move to the right with the car (red star), as in the lower figure of Figure 8.46. Now the child's arm is seen to move up-and-down relative to the moving reference frame.

This example illustrates that many percepts of moving object parts obey a rule of *vector decomposition*, whereby the global motion appears to be subtracted from the true

**HOW DO WE PERCEIVE
THE RELATIVE MOTION OF OBJECT PARTS?**

FIGURE 8.46. How do we determine the relative motion direction of a part of a scene when it moves with a larger part that determines an object reference frame?

motion path of localized stimulus components, so that objects and their parts are seen as moving relative to a common reference frame. In the lower image of Figure 8.46, when the rightward motion of the car is subtracted from the oscillatory motion of the arm, what remains is an up-and-down motion relative to the car.

How is such vector decomposition achieved by the brain? You already have all the mechanisms that we need to explain this, but you do not yet know it! One reason that the answer may not immediately leap into your mind is that vector decomposition is an emergent property of all the mechanisms that I have described to you so far, including multiple-scale and multiple-depth interactions within and between the form and motion processing streams in the V1-V2-MT-MSTv feedback circuit, including processes of form grouping, form-to-motion capture, figure-ground separation, and object motion capture. In particular, these mechanisms solve the aperture problem, group spatially disjoint moving objects via illusory contours, capture object motion direction signals on real and illusory contours, and use inter-depth directional inhibition asymmetrically from near to far. When they act together, they also cause vector decomposition.

Gaussian algebra: Peak shifts and G-waves. Vector decomposition occurs when the motion direction of a moving frame at a nearer depth suppresses this direction at a farther depth. As I will explain in detail in a moment, suppressing the direction of the moving frame causes a *peak shift* in the perceived directions of object parts moving relative to the reference frame. I claim that such a peak shift causes the percept of the child waving up-and-down as you track the motion of the car.

This is not the first time in this book that a peak shift has been of use. Recall that I told you in Chapter 1 about a peak shift that occurs, along with behavioral contrast, during operant conditioning (Figure 1.12). The peak shift that occurs during part motion of a moving object illustrates that the peak shift mechanism is exploited in many parts of the brain. And why not? A peak shift occurs *whenever* you subtract one Gaussian receptive field from a second Gaussian receptive field that is spatially displaced from it, and both receptive fields compete via a recurrent shunting on-center off-surround network, which happens just about everywhere in the brain.

Said in another way, a peak shift is part of the repertoire of properties that may be lumped together under the heading of *Gaussian algebra*. When you

subtract one Gaussian from another that is spatially displaced from it at a fixed time, you get a peak shift. When you *add* one Gaussian to another at successive times, you get a G-wave. Adding and subtracting Gaussians in response to two or more inputs occurs all over our brains.

Johannson dot motions relative to a moving frame

Two famous examples of vector decomposition are shown in Figure 8.47. The top example was described in 1950 by Gunnar Johansson (Johansson, 1950), whereas the bottom example was described in 1929 by Karl Duncker (Duncker, 1929/1938). Much more complex motions may also be understood from my explanations of these percepts, including how a human observer can perceive another person walking, dancing, or performing athletic feats in the light, or even in the dark when the only visible cues are lights attached to the person's joints. It will be obvious how to explain such percepts of "light-point motion" by humans after the first two percepts are explained. A nice video of these motions can be found at https://www.youtube.com/watch?v=1F5ICP9SYLU.

The upper left image in Figure 8.47 depicts the visual stimulus presented to the subject. Here, two dots oscillate in perpendicular directions, one moving vertically up and down, and the other moving horizontally left and right,

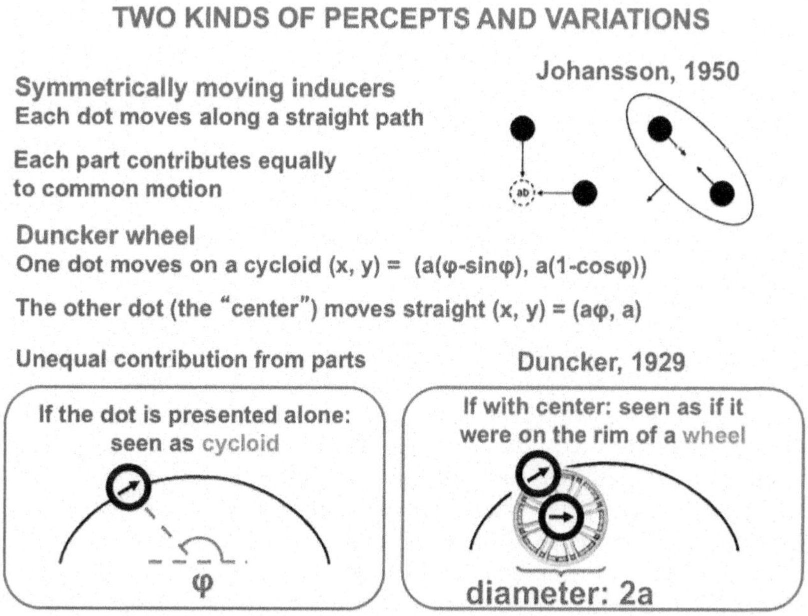

TWO KINDS OF PERCEPTS AND VARIATIONS

Symmetrically moving inducers
Each dot moves along a straight path

Each part contributes equally
to common motion

Johansson, 1950

Duncker wheel
One dot moves on a cycloid $(x, y) = (a(\varphi-\sin\varphi), a(1-\cos\varphi))$

The other dot (the "center") moves straight $(x, y) = (a\varphi, a)$

Unequal contribution from parts

If the dot is presented alone:
seen as cycloid

φ

Duncker, 1929

If with center: seen as if it were on the rim of a wheel

diameter: 2a

FIGURE 8.47. Two classical examples of part motion in a moving reference frame illustrate the general situation where complex objects move while their multiple parts may move in different directions relative to the direction of the reference frame.

HOW VECTOR DECOMPOSITION CAN EXPLAIN THEM

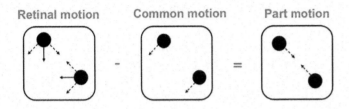

FIGURE 8.48. How vector subtraction from the reference frame motion direction computes the part motion directions.

with their trajectories meeting at one endpoint (point *ab*). This motion can induce a percept of two dots oscillating towards and away from each other along a common diagonal axis, denoted by the ellipse in the upper right image in Figure 8.47, which itself oscillates along the orthogonal direction. In other words, the dots are seen as moving relative to a common reference frame, the diagonal axis. That this is an example of vector decomposition is clarified by Figure 8.48.

The leftmost image in Figure 8.48 shows the vector components into which the retinal downward and leftward motions, respectively, of the two individual dots can be decomposed. For example, the downward vertical motion of the left dot can be decomposed into downward diagonal motions that point to the left and the right of the vertical downward motion. Likewise, the leftward motion of the right dot can be decomposed into leftward diagonal motions that point above and below the horizontal leftward motion.

Suppose that the moving frame captures the common diagonal down-and-left direction of the two dots, as in the middle image of Figure 8.48. If this common diagonal direction is subtracted from the retinal motion directions of the two dots, then the individual dots are left with components that oscillate towards and away from each other, as in the rightmost image of Figure 8.48.

How does such a vector decomposition occur? Figure 8.49 describes one key step in this process. This figure shows how a *directional peak shift* occurs *if* the common diagonal motion has already been computed. The left image in this figure color-codes the leftward "part" motion direction of the right dot in blue, the common diagonal motion in green, and the relative motion of the two dots in red. The right image represents these different motion directions in a *motion direction hypercolumn*. Directional hypercolumns represent motion directions *at each position* of directional maps within cortical areas MT and

MST. Chapter 11 will describe orientational hypercolumns wherein the orientations of visual forms at each position occur in maps within cortical areas V1 and V2 (Figure 11.28). Cells compete within each hypercolumn in both the form and motion cortical streams, with the maximum inhibition occurring between cells whose directional preference differs by 180 degrees in the motion stream, and between cells whose orientational preference differs by 90 degrees in the form stream. These inhibitory interactions are the basis of the waterfall and MacKay illusions that were summarized in Figure 8.3.

It is assumed in Figure 8.49 that the part motion direction generates Gaussianly distributed excitatory inputs across the directional hypercolumn (in red), whereas the common motion direction generates Gaussianly inhibitory inputs (in green). This is exactly what happens in the example of peak shift and behavioral contrast during operant conditioning (Figure 1.12)! When it happens within a directional hypercolumn, it causes a peak shift and behavioral contrast whose maximal activity is centered at the direction of the part motion direction. That is why common diagonal motion of the reference frame coexists with part motion back-and-forth between the pair of dots.

In order for vector decomposition to work, the reference frame of the common motion must first be created, so that its diagonal motion direction can be computed. Figure 8.50 notes that, because both dots move in a common motion direction, the form stream can create an illusory contour between the two dots. This illusory contour can, moreover, persist through time as it moves with the dots. This illusory contour is generated in cortical area

WHAT IS THE MECHANISM OF VECTOR DECOMPOSITION?
Grossberg, Leveille, and Versace, 2011

Prediction: DIRECTIONAL PEAK SHIFT!

...specifically, a peak shift due to Gaussian lateral inhibition

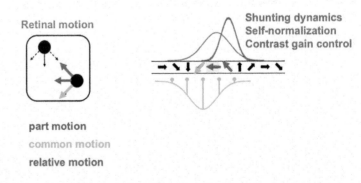

FIGURE 8.49. A directional peak shift in a directional hypercolumn determines the part directions relative to a moving reference frame.

HOW IS COMMON MOTION DIRECTION COMPUTED?

Retinal motion

Bipole grouping in the form stream creates
Illusory contours between the dots

V2-MT formotion interaction injects the
completed boundaries into the motion stream
where they capture consistent motion signals

Motion of illusory contours is computed in
the motion stream; cf., Ramachandran

FIGURE 8.50. The common motion direction of the two dots builds upon illusory contours that connect the dots as they move through time. The common motion direction signal can flow along these boundaries.

V2 (Figure 4.29). Once generated, the illusory contour can be injected into MT via a V2-to-MT formotion interaction (Figure 8.26). Then the diagonal motion direction of the dots can travel along the entire length of the illusory contour as the motion capture process unfolds through time, just as it does in traveling along a moving tilted line in Figure 8.36. This motion capture process also uses the feedback loop between MT· and MSTv (Figure 8.26).

In order to create the illusory contour between the two moving dots, a large spatial scale in V2 is needed with bipole cells whose receptive fields are big enough to bridge the distance between the dots, just as bipole cells bridge the ambiguous region between the two bars in the chopsticks illusion (Figure 8.44). Bipole cells with a small spatial cannot bridge this distance. They can only create boundaries around each dot. Both of these types of boundaries are injected topographically, and in a scale-specific way, from V2 to MT·. Figure 8.51 shows a computer simulation of these boundaries and the direction fields that they generate in MT· at the beginning of a motion, and before the MT·-MSTv feedback loop can carry out motion capture and solve the aperture problem. These and other simulations of these phenomena were carried out with my PhD student Jasmin Leveille (Grossberg, Leveille, and Versace, 2011).

The illusory contour that forms in the large scale (Figure 8.51, left image) occurs around the outside borders of

each dot, without complete dot boundaries within it, because spatial competition from the illusory contour inhibits these interior dot boundaries (Figure 4.25). Thus, only the boundaries of the illusory contour can influence the motion directions that are computed in the large scale. In contrast, only boundaries around the individual dots can form within the small scale (Figure 8.51, right image) because this scale cannot bridge the distance between the dots to form an illusory boundary. The left image also shows a field of noisy diagonal directional motion signals that is induced by the illusory contour. In the right image, noisy downward and leftward directional motion signals, respectively, are induced by the left and right dots. The header says "MT 2/3" because this simulation is carried out in a *laminar* cortical model whereby boundaries are interpreted to form in layer 2/3.

These motion signals can then propagate topographically from MT· to MSTv, whence the feedback loop from MSTv to MT· closes and the motion capture cycle unfolds. Just as in the explanation of the chopsticks illusion, however, there is an *asymmetry between near and far* from the larger to the smaller spatial scales *within* MSTv (Figure 8.41, lower image). This interaction occurs rapidly, before its results can propagate downwards to MT·. We are now ready to observe how the common motion and part motion directions of the two dots in Figure 8.49 (left image) are represented across the directional hypercolumns that exist within MSTv *before the results* of their interaction propagate to MT·. As in Figure 8.49 (right image), the part motion

INITIAL LONG-RANGE FILTER ACTIVITIES IN MT 2/3

Large scale: NEAR

Can bridge gap between dots
to form illusory contours
Spatial competition inhibits inner
dot boundaries

Small scale: FAR

Forms boundaries around dots

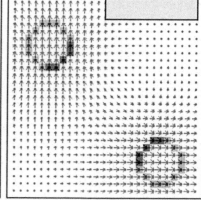

FIGURE 8.51. Large and small scale boundaries differentially form illusory contours between the dots and boundaries that surround each of them respectively. These boundaries capture the motion signals that they will support via a V2-to-MT formotion interaction. The MST-to-MT directional peak shift has not yet occurred.

SIMULATION OF MOTION VECTOR DECOMPOSITION

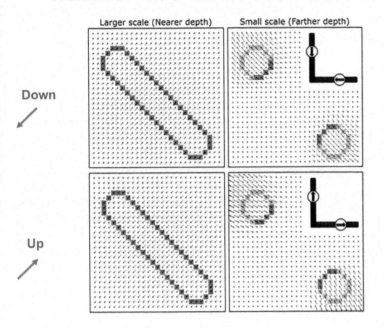

FIGURE 8.52. Direction fields of the object frame (left column) and of the two dot "parts" (right column) show the correct motion directions after the peak shift top-down expectation acts.

in the small scale is represented by a Gaussian *excitatory* kernel that is centered above the part direction and, due to the asymmetry between near and far, the common diagonal motion direction is represented by a Gaussian *inhibitory* kernel. This interaction choices the relative motion direction, thereby giving rise to a percept of the dots back-and-forth within the moving reference frame of the illusory contour. Figure 8.52 summarizes a computer simulation of the direction fields that are created as the MT⁻-MSTv feedback loop cycles through time. Sharp diagonal motion directions of the reference frame are seen to coexist with back-and-forth dot motion directions as the dots move closer together and then further apart.

One more property that contributes to the percept of relative motion should also be noted. Figure 8.50 illustrates how a diagonal motion direction gets computed along the illusory contour that formed between the two dots, and propagates with them through space. The feature contour signals that exist along the entire length of the illusory contour compute the same diagonal motion direction at every time. This directional signal can thus be strengthened at the directional short-range filter stage (Figure 8.31) by accumulating consistent diagonal direction evidence through time. The directional long-range filter further strengthens this diagonal motion direction signal.

The same kind of accumulation of directional evidence occurs at the directional short-range filter for the retinal up-down and left-right motion directions of the individual dots (Figure 8.48). The growing activity at the directional short-range filter stage of the downward vertical motion direction signal of the left dot can be seen in the computer simulation of Figure 8.53. These strong diagonal and vertical motion direction signals enable the peak shift that is schematized in Figure 8.49 (right image) to work well.

This explanation predicts that the relative depth of the perceived dot motions is slightly farther away than the common motion of the reference frame. It will be difficult to measure such a small difference, but it is worth keeping in mind until someone figures out how to test this model prediction.

Duncker motion: Cycloid motion or rotation around a moving wheel?

Now let us turn to the lower images in Figure 8.47. In both of these images, a dot moves along the shape of a cycloid. In the left image, only one dot occurs, so that an observer can clearly see the cycloid trajectory as it evolves through time. Figure 8.54 summarizes a simulation that the model computes of the

SIMULATION OF AMPLIFICATION OF DOWNWARD VERTICAL DIRECTION

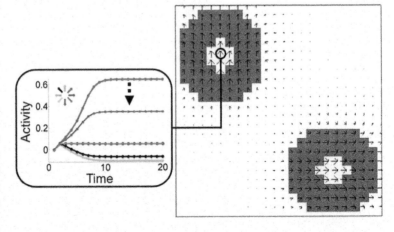

FIGURE 8.53. Simulation of the various directional signals of the left dot through time. Note the amplification of the downward directional signal due to the combined action of the short-range and long-range directional filters.

CYCLOID

**Motion directions of a single dot
moving along a cycloid curve through time**

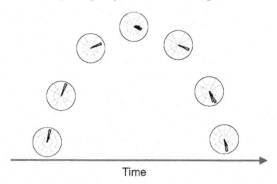

Time

FIGURE 8.54. The simulated part directions of the rotating dot through time after the translational motion of the frame does its work via the top-down peak shift mechanism.

motion directions of this dot. In the right image, a second dot moves at a constant speed towards the right. In this case, the first dot appears to rotate around the moving frame that is defined by the translating dot. This latter percept would be generated, for example, if a bicycle traveled to the right in the dark with a light attached to the center of a wheel and a second light attached to its rim. This percept can be seen in the video. It can be explained as follows using the same mechanisms as I used to explain Johansson motion.

Figure 8.55 summarizes a model simulation of three critical properties of this simulation. The first property is that the center dot moves with a consistent horizontal motion direction to the right. As a result, the horizontal

DUNCKER WHEEL: LARGE SCALE

Cycloid velocity
$\vec{v} = (a - a\cos\varphi, a\sin\varphi)$
Center velocity
$\vec{v} = (a, 0)$

Rightward common velocity
$\vec{v} = (a, 0)$

Stable rightward motion at the center captures motion at the rim

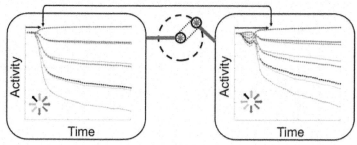

FIGURE 8.55. The rightward motion of the dot that determines the frame propagates along the illusory contour between the dots and thereby dominates the motion directions along the rim as well, thereby setting the stage for the peak shift mechanism.

motion of this dot can strengthen the response to the horizontal motion direction at the directional short-range filter relative to all the other directional motion signals of this dot, as shown in the left simulation in this figure. The horizontal motion direction of the center dot can thereby inhibit other motion directions of the dot at the model's competition stages (Figure 8.31), before it is even further strengthened at the directional long-range filter.

The second property is that the two dots can form an illusory contour between them using the large spatial scale. This illusory contour continues to connect the two dots as they move continuously through time.

The third property is that the horizontal motion direction of the center dot can travel along, and thereby capture, the horizontal motion direction throughout the length of the illusory contour between the two dots, in just the same way as the diagonal motion travelled along the illusory contour between the two dots in Figure 8.50. As in Figure 8.50, this motion capture process takes place in the large scale that maintains the illusory contour. The motion directions that are initially computed at the exterior dot are overwhelmed by the horizontal direction from the center dot because they change continuously through time, and thus cannot accumulate a single consistent directional signal through time at the directional short-range filter. As a result, the dominant motion direction at the exterior dot within the large scale is the horizontal direction.

The fourth major property of the simulation is the directional vector subtraction from the large scale to the small scale due to the asymmetry between near and far. This subtraction causes a peak shift away from the horizontal motion direction at the small scale. The result is plotted in two ways in Figure 8.56. The left image show the temporal processing of activity in eight directions through time. The right image shows the circular directions of the winning motion directions when they are aligned with the rotations of the wheel.

Even very complex point-light natural motions can be explained by these mechanisms, or more generally the relative motions within naturally moving objects for which only a sufficient subset of moving object features can be glimpsed through time.

Converting Motion into Action during Perceptual Decision-Making

From solving the aperture problem to motion-based probabilistic decision-making. By solving the global aperture problem (Figures 8.4, 8.5, 8.30, and 8.31), the 3D FORMOTION model (Figure 8.26) creates a representation of unambiguous object

DUNCKER WHEEL: SMALL SCALE

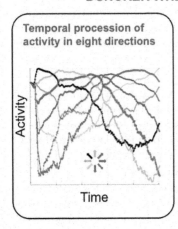

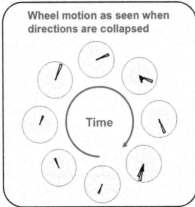

FIGURE 8.56. Simulation of the Duncker wheel motion through time. See the text for details.

motion direction and speed in response to ambiguous aperture-limited motion inputs. This model can then serve as the front end for many subsequent tasks that require additional processing of the object direction and speed information, as we have seen in my earlier comments about visually-based navigation to a target while avoiding obstacles (Figure 8.34).

Another process of this kind is perceptual decision-making that bases its decisions on motion signals. In particular, how do our eyes know where to look in response to motion cues? How does this happen, moreover, if the cues are defined probabilistically, as is often the case in naturalistic settings? In order to accomplish this, a coordinate change is needed that converts object *motion* direction into a commanded eye *movement* direction.

The main conclusion from this modeling study is that the same 3D FORMATION model that has been used to explain many other kinds of motion data can also be used as to process the motion stimuli in motion decision-making experiments. The output from MST in this model then inputs to a circuit that converts the motion direction in cortical MST into a saccadic eye movement direction in LIP, whose cell activations are gated by the basal ganglia (Figure 8.57). My PhD student Praveen Pilly and I called this model the MOtion DEcision model both because its name describes its function and because the model acronym, MODE, emphasizes that it works well in response to probabilistic motion signals, as in the *mode* of a statistical sample,

which describes the value in a probabilistic set of data that appears most often or, in other words, where its probability function takes on its maximum value (Grossberg and Pilly, 2008).

The MODE model combines the solution of two previous design problems into a single neural architecture that can solve problems of probabilistic decision-making. The 3D FORMOTION model preprocessing stages are the same ones that I used earlier to solve the *aperture problem* (Figures 8.4, 8.5, and 8.31). The circuit that converts a motion direction into a movement direction solves the *noise-saturation dilemma* (Figures 1.5, 2.15, and 2.16), namely a nonrecurrent or recurrent on-center off-surround network (Figures 1.7-1.9 and 2.23). In the MODE model, a recurrent on-center off-surround network, much like the one that stores a list in STM (Figure 1.7), transforms the distributed representation of motion directions in MST into a directional movement command in LIP and stores it in STM until the command is executed. The ability of such a recurrent shunting network, or recurrent competitive field, to normalize its total activity enables it to maintain a stable operating range in response to motion input patterns that can vary wildly in the number of MST cells that are active through time. How our brains use the basal ganglia, notably the substantia nigra pars reticulata, or SNr, to gate

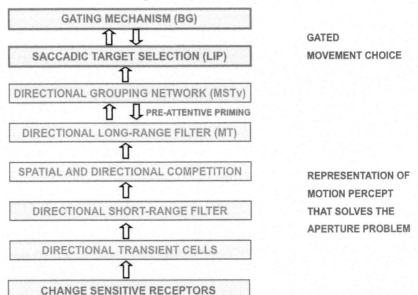

FIGURE 8.57. The MODE model uses the Motion BCS as its front end, followed by a saccadic target selection circuit in the model LIP region that converts motion directions into movement directions. These movement choices are also under basal ganglia (BG) control. More will be explained about the BG in Chapters 13 and 15.

the activity of circuits ON and OFF will be explained in Chapters 12 and 15. In the present situation, this gating reflects the different tasks that monkeys are expected to perform in the two tasks that are simulated by the model.

Probabilistic motion-based decision-making in monkeys. The speed and accuracy of decisions varies with the ambiguity of environmental information (Gold and Shadlen, 2007; Luce, 1986). How this process works has been studied in the laboratory using a paradigm that can precisely calibrate the ambiguity of information and measure an animal's responses with both psychophysical and neurophysiological measures. Such a paradigm for studying decision-making using psychophysics and neurophysiology has been developed by William Newsome, Michael Shadlen, and their colleagues (e.g., Roitman and Shadlen, 2002; Shadlen and Newsome, 2001). This research studies how macaque monkeys discriminate the motion direction of random dot motion stimuli in which, across experimental conditions, a different proportion of the dots move in the same direction, chosen to be either to the left or to the right. The data clarify how the monkeys' responses, with a saccadic eye movement to the left or to the right, vary with the degree of motion coherence, or fraction of the dots that move in a given direction while the other dots move in random directions. In particular, the experiments record the percent accuracy and reaction time of these movements as a function of motion coherence. At the same time, the investigators use electrodes to record the responses of neurons in the monkeys' lateral intraparietal (LIP) area, a part of the parietal cortex, while the monkeys are making these saccadic eye movements (Figures 1.19 and 1.21).

In these experiments, two kinds of tasks were employed: *fixed duration* (FD) and *reaction time* (RT) tasks. Macaques were trained to discriminate net motion direction and report it via a saccade. Random dot motion displays, covering a 5° diameter aperture centered at the fixation point on a computer monitor, were used to control motion coherence. The fraction of dots moving non-randomly in a particular direction changed from one frame to the next in each of the three interleaved motion sequences. Varying the motion coherence provides a quantitative way to manipulate the ambiguity of directional information that the monkey uses to make a saccadic eye movement to a peripheral choice target in the judged motion direction, and thus the task difficulty. More coherence resulted in better accuracy and faster responses.

In the FD task (Roitman and Shadlen, 2002; Shadlen and Newsome, 2001), monkeys viewed the moving dots for a fixed duration of 1 second, and then made a saccade to the target in the judged motion direction after a variable delay.

In the RT task (Roitman and Shadlen, 2002), monkeys had theoretically unlimited viewing time, and were trained to report their decision as soon as the motion direction was determined. The RT task allowed measurement of how long it took the monkey to make a decision, which was defined as the time from the onset of the motion until when the monkey initiated a saccade. The two monkeys in the Roitman and Shadlen (2002, p. 9476) were shaped during RT task training to initiate the choice saccade within "~ 1 sec" after the dots turn on. In each RT task trial, the monkeys had to wait for a minimum of about 1 second (one monkey: 800 msec, and the other: 1200 msec) after motion onset to receive a reward however rapidly they responded. Human subjects in a similar RT task usually respond around 1 second from motion onset for the weakest coherence without any speed instruction (Palmer, Huk, and Shadlen, 2005, p. 385).

Neurophysiological recordings were done in LIP while the monkeys performed these tasks. The recorded neurons had receptive fields (RF) that encompassed just one target, and did not include the circular aperture in which the moving dots were displayed. Also, they were among those that showed sustained activity during the delay period in a memory-guided saccade task. It was found that the speed and accuracy of perceptual decisions covaried strongly with the rate of evidence accumulation by these LIP cells.

MODE simulations of saccadic accuracy and RT, and of LIP neural responses. Figures 8.58-8.62 summarize some of the psychophysical data (Figures 8.60 and 8.61) and neurophysiological data (Figures 8.58, 8.59 and 8.62) about probabilistic motion decision-making alongside model simulations of them. The headers describe what the data and

LIP RESPONSES DURING RT TASK CORRECT TRIALS

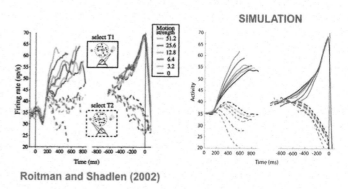

Roitman and Shadlen (2002)

More coherence in favored direction causes:
Faster cell activation

More coherence in opposite direction causes:
Faster cell inhibition

Coherence stops playing a role in the final stages of LIP firing

FIGURE 8.58. Neurophysiological data (left image) and simulation (right image) of LIP data during correct trials on the RT task. See the text for details.

LIP RESPONSES FOR THE FD TASK
DURING BOTH CORRECT AND ERROR TRIALS

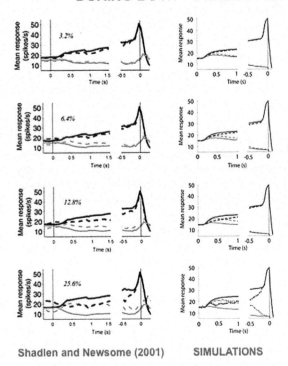

Shadlen and Newsome (2001) SIMULATIONS

LIP encodes the perceptual decision regardless of the true direction of the dots

Predictiveness of LIP responses on error trials decreases with increasing coherence

FIGURE 8.59. Neurophysiological data (left column) and simulations (right column) of LIP responses for the FD task during both correct and error trials. See the text for details.

This can be understood by considering how the mechanism of *motion capture* works to both solve the aperture problem and to determine the motion of a probabilistically defined set of moving dots. In order to solve the aperture problem, the brain needs to ensure that a sparse set of unambiguous feature tracking motion signals can gradually capture a vastly greater number of ambiguous motion signals to determine the global direction and speed of object motion. In the case of random dot motion discrimination tasks, the signal dots at any coherence level produce unambiguous, though short-lived, motion signals. Thus, individual dots do not experience an aperture problem.

Despite this difference, the MODE model shows how the same motion capture process can also enable a small number of coherently moving dots to capture the motion directions of a large number of unambiguous, but incoherently moving, dots. Thus, although individual dots do not experience an aperture problem, a sufficient number of randomly moving dots create *informational*

simulations describe. Even without going into details about the particulars of the data and simulations, the excellent fits to the data are immediately striking, even remarkable, all the more so because the model processes from which they are derived were not developed in order to explain these data. It also needs to be emphasized that these data fits are emergent properties of the model in response to the moving dot stimuli that the experimentalists used in their experiments.

How can sets of moving dots have an aperture problem while individual dots do not? The MODE model's successful simulations of perceptual decision-making data support the hypothesis that the brain designs that solve the aperture problem and noise-saturation dilemma also underlie perceptual decision-making during random dot motion direction discrimination tasks. But how can a neural circuit that solves the aperture problem be used to explain data about moving dots, given that individual moving dots do not experience an aperture problem?

BEHAVIORAL DATA: ACCURACY

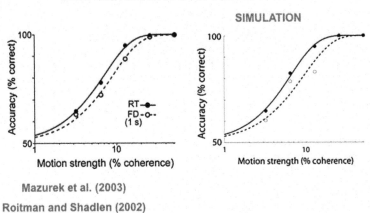

Mazurek et al. (2003)

Roitman and Shadlen (2002)

More coherence in the motion causes more accurate decisions

RT task accuracy at weaker coherence levels is slightly better than FD task accuracy

FIGURE 8.60. Behavioral data (left image) and simulation (right image) about accuracy in both the RT and FD tasks. See text for details.

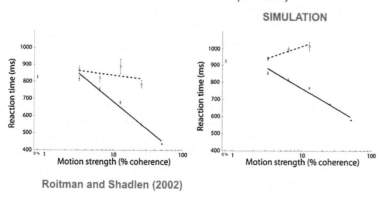

FIGURE 8.61. Behavioral data (left image) and simulation (right image) about speed in correct and error trials of the RT task. See text for details.

uncertainty that creates a similar computational problem for the visual system to solve. The intuitive idea is that the MT-MST feedback loop needs more time to capture the incoherent motion signals when there are more of them, and cannot achieve as high a level of asymptotic response magnitude when more of them compete with the emerging winning direction (Figure 8.58). In other words, the effectiveness of the motion capture process depends on input coherence. LIP then converts the distributed motion directional inputs from MST into a directional eye movement command (Figure 8.62), and thereby enables the monkey to report its decision via a saccade.

Are decisions by our brains Bayesian? The probabilistic nature of decision-making has led to the proposal that classical statistical concepts, such as the Bayes rule, may apply to probabilistic decision-making in the brain (Gold and Shadlen, 2001, 2007; Knill and Pouget, 2004; Pouget, Dayan, and Zemel, 2003). It is typically argued that variability in neuronal responses and the fact that prior knowledge or information influences what we see and how we behave implies explicit Bayesian inference in the brain. Bayesian and other general statistical concepts formalize aspects of the *unconscious inference* hypothesis of Helmholtz; namely, that the visual system works by making inferences about the world based upon probable interpretations of incomplete or ambiguous data. Kanizsa and his disciples have, in contrast, described many visual percepts that cannot be explained by unconscious inference (e.g., Figures 1.4 and 3.2). The Helmholtz vs. Kanizsa perspectives exemplify top-down vs. bottom-up approaches to visual perception, as two extremes in a continuum. The MODE neural model characterizes and joins together both bottom-up and top-down processes to explain challenging behavioral and brain data.

The Bayes rule, and related statistical concepts, are so general that they may be applied to problems in any science. In particular, the Bayes rule follows from writing the probability of any two events *I* and *S*, namely *p(I,S)*, in two different ways and then dividing both sides of this identity by a term on one side of the equation, as I will illustrate below. This generality is part of the broad appeal of Bayesian concepts, but is also its weakness in not providing enough constraints to discover new models of any particular science.

The Bayes equation is a mathematical truism that holds for any two events, whether or not they are in nature. In itself, it does not help to discover the natural laws that distinguish different processes in physics, or chemistry, or biology. Because the Bayes rule does not embody such natural laws, one can learn a lot of physics, chemistry, and biology without ever learning about it.

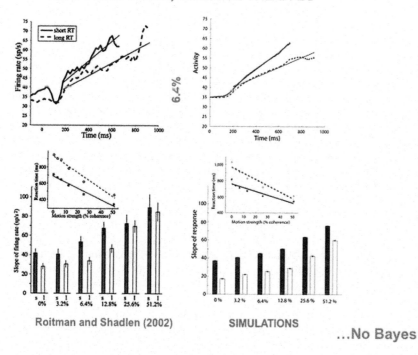

FIGURE 8.62. More remarkable simulation fits (right column) to LIP neurophysiology data (left column) about both where and when to move the eyes.

The same lack of Bayesian explanatory power holds when it comes to trying to discover the brain design principles and mechanisms that can effectively process ambiguous motion stimuli. In contrast, the MODE model proposes how the brain may make perceptual decisions in response to motion stimuli by using organizational principles and detailed neuronal mechanisms that do not invoke the Bayes rule, yet also clarify why a Bayesian approach may initially seem so appealing.

Because Bayesian concepts are so simple, and correspondingly popular with some psychologists and neuroscientists, I will describe the most basic Bayesian equation mathematically to discuss it with precision: In the Bayesian framework, given a stimulus I which falls on the retina, the Bayesian model, or ideal observer, asks what percept S is most likely to have caused it. The basic idea is to find the S that maximizes the posterior probability $p(S / I)$ via the Bayes rule:

$$p(S / I) = \frac{p(I / S)p(S)}{p(I)} \qquad (1)$$

To derive Equation (1), the probability $p(I, S)$ of the events I and S is written in two different ways:

$$p(I,S) = p(I / S)p(S) = p(S / I)p(I) \qquad (2)$$

where $p(I / S)$ is just the probability of I given S, $p(S)$ is the probability of S, $p(S / I)$ is the probability of S given I, and $p(I)$ is the probability of I. Then both sizes of Equation (2) are divided by $p(I)$ to derive Equation (1).

The specific usage depends on which of I and S is observable. I could be a spatial input (static image), or a spatio-temporal input (video). S could be either a distributed pattern of neuronal firing in some low or mid-level brain region (contour, motion, or depth perception, etc.), or a symbolic percept in some high-level brain region (face, house, or object recognition, etc.). Typical psychophysical experiments require subjects to detect or discriminate a perceptual feature and/or estimate its strength. The likelihood $p(I/S)$ assigns a probability to each percept S depending on the amount of consistency with the image I, the prior $p(S)$ is the probability of the scene description S, and $p(I)$ acts as a normalizing factor (Kersten, Mamassian, and Yuille, 2004; Kersten and Yuille, 2003). For example, Bayesian models of speed perception assume a prior that slower speeds are more frequently perceived (Stocker and Simoncelli, 2006; Weiss, Simoncelli, and Adelson, 2002).

This simplicity is accompanied by serious weaknesses. For one, Bayesian and other general statistical approaches do not address how the *units* of stimulus I are made available to the brain, such as boundary groupings and filled-in surfaces, which are emergent properties not explicit in the luminance levels of an inducing image. Bayesian models also do not explain percepts of environments whose statistics change rapidly through time, where there is no obvious likelihood $p(I/S)$, or of novel rare events, where there is no obvious prior $p(S)$. Most importantly, Bayesian models do not explain the brain design principles, mechanisms, circuits, and architectures whereby we see. My 2008 article with Praveen goes on to discuss in considerable detail how Bayes concepts have been applied, as well as several other types of models, and to compare these proposals with the models that I have described for the corresponding phenomena.

In particular, non-Bayesian models for probabilistic motion-based decision-making also exist (Ditterich 2006a, 2006b; Mazurek et al., 2003; Wang, 2002b), but none of them explains how the perceptual ambiguity that is created by the randomly moving dots is gradually transformed by the brain into a perceptual decision in response to subsets of non-randomly moving dots. These models have missed important brain principles and mechanisms that are at play in the dots task by ignoring the motion processing that extracts a dynamic neural representation of the directional uncertainty inherent in the random dot motion stimulus. They model decision-making properties only after assuming that the neural code of sensory uncertainty is provided in advance. In contrast, the MODE model achieves its strikingly accurate simulations of both psychophysical and neurophysiological data as it responds in real time to the dynamically changing visual stimuli that were used in the experiments.

I hope that my explanations above of a range of challenging motion data using the same small set of design principles and neural mechanisms will interest the reader in trying to explain even more data using this foundation. I will continue to apply the same concepts below to explain, for example, in Chapter 9 how we can navigate in space using the same model to process moving visual inputs before they activate navigational circuits at higher levels of brain processing (Figure 8.34). This application will also provide examples where the 3D FORMOTION model successfully processes motion signals from natural scenes, rather than from the laboratory stimuli that were used in the current chapter to highlight basic problems about motion perception that our visual systems have solved.

Target Tracking, Navigation, and Decision-Making

Visual tracking and navigation obey complementary laws

Target tracking and optic flow navigation use complementary cortical streams

Motion processing plays several essential roles in our lives. For starters, it provides useful cues with which to recognize moving objects. We can all, for example, remember having recognized a moving friend from a glimpse of how she walks, even if she is silhouetted in front of a bright light that obscures her facial features and clothing details. This capability involves an interaction from the motion representations of the Where cortical stream to regions of the What cortical stream where recognition categories are learned, including regions like the posterior superior temporal sulcus (STSp) that respond selectively to biological motion (Grossman and Blake, 2002).

More generally, motion signals play a key role when we visually track an object that moves relative to us, or navigate as we move relative to the world. Navigation often occurs in a world that is cluttered with objects at multiple depths from a moving observer. Successful navigation requires the ability to approach goals along an efficient route, while also avoiding obstacles along the way.

Recall from Figure 8.34 the macrocircuit of the ViSTARS (Visually-guided Steering, Tracking, Avoidance, and Route Selection) neural model that I published with my PhD student Andrew Browning in 2009 (Browning, Grossberg, and Mingolla, 2009a, 2009b). This model summarizes how circuits for both object tracking and visually-guided navigation receive bottom-up inputs from motion processing cortical networks that were explained in Chapter 8. ViSTARS models the cortical processing stream for object tracking that goes through MT$^-$-MSTv, and for optic flow navigation that goes through MT$^+$-MSTd. Figure 9.1 shows where in the macrocircuit of the visual system these complementary processing streams occur. The current chapter will explain how these processes work.

Conscious MIND Resonant BRAIN. Stephen Grossberg, Oxford University Press. © Oxford University Press 2021.
DOI: 10.1093/oso/9780190070557.003.0009

How does a moving observer use optic flow to navigate while tracking a moving object?

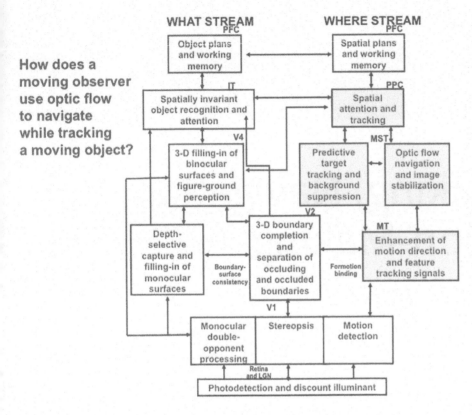

WHAT STREAM
PFC

Object plans and working memory

IT

Spatially invariant object recognition and attention

V4

3-D filling-in of binocular surfaces and figure-ground perception

Depth-selective capture and filling-in of monocular surfaces

Boundary-surface consistency

V2

3-D boundary completion and separation of occluding and occluded boundaries

V1

Monocular double-opponent processing

Stereopsis

Motion detection

Retina and LGN

Photodetection and discount illuminant

WHERE STREAM
PFC

Spatial plans and working memory

PPC

Spatial attention and tracking

MST

Predictive target tracking and background suppression

Optic flow navigation and image stabilization

Formotion binding

MT

Enhancement of motion direction and feature tracking signals

FIGURE 9.1. The brain regions that help to use visual information for navigating in the world and tracking objects are highlighted in yellow.

In what sense do target tracking and optic flow navigation use complementary computations? One key distinction is that target tracking uses *subtractive* processing, indeed specialized on-center off-surround networks, to extract an object's boundaries as they move relative to its background, whereas optic flow computations use *additive* processing to compute properties, such as an observer's heading, that are derived from motion signals across a whole scene. More will be said below about what these properties are and how they are computed.

Optic flow and heading. I will start with an exposition of optic flow navigation. Speaking roughly, optic flow navigation exploits the fact that, as an animal moves through its environment, the positions at which environmental features activate the retinas change through time in a way that implicitly contains information about its navigational trajectory, such as its *heading direction*, or the direction in which the animal is moving. This direction is sometimes also called the self-motion direction. The patterned streaming of environmental features that is caused by self-motion is called optic flow. A central goal of visually-based navigation is to extract useful information for choosing movement trajectories from the structure of these streaming motion signals. One of the main problems in using optic flow to determine heading is that eye and head movements during navigation can distort the streaming pattern. This chapter will explain

how visually-based navigation can compute and exploit optic flow despite the distortions that are caused by eye movements.

The great American psychologist James Gibson pioneered our understanding of how optic flow enables visual navigation, without requiring additional cognitive processing, in his classical 1950 book on *The Perception of the Visual World* (Gibson, 1950). Gibson noted that heading can be determined from optic flow (or the instantaneous vector field), but not necessarily from retinal flow, by finding the focus of expansion (FoE). The FoE is the origin of the radial motion pattern that is created when a navigator translates through space in a stationary environment, as illustrated in Figure 9.2. In this figure, the optic flow field of an airplane that is about to land is depicted by the red arrows that radiate outwards from the FoE. The FoE is itself depicted by a green dot. Heading in this case is defined as the direction that the observer is traveling through the environment, which in this case is towards the green dot.

When our eyes rotate in their orbits, they change the optic flow pattern. As noted in Figure 9.3, when an observer moves linearly forward in an environment, a radially expanding flow field is caused, just as in Figure 9.2.

HEADING AND OPTIC FLOW

Optic flow: Scene motion generates a velocity field
Heading: Direction of travel: self-motion direction

Heading from optic flow
Focus of expansion
Gibson, 1950

Humans determine heading accurately within 1-2 degrees

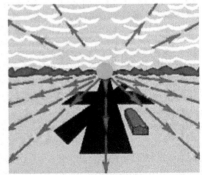

adapted from Gibson, 1950

FIGURE 9.2. Heading, or the direction of self-motion (green dot), can be derived from the optic flow (red arrows) as an object, in this case an airplane landing, moves forward.

OPTIC FLOW DURING NAVIGATION

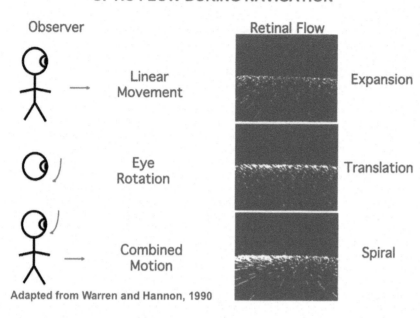

Adapted from Warren and Hannon, 1990

FIGURE 9.3. When an observer moves forward, an expanding optic flow is caused. Eye rotations cause a translating flow. When these flows are combined, a spiral flow is caused. How do our brains compensate for eye rotations to compute the heading of the expanding optic flow?

If the observer is stationary when rotating its eyes, then that causes a translation of the environment in the opposite direction. If the same eye rotation is made while the observer moves linearly forward, then the two flow fields add. The combined motion is a spiral flow field (Figure 9.3). This result raises the basic questions: How does an observer estimate heading if its eyes are rotating when it is moving in an environment? And does an observer even *need* to estimate heading in order to successfully navigate?

In 1992, James Cutting, Ken Springer, Paul Braren, and Scott Johnson (Cutting et al., 1992) estimated that humans require heading estimates that are accurate within 1-3 degrees in order to successfully navigate around cluttered environments. This kind of accuracy is well within normal human capabilities. Indeed, humans have been shown capable of determining heading from optic flow to within 1-2 degrees accuracy even in response to random dot displays (Figure 4.52; Warren and Hannon, 1988). When real eye movements are made, this level of accuracy is not affected (Royden, Crowell, and Banks, 1994; Warren and Hannon, 1990). However, when the same eye rotations are simulated in computer-generated psychophysics stimuli, with no real eye movement occurring, the result is totally different: The resulting displays are almost indistinguishable from those produced by a curvilinear path through the environment. Heading in this case is ambiguous (Warren and Hannon, 1990).

Human heading accuracy is maintained in the presence of simulated eye rotations of up to 1 degree per second at translation speeds of around 2 meters per second (Banks et al., 1996; Royden, Banks, and Crowell, 1992; Royden, Crowell, and Banks, 1994; Warren and Hannon, 1990). At these speeds, humans cannot distinguish between translation alone and translation with simulated eye rotation (Royden and Vaina, 2004). For faster simulated eye rotations, heading accuracy decreases (Banks et al., 1996; Royden, Banks, and Crowell, 1992; Royden, Crowell, and Banks, 1994; van den Berg, 1993; van den Berg and Brenner, 1994). The ratio of rotation rate to translation rate defines the absolute amount of rotation that can be tolerated in the flow field before heading errors accrue (Li, Sweet, and Stone, 2006).

There is no consensus about the precise nature of the error increase, and studies show large inter-observer differences (Banks et al., 1996; van den Berg and Brenner, 1994). Indeed, the use of heading for navigation has been contested by Rushton et al. (1998) and Wilkie and Wann (2003, 2006) who claim that goal position information in relation to self is sufficient to explain human steering data. Warren et al. (2001) have helped to resolve this debate by showing that humans can make use of both strategies and suggesting that, in featureless environments where heading is hard to estimate, egocentric goal position information is used, but in richer environments, heading is used.

The above examples illustrate how challenging it can be to derive precise psychophysical measures to characterize the behavior of a moving observer in different kinds of environments. The modeling literature is correspondingly complex, with some models using computations that are not neurobiologically plausible. Here, I will just

EYE ROTATIONS

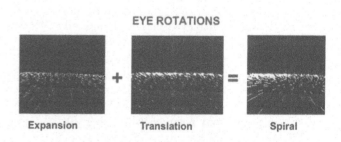

Eye rotations add a uniform translation to a flow field

Resulting retinal patterns are spirals

FIGURE 9.4. This figure emphasizes that the sum of the expansion and translation optic flows is a spiral optic flow. It thereby raises the question: How can the translation flow be subtracted from the spiral flow to recover the expansion flow?

SUBTRACTING EFFERENCE COPY

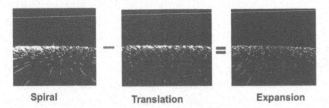

Spiral   Translation   Expansion

Many experiments suggest that the brain internally subtracts the translational component due to eye movements

Efference Copy subtracts the translational component using pathways that branch from outflow movement commands to the eye muscles

FIGURE 9.5. An outflow movement command, also called efference copy or corollary discharge, is the source of the signals whereby the commanded eye movement position is subtracted from spiral flow to recover expansion flow and, with it, heading.

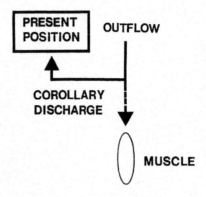

FIGURE 9.6. Corollary discharges are computed using a branch of the outflow movement commands that move their target muscles.

summarize how our psychophysically and neurophysiologically supported ViSTARS model, and its precursors, unifies the computation of object tracking and optic flow navigation using heading.

Compensating for eye rotation with a corollary discharge. There is considerable experimental evidence to support the idea that our brains process a spiral optic flow field by subtracting the effect of the eye movement that caused it in order to generate a radial flow field from which heading can be estimated. Figure 9.5 illustrates how this could happen, at least from a conceptual viewpoint. How it could happen using brain circuits requires further analysis.

The effect of an eye movement is derived from a *corollary discharge*, or *efference copy*, signal that is computed from an outflow movement command to the eye muscles via a parallel pathway (Figure 9.6). However, before the brain can try to subtract a corollary discharge from the spiral flow field, it has to deal with another source of distortion, albeit one that makes this task easier. Recall from Chapter 6 that retinal inputs are distorted by the cortical magnification factor on their way to visual cortical area V1 (Figure 6.10). The cortical magnification factor can be approximated by a log polar mapping that converts Cartesian coordinates (x.y) into polar coordinates (r, θ), where x and y are the horizontal and vertical coordinates of a point on the retina, and r and θ are the radial distance and angle of that point when it is projected onto the cortex. Figure 9.7 shows how the log polar map makes it easier to compute spiral optic flow fields, because *any* combination of expansion and circular motion that is centered on the fovea is transformed by the log polar map

into a cortical flow with a *single direction*! Figure 9.7 clarifies why this is so. The top row of this figure shows how a radial flow field on the retina gets converted into a horizontal flow on the cortex because the angle θ of each flow vector is constant. The bottom row shows how a rotational flow field on the retina gets converted into a vertical flow field on the cortex because the radius r of each flow vector is constant. From this it is easy to see why, in the middle row of the figure, a spiral flow field, which adds a radial and rotational flow field, is represented by a diagonal direction on the cortex. This transformation makes it easy for directionally-selective receptive fields to estimate the optic flow direction in MSTd, much like the directional filters in Figures 8.1, 8.35, and 8.36 estimate the object motion direction in MT⁻ and MSTv.

LOG POLAR REMAPPING OF OPTIC FLOW

Any combination of expansion and circular motion centered on the fovea maps to cortex as a single direction:

Retinal Cartesian coordinates (x, y) map to cortical polar coordinates (r, Θ)

This makes it easy to compute directional receptive fields in the cortex!

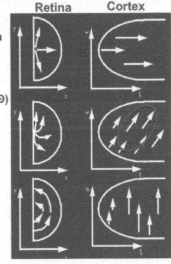

Retina   Cortex

FIGURE 9.7. Log polar remapping from the retina to cortical area V1 and beyond converts expansion, translation, and spiral flows on the retinal into parallel flows, with different orientations, on the cortical map.

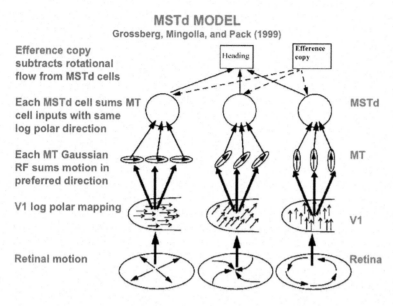

MSTd MODEL
Grossberg, Mingolla, and Pack (1999)

Efference copy subtracts rotational flow from MSTd cells

Heading — Efference copy

Each MSTd cell sums MT cell inputs with same log polar direction — MSTd

Each MT Gaussian RF sums motion in preferred direction — MT

V1 log polar mapping — V1

Retinal motion — Retina

FIGURE 9.8. How the various optic flows on the retina are mapped through V1, MT, and MSTd to then compute heading in parietal cortex was modeled by Grossberg, Mingolla, and Pack (1999), using the crucial transformation via V1 log polar mapping into parallel cortical flow fields.

Additive processing by MSTd to compute heading.

With this background, we can now consider properties of cortical area MSTd and how they contribute to the computation of heading. MSTd cells in monkeys are known to respond to patterns that occur during self-motion through the environment (Duffy, 1998; Grossberg, Mingolla, and Pack, 1999; Stone and Perrone, 1994). The human homolog of monkey MST, the human motion complex hMT+ (Dukelow et al., 2001; Huk, Dougherty, and Heeger, 2002), is also implicated in heading detection tasks (Beardsley and Vaina, 2001; Peuskens et al., 2001). MSTd cells are tuned to planar, radial, and spiral motion (Duffy and Wurtz, 1995; Graziano, Andersen, and Snowden, 1994; Saito et al., 1986), as in Figure 9.7. Heading appears to be represented as a distributed population code in both primate MSTd and human hMT+ (Beardsley and Vaina, 2001; Page and Duffy, 1999).

Figure 9.8 describes a simple model of how heading may be computed in MSTd by exploiting the simplification of receptive field structure that is realized by the log polar map. This heading model was developed with my PhD student Christopher Pack and published in 1999 (Grossberg, Mingolla, and Pack, 1999). In it, retinal optic flow motions are transformed in cortical area V1 by a log polar map. Then each model MT⁺ cell (just denoted by MT in Figure 9.8) sums motion in its preferred direction via a Gaussian receptive field. Each MSTd cell, in turn, sums MT⁺ cell inputs with the same log polar directional tuning over a larger cortical

region. It is this large-scale summation that characterizes the computation of optic flow and heading as an additive process. Then an efference copy, or corollary discharge, signal is subtracted from these MSTd estimates to yield a final prediction of heading.

Figure 9.9 summarizes data that were reported in 1994 by Michael Graziano, Richard Anderson, and Robert Snowden from neurophysiological recordings in MSTd of rhesus monkeys (Graziano, Andersen, and Snowden, 1994). The left image shows the tuning curve of an MSTd cell that is tuned best to a clockwise contracting spiral. The tuning curve shows how much the cell responds to the different optic flows that are depicted on the abscissa. This kind of data supports the ViSTARS hypothesis that heading is represented as an activity distribution across MSTd cells. Such a distributed representation of heading has been described in both primates and humans (Beardsley and Vaina, 2001; Page and Duffy, 1999) with the peak of this tuning curve estimating the direction of heading. The right image shows the preferred spiral directions for 57 MSTd cells. Each arrow represents a different cell. Each cell's preferred direction was found by fitting its tuning curve with a Gaussian function, as in the left image. A preponderance of cells was tuned to expansion, or near-expansion, flow fields.

Figure 9.10 summarizes a model simulation that illustrates how these tuning curves can be used to estimate heading for the case of an observer moving over a ground plane, with no eye movements. The left column of the figure shows typical optic flow stimuli corresponding to

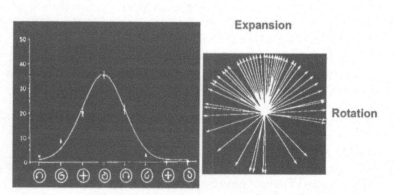

CORTICAL AREA MSTd

Expansion

Rotation

MSTd cells are sensitive to spiral motion as combinations of rotation and expansion

Adapted from Graziano, Andersen, and Snowden, 1994

FIGURE 9.9. Responses of MSTd cells that are used to compute heading. See the text for details.

HEADING IN LOG POLAR SPACE

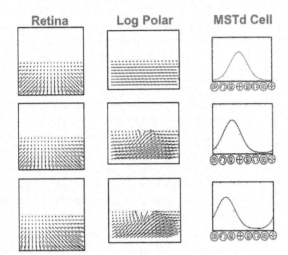

Log polar motion direction correlates with heading eccentricity

FIGURE 9.10. Model simulations of how the peak of MSTd cell activation varies with changes of heading.

various heading directions. The middle column shows that the dominant direction of motion in log polar coordinates changes systematically with heading direction. The right column shows how cells tuned to particular directions of log polar motion can be used to estimate the heading angles shown in the left column. In particular, the dominant directions of log polar motion in the middle column are transformed in the right column into Gaussian profiles that peak at different spiral preferences. The progression down the rows of the left column from a centered heading angle to a progressively eccentric heading angle is transformed in the rows of the right column into a progression from expansion to spiral to circular motion.

Figure 9.11 summarizes psychophysical data from Warren and Hanson (1990) about heading perception for movement towards a wall while fixating a stationary object. The upper curve shows that heading estimation keeps improving as heading angle increases when there are real eye movements. The lower curve showing that heading estimation is poor with simulated eye movements and continues to deteriorate as heading angle increases. The model simulation illustrates that the model competently captures key properties of human heading performance.

Reconciling space-variance with position invariance in MSTd. A surprising source of support for the model arose from the fact that the log polar mapping defines a *space-variant* system. This means that the interpretation of a motion direction depends on where in the visual field the

stimulus occurs. Figures 9.12 and 9.13 illustrate space-variance of the log polar map that carries out cortical magnification. In Figure 9.12, two views of the Simpsons are shown, along with how they are transformed by the log polar map. These images vividly illustrate how the visual field is distorted when a new fixation point is chosen. Figure 9.13 illustrates this same property during unsupervised scanning of three different kinds of pears. From images of the pears that are transformed by the log polar map in the right column of this figure, it is hard to say whether the eyes stay on one, two, or all three of the pears during these five eye movements. Our brains must somehow figure out how to learn about multiple views of a single pear as the eyes move across it, yet stop learning about that pear to enable learning about a new pear when the eyes move to look at it instead. How this View-to-Object Binding problem is solved by the brain so that it can learn view-invariant object categories was explained in Chapter 6, where the concept of surface-shroud resonance played an essential role. Chapter 6 did not emphasize the fact that the categories are learned from visual representations which are computed in log polar coordinates, if only because ARTSCAN can learn invariant categories of representations that are computed in any reasonable coordinate system.

How the brain reconciles space-variance with position invariance: A subtle tradeoff. The analysis with

HEADING: MOVE TO WALL AND FIXATE STATIONARY OBJECT

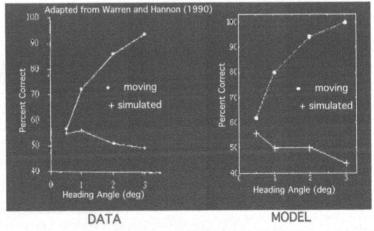

Inaccurate for simulated eye rotation
Accurate for real eye rotation
Need compensation by efference copy!

FIGURE 9.11. Psychophysical data (left panel) and computer simulation (right column) of the importance of efference copy in real movements. See the text for details.

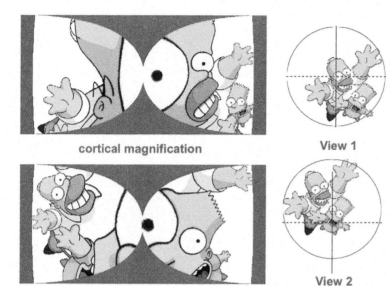

cortical magnification

View 1

View 2

How do we know if we are still fixating the same object?!

FIGURE 9.12. Transforming two retinal views of the Simpsons into log polar coordinates dramatizes the problem that our brains need to solve in order to separate, and recognize, overlapping figures.

Christopher Pack of how optic flow navigation is achieved revealed unexpected properties of how each brain may develop the parameters that characterize its log polar mapping. This analysis suggests how the property of *space-variance*, which was used to explain a number of

VIEW-INVARIANT OBJECT LEARNING AND RECOGNITION

During unsupervised scanning and learning about the world, no one tells the brain what views belong to which objects while it learns view-invariant object categories

Cortical magnification in V1

a

b

c

d

e

Three pears: Anjou, Bartlett, Comice
Which is the Bartlett pear?

FIGURE 9.13. When one scans the three different types of pears in the left image, as illustrated by the jagged blue curve with red movement end positions, and transforms the resulting retinal images via the cortical magnification factor, or log polar mapping, the result is the series of images in the right column. How do our brains figure out from such confusing data which views belong to which pear?

paradoxical findings about optic flow sensitivity in MSTd, could be reconciled with other data of Graziano, Andersen, and Snowden (1994) that reported *position invariance* of MSTd cells. These conflicting properties could not be ignored, because position invariance might have prevented MSTd cells from calculating self-motion. This is because the heading angle is determined by the position of the focus of expansion, so changes in heading would need to be registered as changes in the position of an expansion stimulus. A position-invariant cell would be incapable of registering these changes, as it would respond similarly to the presence of an expansion motion regardless of the locus of stimulation.

The current model illustrates how MSTd cells can process self-motion information while maintaining some degree of position invariance. In particular, the model suggests that evolution may have discovered log polar map parameters that optimize a tradeoff between space-variance and position invariance. This tradeoff was studied by plotting the average standard deviation of spiral tuning as a function of the tuning width σ of model MT cells. In 1984, Tom Albright (Albright, 1984) reported from his neurophysiological data about MT that the average standard deviation of MT cell tuning width is 38°. This estimate was derived by fitting MT tuning curves with a Gaussian receptive field, leading to the estimated Gaussian standard deviation of σ = 38°. Figure 9.14 (top row, left column) shows that, when this MT tuning width is used in the model, then the average standard deviation of spiral tuning in MSTd is approximately 61°, which is the spiral tuning width that was reported in the MSTd neurophysiological data of Graziano et al. (1994)!

This correspondence between model and neurophysiological MT and MSTd parameters was reassuring, but it led to a surprising consequence that implies a remarkable property of cortical evolution and development which warrants a great deal more study. Indeed, Figure 9.14 (bottom row, left column) shows the surprising model prediction that the spiral tuning of 61° found by Graziano et al. (1994) *maximizes the position invariance of MSTd receptive field cells*. The model simulation in Figure 9.14 (top row, right column) shows, moreover, that this occurs without impairing heading sensitivity.

A critical issue here is whether model cells that are tuned to log polar motion

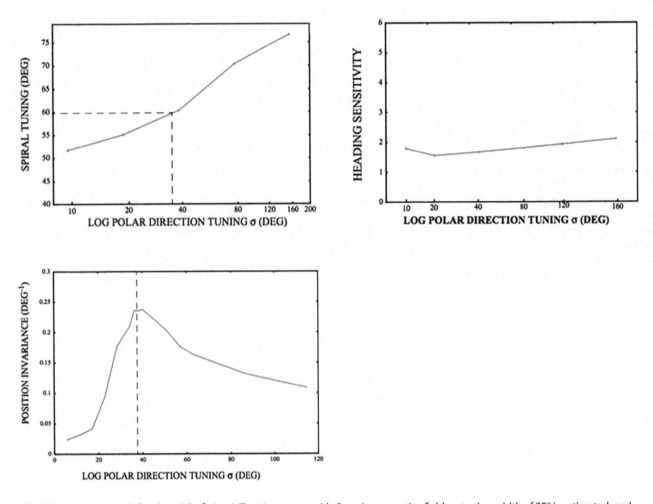

FIGURE 9.14. (top row, left column) By fitting MT tuning curves with Gaussian receptive fields, a tuning width of 38° is estimated, and leads to the observed standard spiral tuning of 61° in MSTd. (bottom row, left column) The spiral tuning estimate in Figure 9.16 maximizes the position invariant of MSTd receptive fields. (top row, right column) Heading sensitivity is not impaired by these parameter choices.

directions that are defined with respect to the fovea could produce tuning curves for stimuli centered on cell receptive fields at non-foveal positions. Because of the maximization depicted in 9.14 (bottom row, left column), the model's optic flow selectivity matches that of MSTd cells, even for physiological studies in which optic flow stimuli were not centered on the fovea. In addition, with regard to those position-varying responses that do occur, the properties of the model quantitatively fit those found in MSTd (Graziano et al., 1994; Duffy and Wurtz, 1995; Lappe et al., 1996; Lappe, Bremmer, and van den berg, 1999).

These results also raise fascinating questions about possible relationships that may exist between the tuning curve parameters that control the complementary processes of object tracking and optic flow navigation (Figure 8.34), notably whether the long-range motion filter that is predicted to occur between V1 and MT for tracking moving objects (Figures 8.26 and 8.31) may have parameters that may be usefully compared with those described above for optic flow navigation.

From Heading to STARS and ViSTARS. Despite its successes in explaining how heading contributes to visually-based navigation, the heading model did not explain how target tracking occurs. Nor did it model how heading is used to determine routes for navigating towards a goal object while successfully avoiding obstacles. In addition, it did not base its heading estimates on raw visual inputs through time. These accomplishments were modeled in stages, first with the STARS (Steering, Tracking, And Route Selection) neural model that I developed with my PhD student David Elder (Elder, Grossberg, and Mingolla, 2009), and then with the ViSTARS model (Figure 8.34) that I developed with my PhD student Andrew Browning (Browning, Grossberg, and Mingolla, 2009a, 2009b).

The ViSTARS model built upon the 3D FORMOTION model and the STARS model. In ViSTARS, the processing of complex naturalistic imagery by a 3D FORMOTION front end was fed into STARS processing stages. The STARS model, as its name attests, did model how routes can be navigated to reach desired goal objects while avoiding obstacles. To do so, it also modeled how moving objects are separated from their backgrounds by their relative motion so that they can serve as navigation goals or obstacles. However, the STARS model used artificially constructed motion vectors as its inputs. ViSTARS overcame this limitation by replacing the artificial motion vectors with outputs from the 3D FORMOTION model, which processed raw visual inputs of moving objects in scenes. Hence the Vi in ViSTARS.

In the original work on the 3D FORMOTION model with Julia Berzhanskaya (Berzhanskaya, Grossberg, and Mingolla, 2007), only data collected in response to the motion stimuli that were used in psychophysical experiments on humans were modeled. These data were invaluable in guiding the discovery of model principles and mechanisms, but the final step to test their ability to process natural moving scenes was not taken. ViSTARS took this final step to test model competence on stimuli ranging from random dot stimuli, through Open GL (Open Graphics Library) sequences of scenes of Yosemite National Park, to videos taken by Andrew Browning driving his car in Boston. My goal here is just to explain the highlights of how these models work, notably the design principles that underlie their competences and key mechanisms that instantiate them.

The STARS model uses parallel cortical streams to carry out the additive processing between MT⁺ and MSTd that accomplishes optic flow navigation and the subtractive processing between MT⁻ and MSTv that enables moving objects to be segmented from their backgrounds (Figure 8.34). Subtractive processing in MT⁻ uses double opponent directional receptive fields (Figure 9.15). For example, a cell whose on-center is tuned to rightward motion (green arrow in on-center) receives inhibitory signals from off-surround cells with the same directional selectivity (red arrows in off-surround). This simple opponency becomes double opponency because the same cell is inhibited by leftward motion in its on-center (red arrow) and is excited by leftward motion in its off-surround. These directional double opponent cells are homologous to the double opponent cells in the form stream that select feature contours for filling-in of lightnesses and colors (Figure 4.47).

Smooth pursuit of a moving target. An observer can track a moving object with eye movements, or navigate towards the object, or carry out a combination of both. As I have already noted in Chapter 3 (see Figure 3.4), the visual acuity of humans and other primates is marked by a central foveal region of high acuity and concentric regions of decreasing acuity. It is thus important to keep the fovea fixed on an object as it moves relative to the observer. This can be accomplished if the eye rotates at a speed equal to that of the target. Such a rotation is called a *smooth pursuit eye movement,* or SPEM. Humans can execute accurate SPEMs for target motion in excess of 30° per second (Lisberger, Morris, and Tychsen, 1987). A SPEM is distinct from a saccadic eye movement, or SAC, by which our eyes ballistically jump from one fixation point to another as fast as they can. SACs also keep the fovea focused upon different objects of interest, which may or may not themselves be moving. As I explained in Chapter 6 during my explanation of how we learn invariant object categories (e.g., Figures 6.14-6.16), SACs are used to move our foveas to search and learn about the scenes that we experience throughout life, including multiple views of individual objects.

It is not, however, sufficient to study either SACs or SPEMs in isolation. When an object moves unpredictably with a rapidly changing speed and direction, smooth pursuit movements may lag behind it until compensatory saccades catch up to it. The brain uses information from the how the smooth pursuit system was keeping up with the object to calibrate the size and direction of the next compensatory saccade with which to catch up to it. The system that coordinates SAC and SPEM movements uses interactions between many brain regions, as illustrated in Figure 9.16. This figure summarizes the macrocircuit of the SAC-SPEM neural model for coordinating saccadic and smooth pursuit movements that I developed with my PhD student Krishna Srihasan and my colleague Daniel Bullock (Grossberg, Srihasam, and Bullock, 2012; Srihasam, Bullock, and Grossberg, 2009). The figure caption labels

MOTION OPPONENCY IN MT

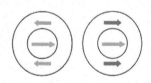

Motion opponent Grossberg et al
Differential motion Royden et al
Subtractive motion cells Neumann et al

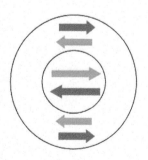

ON center directionally selective
Excited by motion in one direction
Inhibited by motion in opponent direction

OFF surround directionally selective
Excited by motion in opponent direction
Inhibited by motion in center direction

Born and Tootell, 1992

FIGURE 9.15. Double opponent directional receptive fields in MT are capable of detecting the motion of objects relative to each other and their backgrounds.

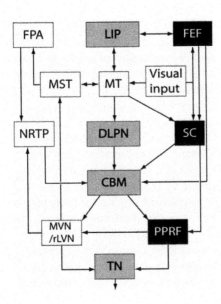

FIGURE 9.16. A macrocircuit of some of the main brain regions that are used to move the eyes. Black boxes denote areas belonging to the saccadic eye movement system (SAC), white boxes the smooth pursuit eye movement system (SPEM), and gray boxes, both systems. The abbreviations for the different brain regions are: LIP—Lateral Intra-Parietal area; FPA—Frontal Pursuit Area; MST—Middle Superior Temporal area; MT—Middle Temporal area; FEF—Frontal Eye Fields; NRTP—Nucleus Reticularis Tegmenti Pontis; DLPN—Dorso-Lateral Pontine Nuclei; SC—Superior Colliculus; CBM—cerebellum; MVN/rLVN—Medial and Rostro-Lateral Vestibular Nuclei; PPRF—a Peri-Pontine Reticular Formation; TN—Tonic Neurons.

the regions that control saccadic eye movements (SAC) and smooth pursuit eye movements (SPEM) in the brain and the model. Although an analysis of how this system works is beyond the scope of this book, the macrocircuit does serve as a reminder that seemingly effortless behavioral competences are often emergent properties of beautifully coordinated brain dynamics among multiple brain regions with different functional roles to play.

How tracking continues after the eyes catch up: Predictive SPEMs. The maintenance of SPEMs is often characterized in terms of a negative feedback system, whereby the oculomotor system continuously attempts to match the velocity of the eye to that of the target. However, this description cannot be complete for a simple reason: A successful SPEM stabilizes the target near the fovea. As a result of successful foveation, there is often little or no motion of the target on the retina, even while the target continues to move in the same speed and direction. Therefore, the pursuit system cannot rely on retinal target velocity to drive a SPEM. This state of affairs raises a basic question: What signals *does* the brain use to maintain fixation on a moving target after it has been foveated?

A number of additional signals have been hypothesized to guide pursuit, including target position, target acceleration (Lisberger et al., 1987), and a "memory" of target

velocity (Young et al., 1968), which is often described in terms of an oculomotor efference copy of eye velocity (Figure 9.6; von Holst, 1954). As I noted to explain how spiral optic flows eliminate the effects of eye movements, an efference copy duplicates the neural signal sent to the muscles that move the eye, and thus carries information about the movement of the eye that is independent of the retinal image. The efference copy can hereby maintain a prediction of pursuit velocity from moment to moment. Thus, the brain may combine retinal information about target motion on the retina with extraretinal information about the velocity of eye rotation.

There is still another source of visual information that does not depend upon the relative motion of the moving target. This is the motion of the visual background. A SPEM is often made as a target moves across a visual scene that contains stationary objects. As the SPEM tracks the moving target, stationary background objects sweep across the retinal image with a velocity opposite that of the target. This results in large-field coherent motion across the retina. Such a large-field motion normally triggers an involuntary eye rotation known as optokinetic nystagmus, or OKN. When it is allowed to occur, OKN causes the eye to move in the *same* direction as the large stimulus that causes it. However, an OKN movement that tracks retinal motion of a visual background during pursuit would be in the opposite direction of the ongoing target pursuit movement. It is therefore crucial that optokinetic signals be suppressed during execution of a SPEM.

Here we have one of those delightful design puzzles of how a brain can Have Its Cake and Eat It Too: On the one hand, the visual motion of the background can cause a disruptive OKN. On the other hand, the visual motion of the background can provide information about the velocity of an ongoing SPEM, even when the pursuit target is relatively stable on the retina. Such a background signal could therefore be used to generate a prediction of target velocity that maintains the SPEM during sustained foveation of the target. The visual motion of the background therefore has contradictory effects on the pursuit system, providing a potentially useful signal for pursuit maintenance, and a potentially destructive OKN signal. Our model explains how background motion maintains a predictive SPEM even while it suppresses OKN.

These processes influence what observers perceive visually. During an accurate SPEM, retinal target motion is very small, while objects in the background move across the retina. Psychophysical experiments indicate that human subjects are able to estimate the velocity of objects during a SPEM, but that observers underestimate the velocity of a moving target during a SPEM when no visible background is present (the Aubert-Fleischl phenomenon: Aubert, 1886), and perceive slight motion of a stationary visual background during a SPEM (the Filehne illusion: Filehne, 1922). More generally, distinguishing between the retinal motion caused by the movement of external objects and that caused by eye rotation is of primary importance for navigation and object tracking, as evidenced by the behavioral deficits that occur when localized cortical lesions disrupt this ability (Haarmeier et al., 1997).

These three types of information have neural data to support them: Neural signals related to target motion, background motion, and an oculomotor efference copy have been found in single cells in the superior temporal sulcus of monkey cortex. Within this sulcus, the medial temporal (MT) area contains cells that are selective for the direction and speed of motion, as I discussed in Chapter 8; e.g., Figures 8.26 and 8.31-8.33. The ViSTARS macrocircuit in Figure 8.34 also summarizes the fact that these MT cells, and their projections in MST, can be broadly subdivided into two types, based on physiological properties and anatomical clustering (Born and Tootell, 1992). One type of cell is found in MT⁻ and MSTv and responds best to small moving stimuli, and is suppressed by large motion patterns. The other kind of cell is found in MT⁺ and MSTd and responds best to large stimuli moving across the receptive fields. The MT⁺-MSTd cell properties are useful for computing retinal motion of the background during self-induced motion, while the MT⁻-MSTv cells are useful for computing the motion of potential pursuit targets (Born and Tootell, 1992; Eifuku and Wurtz, 1998).

Lesion studies have confirmed that areas MT and MST are involved in the control of SPEMs. Lesions of MT create a retinotopic deficit in pursuit initiation, meaning that the monkey's ability to execute a SPEM is impaired when the target moves in a particular part of the visual field (Dursteler, Wurtz, and Newsome, 1987), irrespective of target direction. Lesions of MST create a directional deficit, impairing the animal's ability to execute a SPEM when the target moves toward the lesioned hemisphere, irrespective of position in the visual field (Dursteler and Wurtz, 1988). A similar deficit is seen for OKN movements, indicating that the two behaviors share common neural pathways. Further evidence for the role of MST in controlling SPEMs comes from studies indicating that microstimulation within MST influences the velocity of SPEMs (Komatsu and Wurtz, 1989). It is also known that cells in MST receive an oculomotor efference copy, since they continue to respond during a SPEM when the target is momentarily extinguished or stabilized on the retina (Newsome, Wurtz, and Komatsu, 1988).

Chris Pack and I developed a model to explain how these three kinds of signals combine to enable SPEMs to be sustained after they foveate their target (Pack, Grossberg, and Mingolla, 2001). SPEMs hereby can be said to be *predictive*, since they anticipate where the eye will be and move accordingly to maintain fixation upon it. Figure 9.17 depicts a leftward eye movement channel and Figure 9.18 depicts the model's MST connectivity. The connections in Figure 9.17 are all excitatory. The Retinal Image is processed by two kinds of MT cells: MT⁻ cells with inhibitory surrounds (Figure 9.15) connect to MSTv cells, with

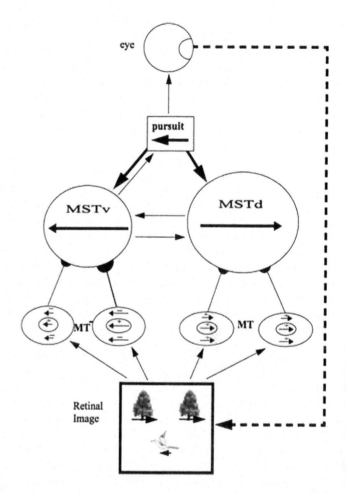

FIGURE 9.17. The leftward eye movement control channel in the model that I developed with Christopher Pack. See the text for details.

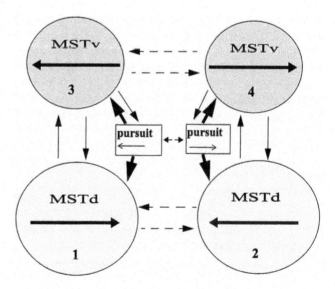

FIGURE 9.18. These circuits between MSTv and MSTd enable predictive target tracking to be achieved by the pursuit system, notably when the eyes are successfully foveating a moving target. Solid arrows depict excitatory connections, dashed arrows depict inhibitory connections.

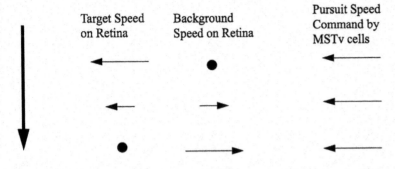

| Target Speed on Retina | Background Speed on Retina | Pursuit Speed Command by MSTv cells |

FIGURE 9.19. How a constant pursuit speed that is commanded by MSTv cells starts by using target speed on the retina and ends by using background speech on the retina in the reverse direction during successful predictive pursuit.

MT⁻ cells that prefer higher speeds weighted more heavily, as represented by the thicker synaptic knob at the end of its connection. MT⁺ cells with excitatory surrounds connect to MSTd cells. The MT and MST cells are drawn to approximate their relative receptive field sizes.

This circuit works in the following way: Model MSTd cells integrate the responses of MT⁺ cells with excitatory surrounds, thereby enabling them to respond well to global motion of the background. Model MSTv cells integrate the responses of MT⁻ cells with inhibitory surrounds, thereby enabling them to respond well to discrete moving targets. The connections from MT⁻ to MSTv are weighted such that MT⁻ cells preferring higher speeds (cf. Figure 8.33) generate larger responses in the MSTv cells to which they connect. This generates a graded response from MT⁻ cells in MSTv that covaries with target speed. MSTv cells drive pursuit eye movements in their preferred direction via the connection from MSTv to the Pursuit processing stage. This response is used to drive pursuit eye movements.

Leftward eye rotation causes rightward retinal motion of the background. As the eye catches up to the target, the leftward target speed on the retina decreases, but the rightward background speed increases in a compensatory way (Figure 9.19), so as MSTv cells get smaller inputs from MT⁻, MSTd cells get bigger inputs from MT⁺. MSTv cells also have excitatory connections with MSTd cells that prefer opposite directions. The excitatory connections from MSTd to MSTv enable increasing relative background motion to supplement decreasing relative target motion as the speed of the eye approaches that of the target. Thus model cells in MSTv can hereby code the *predicted* target speed, rather than the speed of the target on the retina. This sustained signal maintains an accurate smooth pursuit speed even after the target has been foveated.

But what happens if there are no objects in the background that can cause background inputs to MSTd? How is the predictive Pursuit signal maintained then? Efference copy signals that are fed back to MSTv and MSTd from the Pursuit stage via the thick connections, combined with the feedback signals from MST back to the Pursuit stage,

maintain this predictive signal even if there are no objects in the background that can create background motion signals (Figures 9.17 and 9.18).

Figure 9.18 also shows that the leftward and rightward Pursuit and MSTv stages compete with each other in a push-pull way via their reciprocal dashed connections, as do the leftward and rightward MSTd stages. All these connections, taken together, maintain activity in the Pursuit stage for predictive smooth pursuit *and* inhibit OKN due to background motion. Indeed, competition between channels encoding opposite directions of eye movement allows the model cells to suppress stimuli that would normally trigger a disruptive movement to track the retinal motion of the background. This mechanism is sufficient to suppress at least the cortical portion of the OKN response, and may reflect a general strategy used by the oculomotor system, since similar cell types are found in a number of subcortical structures. It should also be noted that, in order to make these transformations work, the model computes how signals in retinotopic coordinates are transformed into head-centered coordinates using both eye position efference copy signals via gain fields, and eye velocity efference copy signals via gain fields; cf. Figures 6.14-6.16. These details will not be summarized here.

In addition to realizing accurate predictive pursuit under normal conditions, the model simulates cortical neurophysiological data about SPEMs, MSTv, and MSTd, as well as perceptual phenomena such as the Filehne illusion and the Aubert-Fleischl phenomenon as emergent properties of the model MSTv and MSTd interactions that control predictive SPEMs.

Goal approach and obstacle avoidance via attractor-repeller control. How do human observers use the kinds of information that are computed from optic flow in order to navigate towards goal objects while avoiding obstacles along the way? David Elder and I studied a lot of psychophysical data about this competence before arriving at the conclusion that, in some way, goal objects acted to *attract* a navigator while obstacles acted to *repel* the navigator. At just around this time, we were delighted to find out that Brett Fajen and William Warren had earlier come to a similar conclusion from their own beautiful navigation data that were collected from humans navigating in a virtual reality environment that gave them a lot of control over the goal and obstacle stimuli (Fajen and Warren, 2003). Moreover, they modeled the routes that their human subjects chose with a mass-spring model that incorporated plausible properties of how the spring would react as a navigator moved among goals and obstacles. Nice fits to their data were made with this model, and thereby demonstrated that "route selection may emerge from on-line steering dynamics, making explicit path planning unnecessary" (p. 343).

STEERING FROM OPTIC FLOW

Fajen and Warren, 2003

Goals are attractors
Obstacles are repellers

Damped spring model explains
human steering data

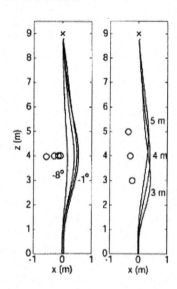

FIGURE 9.20. Using virtual reality displays (left image), Fajen and Warren (2003) collected data (right two images) about how observers avoid obstacles (open circular disks) as a function of their distance and angular position as they navigate towards a fixed goal (x). These data illustrated how goals act as attractors while obstacles act as repellers.

The lower left image in Figure 9.20 depicts one of the virtual reality scenes that they used, with the nearer pole acting as an obstacle on the way to reaching the further pole. Different movement trajectories were caused on the way to the further pole as the nearer pole was moved around the virtual reality environment. Consider, for example, the two images to the right in Figure 9.20. The leftward image shows how movement trajectories are repelled further to the right as the nearer pole is moved progressively to the right (marked with circles) without changing the position of the further pole (marked with x). The rightward image shows how the trajectories veer to the right later in the trajectory as the obstacle is moved progressively towards the goal. These manipulations provided a vivid way to visualize the repulsive region of space that surrounds an obstacle.

Steering with Gaussian peak shifts. Despite the importance of this experimental and modeling contribution, the mass-spring model sheds no light on the brain mechanisms that create attractor-repeller trajectories. This mechanistic gap was filled with the processes in the STARS model, which showed that the familiar

neural mechanism of *peak shift* due to the interaction of Gaussian receptive fields is sufficient to simulate the Fajen and Warren data about attractor-repeller dynamics during route selection (Figures 9.21 and 9.22). Recall that peak shifts also helped to explain data about peak shift and behavioral contrast during operant conditioning (Figure 1.12) and vector decomposition during the relative motion of object parts (Figure 8.49). A peak shift mechanism is also natural for explaining route selection via attractor-repeller dynamics because the direction of heading is represented by the peak of a Gaussian receptive field (Figures 9.21 and 9.22).

Steering can thus be conceptualized by interactions between three Gaussians that represent (1) current heading, (2) a goal, and (3) an obstacle. In this conception, to move the heading direction closer to the goal, a *steering Gaussian* is defined by adding a Gaussian that represents the goal direction to the Gaussian that represents the heading direction. Figure 9.21 summarizes how this happens. In the upper figure, the light blue Gaussian is the sum of the goal and heading Gaussians. It generates the steering direction signal, which is closer to the goal direction than the initial heading

STEERING DYNAMICS: GOAL APPROACH

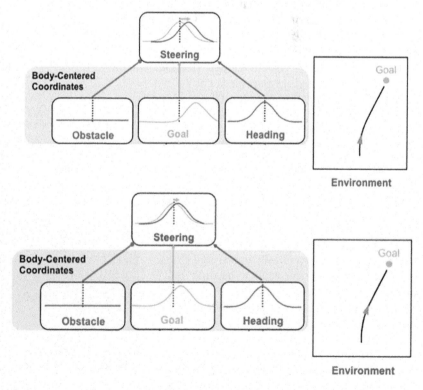

FIGURE 9.21. How attractor-repeller dynamics with Gaussians change the net steering gradient as the goal is approached.

STEERING DYNAMICS: OBSTACLE AVOIDANCE

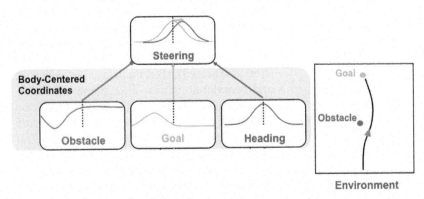

FIGURE 9.22. How the negative Gaussian of an obstacle causes a peak shift to avoid the obstacle without losing sight of how to reach the goal.

direction alone. As steering towards the goal progresses, the peak of the light blue Gaussian shifts closer to the goal direction because the heading moves closer to the goal direction, as illustrated in the lower figure of Figure 9.21.

To move heading away from an obstacle, obstacles are represented by inverted Gaussians. As illustrated in Figure 9.22, when there is an obstacle, the three Gaussians add to determine the steering direction, which is again depicted in light blue. In this case, however, the obstacle Gaussian, being inverted, cause a peak shift of the steering direction away from the obstacle's current direction, thereby causing the trajectory to veer away from it.

Here we note a remarkable similarity with the peak shift that occurs due to punishment during operant conditioning (Figure 1.12) and the peak shift that occurs due to an obstacle during visually-guided steering. During operant conditioning, a punished cue causes an inverted Gaussian to form. During steering, an obstacle is a potentially aversive cue, and also causes an inverted Gaussian to form. But how does one define an obstacle, given that an object that is an obstacle on one route may be the goal on another route? In the STARS and ViSTARS models, an obstacle is any object that is nearer to the observer than the fixation plane where the goal object is represented. This hypothesis works, and enables obstacles for one route to become goals for another route.

On the other hand, the hypothesis that an obstacle causes an inverted Gaussian does raise as yet unanswered questions about the interactions between regions like the ventral intraparietal area, or VIP, in the parietal cortex where attractor-repeller is predicted to occur and the subcortical regions, such as the amygdala, where

affective representations are computed, as described in Chapter 13. Answering these questions will doubtless be a subject of an interesting future investigation.

Solving the aperture problem for heading in natural scenes using the ART Matching Rule. Although STARS showed how attractor-repeller dynamics could control steering to a goal while avoiding obstacles, the inputs to the STARS model were not raw visual inputs from the real world, but rather were a vector field representation that was constructed from visual inputs. ViSTARS overcame this deficiency by feeding visual imagery directly into a 3D FORMOTION front end that input to the STARS control circuitry (Figure 8.34).

I will end this chapter by summarizing highlights of how the ViSTARS model computes heading from videos from driving a car through Boston. This summary will highlight that the MT+-MSTd cortical stream solves an aperture problem for computing a navigator's heading, just as the MT--MSTv cortical stream solves an aperture problem for computing a target object's position, direction, and speed of motion (Figure 8.34). Moreover, both streams share 3D FORMOTION neural mechanisms at their early processing stages and use strikingly homologous mechanisms at their later processing stages to solve their respective problems. How these homologs arise during brain evolution and development is a subject that warrants more study.

Figure 9.23 shows the responses of unidirectional transient cells as a car moves along the road. These

UNDIRECTIONAL TRANSIENT CELLS

Transient cells respond to leading and trailing boundaries

Baloch and Grossberg, 1997; Berzhanskaya, Grossberg, and Mingolla, 2007

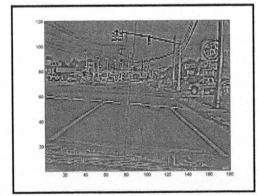

Transient cell response, driving video

FIGURE 9.23. Undirectional transient cells respond to changes in all image contours as an auto navigates an urban scene while taking a video of it.

DIRECTIONAL TRANSIENT CELLS

8 directions, 3 speeds

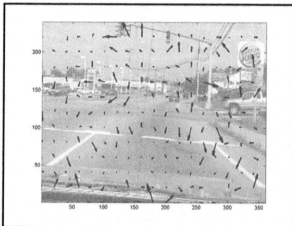

FIGURE 9.24. Directional transient cells respond most to motion in their preferred directions.

change-sensitive cells use habituative transmitter gates to generate their responses to changes in the scene at their positions. The unidirectional transient cell responses then input to directional transient cells that respond most vigorously to motion in their preferred directions (Figure 9.24). Both of these processing stages are part of the usual 3D FORMOTION model preprocessing of visual inputs

MT⁺ COMPUTES GLOBAL MOTION ESTIMATE

Estimate global motion from noisy local motion estimates

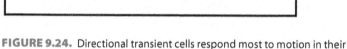

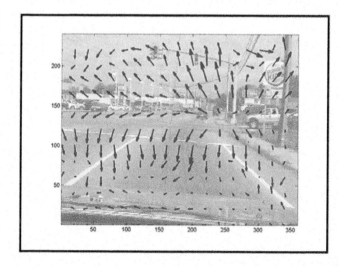

FIGURE 9.25. By the time MT⁺ is reached, directional transient cells and directional filters have begun to extract more global directional information from the image.

(Figure 8.31). The directional filters in MT⁺ use these directional transient responses to begin to estimate global motion directions (Figure 9.25).

Just as the aperture problem for target tracking is solved by feedback interactions between MT⁻ and MSTv (Figure 8.31), the aperture problem for heading is solved by feedback interactions between MT⁺ and MSTd. The top-down feedback from MSTd to MT⁺ uses learned prototypes, or templates, that are derived from previous experiences with optic flow. How such templates can be learned was simulated in a 1998 article with my PhD student Seth Cameron and colleague Frank Guenther (Cameron, Grossberg, and Guenther, 1998).

After the heading cells in MSTd compete, the winning cell population in MSTd feeds back its heading template to MT⁺. These templates were matched against MT⁺ cell activities using the ART Matching Rule, thereby selecting the cells in MT⁺ whose directions are consistent with the winning heading direction in MSTd. Because of this shared use of the ART Matching Rule in both MSTd and MSTv (Figure 8.35), one can interpret the solution of the aperture problem for computing heading as an emergent property of how the learning of heading directions is stabilized, just as one can interpret the solution of the aperture problem for computing object direction as an emergent property of how the learning of object motion directions is stabilized.

The winning cell population in MSTd represents heading accurately, as can be seen from the beautiful heading flow field that is selected in MT⁺ after the chosen MSTd template is matched there against bottom-up inputs to MT⁺. Figure 9.26 depicts this flow field, and also summarizes the excellent heading accuracy that is computed by this process in response to random dot, OpenGL, and car driving video, with all accuracies within the human range of performance.

In summary, ViSTARS provides a neural model of visually-based navigation and tracking that is competent to explain and quantitatively simulate challenging data about these important capabilities, and does so in a computationally parsimonious way. Future research will enable us to better understand the evolutionary and developmental forces that cause the MT⁻-MSTv cortical stream to use subtractive processing of visual motion inputs, and the MT⁺-MSTd stream to use computationally

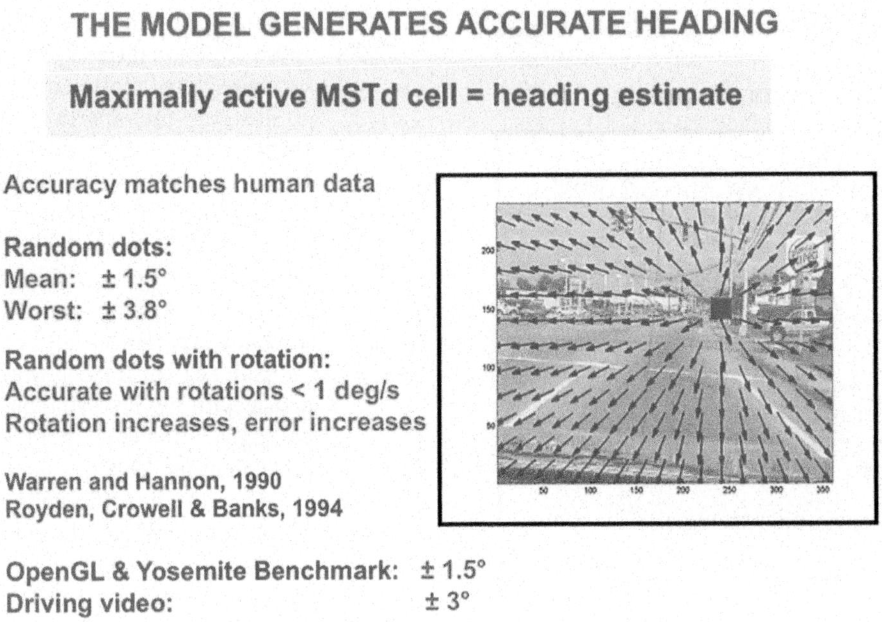

THE MODEL GENERATES ACCURATE HEADING

Maximally active MSTd cell = heading estimate

Accuracy matches human data

Random dots:
Mean: ± 1.5°
Worst: ± 3.8°

Random dots with rotation:
Accurate with rotations < 1 deg/s
Rotation increases, error increases

Warren and Hannon, 1990
Royden, Crowell & Banks, 1994

OpenGL & Yosemite Benchmark: ± 1.5°
Driving video: ± 3°

FIGURE 9.26. The final stage of the model computes a beautiful expansion optic flow that permits an easy estimate of the heading direction, with an accuracy that matches that of human navigators.

complementary additive processing of visual motion inputs (Figure 8.34 and Table 1.1). Once we better understand how the split into complementary streams develops, then the fact that both streams use ART Matching Rule circuits will immediately clarify how these developing circuits are dynamically stabilized. The fact that these dynamically stabilized cells can regulate target tracking and optic flow navigation once again affirms the power of design principles like complementary computing and adaptive resonance when they interact together in response to the different statistical properties of real world input streams.

Laminar Computing by Cerebral Cortex

Towards a unified theory of biological and artificial intelligence

Why does the entire cerebral cortex use variations of a canonical laminar circuit?

So far in the book, I have explained some of the important processes that occur when a brain sees, attends, and learns to recognize and predict objects and events. All of these processes involve parts of the cerebral cortex, including the visual, inferotemporal, and prefrontal cortices. The cerebral cortex, which is the mantle of gray matter that covers much of the brain's surface, is the seat of the highest forms of biological intelligence in all sensory and cognitive modalities, not just vision. The cells in the gray matter are organized into circuits that form six distinct cortical layers (Brodmann, 1909; Martin, 1989) in essentially all cortical areas that carry out perception and cognition, as illustrated in Figures 1.20, 4.39, and 5.38. Variations in properties of the cells of these layers and the connectivity between them have been used to classify the cerebral cortex into more than fifty divisions, or areas, to which distinct functions have been attributed. Why the cortex has a laminar organization for the control of behavior has, however, remained a mystery until recently. It has remained equally mysterious how variations on this ubiquitous laminar cortical design can give rise to so many different types of intelligent behavior. We are thus faced with the following enormous problem: How does *Laminar Computing* contribute to biological intelligence? How do layered circuits of cells help to support all the various kinds of higher-order biological intelligence, including vision, language, and cognition?

The models that I summarized above have several distinct processing stages, but they were not originally developed with the goal of mapping directly onto the laminar circuits of cerebral cortex. Despite this limitation, these models clarified, and helped to solve, several of the fundamental problems that advanced brains face in order to see, and the kinds of circuits that they use during vision, learning, and recognition. Given this background, one additional set of observations led me and my PhD student William Ross in 1997 to a breakthrough that began to clarify why the cerebral cortex has a laminar organization. Subsequent modeling work revealed how this laminar design can be specialized to support intelligent behaviors that seem on the surface to be quite different.

In particular, specializations of the same canonical laminar circuitry have been used in the 3D LAMINART model for 3D vision and figure-ground separation (Bhatt, Carpenter, and Grossberg, 2007; Cao and Grossberg, 2005, 2012; Fang and Grossberg, 2009; Grossberg, 1999; Grossberg and Howe, 2003; Grossberg, Srinivasan, and Yazdanbakhsh, 2014; Grossberg and Swaminathan, 2004; Grossberg and Yazdanbakhsh, 2005; Grossberg, Yazdanbakhsh, Cao, and Swaminathan, 2008; Leveille, Versace, and Grossberg, 2010; Raizada and Grossberg, 2001, 2003), the cARTWORD model for conscious speech perception, learning, and recognition (Grossberg and Kazerounian, 2011, 2016; Kazerounian and Grossberg, 2014), and the LIST PARSE model for cognitive working memory and the learning of cognitive plans (Grossberg and Pearson, 2008; Silver, Grossberg, Bullock, Histed, and Miller, 2011). These models clarify how specializations of the same canonical design for neocortical circuits can be specialized to accomplish many different perceptual and cognitive tasks, in keeping with the experimental evidence that all sensory and cognitive neocortical areas share many basic anatomical properties of circuit design and connectivity (Felleman and van Essen, 1991; Van Essen and Maunsell, 1983). These models constitute an existence proof that future researchers will be able to develop a unified theory of biological intelligence. They also point the way to how VLSI chips with a similar canonical circuit design can be specialized to carry out different types of intelligence in future applications in engineering and technology, and how these chips can be assembled into controllers of increasingly autonomous adaptive agents. These developments will require a great deal of investment, intelligence, and hard work by many people, but the foundations have been laid and point the way to how to proceed.

The breakthrough that led to greater understanding of the functional utility of laminar neocortical circuitry began with a synthesis of concepts and mechanisms that were developed in two parallel, but previously non-intersecting, research streams. The first stream developed the Boundary Contour System (BCS) model for perceptual grouping, which particularly emphasizes the bottom-up filtering and horizontal bipole grouping interactions that form emergent boundary representations during preattentive vision in visual cortical areas such as V1 and V2 (Figure 4.32). The second stream developed Adaptive Resonance Theory (ART) model for attentive learning of recognition categories, which particularly emphasizes interactions between bottom-up and top-down processes in cortical areas such as the visual cortical areas V2 and V4 with the inferotemporal, or IT, cortex (Figure 5.19).

The breakthrough of Laminar Computing clarifies how bottom-up, horizontal, and top-down interactions are combined in a parsimonious and beautiful way at *all* levels of perceptual and cognitive neocortex. In particular, the ART Matching Rule for object attention (Figure 1.25), that was predicted to be realized by a top-down, modulatory on-center, off-surround network, could now be seen to have a clear anatomical realization using identified neocortical cells in a circuit that crosses multiple cortical layers (Figure 10.1), from layer 6 in a higher cortical area, such as V2, to layer 1-then-5-then-6-then-4 of a lower cortical area such as V1, thereby forming a top-down, modulatory on-center, off-surround circuit, as predicted by the ART Matching Rule. This basic fact is one reason why I have called this laminar family of models for 2D perceptual grouping and attention the LAMINART model, and its generalization to 3D vision the 3D LAMINART model.

LAMINART proposes how bottom-up, horizontal, and top-down interactions work together within the cortical layers to enable the visual cortex to realize: (1) the developmental and learning process whereby cortex shapes its circuits to match environmental constraints, and dynamically maintains them thereafter in a stable way; (2) the binding process whereby cortex groups distributed data into coherent object representations; and (3) the attentional process whereby cortex selectively processes important events. As noted above, I have already reviewed aspects of (1) and (3) using ART, and (2) using the BCS. One of the model's remarkable conclusions is that the mechanisms that achieve property (1) imply properties (2) and (3). That is, constraints that control stable cortical self-organization in the infant strongly constrain properties of

TOP-DOWN ATTENTION AND FOLDED FEEDBACK

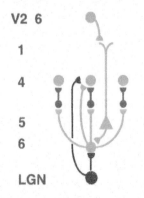

Attentional signals also feed back into 6-to-4 on-center off-surround

1-to-5-to-6 feedback path
Macaque: Lund & Boothe, 1975
Cat: Gilbert & Wiesel, 1979

V2-to-V1 feedback is on-center off-surround and affects layer 6 of V1 the most
Bullier et al., 1996
Sandell & Schiller, 1982

Attended stimuli enhanced Ignored stimuli suppressed

This circuit supports the predicted **ART MATCHING RULE!**

FIGURE 10.1. The laminar cortical circuit that realizes how we pay attention to an object sends signals from layer 6 of a higher cortical level to layer 6 of a lower cortical level and then back up to layer 4. This "folded feedback" circuit realizes a top-down, modulatory on-center, off-surround circuit that realizes the ART Matching Rule.

perceptual grouping, attention, and learning in the adult. These are not three separate problems, but rather a single problem with a unified solution within a laminar cortical setting. With this canonical laminar circuitry as a foundation, the cARTWORD and LIST PARSE models show how specializations of the horizontal connections that carry out perceptual groupings in visual cortex may carry out different tasks in other cortical areas, notably category learning during speech and cognition.

Where preattentive and attentive processes meet

To summarize how LAMINART works, I want to be sure that all the pertinent information is fresh in your minds. I will therefore briefly review some salient properties of perceptual grouping and attention.

Perceptual grouping and attention: Interactions, similarities, and differences. Recall that *perceptual grouping* enables our brains to organize image contrasts into emergent boundary structures that segregate objects and their backgrounds in response to edge, texture, shading, and depth cues in scenes and images. Perceptual grouping is thus a basic step in solving the "binding problem" whereby spatially distributed features are bound into representations of objects and events in the world. Vivid perceptual groupings, such as illusory contours, can form over image positions that do *not* receive contrastive bottom-up inputs from an image or scene. Just think about a Kanizsa square (Figure 3.3). Apart from the inducing pac-man figures, the entire square forms over positions that receive no contrastive bottom-up inputs. Indeed, being able to form a grouping over spatial positions that receive no contrastive inputs is a defining property of an illusory contour. Perceptual groupings can also form *preattentively* and automatically, without requiring the conscious attention of a viewing subject (Moore and Egeth, 1997).

Attention, on the other hand, enables humans and other animals to selectively process information that is of interest to them. In contrast to perceptual grouping, top-down attention does not usually generate visible percepts over positions where no contrastive bottom-up inputs are received. Attention can modulate, sensitize, or prime, an observer to expect an object to occur at a given location, or with particular stimulus properties (Duncan, 1984; Posner, 1980). But were attention, by itself, able to routinely generate fully-formed perceptual representations at positions that did not receive bottom-up inputs, then we could not tell the difference between external reality and internal fantasy. In fact, as I discussed in Chapter 5, when attention fails to be modulatory, hallucinations can occur.

When schizophrenic patients experience such hallucinations, they cannot tell the difference between external reality and internal fantasy.

Despite these differences between perceptual grouping and attention, the history of visual perception has been full of controversies in which distinguished thinkers have assumed that top-down processes are critically important for perceptual grouping. Perhaps the most distinguished perceptual scientist to think this was the great Helmholtz himself, whose concept of *unconscious inference* describes a top-down expectation that helps to shape every percept. Why has this controversy been so enduring between individuals who share beliefs similar to those of Helmholtz or Kanizsa concerning how vision works, with followers of the Kanizsa camp emphasizing bottom-up and horizontal interactions that can be carried out automatically and preattentively, and followers of the Helmholtz camp emphasizing top-down attentive interactions? In the new laminar synthesis (Figure 10.2), one can better understand that these processes for seeing vs. knowing indeed operate a different levels of the brain using specialized circuits. However, these specialized circuits are variations of the same cortical designs and interact via feedback, so cannot be easily separated from one another. The LAMINART model hereby shows that, although these processes are distinct, they are also intimately linked, and their particular linkage gives rise to powerful properties that are important to our survival. The remainder of this chapter clarifies how these circuits work and interact at multiple levels of the visual cortex.

The intermingling of perceptual grouping and attention may be further understood by noting the following facts: Various data have shown that both perceptual grouping

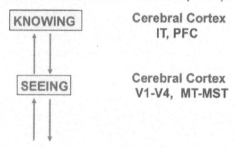

SEEING vs. KNOWING

SEEING AND KNOWING
   operate at different levels of the brain
   use specialized circuits
but they
   interact via feedback
   use similar cortical designs
   feedback is needed for conscious perception

FIGURE 10.2. Distinguishing processes of seeing vs. knowing has been difficult because they interact so strongly.

and attention can simultaneously occur within the same circuits of the visual cortex, notably in cortical areas V1 and V2. In addition, both processes share many properties: they enhance weak stimuli, but have a neutral or even suppressive effect on stimuli that are already strong; they also suppress rival stimuli. Finally, although groupings may arise preattentively, attentional task demands can influence which of several possible alternative groupings actually form. These groupings, in turn, can affect attentional phenomena such as the formation of illusory conjunctions (when the wrong colors and forms are seen together) or reaction times in visual search tasks. It has also been shown that attentional enhancement can propagate along both real and illusory contours, thereby selectively enhancing whole objects that interest us. Various of these phenomena will be explained later in this chapter, and others are described in the archival modeling articles (e.g., Grossberg, 1999; Grossberg and Raizada, 2000).

How is it possible for grouping and attention to share such important properties and intimately interact, yet also obey such different constraints? In particular, how does cortical circuitry form perceptual groupings that *can* complete a boundary grouping over locations that receive no bottom-up visual inputs (Figure 3.3), whereas top-down attention *cannot* do so, because the ART Matching Rule has a modulatory on-center (Figure 1.25)? More generally, why *should* attention be deployed throughout the visual cortex, including early visual cortical areas, such as V1 and V2, which until recently were thought to accomplish purely preattentive processing? An answer can be found by exploring the link between attention and learning, as it is described in the LAMINART model.

Before providing these explanations, let me summarize from a higher vantage point computational properties of laminar neocortical circuits, as revealed by LAMINART and its generalizations, that I believe will have a revolutionary impact on many aspects of future computing applications. Figures 10.3 and 10.4 summarize these properties.

Three basic properties of Laminar Computing. Figure 10.3 summarizes three basic computational properties of Laminar Computing. Property (1) asserts again that laminar cortical circuits can support self-stabilizing development and learning, and thus solve the stability-plasticity dilemma. Property (2) notes that the laminar circuits can consistently fuse, or merge, the demands of preattentive and automatic bottom-up processing with those of attentive and task-selective top-down processing. These distinct constraints are brought together and reconciled using a competitive decision circuit that exists in layers 6-to-4 of multiple cortex processing stages. Property (3) asserts that the laminar circuits have the property of *analog coherence*. In other words, they can choose and coherently sustain perceptual groupings without a lose of analog sensitivity. I discussed this property in Chapter 4, where I noted that

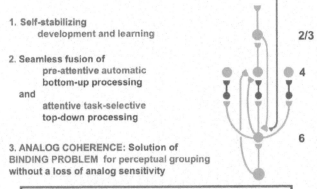

WHAT DOES LAMINAR COMPUTING ACHIEVE?

1. Self-stabilizing development and learning

2. Seamless fusion of pre-attentive automatic bottom-up processing and attentive task-selective top-down processing

3. ANALOG COHERENCE: Solution of BINDING PROBLEM for perceptual grouping without a loss of analog sensitivity

Even the earliest visual cortical stages carry out active adaptive information processing: LEARNING, GROUPING, ATTENTION

FIGURE 10.3. Laminar computing achieves at least three basic properties of visual processing that have analogs in all biologically intelligent behaviors. These properties may be found in all cortical circuits in specialized form.

the strength, or salience, of perceptual groupings should covary with the amount of evidence for them, but that the excitatory feedback loops that are used to choose winning grouping could all too easily make winner-take-all choices in which the winning cells had maximal activity. LAMINART circuits form groupings with a strength that covaries with the amount of evidence in their inducers, as I illustrated with computer simulations of analog grouping strength in Figure 4.37.

Laminar Computing unifies opposing design constraints. Figure 10.4 summarizes that Laminar Computing unifies design constraints that seem to be incompatible in some systems.

First, Laminar Computing combines the *best properties of fast feedforward processing and feedback processing*. When input data are unambiguous, and support only one possible grouping, then signals can be rapidly relayed bottom-up from layers 4-to-2/3 in one cortical area, then on to layers 4-to-2/3 in the next cortical area, and so on. However, when there are multiple possible groupings of the input data, processing automatically slows down long enough to contrast-enhance and amplify the grouping with the most evidence—to the degree that is supported by the input evidence—before feedforward processing resumes to subsequent cortical areas. This automatic slowing down occurs because competition within these circuits is realized by on-center off-surround *shunting* networks which, as I noted in Chapter 1 (see Figure 1.7), tend to *normalize* their total activity. Thus, if there are multiple competing groupings, each grouping gets less activity, and can consequently exceed output thresholds more slowly. As a grouping with the most evidence gets contrast-enhanced

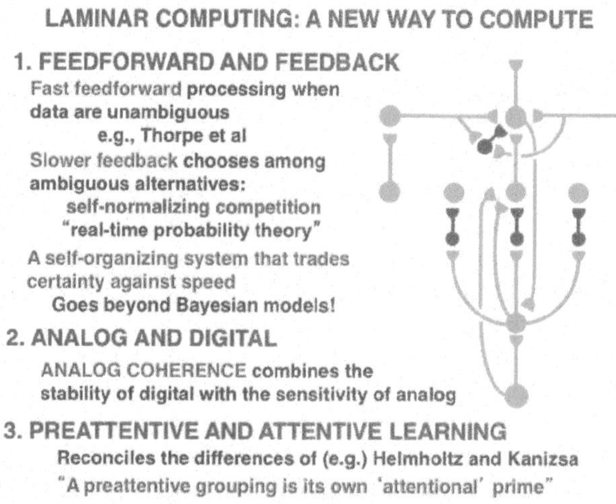

LAMINAR COMPUTING: A NEW WAY TO COMPUTE

1. FEEDFORWARD AND FEEDBACK
Fast feedforward **processing** when
data are unambiguous
    e.g., Thorpe et al
Slower feedback **chooses** among
ambiguous alternatives:
    self-normalizing competition
    "real-time probability theory"
A self-organizing system that trades
certainty against speed
    Goes beyond Bayesian models!

2. ANALOG AND DIGITAL
    ANALOG COHERENCE combines the
    stability of digital with the sensitivity of analog

3. PREATTENTIVE AND ATTENTIVE LEARNING
    Reconciles the differences of (e.g.) Helmholtz and Kanizsa
    "A preattentive grouping is its own 'attentional' prime"

FIGURE 10.4. Laminar Computing achieves its properties by computing in a new way that synthesizes the best properties of feedforward and feedback interactions, analog and digital computations, and preattentive and attentive learning. The property of analog coherence enables coherent groupings and decisions to form without losing sensitivity to the amount of evidence that supports them.

and amplified while weaker groupings get suppressed, the winning grouping can more quickly exceed its output threshold, and feedforward processing resumes. This is thus a *self-organizing system that trades certainty against speed*. It runs as fast as it can, given the amount of evidence that is available with which to make its decisions.

Second, Laminar Computing combines the *best properties of analog and digital computing*. That is because the property of analog coherence combines the *stability* of digital computing—due to the way in which feedback loops enhance and store decisions in STM—without sacrificing the *sensitivity* of analog computing.

Third, Laminar Computing combines the *best properties of preattentive and attentive learning* by reconciling the necessary properties of bottom-up adaptive filtering and horizontal grouping with the stabilizing and task-selective properties of top-down learned expectations and attention.

Infant development and adult learning use similar laws: A universal developmental code

My discussions of ART in Chapters 5 and 6 showed how top-down attention may be a key mechanism that is used by the brain to solve the stability-plasticity dilemma, whereby our brains can rapidly learn throughout life, without just as rapidly forgetting what they already know. Brains are *plastic* and can rapidly learn new experiences, without losing the *stability* that prevents catastrophic forgetting. The generality of the stability-plasticity analysis suggests that suitable top-down mechanisms should be present in *every* cortical area wherein self-stabilizing learning can occur, since without top-down learned expectations that focus attention via the ART Matching Rule, any such learned memories could easily be degraded due to catastrophic forgetting. We are therefore led to ask: How are such attentive processes realized within the laminar circuits of the visual cortex in order to stabilize its learning through time?

ART mechanisms that dynamically stabilize learned memories should also apply to the perceptual grouping process, because the cortical horizontal connections that support perceptual grouping in cortical areas like V1 and V2 develop through a learning process that is influenced by visual experience (Antonini and Stryker, 1993; Calloway and Katz, 1990; Lowel and Singer, 1992). It is also known that many developmental and learning processes, including those that control horizontal cortical connections, are stabilized dynamically, and can be reactivated by lesions and other sources of cortical imbalance (Das and Gilbert, 1995; Gilbert and Wiesel, 1992) in order to embody the environmental statistics to which the new cortical substrate is exposed.

Moreover, adult learning often seems to use the same types of mechanisms as the infant developmental processes upon which it builds (Kandel and O'Dell, 1992). This was one of the guiding themes behind early ART predictions about how brain circuits that form during infant development can support later learning in the child and the adult that refine these early circuits. Indeed, I published two long articles in 1978 that were published back-to-back in *Progress in Theoretical Biology*. One article is called "Communication, Memory, and Development" (Grossberg, 1978c), a sweeping title that underscored the article's theme that there is a universal developmental code *whose mathematical laws are often formally the same* as those that control later learning, albeit realized by different physical mechanisms; e.g., directed growth of connections during development vs. learned tuning of synaptic connections during adult learning. I discuss this theme in Chapter 17. The other is called "A Theory of Human Memory: Self-organization and Performance of Sensory-motor Codes, Maps, and Plans" (Grossberg, 1978a), which made numerous contributions to ART, among other topics. Both articles laid theoretical foundations for many additional model developments during the subsequent decades.

How is this kind of dynamical stability embodied in laminar cortical circuits? Why is a laminar design a natural one in which to achieve this property?

Escaping an infinite regress: The Attention-Preattention Interface Problem

When we ask this question with perceptual grouping in mind, a whole new way of thinking about the problem reveals itself. Indeed, we can immediately see that an improper solution to the stability-plasticity problem could easily lead to an *infinite regress*, by which I mean the following: Perceptual groupings can form preattentively, and they provide the neural substrate upon which higher-level attentional processes can act. But how can the preattentive grouping mechanisms develop in a stable way, before the higher-order attentional processes can develop with which to stabilize them? In particular, how do horizontal connections in cortical area V1 develop before they can be modulated by top-down attention from cortical area V2? If such preattentive mechanisms cannot deliver reliable signals to the higher cortical areas, then any top-down signals from these higher areas may be of little use in stabilizing their own development.

In summary, the dreaded infinite regress would be this: How can attentional top-down mechanisms from a higher cortical area stabilize the formation of preattentive horizontal grouping circuits at a lower cortical area, if these attentional mechanisms cannot develop until the preattentive grouping mechanisms do? I call this the *attention-preattention interface problem* because its solution exploits the fact that laminar cortical circuits include layers (the *interface*) where both preattentive and attentive mechanisms come together, notably layers 6-to-4 in Figure 10.3.

A preattentive grouping is its own attentional prime. In fact, the laminar circuits are beautifully designed to enable preattentive groupings within a cortical area to use some of the same circuitry that top-down attention from a higher cortical area uses, in order to stabilize their own cortical development and learning. Figure 10.4 summarizes this circuitry, along with a phrase that I like to use to describe it: "A preattentive grouping is its own attentional prime". I will explain how it works later in this chapter. It is because such an interface exists that attention can influence which "preattentive" grouping will actually form. I believe that it is because of this kind of cortical interface that various scientific thinkers have struggled to differentiate preattentive and attentive processes, as illustrated by the vigorous debates between the followers of Helmholtz and Kanizsa.

The solution proposed herein to the Attention-Preattention Interface Problem builds upon earlier efforts to solve the stability-plasticity dilemma using the ART Matching Rule. The problem that we need to solve is this: How can the ART Matching Rule be implemented, not only as top-down attention between cortical areas, but also within a cortical area when a preattentive grouping circuit is being formed?

Intracortical but interlaminar feedback also carries out the ART Matching Rule. This is a challenging problem for perceptual groupings because they can generate suprathreshold responses over positions that do *not* receive bottom-up inputs, such as when the grouping is an illusory contour. They therefore seem to *violate the ART Matching Rule*! Recall, in this regard, that the ART Matching Rule forbids a cell to get activated without bottom-up input in order to achieve stable learned memories, but that is precisely what happens whenever an illusory contour forms. How, then, can the horizontal connections that generate perceptual groupings maintain themselves in a stable way? Why are they not washed away whenever an illusory contour forms over positions that do not receive a bottom-up input? If this were true, then sustained viewing of a Kanizsa square could destabilize the circuits of your visual cortex. The very absurdity of this prospect reveals how fundamental are the issues that I am now discussing. LAMINART proposes an answer to this question that clarifies how attention, perceptual grouping, development, and perceptual learning are intimately bound together within the laminar circuits of visual cortex.

I will summarize the proposed solution of Attention-Preattention Interface Problem in eight steps. The first four steps describe how the visual cortex, notably areas V1 and V2, uses its laminar circuits to generate perceptual groupings that maintain their analog sensitivity to environmental inputs, and thereby achieve the property of *analog coherence*. These four steps illustrate how the main processing stages of BCS model of perceptual grouping can be embedded, albeit with refinements and a more parsimonious design, within the laminar circuits of visual cortex. Four additional circuit properties will then be summarized whereby ART principles of attention, development, and learning are integrated into this laminar design. Each of these design constraints is supported by psychophysical, anatomical, and neurophysiological data, and indeed anticipated the discovery of various of these data.

Laminar mechanisms of preattentive perceptual grouping

Analog sensitivity to bottom-up sensory inputs. Bottom-up inputs from the retina go through the Lateral Geniculate Nucleus (LGN) on their way to the visual cortex. LGN outputs directly excite cells in cortical layer 4 (Figure 10.5; Blasdel and Lund, 1983; Ferster, Chung, and Wheat, 1996). These are the *simple cells*, the oriented contrast-sensitive cells that are sensitive to a particular contrast polarity, as discussed in Chapter 4; e.g., Figures 4.15 and 4.16. There

HOW ARE LAYER 2/3 BIPOLE CELLS ACTIVATED?

DIRECT BOTTOM-UP ACTIVATION OF LAYER 4

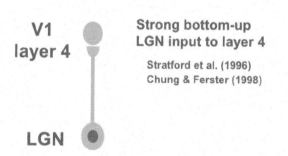

V1
layer 4

**Strong bottom-up
LGN input to layer 4**

Stratford et al. (1996)
Chung & Ferster (1998)

LGN

(Many details omitted!)

FIGURE 10.5. Activation of V1 is initiated, in part, by direct excitatory signals from the LGN to layer 4 of V1.

BOTTOM-UP CONTRAST NORMALIZATION

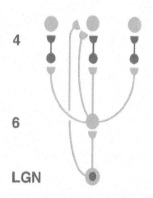

4

6

LGN

**Together, direct LGN-to-4
path and 6-to-4 on-center
off-surround provide
contrast normalization
if cells obey shunting or
membrane equation
dynamics**

Grossberg, 1968, 1973
Sperling and Sondhi, 1968
Heeger, 1992
Douglas et al., 1995
Shapley et al., 2004

FIGURE 10.7. The two bottom-up pathways from LGN to layer 4 of V1 can together activate layer 4 and contrast-normalize layer 4 responses.

is also a new feature in the laminar cortical circuits: LGN inputs also excite layer 6 (Blasdel and Lund, 1983), which then projects to layer 4 via an on-center off-surround network of cells (Ahmed et al., 1997; Callaway, 1998; McGuire et al., 1984; Stratford et al., 1996), as in Figure 10.6. The net effect of LGN inputs on layer 4 simple cells is thus via an on-center off-surround network. Such a feedforward on-center off-surround network of cells can preserve the analog sensitivity of, and contrast normalize, the activities of the simple cells, if these cells obey the membrane equations of neurophysiology (Figure 10.7), as noted in Chapter 4. Such an on-center off-surround network thus enables the layer 4 simple cells to react in a graded fashion (that

ANOTHER BOTTOM-UP INPUT TO LAYER 4: *WHY?*

LAYER 6-TO-4 ON-CENTER OFF-SURROUND

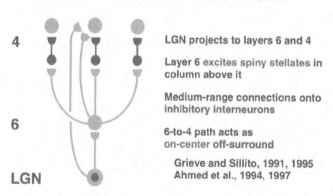

4

6

LGN

LGN projects to layers 6 and 4

**Layer 6 excites spiny stellates in
column above it**

**Medium-range connections onto
inhibitory interneurons**

**6-to-4 path acts as
on-center off-surround**

Grieve and Sillito, 1991, 1995
Ahmed et al., 1994, 1997

FIGURE 10.6. Another, albeit indirect, pathway from LGN exists that can also excite layer 4 of V1. Why are not these two pathways redundant? The answer, ultimately, how to do with how cortex learns, as well as with how it pays attention. See the text for details.

is, preserves their analog sensitivity) in response to LGN inputs that may vary greatly in intensity.

Layer 6-to-4 on-center is modulatory. This particular on-center off-surround network also raises the following perplexing question: Why is a direct excitatory pathway from LGN to layer 4 of V1 needed, when there already exists an indirect excitatory pathway from LGN to layer 4? Why not just use the on-center off-surround network that is mediated by layer 6 to activate and contrast-normalize the activities of layer 4 simple cells? Why is not the direct pathway a huge waste of "wire", particularly since this same dual input design seems to exist in many different sensory and cognitive neocortical areas?

The simple, but subtle, answer to this question will be justified below: The layer 6-to-4 on-center pathway is *modulatory* (Figure 10.8). It cannot, by itself, activate layer 4 cells. That is why the *direct* excitatory LGN-to-4 pathway is needed to do so. As we will see, the layer 6-to-4 pathway is modulatory because it is part of the modulatory on-center in the top-down attentional pathway (Figure 10.1). In addition, it is part of the *intra*cortical, but *inter*laminar, pathway from layer 2/3-to-6-to-4, and then back from layer 4-to-2/3 whereby developing layer 2/3 grouping circuits dynamically stabilize their own development, without requiring top-down attention from higher cortical levels to do so. In other words, this circuit explains how "a preattentive grouping is its own attentional prime". In order to fully make this argument, I first need to tell you how grouping occurs within the laminar circuits of visual cortex.

Let me also note in passing that I am omitting details about how the simple cell circuit achieves its orientational tuning. These details can be more easily added after the basic laminar circuit design for the early stages of stereo vision is presented in Chapter 11.

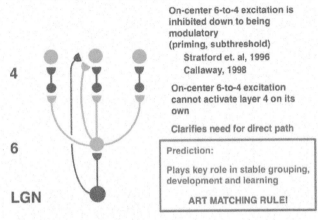

MODULATION OR PRIMING BY 6-TO-4 ON-CENTER

On-center 6-to-4 excitation is inhibited down to being modulatory
(priming, subthreshold)
Stratford et. al, 1996
Callaway, 1998

On-center 6-to-4 excitation cannot activate layer 4 on its own

Clarifies need for direct path

Prediction:

Plays key role in stable grouping, development and learning

ART MATCHING RULE!

FIGURE 10.8. The bottom-up on-center off-surround from LGN-to-6-to-4 has a modulatory on-center because of its role in realizing the ART Matching Rule and, with it, the ability of the cortical to dynamically stabilize its learned memories.

Bipole boundary grouping: Balancing excitation and inhibition during development. In order to initiate boundary grouping, active layer 4 cells input to pyramidal cells in layer 2/3 (Callaway and Wiser, 1996; Fitzpatrick, Lund, and Blasdel, 1985). These cells pool together inputs from like-oriented simple cells that are sensitive to opposite contrast polarities. They thus have complex cell properties, as discussed in Chapter 4; see Figures 4.17 and 4.25. These layer 2/3 cells initiate the formation of perceptual groupings. For present purposes, whether complex cells or hypercomplex cells initiate the formation of perceptual groupings will not be important. The main important property is that boundary groupings can form between input inducers that respond to opposite contrast polarities (Figures 3.3b and 3.7).

One way in which hypercomplex cells come into the grouping story can be understood by putting together two observations. The first observation is that the kind of long-range boundary completion using bipole cells that generates illusory contours and helps to group shading and texture, as in Figure 3.21, occurs in layer 2/3 of cortical area V2, as shown by von der Heydt and his colleagues in articles beginning in 1984 (von der Heydt, Peterhans, and Baumgartner, 1984; Peterhans and von der Heydt, 1989). The second observation is that the laminar organization that I have been describing repeats itself, albeit with specializations, in multiple cortical areas. Thus, layers 6-to-4 of V2 includes a short-range spatial competition, just as it does in V1 (Figure 10.6). This plays the role of the first competitive stage in the BCS (Figure 4.25). The second competitive stage can then occur due to competition across orientations in layer 4, or indeed any layer between 4 and 2/3. A key property of the second competitive stage is that the mutual inhibition between orientations at each position is tonic, and is disinhibited by a large enough

input to one or more of these competing orientations at a given position.

Within the laminar circuits of visual cortex, boundary groupings form among layer 2/3 cells via monosynaptic long-range excitatory connections that remain within layer 2/3 (Figure 10.9). These long-range excitatory connections are also said to be "horizontal" connections, "horizontal" in the sense of propagating horizontally within layer 2/3, and not in the sense of having a horizontal orientational preference. Long-range horizontal connections also excite short-range disynaptic inhibitory connections (Figure 10.9). Converging signals from long-range direct excitatory connections and short-range disynaptic inhibitory connections at target layer 2/3 cells are predicted to realize the *bipole property* for perceptual grouping that was predicted by the BCS (Figure 4.28) and, as noted in Chapter 4, is supported by neurophysiological, anatomical, and psychophysical data from several labs; e.g., Figures 4.29-4.31. The horizontal interactions in layer 2/3 are thus predicted to support *inward* perceptual groupings between two or more boundary inducers (Figure 10.10), as in the case of illusory contours, but not *outward* groupings from a single inducer, which would fill the visual field with spurious groupings.

The LAMINART model proposes how the bipole property is realized by these interactions among layer 2/3 complex cells: When a single active pyramidal cell sends horizontal monosynaptic excitation to other pyramidal cells, it also generates a similar amount of disynaptic inhibition, thereby cancelling its own excitation at target pyramidal cells, so that excitation cannot propagate outwards from individual cells in an uncontrollable way. This is a case of "one-against-one." My PhD student James Williamson and I modeled in 2001 that such an

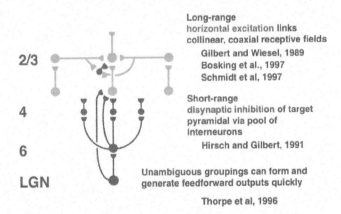

GROUPING STARTS IN LAYER 2/3

Long-range horizontal excitation links collinear, coaxial receptive fields
Gilbert and Wiesel, 1989
Bosking et al., 1997
Schmidt et al, 1997

Short-range disynaptic inhibition of target pyramidal via pool of interneurons
Hirsch and Gilbert, 1991

Unambiguous groupings can form and generate feedforward outputs quickly
Thorpe et al, 1996

FIGURE 10.9. Perceptual grouping is carried out in layer 2/3 by long-range horizontal excitatory recurrent connections, supplemented by short-range disynaptic inhibitory connections that together realize the bipole grouping properties that are diagrammed in Figure 10.10.

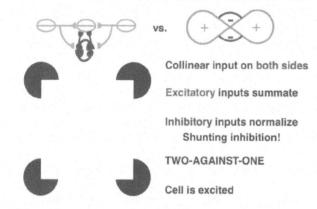

BIPOLE PROPERTY CONTROLS PERCEPTUAL GROUPING

vs.

Collinear input on both sides

Excitatory inputs summate

Inhibitory inputs normalize
Shunting inhibition!

TWO-AGAINST-ONE

Cell is excited

FIGURE 10.10. Bipole grouping is achieved by long-range horizontal recurrent connections that also give rise to short-range inhibitory interneurons which inhibit nearby bipole cells as well as each other.

approximate balance between excitation and inhibition develops during the growth of horizontal connections in a laminar cortical model of an infant brain, and that this excitatory-inhibitory balance can dynamically stabilize this growth (Grossberg and Williamson, 2001). If excitation is too much stronger than inhibition, then excitatory activation could spread uncontrollably, as happens during an epileptic seizure. If excitation is too much weaker than inhibition, then no cells could ever get activated. The synaptic learning laws that establish a balance between excitation and inhibition during development are just the instar and outstar learning laws that were mentioned in Chapter 5 as part of the discussion of competitive learning and self-organizing maps; see Figures 5.10-5.15. Thus the same kinds of laws that guide cortical development in the infant also regulate later cortical learning in the adult.

Bipole grouping: Balanced excitation and inhibition and total inhibitory normalization. A different result obtains when two or more pyramidal cells are activated at positions that are located at opposite sides of a target pyramidal cell, and are sensitive to approximately the same orientation and located at approximately collinear positions across space. Then excitation from the active pyramidal cells summates at the target cell, thereby generating a larger total excitatory input than a single pyramidal cell could. These active cells also excite a single population of disynaptic inhibitory interneurons (Figure 10.10). The inhibitory interneurons mutually inhibit each other, which causes their total activity to be approximately normalized, in just the same way that the on-center off-surround network from layer 6 to layer 4 has a normalizing effect. The total inhibition from the inhibitory interneurons to the pyramidal cell is hereby normalized. As a result, the total excitation is bigger than the total inhibition that converges

on target layer 2/3 cells. This is a case of "two-against-one." As a result, inward grouping between pairs or greater numbers of similarly oriented and positionally aligned layer 2/3 cells can occur.

In summary, the combination of balanced excitation and inhibition, along with normalization of the total inhibitory output, realizes the bipole property in layer 2/3 of a laminar cortical model of grouping. Layer 2/3 pyramidal cells may hereby be activated by direct bottom-up inputs from layer 4, or by horizontal boundary grouping inputs that form in response to recurrent signals from other active layer 2/3 cells, or by a combination of bottom-up and horizontal inputs.

The inhibitory interneurons within layer 2/3 can also inhibit groupings that attempt to form within layer 2/3 at their own location but with a different orientation. This orientational competition between groupings can give rise to binocular rivalry in response to differently oriented inputs to the two eyes, as I will explain in Chapter 11. Orientational competition can also cause monocular rivalry when two different images to the same eye are optically superimposed. Thus, there are at least three different types of inhibition going on across the cortical layers: The spatial competition that occurs between layer 6 and 4, and the orientational competitions that can occur within layers 4 and 2/3.

Folded feedback and analog coherence. Cells with horizontal connections in layer 2/3 can form groupings on their own in response to unambiguous visual inputs, such as a single curve within a given region of space. These unambiguous groupings can form quickly and in a feedforward way, thereby leading to rapid recognition in inferotemporal cortex, as Simon Thorpe and his colleagues reported in 1996 (Thorpe, Fize, and Marlot, 1996).

In response to scenes wherein multiple groupings can form in layer 2/3, but only one, or a few, of them are correct, further processing is needed to select and enhance the strongest groupings and to suppress the weaker possible groupings. The cortex does this in an ingenious way, as I briefly noted when introducing Figure 10.4. In particular, intracortical feedback helps to select the strongest grouping, while binding its cells together into a synchronously firing ensemble. This feedback is proposed to occur as follows: Active layer 2/3 cells send excitatory feedback to layer 6 (Blasdel, Lund, and Fitzpatrick, 1985; Kisvarday et al., 1989), either directly or via layer 5, as in Figure 10.11. Layer 6 then activates the on-center off-surround network from layer 6 to 4. This feedback process is called *folded feedback*, because feedback signals from layer 2/3 to layer 6 get transmitted in a feedforward fashion back to layer 4. The feedback is hereby "folded" back into the feedforward flow of bottom-up information within the laminar cortical circuits.

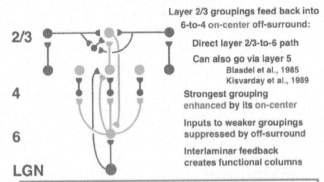

HOW IS THE FINAL GROUPING SELECTED?
FOLDED FEEDBACK

Layer 2/3 groupings feed back into
6-to-4 on-center off-surround:

Direct layer 2/3-to-6 path

Can also go via layer 5
Blasdel et al., 1985
Kisvarday et al., 1989

Strongest grouping
enhanced by its on-center

Inputs to weaker groupings
suppressed by off-surround

Interlaminar feedback
creates functional columns

Activities of conflicting groupings are reduced by self-normalizing
inhibition, slowing processing; intracortical feedback selects and
contrast-enhances the winning grouping, speeding processing

FIGURE 10.11. Feedback between layer 2/3 to the layer 6-to-4-to-2/3 feedback loop chooses the strongest grouping in cases where there is more than one. If only one grouping exists, then the circuit can function very quickly in a feedforward manner. When multiple groupings exist, the cortex "runs as fast as it can" to select the one with the most evidence to support it using the self-normalizing inhibition in the layer 6-to-4 off-surround.

Folded feedback turns the cortex into a feedback network that binds the cells throughout layers 2/3, 4, and 6 into the kind of functional columns that Vernon Mountcastle described in 1957 (Mountcastle, 1957). It was noted in Chapter 1 (e.g., Figures 1.7 and 1.9) that a recurrent on-center off-surround network whose cells obey shunting dynamics can contrast enhance the pattern of activities across a network of cells. In the present case, just as in the non-laminar version of the BCS, this contrast enhancement property helps to select the strongest groupings that are formed in layer 2/3 and to inhibit weaker groupings, while preserving the analog values of the selected groupings. In particular, the on-center signals from layer 6-to-4 support the activities of those pyramidal cells in layer 2/3 that are part of the strongest horizontal groupings. The off-surround signals in the spatial competition from 6-to-4 can inhibit inputs to layer 4 that were supporting less active groupings in layer 2/3. In this way, signals from layer 4 to the less active groupings in layer 2/3 are removed, and thus these groupings collapse. I like to say that the inhibition from layer 6 to 4 "cuts the legs off" of the weaker groupings, therefore forcing them to collapse. It is also useful to think about the layer 6-to-4 circuit as a "choice" or "decision" circuit for selecting correct perceptual groupings.

One might ask: When there are multiple groupings all contending for dominance, why do not all of these groupings get transmitted from layer 2/3 to higher levels of cortex even before a winning grouping is selected, much as happens when an unambiguous grouping occurs? The answer is that, when multiple groupings start to form on their way from layers 4 and 6 to layer 2/3, they compete

among each other using the spatial competition between layer 6 and 4, and the orientational competitions within layers 4 and 2/3. Because shunting competition tends to normalize total activity, all of the contending cells initially get much less activated than in the case of an unambiguous grouping (Figure 10.11). Their small activities translate into weak and slow activation of higher cortical areas.

One, or at most a few, cycles of feedback between layers 2/3, 6, and 4 suffice to contrast-enhance and amplify the winning groupings and to suppress weaker groupings. As soon as the winning groupings get more active, they can more quickly be transmitted to higher cortical areas. Even if some weak initial activity propagated upwards initially, the strong burst of activation when the final grouping is selected can rapidly catch up with it and overwhelm it. A variant of this kind of catch-up occurs during the phenomenon of *metacontrast masking* that was reported in 1910 by Robert Stigler (Stigler, 1910) and has been effectively modeled starting in 1997 by my PhD student Gregory Francis, who is now a full professor at Purdue University, using the BCS/FCS model (Francis, 1997, 2000). Thus the cortex realizes a *temporally self-regulating decision machine that trades certainty against speed.* This discussion predicts that, in response to suitably designed images with multiple groupings, there may be an initial stage of ambiguous and weak cortical output from layer 2/3 of V2 followed soon by a larger burst of activation that can more quickly propagate to higher cortical areas.

Self-similar hierarchical boundary processing. The preceding remarks have focused on cortical area V1. Converging evidence suggests that area V2 replicates aspects of the structure of area V1, but at a larger spatial scale (Figure 10.12). Each cortical area also is specialized to carry out additional processes. For example, area V2 contains specializations for 3D figure-ground separation that I mentioned in Chapter 4 (e.g., Figures 4.54-4.56) and will further discuss in Chapter 11. For now, let me just note that layer 2/3 in area V1 sends bottom-up inputs to layers 4 and 6 of area V2, much as LGN sends bottom-up inputs to layers 4 and 6 of area V1 (Felleman and Van Essen, 1991; Van Essen and Maunsell, 1983). This input pattern from V1 to V2 can preserve the analog sensitivity of layer 4 cells in V2 for the same reason that the LGN inputs to V1 can preserve the analog sensitivity of layer 4 cells in V1.

The shorter perceptual groupings in layer 2/3 of area V1 (Grosof, Shapley, and Hawken, 1993; Redies et al., 1986) are proposed to group together, and enhance the signal-to-noise ratio of, nearby V1 cells with similar orientation and disparity selectivities. The longer perceptual groupings in area V2 (Peterhans and von der Heydt, 1989; von der Heydt, Peterhans, and Baumgartner, 1984) are proposed to build long-range boundary segmentations that separate figures from each other and their background; generate 3D groupings of the edges, textures, shading, and stereo

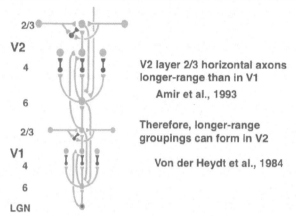

V2 REPEATS V1 CIRCUITRY AT LARGER SPATIAL SCALE

V2 layer 2/3 horizontal axons longer-range than in V1

Amir et al., 1993

Therefore, longer-range groupings can form in V2

Von der Heydt et al., 1984

FIGURE 10.12. The same laminar circuit design repeats in V1 and V2, albeit with specializations that include longer horizontal grouping axons and figure-ground separation interactions.

information that go into object representations; and complete boundaries across gaps in bottom-up signals that are caused by internal factors such as the retinal blind spot and veins, or external factors such as occlusions due to the geometry of 3D space (Grossberg, 1994; Lamme, Supèr, and Spekreijse, 1998).

Laminar mechanisms of attention, development, and learning

The following four circuit properties are proposed to integrate ART-like top-down attention and stabilization of learning into the laminar cortical circuits:

Top-down feedback from V1 to LGN. As illustrated in Figures 5.38 and 5.39, layer 6 of area V1 sends a top-down on-center off-surround network to the LGN. This top-down pathway automatically "focuses attention" on those LGN cells whose activities succeed in activating V1 cells. Remarkable neurophysiological data of Adam Sillito and his colleagues from 1994 (Sillito et al., 1994) were reviewed in Chapter 5, with supporting simulations in Figures 5.5-5.9, that support my prediction from 1976 that this feedback obeys the ART Matching Rule, and thus can only subliminally activate, or modulate, LGN cells when it acts alone. Matched bottom-up inputs are needed to supraliminally activate, gain amplify, and synchronize the firing of LGN cells while top-down signals are active. This process is predicted to help stabilize the bottom-up development and learning of receptive fields in V1, including disparity-tuned complex cells, during the visual critical period, as

well as the development and learning of the top-down expectation signals from V1 to LGN. Data of Penelope Murphy, Simon Duckett, and Sillito from 1999 (Murphy, Duckett, and Sillito, 1999) were also reviewed in Chapter 5 showing that corticogeniculate feedback selectively activates LGN cells at positions that match the orientation of the cortical cells that caused the feedback. These data strongly support the prediction that top-down learning is responsible for this selectivity. Additional studies of the biophysics and biochemistry of this learning process are much to be desired.

Folded feedback from layer 6 of V2 to layer 4 of V1. A similar top-down process seems to occur from all higher to lower stages of visual cortex, and probably beyond: Layer 6 in a given cortical area, such as V2, generates top-down cortical signals to layer 6 of lower cortical areas, such as V1, where they activate the layer 6-to-4 folded feedback network in the lower area (Figure 10.12). One such known top-down pathway exits layer 6 in V2 and activates V1 via layer 1 apical dendrites of layer 5 cells (Rockland and Virga, 1989), which in turn activate layer 6 cells (Gilbert and Wiesel, 1979; Lund and Boothe, 1975), as shown in Figures 5.38 and 10.1. Top-down intercortical feedback can hereby activate a top-down, modulatory on-center, off-surround circuit, as required by the ART Matching Rule. Intercortical attention is hereby predicted to use outputs from layer 6 of a given cortical area to activate layer 4 of a lower cortical area via layer 6-to-4 folded feedback, and this is predicted to occur between multiple cortical regions.

A critical conclusion of this analysis is that preattentive grouping within a cortical area and top-down attention between cortical areas *both use the same selection, or decision, circuit between layers 6 and 4* (Figures 10.13-10.14). This is the interface that solves the Attention-Preattention Interface Problem!

Layer 6-to-4 excitatory signals are modulatory: Inhibition learns to balance excitation. Having identified a possible anatomical substrate for the ART Matching Rule, this Rule also predicts an important neurophysiological property; namely, that this top-down pathway modulates, or subliminally activates, cells in layer 4. This modulatory property is predicted to be due to the fact that the excitatory and inhibitory signals within the on-center from layer 6-to-4 are approximately balanced, so that at most a weak excitatory effect occurs after activating the circuit via top-down feedback. Neurophysiological data have supported this prediction by showing that "feedback connections from area V2 modulate but do not create center-surround interactions in V1 neurons" (Hupé et al., 1997, p. 1031) and that top-down connections have an on-center off-surround organization (Bullier et al., 1996). This prediction is also consistent with neurophysiological data showing that layer

BOTTOM-UP FILTERS AND INTRACORTICAL GROUPING FEEDBACK USE THE SAME 6-TO-4 DECISION CIRCUIT

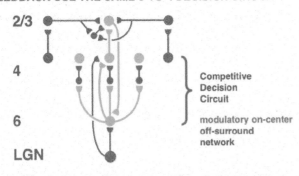

TOP-DOWN INTERCORTICAL ATTENTION ALSO USES THE SAME 6-TO-4 DECISION CIRCUIT!

FIGURE 10.13. The bottom-up adaptive filter, intracortical grouping circuit, and intercortical top-down attentional circuit all use the same competitive decision circuit between layers 6 and 4, called the attention-preattention interface, with which to select the featural patterns that will be further processed.

4 activation that is elicited by layer 6 stimulation is much weaker than that caused by stimulation of LGN axons or of neighboring layer 4 sites (Stratford et al., 1996), and with data showing that binocular layer 6 neurons synapse onto monocular layer 4 cells of both eye types without reducing these cells' monocularity (Callaway, 1998, p. 56).

The mechanistic and functional meanings of these neurophysiological data are clarified by LAMINART model simulations of cortical development that Jim Williamson and I published in 2001 (Grossberg and Williamson, 2001).

EXPLANATION: GROUPING AND ATTENTION SHARE THE SAME MODULATORY DECISION CIRCUIT
Layer 6-6-4-2/3 pathway shown; also a layer 6-1-2/3 path

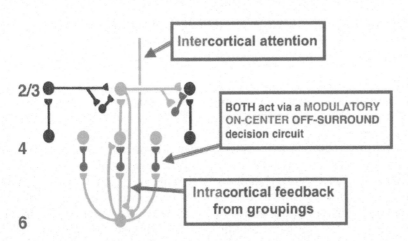

FIGURE 10.14. This figure emphasizes how preattentive intracortical groupings and top-down intercortical attention share the same modulatory on-center, off-surround layer 6-to-4 decision circuit.

These simulations predict how a modulatory on-center develops at layer 4 cells as a result of the layer 6-to-4 input, and how the bipole grouping property develops in layer 2/3. In the former case, excitation of layer 4 via layer 6 is balanced by learning of short-range on-center inhibition within layer 4. In the later case, excitation via long-range horizontal connections within layer 2/3 is balanced by learned disynaptic inhibition within layer 2/3. Thus a balance between excitation and inhibition is needed in multiple cortical layers, and achieves multiple functional roles. How cortical inhibition adapts through time to balance excitation remains a topic of current research interest; e.g., Dorrn et al. (2010) and Vogels et al. (2011).

The modulatory on-center, off-surround network from layer 6 to 4 can have major effects both during preattentive grouping and attentive priming when the cortex is activated bottom-up by visual inputs (Figure 10.13). During preattentive grouping, it can use its off-surround, which is *not* modulatory, to strongly inhibit the activities of layer 4 cells whose layer 2/3 cell projections would otherwise form weak groupings. It can also use the slight on-center bias in its modulatory on-center to selectively amplify the strongest groupings, while inhibiting weaker ones through its driving off-surround, thereby enabling the stronger ones to be contrast-enhanced and resonate. During top-down attentive priming, higher-level influences such as figure-ground separation constraints can use the same modulatory on-center, off-surround circuit, via the folded feedback pathway (Figure 10.1), to bias the cortex to select consistent groupings at lower cortical levels.

Propagating task-selective attentional primes through the entire cortical hierarchy. It is also useful to note that the processes of automatic and task-selective attention may not be independent *in vivo*. This is because higher-order attentional constraints, that may be under task-selective volitional control can propagate downwards through successive cortical levels via layer 6 to layer 6 linkages (Figure 10.12). Because the layer 6-to-4 on-centers are *modulatory*, top-down signals can leap top-down between the layers 6 of multiple cortical areas to prime a whole cascade of cortical areas, without fully activating the corresponding layers 4 unless they also receive consistent bottom-up inputs. For example, task-selective constraints from the prefrontal and inferotemporal cortices that are involved in object and event recognition may propagate their modulatory constraints to lower cortical areas that are involved in perception. System-wide attentive priming—without hallucination!—is thus a beautiful and extremely useful property of these cortical laminar circuits. How the strength of such top-down modulatory influences depends upon the number of synaptic steps from their source to their target cortical area is a topic that would benefit from a systematic study.

ART Matching Rule in multiple cortical modalities. Chapter 5 summarized other psychological, neurophysiological, and anatomical experiments that support the hypothesis that object attention is realized by a top-down, modulatory on-center, off-surround network. When experiments are combined from multiple brain regions, ranging from the V1-to-LGN top-down circuit to studies of the attentional modulation by prefrontal cortex of inferotemporal cortex during visual object recognition, it may be concluded that ART-like top-down matching occurs throughout the brain's visual system. Chapter 5 also mentioned some experiments from non-visual parts of the brain, including the auditory and somatosensory cortices, which all seem to use top-down attentional priming of the same type. This review mentioned just a subset of these experiments. Also of note are the positron emission tomography (PET) experiments on humans that were reported by 1995 by Wayne Drevets, Harold Burton, Tom Videen, Abraham Snyder, Joseph Simpson Jr. and Marcus Raichle (Drevets et al., 1995). In these experiments on human primary and secondary somatosensory cortices, attending to an impending stimulus to the fingers caused a reduction in blood flow of nearby cortical cells that code for the face, but not cells that code the fingers. Likewise, priming of the toes produced reduction in blood flow of nearby cells that code for the fingers and face, but not cells that code for the toes. It would be useful to work out the laminar organization of these on-center, off-surround attentional circuits in animals.

Two bottom-up input sources to layer 4. With the central role in mind of the ART Matching Rule in dynamically stabilizing cortical development and learning in multiple modalities, a simple but computationally fundamental functional explanation can now be given of a cortical design constraint which could otherwise seem quite mysterious; namely, why there are direct bottom-up inputs to layer 4, as well as indirect bottom-up inputs to layer 4 via layer 6 (e.g., Figures 10.6-10.8). Why are not these two separate input pathways redundant? In particular, why is not the indirect layer 6-to-4 pathway sufficient to fully activate layer 4 cells *and* to maintain their analog sensitivity using its on-center off-surround network? The proposed explanation is that the indirect layer 6-to-4 inputs need to be modulatory to preserve the stability of cortical development and learning. Direct inputs to layer 4 are therefore needed to turn on layer 4 cells.

Taken together, these eight cortical design principles lead to the circuit diagram in Figure 10.12 for perceptual grouping, attention, and learning within and between areas LGN, V1, and V2. The generality of the constraints which lead to this design, together with the known generality of laminar circuitry in all sensory and cognitive neocortex, leads to the prediction that the same cortical circuits, suitably specialized, may explain data at multiple levels and modalities of neocortical sensory and cognitive processing. As remarked above, this belief has been supported by the fact that the 3D LAMINART model for 3D vision and figure-ground perception, the cARTWORD model for speech learning, perception, and recognition, and the LIST PARSE model for cognitive working memory and planning all use variants of the same canonical laminar circuitry.

A preattentive grouping is its own attentional prime, revisited. These circuit constraints suggest how the horizontal connections within cortical areas V1 and V2 can develop and learn stably in response to visual inputs, thereby proposing the following solution to the Attention-Preattention Interface Problem: Both preattentive perceptual groupings within V1 and attentive feedback from V2 to V1 generate feedback signals to layer 6 of V1 (Figures 10.13 and 10.14). Both types of feedback activate the folded feedback "decision circuit" from layer 6-to-4. Top-down attention uses this circuit to focus attention within V1 by inhibiting layer 4 cells that are not supported by excitatory 6-to-4 feedback. Perceptual groupings use it to select the correct grouping by inhibiting layer 4 cells that would otherwise form incorrect groupings. In both cases, folded feedback prevents the wrong combinations of cells in layers 4 and 2/3 from being active simultaneously. In the adult, this selection process defines perceptual grouping properties. In the infant, and also during adult perceptual learning, it is predicted to prevent incorrect horizontal connections from being learned, since "cells that fire together wire together".

The potential conflict between preattentive grouping properties and top-down attention properties is resolved by the following considerations: The folded feedback circuit from layer 6-to-4 gets activated by perceptual grouping signals from layer 2/3 at *all* positions of the grouping, even positions that do not receive bottom-up inputs (Figure 10.11), as happens when an illusory contour forms. The ART Matching Rule is thus satisfied at all positions, and the source of the "top-down expectation" is the perceptual grouping itself. I like to say that the *preattentive grouping is its own attentional prime* because it can use the modulatory 6-to-4 selection circuit to stabilize its own development using *intra*cortical feedback, even before attentional *inter*cortical feedback can develop.

This sharing of the layer 6-to-4 selection circuit by both grouping and attention clarifies how attention can bias the selection of which grouping will be facilitated in an ambiguous situation. For example, it can explain neurophysiological data from cortical area V1 of macaque monkeys about how attention can propagate along a boundary grouping, and thereby selectively activate the grouping that defines an entire object. The data of Pieter Roelfsema, Victor Lamme, and Henk Spekreijse that were published in 1998 demonstrate this property (Figures 6.5 and 6.6; Roelfsema, Lamme, and Spekreijse, 1998), and were simulated by the LAMINART model in 2000 with my PhD student Rajeev Raizada. These data can be explained using the laminar circuit in Figure 10.14. This circuit illustrates how an attentional spotlight at one position can activate cells in layer 6 which, when also activated by grouping signals from layer 2/3-to-6, can further activate the grouping through layer 6-to-4-to-2/3 feedback, whence this enhanced activation can propagate along the grouping, as it does in Figure 6.6.

Attention can also bias the percept that is seen in response to an image like that in Figure 3.14 (bottom row). In this percept, a grouping is generated, as the best global compromise, from end cuts that are not perpendicular to their inducing line ends, and are thus not the locally preferred orientations. Focusing attention on a particular position between pairs of the inducing line ends can bias the percept to be more or less circular using the same circuit as in Figure 10.14.

A unified view of developmental, neurophysiological, and perceptual processes and data

From cortical development in infants to adult grouping and attention. As I noted above, my PhD student Jim Williamson and I modeled in 2001 how an approximate balance between excitation and inhibition can develop in both layer 4 and 2/3 (Grossberg and Williamson, 2001). An additional exciting feature of this modeling work was that Jim and I used the receptive fields that were learned during development in order to simulate psychophysical and neurophysiological data collected from adult human and animal observers. In articles with my PhD student Rajeev Raizada in 2000 and 2001 (Grossberg and Raizada, 2000; Raizada and Grossberg, 2001), these learned receptive fields were used in the same model to simulate additional neurophysiological data during perceptual tasks from adult animals. These studies hereby started to mechanistically unify processes of cortical development in the infant with processes of cortical grouping and attention in the adult.

Using this linkage, the model has been able to provide a unified explanation, and also to quantitatively simulate, several different types of developmental, neurophysiological, and perceptual data. I briefly mention some of these data now to illustrate this explanatory range. I then summarize a few of these data in greater detail. Jim Williamson and I simulated developmental data about the projection range of pyramidal cells in cat striate cortex as a function of age (Galuske and Singer, 1996) and the orientation bias in ferret striate cortex as a function of age (Ruthazer and Stryker, 1996). After model development stabilized, it simulated anatomical data about the projection field of adult tree shrew striate cortex (Fitzpatrick, 1996) and the cortical point spread function in macaque V1 (Grinvald et al, 1994); and psychophysical data about the strength of illusory contours as a function of their support ratio (Shipley and Kellman, 1992) and the density of their inducers (Lesher and Mingolla, 1993), as well as the detection thresholds for Gabor patches as a function of the distance between collinear flankers (Polat and Sagi, 1993). In an earlier 1997 study with William Ross and Ennio Mingolla (Grossberg, Mingolla, and Ross, 1997), the model was used to simulate how certain input patterns can cause illusory contours to form in both macaque V1 and V2 (Grosof, Shapley, and Hawken 1993) while others, with more widely separated inducers, can cause illusory contours to form in V2 but not V1 (von der Heydt, Peterhans, and Baumgartner, 1984); how horizontal orientations can compete with a vertical grouping (Kapadia et al., 1995); and how Gestalt grouping laws may arise.

The articles with Raj Raizada in 2000 and 2001 used the learned receptive fields from the article with Jim Williamson to simulate neurophysiological data about how attention can protect macaque neurons from masking by nearby stimuli (Reynolds, Chelazzi, and Desimone, 1999), as in Figure 10.15; how collinear flanking Gabor stimuli can enhance the response of a low-contrast Gabor patch while inhibiting the response of a high-contrast Gabor patch relative to the response of a Gabor patch with no flanking stimuli in cat area 17 (Polat et al., 1998), as in Figure 10.16; how attention can enhance responses along both real and illusory contours (Moore, Yantis, and Vaughan, 1998; Roelfsema, Lamme, and Spekreijse, 1998), as in Figures 6.5 and 6.6; how attention can have a larger effect on low contrast than high contrast stimuli in macaque monkeys (DeWeerd et al., 1999), as in Figure 10.17; and how orientation contrast can occur in response to a surround with bars oriented perpendicular to a target bar (Knierim and Van Essen, 1992), as in Figure 10.18. Taken together, these simulations utilize all of the model mechanisms, and removing any one of them would prevent the model from simulating some of the data.

When attention is not needed to learn: Perceptual learning without awareness. As I have just reviewed,

ATTENTION PROTECTS TARGET FROM MASKING STIMULUS

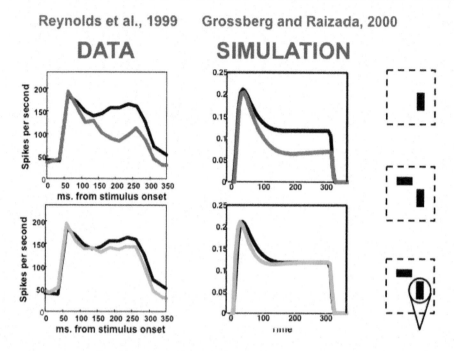

FIGURE 10.15. Data (left column) and simulation (right column) of how attention prevents a masking stimulus from inhibiting the response to the on-center of the cell from which the recording was made.

many data have supported a critical role for attention in visual processing. Chapter 5 has, moreover, discussed how learned expectations that focus attention can help to solve the stability-plasticity dilemma during recognition learning. Remarkably, however, attention is not always needed to learn during perceptual learning, as was first shown in a remarkable experiment of Takeo Watanabe, José Náñez, and Yuka Sasaki (Watanabe, Náñez, and Sasaki, 2001) that I mentioned in Chapter 1. Why and how does this happen? Why do these data not contradict the foundational ART hypothesis about the link between attention and learning?

Although earlier versions of ART could not explain these data, the LAMINART model can. Let me immediately make two points about this state of affairs before sketching how the LAMINART model explains them. First, this state of affairs vividly shows that incremental developments of neural models genuinely expand their explanatory and predictive range. The extension of ART to LAMINART does not just "prettify" ART by showing how it can also explain data about laminar circuits. Rather, it genuinely extends the model's conceptual and explanatory range. Second, I was relieved that LAMINART was first published in 1999 (Grossberg, 1999), two years before the the first Watanabe et

FLANKERS CAN ENHANCE OR SUPPRESS TARGETS

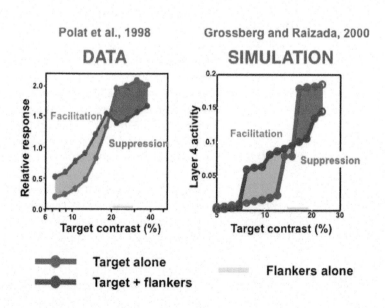

FIGURE 10.16. Neurophysiological data (left image) and simulation (right image) of how a low-contrast target can be facilitated if it is surrounded by a paid of colinear flankers, and suppressed by them if it has high contrast.

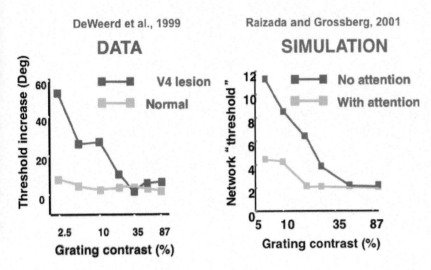

FIGURE 10.17. Neurophysiological data (left image) and simulation (right image) showing that attention has a greater effect on low contrast than high contrast targets.

al. experiment about this subject. Thus, I could immediately see how LAMINART predicted the data. And since Takeo Watanabe was a close colleague of mine at Boston University at that time, I could present this explanation to him and his colleagues in a small seminar about this.

How does LAMINART explain these data? Recall that LAMINART identifies intercortical and *interlaminar*

circuits that can realize top-down, modulatory on-center, off-surround feedback. This additional step clarified how both preattentive grouping and top-down attention may share the same modulatory on-center, off-surround decision circuit from layer 6-to-4 with each other, and also with feedforward pathways that automatically activate cells in response to bottom-up inputs (Figures 10.13 and 10.14). Because a "preattentive grouping is its own attentional prime," these intracortical feedback loops also solve a basic problem that previous versions of ART could not. The Watanabe et al. data follow directly from this solution in the following way.

With Figures 10.13 and 10.14 in mind, recall the ART prediction that, in order to prevent unstable development and learning, only bottom-up inputs can supraliminally activate brain sensory and cognitive cells that are capable of learning, since top-down attention is typically modulatory, except when volition enables top-down attention to generate visual imagery or internal thoughts (Figure 1.25). How, then, can illusory contours form without destabilizing brain circuits? Because a "preattentive grouping is its own attentional prime," it can use the layer 6-to-4 competitive decision circuit to select the correct grouping cells for learning, even without top-down attention. This refinement of the ART prediction implies that, although top-down attention is needed for fast and stable learning of conscious experiences to occur, learning can also occur if a preattentive grouping competitively selects the correct cells with which to "resonate," and thereby synchronize, for a sufficiently long time using its intracortical 2/3-6-4-2/3 feedback circuit. Such learning may be slow and inaccessible to consciousness. I predict that the Watanabe et al. (2001) experiments have engaged this circuit with the stimuli that they used to demonstrate very slow perceptual learning without focused attention or conscious awareness.

In this experiment, 10 letters were presented serially through time within a circular region in the center of a visual display. The task of the subjects was to recognize a target letter when it appeared amid distractor letters that occurred before

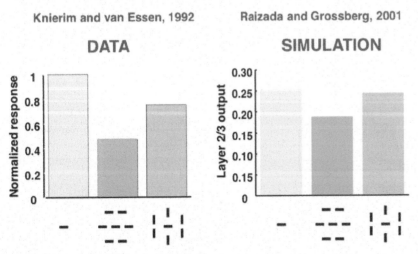

FIGURE 10.18. Neurophysiological data (left image) and simulation (right image) of relative on-cell activities when the input to that cell may also be surrounded by iso-orientation or perpendicular textures.

and after it. Two target letters typically occurred; e.g., V and D. Because this was a demanding task, attention was focused on the center of the display. Each display also contained an annulus of moving dots around the central target zone. Whereas almost all of the dots moved in random directions, 5% of them moved in the same direction. Said in another way, there was 5% directional motion coherence in the background. Chapter 8 has already explained how we can see and track coherent motion direction even if most of the dots move in random directions; cf. Figures 8.57-8.62.

In contrast to the experiments about motion perception whose data were explained in Chapter 8, Watanabe et al. went to great lengths to ensure that subjects did not pay attention to the moving dots, and were not consciously aware of their motion directions. Indeed, the foveal recognition stimuli within the central disk primarily activated the What cortical stream, while the extra-foveal motion stimuli within the surrounding annulus primarily activated the Where cortical stream. This property enabled the motion cues to the Where stream to avoid the off-surround inhibition due to the foveal task-related attention in the What stream. In addition, the extra-foveal resonance that enables a preattentive grouping to be its own attentional prime was not included in the foveal multi-level surface-shroud resonance that brought the foveal task into conscious awareness.

Despite this lack of extra-foveal attention and awareness, the subjects' brains could use their extra-foveal resonances to drive perceptual learning of the coherent motion direction, as illustrated in Figure 10.19, and explained by

the fact that "a preattentive grouping is its own attentional prime".

From non-laminar models of 2D vision to laminar cortical models of 3D vision. When the LAMINART model described above was first proposed, I did not yet know how laminar cortical circuits are organized to perceive objects in depth. Nor did I know how laminar cortical circuits separate multiple objects from one another and their backgrounds during figure-ground separation. By 2001, my students and I had already introduced the non-laminar FACADE, or Form-And-Color-And-DEpth, neural model of 3D vision and figure-ground separation (e.g., Grossberg, 1994, 1997; Grossberg and Kelly, 1999; Grossberg and McLoughlin, 1997; Grossberg and Pessoa, 1998; Kelly and Grossberg, 2000; McLoughlin and Grossberg, 1998). But I did not yet know whether FACADE mechanisms could be embedded into a 3D version of the LAMINART model, or if such an embedding would enable an expansion of their explanatory and predictive range, as occurred when the non-laminar BCS/FCS and ART models were extended by LAMINART. Chapter 11 shows that, to my delight, the BCS/FCS model could be extended in a consistent way to the FACADE model and how, with these insights about 3D vision in hand, LAMINART could be generalized to a 3D LAMINART model in which all of these hopes were realized.

Towards a synthesis of biological and artificial intelligence. As I noted at the beginning of this chapter, the same canonical design for neocortical circuits can be specialized to accomplish many different perceptual and cognitive tasks. This claim has been partially realized by the 3D LAMINART model for 3D vision and figure-ground perception; the cART-WORD model for conscious speech perception, learning, and recognition; and the LIST PARSE model for cognitive working memory and planning. These models provide a foundation for a future unified theory of biological intelligence. They also illustrate how software and hardware with a similar canonical circuit design can be specialized to carry out different types of intelligence in future engineering and technological applications. Because of their compatible design, these software and hardware circuits can be assembled into the "brain" of increasingly autonomous adaptive agents. If and when this happens, biological and artificial intelligence will be able to seamlessly interact, and complement each others' strengths and weaknesses.

UNCONSCIOUS PERCEPTUAL LEARNING OF MOTION DIRECTION

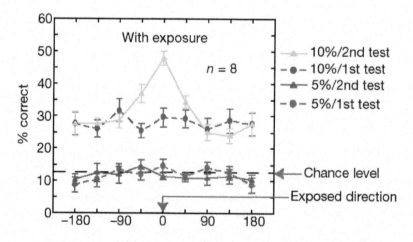

FIGURE 10.19. Data from Watanabe et al. (2001) showing perceptual learning of the coherent motion direction, despite the lack of extra-foveal attention and awareness of the moving stimuli.

11

How We See the World in Depth

From 3D vision to how 2D pictures induce 3D percepts

Several earlier chapters have described key data, concepts, and mechanisms about 3D vision and figure-ground perception. I have delayed until now to present a full chapter to further discuss this crucial topic because many of the brain mechanisms of 3D vision can be better understood in terms of how visual cortical layers are organized for this purpose. Chapter 10 provided a foundation for understanding how cortical layers contribute to 2D vision. I began to develop concepts about 3D vision in the mid-1980s, before I had any systematic understanding of the functional meaning of the cortical layers. These 3D concepts and mechanisms built upon the 2D boundary and surface dynamics of the Boundary Contour System and Feature Contour System. I could not know in advance whether the 2D models would generalize to 3D. Nor could I know if the non-laminar 3D boundary and surface theory that resulted would be consistent with what we later learned about cortical layers.

As I discussed in Chapters 1 and 2, the Method of Minimal Anatomies, and the modeling cycle that operationalizes it (Figure 2.37), insists that these 2D models *must* generalize to 3D, and the non-laminar 3D models *must* generalize to 3D laminar models, or else I committed a basic error that would have to be corrected either by revising the 2D theory or, if necessary, abandoning it entirely and starting over. The 2D results led to so many successful explanations and predictions that I was hopeful that this would not happen.

And indeed it did not! The 2D BCS/FCS model beautifully supported the non-laminar FACADE model of 3D vision and figure-ground perception. With key concepts and mechanisms of FACADE in hand, I could then derive the laminar 3D LAMINART model. As I noted in Chapter 10, 3D LAMINART is not just a pretty version of FACADE. Rather, its development enabled me to solve a basic conceptual problem that the non-laminar models could not handle—namely, the Attention-Preattention Interface Problem—and led to a vastly expanded explanatory and predictive range, including explanations of subtle data about the laminar organization of visual cortex that would have otherwise remained mysterious.

Conscious MIND Resonant BRAIN. Stephen Grossberg, Oxford University Press. © Oxford University Press 2021.
DOI: 10.1093/oso/9780190070557.003.0011

The naturalness of the 3D model development is illustrated by the fact that my colleagues and I published foundational models about 2D vision between 1984 and 1988 (Cohen and Grossberg, 1984; Grossberg, 1984a; Grossberg and Mingolla, 1985a, 1985b; Grossberg and Todorovic, 1988), yet I was already able to publish my first articles about 3D vision by developing the FACADE model starting in 1987 (Grossberg, 1987a, 1987b, 1994, 1997). These foundational articles were followed by a series of articles with multiple PhD students and postdocs over the next decade that further developed FACADE to explain and simulate data about many aspects of 3D vision and figure-ground perception. The laminar models took longer to discover, with the first ones appearing in the late 1990s (e.g., Grossberg, 1999; Grossberg, Mingolla, and Ross, 1997).

I like to begin a discussion of FACADE theory with a *New Yorker* cartoon that I received from my distinguished colleague and friend, Professor Christopher Ricks (Figure 11.1), after I gave the 1989-1990 annual University Lecture at Boston University on the topic *Human Vision and Neural Computation: Illusion and Reality in the Mind's Eye*. I included a discussion of FACADE theory in the lecture, which inspired Christopher to send the cartoon to me, since it vividly illustrates how a facade can hide a system's underlying machinery. We had not yet met, but I am forever grateful to him for providing me with an excuse to meet him. He has been Sir Christopher Ricks since 2009.

As Christopher realized, the *New Yorker* cartoon vividly raises a basic question about 3D vision: How can the world look so real without assuming Naive Realism? As I noted in Chapter 4, Naive Realism asserts that the world looks so real because our senses provide us with direct awareness of objects as they really are. The cartoon reminds us that the world's "real" appearance does not necessarily reveal the mechanisms or perceptual representations whereby we perceive it. Indeed, we have already seen that retinal images are occluded by the blind spot, retinal veins, and other retinal layers before light ever hits the photoreceptors (Figures 3.4 and 3.5), and that our percepts of completed boundaries and surfaces are often constructed in the brain (Figure 3.6) and not derived "directly" from the retina. The model's name FACADE theory, for Form-And-Color-And-DEpth, with hyphens between the individual words, reminds us that the properties of Form and Color and Depth are not computed by independent modules, but are rather multiplexed properties of 3D boundaries and surfaces, whose visible surface representations are predicted to occur in cortical area V4 (Figure 4.56) after multiple stages of preprocessing (Figures 0.1 and 1.21).

Figure 11.1 also summarizes the main technical problem that we now face: How are 3D boundaries and 3D surfaces formed? Figure 11.2 reminds us of a useful way to think of this problem that I also summarized, albeit less colorfully, in Figure 3.22. I now need to explain how these processes work in greater mechanistic detail, along with the new design principles that these details embody.

In particular: How do multiple depth-selective boundaries form? And how do they regulate the filling-in of the corresponding depth-selective surfaces?

Figure 11.2 also notes my predictions that depth-selective, boundary-gated filling-in defines the 3D surfaces that we consciously see, and that a *single* process fills-in lightness, color, *and* depth. This latter claim raises the question: Can a change in brightness cause a change in depth? The phenomenon of *proximity-luminance covariance*, whereby relatively more luminous objects can look closer, illustrates this dependence (Egusa, 1983; Schwartz and Sperling, 1983). I mentioned this perceptual property in Chapter 1 to illustrate that luminance and depth are not computed by independent modules. I will now explain in greater detail how they interact. Figure 11.2 also summarizes my prediction that the interaction between luminance and depth does not cause drastic changes of 3D form when lighting conditions change, because the process of discounting the illuminant limits the amount of change. Chapter 4 discussed how the discounting process eliminates many illumination distortions by computing the reflectances of objects in scenes (e.g., Figures 4.4-4.6), leading to various brightness percepts, notably brightness constancy and brightness contrast (Figures 2.17, 2.18, and 4.7-4.9).

In order to form 3D surfaces, illuminant-discounted feature contour patterns get captured by depth-selective boundaries (Figure 3.22). Basic concepts and mechanisms for doing this were already described in Chapter 4; notably, how boundaries act both as filling-in generators and filling-in barriers (Figure 4.45), and how double-opponent networks determine the output signals that are emitted

3D VISION AND FIGURE-GROUND PERCEPTION

How are
3D BOUNDARIES
and
3D SURFACES
formed?

Form
And
Color
And
DEpth theory

How the world looks so real without assuming naïve realism

Grossberg (1987, 1994, 1997)

Prediction: Visible figure-ground-separated Form-And-Color-And-DEpth are represented in cortical area V4

FIGURE 11.1. FACADE theory explains how the 3D boundaries and surfaces are formed with which we see the world in depth.

3D SURFACE FILLING-IN

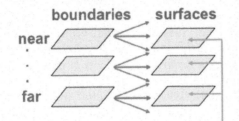

From filling-in of surface

LIGHTNESS and COLOR

to filling-in of surface

DEPTH

Prediction: Depth-selective boundary-gated filling-in
defines the 3D surfaces that we see

Prediction: A single process fills-in lightness, color, and depth

Can a change in brightness cause a change in depth? YES!
e.g., proximity-luminance covariance
Egusa (1983), Schwartz and Sperling (1983)

Why is depth not more unstable when lighting changes?
Prediction: Discounting the illuminant limits variability

FIGURE 11.2. FACADE theory explains how multiple depth-selective boundary representations can capture the surface lightnesses and colors at the correct depths. The fact that both surface qualia and depth are determined by a single process implies that, for example, a change in brightness can cause a change in depth.

from filled-in surfaces (Figures 4.47). Together, these processes enable only boundary contours that are positionally aligned with feature contours to capture them at a particular depth (Figure 4.46), and thereby act as a filling-in generator. These ideas were then illustrated by explanations of challenging 3D percepts like DaVinci stereopsis (e.g., Figure 4.49), whereby we can assign the correct depths to monocularly viewed parts of a scene by using depth-selective filling-in from nearby binocularly viewed scenic regions.

These discussions illustrated the importance of the three hierarchical resolutions of uncertainty that are needed to compute good enough boundary and surface representations whereby to represent the visual world. The first of these discounts the illuminant (Figure 4.5). The second completes boundaries near an object's high curvature positions. It does so using hypercomplex cells (Figure 4.25) to compute end gaps and end cuts (Figures 4.22 and 4.26) to overcome the uncertainty caused by using oriented local contrast detectors like simple cells and complex cells at an earlier processing stage (Figures 4.15-4.17). The third converts a fuzzy initial boundary grouping (Figures 3.15 and 4.31) into a final sharp boundary grouping that optimizes all the constraints on the bipole grouping process (e.g., Figure 3.14).

Chapters 4 and 6 also summarized how cortical areas V2 and V4 are proposed to work together to coordinate critical properties of how we recognize and consciously

see scenes where some objects are partially occluded by others. This interaction prevents all occluders from looking transparent, with V2 enabling conscious amodal recognition of the completed boundary and surface representations of partially occluded objects (Figure 4.55), and V4 supporting conscious seeing and recognition of the unoccluded parts of opaque surfaces (Figure 4.56).

This analysis explained why V4 is predicted to be the earliest cortical stage that generates sufficiently complete, context-sensitive, and stable 3D boundary and surface representations after the three hierarchical resolutions of uncertainty have taken place, including 3D boundaries that are completed and 3D surfaces that are filled in. Chapter 6 could then explain why a surface-shroud resonance (Figure 6.2 and Table 1.4) is assumed to be triggered between V4 and the posterior parietal cortex, or PPC. This resonance can then propagate both top-down to cortical areas like V2 and V1, and bottom-up to cortical areas like prefrontal cortex, or PFC, using the ART Matching Rule (Figures 1.25 and 10.1) to select consistent data and suppress inconsistent data in multiple cortical areas.

While this is happening, the visual qualia of unoccluded regions of the V4 surface representation may become consciously visible. Conscious visibility is proposed to provide an "extra degree of freedom" whereby the brain can utilize the conscious V4 surface representation to help guide orienting eye movements and reaching arm movements; that is, *we see to reach* (Table 1.3). Chapters 4 and 6 also noted that these same circuit mechanisms enable V4 to generate visible surface representations of both opaque and transparent percepts under the circumstances that we experience these different types of percepts in the world (Figure 1.4, bottom row; Figure 4.57), and to explain many data about experiences where one or another form of conscious awareness fails, such as how reaching can be accomplished without knowing what is reached during visual agnosia, and how visual neglect, visual crowding, change blindness, and motion-induced blindness may occur.

Many of these conclusions can be traced to the fact that the laws whereby boundaries are completed and surfaces filled-in are computationally *complementary* (Figure 3.7), and thus cannot be understood, in principle, by any theory that espouses independent modules. The fact of boundary-surface complementary forces one to ask: How is a consistent percept generated by complementary boundary and surface laws? Otherwise expressed, how is *complementary consistency* achieved? As I have sketched in Chapter 4, the feedback interactions between the boundary and surface representations in V2 that ensure consistency also initiate figure-ground separation so that, in this sense, evolution solved figure-ground separation "for free" (Figure 4.51). Figure-ground separation in V4 is augmented by the "asymmetry between near and far", which seems to arise due to the fact that we can walk or run forward, but not backward. This asymmetry helps, in turn, to understand depth-asymmetric processes like boundary enrichment in V4 (Figure 4.56) which enables the V4 representation of the unoccluded parts of opaque surfaces to be computed.

Given so much background, what remains to be done? One major remaining goal is to explain the early processing stages that lead to 3D boundaries, how these processing stages are realized by identified cells in the laminar circuits of visual cortex, and how these various stages and circuits support depth-selective filling-in domains to carry out surface capture in depth.

Correspondence Problem: How our brains know which left and right eye features to fuse. When both of our eyes fixate on an object in the world, it is typically part of a scene that includes many other objects of various shapes, colors, sizes, positions, and depths. Indeed, different parts of the same object may vary in all of these qualities. As I noted in Chapter 4, when both eyes fixate on a particular part of an object, light signals from each of these objects may hit the two eyes at different positions relative to their foveas, as illustrated in Figure 4.18. In Figure 4.18, object A is fixated by both eyes on their foveas, but object B hits the two retinas at different positions relative to each fovea. The brain can begin to estimate the depth of the object relative to the observer by combining signals from these different positions. The size of this positional difference is called *binocular disparity*. These positionally-shifted, disparate signals activate simple cells at different, but nearby, positions in the visual cortex.

This state of affairs immediately raises the question: How does the visual cortex know which pairs of signals from the left and right retinas belong to the same object, indeed the same feature in each object? This Correspondence Problem is solved by our brains using several different kinds of constraints, operating at different stages of cortical processing.

One important constraint is illustrated in Figure 11.3. The upper half of this figure illustrates what is meant by the constraint of *contrast-specific binocular fusion*. If one edge of an object has, say, a dark-light vertical contrast with respect to its background, it will activate simple cells in cortical area V1 that are sensitive to dark-light, but not light-dark, vertical contrasts at its position, as illustrated in Figure 4.15. The same is true with respect to light-dark contrasts. These simple cells occur in layer 4 of V1, and are called *monocular* simple cells because they respond only to inputs from the left or right eye, but not both. The constraint of contrast-specific binocular fusion insists that

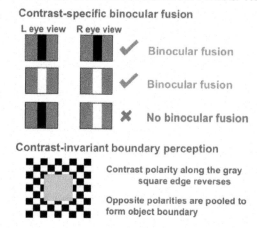

HOW TO UNIFY CONTRAST-SPECIFIC BINOCULAR FUSION WITH CONTRAST-INVARIANT BOUNDARY PERCEPTION?

FIGURE 11.3. Both contrast-specific binocular fusion and contrast-invariant boundary perception are needed to properly see the world in depth.

the *binocular* simple cells in the next cortical processing stage can only binocularly fuse inputs from monocular simple cells that respond to the same contrast polarity, or direction-of-contrast (Figure 11.4).

Contrast-specific processing ensures that an object with an edge of a particular polarity will activate monocular and binocular simple cells with the same polarity (Figure 11.4). By not allowing binocular fusion to occur at a binocular simple cell from pairs of monocular simple cells that are sensitive to opposite polarities, at least some false matches between different features in a scene can be avoided.

Because simple cells come in multiple sizes, matching edges from objects of very different sizes may also be partially reduced, say, if a small object does not produce a large enough input to fire a monocular simple cell with a large receptive field. But clearly, even after these selective properties of monocular simple cells act, there can still be lots of ambiguity at the binocular simple cells about which like-polarity matches belong to the same object.

Contrast-specific binocular vision vs. contrast-invariant boundary perception. The constraint of contrast-specific binocular fusion immediately raises another problem, that is summarized in the bottom half of Figure 11.3. We saw in Chapter 3 (see Figure 3.2) that boundaries need to pool signals from opposite contrast polarities in order to form around objects in front of textured backgrounds. This constraint led us to conclude that "all boundaries are invisible" and to force us towards the conclusion that consciously visible qualia are surface percepts. In the case of 3D vision, this constraint is called *contrast-invariant boundary perception*. I already noted in Chapter 4 that complex cells pool signals from opposite-polarity simple cells in order

MODEL UNIFIES CONTRAST-SPECIFIC BINOCULAR FUSION WITH CONTRAST-INVARIANT BOUNDARY PERCEPTION

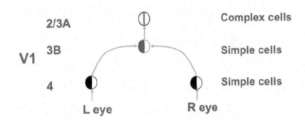

Contrast-specific stereoscopic fusion by disparity-selective simple cells
Contrast-invariant boundaries by pooling opposite polarity binocular simple cells at complex cells in layer 2/3A
Ohzawa et al,. 1990; Grossberg & McLoughlin, 1997

FIGURE 11.4. The three processing stages of monocular simple cells, binocular simple cells, and complex cells accomplish both contrast-specific binocular fusion and contrast-invariant boundary perception.

CONTRAST CONSTRAINT ON BINOCULAR FUSION
Left and right input from same object has similar contrast
Percept changes when one contrast is different:

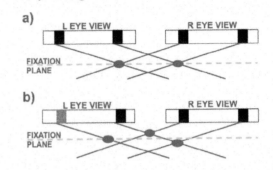

Fusion only occurs between bars of similar contrast
McKee et al., 1994

FIGURE 11.5. The brain uses a contrast constraint on binocular fusion to help ensure that only contrasts which are derived from the same objects in space are binocularly matched.

to form contrast-invariant boundaries (Figure 4.17). I was not then worrying, however, about how to reconcile these properties with contrast-specific binocular fusion. Now I do have to worry about this. How can we have our cake and eat it too?

From the perspective of the laminar organization of cortical cells, this question can be rephrased as follows: Are there cortical layers in which monocular simple cells, binocular simple cells, and complex cells can all be accommodated? The answer, happily, is Yes! When I first did this work, I knew that many monocular simple cells were in layer 4, and complex cells were in layer 2/3. That must mean, if this analysis was correct, that the binocular simple cells may be found in some intervening layer. That layer turns out to be layer 3B (Figure 11.4). As you can imagine, it was immensely satisfying to me that these theoretical constraints called my attention to the functional importance of a cortical layer that I knew nothing about before then.

Contrast constraint on binocular fusion. Now that we have situated these cells within the laminar circuits of visual cortex, let us return to the urgent question: How can the brain further remove the ambiguity about which pairs of edges of objects in the world can be binocularly fused, and thereby solve the Correspondence Problem? The *contrast constraint* on binocular fusion also helps to accomplish this. Figure 11.5 illustrates what this means by summarizing results of a psychophysical experiment by Suzanne McKee, Mary Bravo, Douglas Taylor, and Gordon Legge (McKee et al., 1994). If edges in a left eye and right eye image have the same contrast polarity *and* the same *amount* of contrast, then they can fuse at binocular simple cells in the fixation plane, other things being equal, as

Figure 11.5a illustrates. However, if one edge in a pair has the same contrast polarity as the other, but a very different amount of contrast, then binocular fusion will not occur. Figure 11.5b illustrates this property by showing that the gray-white and black-white contrasts cannot fuse, thereby leading to quite a different percept in which one black-white contrast in the left eye can simultaneously fuse two black-white contrasts in the right eye, while the gray-white contrast is not fused with any other boundary.

There is nothing to stop the binocular simple cells in the circuit depicted by Figure 11.4 from fusing edges with very different absolute contrasts. Fortunately, this is not the entire cortical circuit for binocular fusion. Figure 11.6 includes one of the missing ingredients by showing that, in addition to activating binocular simple cells in layer 3B, monocular simple cells in layer 4 also activate inhibitory interneurons in layer 3B. These inhibitory interneurons, in turn, inhibit the binocular simple cells *and each other*. The entire circuit in layer 3B gives rise to what Gian F. Poggio has called *obligate cells* (Poggio, 1991).

This kind of circuit should ring a bell! It looks very much like the circuit that enables bipole cells in layer 2/3 to respond selectively to two inputs that are on opposite sides of the bipole cell and almost collinear with its preferred orientation, but not to just to inputs on one side (Figure 10.13). The same kind of circuit prevents a binocular simple cell from firing unless its two inputs are of almost the same size; that is, are activated by edges of similar contrast. A psychophysical experiment published in 1995 by Harvey Smallman and Suzanne McKee demonstrated that a straight line can fit data showing how the logarithm of the minimum contrast that allows matching varies with the logarithm of the contrast of the higher contrast bar (Smallman and McKee, 1995). A computer simulation of

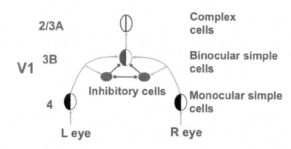

MODEL IMPLEMENTS CONTRAST CONSTRAINT
ON BINOCULAR FUSION

An Ecological Constraint on Cortical Development

Inhibitory cells (red) ensure that fusion occurs when
contrasts in left and right eye are approximately equal
(cf. "obligate" cells Poggio, 1991).

FIGURE 11.6. The contrast constraint on binocular fusion is
realized by obligate cells in layer 3B of cortical area V1.

this relationship quantitatively fit the psychophysical data, using the 3D LAMINART model that I published in 2003 with my PhD student Piers Howe (Grossberg and Howe, 2003). This straight line fit to the data implies that the model successfully embodies the obligate property that was reported in the experiment.

The similarity of the recurrent inhibitory interneuronal networks in layer 3B of V1 for obligate binocular matching, and in layer 2/3 of V2 for bipole grouping, illustrate how the brain can parsimoniously use variations of the same circuit design in multiple places to carry out multiple functions. Figure 11.7 summarizes the 3D LAMINART model that my postdoctoral fellow Yongqiang Cao and I published in 2005 and that includes both the V1 circuit that realizes the obligate property and the V2 circuit that realizes the bipole grouping property (Cao and Grossberg, 2005). This circuit also includes both monocular and binocular simple cells in layers 4 and 3B of V1, respectively, among other cortical features that I will now discuss to continue my explanation of how the visual cortex solves the Correspondence Problem.

Figure 11.8 notes that the two polarity constraints that have already been satisfied are not enough to solve the Correspondence Problem. *All* binocular combinations of the left and right eye like-polarity edges with similar contrasts would still be fusable in response to the stimulus depicted in this figure if no other constraints existed. The stimulus in

this case is just a pair of black rectangles on a white background. Imagine how many false matches could be generated by a more realistic image! Figure 11.9 makes the same point with images composed of three black rectangles on a gray background. Here there are nine possible matches. Only the three matches in blue represent the correct depths of the rectangles. How can the remaining six false matches be eliminated? Figure 11.9 suggests a solution by noting a possible role of inhibition between the cells that carry out binocular matches along the same monocular line-of-sight (shown in green). I will now illustrate with an analysis of several 3D percepts how line-of-sight inhibition can solve the Correspondence Problem when it is combined with the other processing stage in the 3D LAMINART model, including the surface-to-boundary surface contour feedback signals in V2 that assure perceptual consistency and initiate figure-ground perception (Figure 4.51).

3D perceptual grouping circuit also includes a disparity filter that eliminates false matches. Before turning to these examples, let me say where Yongqiang Cao and I predict this line-of-sight inhibition to occur in the visual cortex. Figure 11.10 suggests that it happens within a network that is called the *disparity filter*. The disparity filter is predicted to occur in layer 2/3 of cortical area V2 as part of the network of recurrent inhibitory interneurons that also realizes the bipole grouping property.

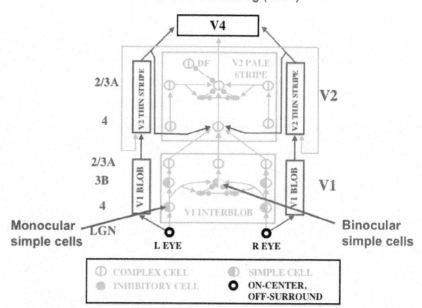

FIGURE 11.7. The 3D LAMINART model uses both monocular and binocular simple cells to binocularly fuse like image contrasts. The remainder of the model generates 3D boundary and surface representations of multiple kinds of experiments as well as of natural scenes.

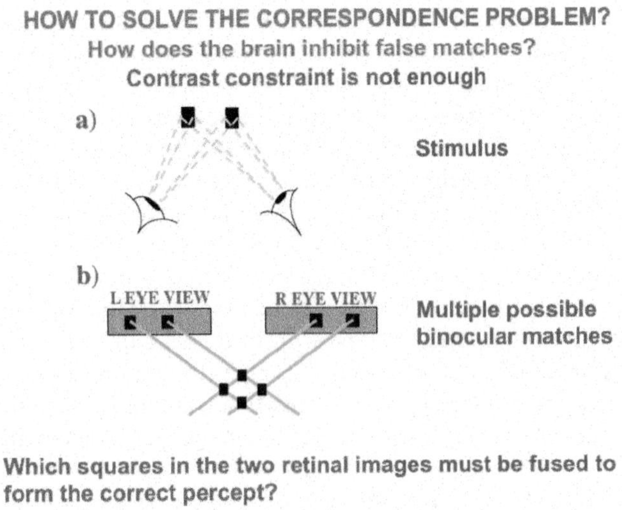

HOW TO SOLVE THE CORRESPONDENCE PROBLEM?
How does the brain inhibit false matches?
Contrast constraint is not enough

a)

Stimulus

b)

L EYE VIEW   R EYE VIEW   Multiple possible
                                 binocular matches

Which squares in the two retinal images must be fused to
form the correct percept?

FIGURE 11.8. The contrast constraint on binocular fusion is not
sufficient to prevent many of the false binocular matches that
satisfy this constrain.

This hypothesis is not the first appearance in one of
my vision models of a disparity filter with which to solve
the Correspondence Problem. It was first proposed in a
1997 article on 3D surface perception with my PhD student
Niall McLoughlin (Grossberg and McLoughlin,
1997) as part of FACADE theory, before we knew anything
about how the laminar circuits of visual cortex carry out
3D vision. A disparity filter was next used in the laminar
3D LAMINART model that I published with Piers Howe
in 2003. Finally, Yongqiang and I were able to see how to
simplify this model by proposing that the disparity filter

**MODEL V2 DISPARITY FILTER
SOLVES THE CORRESPONDENCE PROBLEM**
An Ecological Constraint on Cortical Development

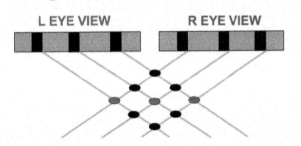

L EYE VIEW   **R EYE VIEW**

False matches (black) suppressed by
line-of-sight inhibition (green lines)

"Cells that fire together wire together"

FIGURE 11.9. The disparity filter in V2 helps to solve the correspondence problem by eliminating spurious contrasts using line-
of-sight inhibition.

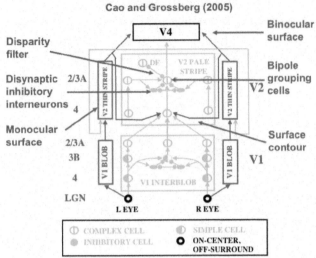

3D LAMINART MODEL
Cao and Grossberg (2005)

FIGURE 11.10. The 3D LAMINART model shows how the disparity filter can be integrated into the circuit that completes 3D
boundary representations using bipole grouping cells. It also
explains how surface contours can strengthen boundaries that
succeed in generating closed filling-in domains.

is part of the recurrent inhibitory network in layer 2/3 of
V2 that is also used for 3D perceptual grouping. This hypothesis hereby links a solution of the Correspondence
Problem to the Gestalt grouping problem; cf. Figures 3.17
and 3.18. This parsimonious hypothesis once again shows
how allowing the inhibitory interneurons in layer 2/3 to
recurrently contact a profusion of nearby cells can carry
out more than one important perceptual function.

The hypothesis that 3D perceptual grouping includes
the elimination of false matches was not concocted out of
thin air. It was motivated by properties of psychophysical
data. One particularly important fact is the following one:
It is often the case that the perceived depths of perceptual
groupings covary with the disparities of the image contrasts
from which they are generated. However, when this is not
the case, then the perceived depth of emergent perceptual
groupings can override the local image disparities from
which they are generated, a fact that has been known for
over 60 years (Ramachandran and Nelson, 1976; Tausch,
1953; Wilde, 1950). Said in another way, a winning 3D
grouping can suppress "false matches" that are derived from
the real local disparities of their generating features in the
outside world. In summary, by realizing the disparity filter
using recurrent inhibitory interneurons of the 3D grouping
process, this process can, in addition to realizing the bipole
grouping property in 3D, suppress false binocular matches
to solve the Correspondence Problem *and* suppress disparities that are incompatible with the emerging 3D grouping.

**How does monocular information contribute to depth
perception?** Due to the lateral displacement of our eyes

in our heads, an object's edge that is seen by one eye may be occluded in the view that is seen by the other eye. We earlier saw an example of this when I mentioned DaVinci stereopsis in Chapter 4. For example, in Figure 4.49, the red region between B and C is seen only by the left eye because it is on a wall between A and C that is farther away than the wall between C and D. Despite this lack of binocular information, the monocularly viewed region between B and C is seen to have the same depth the binocularly viewed surface between A and B. The brain can thus utilize monocular information to build up seamless 3D percepts of the world. I described some of the concepts and mechanisms that contribute to this result in Chapter 4. My goal there was, however, not to explain 3D vision, but rather to clarify how figure-ground perception is initiated. I will complete the explanation here.

Once monocular information is included, the problem immediately arises of how to combine monocular and binocular boundaries. This is a problem because monocular boundaries do not have a definite depth associated with them. How, then, can we decide to which depth they should be assigned? I proposed a solution to this Monocular-Binocular Interface Problem in the 1990s to explain data about 3D figure-ground perception (Grossberg, 1994, 1997). This proposal, and explanations of key figure-ground properties, have already been discussed in Chapter 4. This hypothesis was computationally implemented in my article with Piers Howe in 2003 (Grossberg and Howe, 2003) to help explain many data about 3D surface perception.

The proposal is, as I noted in Chapter 4, that monocular boundaries—or more exactly, the outputs of monocular boundary cells—are added to *all* depth planes in the pale stripes of cortical area V2 along their respective lines-of-sight, as in Figure 4.51. In Figure 11.10 (see also Figure 11.12 below), this happens where the monocular boundary cells *and* the binocular boundary cells in layer 2/3A of V1 send converging output signals to the same boundary cells in layer 4 of V2. Not all of the boundary cells in layer 4 of V2 that receive outputs from monocular boundary cells will receive an output from a binocular boundary cell, because not all pairs of monocular boundaries can be binocularly fused by a binocular boundary cell. As I will show below, the disparity filter in layer 2/3A of V2 selects the strongest boundaries that are created in this way, while eliminating weaker boundaries along their shared lines-of-sight. Some monocular boundaries are not suppressed by inhibition within the disparity filter. These boundaries help to close 3D boundaries that would otherwise remain open and thus unable to contain filling-in, as illustrated in Figure 4.50. After using this solution of the Monocular-Binocular Interface Problem to explain challenging 3D surface data, notably data about variants of DaVinci stereopsis (Figure 4.49), it will also become clear how to solve the Correspondence Problem when there are many false

binocular matches, and to do so in a way that does not undermine the other explanations.

Explaining challenging 3D percepts using interactions between a few simple mechanisms. Explanations of challenging psychophysical data about 3D vision will be given below using the concepts and mechanisms that I have just summarized. In all of these explanations, several simple mechanisms work together to generate the percepts that are consciously seen. The text will describe in words how each of these mechanisms responds to a visual image or scene, and how interactions between the mechanisms generate percepts that would seem quite mysterious without them. Although each mechanism is simple, the reader needs to follow an entire explanation to understand the final percept. Once one percept is explained using these mechanisms, then lots of different percepts can be understood in the same way.

My advice to readers is to at least try to get the gist of the explanations. Readers who do this, but who want to skip the details, especially on a first reading, should feel free to do so because the details are not needed to read with comprehension what follows them.

The percept that is generated by the DaVinci stereopsis display in Figure 11.11 will be used to summarize several of the main challenges that we face when viewing scenes in depth. This display was published by Barbara Gillam, Shane Blackburn, and Ken Nakayama in 1999 (Gillam, Blackburn, Nakayama, 1999). In this display, the left eye view is composed of an unbroken rectangular shape that is derived from two rectangles at different depths. A single rectangle is seen because the right bounding edge of the left rectangle occurs along the same line of sight to the left eye as the left bounding edge of the right rectangle. The right

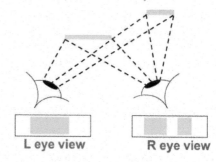

HOW DOES MONOCULAR INFORMATION CONTRIBUTE TO DEPTH PERCEPTION?

DaVinci Stereopis

L eye view   R eye view

Only by utilizing monocular information can visual system create correct depth percept (Gillam et al,. 1999)

FIGURE 11.11. DaVinci stereopsis phenomena occur when only one eye can receive visual inputs from part of a 3D scene due to occlusion by a nearer surface.

eye receives depth information from both bounding edges of each rectangle. Given this ambiguity in the left eye view, how does the brain manage to represent the two rectangles at their correct depths? I will explain how this occurs below while using the same 3D LAMINART mechanisms to explain other ingenious DaVinci displays that Gillam, Nakayama, and Shinsuke Shimojo have contributed to the perceptual literature, as well as many other 3D percepts.

Explaining DaVinci stereopsis percepts without invoking an ecological optics hypothesis. Before beginning these explanations, I want to mention an alternative hypothesis that was advanced by Nakayama and Shimojo in 1990 in order to explain their DaVinci stereopsis data (Nakayama and Shimojo, 1990). They proposed what they call an Ecological Optics hypothesis; namely, that the visual system can correctly interpret a DaVinci display because it has learned about occlusion relationships from experiencing many scenes. This hypothesis is in the grand tradition of Helmholtz and his claim that many percepts are completed by learning unconscious inferences. I mentioned this hypothesis in Chapter 1, where I also noted that it has achieved renewed vigor recently in the hands of scientists who espouse the Bayesian approach to vision. Many of these scientists claim that even high-level percepts depend upon prior learning about the statistics of visual scenes.

This book shows that many such percepts can be explained without resorting to this kind of hypothesis. My explanations emphatically do not deny that learning is crucially important for successful adaptation to a changing world. Adaptive Resonance Theory is just one of many examples of how learning may profoundly influence brain dynamics. To explain DaVinci percepts, however, I do not need to assume that the brain has explicit knowledge of occlusion relationships. I do need properties of line-of-sight inhibition and disparity-tuned complex cells, both of which develop with guidance from visual statistics. But both of these mechanisms are low-level visual processes that do not need global knowledge about occlusion relationships in a scene in order to work flawlessly.

Figure 11.12 summarizes the circuits within 3D LAMINART that compute monocular information and its interactions with binocular information that will form part of these explanations. Note again that there are separate pathways for monocular and binocular complex cells in layer 2/3A of V1 that combine at binocular complex cells in layer 4 of V2.

I will first explain a version of DaVinci stereopsis that was reported in the 1990 article by Nakayama and Shimojo. Figure 11.13 summarizes how the processing stages in 3D LAMINART begin with the left and right eye inputs that are summarized in the bottom row, and end with the 3D surface percept in the top row. This DaVinci display is a variant of the Gillam et al. display, which will also be discussed below.

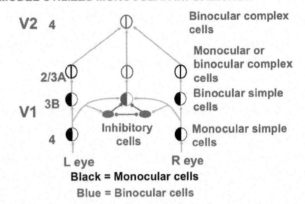

MODEL UTILIZES MONOCULAR INFORMATION

In V2, monocular inputs add to binocular inputs along the line of sight and contribute to depth perception

FIGURE 11.12. How monocular and binocular information are combined in V1 and V2 in the 3D LAMINART model.

First, the left monocular boundary (bottom row, left column) and the right monocular boundary (bottom row, right column) are computed in V1 layer 4. Each of the five columns in the next four rows of the figure depict boundaries or surfaces that occur at one of five depths (Very Near, Near, Fixation Plane, Far, Very Far). Although only five depth planes are computed in this simulation, for simplicity, *any* number of depth planes can be computed using the same mechanisms.

The next-to-last row in Figure 11.13 depicts the two sets of binocular boundaries that are computed from binocular matching of the monocular boundaries in V1 layer 3B (Figure 11.12). The pair of boundaries in the second column from the left is derived by matching the left and right monocular boundaries of the thick rectangle in the left image with the left and right monocular boundaries of the thick rectangle in the right image. The binocular disparities of these edges place them in the Near depth plane of the model. The individual binocular boundary in the fourth column from the left is derived by matching the right monocular boundary of the thick rectangle in the left image with the right monocular boundary of the thin rectangle in the right image. Their binocular disparity places this boundary in the Far depth plane of the model.

The third row from the bottom shows all the boundaries that initially result when the monocular and binocular boundaries are added together at V2 layer 4. The binocular boundaries remain in the same positions as in the second row from the bottom. The monocular boundaries are added to all depth planes along the left eye and right eye lines-of-sight. This array of boundaries may look confusing at first glance, but is easy to interpret if you first look for how pairs of widely separated monocular vertical boundaries from the thick rectangle in the left image shift across each depth plane together, due to line-of-sight shifts,

DA VINCI STEREOPSIS
Nakayama and Shimojo (1990)
An emergent property of the previous simple mechanisms working together

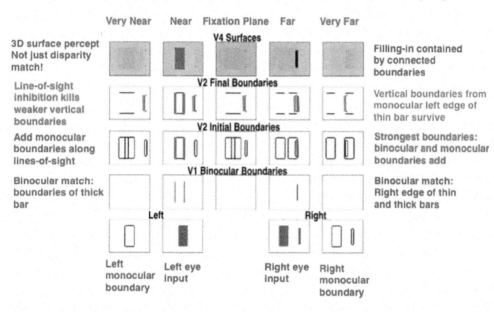

FIGURE 11.13. How the 3D LAMINART model explains DaVinci stereopsis. All the stages of boundary and surface formation are color coded to clarify the explanation. Although each mechanism is very simple, when all of them act together, the correct depthful surface representation is generated. See the text for details.

before then checking how the vertical monocular boundaries from both the thick rectangle and the thin rectangle in the right image shift across each depth plane together, but in the reverse direction. The horizontal boundaries connect the vertical boundaries of the corresponding rectangles. The red vertical boundaries mark where both binocular and monocular boundaries are added at the same positions. These are the strongest boundaries that form.

These initial V2 boundaries then project to the disparity filter in V2 layer 2/3 (Figure 11.10), where they compete along their respective lines-or-sight to choose the final V2 boundaries. These final boundaries are shown in the fourth row from the bottom. Three of the winning vertical boundaries (again in red) are the boundaries where monocular and binocular boundaries add. They inhibit all the monocular boundaries along their lines-of-sight. One vertical monocular boundary also survives at every depth because it has no competitors. These boundaries are shown at every depth in green. They are derived from the vertical boundary at the left edge of the thin bar in the right image. The boundary of this left edge is unmatched because, as shown in the second row from the bottom, only the right boundary of the thin bar matches an edge from the thick bar to form a binocular boundary. The left boundary thus has no binocular competitor.

If you now look carefully at the final V2 boundaries in the fourth row from the bottom, you will see a remarkable

fact: There are only two closed boundaries! The one in the Near depth plane is surrounded by a pair of vertical red boundaries. These vertical red boundaries are the result of binocular matches of both edges of the thick rectangle. The horizontal boundaries that close this figure are due to adding horizontal boundaries to all the depth planes along their lines-of-sight (cf. Figure 4.50). The other closed rectangle is in the Far depth plane. It uses monocular boundaries in a striking way. In addition to the horizontal boundaries, the left vertical boundary of this figure is also a monocular boundary (in green) whereas the right vertical boundary of the figure is binocular (in red). Here is where the ambiguity of the DaVinci display is overcome, and a vertical *monocular* boundary is needed to do it!

Finally, the top row shows how V4 successfully fills in only these two closed boundaries. I explained how this happens in Chapter 4 as part of my explanations of figure-ground percepts. See Figure 4.48 in particular. When this V4 surface representation resonates with the model's posterior parietal cortex, or PPC, as part of a surface-shroud resonance (Figure 6.2), a conscious surface percept of a thick rectangle in the near plane and of a thin rectangle in the far plane is generated. This is also the percept that human observers see in response to this stimulus.

Figure 11.14 explains the conscious surface percept that humans see when presented with a polarity-reversed DaVinci stereopsis stimulus. The surface percept includes the different brightnesses that are induced by the polarity-reversed stimuli. A main point to keep in mind when tracking the boundaries that form is that the left boundary of the white thick rectangle on the gray background has a dark-light contrast, whereas the left boundary of the black thin rectangle has a light-dark contrast. These opposite polarities cannot be matched. However, the left boundary of the white thick rectangle in the left image can match the right boundary of the black thin rectangle in the right image. The rest of the explanation then proceeds as before. Despite this difference, the final surface percept is again of a thick rectangle in the Near depth and a thin rectangle in the Far depth, but here they are seen to have opposite contrast polarities.

POLARITY-REVERSED DA VINCI STEREOPSIS
Nakayama and Shimojo (1990)

Same Explanation!

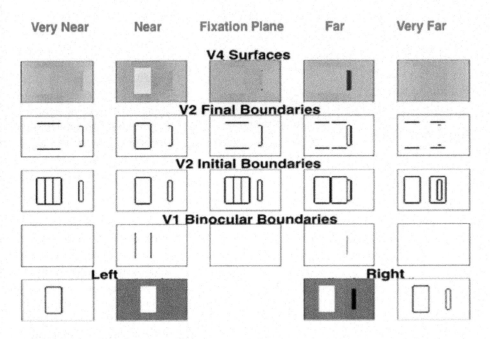

FIGURE 11.14. The model explanation of DaVinci stereopsis when the input stimuli have opposite contrast polarities.

thin bars generate only monocular boundaries because they cannot be matched to either of the edges of the thick bar, either due to the edge pairs having opposite contrast polarity, or to being too disparate from each other across space.

As usual, the V2 layer 4 initial boundaries in the third row from the bottom are the result of adding the two V1 binocular boundary representations at their respective positions with the V1 monocular boundary representations to all depth planes in V2 layer 4 along their respective lines-of-sight. In this way, monocular and binocular vertical boundaries add to form the leftmost vertical boundary in the Near depth and the rightmost vertical boundary in the Far depth. The resulting binocular-plus-monocular boundaries are the two strongest vertical boundaries across all the depths. All boundaries in V2 layer 4 then input into V2 layer 2/3, where the disparity filter can begin to choose the strongest boundaries along lines-of-sight to form the V2 Final Boundaries that are shown in the fourth row from the bottom.

The boundaries in V2 layer 2/3 control the filling-in of monocular surfaces in the V2 thin stripes (Figure 11.10). These monocular surfaces generate the surface-to-boundary surface contour feedback signals that I discussed in Chapter 4 to explain figure-ground data (Figure 4.51). Initially all closed boundaries receive these feedback signals, as the V2 layer 2/3 disparity filter also starts to work. The strongest binocular boundaries in the Near and Far depth planes eliminate all the weaker vertical boundaries that share any of their lines-of-sight via the disparity filter. They do not, however, inhibit the vertical monocular boundaries originating from the two unmatched edges of the thin bars, because these vertical boundaries do not share any of their lines-of-sight.

We have now reached the point where the surface contours play a role. Other things being equal, the vertical boundary representations of the unmatched edges in the Near and Far depth planes could have been inhibited by the corresponding boundaries in the Fixation plane. This is

Surface-to-boundary surface contours and fixation plane bias contribute to DaVinci percepts. So far, my explanation of DaVinci stereopsis percepts has depended only on interactions within the boundary stream, and from the boundary stream to the surface stream. In actuality, surface-to-boundary feedback is always acting as well, but has not to this point changed the result. This is no longer the case when explaining the DaVinci percept that arises from the 1999 display of Gillam, Blackburn, and Nakayama in Figure 11.15 (Gillam, Blackburn, and Nakayama, 1999).

Figure 11.15 summarizes the main processes that are sufficient to explain this percept. This display raises additional issues if only because only two binocular boundaries can form, one in the Near depth plane and the other in the Far depth plane, as can be seen in the next-to-last row of this figure. These binocular boundaries arise when the left edge of the thick bar to the left eye fuses with the left edge of the left thin bar to the right eye in the V1 Near disparity plane, and the right edge of the thick bar to the left eye fuses with the right edge of the right thin bar to the right eye in the V1 Far disparity plane. These binocular fusions can occur because both pairs of edges have the same contrast polarity and contrast, and are not too disparate from each other. The two other vertical edges of the

DA VINCI STEREOPSIS
Gillam, Blackburn, and Nakayama (1999)

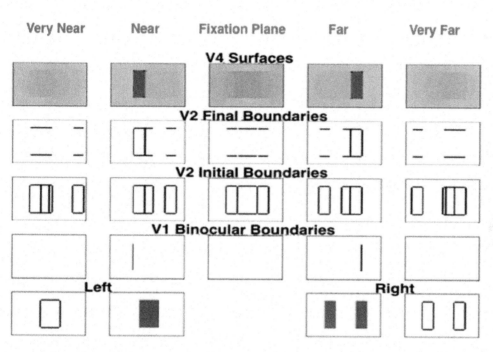

FIGURE 11.15. The same model mechanisms explain the surface percept that is generated by the variant of DaVinci stereopsis that Gillam, Blackburn, and Nakayama studied in 1999.

due to a property of the disparity filter, called *fixation plane bias*, that has not yet been discussed. This property assumes that the fixation plane can inhibit other depth planes more strongly than conversely along their lines-of-sight. This bias is assumed to arise during development due to the frequency with which our eyes foveate the fixation plane, and thereby persistently activate cell populations there. This kind of activity-dependent enhancement influences many properties of cortical map development. For example, I mentioned in Chapter 1 that, due to our experiences with lots of vertically and horizontally oriented structures in an urban environment, the cells that represent these orientations may have a stronger representation than the cells that represent oblique orientations in visual cortical maps. As a result, the orientations of lines that are close to vertical or horizontal may be perceived, during sustained viewing, as being closer to these "norms", leading to the percept of *line neutralization* that was reported by James Gibson and Minnie Radner in 1937 (Gibson and Radner, 1937).

Fixation plane bias does not inhibit the unmatched edges in the Near and Far depth planes in the present situation due to the action of surface contours. This happens in the following way: The boundaries in the V2 layer 2/3 Fixation plane at the positions of the stronger binocular

boundaries in the Near and Far planes are quickly eliminated. The closed boundaries in the Fixation plane that included the two thin bars are hereby both destroyed. Without closed boundaries, the corresponding monocular surfaces cannot be filled in, and thus do not receive surface-to-boundary feedback from surface contours (Figure 11.10). In contrast, the strong binocular boundaries of the thick bar are part of closed boundaries that can fill-in their monocular surfaces in the Near and Far depth planes. Thus they *can* generate surface-to-boundary surface contour signals. These surface contour signals strengthen both of the closed boundaries that led to their formation, including their unmatched monocular boundaries, as illustrated by Figure 4.51. The boundary representations of the two monocularly viewed edges of the right input in the Near and Far depth planes are then strong enough to survive the Fixation plane bias. The final V2 boundary representations are shown in the fourth row from the bottom in Figure 11.15.

As usual, V4 fills-in surfaces in those regions that are completely enclosed by connected boundaries, resulting in the surface percept of a thin Near bar and a thin Far bar in the top row of Figure 11.15, which is the percept that was reported experimentally by Gillam, Blackburn, and Nakayama.

The same mechanisms can explain another example of DaVinci stereopsis that Gillam, Blackburn, and Nakayama reported in the same article (Figure 11.16). In this display, there are three thin rectangles in the right image, rather than two. Again there is a single binocular boundary in the Near and Far depth planes. Apart from some extra matching possibilities to take into account, the explanation proceeds just as before, and leads to a surface percept with one thin bar in each of the Near, Fixation plane, and Far depths.

Venetian blind effect and Panum's limiting case. The same 3D LAMINART mechanisms can also explain many other percepts that arise during 3D vision and

DA VINCI STEREOPSIS
Gillam, Blackburn, and Nakayama (1999)

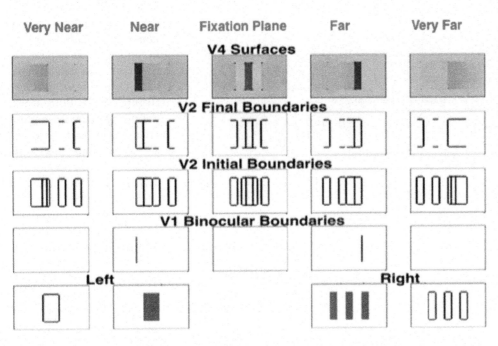

Very Near   Near   Fixation Plane   Far   Very Far

V4 Surfaces

V2 Final Boundaries

V2 Initial Boundaries

V1 Binocular Boundaries

Left   Right

FIGURE 11.16. The version of DaVinci stereopsis wherein three narrow rectangles are binocularly matched with one thick rectangle can also be explained in a similar way.

Figure 11.17 displays the V1 and V2 boundaries and the V4 surfaces. Figure 11.18 displays the V2 monocular surfaces and surface-to-boundary feedback signals. As in previous explanations, Figure 11.17 should be read from the bottom up, with the bottom two rows representing the input (inner pair of figures with black bars on white background) and the V1 boundary representations (white boundaries on black background), the next two rows representing the V2 boundary representations before (V2 Initial Boundaries) and after (V2 Final Boundaries) surface-to-boundary feedback acts, and the top row representing the V4 surface representations. In Figure 11.18, the bottom four rows represent, respectively, in ascending order, the following quantities corresponding to the left eye: the Initial Monocular Surfaces before any feedback interactions occur, the Initial Surface-to-Boundary Signals generated by these surfaces, the Left Final Monocular Surfaces after the Surface-to-Boundary Signals have their effect, and the Final Surface-to-Boundary Signals that are caused by the Final Monocular Surfaces. The top four rows represent the same quantities for the right eye.

As noted above, every second bar of the left input is in retinal correspondence with every third bar of the right input (bottom row). Figure 11.17 makes the network dynamics easier to track by marking these bars in red (the middle two plots of the bottom row), as are their monocular vertical boundaries (the left-most and right-most plots of the bottom row). Because of the retinal correspondence, their vertical boundaries are matched in the Fixation plane to form V1 binocular boundaries, which are marked in red in the middle plot of the next-to-last row. As always, the initial boundaries in V2 layer 4 add the binocular boundaries and the monocular boundaries along the lines-of-sight to create the V2 initial boundaries in the third row from the bottom.

The fixation plane bias now plays an important role in determining the final boundaries in V2 layer 2/3. As a result, every vertical boundary in the line-of-sight of the

figure-ground perception. Among the percepts that the model can simulate is the Venetian blind percept that was described in Figure 6.21 of the classical 1995 book of Ian Howard and Brian Roberts called *Binocular Vision and Stereopsis* (Howard and Rogers, 1995). This version of the Venetian blind stimulus consists of two gratings, a low spatial frequency grating with four thin bars that is presented to the left eye, and a higher spatial frequency grating with six thin bars that is presented to the right eye (Figure 11.17, bottom row, second and fourth columns). When binocularly fused, the frequency of the gratings are such that every second bar of the left grating is in retinal correspondence with every third bar of the right grating. This stereogram produces a percept of short ramps, each containing three bars, sloping up from left to right interspaced with step returns, as shown in the V4 surface percept in Figure 11.17 (top row). In particular, reading positions from left to right, the first bar of the percept is in the zero disparity plane (Fixation plane; third column). The second is in the Near disparity plane (second column). Then there is a step return to the third bar which is located in the Far disparity plane (fourth column), after which the pattern repeats. The total percept is thus of a Venetian blind.

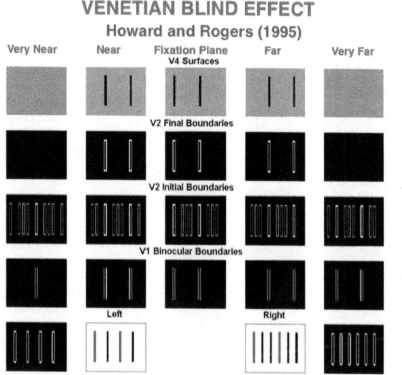

VENETIAN BLIND EFFECT
Howard and Rogers (1995)

Very Near Near Fixation Plane Far Very Far
V4 Surfaces

V2 Final Boundaries

V2 Initial Boundaries

V1 Binocular Boundaries

Left Right

Every second bar on L in same position as every third bar on R
These bars are marked in RED; see them match in Fixation Plane

FIGURE 11.17. The bars in the left and right images that are in the same positions are marked in red to simplify tracking how they are processed at subsequent stages.

are binocularly matched with non-zero disparities. Note that the right eye receives twice the number of these bars as the left eye. This is therefore an example of the classical phenomenon called *Panum's limiting case*, which considers when and how one bar in one eye can be matched against two bars in the other eye. Panum's limiting case (Panum, 1858) contradicts theories of binocular fusion that insist on *unique matching* of only one boundary in the left eye with one boundary in the right eye, as in the influential stereopsis models of W. E. L. Grimson (Grimson, 1981) and of David Marr and Tomaso Poggio (Marr and Poggio, 1976) in their proposals to try solving the Correspondence Problem.

The 3D LAMINART model solves the Correspondence Problem by using a disparity filter that *encourages* unique matching, via line-of-sight inhibition, but does not insist upon it. As a result, each bar of the left input can fuse with two bars of the right input to generate the percept shown in the V4 surface representation in the top row of Figure 11.17. In effect, this V4 surface representation consists of two side-by-side Panum's limiting cases. I will explain the Panum's limiting case percept in greater detail in a moment. Adding together the percepts shown in top row of Figure 11.17 yields the complete Venetian blind V4 surface percept.

In summary, the Venetian blind percept may be viewed as just a more complicated version of Panum's limiting case, when it is fully analyzed by combining early stereo matching, later boundary selection by a disparity filter that is part of the 3D boundary grouping process, surface-to-boundary signals that enhance closed boundaries, and surface filling-in of those regions that are completely enclosed by surviving closed boundaries after the disparity filter acts.

binocular fixation plane boundaries will be inhibited, whether binocularly matched or not. In particular, vertical boundaries in the Very Near and Very Far depths (the first plot and the last plot of the second row) are eliminated. The binocular vertical boundaries in the Near and Far depths (the second plot and the fourth plot of the second row) survive this inhibition because the corresponding monocular boundaries are matched with non-zero disparities, and are thus not in the lines-of-sight of the binocular fixation plane boundaries.

In order to further simplify the explanation, it is useful to think of the stimulus as being divided into two components that can be analyzed separately. As noted above, the bars in retinal correspondence are shown in red in the middle two plots of the first row of Figure 11.17. Since the red bars in the left and right inputs of this figure are in retinal correspondence, the model correctly predicts that they will generate surface percepts in the fixation plane, as shown by the two bars in the V2 surface representation of the top row. The specific binocular matches are shown in red at the V1 binocular boundaries.

Unique binocular matching vs. disparity filter selection. The remaining bars generate monocular boundaries that

From dichoptic masking to Panum's limiting case. I will now explain some percepts that variants of the Panum's Limiting Case display induces. It is instructive to think about these explanations in terms of the phenomenon

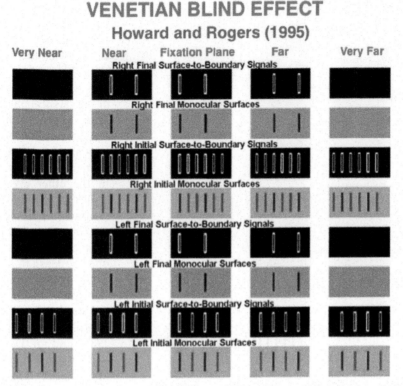

VENETIAN BLIND EFFECT
Howard and Rogers (1995)

Very Near   Near   Fixation Plane   Far   Very Far

Right Final Surface-to-Boundary Signals

Right Final Monocular Surfaces

Right Initial Surface-to-Boundary Signals

Right Initial Monocular Surfaces

Left Final Surface-to-Boundary Signals

Left Final Monocular Surfaces

Left Initial Surface-to-Boundary Signals

Left Initial Monocular Surfaces

Every second bar on L in same position as every third bar on R
PERCEPT: 3-bar ramps sloping up from L to R with step returns

FIGURE 11.18. Surface and surface-to-boundary surface contour signals that are generated by the Venetian blind image.

of *dichoptic masking*. In the basic paradigm of dichoptic masking that was studied by Suzanne McKee, Mary Bravo, Harvey Smallman, and Gordon Legge in 1994 (McKee et al., 1994), the contrast threshold for detecting a low contrast bar that is presented to one eye increased radically when a high contrast bar was presented to the other eye. In other words, the high contrast bar *masked* the low contrast bar. Furthermore, it was not necessary for the two bars to be registered at the same retinal positions. The model explains this percept in the following way.

In Figure 11.19, the high contrast bar is presented to the left eye and the low contrast bar to the right, as shown by the middle two plots in the bottom row. The outer two plots of the bottom row show the simulated monocular boundary representations. Since their contrasts differ greatly, these two bars cannot be stereoscopically fused in V1, due to the contrast constraint on binocular fusion (Figure 11.5) and its realization by the obligate property in layer 3B binocular simple cells (Figure 11.6). This accounts for the absence of V1 binocular boundary representations in the second row from the bottom of Figure 11.19.

The monocular boundaries are added to all depth planes in V2 along their respective monocular lines-of-sight, as shown in the third row from the bottom.

Critically, the left and right monocular boundaries coincide in the Near depth plane. These boundaries are consequently stronger than those in the other four depth planes, which they suppress via the line-of-sight inhibition of the V2 disparity filter. The final V2 boundary representations are shown in the fourth row from the bottom. All horizontal boundaries survived because the disparity filter only inhibits vertical boundaries. The only closed boundary in V2 thus lies in the Near depth plane. As a result, only a single bar in the Near depth plane forms a visible surface percept in V4, in the top row of the figure. Importantly, this bar fills in the contrast of the high contrast bar that inputs to the left eye. The low contrast bar that inputs to the right eye does not influence this filling-in event. This simulation hereby shows how the left and right monocular input rectangles can form a single rectangular percept in V4 using the higher contrast to fill in the final percept in the Near depth plane, even though their contrasts are so different that they cannot be fused by binocular cells in V1.

Panum's limiting case as an example of dichoptic masking. We can now understand how Panum's limiting case can be understood as an example of dichoptic masking. The Panum stimulus presents a single vertical bar to the left eye and two disparate vertical bars to the right eye, as shown by the middle two plots of the bottom row of Figure 11.20. The resultant monocular boundaries are shown by the outer two plots of this row. V1 binocular boundary cells fuse the bar of the left input with both bars of the right input, to form binocular boundaries in both the Near and the Far depth planes, represented by the second and fourth plots of the next-to-last row.

The monocular boundaries are added to all disparity planes in V2 along their respective lines-of-sight, as shown by the third row from the bottom. The left eye monocular boundary forms the left bar representations in the first two plots, from left to right, in the third row; the middle

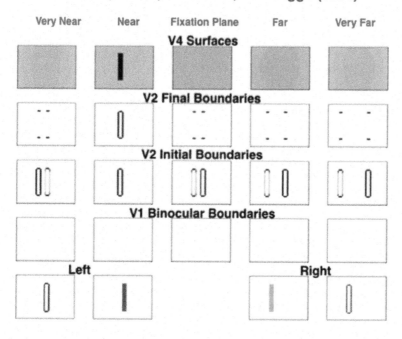

FIGURE 11.19. Dichoptic masking occurs when the bars in the left and right images have sufficiently different contrasts.

are hereby suppressed that receive only monocular inputs and share one of their lines-of-sight.

Here is a critical point about dichoptic masking: The binocularly matched boundaries in the Near and Far depths are also in the same line-of-sight, but they have the same strength, and therefore do not inhibit each other, unlike the situation in Figure 11.19. This is thus a good example of how the disparity filter *encourages* unique matching via line-of-sight inhibition, but does not always *enforce* it.

The surviving V2 boundary representations are shown in the fourth row from the bottom. Those regions in V2 that are enclosed by a closed boundary give rise to the surface percept in V4, as shown in the top row. The model thus correctly predicts that the bar of the left input is matched with both bars of the right input, and so masks them both equally (McKee et al., 1995).

The 3D Craik-O'Brien-Cornsweet Effect. Many variants of dichoptic masking and

bar representation in the third plot; and the right bar representations in the fourth and fifth plots. Similarly, the two right eye monocular boundaries the two right bar representations in the first two plots, again from left to right, in the third row; the outer two bar representations in the third plot; and the leftmost two bar representations in the fourth and fifth plots. The V1 binocular boundaries are also added to the monocular boundaries in V2 in the third row. They coincide with the vertical boundaries of the left bar representation in the second plot from the left, and the right bar representation in the fourth plot from the left. Because these boundaries receive both binocular and monocular inputs, they are stronger than the other vertical boundaries, and consequently suppress them via the disparity filter. All V2 vertical boundaries

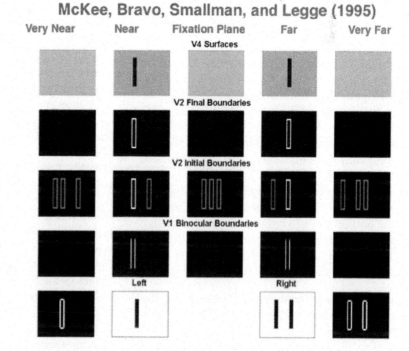

Panum's limiting case is a simplified version of the Venetian blind effect!

FIGURE 11.20. Dichoptic masking occurs in Panum's limiting case for reasons explained in the text.

CRAIK-O'BRIEN-CORNSWEET EFFECT
Can the model simulate other surface percepts? e.g., surface brightness

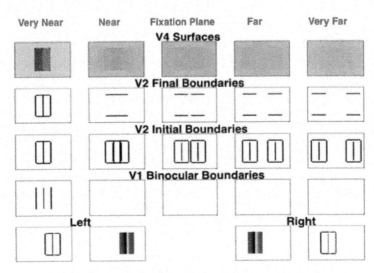

The 2D surface with the image on it is viewed at a very near depth
Adapts Grossberg and Todorovic (1988) to 3D

FIGURE 11.21. A simulation of the Craik-O'Brien-Cornsweet Effect when viewed on a planar surface in depth.

related facts about stereopsis are explained and simulated by the 3D LAMINART model in articles like Cao and Grossberg (2005), Fang and Grossberg (2009), and Grossberg and Howe (2003). Here, I will just explain two additional types of data.

The first kind of data emphasizes that the 3D surface percept in V4 multiplexes Form-*And-Color*-And-DEpth. Accordingly, Figure 11.21 summarizes a simulation of the Craik-O'Brien-Cornsweet Effect, or COCE, when a 2D image of this stimulus is viewed at a Very Near depth. I already discussed this percept in 2D in Chapter 4 to illustrate concepts about 2D boundary completion and surface filling-in; see Figures 4.2 and 4.12.

When viewed at a Very Near depth, the left and right eye images of the COCE are registered in the manner shown in the bottom row of Figure 11.21. Going through the usual analysis leads to a V4 surface percept in the Very Near depth, in the top row of the figure. Note that the proper relative brightnesses of the COCE are filled in here.

3D surface and figure-ground percepts from Julesz stereograms. *Random-Dot-Stereograms* (RDS) have been used to study stereopsis and 3D vision since Bela Julesz introduced them in his seminal 1971 book (Julesz, 1971) to show how binocular disparity can induce 3D percepts without any help from monocular cues. The simplest kind of RDS is constructed as follows: Start with an image that is filled with black dots that are randomly placed on a white

sheet of paper. Imagine a shape that covers a definite region of the first sheet of paper. Lift that shape, keeping all of its dots in their original positions, and place it on a second sheet of paper in a position that is slightly shifted to the right with respect to their positions in the first sheet of paper. Now place all the random dots in the first sheet of paper that have not yet been moved in the same positions in the second sheet of paper as they have in the first sheet, except for the dots that would cover the shifted shape. Because the shape is shifted relative to the first image, there will also be a region that has not yet been filled with random dots. Now fill that region too with random dots. The result is a second image that is filled with random dots with essentially the same background dots as in the first image, but with a hidden shape that is shifted with respect to the first image. The 3D LAMINART model can discover this hidden shape and generate a 3D surface representation in which it, and its constituent dots, are seen in depth with respect to the background of random dots. Previous stereopsis models were not able to do this.

A 2009 article with my PhD student Liang Fang (Fang and Grossberg, 2009) used 3D LAMINART to simulate three types of 3D surface percepts that can be generated by RDS. These RDSs will be illustrated by images constructed from black dots on a white background, but the same mechanisms work for many other matchable features.

Dense RDS. The first kind of RDS contains densely-packed features that make the Correspondence Problem hard to solve by including many false binocular matches. Figure 4.52 (top row) shows a typical dense RDS. The images in the bottom row of this figure show how the 3D LAMINART model separates the hidden object surfaces in depth, along with the surface lightnesses of their dot patterns. Only Near, Fixation, and Far planes were simulated because the RDS only induced figures at these three depths. The Fixation plane contains a letter L that is composed of random dots, the Near plane contains an inverted letter L, and the Far plane is composed of the remaining random dots.

Boundary, Near, V1   Boundary, Fixation, V1   Boundary, Far, V1

Boundary, Near, V2   Boundary, Fixation, V2   Boundary, Far, V2

Boundary, Near, V2   Boundary, Fixation, V2   Boundary, Far, V2

FIGURE 11.22. Simulation of the boundaries that are generated by the Julesz stereogram in Figure 4.59 (top row) without (second row) and with (third row) surface contour feedback.

Figure 11.22 summarizes a computer simulation that explains how this RDS percept is formed. The top row shows the results of binocular matching the vertical RDS boundaries at black-white and white-black contrast changes at V1 complex cells. The middle row shows the V2 layer 4 cell responses after adding these binocular boundaries and the horizontal boundaries along their lines-of-sight, but before the surface-to-boundary surface contour feedback signals operate. Recall that surface contours form only at the bounding contours of successfully filled-in closed boundaries. The bottom row shows the boundaries that survive surface-to-boundary feedback after the disparity filter in V2 layer 2/3 inhibits the weaker boundaries across all depths along the lines-of-sight. The surviving boundaries are the closed boundaries at the "correct" depths. These boundaries generate the V4 surface representation in Figure 4.52 (bottom row).

Sparse RDS. The second kind of RDS contains a much smaller number of widely separated black dots (Figure 11.23, top row). Such a RDS presents a different computational challenge, because there are large white background

regions with no dots in them. Somehow these large white backgrounds are broken up and captured into different depth planes due to the configuration of the sparse black dots among them. This is a RDS version of the same kind of problem that was illustrated by Figure 1.4 (top row), in which the ambiguous white regions where the cross and square overlap are "captured" by the figure that appears in front.

In response to the RDS in Figure 11.23, local filtering of contrast features by simple and complex cells (Figure 11.6) can compute binocular disparities only at the matched edges of the sparse image features. Depth-selective 3D boundary completion by bipole cells (Figure 11.10) responds to the filtered features to form connected large-scale boundaries at multiple depths. These boundaries act as filling-in generators and barriers of surface filling-in at different depths (Figures 3.22 and 11.2).

The simulated V4 surface representation in response to the sparse RDS in Figure 11.23 (top row) is shown in Figure 11.23 (bottom row). The gray color at the near depth corresponds to zero neural activity in the V4 cells. The hidden square figure is at the fixation depth, and the background is at the far depth. The filled-in regions contain black dots and white backgrounds, although the white does not print too clearly across the entire surface.

Figure 11.24 shows more details about how the model explains this sparse RDS percept. When the images in Figure 11.23 (top row) are binocularly fused, boundaries are completed within the central square region at the Fixation depth, and also throughout the complementary background region at the Far depth (Figure 11.24, top row). This occurs in layer 2/3 of the V2 interstripes (Figures 1.21 and 11.10). At the Fixation depth, the complete 3D boundaries project to the V2 thin stripes to contain filling-in of black within the dots, and of white outside the dots, of the central square region (Figure 11.24, bottom row). At the Far depth, the same thing happens within the background surface. Filling-in at only the correct depths is further supported by surface contour feedback, which strengthens the closed boundaries at the correct depths, and thereby enables the disparity filter to better inhibit any boundaries that may exist at other depths. With no boundaries to support filling-in at the far depth within the central square region, the central square at the fixation depth looks opaque. V4 surfaces control similar filling-in events,

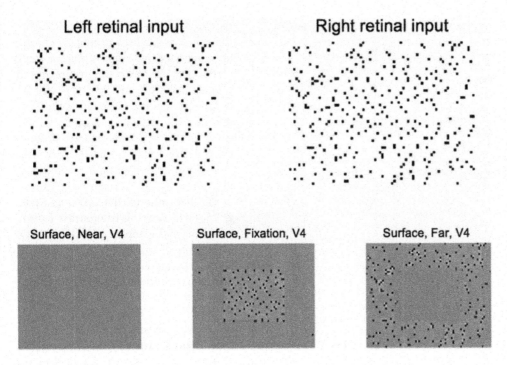

Left retinal input

Right retinal input

Surface, Near, V4   Surface, Fixation, V4   Surface, Far, V4

FIGURE 11.23. Simulation of the surface percept that is seen in response to a sparse stereogram. The challenge is to assign large regions of ambiguous white to the correct surface in depth.

simulated by showing how both small-scale and large-scale bipole cells can work together to accomplish both goals. The large-scale bipole cells can group image contrasts over larger distances. This issue brings us face-to-face with the problem of how multiple scales support percepts of forms in depth, a topic to which I now turn.

Multiple-scale, depth-selective boundary groupings determine perceived depth. How do our brains determine how far away objects are from us? The size of an object's image on our retinas cannot be the only cue to depth, if only because an image on the retina can be large either because it is derived from a small object that is nearby, or from a large object that is farther away. One way to distinguish these different causes of the same retinal image is to use receptive fields with multiple sizes. This insight has been used since at least the Renaissance to signal depth in 2D pictures using perspective, as illustrated by the upper left image in Figure 3.40. In this spirit, Chapter 3 suggested how multiple-scale boundary webs generate the depthful

leading to a percept of a central dotted opaque square in the Fixation plane, surrounded by a dotted background at the Far depth.

Dense RDS that induce perceptual completion of partially occluded objects. The third kind of RDS supports amodal completion of a partially occluded object behind an occluder, even when all the "objects" are constructed from from a dense stereogram that is composed of small black dots on a white background. The model simulate this kind of percept in response a RDS that induces a percept of a horizontal bar that partially occludes a vertical bar, as in Figure 1.3. This kind of percept creates an additional challenge because the small-scale bipole cells whose boundaries surround the individual dots, and separate their surfaces in depth, are not big enough to bridge the distance behind the horizontal bar to amodally complete the boundary of the vertical bar. This percept was

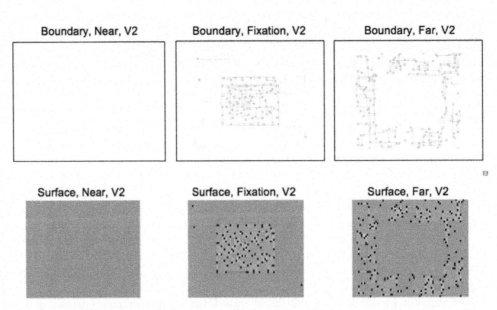

Boundary, Near, V2   Boundary, Fixation, V2   Boundary, Far, V2

Surface, Near, V2   Surface, Fixation, V2   Surface, Far, V2

FIGURE 11.24. Boundary groupings capture the ambiguous depth-ambiguous feature contour signals and lift them to the correct surface depths to trigger surface filling-in there.

3D VISION AND FIGURE-GROUND SEPARATION
Multiple-scale, depth-selective boundary webs

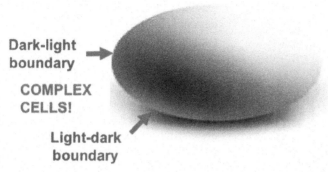

Dark-light boundary

COMPLEX CELLS!

Light-dark boundary

If boundaries were just edge detectors, there would be just a bounding edge of the ellipse. After filling-in, it would look like this:

FIGURE 11.25. Boundaries are not just edge detectors. If they were, a shaded ellipse would look flat, and uniformly gray.

percepts of the textured disk and shaded ellipse in the bottom half of Figure 3.21 by capturing lightness and color in their depth-selective filling-in domains, as diagrammed in Figure 3.22.

The examples of the textured disk and shaded ellipse are sufficiently important conceptually to flesh out how we see them a little more here than I could in Chapter 3. Figure 11.25 begins this analysis by making two observations. First, when the bounding contour of the shaded ellipse at the top of the figure is traversed, its contrast polarity reverses between light-dark and dark-light. The continuity of the boundary that surrounds the ellipse benefits from the fact that complex cells pool output signals from opposite-polarity simple cells at each position (see Figures 4.17, 4.19, and 4.25). However, this boundary that surrounds the entire ellipse is not the only boundary that is generated when we consciously see a shaded ellipse. If boundaries did act just like edge detectors, then the gray contrasts within this boundary could spread in all directions within the ellipse until it hit this boundary, thereby creating the percept of a flat, uniformly gray ellipse, as depicted at the bottom of Figure 11.25. This is not, however, what we see.

Instead, the shaded ellipse is filtered by simple and complex cell populations whose receptive fields have different sizes, or scales. These filtering cells generate multiple-scale,

depth-selective boundary webs that respond maximally to different parts of the shaded ellipse image. When all of these boundary webs capture the gray ellipse contrasts at their positions, the totality of all these filled-in depth-selective Filling-In Domains, or FIDOs, gives rise to the percept of a shaded ellipse-in-depth. To better understand how this works, a few more observations need to be made about how multiple scales contribute to the percept of multiple depths.

If only because the retinal image of a *single* object increases in size we approach the object, or conversely, there is a tendency for "big" scales to signal "near" depths. The two images in Figure 11.26 illustrate that this is sometimes, but not always, true. The left figure is a picture of a sinusoidal grating whose spatial period increases from left to right. Under good viewing conditions, the right half of this figure can look a little closer than the left half, just as in the picture with perspective in Figure 3.40.

The right figure in Figure 11.26 is, however, a picture that generates the opposite result! This picture was published in 1988 by James Brown and Naomi Weisstein (Brown and Weisstein, 1988). When viewing it, the high spatial frequency sinusoidal grating looks nearer, whereas the low spatial frequency sinusoid looks farther away, at least most of the time. Then a perceptual switch can suddenly occur, after which the low spatial frequency looks closer and the high spatial frequency farther away. These percepts can then alternate bistably through time. This figure is one of many possibilities that show the same result. Because the high spatial frequencies look closer most of the time in this figure, it is not always true that large scales code for closer. Because the figure is reversible, it is clear that the same scale may code for more than one depth.

Why does the bigger scale looks closer in the left image of Figure 11.26, but not in the right one? One possibility is that the different scales are organized into different groupings in the two pictures. I will show below that grouping is, indeed, a major factor in determining the relative depths

MULTIPLE-SCALE DEPTH-SELECTIVE GROUPINGS DETERMINE PERCEIVED DEPTH

As an object approaches, it gets bigger on the retina

Does a big scale (RF) always signal NEAR? NO!

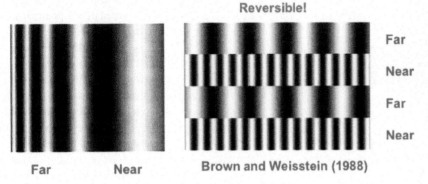

The same scale can signal either near or far

Some scales fuse more than one disparity

FIGURE 11.26. Although larger scales sometimes look closer (left image), that is not always true, as the right image of Brown and Weisstein (1988) illustrates. The latter percept is, moreover, bistable. These images show the importance of interactions between groupings and multiple scales to determine perceived surface depth.

of what we see. Near and far are thus not just properties of multiple spatial scales. Rather, they are properties of *how multiple spatial scales are organized into depth-selective groupings*.

This conclusion is supported by the following thought experiment: Imagine that the low spatial frequency sinusoid in the Brown and Weisstein picture of Figure 11.26 is used as the high spatial frequency in a new picture, in which the spatial frequency of the other sinusoid is even lower. Then the low spatial frequency would look closer most of the time in this new picture even though, within Figure 11.26, it looks further away most of the time. This comparison again shows that a single spatial frequency can code for more than one relative depth. It also shows that the *grouping* that organizes the two spatial scales is very important in determining what we consciously see, since the same grouping can generate the same qualitative result in both pictures, even if a spatial scale that is used in them both is seen at opposite relative depths in them.

Size-Disparity Correlation: How do multiple scales get converted into multiple depths? With this background, I can now propose an answer to the question: *How do multiple scales get transformed into multiple depths?* More specifically, how do populations of cells that include multiple spatial scales get used to form groupings that are selective for different depths? This analysis will clarify how cells of a single scale can contribute to multiple depth-selective groupings, as in the Brown-Weisstein effect, despite the

tendency for larger scales to look closer, at least most of the time.

Figure 11.27 illustrates a basic reason why multiple scales contribute to multiple depths. As illustrated in the left image, simple cells come in multiple sizes, or scales, that are used to binocularly fuse pairs of monocular representations from the left and right eyes that are derived from objects in the world. This image shows that bigger scales can, other things being equal, fuse a bigger range of binocular disparities, including both smaller and larger disparities, than small scales. It also shows that a given disparity can be fused by multiple scales, especially the smaller disparities. This is a basic reason why disparity alone does not code for relative depth.

The image to the right of Figure 11.27 suggests why this is so. It shows a schematic cross-section of the responses of simple cells when an object feature is registered by the left and right eyes at different positions on the cortical map in V1. The activity profiles of simple cells with a larger spatial scale are shown to the left, and of simple cells with a smaller spatial scale are shown to the right. Left and right eye responses alternate with each other across space in the cortical map. This alternation occurs within the ocular dominance columns in V1. Figure 11.28 (left image) shows a top-down view of these ocular dominance columns, as seen in a reconstruction of a flattened piece of cortex that has been stained for cytochrome oxidase. The black regions are activated by one eye, and the white regions by the other eye. Figure 11.28 (right image) provides a schematic diagram of how left and right eye responses of the lateral geniculate nucleus, or LGN, at a given position are interleaved within the cortical map, and nearby positions in the world are represented by nearby positions in the map (Schmolesky, M. Visual Cortex. Webvision http://webvision.med.utah. edu/book/part-ix-psychophysics-of-vision/the-primary-visual-cortex/)

Coming back to Figure 11.27 (right panel), note that the activities of simple cells that respond to the left (right) eye input are drawn as open (filled) rectangles whose heights covary with the cell activity at that position. The distance between the left and right eye inputs to the map (red bars) covaries with their binocular disparity. Larger scale cells can continue to respond at positions that are further from the position of their inducing stimulus than do smaller scale cells. Given the particular binocular disparity that the two inputs in the figure represent, the activity profiles of the larger scale simple cells overlap, but the activity profiles of the smaller scale simple cells do not.

MULTIPLE-SCALE GROUPING
AND SIZE-DISPARITY CORRELATION

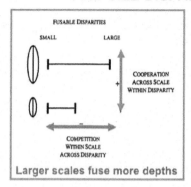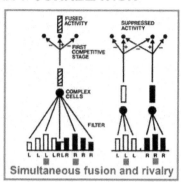

Larger scales fuse more depths | **Simultaneous fusion and rivalry**

Depth-selective cooperation and competition among multiple
scales determines perceived depth

BOUNDARY PRUNING using SURFACE CONTOURS:
Surface-to-boundary feedback from the nearest surface that is
surrounded by a connected boundary eliminates redundant boundaries
at the same position and further depths

FIGURE 11.27. (left image) Each scale can binocularly fuse a subset of spatial scales, with larger scales fusing more scales and closer ones than small scales. (right image) Cortical hypercolumns enable binocular fusion to occur in a larger scale even as rivalry occurs in a smaller scale.

Let us assume for definiteness that the activities caused by the left and right eye inputs induce (spatially discrete) Gaussian activity profiles across the cortical map. The output signals from all the simple cells input via an adaptive filter to complex cells at the next processing stage, after which they compete across map positions (Figure 4.25). As a result, in response to inputs from the larger-scale simple cells, a single complex cell population receives the largest input and wins the competition. This happens because the *sum* of the left and right eye Gaussian activity profiles has its maximum at a position halfway between the left and right eye inputs. The winning complex cell hereby binocularly fuses its left and right eye inputs, and can send a topographic output signal to the first competitive stage and beyond.

In contrast, the input patterns to complex cells from the smaller scale simple cells peak at the positions of each monocular input. After competition acts, these inputs activate two populations of complex cells that lie at the monocular positions of the left and right eye inputs. The output signals from these complex cells, being spatially disparate, then compete at the first competitive stage, and hereby initiate binocular rivalry.

In summary, when multiple scales filter disparate left and right eye inputs, they can generate simultaneous fusion (by the larger scale) and rivalry (by the smaller scale). The properties of this relationship between size and disparity is called the *size-disparity correlation*, and such simultaneous fusion and rivalry is known to occur in response

to many stereograms (Julesz and Schumer, 1981; Kulikowski, 1978; Richards and Kaye, 1974; Schor and Tyler, 1981; Schor and Wood, 1983; Schor et al., 1984; Tyler, 1975, 1983). Filtering disparate visual data using multiple scales hereby begins to distinguish between images on the retina that are large because they are nearby, or are large because they come from very large objects that are further away.

Explaining why a shaded ellipse does not look flat: Scale-to-depth and depth-to-scale maps. I can now return to continue my explanation of why a shaded ellipse does not look flat (Figure 11.25) by also explaining how the size-disparity correlation is used by subsequent processing stages to overcome some remaining ambiguities about where objects are in depth. As noted in Figure 11.27, multiple scales can respond to smaller disparities. Figure 11.27 suggests that the groupings that form in response to multiple scales help to resolve this ambiguity, but did not explain how this works with any precision. Consideration of shaded ellipses points the way to greater clarity.

In particular, Figure 11.29 notes that, whereas smaller scales that are aligned with an ellipse's shading can respond well at positions near the ellipse's bounding edge, only larger scales can respond more deeply into the ellipse as the shading gradient becomes more gradual. This fact is represented in Figure 11.29 in a simplified way by coloring the regions red whose oriented simple and complex cell scales respond well. How do these multiple scales interact with boundary groupings that selectively represent different depths, and then control the depth-selective filling-in of their corresponding surface representations, as in Figure 3.22?

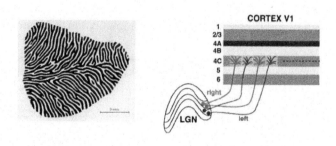

FIGURE 11.28. (left image) Ocular dominance columns respond selectively to inputs from one eye or the other. (right image) Inputs from the two eyes are mapped into layer 4C of V1, among other layers.

3D VISION AND FIGURE-GROUND SEPARATION
Multiple-scale, depth-selective boundary webs

Instead, different size detectors generate dense boundary webs at different positions and depths along the shading gradient

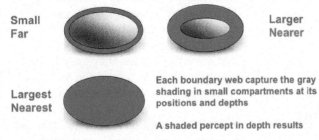

Small
Far

Larger
Nearer

Largest
Nearest

Each boundary web capture the gray shading in small compartments at its positions and depths

A shaded percept in depth results

FIGURE 11.29. Boundary webs of the smallest scales are closer to the boundary edge of the ellipse, and progressively larger scale webs penetrate ever deeper into the ellipse image, due to the amount of evidence that they need to fire. Taken together, they generate a multiple-scale boundary web with depth-selective properties that can capture depth-selective surface filling-in.

I proposed in my foundational article about 3D vision and figure-ground separation in 1994 (Grossberg, 1994) how scale-to-depth and depth-to-scale maps could form during development; namely, how different combinations of multiple-scale filters could input to depth-selective groupings, and conversely, thereby giving rise to percepts of curved shapes in depth. Whereas this idea helped to qualitatively explain a lot of data, as illustrated above, it was not until I worked with my PhD student Levin Kuhlmann to quantitatively simulate challenging data about depth-from-texture percepts that are experienced in response to pictures like those in Figure 3.21c that a rigorous computational model was developed and used to quantitatively simulate challenging depth-from-texture psychophysical data.

HOW MULTIPLE SCALES VOTE FOR MULTIPLE DEPTHS
Scale-to-depth and depth-to-scale maps

Smallest scale projects to, and receives feedback from, boundary groupings that represent the furthest depths

Largest scale connects to boundary groupings that represent all depths

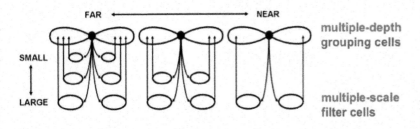

FAR ← → NEAR

SMALL

LARGE

multiple-depth
grouping cells

multiple-scale
filter cells

FIGURE 11.30. Multiple scales interact with bipole cells that represent multiple depths, and conversely. See the text for details.

This LIGHTSHAFT (LIGHTness-and-SHApe-From-Texture) model was published in 2007 (Grossberg, Kuhlmann, and Mingolla, 2007). Levin and I extensively modeled three variations of the same concepts that could all simulate the data well. I find it instructive to develop models in parallel if all available concepts, mechanisms, and data cannot yet distinguish them, and they all have similar explanatory power. With all the models and their explanations clearly in mind, it is easier to test them, and to select the correct one as more data become available.

Figure 11.30 schematically shows how multiple filter scales can vote for multiple depth-selective groupings, with the smallest scales restricted to the furthest depth-selective groupings, and the largest scale contributing to all depth-selective groupings. For example, in response to a shaded ellipse (Figure 11.29), the smaller scales vote for further depths, whereas the larger scales vote for nearer depths. Figure 11.31 shows the kind of data that LIGHTSHAFT quantitatively simulated. These data were collected in a series of remarkable psychophysical experiments by James Todd and Robin Akerstrom (Todd and Akerstrom, 1987). Jim and Robin carefully measured the depth judgements of human observers in response to computer-generated shape-from-texture images that could vary from highly curved in appearance (to the left) to flat in appearance (to the right). The data curves for the different stimuli are also shown, and were closely fit by the model. Thus, when multiple-scale boundary webs properly transform scale-to-depth and back, a lot can be understood about shape judgements by humans.

Simultaneous fusion and rivalry percepts from viewing Kulikowski and Kaufman stereograms. Simultaneous fusion and rivalry can also occur in response to stereograms where the rivalry is due to multiple-scale 3D filtering and grouping of the stereogram, as in Figure 11.27 (right panel) and/or due to the competition that occurs across orientations at each position (Figure 4.25). The former type of stereogram (Figure 11.32) was published by Janus Kulikowski in 1978 (Kulikowski, 1978). The second type of stereogram (Figure 11.33) was published by Lloyd Kaufman in his seminal 1974 book called *Sight and Mind* (Kaufman, 1974). Lloyd's book had a profound influence on my interest in studying vision.

The percepts that are caused by the Kulikowski and Kaufman stereograms provided me with early evidence that the BCS/FCS model of 2D vision would generalize in a natural way to 3D vision. I arrived at this conclusion because the percept of the Kulikowski stereogram can be explained by how the first competitive stage

FACTORS DETERMINING DEPTH-FROM-TEXTURE PERCEPT

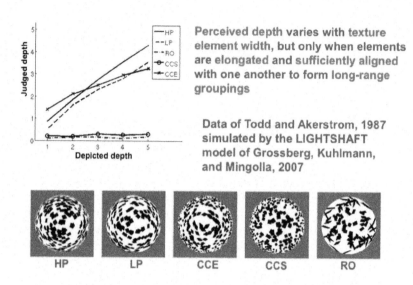

Perceived depth varies with texture element width, but only when elements are elongated and sufficiently aligned with one another to form long-range groupings

Data of Todd and Akerstrom, 1987 simulated by the LIGHTSHAFT model of Grossberg, Kuhlmann, and Mingolla, 2007

FIGURE 11.31. Todd and Akerstrom (1987) created a series of 2D images from discrete black patches on a white disk and showed how perceived depth varies with the factors summarized in the figure. The LIGHTSHAFT model quantitatively simulated their data.

interacts with bipole grouping (Figure 4.25) when these mechanisms are generalized to multiple-scale 3D filtering and grouping. Explaining the percept of the Kaufman stereogram required both the first and second competitive stages interacting with bipole grouping (Figure 4.25), again generalized to multiple-scale 3D filtering and grouping. In other words, these stereograms encouraged my belief that the BCS/FCS 2D circuits for early processing of images and scenes by simple, complex, hypercomplex, and bipole cells could be naturally extended to explain many challenging data about 3D vision. I will now sketch these explanations so that you can see how naturally the 2D BCS/FCS model generalizes to the 3D FACADE model to explain 3D percepts of simultaneous fusion and rivalry that are derived from stereograms.

The stereograms in Figures 11.32a and 11.32b contain pairs of short vertical lines outside the frame of each image. These lines are binocularly fused to set the stage for fusion or rivalry of the images within the frames. The stereogram in Figure 11.32a is composed of low spatial frequency sinusoids, whereas the stereogram in Figure 11.32b is composed of rectangles. The stimuli to the left eye across both figures are in phase

with one another, as are the stimuli to the right eye across both figures. The stimuli to the left and right eyes are, however, shifted in space with respect to each other, thereby creating a binocular disparity. This disparity is chosen so that the stereogram in Figure 11.32a can be binocularly fused to yield a percept of a sinusoid in depth with respect to its bounding frame.

The main reason to compare sinusoids with rectangles at the same retinal positions is that the rectangles can activate both low spatial frequency and high spatial frequency simple cells. The percept that is generated by Figure 11.32b thus includes a binocularly fused low frequency percept that is seen in depth, analogous to the percept in response to Figure 11.32a which uses the mechanism of binocular fusion by a large scale in Figure 11.27 (right panel). This stereogram also induces binocular rivalry between the high spatial frequency edges of the rectangles, analogous to the binocular rivalry caused by the small scale in Figure 11.27 (right panel). Similar percepts are caused in response to Figure 11.32c when a single sinusoidal or rectangular bar occurs in each stereogram frame. In summary, the rectangular inputs in the Kulikowski stereogram generate simultaneous fusion and rivalry due to the way in which large scale and small scale simple-complex-hypercomplex-bipole cells simultaneously respond to them.

In response to the left and right eye images in the Kaufman stereogram of Figure 11.33 (left panel), simultaneous fusion and rivalry is created in a different way. First, the positions where the straight lines in each image have corners generate emergent illusory square boundaries due to the way in which end cuts are formed (Figure

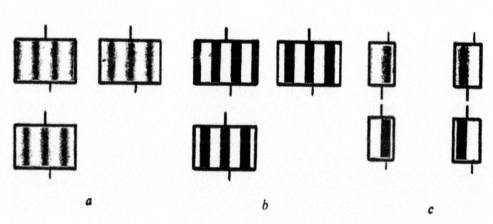

a   *b*   *c*

FIGURE 11.32. Kulikowski stereograms involve binocular matching of out-of-phase (a) Gaussians or (b) rectangles. The latter can generate a percept of simultaneous fusion and rivalry. See the text for why.

3D GROUPINGS DETERMINE PERCEIVED DEPTH
Kaufman stereogram (1974)

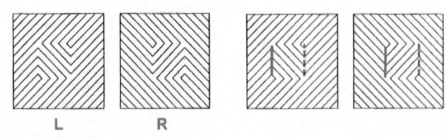

L   R

Vertical illusory contours are at different disparities than those of bounding squares

Illusory square is seen in depth

Vertical illusory contours are binocularly fused and determine the perceived depth of the square

Thin oblique lines, being perpendicular, are rivalrous: simultaneous fusion and rivalry

FIGURE 11.33. The Kaufman stereogram also creates a percept of simultaneous fusion and rivalry. The square in depth remains fused and the perpendicular lines in the two images are perceived as rivalrous.

4.22), which can then be collinearly grouped by bipole cells (e.g., Figures 3.18d. 3.18f, and 4.27). As part of these emergent square boundaries, vertical boundaries are generated by the left and right eye images, with corresponding boundaries denoted by solid and dashed red lines, respectively, in Figure 11.33 (right panel). These pairs of emergent boundaries are positionally displaced by an amount that can be binocularly fused, as in Figure 11.27 (right panel). They can therefore induce a percept of a square in depth, in the same way that any sparse stereogram does (Figures 11.23 and 11.24).

Coexisting with this fused percept is a percept of rivalry due to the fact that the lines in each stereogram image are perpendicular to each other at each position. These perpendicular lines are rivalrous because of the competition between orientations at each position that occurs at the second competitive stage (Figure 4.25). For this explanation to work, the second competitive stage must occur after the inputs from both eyes are combined in the visual cortex to form binocular cells, as illustrated by Figures 11.27, 11.28, and 4.25. Once enough collinear segments of a given orientation wins the orientational competition, they can form a boundary between them inwardly, along their entire line, via bipole grouping (Figures 3.7 and 4.29-4.32), and thereby suppress the perpendicularly oriented boundaries that abut the line (Figures 4.35 and 4.58). In this way,

boundaries with just one orientation can win in an extended region of the image, not just locally. The winning boundaries can then use the mechanisms for surface capture that are summarized in Figures 4.45-4.47 to trigger filling-in of surface lightnesses from feature contours that abut and are collinear with them, while suppressing feature contours that are not. In this way, only the winning boundaries can support conscious percepts of visible surface qualia via a resulting surface-shroud resonance (Figure 6.2).

How to explain both binocular rivalry and stable 3D vision in a unified way? In general, binocular rivalry is caused by presenting dissimilar images to corresponding regions of the two eyes. The two images compete for perceptual dominance, and one image can dominate conscious awareness for several seconds at a time, after which the previously suppressed image can be perceived. Rivalry has been described and analyzed for several hundred years (Blake and Logothetis, 2002; Fox, 1991) during which psychophysical and neurobiological studies have identified a wide range of rivalry properties under different experimental conditions.

Under natural viewing conditions, however, a single depthful percept of the world is consciously seen. A major question for neuroscience thus is: How do the same brain mechanisms that generate a single depthful percept of the world also cause perceptual bistability, notably binocular rivalry? What properties of brain representations correspond to consciously seen percepts? The above percepts and their explanations by the 3D LAMINART and ARTSCAN models provide principled answers to these equations. In particular, the same kind of processes that realize the three hierarchical resolutions of uncertainty that are needed to generate stable conscious percepts of the visual world, such as neon color spreading (Figures 3.10 and 3.11), also cause binocular rivalry when stimuli that are known to cause rivalry are presented to the model.

Most models of binocular rivalry (Figure 11.34) typically describe a circuit with two populations of

COMPARISON OF RIVALRY MODELS

Author	Levelt (1967) Data	Muller and Blake (1989) Data	Does both eye rivalry and stimulus rivalry	Explains patchy percepts	Explains rivalry from normal 3-D vision*	Explains rivalry-based V1 modulation	Uses visual input patterns
Matsuoka (1984)	No	No	No	No	No	No	No
Mueller (1990)	No	Yes	No	No	No	No	No
Laing and Chow (2002)	Yes	No slope simulation	No	No	No	No	No
Stollenwerk and Bode (2003)	Yes	Only CC paradigm	No	Yes	No	No	No
Wilson (2003)	Claims it would work if noise added	No	Yes	No	No	No	No
Freeman (2005)	Partially (Very long dominance durations)	Only CC paradigm	Yes	No	No	No	No
Lankheet (2006)	Yes	No	No	No	No	No	No
Grossberg et al (Our model)	Yes	Yes	Yes	Yes	Yes	Yes	Yes

*Explains how binocular rivalry emerges from cortical mechanisms of normal and fused 3-D vision.

FIGURE 11.34. A comparison of the properties of other rivalry models with those of the 3D LAMINART model (surrounded by red border). Significantly, only 3D LAMINART explains both stable vision and rivalry (green border).

competing cells that oscillate with respect to one another with temporal properties similar to rivalry oscillations (e.g., Arrington, 1993; Freeman 2005; Laing and Chow, 2002; Lankheet, 2006; Matsuoka, 1984; Mueller, 1990; Mueller and Blake, 1989; Stollenwerk and Bode 2003; Wilson 2003, 2005). These models typically are not designed to receive visual images and do not have an internal representation of a visual percept. A stronger test of a correct explanation of rivalry is to show how a model of normal 3D vision, which explains and simulates visual percepts under normal viewing conditions wherein a single percept persists through time, can also undergo binocular rivalry when certain visual stimuli occur.

This weakness of many models of binocular rivalry is similar to the weakness of many models of animal or human locomotion. These locomotion models can only oscillate with movement gaits. In contrast, animals spend at least as much time in positions of stable posture, such as sitting and lying down, as they do carrying out oscillatory movements. The challenge for all such models is to explain when, how, and why they are, or are not, oscillating.

As the above examples of stable and rivalrous percepts illustrate, the ability to explain both stable and rivalrous vision is what the 3D LAMINART model achieves (Grossberg, 1987b; Grossberg, Yazdanbakhsh, Cao, and Swaminathan, 2008). 3D LAMINART proposes that the circuits which trigger rivalrous and bistable percepts are the ones that complete boundaries in layer 2/3 of cortical area V2, as summarized in Figures 10.9-10.11. These boundary representations, in turn, interact with other circuits throughout cortical areas V1, V2, V4, and PPC to generate visible surface percepts. As in many explanations in this book, these circuits were not derived from postulates about rivalry, or to explain data about rivalry. Instead, they were derived and used to explain data about processes of cortical development, perceptual grouping, and figure-ground perception that typically lead to stable percepts, but happen to generate rivalrous percepts when they process stimuli that are known to induce rivalry.

Why binocular rivalry percepts involve many parts of the visual cortex. I will explain in a moment how three basic properties of the layer 2/3 boundary grouping circuits in V2 are sufficient to generate many quantitative properties of rivalry data as emergent properties. However, although boundary grouping properties may underlie the oscillations that drive binocular rivalry, they are not the processes that generate the conscious surface percepts that occur during binocular rivalry, for the same reason that *no* visual qualia can be seen except as surface percepts that are rendered consciously visible via a surface-shroud resonance.

How three basic properties of boundary grouping generate binocular rivalry. With this major caveat in mind, let us consider the three properties of boundary grouping that can generate binocular rivalry. These properties are summarized in Figure 11.35. The first property is *bipole grouping* (Figure 10.10). This ensures that boundary groupings determine the perceived relative depths of objects as they resolve the multiple constraints implicit in the spatial organization of disparity-sensitive hypercomplex cells across an entire scene. The second property is *orientational competition*. This property operates at several cortical stages, as indicated in Figure 4.58. An image like the Kaufman stereogram can activate orientational competition at all these stages, but the competition in layer 2/3 of V2 among bipole cells enables entire groupings to compete.

The third property is *activity-dependent habituation*. This is the same habituative gating process, or medium term memory (Figure 2.11), that enables our brains to get rapidly reset in response to changing images and scenes (Figure 7.1), as illustrated by properties of visual persistence (Figures 7.2-7.6). Even before adult neocortex forms, activity-dependent habituation plays a critical role in the development of the V1 cortical map, including its ocular dominance columns (Figure 11.28). During both developmental and adult cortical dynamics, habituative transmitters gate, or multiply, the signals between cells and habituate in an activity-dependent way. They prevent the earliest cells that win the competition during learning of the emerging cortical map from persistently dominating network dynamics in response to subsequent inputs (Grossberg and Seitz, 2003). By weakening the inputs to these cells in an activity-dependent way, other as yet uncommitted cells can also get activated and enable map learning to spread across the entire cortex. During binocular rivalry, visual inputs are approximately balanced in a way that enables more than one boundary grouping to try to form (e.g., Figures 11.32 and 11.33). When a winning grouping is weakened sufficiently by activity-dependent competition, then the unhabituated inputs to the other possible grouping enable it to win, thereby initiating the rivalry cycle through time.

Figure 11.36 summarizes a computer simulation of how the model responds when arrays of perpendicular lines are presented to its left and right eyes, respectively (top row). The last two rows illustrate how one or another boundary orientation wins at any time, how the winning boundary propagates across the entire image (times t1-to-t2 for the vertical orientation and t3-to-t4 for the horizontal orientation), and how the perpendicular orientation begins to win when the previous winning grouping is weakened enough by activity-dependent habituation (between times t2 and t3).

In summary, all three of the main properties that enable boundary groupings to trigger binocular rivalry also play basic roles in infant and adult processes of stable visual development, learning, and perception. Here again, a curious property of perception is seen to arise from properties that are essential for survival.

Stimulus rivalry vs. eye rivalry? Many psychophysical and neurobiological experiments have been done to characterize properties of binocular rivalry. Given how many brain areas are are measured in these experiments, and whose mechanistic and functional properties are explained by 3D LAMINART, it is perhaps not surprising that debates continue about where in the brain rivalry is caused and perceived.

Any theory that hopes to bring order to this diverse literature must thus provide a unified explanation of many rivalry data, and must do so using brain mechanisms that also explain lots of data about stable vision. To this end, a 2008 article with my colleagues Arash Yazdanbakhsh, Yongqiang Cao, and Guru Swaminathan (Grossberg et al., 2008) applied 3D LAMINART to explain and simulate rivalry data with the following descriptions: influences of contrast changes that are synchronized with switches in the dominant eye percept, gamma distribution of dominant phase durations, piecemeal percepts, coexistence of eye-based and stimulus-based rivalry, effects of object attention on switching between superimposed transparent surfaces, monocular rivalry, Marroquin patterns, the spread of suppression during binocular rivalry, binocular summation, fusion of dichoptically presented orthogonal gratings, general suppression during binocular rivalry, and pattern rivalry.

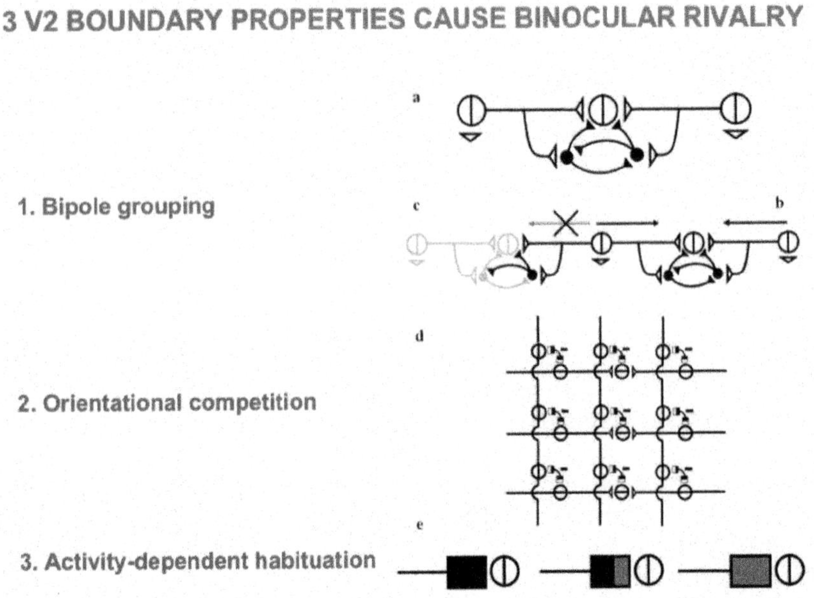

3 V2 BOUNDARY PROPERTIES CAUSE BINOCULAR RIVALRY

1. Bipole grouping

2. Orientational competition

3. Activity-dependent habituation

FIGURE 11.35. Three properties of bipole boundary grouping in V2 can explain how boundaries oscillate in response to rivalry-inducing stimuli. Because all boundaries are invisible, however, these properties are not sufficient to generate a conscious percept of rivalrous surfaces.

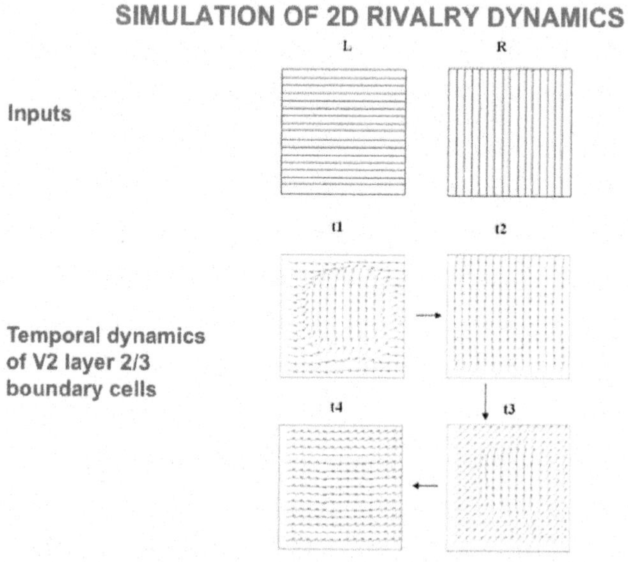

SIMULATION OF 2D RIVALRY DYNAMICS

FIGURE 11.36. Simulation of the temporal dynamics of rivalrous, but coherent, boundary switching.

In particular, the model simulates percepts of both *stimulus rivalry* (Logothetis et al., 1996) and *eye rivalry* (Lee and Blake, 1999) percepts that are caused by swapping perpendicular gratings between the two eyes at different stimulus contrasts and swapping rates. These experiments were designed to test a leading concept about how rivalry works, moreover a concept that already had significant experimental data to back it up. Responding to this experimental challenge, various binocular rivalry modelers added specific hypotheses to their oscillation models in order to explain stimulus rivalry data, but still could not simulate eye rivalry (e.g., Freeman, 2005; Wilson, 2003). Both phenomena were naturally explained and simulated by 3D LAMINART, as I will show below. The following exposition reviews some of the earlier experiments, and the concepts that motivated them, before sketching how 3D LAMINART explains both sets of data.

Many experiments had reported data showing that multiple brain areas may oscillate with rivalry percepts. For example, using fMRI techniques, Polonsky et al. (2000) and Lee and Blake (2002) showed that modulated activity of V1 is related to the perceptual switch. Such data are consistent with the models of Blake (1989), Mueller (1990), and Lumer (1998), which assume that *monocular competition* causes rivalry, and therefore that the generative rivalry circuit may be in V1, because V1 contains monocular cells, such as monocular simple cells (Figure 11.6). In 1989, Randolph Blake (Blake, 1989) published a thorough description of how monocular competition could work within "a neural theory of binocular rivalry that treats the phenomenon as the default outcome when binocular correspondence cannot be established. The theory posits the existence of monocular and binocular neurons arrayed within a functional processing module, with monocular neurons playing a crucial role in signaling the stimulus conditions instigating rivalry and generating inhibitory signals to implement suppression. Suppression is conceived as a local process happening in parallel over the entire cortical representation of the binocular visual field. The strength of inhibition causing suppression is related to the size of the pool of monocular neurons innervated by the suppressed eye, and the duration of a suppression phase is attributed to the strength of excitation generated by the suppressed stimulus" (p. 145).

Blake was led by several lines of psychophysical evidence to conclude that eye dominance, not stimulus dominance, causes rivalry. For example, during an eye swapping procedure, observers depress a switch when the pattern shown to one eye is dominant in its entirety, while the other pattern is completely suppressed from conscious vision (cf. Figure 11.36). This key press causes the immediate interchange of the left-eye and right-eye input patterns, so that the previously dominant pattern will now be shown to the previously suppressed eye, and vice versa. Blake, Westendorf, and Overton (1980) showed that, when this happens, the dominant pattern abruptly becomes invisible and the previously suppressed pattern becomes dominant, leading them to conclude that it is an eye that dominates, not a particular stimulus. The same conclusion was drawn from experiments using a stimulus change procedure. Here, the orientation, spatial frequency, or the direction of motion of a stimulus is changed while that stimulus is suppressed. These changes are not noticed until seconds later when the suppressed eye returns to dominance, thereby showing, once again, that it is an eye that is suppressed, not a particular pattern (Blake and Fox, 1974; Blake, Yu, Lokey, and Norman, 1998).

However, other experiments showed that the Blake account was incomplete. For example, by recording from single neurons in V1, V2, and V4, while using a perpendicular grating stimulus, Leopold and Logothetis (1996) found many cells, particularly in V4, have activity modulations related to the perceptual switch, thereby supporting a stimulus rivalry account. Logothetis (1998) reported that such cells are almost exclusively binocular and that their proportion increases in the higher processing stages of the visual system, as may be expected from the 3D LAMINART and ARTSCAN explanations of how a surface percept in response to a rivalry stimulus is constructed and becomes conscious.

The early data of Diaz-Caneja (1928) also showed that rivalry may not just follow competition between the two eye views. Rather, it can also follow cross-ocular groupings that are induced between the two eyes, and thereby implicate perceptual grouping in the rivalry process. This observation does not reject monocular channel competition, but it does implicate higher-level competition as well. Polonsky et al. (2000) used different contrasts as ocularity tags, and found that fMRI responses of later visual areas, such as V2, V3, V3A, and V4, fluctuate strongly between higher and lower contrasts, even as V1 activity also fluctuates between higher and lower contrasts.

The stimulus rivalry paradigm was developed, in part, to challenge the monocular channel hypothesis. In order to explain what the stimuli are that are used in this paradigm, and how the percepts that they cause can be explained, it is convenient to use the standard notation Hz for Hertz, where 1 Hz is an oscillatory cycle that lasts for 1000 milliseconds, or one second. The stimulus rivalry, or Flicker and Swap (F&S), paradigm of Logothetis, Leopold, and Sheinberg (1996) used a variant of the eye interchange technique. They repetitively exchanged perpendicular gratings to the two eyes every 333 milliseconds. In addition, the gratings were rapidly flickered at 18 Hz. While viewing relatively low contrast gratings, their observers reported that fluctuations in visibility between the rival targets followed a slow, irregular rhythm with dominance durations of about 2.35 seconds, which span approximately 7 swaps. This switching rate resembles that of conventional rivalry. Logothetis et al. called this *stimulus* rivalry because the extended durations of exclusive dominance were longer than the exchange rate. They more generally concluded that rivalry under conventional conditions, wherein stimuli are not swapped between the eyes, entails alternations in dominance between competing stimuli, not between competing eyes.

Lee and Blake (1999) showed, however, that the F&S stimulus rivalry effect in Logothetis et al. (1996), unlike conventional binocular rivalry, occurs only when stimulus contrast is low and swapping is fast. These conditions are known to disrupt conventional binocular rivalry. With high contrast and slow swapping, subjects reported rapid rivalry alternations, or eye rivalry.

Explaining stimulus rivalry and eye rivalry data in a unified way: Habituation again! 3D LAMINART simulations exhibit the same results as *all* of these experimental data and, in so doing, clarify how stimulus rivalry and eye rivalry properties can coexist. As in the experiment of Logothetis et al. (1996), the model inputs were perpendicular monocular gratings that were flickered on and off at 18 Hz. Figure 11.37 shows the simulation results for non-reversal trials, in which the orientations of stimuli remained unchanged in each eye, with a vertical grating presented to the right eye and a horizontal grating presented to the left eye throughout the trial. The binocular cell activities in Figure 11.37a oscillate in response to the rivalrous, but sustained, left and right eye inputs to them at a dominance duration of around 2.3 seconds. Figure 11.38 shows the result for reversal trials, in which the flickering gratings were exchanged between the two eyes every 333 ms. Here, the dominance duration of the binocular cells in Figure 11.38a is again around 2.3 seconds. In addition, this duration spans about seven swaps, as seen in the monocular cell responses in Figures 11.38b and 11.38c, thereby simulating the main effects that were reported by Logothetis et al. (1996).

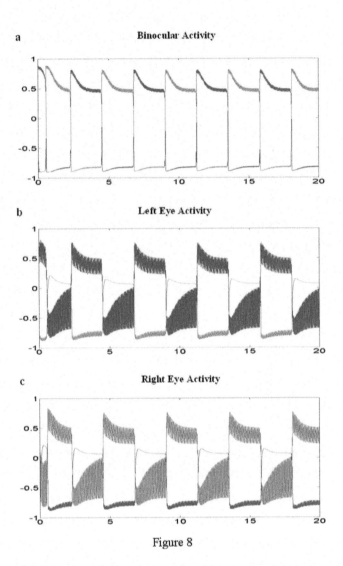

Figure 8

FIGURE 11.37. Simulation of the no swap baseline condition of Logothetis, Leopold, and Sheinberg (1996).

In the next simulation, as in the experiment of Lee and Blake (1999), the stimulus contrast of the grating stimuli was doubled and presented at a slower swapping rate. The simulation result is shown in Figure 11.39. Here, rapid eye rivalry alternations occur in the binocular cells (Figure 11.39a), rather than the slow, irregular changes that are characteristic of stimulus rivalry (Figure 11.38a).

How does the 3D LAMINART model generate these results? To explain this, I will first review relevant cortical anatomy before explaining the dynamics. A main theme is that both monocular and binocular cells are needed to understand 3D vision, as I showed to explain DaVinci stereopsis (e.g., Figure 11.13). Accordingly, the model circuits within Figures 4.58 and 11.10 includes both monocular simple and complex cells from layers 6 through 2/3A of V1, and binocular grouping cells in layer 2/3 of V2. These V2 binocular grouping cells receive inputs from V2 layer 4 cells that sum all monocular and binocular inputs from

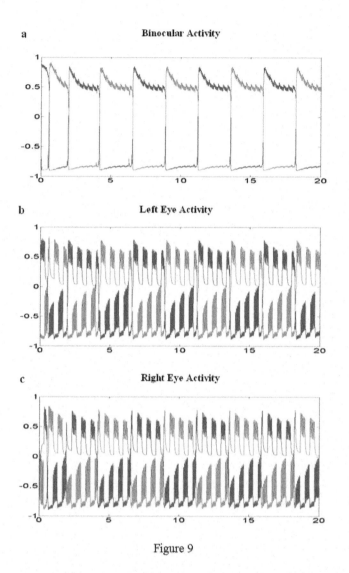

Figure 9

FIGURE 11.38. Simulation of the swap condition of Logothetis, Leopold, and Sheinberg (1996).

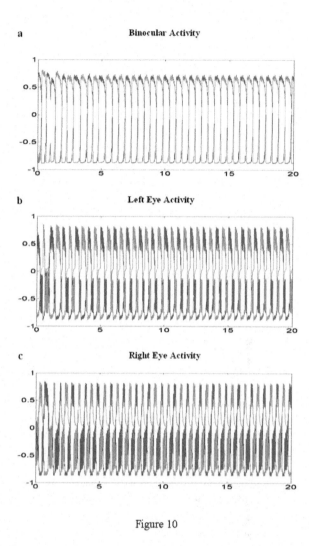

Figure 10

FIGURE 11.39. Simulation of eye rivalry data of Lee and Blake (1999).

V1. The bottom-up monocular pathways in layers 6-to-4 of V1 can also be modulated by feedback from binocular groupings in V2 layer 2/3 that reach V1 layer 6 and then propagate up to V1 layer 4 (Figure 11.12). Both intraocular orientational competition within V1 monocular channels and interocular competition between V1 monocular channels occur, where eye rivalry can originate.

The dynamics of stimulus rivalry and eye rivalry may be intuitively explained as follows. When a vertical grating in the left eye wins, its habituative transmitter gate will deplete, while the habituative transmitter gate of the losing horizontal grating accumulates. Slow swapping allows transmitter depletion and accumulation processes to progress sufficiently between swaps. When, for example, a swap from a vertical grating to a horizontal grating in the left eye occurs, then the horizontal grating can win quickly because of its accumulated habituative transmitter value. A high contrast can greatly enhance this process, because

the habituation rate is activity-dependent, as occurs during rapid eye rivalry. On the other hand, when a swap is too fast, the habituative transmitters cannot deplete and accumulate sufficiently between swaps, so that the swap cannot make the opposite grating win. As a result, it looks like the swap never happened. This generates the slow stimulus rivalry case. A low contrast will help the slow stimulus rivalry process by further slowing the rate of transmitter depletion and accumulation.

It cannot be overemphasized that these properties of habituative transmitters clarify how the brain resets cortical representations in response to *all* changing perceptual stimuli. Binocular rivalry is just one case of such a reset phenomenon. As noted above, another case where the sensitivity of habituation rate to stimulus contrast plays a role is in controlling the duration of visual persistence (Figures 7.2-7.6; Bowen, Pola, and Matin, 1974; Meyer, Lawson, and Cohen, 1975; Meyer and Ming, 1988), many properties of which have also been quantitatively simulated by interactions of bipole grouping, orientational competition, and habituative transmitters (Francis and Grossberg, 1996; Francis, Grossberg, and Mingolla, 1994).

The model explanation of how stimulus rivalry and eye rivalry can coexist is also consistent with data showing that, for stimuli rapidly swapped between the eyes, rivalry shifts gradually from eye rivalry to stimulus, or pattern, rivalry when pattern coherence, as reflected by properties such as texture uniformity and contour smoothness, is increased (Bonneh and Sagi, 1999; Bonneh, Sagi, and Karni, 2001). More generally, such data support the prediction that perceptual grouping plays a key role in binocular rivalry, just as it does in explaining many data about normal non-rivalrous 3D vision within the 3D LAMINART model.

Explaining stable and bistable percepts of slanted surfaces in depth: Necker cube. The topic of 3D vision is as inexhaustibly rich as our visual experiences of the world. The topics that I have discussed so far were chosen for their intrinsic interest, as well as because they illustrate important foundational properties of these experiences, and the design principles and neural mechanisms whereby the visual brain has enabled them. One more topic will be described, both because it extends the above analyses of how stable and rivalrous vision coexist, and also because it points to how we experience objects that are curved and slanted in 3D. A good example for focusing ideas about these themes is the famous Necker cube that was already depicted in Figure 4.43b. Although the Necker cube stimulus is a 2D picture, it can induce two different percepts of 3D parallelopipeds that can oscillate bistably through time. The sides of these parallelopipeds are, moreover, slanted in depth.

As with so many examples of how we see, the Necker cube points to a quite different kind of geometry of space than we typically learn about in school. I already noted in Chapters 1 and 3 that the processing of boundary grouping by bipole cells embodies a different kind of geometry than the classical Euclidean geometry of points and lines. Instead of points and lines, our brains compute coherent context-sensitive boundary groupings that may be rendered visible as filled-in surfaces. The same is true of how our brains compute end gaps and end cuts at the ends of lines and other high curvature points (Figures 4.22 and 4.24).

Figure 11.40 illustrates yet another way in which the geometrical representations of our brains differ dramatically from those that are taught in school about classical geometrical concepts. This figure shows how three different planar surfaces,

shown in red, green, and blue, can be combined in different ways to generate two images that are perceived as parallelopipeds slanted in depth. Consider the long edges of the green parallelogram that forms one side of each parallelepiped. The long green edge in the left parallelopiped appears to go from far-to-near. In contrast, the *same* long green edge of the right parallelopiped appears to go from near-to-far! This example shows, in a dramatic way, that our percepts of geometrical features, such as lines, that we may think are locally defined, are really the result of subtle context-sensitive interactions.

What kind of contextual information distinguishes the left parallelopiped from the right one? One important factor is the angles that the edges of each parallelogram makes with the other parallelograms in the figure. These angles help to determine which edges in each parallelogram look flat in depth, and which look slanted. The edges that look flat may be grouped by the types of collinear bipole cells with which we are already familiar. Slanted straight edges may be said to fall along a colinear *disparity gradient*, either from far-to-near or from near-to-far. Arguing from "flat" bipole cells, one might expect that there are also collinear "disparity-gradient" bipole cells that can group along slanted straight edges between multiple depths. How about the groupings that involve angles? Do angle cells also exist? And if they do, are they related to collinear bipole cells and, if so, how?

To understand these issues, two things are worth keeping in mind: First, each bipole cell has two "poles" along which it receives its inputs. If these poles are collinear and flat, then the result is the usual bipole cell. If they are

3D REPRESENTATION OF 2D IMAGES

Monocular cues (e.g angles) can interact together to yield 3D interpretation

Monocular cues by themselves are often ambiguous

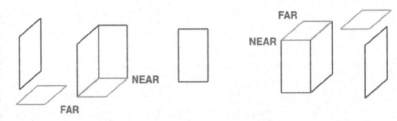

SAME ANGLES AND SHAPES, DIFFERENT SURFACE SLANTS

How do these ambiguous 2D shapes contextually define a 3D object form?

FIGURE 11.40. When planar 2D parallelograms are juxtaposed, the resultant forms generate 3D percepts that are sensitive to the configuration of angles and edges in the figure. See the text for why.

collinear along a disparity gradient, then the result is a disparity-gradient bipole cell. If, however, the poles are not collinear, then the result is an angle cell.

The second thing worth keeping in mind is this: Even a flat bipole cell does not group along a straight line on the cortical map! This is because the cortical map is computed in log polar coordinates, not Euclidean coordinates (Figure 6.10). Thus, even a flat bipole cell is an "angle" cell on the log polar cortical map! If even flat bipole cells are angle cells, then so too are disparity-gradient bipole cells. In addition, what we have called angle cells need to exist with multiple angular sizes in order to represent the multiple 3D shapes to which an individual may be exposed through his or her life.

Once it is realized that all three types of cells are, mechanistically speaking, angle cells, albeit with "angles" of different sizes, then it becomes clear that the particular angles that they represent must be learned. I showed how this can happen in a unified way for all three kinds of cells in a 2004 article with my PhD student Guru Swaminathan (Grossberg and Swaminathan, 2004). Perhaps not surprisingly, the same combination of instar and outstar learning embedded in a competitive network (Figures 5.11-5.18) that had earlier been used to explain basic data about cortical map formation (e.g., Grossberg and Seitz, 2003; Grossberg and Williamson, 2001) was also able to explain how bipole, disparity-gradient, and angle cells could develop from the same set of developmental learning laws when they respond to different visual statistics.

Two more questions immediately come to mind: Do bipole, disparity-gradient, and angle cells exist in visual cortex? And how, exactly, can they be used to explain percepts of slanted 3D shapes, as in the percepts generated by Figure 11.40? My article with Guru reviews ample neurobiological data that answer the first question in the affirmative. More generally, my work with Guru extended the 3D LAMINART model in a consistent way to incorporate flat bipole cells, angle cells, and disparity-gradient cells (Figure 11.41), as a natural generalization of the more familiar bipole cells. In order to explain how these various cell types could fit, or be multiplexed, into the cortical map, Guru and I drew a speculative diagram of a hypothetical cortical hypercolumn that could accommodate the required richness of cell types (Figure 11.42). Hopefully, this diagram will inspire more experiments on this topic, if only to refine or even disconfirm it.

The enhanced 3D LAMINART model in Figure 11.41 also explains the slanted percepts generated by Figure

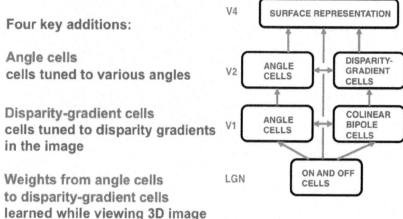

3D LAMINART MODEL

Four key additions:

Angle cells
cells tuned to various angles

Disparity-gradient cells
cells tuned to disparity gradients in the image

Weights from angle cells
to disparity-gradient cells learned while viewing 3D image

Colinear grouping
between angle cells and disparity-gradient cells disambiguates ambiguous groupings

FIGURE 11.41. The 3D LAMINART model proposes how angle cells and disparity-gradient interact through learning to generate 3D representations of slanted objects.

11.40. The basic idea is that angle cells can get associated with combinations of flat bipole cells and/or disparity-gradient cells, again using the same learning laws when they are driven by the statistics of the visual environment. For example, one pair of angle cells may be associatively linked with a flat vertical or horizontal collinear bipole cell. Another combination of angle cells might be associatively linked with a far-to-near disparity-gradient cell. And so on.

HYPERCOLUMN REPRESENTATION OF ANGLES

FIGURE 11.42. A hypothetical cortical hypercolumn structure proposes how angle cells and disparity gradient cells, including bipole cells that stay within a given depth, may self-organize during development.

Our most delightful explanatory target was to simulate how the two different 3D boundary and surface representations of the Necker cube form, and how they oscillate bistably through time. It should now be no surprise that the same activity-dependent habituative transmitters that help to explain binocular rivalry data also help to explain the bistability of the Necker cue. We also showed how paying attention to one edge of the cube could

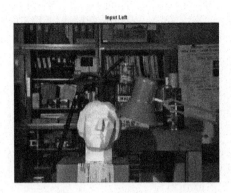

FIGURE 11.43. A pair of disparate images of a scene from the University of Tsukuba Multiview Image Database.

cause it to pop forward in depth, and thereby force a switch to that 3D representation of the cube. This explanation uses the same mechanisms of how spatial attention flows along a boundary, with its attendant enhancement of boundary strength (Figures 6.5 and 6.6), end cutting (Figure 4.43a), and figure-ground separation (Figures 4.51 and 4.54), that were used to show how many other 3D percepts pop forward in depth when enhanced by spatial attention; e.g., the bistable percept of Peter Tse in Figure 4.43c. To the best of my knowledge, our simulation of the Necker cube is still the only one that explains its perceptual properties.

3D boundary and surface representations of natural scenes. The 3D LAMINART model was developed with inspiration from large numbers of psychophysical experiments. Most of its simulations have accordingly offered explanations of the percepts that are generated by visual stimuli in the laboratory. Our ultimate goal, of course, is to understand how our brains see in the real world. Accordingly, the 3D LAMINART has also been used to automatically generate 3D boundary and surface representations of natural scenes. Yongqiang Cao and I were in the midst of this study just before he left to join the research staff of HRL Laboratories in Malibu, California in 2014, after which he left with several colleagues to go to Intel Labs, so it took longer to finish that would otherwise have been the case (Cao and Grossberg, 2019).

Although a great deal more research can profitably be done on this huge research topic, the model in its current form already does a creditable job, as illustrated by its reconstruction of a famous

scene from the University of Tsukuba Multiview Image Database. The left and right eye images of this scene are shown in the top row of Figure 11.43. Figure 11.44 summarizes a computer simulation of the model's 3D surface

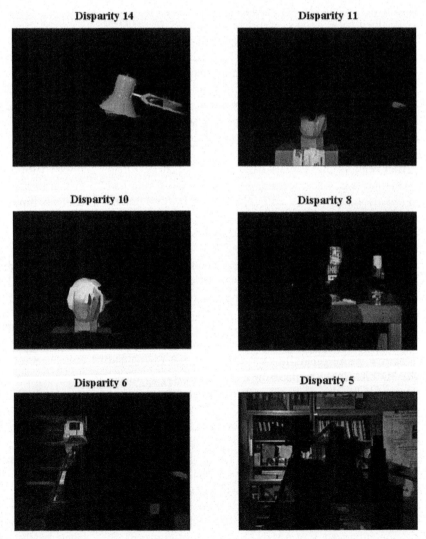

FIGURE 11.44. 3D scenic reconstruction of the image in Figure 11.43 by the 3D LAMINART model.

lightness representation. Each major part of the scene (lamp, statue of head, bottle, table, camera, bookcase and other background featural details) are correctly separated in depth and filled-in. Drs. Y. Ohta and Y. Nakamura kindly provided us with the ground truth data from the University of Tuskuba. With this information, we constructed a disparity map of the model's 3D surface representation and compared it with the ground truth data. Our best estimated disparity map for this reconstruction had an accuracy of 96.2%. This accuracy is comparable to the top-of-the-line machine vision results of Zitnick and Kanade (2000) that produced only a disparity map, not a reconstruction of surface lightnesses, and did not use mechanisms that are biologically plausible to do so (Zitnick and Kanada, 2000)

Successful processing of natural 3D scenes added to the list of natural images that our models could handle, including images of natural scenes that were acquired with artificial sensors, such as the kind of SAR image that is summarized in Figure 3.24. It is perhaps worth noting that our processing of SAR images used multiple boundary and surface scales which, as I noted in Figures 11.29 and 11.30, is often important for preprocessing 3D information. Figure 11.45 shows the multiple-scale boundaries and surfaces that were generated by the SAR image in Figure 3.24 (top row, left column). Each of the three boundary scales in the image (small, medium, large) groups together image data that have enough statistical regularity relative to its scale. The boundaries before and after bipole boundary completion are shown in the top and middle rows. Note that the small boundary scale can sense details like the individual posts on the bridge, whereas the large boundary scale senses more global bridge structure. Each of these emergent boundary webs creates the compartments to which surface filling-in is restricted. The bottom row shows how the filled-in surfaces reflect the corresponding boundary compartments. The final image reconstruction in Figure 3.24 (bottom

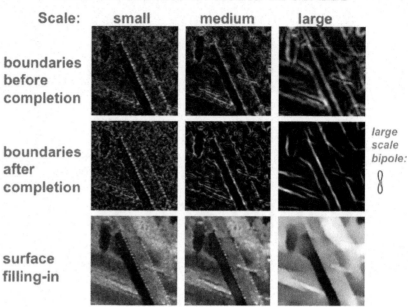

FIGURE 11.45. The multiple boundary and surface scales that were used to simulate a reconstruction of the SAR image in Figure 3.24.

row, right column) is a weighted average of all three scales of boundary and surface representation. Another example of how our models successfully process natural scenes was summarized in Figures 9.23-9.26, which showed how they could extract heading information from video during optic flow navigation.

The field of 3D vision is as vast as our experiences with the real world, the artistic representations of the world that myriad artists have created, and all the pictorial representations that our entertainment and technology industries present us with, knowing that our brains can effortlessly generate 3D representations of their 2D images. I hope that I have summarized enough design principles, mechanisms, data explanations, and technological applications to interest you in further studying the FACADE, 3D LAMINART, and 3D FORMOTION models to learn more about what has already been explained, and for those who can, to further develop these theories to enable modeling insights about how we see to transform many aspects of our lives in a constructive way.

12

From Seeing and Reaching to Hearing and Speaking

Circular reaction, streaming, working memory, chunking, and number

What and Where/How Streams for Audition

Ventral sound-to-meaning vs. dorsal sound-to-action: Complementary invariants. The concepts and processes that have helped to understand aspects of conscious visual perception are also useful towards explaining properties about conscious auditory perception. This is true because there are strong homologs between the cortical streams that process vision and audition. Just as there are What and Where/How cortical streams for visual processing (Figure 1.19), What and Where/How cortical streams for auditory processing have also been described, notably by Josef Rauschecker and his colleagues (e.g., Rauschecker, 1998; Rauschecker and Tian, 2000). There is a ventral pathway into anterior temporal cortex that carries out identification of complex auditory patterns or objects, and a dorsal pathway into posterior parietal cortex that carries out spatial processing, with primary visual cortex V1 replaced by primary auditory cortex A1 (Figure 12.1). Gregory Hickok and David Poeppel (Hickok and Poeppel, 2007) have summarized this dichotomy by linking the ventral pathway with *sound-to-meaning* and the dorsal pathway with *sound-to-action*. In other words, auditory as well as visual processes are organized into computationally complementary cortical processing streams (Table 1.1).

How complete is the homolog that is suggested by the fact that both auditory and visual processing use temporal and parietal cortices? If the homology is strong, what types of auditory properties should we expect from it? In attempting to answer this question, one needs to acknowledge that both auditory and visual processing compute *invariants* to be effective. For example, as I summarized in Chapter 6, conscious seeing uses retinotopic surface representations and head-centered shrouds to maintain perceptual stability during eye movements, thereby both stabilizing conscious percepts of visual qualia as the eyes move, and enabling visual recognition categories to be learned that are significantly invariant under changes in object view, position, and size. What mechanisms maintain perceptual stability of auditory conscious percepts, and what

Conscious MIND Resonant BRAIN. Stephen Grossberg, Oxford University Press. © Oxford University Press 2021.
DOI: 10.1093/oso/9780190070557.003.0012

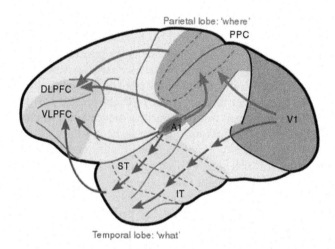

FIGURE 12.1. A What ventral cortical stream and Where/How dorsal cortical stream have been described for audition, no less than for vision.

kinds of invariants are learned by auditory recognition categories?

In the auditory domain, any mechanistically satisfying answer to this question would address, at least in part, the following phenomena that I will discuss below: How can a young child babble sounds in one set of acoustic frequencies and use them to learn how to imitate sounds from teachers, including parents, who speak using different frequencies? How can codes for speech and language meanings be coded in a speaker-invariant and rate-invariant way in order to prevent a combinatorial explosion of stored memories, for much the same reason that learned visual object recognition codes are invariant under view, position, and size? How does the brain compute these speaker and rate invariants, despite the fact that they are not present in acoustic signals? Given that the brain learns to recognize speech and language meanings in a speaker-invariant way, how can speaker identity nonetheless be learned too, so that different voices can be consciously heard and recognized? Moreover, how do our brains join together these two kinds of information? Most importantly, how do speaker-invariant and speaker-sensitive representations interact to understand the meaning and identity of an identifiable acoustic source? Given that codes for speech and language meaning are stored in a rate-invariant way, how can these meanings be performed from memory at variable rates that are under volitional control? In particular, how can rate-invariant codes be performed as the lyrics of songs with different rhythms and pitches?

The sections below propose answers to these questions that illustrate complementary processes and ART resonances operating at multiple levels of the auditory system, just as they do in the visual system. As in the visual system, these ART resonances support conscious auditory experiences while stabilizing learning and memory of auditory

representations along the way. The text outlines an emerging unified neural system that combines modeling discoveries that have been developed to explain distinct databases about audition, speech, and language. In order to achieve this synthesis, new ideas about the mechanistic neural substrates of conscious auditory experiences are proposed, and explanations of many additional data are offered to support these ideas.

Despite all this progress, a great deal of additional experimental and theoretical work can profitably be done to further develop this theoretical foundation. Studies of auditory brain processes have tended to lag behind those of visual processes if only because all auditory processing is fleeting in time, whereas many aspects of vision are more static, such as the processing of boundaries and surfaces in response to unmoving visual stimuli. Both the study of motion perception in vision and the study of auditory perception in general needed to await technological methods that could control processes which change rapidly through time before these fields could take off experimentally.

Circular reactions in vision and audition: Babbling to reach and to speak. A helpful way to understand auditory-visual homologs is to consider the perception-action *circular reactions* that occur during auditory and visual development, and to whose understanding the pioneering Swiss clinical and developmental psychologist Jean Piaget so richly contributed (e.g., Piaget, 1945, 1951, 1952). All babies normally go through a *babbling phase*, and it is during such a babbling phase that a circular reaction can be learned. In particular, during a visual circular reaction, babies endogenously babble, or spontaneously generate, hand/arm movements to multiple positions around their bodies. As their hands move in front of them, their eyes automatically, or reactively, look at their moving hands. While the baby's eyes are looking at its moving hands, the baby learns an associative map from its hand positions to the corresponding eye positions, *and* from eye positions to hand positions. Learning of the map between eye and hand in both directions constitutes the "circular" reaction.

After map learning occurs, when a baby, child, or adult looks at a target position with its eyes, this eye position can use the learned associative map to activate a movement command to reach the corresponding position in space. If "the will to act" is activated by opening the correct basal ganglia gate (Figure 6.13), then the hand/arm can reach to the foveated position in space under volitional control. In this way, the babbled movements endogenously sweep out the "work space" within which a baby can reach, and the learned associations between looking and reaching that are thereby established can be used to control reaching under volitional control, as when a baby looks at her toes and then moves her hands to hold them. Because our bodies continue to grow for many years as we develop from babies into children, teenagers, and adults, these maps need to continue updating themselves, and they must do so without becoming catastrophically destabilized. I will explain how this may be achieved later in this chapter.

There is also an auditory circular reaction that occurs during its own babbling phase. During an auditory circular reaction, babies endogenously babble simple sounds that sweep out the "work space" of sounds that they can create. They also hear the sounds that they create in this way. When the motor commands that caused the sounds and the auditory representations of the heard sounds are simultaneously active in the baby's brain, it can learn a map between these auditory representations and the motor commands that produced them. This map is also "circular" in a sense that I will explain below.

After a sufficient amount of map learning occurs, a child can use the map to imitate sounds from adult speakers, and thereby begins to learn how to speak using increasingly complicated speech and language utterances, again under volitional control.

For either of the visual or auditory circular reactions to be able to support future volitional behaviors of reaching or speaking, multiple design problems need to be solved by the brain, as I will now explain.

Vector Integration to Endpoint control of arm movement trajectories. Chapter 6 explained how and why visual surface representations that can become conscious are well-positioned in the brain to control eye movements and arm reaches. To what extent do similar conclusions hold for the relationship between auditory consciousness and speech production? In particular, are *reaching* and *speech production* controlled by homologous neural systems? I now summarize evidence that the answer is Yes.

During a visual circular reaction, the brain learns to associate hand positions with eye positions and eye positions with hand positions. Visual cues enter the brain through the retina, but the eyes move in the head and the hand/arm system moves in the body. This learning process thus includes learned coordinate transformations from retinotopic visual coordinates to head-centered coordinates, which the eyes use to look at the object, and to body-centered motor coordinates, which the hand/arm uses to reach towards it. All of these coordinate changes are learned during the visual circular reaction, and are later refined as the body grows to be able to continue to generate accurate looking and reaching movements, under basal ganglia control, towards valued goal objects.

In order for me to explain in greater detail how a visual circular reaction enables reaching to occur, I need to review how a reaching movement is controlled by the brain. I will do this starting with the simplest neural model of this process, and then gradually generalize it until I have enough concepts before us to complete the explanation.

In particular, when a desired goal object is visually attended, the learned mapping due to the visuo-motor

circular reaction can activate a desired hand/arm *target position vector*, or T, with which to reach it (Figure 12.2). The target position vector represents the position to which the brain wants the arm to move. This target position representation is compared to the current hand/arm position, called the *present position vector*, or P. The present position vector is computed from the outflow movement command that is currently holding the arm in its current position, and will be used to move it as the present position vector changes. In order to both command the arm to move, and to represent the position at which the arm currently is, the brain uses two parallel pathways. The first pathway holds the arm in place. The second path represents the position in which the arm currently is. This latter pathway is called an *efference copy* or *corollary* discharge (Figure 9.6). Johann Georg Steinbuch and Herman von Helmholtz are two of the scientists who first realized its importance in motor control (Helmholtz, 1924; Steinbuch, 1811). Helmholtz asserted that the world looks stable when your eyes move because an efference copy compensates for your eye movement. In contrast, if you use your fingers to externally jiggle your eye ball back and forth, then the world also seems to move because there is no efference copy to compensate in that case. I discussed in Chapter 6 how the brain uses efference copies to explain how we learn invariant object categories (see Figure 6.16), as well as to explain how we experience a stable visual world as we move our eyes, as Helmholtz had noted (see Figures 6.25 and 6.26).

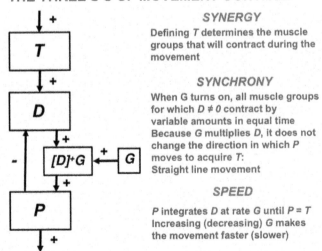

THE THREE S'S OF MOVEMENT CONTROL

SYNERGY
Defining *T* determines the muscle groups that will contract during the movement

SYNCHRONY
When G turns on, all muscle groups for which *D ≠ 0* contract by variable amounts in equal time Because *G* multiplies *D*, it does not change the direction in which *P* moves to acquire *T*: Straight line movement

SPEED
P integrates *D* at rate *G* until *P = T* Increasing (decreasing) *G* makes the movement faster (slower)

FIGURE 12.2. The Vector Integration to Endpoint, or VITE, model of arm trajectory formation enables the three S's of a movement to be realized: Synergy formation, Synchrony of muscles within a synergy, and variable Speed that is under volitional control (G). This is accomplished by subtracting a present position vector (P) from a target position vector (T) to form a difference vector (V) which moves P towards T at a speed that is determined by G.

The concept of efference copy has a long and complicated history in psychology and neuroscience, as illustrated by the fact that Nobel laureate Roger Sperry first introduced in 1950 the equivalent name of corollary discharge for it as part of his study of the optokinetic reflex (Sperry, 1950). This reflex enables an individual to follow a moving object with her eyes until it moves out of the field of vision. Then the eyes move back to the position they were in when the object was first seen. Sperry studied why animals with inverted vision that is caused by surgical eye rotation lose this stability. Instead, they tend to turn continuously in circles. Sperry was led by these experiments to reassert the importance of the corollary discharge in maintaining visual and postural stability during normal circumstances.

An efference copy, or corollary discharge, is also used to move an arm to a desired new target position. To accomplish this, the efference copy defines the present position vector that is subtracted from the target position vector to compute a *difference vector*, or D (Figure 12.2). The difference vector codes the direction and distance that the hand/arm needs to move from its present position to the desired target position. In the 1980s, Apostolos Georgopoulos and his colleagues published beautiful neurophysiological data showing how populations of cells in the motor cortex compute difference vectors with which to control arm movements (Figure 12.3; Georgopoulos et al., 1982; Georgopoulos, Schwartz, and Kettner, 1986). Figure 12.3 (left panel) shows an orderly variation in the frequencies of discharge, shown as time series of spikes, of a single

motor cortical cell as the directions of movement are varied. The arrows in the center of the figure point in each movement direction. This particular cell fires more for movement directions between 90 and 235 degrees. Clearly its directional selectivity, acting alone, is insufficient to determine a movement direction with sufficient precision. In contrast, Figure 12.3 (right panel) summarizes the firing patterns of all the cells in a motor cortical population, and shows how the vector average of these patterns accurately predicts the actual direction of the arm movement (compare the dashed and solid arrows).

The computation of difference vectors in the Where cortical stream illustrates one of the computationally complementary properties of the What and Where cortical streams (Table 1.2). Whereas a good match between a top-down expectation and a bottom-up input pattern in the What cortical stream can lead to an ART-like excitatory resonance, a good match in the Where cortical stream between a target position vector and present position vector leads to a zero difference vector, and is thus inhibitory. That is why, among other differences, ART-like matching in the What stream can solve the stability-plasticity dilemma, and thereby enable us to learn increasing expertise about the world. In contrast, Where stream inhibitory matching, which I call VAM-like matching, after the Vector Associative Map model (Gaudiano and Grossberg, 1991), leads to continual relearning of sensory-motor maps and commands with which to accurately control our current bodily parameters, as I will explain shortly.

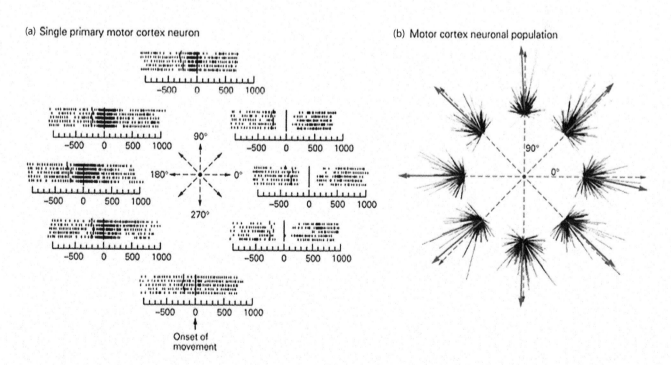

(a) Single primary motor cortex neuron

(b) Motor cortex neuronal population

Onset of movement

FIGURE 12.3. Neurophysiological data showing how motor cortical cells code different vectors that are sensitive to both the direction of the commanded movement and its length.

A difference vector can be large without any overt movement occurring. Said in another way: We can be *ready*, or *primed*, to launch a movement before we volitionally will the movement to occur. A volitional *GO signal*, or G, from the basal ganglia (Prescott, Gurney, and Redgrave, 2003) gates, or multiplies, the difference vector to determine which arm will move and the speed with which it will approach the target position. An overt movement can occur only when the GO signal is positive, and movement speed increases as the GO signal becomes larger.

To explain how arm movement trajectories are controlled by the brain, I published the Vector Integration to Endpoint, or VITE, model (Figure 12.2), in 1988 with Daniel Bullock, who was then my postdoctoral fellow and is now a senior faculty colleague (Bullock and Grossberg, 1988). The VITE model circuit is homologous to a circuit for the control of saccadic eye movements that I had just published in a book about many aspects of eye movement control with my postdoctoral fellow Michael Kuperstein in 1986 (Grossberg and Kuperstein, 1986). There are similarities and differences between the eye and arm movement controllers that I will not dwell upon here, except to note two striking and immediately relevant differences: Whereas saccadic eye movements tend to move our eyes as quickly as possible to each movement target, arm movements can be carried out with variable speeds that are under volitional control. Whereas eye movements are never burdened by unexpected loads, arm movements are designed to move around loads that may differ greatly in their weight. These functional differences lead to differences in the VITE and related circuits that control arm movement trajectories.

The three S's of movement control: Synergy, Synchrony, and Speed. The VITE model uses the T, P, and D vectors to clarify how the Three S's of reaching—Synergy, Synchrony, and Speed—are carried out. The first S is the flexible choice of a motor Synergy. In other words, T defines the collection, or Synergy, of muscle groups that will contract to carry out the desired arm movement. The second S controls the Synchronous performance of this arm movement. In other words, the muscles in the chosen Synergy contract together during the same time interval, even if they contract by different amounts. Finally, the third S enables the VITE model to cause the same arm movement trajectory to be executed at variable Speeds. Increasing the GO signal translates into a faster performance speed.

Because of the three S's, the VITE model can explain how a simple reaching movement by an arm can be carried out in an approximately straight movement trajectory through space. Then sequences of arm movements can be combined to carry out more complex motor skills.

The three S's of reaching follow from the fact that the volitional GO signal G *multiplies* the difference vector D, or more precisely the thresholded difference vector

$[D]^+ = \max(D, 0)$, to form the product $[D]^+ G$ in Figure 12.2. Multiplication by G does not change the direction in which the arm moves, so the same arm movement trajectory can be traversed in response to any positive value of G. The product $[D]^+ G$ is integrated through time by P until P equals T. When this happens, the arm has attained the desired target position. Multiplying by G hereby ensures that all the muscles in the Synergy get integrated with velocities that scale proportionally with the distances that they have to travel, and thus ensure that contractions within the Synergy are Synchronous during the movement. Indeed, just as P is the outflow present position vector of the VITE circuit, $[D]^+ G$ is the *outflow velocity vector* of the circuit. Because this vector is integrated by P, changing G changes the rate at which P approaches T, and thus the velocity of movement, with smaller Gs causing slower movements, and bigger Gs causing faster movements. Finally, the model's name, Vector Integration to Endpoint, describes the fact that the difference vector D is integrated at a G-modulated rate until P equals the desired endpoint T.

Variant and invariant properties of arm movement trajectories under size and speed changes. Although the neural processes that are modeled by VITE are conceptually and computationally very simple, they enabled Dan Bullock and me to quantitatively explain and simulate a remarkable amount of challenging psychophysical data about reaching behaviors, and the anatomical and neurophysiological data about the brain regions that carry them out. These simulations included the neurophysiologically recorded response profiles of the population activity that controls an arm movement (Figure 12.4); how the shape of the velocity profile is approximately preserved as the size of a movement increases if its GO signal remains the same, as illustrated in the VITE simulation summarized in Figure 12.5; how the shape of the velocity profile become more symmetric through time (e.g., Atkeson and Hollerbach, 1985; Beggs and Howarth, 1972; Zelaznik et al., 1986) when the arm movement is carried out at a faster speed; and how arm movement velocity can get amplified to up to three times the maximum speed that is attained by a single movement if a second target position is turned on while the arm is moving to a first movement target (Georgopoulos, Kalaska, and Massey, 1981), thereby causing the arm to switch towards the second target before it reaches the first target, as shown in Figure 12.6, and simulated by the VITE model in Figure 12.7.

Figure 12.4 (top image) shows the population activity of movement vector cells, above six raster plots of the spikes that go into the population response from six of the contributing cells. Our simulation of this result shows the plots through time of the difference vector V, GO signal G, present position vector P, and outflow velocity

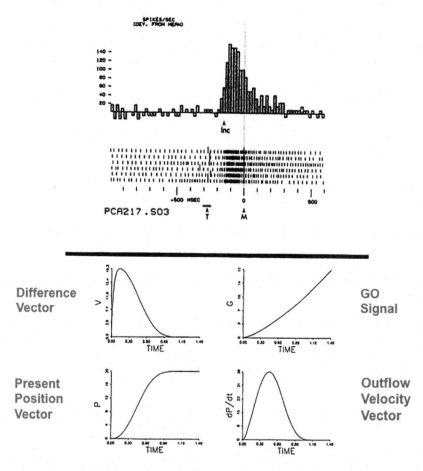

FIGURE 12.4. (top half) Neurophysiological data of vector cell responses in motor cortex. (bottom half) VITE model simulations of a simple movement in which the model's difference vector simulates the data as an emergent property of network interactions.

computes the ratio of the time it takes to move half the distance, to the time it takes to complete the trajectory. SR can become greater than .5 if the GO signal is increased even more, as also occurs in the data. This is due to the fact that faster GO signals grow faster and thus reduce the amount of asymmetry that otherwise would be caused by their initially small values. These results about velocity profile asymmetry follow easily from VITE model mechanisms, but are incompatible with many other models of arm movement control, notably models that depend upon global optimization principles such as minimal jerk (e.g., Hogan, 1984), which also have conceptual properties that are hard to realize biologically, such as the imposition of a global optimization constraint over an entire movement trajectory, even before it has begun to be performed.

Figure 12.6 shows one movement that can reach the first target (marked with a + sign diagonally to the right), after which it moves to the second target (marked with a + sign diagonally to the left). The second movement occurs when the onset of the second target occurs 300 milliseconds after the first target, thereby allowing the first arm movement to be completed before the second arm movement begins. The two other trajectories that are shown occur with the onset of the second target occurring only 100 and 30 milli-

vector dP/dt. The neurophysiological population response is compared with the difference vector V. Note that, because G starts out at a value of zero, when it multiplies V and the product is integrated by P, the resulting velocity vector dP/dt is more symmetric through time than the shape of V alone, since V times G at early times is smaller than V alone is.

The velocity profiles dP/dt in Figure 12.5a (bottom row) and Figures 12.5b (bottom row) have the same shape—that is, are invariant—because, although their difference vectors V start out different in order to create movements of different size, they are multiplied at each time by the same GO signal G. As a result, the larger trajectory moves proportionally faster than the smaller trajectory, without changing its overall shape. When the two velocity profiles dP/dt have their size axes rescaled to match, they are identical, as also occurs in psychophysical data.

In both the data and VITE, the velocity profiles get more symmetric as the speed of movement is increased by increasing the size of the GO signal. The amount of symmetry is measured by the Symmetry Ratio, or SR, which

second delays after the first target position appears. In these two cases, the arm smoothly swerves from moving in the direction of the first target to that of the second target in mid course, and reaches the second target after reaching a higher maximum velocity than it did when it made a movement to a single target. Velocity amplification during a switch to a second target position in Figure 12.7 shows that this velocity amplification can occur for a simple reason within the VITE model; namely, whereas a first target position vector is initially multiplied by a small, but growing, G (Figure 12.7a, top row), the second target position vector is, from the very start, multiplied by the large G values that were attained during the movement towards the first target (Figure 12.7b, top row), and hence is driven by a GO signal that is generally bigger than the one that drove the first movement. As a result, in this simulation, the peak velocity of the switched target whose GO signal begins at a positive value (Figure 12.7b, bottom row) is 2.3 times larger than that of the peak velocity that is attained with a GO signal begins at zero.

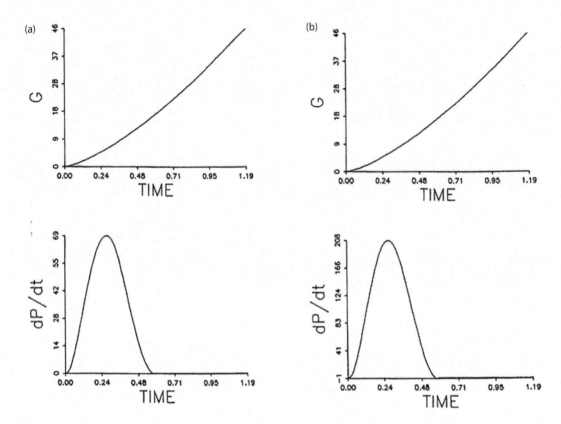

FIGURE 12.5. VITE simulation of velocity profile invariance if the same GO signal gates shorter (a) or longer (b) movements. Note the higher velocities in (b).

Dan Bullock and I chatted with Apostolos Georgopoulos about our explanation and simulation of this striking fact during one of his visits to our department to give a lecture. Apostolos told us that no one but us seemed to be interested in this fact, which to us was diagnostic of how a GO signal G changes through time as it multiplies a difference vector V to determine an outflow velocity command. Other simulated properties by the VITE model include challenging properties of isotonic arm movement properties before and after de-afferentation, Fitt's law, why the position of maximal curvature and the time of minimal velocity are correlated during two-part arm movements, and the 2/3 Power Law of Lacquiniti. These properties, among others, are also explained in Bullock and Grossberg (1988), wherein citations of the relevant experimental articles are also provided.

Despite its impressive explanatory range for a model that uses such a small number of simple concepts and mechanisms, the VITE model was just a first step in clarifying the neural mechanisms of arm movement trajectory control. Indeed, every model can only hope to articulate *necessary* conditions towards explaining a class of phenomena. Necessary and sufficient conditions would be tantamount to having a complete theory. Science typically progresses towards such a goal in stages, sometimes small ones, and sometimes in surprising, indeed conceptually shocking, leaps, such as the discovery of general relativity theory in physics. The goal of deriving a complete theory generally takes a long time to even approximate.

VITE itself contains some additional details that are needed for it to work properly. In particular, muscle

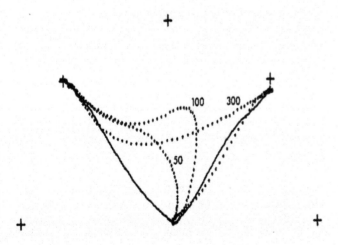

FIGURE 12.6. Monkeys seamlessly transformed a movement initiated towards the 2 o'clock target into one towards the 10 o'clock target when the later target was substituted 50 or 100 msec after activation of the first target light.

HIGHER PEAK VELOCITY DUE TO TARGET SWITCHING
VITE simulation of higher peak speed if second target rides on first GO signal

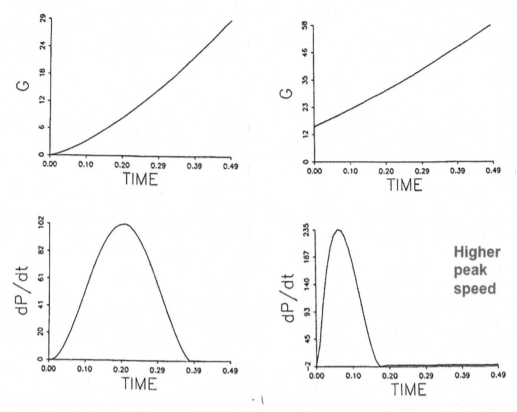

FIGURE 12.7. The left column simulation by VITE shows the velocity profile when the GO signal (G) starts with the movement. The right column shows that the peak velocity is much greater if a second movement begins when the GO signal is already positive.

groups are organized into agonist-antagonist pairs with, say, an agonist muscle like the biceps muscle in your arm contracting while an antagonist muscle like the triceps muscle relaxes. Corresponding, the VITE model circuit organizes its T, P, and V computations into mutually competing agonist-antagonist commands (Figure 12.8).

From VITE to VAM: How a circular reaction drives mismatch learning to calibrate the model. One elaboration of VITE, called the Vector Associative Map, or VAM model that I published with my PhD student Paolo Gaudiano in 1991 and 1992 (Gaudiano and Grossberg, 1991, 1992) shows how the signals used in VITE may be calibrated by learning to ensure that they actually work the way that they are supposed to work. In particular, the inputs to D from T and from P come from different cell populations and are carried by different pathways. It is too much to expect that the activities of these two networks of cells, and the gains of the pathways that carry their signals to D, become perfectly matched without the benefit

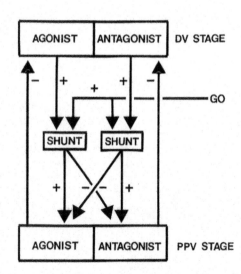

FIGURE 12.8. Agonist-antagonist opponent organization of difference vector (DV) and present position vector (PPV) processing stages and how GO signals gate them.

of some kind of learning. The VAM model demonstrates how these irregularities can be corrected by a form of mismatch learning that adaptively changes the gains in the T-to-D pathways until they match those in the P-to-D pathways.

The VAM model does this using a circular reaction that generates reactive movements which create a situation in which both T and P represent the same position in space. If the model were perfectly calibrated, the excitatory T-to-D and inhibitory P-to-D signals that input to D in response to the same positions at T and P would cancel, causing D to equal zero, since then the model has already moved the arm to where it wants it to be. If D is not zero under these circumstances, then the signals are not properly calibrated. VAM uses such non-zero D vectors as mismatch teaching signals that adaptively calibrate the T-to-D signals. As perfect calibration is achieved, D approaches zero, at which time mismatch learning self-terminates.

Figure 12.9 summarizes how this VAM circular reaction works. In this model, target position vectors (TPV) and present position vectors (PPV) are called target position commands (TPC) and present position commands (PPC), respectively. It took us awhile to settle down on the former names, since all the variables are, in fact, vectors. In Figure 12.9 (top row, left column), the circular reaction is turned on when the Endogenous Random Generator, or ERG+, sends random signals to the PPC that cause the arm to automatically babble a movement in its workspace. This movement is not under volitional control. When PPC gets

activated, in addition to causing the arm to move, it sends signals that input an inhibitory copy of the PPC to the DV.

The ERG, just like all VITE and VAM motor commands, has an opponent organization. It is the ERG ON, or ERG+, component that energizes the babbled arm moment. When ERG+ momentarily shuts off, ERG OFF, or ERG-, is disinhibited (Figure 12.9, top row, right column) and opens a Now Print, or NP, gate. This open gate enables a representation of the current arm position generate an excitatory input from the PPC to the TPC, where it is stored. At this moment, both TPC and PPC represent the same position in space.

When the TPC is activated, it sends excitatory signals to DV (Figure 12.9, bottom row, left column). These signals are adaptive, because they are multiplied by adaptive weights, or long-term memory (LTM) traces, before they reach DV. As this happens, the PPC inhibitory signals are subtracted from the TPC adaptive excitatory signals. If the DV does not equal zero, then the two sets of signals are not properly calibrated.

The LTM traces learn by a mismatch learning law that uses the DV as an error, or teaching, signal. This teaching signal has the effect of altering the LTM traces through learning until the DV shrinks to zero (Figure 12.9, bottom row, right column). After the DV equals zero in response to a representative set of babbled movement positions, then the VAM circuit is correctly calibrated to be able to generate accurate movements under volitional control. In particular, when the model volitionally inputs to DV a different TPC than the current PPC, then the non-zero DV that is computed correctly represents the direction and distance of the desired new movement. This movement can occur when a volitionally-controlled GO signal, which is a later developmental variant of the ERG, multiplies the DV and initiates its integration by the PPC until the new TPC is attained.

The VAM model includes all the circuits that are needed for the ERGs and all other circuit elements to work well on their own. Model simulations demonstrate how the model samples the work space during the critical period and learns the correct LTM traces with which to enable accurate later volitional movements to be made.

This kind of DV-mediated mismatch learning instantiates one of the kinds of mismatch learning in the Where cortical stream that is summarized in Table 1.2. Mismatch learning allows our spatial and movement control systems to adjust to our changing bodies through time. It is not the only kind of mismatch learning that occurs in these systems.

VECTOR ASSOCIATIVE MAP MODEL

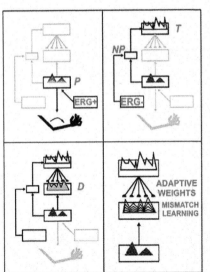

During critical period, Endogenous Random Generator (*ERG+*) turns on, activates *P*, and causes random movements that sample workspace

When ERG+ shuts off, posture occurs

ERG- then turns on (rebound) and opens Now Print (*NP*) gate, that dumps *P* into *T*

Mismatch learning enables adaptive weights between *T* and *D* to change until *D* (the mismatch!) approaches 0

Then *T* and *P* are both correctly calibrated to represent the same positions

FIGURE 12.9. How a Vector Associative Map, or VAM, model uses mismatch learning during its development to calibrate inputs from a target position vector (T) and a present position vector (P) via mismatch learning of adaptive weights at the difference vector (D). See the text for details.

Chapter 15 will discuss how a different kind of error-driven learning system occurs in the hippocampus, cerebellum, and basal ganglia to control adaptively-timed motivated attention, adaptively-timed motor control, and adaptively-timed reinforcement learning signals. All of these brain regions seem to have similar circuits and underlying biochemical mechanisms, despite their different behavioral functions.

I already noted in Chapter 5 how the hippocampus may also be involved in the control of memory consolidation during ART category learning. Each part of the brain may carry out several different functions, and it is always interesting to understand why those particular functions are segregated together anatomically. Chapter 16 will, towards this end, offer a unified explanation of why and how a particular set of functions is carried out in the hippocampal system, including two kinds of memory consolidation, spatial navigation, and adaptively-timed motivated attention that supports timed action via the cerebellum.

From Platonic plans to Newtonian force and obstacle compensations. Another refinement of VITE showed how arm movements can compensate for variable loads and obstacles (Figure 12.10). This model development enabled the Platonic plans of the cortical VITE circuit to begin to effectively control the Newtonian forces and obstacles that a physical arm has to deal with when moving in the real world. I developed this extension of the VITE model with my PhD student Paul Cisek, who is now a leading motor control neuroscientist and modeler in his own right, and Dan Bullock, who was by then a professor in our department (Bullock, Cisek, and Grossberg, 1998; Cisek, Grossberg, and Bullock, 1998). This model development enabled the model arm trajectory to be carried out while compensating for variable loads, such as heavy or light objects to carry, and to accurately compute its position when it unexpectedly hits an obstacle. Because the hand/arm can hit an obstacle on the way to its desired target position, the model needed to distinguish a perceived position vector (PPV) in parietal cortical area 5 from an outflow position vector (OPV) in motor cortical area 4. Signals to and from the spinal cord and cerebellum were also needed to inform the cortical trajectory generator about the current status of muscle contractions relative to desired positions, and thus to be able to control them better.

With these added capabilities, the model's trajectory formation stages can explain the temporal dynamics during reaching behaviors of identified cells in the motor and parietal cortical areas 4 and 5. Examples of these neurophysiological data and model simulations of them are provided in Figure 12.11. These model explanations and data fits began to explain why so many different cell types are needed to control arm movement trajectories under real-world conditions, each of them carrying out an important function that is an emergent property of its circuit acting as a whole in a feedback loop with its inputs and outputs.

The VITE circuit cannot, by itself, maintain a desired trajectory under variable force and loading conditions. It needs to interact with suitably designed cerebellar and spinal cord circuits to accomplish this feat. Dan Bullock and I developed the Factorization-of-LEngth-and-TEnsion, or FLETE, model, to show how the trajectories that are computed by the cortical VITE model could be used to generate accurate movements of an arm under conditions of variable speed and force (Bullock and Grossberg, 1989, 1991). The FLETE model enabled us to explain and simulate many data about how identified cells and circuits in the spinal cord work together with the motor and parietal cortex to achieve these goals. These cortical VITE and spinal FLETE model circuits were joined with circuits of the cerebellum to show how, working all together, they could use cerebellar learning to control a multi-joint arm model with antagonistic muscles (Figure 12.12). This model extension was developed with our PhD student Jose Contreras-Vidal (Contreras-Vidal, Grossberg, and Bullock, 1997), who is now also a distinguished motor control scientist in his own right. These circuit designs could profitably be incorporated

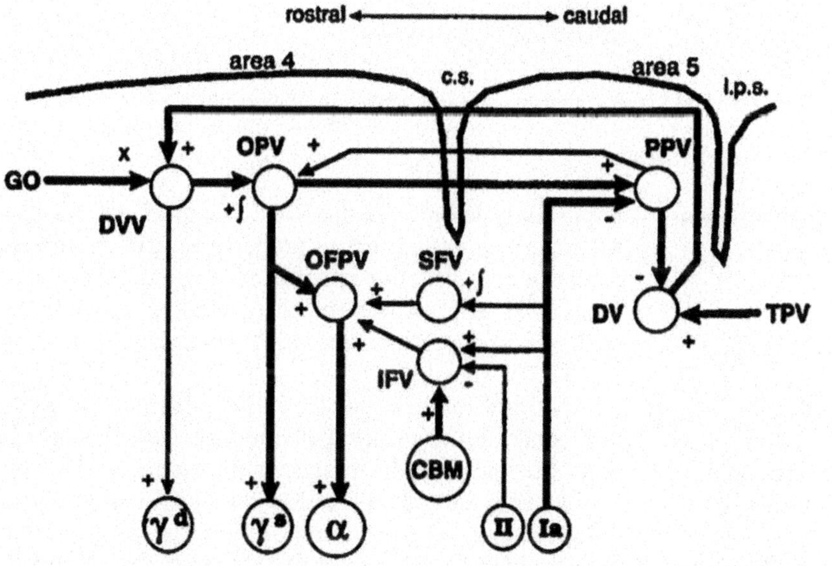

FIGURE 12.10. Processing stages in cortical areas 4 and 5 whereby the VITE model combines outflow VITE trajectory formation signals with inflow signals from the spinal cord and cerebellum that enable it to carry out movements with variable loads and in the presence of obstacles. See the text for details.

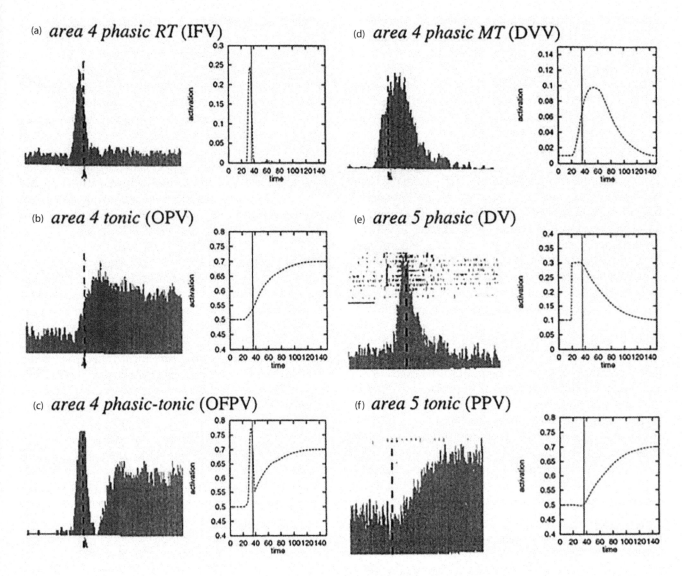

FIGURE 12.11. Neurophysiological data from cortical areas 4 and 5 (every other column) and simulations thereof (other columns) during a reach.

into designs for robotic arms that exploit the many benefits of agonist-antagonist motor control.

Motor-equivalent reaching and tool use

The VITE model refinement that sheds the most light on auditory-visual homologs of reaching and speaking circuits is called the DIRECT model (Figure 12.13), which I published in 1993 with my PhD student Frank Guenther and Dan Bullock (Bullock, Grossberg, and Guenther, 1993). Just like the VAM model, DIRECT also begins to learn by using a circular reaction that is energized by an Endogenous Random Generator, or ERG. More

importantly, learning in the DIRECT model clarifies how a crucial *motor-equivalence* property of arm movement control is achieved. In particular, during movement planning, either arm, or even the nose, could be moved to the goal object, depending on which movement system receives a GO signal.

This fact implies that trajectory planning does not just combine the position of the target on the retinas with the motorically-computed positions of the eyes in the head, and of the head in the body, to compute a body-centered representation of the target position that can command a movement of an arm. Motor control is emphatically not just a matter of combining visual and motor information! Instead, these visual and motor signals are first combined to learn a representation of the *space* around the actor.

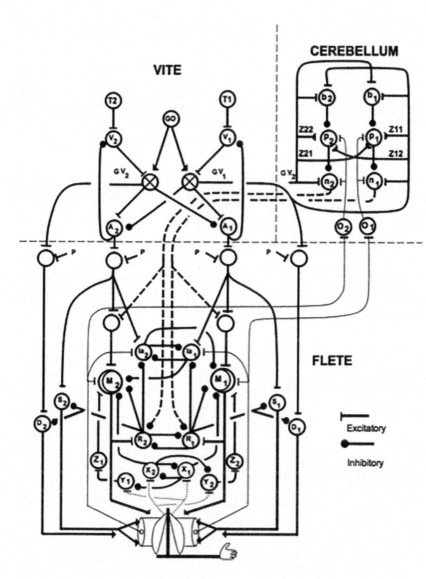

FIGURE 12.12. The combined VITE, FLETE, cerebellar, and multi-joint oppo-nent muscle model for trajectory formation in the presence of variable forces and obstacles.

Position-Direction Map. In particular, cells in the Position-Direction Map join together motor information about the arm's current position, from the Motor Present Position Vector, with informa-tion about the desired direction of move-ment in space, from the Spatial Direction Vector. This position-direction informa-tion fusion is realized in the model using a self-organizing map (Figures 5.16-5.18). Information fusion is needed to move a limb correctly, because if the limb begins a movement in a different position in space, then it may need to move in a dif-ferent direction to reach the desired target position.

By controlling the Motor Direction Vector using both kinds of information, this spatial-to-motor transformation can command the correct direction needed to reach the target position starting at different positions of the workspace. This learned spatial-to-motor transforma-tion thus enables different limbs, which always move from different positions in space due to their different insertions in the body, to generate different motor trajectories whereby they can reach the same target position in space. To enable this downloading process, DIRECT, which stands for Direction To Rotation Effector Control Transform, learns to map visual motion *directions* into joint *rotations* during reaching move-ments, as embodied in the transforma-tion from the model's Spatial Direction Vector to its Motor Direction Vector in Figure 12.13.

Movements other than arm reaching movements also depend upon spatial rep-resentations. For example, neurophysiological data (e.g., Andersen, Essick, and Siegel, 1985, 1987; Bisley, Krishna, and Goldberg, 2004) and neural models (e.g., Gancarz and Grossberg, 1999; Grossberg and Kuperstein, 1986; Silver et al., 2011) about saccadic eye movement control both support the hypothesis that head-centered spatial repre-sentations in the parietal cortex help to select movement targets. This is again a subtle issue, as illustrated by the earlier discussions (see Figures 6.14-6.16, 6.25, and 6.26) of how both retinotopic and spatial representations are both needed to move the eyes during learning of invariant rec-ognition categories.

Remarkably, after the DIRECT model uses its circular reaction to learn its spatial representations and transforma-tions, its motor-equivalence properties enable it, not only to

In this regard, note the *Spatial* Present Position Vector and the *Spatial* Target Position Vector in Figure 12.13. These spatial representations are computed in the pari-etal cortex. Because the Spatial Present Position Vector is delayed relative to the Spatial Target Position Vector by going through the Spatio-Motor Present Position Vector before being subtracted from the Spatial Target Position Vector, the result of this subtraction is a Spatial Direction Vector. The Spatio-Motor Present Position Vector and the Position-Direction Vector are two model stages where spa-tial and motor information are fused to enable both to de-termine the correct movement directions.

For example, the Spatial Direction Vector towards the target in *spatial coordinates* is converted into *motor coordinates* in the Motor Direction Vector. This trans-formation is learned during the circular reaction via the

DIRECT model
Bullock, Grossberg, and Guenther, 1993

learns by circular reaction

learns spatial representation
to mediate between vision and
action

motor-equivalent reaching

can reach target with clamped
joints

can reach target with a
TOOL on the first try under
visual guidance

HOW DID TOOL USE ARISE?!

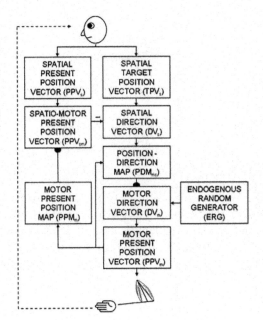

From motor-equivalent reaching to motor-equivalent speech production and coarticulation

FIGURE 12.13. The DIRECT model learns, using a circular reaction that is energized by an Endogenous Random Generator, or ERG, to make motor-equivalent volitionally-activated reaches. This circular reaction learns a spatial representation of a target in space. It can hereby make accurate reaches with clamped joints and on its first try using a tool under visual guidance; see Figure 12.16.

This background helps to propose solutions to problems that are relevant to both auditory and visual consciousness. As Figures 6.14-6.16 illustrate, spatial attention in the visual system helps to control eye and arm movements, while also supporting visual consciousness through surface-shroud resonances. Does their auditory homolog help to support auditory consciousness, keeping in mind

accurately move an arm for the first time when its joints are clamped, but also enable it to manipulate a tool in space. The conceptual importance of this result cannot be overemphasized: Without measuring tool length or angle with respect to the hand, the model can move the tool's endpoint to touch the target's position correctly under visual guidance *on its first try*, in a single reach without later corrective movements, and without additional learning! In other words, the *spatial affordance* for tool use, a critical foundation that supported the rapid development of human societies, follows directly from the brain's ability to learn a circular reaction for motor-equivalent reaching. Figure 12.14 summarizes model simulations of these competences, among others. We will see below that the spatial affordance which enables tool use during reaching is analogous to an affordance for speaking which enables coarticulation of speech sounds to occur.

COMPUTER SIMULATIONS OF DIRECT REACHES

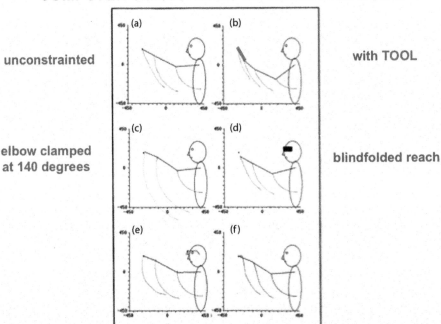

FIGURE 12.14. Computer simulations of DIRECT reaches with (b) a tool, (c) a clamped elbow, and (d) with a blindfold, among other constraints.

the caveat that auditory information enters the brain in head-centered coordinates, and not in retinotopic coordinates? Does auditory spatial attention support conscious auditory states in brain networks that input to motor representations for *speech production*, as would be expected if Piagetian circular reactions for vision and speech are embodied using homologous brain circuits?

From eating to speaking. During the development of the DIRECT model with Frank Guenther and Dan Bullock (Bullock, Grossberg, and Guenther, 1993), an evolutionary rationale was noted for why both the hand/arm and speech articulator systems may use homologous neural circuits. Namely, eating preceded speech during human evolution (MacNeilage, 1998), and skillful eating requires movements that coordinate hand/arm and mouth/throat articulators, including motor-equivalent solutions for reaching and chewing. If the behaviors of reaching and eating are part of an integrated sensory-motor system, then these component processes may be expected to use similar circuit mechanisms.

With this insight in mind, after he finished working with me as a PhD student and a postdoctoral fellow, Frank Guenther was hired as an assistant professor by our department. He and his colleagues then adapted the DIRECT model to develop the DIVA model for motor-equivalent speech production using circuits homologous to DIRECT reaching circuits (Figure 12.15). DIVA stands for Directions Into Velocities of Articulators, which is the analog for speaking of the direction-into-rotation transform that DIRECT models for reaching. DIVA showed how babbled speech articulator movements may be used to learn volitionally controlled speech sounds that are capable of motor-equivalent articulator movements, such as those that occur during coarticulation (Guenther, 1995; Guenther, Hampson, and Johnson, 1998). Coarticulation during speech means that a speech sound is influenced by, and becomes more like, a preceding or following speech sound, often due to motoric constraints on the sequential production of these sounds within an extended speech utterance.

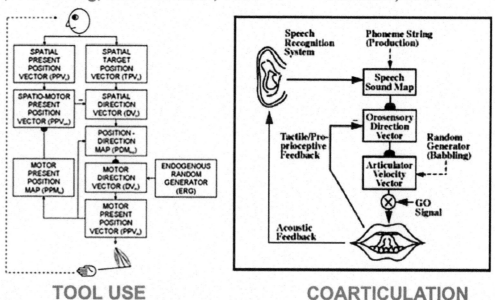

FIGURE 12.15. The DIRECT and DIVA models have homologous circuits to learn and control motor-equivalent reaching and speaking, with tool use and coarticulation resulting properties. See the text for why.

As with the VITE and DIRECT models, the DIVA model was incrementally developed, and is now broadly regarded as a leading neural model of speech production. One of these influential developments, by Guenther, Satrajit Ghosh, and Jason Tourville in 2006 (Guenther, Ghosh, and Tourville, 2006), led to an anatomical interpretation of model computational stages in terms of identified anatomical regions and their functions (Figure 12.16).

With this background in hand, homologs between auditory and visual brain processes underlying consciousness can now be discussed, including neural mechanisms and psychological competences that go beyond the explanatory range of DIRECT and DIVA.

Auditory neglect and speech production deficits

The following data support the hypothesis that visual and auditory consciousness arise from similar circuit designs, modulo their different learned invariants. As in the case of visual neglect that I discussed in Chapter 6, auditory neglect can be produced by lesions of the inferior parietal lobule, or IPL, particularly in the right hemisphere (e.g.,

Bellmann, Meuli, and Clarke, 2001; Clarke and At, 2013; Driver and Mattingly, 1998; Gutschalk and Dykstra, 2015; Marshall, 2001). Deficits in perception of auditory space can be severe, including a spatial bias in sound localization to the ipsilesional side of the lesion, and marked left ear perceptual extinction during dichotic listening tasks with pairs of simultaneous disyllabic words. This deficit includes a systematic bias in auditory space representation with respect to the body. It also often includes impairment in maintaining sustained attention (Robertson et al., 1997), as reflected by impaired auditory target detection during continuous stimulation. This link between auditory space representation and sustained attention is reminiscent of how surface-shroud resonances sustain spatial attention in the visual system. I propose that *stream-shroud resonances* seem to play the role for audition that surface-shroud resonances do for vision (Table 1.4), including their ability to sustain spatial attention upon consciously perceived and recognized auditory events.

Why there are also problems with speech production after parietal lesions is clarified by the DIVA model anatomy of Figure 12.16. The model's proposed anatomy implies that damage to the inferior parietal cortex could disrupt or destroy its Somatosensory State Map and/or Somatosensory Error map, and thereby lead to problems in learning correct speech productions of articulatory

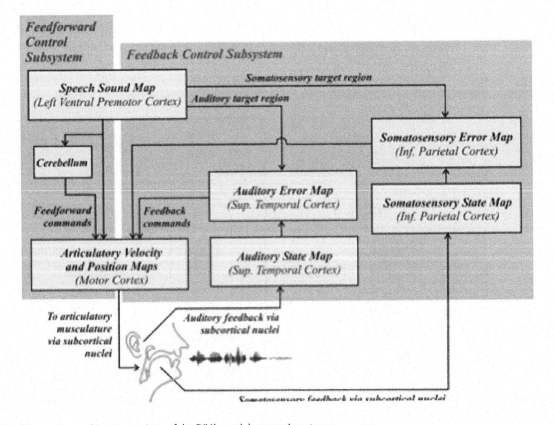

FIGURE 12.16. Anatomical interpretations of the DIVA model processing stages.

velocity and position maps in the Motor Cortex. Thus, just as damage to visual representations in the inferior parietal cortex can undermine surface-shroud resonances that can lead to problems in eye movement control and reaching, damage to auditory representations in the inferior parietal cortex can lead to problems in speech production when their stream-shroud resonances are undermined.

Discussions of lesions in auditory spatial representations and how they may lead to neglect and deficits in sustained attention and production will continue in the next section as I continue to explore the complementary global organization of auditory processing into What and Where/How cortical streams in human and monkey brains. These results will show that ART resonances exist at multiple levels of the auditory system, where they enable fast learning and stable memory of several different types of auditory recognition categories.

Stream-shroud resonances for conscious hearing of auditory qualia

Auditory scene analysis: Tracking sound sources through noise and overlapping frequencies. Auditory resonances occur in cortical regions that support conscious percepts of auditory sounds as parts of auditory streams. The process that forms auditory streams has been called *auditory scene analysis* by Albert Bregman, whose 1990 book of the same name is a veritable bible of streaming data and concepts (Bregman, 1990). Auditory scene analysis enables our brains to separate multiple sound sources, such as voices or instruments, into trackable auditory streams, even when these sources may contain harmonics that overlap and are degraded, or even totally occluded, by environmental noise.

Auditory scene analysis hereby helps to solve the so-called *cocktail party problem*, which occurs when listening to a friend at a noisy cocktail party or other social occasion. Such an analysis can separate overlapping frequencies that are due to different acoustic sources into distinct auditory streams. This separation process enables our brains to track each stream through time. In particular, each stream has the coherence that is needed to bridge across spectrally ambiguous sounds. For example, bursts of noise may occlude some of a speaker's sounds during a cocktail party that is taking place in a crowded, reverberant room. An auditory stream can bridge across these noisy intervals and complete the noise-occluded speaker sounds. It is only after

sounds are broken up into streams and these occlusions overcome that our brains learn to recognize the meaning of these streams and the identities of the sounds, whether the sound source is a speaker, a musical instrument, or a natural phenomenon like a crashing waterfall or the rustling of leaves in a forest.

The formation of multiple, distinct auditory streams may be compared with the process of 3D figure-ground separation during vision. In both cases, distinct auditory or visual "objects" are separated from one another to facilitate their perception and recognition. As I noted in Chapter 6, visual figure-ground separation seems to be completed in cortical area V4, from which its 3D surface representations can resonate in surface-shroud resonances that can reach conscious awareness. Before discussing the analogous stream-shroud resonances, I need to tell you more about how ART mechanisms form auditory streams.

Auditory continuity illusion and spectral-pitch-and-timbre resonances. The *auditory continuity illusion* (Bregman, 1990) illustrates that ART properties play a critical role during auditory streaming. These properties of ART are adapted to deal with events that are rapidly changing through time, as occurs in all acoustical phenomena. The auditory continuity illusion illustrates how an auditory stream can complete the representation of an auditory event even if it is partially occluded by a loud noise.

This illusion can be experienced, for example, when a steady tone occurs both before and after a burst of broadband noise (Figure 12.17, top row, left column). Under appropriate temporal and amplitude conditions, a percept

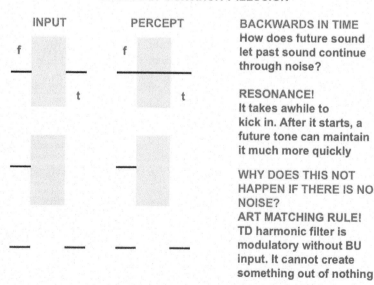

FIGURE 12.17. The auditory continuity illusion illustrates the ART Matching Rule at the level of auditory streaming. Its "backwards in time" effect of future context on past conscious perception is a signature of resonance.

is consciously heard in which the tone continues through the noise (Figure 12.17, top row, right column), and the residual noise sounds like it occurs in a different stream. In other words, the brain is able to restore the partially occluded tone so that it can be heard over the noise. However, if a second tone does not follow the noise burst (Figure 12.17, middle row, left column), then the tone is not heard continuing through the noise (Figure 12.17, middle row, right column). The brain can hereby distinguish between a sound that is partially occluded by noise and one that ends before the noise begins.

Comparing these two cases in Figure 12.17 discloses a remarkable fact: Until the second tone occurs, the two sets of stimuli are identical. Somehow the second tone operates "backwards-in-time" to create a conscious percept of the first tone continuing through the noise. Without the second tone, this "backwards-in-time" effect does not occur.

Noise is critical for this percept to occur. If two tones are played before and after a period of silence, with no noise between them (Figure 12.17, bottom row, left column), then silence is heard between them (Figure 12.17, bottom row, right column). The brain can hereby distinguish between two different acoustic events that are separated by silence, and one event that is partially occluded by noise.

These are all properties of the ART Matching Rule (Figure 1.25) acting through time at the level of auditory scene analysis! If indeed ART helps to process auditory streams, then we should expect it to be dynamically stabilizing the learning of some kind of auditory category. What kind of category is being learned during auditory streaming that requires such dynamical stabilization?

SPINET and ARTSTREAM: Resonant dynamics during auditory streaming. Streaming phenomena like the auditory continuity illusion, and the functional reason why ART is operating on them at all, are explained and modeled by the ARTSTREAM model (Figure 12.18) that I published in 2004 with my colleagues Krishna Govindarajan, Lonce Wyse, and Michael Cohen (Grossberg et al., 2004). Looking ahead, let me note that ARTSTREAM proposes how *spectral-pitch-and-timbre resonances* occur between logarithmic spectral representations of sound frequency patterns and recognition categories that code for pitch (Table 1.4). I will now explain what this sentence means.

ARTSTREAM shows how the brain may stably learn categories that represent the pitch of a sound. The *pitch* of a sound and its *position in space* are two important kinds of information that our brains compute in order to track a sound source via an auditory stream (Bregman, 1990). A sound's pitch enables listeners to judge the relative position of a sound, from lower to higher, on a musical scale. Although pitch tends to covary with a sound's frequency, the two measures are not equivalent. A percept of pitch arises from many sounds, such as musical sounds and vowels, whose pressure wave in the air is approximately periodic in time. The *fundamental frequency* of such a sound is the number of cycles of the waveform per second. Many periodic tones also contain frequencies that are integer multiple of the fundamental frequency, which are called *harmonics*. The pitch that is perceived tends to covary with a sound's fundamental frequency. As the fundamental frequency increases, the pitch sounds "higher".

How ARTSTREAM mechanistically distinguishes a sound's pitch from the acoustic frequencies that define the sound will be explained below. A sound's pitch and loudness are, however, not sufficient to identify all naturally important sounds. *Timbre* describes more complex sound qualities. It is sensitive to properties of a sound such as its entire frequency spectrum and envelope. A sound's *frequency spectrum* is a representation of the amount of sound pressure, or amplitude, in each of the sound frequencies

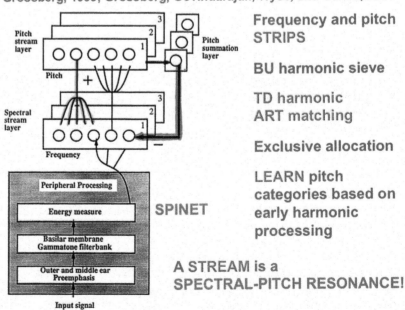

FIGURE 12.18. The ARTSTREAM model explains and simulates the auditory continuity illusion as an example of a spectral-pitch resonance. Interactions of ART Matching Rule and asymmetric competition mechanisms in cortical strip maps explain how the tone selects the consistent frequency from the noise in its own stream while separating the rest of the noise into another stream.

that are active during the occurrence of that sound, where frequency measures the number of vibrations per second (called hertz, or Hz) or thousands of vibrations per second of the sound (called kilohertz, of kHz). A sound's *envelope* is a smoothed total amplitude of a sound wave. Properties of a sound's spectrum and envelope enable listeners to distinguish different voices and musical instruments, even when these sounds may have the same pitches and loudnesses. ARTSTREAM clarifies how a listener can track these important cues to a sound source's identity, even when they are interrupted by occluding noise bursts.

I will begin my explanation of how ARTSTREAM works by first heuristically explaining properties of the auditory continuity illusion using *pitch categories* and the ART Matching Rule whereby they are learned. After that, I will say more about how sounds are preprocessed before they reach these streaming mechanisms.

First, why does the tone continues through the noise when the noise is followed by a subsequent tone, but not otherwise, as in the first two rows of Figure 12.17? This difference can be explained by the fact that it takes a resonance awhile to fully kick in. As in every ART category learning model, a resonance develops between a feature level and a category level (Figures 5.13 and 5.19), and eventually triggers a feature-category resonance (Table 1.4). In ARTSTREAM, such a resonance develops between a feature level that represents the tone's auditory frequency spectrum (the *spectral stream layer* in Figure 12.18), and a category level that selectively responds to the pitch of this spectrum (the *pitch stream layer* in Figure 12.18).

It takes awhile for the following events to occur: First, a pitch category is activated in response to the tone input at the frequency spectrum level. Second, the activated pitch category feeds back a top-down expectation that amplifies the frequency of the tone input, while inhibiting other frequencies, using the ART Matching Rule (see the green top-down on-center and the red top-down off-surround). Third, this bottom-up/top-down interaction cycles until the mutually reinforcing signals exceed a resonance threshold. Then a *spectral-pitch-and-timbre resonance* is generated that can support a conscious recognition of the auditory stream.

How does a second tone create the percept of a tone continuing through the noise? Once the spectral-pitch-and-timbre resonance is underway, it takes much less time for the second tone to add to the resonant activity, and to thereby keep it above threshold, than it did to exceed the resonance threshold from scratch. This rapid boost to the resonant activity enables its top-down expectation to continue selecting the tone from the noise, and maintaining a percept of a tone continuing through the noise. For this "backwards-in-time" effect to occur, the noise duration cannot be too long, or else the second tone will not arrive until after the noise interval is consciously

perceived. This duration can be used to estimate the amount of time needed to trigger a spectral-pitch-and-timbre resonance.

The fact that a tone followed by noise, with no subsequent tone, sounds just like a tone followed by noise is due to the fact that there is no backwards-in-time boost of the resonance due to the occurrence of a second tone.

The fact that two temporally separated tones are not completed over the intervening silence (Figure 12.17, third row) is explained by the fact that top-down expectations that obey the ART Matching Rule are modulatory and cannot create a conscious experience when there is no bottom-up signal. The modulatory one-against-one property in the top-down on-center of the ART Matching Rule circuit is realized in the ARTSTREAM model of Figure 12.18 by the balanced excitation in the top-down (green) on-center and inhibition in the top-down (red) off-surround.

One implication of this explanation is that conscious percepts can lag in time behind their generative stimuli. Many examples are known of temporal lags between inducing stimuli and the conscious events that they induce. A particularly famous example is the *cortical readiness potential*, which was described in a classical 1983 study of Benjamin Libet, Curtis Gleason, Elwood Wright, and Dennis Pearl (Libet et al., 1983). The cortical readiness potential typically precedes a voluntary motor act. In the Libet et al. study, the onset time of the cerebral activity that represents the readiness potential was compared with the reportable time of the subject's subjective experience of intending to act. The reportable time generally occurred between 150 to 300 milliseconds after the onset of the readiness potential.

In addition to proposing how a *spectral-pitch-and-timbre resonance* can support pitch category learning and recognition, ARTSTREAM also explains how this process can trigger the formation of multiple parallel auditory streams, notably how the frequency components that correspond to a given acoustic source may be coherently grouped together into a distinct auditory stream based on the pitch and spatial location of an acoustic source. For now, just note that the rapid cycles of bottom-up and top-down exchanges of excitatory signals that sustain a resonance through time allow individual sound sources to be tracked through a noisy multiple-source environment. Various popular methods of stream segregation in engineering and technology, such as independent component analysis, do not exhibit this sort of temporal coherence (Comon, 1994; Hyvärinen and Oja, 2000). The ARTSTREAM circuit that models the interaction between pitch-induced auditory streams and their spatial locations is summarized in Figure 12.19. As shown in this figure, the computation of spatial location needs input from both ears for a reason that I will explain below.

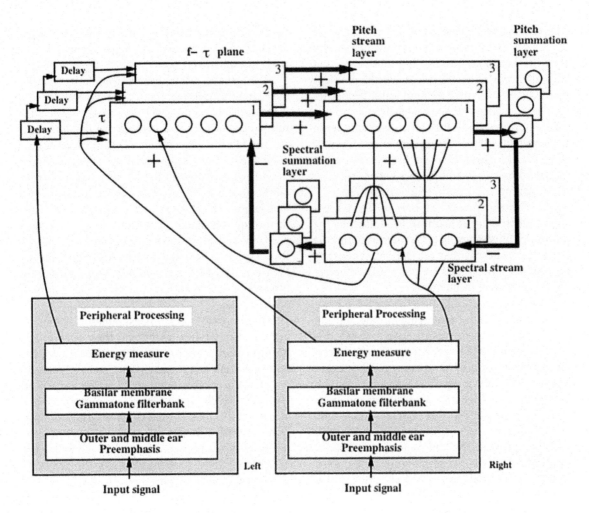

FIGURE 12.19. The ARTSTREAM model includes mechanisms for deriving streams both from pitch and from source direction. See the text for details.

From SPINET processing of sound spectra to ARTSTREAM creation of multiple streams. Sequences of sounds need to be properly preprocessed before they are in a suitable form for being broken into distinct auditory streams, In ARTSTREAM, acoustic input signals are preprocessed by multiple stages that together comprise the Spatial PItch NETwork, or SPINET, model (Figure 12.20) that I published in 1995 with my colleagues Michael Cohen and Lonce Wyse (Cohen, Grossberg, and Wyse, 1995). SPINET has been used to quantitatively simulate many human psychophysical data about pitch perception. These include properties with names such as the phase of mistuned components, shifted harmonics, dominance region, octave shift slopes, pitch shift slopes, pitch of narrow bands of noise, rippled noise spectra, tritone paradox, edge pitch, and distant modes. Figure 12.21 summarizes human psychophysical data of how a pitch percept changes when there are component shifts of various sizes in its inducing frequency, along with a SPINET simulation of these data. This impressive explanatory range is what gave me confidence

that SPINET provides a stable foundation to provide inputs to streaming processes within ARTSTREAM.

A critical property that enables SPINET to support streaming processes is that it creates a *spatial representation* of sound frequency spectra and pitch categories *within a cortical map*, rather than just the kind of formal algebraic autocorrelation measure of these quantities that many other models compute. This Spatial Pitch representation can be exploited by the brain to break sounds up into multiple streams whose frequencies may be grouped by pitch, timbre, and position cues that separate and resonantly track multiple sound sources.

The first few SPINET processing stages just emulate standard properties of early acoustic processing by the inner ear and related brain mechanisms, such as the Gamma-Tone Filter bank (Patterson et al., 1987) in Level 2 of the model (Figure 12.20). These processing stages generate a sound frequency spectrum that is represented in logarithmic frequency coordinates at Level 6 of the model. The final processing stage, Level 7, selects a pitch category.

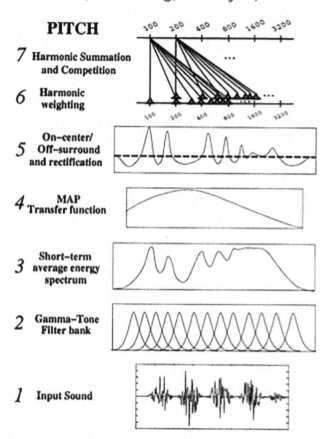

SPINET MODEL
Spatial PItch NETwork
Cohen, Grossberg, and Wyse, 1995

PITCH

7 Harmonic Summation and Competition

6 Harmonic weighting

5 On-center/ Off-surround and rectification

4 MAP Transfer function

3 Short-term average energy spectrum

2 Gamma-Tone Filter bank

1 Input Sound

FIGURE 12.20. The Spatial Pitch Network, or SPINET, model shows how a log polar spatial representation of the sound frequency spectrum can be derived from auditory signals occurring in time. This spatial representation allows the ARTSTREAM model to compute spatially distinct auditory streams.

As in all self-organizing map models (Figure 5.10), this Pitch Stream Layer gets activated by the Spectral Stream Layer via a bottom-up adaptive filter. The cells in this filter are activated by the frequency harmonics of the currently active sound. Harmonics activate the Spectral Stream Layer due to the way in which a sound is broken up into harmonics when it is peripherally processed by the cochlear nucleus of the inner ear (Figure 12.22). The adaptive filter thus acts like a "harmonic sieve" that selectively processes the spatial pattern of harmonic frequencies to activate a pitch category. Because harmonics of a simple sound, like a pure tone, highly correlate through time, the adaptive filter can select and learn pitch-sensitive category cells at the Pitch Stream Layer.

As in any self-organizing map model, however, learning of pitch categories in response to a sufficiently complex and non-stationary input series of sound frequency

spectra could cause catastrophic forgetting of previously learned categories; see Figures 5.16-5.18. Here is where ART top-down learned expectations can come into the act to dynamically stabilize the learning of pitch categories (Figures 5.18 and 5.19). Along the way, these top-down expectations can automatically control the formation of multiple auditory streams if the rest of the network is appropriately designed.

How multiple auditory streams are formed: Strip maps and spectral-pitch resonances

How does the brain convert a frequency spectrum into a spatial map that can represent *multiple* auditory streams? This is a kind of one-to-many transformation where a single spectral representation of a sound needs to be potentially available for being incorporated into more than one auditory stream. To create this "extra space" for forming multiple streams, after the auditory signal is preprocessed by SPINET mechanisms, each frequency activates a *strip* of cells in the spatial map, thereby forming a *strip map*. Thus, when SPINET is embedded into ARTSTREAM, each of its sound frequencies is broadcast in a one-to-many manner to an entire *strip* of cells in the Spectral Stream Layer, labeled 1, 2, 3 in Figures 12.18 and 12.19. This strip is perpendicular to (or at least cuts across) the spatial layout of the frequency spectrum. Since each frequency is represented by an entire strip of cells, the entire frequency spectrum is redundantly represented across the strips. The main idea of ARTSTREAM is that multiple streams can be chosen within these strips. ARTSTREAM shows how the ART Matching Rule can select and maintain streams within these multiple strips. This happens in the following way.

The parallel copies 1, 2, 3, . . . of the Spectral Stream Layer can each activate their own pitch categories within the corresponding parallel copies 1, 2, 3, . . . of the Pitch Summation Layer. Each such pitch category can categorize the sound frequency harmonics corresponding to the pitch of a single acoustic source.

In order to choose which pitch category will win within the first stream that forms, the Pitch Stream Layer competes *across* pitch categories but *within* a single strip or stream. In order to determine which stream will be the first to form, a *spatially asymmetric competition* occurs across streams, and favors strip 1. Thus, the asymmetric cross-stream competition within the Pitch Stream Layer is stronger from strip 1 to strips 2 and 3, and from strip 2 to 3, than in the opposite direction. Such spatially

PITCH SHIFTS WITH COMPONENT SHIFTS
Patterson and Wightman, 1976; Schouten, 1962

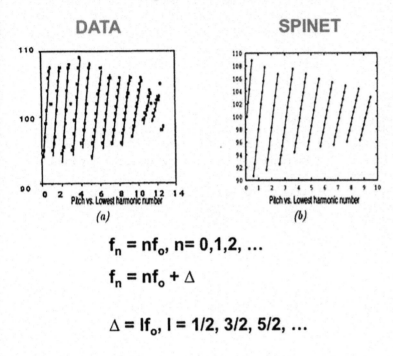

$$f_n = nf_o, \ n = 0, 1, 2, \ldots$$

$$f_n = nf_o + \Delta$$

$$\Delta = |f_o, | = 1/2, \ 3/2, \ 5/2, \ \ldots$$

FIGURE 12.21. One of the many types of data about pitch processing that are simulated by the SPINET model. See the text for details.

asymmetric competition across strips is, in fact, common in the auditory system, where it helps to break the following kind of symmetry: Other things being equal, if the same frequency spectrum is redundantly activated across multiple streams, the asymmetric cross-stream

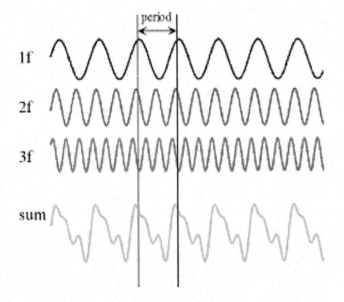

FIGURE 12.22. Decomposition of a sound (bottom row) in terms of three of its harmonics (top three rows).

competition enables a pitch category in the first stream to be chosen, at the same time that it inhibits the corresponding pitch categories in the other streams.

The winning pitch category in strip 1 of the Pitch Stream Layer then reads out a top-down expectation that obeys the ART Matching Rule to strip 1 of the Spectral Stream Layer. In particular, the top-down, modulatory on-center of the top-down expectation selects and enhances the harmonics of the winning pitch, at the same time that its off-surround inhibits all the other frequencies that may be receiving inputs from other sound sources in strip 1. Only frequencies that are harmonics of the winning pitch can survive this competition. In this way, the winning pitch in a pitch stream selects and amplifies those harmonics in its stream that are consistent with it. This resonant feedback loop realizes the temporal coherence that will be needed to sustain a percept across an interval of occluding noise.

As this first stream and its pitch are being chosen, the amplified spectral frequencies of the chosen harmonics in the Spectral Stream Layer of strip 1 can use the asymmetric spatial competition that exists across the Spectral Stream Layer to inhibit the same frequencies in the other strips, or streams, by using competitive off-surround interactions that occur *within* the frequency of that strip, but *across* streams. Inhibiting such redundant activations of the same frequency in other streams, when it is complete (which is not always the case!), achieves the property that Bregman calls *exclusive allocation* of a given frequency to one stream at a time (Bregman, 1990).

Another important cross-stream property occurs because the first winning pitch uses its top-down off-surround to inhibit frequencies within the Spectral Stream Layer of stream 1 that are not its harmonics. These inhibited frequencies can then no longer inhibit the same frequencies in other streams using asymmetric competition. These disinhibited frequencies can then select a pitch in a different stream, notably in strip 2. The asymmetric competition within the Pitch Stream Layer then enables a second stream to form in strip 2, and only in that strip, to represent the pitch of a different sound source. The process can then continue to rapidly propagate across streams in this way. Multiple simultaneously occurring spectral-pitch-and-timbre resonances can hereby emerge.

Some simulated auditory streaming data. ARTSTREAM is not yet a complete theory of auditory scene analysis. However, it has successfully simulated some key streaming data, and it is clear how the model would need to be extended to expand its explanatory and predictive range in a principled way. Among simulated phenomena are key properties of the auditory continuity illusion itself (Figure 12.23, left column), as well as variants of it (Figure 12.23, right column). For example, Figure 12.23 (left column, top row) depicts a simulation in which no noise fills the silent gap between two pure tone stimuli. As a result, the pitch category is not activated during this interval of silence, so no spectral-pitch-and-timbre resonance develops then, and no conscious recognition of that pitch will then occur. Only the two pure tone stimuli will be recognized. Figure 12.23 (left column, bottom row) shows, in contrast, that adding a broad-band noise spectrum between the same two tones enables a spectral-pitch-and-timbre resonance to be generated across the noise-filled interval in stream 1, and for the remaining broad-band noise spectral components to be segregated to stream 2 during that interval.

ARTSTREAM has simulated additional streaming data from psychophysical grouping experiments, such as how a tone sweeping upwards in frequency that intersects a tone sweeping downwards in frequency creates a bounce percept whereby the higher tones group together separately from the lower tones, which also group together (Figure 12.23 (right column, row 5)). This bounce occurs due to the proximity of the grouped frequencies even if noise replaces the tones at their intersection point (Figure 12.23 (right column, row 7)) but, just as in the auditory continuity illusion, no bounce occurs if the sweeps are replaced by silence when their frequencies are close together (Figure 12.23 (right column, row 6)). Other simulated streaming data include the illusion of Howard Steiger (Steiger, 1980; Steiger and Bregman, 1981) whereby upward and downward frequency sweeps that are joined by downward and upward frequency sweeps break up into a percept of two streams that segregate the upper from the lower frequencies (Figure 12.23 (right column, row 8)), even if the intersecting frequencies are replaced by broad-band noise (Figure 12.23 (right column, row 9)), and the scale illusion of Diana Deutsch (Deutsch, 1975) whereby downward

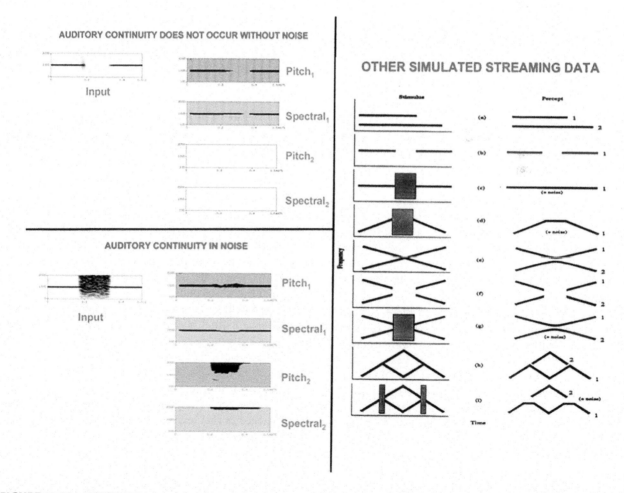

FIGURE 12.23. ARTSTREAM simulations of the auditory continuity illusion and other streaming properties (left column, top row) When two tones are separated by silence (Input), a percept of silence also separates them in a spectral-pitch resonance. (left column, bottom row) When two tones are separated by broadband noise, the percept of the tone continues through the noise in one stream (stream 1) while the remainder of the noise occurs in a different stream (stream 2). (right column) Some of the other streaming properties that have been simulated by the ARTSTREAM model.

and upward scales presented alternately to the two ears are regrouped based on frequency proximity, leading to a bounce percept.

Although these simulations only begin to explain the rich literature on streaming, they do illustrate how pitch categories can help to define multiple coherent streams. Once these streams can form, they create distinguishable auditory sources whereby higher speech and language processing levels can begin to extract and learn language meanings. As I will explain below, all of these streaming, speech, and language processing levels obey ART dynamics to enable them to rapidly learn and stably remember their respective categories. As a result, all of them can resonate together to generate context-sensitive conscious speech and language, just as multiple levels of the visual system can resonate together to generate context-sensitive conscious visual objects and scenes.

Generalizing ARTSTREAM to include timbre and voice categories: From item to list chunks. Pitch categories must be learned. ARTSTREAM indicates how this may occur using spectral-pitch-and-timbre resonances that enable the learned pitch categories to solve the stability-plasticity dilemma and thereby dynamically stabilize themselves via the ART Matching Rule (Figure 12.18).

Not only pitch categories can be learned by this resonant process. *Any* acoustic frequency patterns that occur with sufficient statistical consistency through time can be learned and categorized. Pitch categories compress relatively simple, harmonically-related spectral frequencies within a given time interval. A pitch category is thus a special case of *item category*, or *item chunk*. As I will explain below, item chunks are computed at multiple levels of the auditory system. An item chunk is any learned recognition category that selectively responds to a spatial pattern of activation across a network of auditory feature detectors during a brief time interval. In the special case of a pitch category, these auditory feature detectors are the harmonics of simple sounds.

Timbres are perceived in response to more complex sounds that can also include frequency sweeps, different onset and offset times, and different relative amplitudes in different frequency bands (Grey, 1977; McAdams, 2013). Representing a timbre thus requires that the feature detectors of the model be able to selectively respond to sequences of acoustical signals that change through time, notably transient changes in sounds such as frequency sweeps that can rapidly ascend or descend through time across multiple frequencies. Figure 12.24 shows the transient frequency changes that support percepts of the consonant sounds /b/ and /p/ as part of the sounds /ba/ and /pa/. Also recall the spectrogram of the word "legislatures" in Figure 1.22, including the consonant sound /t/. ARTSTREAM does not include this kind of transient detector in its SPINET front end.

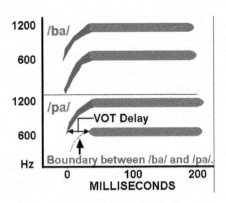

FIGURE 12.24. Spectrograms of /ba/ and /pa/ show the transient and sustained parts of their spectrograms.

Because of its more complex spatiotemporal structure, a timbre cannot be classified by a category that is as simple as a pitch category. It requires a category that can selectively respond to information that changes sequentially through time. Such a category is called a *list category*, or *list chunk*. In order to learn a list chunk, a model must first be able to temporarily store representations of the sequence, or list, of sounds that will activate the list chunk. A network that can temporarily store a sequence of temporally-occurring events is called a *working memory*. How working memories are designed to enable stable chunk learning to occur is a major issue in neuroscience, and one to which I will return later in this chapter. For the moment, let me just note that the characteristic sounds of voices and instruments (e.g., Belin et al., 2000; Goldinger, 1996; Palmeri, Goldinger, and Pisoni, 1993) may be stored by working memories and categorized by list chunks. Such a working memory is called a *spectral working memory* to emphasize that it supports the recognition of spectral characteristics of acoustic sources. The widely varying spectral properties of this full range of sounds may cause their adaptive filters to selectively activate different cortical areas (e.g., Belin et al., 2000; Fecteau et al., 2004). No matter how complicated these item and list chunks may be, they may be segregated into distinct auditory streams to identify sources upon which later speech and language processes can build.

Multiple working memories and list chunking networks exist in the What and Where/How auditory cortex, some devoted to representing frequency-sensitive and rate-sensitive information like voices and instruments, using categories that learn to identify a source, and others devoted to representing processes that are frequency-invariant and rate-invariant, using categories that learn to recognize speech and language meanings. I will suggest below that all of these networks obey similar ART design principles that are embodied by specializations of similar types of circuits, so that each can learn to categorize and recognize different types of acoustic information rapidly and stably through time.

When the totality of these working memories resonates with the logarithmic representations of sound frequency patterns, the ensuing resonance is called a *spectral-pitch-and-timbre resonance* to emphasize that acoustical categories other than pitch categories can drive it. A spectral-pitch-and-timbre resonance can support conscious recognition of a complex sound in an auditory stream (Table 1.4).

Stream-shroud resonances for conscious perception of auditory objects in streams.   Chapter 6 explained why and how a surface-shroud resonance may support conscious percepts of visual qualia. A surface-shroud resonance is proposed to be triggered at the cortical stage that completes the process of 3D figure-ground separation of visual surfaces. Because of the mechanistic homolog that is proposed to exist between visual figure-ground separation and auditory streaming, an analogous process of *stream-shroud resonance* is proposed to be triggered at the cortical stage that completes auditory streams, where this resonance is predicted to support percepts of conscious auditory qualia, notably qualia of auditory objects in streams (Table 1.4).

A surface-shroud resonance enables sustained spatial attention to focus on a visual object as its qualia become visible. An auditory shroud cannot represent *spatial* attention unless it can represent the attended position of a sound in space. The position in space of auditory sources is computed from interaural time differences (ITD) and interaural level differences (e.g., Bronkhorst and Plomp, 1988; Darwin and Hukin, 1999; Rayleigh, 1907). An *interaural time difference* is the difference in arrival time of a sound between the two ears of an animal or human. It provides a cue to the direction of the source relative to the head, since an earlier arrival time is expected if the sound source is on the side of that ear. An *interaural level difference* is the difference in sound pressure level in one ear than the other, due in part to the fact that, say, a sound to the right of the head is shadowed, and thereby attenuated, by the head before it reaches the left ear. Each of these cues has its own strengths and weaknesses as a source of information about the position of the sound in space. In general, for low frequencies of sound, interaural temporal differences may dominate a judgement of sound source direction, whereas for high frequencies, interaural level differences may dominate the judgment. Without going further into these details, it is nonetheless clear that auditory spatial attention in humans does not appear to have a map structure (e.g., Kong et al., 2012). Instead, it seems to be represented by an opponent process whose neurons are tuned to (e.g.) ITDs (Magezi and Krumbholz, 2010).

The ARTSTREAM model in Figure 12.19 proposes how both pitch and ITD spatial position information can cooperate during auditory scene analysis to identify sound sources for streaming. Such a cue combination is well-known to often play a role in determining streaming properties (Bregman, 1990). In Figure 12.19, stream selection is modulated by information about source position using the so-called $f - \tau$ plane (Colburn, 1973, 1977), wherein individual frequencies f are assigned to a radial τ direction that is computed from ITDs.

The representation of auditory space that is generated by ITD and ILD cues, among others, is assumed to interact with auditory spatial attention via excitatory feedback interactions to generate a *stream-shroud resonance*. Because of their intersection at shared auditory streams, an auditory stream-shroud resonance for conscious hearing can synchronize with a spectral-pitch-and-timbre resonance for conscious recognition of auditory objects in streams. In this way, observers can consciously hear objects in streams even as they can recognize them.

This synchronizing event is proposed to occur in much the same way that a surface-shroud resonance and a visual feature-category resonance may synchronize during conscious seeing and recognition (Figure 6.27). Indeed, a spectral-pitch-and-timbre resonance is a type of "feature-category resonance" in the What cortical stream, albeit one that builds upon auditory, rather than visual, features. Just as visual agnosias can occur when the visual feature-category resonance in the What cortical stream is lesioned, so that visual objects can be seen without being recognized, there are auditory agnosias that occur when the auditory spectral-pitch-and-timbre resonance in the What cortical stream is lesioned, so that auditory objects can be consciously heard without being recognized. Further experimental and theoretical analysis of how these two types of auditory resonances interact is much to be desired, especially because psychophysical data about audition is generally much scarcer than comparable data about vision.

From streaming to speech: Learning to imitate speech requires speaker normalization

From circular reactions to language imitation: Speaker normalization and imitative maps.   How does a baby start to imitate sounds that are spoken by her parents? Parents typically use different sound frequencies than babies when they talk. How do babies bridge this frequency gap?

The fact that babies, women, and men may speak using a different range of acoustical frequencies illustrates that the auditory signals of speech are speaker-*dependent*. In contrast, representations of language meaning are speaker-*independent*. If, instead, we had to separately learn the meaning of every language utterance for each speaker, then we could never transfer the language learning that we acquire from one speaker to understand another speaker.

The process whereby a speaker-independent representation is formed is called *speaker normalization*. Speaker normalization is a critical transformation that occurs in our brains at a processing stage *after* the selection and attentive tracking of an auditory stream, but *before* the stage where the meaning of what the speaker is saying is extracted. As a result, we can begin to learn to understand the meanings of many speakers by learning language from just a few, including our parents.

Speaker normalization allows language learning to get started after a baby goes through its own verbal *circular reaction*. As I noted earlier in the chapter, this circular reaction occurs, during a critical period, from the motor apparatus that generates a baby's endogenously babbled sounds to the sounds that the baby hears itself

emit. Speaker normalization transforms the babbled sounds that the baby hears into a normalized auditory representation. Then the baby can learn an associative map, called an *imitative map*, between the normalized auditory representations of its own heard babbled sounds to the motor commands that caused them (Figure 12.25, left figure). When the baby later hears adults speak, the adult utterances are also transformed into normalized auditory representations. This speaker-normalized representation reduces or eliminates the frequency differences of adult and baby speakers. Adult normalized sounds can then also be filtered by the imitative map and used to simultaneously activate a composite of the simpler motor commands that the baby was able to endogenously generate. The sounds that the baby can utter using these composite commands are closer to the sounds that the adults made than its own babbled sounds. In this way, the baby can begin to imitate and refine heard sounds in its own language productions.

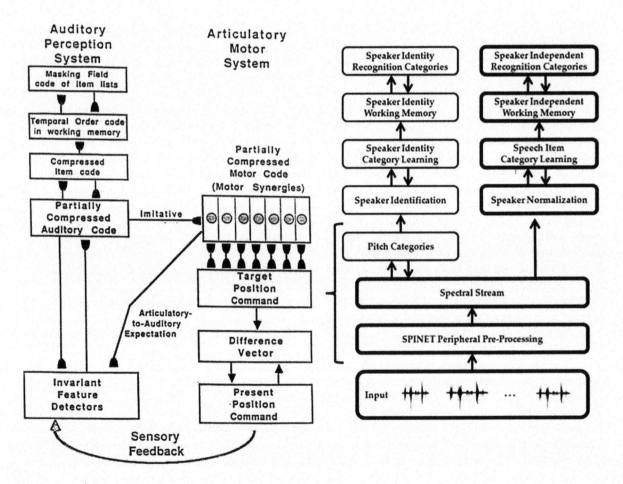

FIGURE 12.25. (left architecture) Auditory-articulatory feedback loop whereby babbled sounds activate learning in an imitative map that is later used to learn to reproduce the sounds of other speakers. An articulatory-to-auditory expectation renders learning possible by making the auditory and motor data dimensionally consistent, as in the motor theory of speech. (right architecture) Parallel streams in the ARTSPEECH model for learning speaker-independent speech and language meaning, including a mechanism for speaker normalization (right cortical stream) and for learning speaker-dependent vocalic qualities (left cortical stream).

Speaker normalization has related roles as well. Throughout life, it enables language meanings that were learned from one teacher's voice to be readily understood when heard from another speaker. It hereby overcomes a combinatorial explosion that would otherwise occur if the brain needed to store every instance of every speaker's utterance in order to understand language meaning. Speaker normalization thus helps to ensure *speaker*-independent imitation and understanding while other processing stages help to ensure *rate*-invariant learning and understanding. I will propose how rate-invariance is achieved right after explaining how speaker-normalization is achieved.

Learning in such an imitative map needs to remain possible for many years in order to enable an individual's changing voice through puberty and adulthood to continue to activate and revise the map. This fact raises two design problems: What process *dynamically stabilizes* the map learning process, while also allowing the map to undergo controlled changes? Another equally important problem is how to learn a map between two such different kinds of information; namely, auditory feature patterns and motor commands? In other words, what process ensures *dimensional consistency* of the auditory speech representations and motor speech commands that are linked by the map, so that the map can, in fact, be learned?

The ART speech-learning architecture in Figure 12.25 (left panel) incorporates a solution to both problems. In it, babbled sounds are generated by a VITE motor trajectory generator circuit (Figure 12.2) when it is activated by an Endogenous Random Generator, or ERG, during a speech circular reaction. The ERG is not drawn in this figure, but operates much as it does in the VAM circuit of Figure 12.9. These babbled sounds create auditory feedback that activate acoustic feature detectors. At the time that this circuit was published in 1988 with my colleagues Michael Cohen and David Stork (Cohen, Grossberg, and Stork, 1988), it was not yet understood how speaker normalization might occur, so these acoustic features were simply said to be invariant—that is, speaker-normalized—at the model's Invariant Feature Detectors level. These speaker-normalized feature patterns are partially compressed into multiple auditory item chunks (at the model's Partially Compressed Auditory Code level), which are then associated through learning via the imitative map with the still-active motor synergy commands that produced the babbled sounds (at the model's Partially Compressed Motor Code level). This learned auditory-to-motor imitative map is rendered dimensionally consistent and temporally stable by motor-to-auditory learned expectations that use the ART Matching Rule (Figure 1.25) to attentively select and learn auditory feature patterns that are dimensionally consistent with the active motor commands.

From imitative map stabilization to the Motor Theory of Speech Perception. This top-down motor-to-auditory attentive selection process explicates one possible mechanistic basis for the Motor Theory of Speech Perception (Galantucci, Fowler, and Turvey, 2006; Liberman and Mattingly, 1985). The Motor Theory hypothesizes that people perceive spoken words by identifying the vocal tract gestures with which they are produced, rather than by identifying the sound patterns that are generated by speech. The feedback circuit in Figure 12.25 (left panel) links auditory feature patterns, the auditory categories whereby they are recognized, and the motor commands that control vocal tract gestures. This loop does not replace speech categorization with vocal tract gestures, but it does show how both types of information intimately interact and shape each other.

The subsequent processing stages in Figure 12.25 (left panel) for learning item chunks, storing sequences of item chunks in working memory, and learning list chunks of these stored sequences use cognitive mechanisms whose designs are explained below. These sequence processing stages occur after the speaker normalization stage, and thus enable language meanings that were learned from one teacher's voice to be understood when uttered by another speaker.

NormNet: A shared design for auditory streaming and speaker normalization. How did speaker normalization evolve in the brain? How could brain evolution be smart enough to discover what seems to be such a specialized process? We confront this same type of evolutionary question when we try to understand how tool use arose, or where numbers came from, or how written script can be effortlessly performed with multiple sizes and styles at multiple speeds. In every case so far where I have faced this sort of dilemma, our models have led us to an intuitively simple answer. The same is true for speaker normalization.

I published the Neural Normalization Network, or NormNet, model in 2008 with my PhD student Heather Ames (Ames and Grossberg, 2008) to explain how speaker normalization may be accomplished in our brains. NormNet showed how the network that carries out speaker normalization may have arisen during evolution from an elaboration and specialization of the more primitive mechanisms that accomplish auditory streaming. If this is indeed true, then it also clarifies how speaker normalization could occur right after the stage where multiple auditory streams are formed and separated, and thereby set the stage for speech and language classification and meaning extraction from these streams.

This proposal offers a parsimonious solution to the speaker normalization problem because it is only after acoustic sources, including speakers, have been separated from one another by streaming that they can be speaker-normalized, just as it is only after visual figure-ground separation occurs that invariant visual object categories can be learned (Figures 6.14-6.16). NormNet hereby predicts that speaker normalization is accomplished by specializing streaming mechanisms at the next processing stage.

The phonetic processes that occur after speaker normalization is accomplished—notably the working memories and list chunks that derive their information from speaker-normalized auditory representations—would not be expected to be as sensitive to frequency harmonics as are the spectral-pitch resonances that separate and track the speaker sources within their auditory streams. Consistent with this expectation, Robert Remez and his colleagues have shown that harmonics are more important during auditory streaming than during phonetic perception (Remez, 2003; Remez et al., 1994, 2001). They distinguished these two types of processes experimentally by using a variety of stimuli, ranging from synthetic speech to sine wave analogs of speech. They also concluded from their experiments that "divergent auditory and phonetic organizations are sustained simultaneously" (p. 29, Remez et al., 2001).

In particular, our brains also preserve the frequency content of the streams for purposes of speaker identification. The ARTSPEECH architecture that is summarized in Figure 12.25 (right panel) illustrates how, even as speaker-independent phonetic processing occurs after the speaker normalization stage (right cortical processing stream), speaker-dependent identity processing can occur concurrently in a parallel cortical stream (left cortical processing stream).

I should immediately note that NormNet is not just a fond wish for a future theory of speaker normalization.

NormNet was able to learn speaker-normalized steady-state vowel categories from the classical Peterson and Barney (1952) vowel database using an ART classifier (Figure 12.26c). These simulations achieved accuracy rates similar to those achieved by human listeners. This promising proof of principle will, however, require a lot more research to be developed into a speaker normalization network for processing naturally-occurring variable-rate speech from multiple speakers. Some of the additional network designs and circuits that will be needed to simulate such a general-purpose architecture will be described right after I take a few moments to explain how NormNet works.

Strip maps and asymmetric competition for auditory streaming and speaker normalization. What kind of mechanisms are shared by streaming and speaker normalization processes? Both the ARTSTREAM and NormNet models use neural circuits that are called *strip maps* and *spatially asymmetric competitive maps*. In all examples of strip maps, they enable the brain to create the "extra space" that is needed to represent multiple features of one kind of another. In strip maps for auditory streaming, different portions of each frequency-specific strip are devoted to different streams within the parallel copies 1, 2, 3,. . . of the Spectral Stream Layer of Figure 12.28. In strip maps for speaker normalization, they help to create representations of speech in different frequency ranges. In particular, different portions of each frequency-specific strip in NormNet shift the frequency range of heard sounds by a

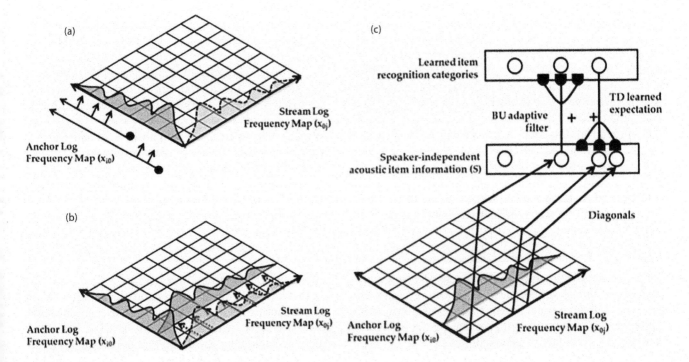

FIGURE 12.26. The NormNet model shows how speaker normalization can be achieved using specializations of the same mechanisms that create auditory streams. See the text for how.

different amount (Figure 12.26). The spatially asymmetric competition in ARTSTREAM helps to separate streams in an orderly way, and to achieve "exclusive allocation" of frequencies to just one stream. The same mechanism in NormNet helps to choose an "anchor frequency" (Figure 12.26a) that determines how much the frequency representation of a speaker will be shifted by a coincidence detection mechanism in order to be properly normalized (Figure 12.26b). As in ARTSTREAM, asymmetric competition in NormNet also accomplishes a kind of "exclusive allocation," albeit one that achieves speaker normalization, rather than stream selection. Thus, speaker normalization circuits may have arisen during evolution from an elaboration and specialization of auditory streaming circuits.

Strip maps as a general principle of brain design. Having gone this far, we can go further to ask: How generally do strip maps and asymmetric competitive circuits occur throughout the brain? Are these circuits general brain designs? The answer seems to be Yes. Strip maps seem to be a design that enables more cells to be devoted to representing a given feature, so that these cells can compete in a way that enables the feature to be shared across several related representations. A classical example of how the brain provides "extra space" is the *ocular dominance columns* that David Hubel and Thorsten Wiesel discovered as part of their Nobel-prize winning work on the development and organization of cortical area V1 (Hubel and Wiesel, 1968). As illustrated in Figure 12.27, each ocular dominance column is sensitive to inputs from one eye at each position, but individual cells within a "strip" of such

cells can respond selectively to differently oriented visual features at that position. Readers who want to understand how these ocular dominance columns develop may want to read a neural model about this that my PhD student Aaron Seitz and I published in 2003 (Grossberg and Seitz, 2003). This article simulates how ocular dominance and orientation columns, among other cortical map features, develop within the kind of *laminar* cortical model of V1 that I described in Chapter 10.

Where do numbers come from? Motion and space processing in parietal cortex

Strip maps and asymmetric competition for numerical estimation. Strip maps and asymmetric competition also seem to play a critical role in modeling how humans represent numbers. Any discussion of our numerical estimation abilities inevitably raises the question: Where do numbers come from?! Here too we need to ask if evolution needed to discover a special "trick" to achieve a brain's ability to estimate numbers? This possibility seems less likely as soon as one realizes that many animals other than humans can also estimate numerical quantities. You might at first wonder why animals need this competence. This is easily rationalized by considering the evolutionary advantages of a foraging animal who can choose a tree with more pieces of fruit, or a nest with more eggs, to eat. A striking example of this competence was reported in 1991 by David Washburn and Duane Rumbaugh (Washburn and Rumbaugh, 1991). In their experiment, chimpanzees were presented with two piles of chocolate bits. Each pile consisted of several smaller piles. The chimps were able to choose the pile with the bigger total number of bits, even though its individual piles had fewer bits than the largest pile in the other alternative. To fix ideas, this would be like choosing a pile with 11 bits, made up of two individual piles with 5 and 6 bits, over a pile with 9 bits, made up of two individual piles with 1 and 8 bits.

Moreover, all of these species show similar properties of numerical estimation: For both humans and animals, the processing of larger numerical quantities is increasingly difficult, and leads to larger reaction times and error rates, a finding known as the Number Size effect (Dehaene, 1992). In addition, the detection of the difference between two groups of objects that differ only in amount becomes easier, as reflected by faster reaction times and less

ADULT ORGANIZATION OF V1

Ocular Dominance Columns (ODCs)

  Alternating stripes of cortex respond preferentially to visual inputs of each eye (R/L corresponds to Right and Left eye inputs in the figure)

Orientation Columns

  A smooth pattern of changing orientation preference within each ODC
  Organized in a pinwheel like fashion

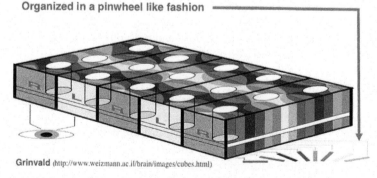

Grinvald (http://www.weizmann.ac.il/brain/images/cubes.html)

FIGURE 12.27. The strip maps that occur in ARTSTREAM and NormNet are variants of a cortical design that also creates ocular dominance columns in the visual cortex.

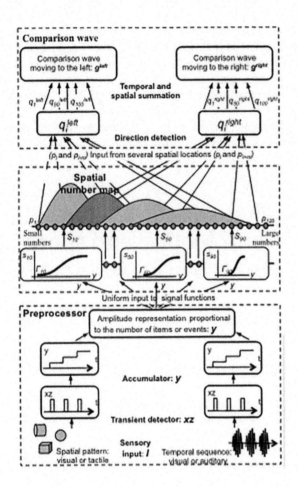

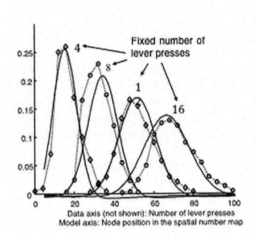

FIGURE 12.28. (left image) The SpaN model simulates how spatial representations of numerical quantities are generated in the parietal cortex. (right image) Behavior numerosity data and SpaN model simulation of it.

errors, as the difference between the number of objects increases, a finding known as the Numerical Distance effect (Dehaene, 1997).

Given that many species can estimate numerical quantities, on what evolutionary pillars does this ability build? My PhD student Dmitry Repin and I published the Spatial Number Network, or SpaN, model (Figure 12.28) in 2003 to answer this question and to simulate psychological data about numerical estimation (Grossberg and Repin, 2003). We showed that the kind of numerical estimation that we share with animals may arise from specializations of basic processes of motion perception and spatial representation are well-known to occur in the Where cortical stream of the brain that I discussed in Chapters 6 and 8. In particular, temporal integration of transient cell responses, a property of the cortical motion stream that is used to solve the aperture problem, is also used to form a number map. This hypothesis is consistent with neural data showing that a number map exists in the inferior parietal cortex, a part of the Where stream that also computes properties of visual motion. The SpaN model proposed how a "number line" of cells in parietal cortex could respond selectively

to increasingly large numbers (Figure 12.28). Responses to larger numbers hereby occurred at more distal positions on the number line. The number line adds, or integrates, inputs from the transient cells, with more inputs creating a larger total input to the number line. A larger total input generates an activity profile whose maximum occurs at a more distal position on the number line. Dmitry and I were pleased when my colleague Earl Miller and his postdoctoral fellow Andreas Nieder published neurophysiological data that are consistent with our SpaN predictions (Nieder and Miller, 2003, 2004).

Strip maps and numerical language categories in place-value number systems. Although many foraging animal species can estimate small numerical quantities, the human capacity for using numbers far exceeds that of any other species. There is no analog of arithmetic, higher mathematics, and mathematically-based sciences in other species. What foundational abilities do we have they they do not? I believe that one advantage of humans is that we use strip maps in combination with numerical language categories (Figure 12.29). Thus, the development of language in humans also set the stage for the ability of humans to exceed the numerical capabilities that they share with various animal species.

It is well known that human superiority in forming numerical estimates depends on using symbolic notation, such as number names. If unable to use a symbolic notational system, humans may perform no better than animals in certain estimation and comparison tasks. Historically, however, it was not written symbolic notation, but spoken language that brought the concept of number into human civilization, and numerical systems were developed independently by many civilizations in different parts of the world. Long before the appearance of the first concise numerical notation, from the third millennium BC, the Sumerians, who inhabited the southern part of Mesopotamia, based their system on gradations of the number 60, an influence that can be seen today in how time is measured in minutes and seconds. The Celts in Europe, as well as the Maya and the Aztecs in Mesoamerica, used a vigesimal, or base-20, numerical system. Modern French still bears the legacy of the base-20 that interferes with its number-naming base-10 structure. Our modern numerical competence has a decimal system in its foundation that originated from Arab and Indian cultures. Numerical systems that have such a base are called *place-value* number systems. Our contemporary use of number words like "hundred", "thousand", "million", and so on enable humans to describe arbitrarily large numbers with high precision in a base-10 structure.

Dmitry Repin and I proposed how to generalize the SpaN model to an Extended SpaN, or ESpaN model. The ESpaN model proposes how number categories and their names—such as "one", "two", "hundred", "thousand"—are learned in the What cortical processing stream as part of the normal course of language learning, as modeled by ART category learning networks (Figure 5.19). ESpaN further proposes, and simulates, how number categories in the What processing stream are associated through learning with the spatial numerical representation in the Where processing stream, and how this association naturally activates representations of place-value number representations that are much larger than those that other animals can represent (Figure 12.29).

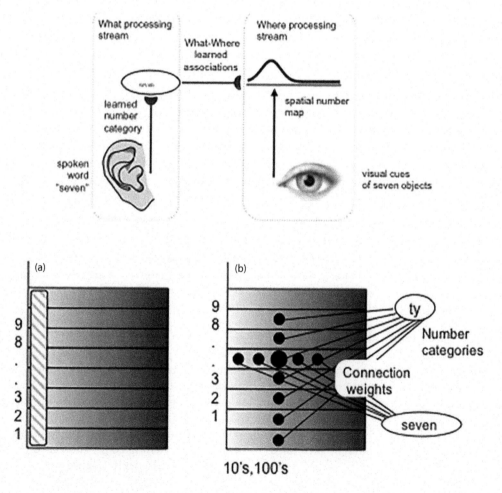

FIGURE 12.29. Learning of place-value numbers maps language categories in the What cortical stream into numerical strip maps in the Where cortical stream. See the text for details.

Where do strip maps and asymmetric competition come into this picture? The analog representation of number in the parietal cortex, which we share with other animals, is extended from the number line of SpaN into a *number strip map* in ESpaN. The *primary number line*, which humans share with other animals, occurs as a bounding edge of the number strip map (Figure 12.29, lower row (a), the leftmost vertical strip). As in SpaN, the number line continues to represent small numbers, such as "one", "two", "three", and so on. In addition, the model inputs that activate the numerical representations in the primary number line also activate the entirety of the corresponding number strips. All this happens without language. When number categories from language are associated with these strips, place-value number representations emerge.

The main idea about how this happens is that the number strips will be broken up by learning into "number streams" (Figure 12.29), much as the frequency strips during auditory streaming are broken up into auditory streams (Figure 12.18). Thus, in addition to representing the number "one" in the primary number line, or stream, other positions in the same number strip will represent larger numbers, such as "one hundred", "one thousand", and so on. In particular, adjacent to the primary number stream is the "ty" number stream, and adjacent to that is the "hundreds" number stream, and so on, all part of the strip corresponding to "one". ESpaN models how these different number streams, each corresponding to a different place value, such as "ty" or "hundred", emerge through learning as the model associates number categories, that are learned in the What cortical stream, with activations of the different strips in the Where cortical stream. A position within the strip map that is maximally activated by, say, converging learned signals from the "seven" and the "ty" number name categories in the What stream, would represent the number "70" in this strip map. Asymmetric competition across this strip map helps to organize the learned place value numbers so that, as one migrates further away from the primary number line, the place values increase in a regular manner, just as asymmetric competition causes stream selection in the order from 1 to 2 to 3 in Figure 12.18.

In summary, the emergence of place-value number systems in many human cultures is proposed to be an example of learned What-to-Where stream information fusion. There is, of course, a finite upper bound on how big a number can be represented by any spatial map in the brain. With this foundation built on numerical representations that can be associated with perceptual experiences, higher cognitive processes can learn to develop purely symbolic representations of even larger numbers, notably the algorithmic mathematics that represent arbitrarily large numbers.

Zeno's Dichotomy Paradox: Infinitely many steps to get anywhere means you never get there. Thus, once the

foundation for mathematics is laid, language can use the place value number system as a foundation for inventing numerical systems that go beyond perceptual experiences with numbers in space. In particular, the analog parietal number line has its resolution limited by properties such as the Number Size Effect. Formal mathematical number systems need have no such restrictions in the resolution of numbers. Conflicts between our understanding of space, as built up from the parietal number line, and more abstract concepts of number can be understand from this difference between Where and What stream representations of numerosity.

The philosopher Zeno of Elea who lived between 490 and 430 BC proposed nine paradoxes, one of which, the Dichotomy Paradox, vividly illustrates how conflicts can arise between our analog understanding of space and formal mathematical concepts about space (https://en.wikipedia.org/wiki/Zeno%27s_paradoxes#Dichotomy_paradox). In this paradox, one supposes that an individual wants to walk to the end of a path. Before he can get there, he must get half way there. Before he can get half way there, he must get a quarter of the way there. Before reaching a quarter of the way there, he must travel one-eighth, then one-sixteenth, and so on ad infinitum. Because one must complete an infinite number of tasks to get to the end of the path, and we can only carry out finitely many tasks during our finite lives, Zeno concludes that it is impossible to do this.

Another way to say this is that, because there is no first distance to walk, the trip cannot even begin, so all motion must be an illusion!

What-to-Where interactions in formotion tracking, Where's Waldo search, and synesthesia. Are there other processes in our brains that depend upon learned interactions from the What to the Where cortical stream? The answer is emphatically Yes! I will illustrate the diversity of such useful interactions with three examples.

Formotion tracking. My discussion of formotion dynamics in Chapter 8 illustrated one important What-to-Where stream interaction. In this example, *complementary* properties of visual form and visual motion are processed within the What and Where cortical streams, respectively (Tables 1.1 and 1.2). The What stream can process good estimates of an object's depth, but not good estimates of its motion direction. The Where stream can process good estimates of an object's motion direction, but not of its depth. Learned formotion associations from cortical area V2 in the What stream to cortical area MT in the Where stream overcome the complementary deficiencies of each stream acting alone, and enable the brain to track a moving object in depth (Figure 8.26).

Where's Waldo search. Searching for a desired object in a cluttered scene also uses What-to-Where stream interactions, even when that person or object is not moving. This competence is sometimes said to solve the Where's Waldo Problem, where Waldo is the person being sought. I have already briefly mentioned this problem in Chapter 6 and will discuss it more fully in Chapter 14.

Synesthesia. The third example of What-to-Where interactions in the brain is *synesthesia*. Synesthesia is a phenomenon in which stimulation of one sensory or cognitive pathway leads to automatic, involuntary experiences in another sensory or cognitive pathway. For example, in *number form synesthesia*, which was first described in 1881 by Sir Francis Galton (Galton, 1881), numbers, days of the week, or months of the year, that are represented by verbal categories within the What cortical stream, may trigger activation of positions in space, that are represented in the Where cortical stream. For example, 1970 may be "farther away" than 1980. Alternatively, both numbers may appear in a clockwise or counter-clockwise three-dimensional map. During *grapheme-color synesthesia*, letters or numbers are perceived as colored (Rich and Mattingley, 2002; Hubbard and Ramachandran, 2005).

Mechanistic unifications of psychologically diverse data. I find it instructive to think about such synesthesia experiences as the result of the brain's need for inter-stream interactions to overcome the complementary computational deficiencies of each cortical stream acting alone. In the case of synesthesia, it seems that there is a more exuberant proliferation of inter-stream interactions than in most of us. Indeed, number form synesthesia shares some striking similarities with the What-to-Where stream interactions that seem to subserve the learning of place-value number systems (Figure 12.29). And grapheme-color synesthesia may benefit from an exuberant variant of the ubiquitous Boundary-to-Surface interactions that control the filling-in of surface colors (Figures 3.10, 3.11, and 4.1). This suggestion will doubtless not end the vigorous experimental investigations and theoretical discussions aimed at ruling out alternative explanations of synesthesia, but it does suggest additional constraints for further thought and testing.

I have included the strip maps that compute ocular dominance columns and place value numbers in order to make several points. The first point is that, in every case, a strip map provides "extra space" in the map for organizing finer map structures, whether they are ocular dominance columns, place value numbers, auditory streams, or speaker-normalized sounds. The second point is that such a unification enables us to think about these seemingly radically different kinds of psychological processes as examples of a unified theory. The third point is that, once mechanistically unified in this way, these models go on clarify yet other kinds of psychological processes that would have remained mysterious without them. For example, in the next part of this chapter, I will show you how the parietal number map helps to construct *working memories* that can store the same item multiple times in a list; e.g., the items A and B in the list ABACBD. Such are the explanatory benefits of getting the foundational design principles and computations right! They launch you into unexpected territories that you could never have understood without them. I like to call this The Gift That Keeps on Giving.

From streaming to speech: How working memory and list chunking nets are designed

Short-term storage of item chunk sequences in working memory and learning of list chunks. ART mechanisms also operate at higher cortical levels of the auditory system, where they enable speech and language to be rapidly learned, stably remembered, flexibly performed, and consciously heard. To explain how this happens, ART models have been developed as part of an emerging neural theory of speech and language learning, perception, recognition, and recall whose increasingly developed models have names such as PHONET, ARTPHONE, ARTWORD (Figure 1.24), and conscious ARTWORD, or cARTWORD (Figure 12.30). The subsequent text will clarify the speech and language design principles and mechanisms that go into these models, and how they interact with the stream-shroud circuits that determine conscious hearing, and the spectral-pitch-and-timbre resonances that recognize the auditory objects that occur in these streams. These interactions among these multiple processing levels are possible because they all embody ART design principles within laminar cortical circuits that are variations of the same underlying canonical circuit design.

The design principles and mechanisms that support speech and language are also used, in specialized form, to control many other types of complex predictive behaviors. This is true because all such behaviors depend upon the capacity to think about, plan, execute, and evaluate *sequences* of events. In order for event sequences to determine future predictive behaviors, they are stored temporarily in a *working memory*.

Working memory is a form of short-term memory, or STM (see Chapter 1). For example, when you hear a telephone number for the first time, it is stored in STM. If you are distracted before trying to dial the number, you may not be able to dial it because its storage in working memory has been inhibited, or *reset*, by the distracting event. In

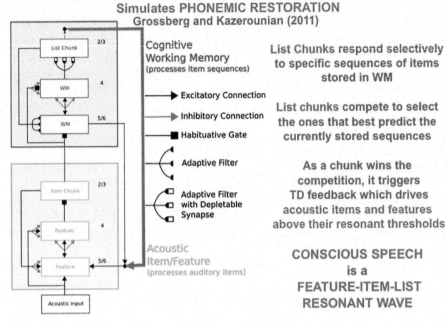

cARTWORD: LAMINAR CORTICAL MODEL MACROCIRCUIT
Simulates PHONEMIC RESTORATION
Grossberg and Kazerounian (2011)

Cognitive
Working Memory
(processes item sequences)

→ Excitatory Connection
→ Inhibitory Connection
■ Habituative Gate
Adaptive Filter
Adaptive Filter with Depletable Synapse

Acoustic
Item/Feature
(processes auditory items)

List Chunks respond selectively to specific sequences of items stored in WM

List chunks compete to select the ones that best predict the currently stored sequences

As a chunk wins the competition, it triggers TD feedback which drives acoustic items and features above their resonant thresholds

CONSCIOUS SPEECH
is a
FEATURE-ITEM-LIST
RESONANT WAVE

FIGURE 12.30. The conscious ARTWORD, or cARTWORD, laminar cortical speech model simulates how future context can disambiguate noisy past speech sounds in such a way that the completed percept is consciously heard to proceed from past to future as a feature-item-list resonant wave propagates through time.

contrast, you can tell someone your name even after you are distracted, because your name has been learned and stored in long-term memory, or LTM.

I follow the tradition in cognitive science of using the term working memory only to describe brain processes that can temporarily store event *sequences*, and not just store a single event. The latter property is called *persistence* in this book, as illustrated by the persistent storage of activities by some cells in inferotemporal cortex (Figure 6.17). As these event sequences are stored in working memory, they are grouped, or chunked, through learning into unitized plans, or *list chunks*, that can later be performed at variable rates under volitional control. List chunks can, for example, represent familiar words, navigational routes, and motor skills.

When considering the design of working memories and their learned list chunks, we are again confronted with the usual evolutionary question: How could evolution be smart enough to discover a working memory? As with so many other cases, it will turn out that working memories specialize an ancient and ubiquitous brain design that evolution has opportunistically exploited to support yet another important psychological function.

Why is storage of temporal order information so imperfect? Bowing during free recall. What this design may be is not immediately obvious, if only because temporary storage of event sequences exhibits properties that, at least at the outset, may not seem to be particularly adaptive. If items that are stored in working memory could always be recalled in their correct order, the earlier items would be recalled first, and only then the later items. However, this is not what actually happens. Figure 12.31 summarizes the kind of data that is ubiquitously observed in free recall experiments. In a free recall experiment, a human subject is presented once with a list of items that the subject is instructed to recall in the order in which the list items come to mind. The left graph in this figure shows that items from the beginning and the end of the list are recalled with higher probability than items in the middle. The right graph shows that items from the beginning and the end of the list are recalled earlier than items in the middle. Figure 12.32 summarizes a free recall data curve from a 1962 article of Bennet Murdock (Murdock, 1962). These bowed serial

WORKING MEMORY

How to design a WORKING MEMORY to code TEMPORAL ORDER INFORMATION in STM before it is stored in LTM?

Speech, language, sensory-motor control, cognitive planning e.g., repeat a telephone number unless you are distracted first

Temporal order STM is often imperfect, e.g.: FREE RECALL

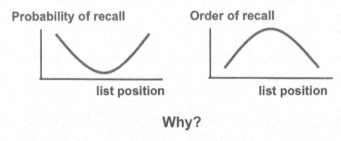

Probability of recall

list position

Order of recall

list position

Why?

FIGURE 12.31. Working memories do not store longer sequences of events in the correct temporal order. Instead, items at the beginning and end of the list are often recalled first, and with the highest probability.

SERIAL POSITION FUNCTION FOR FREE RECALL

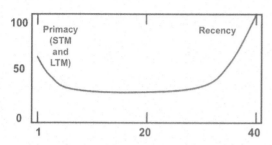

Position of word on a 40-word list

Data after Murdock, JEP, 1962, 64, 482-488

Primacy gradient can be a mixture of STM and LTM read-out

FIGURE 12.32. Data from a free recall experiment illustrate the bowed serial position curve.

position curves, which arise after a single presentation of a list, may be compared with the bowed curves that arise due to multiple learning trials during serial learning of a list (Figure 2.5). All of these examples show that lists are typically not recalled in their correct order, even in situations as simple as free recall. Why not?

I proposed an answer to these questions in 1978 when I introduced concepts and model mechanisms for a working memory model that subsequent psychological and neurobiological data have supported, and upon which recent models have built (Grossberg, 1978a, 1978b). Such an *Item-and-Order* working memory model posits that a temporal stream of inputs is stored through time as an evolving spatial pattern of activity across a network of content-addressable item representations (Figures 1.6 and 12.33). Inputs to this working memory are unitized item chunks of individual sounds. As I noted above, an item chunk is a learned recognition category that selectively responds to a spatial pattern of activation across a network of feature detectors during a brief time interval. Such an item chunk may represent a sufficiently simple auditory phoneme or letter category, an invariant visual object category, or even a simple motor synergy. As I will clarify in Chapter 15, such item chunks may benefit from having enough adaptively-timed incentive motivational support to be persistently activated, say in the orbitofrontal part of the prefrontal cortex, before they are stored in a working memory within the prefrontal cortex.

The temporal-to-spatial transformation from sequences of item chunks to a stored working memory representation converts the input sequence into a temporally evolving spatial pattern of activity, or *activity gradient*, across item-selective cells (Figures 1.6 and 12.33). The *relative activities* of different cell populations code the temporal order in which the items will be recalled, with the largest activities recalled earliest; hence, the name *Item-and-Order* working memory for this class of models.

A *primacy gradient*, in which the first item stored has the largest activity, the second the next largest activity, and so on, can be recalled in the correct order. Recall occurs when a nonspecific rehearsal wave opens all the output gates of the network (Figure 1.6). The most active item chunk is read-out first because it can exceed its output threshold fastest. As it is read out, it self-inhibits its stored activity, thereby enabling the next item chunk to be read out, and so on until the entire stored list is performed. This self-inhibition process is often called *inhibition of return*. It prevents the perseverating performance of the same item, over and over, from the working memory.

A more recent name for this class of models is *competitive queuing* (Houghton, 1990; Hartley and Houghton, 1996), which emphasizes the Item-and-Order property that the most active stored item representation is chosen by a competition that decides which item to recall next.

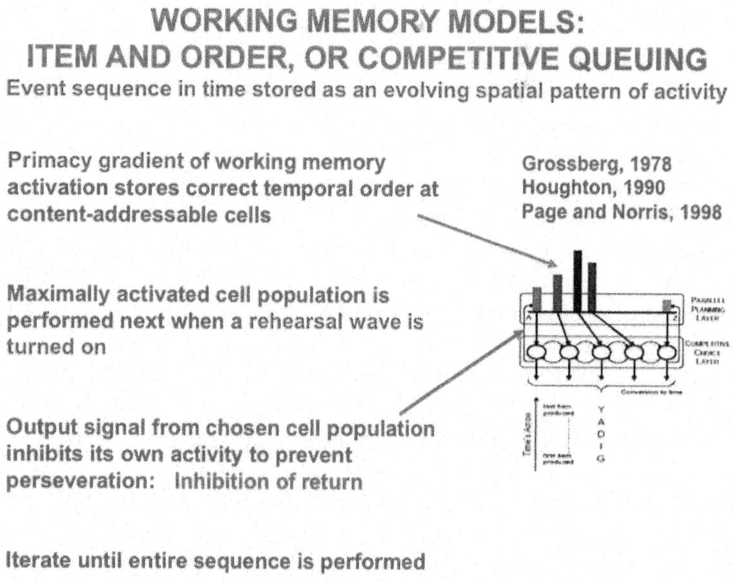

WORKING MEMORY MODELS:
ITEM AND ORDER, OR COMPETITIVE QUEUING

Event sequence in time stored as an evolving spatial pattern of activity

Primacy gradient of working memory activation stores correct temporal order at content-addressable cells

Grossberg, 1978
Houghton, 1990
Page and Norris, 1998

Maximally activated cell population is performed next when a rehearsal wave is turned on

Output signal from chosen cell population inhibits its own activity to prevent perseveration: Inhibition of return

Iterate until entire sequence is performed

FIGURE 12.33. Item and Order working memory models explain free recall data, as well as many other psychological and neurobiological data, by simulating how temporal series of events are stored as evolving spatial patterns of activity at content-addressible item categories. The categories with the largest activities are rehearsed first, and self-inhibit their activity as they do so in order to prevent them from being rehearsed perseveratively. The laws whereby the items are stored in working memory obey basic design principles concerning how list categories, or chunks, of sequences of stored items can be stably remembered.

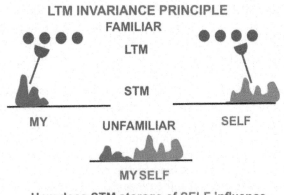

LTM INVARIANCE PRINCIPLE

How does STM storage of SELF influence
STM storage of MY?

It should not recode LTM of either MY or SELF!

FIGURE 12.34. The LTM Invariance Principle insists that words being stored in working memory for the first time (e.g., MYSELF) do not cause catastrophic forgetting of the categories that have already been learned for their subwords (e.g., MY, SELF, and ELF) or other subset linguistic units.

All working memories obey the LTM Invariance Principle and Normalization Rule. What properties recommend Item-and-Order working memories more than other possible alternatives, over and beyond their broad explanatory and predictive range? I proposed in 1978 (Grossberg, 1978a) that all Item-and-Order working memories satisfy two postulates which ensure that speech and language can be learned in a stable way through time: the LTM Invariance Principle and the Normalization Rule.

The LTM Invariance Principle is the main postulate (Figure 12.34). It makes precise the idea that there is no point in storing novel sequences of events in working memory if the brain cannot stably learn to unitize the sequences into list chunks that can control future skillful performance. The LTM Invariance Principle claims that working memories are *designed* to enable such stable list chunking to occur.

The LTM Invariance Principle guarantees, for example, that the first time a novel word, such as MYSELF, is stored in working memory, it does not force the forgetting of previously learned list chunks that code for its familiar subwords MY, ELF, and SELF. Without such a property, longer chunks (e.g., for MYSELF) could not be stored in working memory without risking the catastrophic forgetting of previously learned memories of shorter chunks (e.g., for MY, SELF, and ELF). Language, motor, and spatial sequential skills would then be impossible. As a consequence of LTM Invariance, as new items are stored through time in working memory, smaller stored sequences of items can continue to activate their familiar list chunks until they are inhibited by longer, and more predictive, list chunks; e.g., until MY is supplanted by competition from MYSELF through time.

The LTM Invariance Principle is achieved by preserving the *relative activities*, or ratios, between previously stored working memory activities as new list items are stored in the working memory through time. Newly arriving inputs may, however, alter the *total activity* of each active cell across the working memory. In this way, the previous *learning* of chunk MY is not undermined, but the *current activation* of the chunk MY can be inhibited by MYSELF.

How does preserving activity ratios help to stabilize previously learned categories? These activities send signals to the next processing stage, where the category cells are activated (Figures 5.10 and 5.11). The signals are multiplied by adaptive weights, or LTM traces, before the net signals activate their target categories (Figures 5.16 and 5.17). The total input to a category multiplies a *pattern*, or vector, of activities times a *pattern*, or vector, of LTM traces. By preserving relative activities, the relative sizes of these total inputs to the category cells do not change through time. Thus, nor do the corresponding LTM patterns that track these activities when learning occurs at their category cells.

Consider for example, what happens as bottom-up acoustic inputs arrive in time, activating their corresponding chunked (word) representations. As these inputs arrive, a chunk such as MY may become active once it receives its expected bottom-up input. If the acoustic inputs are then followed immediately by silence, the chunked representation of MY could stably learn from the stored STM pattern of activity that supported it. On the other hand, as is often the case, the acoustic inputs might not simply be followed by silence, but rather by further acoustic information (e.g., the inputs corresponding to the superset word or chunk MYSELF). In this case, the newly arriving inputs could drastically alter the pattern of activation reverberating in STM if the LTM Invariance Principle did not hold. As a result, the chunked representation for MY would begin to degrade as the weights to MY change in response to the now altered STM pattern in working memory. If however, the newly arriving inputs (corresponding to SELF) leave intact the relative pattern of activity in STM of the already occurring acoustic inputs (corresponding to MY), a new chunk for the full superset word (in this case, MYSELF) could be learned without destabilizing the already learned LTM pattern for its subset components (e.g., MY).

The Normalization Rule assumes that the *total activity* of the working memory network grows to a maximum that is (approximately) independent of the total number of actively stored items (Figure 12.35). Thus, if more items are stored in working memory, then each item tends to be stored with less activity. In other words, working memory has a *limited capacity* and activity is redistributed, not just added, when new items are stored.

NORMALIZATION RULE
Grossberg, 1978

Total STM activity has a finite upper bound independent of the number of items (limited capacity of STM)

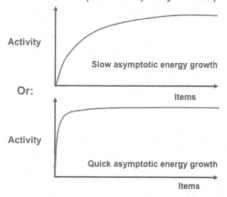

FIGURE 12.35. The Normalization Rule insists that the total activity of stored items in working memory has an upper bound that is approximately independent of the number of items that are stored.

Item and order working memories are recurrent shunting on-center off-surround networks. Are postulates such as the LTM Invariance Principle and the Normalization Rule too sophisticated to be discovered by evolution? I fortunately already knew in 1978 when I published the first Item-and-Order model that the answer is: Emphatically not! Indeed, both the LTM Invariance Principle and the Normalization Rule are properties of a ubiquitous neural design, and I knew this because I had published a model of the type of ubiquitously occurring neural network that embodies it, and proved its mathematical properties, in an article that was published in 1973 (Grossberg, 1973). This model is a recurrent on-center off-surround network of cells that obey the membrane equations of neurophysiology, otherwise called shunting dynamics (Figure 1.6).

Excitatory feedback due to recurrent on-center interactions in such a network helps to store an evolving spatial pattern of activities in response to a sequence of inputs (Figure 12.36 (1)). The recurrent shunting off-surround, in concert with the on-center, helps to preserve the relative activities that are stored (Figures 12.36 (2) and (3)).

ITEM AND ORDER WORKING MEMORIES

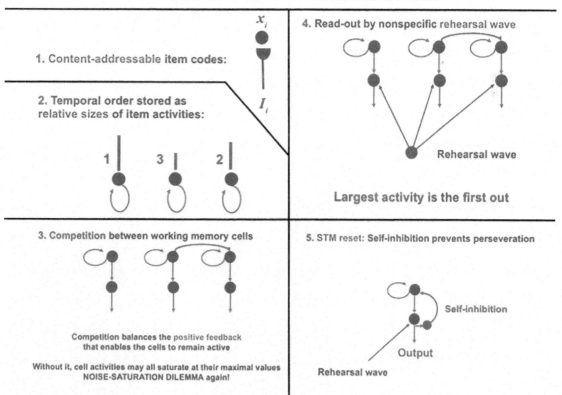

FIGURE 12.36. (1) Inputs to Item and Order working memories are stored by content-addressible item categories. (2) The relative activities of these item categories code the temporal order of performance. (3) In addition to excitatory recurrent signals from each working memory cell (population) to itself, there are also inhibitory recurrent signals to other working memory cells, in order to solve the noise-saturation dilemma. (4) A nonspecific rehearsal wave allows the most active cell to be rehearsed first. (5) As an item is being rehearsed, it inhibits is own activity using a feedback inhibitory interneuron. Perseverative performance is hereby prevented.

A volitional rehearsal wave from the basal ganglia enables the highest stored activity to be read out first (Figure 12.36 (4)), and self-inhibitory feedback prevents perseverative performance of this most highly activated cell population, thereby enabling less active populations to be performed (Figure 12.36 (5)), while the network as a whole gradually renormalizes its activity through time. Prevention of perseverative performance is sometimes also called *inhibition of return* (Posner et al., 1985).

In order to convert a recurrent shunting on-center off-surround network into a working memory, all one needs to do is to add a rehearsal wave and self-inhibitory feedback. These latter mechanisms also occur ubiquitously in the brain.

Stable chunking implies primacy, recency, or bowed gradients in working memory. How do the LTM Invariance Principle and Normalization Rule imply bowed performance curves like the ones that occur during free recall (Figures 12.31 and 12.32)? More generally, why are there limits to the number of items that can be stored in working memory in the correct temporal order? In an Item and Order working memory, it can be mathematically proved that, under constant attentional conditions, the pattern of activation that evolves in an Item and Order working memory is one of three types, depending on how network parameters are chosen (Bradski, Carpenter and Grossberg, 1992, 1994; Grossberg, 1978a, 1978b):

Primacy gradient. Here, the first item to be stored has the largest activity and the last item to be stored has the smallest activity. A primacy gradient allows the stored items to be rehearsed in their presented order.

Recency gradient. Here the first item is stored with the smallest activity and the last item with the largest activity. Rehearsal of a recency gradient recalls the most recent item first and the first item last.

Bowed gradient. Here, the first and last items to be stored have larger activities, and thus are earlier rehearsed, than items in the middle of the list, just as during free recall.

From primacy to bowed gradient. I also proved that, as more and more items are stored, a primacy gradient becomes a bowed pattern whose recency part becomes increasingly dominant. Figure

12.37 summarizes a computer simulation in which a primacy gradient is transformed into a bowed gradient as more items are stored in working memory. Note also that, when more items are stored, each is stored with less activity due to the Normalization Rule. This last result predicts why bowed gradients are found in many types of serially ordered behavior: The property of stable learning and memory of list chunks thus imposes a severe limitation on the number of items that can be recalled in the correct temporal order from working memory, because a bow necessarily occurs in the stored gradient of sufficiently long lists.

An algebraic working memory model explains primacy, recency, and bowed gradients. My 1978 articles introduced Item-and-Order working memories using a simple algebraic model that made its concepts clear and its results easy to prove. I will summarize some of the main ideas here using that model for readers who might find that helpful. Other readers can skip to the next section without missing crucial new ideas. The next few figures make the main points.

The first important point is that the LTM Invariance Principle preserves the relative activities of previously stored items so that the adaptive filters that respond to their activities and activate their target list chunks can

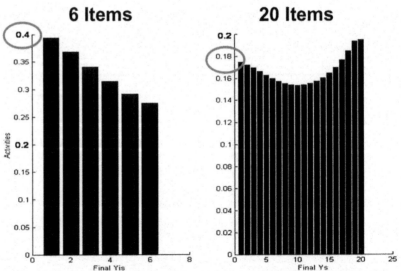

FIGURE 12.37. Simulation of a primacy gradient for a short list (left image) being transformed into a bowed gradient for a longer list (right image). Activities of cells that store the longer list are smaller due to the Normalization Rule, which follows from the shunting inhibition in the working memory network.

preserve their previously learned LTM pattern (Figure 12.38). Figure 12.39 (left column, top row) goes on to show the stored activities using the simplest assumptions that the total activity is the constant value 1, and that previously stored activities are multiplied, or shunted, by the same factor w, which is chosen less than 1, as each new item is stored. Figure 12.39 (right column, top row) goes on to show that, if w is chosen greater than ½, then the stored activity pattern starts to bow when the third item is stored in working memory.

Figure 12.39 (left column, bottom row) starts to analyze more general conditions under which such a bowed gradient will occur. In this case, the ith item is stored with its own initial activity u_i. When it is stored, all previously stored items are shunted by w_i, which can be different as each new item is stored. Each stored activity hereby gets multiplied by more and more shunting terms as more items are stored. The total activity S_i after the ith item is stored is thus a sum of these products.

Figure 12.39 (right column, bottom row) posits that the total activity can grow in perhaps rather complicated ways to its maximum value M. A remarkable behavioral index of such a gradually growing working memory load was described by Daniel Kahneman and Jackson Beatty in 1966 (Kahneman and Beatty, 1966). They showed that the pupil diameter of the eye increases as more items are stored in working memory, and decreases as the stored items are rehearsed.

Remarkably, one can explicitly solve, using just elementary algebra, for the activity $x_i(j)$ of the ith item in the list after the jth item is stored. This equation is at the top of Figure 12.40. I then assumed that steady attention is paid to all the items as they are stored, but I allowed successive items to possibly get stored with less activity, if only because of competition from already-stored items. Even under rather general conditions on such possible decreases in steady attention, I was able to prove that only three possible activity gradients could be stored: a primacy gradient, recency gradient, or bowed gradient for sufficiently long lists.

In summary, long sequences of items are not stored in working memory with their correct temporal order because such storage must also support stable learning and memory of the list chunks that are needed to use the stored sequences to represent the world and to predictively control the next behaviors.

Later modeling work with collaborators such as Gail Carpenter, Gary Bradski, and Lance Pearson (e.g., Bradski, Carpenter, and Grossberg, 1992, 1994; Grossberg and Pearson, 2008) showed how these algebraic properties translate into the dynamics of recurrent shunting on-center off-surround networks with rehearsal waves and self-inhibition.

Psychological and neurophysiological data support predicted working memory properties. These properties of Item and Order working memories have been supported by many subsequent psychological and neurobiological experiments. For example, in 2004, Simon Farrell and Stephan Lewandowsky (Farrell and Lewandowsky, 2004) concluded from their human psychophysical data that: "Several competing theories of short-term memory can explain serial recall performance at a quantitative level. However, most theories to date have not been applied to the accompanying pattern of response latencies . . . these data rule out three of the four representational mechanisms. The data support the notion that *serial order is represented by a primacy gradient that is accompanied by suppression of recalled items*" [italics mine]. Earlier, in 1998, Michael Page and Dennis Norris (Page and Norris, 1998) adapted the Item and Order working memory to describe a Primacy Model, which they used to fit human psychophysical data about immediate serial recall, notably the effects of word length, list length, and phonological similarity.

The predicted properties of the Item-and-Order model were strikingly supported by direct neurophysiological experiments of Bruno Averbeck working

LTM INVARIANCE PRINCIPLE

Choose STM activities so that newly stored STM activities may alter the SIZE of old STM activities without recoding their LTM patterns. In particular:

New events do not change the RELATIVE activities of past event sequences, but may reduce their ABSOLUTE activities

Why? Bottom-up adaptive filtering uses dot products:

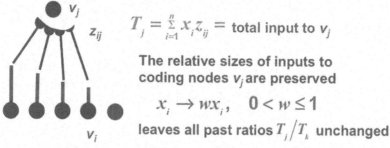

$$T_j = \sum_{i=1}^{n} x_i z_{ij} = \text{total input to } v_j$$

The relative sizes of inputs to coding nodes v_j are preserved

$$x_i \to w x_i, \quad 0 < w \le 1$$

leaves all past ratios T_j / T_k unchanged

FIGURE 12.38. The LTM Invariance Principle is realized if the relative sizes of the inputs to the list chunk level stay the same as more items are stored in working memory. This property, in turn, follows from shunting previously stored working memory activities when a new item occurs.

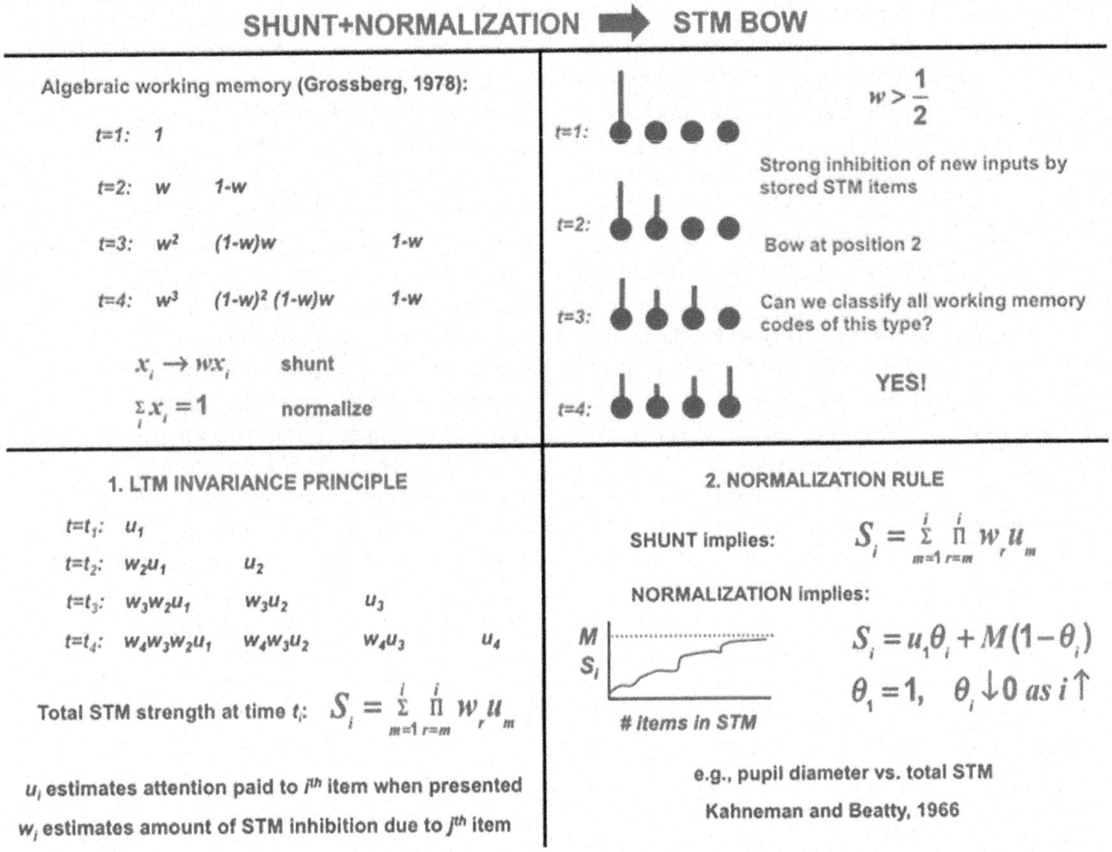

SHUNT+NORMALIZATION ➡ STM BOW

Algebraic working memory (Grossberg, 1978):

$t=1$:   1

$t=2$: w $1-w$

$t=3$: w^2 $(1-w)w$ $1-w$

$t=4$: w^3 $(1-w)^2$ $(1-w)w$ $1-w$

$x_i \to wx_i$ shunt

$\sum_i x_i = 1$ normalize

$t=1$:

$t=2$:

$t=3$:

$t=4$:

$w > \dfrac{1}{2}$

Strong inhibition of new inputs by stored STM items

Bow at position 2

Can we classify all working memory codes of this type?

YES!

1. LTM INVARIANCE PRINCIPLE

$t=t_1$: u_1

$t=t_2$: w_2u_1 u_2

$t=t_3$: $w_3w_2u_1$ w_3u_2 u_3

$t=t_4$: $w_4w_3w_2u_1$ $w_4w_3u_2$ w_4u_3 u_4

Total STM strength at time t_i: $S_i = \overset{i}{\underset{m=1}{\Sigma}} \overset{i}{\underset{r=m}{\Pi}} w_r u_m$

u_i estimates attention paid to i^{th} item when presented

w_j estimates amount of STM inhibition due to j^{th} item

2. NORMALIZATION RULE

SHUNT implies: $S_i = \overset{i}{\underset{m=1}{\Sigma}} \overset{i}{\underset{r=m}{\Pi}} w_r u_m$

NORMALIZATION implies:

M

S_i

items in STM

$S_i = u_1\theta_i + M(1-\theta_i)$

$\theta_1 = 1, \quad \theta_i \downarrow 0 \text{ as } i \uparrow$

e.g., pupil diameter vs. total STM

Kahneman and Beatty, 1966

FIGURE 12.39. (left column, top row) How a shunt plus normalization can lead to a bow in the stored working memory spatial pattern. Time increases in each row as every item is stored with activity 1 before it is shunted by w due to each successive item's storage, and the total working memory activity in each row is normalized to a total activity of 1. (right column, top row) When the working memory stored pattern is shunted sufficiently strongly (w > 1/2), then the pattern bows at position 2 in the list as more items are stored through time. (left column, bottom row) LTM Invariance can be generalized to consider arbitrary amounts of attention u_i being paid when the i_{th} item is stored with an arbitrary amount of shunting w_j to the j_{th} item. (right column, bottom row) The Normalization Rule can also be generalized to approach the maximum possible normalized total activity that is stored across all the working memory cells at different rates.

LTM INVARIANCE + NORMALIZATION

Given (1) and (2), the x_i can be computed:

$$x_i(j) = u_i \prod_{k=i+1}^{j} \left[\frac{u_1\theta_k + M(1-\theta_k) - u_k}{u_1\theta_k + M(1-\theta_{k-1})} \right]$$

How to choose attention weights u_i?

Assuming steady attention, $u_i \geq u_{i+1}$

e.g., $u_i = u_1\phi^{i-1} + u_\infty(1-\phi^{i-1}), 0 \leq \phi \leq 1$

More generally, let $\dfrac{du}{dt} \leq 0, \quad \dfrac{\partial^2 u}{\partial t^2} \geq 0, \quad$ set $\quad u_i = u(i)$

Then the x_i can ONLY form: Primacy gradient

Recency gradient

Unimodal bow

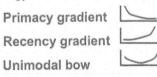

FIGURE 12.40. Given the hypotheses in Figure 12.39 (right column, bottom row) and a generalized concept of steady, albeit possibly decreasing, attention to each item as it is stored in working memory, only a primacy, recency, or bowed gradient of activity across the working memory items can be stored.

with multiple collaborators in the laboratory of Apostolos Georgopoulos (Averbeck et al., 2002, 2003a, 2003b). In their experiments, monkeys were trained to draw copies of geometrical shapes, such as triangles, squares, trapezoids, and inverted triangles, that were presented on a video monitor. The monkeys performed these copying movements by using a joystick while single cell activity was recorded in their prefrontal cortex. Figure 12.41 summarizes some of their data. You can see in each of the graphs for Triangle, Square, and Inverted Triangle the primacy gradient of activity across multiple cells. The cell with the highest activity is performed first, then self-inhibits, before the next most active cell is performed, and so on. Note that, in every case, the last cell to be performed has the highest activity. This can be explained by the fact that all the cells interacted within a recurrent on-center off-surround network. After all the other cells self-inhibited, all inhibition from the off-surrounds of these cells was removed, so the final cell was free from their inhibition and could fire more vigorously than any of the previous ones.

NEUROPHYSIOLOGY OF SEQUENTIAL COPYING

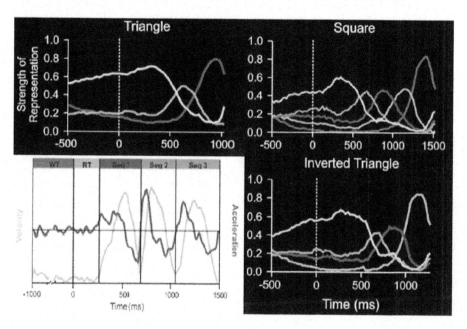

FIGURE 12.41. Neurophysiological data from the Averbeck et al. sequential copying experiments show the predicted primacy gradient in working memory and the self-inhibition of activity as an item is stored. When only the last item remains stored, it has the highest activity because it has been freed from inhibition by earlier items.

LIST PARSE: A laminar model of variable-rate performance of variable-length sequences. These neurophysiological data have been simulated by an Item-and-Order model that is called the LIST PARSE model (Figure 12.42). LIST PARSE was published with my PhD student Lance Pearson in 2008 (Grossberg and Pearson, 2008). The model has several remarkable properties that are of general importance.

For one, LIST PARSE is a *laminar* cortical model of working memory and list chunking. Indeed, its working memory and list chunking circuit is a variant of the same laminar cortical circuit that was used to model 3D vision and figure-ground separation using the 3D LAMINART model that I described in Chapter 11. In both LIST PARSE and 3D LAMINART, the deep layers, such as layers 6 to 4, of the cortex carry out item storage, activity normalization, and contrast enhancement of cell activities, whereas the superficial layers, such as layer 2/3, carry out grouping across processing channels. In 3D LAMINART, these deeper layer properties accomplish oriented filtering of image contrasts, while the superficial layers in V1 and V2 carry out binocular matching and perceptual grouping of oriented image features. By comparison, the deeper layers in LIST PARSE realize a working memory for short-term memory storage of event sequences, whereas the superficial layers carry out list chunking and long-term memory coding of familiar event sequences (Figure 12.43), including sequences of the individual stored items when no

longer sequences have been learned. Resonance between the superficial and deeper layers can maintain stored event sequences in working memory.

Also recall from Chapter 5 the discussion of neurophysiological data from the laboratory of Earl Miller (e.g., Bastos et al., 2018; Lundqvist et al., 2018) about how the superficial and deeper layers of prefrontal working memory circuits realize the predicted gamma/beta match/mismatch dichotomy of laminar cortical dynamics that was predicted by the SMART model of Grossberg and Versace (2008).

There are multiple working memory circuits in the prefrontal cortex. For starters, LIST PARSE (Figures 12.42 and 12.43) proposes that laminar circuits in the deeper layers of ventrolateral prefrontal cortex (VLPFC) may embody a cognitive Item-and-Order working memory, whereas VLPFC superficial layers are predicted to learn list chunks. These list chunks, in turn, control inputs to a motor working memory in dorsolateral prefrontal cortex (DLPFC) whose outputs are gated by a basal ganglia (BG) adaptively-timed volitional control system. When all of these circuits interact, LIST PARSE is able to store and learn event sequences of variable length and to perform them at variable speeds under volitional control. I will say more about how performance is realized at variable speeds later in this chapter.

Thus LIST PARSE and 3D LAMINART illustrate the central theme of Laminar Computing that variations of

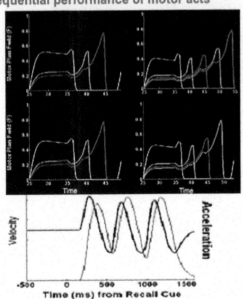

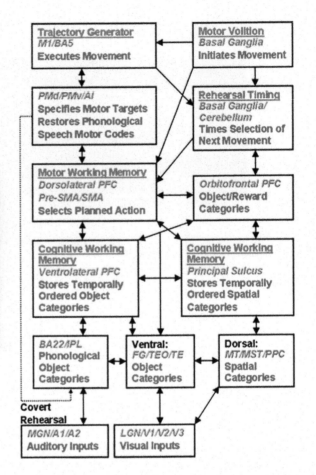

FIGURE 12.42. The LIST PARSE laminar cortical model of working memory and list chunking that I published with Lance Pearson in 2008 simulated the Averbeck et al. data in Figure 12.41, as in the left column of the figure. It also simulated cognitive data about working memory storage by human subjects. See the text for details.

the same canonical cortical circuit can be used to support seemingly very different kinds of biological intelligence.

The second remarkable property of LIST PARSE is that it can quantitatively simulate both psychological data about human verbal behavior, and neurophysiological data about monkey motor behavior. As summarized in Figure 12.42, LIST PARSE simulates human data, using the same set of parameters, about immediate serial recall, during which subjects try to recall items in the order that they were heard, as well as about immediate free recall, delayed free recall, and continuous distractor free recall, which are all variations of the free recall paradigm that I have already discussed. Some of the simulated human data are summarized in Figures 12.44 and 12.45 to show how good these data fits are.

A universal design for linguistic, spatial, and motor working memories. The LIST PARSE simulations of both human verbal data and monkey motor data illustrate the success of a prediction that I made when I introduced Item-and-Order working memories. This prediction asserts that *all linguistic, spatial, and motor working memory*

networks have a similar design, because they all must obey the LTM Invariance Principle and Normalization Rule. In particular, LIST PARSE uses a prefrontal *linguistic* working memory to quantitatively simulate psychophysical data about immediate serial recall, and immediate, delayed, and continuous distractor free recall; and a similarly designed prefrontal *motor* working memory to quantitatively simulate neurophysiological data about sequential recall of stored motor sequences. As I will summarize more completely below, the lisTELOS model that I published in 2011 with my PhD student Matthew Silver and several other collaborators (Silver et al., 2011) used a similarly designed prefrontal *spatial* working memory to quantitatively simulate neurophysiological data about the learning and planned performance of saccadic eye movement sequences.

If indeed all working memories, whether they store linguistic, spatial, or motor item sequences, are realized by similarly designed neural circuits, then they should all exhibit similar data properties, such as error distributions. Many experiments have supported this prediction. Here are a few of them:

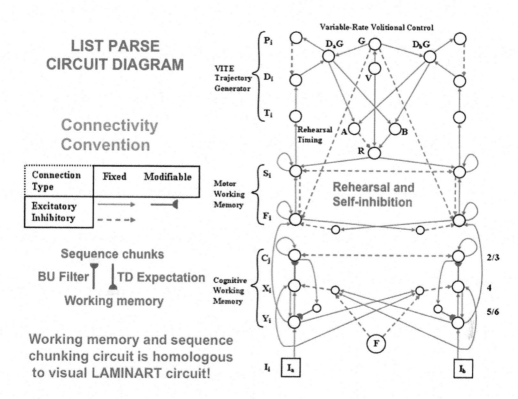

LIST PARSE CIRCUIT DIAGRAM

FIGURE 12.43. The LIST PARSE laminar cortical Cognitive Working Memory circuit, that is proposed to occur in ventrolateral prefrontal cortex, is homologous to the LAMINART circuit that models aspects of how visual cortex sees. The Motor Working Memory, VITE Trajectory Generator, and Variable-Rate Volitional Control circuits model how other brain regions, including dorsolateral prefrontal cortex, motor cortex, cerebellum, and basal ganglia, interact with the Cognitive Working Memory to control working memory storage and variable-rate performance of item sequences.

In 1995, Dylan Jones, Paul Farrand, George Stuart, and Neil Morris (Jones et al., 1995) reported data from a *spatial* serial short-term memory recall task in which visual locations were remembered. These data show similar performance characteristics to data from serial recall during *verbal* short-term memory tasks, including "a marked increase in error with increasing list length, a modest rise in error as retention interval increased, and bow-shaped serial position curves" (p. 1008).

In 2005, Yigal Agam, Daniel Bullock, and Robert Sekuler (Agam et al., 2005) reported psychophysical evidence of Item-and-Order working memory properties in humans as they performed sequential *motor* copying movements. These results included "a strong primacy effect and a moderate recency effect, . . . transposition errors . . . between adjacent segments that, along with the serial position effects, support a competitive queuing model of sequencing . . . " (p. 2832).

In 2007, Yigal Agam, Henry Galperin, Brian Gold, and Robert Sekuler (Agam et al., 2007) reported data consistent with the formation of list chunks as arm movement sequences are practiced, thereby supporting the prediction that working memory networks are designed to interact

closely with list chunking networks. In particular, these authors noted that "with learning, multiple segments in memory are grouped into more compact representations." A number of psychophysics experiments about speech perception have also been carried out to demonstrate the link between short-term working memory and learning of list chunks in long-term memory (e.g., Auer and Luce, 2008; Goldinger and Azuma, 2003; Luce, and McLennan, 2008; McLennan, Conor, and Luce, 2005; McLennan, Luce, and Charles-Luce, 2003; Vitevitch and Luce, 1999).

The similar designs of linguistic, spatial, and motor working memories make it easier to understand how complex behaviors that use more than one modality at a time may be learned and performed. For example, because of this shared design, it becomes easier to understand how verbal language in young children can begin to develop in a way that parallels the motor behaviors of their adult teachers during mutual play, as described in classical studies of Jerome Bruner (Bruner, 1975), or how hearing adults can coordinate their verbal speaking with their motor sign language gestures (Newman et al., 2002). All of these behaviors can benefit from a great deal more experimental and theoretical research that probes their shared working memory designs and how they are coordinated.

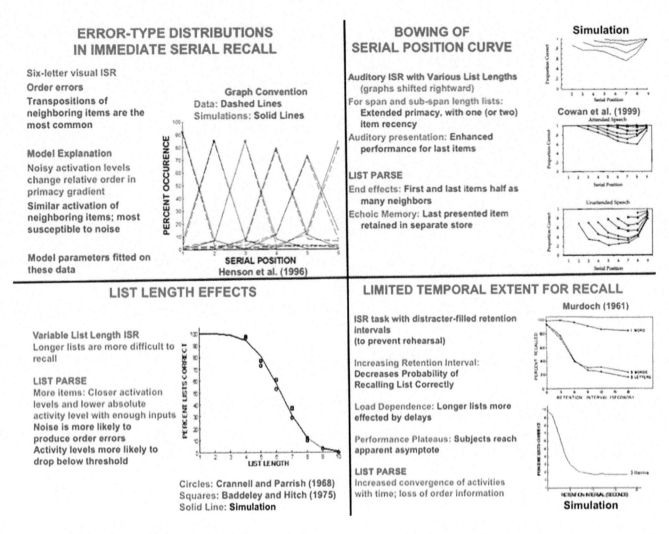

FIGURE 12.44. (left column, top row) LIST PARSE can model linguistic data from human subjects. In this figure, model parameters are fixed to enable a close fit to data about error-type distributions in immediate free recall experiments, notably transposition errors. (right column, top row) Simulation and data showing bowing of the serial position curve, including an extended primacy gradient. (left column, bottom row) The simulation curve overlays data about list length effects, notably the increasing recall difficulty of longer lists during immediate serial recall (ISR). (right column, bottom row) Simulation (bottom image) and data (top image) of the limited temporal extent for recall.

The Magical Numbers Seven and Four: Transient and immediate memory spans. The prediction that primacy gradients become bows for longer lists (Figure 12.37) provides a conceptually satisfying explanation of what have come to be called the Magical Number Seven Plus and Minus Two, and the Magical Number Four Plus and Minus One.

The Magical Number Seven concerns the well-known *immediate memory span* (IMS) of 7+/-2 items that was described in 1956 in a seminal article by George Miller (Miller, 1956). This fact asserts that 7+/-2 chunks can typically be recalled in the correct order during free recall experiments. In addition to explaining the limited span of free recall, Item-and-Order models also explain how a bowed working memory gradient translates

into both *relative order* and *probability of recall*, with items from the beginning and end of a list recalled earlier and with larger probability (Figures 12.31 and 12.32). *Transposition errors* also have a natural explanation. These errors occur when an item is performed just before or after its correct position in a list. They are easily explained by the fact that stored items with similar activity levels will transpose their relative activities, and thus their rehearsal order, more easily than items with very different activity levels if noise perturbs these levels through time.

If attention varies across items, then multimodal bows, or what is typically called von Restorff effects, are also easily explained. These effects were reported in the classical 1933 article on this topic of Hedwig von Restorff (von

TEMPORAL GROUPING AND PRESENTATION VARIABILITY

Temporal Grouping
Inserting an extended pause leads to inter-group bowing
Significantly different times of integration and activity levels across pause; fewer interchanges

Prediction
Increasing IOIs while effectively preventing rehearsal
Enhances performance of recency items, weakens primacy?

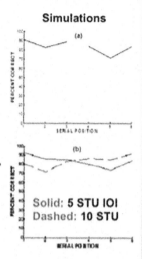

Solid: **5 STU IOI**
Dashed: **10 STU**

IMMEDIATE FREE RECALL
and delayed and continuous-distracter free recall

Overt Rehearsal IFR Task with Super-span (i.e. 20 Item) Lists
Extended recency; even more extended with shorter ISIs
Increased probability of recall with diminished time from last rehearsal
Early items in list rehearsed most

LIST PARSE (Unique)
For long lists:
Incoming items form recency gradient
Rehearsal (re-presentation) based upon level of activity

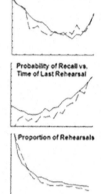

Dashed: **Data**
Solid: **Simulation**

FIGURE 12.45. (left column) LIST PARSE simulations of the proportion of order errors as a function of serial position for 6 item lists with (a) an extended pause of 7 time units between the third and fourth items, and (b) pauses of 5 time units (solid curve) and 10 time units (dashed curve) between all items. (right column) Simulations (solid curves) and data (dashed curves) illustrating close model fits in various immediate free recall tasks.

Restorff, 1933) wherein a distinctive item in a list "stands out like a sore thumb" and is thus more likely to be remembered than other list items. For this reason, such effects are also sometimes called isolation effects (Hunt and Lamb, 2001). Just choose the initial activity u_i larger of the ith item in Figure 12.39 (left column, bottom row) to cause such an effect. Von Restorff effects can also be caused by rate differences and feature-similarity differences across items. Von Restorff effects also occur during serial verbal learning (Grossberg, 1969c, 1974) and can be traced to associative and competitive mechanisms that are consistent with the Item-and-Order working memory model explanation.

What is the difference between the Magical Number Seven Plus or Minus Two, and the Magical Number Four Plus or Minus One? In my 1978 article on human memory (Grossberg, 1978a), I distinguished between the classical *immediate memory span* (IMS) of Miller (1956) and the then new concept of *transient memory span* (TMS). The TMS was predicted to be the result of purely bottom-up processes of short-term working memory storage and recall, without a significant top-down long-term memory (LTM) component from ART mechanisms. The TMS is, accordingly, the longest list length for which a working memory can store a primacy gradient in response to only bottom-up inputs. In contrast, the IMS was predicted to be the result of combining bottom-up inputs and read-out of learned top-down expectations (Figure 5.13). These top-down expectations were assumed to be read out from list chunks that received bottom-up signals from the active working memory item chunks. I was able to mathematically prove that the read-out of list chunk top-down expectations into working memory at the beginning of a list (see Figure 12.32) could generate a longer primacy gradient in working memory, and thus a longer list that could be recalled in the correct order.

Thus, ART top-down feedback to an Item-and-Order working memory leads to an IMS that is longer than the TMS. Estimating the IMS at seven, I was led to expect that the TMS would be around four. Supportive data were published in a seminal 2001 article by Nelson Cowan (Cowan, 2001) that reported a four plus-or-minus one working memory capacity limit when learning and grouping influences are minimized. In addition, it has been shown that long-term memory (LTM) does bias working memory toward more primacy dominance (e.g. Knoedler, Hellwig, and Neath, 1999), and its influence can be difficult to limit. Cowan's 2001 article reviewed proposals for limiting LTM influence, such as using novel sequence orderings of well-learned items that are difficult to group.

Learning chunks of variable lengths and sequences of repeated words

Why is the Magical Number Seven magical? The remarkable property that justifies the name *Magical* Number Seven is that, as noted by Miller, "the memory span is a fixed number of chunks". In other words, within a reasonable range, whether each chunk represents a short or a long list of items, one can simultaneously store in working memory around the same number of chunks of the same length. This fact clarified the critical role of learning in supporting all complex planned behaviors by showing that one could remember and perform more information if it is encoded into longer familiar chunks.

A Masking Field working memory chunks lists of variable length. In order to explain a property like the Magical Number Seven, one needs to understand how the brain can learn list chunks that represent lists of variable length. One also needs to understand how sequences of list chunks of variable length can simultaneously be stored in working memory in a way that explains the Magical Number Seven. Finally, as illustrated by the LTM Invariance Principle, one needs to understand how such a storage process can preserve previously learned memories of shorter familiar chunks, even if longer familiar chunks are chosen to best represent a given environment.

A neural explanation of the Magical Numbers Four and Seven was first given using an Item-and-Order working memory that I have called a Masking Field (Figure 12.46; Grossberg, 1978a, 1984d, 1986). A Masking Field is a specialized type of Item-and-Order working memory. As with all Item-and-Order working memories, it is defined by a recurrent on-center off-surround network whose cells obey the membrane equations of neurophysiology, or shunting laws. In a Masking Field, however, the "items" are themselves *list chunks* that are selectively activated, via a bottom-up adaptive filter, by prescribed sequences of items that are stored in an Item-and-Order working memory at an earlier processing level (Figure 1.24). In other words, Masking Field cells represent list chunks because each of them is activated by a particular temporal sequence, or list, of items that is stored within the Item-and-Order working memory at the previous processing level. Thus, both levels of the item and list processing hierarchy are composed of working memories that obey similar laws.

In order for Masking Field list chunks to represent lists (e.g., syllables or words) of multiple lengths, its cells interact within and between multiple spatial sizes, or scales, with the cells of larger sizes capable of selectively representing item sequences of greater length, and of inhibiting smaller Masking Field cells that represent item sequences of lesser length (Figures 12.46 and 12.47). As items are stored in working memory, an adaptive filter activates the learned Masking Field list chunks that represent the

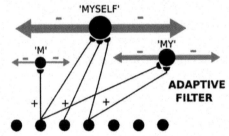

HOW TO CODE VARIABLE LENGTH LISTS?
MASKING FIELDS code list chunks of variable length
Cohen and Grossberg (1986, 1987); Grossberg and Kazerounian (2011, 2016);
Grossberg and Myers (2000); Grossberg and Pearson (2008)

Multiple-scale self-similar WM MASKING FIELD

'MYSELF'
'M'   'MY'
ADAPTIVE FILTER

VARIABLE LENGTH CODING: Masking fields select list chunks that are sensitive to WM sequences of variable length

SELECTIVITY: Larger cells selectively code longer lists

ASYMMETRIC COMPETITION: Larger cells can inhibit smaller cells more than conversely Magical Number 7!

TEMPORAL ORDER: Different list chunks respond to the same items in different orders e.g., LEFT vs FELT

FIGURE 12.46. A Masking Field working memory is a multiple-scale self-similar recurrent shunting on-center off-surround network. It can learn list chunks that respond selectively to lists of item chunks of variable length that are stored in an item working memory at the previous processing stage. Chunks that code for longer lists (e.g., MY vs. MYSELF) are larger, and give rise to stronger recurrent inhibitory neurons (red arrows).

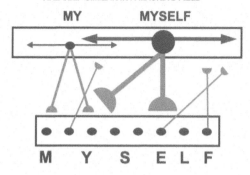

FIGURE 12.47. This figure illustrates the self-similarity in a Masking Field of both its recurrent inhibitory connections (red arrows) and its top-down excitatory priming signals (green arrows) to the item chunk working memory.

most predictive item groupings at any time, while its recurrent inhibitory interactions suppress less predictive list chunks. My PhD student Sohrob Kazerounian and I simulated in 2014 how variable-length list chunks of a Masking Field can be learned as lists of items are stored in working memory in real time (Kazerounian and Grossberg, 2014).

Each item that inputs to a Masking Field, just like to any working memory, is an *item chunk*. Each item chunk responds selectively to a briefly active spatial pattern of activity across acoustical feature detectors. A bottom-up adaptive filter responds to this feature pattern by activating the item chunk (Figure 5.13). The prescribed time interval is short, and is commensurate with the duration of the shortest perceivable acoustic inputs, of the order of 10–100 msec. Each item chunk is learned using an ART network in order to dynamically stabilize its learning and memory. Thus, in addition to the bottom-up adaptive filter learning, there is also top-down expectation learning. As a sound stream evolves, new acoustic feature patterns arrive and will mismatch the previously active item chunk. It is then reset in order to enable the next item chunk to be processed (Figure 5.19). As this process evolves through time, the cells in the working memory at the bottom of Figures 12.46 and 12.47 are activated by sequences of item chunks before a second adaptive filter responds to sequences of these stored item chunks by activating list chunks in the Masking Field.

Temporal Chunking Problem: Learning words of variable length. In order for such a sequence of events to be possible, the brain first needs to solve several basic problems. All of these problems, in one form or another, ask the same question: How does the process even get started, assuming that it will be operating autonomously, and without help from an external teacher? In particular, Masking Fields were introduced to solve the Temporal Chunking Problem (Cohen and Grossberg 1986, 1987; Grossberg 1978a, 1986). The Temporal Chunking Problem concerns how a new

word gets learned that is composed of syllables that are themselves already familiar words. The problem is: Why is not the brain forced to process the new word as a sequence of smaller familiar words? How does a not-yet-established word representation overcome the salience of already well-established phoneme, syllable, or word representations to enable learning of the novel word to occur?

For example, suppose that the words MY, ELF, and SELF have already been learned, and have their own list chunks. When the novel word MYSELF is presented for the first time, all of its familiar subwords also get presented as part of this longer sequence. What mechanisms prevent the familiarity of MY, ELF, and SELF, which are trying to activate their own list chunks, from forcing the novel longer list MYSELF from being processed as a sequence of these smaller familiar chunks, rather than eventually as a newly learned unitized whole? If this did happen, then longer words could never be learned. Nor could longer navigational routes that include familiar subroutes, or more complex motor skills that include familiar gestures. We would be led to a *reductio ad absurdum*.

Self-similar growth and length-sensitive competition solve the Temporal Chunking Problem. A Masking Field overcomes the Temporal Chunking Problem by using cells with multiple receptive field sizes, or scales (Figures 12.46 and 12.47). These cells are related to each other by a property of *self-similarity*; that is, each scale's properties, including its cell body sizes and their excitatory and inhibitory connection lengths and interaction strengths, are (approximately) a multiple of the corresponding properties in another scale. In 1986 and 1987, Michael Cohen and I showed that this self-similarity property can develop as a result of simple activity-dependent growth laws in the following way (Cohen and Grossberg 1986, 1987):

Many connections in the developing brain are formed initially by an activity-dependent process. Assume that such an activity-dependent process helps to control the formation of connections between the two cortical levels that are depicted in Figure 12.46. In particular, the cells in the cortical level that will eventually represent item chunks are endogenously active during a critical period of development. During this active phase, these cells send growing connections to the cortical level that will eventually represent the Masking Field. Suppose for simplicity that these growing connections are distributed randomly across the Masking Field, constrained possibly by obstructions to unfettered growth that may occur due to their density. As a result of this growth, different Masking Field cells will receive different numbers of connections. Due to the endogenous activity, Masking Field cells that receive more connections will, on the average, receive a larger total input activity through time.

The second assumption is that, during the critical period, activating Masking Field cells above a fixed threshold can cause their cell bodies *and* their connections to grow approximately proportionally. The property of proportional growth is called *self-similar growth*. Cell growth terminates when the cell bodies become large enough to dilute their activities sufficiently in response to their inputs so that these inputs no longer exceed the growth-triggering threshold. Because they receive larger total inputs through time, cells that receive more input connections grow larger than cells that receive fewer input connections. The effects of individual inputs are thus smaller on the firing of larger cells. In this way, self-similar growth *normalizes* the total effect of all the inputs that converge on a Masking Field cell. Consequently, a Masking Field cell will only fire vigorously if it receives active inputs from all of its item chunk cells. In other words, self-similar growth ensures that each Masking Field cell responds *selectively* to the input sequence that it codes. A similar kind of normalization enables multiple scales of cells in the motion cortical stream to respond selectively to different object speeds (Figures 8.32 and 8.33).

Due to self-similar growth, larger list chunks selectively represent longer lists because they need more inputs, and thus more evidence, to fire. Once they fire, their stronger inhibitory interaction strengths than those of smaller list chunks can inhibit the smaller list chunks more than conversely. This is thus yet another example of *asymmetric competition*. The intuitive idea is that, other things being equal, the longest lists are better predictors of subsequent events than are shorter sublists, because a longer list embodies a more unique temporal context. The stronger inhibition from list chunks of longer, but unfamiliar, lists (e.g., MYSELF) enables them to inhibit the chunks that represent shorter, but familiar, sublists (e.g., MY), more than conversely, thereby providing a solution of the Temporal Chunking Problem.

Self-similarity clarifies the Magical Number Seven and the word superiority effect. The Masking Field self-similarity property helps to explain several kinds of challenging cognitive data, including the Magical Number Seven and word length effect in word superiority studies.

The Magical Number Seven results from the properties of self-similarity and asymmetric competition. To understand why, think of a Masking Field as being composed of multiple interacting networks, such that each network consists of cells with the same scale. All cell body and connection parameters are chosen across scales in a self-similar way to ensure that all Masking Field cells respond selectively to the input sequences that they experience. In addition, due to self-similarity and asymmetric competition, the largest fully-activated chunks are chosen by asymmetric competition in response to any input sequence (Figure 12.46). Because each single-scale network within the Masking Field is self-similar with every other single-scale network, the same number of winning chunks

will tend to be activated, no matter how big their chunks may be. This explains why "the memory span is a fixed number of chunks". Why that number tends to be Seven Plus-or-Minus-Two depends upon parameter choices that define these working memory networks. Bradski, Carpenter, and Grossberg (1994) provide a mathematical analysis of how such parameter choices influence a network's memory span.

The *word length effect* was reported in 1982 by Arthur Samuel, Jan van Santen, and James Johnston (Samuel et al., 1982, 1983). These authors showed that a letter is progressively better recognized when it is embedded in longer words of lengths from 1 to 4. The word length effect is relevant to self-similarity because larger list chunks are more potent and predictive than smaller list chunks in a Masking Field. However, self-similarity implies that the list chunk of a familiar multi-letter word can *inhibit* the list chunk of a familiar letter within the Masking Field. This fact seems to contradict the property that the word can *facilitate* perception of its constituent letters, which is the main result of word superiority studies.

This problem is resolved in an ART systems with item chunk and list chunk processing levels, if the list chunks occur in a Masking Field. In particular, although chunks that represent lists of multiple lengths *compete within the Masking Field* that categorizes list chunks, the top-down *expectations from the list chunk level to the item chunk level are excitatory* (Figure 12.47). By self-similarity, list chunks that represent longer words generate larger recurrent inhibitory signals within the chunk level *and* larger top-down excitatory priming signals to the item chunk level. As a result, letters in longer words get larger excitatory top-down priming signals, and are thus better recognized than letters in shorter words.

These explanations of the Magical Number Seven and the word length effect provide further support for the ART prediction that item chunk and list chunk levels process speech and language (Grossberg, 1978a, 1984d, 1986), rather than the phoneme, letter, and word levels that were used in other popular cognitive models, notably the Interactive Activation Model that James McClelland and David Rumelhart published in 1981 (McClelland and Rumelhart, 1981, 1982).

All familiar letters activate item chunks and list chunks. The word length property is only one of the many language properties that support the hypothesis that speech and language properties build upon processing levels in which item chunks and list chunks are the basic functional units, rather than phoneme, letter, and word levels. One additional kind of data is worth mentioning. If one believes that distinct letter and word levels exist, then familiar letters that are not words, such as E and F, should be recognized worse than letters, such as A and I, that are also words. This conclusion would follow from the hypothesis that top-down matching from the word level to the letter level could support the recognition of A and I in a way that would not happen for letters like E and F. This is not, however, true. Daniel Wheeler reported in 1970 (Wheeler, 1970) that letters such as A and I are not recognized more easily than letters such as E and F.

This fact is easily explained if there are item chunk and list chunk levels: *All* familiar letters, whether or not they are words, have item chunk and list chunk representations. They therefore can all benefit from top-down matching from the list level to the item level. Hence, there should be no difference in recognition simply due to the fact that some letters are words but others are not. The fact that list chunks for familiar letters may not be strongly activated when these letters are part of multi-letter words is clarified by Masking Fields, which show how the most predictive list chunk for the word can inhibit less predictive syllabic chunks, including the list chunks for the words' individual letters. As I noted above when explaining the word superiority effect, even when the list chunk of a familiar letter is inhibited, the winning list chunk that represents the word can enhance the processing of the inhibited letter's item chunk.

This difference between the two hypotheses about processing levels is only one of the problems faced by a theory that posits separate levels for phonemes, letter, and words. A much more serious problem is that the units within these levels cannot stably self-organize during development, hence language could never be learned.

From streaming to speech: Item-list resonances for recognition of speech and language

Top-down attentive matching during speech and language using the ART Matching Rule. Given that top-down attentive priming helps to explain data like the word superiority effect, what evidence supports the hypothesis that this top-down circuit obeys the ART Matching Rule? Below some of the data that support this hypothesis will be reviewed. Assuming that it is true, I can look ahead to draw the following conclusions:

Top-down expectation signals from the list chunks are activated as the items are being stored in working memory through time. If these top-down expectations satisfy the ART Matching Rule, they can select consistent item sequences, while inhibiting inconsistent ones, to create a temporally-evolving attentional focus. As the cycle between bottom-up activation of list chunks and top-down

attentive matching of item sequences continues through time, an *item-list resonance* can develop whose list chunks represent the best prediction of what item chunk sequences are attended at any given time within the working memory. Such an item-list resonance is proposed to support conscious recognition of attended speech and language representations (Table 1.4) when it interacts with lower-level resonances, such as stream-shroud and spectral-pitch-and-timbre resonances.

Phonemic restoration: How the future can influence what is consciously heard in the past. One striking phenomenon that illustrates how the ART Matching Rule operates during speech and language processing is *phonemic restoration*, that I discussed briefly in Chapter 1. Phonemic restoration was described by Richard Warren and his colleagues in the 1970s (e.g., Warren and Sherman, 1974). It illustrates the operation of ART mechanisms during speech perception in much the same way as the auditory continuity illusion represents them during auditory streaming (Figure 12.17). Suppose that broadband noise replaces the phonemes /v/ and /b/ in the words "delivery" and "deliberation", respectively. Despite the identical initial portion of these words ("deli-"), if the broadband noise is immediately followed by "ery" or "eration", listeners hear the /v/ or /b/ as being fully intact. However, if the noise is replaced by silence, then restoration does not occur.

These properties of phonemic restoration follow from properties of top-down matching by the ART Matching Rule (Figure 1.25). For example, why is not the noise in "deli-noise-[ery/eration]" heard before the last portion of the word is presented? This may be explained by the fact that, if the resonance for the first part of the word has not developed fully before the last portion of the word is presented, then the last portion can influence the top-down expectations that determine the conscious percept. These expectations convert the noise in "deli-noise-[ery/eration]" into a conscious percept of /v/ or /b/ by selecting expected feature clusters for attentive processing while suppressing unexpected ones. In the "deli-noise-[ery/eration]" example, spectral components of the noise are suppressed that are not part of the expected consonant sound.

If the /v/ or /b/ in "delivery/deliberation" is replaced by silence, why is the silence perceived as silence despite the fact the disambiguating cue would have influenced the percept were these phonemes replaced by noise? This property follows from the fact that the on-center of the ART Matching Rule is *modulatory*. This matching process can select feature components that are consistent with its prototype, but it cannot create something out of nothing.

Thus, phonemic restoration properties illustrate attentive matching properties of the ART Matching Rule that enable speech and language to be learned quickly, without risking catastrophic forgetting. In the case of speech perception, the categories that are learned are list chunks of phonemes, syllables, and words, rather than the pitch-and-timbre categories that are learned during auditory streaming.

A variation of this experiment uses a reduced set of spectral components in the noise stimulus. This leads to hearing a correspondingly degraded consonant sound, since the expected speech formants are not fully present in the available noise spectrum. This effect was reported in 1981 by Arthur Samuel (Samuel, 1981a, 1981b). Phonemic restoration is thus not merely a symbolic reconstruction of an expected sound. Rather, it creates a phonetic experience of this sound.

Further evidence for phonemic restoration as a perceptual phenomenon comes from experiments that Makio Kashino published in 2006 (Kashino, 2006). The stimuli in this study contained multiple deletions of the speech signal "Do you understand what I am saying" such that the signal would alternate with silence intervals every 50, 100, or 200 milliseconds. In these examples, stimuli with silence intervals that are not filled with broadband noise sound disjoint and are either difficult or impossible to understand. Filled with broadband noise, however, the speech signal sounds more natural and continuous, and becomes easily understandable. Because the earliest studies relied on just a single excised portion of the speech signal, the utterance remained relatively intact and understandable regardless of whether or not noise was presented in place of the silence, making response strategies susceptible to bias. In the Kashino stimuli, however, it would be very difficult to alter response strategies, since a subject cannot force understanding of an otherwise unintelligible acoustic stream.

Conscious speech is a resonant wave: Coherently grouping the units of speech and language. As in the case of the auditory continuity illusion, future events during phonemic restoration can influence past events without smearing over all the events that intervene, including the silence intervals between words. Again this is due to the fact that the top-down attentive matching process is modulatory.

The opposite concern is also of importance: How can sharp word boundaries be perceived even if the sound spectrum that represents the words exhibits no silence intervals between them? ART proposes that "conscious speech is a resonant wave" and that "perceived silence is a temporal break in the rate at which the resonant wave evolves". These revolutionary claims shed light on how the top-down matching process coherently groups familiar linguistic units together

through time, even if they are not separated by silence intervals in the input stream. In particular, the "resonant wave" that embodies the properties of phonemic restoration illustrates how the conscious percepts of speech sounds can proceed from past to future, even if sounds that are heard in the past may be disambiguated by future contextual information.

When is a "gray chip" a "great ship"? There are many examples of such "backward effects in time" in the speech and language perception literature. They are an important type of data because they challenge classical ideas about what the functional units of speech and language are and how they are formed in the brain, while also providing valuable clues about how these functional units form through time.

Many other examples of how contextual interactions across time can change the perceived units of speech and language have been explained as emergent properties of ART interactions. These examples all illustrate the dynamic nature of the process whereby the brain coherently groups item sequences, using item-list resonances, into the emergent auditory objects that have meaning in speech and language.

Striking examples of such dynamism in language were published in 1978 by Bruno Repp, Alvin Liberman, Thomas Eccardt, and David Pesetsky (Repp et al., 1978). These authors used a recording of the sentence "Did anyone see the gray ship?" to show that variations in the durations of individual speech sounds and the silence intervals between them can produce strikingly different perceived consciously heard words (Figure 12.48 (left column)). Keep in mind throughout this discussion that both of the relevant words "gray" and "ship" are short,

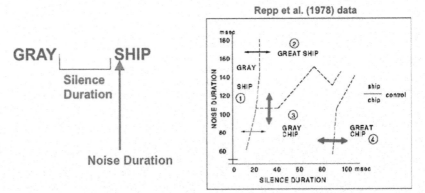

FIGURE 12.48. (left column) In experiments of Repp et al. (1978), the silence duration between the words GRAY and SHIP was varied, as was the duration of the fricative noise in S, with surprising results. (right column) The red arrows direct our attention to surprising perceptual changes as silence and noise durations increase. See the text for details.

unambiguous, and highly familiar. Despite this fact, increasing the silence interval between the words "gray" and "ship" can cause listeners to perceive them as "gray chip", or at even longer silence intervals as "great chip" (Figure 12.48 (right column)).

Why should *increasing* the silence interval between words—which from a naïve point of view should separate them more completely in time—cause the initial fricative noise in "chip" to leap backwards in time over a silence interval of 100 milliseconds to supplant a perfectly legal word "gray" with the word "great" that is not represented in the speech signal, thereby changing the conscious percept from "gray chip" to "great chip"? Further, increasing the duration of the initial fricative noise of the word "chip" can induce a switch in the perception of "gray chip" to "great ship", thus again changing the percept of the first word by altering its final sounds, but also changing the percept of the second word too. Why should increasing the duration of the fricative noise at the beginning of the second word "chip" cause it to leap backwards in time over 30–80 milliseconds of silence to supplant the first word "gray" by "great" *and* at the same time detach itself entirely from the word "chip" to which it belonged, leaving behind the word "ship"?

These processes were quantitatively simulated in an article that I published in 2000 with my PhD student Christopher Myers (Grossberg and Myers, 2000). This article describes an ART-based model that we called the ARTWORD model (Figure 12.49). We gave this variant of

the ARTPHONE model the name ARTWORD because it shows how backward effects can cross over word boundaries to change consciously heard word percepts. Indeed, all of the paradoxical data properties could be traced to intuitively simple properties of how resonant waves develop between working memories and list chunking networks. In particular, ARTWORD has a working memory to store sequences of item chunks, a Masking Field to store list chunks of variable length, a bottom-up adaptive filter, a top-down expectation whose pathways obey the ART Matching Rule, and activity-dependent habituative transmitter gates in its pathways to prevent storage of any list chunk from perseverating through time.

Resonant transfer from "gray" to "great": Longer silence intervals allow greater habituation. The ARTWORD neural model qualitatively explains how these percepts arise naturally from ART concepts, and quantitatively simulates these context-sensitive speech data. These explanations follow directly from the ARTWORD perception cycle. Proceeding from (a) to (d) in Figure 12.50: First, bottom-up inputs try to activate their list chunks, which compete for dominance. The list chunk that has the most support from its item chunks typically wins the competition, even as it resonates with these item chunks. As this item-list resonance persists, it begins to collapse due to the activity-dependent habituative transmitter gates in its active bottom-up and top-down pathways. A longer silence interval before activating the fricative noise will

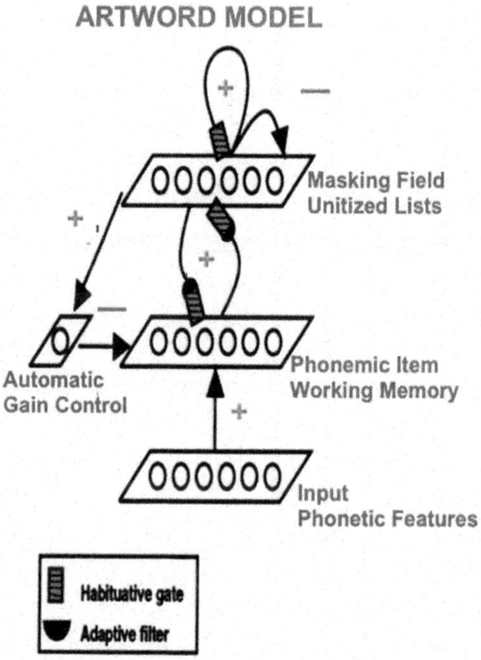

FIGURE 12.49. The ARTWORD model that I published in 2000 with my PhD student Christopher Myers simulates data such as the Repp et al. (1978) data in Figure 12.68. See the text for details.

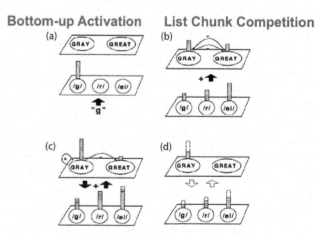

FIGURE 12.50. The ARTWORD perception cycle shows how sequences of items activate possible list chunks, which compete among each other and begin to send their top-down expectations back to the item working memory. An item-list resonance develops through time as a result.

therefore create a /t/ input to the list chunks when the GRAY chunk's activation is significantly weakened due to activity-dependent habituation in the pathways that lead to and from it (Figure 12.51 (left column)). In contrast, the pathways that link the chunk GREAT to the working memory items are not as habituated. As a result, the GREAT chunk can now win the competition, leading to a "resonant transfer" from list chunk GRAY to list chunk GREAT, along with an item-list resonance that supports a percept of GREAT, rather than GRAY.

Figure 12.51 (right column) shows a computer simulation of a resonant transfer from list chunk GRAY to list chunk GREAT as the silence interval between the acoustic inputs for "gray" and "chip" increases. The figure summarizes four simulations of the network response, labeled (A) – (D). The bottom figure in each of these simulations shows three temporally-contiguous inputs corresponding to "gray", shown as abutting alternating green and red rectangles, followed after an interval of silence by an input in red

corresponding to the fricative noise in "chip". Each figure presents the fricative noise at a longer delay. The response in (A) in the top figure shows that chunk GRAY initially wins over chunk GREAT. However, the responses in (B) and (C) show that the chunk GREAT wins over chunk GRAY due to the longer delays, and thus weaker GRAY resonances when the fricative noise is turned on. When the silence interval becomes too long, as in (D), the fricative noise no longer has any effect during the resonance time scale, so that the GRAY chunk continues to win the competition.

Phonemic restoration in a laminar cortical model of speech perception. I explained above how the ART Matching Rule can select expected formants in a sound stream when they are occluded by noise, but not when they are replaced by silence (Figure 1.22). This argument is not, however, sufficient to explain how we consciously recognize the restored sounds in the correct temporal order, from past to future, even if the phonetic context that

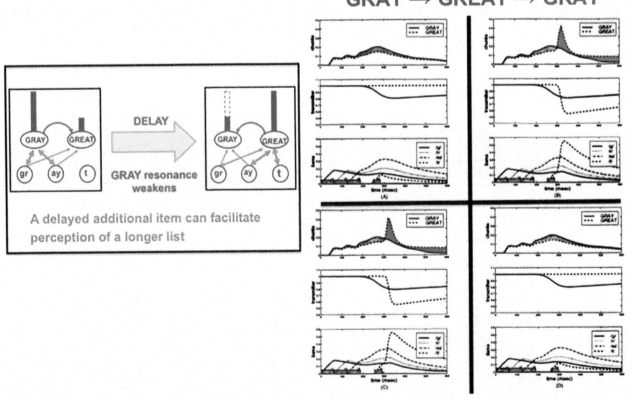

FIGURE 12.51. (left column) Even as a resonance with the list chunk GRAY begins to develop, if the delay between "gray" and "chip" is increased, greater habituation of this resonance may allow the GREAT chunk to begin to win, thereby smoothly transferring the item-list resonance from GRAY to GREAT through time. (right column)
Simulation of a resonant transfer from GRAY to GREAT, and back again as the silence interval between the words "gray" and "chip" increases. The red region between the GRAY and GREAT curves calls attention to when GREAT wins. See the text for details.

enables this restoration occurs after the occluded sounds are presented. The *conscious ARTWORD*, or cARTWORD model that I published in 2011 with my PhD student Sohrob Kazerounian provides a qualitative explanation and computer simulations of this kind of restoration (Figure 12.30; Grossberg and Kazerounian, 2011, 2016; Kazerounian and Grossberg, 2014) To the best of my knowledge, cARTWORD provides the only available neural model that simulates how, during phonemic restoration, future acoustic context can disambiguate noise-occluded speech sounds that occurred earlier, yet generate a completed percept that is consciously heard in the correct temporal order from past to future. How does cARTWORD explain this?

In cARTWORD, a hierarchy of coordinated resonances can generate this conscious percept. This is accomplished within *laminar* cortical circuits that, remarkably, are specializations of laminar cortical circuits that have also been used to model 3D vision and figure-ground perception in the 3D LAMINART model that I described in Chapter 11.

A main insight of cARTWORD is that active list chunks, which represent the most predictive representation of the current linguistic context, trigger the conscious recognition process. These list chunks are chosen within the highest level of cARTWORD, which would occur in the prefrontal cortex of a living brain. Once such a list chunk wins the competition for activation, it does several things. One thing that it does is activate the usual ART Matching Rule top-down expectation signals to prime

item chunks in its learned prototype that are stored in working memory. In addition, it sends out a parallel top-down signal (shown in purple in Figure 12.30) that can open basal ganglia gates (Figure 6.13) that enable the entire hierarchy of cARTWORD processing stages to start resonating. This multi-level resonance triggers a resonant wave that includes acoustic features, item chunks, working memory activity patterns, and list chunks. The unfolding through time of this resonant wave simulates the consciously recognized, phonemically restored, speech representations progressing in their correct temporal order from past to future.

Figure 12.52 through Figure 12.55 summarize computer simulations of the wave through time. In particular, Figure 12.52 shows the dynamics of multiple cARTWORD processing stages through time in response to a normal sequence of three items that are, for simplicity, labeled /1/, /2/, and /3/. The processing level that is surrounded by a red rectangle shows the resonating activities of all three items that support conscious recognition. Figure 12.53 shows the response to the two items /1/ and /3/ that are separated by a silence interval. The corresponding resonance also has a gap in it where the silence is perceived. Figure 12.54 shows the dynamics in response to a list with items /1/ and /3/ separated by noise. The network restores the item /2/ instead of the noise. Figure 12.55 shows the dynamics in response to a list with items /1/ and /5/ separated by noise. Here, the correct restoration is item /4/. Thus, despite the

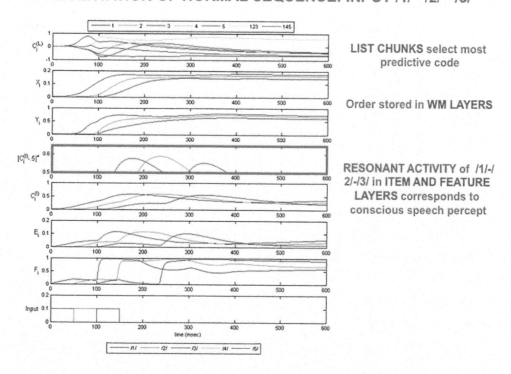

PRESENTATION OF NORMAL SEQUENCE: INPUT /1/ - /2/ - /3/

LIST CHUNKS select most predictive code

Order stored in **WM LAYERS**

RESONANT ACTIVITY of /1/-/2/-/3/ in **ITEM AND FEATURE LAYERS** corresponds to conscious speech percept

FIGURE 12.52. Simulation of cARTWORD dynamics in response to the complete list /1/ - /2/ - /3/. The relevant responses are surrounded by a red box.

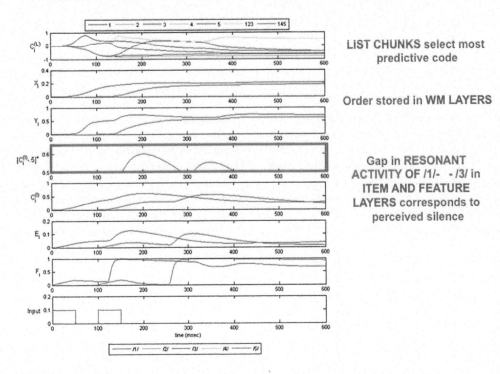

FIGURE 12.53. Simulation of cARTWORD dynamics in response to the partial list /1/ - -/3/ with /2/ replaced by silence. Only the representations of these items can be seen in the red box.

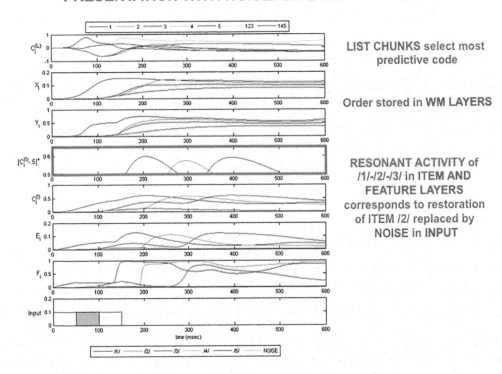

FIGURE 12.54. Item /2/ is restored in the correct list position in response to the list /1/ - NOISE - /3/.

PRESENTATION WITH NOISE: INPUT /1/ - NOISE - /5/

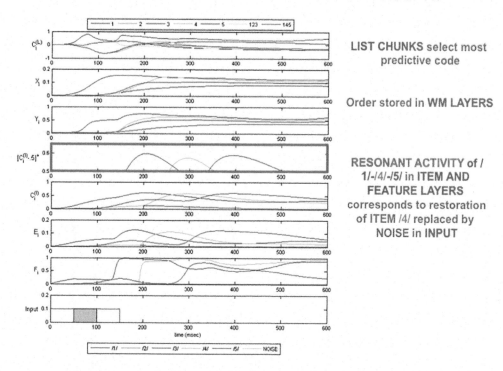

LIST CHUNKS select most predictive code

Order stored in WM LAYERS

RESONANT ACTIVITY of /1/-/4/-/5/ in ITEM AND FEATURE LAYERS corresponds to restoration of ITEM /4/ replaced by NOISE in INPUT

FIGURE 12.55. Item /4/ is restored in the correct list position in response to the list /1/ - NOISE /5/. This and the previous figure show how future context can disambiguate past noisy sequences that are otherwise identical.

fact that the initial lists "/1/-noise" are identical in the two cases of restoration, the final item /3/ or /5/ can restore the contextually-correct noise-occluded item.

Simple item inputs were used in this first demonstration of phonemic restoration, in order to get the hierarchical dynamics correct for acoustic feature, item chunk, working memory, and list chunk interactions. Future work on cARTWORD should focus on, among other improvements, including more realistic auditory features in its items.

In summary, figure-ground separation in vision may be compared with streaming in audition and speech perception. If these visual and auditory processes have homologous brain designs, then the auditory analog of V4 in visual surface representation may be sought by future research in the anatomical substrate of auditory streaming, notably in the auditory cortex A1 and beyond (Figure 12.1; Gutschalk, Rupp, and Dykstra, 2015; Micheyl, Carlyon, Gutschalk, Melcher, Oxenham, Rauschecker, Tian, and Wilson, 2007). A spectral-pitch-and-timbre resonance has some of the required properties to support conscious percepts of auditory streams, but the resonances that support conscious hearing cannot be restricted only to the sustained sounds that support pitches. As explained below in this chapter, both transient and sustained feature detectors are needed to consciously hear, understand, and perform the sounds of the world.

Item-Order-Rank working memories: From numerical to positional coding

Storing sequences of repeated items in working memory. Before discussing how the feature detectors that input to early auditory processing can be enriched with transient detectors and related refinements, I will describe how Item-and-Order working memories can be generalized to store event sequences whose items may be repeated several times at different positions, or *ranks*, in the sequence; e.g., ABACBD.

Both psychophysical and neurobiological data indicate that rank information may be explicitly coded by the brain. For example, when a list is presented multiple times, there is an increased likelihood of intrusions from items at similar list positions across trials (reviewed in Henson, 1998a, 1998b). Moreover, repetitive presentation of an item in the same absolute serial position when lists are repeated with otherwise different list orderings leads to a statistically significant increase in learning of that item (Conway and Christiansen, 2001). There is also a statistically small, but significant, class of errors called "protrusions", in which interchanges between items in similar serial positions of different temporal groupings in a list are more common than interchanges between items in different serial positions (Henson, 1998a, 1998b). That is, when presented with the sequence ABC (pause) DEF, interchanges between items at B and E are more common than interchanges between items at B and F. The well-known "slip of the tongue" error of "spoonerisms" illustrates a similar effect. Here, phonemes or syllables in similar positions in different words are selectively interchanged (e.g., "hissed my mystery lesson").

On the neurobiological side, it is also known that there are cells in the brain that are sensitive to rank. For example, a cell may respond to any target in the initial, middle or final ordinal position in a sequence, or the first, second, third, etc. positions. These cells are said to exhibit *rank order*, also called temporal selectivity or position specificity, while other cells may exhibit selectivity to *conjunctive coding* of item and ordinal position. Such a cell may respond to a specific target presented in a specific ordinal position (Averbeck et al., 2003a; Funahashi et al., 1997; Inoue and Mikami, 2006).

Positional theories due to scientists like Neil Burgess, Graham Hitch, and Richard Henson (e.g., Burgess, 1995; Burgess and Hitch, 1992; Henson, 1988a, 1988b) posit that positional information is explicitly maintained to establish recall order. Such positional information may be absolute, or relative to the beginning and/or end of lists. However, these models do not explain critical data about how the brain stores item repetitions in working memory. For example, I have already reviewed psychophysical data of Farrell and Lewandowsky (Farrell and Lewandowsky, 2004) about error latencies which led them to conclude that recall from working memory involves a primacy gradient modulated by self-inhibition of recalled items, which are bedrock Item-and-Order properties. I have also described the monkey neurophysiological data of Averbeck et al. (Averbeck et al., 2002, 2003a, 2003b) about serial performance of arm movements (Figure 12.41) in which a primacy gradient with self-inhibition of recalled items can vividly be seen. These latter data also include a property that I did not earlier mention, namely rank-selectivity of the recorded cells.

Our task is thus to show whether and how Item-and-Order working memories can be generalized to Item-Order-Rank working memories without undermining my previous explanations of data that did not require rank selectivity. In fact, if an Item-Order-Rank working memory was used in all the above explanations and simulations, instead of an Item-and-Order working memory, it would have yielded the *identical* results, since the inputs used in these simulations included no repeated items. I will now explain why this is true.

From parietal numerical representations to prefrontal Item-Order-Rank working memory. The incorporation of rank information into Item-and-Order models was done in stages. In 1994, my PhD student Gary Bradski, working with my colleague Gail Carpenter and me, proposed the first Item-Order-Rank working memory model that incorporated rank-order coding into an Item-and-Order working memory (Bradski, Carpenter, and Grossberg, 1994). In 2010, Jason Bohland, Daniel Bullock, and Frank Guenther developed the Gradient Order DIVA, or GODIVA, model to explain how speech sequences with repeated items might be performed (Bohland et al., 2010), but noted that their proposal for how this may be achieved "requires some ad hoc machinery". Also in 2010, Colin Davis (Davis, 2010) proposed a related concept to model letter repetitions during visual word identification.

The LIST PARSE model that I published in 2008 with Lance Pearson (Grossberg and Pearson (2008) proposed how repeated elements could be stored in an Item-Order-Rank working memory, without "ad hoc machinery", by suggesting where and how such rank order coding may arise in the brain, and how it gets represented in working memory. This model predicted how an Item-Order-Rank working memory can be created in prefrontal cortex by deriving its rank selectivity from the analog spatial representations of numbers in the parietal cortex via parietal-prefrontal projections (Figure 12.56). This prediction, in turn, built upon the Spatial Number Network, or SpaN, model that I published in 2003 with Dmitry Repin (Grossberg and Repin, 2003) which simulated how the known analog map of ordered numerical representations in inferior parietal cortex may control the ability of animals and humans to estimate and compare sufficiently small numerical quantities. The predicted properties of SpaN model parietal neurons were supported by neurophysiological data published the next year by Andreas Nieder and Earl Miller (Nieder and Miller, 2004), who also reported prefrontal projections of these parietal numerical representations. However, they did not explain how these prefrontal projections could support an Item-Order-Rank working memory.

In such an Item-Order-Rank working memory, a spatial gradient of activity still represents temporal order, with the most active cell population being performed first. To enable the storage of the same item at multiple list positions in this gradient, the parietal-prefrontal projection of the analog spatial map of parietal numerical representations embeds *numerical hypercolumns* into the prefrontal working memory, so that each item is stored in a different position in its hypercolumn if it is repeated in the list more than once (Figure 12.56). A single numerical hypercolumn that represents a particular list item can store that item in multiple list positions, just as a positional hypercolumn in the visual cortical map of the primary visual cortex can selectively respond to multiple orientations at that position (Figure 12.27; Hubel and Wiesel, 1962, 1968), or a strip map can store multiple

ITEM-ORDER-RANK WORKING MEMORY
Rank information from parietal numerosity circuit
Grossberg and Pearson, 2008

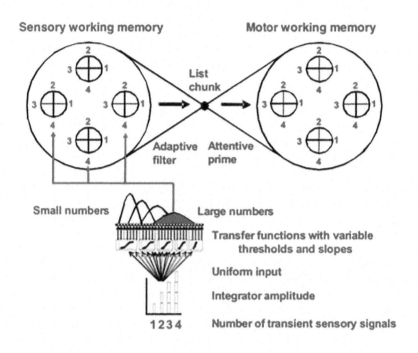

Grossberg and Repin, 2003

FIGURE 12.56. Grossberg and Pearson (2008) proposed that the ability of working memories to store repeated items in a sequence represents rank information abut the position of an item in a list using numerical hypercolumns in the prefrontal cortex (circles with numbered sectors: 1, 2, 3, 4). These numerical hypercolumns are conjointly activated by inputs from item categories and from the analog spatial representation of numerosity in the parietal cortex. These parietal representations (overlapping Gaussian activity profiles that obey a Weber law) had earlier been modeled by Grossberg and Repin (2003). See the text for details.

auditory streams (Figures 12.18) or place value numbers (Figure 12.29). For example, to store and perform in its correct order the short list ABAC, item A would be stored in two different positions—namely, positions 1 and 2—within its hypercolumn, whereas items B and C would be stored only in one position—namely, position 1—in their respective hypercolumns. A primacy gradient of activity would still represent the temporal order of a short stored list, whether or not it had repeated items.

In addition, the recurrent on-center off-surround network that stores items in an Item-Order-Rank working memory can still have the same simple anatomy as it does for an Item-and-Order working memory that does not store repeats: self-excitatory feedback from each cell population to itself, and a broad off-surround that equally inhibits all other populations in the working memory.

An Item-Order-Rank Masking Field hierarchy chunks lists of repeated words

With this background in mind, it is easy to explain how ART dynamics can store and chunk lists of repeated words. This can be accomplished by a three-level network (Figure 1.24): Each processing level in this network is an Item-Order-Rank, or IOR, working memory that can store sequences with repeated items in short-term memory. The second and third IOR working memories are, in addition, multiple-scale Masking Fields that can chunk input sequences of variable length, and choose the sequence, or sequences, for storage that receive the most evidence from its inputs. Each level receives its bottom-up inputs from an adaptive filter and reads-out top-down expectations that focus attention on the feature patterns in their learned prototypes at the previous level. The first level stores sequences of item chunks. The second level stores sequences of list chunks. The individual list chunks of the third level thus represent sequences of list chunks at the second level, including sequences with repeated words, as in the sentence "DOG EATS DOG".

lisTELOS: Storing, learning, planning, and performing eye movement sequences

Perhaps the currently most advanced neural architecture that includes an Item-Order-Rank working memory with which to control a biologically important behavior is the lisTELOS model. Published in 2011 with my PhD student Matthew Silver and several other collaborators (Silver et al., 2011), lisTELOS is a comprehensive model of how sequences of eye movements may be stored, learned, planned, and performed (Figure 12.57). I have been fascinated by eye movements for many years, having published

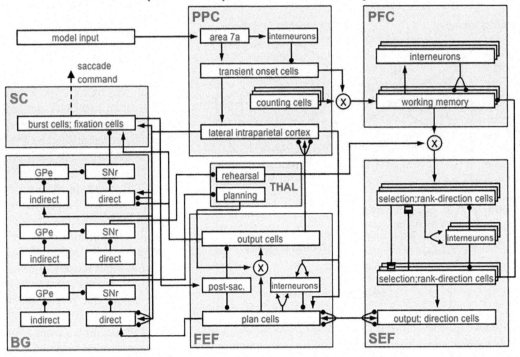

lisTELOS Model: SPATIAL working memory
Silver, Grossberg, Bullock, Histed, and Miller, 2011
Simulates how PPC, PFC, SEF, FEF, and SC interact with 3 BG loops
to learn and perform sequences of saccadic eye movements

FIGURE 12.57. The lisTELOS architecture explains and simulates how sequences of saccadic eye movement commands can be stored in a spatial working memory and recalled. Multiple brain regions are needed to coordinate these processes, notably three different basal ganglia (BG) loops to regulate saccade storage, choice, and performance, and the supplementary eye fields (SEF) to choose the next saccadic command from a stored sequence. Because all working memories use a similar network design, this model can be used as a prototype for storing and recalling many other kinds of cognitive, spatial, and motor information. See the text for details.

a book about saccadic eye movements in 1986 with my postdoctoral fellow Michael Kuperstein (Grossberg and Kuperstein, 1986/1989). When Michael and I started working together, we did not initially plan to publish a book about them. But as we modeled an ever-longer list of processes that were needed to adaptively control eye movements in a biologically relevant way, it gradually became clear that the resulting text was too long to publish in any journal. This is perhaps to be expected from the fact that processes that control eye movements involve a remarkably large number of brain regions.

Eye movements are often launched in response to visual information before any other movements, such as head, arm, and body movements, are made. Eye movements can be made reactively, and very quickly, in response to unexpected visual events. The eye movement system is thus an interface of great survival importance between seeing and doing. The psychological and neurobiological literatures about eye movements are correspondingly large, and provide a great deal of guidance when trying to figure out how this system works.

In order to convert a visual signal into an eye movement command, a coordinate transformation must occur. Moreover, this transformation must be learned in order to compensate for bodily growth over a period of years. There are many parts to the adaptive coordinate transformation problem, depending upon what limb is being controlled and by what sensory information. For example, we have already seen during my review of the ARTSCAN model (Figures 6.14-6.16) and the ARTSCAN Search model (Figures 6.3 and 6.4) how important adaptive coordinate changes are in enabling humans to learn about, and search for, objects as they scan a scene with saccadic eye movements.

Spatial Item-Order-Rank working memory stores sequences of saccadic target positions. The lisTELOS model's name derives from the fact that it unifies and further develops concepts and mechanisms from two sources, the LIST PARSE and the TELOS models. First, it built upon the qualitative proposal from the LIST PARSE model in Figure 12.56 of how to use the parietal numerical representation to create an Item-Order-Rank working memory. lisTELOS converted this proposal into a mathematically rigorous theory of how to design a *spatial* working memory as a basis for storing, learning, planning, and performing sequences of saccadic eye movements. The activity gradient of stored positions in the working memory determines the target positions of the saccades *and* the temporal order in which they will occur. lisTELOS was used to quantitatively simulate behavioral, electrophysiological, anatomical, and microstimulation data about rank-selective working memory storage in prefrontal cortex (PFC) as it interacts with multiple brain regions, including the posterior parietal cortex (PPC), frontal eye fields (FEF), supplementary eye fields (SEF), and superior collicular (SC), all regulated by three basal ganglia (BG) loops that coordinate the storage, selection, and performance of eye movement sequences. Taken together, the LIST PARSE and lisTELOS models simulate linguistic, spatial, and motor working memory data, thereby illustrating how all working memories may exploit variations of a shared underlying network design to satisfy the LTM Invariance Principle and Normalization Rule.

How does the brain know before it knows? Balancing reactive vs. planned movements. Second, lisTELOS incorporates properties from the TELOS model of how our brains balance the demands of reactive vs. planned movements that I developed with my PhD student Joshua Brown and my colleague Daniel Bullock (Brown, Bullock, and Grossberg, 1999, 2004). In particular, rapid reactive movements are needed to ensure survival in response to unexpected dangers, such as an automobile that goes through a stop light while we are crossing the street. In particular, a fast reactive saccade may be made to foveate our eyes upon such a sudden and unexpected visual stimulus registered in a right or left extrafoveal region (Figure 3.4). Planned movements often take longer to elaborate, since their visual cues may need to be processed by more brain regions before a movement decision is made. For example, a familiar discriminative cue registered in a right or left extrafoveal region may trigger escape movements in the opposite direction, rather than a reactive movement towards the cue. How does the brain prevent reactive movements from being prematurely triggered, and wasting precious time, in situations where a contextually-appropriate planned movement would be more adaptive?

Every movement is gated by an appropriate basal ganglia loop (Figure 6.13).

In order for any saccadic eye movement to be made, the basal ganglia need to open a movement gate in the superior colliculus (or SC in Figure 12.57) that codes for that saccade's target position. These gates solve the following challenging balancing act: When a sensory cue occurs, such as an extrafoveal flashing light on the retina, the fastest response would be an orienting response to look at it. For this to happen, the cue needs to open the appropriate basal ganglia gate to enable the reactive movement to occur. However, if the cue is a discriminative cue to do a different learned action, especially an action that requires rapid execution, then the reactive response is not adaptive. The main problem is: How does the brain know that a plan is being elaborated, even before it is chosen, so that it can keep the reactive gate shut? *How does the brain "know before it knows"?* In addition, how does the brain prevent a reactive movement command from opening its gate before a planned movement command is ready to open a different gate, yet also allow a reactive movement command to open its gate as rapidly as possible when no planned movement command is being selected?

The TELOS model was developed to explain and simulate how the brain may achieve this sort of balance between reactive and planned movements as it controls the

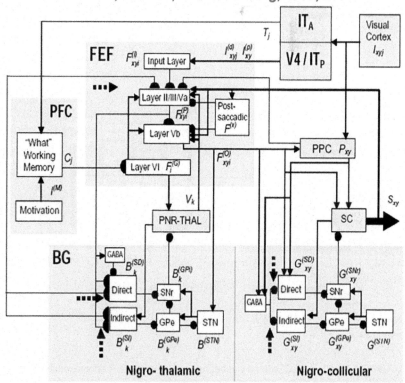

FIGURE 12.58. The lisTELOS model built upon key processes that were earlier modeled by the TELOS model. See the text for details.

learning and performance of saccadic eye movements. The acronym TELOS, or TElencephalic Laminar Objective Selector, for the model was inspired by the ancient Greek word *telos* for goal, end, or completion of a plan.

Choosing reactive and planned movements using frontal–parietal resonances. According to TELOS, the brain "knows before it knows" in the following way: Before the appropriate movement plan is selected, there can be multiple stimuli converging on the basal ganglia to open one or another movement gate (Figure 12.59aA). The model predicts how the distribution of excitation and inhibition that converges on the basal ganglia enables the corresponding gate to rapidly open when only one target position is active

(Figure 12.59aB). In contrast, when a plan is being elaborated that is different from the reactive cue, it can keep the reactive gate closed (Figure 12.59aC) by changing the balance of inputs to the basal ganglia from favoring excitation to favoring inhibition. When a movement plan is finally chosen, there is agreement between cells in the frontal eye fields (FEF) and the posterior parietal cortex (PPC) that represent the same target position (Figure 12.59aD).

Then mutually reinforcing excitatory feedback develops between the FEF and PPC into a synchronous *frontal-parietal resonance*. TELOS predicted how the balance of excitation and inhibition then enables the appropriate basal ganglia gate to open and release the planned movement (Figure 12.59aD). Neurophysiological data consistent

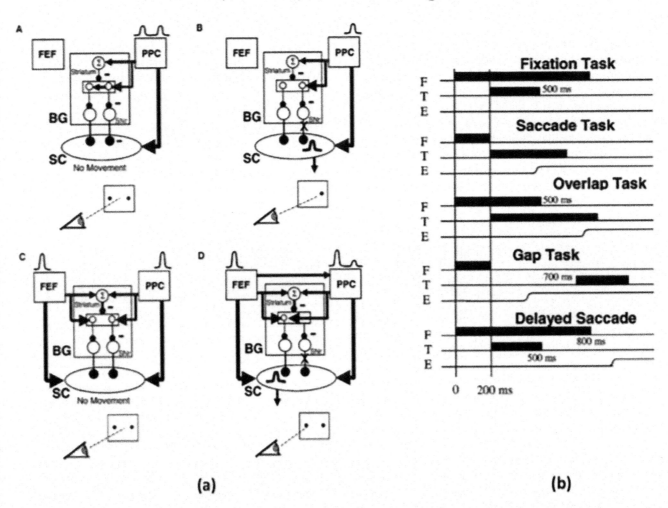

BALANCING REACTIVE VS. PLANNED MOVEMENTS
Brown, Bullock, and Grossberg, 2004

(a)

(b)

FIGURE 12.59. The TELOS model clarifies how reactive vs. planned eye movements may be properly balanced against one another, notably how a fast reactive movement is prevented from occurring in response to onset of a cue that requires a different, and more contextually appropriate, response, even if the latter response takes longer to be chosen and performed. The circuit explains how "the brain knows before it knows" what this latter response should be by changing the balance of excitation to inhibition in the basal ganglia (BG) to keep the reactive gate stays shut until the correct target position can be chosen by a frontal-parietal resonance.

with the predicted role of a synchronous frontal-parietal resonance in triggering an eye movement was published in 2007 by Timothy Buschman and Earl Miller (Buschman and Miller, 2007). In addition, Anitha Pasupathy and Miller showed in 2004 (Pasupathy and Miller, 2004) that there are different time courses of learning-related activity in the prefrontal cortex and basal ganglia that are consistent with the TELOS model prediction of how basal ganglia-mediated gating of prefrontal cortical plans is learned.

TELOS concepts and circuits were further supported by showing how the model can learn how to perform eye movements in five different type of movement tasks: fixation, single saccade, overlap, gap, and delay (memory-guided) saccade tasks. These tasks are defined in Figure 12.59b, where F designates the time interval when the fixation cue is on, T the time interval when the target cue is on, and E plots the time course of a typical saccade. After learning occurs, model cell activation dynamics quantitatively simulate, and predict functional roles for, the neurophysiologically-recorded dynamics of 17 types of identified neurons during performance of these tasks. This striking fact both supports model hypotheses and illustrates the complexity of brain circuits that are capable of autonomously learning and performing movement tasks.

From TELOS to lisTELOS: Basal ganglia coordination of multiple brain processes

I am reviewing highlights of lisTELOS to emphasize that a working memory, by itself, is only a part of any brain system whereby our brains can store, learn, plan, and perform sequences of behaviors, whether they be words, navigational movements, or skilled actions. In particular, lisTELOS shows how rank information, originating in PPC, may support rank-selective storage of items in an Item-Order-Rank working memory in PFC. Figure 12.60 (left image) shows rank-selective cell responses in PFC that were recorded when a second arm movement to the left was generated as a monkey drew a square or inverted triangle during the Averbeck et al. (2003a, 2003b) experiments (see Figure 12.41). lisTELOS also explains and simulates how the SEF chooses the next saccade to be performed from those that are currently stored in working memory using a variant of the Item-and-Order mechanisms

that are summarized in Figure 12.36. The SEF is an oculomotor area in the dorsomedial frontal cortex (Schlag and Schlag-Rey, 1987) that is heavily interconnected with the PFC (Barbas and Pandya, 1987; Huerta and Kaas, 1990) and which also exhibits rank-related activity (Berdyyeva and Olson, 2009; Isoda and Tanji, 2002, 2003). Figure 12.60 (right image) shows some rank-selective responses of SEF cells during experiments in 2002 by Masaki Isoda and Jun Tanji (Isoda and Tanji, 2002).

SEF is both anatomically and physiologically well-suited to interact with a rank-selective working memory. Its role in the selection of saccadic targets is consistent with many data. For example, patients with lesions in what was at the time called the supplementary motor area (Gaymard, Pierrot-Deseilligny, and Rivaud, 1990; Gaymard, Ploner, Rivaud, and Pierrot-Deseilligny, 1999) have mostly intact performance for visually-guided saccades, anti-saccades, and single memory-guided saccades, but greatly degraded performance for *sequences* of memory-guided saccades. In addition, activation of SEF during sequential saccade tasks has been observed with positron emission tomography (Petit et al., 1996) and during a functional magnetic resonance imaging study (Heide et al., 2001) whose authors concluded that "the supplementary eye field essentially controls the triggering of memorized saccade sequences".

The competence of the lisTELOS model was tested by simulating data collected from several different paradigms, including visually-guided and memory-guided saccade tasks and several sequential saccade tasks, notably using the immediate serial recall task; cf. Figure 12.44. The model also reproduces behavioral and electrophysiological data when SEF activity is

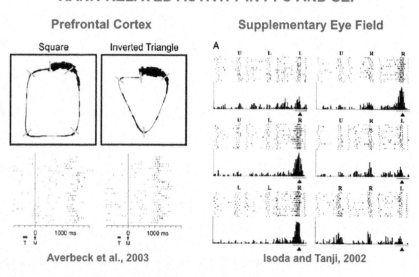

RANK-RELATED ACTIVITY IN PFC AND SEF

Prefrontal Cortex

Square   Inverted Triangle

1000 ms   1000 ms

Averbeck et al., 2003

Supplementary Eye Field

A

Isoda and Tanji, 2002

FIGURE 12.60. Rank-related activity in prefrontal cortex and supplementary eye fields from two different experiments. See the text for details.

Microstimulation Causes Habituation

Stimulation caused habituation

Cells close to the stimulation site habituate most strongly

Grossberg, 1968

Stimulation Biases Selection

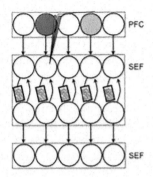

Activity gradient in working memory

Microstimulation causes habituation

During selection habituated nodes are less likely to win the competition

The weaker representation may be excited in SEF output layer

PFC

SEF

SEF

FIGURE 12.61. (left column) A microstimulating electrode causes a spatial gradient of habituation. (right column) The spatial gradient of habituation that is caused by microstimulation alters the order of saccadic performance of a stored sequence, but not which saccades are performed, using interactions between the prefrontal cortex (PFC) working memory and the supplementary eye field (SEF) saccadic choice.

perturbed by microstimulation under two quite different experimental protocols (Histed and Miller, 2006; Yang, Heinen, and Missal, 2008). Microstimulation data provide particularly strong support for the concept of a *spatial* Item-Order-Rank working memory, because of how microstimulation alters the *temporal order*, but not the *target positions*, of the saccades that are performed.

Figure 12.61 summarizes how SEF is proposed to choose the next saccadic eye movement target position during the microstimulation experiment of Mark Histed and Earl Miller (Histed and Miller, 2006). Figure 12.61 (left column) shows that a microstimulating electrode habituates an activity-dependent transmitter gate (cf. Figures 1.14 and 1.15) at the stimulation site more than it does the gates of nearby cells. Figure Figure 12.61 (right column) situates the electrode within the network that includes both the PFC working memory and the SEF choice network. Selective habituation of an output pathway from PFC through SEF weakens the net output that is caused by the corresponding stored PFC activity.

Thus a target position that is stored with high activity may have a small output if its SEF gate has been significantly habituated, thereby causing that target position to be foveated later than it otherwise would. Figure 12.62 shows that the net effect on performance order, but not on the target positions that are foveated, is to ensure that the most highly stimulated map position is foveated last. Figure 12.63 shows that the model does a good job of simulating the entire pattern of microstimulation data.

Three basal ganglia gates regulate saccadic sequence storage, choice, and performance. To explain learning and performance of eye movement sequences, and by extension other kinds of cognitive and movement sequences, the lisTELOS model simulates in considerable cellular detail how three loops through the basal ganglia (Middleton and Strick, 2000) control the flow of information within and between brain areas that are simulated by the model (Figure 12.57, see BG: lower left corner; also see Figures 15.33 and 15.34). It is not too much of an exaggeration to claim that the expression of our selfhood depends critically on the proper coordination of multiple basal

THE MOST HABITUATED POSITION IS FOVEATED LAST

For each pair of cues, the cue closest to the stimulation site is most habituated -- and least likely to be selected

Because stimulation spreads in all directions, saccade trajectories tend to converge

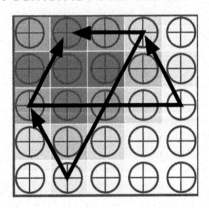

FIGURE 12.62. The most habituated positions have their neuronal activities most reduced, other things being equal, as illustrated by the gradient from deep habituation (red) to less habituation (pink). The saccadic performance orders (black arrows) consequently tend to end in the most habituated positions that have been stored.

SACCADE TRAJECTORIES CONVERGE TO A SINGLE LOCATION IN SPACE

Microstimulation biased selection so saccade trajectories converged toward a single location in space

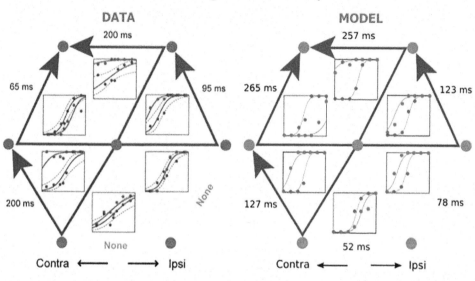

FIGURE 12.63. Neurophysiological data (left image) and lisTELOS stimulation (right figure) showing how microstimulation biases saccadic performance order but not the positions to which the saccades will be directed. See the text for details.

ganglia gates. One has only to study the devastating deterioration of both cognition and movement in individuals who are afflicted with Parkinson's disease to realize how much proper basal ganglia functioning supports every thought and action (Dubois et al., 2007). This gating function of the BG is controlled by the substantia nigra pars reticulata, or SNr (Alexander and Crutcher, 1990; Alexander, DeLong, and Strick, 1986; Grahn, Parkinson, and Owen, 2009; Hikosaka and Wurtz, 1983, 1989).

Each of the three BG loops in lisTELOS is based on the BG implementation used in the TELOS model (Figure 12.58). These TELOS hypotheses are, in turn, consistent with the experimental and modeling work of many other researchers (e.g., Alexander and Crutcher, 1990; Bullock and Grossberg, 1988, 1991; Gancarz and Grossberg, 1999; Grossberg, Roberts, Aguilar, and Bullock, 1997; Hikosaka and Wurtz, 1983; Mink, 1996). As in the brain, BG gate opening in the model relies on opposing forces between the direct and indirect pathways (Brown et al., 2004; Frank, 2005; Frank, Loughry, and O'Reilly, 2001; Mink, 1996). The details about how these pathways work individually and together are quite technical. They are described in detail in Silver et al. (2011). The main idea is that the indirect pathway acts in opposition to the direct pathway. The direct pathway activation excites cells in the thalamus or SC. It functions as a GO signal and uses a D1 dopaminergic transmitter.

In contrast, the indirect pathway activation inhibits these cells. It functions as a STOP signal and uses a D2 dopaminergic transmitter. These opposing processes of disinhibition and inhibition determine how and when BG gates open and close. Chapter 15 further discusses how sustained opening of BG gates can support repetitive behaviors in normal individuals under volitional control, and involuntarily in autistic individuals when the direct and indirect pathways become imbalanced in prescribed ways.

The three BG gates in the lisTELOS macrocircuit in Figure 12.57 are marked by x's. The first BG gate restricts the flow of information from the PFC working memory to the SEF. The second gate controls the flow of information between the FEF plan layer and the FEF output layer. The third gate controls outputs from the SC. For present purposes, it is sufficient to realize the following: The three BG loops hold the model in a state of preparedness as information important for guiding its future responses is being presented, and detect the task conditions that signal when it is time to utilize the stored information to drive behavior. In the experiments under consideration, this process depends on the presence or absence of a fixation cue (see F in Figure 12.59b). When a fixation cue is present, the rehearsal and collicular gates are held shut and task-relevant cues are simply stored in memory. When the fixation cue shuts off, SEF can select saccade targets from WM and excite corresponding representations in FEF. Provided that the selected saccade plan is not inconsistent with any external cues represented in LIP, the FEF and collicular BG loops open their gates and allow plan signals to flow to SC, which generates the saccadic response.

In summary, the above mechanisms propose how an Item-Order-Rank spatial working memory can be used to store arbitrary spatial sequences, and how three distinct BG gates enable SEF to select spatial targets from WM and excite corresponding representations in downstream oculomotor areas such as SC that are responsible for saccade production.

Learning and storage of speaker-invariant and rate-invariant working memories

The previous examples illustrate that multiple working memories and list chunking networks in the What and Where/How auditory cortices are used to encode sounds. Some of these working memories and list chunking networks embody frequency-specific and rate-sensitive processes like voice, instrument, and speaker identification, whereas others embody frequency- and rate-invariant processes, such as speech and language recognition and meaning (Figure 12.25, right panel). These several working memory and list chunking networks obey similar design principles, notably the LTM Invariance Principle and Normalization Rule, that are realized by similar types of circuits which rapidly learn and stably remember different kinds of acoustic information through time.

Below are summarized key preprocessing stages that are needed to more fully understand conscious experiences of hearing and knowing. In particular, how does the brain learn and understand the speech and language meanings of multiple speakers as they speak at variable rates (speaker-independence and rate-invariance), while also being able to consciously hear and identify the voices of individual speakers (speaker-dependence and rate-sensitivity)?

From speaker normalization to rate normalization: Transients and two kinds of gain control. I have already described how speaker normalization may occur by using a variant of the strip maps and asymmetric competitive networks that are used to form auditory streams (Figure 12.26). Learned codes for speech and language meaning need also to be *rate-invariant* to enable us to understand multiple speakers talking at variable rates. Many features of speech signals are, however, not preserved as speech rate changes, so rate-invariant representations must be actively constructed by the brain.

Human listeners can also consciously hear and understand particular voices speaking at variable rates, and human speakers can use their speaker- and rate-invariant representations of meaning to speak or sing in their own voices and at their own volitionally-controlled rates. How the brain accomplishes these various variant and invariant competences, and how they are coordinated to support consciously hearing and recognition will be proposed below.

Three additional design features are needed to solve the rate-invariance problem:

(1) *Sustained and transient streams.* Parallel cortical streams exist for processing sustained (S) vs. transient (T)

acoustic features to represent all the sounds that occur during audition, speech, and music.

(2) *Intra-word rate-invariance.* Gain control signals from the T stream to the S stream compensate for non-invariant changes *within* syllables, such as pairs of consonants and vowels, also called CV pairs, as speaking rate changes. This T-to-S stream gain control process creates more invariant S/T ratios across rates.

(3) *Inter-word rate-invariance.* A different rate-dependent gain control process adjusts the integration rates of working memory and list chunking networks as the overall speech rate changes *across* syllables. This process generates more rate-invariant storage of speech and language representations in working memories and list chunking networks.

Each process will be briefly discussed in turn. Each provides more examples of how Item-List resonances support conscious recognition of speech and language.

Transient and sustained processing steams in audition and speech. Both psychoacoustic and neurophysiological evidence support the idea that the auditory system uses distinct neural mechanisms for coding *transient* sounds, like the consonants /b/ or /w/, and *sustained* sounds, like the vowel /a/, that have steady acoustic energy concentrated in several narrow bands in frequency space that are called formant frequencies (Phillips, 1993; Pickles, 1988). However, acoustic segments do not necessarily correspond directly to consciously perceived phonetic percepts. For example, consonants cannot usually be perceived as phonemes independent of the vowel context. The vowel sound that precedes or follows the consonant is perceived as a vowel while simultaneously contributing to the percept of the consonant. Without such a vowel context, isolated consonants often sound like chirps!

Another complicating factor is that motor articulations that are associated with phonemes like /w/ are often distributed in time and interleaved with the articulations of past or future speech sounds like /a/, a property called *coarticulation*. Speech sounds are thus integrated, or grouped, across time to derive phonetic percepts. As noted above, this grouping process operates on the local time scale of individual acoustic segments, roughly 10-100 milliseconds, and is sensitive to temporal information that is *intrinsic* to these segments, such as segment durations (Miller, 1980; Repp, 1978). This type of grouping occurs at an earlier stage of acoustic processing than the working memory and list chunking networks that I discussed above. Grouping of working memory item sequences into list chunks operates on the time scale of syllables and is sensitive to *extrinsic* temporal information like the global speech rate.

Thus, in order to represent all ecologically useful sounds, the brain's auditory system includes sustained cells (S) that are sensitive to particular frequencies over time, and transient cells (T) that are sensitive to frequency-modulated, or FM, sweeps that activate multiple frequencies with a particular rate and direction of frequency change, as in Figure 12.24 (e.g., Atzori et al., 2001; Britt and Starr, 1976; Delgutte and Kiang, 1984a, 1984b, 1984c; Mendelson et al., 1993; Moller, 1983; Phillips, 1993; Pickles, 1988; Rhode and Smith, 1986a, 1986b; Sachs and Young, 1979; Tian and Rauschecker, 1994; Young and Sachs, 1979). In 1997, Michael Cohen and I (Cohen and Grossberg, 1997) modeled how coarticulated consonants and vowels may activate distinct, but parallel, T and S channels, and how this selectivity helps to explain data about how the auditory nerve processes sounds through time. The S channel can discriminate synchronous vocalic quality, as occurs during steady-state vowels like /a/ or /e/, while suppressing transient speech signals like /p/ or /t/. The parallel T channel can discriminate onsets and offsets of fricatives and stop consonants, as well as detect vowel onsets and offsets. In 2000, Josef Rauschecker and Biao Tian (Rauschecker and Tian, 2000) reviewed cortical regions that include S and T cells, including the core and lateral belt regions (Figure 12.64), respectively.

Transient and sustained cell responses also occur within the visual system, where sustained and transient cells tend to process form percepts and motion percepts, respectively, as illustrated by the surface-shroud resonances (S) and change blindness (T) that are discussed in Chapter 6.

PHONET: Asymmetric T-to-S gain control creates within-syllable rate invariance. A faster speech rate may more strongly activate transients in the speech signal, but leaves less time to integrate, and thereby strengthen, sustained signals. For example, buildup cells in the cat cochlear nucleus integrate up to a maximum spike rate over the

duration of a pure tone (Britt and Starr, 1976; Rhode and Smith, 1986a, 1986b). Thus, faster rates can change the relative activities of T and S cells, with T cells being favored. Such rate-dependent changes in relative T and S activities could cause serious problems for learning speech codes because the bottom-up adaptive filter pathways tend to activate the same set of chunks when their *relative* activities across the network are preserved (Figures 5.10, 5.11, and 5.16-5.18).

Robert Port and Jonathan Dalby described psychophysical experiments in 1982 (Port and Dalby, 1982) which emphasize that "consonant/vowel ratio serves as a primary acoustic cue" (p. 141) for voicing in English, and noted that their data suggest that "this ratio possibly is directly extracted from the speech signal" (p. 141). The burning question is: How?

A more rate-invariant T/S ratio can be created by letting T and S inputs activate their own working memories, after which excitatory signals from the T working memory increase the integration rate of the S working memory, thereby compensating for the relative strengthening of T relative to S activation as speaking rate increases (Figure 12.65, left column, upper row). These rate-dependent changes help to maintain a constant *ratio* of activities across the T and S working memories as speech rate changes. This ratio represents a stable phonemic code because it will be processed in the same way at different speaking rates by the adaptive filters that respond to the pattern of activation across the T and S working memories by choosing the same list chunks at subsequent processing levels.

In particular, as the speech rate speeds up, transient cells that are activated by consonants like /w/ may be more strongly activated, whereas sustained cells that are activated by vowels like /a/ have less time to integrate their sustained inputs. If the transient working memory compensates for this lack of invariance by controlling the gain with which activity is integrated by the sustained working memory, then a faster integration rate can compensate for a shorter duration of integration. Several psychophysical experiments have supported this hypothesis by reporting such asymmetric vocalic context effects from T to S, but not conversely (Kunisaki and Fujisaki, 1977; Mann and Repp, 1980).

I published the PHONET model in 1999 with my PhD students Ian Boardman and Christopher Myers, and my colleague Michael Cohen, to quantify how T and S working memories can use asymmetric T-to-S gain control to create rate-invariant representations of individual speech syllables or words (Boardman et al., 1999). PHONET was tested by quantitatively simulating some remarkable data that illustrate the importance of the T/S ratio in determining a conscious speech percept. For example, Joanne Miller and Alvin Liberman showed in 1979 that, when listening to consonant-vowel (CV) syllables such as /ba/ and /wa/ (Figure 12.66 (left column)),

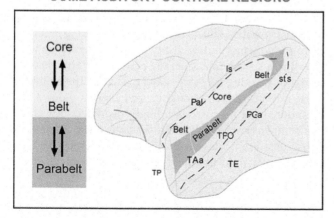

SOME AUDITORY CORTICAL REGIONS

FIGURE 12.64. Some of the auditory cortical regions that respond to sustained or transient sounds. See the text for details.

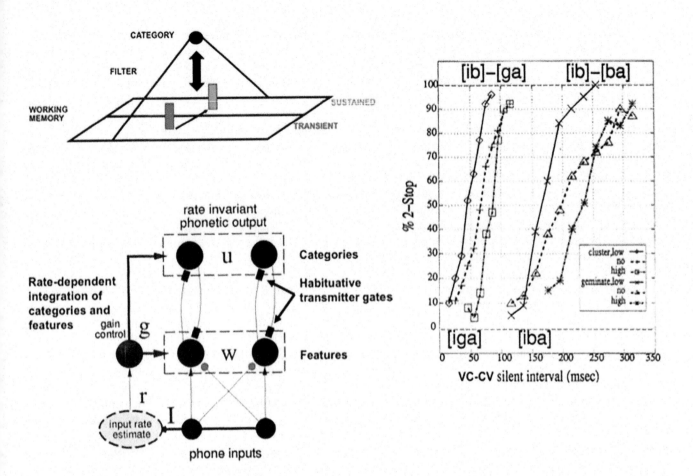

FIGURE 12.65. Linguistic properties of the PHONET model and some of the data that it simulates. The upper left image summarizes the asymmetric transient-to-sustained gain control that helps to create invariant intraword ratios during variable-rate speech. The lower left image summarizes the rate-dependent gain control of the ARTPHONE model that creates rate-invariant working memory representations in response to sequences of variable-rate speech. The right image summarizes the kind of paradoxical VC - CV category boundary data of Repp (1980) that ARTPHONE simulates. See the text for details.

an increase in duration of vowel /a/ can switch the percept of the preceding consonant from /w/ to /b/ (Miller and Liberman, 1979). This switch does not occur if the relative durations of these sounds are preserved as their absolute durations are changed. In 1981, Eileen Schwab, James Sawusch, and Howard Nusbaum (Schwab, Sawusch, and Nusbaum, 1981) showed that, even if the relative durations of these sounds are preserved, a change in their frequency extent, or total frequency change, can also influence the /b/-/w/ distinction (Figure 12.66 (right column)). That is the kind of consonant enhancement that could be due, for example, to an increase in speaking rate. By modeling how sustained and transient detectors respond to speech at variable rates, followed by asymmetric T-to-S control (Figure 12.67), PHONET was quantitatively fit 99.3% of the variance in both data sets with the same parameters.

ARTPHONE: Rate-sensitive gain control creates rate-invariant working memories.

Rapidly-acting T-to-S gain control is only part of the story whereby our brains

can compensate for changes in speech characteristics as speech rate changes. In particular, such an *intra*-syllabic transformation cannot compensate for speech properties that change with speech rate across multiple words. As speech rate increases, each feature pattern and its item chunks have less time to be stored in working memory. The same problem afflicts the list chunk working memory. If working memory integration rates do not keep up with changes in speech rate, then the activity patterns that are stored in working memory may be altered. The ability to learn rate-invariant list chunks and their top-down expectations will be correspondingly degraded. An effective compensatory mechanism needs to speed up or slow down integration rates across all working memory and list chunking networks to mirror changes in speech rate.

Taken together, these two sorts of gain control, one acting within individual words and the other acting across sequences of words, begin to explain how a rate-invariant speech representation may be created internally by brain dynamics from variable-rate speech signals that do not

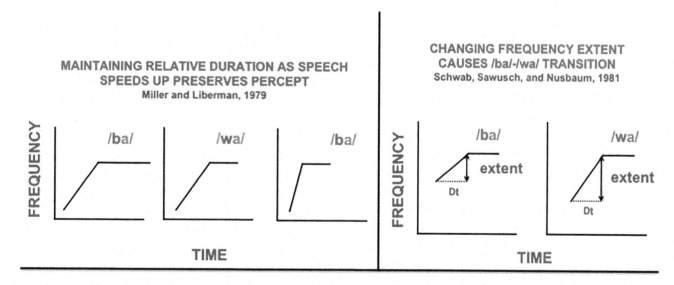

FIGURE 12.66. (left column) A schematic of how preserving relative duration, as in the first and third images, of consonant and vowel pairs can preserve a percept, in this case of /ba/, but not doing so, as in the first and second images, can cause a change in percept, as from /ba/ to /wa/, as in the data of Miller and Liberman (1979) that PHONET simulates. (right column) Changing frequency extent can also cause a /ba/ - /wa/ transition, as shown in data of Schwab, Sawusch, and Nusbaum (1981) that PHONET also simulates.

themselves exhibit properties of invariance. How rate-dependent productions and their conscious percepts via auditory feedback can be created from these rate-invariant representations will be described later in this chapter.

But first I need to explain how a rate-dependent gain control mechanism can act across sequences of words to compensate for variations in speech rate. Then I need to

show how this mechanism can explain and quantitatively simulate psychophysical data that would otherwise seem to be quite mysterious. I published the ARTPHONE model (Figure 12.65, left column, lower row) with Ian Boardman and Michael Cohen in 1997 (Grossberg, Boardman, and Cohen, 1997) to realize both of these goals. Its gain control mechanism can, moreover, be readily be incorporated into other speech models that include Item-Order-Rank working memories and list chunks, notably the ARTWORD (Figure 12.49) and cARTWORD models (Figure 12.30).

In ARTWORD, a rate-dependent gain control processing stage (variable g in 12.65 (left column, lower row)) time-averages the number of transient signals through time (from the input rate estimate), and thus depends in yet another way on the T stream. More transient signals per unit time occur at faster speech rates. They are integrated, or added, as they occur through time to create a larger gain control signal. Gain control signals multiply the rates at which the working memory and list chunk processing levels respond to their inputs and recurrent signals. Larger gain control signals hereby speed up these rates more

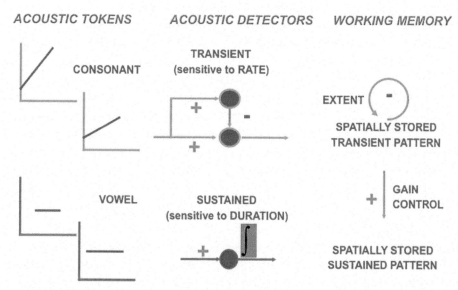

FIGURE 12.67. PHONET contains transient and sustained cells that respond to different kinds of sounds, notably the transients of certain consonants and the sustained sounds of certain vowels. It then uses the transient working memory to gain control the integration rate of the sustained working memory to which these different detectors input.

than smaller signals and thereby keep up with changes in speech rate.

Category boundary shifts due to gain control by average speech rate. This kind of gain control helps to explain paradoxical properties of psychophysical data about conscious speech perception and recognition. Although the data may appear to be paradoxical, they arise because of a simple reason: Listener percepts tend to be invariant under changes in the speed with which speech is heard. How does this happen? The speech rate is inversely proportional to the durations of silence intervals in the speech. Changing the mean silence interval changes the number of T-cell activations per unit time, which thereby changes the T-sensitive gain, and thus the working memory and list chunking network integration rates. What is paradoxical is that these *rate-invariant* percepts can produce *rate-dependent* category boundaries of heard speech.

Resonant fusion and reset during speech: [ib]-[ga] vs. [ib]-[ba]. A classical example of this phenomenon was reported in 1980 by Bruno Repp (Repp, 1980). Repp constructed VC-CV syllables from the syllables [ib], [ga], and [ba] to form [ib]-[ga] and [ib]-[ba]. The durations of the silence intervals between these syllables were varied.

Part of the data were not surprising at all: A longer silence interval increases the probability of hearing two syllables instead of one. For example, increasing the silence interval makes it more probable to hear [ib]-[ga] than [iga], and [ib]-[ba] than [iba]. This intuitive finding is represented by S-shaped category boundary curves that measure the probability of hearing two syllables at each silence interval for each of these VC-CV syllables.

However, if one looks more closely at the data that are summarized in Figure 12.65 (right column), then one notices something very remarkable indeed: the transition from a fused percept of [iba] to one of [ib]-[ba], with a perceived silence between [ib] and [ba], occurs after a silence duration that is 100-150 milliseconds longer than for the transition from [iga] to [ib]-[ga]. In other words, humans hear silence between [ib] and [ga] at the same silence duration at which they hear the continuous sound of [iba] in response to the input [ib]-[ba]! This is surprising because it shows that the brain can interpolate sound over rather long time intervals where no sound is present in the input signal. It is also surprising because the brain does this only in response to changes in *future* sounds: both [ib]-[ba] and [ib]-[ga] begin with [ib]. In fact, the *only* difference between these two VC-CV syllables is that one of them includes two consonants and the other only one consonant.

Why did switching from the different consonant /g/ to the same consonant /b/ in the CV syllable shift the latter category boundary curve to the right by 125 milliseconds? Given that the consonant switch is the only difference between the VC-CV syllables, why was silence heard

between [ib] and [ga] at some of the same times that /b/ was continuously heard in response to [iba]? These data hereby illustrate yet another way in which future context can influence a past conscious percept, just as in phonemic restoration. Finally, the sheer size of the shift in the curves is noteworthy: a duration of 100-150 milliseconds is a very long time relative to the time scale at which individual neurons can be activated, which is an order of magnitude faster. Why is this shift so large?

Before sketching an explanation of these data, I want to emphasize a major implication of them: Perceived silence is not a passive property of the external speech signal. Under certain circumstances, internal brain dynamics can convert external silence into an internal perception of sound. Indeed, this property illustrates my hypothesis that *"Perceived silence is a discontinuity in the rate at which the resonant wave evolves."* If the resonant wave stops, then we hear silence. Otherwise, we hear the sound that the resonance energizes. This hypothesis is radically different from that in more traditional approaches to speech perception. For example, the popular TRACE model of speech perception that was published by James McClelland and Jeffrey Elman in 1986 (McClelland and Elman, 1986) cannot explain data of this type because it postulates that silence directly activates "silence nodes" that represent the silence interval. Why, then, do we not always hear silence during the long silence intervals between [ib] and [ba]?

Although these data properties seem weird if you have no theory to explain them, they follow naturally from the the ART dynamics that control interactions between working memories and their list chunking networks (Figure 12.68). In particular, the separate syllables [ib] and [ga] in [ib]-[ga] are heard at shorter silent intervals because /g/ mismatches, and thereby inhibits, /b/ at these times using the mechanism of *mismatch reset* that occurs in all ART models (Figures 5.19c and 12.68B top row). In contrast, as in the auditory continuity illusion (Figure 12.17) and phonemic restoration (Figure 1.22), it takes more time for a resonance to reach threshold in response to a given cue than for a second occurrence of that cue, in this instance /b/ in [ib]-[ba], to keep the resonance active (Figure 12.68A, bottom row). Thus, the second occurrence of /b/ keeps the resonance active for much longer than one would expect if only feedforward neuronal processing were involved. As a result, [iba] is heard for much longer silence intervals than [iga]. The Repp (1980) data may thus be understood as an example of *resonant reset* vs. *resonant fusion*.

Why don't sounds last forever? Habituative collapse via activity-dependent transmitter gates. This explanation raises a potential problem: If [ib] can fuse across time with [ba], then how do we ever hear distinct [ib] and [ba] sounds when the silence interval gets long enough? Why does not the resonance continue forever? More generally, if positive feedback between a working memory and a list chunking

MISMATCH VS. RESONANT FUSION

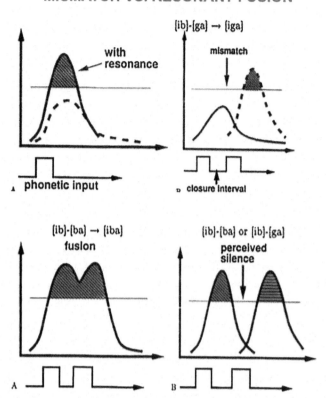

FIGURE 12.68. A mismatch reset of /b/ in response to the /g/ in [ib] - [ga] can rapidly shut off the [ib] percept, leading to the percept of [ga] after an interval of silence. In contrast, resonant fusion of the two occurrences of /b/ in [ib] - [ba] can cause a continuous percept of sound [iba] to occur during times at which silence is heard in response to [ib] - [ga].

network maintains a resonance, as it does in Figure 12.65 (left column, lower panel), then, if there is no active reset, why could not *every* such resonance last forever, leading to an indefinitely long perseverative ringing of many sounds that we hear?

My proposed solution to this problem is the same as the one that I proposed for limiting the duration of visual persistence in Chapter 7. Recall that positive feedback is used to select and maintain correct perceptual groupings during visual perception. In the perceptual grouping circuit, I proposed that habituative chemical transmitters exist within the pathways that maintain the resonance via reciprocal bottom-up and top-down signals; e.g., Figure 7.1. I propose that they also exist within the pathways that maintain a speech resonance.

Such habituative chemical transmitters play the role of a medium-term memory (MTM) trace whose response rate is slower than the short-term memory (STM) traces that define cell activation, and faster than the long-term memory (LTM) traces that are embodied in learned adaptive weights. The square synapses in the bottom-up and top-down pathways of the ARTPHONE model (Figure

12.65, left column, lower panel) contain these MTM traces. As a result, the *net* signals that pass through these pathways become smaller through time as their gating transmitters habituate. Thus, after a resonance develops fully, it spontaneously collapses after awhile due to activity-dependent habituation of the transmitters within the pathways that maintain the resonance. If the silence interval is chosen long enough for resonant collapse of [ib] to occur, then a distinguishable [ba] resonance can subsequently develop and be heard after an interval of perceived silence, as in Figure 12.68B (bottom row).

In summary, there are at least two ways to reset a resonance: *mismatch reset*, which can act quickly whenever bottom-up and top-down information do not match, and *habituative collapse*, which can act more slowly when activity-dependent transmitters habituate enough to terminate an ongoing resonance.

Varying the integration rate to preserve rate-invariant speech codes. Finer aspects of the Repp (1980) data illustrate how speech percepts can keep up with variable rates of heard sounds using rate-dependent gain control in order to create working memories and list chunks that can learn rate-invariant language meanings (Figure 12.65, left column, bottom row). This kind of invariance is reflected in the Repp (1980) data that measured three category boundary curves for each of the VC-CV syllables [ib]-[ga] and [ib]-[ba] (Figure 12.65, right column): A *low anchor* condition had its distribution of silence intervals skewed to be shorter, a *high anchor* condition had them skewed to be longer, and a *no anchor* condition had no skew. The three curves for each VC-CV syllable show that listeners track the mean physical silence interval to make their judgments in response to their conscious percepts. These *rate-dependent* category boundary shifts thus emerge from rate-sensitive integration of working memory and chunking networks to create *rate-invariant* working memory and list chunk integration!

These six data curves were simulated as emergent properties of model dynamics. Many other data about conscious speech percepts can also be explained by using this combination of Item-List resonant feedback, rate-dependent gain control of working memory integration rate, and habituative transmitter gating of the feedback signals that support resonance.

Data supporting MTM by activity-dependent habituative transmitter gates. Such a habituative or MTM process has been used to explain many other data about the reset of visual, auditory, cognitive, emotional, or motor representations in response to rapidly changing events, including the reset that takes place during the ART category learning and search cycle (Figure 5.19). I was finally able to get the mathematical equation for MTM published in 1968 in the *Proceedings of the National Academy of Sciences*, along with laws for STM and LTM that are still in use today (Grossberg, 1968d), and then again in 1969 in the *Journal of Theoretical Biology* (Grossberg, 1969b). I write "finally" because the laws were first derived when I was a college Freshman in 1957–58. Since that time, it has found its way into the explanation of many different kinds of data, often as part of gated dipole opponent processing circuits (e.g., Figures 11.4, 1.15, and 7.1).

It took a long time before MTM became a fashionable concept. In 1997, Larry Abbott and his colleagues reported data from visual cortex that they modeled using the same activity-dependent habituative law, which they derived from data properties in their own experiments on the visual cortex that had been theoretically explained in my earlier publications (Abbott et al., 1997). They called the MTM mechanism a *depressing synapse*. Also in 1997, Misha Tsodyks and Henry Markram derived a similar law to explain their data from the somatosensory cortex. They called the MTM mechanism a *dynamic synapse* (Tsodyks and Markram, 1997).

One reason why such a habituative law may be found so ubiquitously across brain systems is because it helps to rapidly reset and rebalance neural circuits in response to rapidly changing input conditions, often as part of a gated dipole opponent process, as it does during a memory search in ART (Grossberg, 1980). MTM also has other important properties, including the ability to adapt a cell's sensitivity to the ambient level of input through time. This latter property is just another way of saying that the cell's response amplitude habituates to the input intensity through time. This property was exploited in a 1981 article by Gail Carpenter and myself that quantitatively simulates data about how vertebrate photoreceptors adapt their sensitivity to varying intensities of light (Carpenter and Grossberg, 1981). For example, when we walk from a brightly lit room into a dark room, the retina adapts its sensitivity so that we can soon see better again despite the much lower light level. Adaptation properties were also reported in the visual cortical data of Larry Abbott and his collaborators in 1997.

How can continuous sound be heard during 125 milliseconds of silence? In summary, the data of Bruno Repp from 1980 show that the duration of a consciously perceived interval of silence is sensitive to the phonetic context into which the silence is placed. Indeed, phonetic context can generate a conscious percept of continuous sound across more than 100 milliseconds of silence! For example, consider the silent interval of 125 milliseconds in Figure 12.65. Here human listeners hear the single continuous syllable [iba] with high probability *and* the two distinct syllables [ib] and [ga], that are separated by silence. My explanation of these data in terms of the maintenance of resonance in one case, but its rapid reset in another, is consistent with a simple, but revolutionary, definition of consciously heard sound and the silences within it: *Conscious speech is a*

resonant wave, and *perceived silence is a temporal discontinuity in the rate with which the resonance evolves.*

These data also raise a potentially serious problem: Does the fact that [iba] can be heard as perceived sound during a silence interval of 125 milliseconds contradict the ART Matching Rule? Recall that the ART Matching Rule claims that bottom-up inputs are needed to drive a resonance, and that top-down feedback, on its own, plays a merely modulatory, or priming, role? If the ART Matching Rule is correct, then how can sound be heard during a 125-millisecond interval of silence during which there is no bottom-up input?

Here one needs to realize that working memory cells are designed to maintain their activation for awhile after their bottom-up inputs shut off. The resonance that develops is between the activities of items stored in working memory and the top-down expectations from the list chunking network (Figures 12.30 and 12.43). The signals from the list chunking network to the working memory are modulatory signals, but the working memory cells are active when they occur. The top-down signals can then select and amplify those working memory activities that are consistent with them, and suppress those that are not.

Adaptive resonance in lexical decision tasks: Error rate vs. reaction time data

The resonant fusion and reset mechanisms that help to explain the Repp data on category boundary shifts also helps to explain many other data about how humans carry out perceptual and cognitive tasks. I will review one more kind of experiment to illustrate the broad explanatory power of these ideas.

One important class of tasks is called a *lexical decision task*. In such a task, the basic procedure involves measuring how accurately and quickly people classify stimuli as words or non-words when these targets follow semantically related (R), neutral (N, a string of s's), or unrelated (U) word primes. Crucially, the R and U primes are *semantically* related to the word and non-word targets, rather than in terms of similarity to their visual features. For example, the word CAR is semantically related to words like ROAD, DRIVING, and BUS, even though these words bear little similarity to CAR in terms of their visual features. Thus a lexical decision task probes how the *meaning* of *previous* auditory cues may influence the the lexical units that are chosen by our brains. A lexical decision task also clarifies the kind of contextual processing that occurs *after* the word or non-word targets have already occurred.

Non-words are strings of letters that vary in their similarity to words. Both words and non-words may be similar to words that may compete with them before a final decision is made. For example, the words BUTTER and BETTER may compete, or the non-word TIGAR may compete with the word TIGER. One of the manipulations that can influence error rates and reaction times during lexical decision tasks is to present a masking stimulus at a fixed time after a word or non-word target is presented. The masking stimulus terminates the processing of that target by the brain. If a mask causes a major change in accuracy or reaction time, then we can infer that it interrupted a brain process that normally takes longer to occur.

In classical lexical decision experiments that were published in 1981, Roger Schvaneveldt and James McDonald (Schvaneveldt and McDonald, 1981) presented word and non-word targets after R, N, or U word primes. Each prime remained on for 750 milliseconds and was followed by a blank interval of 500 milliseconds before a word or non-word was presented. A non-word target was constructed by changing one of the interior letters of a word target that is in the designated relation R, N, or U to a prime. Subjects were told that the prime was to prepare them to respond to the target stimulus, but that no response to the prime was required.

Semantic vs. visual similarity. Because primes are semantically related to word and non-word targets, R, N, and U primes cause equal amounts of interference, on average, with the bottom-up registration of word and non-word targets. Their different effects are due essentially entirely to the matching process that more slowly unfolds between the bottom-up inputs and the top-down signals from the categories that the primes earlier activated. That is why a sufficiently early masking stimuli can have a big effect on the data.

Two kinds of data were reported: *Error rates* in tachistoscopic experiments with a backward mask (Figure 12.69a), and *reaction times* in non-masked conditions (Figure 12.69b). In the tachistoscopic experiments, the target was displayed for approximately 33.3 msec and was followed by a masking pattern consisting of a string of number signs (#) that blocked further processing of the target. In the reaction time experiments, the target remained visible until the subject responded. The subjects were instructed to respond as rapidly and accurately as possible. The error rates are also shown for each reaction time condition.

The data in Figure 12.69 exhibit a number of striking properties, including the following two: First, there was *no increase in reaction time* on word trials due to a U prime relative to an N prime in the unmasked condition (lower curve in Figure 12.69b), even though a U prime *increased the error rate* relative to an N prime in response to a word target in the masked condition (lower curve in Figure 12.69a). Second, an R prime *decreased reaction time* relative to an N prime in response to a non-word target in the unmasked condition (upper curve in Figure 12.69b), even

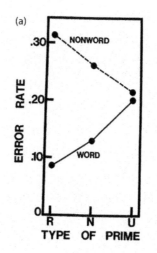
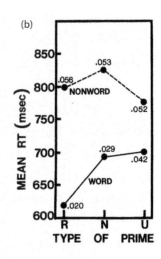

FIGURE 12.69. Error rate and mean reaction time (RT) data from the lexical decision experiments of Schvaneveldt and McDonald (1981). ART Matching Rule properties explain these data in Grossberg and Stone (1986).

though an R prime *increased error rate* relative to an N prime in response to a non-word target in the masked condition (upper curve in Figure 12.69a). These results illustrate how powerfully the interruption of lexical processing after the cues terminate can influence both the speech and accuracy of responses, and in different ways.

My postdoctoral fellow Gregory Stone and I showed in 1986 (Grossberg and Stone, 1986b) how specific properties of the ART Matching Rule contribute to an explanation of these data. In particular, in tachistoscopic experiments with a backward mask, a top-down expectation that is activated by a priming stimulus cannot act rapidly enough to significantly match or mismatch a target word or non-word target before the mask aborts further processing of the target. In the unmasked condition, word vs. non-word primes can have different effects on reaction times because their top-down expectations have enough time match or mismatch target words or non-words.

Auditory-visual interactions are needed to model semantic relatedness. Greg and I used the model macrocircuit in Figure 12.70 to explain all the Schvaneveldt and McDonald data. Figure 12.70 uses many of the same processing stages as in Figures 12.25 (left panel) and 12.49. Each of these macrocircuits emphasizes different aspects of speech and language learning and performance. A key fact is that the processing levels consist of item chunks and list chunks that are stored in Item-and-Order working memories. These working memories are called sensory STM and motor STM in Figure 12.70, depending upon whether it stores sequences of auditory signals or motor commands Figure 12.70 also includes both auditory and visual cortical processes in order to represent list chunks that code semantic information. This semantic network

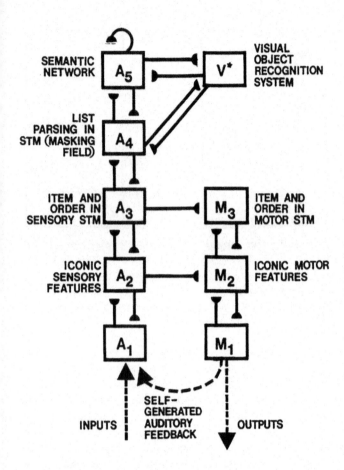

FIGURE 12.70. The kind of model macrocircuit that was used in Grossberg and Stone (1986) to explain lexical decision task data.

can be visually activated by list chunks of familiar words via the visual object recognition system. Once activated, semantic list chunks can then trigger top-down expectations that prime semantically related words.

Explaining data from the tachistoscopic condition using ART. It is easiest to understand the data patterns in Figure 12.69 by comparing pairs of data points. Let us start with word targets in the tachistoscopic condition (Figure 12.69a, bottom curve). Each tachistoscopic condition is identified by prime type followed by target type. For example. **R/W-N/W** denotes a comparison between an R prime followed by a word target vs. an N prime followed by a word target. Target words receive equal interference on the item level from prior R and N primes because relatedness is defined semantically, not in terms of visual similarity. By contrast, the R prime strongly activates list chunks of the word target because of their semantic relatedness. When the word target occurs after an R prime, its input to its list chunk augments the prior activation that has lingered since the R prime presentation. The N prime does not significantly activate the list chunks of target words. Hence the R prime facilitates recognition more

than does the N prime, so there are more N/W errors than R/W errors.

In the **N/W-U/W** comparison, the N and R primes again cause equal amounts of interference on the item level. The N prime does not significantly activate the list chunk representations of any target words. The U prime activates list chunks that competitively inhibit the list chunks of the word target, because of the recurrent lateral inhibition between list chunks within a Masking Field (Figures 12.46 and 12.47). Hence a target word can activate its list chunk more effectively after an N prime occurs than after a U prime occurs, so there are more U/W errors than N/W errors.

Why do the primes show the opposite effect when non-words are the targets (Figure 12.69a, upper curve)? Here it is important to keep in mind that a non-word target is constructed from a word target by changing one of its interior letters, and that the relatedness (R, N, and U) of the primes is determined by the original word. With this in mind, consider the **R/Nw-N/Nw** comparison, where Nw means non-word. The R prime significantly activates the same list chunk that the subsequent target non-word activates, whereas the N prime does not significantly activate the list chunk level. Thus the non-word target is more often *misidentified as a word* after an R prime than after an N prime, so there are more R/Nw errors than N/Nw errors.

Now consider the **N/Nw-U/Nw** comparison. The N prime does not significantly activate the list level, but the subsequent non-word target activates the corresponding word chunk on the list level. The non-word target does not activate the word chunk as strongly when it is preceded by a U prime, because the U prime activates word representations that inhibit this word chunk. Thus there will be more misidentification errors in the N/Nw condition than the U/Nw condition.

Why are there more non-word target errors than word target errors? Because of the masking stimulus, there is not enough time for significant top-down matching and a fully blown resonance to develop. Instead, subjects must rely upon transient bursts of bottom-up activation that are caused by the word and non-word targets. The relative sizes of these bursts vary across the priming conditions in the manner that I have just described, and determine whether the error curves decrease or increase across R, N, and U prime conditions. Because subjects may require resonance in order to confidently respond "word", they will also be biased to respond "non-word" in all conditions, hence leading to higher error rates for non-words than words.

Explaining data from the reaction time condition using ART: List-item error trade-off. I will now trace the differences between the reaction time data (Figure 12.69b) and of the tachistoscopic condition (Figure 12.69a) to the action of top-down expectations from list to item representations. To emphasize these differences, I will compare pairs of data points in the reaction time condition with the corresponding pairs of data points in the tachistoscopic condition. These explanations depend on a trade-off between an initial tendency to misidentify a word at the list level and the ability of this initial list activation to generate an error-correcting mismatch at the item level before false recognition can occur. I call this property the *list-item error trade-off*.

Two changes in the reaction time data are of particular interest. First, there was no increase in reaction time on word trials due to a U prime relative to an N prime (Figure 12.69b, lower curve), although a U prime increased error rate relative to an N prime in the tachistoscopic experiment (Figure 12.69a, lower curve). Second, an R prime decreased reaction time relative to an N prime on non-word trials (Figure 12.69b, upper curve), whereas an R prime increased error rate relative to an N prime in the tachistoscopic experiment (Figure 12.69a, upper curve). I will again make pairwise comparisons of the data points.

Each reaction time condition is again identified by prime type followed by target type with unmasked targets indicated by an apostrophe: For example, N/W' denotes an N prime followed by an unmasked W target. The comparison of R/Nw'-U/Nw' with R/Nw-U/Nw explains the large difference between the error rates for R/Nw and U/Nw in the tachistoscopic condition (Figure 12.69a, upper curve) and the insignificant difference between both the reaction times and error rates of R/Nw' and U/Nw' in the reaction time condition (Figure 12.69b, upper curve).

I begin with the **R/Nw-R/Nw'** comparison. In R/Nw (Figure 12.69a, upper curve), both the R prime and the non-word target activate the list representation of the word from which the non-word was derived. Hence the non-word target generates a relatively large number of word misidentifications because the mask prevents any top-down corrections from occurring, leading to the highest error rate of any target-prime combination. The processing in R/Nw' starts out just as it does in R/Nw. In R/Nw', however (Figure 12.69b, upper curve), the conjoint activation of the word's list representation by both the R prime and the non-word target can generate large top-down feedback signals from the word list representation to the non-word item representation. Thus the very factor that causes many false word identifications of the non-word target in R/Nw leads to strong feedback with which to disconfirm this misidentification in R/Nw'.

In particular, a mismatch is caused by the ART Matching Rule between the word's top-down feedback prototype and the non-word's item representation. This mismatch suppresses the non-word item representation and thereby causes a significant collapse in the item-to-list signals that were supporting the word's list representation. Thus the number of word misidentifications of the non-word target in R/Nw' is significantly reduced relative to those in R/Nw, leading to a much-reduced error rate.

Moreover, the fact that the word list representation is active because of the R prime when the non-word target is presented speeds up as well as amplifies the read-out of the word's top-down expectation, thereby causing a speed-up in the reaction time.

Now let us compare how different primes affect non-word processing when no mask occurs (Figure 12.69b, upper curve), starting with R/Nw' and U/Nw'. We need to explain how both the error rate and reaction time of R/Nw' and U/Nw' are similar in Figure 12.69b (upper curve) despite the large difference in error rate between R/Nw and U/Nw in Figure 12.69a (upper curve). In contrast with R/Nw', in U/Nw' the U prime inhibits the list representation of the word that the non-word target activates. Thus the net activation of the word's list representation by a non-word target is weaker in U/Nw' than it is in R/Nw'. Consequently, the word template that is read out by the list representation in U/Nw' is weaker than that read out in R/Nw'. The U/Nw' template is therefore less effective than the R/Nw' template in mismatching the non-word item representation. Again, a list-item error trade-off exists between the initial tendency toward word misidentification at the list level and the ability of this initial tendency to trigger ART Matching Rule feedback that can correct this tendency before erroneous recognition can occur.

The two factors, degree of incorrect initial list activation and degree of item mismatch, tend to cancel each other out. This trade-off holds for both activity levels and rates of activation. Concerning rate, a large prior activation of the word's list representation by the R prime helps to cause a more rapid initial read-out of the word template. This rapid reaction elicits a stronger item mismatch that is better able to undercut the large initial activation of the word's list representation. The greater initial speed is hereby compensated for by the larger activation that can more quickly inhibit it. Thus in both error rate and reaction time, R/Nw' and U/Nw' are similar despite the large difference in error rate between R/Nw and U/Nw.

Why in the reaction time paradigm is U/Nw' reliably faster than N/Nw' even though their error rates are comparable (Figure 12.69b, upper curve), whereas in the tachistoscopic paradigm, the error rate in U/Nw is reliably less than that of N/Nw (Figure 12.69a, upper curve)? Again the main reason boils down to how the ART Matching Rule in the N/Nw'-U/Nw' comparison alters the N/Nw-U/Nw dynamics of the tachistoscopic case. Once again, a list-item error trade-off occurs between the amount and timing of list representation activation and its effects on the amount and timing of item mismatch.

In particular, an N prime does not activate the list representations nearly as much as a R prime does. Hence a non-word target can modestly activate its word representation without major interference or augmentation from its prior N prime. The word's list representation then reads out a top-down expectation whose ability to mismatch the non-word's item representation depends on how strongly the non-word was able to activate the word's list representation. Thus the size of the initial tendency to misidentify the non-word target again covaries with the ability of the feedback template to correct this error.

This balance between initial list activation and subsequent item mismatch also occurs in the U prime condition. In this condition, however, the U prime inhibits the word list representation that the non-word target activates. This list representation is thus activated by the non-word less after a U prime than after an N prime. The weaker tendency to misidentify the non-word as a word after a U prime leads to a weaker top-down read-out and a weaker item mismatch with the non-word's item representation. The similar error rates in the N and U non-word conditions can thus be traced to the list-item error trade-off.

Why then is the reaction time in the U/Nw' condition reliably faster than in the N/Nw' condition? A major factor is that, in the U prime condition, the non-word target causes a relatively small initial activation of the word level because of the prior inhibitory effect on the word level of the U prime. This relatively small initial activation tends to cause a relatively weak item mismatch that can only cause the initial list activation to become even smaller. The absence of a large rate or amount of activation within the list level at any time provides a relatively rapid cue that a non-word has occurred, thereby leading to a fast non-word decision.

By contrast, within the N prime condition, the non-word target can cause a relatively large initial activation of the list level. Although the large top-down read-out that is caused by this activation can compensate for it via list-item error trade-off, more time is required to inhibit this initial activity surge than is required to register the absence of such a surge in the U prime condition. Thus the reaction time tends to be longer in the N prime condition than in the U prime condition.

All the remaining comparisons can be explained using similar combinations of mechanisms. These various cases provide strong evidence for how bottom-up and top-down processes work together to choose speech and language units.

Adaptive Resonance in word frequency and related tasks

Greg Stone and I used a similar combination of mechanisms to explain paradoxical data about *word frequency effects* in recognition and recall that were described by Benton Underwood and Joel Freund in 1970 (Underwood and Freund, 1970). Word frequency manipulations can have different effects on recall than on recognition of the

prior occurrence of a word. In particular, Underwood and Freund presented a list of 50 low-frequency (L) words or a list of 50 high frequency (H) words. Then subjects were shown pairs of words. One word in each pair was chosen from the list of study words. The other word in each pair was chosen from a list of either H words or from a list of L words. Thus, subjects fell into one of four categories, L-L, L-H, H-L, or H-H, in which the first letter designated whether the study list was composed of L or H words, and the second letter designed whether the distractor word in each pair was chosen from an L or H list. The subjects were instructed to identify the word in each pair that they had seen on the study trial.

Unlike a lexical decision judgment, a judgment of word frequency compares only words with words, and not words with non-words. Judgments of word frequency go by different names in the literature, including "familiarity" (Juola et al., 1971; Kintsch, 1967; Mandler, 1980) and "encoding specificity" (Tulving, 1976; Tulving and Thomson, 1973).

These data are summarized in Figure 12.71. They show that forced choice recognition of (old-new) word pairs leads to more errors for old high-frequency words paired with new high-frequency words (H-H) than for old low-frequency words paired with new low-frequency words (L-L), yet more errors occur for old low-frequency words paired with new high-frequency words (L-H) than for the converse (H-L). Greg Stone and I explained these data as well in our article using ART mechanisms. Various other lexical decision and word frequency data have also been explained using ART concepts by other authors (e.g., Dunbar, 2012; Glotin et al., 2010; McLennan, Luce, and Charles-Luce, 2003; Vitevitch and Donoso, 2011).

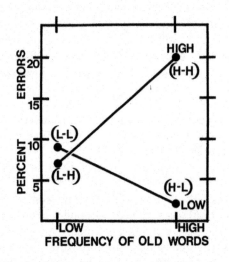

FIGURE 12.71. Word frequency data of Underwood and Freund (1970) that were explained in Grossberg and Stone (1986). See the text for details.

From invariant working memory storage to volitionally-variant percepts and productions

The previous sections aimed to show how ART mechanisms can explain challenging cognitive data about speech and language processing. I will now discuss how basic capabilities that are taken for granted during speech and language learning and performance are realized in ART architectures. In particular, I will discuss how speaker-invariant and rate-invariant working memories and list chunking networks can recall their learned representations as voice-specific and rate-variant productions that are matched against auditory top-down expectations, and consciously heard when a stream-shroud resonance develops in response to a good enough match. The networks are successively generalized to enable variable-rate productions without and with a learned rhythm, and without and with a singing voice. Further development of these modeling concepts and mechanisms will be needed to process realistic speech and music.

Back to LIST PARSE: Volitionally-controlled variable-rate sequential performance. The first example proposes how recall from working memory can occur in an individual's usual speaking voice with the production rate controlled by a volitional GO signal from the basal ganglia. This example uses the LIST PARSE model that I discussed earlier in this chapter (Figures 12.42 and 12.43; Grossberg and Pearson, 2008). LIST PARSE illustrates how multiple processing stages work together to enable variable-rate production from rate-invariant working memory and list chunking networks. In order to achieve variable-rate performance that is under volitional control, the dynamics of these processing stages need to be coordinated, even though none of them knows what the other stages are doing. For example, read-out rates of stored item sequences from the cognitive working memory in ventrolateral prefrontal cortex, to the motor working memory in dorsolateral prefrontal cortex, need to be coordinated with the current production that the motor working memory activates, so that the next command does not occur before the current production is sufficiently executed, or too long after it is fully executed.

For example, to coordinate performance of a dance, the command for the next dance step needs to be read-out at just the right time to smoothly interpolate the previously performed step, even if the dancer decides on a moment-to-moment basis to perform the steps with a different rhythm than in the past. The same problem is faced by all examples of variable-rate volitional control of stored sequences. In the case of speech and language performance, read-out of an ART sensory expectation needs to be coordinated with the expected time that auditory feedback from the production will be consciously heard, or in the case of vision, with the expected time that a familiar scene will be consciously seen after an eye movement.

How does the state of a current production influence the timing of the next working memory read-out, given that these two processes occur in separate networks and compute different kinds of information? The VITE model (Figure 12.2) and DIRECT model (Figure 12.13) describe how a motor trajectory approaches its target position as its difference vector (D) approaches zero. However, the difference vector does not include information about the speed with which the movement is being made. The outflow velocity vector (DG) that multiplies D with the GO signal G does incorporate this information (Figures 12.2 and 12.4). (I have omitted the rectification $[D]^+$ of D for simplicity.) However, DG can be small at both the beginning and the end of a movement, since G can grow from zero when a movement is launched, and D approaches zero as it ends. How does the network distinguish between a small DG at the beginning vs. the end of a movement?

LIST PARSE proposes that the network makes this distinction by computing the *deceleration* of the trajectory velocity profile as D, and DG, both approach zero (Figure 12.4). In VITE, DIRECT, and LIST PARSE, DG inputs to the present position command P, where it is integrated to reach the target position T. In addition, in LIST PARSE, DG also inputs to two additional cell populations in order to estimate deceleration (Figure 12.43): It is slowly integrated through time by the activity of cells B and more rapidly integrated through time by the activity cells A. Then B excites the rehearsal wave stage R, while A inhibits it.

During the beginning of a movement, the bell-shaped velocity curve increases. Hence activity A is greater than activity B, because fast cells better track the increasing velocity signal, whereas slow cells still remember smaller velocity signals. At the end of a movement, the bell-shaped velocity curve decreases. Here, activity A is less than activity B, because fast cells better track the smaller velocities, whereas slow cells still remember the larger velocities from when the bell-shaped velocity profile was still increasing.

Outputs from A are subtracted from outputs from B at the cells that control the rehearsal gate R (Figure 12.43). At the beginning of a movement, the difference signal (B – A) is negative, thereby shutting off the rehearsal gating signal, R, and preventing premature read-out of the next motor item. At the end of movement, (B – A) is positive and can open the rehearsal gate to initiate the next movement before the present movement is over. Since (B – A) is derived from the bell-shaped velocity profile, it is sensitive to the rate of movement and can control seamless performance of a movement sequence at variable speeds.

The difference signal (B – A) hereby estimates the deceleration, and causes a rehearsal wave to read out the next command from the working memory at the appropriate time. The entire command hierarchy can then coordinate variable-rate read-out of working memory commands with trajectory generator dynamics to control smooth sequential productions.

The inputs to the cognitive working memory in LIST PARSE (I_i in Figure 12.43) do not include the speaker-invariant (Figures 12.25 and 12.26) and rate-invariant (Figures 12.65 and 12.67) pre-processing stages that I discussed earlier in this chapter. These preprocessing networks can readily be joined to the front end of LIST PARSE.

Various of the capabilities of LIST PARSE were strengthened in the lisTELOS model that I discussed earlier in this chapter. In particular, lisTELOS extended TELOS to explain and predict how sequences, or lists, of eye movements can be carried out, while continuing to simulate everything that TELOS could. To accomplish this extension, lisTELOS models how a sequence, or list, of eye movement target positions can be stored in an Item-Order-Rank *spatial* working memory, and how three different basal ganglia loops are coordinated for the planning, selection, and release of such an eye movement sequence.

Saccadic eye movements are typically performed in a stereotyped way, and without the fine control of performance speed that is characteristic of arm or leg movements. lisTELOS thus does not include volitional control of performance speed. Despite this simplification, the lisTELOS demonstration of how the basal ganglia control planning, choice, and performance of item sequences is relevant to speech and language, and thus to the timed read-out of sensory expectations that will be matched during conscious hearing. Its relevance is due both to the fact that all linguistic, spatial, and motor working memories have a similar design (Figure 1.6), and to the fact that all basal ganglia loops have a homologous anatomical organization (Figure 6.13; Alexander, DeLong, and Strick, 1986). When multiple basal ganglia loops are used to simulate the coordinated gating through time of perceptual, cognitive, and affective processes, a more complete description becomes possible of how several consciousness-supporting resonances evolve through time while a self is engaged with its world.

From learning of invariant lists to rhythmic intonated performance

LIST PARSE, and its various extensions, clarify how changing the amplitude of a volitional signal can, on a moment-by-moment basis, vary the speed with which stored sequences are performed (Figures 12.42 and 12.43). Albeit useful, this simple form of rhythmic performance is insufficient to explain the more sophisticated rhythms that occur during natural speech and singing. This book does not include a comprehensive analysis of the many fascinating facts that have been experimentally reported about rhythm and rhythmic performance (e.g., Ackermann, 2008; Deutsch, 2013; Fraisse, 1982; Krumhansl, 2000; Ladefoged and Disner, 2012), notably the role of beat in music. However, see Grossberg (2021). On the other hand, the book does propose how parallel neural mechanisms for rate-invariant and speaker-normalized representations of speech meaning, and for pitch-dependent and rhythm-dependent speech intonation (Ladefoged and Disner, 2012), may interact to achieve "online sequencing of syllables into fast, smooth, and rhythmically organized larger utterances" (Ackermann, 2008, p. 265). This analysis also proposes how these several kinds of information are learned, stored, and combined during fluent performance and conscious awareness thereof; and how speaker-normalized representations may be sung with multiple tunes. These neural design principles and their mechanistic realizations extend and complement the discoveries of processing streams, components, and their interactions that have been already been proposed, without mechanistic neural realizations, by other authors (e.g., Armony et al., 2015; Norman-Haignere, Kanwisher, and McDermott, 2015; Rauschecker and Scott, 2009; Rauschecker and Tian, 2000; Sleve and Okada, 2015).

Factorization of order and rhythm. These competences depend upon a brain design that supports a flexible relationship between stored order information and the pitch and rhythm with which it is performed. In particular, when a listener hears a sufficiently short segment of novel speech that is uttered with one rhythm, he or she can immediately perform it with the same rhythm, or with a different rhythm that the listener chooses. For example, after hearing the sentence "How ARE you TODAY?", where the capital letters indicate a slower and more stressed pronunciation of the words ARE and TODAY, I can repeat it as "HOW are YOU today?" Thus, the rate-invariant order information in the sequence can flexibly be decoupled from, and later recoupled with, one of several possible rhythmic productions.

I like to call this property *factorization of order and rhythm* (Grossberg, 1986) for the following reasons: The speech items and their order can be stored in a rate-invariant Item-Order-Rank working memory that is an early stage in representing the meaning of the stored sequence. The fact that a sufficiently short, stored order sequence, after one hearing, can be performed with the same rhythm, or with a different rhythm, shows that a separate system with working memory properties exists for storing the rhythm. The fact that the stored rhythm does not have to be used for the performance shows that these parallel order and rhythm working memories can operate independently from each other, under volitional control.

Independence of lyrics and tunes. This property is related to the so-called *independence of lyrics and tunes* that occurs when hearing and performing vocal music (Besson et al., 1998; Bonnel et al., 2001). A big caveat to such "independence" is that these two types of information interact during storage—when the heard order information of a lyric influences the perceived timing and storage of a tune's pitch contours and rhythm—and again during production—when order, pitch, and rhythm information are combined to yield the final performance (Sammler et al., 2010; Sleve and Okada, 2015). These interactions are the reason why I prefer the term "factorization" to "independence" of order, pitch, and rhythm. Indeed, the learned list chunks that are activated by the items that are stored in a rate-invariant working memory *group these items together into emergent units*. These emergent units help to determine what rhythm is perceived and then stored, much as the learned chunks of a familiar language may influence its perceived rhythm.

From speaking to singing

One more interaction between complementary processing streams will now be briefly noted. Order and rhythm information are stored within parallel working memories whose inputs are speaker-normalized. These working memories read out their commands to representations that control the speaking voice of the performer. This interstream interaction between hearing and saying builds upon the learned circular reaction between speaking and hearing that occurs throughout life (Figure 12.15, right panel).

Learning also goes on throughout life of a parallel circular reaction that links learned pitch-and-timbre categories for the recognition of heard sounds (Table 1.4), which are not speaker-normalized, to the motor synergies (Figure 12.2) that control the pitches generated by the vocal folds, or vocal cords (Sundberg, 1977). The vocal folds are open when inhaling and closed when swallowing or holding one's breath. They are held apart slightly for speech or singing, during which they vibrate to modulate the expelled airflow from the lungs. A person's voice pitch is determined by the resonant frequency of vibration by the vocal folds.

The pitch of a person's voice changes during the singing of a song due to modulation of the singer's vocal fold vibrations. The auditory feedback due to these sounds leads to the activation of a sequence of pitch-and-timbre item chunks that can be stored in a spectral working memory. A spectral working memory can store a rate-invariant representation of the melody of a song, just as a rate-invariant *and* speaker-invariant working memory can store its lyrics. Production of a remembered song can be accomplished when the three types of working memory that have stored different aspects of the song are read out in a coordinated way: the invariant working memory of the song's lyrics, the spectral working memory of its melody, and the rhythm working memory. The spectral working memory of the melody directly modulates the vocal fold vibrations with which the lyrics are performed. All three of these working memory productions are coordinated by the basal ganglia. The song can be performed with a different rhythm by exploiting the factorization of order and rhythm. Much more modeling needs to be done to carry out large-scale simulations of such coordinated resonances during the control of real-world auditory behaviors. The above summary is aimed at illustrating this particularly important example of how all working memories share a similar circuit design, which makes their coordination possible.

Conscious audition is achieved if these working memories read out production commands at the same time as they read out top-down sensory expectations of the sounds that are predicted to be heard. When these expectations are matched by the auditory feedback of the productions (e.g., Figure 12.25, left panel), the song is consciously heard by coordinated stream-shroud and spectral-pitch-and-timbre resonances (Table 1.4).

This has been a particularly long chapter! Its many distinct but related threads create a vibrant tapestry of fascinating themes that intertwine in complex ways during auditory cognition and consciousness. I have tried in this chapter to introduce you to this tapestry by outlining a principled conceptual and computational foundation of brain design principles and models upon which many years of fruitful additional research can be built, ranging across the full gamut of topics from audition, through speech and language, to music understanding and performance.

From Knowing to Feeling

How emotion regulates motivation, attention, decision, and action

Cognitive-emotional dynamics: Beyond Chomsky and Skinner

Resonating object, value, and object-value categories: The "feeling of what happens". The visual and auditory processes summarized in the previous chapters represent external information about the world, but do not evaluate how important this information is for survival or success. Interactions between perceptual/cognitive and evaluative reinforcement/emotional/motivational mechanisms accomplish this. What kind of resonance supports a conscious emotion? What kind of resonance enables an emotion to generate the kind of conscious "feeling of what happens" that Antonio Damasio has described (cf. Chapter 1; Damasio, 1999), knowing the source of that feeling, and being able to behave appropriately in response to it? In particular, how does an emotion generate motivation that may help us to search for, and acquire, goal objects that can satisfy that emotion? Under what circumstances can emotions affect behavior without being conscious? How do emotions contribute to behaviors that are properly timed to achieve desired goals? How do breakdowns in the resonances that support conscious feelings lead to prescribed mental disorders, such as autism and schizophrenia, and how does the affective meaning of familiar objects and events fail to organize behavior in a context-appropriate way when this happens?

A study of cognitive-emotional interactions, and the conscious resonances that they support, is needed to propose answers to these questions. Such resonances focus *motivated attention* upon valued objects in an adaptively timed way, and thereby supports the release of appropriately timed actions that are directed towards these objects. Unlike visual and auditory conscious percepts, emotions or feelings do not represent *external* sensory cues, such as sights and sounds. Rather, they represent *internal* affective states of fear, pleasure, pain, happiness, sadness, and the like, that may be activated by a variety of external and internal signals.

When conscious emotions are triggered by viewing affectively meaningful visual scenes, *cognitive-emotional resonances* are proposed to support these feelings, our knowledge of them, and our ability to respond appropriately. These resonances occur

Conscious MIND Resonant BRAIN. Stephen Grossberg, Oxford University Press. © Oxford University Press 2021.
DOI: 10.1093/oso/9780190070557.003.0013

using feedback interactions (Figure 13.1) between *invariant object categories* for recognition of objects in temporal cortex (Chapter 6); *value categories*, or drive representations, in the amygdala, where reinforcing and homeostatic inputs converge and from which motivational signals emerge (Aggleton, 1993; Aggleton and Saunders, 2000; Barbas, 1995, 2007; Bower, 1981; Davis, 1994; Gloor et al., 1982; Halgren et al., 1978; LeDoux, 1993); *homeostatic representations* in the hypothalamus (not labeled in Figure 13.1) that register and control autonomic and other affective reactions; and *object-value categories* in orbitofrontal cortex to which object categories and value categories both send their output signals. The object category representations may, in turn, synchronously interact with surface-shroud and stream-shroud resonances that support conscious awareness of the visual or auditory events that activate object categories (Chapters 6 and 12). Finally, *motor representations* (M) control discrete adaptive responses. They include multiple brain regions, including motor cortex and cerebellum (Evarts, 1973; Ito, 1984; Kalaska, Cohen, Hyde, and Prud'homme, 1989; Thompson, 1988). Some of the more complete models of the internal structure of motor representations and how they generate movement trajectories were summarized in Chapter 12. More about these and related models is described in a serial of archival papers (e.g., Bullock, Cisek, and Grossberg, 1998; Bullock and Grossberg, 1988; Cisek, Grossberg, and Bullock, 1998; Contreras-Vidal, Grossberg, and Bullock, 1997; Fiala, Grossberg, and Bullock, 1996; Gancarz and Grossberg, 1998, 1999), and can readily be incorporated into CogEM model extensions.

Separate and antagonistic historic movements studied cognition and emotion. I began to introduce neural models of cognitive-emotional resonances in 1971 (Grossberg, 1971a, 1972a, 1972b, 1975) at a time when

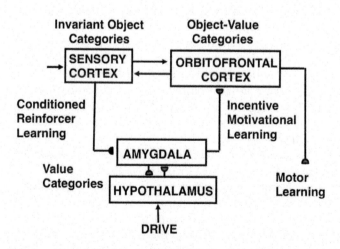

FIGURE 13.1. Macrocircuit of the functional stages and anatomical interpretations of the Cognitive-Emotional-Motor, or CogEM, model.

there was a major split between studies of cognition, as exemplified by the work on linguistics of Noam Chomsky in 1975 (Chomsky, 1957), and of emotion, as exemplified by the work on instrumental, or operant, conditioning of B. F. Skinner in 1938 (Skinner, 1938). *Instrumental conditioning* concerns how animals learn about their environments by emitting actions and receiving rewards or punishments in response to them. Skinner and his colleagues described important properties of animal learning under different schedules of reward and punishment that could be tightly controlled in experimental chambers that were called Skinner boxes. One example of a Skinner box is the two-way shuttle box that was described in Chapter 1. The phenomenon of peak shift and behavioral contrast (Figure 1.12) was just one of hundreds of fascinating facts about behavior that Skinner and his colleagues described.

A dramatic counterpoint to this seminal experimental contribution was Skinner's radical behaviorist anti-theoretical stance that opposed any model that describes internal mental states, including states like emotions. Instead, Skinner tries to explain everything in terms of observable behaviors. Chomsky embraced the modeling of mental states by advocating, along with pioneers like Donald Broadbent and George Miller, what many scientists called the *cognitive revolution*. However, Chomsky's universal grammar formalism included no dynamics, let alone learning dynamics, and was devoid of any allusion to emotion. Instead, cognition and emotion studies were often antagonistic to each other, as illustrated by the influential critique of Skinner's behaviorism that Chomsky published in 1959 (Chomsky, 1959).

Divided concepts of cognition and emotion have persisted during many historical periods. A particularly vivid period was described in the book *Wittgenstein's Vienna* that Allan Janik and Stephen Toulmin published in 1973 (Janik and Toulmin, 1973). This important book reviewed beliefs in the Austro-Hungarian empire just before the First World War—a time and place that boasted geniuses like Wittgenstein, Freud, Viktor Adler, and Arnold Schoenberg—that men were endowed with reason and logic, whereas women were emotional creatures and, not infrequently, hysterical ones. In reality, as this book has documented, and will continue to do so in the present chapter, cognition and emotion interact intimately in each of our brains in order to support lives that are worth living.

My own articles about cognitive-emotional interactions began a mechanistic synthesis of cognition and emotion by showing how the same kinds of neural equations and modules, suitably specialized, could be used to describe both the cognitive and the emotional processes that interact during a cognitive-emotional resonance to join *what we know* with *what we feel*. As illustrated below, the emergence of the field of *affective neuroscience* in the intervening years has supported all the predictions that grew out of this synthesis. In fact, I viewed Skinnerian data as a rich source of information about cognitive processes, including data about peak shift and behavioral contrast (Figure 1.12). These data imply the existence of brain maps wherein nearby cells code similar features of external stimuli, and interact via recurrent competitive networks that tend to conserve their total activity. These and related data forced me to derive the laws for networks whose cells interact via shunting on-center off-surround interactions that play such an important role in understanding the perceptual and cognitive processes that I discussed in earlier chapters.

In this chapter, I will first discuss some basic data about cognitive-emotional interactions and how neural models explain them. I will do this for data about normal individuals as well as data about clinical patients with mental problems like autism and schizophrenia. Then I will show how these neural models can be derived from a simple gedanken, or thought, experiment that uses for its hypotheses very simple facts of daily life that no one would deny. The two main hypotheses are that (1) stimuli may learn to predict rewards or punishments that occur after variable time delays, and (2) this kind of learning is possible. No one would deny such trivialities. Despite the simplicity of these theoretical foundations, the model mechanisms to which they lead are capable of explaining highly paradoxical data that currently seem to have no explanation without them. This demonstration again illustrates the power of models to clarify how our minds work.

Reinforcement learning: Conditioned reinforcer and incentive motivational learning

Classical conditioning. Many visual cues do not initially have affective meaning to an individual. These cues can acquire affective significance through reinforcement learning, whereby the pathways between the object, value, object-value, and homeostatic representations can be altered (Figure 13.1). For definiteness, I will start by considering the other main kind of reinforcement learning to instrumental, or operant, conditioning. This alternative learning paradigm is called Pavlovian, or classical, conditioning after the pioneering work of Ivan Pavlov in Russia in the early part of the twentieth century (Kamin, 1968, 1969; Pavlov, 1927). Although classical conditioning may at first seem too simple to apply to important real-life learning experiences, I will show you below that it is a valuable probe of how animals and humans learn what cues in the environment predict, indeed cause, important

affective consequences. There are few processes in life that are more important than the ones that enable us to discover the causes of our experiences, for only then can we take whatever steps are necessary to encourage those causes, or change them when necessary.

During classical conditioning, a conditioned stimulus, or CS, that initially may have no emotional significance, is paired with an unconditioned stimulus, or US, that can from the start generate a strong emotional response. The conditioned response, or CR, is a version of the response that the US caused. For example, during eyeblink classical conditioning, the CS is a neutral tone or light, the US is a puff of air to the eye or a shock to the eye's orbital muscle, and the CR is an adaptively timed closure of the eyelid in a human, or the analogous nictitating membrane reflex in a rabbit. One reason why eyeblink conditioning is studied so much is that the brain circuits that underlie it have been worked out in considerable detail.

Before conditioning occurs, when a familiar CS occurs, the CS can selectively activate an object category. For example, a tone would activate an auditory category, and a light would activate a visual category. The object category can, in turn, send priming signals to most or all of the value categories (Figure 13.1), but cannot vigorously fire any of them. It can also send priming signals to its object-value category. Neither the object-value category nor the value categories can fire vigorously in response to a CS before reinforcement learning occurs.

Learning to become a conditioned reinforcer and source of incentive motivation. When a CS is suitably paired in time with a US, reinforcement learning can begin. The US can activate the amygdala value category and the hypothalamic homeostatic representations that correspond to the emotion that it incites. As a result, the CS-activated object category and US-activated value category are simultaneously activated, so that learning can occur in the pathways from the active object category to the active value category, thereby strengthening the learned connections between them. After sufficiently many learning trials occur, the CS can activate that value category. When this happens, the CS is said to have become a *conditioned reinforcer* (Figure 13.1), because it has acquired, through conditioning, the ability to trigger many of the affective responses that the US does, and can also be used as a reinforcer with which to condition other CSs.

As a conditioned reinforcer is being learned, the value category that is activated by the US is able to send signals, called *incentive motivation* signals, to many object-value categories, including the object-value category of the CS (Figure 13.1). When this occurs, convergent signals from both the object category and the value category converge on the object-value category. Such convergent signals are sufficient to activate the object-value category (Figure 13.2). Now both the value category and an object-value category

Cognitive-Emotional-Motor (CogEM) model

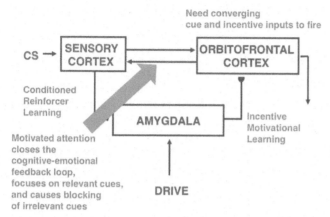

FIGURE 13.2. The object-value categories in the orbitofrontal cortex require converging specific inputs from the sensory cortex and nonspecific incentive motivational inputs from the amygdala in order to fire. When the orbitofrontal cortex fires, it can deliver top-down ART Matching Rule priming signals to the sensory cortical area by which it was activated, thereby helping to choose the active recognition categories there that have the most emotional support, while suppressing others, leading to attentional blocking of irrelevant cues.

are simultaneously active, so learning can occur in the pathway from the value category to the object-value category, further strengthening it, while weakening pathway connections to inactive object-value categories. This strengthening is called *incentive motivational learning*.

Suppose that both conditioned reinforcer learning and incentive motivational learning have already occurred, Then, when a conditioned reinforcer CS turns on, it can activate its object category, as it already could before conditioning occurred. It can also prime its object-value category, again just as it could before conditioning occurred. However, unlike the situation before conditioning occurred, a conditioned reinforcer stimulus can, by itself, activate its value category using the pathway that was strengthened by conditioned reinforcer learning. Then convergent input to the object-value category from both the object category and the activated value category can fully activate the object-value category and, with it, motivated behaviors.

Anatomical substrates of object, value, and object-value categories. Do these model processing stages actually occur in our brains? The anatomical interpretations of the sensory cortical, amygdala, and orbitofrontal cortical brain regions that are shown in Figure 13.2 for the object, value, and object-value categories, respectively, have been supported by extensive anatomical data, as Figure 13.3 from a 1995 article by the distinguished anatomist Helen Barbas illustrates (Barbas, 1995). More will be said below about this anatomical interpretation.

After a value category is conditioned to sufficiently many CSs, activating just a value category can generate an *emotional set* by priming all of the object-value categories with which it was associated in the past. This is how, when we are hungry, our minds tend to think about good things and places to eat.

Cognitive-emotional resonance and attentional blocking. After an object-value category in the orbitofrontal cortex gets activated, it can generate top-down priming signals to its object category in the sensory cortex via the ART Matching Rule (Figures 13.1 and 1.25). The importance of this feedback pathway can be seen by considering situations where multiple visual cues simultaneously activate the sensory cortex. Suppose that, after competition occurs between the object-value categories, one object-value category wins the competition between them due to the incentive motivational signals that it receives from the value category in the amygdala. This object-value category is then the most motivationally salient object-value category at that moment. It can then read-out a strong top-down attentional signal to the corresponding currently active object category, whose activity is thereby amplified by motivated attention, while the competitive interactions in the off-surround of the ART Matching Rule attentionally *block* object categories of motivationally-irrelevant sensory cues (Grossberg and Levine, 1987; Pavlov, 1927). In other words, the top-down feedback enables motivated attention to bias, and thereby help to choose, motivationally consistent object categories for further processing. I mentioned attentional blocking in

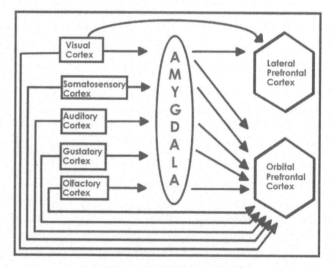

Adapted from Barbas (1995)

FIGURE 13.3. The predicted processing stages of CogEM have been supported by anatomical studies of connections between sensory cortices, amygdala, and orbitofrontal cortex.

COGNITIVE-EMOTIONAL RESONANCE
Basis of "core consciousness" and "the feeling of what happens"
Damasio (1999) derives heuristic version of CogEM model from his
clinical data

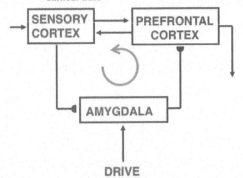

DRIVE

HOW IS THIS RESONANCE MAINTAINED LONG
ENOUGH TO BECOME CONSCIOUS?!

FIGURE 13.4. The top-down feedback from the orbitofrontal cortex closes a feedback loop that supports a cognitive-emotional resonance. If this resonance can be sustained long enough, it enables us to have feelings at the same time that we experience the categories that caused them.

Chapter 1. Recall that attentional blocking helps to choose the cues that predict learned consequences. The attentive feedback from the object-value category to object categories hereby helps to explain how cues that are affectively predictive in a given situation can grab our attention.

Activation of the feedback circuit that is defined by temporal-amygdala-orbitofrontal interactions can create a *cognitive-emotional resonance* that focuses and maintains motivated attention upon a motivationally salient object category (Figure 13.4). If this resonance is sustained long enough, it can also support conscious feelings about this object, and enable the release of motivationally-compatible actions (Tables 1.3 and 1.4). I will explain how this is proposed to happen later in this chapter.

CogEM: Cognitive-Emotional-Motor model of conditioning

I first predicted the existence of this kind of cognitive-emotional resonance in 1971 when I introduced the Cognitive-Emotional-Motor, or CogEM, model (Grossberg, 1971a, 1972a, 1972b, 1982, 1984c) whose basic circuit is summarized in Figures 13.1-13.4. CogEM enabled me and my colleagues to explain and simulate properties of many cognitive-emotional data as consequences of simple evolutionary design constraints, including data about primary and secondary excitatory and inhibitory conditioning and extinction (Grossberg and Schmajuk, 1987), attentional blocking and unblocking (Grossberg,

1975a, 1982; Grossberg and Levine, 1987), adaptively timed conditioning (Grossberg and Schmajuk, 1989; Grossberg and Merrill, 1992, 1996), and decision making under risk (Grossberg and Gutowski, 1987). Predictions of CogEM and its extensions have been supported by many subsequent data, including data concerning the anatomy and neurophysiology of the brain regions that the model interactions use to explain psychological data. Let's turn now to explanations of some of these phenomena.

Classical conditioning and non-stationary prediction. Figure 13.5 depicts an important property of classical conditioning: The CS needs to start before the US in order for good conditioning of a CR to occur. It can happen that the conditioned response, or CR, resembles in all respects the unconditioned response, or UR, that the US excites, but sometimes the CS predicts only a subset of US properties, which is why the CR is distinguished from the UR. This figure also depicts the sense in which classical conditioning is a form of *associative learning*, or learning that *associates* a stimulus event A with a predicted event B. Because learning enables A to predict B, it is also a kind of *nonstationary* prediction, which is the kind of prediction where the probability that one event predicts another changes through time, in this case due to learning. Here the question of whether A predicts only a subset of B's properties will not be considered.

One of the paradoxical properties of classical conditioning is that conditioning is best if the CS starts a little while before the US starts. Let us call the delay between CS and US onset the interstimulus interval, or ISI. Figure 13.6 (left column) illustrates the remarkable fact that the strength of a learned CR is an inverted-U function of the ISI, with conditioning poor at either a long ISI or a zero ISI.

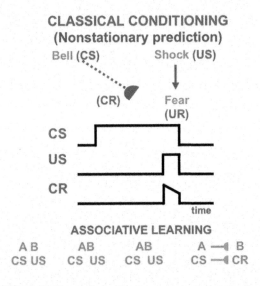

CLASSICAL CONDITIONING
(Nonstationary prediction)

Bell (CS)   Shock (US)

(CR)   Fear
              (UR)

CS

US

CR

                              time

ASSOCIATIVE LEARNING

| A B | AB | AB | A ◀ B |
| CS US | CS US | CS US | CS ◀ CR |

FIGURE 13.5. Classical conditioning is perhaps the simplest kind of associative learning.

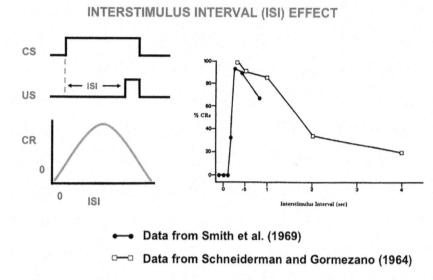

Data from Smith et al. (1969)

Data from Schneiderman and Gormezano (1964)

FIGURE 13.6 (left column) An Inverted-U occurs in conditioned reinforcer strength as a function of the ISI between the CS and the US. Why is learning attenuated at 0 ISI? (right column) Some classical conditioning data that illustrate the Inverted-U in conditioning as a function of the ISI.

The fact that conditioning is poor if the ISI is sufficiently large makes perfect sense. If a bell rings today and I get shocked a week later, there is no reason to associate the bell with the shock. However, the fact that conditioning is poor at a zero ISI is not so obvious, because then the CS and US are perfectly correlated in time. Figure 13.6 (right column) summarizes some data about classical conditioning that illustrate this inverted-U. Why is there an inverted-U as a function of the ISI? Why doesn't conditioning get better and better as the ISI gets smaller and smaller?

Learning causality: ISI inverted-U, secondary conditioning, and attentional blocking. This property follows from the ability of animals, and of the CogEM model, to focus attention upon cues that causally predict expected consequences. Before explaining how this happens, let me review two basic facts that I already mentioned in Chapter 1. The first fact is secondary conditioning. This occurs when a CS, call it CS_1, that is already a conditioned reinforcer due to previous learning, is used to condition a different CS, call it CS_2, to also become a conditioned reinforcer (Figure 13.7). As I noted in Chapter 1, secondary conditioning affects our lives in myriad ways, ranging from enabling us to learn that the sight of food predicts that it will be a source of nourishment, to our susceptibility to the inducements of the multi-billion dollar advertising industry.

The second basic fact is *attentional blocking* (Figure 1.10). Attentional blocking is important to understand because it is one of the main ways that animals and humans can discover, without the use of higher cognition and language, what events *cause* subsequent events,

and what events are just accidentally correlated with them. In order to fully understand how blocking works, we need to also understand one additional fact that is summarized in Figure 13.9. This picture shows that *if t*wo stimuli, like a bell and light, are carefully chosen to be equally salient to a learner, then when they are simultaneously presented before a US, each of them can be conditioned to generate a CR. In other words, parallel processing of multiple cues is possible during conditioning. On the other hand, this is a big "if" because more salient cues can *overshadow* learning with respect to less salient cues.

Blocking can be viewed as an extreme version of overshadowing (Figure 13.8). During Phase 1 of a blocking experiment. CS_1 is presented before a US until it becomes a conditioned reinforcer. During Phase 2 of the experiment, CS_1 is presented simultaneously with another CS, call it CS_2, before the same US occurs. Despite the fact that equally salient CSs can separately be associated with a subsequent US, as in Figure 13.9, prior conditioning of the US to CS_1 can prevent CS_2 from learning the CR. In other words, prior learning by CS_1 has *blocked* learning by CS_2 of the CR.

Classical conditioning shows that we are minimal adaptive predictors. As illustrated by Figure 13.8 (left column) and discussed in Chapter 1 (see Figure 1.10), blocking prevents irrelevant stimuli from predicting affective consequences. Blocking hereby illustrates in a dramatic way that classical conditioning is not just a simple

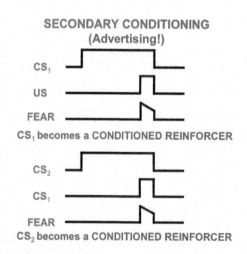

FIGURE 13.7. The paradigm of secondary conditioning. See the text for details.

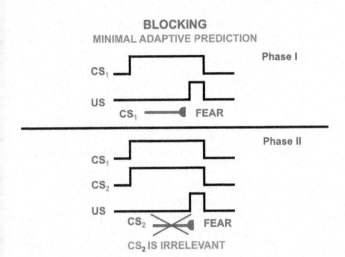

FIGURE 13.8. The blocking paradigm illustrates how cues that do not predict different consequences may fail to be attended.

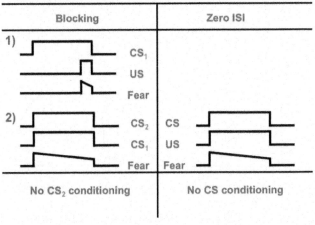

FIGURE 13.10. Blocking follows if both secondary conditioning and attenuation of conditioning at a zero ISI occur.

passive process. Rather, conditioning enables animals and humans to behave like *minimal adaptive predictors* who discover a sufficient set of stimuli to predict important affective consequences, while allowing us to ignore stimuli that are predictively irrelevant.

Each of us may discover different combinations of environmental features that can successfully predict behavioral outcomes. We can hereby each learn a uniquely personal way to attend and understand an environment. It is only when our different attended critical features lead to disconfirmations due to the predictions based on others' features that we can begin to discover our different understandings of the world.

Blocking follows when the Inverted-U is combined with secondary conditioning. What Chapter 1 did not

do was to explain how attentional blocking occurs. This I will now do. Figure 13.10 begins this explanation by showing that blocking follows from the combination of two simpler properties: secondary conditioning (Figure 13.7), and the inverted-U in conditioning as a function of ISI (Figure 13.6). In the left hand column of Figure 13.10, the two phases of the blocking paradigm are shown. The first phase just describes conditioning of CS_1 to the US. The second phase describes secondary conditioning of CS_2 using CS_1 as the conditioned reinforcer. However, this conditioning occurs at a zero ISI in the blocking paradigm. The right hand column reminds us that no conditioning occurs at zero ISI, at least in the case of conditioning a CS to a primary US. The same thing happens if a conditioned reinforcer like the CS_1 is used instead of a primary reinforcer like the US. In order to explain blocking, we therefore only need to explain secondary conditioning and the inverted-U in conditioning as a function of the ISI. The CogEM model provides an easy explanation of both these properties.

Before turning to this explanation, let me note how properties of unblocking (Figure 1.10, right column) support the interpretation of blocking as an example of minimal adaptive prediction (Figure 13.8). The unblocking paradigm differs from the blocking paradigm only by using a different US after CS_2 is presented—call it US_2—from the one that occurred after CS_1 was presented—call it US_1. As a result of this change in predicted consequences, CS_2 is no longer a redundant, or predictively irrelevant, stimulus. CS_2 can then learn to predict the changed outcome, thereby expanding the set of stimuli that are predictively relevant.

Unblocking also shows that there is a difference between the *novelty* of an outcome and the *affective sign* that it predicts. For example, suppose that US_1 is a shock of a given intensity. We can define US_2 to either increase

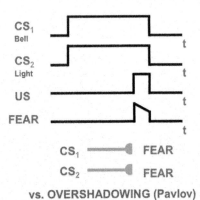

FIGURE 13.9. Equally salient cues can be conditioned in parallel to an emotional consequence.

or decrease shock intensity by an amount that is carefully chosen to be equally novel in either case. Increasing shock will typically cause CS_2 to become a conditioned reinforcer of *fear*, which is a negative reinforcer, whereas decreasing shock will typically cause CS_2 to become a conditioned reinforcer of *relief*, which is a positive reinforcer. Thus, at the moment when an unexpected consequence occurs, at least two different processes will take place, one devoted to calibrating how novel the consequence is, and the other to its affective sign, with the amount of novelty helping to determine to what extent the change in affective sign will be learned.

Key properties of blocking and unblocking enable us to better understand how conditioning regulates the set of stimuli that motivated attention selects, while suppressing redundant stimuli. First, conditioning enables us to pay attention to, and learn about, relevant cues, much as CS_1 learns to predict US_1 in the first stage of an unblocking paradigm in Figure 1.10 (right column). Second, *unexpected consequences* can redefine the set of relevant cues, much as changing US_1 to US_2 makes CS_2 a relevant stimulus. Just how remarkable this property is can be appreciated by remembering that, if the US did not change, then CS_2 *would* be blocked by CS_1. The brain does not, however, know that the US will change until it changes! And this does not happen until CS_2 has already occurred, may no longer even be on, and has already begun to be blocked by CS_1!

We are hereby led to ask: How does an unexpected consequence like US_2 unblock the internal representation of a stimulus like CS_2 that has already begun to be blocked? Chapter 1 summarized the crucial importance of this state of affairs by calling the time at which US_2 occurs *The Disconfirming Moment*. At The Disconfirming Moment, the brain has no idea what set of internally stored stimuli *should* have been used to predict the unexpected outcome. In order to discover these stimuli, and thereby enable them to learn to predict the outcome, the US_2 triggers an internal event that can alter the processing of *all* previously stored stimuli. I call this a *nonspecific* event. I furthermore call it *nonspecific arousal* because unexpected, or novel, events are arousing.

In order for an outcome to be unexpected, the brain has to learn an expectation of what outcome to expect, and this expectation needs to be mismatched by a current outcome. This line of reasoning about unblocking led me in the 1970s to realize that mismatch of a learned expectation triggers nonspecific arousal that can drive a memory search which can unblock previously blocked internal representations of recently occurring stimuli. The requirements of unblocking during classical conditioning, properly analyzed,

hereby motivated me to develop a cognitive theory about how our brains learn expectations and use their mismatch to drive memory searches to discover and learn recognition categories that can more successfully predict outcomes in the world. The result was Adaptive Resonance Theory, that I already discussed in Chapter 5; e.g., Figure 5.19. This connection clarifies why I was able to publish a major article about cognitive-emotional interactions, including blocking and unblocking, in the *International Review of Neurobiology* in 1975 (Grossberg, 1975a), and the first articles about Adaptive Resonance Theory in *Biological Cybernetics* in 1976 (Grossberg, 1976a, 1976b).

These processes and their interactions clarify how the brain distinguishes novelty from emotional sign, and uses interactions between these cognitive ART and cognitive-emotional CogEM processes to choose the emotional sign that a conditioned reinforcer will learn in order to correctly motivate, and thereby support, appropriate actions in a changing world.

How CogEM explains attentional blocking. Figure 13.11 summarizes the main mechanisms whereby the CogEM model explains attentional blocking. This simplified circuit summarizes three kinds of internal representations (sensory, drive, motor) and three kinds of conditioning (conditioned reinforcer, incentive motivational, motor). A comparison with Figure 13.1 shows that the invariant object categories that CSs activate are also called sensory representations and that the value categories are also called drive representations. In Figure 13.11, object-value categories are also identified with invariant object categories, a simplification that will need to be revised after my

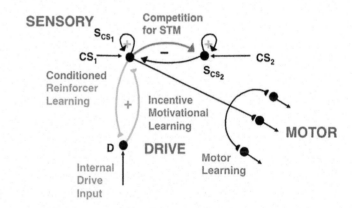

CogEM EXPLANATION OF ATTENTIONAL BLOCKING

1. Sensory representations compete for LIMITED CAPACITY STM
2. Previously reinforced cues amplify their STM via POSITIVE FEEDBACK
3. Other cues lose STM via COMPETITION

FIGURE 13.11. The three main properties of CogEM that help to explain how attentional blocking occurs.

first explanation is made. This explanation will clarify why object categories and object-value categories must be distinct representations in our brains, and how to make them work together properly.

First, sensory representations that are activated by CSs compete for an approximately conserved *total* amount of cell activation via a recurrent shunting on-center off-surround network. Recall that this kind of network first came up when I was discussing Figure 1.6. Recall also that the normalization property that such a network embodies is often called the *limited capacity* of short-term memory by many cognitive scientists. Second, a conditioned reinforcer can amplify its own activity, and thereby draw attention to itself, via a positive feedback loop that passes through conditioned reinforcer and incentive motivational pathways. These properties are described moment-by-moment in Figure 13.12 (left column). Finally, because total activity across the sensory representations tends to be conserved, the enhanced activity of a conditioned reinforcer can drive down the activity of other sensory representations, as illustrated by Figure 13.12 (right column). These losing cues do not have enough activity to sample affective consequences, so are blocked.

In response to two CS inputs with the same intensity and duration, the activity of their sensory representations begins to grow at the same rate, whether or not they are conditioned reinforcers. However, after positive feedback arrives from its drive representation, the activity of the sensory representation of a US or conditioned reinforcer starts to get amplified to a much higher level than it would otherwise reach.

If, now, two sensory representations are simultaneously activated by CSs that are matched in intensity and duration, then they both begin to grow at the same rate. However, if one of them is a US or conditioned reinforcer, then its amplified activity can quickly inhibit the activity of the other sensory representation due to the limited capacity of STM (Figure 13.12 (right column)). Computer simulations with my PhD student Daniel Levine in 1987 (Grossberg and Levine, 1987) showed that this suppression is sufficient to prevent the blocked stimulus from acquiring conditioned reinforcer properties. Dan is now a senior cognitive neuroscientist researcher and author in his own right (e.g., Levine, 2018).

If a US or conditioned reinforcer can suppress other sensory representations, then how does successful conditioning occur if a new CS precedes a US? Figure 13.13 (left column) explains how this can happen. By the time that the US occurs, the CS activity S_{CS} is already large, and is already inhibiting the sensory representation of the US. The motivational amplification of the US sensory representation can nonetheless take hold and, as it does so, it can eventually suppress the activity of the CS. However, during the crucial time interval when the CS and US are both active, shown in yellow in Figure 13.13 (left column), the CS conditioned reinforcer and incentive motivational pathways can sample and learn from the US-activated representations, thereby supporting conditioning during a range of positive ISIs between the CS and US. Taken together, Figures 13.12 (right column) and 13.13 (left column) illustrate the importance of thinking about how events occur in real time when trying to understand conditioning data, or indeed any other kind of mind and brain data.

This heuristic description leaves open the question of how big an ISI can still support conditioning. Conditioning fails at very large ISIs because the sensory representation of the CS is no longer active when the US occurs. Figure 13.13 (bottom row) depicts a computer simulation of the resulting inverted-U in conditioning as a function of the ISI using the CogEM model. This simulation was published as part of a

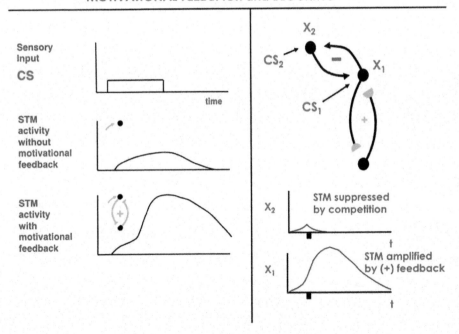

MOTIVATIONAL FEEDBACK and BLOCKING

FIGURE 13.12. (left column) How incentive motivational feedback amplifies activity of a sensory cortical cell population. (right column) A sensory cortical cell population whose activity is amplified by incentive motivational feedback can suppress the activities of less activated populations via self-normalizing recurrent competitive interactions.

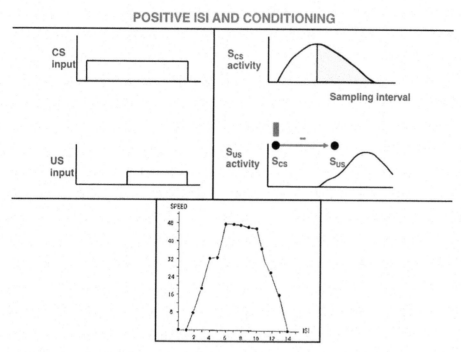

FIGURE 13.13. (top row) If a positive ISI separates onset of a CS and US, then the CS can sample the consequences of the US during the time interval before it is inhibited by it. (bottom row) A CogEM simulation of the Inverted-U in conditioning as a function of the ISI between CS and US.

larger study of CogEM that Dan Levine and I published in 1987 (Grossberg and Levine, 1987). The lack of conditioning at zero ISI can now be understood as a result of attentional blocking in a CogEM network.

A polyvalent orbitofrontal processing stage helps CogEM to work properly. The circuit in Figure 13.11 helps to qualitatively explain paradoxical data about properties like attentional blocking. However, without further refinement, this circuit may not be able to do its job well in lots of situations. This is true because, after a CS activates its sensory representation, it can immediately activate a motor response even before incentive motivation has a chance to feed back to the sensory representation. Without incentive motivational support, any CS, no matter how motivationally irrelevant in a given situation, can generate a motor response using this circuit.

The circuit refinement in Figure 13.14 prevents signals from triggering an action until the circuit can determine whether this action is valued in the current situation. In Figure 13.14, each sensory representation has two successive processing stages. The first stage is activated by the CS, which then sends signals to the second stage. The second stage is labeled with a ? in the figure until we can interpret it functionally and neurally. The second stage cannot, however, fire until it also receives incentive motivational feedback from a drive representation. The second stage thus consists of *polyvalent* cells that require a convergence of two signals in order to fire: a sensory signal and an incentive motivational signal. As a result, only motivated actions can be triggered by the second sensory processing stage, which is the stage that can activate motor responses further downstream.

Delivering incentive motivation to the polyvalent cell stage also imposes the requirement that the polyvalent cell stage send excitatory feedback to the first sensory processing stage to help amplify, and thereby select via limited-capacity competition, sensory representations that are motivationally salient at that time.

Interactions between sensory cortices, amygdala, and orbitofrontal cortex. Figure 13.14 has the same anatomy as the CogEM circuit in Figure 13.1, with the first sensory processing stage occurring in a sensory cortex such as inferotemporal cortex, the second sensory processing stage occurring in the orbitofrontal cortex, and the drive representation occurring in the amygdala. Many experiments have supported the prediction that drive-sensitive value category cells are found in the amygdala (e.g., Aggleton, 1993; LeDoux, 1993; Pessoa, 2008, 2009; Pessoa and Adolphs, 2010). Amygdala cells that are sensitive to hunger and satiety signals (Muramoto et al., 1993; Yan and Scott, 1996) and that respond in proportion to the value of a food reward have been extensively studied in the primate and rodent (Nishijo, Ono, and Nishino, 1988a; Toyomitsu et al., 2002). Activated value categories in the drive representation can send excitatory signals the orbitofrontal cortex via learned incentive motivational pathways. Neurobiological experiments have supported the prediction that an object-value category in orbitofrontal cortex receives a direct input a from an object category in a sensory cortex, and incentive motivational inputs from the amygdala (e.g., Figure 13.3; Barbas, 1995), and that the strength of the incentive motivational input determines how vigorously an object-value representation is activated in response to its object category input (e.g., Baxter et al., 2000; Hikosaka and Watanabe, 2000; Roesch and Olson, 2004; Rolls, 1999, 2000; Schoenbaum et al., 2003; Thorpe et al., 1983). In addition to neocortical inputs to the amygdala, a parallel pathway also includes direct subcortical inputs to the amygdala (LeDoux, 1996).

MODEL OF COGNITIVE-EMOTIONAL CIRCUIT

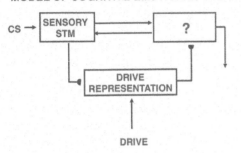

FIGURE 13.14. In order for conditioning to work properly, the sensory representation needs to have at least two successive processing stages. See the text for why.

CogEM type circuits are an ancient design! How long ago did evolution discover a circuit like CogEM? Figure 13.15 shows that it is an ancient design. This figure summarizes a circuit from *Aplysia californica*, which is a sea slug, or marine gastropod mollusk. Eric Kandel and his colleagues studied conditioning in *Aplysia*, notably learning that takes place in its gill and siphon withdrawal reflex. Kandel won the Nobel Prize in 2000 for their discoveries about this conditioning process. The circuit in Figure 13.15 was modeled by Dean Buonomano, Douglas Baxter, and John Byrne in 1990 to explain *Aplysia* data (Buonomano et al., 1990).

As in Figure 13.11, CS inputs in Figure 13.15 activate sensory neurons (SN). The SN, in turn, mutually inhibit each other via inhibitory interneurons (IN), as they send excitatory signals to a facilitator neuron (FC). The FC also receives excitatory input from a US, and thus acts like a drive representation. The FC then sends excitatory signals

APLYSIA

Buonomano, Baxter, and Byrne, *Neural Networks*, 1990
Grossberg, *Behavioral and Brain Sciences*, 1983

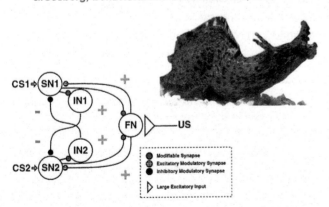

FACILITATOR NEURON ~ DRIVE REPRESENTATION

FIGURE 13.15. The CogEM circuit is an ancient design that is found even in mollusks like *Aplysia*. See the text for details.

back to the SN cells, thereby completing a positive feedback loop between SN cells and FC cells that is analogous to the motivational feedback loop in higher organisms.

Why did CogEM-type circuits emerge so early in the evolutionary process? I believe that this is due to the fact that this kind of circuit embodies solutions to ubiquitous environmental problems that all terrestrial animals must solve in order to survive.

Universal evolutionary constraints: The Synchronization and Persistence Problems

Two of these problems are called the Synchronization Problem and the Persistence Problem (Grossberg, 1975a, 1982). Both represent ubiquitously occurring situations in Nature. Without further analysis, one might easily pass them by without realizing that they impose urgent problems that terrestrial animals must solve in order to survive.

The Synchronization Problem simply observes that, under naturally occurring conditions, the time lags between CS and US on successive learning trials may not be the same. Conditioning must nonetheless be possible for a range of ISIs, as the inverted-U in conditioning depicted in Figure 13.13 (right column).

The Persistence Problem observes that humans and animals frequently experience environments in which more than one CS may occur, and different CSs may have different motivational significance. I will use a gedanken, or thought, experiment below to show how both of these problems may be solved by CogEM circuits.

The Turkey-Lover Fiasco: Feedforward interactions cannot prevent affective short circuits. Before turning to the gedanken experiment, I will say a little more about why the Persistence Problem can cause a lot of trouble if it is not properly solved. A simple feedforward circuit illustrates what can go wrong. This feedforward network sends connections from each of two CS_i-activated cells to both of two learned CR_i output pathways, where i = 1, 2. If no other interactions occurred in this network, then pairing CS_1 with CR_2 would enable CS_1 to learn to elicit CR_2 as well as the previously learned CR_1. Likewise, pairing CS_2 with CR_1 would enable CS_2 to learn to elicit CR_1 as well as the previously learned CR_2.

The absurdity of this outcome is illustrating by assuming that it happens when you are having Thanksgiving dinner with your lover. Let CS_1 be the lover's face, CR_1 be actions that support having sex with your lover, CS_2 be the sight of the Thanksgiving turkey on the dinner plate, and CR_2 be actions that support eating the turkey. During dinner, you cyclically look at your lover's face and at the turkey. If you learned using only a feedforward circuit, you could experience rapid cross-conditioning during dinner. After dinner, you could have acquired the fetish of wanting to have sex with turkeys, and the even more problematic desire of wanting to eat your lover!

This Turkey-Lover Fiasco is both crude and unforgettable. It calls attention to the fundamental problem that, without additional interactions, persistence of learned meanings during parallel processing of motivationally incompatible actions would not be possible. These interactions include the feedback pathways from a sensory cortex to amygdala, then to orbitofrontal cortex, and then back to sensory cortex (Figure 13.1). When incentive motivational feedback amplifies one set of motivationally compatible stimuli in the sensory cortex, it also attentionally blocks stimuli that could otherwise learn to activate motivationally incompatible responses. Attentional blocking hereby solves the Persistence Problem by enabling *motivationally-selective attention switching* to occur between stimuli with different motivational significance. This solution also emphasizes the crucial role of positive feedback circuits during the regulation of cognitive-emotional processes, no less than of perceptual-cognitive processes. Feedforward circuits are insufficient for autonomous learning in the real world, including the feedforward circuits of popular AI algorithms like back propagation and its more recent variant, Deep Learning.

A thought experiment about cognitive-emotional interactions that leads to CogEM

Starting in the middle: Outstar learning and stimulus sampling. Every gedanken experiment about a self-organizing mind needs to begin its story in the middle. *Something* needs to be assumed to avoid an infinite regress and get off the ground. This particular thought experiment assumes two simple properties about associative learning that were discussed in Chapter 1.

The first property is that the unit of long-term memory, or LTM, is a *spatial pattern*. This property can be understood in outstar circuits and their generalizations (Figure 5.15). In an outstar, when a sampling cell, denoted by v_0, is activated, it can send out diverging pathways, or axons, whose adaptive weights, or LTM traces, can learn from the patterns of STM activity that fluctuate through time at sampled cells $v_1, v_2, \ldots, v_n$ that these weights abut. In particular, during classical conditioning, a CS can activate the sampling cell and a US can activate the sampled cells.

The second property is that there is a *stimulus sampling operation* that controls this learning process. This means that the sampling cell can only learn about a STM activity pattern when it sends a *sampling signal* to its LTM traces. These LTM traces can then track the STM activity patterns that are active across the network of sampled cells while the sampling signal is on. As a result, the pattern of LTM traces learns to encode a weighted average of the STM activity patterns that occur during the sampling interval.

Chapters 1 and 5 discussed a learning law that has these properties. This *outstar learning* law is displayed in Figure 5.14. As noted in Chapter 5, it is called outstar learning because the network can be redrawn in a star-like shape with its LTM traces at the ends of each branch of the star, as in Figure 5.15. Outstar learning is a kind of *gated steepest descent* learning because, after the learning gate opens, each LTM trace tracks the activity at its abutting cell. The LTM traces can, in this way, learn *any* spatial pattern because each individual LTM trace can get bigger or smaller due to conditioning, depending on whether its sampled cell is more or less active.

After this learning process occurs, a CS-activated sampling signal is multiplied by the LTM trace in each pathway. The resulting LTM-gated signals that are received across all the sampled cells are proportional to the pattern of LTM traces. The CS can hereby reproduce the STM pattern that was originally generated by the US. In other words, the CS has generated a CR which, in this most simple case, replicates the US.

With this background in mind, let us now turn to the gedanken experiment.

Learning with variable CS-US delays is possible! We are now ready to consider the two new hypotheses of the gedanken experiment. The first new hypothesis, numbered (3), is that the time intervals between CS and US presentations on successive learning trials can differ. This is frequently the case in real life, where cues may predict consequences after variable delays. The second new hypothesis, numbered (4), is the obvious fact that learning is possible under these conditions. In other words, presenting the CS alone after it has become a conditioned reinforcer can elicit a CR. Our immediate acceptance of these hypotheses indicates how fundamental they are. The fact, moreover, that the CogEM model circuit can be derived from them, and with it explanations of many challenging, and highly non-obvious, psychological and neurobiological data about conditioning across multiple species, suggests that CogEM embodies basic brain designs that have been shaped by ubiquitous evolutionary pressures.

In order to understand how these obvious constraints imply non-obvious consequences, let us imagine trying to learn from the Blooming Buzzing Confusion of a continuous stream of events. In particular, suppose that an outstar O_i attempts to learn a prescribed US spatial pattern

$\theta^{(i)}$ which is embedded within a sequence $\theta^{(1)}$, $\theta^{(2)}$, $\theta^{(3)}$, . . . of spatial patterns that activates the outstar border B_i through time. Denote the sampling population, or source, of O_i by S_i and the sampled cells v_1, v_2, . . . , v_n, or border, of the outstar by B_i. The main question is: How does S_i know when to sample B_i in order to learn $\theta^{(i)}$, and how can this learning be incrementally strengthened on successive learning trials?

If hypothesis (3) holds, then the time lag between the CS that excites S_i and the US pattern $\theta^{(i)}$ at B_i is different on successive learning trials. If S_i samples B_i a fixed time after it is itself activated on successive learning trials, due to the constant delay for transmitting a signal from S_i to B_i, then the outstar will learn a weighted average of *all* the patterns that activate B_i during these times, rather than the desired pattern $\theta^{(i)}$. To avoid this problem, S_i must somehow know when to sample only the "important" US pattern $\theta^{(i)}$ at B_i.

To accomplish this, the onset of sampling by S_i and the arrival of the US at the border B_i of sampled cells must be *synchronized* so that S_i can sample $\theta^{(i)}$, and only $\theta^{(i)}$, on successive learning trials. The following conclusions can now be drawn:

US-activated nonspecific arousal at polyvalent sensory cells. First, the CS on its own must be insufficient to elicit a sampling signal from S_i.

Second, the US must let S_i know when it will arrive at B_i by sending a signal to S_i. Only in this way can S_i know when the US will arrive at B_i.

Third, S_i must be prevented from eliciting a sampling signal unless large CS *and* US signals converge simultaneously at S_i. S_i is thus *polyvalent*!

Fourth, the US signal must arrive at S_i *before* the US pattern activates B_i so that S_i can send a signal to B_i in time to sample $\theta^{(i)}$. The US-activated signal hereby *arouses* S_i to get ready for the US.

In order to realize these constraints, the US activates a bifurcating pathway (Figure 13.16 (left column)): One branch arouses S_i; that is, it gets S_i ready to sample the US that will soon activate B_i. When the US-activated arousal combines with the CS-activated input, S_i can fire. The other branch delivers the US pattern to B_i a little while later, while the sampling signal S_i is active at B_i. As a result of this polyvalent constraint on the firing of the outstar sampling signal, the outstar can learn about the US, and only the US.

Several additional conclusions are implicit in the previous analysis:

Fifth, the US does not know to which CS it will be paired. It could be paired with *any* CS that can, in principle, learn to predict the CR. Thus the US must be able to arouse the sampling cells of every outstar that is activated by any CS. In other words, the US *nonspecifically arouses* the entire field of sampling cells just before it delivers its pattern to B_i (Figure 13.16 (right column)).

Conditioned reinforcer learning: CS-activated conditioned arousal at drive representations. We are now ready to switch to hypothesis (4); namely, that learning is possible. Out of context, this hypothesis seems to be completely trivial, since all it demands is that the CS alone can elicit a CR on performance trials. But how is this possible if the outstar sampling cell is polyvalent?! In particular, if S_i can fire only when a specific CS signal *and* a nonspecific

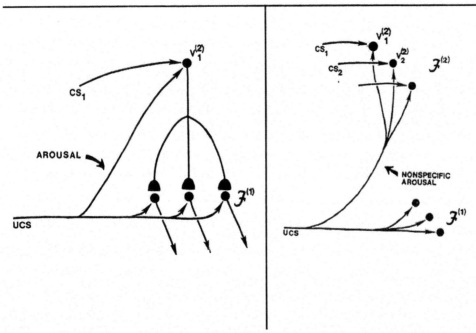

POLYVALENT CS SAMPLING and US-ACTIVATED NONSPECIFIC AROUSAL

FIGURE 13.16. (left column) In order to satisfy all four postulates, there needs to be UCS-activated arousal of a polyvalent CS-activated sampling neuron. (right column) The arousal needs to be nonspecific in order to activate any of the CSs that could be paired with the UCS.

US-derived arousal signal converge on S_i, then how can the CS alone fire S_i *after* learning occurs, when the US is no longer presented?

Only one conclusion is possible (Figure 13.17, top row): Two kinds of learning go on simultaneously during classical conditioning. Learning must surely enable the CS to learn the US pattern at B_i, so that it can perform the CR. But learning must also occur at the source of nonspecific arousal, so that the CS can learn to activate arousal. After conditioning occurs, the CS can arouse its sampling signal and thereby satisfy the polyvalent constraint, all by itself, so that it can trigger read-out of the learned CR, even with no presentation of the US.

In order for this to work, there must exist cells, other than the sampling and sampled cells of outstars, where a CS can learn to control arousal during the conditioning process (Figure 13.17, bottom row). I call these cells *drive representations* for reasons that will become clear in a moment.

With the addition of drive representations at which a CS can learn to activate nonspecific arousal on its own, both postulates (3) and (4) are realized. When a CS is able to do this, it is called a *conditioned reinforcer*, and the learning through which a CS can learn to activate nonspecific arousal is called *conditioned reinforcer learning*. The nonspecific arousal signals themselves are called *incentive motivation*. Figure 13.17 (bottom row) hereby sheds new light on why a conditioned reinforcer can activate incentive motivation with which to draw motivated attention to valued objects. Using just hypotheses (3) and (4), we have hereby derived the main properties of the CogEM circuit in Figure 13.11. The remainder of the derivation makes explicit properties that are implicit in this circuit.

Polyvalent object-value cells control conditioned actions. Although Figure 13.11 defines the main processes of the CogEM circuit, it cannot work well without further refinements. One such refinement requires that the CS activate a sensory representation that contains (at least) two successive processing stages. Why this is necessary is clarified by the varieties of CogEM circuits that are summarized in Figure 13.18. As noted in this figure, a CS can activate its sampling cells S_i on recall trials only if the sampling cells also receive incentive motivational feedback from the arousal cells A. However, on *recall* trials, the arousal cells are also activated by the CS. This cannot happen in the CogEM circuits of Figures 13.11 and 13.18a because the cell (population) $v_{i2}^{(2)}$ can receive a signal from A only after it already has fired, which is logically impossible. The circuit in Figure 13.18b is impossible for a similar reason, even though its sensory representation has two processing stages $v_{i1}^{(2)}$ and $v_{i2}^{(2)}$: In order to fire the polyvalent stage $v_{i2}^{(2)}$, converging signals from $v_{i1}^{(2)}$ and A would be needed. But A can only fire *after* $v_{i2}^{(2)}$ fires and activates it.

Both of the circuits in Figures 13.18c and 13.18d are possible because a CS can activate both $v_{i1}^{(2)}$ and A. However, the circuit in Figure 13.18d has a huge additional advantage, which Figure 13.18e summarizes. Only this circuit enables a short-term memory (STM) trace of the CS to be stored after the CS shuts off *and* this STM trace can activate the polyvalent stage $v_{i2}^{(2)}$ to control read-out of a CR. This version of the CogEM circuit can thus learn during trace conditioning, operant conditioning, and other experiments during which the US may turn on only after the CS shuts off.

The main processing stages of the CogEM model shown in Figure 13.2 have hereby been derived from first principles, with the first sensory representation $v_{i1}^{(2)}$ in a sensory cortex like inferotemporal cortex, the second sensory representation

LEARNING NONSPECIFIC AROUSAL AND CR READ-OUT

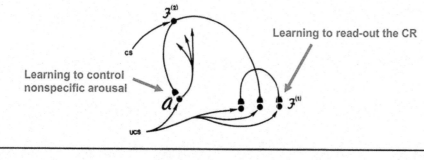

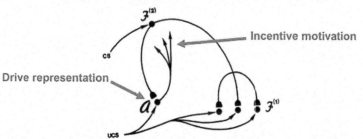

FIGURE 13.17. (top row) Overcoming the ostensible contradiction that seems to occur when attempting to simultaneously realize hypotheses (3) and (4). (bottom row) The problem is overcome by assuming the existence of US-activated drive representation to which CSs can be associated, and that activate nonspecific incentive motivational feedback to sensory representations.

LEARNING TO CONTROL NONSPECIFIC AROUSAL
AND READ-OUT OF THE CR: TWO STAGES OF CS

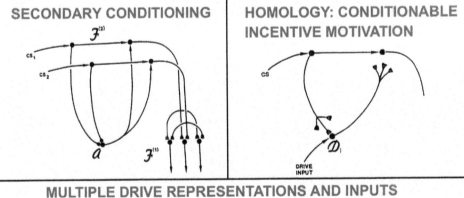

FIGURE 13.18. Realizing the above constraints favors one particular circuit. Circuits (a) and (b) are impossible. Circuit (d) allows previously occurring sensory cues to be stored in STM. Circuit (e) in addition enables a CS can be stored in STM without initiating conditioning in the absence of a US.

Internal drive inputs: Eating when hungry. A refinement of the drive representations must also be made, for the same reason that sensory representations have at least two successive processing stages. In the CogEM circuit as it currently stands, a conditioned reinforcer CS can always fire a drive representation. The ensuing incentive motivational signal can thereby energize a CR. This can happen even if the drive in question has already been satisfied. As a result, without further constraints, such a circuit would continue to elicit eating behavior until all available food was eaten, with possibly disastrous consequences that could include a burst stomach.

$v_{i2}^{(2)}$ in the orbitofrontal cortex, and the drive representation including the amygdala.

When this CogEM circuit includes more than one CS sensory representation, it enables secondary conditioning to occur (Figure 13.7), as illustrated in Figure 13.19 (left column, top row). This is because, after a CS (e.g., CS₁ in Figure 13.19 (left column, top row)) becomes a conditioned reinforcer, it can activate both conditioned *nonspecific* arousal (cf. Figure 13.16 (right column)), which is received by the polyvalent sensory representations of multiple CSs, *and* the pattern to be learned at the outstar border that is shared by these CSs (e.g., CS₁ and CS₂ in Figure 13.19 (left column, top row)). In this way, the conditioned reinforcer CS₁ can teach CS₂ to also become a conditioned reinforcer, much as occurs in many advertising campaigns.

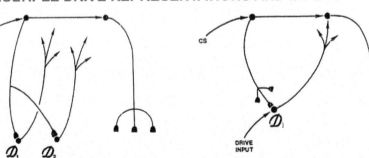

FIGURE 13.19. (left column, top row) Secondary conditioning of both arousal and a specific response are now possible. (bottom row) The CogEM circuit may be naturally extended to include multiple drive representations and inputs. (right column, top row) The incentive motivational pathway is also conditionable in order to enable motivational sets to be learned.

Clearly, a conditioned reinforcer, by itself, should not always be allowed to fire its drive representation, any more than a sensory representation, by itself, should not always be allowed to fire its orbitofrontal representation. A sufficient large *drive input* is also needed to fire a drive representation. Drive representations, just like orbitofrontal sensory representations, are thus *polyvalent*. As depicted in Figure 13.19 (bottom row), there are multiple drive representations to satisfy different drives (e.g., hunger, thirst, sex), and each of them receives drive inputs that grow to the extent that the drive has not been satisfied. When a drive, like hunger, is satiated, its drive input becomes small, so its drive representation cannot fire.

Conditioned incentive motivation. Given this emerging homology between sensory representations and drive representations, it is natural to ask: Are incentive motivational pathways, just like conditioned reinforcer pathways, conditionable? The answer is Yes (Figure 13.19 (right column, top row)) in order to avoid some potentially fatal consequences. For example, suppose that CS_1 in Figure 13.19 (left column, top row) has a weak drive input and is conditioned to a CR, whereas CS_2 has a strong drive input, but is not yet conditioned to a CR. If incentive motivation is not conditionable, then turning CS_1 and CS_2 on simultaneously allows CS_2 to motivate performance of the CR that was learned by CS_1. Moreover, this situation cannot change due to refinement by learning of which cues CS_2 can arouse. For example, if CS_1 is activated by the sight of food and controls an eating response CR, and CS_2 is activated by sexual arousal, then turning both cues on simultaneously could trigger eating behavior, even when not hungry. Moreover, because the sexual arousal is not satisfied by eating behavior, this eating behavior can persist voraciously, without limit.

These constraints make it possible for a single CS to become conditioned to more than one drive representation, and to elicit different motivated behaviors in response to the CS when different drives rise and fall through time.

Homologous sensory and drive representations: Evolutionary precursors?

In summary, sensory and drive representations have remarkably homologous designs. Both types of representations require a specific input and a nonspecific input in order to fire. The specific inputs that activate sensory representations are external sensory cues, whereas the specific inputs that activate drive representations are internal homeostatic cues. The nonspecific inputs that activate sensory representations are incentive motivational inputs, whereas the nonspecific inputs that activate drive representations are conditioned reinforcer inputs. These results suggest that the orbitofrontal cortex and amygdala may be variants of the same circuit design, albeit located in different relative positions within a CogEM circuit. This possibility makes it easier to imagine how these representations evolved.

Additional experiments would be of great interest that explore this predicted homology during evolution and development, notably to determine if the corresponding anatomical cell types and connections represent variations on a shared developmental design. Such results would illuminate supportive data about the close interactions between the orbitofrontal cortex and basolateral amygdala that are known to occur to realize valued outcomes (e.g., Arana et al., 2003; Gottfried, O'Doherty, and Dolan, 2003; Schoenbaum, Chiba, and Gallagher, 1998; Schoenbaum et al., 2003).

An ancient design: Avalanche circuits for sequence learning

What is the smallest network that can learn an arbitrary act? This homology gains additional interest when we notice that the convergence of specific and nonspecific inputs at polyvalent cells is an ancient design, going back at least to similar circuits in crustacea. It raises the fascinating question of whether, and how, these early circuits got modified and refined during eons of evolutionary experimentation and refinement.

This ancient design can be understood as an answer to the following basic questions: What is the simplest network that can learn to perform an arbitrarily complicated sequence of actions, such as a piano sonata, dance, or other skilled sequence of actions. What is the minimum number of cells needed to do this?

The answer is: ONE!

This surprising answer leads to an immediate insight and to another basic question. The insight is that small brains, with relatively few neurons, can carry out complex reflexes, as occurs in many relatively simple organisms. For example, *Wikipedia* notes that the brain of a medicinal leech contains 10,000 neurons, that of a lobster contains 100,000 neurons, and that of an ant contains 250,000 neurons. In contrast, human brains contain 86,000,000,000 neurons. This comparison urges us to ask the question: Why do humans need such big brains? What do the extra neurons do?

Ritualistic learning of a movie as a series of still pictures. Without getting into sophisticated answers such as the demands of language and higher cognition, there is a more basic answer that becomes evident when we consider how a single neuron can encode the performance of, say, the Appassionata Sonata of Beethoven. The *avalanche* cell in Figure 13.20 (top image) can learn and perform *any* space-time pattern, including a sonata. It does so by learning the space-time pattern as an ordered series of spatial patterns. To do so, the avalanche has a long axon that gives rise to branches at regular intervals. Each branch defines an *outstar*. As described in Chapter 5 and illustrated in Figures 5.14 and 5.15, an outstar can learn an arbitrary spatial pattern when its sampling signal is active. The sampling signal in an avalanche travels along its axon and briefly activates learning in each of its sequentially arrayed outstars, which are hereby activated in rapid succession. The adaptive weights, or LTM traces, of each outstar can hereby learn a spatial pattern that forms part of the total space-time pattern that needs to be learned. After learning of the space-time pattern occurs, reactivating the sampling signal can read-out from LTM the space-time pattern as a series of spatial patterns. These spatial patterns are smoothly interpolated by the activities of the output cells. An avalanche hereby performs a space-time pattern much as we see a movie as a sequence of still pictures.

Why do we need big brains? If avalanches can perform arbitrarily complicated actions, then why do we need such big brains? This is because the avalanche is totally insensitive to environmental feedback. After performance by an avalanche begins, there is no way to stop it until it performs the entire space-time pattern. If you learned the Appassionata Sonata using an avalanche, and were in the midst of your recital in Carnegie Hall when someone shouted Fire!, you would have to keep playing it to the bitter end, even while the flames consumed you and the piano!

When we study how avalanches can adapt to environmental feedback of various kinds, lots more cells are needed, and the networks comprised of these cells incrementally embody the kinds of perceptual, cognitive, emotional, and sensory-motor processes that are summarized in this book. Indeed, after I discovered outstars and avalanches in the late 1960s, one of my pathways towards discovering these processes was to incrementally unlump avalanches, using my Method of Minimal Anatomies (Figure 2.37). This unlumping process has continued to the present day. In the next few paragraphs, I illustrate how such an unlumping process can naturally lead to a study of cognition and emotion.

Avalanche cells are polyvalent cells where specific and nonspecific arousal signals converge. How can we stop performance of an avalanche at any stage of its recall, to at least have a chance to escape from the flames in the recital hall? Clearly, the avalanche must be composed of lots of cells, with each such cell being the sampling cell of an outstar. As shown in Figure 13.20 (bottom image), such an avalanche can still learn and perform an arbitrary space-time pattern as a sequence of spatial patterns. At least now there is the possibility of stopping performance at the sampling cell of any of the outstars.

In order to stop performance, however, input from a previous outstar cannot be sufficient to fire the next outstar. Otherwise, after the first outstar fires, *all* the outstars would be forced to fire in their correct order, just as before.

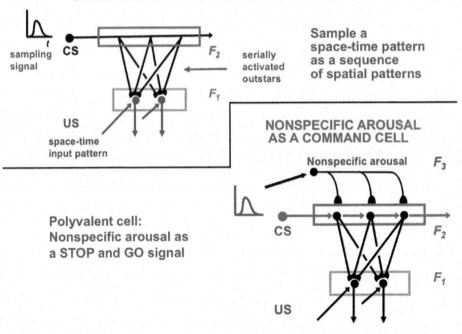

SPACE-TIME PATTERN LEARNING: AVALANCHE

Sample a space-time pattern as a sequence of spatial patterns

serially activated outstars

sampling signal   CS F_2 F_1

US
space-time input pattern

NONSPECIFIC AROUSAL AS A COMMAND CELL

Nonspecific arousal F_3

CS F_2 F_1

US

Polyvalent cell:
Nonspecific arousal as a STOP and GO signal

FIGURE 13.20. (top image). A single avalanche sampling cell can learn an arbitrary space-time pattern by sampling it as a temporally ordered series of spatial patterns using a series of outstars. Once an avalanche's sampling cell starts to fire, there is no way to stop it from performing the entire space-time pattern, no matter how dire the consequences. (bottom image) If nonspecific arousal and a specific cue input are both needed to fire the next cell in an avalanche, then environmental feedback can shut off avalanche performance at any time, and volition can speed up or slow down performance.

An additional input source must also be required to fire each outstar sampling cell, one that could be withdrawn at any time. In the simplest version of this idea, a single additional cell provides *nonspecific arousal* signals simultaneously to all of the outstar sampling cells, and each outstar cell can fire only it receives a specific input from the previous outstar *and* a nonspecific arousal signal (Figure 13.20 (bottom image)). In other words, each outstar sampling cell is *polyvalent*! Now, if arousal is suddenly removed, performance can be stopped dead in its tracks. Arousal thus functions as both a GO and STOP signal. Another benefit of nonspecific arousal is that a larger arousal level enables each outstar to exceed its firing threshold more quickly, whereas a smaller arousal level forces it to fire more slowly, with zero arousal being the limit of no firing at all. In this way, nonspecific arousal can support performance of the space-time pattern at variable speeds.

We have hereby shown that avalanches that can be stopped in the middle of a performance are composed of polyvalent cells that respond to a combination of CS-activated specific inputs *and* nonspecific arousal inputs. Sound familiar?! These are the same requirements that constrain key circuits in the CogEM model.

Arousal-modulated avalanches: A conserved design from crustacea to songbirds. Even the simple kind of avalanche circuit in Figure 13.20 (bottom image) is found in multiple species, and is thus a conserved design through multiple evolutionary epochs. This fact provides strong additional support for how long ago basic circuits like outstars and avalanches, and their stimulus sampling dynamics, arose during brain evolution.

One ancient variant of arousal-modulated avalanches occurs in the crayfish swimmeret system, whereby this crustacean contracts multiple swimmerets in the correct temporal order in order to swim through its environment (Figure 13.21 (left column)). In crustacea, such a nonspecific arousal source is called a *command cell* because it turns on the swimming, or other, behavior (Stein, 1971). Much later in the evolutionary process is the songbird pattern generator (Figure 13.21 (right column)), which controls learning and performance of songs in these birds. Here, the avalanche takes place in the HVC (hyperstriatum ventale, pars caudalis; or high vocal center) of the songbird brain, which reads-out

the successive spatial patterns to its RA (robust nucleus of the arcopallium) for further processing and performance (Hahnloser, Kozhevnikov, and Fee, 2002).

From avalanches to emotion and cognition. With these insights in hand, one needs to ask: How do these command cells and their links *self-organize* in higher species, so that the sampling cells and their connections in more advanced species do not need to be pre-wired by evolution, but can rather be learned from experience? For example, in order for a command cell to have the desired effect on behavior, it should only fire in response to appropriate signals. In particular, it would be maladaptive for a crustacean to try to "escape" from a source of food. Food should usually be approached, not avoided. Such selective firing requires that command cells be able to filter environmental signals so that they fire only in appropriate contexts. Such a filter could, in principle, be pre-wired, but if the animal can learn about a variety of possible food sources, then an *adaptive* filter is needed that can learn from experience (Figure 13.22 (left column, top row)). This kind of constraint naturally leads to instar adaptive filter circuits (Figure 5.11), competitive learning circuits (Figures 5.10 and 5.16-5.18), and adaptive resonance circuits (Figures 5.13 and 5.19) in progressively more complex organisms, and hereby paves a path towards perceptual and cognitive dynamics.

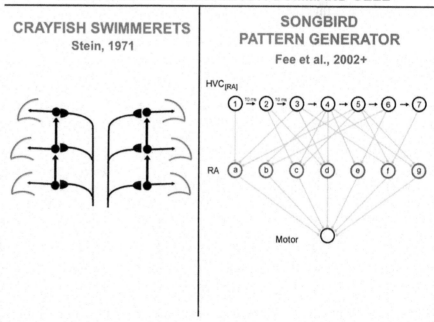

FIGURE 13.21. (left column) An early embodiment of nonspecific arousal was as a command cell in such primitive animals as crayfish. (right column) The songbird pattern generator is also an avalanche. This kind of circuit raises the question of how the connections self-organize through development and learning.

ADAPTIVE FILTERING and CONDITIONED AROUSAL

Towards COGNITION:
Need to FILTER inputs
to the command cell

Towards EMOTION:
IMPORTANT signals turn
arousal ON and OFF

CONDITIONED AROUSAL AND DRIVE REPRESENTATIONS

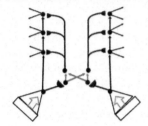

Competition between
conditioned arousal sources
at drive representations
e.g., amygdala

FIGURE 13.22. (left column, top row) Adaptive filtering and conditioned arousal are both needed to regulate what cues can learn to activate particular space-time patterns. These developments lead inexorably to basic cognitive abilities, as embodied in the 3D LAMINART models for 3D vision and figure-ground perception (Chapter 11) and the 3D ARTSCAN SEARCH model for invariant object learning, recognition, and 3D search (Chapter 6). (right column, top row) Conditioned arousal enables only emotionally important cues to activate a motivationally relevant space-time pattern. (bottom row) Conditioned arousal and drive representations arise naturally from the unlumping of avalanche circuits to make them selective to motivationally important cues. The MOTIVATOR model is a natural outcome of this unlumping process (this chapter).

Likewise, only important signals should be able to turn arousal ON or OFF. Thus the link from the adaptive filter to the arousal source also needs to be capable of learning (Figure 13.22 (right column, top row)). This requirement naturally leads to the notion of *conditioned arousal* and raises the question: How is reinforcement learning related to a cue's ability to activate conditioned arousal? Learning of conditioned arousal is a primitive version of conditioned reinforcer learning in a CogEM model (Figure 13.2). Pursuing this line of thought leads to a better understanding of the role of emotion in guiding actions towards valued goals.

Indeed, if an organism needs to satisfy more than one drive to survive, it is not enough to have just one command cell and one source of conditioned arousal. Different adaptive filters will learn to be sensitive to different combinations of environmental cues, and to activate different command cells to satisfy their respective drives (Figure 13.22 (bottom row)). These distinct conditioned arousal sources evolve into different drive representations in a CogEM circuit (Figure 13.2), and the competition between the different drive representations inexorably leads to the concept of a sensory-drive heterarchy (Figure 1.17).

This conclusion illustrates the much more general fact that many decisions, whether they be cognitive, emotional, or motor, emerge from parallel circuits that compete for dominance before choosing the most salient one in each specific context. I summarized in Chapter 1 (Figure 1.7) how a recurrent shunting on-center off-surround network can achieve such a choice among multiple alternatives. This is just one of many uses of such networks summarized throughout the book that may all be viewed as variations on the theme of how cellular tissues solve the noise-saturation dilemma (Figure 1.5).

In addition to adaptive filtering by instars and spatial pattern learning by outstars, a self-organizing avalanche needs to also learn the order in which its successive links should be activated (Figure 13.23 (left column)). This last kind of learning is one of many examples of *serial list learning* by which associations can be learned within a recurrent neural network in response to a temporally ordered series of inputs, marked 1, 2, 3, and 4 in Figure 13.23 (right column). Serial verbal learning (Figures 2.4-2.8) is another example of list learning, and the bowed serial position curve that occurs during serial verbal learning (Figure 2.5) can occur during other forms of list learning as well.

How gated dipole opponent processes work: Learning of opponent emotions

The above overview illustrates how each stage of modeling, and the data that it can and cannot explain, generates conceptual pressures that force one to think about what is missing, and provides strong clues about how to include it using the Method of Minimal Anatomies. We are now ready to further unlump the CogEM model by considering finer aspects of how drive representations are designed and work.

Two important features of drive representations were discussed in Chapter 1. The first is the need for opponent processing channels (Figure 1.13) to represent interactions between competing GO and STOP drive inputs, such as hunger and satiety inputs. The second is the organization of these opponent processes in a *sensory-drive heterarchy* instead of a *drive hierarchy* (Figure 1.17). Recall that a sensory-drive heterarchy enables the most active *combination* of available external sensory cues *and* internal drive inputs to generate incentive motivational outputs, and thus actions to achieve valued goals. This property avoids the risk of being frozen in inaction that

SELF-ORGANIZING AVALANCHES

SERIAL LIST LEARNING

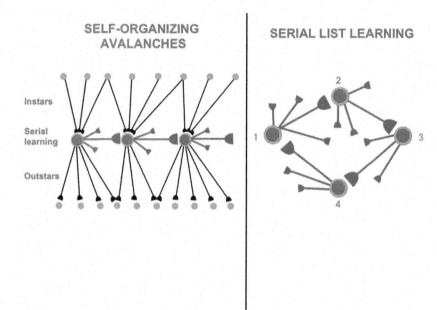

FIGURE 13.23. (left column) Self-organization in avalanches includes adaptive filtering by outstars, serial learning of temporal order, and learned read-out of spatial patterns by outstars. (right column) Serial learning of temporal order occurs in recurrent associative networks.

Fear, relief, and their antagonistic rebounds. Basic properties of the opponent emotions that are represented in gated dipoles provide a foundation for explaining many other properties of reinforcement learning. First, why is onset of a shock a source of fear that is negatively rewarding? Second, why is offset of the shock a source of relief that is positively rewarding?

Onset of a shock can trigger a feeling of fear by activating suitable hypothalamic and amygdala cells, whereas offset of the shock can trigger an antagonistic rebound that supports a feeling of relief by activating a different set of hypothalamic and amygdala cells. Such antagonistic rebounds are ubiquitous across modalities. For example, as I already noted in Chapter 8, after looking at an array of radial lines for awhile, looking at a blank wall triggers an antagonistic rebound that is seen as a negative aftereffect of concentric circles, and is called the MacKay illustration. Figure 8.3 also shows that, after looking at a downward flow of water for awhile, looking at a blank well triggers an antagonistic rebound that is seen as an aftereffect of upward motion, as in the waterfall illusion. These aftereffects are there to dynamically reset ongoing activity as stimuli change through time so that our brains can try to respond to the "blooming buzzing confusion" of event sequences with as little bias as possible.

Both emotional responses to stimuli and their antagonistic rebounds can trigger new reinforcement learning. The left hand side of Figure 13.24 summarizes the paradigm of primary *excitatory* conditioning in which a CS is paired with a later occurring shock until it becomes a conditioned reinforcer that can elicit fear. For this to occur, the CS-activated sensory representation sends a conditionable pathway to the fear center whose LTM trace is strengthened by conditioning. The right hand side of Figure 13.24 summarizes the paradigm of primary *inhibitory* fear conditioning. Here the offset of a shock is followed by the CS. The onset of the shock directly activates a fear response, but its offset activates an *antagonistic rebound of relief*. The CS can then get associated with the relief rebound that is occurring at the relief center. Thus, a single CS can learn to become either a source of conditioned fear or of relief by sending conditionable pathways to both the fear and relief centers. In order for relief to be reliably activated by offset of the shock, these activities are organized in (fear, relief) gated dipoles so that offset of shock can cause an antagonistic rebound of relief.

could occur in a drive hierarchy when a prepotent drive input occurs without compatible sensory cues with which to satisfy it.

Chapter 1 also outlined why opponent processes are embodied by *gated dipole* circuits (Figures 1.14 and 1.15) that can generate *antagonistic rebounds* in response to unexpected events. In this way, reinforcement learning can react flexibly to arbitrary combinations of expected and unexpected events, and thereby better learn to generate actions that elicit expected consequences in changing environments. Although antagonist rebounds are essential for doing this, reinforcement learning cannot discover predictive events perfectly, any more than the visual cortex can avoid sometimes seeing visual illusions. Even with antagonistic rebounds to strengthen the learning of predictive consequences, "maladaptive, irrational, and even bizarre behaviors" can be elicited "when they interact with the wrong environments," as I noted in Chapter 1, such as peak shift and behavioral contrast (Figure 1.12), partial reinforcement acquisition effect, learned helplessness, and self-punitive behaviors.

Although Chapter 1 explained qualitatively how a gated dipole circuit can generate an antagonistic rebound (Figure 1.14), it did not do so quantitatively. Because it is so simple to mathematically explain how an antagonistic rebound occurs, and the equally important inverted-U in performance (Figure 1.18), they will now be discussed in greater detail, along with other properties of cognitive-emotional learning that we depend upon to achieve our valued goals.

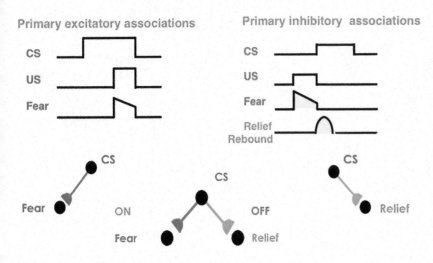

OPPONENT PROCESSING
Cognitive-Drive Associations

FIGURE 13.24. Both primary excitatory and inhibitory conditioning can occur using opponent processes and their antagonistic rebounds.

Chemical transmitters as unbiased transducers

I already explained heuristically in Chapter 1 how a gated dipole can cause an antagonistic rebound in its OFF channel in response to offset of a phasic cue like a shock to its ON channel (Figure 1.14). I can now explain in greater detail, using very simple mathematics, how such antagonistic rebounds are generated in gated dipole circuits. I will then use these equations to explain some important properties of learning and behavior that would be hard to understand without them.

A thought experiment about unbiased transmission leads to antagonistic rebounds. The main properties of antagonistic rebounds follow from a simple thought experiment about unbiased transmission between cells. This particular thought experiment readily leads to equations for how chemical transmitters work in an opponent processing circuit. A signal coming down an axon releases some of the chemical transmitter from the synapse where it is produced and stored. The released transmitter can then alter the activity, or potential, of the postsynaptic cell (Figure 13.25). Here, only the simplest properties of such a transmitter will be described.

Let me start with the observation that our goal here is to generate an *unbiased* response T to the axonal signal S. The simplest unbiased transduction from signal S to response T is just T = SB, where B is a constant. In other words, the response is proportional to the signal, and B is the sensitivity, or *gain*, of the response to this signal.

Now let me impose the constraint that response T is due to the release of a chemical transmitter y at the synapse into the synaptic cleft, where it can influence the postsynaptic cell. To maintain the property of unbiased transduction, T = SB is changed to T = Sy, where y tries to maintain the value B, so that sensitivity is not lost.

The law T = Sy says that transmitter y is *released* at a rate proportional to S. As a result, either a bigger signal S, or more accumulated transmitter y, can cause a bigger response T. A law like T = Sy, where two quantities are multiplied together, is called a *mass action* law. In other words, S generates T via a mass action interaction with transmitter y.

The property that transmitter y tries to maintain the value B can be interpreted as a process whereby y *accumulates* until it reaches the target gain B.

Transmitter accumulation and release: Infinity does not exist in biology! Physical processes like transmitter accumulation and release cannot occur infinitely fast. They can only occur at a finite rate. I therefore need to translate the two sets of constraints: T = Sy for transmitter release, and y = B for transmitter accumulation, into a process that occurs at a finite rate. Using a differential equation is the right way to do this, because differential equations provide the language, in all sciences, for describing processes that take some time to occur.

The simplest differential equation that achieves this for transmitter accumulation and release is shown in Figure 13.26. Term $\frac{dy}{dt}$ on the left hand side of the equation is just the rate of change of y through time. This rate is determined by the sum of two terms on the right hand side of the equation. The first term A(B − y) defines the rate of accumulation of y. The amount of transmitter y can never exceed B, so term A(B − y) is non-negative, which *increases* the rate of change of y until y = B. Accumulation then stops because the accumulation term is then zero. This term ensures that y accumulates to B, but does so at a finite rate.

The second term −Sy says that transmitter is released, or inactivated, at a rate proportional to the rate T = Sy of transmitter release. The minus sign in this term causes the rate of change of y to *decrease*.

Unbiased transduction, medium-term memory, depressing synapses, and dynamic synapses. These simple finite-rate equations for unbiased transduction, which I first published in 1968 (Grossberg, 1968d) and again, in

UNBIASED TRANSDUCER
Grossberg (1968)

S = input
T = output
T = SB   B is the gain

Suppose T is due to release of chemical transmitter y at a synapse:

S   y   T

RELEASE RATE: T = S y (mass action)
ACCUMULATION: y ≅ B

FIGURE 13.25. When an unbiased transducer is embodied by a finite rate physical process, mass action by a chemical transmitter is the result.

greater detail, in Grossberg (1969b), have been supported by subsequent data and modeling. They are, in fact, the equations for a habituative transmitter gate, or medium-term memory, that I summarized in Figure 2.11. It took quite awhile for other modelers to realize the importance of medium-term memory. For example, as I noted earlier in the book, it occurs in the 1997 model of *depressing synapses* by Larry Abbott and his colleagues to simulate their neurophysiological data from visual cortex (Abbott et al., 1997), and in the model of *dynamic synapses*, also in 1997, by Mischa Tsodyks and Henry Markram to simulate their neurophysiological data from somatosensory cortex (Tsodyks and Markram, 1997). These simple equations are also sufficient to cause an antagonistic rebound *and* an Inverted-U as a function of arousal level, among many

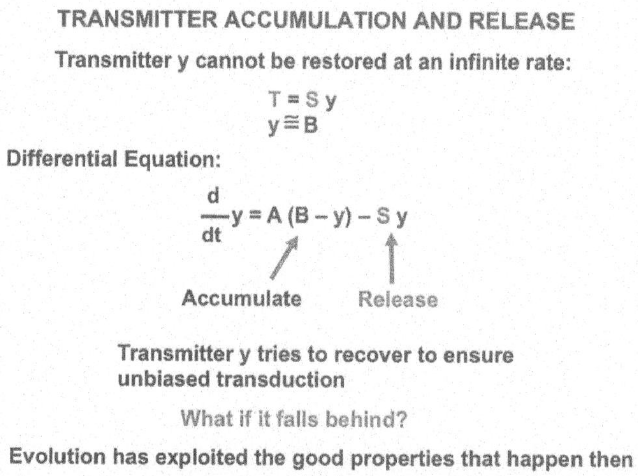

TRANSMITTER ACCUMULATION AND RELEASE

Transmitter y cannot be restored at an infinite rate:

T = S y
y ≅ B

Differential Equation:

$$\frac{d}{dt}y = A(B - y) - S y$$

Accumulate   Release

Transmitter y tries to recover to ensure unbiased transduction

What if it falls behind?

Evolution has exploited the good properties that happen then

FIGURE 13.26. A simple differential equation describes the processes of transmitter accumulation and release that do their best, at a finite rate, to carry out unbiased transduction.

other useful properties, when these transmitters operate within a gated dipole. I need to make just one more observation to prove how this happens.

A minor mathematical miracle: Transmitter gating and the importance of brain nonlinearity. One might worry that, as the input signal S increases, it would inactivate more transmitter y and, as a result, the output signal T would also decrease. This would not be a desirable outcome, since increasing S should activate its postsynaptic cell more, not less. A decreasing output does not occur, however, due to mass action. I call it a Minor Mathematical Miracle because, albeit simple, it has so many functionally useful consequences.

Figure 13.27 explains this Minor Mathematical Miracle. It assumes that the signal S is held constant, and then solves for the steady-state, or equilibrium, value of transmitter that is caused by it. Setting $\frac{dy}{dt}$ equal to zero lets us solve for the equilibrium value of y. This result follows by moving both terms –Ay and –Sy that have a minus sign on the right hand side of the equation to the left hand side of the equation. They now have a plus sign; namely, Ay + Sy = AB. Both terms on the left hand side have a common factor y in them. Factor out y to find (A + S)y = AB. Now divide both sides of the equation by (A + S), yielding the desired result. The second equation gives the answer.

If S is increased in this equation, then y decreases, as expected. So why doesn't the *output* decrease as S increases? This is true because the output is the product Sy, not just y. The equation for Sy is derived just by multiplying the equation for y by S on both sides. Then, as the third equation in Figure 13.27 shows, an increase of S *increases* the output signal T = Sy, even while the amount of transmitter y *decreases*. Mass action, in this case *transmitter gating*, causes this result, which is the Minor Mathematical Miracle. This example, albeit mathematically simple, provides one of many examples of the need for nonlinear operations, like multiplication, to understand how our brains work. The Method of Minimal Anatomies highlights where nonlinearities are essential by trying to derive the simplest, and thus most linear, models possible, and thereby shining a bright light on where linear interactions are not sufficient, why they are not, and what nonlinearities to include.

Fast signaling and slow habituation lead to overshoot, habituation, and undershoot. Figure 13.28 shows how these equations operate in time. The first row of the figure plots S through time. S starts with a low intensity, jumps quickly to a higher intensity and maintains it for awhile, and then jumps back to the original low intensity. These jumps are intended to illustrate that S can react quickly through time, just as cell activities, or potentials, can.

The jumps in S are separated in time long enough for y to habituate to them. The second row of the figure shows y

MINOR MATHEMATICAL MIRACLE

At equilibrium:

$$0 = \frac{dy}{dt} = A(B - y) - Sy$$

Transmitter y decreases when input S increases:

$$y = \frac{AB}{A + S}$$

However, output Sy increases with S!

$$Sy = \frac{ABS}{A + S} \quad \text{(gate, mass action)}$$

FIGURE 13.27. Despite the fact that less transmitter y is available after persistent activation by a larger input signal S, the gated output signal Sy is larger due to the mass action gating of S by y.

habituating to these values of S. When S is small, y is large. When S jumps quickly to a high intensity, y decreases gradually to a lower value due to habituation. Thus S is a "fast" variable and y a "slow" variable.

The output T is a product of these fast and slow changes, When the top two curves are multiplied together, the result is the output curve in the third row of the figure. This curve

HABITUATIVE TRANSMITTER GATE

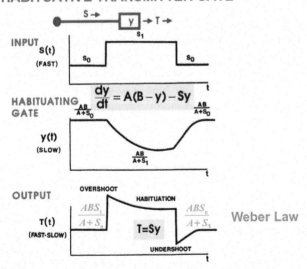

FIGURE 13.28. Fast increments and decrements in an input S lead to slow habituation of the habituative gate, or medium-term memory, transmitter y. The output T is a product of these fast and slow variables, and consequently exhibits overshoots, habituation, and undershoots in its response.

first overshoots after S increases, gradually habituates with y to an intermediate level, and then undershoots when S decreases again. It turns out that these properties are all that we need to explain antagonistic rebounds in the gated dipole circuit of Figure 1.14. The explanation that was given there explained everything but how the shape of the tonic arousal input I plus the phasic input J in the ON channel at activity x_1 is converted into an overshoot-habituation-undershoot sequence of events in activity x_3. This follows immediately from Figure 13.28, where the step response in S is converted into an overshoot-habituation-undershoot sequence in T. The transient antagonistic rebound in the OFF channel is just the inverted shape of this sequence, after it is thresholded to generate an output signal.

Antagonistic rebounds to phasic cue decrements: Frustration and the relaxation response. In summary, antagonistic rebounds follow automatically when tonically-aroused opponent channels are gated by transmitters that try to generate unbiased outputs, but can fall behind the response rate of their input signals.

It is also easy to show this mathematically. One might ask: Why bother, since figures like Figure 1.14 and Figure 13.28 already show this property in pictures? The reason is that mathematical analyses of gated dipole properties also lead to several surprising and important properties. These properties include how an unexpected event can cause a rebound, and thereby quickly reset a motivated behavior that leads to an unwelcome unexpected consequence; and how an Inverted-U, or Golden Mean, in affective responsiveness can occur as a function of arousal level (Figure 1.18) with surprising properties that enabled me to begin explaining clinical data about autism and schizophrenia. Once again, simple hypotheses, when correctly formulated to embody key biological designs, can lead to emergent properties that are not obvious using intuition alone, but become obvious with a little help from simple mathematics.

There are many examples of how antagonistic rebounds facilitate tracking and learning about changing reinforcement contingencies. For example, either a sudden reduction of a fearful shock, or the non-occurrence of an expected shock, can cause a rebound of *relief* (Denny, 1971; Masterson, 1970; Reynierse and Rizley, 1970). The concept of a relief or relaxation response was developed in the 1960s and 1970s into what was called *elicitation theory* and was used to explain how the positive motivation arises that can support escape behaviors from fearful cues. In particular, if the sudden reduction of a fearful shock is due to a successful escape behavior, then the relief rebound can trigger new conditioned reinforcer learning and incentive motivational learning (Figure 13.1), using relief to motivate that escape behavior in the future. Because the ability to "escape" from persistent learned fear is of therapeutic value, elicitation theory was also applied to behavior therapy, where it could help people to cope with phobias. Dr. Herbert Benson popularized the term Relaxation Response starting in 1975. I personally like to think of relief or relaxation when considering what happens to individuals when they enter a deep meditative state.

The unexpected non-occurrence of food can, in contrast, cause a frustrative rebound (Amsel, 1962, 1992). The frustrative rebound that occurs after expected food does not occur can drive forgetting, or extinction, of motivational support for the consummatory actions that no longer lead to food, thereby releasing exploratory behaviors to search for more productive sources of food. In summary, antagonistic rebounds can occur from negative to positive affects, such as from fear to relief, or from positive to negative affects, such as from hunger to frustration. They enable our brains to quickly adapt to changing reinforcement contingencies.

As I noted in Chapter 8, opponent processing circuits with gated dipole rebound properties also occur in perceptual and cognitive brain regions, and reflect the ability of these representations to be rapidly reset, and indeed reversed, when stimulus conditions change. For perceptual examples of how a change in stimulus level can cause a rebound, I mentioned negative aftereffects of form and motion (Figure 8.3): Offset of sustained viewing of intersecting radial lines leads to an opponent MacKay negative aftereffect of concentric circles, whereas offset of sustained viewing of a video of water flowing downwards leads to an opponent waterfall aftereffect of motion upwards. In addition, offset of sustained viewing of a red surface leads to an opponent green surface aftereffect. In 1996, my PhD student Gregory Francis and I modeled psychophysical data about various negative aftereffects (Francis and Grossberg, 1996). Greg has gone on to have a successful research career that combines psychophysical experiments and neural models of them as part of his work as a professor.

For another example of a rebound that occurs in perceptual and cognitive brain regions, consider the task of pushing a buzzer as fast as possible when a red light shuts off. If the only thing that happened in the brain when the light shuts off was the termination of activity within a category that codes for red (among other features), then there would be no internal signal at stimulus offset to control the buzzer press. If, however, offset of the ON cell (population) that codes for red triggers an antagonistic rebound in an associated OFF cell (population), then activation of the OFF cell can learn to be associated with the buzzer press command.

Figure 13.29 derives an equation which explains how a gated dipole responds to onset of the phasic input J. Figure 13.30 shows how the dipole subsequently responds with an antagonistic rebound to offset, or at least a sufficient reduction, of J.

Figure 13.29 labels the ON channel's input signal S, habituative transmitter gate y, and output signal $T = Sy$ with

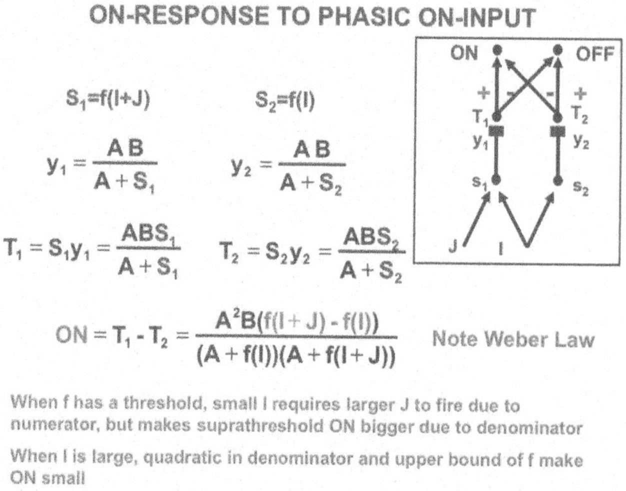

ON-RESPONSE TO PHASIC ON-INPUT

$$S_1 = f(I+J) \qquad S_2 = f(I)$$

$$y_1 = \frac{A B}{A + S_1} \qquad y_2 = \frac{A B}{A + S_2}$$

$$T_1 = S_1 y_1 = \frac{ABS_1}{A + S_1} \qquad T_2 = S_2 y_2 = \frac{ABS_2}{A + S_2}$$

$$ON = T_1 - T_2 = \frac{A^2 B(f(I+J) - f(I))}{(A + f(I))(A + f(I+J))}$$

Note Weber Law

When f has a threshold, small I requires larger J to fire due to numerator, but makes suprathreshold ON bigger due to denominator

When I is large, quadratic in denominator and upper bound of f make ON small

FIGURE 13.29. The ON response to a phasic ON input has Weber law properties due to the divisive terms in its equilibrium response, which are due to the habituative transmitter.

the subscript "1". The subscript "2" labels these variables in the OFF channel. All the equations are solved at equilibrium before the net dipole ON output, after opponent competition, is computed by $T_1 - T_2$. This computation uses an arbitrary signal function f(w), that increases with its input w, to transform I and $I + J$ into cell activities $f(I)$ and $f(I + J)$, respectively. You can see that the ON dipole response is positive because all the terms in the right hand side of its equation are positive. You can also see an important additional fact: There are terms in the denominator of this output. These terms are due to the habituated levels of the transmitters in the ON and OFF channels. These terms define a Weber law.

Habituative transmitters, in one form or another, can generate Weber law properties in processes that occur in multiple brain regions. For example, in Chapter 2, I commented about how a Weber law in time occurs within vertebrate photoreceptors as they undergo adaptation to the ambient light level. The denominators in the equilibrium values y_1 and y_2 of the transmitters in Figure 13.29 approximate such equilibrium values. As in photoreceptors, they divide the current signals S in the output signals $T = Sy$.

The same kind of analysis explains how an antagonistic rebound occurs in response to sudden offset, or sufficient reduction, in the phasic input J. Figure 13.30 summarizes how this can happen. Here the fact that the transmitters y react more slowly than the signals S is critical. This property implies that the transmitters "remember" their values when J was on for awhile after J shuts off. That is why they are called a type of *medium-term memory* that operates at a slower time scale than short-term memory, but a faster time scale than long-term memory. These values of y_i are shown in their approximations ($\cong$) to their previous habituated values. Only the habituated values y_1 and y_2 in the

OFF-REBOUND DUE TO PHASIC INPUT OFFSET

Shut off J (Not I!). Then: $S_1 = f(I)$ and $S_2 = f(I)$

$$y_1 \cong \frac{AB}{A + f(I + J)} < y_2 \cong \frac{AB}{A + f(I)}$$

y_1 and y_2 are SLOW

$$T_1 = S_1 y_1 \qquad\qquad T_2 = S_2 y_2$$

$$T_1 < T_2$$

$$\text{OFF} = T_2 - T_1 = \frac{AB f(I)(f(I + J) - f(I))}{(A + f(I))(A + f(I + J))}$$

Note Weber Law due to remembered previous input

Arousal sets sensitivity of rebound: $\dfrac{\text{OFF}}{\text{ON}} = \dfrac{f(I)}{A}$

Why is the rebound transient? **Note equal f(I) inputs**

FIGURE 13.30. OFF rebound occurs when the ON-input shuts off due to the imbalance that is caused by the ON input in the habituation of the transmitters in the ON and OFF channels. The relative sizes of ON responses and OFF rebounds is determined by the arousal level I.

ON and OFF channels, respectively, are used to compute the OFF response that transiently occurs when J shuts off. This OFF response occurs because y_1 habituates more than y_2 due to the fact that y_1 responded to $f(I + J)$, whereas y_2 responded to only $f(I)$. The OFF response is computed as $T_2 - T_1$. It is positive until y_1 "forgets" J and equilibrates to the value imposed by the tonic arousal level I. Since arousal is equal in both the ON and OFF channels, after both y_1 and y_2 equilibrate to I, the rebound terminates, hence is transient.

In summary, a transient antagonistic rebound is due to a combination of arousal, habituative transmitter gating, competition, and thresholding.

When food is frustrating and fear causes relief. I will now describe additional unanticipated properties. It is important for an antagonistic rebound in the OFF channel to be large enough to inhibit the ON channel. To prove this, one needs to compute the ratio of OFF to ON responses. Surprisingly, as shown in the lower right equation in Figure 13.30, this ratio increases with the signal $f(I)$.

This fact raises an urgent question: Under what conditions is the OFF rebound enough larger than the ON response to drive relearning of unsuccessful behaviors? In particular, is the ratio OFF/ON bigger than one in a range of ON and OFF responses that are large enough to have behavioral consequences; that is, which occur near the peak of the Inverted-U (Figure 1.18)? I was delighted to be able to mathematically prove that the answer is Yes in the 1972 article about the neural dynamics of punishment and avoidance behaviors that introduced the gated dipole model (Grossberg, 1972a, 1972b).

BEHAVIORAL CONTRAST: REBOUNDS!

1. A sudden DECREASE in frequency or amount of FOOD can act as a NEGATIVE reinforcer: Frustration

2. A sudden DECREASE in frequency or amount of SHOCK can act as POSITIVE reinforcer: Relief

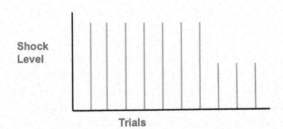

FIGURE 13.31. Behavioral contrast can occur during reinforcement learning due to decreases in either positive or negative reinforcers. See Figure 13.32 for illustrative operant conditioning data.

One additional set of properties is worth stating right now, since it depends upon the ratio OFF/ON being greater than one. It considers how a suddenly reduced, but not totally eliminated, input to an ON channel can cause an antagonistic rebound in the OFF channel that is big enough to overwhelm it (because OFF/ON is greater than one), but in so doing leads to paradoxical results. Figure 13.31 summarizes the paradox. It notes that a sudden decrease in the frequency or amount of food can cause frustration, and thus act as a *negative* reinforcer. However, even though there is less food, food is still, in itself a *positive* reinforcer that directly activates a hunger channel in a gated dipole for eating. Likewise, a sudden decrease in frequency or amount of shock can cause a relief rebound, and thus act as a *positive* reinforcer. However, even though there is less shock, shock is still, in itself, a *negative* reinforcer that directly activates the fear channel in a gated dipole for emotion. Both of these properties occur because the size of an OFF rebound can be larger than the size of the original ON response.

Graded rebounds to shock reductions in operant reinforcement. This kind of result depends, more generally, upon the ability of a gated dipole to respond in a graded way to the intensity of its inputs. The equations for the ON and OFF channels in Figures 13.29 and 13.30 show that this is true both for responses to the phasic input J and the tonic arousal input I. A vivid classical example of this analog sensitivity during operant conditioning was published in 1968 by George S. Reynolds (Figure 13.32; Reynolds, 1968). The animals in this experiment received no shock for the first five test trials shown in this figure. They had previously been trained to respond on a variable interval (VI) reinforcement schedule before that, leading to the baseline number of responses per minute that is shown in the leftmost part of the data curve during

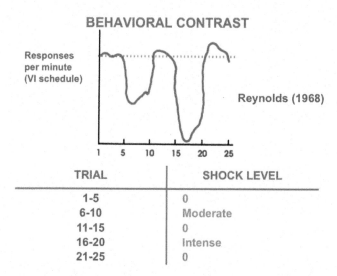

FIGURE 13.32. Response suppression and the subsequent antagonistic rebounds are both calibrated by the inducing shock levels.

trials 1-5. On trials 6-10, a moderate shock level was imposed, causing a suppression of the responses per minute because of the way that the fear channel in a gated dipole suppresses incentive motivation to respond. Then shock was shut off again on trials 11-15, leading to an antagonistic rebound in incentive motivation to respond. When an intense shock level was imposed on trials 16-20, responding was dramatically suppressed. Its offset on trials 21-25 caused an even bigger antagonistic rebound. Thus both the ON responses and the OFF rebounds respond in a graded way to the size of *J*, as Figures 13.29 and 13.30 explain.

Antagonistic rebound to tonic arousal increment: Novel events are arousing! A more surprising consequence of these ON and OFF equations is that a sudden increment in arousal *I*, without a change in *J*, can also cause an antagonistic rebound. This result was a delightful surprise to me when I discovered it around 1970. It led me to ask: What sorts of events can cause a sudden increase in arousal? The answer seemed evident: *unexpected events*. Novel events are arousing! This fact forced me into thinking about what is currently called the *predictive brain* by many neuroscientists, a brain that can continually monitor whether or not it is achieving expected goals, and can reset itself adaptively when it is not. I was also led to ask a more narrowly focused technical question: How does the brain compute when an event is unexpected? And how unexpected must the event be in order to trigger a novelty-driven arousal burst? These questions, among others, led me to discover Adaptive Resonance Theory.

I already discussed in Chapter 1 how paradoxical it is for the non-occurrence of an expected reward or punishment to trigger any reaction, since *nothing is*

happening. This paradox is resolved by explaining how mismatch of a learned expectation can cause an arousal burst (Figure 5.19c) which, in turn, can cause an antagonistic rebound.

Figure 13.33 proves how a rebound in response to an unexpected event can occur. The same strategy as before is used, except now *J* stays fixed and arousal suddenly increases from I to $I^* = I + \Delta I$, where ΔI is the amount by which *I* suddenly increases. The resulting equation for the OFF response $T_2 - T_1$ seems at first too complicated to understand. However, Figure 13.34 shows that the answer is simple to understand when a linear signal function $f(w) = Cw$ is used. The OFF rebound is now easily seen to increase with *J* and with the amount of "novelty" ΔI. Thus, a larger *J* generates a larger ON response *and* a larger OFF rebound when it leads to an unexpected consequence. This makes sense because a larger ON response will contribute more to the behavior that has been disconfirmed, so needs a larger OFF rebound to correct the error. Moreover, there is no rebound unless ΔI is sufficiently novel, which in this case means being greater than the parameter *A*, which is the rate with which transmitter accumulates (Figure 13.28).

Parallel hypothesis testing and memory search in response to unexpected events. Such an antagonistic rebound can occur in *all* the gated dipole circuits that receive the arousal burst, whether they are in perceptual, cognitive, emotional, or motor networks of the brain. This realization naturally leads to consideration of networks where arousal *nonspecifically*, or equally, activates an *arbitrary* number of (ON cell)-(OFF cell) dipoles. Such a nonspecific arousal burst can *selectively reset the entire network* so that more reset occurs of ON

NOVELTY RESET: REBOUND TO AROUSAL ONSET

Equilibrate to I and J: $S_1 = f(I+J)$ $S_2 = f(I)$

$$y_1 = \frac{AB}{A + S_1} \qquad y_2 = \frac{AB}{A + S_2}$$

Keep phasic input J fixed; increase arousal I to $I^* = I + \Delta I$:

OFF reaction if $T_1 < T_2$

$$OFF = T_2 - T_1 = f(I^*+J)\, y_2 - f(I^*)\, y_1$$

$$= \frac{AB(f(I^*) - f(I^*+J)) - B(f(I^*)f(I+J) - f(I)f(I^*+J)}{(A + f(I))(A + f(I + J))}$$

How to interpret this complicated equation?

FIGURE 13.33. An unexpected event can disconfirm ongoing processing by triggering a burst of nonspecific arousal that causes antagonistic rebounds in currently active gated dipoles, whether cognitive or affective.

NOVELTY RESET: REBOUND TO AROUSAL ONSET

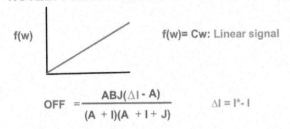

$$f(w)$$

$$f(w) = Cw: \text{Linear signal}$$

$$OFF = \frac{ABJ(\Delta I - A)}{(A + I)(A + I + J)}$$

$$\Delta I = I^* - I$$

OFF > 0 only if there is enough novelty: $\Delta I > A$

OFF response increases with J:
If a given cell has a greater effect on a mismatched expectation, then it is reset more vigorously

Selective reset of dipole field by unexpected event

FIGURE 13.34. With a linear signal function, one can prove that the rebound increases with both the previous phasic input intensity J and the unexpectedness of the disconfirming event that caused the burst of nonspecific arousal.

cells that contributed more to the disconfirmation that triggered the arousal burst. I call such a network of dipoles a *dipole field*. Figure 13.34 shows how selective reset of an entire dipole field by an unexpected event can occur. This property helped me to understand lots more data about cognitive-emotional interactions, notably how reinforcement learning is altered when reinforcement contingencies change. It soon also guided me to an explanation of how Adaptive Resonance Theory circuits carry out parallel hypothesis testing and memory search in response to unexpected events (Figure 5.19), leading to discovery and learning of recognition categories that better predict outcomes in a changing world.

The linear signal function in Figure 13.34 is not sufficient, however, if only because it can amplify noise. As shown in Figure 1.7, a signal function $f(w)$ must be faster-than-linear at small activity values w in order to suppress noise. I therefore also computed the OFF rebound in response to a faster-than-linear signal function. This calculation happily showed that previously attenuated features can be amplified during an antagonistic rebound, even while previously more active features are suppressed by it. This property led to a better understanding of how *attentional unblocking* can occur in response to an unexpected event (Figure 1.10) by shifting attention to include previously attenuated features that may be relevant. Again, a simple mathematical calculation led to a behaviorally important property that unaided intuition could not understand without it.

Three cognitive and emotional processes during learning about a reinforcer

The above discussions implicitly point to several different functional roles for a reinforcing event. These roles clarify that a reinforcing event has cognitive functions that are at least as important as their emotional functions as a reinforcer. Interactions between these cognitive and emotional functions enable us to learn—and unlearn—the predicted effects of the reinforcer as environmental circumstances change.

Consider a shock to fix ideas. Figure 13.35 summarizes three roles for a shock. Item 1 in this figure notes that a shock can, by itself, act as a negative reinforcer, but in some contexts (e.g., Figure 13.31) can trigger a reinforcement sign reversal. Item 2 notes that prior shock levels can be remembered and used to calibrate the effect of a present shock. The LTM traces of a gated dipole (Figures 1.14 and 1.15) enable a cue to become a conditioned reinforcer using these LTM traces (Figure 13.7). A cue can also read out an expectation of a remembered expected shock level. When a shock with a different intensity or timing occurs, it can mismatch the learned expectation and trigger new reinforcement learning. This kind of matching takes place in the basal ganglia, in particular in the substantia nigra pars compacta, or SNc, as Chapter 15 will explain. A shock can function as a reinforcer and as a sensory cue with predictable properties like its intensity and timing. When a

MULTIPLE FUNCTIONAL ROLES OF SHOCK

1. Reinforcement sign reversal
An ISOLATED shock is a negative reinforcer
In certain CONTEXTS, a shock can be a positive reinforcer

2. STM-LTM interaction
Prior shock levels need to be remembered (LTM) and used to calibrate the effect of the present shock (STM)

3. DISCRIMINATIVE AND SITUATIONAL CUES
The present shock level is UNEXPECTED (NOVEL) with respect to the shock levels that have previously been contingent upon experimental cues

1. Shock as a reinforcer
2. Shock as a sensory cue
3. Shock as an expectancy

FIGURE 13.35. A shock, or other reinforcing event, can have multiple cognitive and emotional effects on different brain processes.

situational cue occurs where the shock has previously been experienced, it can read out a previously learned expectation of how intense and at what time the shock is expected. When the shock does occur, its present intensity and timing will be matched or mismatched against this expectation, leading to very different consequences in the two cases, as I will explain in Chapter 15.

Inverted-U and arousal: Golden Mean, depression, autism, schizophrenia, and ADHD

Finally, how do these simple equations prove that an Inverted-U occurs in ON cell dipole output as arousal I is chosen at progressively larger values (Figure 1.18)? The Inverted-U is a consequence of the same mechanisms that enable a gated dipole to trigger antagonistic rebounds and to thereby quickly adapt to changing reinforcement contingencies. That is because the Inverted-U can also be traced to how the state of habituation in the dipole's transmitter gates (square synapses in Figures 1.14 and 1.15) *divide* the effects of signals through the dipole. This division creates a Weber law of dipole responsiveness.

Although I briefly discussed this topic in Chapter 1, I can better explain these properties with the benefit of the ON response equation in Figures 13.29. Suppose that the signal function $f(w)$ has a positive threshold below which it equals zero, as is often the case in biologically plausible signal functions that are faster-than-linear at small activities. Then a small arousal I requires a larger phasic input J to make the term $f(I+J)$ positive in the numerator of the ON response. Thus, the ON response is small for small values of I and J. This explains the small dipole response when I is small. What happens at large I values? Note that there are two terms that include I in the denominator, and that these terms are multiplied together. In contrast, the terms with I in the numerator are not multiplied together. Rather, they are subtracted. As a result of this difference, the denominator grows faster as a function of I than the numerator, thus reducing the ON response at large I values. This explains the small dipole response when I is large. Together these effects explain the Inverted-U.

Additional properties of the Inverted-U can also be read off from the ON equation. In particular, as depicted in Figure 1.18, problems can occur when arousal is either too small or too large. When I is too small, a form of *underaroused depression* occurs. When I is too large, *overaroused depression* can occur. As I will note in a moment, these properties provide insight into emotional symptoms of autism and schizophrenia, respectively.

Let's consider the underaroused case first: Because I is so small, it takes larger J values to generate a positive ON response in term $f(I+J)$. However, because I is also small in the denominator, once J is big enough to generate a response, further increments in J cause greater-than-normal ON responses, because they are divided by a smaller denominator. Thus, an underaroused dipole has an *elevated* response threshold, but is *hyper*excitable above threshold. This property is paradoxical because one might expect a high threshold to imply less excitability above threshold. It is due to the small habituative transmitter terms in the denominator of the ON response. Underaroused depression may thus be understood as a result of the dipole's Weber law properties. The combination of high threshold followed by suprathreshold hyperexcitability helps to explain why autistic individuals may be unresponsive to some emotional stimuli, but can then have intense responses to others.

What happens in the overaroused case? Here, because I is large, a response can be generated by even small values of J in term $[f(I+J) - f(I)]$ of the nominator in the ON response, since the threshold of $f(I + J)$ is easily exceeded. However, because I is also large in the denominator, and terms with I are multiplied together in the denominator, the response will be small for *all* values of J. Thus, an overaroused dipole has a *low* response threshold, but is *hypo*excitable above threshold. This property is also paradoxical because one might expect a low threshold to imply more excitability above threshold. It is also due to the habituative transmitter. The combination of low threshold and hypoexcitability helps to explain why various schizophrenic patients have flat affect and, when embodied within a CogEM model (Figure 13.2), why the ensuing abnormally small incentive motivational signals contribute to a hypofrontal condition that prevents adequate activation of prefrontal executive functions.

In summary, underarousal may be one cause of behavioral symptoms in individuals with autism (Baker et al., 2017; Bujnakova et al., 2016) that are explained in my 2006 *Psychological Review* article with Don Seidman (Grossberg and Seidman, 2006), whereas overarousal may be one cause of behavioral symptoms in schizophrenia (Ban, 1973; Depue, 1974; Haralanova et al., 2011) that are explained in my 2000 *Biological Psychiatry* article (Grossberg, 2000c).

Other mental disorders may also reflect these underaroused and overaroused depressive properties. For example, many individuals with attention deficit hyperactivity disorder, or ADHD, seem to be underaroused; e.g., Mayer, Wyckoff, and Strehl, (2016). The underaroused transmitter has been reported to be dopamine, and it gives rise to the kind of ADHD hypersensitivity that gated dipole affective dynamics predict (Sikström and Söderlund, 2007). Moreover, pharmacological "uppers" like Ritalin are often used to bring individuals with ADHD "down" (e.g., Weyandt et al., 2014). In a gated dipole, this happens because an upper will increase tonic arousal from under-aroused hypersensitivity to a Golden Mean of more moderate sensitivity and threshold reactivity (Figure 1.18).

If in fact these properties follow from how the chemical transmitter influences dipole responses, then what is the transmitter? Large clinical literatures, such as the ADHD literature that I just touched upon, implicate dopamine as a key transmitter in both autism and schizophrenia as well. Gated dipole properties provide a unifying perspective on how these conditions may be influenced by opposite ends of the Inverted-U as a function of dopaminergic arousal of drive representations in the amygdala and related reward-related regions.

READ circuit: REcurrent Associative Dipole

Feedback enables secondary inhibitory conditioning. The nonrecurrent gated dipole must be refined to realize additional properties that are important in the control of learning and behavior. In particular, as is so often the case, feedforward interactions are not sufficient. A *recurrent*, or feedback, gated dipole circuit is needed to realize additional performance and learning properties. I mentioned such a recurrent gated dipole in Figure 1.15. It is called a READ circuit, an acronym for the REcurrent Associative Dipole that I published in 1987 with my postdoctoral fellow Nestor Schmajuk (Grossberg and Schmajuk, 1987),

In the READ circuit, there is recurrent excitatory feedback in both the ON and OFF channels: Activity x_7 reactivates x_1 in the ON channel, while activity x_8 reactivates x_2 in the OFF channel. There are also habituative transmitter gates z_1 and z_2 in the ON and OFF channels, respectively. In addition, there are adaptive weights, or long-term memory (LTM) traces, w_{k7} and w_{k8} within the black hemidisk synapses. These LTM traces sample the ON and OFF channels, respectively, when they are gated by sampling signals S_k that are turned on by different CSs. The CSs learn to become conditioned reinforcers when they are associated with reinforcing USs J at the gated dipole. Any number k of sampling signals, that may be activated by many different kinds of objects and events, can converge on a single READ circuit.

A sleight of hand: Secondary inhibitory conditioning requires recurrent connections. The utility of a recurrent anatomy is vividly illustrated by the case of *secondary inhibitory conditioning*. Suppose that CS_1 is associated with a US shock input J until it becomes a source of conditioned fear. For this to happen, the adaptive weights that CS_1 activates must occur *after* the position in the ON channel where the US input J is registered, so that it can sample the activity caused by the US. After CS_1 has become a source

of conditioned fear, suppose that *onset* of a different CS_2 is associated with the *offset* of CS_1 so that the adaptive weights of CS_2 can sample the antagonistic rebound in the relief channel, and thereby learn how to become a source of conditioned relief. For this to happen, CS_1 must deliver its input *before* the habituative gates, so that its offset can cause the rebound in the OFF channel. In contrast, CS_2 must occur *after* the habituative gates, where it can sample the rebound, and thereby achieve secondary inhibitory conditioning.

What does this have to do with recurrent connections? The following sleight of hand makes this clear: This experiment could have been done with *any* CS_1 and CS_2. If we now interchange the cues that are used as CS_1 and CS_2, then by the above argument, each CS must occur both before *and* after the habituative gates! This can only happen if the network has recurrent connections within the ON and OFF channels, as in a READ circuit.

Stable motivational baseline and rapid motivational switching. A READ circuit supports several other, equally basic, functional properties that enable it to learn and perform motivated behaviors in complex naturalistic environments. These properties were also demonstrated with computer simulations in my 1987 article with Nestor Schmajuk. First, its recurrent pathways can maintain steady motivation while a behavior is being performed, even during sufficiently small environmental distractions. Suppose, for example, that you are eating and put your fork into a piece of food and begin to move the food to your mouth. Why doesn't any distraction force you to switch attention and abort the eating gesture? We could easily starve if this actually happened all the time. The recurrent pathways in the READ circuit convert it into a recurrent on-center off-surround network (cf. Figure 1.15). It is therefore able to store its activity patterns in short-term memory, or STM, just like in any such network. In a READ circuit, these stored activities can maintain incentive motivation, and the motivated attention that it controls (Figure 13.2), whereby to sustain the current motivated behavior until it is complete.

Second, a READ circuit can rapidly switch to support a new behavior with a different motivation if a distraction, or change in conditioned reinforcer cues, or available sources of primary reinforcement, is big enough. This is just a reset of STM in response to external inputs that change enough to overcome the hysteresis caused by the recurrent excitatory feedback. Such a reset can, for example, be caused by a mismatch reset event in response to an unexpected new event, as in ART (Figure 5.19c). READ circuit reset can be caused when an unexpected event triggers an arousal burst to the READ circuit, where it can cause an antagonistic rebound of the currently active motivational signal (Figures 13.33 and 13.34). A switch to another behavior can also be caused directly by competition from another, more salient, combination of sensory cues and drives in the sensory-drive heterarchy (Figure 1.17).

Life-long affective learning without associative saturation or passive forgetting. Third, a READ circuit enables affective learning to remain adaptive in response any number of reinforcing events throughout the lifespan. Its LTM traces do not saturate. This property solves an important problem that is faced by every learning process in our brains, and may be applied to other learning situations. Suppose, for example, that an animal gets shocked a large number of times after receiving a conditioned stimulus CS until the conditioned reinforcer LTM trace from the sensory representation of the CS to its fear center reaches its maximum value (Figure 13.36). Note, in this regard, that every synapse has a maximum value because "infinity does not exist in biology". Now imagine that the learning contingencies change so that the CS no longer predicts shock. Then antagonistic rebounds can activate a relief rebound and the LTM trace from the CS to the relief center can also grow large. In this way, both the fear and relief LTM traces could saturate at their maximal values (Figures 13.37), and no further learning could occur in that affective dipole from that time on. A READ circuit avoids this potential disaster, and enables affective learning to continue throughout the lifespan in response to multiple changes in reinforcement contingencies.

One might at first imagine that LTM saturation does not cause a serious problem because forgetting is passive. As a result, even if LTM traces do saturate at a given time, they will spontaneously decay to smaller values a short time later (Figure 13.36). Passive forgetting is not a tenable solution, however, because if it occurs on a time scale that

is fast enough to enable an animal to respond to rapidly changing environmental contingencies, then everything that we learned would have to be practiced within that time scale to avoid forgetting even the most basic skills. We would then be imprisoned by a life devoted to practicing a small number of menial tasks, ranging from tying our shoelaces to brushing our teeth. Such relentless practice would take up so much time each day that our minds would not be freed to learn more interesting things, and civilization could never have progressed to its present level.

But if neither LTM saturation nor passive forgetting are tenable, then what other options are available?

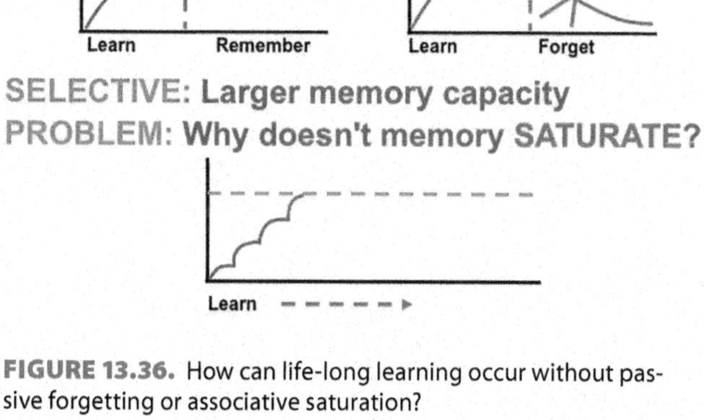

Informational noise suppression prevents LTM saturation. If LTM saturation of the ON and OFF LTM traces in a gated dipole could saturate, then they could read out equal learned signals to the dipole's ON and OFF channels. Recall from Chapter 2 that such a uniform activity pattern is uninformative and cannot be allowed to drive new learning because, if it did, the newly learned LTM traces would all be the same. All previous learned differences would be washed out. A READ circuit solves this problem by causing *informational noise suppression* (Figure 2.30). In other words, when the active LTM traces read out a uniform input pattern, the resulting cell activities equal zero due to information noise suppression. These activities then generate zero *teaching signals* to the LTM traces. As a result, the LTM traces will also be driven to zero. Nothing would be remembered, because nothing informative was experienced. In this way, saturation of LTM traces can never occur in a READ circuit.

This seemingly appealing result does raise a perplexing question: If a READ circuit causes information noise suppression, then how does it manage to learn anything at all?

Dissociating LTM read-out and read-in: Back-propagating dendritic teaching signals. READ circuits accomplish lifelong learning by exploiting two ubiquitous neural designs. The first design is opponent competition, which would, as I just noted, drive the read-out of equal LTM traces in the ON and OFF channels to zero (Figure 13.37). The second is that many inputs to neurons end on dendrites before the dendrites send signals to their neuronal cell bodies (Figures 1.15 and 1.20). The LTM traces that synapse on a READ circuit end on the dendrites (the thick black bars in Figure 1.15) of the READ cells with activities x_7 and x_8. The signals that the CSs read out through their LTM traces on the dendrites cannot, however, immediately serve as teaching signals back to the LTM traces. Instead, the *read-out of old LTM values is dissociated from the read-in of new LTM values*.

This is accomplished by exploiting the *opponent competition* that occurs across the ON and OFF channels. Only *after* these activities compete can they generate teaching signals to the LTM traces in the form of spikes

ASSOCIATIVE LEARNING
FORGETTING

e.g., Remember childhood experiences

Forgetting is NOT PASSIVE
Forgetting is SELECTIVE

SELECTIVE: Larger memory capacity
PROBLEM: Why doesn't memory SATURATE?

FIGURE 13.36. How can life-long learning occur without passive forgetting or associative saturation?

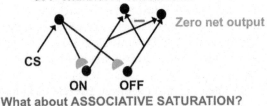

LEARN ON-RESPONSE

Disconfirmed expectation ➝ antagonistic rebound
OFF-channel is conditioned

Zero net output

What about ASSOCIATIVE SATURATION?

FIGURE 13.37. A disconfirmed expectation can cause an antagonistic rebound that inhibits prior incentive motivational feedback, but by itself is insufficient to prevent associative saturation.

in the dendrites. In vivo, these spikes travel from the cell bodies up their dendrites: They are back-propagating calcium spikes (Figure 13.38; Grossberg, 1975a; Markram, Helm, and Sakmann, 1995; Markram et al., 1997; Magee and Johnston, 1997).

Opponent extinction leads to learning of normalized net activities. Because these teaching signals occur only *after* the ON and OFF channels undergo opponent competition, if both ON and OFF channels have the same activity, then their teaching signals will be inhibited to zero, so that the LTM traces that sample them will also approach

zero, thereby preventing LTM saturation. I like to call this process *opponent extinction* because it shows how counterconditioning an OFF channel using antagonistic rebounds can use opponent competition and back-propagating dendritic spikes to force forgetting of ON channel contingencies that are no longer relevant.

No less important, when the ON and OFF channels have different activities, the competition computes teaching signals that are *normalized net activities* in which the smaller activity is inhibited to zero and the larger activity is sensitive to the ratio of the inputs (Figure 13.39). These properties follow from the fact that activities in any recurrent shunting on-center off-surround network, including a READ circuit, are normalized and are sensitive to the relative input sizes. Because the network also carries out informational noise suppression, the smaller activity is zero. The LTM traces can continue to learn these normalized net values throughout life, without ever saturating.

In summary, a READ circuit solves the informational noise suppression problem by using opponent competition, and only letting the net activities after competition drive new learning. Opponent competition may be viewed as a specialized version of competitive decision-making. READ circuits illustrate the general proposition that many learning processes dissociate read-out of old LTM values from read-in of new LTM values by interpolating a context-sensitive competitive decision process whose winners will determine what is learned.

Stable memories and mismatch-mediated active forgetting over the lifespan. Dissociation of LTM readout and read-in also explains the fourth desirable property of a READ circuit: It enables affective memories to be preserved for a long time, even years, until reward or

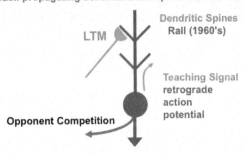

DISSOCIATION OF LTM READ-OUT AND READ-IN
Back-propagating dendritic action potentials as teaching signals

LTM
Dendritic Spines
Rall (1960's)

Teaching Signal
retrograde
action
potential

Opponent Competition

Early Predictions
Ca⁺⁺ currents in learning (1968)
Role of dendritic spines in learning (1975)
Cf., experiments of Häusser, Markram, Poo,
Sakmann, Spruston, etc.

FIGURE 13.38. Dissociation of the read-out of previously learned adaptive weights, or LTM traces, and of the read-in of new weight values enables back-propagating dendritic action potentials to teach the new adaptive weight values.

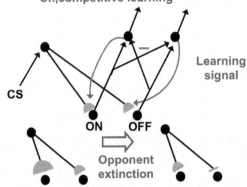

LEARN NET DIPOLE OUTPUT PATTERN
Opponent "decision" controls learning
Cf.,competitive learning

Learning
signal

CS

ON   OFF

Opponent
extinction

FIGURE 13.39. Shunting competition and informational noise suppression in affective gated dipoles, plus back-propagating action potentials for teaching signals, enable the net normalized adaptive weights to be learned. They never saturate!

punishment schedules change, or cognitive expectations are disconfirmed. They can then be quickly modified. Affective memories persist stably between such changes and disconfirmations because, when normalized net LTM traces are read into STM by multiplying the output signals from a recall probe S_k in Figure 1.15, they instate in STM the normalized net pattern that they had learned. This kind of pattern is unchanged by opponent competition. The teaching signals thus reinstate in new LTM the same old LTM pattern that was read out into STM. In other words, unless new learning or a disconfirmed expectation intervene, this LTM-STM-LTM cycle maintains its stability under recall. Forgetting is thus an active process, not a passive one! In summary, these properties help to explain how old affective memories can be triggered by a sensory cue or other memory that we have not experienced for a long time, and how these memories, once reactivated, can be modified by new learning.

Consistent with this explanation, Guang Yang, Feng Pan, and Wen-Biao Gan have shown in their 2009 article in *Nature* that dendritic spines can maintain memories for an entire lifetime in their experimental rats (Yang, Pan, and Gan, 2009). Such stable memories also help a CogEM model with a READ opponent process to explain, in addition to basic phenomena like primary and secondary excitatory and inhibitory conditioning, the persistence of instrumental avoidance behaviors and why Pavlovian conditioned inhibitors do not extinguish, among other conditioning data (Grossberg, 1972a; Grossberg and Schmajuk, 1987; Kamin, Brimer, and Black, 1963; Lysle and Fowler, 1985; Maier, Seligman, and Solomon, 1969; Miller and Schachtman, 1985; Owren and Kaplan, 1981; Solomon, Kamin, and Wynne, 1953; Witcher, 1978; Zimmer-Hart and Rescorla, 1974). It is instructive to summarize how the model explains why Pavlovian conditioned excitators do extinguish, but conditioned inhibitors do not. Before doing so, let me also point out that the dissociation of LTM read-out and read-in also helps to explain a phenomenon that has been the subject of intense experimental study during the past 20 years; namely, how *reconsolidation* of memories occurs when old LTM is read out, and how that may provide a powerful tool for combatting mental disorders like post-traumatic stress disorder, or PTSD.

Reconsolidation and retraining clinical symptoms during disorders like PTSD. When new memories form, they are labile and sensitive to being disrupted before they can consolidate into stable long-term memories; e.g., Dudai (1996, 2004). Many experiments have shown that the consolidation process involves the synthesis of new proteins in neurons; e.g., Davis and Squire (1984). If the protein synthesis inhibitor anisomycin is infused into the lateral and basal nuclei of the amygdala, or LBA, shortly after training with a shock, then the consolidation of fear memories is prevented. The laboratory of Joseph LeDoux has shown,

in addition, the exciting result "that consolidated fear memories, when reactivated during retrieval, return to a labile state in which infusion of anisomycin shortly after memory reactivation produces amnesia on later tests, regardless of whether reactivation was performed 1 or 14 days after conditioning. The same treatment with anisomycin, in the absence of memory reactivation, left memory intact. Consistent with a time-limited role for protein synthesis production in consolidation, delay of the infusion until six hours after memory reactivation produced no amnesia. . . ." (Nader, Schafe, and LeDoux, 2000, p. 722).

Fear conditioning has important uses for surviving dangerous situations, notably to help trigger escape or avoidance behaviors that can be supported by relief (Figure 13.24). However, excessive fear can be crippling, as often occurs during PTSD, due to reliving of a traumatic event, avoiding all cues associated with it, emotional numbing, and elevated arousal (e.g., Foa, Keane, Friedman, and Cohen, 2009). The persistence of such experiences and their ability to interfere with more constructive behaviors can be understood by considering how a trauma can cause abnormal strengthening of the LTM traces that bidirectionally link the fear drive representation to its remembered sensory and cognitive representations via a persistent cognitive-emotional resonance that is hard to reset, and that inhibits other emotions and cognitive possibilities in the sensory cortex, amygdala, and orbitofrontal cortex (Figure 13.2).

Whereas the above results on reconsolidation indicate how application of a protein synthesis inhibitor shortly after presenting a fear-inducing stimulus may lead to erasure of that memory, various pharmacological treatments are toxic in humans. It has, however, also been shown in humans how old fear memories can be updated during the reconsolidation window by presenting non-fearful information during extinction, or forgetting, trials (Schiller et al., 2010), and thereby avoiding pharmacological treatments. Although extinction is a classical method for eliminating fearful memories, as I will describe in the next sections, these experiments emphasize the utility of doing extinction procedures during the labile reconsolidation window. After sufficiently many extinction trials, fear memories are no longer expressed. The effect is, moreover, specific to the expressed fear memory and lasts for at least a year.

It needs also to be kept in mind, however, that fear memories are not the only ones that contribute to PTSD episodes. PTSD experiences are supported by *cognitive-emotional resonances*. Sensory and cognitive memories may persist, but breaking the cognitive-emotional loop by extinguishing conditioned LTM traces to and from the fear representation may make it easier to substitute non-fearful sensory and cognitive experiences that may be able to better inhibit traumatic memories.

Returning to the basic issue of reconsolidation, it also needs to be noted that the process of memory consolidation is a complex one that involves multiple brain regions, including the hippocampus, and brain states like slow wave sleep. Here I will just describe how the process of reconsolidation may be clarified by properties of the dissociation of LTM read-out and read-in. This process in the amygdala is then influenced by all of the extra-amygdaloid consolidation processes, including the cognitive-emotional resonance between amygdala, sensory cortex, and orbitofrontal cortex (Figure 13.4).

As I have just explained, affective learning within a READ circuit reads-out old LTM into a decision-making process that involves recurrent competitive interactions between opponent channels, followed by back-propagating action potentials on cell dendrites (Figures 1.15 and 13.38). The READ circuit hereby suggests that the competitive decision process and dendritic action potentials are the processes where consolidation and reconsolidation are locally controlled. The ability of the READ circuit to *dynamically* maintain an affective memory for years due to the stability of this memory during LTM-STM-LTM dendritic read-out and read-in cycles clarifies the paradox of why, during read-out intervals when sampling signals are still active, new affective inputs can, on a much shorter time scale, alter the previously maintained affective memory.

Consistent with this READ circuit prediction, it has been shown that fear conditioning is associated with increases in protein synthesis throughout amygdala dendrites, as well as increases in synapse size and more frequent appearances on large dendritic spines of a spine apparatus (Ostroff et al., 2010). Moreover, disruption of dendritic translation of calcium/calmodulin-dependent protein kinase IIα (CaMKllα) impairs stabilization of synaptic plasticity and memory consolidation (Miller et al., 2002). Memory consolidation also depends on functional interactions between the basolateral amygdala and the orbitofrontal cortex (Roozendaal et al., 2009), as predicted by the role of cognitive-emotional resonance in affective memory consolidation. Further experimental studies of the entire predicted LTM-STM-LTM read-out and read-in cycle is much to be desired.

Chapter 15 will explain in greater detail how the hippocampus can learn to bridge temporal gaps between CS and US stimuli during conditioning, as occurs during learning paradigms like trace conditioning, and how endogenous hippocampal activity during slow wave sleep, supported by Brain-Derived Neurotrophic Factor, or BDNF, can support the consolidation of memories that were learned during waking hours, including fearful memories in the amygdala.

Why do conditioned excitors extinguish but conditioned inhibitors do not?

I will now explain data about a classical example of extinction, and also related data about an extinction paradigm where extinction does not occur. Said more simply: What sorts of emotional memories do we readily forget, and what sort persist for a long time? These different outcomes will provide more insight into how cognitive processes regulate emotional learning and forgetting.

A conditioned excitor extinguishes. A classical paradigm wherein a conditioned excitor extinguishes is perhaps the simplest example of forgetting after several trials of fear conditioning have occurred. Figure 13.40 shows a learning phase in which a conditioned stimulus CS_1, such as a ringing bell, is paired with a shock until the learner is afraid of the bell. During the extinction, or forgetting, phase, the bell is presented by itself, without shock, and gradually becomes less fearful with successive non-shocked presentations.

A conditioned inhibitor does not extinguish. The paradigm for training a conditioned inhibitor begins in the same way as the paradigm for training a conditioned excitor. In Figure 13.41, a conditioned stimulus CS_1, in this case chosen to be a flashing light, is again paired with shock until the learner is afraid of the light. Then a second learning phase begins, in which two conditioned stimuli, CS_1 and CS_2, are presented together. Here, CS_2 is a ringing bell that is calibrated to have the same sensory salience as the flashing light. These stimuli are followed by no shock. In other words, the two stimuli occur during an extinction phase. Due to the unexpected non-occurrence of the shock, a relief rebound is caused during the no shock interval (Figures 13.33 and 13.37), so that CS_2 becomes a source of conditioned relief. Then CS_2 is presented by itself during a forgetting, or extinction, phase. Remarkably, multiple presentations of the flashing light do not lead to extinction of its potency as a source of conditioned relief.

Comparison of Figures 13.40 and 13.41 point to a paradox that is noted at the bottom of Figure 13.41: In both

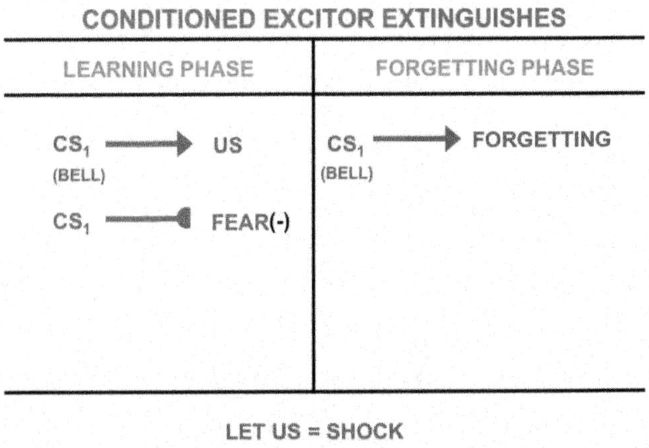

CONDITIONED EXCITOR EXTINGUISHES

LEARNING PHASE	FORGETTING PHASE
$CS_1 \longrightarrow$ US (BELL)	$CS_1 \longrightarrow$ FORGETTING (BELL)
$CS_1 \longrightarrow$ FEAR(-)	

LET US = SHOCK

FIGURE 13.40. A conditioning paradigm that illustrates what it means for conditioned excitators to extinguish.

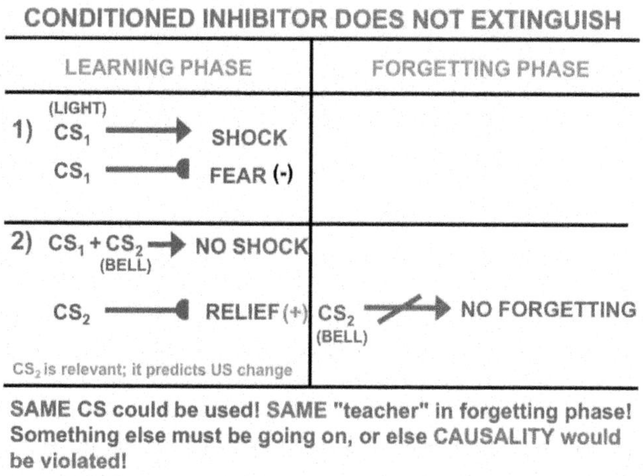

CONDITIONED INHIBITOR DOES NOT EXTINGUISH

LEARNING PHASE	FORGETTING PHASE
1) (LIGHT) CS_1 ⟶ SHOCK CS_1 ⟶ FEAR (·)	
2) $CS_1 + CS_2$ ⟶ NO SHOCK (BELL) CS_2 ⟶ RELIEF (+)	CS_2 (BELL) ⟶ NO FORGETTING

CS_2 is relevant; it predicts US change

SAME CS could be used! SAME "teacher" in forgetting phase! Something else must be going on, or else CAUSALITY would be violated!

FIGURE 13.41. A conditioning paradigm that illustrates what it means for conditioned inhibitors not to extinguish.

forgetting phases, a ringing bell is presented without shock. In the conditioned excitor paradigm, its affective learning extinguishes, but in the conditioned inhibitor paradigm, it does not. Some additional process must be regulating these different outcomes, or else we would have to assume that causality itself does not hold during conditioning, which would be a heavy price to pay and one that could undermine our entire theoretical enterprise.

Extinction due to disconfirmation of a learned expectation. Figures 13.42 and 13.43 describe what was missing. During conditioned excitor learning, in addition to the fear conditioning that occurs at drive representations, CS_1 is also learning to expect a shock (Figure 13.42). Thus, both emotional *and* cognitive learning occur during classical conditioning trials. During the forgetting phase, no shock occurs, so this expectation is disconfirmed. Such

a disconfirmed expectation can trigger an arousal burst that, in turn, drives a rebound from fear to relief in the READ circuit (Figure 13.37). Conditioning of CS_1 to relief begins to compete with the previous fear conditioning. As the learned relief approaches the strength of the learned fear, the bell no longer generates an emotional response. As explained above, informational noise suppression will lead to very small, or even zero, conditioned reinforcement LTM traces to both the fear and relief channels (Figure 13.39). In other words, a *disconfirmed expectation drives emotional forgetting.*

During conditioned inhibitory learning (Figure 13.43), when CS_2 turns on during the second learning phase of the experiment, in addition to sampling the relief rebound due to the non-occurrence of the expected shock, CS_2 also learned to expect an environment with no shock. During the forgetting phase, no shock occurs, so this expectation is confirmed. Because conditioned reinforcer LTM traces to a READ circuit can persist for a long time in the absence of a disconfirmed expectation or other change in reinforcement level, there is no forgetting.

There is no one "engram": Recognition learning is distinct from reinforcement learning. The explanation of why conditioned excitors extinguish but conditioned inhibitors do not dramatizes the fact that there is no single engram. For many years, quite a few investigators in neuroscience behaved as if there was. Instead, one needs, even to explain this particular type of data, to distinguish between recognition learning and reinforcement learning and how these two anatomically and functionally distinct processes mutually influence one another. Even at the level of the individual synapse, one needs to acknowledge that, if only due to complementary computing, different synapses may obey different learning laws (Table 1.2). Despite

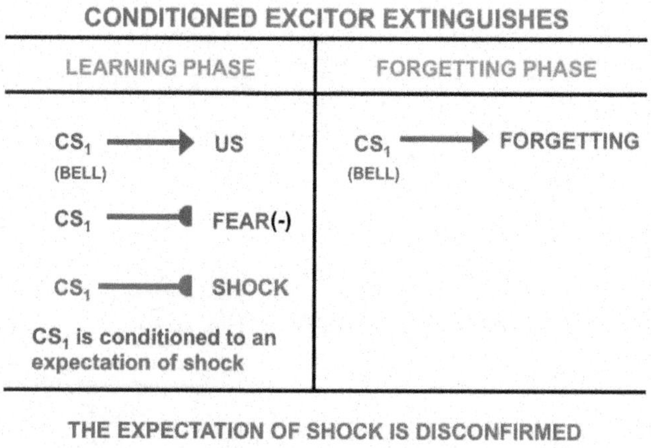

CONDITIONED EXCITOR EXTINGUISHES

LEARNING PHASE	FORGETTING PHASE
CS_1 ⟶ US (BELL) CS_1 ⟶ FEAR(·) CS_1 ⟶ SHOCK	CS_1 ⟶ FORGETTING (BELL)

CS_1 is conditioned to an expectation of shock

THE EXPECTATION OF SHOCK IS DISCONFIRMED

FIGURE 13.42. A conditioned excitor extinguishes because the expectation that was learned of a shock during the learning phase is disconfirmed during the forgetting phase.

CONDITIONED INHIBITOR DOES NOT EXTINGUISH

LEARNING PHASE	FORGETTING PHASE
1) (LIGHT) CS_1 ⟶ SHOCK CS_1 ⟶ FEAR (·)	
2) $CS_1 + CS_2$ ⟶ NO SHOCK (BELL) CS_2 ⟶ RELIEF (+) CS_2 ⟶ NO SHOCK	CS_2 (BELL) ⟶ NO FORGETTING

THE EXPECTATION THAT "NO SHOCK" FOLLOWS CS_2 IS NOT DISCONFIRMED!

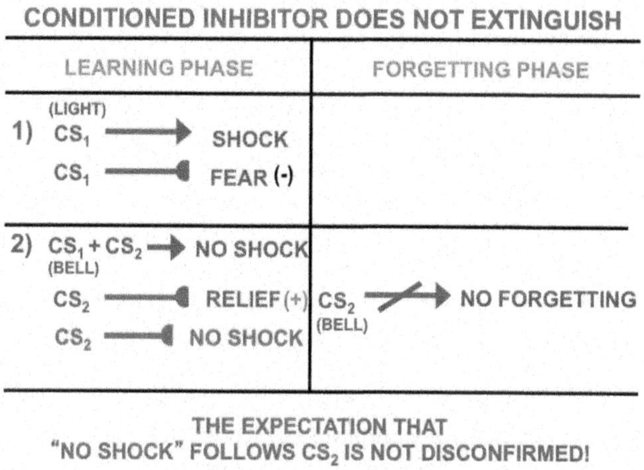

FIGURE 13.43. A conditioned inhibitor does not extinguish because the expectation that was learned of no shock during the learning phase is not disconfirmed during the forgetting phase.

these differences, there is nonetheless a breathtaking simplicity of shared designs underlying behaviors that often seem to be totally unrelated.

A disconfirmed expectation is not an explicit teacher! It also cannot be overemphasized that a disconfirmed expectation is not an explicit teacher. Conditioned excitators extinguish during *unsupervised* learning. At the moment of an unexpected disconfirmation, the correct answer is, by definition, unknown to the system. It is part of the genius of the evolutionary process that the brain mechanisms that have evolved to achieve behavioral success can use a novelty-triggered *nonspecific* arousal burst to drive a search that usually leads to new learning of cognitive and emotional representations with which to better predict what will happen next.

The feeling of what happens, core consciousness, dual competition, and survival circuits

Let us now consider how CogEM dynamics are related to proposals by other theorists about how cognitive-emotional interactions work. In his elegant 1999 book entitled *The Feeling of What Happens*, Antonio Damasio (Damasio, 1999) derived from a large corpus of clinical data his heuristic model of cognitive-emotional dynamics. This heuristic model, for which no equations or data simulations were presented, is nonetheless strikingly similar to the CogEM model in Figure 13.1, which was derived and first used to explain totally different data bases. This convergence of concepts provides additional support to these foundational concepts. Figure 13.44 reprints Figure 6.1 from Damasio's book. Damasio's concept of the "map of object X" corresponds in CogEM to an invariant object category that activates sensory cortex; the "map of the proto-self" corresponds to the value category in amygdala and its multiple interactions with other brain regions such as the hypothalamus; the "second-order map" corresponds to the object-value category in orbitofrontal cortex; and the "map of object X enhanced" corresponds to the object category when it is attentively amplified by feedback from the object-value category (also see Figure 13.2). As this cognitive-emotional resonance develops through the excitatory feedback loop between object, value, and object-value categories (Figure

13.4), the attended object achieves emotional and motivational significance.

This cognitive-emotional resonance binds together complementary properties of object categories and value categories in much the same way that a feature-category resonance binds together complementary properties of distributed features and their object categories (Figure 2.2). In the CogEM model, the invariant object category can classify particular combinations of features in the world, but cannot compute their value to the organism. Activation of a value category sets the stage for thoughts and actions that have a particular emotional and motivational meaning, but does not represent any particular objects or events to which these feelings could be directed. The *bound state* of the cognitive-emotional resonance combines facts about the external world with feelings about and motivations to act from the internal world. As Damasio notes on p. 171 of his book: "Attention is driven to focus on an object and the result is saliency of the images of that object in mind", leading to what Damasio calls *core consciousness*. As a result of such a cognitive-emotional resonance, "the feeling of what happens" can ascribe feelings to particular objects and events in the world, activate sensory expectations of what one would like to happen next, and activate behaviors to achieve valued goals.

Damasio also went on to write on p. 180 that "I do not know how the fusing, blending, and smoothing are achieved . . . ". The CogEM model began to provide mechanistic explanations of how this happens in the

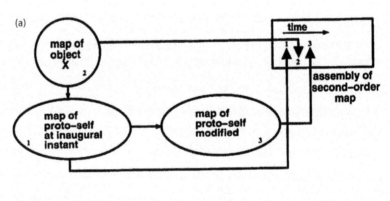

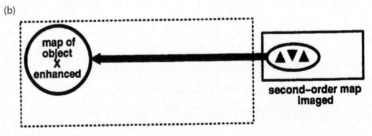

FIGURE 13.44. Analog of the CogEM model in Figure 6.1 of Damasio (1999).

brain in 1971, 28 years before Damasio wrote these words (Grossberg, 1971a).

As in the case of a surface-shroud resonance (Figure 6.2), a CogEM cognitive-emotional resonance is predicted to propagate to other brain regions with which its object, value, and object-value categories interact, including hypothalamus, visual cortex, and additional prefrontal cortical areas, including ventrolateral and dorsolateral prefrontal cortices that control executive planning and action, and that I will discuss in Chapter 14. The hypothalamus controls internal homeostatic states for drives like hunger, thirst, and sex, whose activation patterns correlate with different emotions (Figure 13.1). These homeostatic representations will be discussed in greater detail below when I discuss how the MOTIVATOR model (Figures 13.22 (bottom row) and 14.3) unlumps the CogEM model and shows how it interacts with the basal ganglia, thereby enabling even more data about reinforcement learning and motivated attention to be explained and predicted.

The CogEM model is also consistent with more recent proposals about how emotions work. These include the "dual competition" model of Luiz Pessoa (Pessoa, 2009, p. 160), who writes: "The proposed framework is referred to as the 'dual competition' model to reflect the suggestion that affective significance influences competition at both the perceptual and executive levels—and because the impact is caused by both emotion and motivation." These two competitive stages correspond to the object categories and the object-value stages in CogEM. Competition occurs at both processing stages, as my explanation of attentional blocking (Figures 1.10 (left column), 13.10, and 13.12 (right column)) earlier in this chapter illustrates, and the orbitofrontal object-value categories feed higher-level cognitive processes such as working memory and its unitization into predictive list chunks (Figure 12.42) using Masking Fields (Figures 12.46 and 12.47).

The even more recent "survival circuit" concept that was proposed in 2012 by Joseph LeDoux (LeDoux, 2012, p. 653) "integrates ideas about emotion, motivation, reinforcement, and arousal in the effort to understand how organisms survive and thrive by detecting and responding to challenges and opportunities in daily life". The CogEM model provides detailed mechanistic explanations of how "survival circuit" processes are integrated to generate appropriate learned behaviors in response to unique environmental challenges, especially when they are combined with perceptual, cognitive, and motor circuits in larger systems.

How such larger systems can "survive and thrive" in an embodied system started to get demonstrated in adaptive mobile robots more than 25 years ago. The pioneering adaptive mobile robot MAVIN, or Mobile Adaptive Visual Navigator, that was described in 1991 by Aijaz Baloch and Allen Waxman (Baloch and Waxman, 1991), included a neural system that integrated processes "from visual object learning and recognition to behavioral conditioning." One of Baloch and Waxman's demonstrations used MAVIN to illustrate classical conditioning properties that my colleagues and I had earlier simulated, but they demonstrated them in an end-to-end simulation on the robot that included registration of sensory events. Aijaz Baloch was also one of my PhD students, as was Luiz Pessoa, although we worked on motion perception together, rather than cognitive-emotional dynamics.

Breakdowns during mental disorders: Theory of Mind, autism, and schizophrenia. As I have mentioned above in my review of the Inverted-U as a function of arousal (Figure 1.18), when a CogEM circuit functions improperly, symptoms of mental disorders can result. For example, hypoactivity of amygdala or orbitofrontal cortex can prevent a cognitive-emotional resonance from occurring, thereby causing failures in what are called Theory of Mind processes (Baron-Cohen, 1989; Perner et al., 1989) in both autism and schizophrenia (Grossberg, 2000c; Grossberg and Seidman, 2006). Such failures include problems with activating motivationally directed goals and intentions. This happens in CogEM when a depressed emotional response in the amygdala also depresses the incentive motivational signals needed to activate prefrontal cortex in response to motivationally salient events (Figure 3.1). The prefrontal cortex will then not adequately activate, and a hypofrontal condition can emerge during which working memory representations and plans are degraded, so social goals and plans will not form normally.

Depressed emotional responses to environmental and internally generated cues, including facial expressions, combined with insufficient motivational support for emotionally-appropriate plans and actions, helps to explain why individuals with autism may be unable to understand others' actions and may themselves perform actions that are socially inopportune. Deficiencies in Theory of Mind are not, however, sufficient to explain all aspects of autistic development and behavior, as I have reviewed in my 2006 *Psychological Review* article with Don Seidman about the neural dynamical of autistic behaviors (Grossberg and Seidman, 2006).

From survival circuits to ARTSCAN Search, pART, and the Where's Waldo problem. How survival circuits like CogEM can actually respond "to challenges and opportunities in daily life" is illustrated by how the ARTSCAN Search and predictive ART, or pART, model, of which CogEM forms a part, can solve the Where's Waldo problem; that is, can search for and recognize valued goal objects in multi-object scenes. I will return in Chapter 14 to a proposed solution of the Where's Waldo problem and, more generally, to a unified explanation of how the prefrontal cortex coordinates cognitive and cognitive-emotional interactions using the pART model.

Conscious vs. non-conscious emotions. Chapter 1 pointed out that we do not always know what we will want when confronted with new situations. This human frailty was illustrated by the example of peak shift and behavioral contrast (Figure 1.12), which illustrates how interactions among the category representations of previously rewarded or punished events can cause novel events to have even greater value to us than ones for which we have been rewarded in the past. In this example, at least some of the rewarded or punished events that influence subsequent behaviors were consciously experienced. Many experiments have also shown that emotional processes can influence future decisions without us having any conscious awareness of them. This insight reached a wide audience of readers with Vance Packard's famous 1957 book about *The Hidden Persuaders* (Packard, 1957), which described how advertisements that include subliminal, and thus non-conscious, value-laden cues can guide our product choices. In the current theory, any stimulation that does not cause a sustained cognitive-emotional resonance may lead to a non-conscious outcome. The lack of conscious awareness may be due to insufficient sensory stimulation in terms of intensity or duration, attention-distracting tasks, or any other manipulation that prevents a full resonance from developing and being sustained. In particular, amygdala and hypothalamus can interact without necessarily leading to conscious awareness.

In 2010, Marco Tamietto and Beatrice de Gelder (Tamietto and de Gelder, 2010) reviewed several different kinds of experimental evidence that led them to a similar viewpoint, but without mechanisms of cognitive-emotional resonances to derive mechanistic conclusions. They wrote that "a major difference between the two types of perception [conscious and non-conscious] may be the combined involvement of cortical areas and of cortico-subcortical interactions when stimuli are consciously perceived. *The dichotomy of conscious and non-conscious perception of emotional signals can thus be reformulated in neural terms as the integration of activity in subcortical and cortical structures*" [italics mine], where the amygdala figures prominently in their review of relevant emotional structures. Cognitive-emotional resonances in the CogEM model link subcortical structures, such as the amygdala and hypothalamus, with cortical structures, such as the temporal and orbitofrontal cortices, into a bound state that supports both the feeling of what happens, and the knowledge of what event has caused it.

Our emotional experiences pervade our lives just as fully as our visual and auditory ones do. I have tried in this chapter to lay a foundation whereby you can begin to think independently about emotions, motivations, and the decisions that they guide, as they most influence your own life. I hope that you find the concepts, brain designs, and mechanisms that I have described in this selective review helpful in your own personal reflections and struggles to achieve a better understanding of your life-long odyssey between thought and feeling.

How Prefrontal Cortex Works
Cognitive working memory, planning, and emotion conjointly achieve valued goals

Towards a unified theoretical understanding of prefrontal cortex and its functions

Functional roles of orbitofrontal, ventrolateral, and dorsolateral prefrontal cortex. The prefrontal cortex is needed for us to carry out many of the higher cognitive, emotional, and decision-making processes that define human intelligence, while also controlling the release of actions aimed at achieving valued goals. This chapter will describe a unified theory of prefrontal cortex that explains how it carries out several of its most important functions. This theory builds upon the foundation that I have laid in previous chapters.

The *Wikipedia* article about PFC illustrates the range of its functions: "The most typical psychological term for functions carried out by the prefrontal cortex area is *executive function*. Executive function relates to abilities to differentiate among conflicting thoughts, determine good and bad, better and best, same and different, future consequences of current activities, working toward a defined goal, prediction of outcomes, expectation based on actions, and social 'control' (the ability to suppress urges that, if not suppressed, could lead to socially unacceptable outcomes)." Elliott, Dolan, and Frith (2000) discussed how the PFC contributes to generating behaviors that are flexible and adaptive, notably in novel situations, and to suppressing actions that are no longer appropriate, thereby freeing humans and other primates from being forced to respond reflexively to current sensory inputs. These authors also review the various terms that have been used to describe PFC functions, including planning (Luria, 1966), memory for the future (Ingvar, 1985), executive control (Baddeley, 1986), working memory (Goldman-Rakic, 1987), supervisory attention (Shallice, 1988), and top-down modulation of bottom-up processes (Frith and Dolan, 1997).

Earl Miller and Neal Cohen (Miller and Cohen, 2001) reviewed data that are consistent with these concepts, noting that these functions result "from the active maintenance of patterns of activity in the prefrontal cortex that represent goals and the means

Conscious MIND Resonant BRAIN. Stephen Grossberg, Oxford University Press. © Oxford University Press 2021.
DOI: 10.1093/oso/9780190070557.003.0014

to achieve them. They provide bias signals to other brain structures whose net effect is to guide the flow of activity along neural pathways that establish the proper mappings between inputs, internal states, and outputs needed to perform a given task" (p. 167). Said in yet another way, the PFC is involved with predicting future outcomes and enabling animals and humans to respond adaptively to them.

Stephen Wise (Wise, 2008) espoused a similar view that he vividly summarized as follows: "The long list of functions often attributed to prefrontal cortex may all contribute to knowing what to do and what will happen when rare risks arise or outstanding opportunities knock" (p. 599).

Joachín Fuster has written perhaps the definitive book on the prefrontal cortex. As he notes in the Preface to its Fifth Edition (Fuster, 2015), "what is new in the field of the prefrontal cortex seems to be *novelty* itself, or at least a renewed emphasis on it and on the *future orientation* of prefrontal functions. There is a growing recognition that the cardinal function of this part of the brain . . . is the design and implementation of novel, complex, goal-directed or purposeful actions".

Even this brief heuristic summary of the multiple functions of the PFC illustrates the challenge facing any theorist who wishes to model this, or indeed any, part of the brain. The challenge is that various functionally distinct parts of the PFC are connected to each other in complex ways, in addition to being widely connected with multiple other brain regions. Broadly speaking, the dorsal prefrontal cortex is interconnected with brain regions involved with attention, cognition, and action (Goldman-Rakic, 1988), whereas the ventral prefrontal cortex is interconnected with brain regions involved with emotion (Price, 1999). These facts do not, however, explain how these brain circuits give rise to these distinct psychological functions as *emergent properties* that arise from interactions among brain regions that work together as *functional systems*. My modeling Method of Minimal Anatomies enables these systems to be discovered and characterized as part of its ever-expanding linkage of brain mechanisms to psychological functions (Figure 2.37).

The above conclusions about PFC functions derive from a large number of experimental studies of PFC using a wide range of methods. Some articles have studied the PFC of humans with functional neuroimaging in normal subjects or clinical patients, while others have studied monkeys or rats with neurophysiological or anatomical methods. Important functional conclusions have also been derived by combining selective lesions with behavioral studies in monkeys. Recent studies have, however, shown that different lesion methods can yield quite different results. These results justify a concern that lesion studies have always raised, because it is sometimes not clear what structures a particular lesion may damage. Whereas excitotoxic lesions kill only targeted neurons, other lesion methods may also damage fibers of passage to adjacent cortical areas.

For example, monkeys with selective excitotoxic lesions of the orbitofrontal cortex (OFC), unlike monkeys who have received aspiration lesions that suck out a region of OFC tissue, are unimpaired in learning and reversing object choices based on reward feedback (Rudebeck et al., 2013). In a similar way, neurotoxic lesions of the amygdala (Izquierdo and Murray, 2007) have also led to results that challenge earlier demonstrations using aspiration and radiofrequency lesions that the amygdala is needed for object reversal learning (Aggleton and Passingham, 1981; Jones and Mishkin, 1972; Spiegler and Mishkin, 1981). The fact that OFC activity has been reported during reversal learning (Fellows and Farah, 2003; Morrison et al., 2011; Rolls, 2000; Rolls et al., 1994) suggests that several neuronal regions and pathways may be involved in this behavioral competence.

This picture is complicated further by different definitions of the brain areas that constitute OFC and the ventrolateral prefrontal cortex, or VLPFC. The conclusions above hold if OFC is understood to consist of cortical areas 11, 13, and 14, which are shown in coronal sections A-E in Figure 14.1, which comes from the Wikimedia Commons. If, however, area 12o is also included (Figure 14.1), which overlaps what Chau al. (2015) call the lateral OFC, or lOFC, then various properties of what Rudebeck et al. (2017) would assign to VLPFC get attributed to OFC. Herein, I will assume that OFC consists of areas 11, 13, and 14. Another caveat is that there appear to be species-specific variations. For example, unlike old world monkeys, excitotoxic lesions in new world monkeys such as marmosets (Roberts, 2006) *can* impair these animals on reversal tasks. These variations will not be further discussed in this book.

Because Chapter 12 reviewed and explained some of the fundamental neural designs and data about cognition, and Chapter 13 has done the same for emotion, I can now try to explain to you recent data about how prefrontally-mediated higher-order intelligence works, and how these circuits integrate both types of information. In addition, I will also note where our models anticipated these data, which hereby added to the long list of confirmed predictions over the years.

Predictive Adaptive Resonance Theory: A unified neural theory of prefrontal cortex

These processes are synthesized into a comprehensive neural architecture that mechanistically explains how the

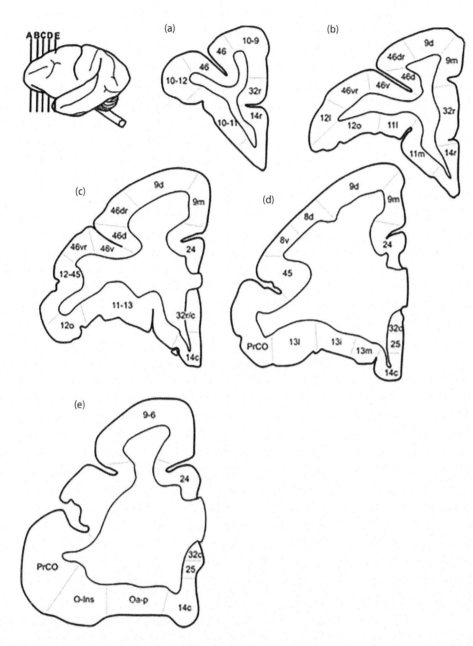

FIGURE 14.1. Coronal sections of prefrontal cortex. Note particularly the areas 11, 13, 14, and 12o.

interactions with multiple brain regions. This article further develops a unified neural architecture that explains many recent and classical data about prefrontal function, and makes testable predictions. Prefrontal properties of desirability, availability, credit assignment, category learning, and feature-based attention are explained. These properties arise through interactions of orbitofrontal, ventrolateral prefrontal, and dorsolateral prefrontal cortices with the inferotemporal cortex, perirhinal cortex, parahippocampal cortices; ventral bank of the principal sulcus, ventral prearcuate gyrus, frontal eye fields, hippocampus, amygdala, basal ganglia, hypothalamus, and visual cortical areas V1, V2, V3A, V4, MT, MST, LIP, and PPC. Model explanations also include how the value of visual objects and events is computed, which objects and events cause desired consequences and which may be ignored as predictively irrelevant, and how to plan and act to realize these consequences, including how to selectively filter expected vs. unexpected events, leading to movements towards, and conscious perception of, expected events. Modeled processes include reinforcement learning and incentive motivational learning; object and spatial working memory dynamics; and category learning, including the learning of object categories, value categories, object-value categories, and sequence categories, or list chunks."

PFC interacts with many brain regions to carry out these high mental processes in a coordinated way. I call this the *predictive ART*, or pART, architecture (Figure 14.2). The following Abstract from my 2018 article about pART (Grossberg, 2018) describes the scope of this architecture, all of whose functions are explained here and elsewhere in the book. When I began my work in 1957, I never dreamed that such a synthesis would be possible during my own lifetime:

"The prefrontal cortices play an essential role in cognitive-emotional and working memory processes through

Many, but not all, of the concepts and brain regions that are listed in the abstract have already been discussed in earlier chapters. I will here take the next step in putting them all together.

Updating a predicted outcome's desirability and availability. In particular, this chapter will discuss models that help to explain recent data about the orbitofrontal cortex (OFC), ventrolateral prefrontal cortex (VLPFC), and dorsolateral prefrontal cortex (DLPFC). These explanations shed light on issues that we face every day in our

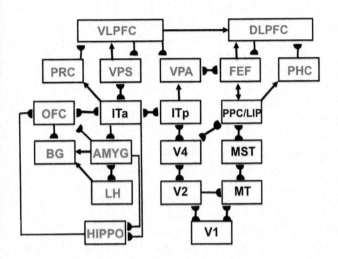

FIGURE 14.2. Macrocircuit of the main brain regions, and connections between them, that are modelled in the unified *predictive Adaptive Resonance Theory* (pART) of cognitive-emotional and working memory dynamics. Abbreviations in red denote brain regions used in cognitive-emotional dynamics, Those in green denote brain regions used in working memory dynamics. Black abbreviations denote brain regions that that carry out visual perception, learning and recognition of visual object categories, and motion perception, spatial representation and target tracking. Arrows denote non-adaptive excitatory synapses. Hemidiscs denote adaptive excitatory synapses. Many adaptive synapses are bidirectional, thereby supporting synchronous resonant dynamics among multiple cortical regions. The output signals from the basal ganglia that regulate reinforcement learning and gating of multiple cortical areas are not shown. Also not shown are output signals from cortical areas to motor responses. V1: striate, or primary, visual cortex; V2 and V4: areas of prestriate visual cortex; MT: middle temporal cortex; MST: medial superior temporal area; ITp: posterior inferotemporal cortex; ITa: anterior inferotemporal cortex; PPC: posterior parietal cortex; LIP: lateral intraparietal area; VPA: ventral prearcuate gyrus; FEF: frontal eye fields; PHC: parahippocampal cortex; DLPFC: dorsolateral hippocampal cortex; HIPPO: hippocampus; LH: lateral hypothalamus; BG: basal ganglia; AMGY: amygdala; OFC: orbitofrontal cortex; PRC: perirhinal cortex; VPS: ventral bank of the principal sulcus; VLPFC: ventrolateral prefrontal cortex. See the text for further details.

lives. For example, how are our preferences for specific foods learned and represented in our brains? How do we choose different foods in response to particular metabolic needs or taste preferences on different days, or different times during the same day? How do we select only valued objects or events for storage in working memory, and use them to learn plans about what will happen next? How do we selectively pay attention to only such valued objects and events? As we go along below, I will call your attention to how model explanations shed light on such day-to-day concerns.

OFC helps to update a predicted outcome's *desirability*, whereas VLPFC is involved in updating its *availability* (Rudebeck et al., 2017). In addition, DLPFC neurons encode a solution of the *credit assignment problem* (Assad et al., 2017). I will explain below that

results on desirability were predicted, indeed simulated, by the MOTIVATOR model of cognitive-emotional interactions (Figure 14.3; Grossberg, Bullock, and Dranias, 2008). The role of VLPFC in updating availability and of DLPFC in providing credit assignment will, in turn, be clarified by the LIST PARSE model of cognitive working memory and list chunking (Figures 12.42 and 12.43; Grossberg and Pearson, 2008). My explanations of these new data will propose how these models function in a larger neural system, whose pART macrocircuit is shown in Figure 14.2. I will say more about the mechanisms and functions of the brain regions in this macrocircuit as I go along. This macrocircuit will also enable me to explain other recent data about PFC, such as data from the laboratory of Robert Desimone at MIT about how PFC contributes to "feature based attention" in monkeys (Bichot et al., 2015) and humans (Baldauf and Desimone, 2014). I have already explained how other brain regions may also contribute to feature-based, or object, attention. These include how prestriate visual cortex and inferotemporal cortex interact to support feature-category resonances (Table 1.4; Figure 2.2). This fact raises the question: What additional functions does the PFC source of attention add?

Cognitive-emotional dynamics and the orbitofrontal cortex

Reinforcement learning, motivated attention, resonance, and directed action. First I will consider how the orbitofrontal cortex tracks the desirability of predicted outcomes (Rudebeck et al., 2017). This conclusion is related to earlier concepts such as the "somatic marker hypothesis" which proposes that decision-making is a process that depends upon emotion (Bechara et al., 1999). To ensure that my explanations are self-contained and do not require too much flipping between this chapter and previous ones, I will start out by reviewing how the Cognitive-Emotional-Motor, or CogEM, model, that was described in Chapter 13 (Figure 13.1) explains how sensory cortex, amygdala, and orbitofrontal cortex interact to make emotionally-modulated decisions (Baxter et al., 2000; Bechara et al., 1999; Schoenbaum et al., 2003; Tremblay and Schultz, 1999). I will then turn to how the MOTIVATOR extension of CogEM clarifies how orbitofrontal cortex contributes to the incentive value of rewards and their sensitivity to reward devaluation (Gallagher, McMahan, and Schoenbaum, 1999).

As I summarized in Chapter 13, the CogEM model explains how *invariant object categories*, in sensory cortical regions like the anterior inferotemporal cortex

(ITa), and *object-value categories*, in cortical regions like the orbitofrontal cortex, interact with *value categories*, in subcortical emotional centers like amygdala and hypothalamus. These brain regions are linked by a feedback loop which, when activated for sufficiently long time, can generate a *cognitive-emotional resonance*. Such a resonance can support conscious feelings while using *conditioned reinforcer learning* pathways (from sensory cortex to amygdala; Gore et al., 2015) and *incentive motivational learning* pathways (from amygdala to orbitofrontal cortex; Arana et al., 2003) to focus motivated attention upon valued object and object-value representations. These attended object-value representations can, in turn, release commands to perform actions that are compatible with these feelings.

It needs to be noted, however, that the CogEM circuit in Figure 13.1 cannot, by itself, maintain motivated attention during an adaptively-timed interval that is sufficiently long to enable reinforcement learning to effectively occur in paradigms where rewards are delayed in time, as happens during trace conditioning and delayed match-to-sample, and to enable a conscious "feeling of what happens" to emerge (Damasio, 1999). The hippocampus is needed to support both of these properties. Chapter 15 will explain how this happens as part of the explanation of how our brains carry out adaptively timed learning over an extended duration that may span hundreds of milliseconds, or even seconds. The next sections say more about these several types of categories and the learned interactions between them.

Category learning and memory consolidation: Effects of lesions. A fourth kind of learning, *category learning*, learns to refine the connections from thalamus to an object category in sensory cortex, and from an object category to an object-value category in orbitofrontal cortex. This category learning process enables external objects and events in the world to selectively activate object and object-value categories. Category learning was not simulated in the original CogEM model, which focused on reinforcement learning, motivated attention, and the release of actions towards valued goal objects. Category learning does play a key role in extensions of CogEM, such as the *neurotrophic Spectrally Timed Adaptive Resonance Theory*, or nSTART, model that I published in 2017 with my PhD student Daniel Franklin (Franklin and Grossberg, 2017).

nSTART augments CogEM to include category learning, as well as adaptively timed learning in the hippocampus. Interactions between these two processes, augmented by all the other processes of CogEM, enable nSTART to explain and simulate how memory consolidation of recognition categories may occur after conditioning ends. This nSTART explanation includes simulations of the complex pattern of disruptions of memory consolidation that occur in response to early vs. late lesions of thalamus, amygdala, hippocampus, and orbitofrontal cortex. I will say more about nSTART in Chapter 15 after explaining how our brains can adaptively time our learned responses to valued goal objects. We can thereby respond to goals at appropriate times, neither too early or too late. This ability is crucially important for successful predation and escape in the wild, no less than in the many social situations of advanced societies where temporally controlled behaviors are necessary for acceptance and success.

Polyvalent constraints and competition interact to choose the most valued options. For reasons that were explained by the thought experiment about cognitive-emotional interactions in Chapter 13, both the CogEM and nSTART circuits need to have two successive sensory processing stages, an invariant object category stage in the temporal cortex, and an object-value category stage in orbitofrontal cortex (Figure 13.1), in order to ensure that the object-value category can release motivated behavior most vigorously if both sensory and motivational inputs are simultaneously received by the object-value category. A *polyvalent constraint* on an object-value category means that it fires most vigorously when it receives input from its invariant object category *and* from a value category. In other words, an object-value category is amplified when the action that it controls is valued at that time. Only when an object-value category wins a competition with other object-value categories can it trigger an action. After learning occurs, a conditioned reinforcer can, by itself, satisfy this polyvalent constraint by sending a signal from its object category directly to its object-value category, and indirectly via the (conditioned reinforcer)-(incentive motivational) pathway using anatomical pathways between sensory cortex and amygdala to the orbitofrontal cortex that are known to exist (Figure 13.3).

The firing of each value category in the amygdala/hypothalamus is also regulated by a combination of polyvalent constraints and competition. Here, the polyvalent constraint (Figures 13.1 and 13.19 (bottom row)) is realized by two converging inputs to each value category: a reinforcing input from a US or conditioned reinforcer CS *and* a sufficiently large internal drive input (e.g., hunger, thirst) that provides excitatory modulation of the reinforcer. Each value category can only then become active enough to reliably win the competition with other value categories via the sensory-drive heterarchy (Figure 1.17), and only a winning sensory-drive combination can generate large incentive motivational output signals to the corresponding object-value categories. In particular, even if visual cues such as a familiar food generate a strong reinforcing signal to a value category, it cannot fire if its internal drive input is reduced by eating a lot, since then the hunger drive input will decrease and the satiety drive input will increase, thereby preventing its value category from winning the competition.

Because both the value categories and the object-value categories obey polyvalent constraints and compete to determine either incentive motivational or motor outputs, a CogEM circuit tends to choose options for action that are currently the most desired ones.

Many issues need to be discussed to better understand how these circuits work in practice. Here are some of them: Why is it called a value category? How does a value category differ from just an internal drive such as hunger? In particular, can value categories represent specific hungers? How is the hypothalamus involved in learning a value category? And are there multiple pathways for expressing valued goals that do not require the amygdala? I will discuss these issues in this chapter, using explanations of recent experiments about the functions of different parts of the prefrontal cortex to organize my exposition.

Orbitofrontal coding of desirability as probed by selective satiation. Rudebeck et al. (2017) did experiments that support the hypothesis that the orbitofrontal cortex (OFC), but not the ventrolateral prefrontal cortex (VLPFC), plays a necessary role in choices that are based on outcome *desirability*. In contrast, the VLPFC, but not the OFC, plays a necessary role in choices that are based on outcome *availability*. The experiment to test desirability (their experiment 2) manipulated the subjective value of different food rewards with a stimulus-based reinforcer devaluation, or satiation, procedure (Málková et al., 1997), while keeping the probability and magnitude of reward stable. This procedure was carried out in the following way: The monkeys were trained with some objects that were associated with food 1, and other objects that were associated with food 2. Following the selective satiation procedure, monkeys were presented with pairs of objects, one object associated with food 1 and the other with food 2. The effects of how and whether the satiation procedure led to devaluation of the satiated food were measured by calculating how much monkeys shifted their choices towards objects associated with a higher-value food, relative to baseline choices.

Both unoperated control monkeys and monkeys that had excitotoxic VLPFC lesions could update and use the current value of food reward to guide their choices. In contrast, monkeys with excitotoxic OFC lesions chose stimuli that were associated with the sated food at a much higher rate. Various tests led unambiguously to the conclusion that this deficit in monkeys with OFC lesions arose from their inability to link objects with the current value of the food to guide their choices.

The same devaluation procedure was carried out on rhesus monkeys 20 years earlier by Málková et al. (1997), but these experiments tested whether excitotoxic lesions of the basolateral amygdala lead to an inability to shift decisions based upon current food value. Their experiments, in turn, followed up even earlier work of Hatfield et al. (1996) and Holland and Straub (1979) in rats.

The results on desirability that were reported by Rudebeck et al., (2017) were earlier predicted, and indeed simulated, by the CogEM model in 2008. In particular, my PhD student Mark Dranias and I, working with Dan Bullock, wrote the following in the caption of Figure 8 in one of our joint articles that year (Grossberg, Bullock, and Dranias, 2008) as part of our explanation of data and simulations about reaction time, choice behavior, and reward value: "Choices made between the two CSs reflect preferences between the different food rewards. Devaluation of a US by food-specific satiety (FSS) shifts the choices of the animal away from cues associated with the devalued rewards (reprinted with permission from Málková et al., 1997). Málková et al. (1997) report the effects of basolateral amygdala lesions using a difference score. The difference score is calculated by measuring the percent of the trials in which the to-be-devalued food is chosen over other foods, before and after FSS. The 'difference score' reflects the difference between these two percentages . . . Using FEF [frontal eye field] activity to determine cue choice, the intact model (CTL) shows a similar shift in CS preference when the US associated with it is devalued by FSS. Food-specific satiety is implemented by lowering selected DRIVE inputs to the LH . . . *The automatic shifting of visual cue preference when an associated US is devalued by FSS is lost after AMYG lesions (AX) and ORBl lesions (OX)*" [italics mine].

How did CogEM explain these data? In the CogEM model, devaluing food 1 reduces the drive input (Figure 13.1) that is needed to activate its value category in the amygdala, thereby reducing its ability to compete with the value category of food 2. The value category of food 2 can hereby win the competition, and release an incentive motivational signal to the OFC, which enables the OFC to choose food 2 with increased probability. Either amygdala or OFC lesions eliminate this pathway to motivated choice of food 2.

How do we learn preferences for specific foods? This explanation explains the data, but only if CogEM model embodies mechanistic answers to the following basic questions about how we choose what to eat: How are our preferences for specific foods learned and represented in our brains? How do we choose different foods in response to particular metabolic needs or taste preferences on different days, or different times during the same day? In order to explain how this happens, I need to use three model properties: (1) How the brain can learn value categories that can be selectively activated by different foods; (2) how internal drive inputs, notably satiety signals, combine with conditioned or unconditioned reinforcing sensory inputs before such sensory-drive combinations compete to determine which value category will be able to emit an incentive motivational output, leading to a food choice; and (3) how frequent viewing of a particular food can habituate its conditioned reinforcer pathway, and thus create progressively smaller inputs with which to activate its value category. When these properties break down due to an amygdala or orbitofrontal lesion, an animal loses its ability to shift its visual cue preference away from a devalued food.

MOTIVATOR: Amygdala and basal ganglia dynamics during conditioning

These three properties are mechanistically embodied within the CogEM model extension that is called the MOTIVATOR (Matching Objects To Internal Values

Triggers Option Revaluations) neural model that I published in 2008 with my PhD student Mark Dranias, and our collaborator Dan Bullock (Figure 14.3; Dranias, Grossberg, and Bullock, 2008; Grossberg, Bullock, and Dranias, 2008).

As in CogEM, the model amygdala and lateral hypothalamus in MOTIVATOR interact to calculate the expected current value of the subjective outcome that the CS predicts, constrained by the current state of deprivation or satiation. The amygdala then relays the expected value information to orbitofrontal cells (ORB in Figure 14.3) that receive visual inputs from anterior inferotemporal cells (ITA). In addition to these visual pathways, MOTIVATOR also models medial orbitofrontal cells (MORB in Figure 14.3) that receive gustatory, or taste-sensitive, inputs from rhinal cortex (RHIN). The activations of all these orbitofrontal cells code the subjective values of objects, whether they be visual or gustatory. These values guide behavioral choices.

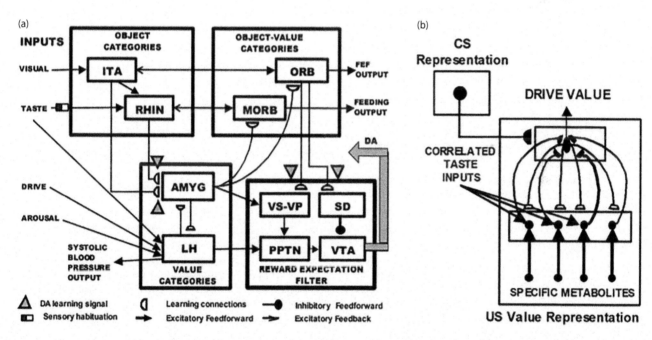

FIGURE 14.3. (a) The MOTIVATOR neural model generalizes CogEM by also including the basal ganglia. It can hereby explain and simulate complementary functions of the amygdala and basal ganglia (SNc) during conditioning and learned performance. The basal ganglia generate Now Print signals in response to *unexpected* rewards. These signals modulate learning of new associations in many brain regions. The amygdala supports motivated attention to trigger actions that are *expected* to occur in response to conditioned or unconditioned stimuli. Object Categories represent visual or gustatory inputs in anterior inferotemporal (ITA) and rhinal (RHIN) cortices, respectively. Value Categories represent the value of anticipated outcomes on the basis of hunger and satiety inputs, in amygdala (AMYG) and lateral hypothalamus (LH). Object-Value Categories resolve the value of competing perceptual stimuli in medial (MORB) and lateral (ORB) orbitofrontal cortex. The Reward Expectation Filter detects the omission or delivery of rewards using a circuit that spans ventral striatum (VS), ventral pallidum (VP), striosomal delay (SD) cells in the ventral striatum, the pedunculopontine nucleus (PPTN) and midbrain dopaminergic neurons of the substantia nigra pars compacta/ventral tegmental area (SNc/VTA). The circuit that processes CS-related visual information (ITA, AMYG, ORB) operates in parallel with a circuit that processes US-related visual and gustatory information (RHIN, AMYG, MORB). (b) Reciprocal adaptive connections between lateral hypothalamus and amygdala enable amygdala cells to become learned value categories. The bottom region represents hypothalamic cells, which receive converging taste and metabolite inputs whereby they become taste-drive cells. Bottom-up signals from activity patterns across these cells activate competing value category, or US Value Representations, in the amygdala. A winning value category learns to respond selectively to specific combinations of taste-drive activity patterns and sends adaptive top-down priming signals back to the taste-drive cells that activated it. CS-activated conditioned reinforcer signals are also associatively linked to value categories. Adaptive connections end in (approximate) hemidiscs. See the text for details.

In addition to these CogEM functions, MOTIVATOR also includes a model (Figure 14.4a) that I published in 1999 with my PhD student Joshua Brown (Brown, Bullock, and Grossberg, 1999) of how a key process in the basal ganglia works. The basal ganglia plays an important role in both the cognitive-emotional and working memory learning that are relevant to explaining PFC functions. Indeed, the amygdala and basal ganglia seem to play computationally *complementary* roles (Grossberg, 2000b), with the amygdala learning to activate incentive motivational signals with which to help acquire *expected* rewards (Figure 13.1). and the basal ganglia triggering Now Print dopaminergic learning signals in response to *unexpected* rewards (Figure 14.4). In particular, as in the CogEM model (Figures 13.1 and 13.4), sustained

feedback between sensory cortex, amygdala, and orbitofrontal cortex causes a cognitive-emotional resonance that maintains motivated attention on the orbitofrontal categories which control actions to acquire an *expected* rewarding event. In contrast, cells of the basal ganglia generate dopamine bursts or dips in response to an *unexpected* rewarding event. These bursts and dips generate widespread dopaminergic Now Print signals to facilitate learning or unlearning of currently active associations, including the conditioned reinforcer and incentive motivational associations that can sustain cognitive-emotional resonances. These learned pathways can continue to support motivated behaviors to achieve expected rewards, even after the Now Print signals end when no more unexpected rewards occur.

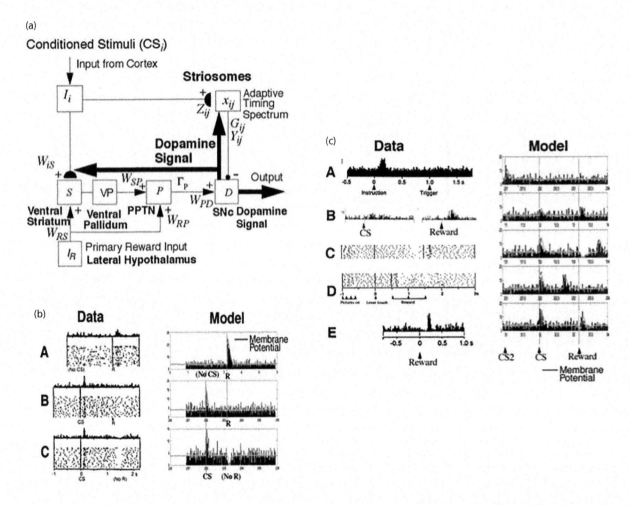

FIGURE 14.4. (a) Model basal ganglia circuit for the control of dopaminergic Now Print signals from the substantia nigra pars compacta, or SNc, in response to unexpected rewards. Cortical inputs (I_i), activated by conditioned stimuli, learn to excite the SNc via a multi-stage pathway from the ventral striatum (S) to the ventral pallidum and then on to the PPTN (P) and the SNc (D). The inputs I_i excite the ventral striatum via adaptive weights W_{iS}, and the ventral striatum excites the PPTN via double inhibition through the ventral pallidum, with strength W_{SP}. When the PPTN activity exceeds a threshold GP, it excites the SNc with strength W_{PD}. The striosomes, which contain an adaptive spectral timing mechanism (x_{ij}, G_{ij}, Y_{ij}, Z_{ij}), learn to generate adaptively timed signals that inhibit reward-related activation of the SNc. Primary reward signals (I_R) from the lateral hypothalamus both excite the PPTN directly (with strength W_{RP}) and act as training signals to the ventral striatum S (with strength W_{RS}) that trains the weights W_{iS}. Arrowheads denote excitatory pathways, circles denote inhibitory pathways, and hemidiscs denote synapses at which learning occurs. Thick pathways denote dopaminergic signals.

Such Now Print signals also play a critical role in the TELOS model, where they modulate learning of multiple eye movement skills. The five dashed arrows in Figure 12.58 designate the several brain regions, including both the basal ganglia and frontal eye fields (FEF), where these Now Print signals act.

The model basal ganglia circuit thus functions like a *reward expectation filter* (Figure 14.3) because it detects errors in CS-activated predictions of the rewards that are expected to occur, including their expected intensity and timing (Ljungberg et al., 1992; Schultz, 1998; Schultz, Apicella, and Ljungberg, 1993; Schultz et al., 1992, 1995, 1997). This predictive capability is achieved using the circuit that is summarized in Figure 14.4. Cells in the substantia nigra pars compacta, or SNc, are the ones that generate Now Print signals when an unexpected reward occurs. The ability to detect and fire in response to unexpected rewards is due to how excitatory and inhibitory signals that converge on SNc cells become imbalanced at particular times.

In particular, *excitatory* reinforcing inputs from the lateral hypothalamus go through the pedunculopontine nucleus (PPTN) to reach the SNc. The SNc also receives adaptively-timed *inhibitory* inputs from model striosomes in the ventral striatum. When a mismatch occurs between the sizes and timing of these excitatory and inhibitory signals due to the occurrence of an unexpected reward, dopaminergic burst or dip Now Print signals are broadcast from the SNc (Figure 14.4). A similar circuit exists in the ventral tegmental area (VTA in Figure 14.3). Learning in cortical and striatal regions is strongly modulated by these Now Print signals, with dopamine bursts strengthening conditioned links that are forming between currently active associations, and dopamine dips weakening them. The data and model simulations in Figure 14.4b and 14.4c will be explained as part of my analysis in Chapter 15 of how adaptively timed learning works.

Learning value categories for specific foods and effects of their removal. I can now begin to explain how our preferences for specific foods may be learned. Figure 14.3b diagrams how the MOTIVATOR model conceptualizes the learning of a value category as a result of reciprocal adaptive interactions between the lateral hypothalamus (LH) and the amygdala (AMYG). Model amygdala cells are called *value categories*, as they have been throughout the book, because they respond selectively to different patterns of activation across hypothalamic drive-selective cells via an adaptive filter. They hereby learn to categorize the patterns of homeostatic signals that occur during different emotions. These value categories also send top-down signals that obey the ART Matching Rule back to their hypothalamic sources, and thereby dynamically stabilize the learned amygdala value categories and attentionally bias homeostatic responses.

The amygdala also relays the expected value information to orbitofrontal cells (ORB in Figure 14.3a) that receive inputs from anterior inferotemporal cells, and to orbitofrontal cells (MORB in Figure 14.3a) that receive gustatory inputs from rhinal cortex. The activation of these orbitofrontal cells by conjoint inputs from object and value categories codes the subjective values of objects, and triggers cognitive-emotional resonances that support behavioral choices via output signals for the active orbitofrontal object-value categories.

Figure 14.3b summarizes how the model embodies a network that calculates the drive-modulated affective value of food unconditioned stimuli (US; Cardinal et al., 2002); notably, how selective responses to different foods can be acquired. The model proposes that, to accomplish this, a value category computes a drive-weighted sum of taste inputs that are excited during consumption of a food reward. Humans and animals have specific hungers that vary inversely with blood levels of metabolites such as sugar, salt, protein, and fat (Davidson et al., 1997). Similarly, the gustatory system has chemical sensitivities to complementary tastes such as sweet, salty, umami, and fatty (Kondoh et al., 2000; Rolls et al., 1999). An AMYG value category learns to respond to particular combinations of these metabolites and tastes in a selective fashion, hence can represent specific hungers.

MOTIVATOR begins its computation of food-specific selectivity with the lower layer of the model's cells in Figure 14.3b. These cells are proposed to occur in the LH. They perform pairwise multiplications, each involving a taste and its corresponding drive level, and are therefore called *taste-drive cells.* LH neurons such as glucose-sensitive neurons provide examples of LH cells that are both chemical- and taste-sensitive. Indeed, glucose-sensitive neurons are excited by low glucose levels, inhibited by high glucose levels, and respond to the taste of glucose with excitation (Karadi et al., 1992; Shimizu et al., 1984).

The activation pattern across *all* of these taste-drive cells implicitly represents a particular food. How does the brain convert this *distributed implicit* information into a *compact explicit* representation of that food? The answer is always the same: through one or another type of category learning. In the present instance, this activation pattern generates output signals via bottom-up pathways that converge at a higher cell layer, where they are summed within an AMYG value category cell. This AMYG value category responds selectively to the current value of the specific food US. These AMYG value category cells are therefore also called *US-value cells* in Figure 14.3b.

Such food-selective US-value representations can be learned using the usual competitive learning process (Figure 5.10; Grossberg, 1976a, 1978a) that associates distributed activation patterns at the taste-drive cells with compressed categorical representations at the US-value cells that survive the competition at the AMYG. The resulting US-value cells in the AMYG help to explain data about neurons in the AMYG that respond selectively to specific foods or associated stimuli in a manner that reflects the expected consumption value of the food (e.g. Nishijo et al., 1988a, 1988b).

Figures 14.3a and 14.3b illustrate the hypothesis that a visual CS becomes a conditioned reinforcer by learning to activate a US-value representation in the AMYG during CS-US pairing protocols. Even if the CS is not actually eaten, so generates no gustatory inputs to the taste-drive cells, the model can use this CS-US association to compute the prospective value of the US, given current drives, during the period between CS onset and the delivery of the food US. The model can do this because the CS-activated US-value representation in the AMYG can, using top-down signals back to LH, prime the taste-drive cells in the LH that have activated it in the past, when the US was being consumed.

As noted in Figures 14.3a and 14.3b, these top-down pathways are adaptive. They act like learned expectations, from US-value cells layer in the AMYG to taste-drive cells in the LH. The resultant bidirectional adaptive signaling between taste-drive LH cells and integrative US-value AMYG cells can prime the taste-value combinations that are expected in response to the conditioned reinforcer CS. In other words, the learning of AMYG value categories is carried out by a specialization of the same kind of Adaptive Resonance Theory, or ART, circuitry that is used to stabilize learned categorical memories throughout the brain (Figures 5.13 and 5.19). Without top-down expectations to dynamically stabilize the learning of value categories, memory instability could become as great a problem in LH-AMYG dynamics as it would be in the learning of invariant object categories by the inferotemporal cortex (Figure 6.3).

When the AMYG is lesioned, its value categories are eliminated, and with them the ability to selectively respond to specific foods. The reduced drive inputs of a satiated food will then not be able to cause a smaller activation of its AMYG value category. Also lost will be the competition among value categories that would determine the choice of a non-satiated food in a normal animal.

In contrast, after a food is visually presented to a normal animal in order to satiate it, then both reduced internal drive *and* external cue inputs could contribute to the choice of a non-satiated food. In particular, eating a lot of food would lead to shrinking appetitive drive inputs and growing satiety drive inputs to the LH. Seeing the food repeatedly during each eating event could also habituate the conditioned reinforcer inputs that activate the corresponding AMYG value category. This latter kind of habituation is what a dessert, with a very different combination of tastes, bypasses after the rest of a meal has been eaten.

Two mismatch-mediated mechanisms for shifting from unsuccessful behaviors. Let me immediately point out

a fact that will be important in some of my data explanations below: Not all responsiveness to reinforcing cues is eliminated by lesions of the AMYG. The basal ganglia can still be fully functional. As illustrated by Figure 14.4a, rewarding inputs from the lateral hypothalamus can still activate Now Print signals from the SNc if these inputs are not inhibited by adaptively timed signals from the striosomes. Lateral hypothalamic inputs can also regulate learning in CS-activated pathways to the ventral striatum that can subsequently also trigger Now Print signals in response to unexpected rewards. These Now Print signals are broadcast to large parts of the brain, including the PFC. I will explain below how these Now Print signals can support learning of PFC working memory representations that are sensitive to the probability of reward over a series of previous trials.

The basal ganglia circuit in the SNc is not the only way that unexpected events are processed by the brain. I explained in Chapter 5 how unexpected events can also be computed by Adaptive Resonance Theory, or ART, circuits when sufficiently big mismatches occur between bottom-up input patterns and currently active top-down expectations of the events that are expected to occur in a given situation, based on past learning. As illustrated in Figure 5.19c, such a mismatch, or disconfirmed expectation, can trigger a burst of nonspecific arousal ("novel events are arousing"). I call it *nonspecific* arousal because it affects all category representations equally, since the orienting system *A* that triggers such an arousal burst has no information about which active categories caused the mismatch, and thus must be reset. A nonspecific arousal burst can reset whatever categories caused the mismatch, and thereby initiate a search for, and choice of, a more predictive category (Figure 5.19d). In this way, rapid switching between the categories that control ongoing behaviors can occur when they no longer cause expected outcomes.

Opponent processing by gated dipoles in object and value categories. How do brain circuits *selectively* respond to a *nonspecific* arousal burst in order to inhibit unpredictive categories and trigger a memory search? As I explained in Chapter 13, nonspecific arousal can cause *antagonistic rebounds* in gated dipole opponent processing circuits (Figures 13.33 and 13.34), and can thereby selectively reset previously active dipole cells that read out a disconfirmed expectation. Such rebounds can occur in perceptual, cognitive, and affective opponent processing circuits. I will now go beyond the analysis of gated dipoles in Chapter 13 using LH-AMYG interactions as an example, because it is these circuits that we need to understand to explain how the PFC predicts an object's desirability.

The LH-AMYG pathways in Figure 14.3 include circuits that control *opponent* emotional states. As in any gated dipole, these opponent circuits can trigger an antagonistic rebound in response to two kinds of input changes:

changes in the amount of reward or punishment, such as a sudden reduction or increase in shock level; or to an unexpected event, such as the non-occurrence of an expected shock. These rebounds can rapidly reset a currently active value category, and the amount of incentive motivation with which it was supporting an ongoing valued behavior, while simultaneously helping to choose more predictive representations with which to learn and perform the new environmental contingency.

MOTIVATOR gated dipoles have been used to simulate neurophysiological data from hypothalamic "opposite cells", including their opponent and rebound properties (Nakamura and Ono, 1986; Ono et al., 1986; Nakamura et al., 1987). The hypothalamic ON and OFF channels within MOTIVATOR dipoles deliver inputs to the amygdala which, in turn, provides incentive motivational signals to object-value categories in the OFC, and thereby influences what actions are taken to achieve valued goals. Animals with an intact AMYG and OFC can use such hypothalamic rebounds to flexibly choose value and object-value categories that can track changing reinforcement contingencies. MOTIVATOR value categories also explain neurophysiological data showing that the primate amygdala contains separate cell populations that respond to positively and negatively valued visual stimuli (Paton et al., 2006), can carry out moment-by-moment tracking of state value (Belova, Paton, and Salzman, 2008; Morrison and Salzman, 2010), and are modulated by unexpected events (Belova et al., 2007).

Affective antagonistic rebounds and reversal learning. Also noted in Chapter 13 is how either a sudden reduction of a fearful shock, or the non-occurrence of an expected shock, can cause a rebound of *relief*, whereas the unexpected non-occurrence of food can cause a rebound of *frustration*. These antagonistic rebounds enable the brain to quickly adapt to changing reinforcement contingencies. For example, if the sudden reduction of a fearful shock is due to a successful escape behavior, then the relief rebound can trigger new conditioned reinforcer learning and incentive motivational learning, using relief to motivate that escape behavior in the future. In the opposite direction, the frustrative rebound that occurs after expected food does not occur can drive forgetting, or extinction, of motivational support for the consummatory actions that no longer lead to food, thereby releasing exploratory behaviors to search for more productive sources of food.

Using the same mechanisms, the unexpected change in reinforcer amplitude in an unblocking experiment (Figure 1.10), or an unexpected change in reward schedule in a reversal experiment, can cause antagonistic rebounds that immediately modify the net incentive motivation that is controlling ongoing behavior, while also triggering rapid relearning of the conditioned reinforcer and incentive motivational pathways that will control subsequent motivated choices. These events can also help reversal learning to occur in circuits that do not involve AMYG and OFC, for example via Now Print bursts and dips from the SNc in response to unexpected rewards.

Working memory, chunking, and reinforcement in prefrontal cortex and related areas

VLPFC lesions cause a deficit in learning probabilistic stimulus-outcome associations. Reinforcement learning also plays a role in explaining how the VLPFC encodes the availability, rather than the desirability, of outcomes. It does so through interactions with prefrontal working memories. In order to arrive at their conclusions about availability, Rudebeck et al. (2017) did experiments in which excitotoxic lesions of the VLPFC led to a profound deficit in the ability of lesioned monkeys to learn probabilistic stimulus-outcome associations. Their Experiment 1 first tested the ability to update likelihood estimates for predicted outcomes. They did this by training a group of unoperated control monkeys and a group of monkeys with excitotoxic OFC neurons to perform a three-choice probabilistic learning task. Four of the unoperated control monkeys completed postoperative testing before they also received excitotoxic VLPFC lesions. This procedure enabled monkeys with OFC lesions to be compared with controls, whereas monkeys with VLPFC lesions were compared with their own preoperative performances.

Each training session consisted of 300 trials on which monkeys were presented with three novel stimuli on a touch screen monitor. Monkeys sampled different stimuli over trials to learn which stimulus was associated with the highest probability of reward. Reward delivery was based on one of four different reinforcement schedules.

They found out in this way that unoperated controls and monkeys with OFC lesions quickly learned what image predicted the highest probability of reward, and could track the predictive image as it changed with the reward schedule on each session. In contrast, the VLPFC-lesioned monkeys were severely impaired on this task, except with the schedule wherein one option had a very high probability of reward compared to the others. Thus the deficit is greatest when the probabilistic difference between the options is small. Unlike unoperated controls and OFC-lesioned animals, VLPFC-lesioned animals were more likely to change their choices between trials than they were before their lesions. In particular, they were more likely to switch choices after a rewarded choice than were controls or OFC-lesioned monkeys.

Rudebeck et al. (2017) traced these effects to a reduced effect of the longer-term effects of reward history. Such longer-term effects are sometimes called *contingent learning*. To demonstrate this effect, choices on the five preceding trials were included in their data analysis. In monkeys with VLPFC lesions, associations between previous choices and the outcomes that contingently followed had essentially no influence on subsequent choices, except when one option consistently had a very high probability of reward. In this last condition, monitoring which previous sequences of stimuli predicted higher reward is not essential to doing the task.

Some classical data about sequential dependencies influencing future choices. The experiments of Rudebeck et al. (2017) contribute to a long history of experiments in psychology and psychobiology that have studied how probabilistic choices are determined by previous sequences of events. Data of this kind are often attributed to the short-term storage of sequences of events in working memory, as described in Chapter 12, and the influence of these stored sequences on current choices.

Studies that are relevant to the Rudebeck et al. (2017) work include the discovery that pupil dilation increases with the number of items that are stored in working memory; e.g., Kahneman and Beatty (1966) and Unsworth and Robison (2015). Oddball experiments also activate working memory. In an oddball paradigm (Banquet and Grossberg, 1987; Squires, Squires, and Hillyard, 1975), a subject receives a series of two types of stimulus in random order. The frequent stimulus typically serves as a distractor, and the rare stimulus serves as the target for which the subject is searching. There are also often unsignalled switches in the probabilities of these stimuli. The subject has to perform a task such as releasing a motor response to each target stimulus, or counting target stimuli. Various measures indicate that a subject tracks the probabilistic sequential dependencies of distractor and target stimuli. These include the P300 event-related potential (Picton, 1992; Sutton et al., 1965), also called the P3b, whose amplitude tends to vary inversely with stimulus probability (Duncan-Johnson and Donchin, 1977; Tueting, Sutton, and Zubin, 1970), so that rarer stimuli elicit larger P3b potentials. In a similar way, longer sequences of distractors elicit larger P300s (Remington, 1969; Squires et al., 1976), and P300 is amplified by practice as an expectation of sequence structure is learned (Banquet and Grossberg, 1987).

The issue of learning reminds us that, after an object or event sequence is stored in working memory, it can activate a bottom-up adaptive filter. Learning by the adaptive weights, or long-term memory (LTM) traces, in such an adaptive filter enables a category to be chosen that responds selectively to that sequence. Such a category is analogous to an object category or a value category, but it codes sequences, or lists, of events rather than objects or

affective values, which is why I call it a *list category*, or alternatively a *list chunk*. I described Masking Field circuits in Chapter 12 (Figures 12.46 and 12.47) in order to explain how list chunks can code working memory sequences of variable length.

Cognitive working memory and list chunks in VLPFC. A large cognitive neuroscience experimental literature has implicated the VLPFC in working memory tasks, notably tasks that engage verbal and language working memory properties (e.g., Awh et al., 1996; Schumacher et al., 1996), as well as shared temporal sequencing properties that are dissociated from the specific stimulus type (Gelfand and Bookheimer, 2003). Nazbanou Nozari, Daniel Mirman, and Sharaon Thompson-Schill (Nozari, Mirman, and Thompson-Schill, 2016) have, for example, reviewed a large number of competences that all require such a temporal sequencing property at their core, whatever other control structures also exist in order to convert the stored sequences into behaviors.

This kind of conclusion is consistent with the proposal that I made in Chapter 12 of why so many cognitive competences may exploit a similar temporal sequencing property, notably why *all* linguistic, spatial, and motor working memories seem to exploit variations and specializations of a similar circuit design (Grossberg, 1978a, 1978b; Grossberg and Pearson, 2008; Silver et al., 2011). I find it helpful to call the kind of working memory that is found in VLPFC as a *cognitive* working memory to distinguish it from the kind of *motor* working memory in DLPFC that converts the VLPFC stored sequences into sequences that are monitored to choose and perform properly ordered and timed sequential behaviors (Petrides, Alivisatos, and Frey, 2002).

List chunks and reinforcement interact in a probabilistic choice environment. In order to discuss the proposal that VLPFC computes target availability, a kind of interaction that was not exploited earlier in the book must be made explicit; namely, a list chunk can be amplified by learned feedback interactions from reinforcement-sensitive midbrain structures, if it has been active when reinforcement occurs. Amplification helps it to win the competition with other possible list chunks. For example, area 12o of macaque monkeys interacts with the lateral hypothalamus (Öngür, An, and Price, 1998), and this area was spared in the excitotoxic OFC lesions of Rudebeck et al. (2017). Interactions with perirhinal cortex may also play a role (Petrides and Pandya, 2002). I will discuss the importance of both perirhinal cortex and parahippocampal cortex in making probabilistic choices below. The winning list chunk can then be preferentially associated with a rewarded stimulus by the Now Print signals that are emitted by SNc when this stimulus unexpectedly occurs (Figures 14.3 and 14.4). In this way, list chunks that are active when the most rewards occur will be favored to win the competition and to determine future choices. On later trials, this list chunk can then be used to prime, and thus help to choose, the next stimulus to be attended and chosen.

On the other hand, when a winning list chunk no longer best represents the correct choice, then a choice of an unexpectedly unrewarded stimulus can cause hypothalamic rebounds that can begin to extinguish its motivational support (Figure 13.33). Likewise, SNc-mediated dopaminergic dips, when a chosen stimulus is unexpectedly non-rewarded, can begin to weaken the association between the list chunk and its learned prime. These positive and negative events are cumulative across learning and performance trials, thereby shifting the list chunk that has the most support, and thus the animal's choices.

In all, when a list chunk influences future choices based on past event sequences and their reinforcement history, it may be said to function as a cognitive plan.

Using these mechanisms, working memory representations and their list chunks in the VLPFC can be amplified by reinforcing events, even if the AMYG and OFC are excitotoxically lesioned. Then animals with AMYG or OFC lesions can compute the availability of a valued outcome, even if they can no longer estimate the desirability of such an outcome.

Different probabilistic reinforcement schedules require that an animal or human be sensitive to, and thus store in working memory, different numbers of preceding rewarded and unrewarded choices. Choosing among lower reinforcement probabilities requires sensitivity to longer preceding sequences, other things being equal. This is where the ability of a Masking Field to code list chunks of variable length sequences in working memory comes in (Figures 12.46 and 12.47). The winning list chunk will have the best combination of cognitive and reinforcement constraints. When reinforcement is increased, and in the limit rewards every choice of a particular image, then tracking previous sequences of choices is no longer needed to make a correct choice on the next trial. This sort of consideration clarifies why a VLPFC working memory is not needed to adapt to a (nearly) deterministic reinforcement schedule.

DLPFC credit assignment by selective and sustained working memory storage. A property of working memory that was not studied in Chapter 12, but that is important for efficient decision-making and planning, is that PFC storage is *selective*. It may be prevented on tasks that do not require storage of visual information, as illustrated by data demonstrating that PFC working memory cells do not fire during such tasks (Fuster, 1973; Kojima and Goldman-Rakic, 1984). Such active gating is also consistent with the observation that, in response to the presentation of identical stimuli, neural selectivity in PFC depends on subsequent task demands (Warden and Miller, 2010). Edward Awh and Edward Vogel (Awh and Vogel,

2008) furthermore noted, using imaging data of McNab and Klingberg (2008), that success on working memory tasks was associated with an individual's ability to selectively identify and store task-related stimuli from a larger sequence of stimuli.

Yoshiaki Tsushima, Aaron Seitz, and Takeo Watanabe (Tsushima, Seitz and Watanabe, 2008) showed that subliminal distracters can damage performance in attention tasks, but that making distracters suprathreshold can alleviate performance deficits, perhaps by facilitating the ability to filter them out. Mototaka Suzuki and Jacqueline Gottlieb (Suzuki and Gottlieb, 2013) showed similarly that, during a memory saccade task (Figure 12.59b) in which a salient distractor was flashed at a variable time and position during the memory delay, responses to the salient distractor were more strongly suppressed and more closely correlated with performance in DLPFC than in LIP. The brain may hereby learn to "blacklist" distracting stimuli before they can be stored in PFC, while allowing all other information to be stored. This ability to select relevant stimuli, when combined with the sustained storage of selected stimuli during the delay period, qualitatively embodies a solution of the structural and temporal credit assignment problem that the DLPFC has been proposed to solve (Assad et al., 2017).

Two processes regulate whether items will be stored in working memory. It is now possible to distinguish two distinct processes that can influence what items will be stored in working memory, even after all earlier preprocessing has taken place. The first process, as noted above, carries out task-sensitive filtering of individual items *before* they reach the working memory. This process selects only those items for storage whose feature combinations are compatible with task requirements; for example, only red objects from a sequence of objects with various colors (cf., Egeth, Virzi, and Garbart, 1984; Grossberg, Mingolla, and Ross, 1994; Treisman and Gelade, 1986; Wolfe, Cave, and Franzel, 1989) How this filtering process works will be discussed below. Along the way, I will provide a mechanistic explanation of proposed roles of the ventral bank of the principal sulcus, or VPS, and the ventral prearcuate gyrus, or VPA, in enabling monkeys to attend and foveate objects that possess task-relevant feature combinations (Bichot et al., 2015), and the related role of the inferior frontal junction, or IFJ, in humans (Baldauf and Desimone, 2014).

The second process enables all the items that get through the filter to be stored *after* they reach the working memory. This corresponds to keeping a basal ganglia gate open during list storage. This process can also rapidly reset, or delete, the entire stored sequence from working memory when there is an attention shift to do a different task. This latter event corresponds to closing the gate. As noted above, this kind of gating is carried out by the SNr, as illustrated by the TELOS (Figure 12.58) and lisTELOS (Figure 12.57) models.

Visual search: Efficient vs. inefficient, bottom-up vs. top-down.

Before decisions can be made about what objects or events are stored in working memory, they must first be discovered in the world. This is accomplished through one or another kind of visual search. Visual attention and eye movements can explore scenes without any goals in mind. Just as often, however, visual searches seek out valued goal objects that are embedded in complex scenes. Common examples include finding a friend in a crowd or locating a menu board in a fast food restaurant.

Neurophysiological data from monkeys that illustrate this distinction have been collected by Tim Buschman and Earl Miller by simultaneously recording from multiple electrodes in the parietal and prefrontal cortices (Buschman and Miller, 2007). Their work was briefly mentioned before during the discussion of the TELOS model, and how a parietal-prefrontal resonance can signal when a choice has been made of a target position. Here I will describe their experiments more fully in order to explain concepts about visual search. In particular, the Buschman and Miller experiments used simple stimulus materials to distinguish bottom-up vs. top-down processes of attentional control whereby to search a scene.

The distinction between a fast automatic bottom-up sweep of activation vs. a slower controlled top-down flow of activation has been described in many publications (e.g., Desimone and Duncan, 1995; Grossberg, Mingolla, and Ross, 1994; Hochstein and Ahissar, 2002; Sarter, Givens, and Bruno, 2001; Treisman and Gelade, 1980). In all conditions of the Buschman and Miller (2007) experiments, a target was randomly located in an array of four stimuli. In the bottom-up, or *pop-out*, condition, the distractors were identical and differed from the target along the dimensions of color and orientation. In this case, the target's salience automatically drew attention to it. In the top-down, or *search*, condition, each distractor differed independently from the target, and the target matched some of the distractors in each dimension. Memory of the target, rather than its salience, had to be used to find it. These two possibilities are illustrated by the search for the tilted green bar in each of the two images with four tilted bars in Figure 14.5 after it was presented for a second in the Sample interval.

In the pop-out condition, LIP neurons in the PPC were activated first, followed by neurons in the FEF and DLPFC. This kind of search thus proceeded in a primarily bottom-up way. In the search condition, the reverse order of activation

was observed, and with a longer latency. Here, search proceeded top-down from prefrontal to lower cortical areas.

In the classical visual search literature, pop-out searches were often called *efficient* searches. These searches typically yielded flat slopes of reaction time (RT) as a function of the number of distractors. The term "pop-out" search indicates that the distractors did not have to be searched before the target was identified. The Buschman and Miller (2007) search task illustrates an *inefficient* search, which in the classical search literature often used targets that are described by a conjunction of features. During an inefficient search, RT increased with the number of distractors (e.g., Treisman and Gelade, 1980).

Albeit suggestive, the dichotomy of efficient versus inefficient search based on RT slopes was later shown to be inadequate by several investigators (e.g., Thornton and Gilden, 2007; Townsend, 1972) because a continuum of flat to steep slopes can be obtained by varying how salient the targets were with respect for the distractors (Wolfe, 1998; Wolfe, Cave, and Franzel, 1989). For example, search efficiency increases with decreased similarity of targets to distractors and increased similarity between distractors (Duncan and Humphreys, 1989). By proper choice of stimuli, a conjunction search can be rendered efficient, and a feature search can be rendered inefficient, all depending on the degree to which a target can be distinguished from distractors.

Before the eyes move to search a scene, its gist can be rapidly identified (e.g., coast, forest, mountain, countryside; Oliva and Torralba, 2001) if the scene contains enough familiar elements. The gist of natural scenes was learned as a large-scale, or coarse, texture category in the model IT cortex of the ARTSCENE model that I developed with my PhD student Tsung-Ren (Tren) Huang (Figure 14.6; Grossberg and Huang, 2009). This category learning process used supervised learning with the usual ARTMAP kind of circuitry (Figure 5.31). Scene identity could then be

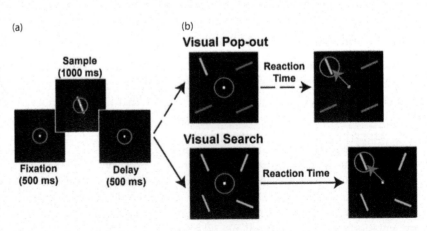

FIGURE 14.5. Displays used by Buschman and Miller (2007) in their visual search experiments. See the text for details.

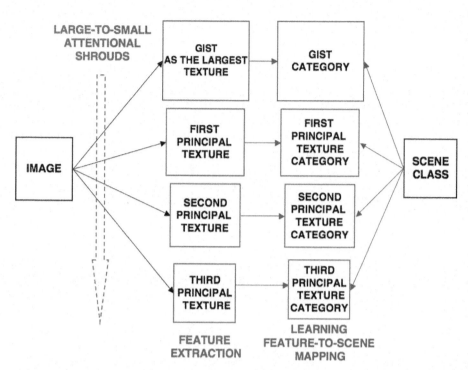

FIGURE 14.6. Classification of scenic properties as texture categories by the ARTSCENE model. See the text for details.

more complex preprocessing that is not biologically plausible.

Object and spatial contexts and reinforcement influence predictive choices. The computation of gist does not require the working memory properties of PFC. Computing gist just begins the process whereby human observers deploy visual attention using attention shifts and eye movements in a global-to-local and coarse-to-fine manner (Navon, 1977; Schyns and Oliva, 1994), thereby accumulating evidence about a scene, including where a target lies within it (Gold and Shadlen, 2007; Grossberg and Pilly, 2008; Heekeren, Marrett, and Ungerleider, 2008; Irwin, 1991; Jonides, Irwin, and Yantis, 1982). As part of this evidence accumulation process, object and spatial *contexts* provide important information that enables PFC working memories and list chunks to carry out more effective visual searches. As evidence accumulation continues, sequences of objects and their spatial positions may be attended, not just

refined by assuming that the eyes randomly looked across the scene, thereby landing in the largest textured regions with highest probability. It was assumed that an attentional spotlight at the position where the eyes landed used top-down excitatory signalling to the attended surface (Figure 6.7) to form an attentional shroud that covered this region (Figure 6.2). Then a finer texture category could be learned of that attended region. This was done for three regions in order to illustrate the search process. Then, recognition performance was determined by letting all the learned texture categories *vote* for the best scenic label (Figure 14.7). At the time ARTSCENE was published, it reduced the error rate of popular alternative scene classification models by 16.15%, even though these models typically used much

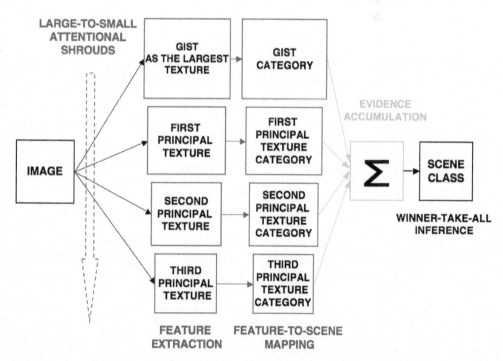

FIGURE 14.7. Voting in the ARTSCENE model achieves even better predictions of scene type. See the text for details.

individual ones. For example, when looking for a friend in a beach picture, our eyes typically fixate the sand at the bottom of the scene before the sky at its top.

Such knowledge about the spatial layout of a scene is called *spatial contextual cueing* (e.g., Chun and Jiang, 1998). Spatial contextual information is not, however, always available in a novel environment. For example, when searching for a beverage in a friend's refrigerator for the first time, we may not even know where the kitchen is located in the house until we glimpse related objects such as a stove and a sink. In this situation, we may have prior knowledge about which objects may be correlated in a scene like a kitchen, so continue to move towards the room where the stove and sink were glimpsed. However, we may not know the position where the refrigerator is located in this particular kitchen. This is an example of *object contextual cueing* (e.g., Chun and Jiang, 1999). The Chun in both of the above references is Marvin Chun of Yale University, who is a leader of contextual cueing research.

Many psychological experiments have described how humans accumulate evidence of spatial and object contexts with which to efficiently search scenes. Such contextual cueing effects are typically measured using the reaction time, or RT, for visually searching a familiar scene, subtracted from the RT for more slowly searching a novel scene, as described more fully below. These data have inspired the development of many visual search models (e.g., Backhaus, Heinke, and Humphreys, 2005; Brady and Chun, 2007; Grossberg, Mingolla, and Ross, 1994; Itti and Koch, 2000; Torralba et al., 2006; Treisman and Gelade, 1980; Wolfe, 1994). My *Psychological Review* article in 2010 with Tren Huang (Huang and Grossberg, 2010) reviews many facts about how search materials are chosen and how different search models differ.

In general, these models typically try to explain where eye movements fixate to discover targets, and how fixated non-targets lead to the next eye movement. I worked with Tren to go beyond this kind of analysis. We developed the ARTSCENE Search neural model (Figure 14.8; Huang and Grossberg, 2010) to propose, in addition, how an eye fixation on an object triggers learning about both the object's identity and its position, while also matching learned top-down expectations against the object and its position to determine whether it is a target or non-target. Sequences of such

scanning eye movements also lead to storage of sequences of object and positional representations.

These *object and spatial contexts* are associated through learning with currently fixated objects as the search continues. The learned associative strength is commensurate with the co-occurrence frequency of the contextual information and the target, and the attentional valence of both the search target/position and a context object/position. Attentional valence is defined as the degree to which an object attracts attention in response to both bottom-up and top-down factors. In this way, each eye movement also helps to *accumulate learned contextual evidence about object and spatial sequential contexts* that can be used to determine where to look next to most efficiently find the target.

Perirhinal and parahippocampal cortices store object and spatial contexts. What brain regions carry out these contextual processes? Not surprisingly, sequences of scanned objects and their spatial positions are proposed to be stored in object and spatial working memories within the model VLPFC and DLPFC, respectively. In addition, however, sequences of fixated objects and their spatial positions are also stored in the model perirhinal cortex (PRC) and parahippocampal cortex (PHC), respectively (Figure

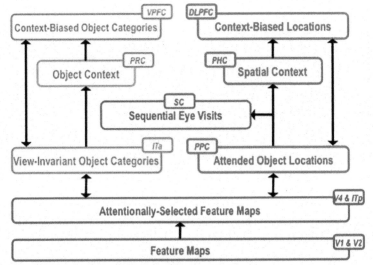

FIGURE 14.8. Macrocircuit of the ARTSCENE Search neural model for learning to search for desired objects by using the sequences of already experienced objects and their locations to predict what and where the desired object is. V1 = First visual area or primary visual cortex; V2 = Second visual area; V4 = Fourth visual area; PPC = Posterior parietal cortex; ITp = Posterior inferotemporal cortex; ITa = Anterior inferotemporal cortex; MTL = Medial temporal lobe; PHC = Parahippocampal cortex; PRC = Perirhinal cortex; PFC = Prefrontal cortex; DLPFC = Dorsolateral PFC; VPFC = Ventral PFC; SC = Superior colliculus.

14.2). Stored PRC and PHC sequences define object and spatial contexts that interact with the VLPFC and DLPFC working memories via bottom-up adaptive filters. The proposed role of PRC and related cortical areas in defining object contexts, and of PHC and related cortical areas in defining spatial contexts, is consistent with neuroimaging data about the dissociation of item and context information by these regions in humans (Aminoff, Gronau, and Bar, 2007; Diana, Yonelinas, and Ranganath, 2007; Libby, Hannula, and Ranganath, 2014).

Learning occurs in the ARTSCENE Search model from a stored object or position in PRC or PHC, respectively, to a stored object or position in VLPFC or DLPFC, respectively. This learning is modulated by a dopamine burst from the model basal ganglia (Figures 14.3 and 14.4) when a target is foveated and reinforced. In this way, predictively successful associations between PRC and VLPFC,

and between PHC and DLPFC (Figure 14.2), can amplify the stored working memory item chunks and list chunks that led to predictive success. The spatial attentional focus can be broadened or narrowed, as task constraints demand, to determine what objects or positions will influence the winning prediction. By modeling these processes, ARTSCENE Search quantitatively simulated key psychophysical data from experiments on contextual cueing, including spatial and object cueing, positive and negative spatial cueing, and local and distant cueing effects (e.g., Brockmole, Castelhano, and Henderson, 2006; Brockmole and Henderson, 2006; Chun, 2000; Chun and Jiang, 1998; Jiang and Wagner, 2004; Lleras and von Mühlenen, 2004; Olson and Chun, 2002). I will summarize here some of these computer simulations in Figure 14.9.

Model interactions of IT, PRC, and VLPFC may also clarify neurophysiological data from monkeys that are

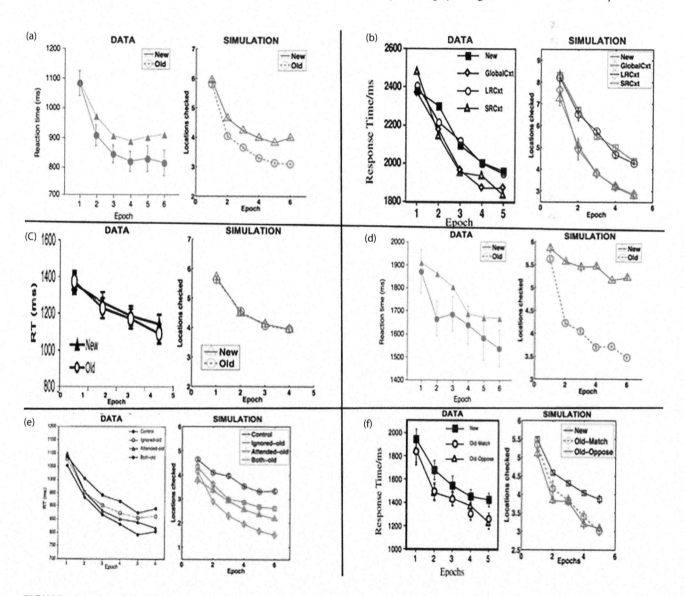

FIGURE 14.9. Search data and ARTSCENE Search simulations of them in each pair of images from (A) to (F). See the text for details.

recorded when they learn, using a delayed match-to-category paradigm, to categorize morphs of image exemplars into two categories; e.g., cats vs. dogs (Cromer, Roy, and Miller, 2010; Freedman et al., 2001, 2003). To carry out this task, monkeys were required to release a lever if two stimuli that were separated by a one second delay were from the same category. Thus a monkey's responses (release or hold) indicated whether there was a match or mismatch between the two stimuli. This procedure allowed the investigators to attribute any neuronal signals that were related to the category of a stimulus to a category learning process, because the behavioral responses of the monkeys did not differentiate between categories. Supervised learning was needed if only because exemplars that are close to the category boundary, but on opposite sides of it, could be visually more similar than stimuli that belonged to the same category; e.g., a cheetah and a housecat.

Contextual cueing using sequences of image exemplars, and of a category-predicting discriminative stimulus in cases where it is also presented, can help to explain these data. In particular, it was found that IT seems to have properties consistent with ART mechanisms of ITp-ITa category learning (Figure 6.3), notably attention to critical features of each exemplar (Figure 1.25), whereas VLPFC seems to have properties consistent with ITa-PRC-VLPFC contextually cued learning (Figure 14.2), notably sustained activity during the delay period before reward, and greater match/mismatch effects. These studies did not, however, record from PRC, or interactions between PRC and VLPFC. Such additional measures are much to be desired.

RTs in behavioral data and simulations about object and spatial searches. As I noted above, in addition to clarifying distinct neurophysiological properties of IT and PFC, ARTSCENE Search quantitatively simulates the much larger psychophysical database about subjects' reaction times, or RT, during positive and negative, spatial and object, and local and distant contextual cueing effects during visual search. Figure 14.9. summarizes six of the many experimental conditions about contextual cueing that ARTSCENE Search has successfully simulated. Each panel in the figure depicts RT data (left) and a computer simulation of it (right). These various data, and their explanations, lead to expectations about what to measure using neurophysiological methods to more deeply probe the brain mechanisms that underlie more complex searches.

Figure 14.9a summarizes RT data and a simulation of positive spatial cueing. Positive spatial cueing effects are the RT reductions for search in a familiar spatial context compared to a new context. In this paradigm, which is due to Marvin Chun and Yuhong Jiang (Chun and Jiang, 1998), a fixed target position was chosen without replacement from a grid search display, and presented in one trial

per block. Across blocks of search trials, a target position was accompanied by either a repeated spatial configuration of distractors (Old condition) throughout the entire experiment, or by a random configuration that was newly generated in each block (New condition). In Figure 14.9a (left panel), the x-axis represents search epochs grouped from blocks of trials, and the y-axis represents search RT for completing a trial. The upper and lower curves in each panel of this figure correspond, respectively, to the New and Old spatial context condition. The separation between these two curves indicates the amount of contextual facilitation in search RT that derives from a regular spatial context. Notice that the RT in the New spatial context condition dropped across epochs, and a further RT reduction in the Old spatial condition also developed as the session progressed.

ARTSCENE Search replicates spatial cueing effects through learning of pairwise associations between a context position and a target position. Specifically, when a search display is presented, the layout of search items forms a spatial scene gist, which activates model PPC and, from there, both DLPFC and PHC as the eyes search a scene. Each context position that is stored in PHC learns to vote for its correlated target positions that are stored in DLPFC (Figure 14.2). These associations collectively build up a spatial representation in DLPFC about the likelihood of seeing a target at each position. Top-down feedback from DLPFC then biases attention and eye movements toward possible target positions given the current scene layout. Where this feedback acts in the brain will be discussed below. As evidence accumulates through time, an eye-scan path becomes more target-based rather than saliency-based. Accordingly, the probability of fixations on salient distractors is reduced, reflected as spatial cueing effects.

Why does the New curve also decrease with increased training? This happens because the strongest pairwise associations learned by the model are typically from a target position to itself due to its perfect self-correlation. Unlike positions where a target never occurs, a target position itself, once it re-appears in a search trial, signifies target presence and strongly attracts overt attention. Therefore, search RT can still decrease during the course of training, even if a target position is presented in combination with a new context.

The five other panels in Figure 14.9 depict other spatial contextual cueing (Figures 14.9b and 14.9c) and object contextual cueing (Figures 14.9d-f) paradigms that the model successfully simulates. The object contextual cueing results depend upon model interactions between the model's IT, VLPFC, and PRC regions (Figure 14.2). These and other successful simulations of the model strongly support its proposed mechanisms. It should, however, be noted that the simulations compute the decreasing number of eye fixations in the New and Old conditions, rather than absolute RTs. By assigning an RT to each fixation duration, a fit to RTs can also be achieved. However, that would still leave open the question about whether each of these fixation steps takes that amount of time in associated brain regions. Such a mixed experimental and modeling study remains to be done.

Where-to-What and What-to-Where interactions learn and search for objects. The ability to carry out a search for a desired object calls attention to a major design problem that sufficiently advanced brains have solved. The What cortical stream learns recognition categories that tend to be increasingly independent of object view, size, and position at higher cortical levels, with ITa cells, among others in the temporal cortex, exhibiting such invariance (Bar et al., 2001; Sigala and Logothetis, 2002; Tanaka et al., 1991). The cortical magnification factor (Figure 6.10) does, however, limit the degree of positional invariance, as reflected by the neurophysiologically-recorded tradeoff between object selectivity and position tolerance in ITa cells (Zoccolan et al., 2007). These data and their simulation using ART have been reviewed in the text around Figure 6.21.

Invariant recognition categories avoid a combinatorial explosion in the number of categories that are needed to represent an object when it interacts with other brain processes, such as processes of reinforcement learning (Figure 13.1) and working memory storage (Figure 12.43). In particular, an invariant object category in ITa may be attended with higher probability if it receives motivated attention via the kind of ITa-AMYG-OFC cognitive-emotional resonance that is simulated by the CogEM model (Figures 13.2 and 13.4) and its extension in the START and nSTART models (Figure 5.37) that I will describe more fully in Chapter 15 as part of my exposition of how adaptively timed learning works.

In becoming positionally invariant, however, ITa recognition categories lose information about the positions in space of the objects that they represent. The Where stream represents target positions and controls actions aimed at acquiring them, but does not represent featural properties of the objects themselves. As I noted in Chapter 1, these What and Where stream properties are computationally complementary (Table 1.2; Grossberg, 2000b, 2013a). Interactions between the What stream and the Where stream overcome these complementary computational deficiencies. By using What-to-Where interactions, invariant object categories in the What stream can use Where stream spatial representations to control actions towards desired goals in space. I propose how this may happen in the next section.

What working memory filtering and activation of Where target positions. After Where-to-What stream interactions help to learn an invariant object category (Figure

6.14-6.16), What-to-Where stream interactions regulate how to foveate the object in a scene. Both the ARTSCAN Search and ARTSCENE Search models proposed a *minimal anatomy* that could carry out this function, while also simulating challenging RT data, such as the data summarized in Figure 14.9, about visual search.

This minimal anatomy proposes how an invariant object representation in the What stream can activate a positional representation in the Where stream that can be used to foveate the object in a scene. However, this proposal did not try to solve the problem of how the brain can *selectively* filter desired targets from a stream that also contains distractors, so that it only attends, stores, and foveates *matched* targets.

Instead, in the minimal anatomy of ARTSCENE Search (Figure 6.4), winning VLPFC activities send a top-down attentional prime to ITa. An open SNr gate lets the primed ITa cells fire. These ITa cells can then prime the positionally-sensitive categories in ITp with which they were associated when ITa was being learned using resonant bottom-up and top-down interactions (Figure 6.3). If one of the primed ITp categories also receives a bottom-up input from an object at its position, then it can fire and activate positional representations in regions like LIP and FEF. These positional representations can move the eyes to the position in space that they represent.

More is needed for VLPFC to also be able to selectively filter desired targets from a stream that also contains distractors, and to enable it to selectively attend, store, and foveate matched targets. Neurophysiological data have been reported in 2015 by Narcisse Bichot, Matthew Heard, Ellen DeGennaro, and Robert Desimone (Bichot et al., 2015, p. 832) about the role of the ventral prearcuate gyrus, or VPA, as "a source for feature-based attention". I believe that these data may be understood in the light of how our brains can selectively filter desired targets from a stream that also contains distractors, so that it only attends, stores, and foveates matched targets. These functional requirements are consistent with the facts that cells in VPA selectively match desired combinations of object features, resonate with a target that matches these features, and then rapidly activate a positional representation in FEF that can command a saccade to this target. These properties were recorded in experiments where monkeys fixated on a central cue object that defined the search target, which was followed by a delay during which the monkeys held a representation of the target in memory. Then an array of eight stimuli appeared in nonfoveal positions. This array contained the search target and seven distractors. The monkeys' task was to find the target using free gaze, and then to maintain fixation on it for 800 msec in order to get a reward.

Bichot et al. (2015) did experiments in which they simultaneously recorded from IT, VPA, and FEF in two monkeys, and the VPS (ventral bank of the principal sulcus), VPA, and FEF in two other monkeys. The following summary proposes a mechanistic explanation, along with functional properties, of these cells, as part of the pART architecture (Figure 14.2), thereby extending the capabilities of the ARTSCENE Search architecture so that matched and mismatched objects are selectively processed in PFC:

1. Both ITp (also called TEO) and ITa (also called TE) project to PFC (Barbas and Pandya, 1989; Tanaka, 1996; Webster et al., 1994).

2. ITp topographically projects to VPA, whose cells exhibit significant sensitivity to extrafoveal positions (Bichot et al., 2015), as do those in ITp (Tanaka, 1996), in keeping with the idea that these positions will become targets for eye movements under the proper conditions.

3. ITa topographically projects to PRC, as in the original ARTSCENE search, and also to VPS, which in turn projects to VLPFC (Figure 14.2). As noted in Bichot et al. (2015), VPS had the largest spatial tuning curve of any of the cells that they recorded, consistent with the idea that these cells exhibit considerable position invariance, as do the ITa cells that project to them.

4. VLPFC outputs send top-down projections across VPS and VPA (Figure 14.2), where they learn modulatory top-down expectations when they are associated with the currently active VPS and VPA cells. These expectations are assumed to obey the ART Matching Rule (Figure 1.25).

5, The activity of cells in VPA that are receiving an active VLPFC-to-VPA prime are enhanced when a currently presented extrafoveal object matches target features in their receptive field, and is suppressed when such an object mismatches expected target features.

6. The enhanced VPA activity during a target match is sufficient to trigger an output signal to the FEF at the corresponding positional representation in FEF (Figure 14.2). This hypothesis is consistent with data of Bichot et al. (2015) showing VPA activating around 20 msec before FEF. FEF can then elicit a saccade to the matched target, leading to the target being foveated. By inhibiting inputs from objects that mismatch the VPA expectation, mismatched objects are not foveated.

    It should, however, also be noted that top-down search for a target is always competing with the onsets and motions of bottom-up visual signals; e.g., Figures 8.26 and 8.31. Sufficiently energetic bottom-up signals can override the top-down prime.

7. The activity of cells in VPS that are receiving an active VLPFC-to-VPS prime are enhanced when an invariant object category from ITa matches their receptive field, and are suppressed when an object mismatches it. When

a match occurs, a synchronous resonance develops that enables the category to be stored in VLPFC. This resonance propagates through multiple cortical areas, in the manner that is described in the next section, and supports a conscious percept of the object.

The mapping between VPA and FEF positions is assumed to have been learned in response to series of objects that have, in the past, activated the What and Where streams in parallel. The kind of learning that can associate corresponding VPA and FEF positions has previously been simulated in the FACADE model of 3D vision and figure-ground perception (Figure 4.44). Indeed, in cortical area V1, the boundary contours that are computed by complex cells in layer 2/3 interblobs are binocular, even though the surface contours that are computed in V1 blobs are still monocular. There are also binocular boundaries and monocular surfaces in V2 interstripes and thin stripes, respectively. The positions on the cortical maps of the binocular cells are shifted with respect to the positions of the monocular cells that code information about the same positions in space, as illustrated by Figures 4.19 and 11.27. I already discussed this process of binocular displacement, or allelotropia, in Chapter 4 when discussing the example of DaVinci stereopsis in Figure 4.49.

In order to successfully act as filling-in generators and barriers, signals between the corresponding positions of boundaries and surfaces need to be aligned, even though they are shifted relative to each other on their respective cortical maps. Such an adaptive alignment as been implicit in all my discussions of how boundaries and surfaces interact; e.g., Figures 4.45 and 4.46.

In 2002, my PhD student Seungwoo Hwang and I, along with my colleague Ennio Mingolla (Grossberg, Hwang, and Mingolla, 2002), showed how to learn such a position-specific associative map between corresponding positions in boundary and surface representations across the interblob and blob cortical streams when they were activated in parallel by a series of objects (Grossberg, Hwang, and Mingolla, 2002). We carried out this simulation in order to explain a challenging visual percept; namely, the long-term, oriented, chromatic aftereffect that is called the McCollough effect, among other percepts. The McCollough effect was discovered by Celeste McCollough in 1965 (McCollough, 1965). For example, if a person alternately looks at a red horizontal grating and a green vertical grating for a few minutes, then a black-and-white horizontal grating will look greenish and a black-and-white vertical grating will look pinkish. Watching the video https://www.youtube.com/watch?v=JOyHsu6MJKk will enable you to see this effect for yourself. The effect is remarkable because it can last several months, so clearly involves some kind of learning. My insight was that the learned mapping between boundaries and surfaces was sufficient—which naturally links boundary orientations and surface colors— when combined with other standard FACADE mechanisms. Using this learned mapping, the 3D LAMINART model succeeded in explaining and quantitatively fitting data from thirteen experiments that probe the nature of achromatic/chromatic and monocular/binocular interactions during induction of the McCollough effect.

Including map learning into 3D LAMINART is thus another example of how the Method of Minimal Anatomics can expand the explanatory and predictive range of neural models whose design principles are sufficiently correct to withstand the new challenge.

Moreover, once one sees how such position-specific associative maps can be learned in one part of the brain, the same mechanisms can learn such maps elsewhere, including the map between VPA and FEF. The rest of the explanation of how selective filtering and working memory storage works then just uses properties that I have already taught you in earlier chapters, just as the rest of the explanation of the McCollough effect just uses standard properties of the 3D LAMINART model.

Synchronization of multiple cortical regions for feature-based attention. The proposed role of VPA for "feature-based attention" should not be conflated with the "feature-based attention" that supports conscious seeing and knowing about a familiar object. In this regard, ART and ARTSCAN predicted, and thereby explained, a lot of data about how percepts of visual qualia may become conscious due to surface-shroud resonances that are triggered between V4 and PPC, before propagating both bottom-up and top-down to other cortical areas; how familiar objects may be recognized due to a feature-category resonance that is triggered between V4 and IT, before propagating both bottom-up and top-down to other cortical areas; and how an observer may consciously see and know about a familiar object when these two types of resonances synchronize (Figure 6.27).

VPA processing carries out a type of top-down "feature-based attention" in a strict mechanistic sense because its circuit seems to embody the ART Matching Rule (Figure 1.25), as do multiple stages of feature-based attention (Grossberg, 2013a, 2017b). Multiple cortical stages that compute "feature-based attention" can synchronize during a match state, as illustrated by MEG and fMRI data of Baldauf and Desimone (2014) in humans. See also Buschman and Miller (2007), Engel, Fries, and Singer (2001), Gregoriou et al. (2009), and Pollen (1999).

The LAMINART model clarifies how multiple cortical stages can synchronize; e.g., Figures 5.38, 5.48, and 10.12. The LAMINART model proposes how *all* granular neocortical areas combine bottom-up, horizontal, and top-down interactions that embody variations of the same canonical laminar cortical circuitry. Because of this shared circuitry across cortical areas, the ART Matching Rule circuit in

Figure 1.25 may be realized using a similar circuit design at multiple stages of cortical processing. For example, in Figures 5.48b and 5.48e, the top-down pathway from layer 6 in V2 projects to layer 6 in V1, which sends bottom-up signals to layer 4. These bottom-up signals are sent via a modulatory on-center (note the balanced excitatory and inhibitory pathways to layer 4) surrounded by a driving off-surround network. The top-down signals from V2 are hereby "folded" at layer 6 in V1 in order to reach layer 4. As I noted in Chapters 5 and 10, this property is called *folded feedback*.

Figures 5.48e and 10.12 illustrate how a top-down, task-selective priming signal from PFC can propagate through multiple lower cortical areas via their layers 6, which can then activate their layer 6-to-4 modulatory on-center, off-surround networks. In this way, an entire cortical hierarchy may get primed to process incoming bottom-up signals to accommodate the bias imposed by the prime. When a matched bottom-up target is received by this cortical hierarchy, multiple processing stages can rapidly go into gamma synchrony, as discussed in Chapter 5 (recall Figure 5.40 and the surrounding text), and support conscious seeing and recognition of the target.

How do we feel when we hear DOG vs. DOG EATS DOG? The above analysis of prefrontal functions clarifies how cognitive processes that are controlled by the prefrontal cortex interact with affective processes in the amygdala, basal ganglia, and related areas. We can now clearly see how, for example, in response to hearing the word "dog" one might have a positive affective response, assuming that one's experiences with dogs in the past have been happy ones, yet have quite a different affective response to a sentence like "dog eats dog" (Figure 1.24). Indeed, these different linguistic sequences will be stored by different item chunk sequences and list chunks in VLPFC, which in turn will resonate with different drive representations in the amygdala.

Concluding remarks. This chapter concludes my description of a unified theory of prefrontal cortex, the predictive ART, or pART, theory. pART explains how cognitive processes and emotional processes work together to guide our highest forms of intelligence. Core cognitive processes include the temporary storage of sequences of events and their encoding in learned plans, or list chunks, that are used to predict and act upon what will happen next. Which plans will be chosen is typically strongly influenced by emotional processes that determine how we impart value to events. Value processes include our emotions and how they motivate us to achieve desired goals or avoid undesired ones.

To achieve these familiar abilities, our brains need several prefrontal cortical areas, including OFC, VLPFC, DLPFC, VPS, VPA, and FEF. These abilities are emergent properties due to interactions among the several prefrontal regions as they interact with many other brain regions, including the amygdala, basal ganglia, cerebellum, V1, V2, V3A, V4, ITp, ITa, MT, MST, LIP, PPC, and SC. In this chapter, I have focused on functional properties such as the computation of desirability by the amygdala and availability by the VLPFC (Rudebeck et al., 2017), a solution of the credit assignment problem by the DLPFC (Assad et al., 2017), and how feature-based attention by VPS and VPA may filter expected vs. unexpected objects and direct saccadic eye movements to expected objects (Baldauf and Desimone, 2014; Bichot et al., 2015).

Many of the processes that I have explained in earlier chapters play an essential role in these explanations. These include cognitive-emotional interactions, including reinforcement learning and incentive motivational learning; object and spatial working memory dynamics; and category learning, including the learning of object categories and of cognitive plans. Several functionally distinct types of attention (prototype, surface, and motivated attention) help to dynamically stabilize these learning processes as well as to predictively prime their target representations. Prototype attention focuses upon the critical feature patterns that are attended during the feature-category resonances that support object recognition; surface attention focuses on an object surface during the surface-shroud resonances that support conscious seeing of its visual qualia; and motivated attention focuses on valued objects during conscious cognitive-emotional resonances and supports conscious feelings about them (Table 1.4).

The preceding chapters have explained in gradual stages the concepts and mechanisms that are needed to cope with the subtlety and complexity of processes like those that the prefrontal cortex carries out. These explanations are at the cutting edge of current understanding in cognitive neuroscience. I hope that some of them have excited and interested you as much as they continue to excite me to further study this fascinating part of our brains, without which many of our most human qualities would not exist.

Adaptively Timed Learning

How timed motivation regulates conscious learning and memory consolidation

How do we learn When to act and Where we are? To fully realize the CogEM model's properties as a "survival circuit", it needs to be embedded in neural systems that can direct appropriate actions towards desired goals. In particular, our brains need to be able to navigate in *space* towards these goals, and to adaptively *time* our actions to acquire them.

Each of these capabilities uses several types of brain designs that are embodied in different brain regions. For example, the ARTSCAN model that was described in Chapter 6 illustrates how the parietal cortex enables *spatial attention* to modulate invariant object category learning, so that we can recognize valued goal objects from multiple vantage points. The LIST PARSE model that was described in Chapters 12 and 14 illustrates how the prefrontal cortex can store the *temporal order* of experienced events in working memory, so that we can use our recent experiences to predict and control subsequent actions that are most likely to realize valued goals.

In addition to spatial and temporal processes like these, the entorhinal and hippocampal cortices play a critical role in representing a different type of spatial and temporal intelligence. Whereas the parietal cortex is activated by visual or auditory inputs, the entorhinal-hippocampal system also receives *path integration* inputs that are activated by an animal's movements through space. This additional source of spatial information helps animals to determine where in space they currently are. Whereas a prefrontal working memory can store the temporal order of a sequence of events, the entorhinal-hippocampal system can learn to adaptively time the performance of an individual action in response to a discriminative cue. This additional source of temporal information helps animals to respond at appropriate times. For humans, such timing is of particular importance in social situations, and its breakdown occurs in people with various mental disorders, such as autism, with negative social consequences.

Understanding these entorhinal-hippocampal capabilities will propose answers to the following basic questions: How do little nerve cells learn to represent big spatial regions, such as large rooms and open fields, so that humans and animals can successfully navigate in them? How do little nerve cells learn to bridge big time intervals of hundreds of milliseconds or even several seconds, and thereby learn to associate events that are separated in time?

This and the next chapter will clarify how the entorhinal-hippocampal system does these things, and will explain why these particular spatial and temporal representations,

Conscious MIND Resonant BRAIN. Stephen Grossberg, Oxford University Press. © Oxford University Press 2021.
DOI: 10.1093/oso/9780190070557.003.0015

unlike spatial attention and working memory, are both in a single part of the brain. I will propose that they are both in the entorhinal-hippocampal system because, remarkably, these spatial and temporal representations seem to be variations of a single brain design. This design enables large spaces to be navigated using a mechanism of *spectral spacing* whereby a "spectrum" of grid cells along a dorsoventral gradient in the medial entorhinal cortex can activate place cells in the hippocampal cortex that can represent large spaces. A variant of the same design also enables large temporal intervals to be bridged using a mechanism of *spectral timing* whereby a "spectrum" of time cells along a dorsoventral gradient in the lateral entorhinal cortex, each with different reaction rates, can learn to match the statistical distribution of expected delays in reinforcement over hundreds of milliseconds, or even seconds. Although each of the cells in such a spectrum reacts briefly at different times, their population response as a whole can bridge a much longer time interval that can be used to associate events that are separated in time.

I will also show that spectral timing in the hippocampus seems to be a variant of a brain design for adaptively timed learning that is also found in the cerebellum and basal ganglia, where it carries out different behavioral functions. Indeed, all of these circuits seem to exploit an ancient design that is found even in non-neural cells, such as HeLa cancer cells. These results suggest once again how our brains opportunistically exploit valuable evolutionary discoveries to parsimoniously carry out a broad range of adaptive behaviors.

In addition to explaining how brain regions like the hippocampus, cerebellum, and basal ganglia learn to adaptively time behaviors, and the multiple consequences for conscious cognition, emotion, and action of these processes, I will also provide more information about another function of the basal ganglia, which is to open and close gates that enable or prevent the expression of cognitive and motor processes. Chapters 12 and 14 already described some of the functions that are carried out by this gating process in the substantia nigra pars reticulata, or SNr. I will also explain some of the fascinating and clinically important functional relationships that exist between these various processes, including failures of adaptive timing in individuals with autism and Fragile X syndrome, and repetitive behaviors in individuals with autism.

After this chapter discusses adaptively timed learning and how it is supported by spectral timing, Chapter 16 will do the same thing for spatial navigation and how spectral spacing enables entorhinal grid cells and hippocampal place cells to support spatial navigation in large spaces.

Conditioning and consciousness: Trace conditioning, hippocampus, and "time cells". Early work interpreted conscious awareness as just another class of conditioned responses (Grant, 1973; Hilgard, Campbell, and Sears,

1937; Kimble, 1962; McAllister and McAllister, 1958). The inadequacy of this perspective is illustrated by the fact that a cognitive-emotional resonance needs to be sufficiently sustained in order to generate a conscious emotion (e.g., Figure 13.4), and thereby support "the feeling of what happens", attentional blocking, and many other behavioral properties of motivated behaviors. But how sustained is "sufficiently sustained"? This issue is dramatized by trace conditioning experiments in humans. Unlike the *delay conditioning* experiments that were discussed using Figures 13.5-13.13, where the CS is still on when the US turns on, during a *trace conditioning* experiment, the CS shuts off before the US turns on (Figure 15.1).

Various experimenters have used trace conditioning to describe a link between conditioning and consciousness, including a role for hippocampus in enabling conditioning to bridge the temporal gap between CS offset and a subsequent US. For example, amnesic patients with hippocampal damage learn at a normal rate during delay conditioning, but not during trace conditioning. Guided by such data, Robert Clark and Larry Squire postulated in 1998 (Clark and Squire, 1998) that normal humans acquire trace conditioning because they have intact declarative and episodic memory, where a *declarative memory* is a memory of facts and events that can be consciously recalled, and an *episodic memory* is a memory of a personal experience that occurred at a particular time and place. If indeed trace conditioning activates these memory resources, that would explain why subjects have conscious knowledge of a temporal relationship between CS and US during trace conditioning, leading the authors to write (p. 79) that "trace conditioning requires the acquisition and retention of conscious knowledge [and] would require the hippocampus and related structures to work conjointly with the neocortex".

Various other studies have also linked trace conditioning and consciousness (Gabrieli et al., 1995; McGlinchey-Berroth, Brawn, and Disterhoft, 1999;

DELAY AND TRACE CONDITIONING PARADIGMS

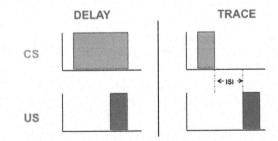

To perform an adaptively timed CR, trace conditioning requires a CS memory trace over the inter-stimulus interval (ISI)

FIGURE 15.1. The timing of CS and US inputs in the delay and trace conditioning paradigms.

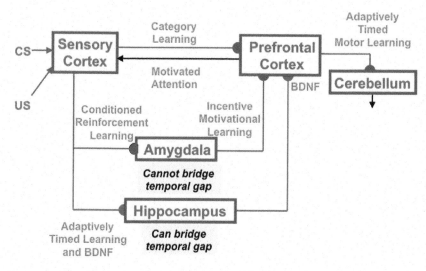

HIPPOCAMPUS CAN SUSTAIN A COGNITIVE-EMOTIONAL RESONANCE
that can support "the feeling of what happens"
and knowing what event caused that feeling

FIGURE 15.2. The neurotrophic Spectrally Timed Adaptive Resonance Theory, or nSTART, model of Franklin and Grossberg (2017) includes hippocampus to enable adaptively timed learning that can bridge a trace conditioning gap, or other temporal gap between CS and US.

McGlinchey-Berroth et al., 1997). For example, trace conditioning is facilitated by conscious awareness in normal control subjects, whereas delay conditioning is not, and amnesics with bilateral hippocampal lesions—the kind of lesion that HM had—perform at a success rate similar to unaware controls for both delay and trace conditioning (Clark, Manns, and Squire, 2001; Manns, Clark, and Squire, 2000; Papka, Ivry, and Woodruff-Pak, 1997). In these and related experiments, amnesics were found to be unaware of experimental contingencies, and poor performers on trace conditioning (Clark and Squire, 1998). An important link between adaptive timing, attention, awareness, and consciousness has hereby been experimentally established within the trace conditioning paradigm. The nSTART model that I will describe below traces the link between consciousness and conditioning to the role of hippocampus in supporting a sustained cognitive-emotional resonance (Figures 13.4 and 15.2) that underlies motivated attention, consolidation of long-term memory, core consciousness, and "the feeling of what happens" (Damasio, 1999).

The nSTART, or *neurotrophic Spectrally Timed ART*, model (Figure 15.2; Franklin and Grossberg, 2017) explains and simulates the link between conditioning and consciousness by embedding the CogEM model into a larger learning circuit that includes the hippocampus. The model hippocampus includes a circuit for adaptively timed learning using a spectral timing circuit. Spectral timing was introduced in the earlier START model that

I developed with my postdoctoral fellows John Merrill and Nestor Schmajuk (Grossberg and Schmajuk, 1989; Grossberg and Merrill, 1992, 1996). START showed how the hippocampus can bridge the temporal gap between a CS and US during a trace conditioning experiment, or indeed during any other experience where a predictive cue and its valued consequence are separated by a temporal gap.

To bridge such a temporal gap, a spectral timing circuit uses a population of cells that have differently timed responses (the "spectrum"). Although none of these cells can individually time the delay between CS and US during a trace conditioning experiment (Figure 15.3a), the population as a whole can do so (Figure 15.3c and 15.3d). The feedback loop between sensory cortex, hippocampus, and prefrontal cortex (Figure 15.2) can "sufficiently sustain" a cognitive-emotional resonance until motivated attention, core consciousness, and "the feeling of what happens" can be fully expressed. Such a sustained cognitive-emotional resonance also drives the five different kinds of learning—category

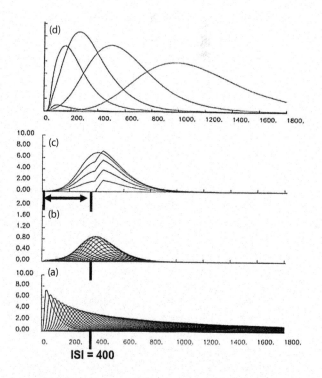

FIGURE 15.3. Stages in the processing of adaptively timed conditioning, leading to timed responses in (d) that exhibit both individual Weber laws and an Inverted U in conditioning as a function of ISI. See the text for details.

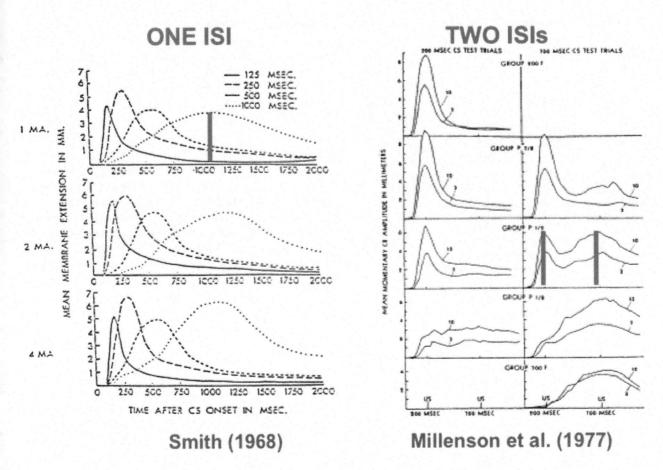

ONE ISI

Smith (1968)

TWO ISIs

Millenson et al. (1977)

Conditioned eye blinks, made with nictitating membrane and/or eyelid, are ADAPTIVELY TIMED: peak closure occurs at expected time(s) of arrival of the US following the CS and obeys a WEBER LAW

FIGURE 15.4. Conditioning data from Smith (1968) and Millenson et al. (1977). The former shows the kind of Weber law and Inverted U that were simulated in Figure 15.3. The latter shows that, if there are two ISIs during an experiment, then the animals learn to adaptively time their responses with two properly scaled Weber laws.

learning, conditioned reinforcer learning, incentive motivational learning, adaptively timed cortico-hippocampal learning, and adaptively timed motor learning—that are described in the nSTART circuit of Figure 15.2. The adaptively timed cortico-hippocampal activity also supports consolidation of these learned memories, and its failure can cause serious problems with future recall.

The existence of a hippocampal spectral timing circuit that can support learning across CS-US temporal gaps is supported by psychological data (e.g., Gibbon, 1991; Millenson, Kehoe, and Gormenzano, 1977; Smith, 1968) and neurophysiological data (e.g., Berger and Thompson, 1978; MacDonald et al., 2011). These data also exhibit the *Weber law* property that larger inter-stimulus intervals between CS and US lead to learned response curves with

broader variances. Weber law properties were reported in the classical psychological literature in a number of experimental paradigms. The conditioned eye blink paradigm was particularly useful. In Figure 15.4 (left column), the Weber law property can be seen when data from multiple experiments, each with a different interstimulus interval, or ISI, are plotted together (Smith, 1968). This property is simulated using spectral timing in Figure 15.3d. In Figure 15.4 (right column), a Weber law can be seen when two ISIs occur within the same experiment (Millenson, Kehoe, and Gormezano, 1977). Figure 15.5 shows a simulation of this double peaked response when a spectral timing circuit learns from CS-US contingencies with two different ISIs. The Weber law property is also called *scalar timing* in the classical psychological literature (Gibbon, 1977).

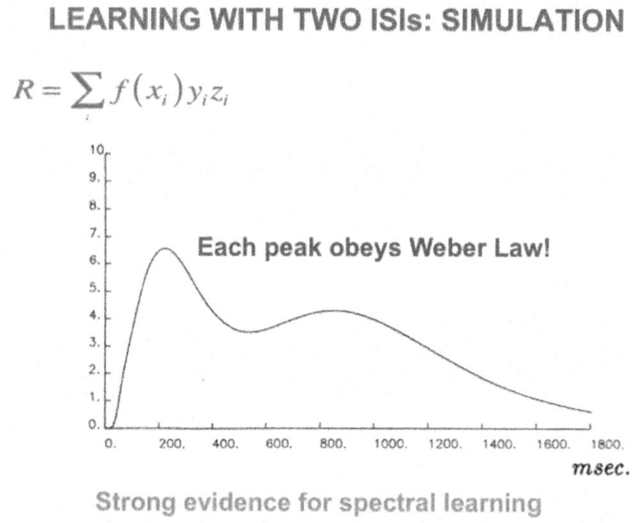

LEARNING WITH TWO ISIs: SIMULATION

$$R = \sum_i f(x_i) y_i z_i$$

Strong evidence for spectral learning

FIGURE 15.5. Simulation of conditioning with two ISIs that generate their own Weber laws, as in the data shown in Figure 15.4.

In all these data and simulations, the Weber law exhibits a property of a *population* response. The classical neurophysiological data from 1978 of Theodore Berger and Richard Thompson also, by and large, exhibited population responses. However, the simulation in Figure 15.3a also shows a Weber law property in the individual cells of the spectrum that gives rise to such a population response. The earliest direct confirmation of this prediction seems to have been published in 1992, three years after I published the first spectral timing model with Nestor. In this report, A. J. Nowak and Theodore Berger (Nowak and Berger, 1992) reported neurophysiological data showing spectra of dentate granule cells, each with its own timed response to a CS, along with "systematic changes in the gradient of entorhinal activation of dentate granule cells in a septal-temporal direction as revealed by . . . a decrease in the peak latency and an increase in the peak amplitude of somatic EPSPs", or excitatory postsynaptic potentials. This is just what our earlier computer simulation in Figure 15.3a predicted.

In addition, an earlier article of Berger, together with Stephen Berry and Richard Thompson (Berger, Berry, and Thompson, 1986) also described that dentate granule cells "increased firing . . . in the CS period . . . the latency . . . was constant". These results also suggested that there is a spectrum of dentate granule cells, each with its own preferred response delay, just as in the simulation of Figure 15.3a. How, then, does the adaptively timed population response occur? A 1978 article of Berger and Thompson (Berger and Thompson, 1978) provided some guidance when they reported an adaptively timed population response at CA3 cells of the hippocampus. Such a population response could be caused if lots of differently timed

dentate granule cells sent converging outputs to individual hippocampal CA3 cells along pathways whose strength could be changed by conditioning (Figure 15.6). The predicted effects of such a transformation can be seen by comparing Figure 15.3a, which shows the simulated activities of cells in the dentate granule cell spectrum, and Figure 15.3b, which shows the simulated outputs of these cells after they are multiplied, or gated, by LTM traces that can learn during classical conditioning experiments. If these gated outputs converge on individual CA3 cells, the resulting CA3 cell activation would look like the adaptively timed response in the simulation shown in Figure 15.3c, which it does. Figure 15.3c also shows the development of an adaptively timed response during four conditioning trials, followed by a single recall trial.

More recent neurophysiological experiments have provided additional evidence for these theoretical and neurophysiological results. In particular, in 2011, Christopher MacDonald, Kyle Lepage, Uri Eden, and Howard Eichenbaum (MacDonald et al., 2011) reported data about a population of hippocampal cells that they call "time cells". These cells have all of the predicted properties of a spectral timing circuit, notably the Weber law property. Indeed, MacDonald et al. (2011) write: " . . . the mean peak firing rate for each time cell occurred at sequential moments, and the overlap among firing periods from even these small ensembles of time cells bridges the entire delay. Notably, the spread of the firing period for each neuron increased with the peak firing time . . ." (p. 3). Their "small ensembles of time cells" are the cells in the spectrum, and the "spread of the firing period . . . increased with the peak firing time" is the Weber law property.

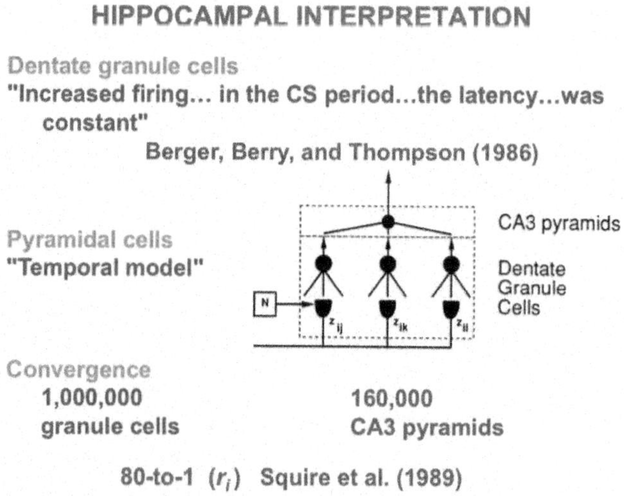

HIPPOCAMPAL INTERPRETATION

FIGURE 15.6. The circuit between dentate granule cells and CA1 hippocampal pyramidal cells seems to compute spectrally timed responses. See the text for details.

How is an adaptively timed response learned by a spectral timing circuit? Does the brain need a complicated learning law to realize the beautifully timed responses that are shown in Figures 15.3c and 15.3d? The answer is emphatically No! Only our old friend, the Gated Steepest Descent Learning law, is needed (Figure 2.11). Figures 15.7-15.13 summarize how this kind of adaptively timed learning may give rise to beautifully timed population responses that obey a Weber law, and that in addition demonstrate the classical Inverted-U property as a function of ISI (Figure 15.3d) that is found in many classical conditioning experiments; cf. Figure 13.6.

Figure 15.7 shows how to derive these properties using the simplest possible CS input, one that jumps quickly to its maximum value, stays there for awhile, and then jumps back down to zero. This CS is rapidly stored and maintained in STM (stored activity I_{cs} in Figure 15.7), which activates a spectrum of cells, or cell sites, whose activities x_i each respond with their own rate r_i through time. These different responses are drawn in the lower right of the figure. The bottom of Figure 15.8 shows that each activity generates an output signal $f(x_i)$ that is multiplied by a habituative transmitter gate y_i before the gated signal $f(x_i)$ y_i can influence its target cell.

As in Figure 2.11, each habituative transmitter gate y_i obeys the top equation in Figure 15.9, with its net change through time dy_i/dt determined by an accumulation term, which is positive, and a gated inactivation, or habituation, term, which is negative. This figure shows that, in response to a step input $f(x_i)$, y_i decays at a slower rate to a smaller equilibrium value. Multiplying these two curves shows that their product, the gated output signal $f(x_i)y_i$, responds with an overshoot that is followed by gradual habituation to an intermediate equilibrium value. This is just the kind of dynamics that explains the overshoot-habituation sequence in a gated dipole (Figure 1.14).

HABITUATIVE TRANSMITTER GATE

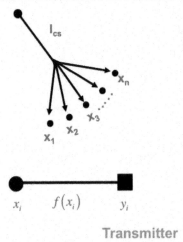

FIGURE 15.8. The spectral activities x_i generate sigmoid signals $f(x)$ before the signals are, in turn, gated by habituative transmitters y_i.

How do these properties look when they are applied to a spectrum of activities $f(x_i)$ that react at different rates? Although all the transmitters y_i obey an equation with the same rate parameters C and D for accumulation and habituation, respectively, they react at different rates because they habituate in response to signals $f(x_i)$ that react at different rates. Figure 15.10 shows a computer simulation of the spectrum of output signals $f(x_i)$ growing at different rates, and the corresponding spectrum of transmitters y_i habituating at different rates in response to these output signals. The gated output signal from each pathway is, as usual, the product $f(x_i)y_i$. The spectrum of these products

SPECTRAL TIMING: ACTIVATION

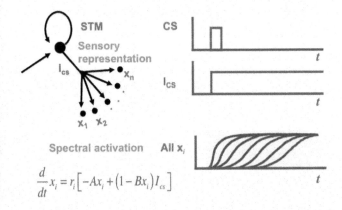

FIGURE 15.7. In response to a step CS and sustained storage by I_{cs} of that input, a spectrum of responses x_i at different rates r_i develops through time.

HABITUATIVE TRANSMITTER GATE
Grossberg, 1968

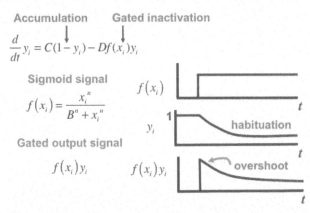

FIGURE 15.9. As always, the habituative transmitter gate y_i increases in response to accumulation and decreases due to gated inactivation, leading to the kinds of transmitter and output responses in the right hand column.

A TIMED SPECTRUM OF SAMPLING INTERVALS

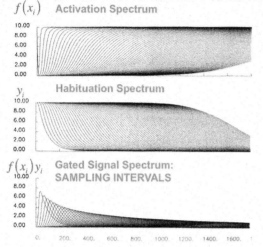

$f(x_i)$ Activation Spectrum

y_i Habituation Spectrum

$f(x_i)y_i$ Gated Signal Spectrum: SAMPLING INTERVALS

FIGURE 15.10. When the activity spectrum x_i generates a spectrum of sigmoid signals $f(x)$, the corresponding transmitters habituative at different rates. The output signals $f(x)y_i$ therefore generate a series of unimodal activity profiles that peak at different times, as in Figure 15.3a.

is shown in the bottom curves of Figures 15.10 and 15.3. So far, there has been no learning.

As depicted in Figure 15.11, the gated output signal from each pathway is also gated by an LTM trace z_i that obeys the Gated Steepest Descent Learning law. Thus the final output signal from each pathway is $f(x_i)y_iz_i$, as shown at the bottom of the figure, The Gated Steepest Descent Learning law says that learning of each LTM trace z_i is gated on and off by the sampling signal $f(x_i)y_i$. No learning occurs when this sampling signal equals zero. The LTM

ASSOCIATIVE LEARNING
Gated Steepest Descent Learning
Grossberg (1969)

steepest descent

$$\frac{d}{dt}z_i = Ef(x_i)y_i\overbrace{\left[-z_i + I_{us}\right]}$$

Read-out of CS gated signal   Read-out of US

Output from each population: $f(x_i)y_iz_i$
Doubly gated signal

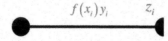

$f(x_i)y_i$ z_i

FIGURE 15.11. The adaptive weight, or LTM trace, z_i learns from the US input I_{us} at times when the sampling signal $f(x)y_i$ is on. It then gates the habituative sampling signal $f(x)y_i$ to generate a doubly gated response $f(x)y_iz_i$.

traces that grow the most have the largest sampling signals when the US is on. At such times, z_i increases by steepest descent towards the US input intensity I_{US}. Cells in the spectrum whose sampling signals are zero, or very small, when the US is on do not change at all, or change very little. Figure 15.12 illustrates these properties with a simulation of the LTM traces of six spectral cells. The cells that sample the US too quickly ("FAST") or too slowly ("SLOW") have small or zero sampling signals when the US is on, so learn very little. The third cell down in the left column samples the US best, so its LTM trace grows the most (marked in green). The two cells with the most similar sampling signals (second cell down in the left column; first cell in the right column) learn more slowly.

Figure 15.3b shows the learned spectrum of all the doubly gated responses $f(x_i)y_iz_i$ after four learning trials. Note how the LTM traces have transformed the sampling signals in Figure 15.3a. Although the learned responses in Figure 15.3b are largest for the cells whose sampling signals are largest when the US occurs, none of these responses, taken individually, is perfectly timed to peak at the ISI when the US occurs. In contrast, when all of these doubly gated signals are added to compute the population response $R = \sum_i f(X_i)y_i\,z_i$, as in Figure 15.13, then the beautifully timed responses shown in Figures 15.3c and 15.3d emerge.

Is episodic learning and memory necessary to consciously experience trace conditioning? These theoretical results suggest that, contrary to the assertion of Clark and Squire (1998), episodic learning and memory may not be *necessary* to consciously experience emotions. All that seems to be necessary is the ability to bridge the trace interval well enough to drive a sustained cognitive-emotional resonance. Such a resonance can support a conscious "feeling of what happens", thereby clarifying the reported connection between conditioning and consciousness. This being said, it also needs to be acknowledged that a cognitive-emotional resonance can also synchronize via its attended invariant object category with a feature-category resonance (Figure 2.4) and a surface-shroud resonance (Figure 6.2) to support conscious seeing, knowing, and feeling about the experienced event. Moreover, both spatial and temporal representations coexist in the hippocampus and, under normal learning conditions, representations of both space and time may be combined in newly learned episodic memories (Eichenbaum and Lipton, 2008; Tulving, 1972). So, episodic learning and memory may occur during trace conditioning experiences, even though they may not be necessary to explain the link between conditioning and consciousness.

Neural relativity: A homology between spectral spacing and spectral timing. As I remarked at the beginning of

COMPUTER SIMULATION OF SPECTRAL LEARNING

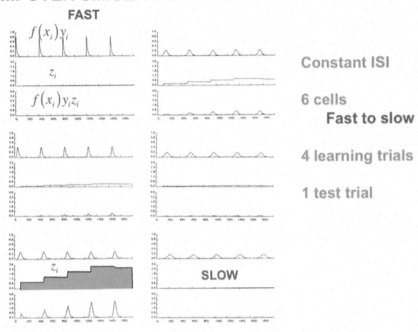

FIGURE 15.12. The adaptive weights z_i in the spectrum learn fastest whose sampling signals are large when the US occurs, as illustrated by the green region in this simulation of conditioning from Grossberg and Schmajuk (1989).

ADAPTIVE TIMING IS A POPULATION PROPERTY

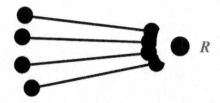

Total output signal: $R = \sum_i f(x_i) y_i z_i$

Adaptive timing is a collective property of the circuit

"Random" spectrum of rates achieves good collective timing

FIGURE 15.13. The total learned response is a sum R of all the doubly gated signals in the spectrum.

15.2). Key aspects of this process seem to occur within the *lateral* entorhinal-hippocampal system. I will propose in Chapter 16 how the *dorsal* entorhinal-hippocampal system uses similar circuitry to represent the large spaces that help us to navigate in space. As I noted at the beginning of this chapter, based on its homology with spectral timing, I call the model of how large spaces are represented the spectral spacing model.

I like to call this exciting homology, which was discovered with my postdoctoral fellows Anatoli Gorchetchnikov and especially Praveen Pilly, *neural relativity* to emphasize its unification of concepts about space and time (Gorchetchnikov and Grossberg, 2007; Grossberg and Pilly, 2012, 2014). The fact that both spatial and temporal representations of this kind occur in the entorhinal-hippocampal system may provide new insights into how episodic learning and memory are supported by this system. A full analysis of how this happens will require additional research. Even in the absence of a mature neural model of episodic learning and memory, it nonetheless seems reasonable to assert once again that, whereas a spectral timing circuit may help to sustain a cognitive-emotional resonance until conscious awareness occurs, the full resources of episodic memory may not be needed to support consciousness during trace conditioning, especially in conditioning paradigms where no spatial navigation occurs.

Balancing exploratory and consummatory behaviors: Functional role of Weber law. What is the functional utility of the Weber law property during adaptively timed conditioning (Figures 15.3-15.5)? Adaptively timed responding is essential for terrestrial animals that actively explore and learn about extended environments, since rewards and other goals are often delayed in time relative to the environmental cues that predict their future occurrence. Adaptive timing of this kind is a double-edged sword: If an animal cannot wait for an expected source of food, then it may be forced to restlessly explore its world seeking immediate gratifications, possibly starving to death along the way if they are not forthcoming sufficiently often. But if it waits too long for food that does not materialize, then it may again starve to death. How long an animal or human waits must thus be adaptively timed to learn the temporal

this chapter, my modeling work with several colleagues proposes that spatial and temporal representations coexist in the entorhinal-hippocampal system because they exploit similar circuit mechanisms. At this point, I can say a little more about this homology, now that we know something about spectral timing. Spectral timing enables the brain to bridge the large times, spanning hundreds of milliseconds or even seconds (Figures 15.3-15.5), that may be needed to associate cues with temporally delayed responses (Figure

constraints of each environment. Said in another way, in order to survive, a terrestrial animal or human needs to properly balance its exploratory and consummatory behaviors. It needs to know when to *excite* exploratory behaviors to discover desired rewards that are not physically present. But it also needs to know when to *inhibit* exploratory behaviors in order to stay in one place long enough to carry out consummatory behaviors when rewards are available, or are expected to become available reasonably soon.

Distinguishing expected vs. unexpected disconfirmations, or non-occurrences, of reward. The START model accomplishes the balancing act between consummatory and exploratory behaviors in an adaptively timed way. It does so by modeling how the brain distinguishes *expected disconfirmations*, also called *expected non-occurrences*, of reward, which should not be allowed to interfere with acquiring a delayed reward, from *unexpected disconfirmations*, also called *unexpected non-occurrences*, of reward, which can trigger the orienting responses that typically follow a predictive failure.

How does this the distinction between expected and unexpected disconfirmations work in practice? Key questions that must be answered to understand this distinction include: What spares an animal or human from erroneously reacting to an *expected* non-occurrence of reward as a predictive failure? In particular, how does the animal continue to attentively wait for a delayed reward that is expected to occur during a future time interval? Why does an animal not become frustrated by the immediate non-occurrence of a reward and prematurely release exploratory behavior aimed at finding the desired reward somewhere else, leading to restless exploration for immediate gratification?

In the opposite direction, suppose that the animal does wait, but the reward does not occur at the expected time. Why does not the animal wait indefinitely, perhaps starving to death, if the reward never appears? How does the animal then react to this *unexpected* non-occurrence of reward with orienting reactions (Figure 15.14), which in this case may be life-saving, such as resetting its working memory to enable it to process new information, shifting its attention to focus upon more likely sources of useful information, becoming frustrated to counter-condition (or extinguish) current motivational support for the unsuccessful behavior, and releasing exploratory behavior to search for better sources of gratification?

How the orienting system stays inhibited during an expected disconfirmation. The key insight is that, if a reward happens to occur earlier than expected, an animal can still perceive it and release a consummatory response, just as a pigeon can eat a pellet that is delivered earlier than expected in a Skinner box. This basic fact implies that the process of registering ART-like sensory matches with incoming sensory events is not inhibited during

UNEXPECTED NON-OCCURRENCE OF GOAL

A Predictive Failure

e.g., reward that does not occur at the expected time

Leads to **ORIENTING REACTIONS:**

Cognitive: STM reset, attention shift, forgetting
Emotional: Frustration!
Motor: Exploratory behavior

What about an expected non-occurrence?

FIGURE 15.14. An individual's survival depends upon being able to process expected non-occurrences, or disconfirmations, of goals differently from expected non-occurrences, or disconfirmations. See the text for details.

either expected or unexpected non-occurrences within a perception-cognitive ART circuit (Figure 5.19). Rather than directly interfering with the matching process, I have predicted that the *effects of mismatches* upon reinforcement, attention, and exploration are prevented by *inhibiting the orienting system* in ART perception-cognition circuits (Figure 15.15).

In particular, a mismatch in the feature-category circuit typically activates the orienting system, other things being equal, by *reducing* the amount of inhibition that it sends to the orienting system while the orienting system is also being excited by a bottom-up feature pattern (Figures 5.19b and 5.19c). This inhibition is then not sufficient to

EXPECTED NON-OCCURRENCE OF GOAL

Some rewards are reliable but delayed in time
Does *not* lead to orienting reactions: How?

Both expected and unexpected non-occurrences are due to mismatch of a sensory event with a learned expectation

Expected non-occurrences do not inhibit sensory matching: e.g., a pigeon can see an earlier-than-usual food pellet

Hypothesis:

Expected non-occurrences inhibit the process whereby sensory mismatch activates orienting reactions

FIGURE 15.15. Expected non-occurrences do not prevent the processing of sensory events and their expectations. Rather, they prevent mismatches of those expectations from triggering orienting reactions.

prevent the bottom-up excitation from activating the orienting system. Other things are not equal at times when the cognitive-emotional network delivers adaptively timed inhibition to the orienting system while an animal is waiting for an expected reward.

The *increase* in adaptively timed inhibition from the cognitive-emotional circuit compensates for the *decrease* of inhibition from the perception-cognitive circuit during a sensory mismatch, thereby preventing orienting reactions from occurring (Figure 15.15). In this way, orienting responses are inhibited in an adaptively timed way during an expected non-occurrence, and with it undesired cognitive, emotional, and motor consequences.

This explanation of how orienting responses are inhibited illustrates a beautiful homology that exists between ART recognition learning systems and CogEM reinforcement learning systems (Figure 15.16). Both systems involve adaptive resonances between a category level F_2 and a "feature" level F_1. In an ART recognition learning system, the feature level typically includes sensory feature detectors in thalamic or cortical regions that are activated by external sensory cues. In a CogEM reinforcement learning system, the feature level typically includes amygdala value categories that are activated by internal drive cues. In both systems, the feature level can inhibit the orienting system, albeit in response to different circumstances. The fact that the *decrease* in inhibition during a perceptual-cognitive mismatch is compensated by an *increase* in inhibition during cognitive-emotional adaptive timing can now clearly be seen as compensatory inputs to the orienting system from homologous circuit designs.

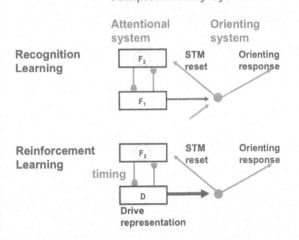

HOMOLOG BETWEEN ART AND CogEM MODEL
complementary systems

FIGURE 15.16. Homologous recognition learning and reinforcement learning macrocircuits enable adaptively timed conditioning in the reinforcement learning circuit to increase inhibition of the orienting system at times when a mismatch in the recognition system would have reduced inhibition of it.

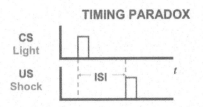

TIMING PARADOX

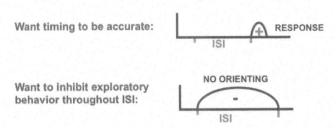

ISI = Interstimulus interval = Expected delay of reinforcer

Want timing to be accurate:

Want to inhibit exploratory behavior throughout ISI:

FIGURE 15.17. The timing paradox asks how inhibition of an orienting response (-) can be spread throughout the ISI, yet accurately timed responding can be excited (+) at the end of the ISI.

Timing paradox: Combining inhibition of orienting responses with adaptively timed responses. The above explanation implies how the brain solves a fascinating *timing paradox*. On the one hand, it is desired that responses are adaptively timed. Thus, in response to a stimulus that predicts a delayed reward (Figure 15.17, top image), one wants the brain to be able to trigger an adaptively timed response at around the time the reward is expected (Figure 15.17, middle image). On the other hand, it is also desired that orienting responses are inhibited throughout the time interval leading up to the delayed reward, so that the animal can actually receive it, and not be distracted by maladaptive orienting responses (Figure 15.17, bottom image). Thus both accurate timing and fuzzy timing are required. How can the brain realize both of these requirements?

A spectral timing circuit solves this problem in the following way: Its timed response begins immediately after its triggering CS stimulus, and builds throughout the interstimulus interval, or ISI, between the CS and US, peaking at the ISI (Figure 15.18, top image). As illustrated in the insert depicting a simplified cognitive-emotional CogEM circuit, such a timed response can both maintain inhibition of the orienting system until the expected time of occurrence of the reinforcing stimulus, yet can also release the learned response with maximal probability at the expected time of the reward. This inhibition would not, however, occur in response to an unexpected non-occurrence because the spectral timing circuit would not be active then. As a result, an unexpected non-occurrence could lead to the usual cognitive, emotional, and motor responses to correct the predictive error.

Why is there a Weber law? The Weber law immediately follows from these properties when the ISI is varied (Figure 15.18, bottom image). In other words, the Weber law solves

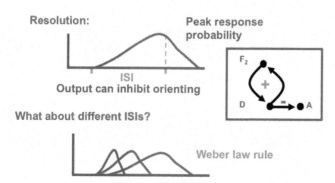

WEBER LAW:
RECONCILING ACCURATE AND DISTRIBUTED TIMING

Resolution:

Peak response probability

ISI

Output can inhibit orienting

What about different ISIs?

Weber law rule

Standard deviation ≈ peak time

FIGURE 15.18. The Weber law solves the timing paradox by creating an adaptively timed response throughout the ISI that peaks at the ISI. Within the reinforcement learning circuit, this response can maintain inhibition of the orienting system A at the same time as it generates adaptively timed incentive motivation to the orbitofrontal cortex.

the Timing Paradox! When this property of a spectral timing circuit is embedded within the architecture of the START model (Figure 5.19), it realizes three critical functional roles that were simulated by this model, and used to explain many data about adaptively timed classical conditioning (Grossberg and Merrill, 1992, 1996; Grossberg and Schmajuk, 1989): By beginning right after its inducing stimulus, spectral timing can inhibit spurious orienting responses throughout its adaptively timed interval (red arrow from the drive representation D to the orienting system A in Figure 15.19). By exciting orbitofrontal

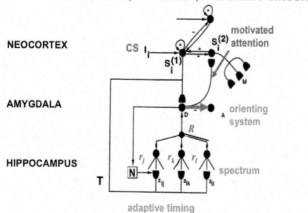

CONDITIONING, ATTENTION, AND TIMING CIRCUIT

NEOCORTEX

CS

motivated attention

$S_i^{(2)}$

$S_i^{(1)}$

M

AMYGDALA

D

orienting system

A

R

HIPPOCAMPUS

r_j r_k r_l

N

spectrum

T

z_{ij} z_{ik} z_{il}

adaptive timing

Adaptive timing circuit **INHIBITS** orienting system
and maintains adaptively timed **MOTIVATED ATTENTION** on the CS

FIGURE 15.19. How the adaptively timed hippocampal spectrum T inhibits (red arrow) the orienting system A as motivated attention in orbitofrontal cortex $S_i^{(2)}$ peaks at the ISI.

object-value categories (with activities $s_i^{(2)}$ in Figure 15.19), the spectral timing circuit can also maintain motivated attention upon the correct orbitofrontal representation throughout this time interval. Finally, by peaking at the expected time of occurrence of the reinforcing cue, it can generate a peak amplitude of motivated attention at the correct time at the orbitofrontal representation that controls learned responses, thereby triggering the learned response with maximal probability at the expected time of occurrence of the reward.

START: Spectrally Timed Adaptive Resonance Theory

Coordinating adaptively timed learning in the hippocampus and cerebellum. Two functionally distinct, but interacting, spectral timing circuits are embedded within the more comprehensive dynamics of the START model. These functions were summarized in 1987 by Richard Thompson and nine other colleagues (Thompson et al., 1987) who distinguished two types of learning that go on during conditioning of the rabbit Nictitating Membrane Response: Adaptively timed "conditioned fear" learning that is linked to the hippocampus, and adaptively timed "learning of the discrete adaptive response" that is linked to the cerebellum.

A unified explanation of why both hippocampus and cerebellum use adaptively timed learning is given by the START model. As noted above, the CogEM model (Figure 13.2) explains how salient conditioned cues can rapidly focus motivated attention upon their object categories via a feedback loop through their associated value categories in the amygdala, and object-value categories through the orbitofrontal cortex. This attentional focus can be maintained during an adaptively timed interval as a sustained cognitive-emotional resonance with the additional support of the hippocampus (Figure 15.2). The Contingent Negative Variation, or CNV, event-related potential is predicted to be a neural marker of adaptively timed motivational feedback (Cant and Bickford, 1967; Irwin et al., 1966; Walter et al., 1964; Tecce, 1972).

Many additional data have been explained using these circuits, notably data from delayed non-match to sample (DNMS) experiments wherein both temporal delays and novelty-sensitive recognition processes are involved (Gaffan, 1974; Mishkin and Delacour, 1975). This task was originally created to study visual recognition memory in monkeys by exploiting their natural preference to choose a novel object over another object that was presented a few seconds or minutes earlier. During experiments of this kind, an animal is presented with a sample stimulus. After a short delay, the sample stimulus is shown again along with a novel alternative. In the non-matching paradigm, the animal is rewarded for selecting the novel stimulus. In the matching variant of this paradigm, the animal is rewarded for selecting the sample stimulus and avoiding the novel stimulus. If different stimuli are used for every trial, then the test measures visual recognition memory. If the same stimuli are used on every trial, then the test measures the animal's ability to remember the most recent item. In either case, hippocampal involvement is required by the delay between sample and text stimuli.

Although hippocampally-mediated adaptive timing can clarify how such temporal gaps may be bridged, this adaptively timed motivated attention does not explain what prevents the actions that are controlled by the orbitofrontal object-value categories from being prematurely released. Indeed, rapid focusing of attention by the amygdala on motivationally-salient object-value categories in the orbitofrontal cortex could rapidly satisfy the polyvalent constraint needed to fire these categories, and thereby prematurely release the motor behaviors that they control. Premature responding can cause multiple problems in both naturalistic and social settings. To explain how premature responding is avoided, adaptively timed motor learning in the cerebellum is also needed.

Achieving three fundamental behavioral competences. When both the hippocampal and cerebellar adaptive timing circuits are combined in the START model, three essential behavioral competences will be achieved:

1. Fast Motivated Attention. Rapid focusing of attention on motivationally salient cues occurs from regions like the amygdala to prefrontal cortex. It is vital for survival to be able to rapidly attend to motivationally salient objects, whether they be food sources or attacking predators. However, as I just noted, without further processing, fast activation of object-value category representations could prematurely release motor behaviors.

2. Adaptively Timed Responding. In the manner that I will explain in a moment, despite the fast activation by motivated attention of object-value categories, adaptively timed read-out of responses can be achieved by cerebellar circuits that are further downstream.

3. Adaptively Timed Duration of Motivated Attention and Inhibition of Orienting Responses. Motivated attention needs to stay focused on these object-value categories while a response is read out at the correct time. Premature reset of active object-value representations by irrelevant cues during task-specific delays is prevented by adaptively timed inhibition of mismatch-sensitive cells in the orienting system of the hippocampus, while adaptively timed support of motivated attention is also maintained, as I have already explained (Figure 15.19). This inhibition

is part of the competition between consummatory and orienting behaviors (Staddon, 1983) that the ability to distinguish expected vs. unexpected non-occurrences assures.

Adaptively timed responding by the cerebellum. Figure 15.20 summarizes how adaptively timed responding by the cerebellum prevents premature responding. This circuit shows that a conditioned stimulus (CS), say via the prefrontal cortical output pathway in Figures 15.2 and 15.19, activates the cerebellum along two different pathways. One pathway activates *parallel fibers* in the cerebellar cortex. The parallel fibers, in turn, synapse on Purkinje cells, which possess perhaps the most remarkable dendritic tree in the entire brain. Figure 15.21 (Watson, Wong, and Becker, 2015) shows a Purkinje cell (PC) and several parallel fibers (PF) passing through it. The other pathway ends in a subcortical, or deep, cerebellar nucleus (Figure 15.20); also see DCN in Figure 15.21. The Purkinje cells are tonically active, and send sustained inhibitory signals to their subcortical cerebellar nuclear targets. Learning via the parallel fibers acts to *weaken* this tonic inhibition in an adaptively timed way.

In particular, the CS-activated parallel fibers activate a spectrum of differently timed intracellular processes at their parallel fiber/Purkinje cell synapses. The unconditioned stimulus (US) activates climbing fibers (Figure 15.20 and CF in Figure 15.21) that deliver a teaching signal to these synapses throughout the Purkinje cell dendritic tree. This teaching signal causes the CS-activated synapses within the parallel fiber spectrum to become weaker if they are active at times when the US teaching signal is also

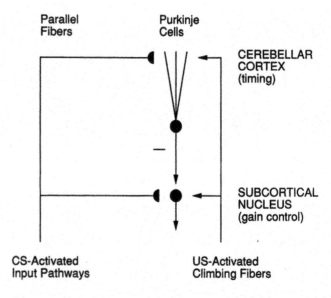

FIGURE 15.20. Adaptively timed conditioning of Long Term Depression, or LTD, occurs in the cerebellum at synapses between parallel fibers and Purkinje cells, thereby reducing inhibition of subcortical nucleus cells and enabling them to express their learned movement gains within the learned time interval. Also see Figure 15.21.

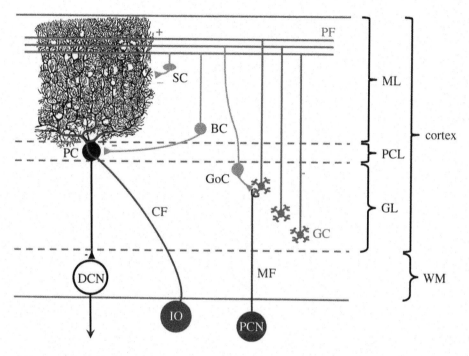

FIGURE 15.21. The most important cell types and circuitry of the cerebellum: Purkinje cells (PC) receive excitatory inputs from climbing fibers (CF) that originate in the inferior olive (IO) and from parallel fibres (PF), which are the axons of granule cells (GC). GCs, in turn, receive inputs from the mossy fibres (MF) coming from the precerebellar nuclei (PCN). The PF also inhibit PC via basket cells (BC), thereby helping to select the most highly activated PC. The PC generate inhibitory outputs from the cerebellar cortex to the deep cerebellar nuclei (DCN), as in Figure 15.20. Excitatory signals are denoted by (+) and inhibitory signals by (-). Other notations: GL, granular layer; GoC, golgi cells; ML, molecular layer; PCL, Purkinje cell layer; SC, stellate cell; WM, white matter.

active. This kind of associative learning is called Long Term Depression, or LTD. Synapses whose CS-activated spectral activity does not overlap the climbing fiber signals become stronger via Long Term Potentiation, or LTP. When a CS is activated after LTD occurs, the Purkinje cells are inhibited during a time interval that includes the ISI of the CS-US learning trials. Because the Purkinje cells tonically inhibit their subcortical nuclear cells, their adaptively timed LTD disinhibits the tonic inhibition of these nuclear cells. In other words, an adaptively timed gate opens and allows the subcortical cells to fire during the learned time interval.

The climbing fiber teaching signal also controls learning of adaptive gains along the subcortical pathways through the nuclear cells. Thus, when the adaptively timed Purkinje cell gate opens, the learned gains can be expressed at the correct times, leading to read-out of the correct amplitude of a correctly timed motor response.

Adaptively timed learning by the metabotropic glutamate receptor system. My PhD student John Fiala and my colleague Daniel Bullock proposed with me in 1996 (Fiala, Grossberg, and Bullock, 1996) a detailed spectral timing model of cerebellar adaptive timing that links

biochemistry, neurophysiology, neuroanatomy, and behavior, and predicts how the metabotropic glutamate (mGluR) receptor system may create a spectrum of delays during cerebellar learning. mGluRs are a form of glutamate receptor that is different from the ionotropic glutamate receptors that support widespread excitatory signalling throughout the brain. Unlike ionotropic glutamate receptors, which directly activate ion channels, mGluR receptors activate biochemical cascades. Spectral timing properties are predicted to be an example of such a biochemical cascade.

John Fiala and I came to this mGluR prediction through an indirect route. I wanted us to discover the biochemical basis of spectral timing, but did not know what it was. I had, however, published a model in 1981 with Gail Carpenter (Carpenter and Grossberg, 1981) of how retinal photoreceptors adapt to changing light levels during the day and night, or when ambient light intensities change during the day. In that situation, too, there was a slowly adapting process whose properties reminded me of spectral timing. Figure 15.22 shows neurophysiological recordings from the turtle retina that were reported in 1974 by Denis Baylor and Alan Hodgkin (Baylor and Hodgkin, 1974). These data show how a cone in the turtle retina responds to brief flashes of light as the light intensity is increased. Note that all the responses start at the same time, but that higher light intensities generate more intense responses that peak at later times. In the retina, the habituative transmitter is calcium. In a spectrum of cells, different cells have

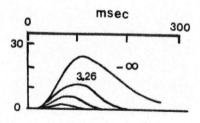

FIGURE 15.22. Responses of a retinal cone in the turtle retina to brief flashes of light of increasing intensity.

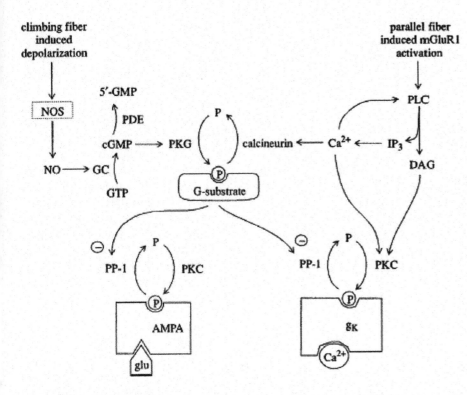

FIGURE 15.23. Cerebellar biochemistry that supports the hypothesis of how mGluR supports adaptively timed conditioning at cerebellar Purkinje cells. AMPA, Amino-3-hydroxy-5-methyl4-isoxazole propionic acid-sensitive glutamate receptor; cGMP, cyclic guanosine monophosphate; DAG, diacylglycerol; glu, glutamate; GC, guanylyl cyclase; gK, Ca2+ -dependent K+ channel protein; GTP, guanosine triphosphate; IP 3'inositol,4,5-trisphosphate; NO, nitric oxide; NOS, nitric oxide synthase; P, phosphate; PLC, phospholipase C; PKC, protein kinase C; PKG, cGMP-dependent protein kinase; PP-I, protein phosphatase-i.

different rates that accomplish the property that variable light levels achieve in the retina. I wondered if the brain had also discovered how a calcium gradient could create different reaction rates across a spectrum of cells.

I therefore asked John to search the literature on retinal light adaptation for hints about how the light adaptation process was controlled. To my delight, he found data that implicated mGluR *and* a calcium gradient. When we then turned to the cerebellum, more mGluR and calcium data were found, and had properties that were consistent with what we needed to explain the biochemistry of spectral timing. A summary of the key biochemical processes that we needed to explain and simulate data about adaptively timed cerebellar dynamics is provided in Figure 15.23. The model proposes in detail how mGluR1-induced delayed calcium (Ca^{2+}) release enables the temporal coincidence of CS-activated parallel fiber signals and US-activated climbing fiber teaching signals to control learning. A gradient of calcium concentrations across the cell spectrum causes different response delays to occur, as in Figures 15.7 and 15.10.

Our 1996 prediction of a role for mGluR and calcium gradients in adaptively timed cerebellar learning is consistent with data about mGluR and calcium signalling in

cerebellar adaptive timing that was published in several articles in *Nature* and *Science* a few years later (Finch and Augustine, 1998; Ichise et al., 2000; Miyata et al., 2000; Takechi, Eilers, and Konnerth, 1998). The model simulates both normal adaptively timed conditioning data, and data about premature responding when the cerebellar cortex is lesioned (Perrett, Ruiz, and Mauk, 1993), thereby eliminating the adaptively timed gating process. Various individuals with autism, who are known to have cerebellar deficiencies, also perform short-latency responses in the eye blink conditioning paradigm (Grossberg and Seidman, 2006; Sears et al., 1994).

The prediction of a role for mGluR in adaptively timed learning hereby raised the question of whether the mGluR system is not functioning normally in some people who have various mental disorders. I will come back to this issue below when I discuss how our prediction explains data about abnormal timing in autistic individuals, as well as data about the related Fragile X syndrome, notably the role of mGluR in causing it, and the failure of adaptively timed trace conditioning in individuals who are living with this problem.

nSTART: neurotrophic Spectrally Timed Adaptive Resonance Theory

Hippocampal, amygdala, and orbitofrontal lesions affect memory consolidation. Before discussing autism and Fragile X syndrome, I would like to note in passing that the START model, with one additional refinement, can explain a subtle and challenging database about learning and memory consolidation. These are the kind of data that try to explain the memory deficits of people like the famous amnesic patient Henry Molaison, who I mentioned in Chapter 2, and who was publicly known just as HM in order to protect his privacy until after his death in 2008. HM had a bilateral lesion in his hippocampus when he was 27 years old in order to control his otherwise intractable epilepsy. The data that have been collected since that time by scores of cognitive neuroscientists have studied the effects of lesions in multiple brain regions upon the memory consolidation process.

The START model refinement that can explain such data adds neurotrophic modulation by Brain Derived Neurotrophic Factor, or BDNF, and its ability to help sustain hippocampal firing during the process of memory consolidation, even during sleep. This model refinement is accordingly called the neurotrophic START, or nSTART, model. As a noted above, I published nSTART with my PhD student Daniel Franklin in 2017 (Figure 15.2; Franklin and Grossberg, 2017). Although a generation of cognitive neuroscientists devoted itself to collecting and interpreting this kind of data, no unified mechanistic explanation was given of it until ours.

You will better appreciate why these data have been so hard to explain when I summarize some of the main data properties: Lesions of amygdala, hippocampus, and prefrontal cortex have different effects on memory consolidation depending on the phase of learning when they occur (Figure 15.2); in other words, whether the lesion occurs shortly after, or much after, the learning phase. nSTART explains, for example, why the hippocampus is typically needed for trace conditioning, but not delay conditioning, and what the exceptions reveal; why amygdala lesions made before or immediately after training decelerate conditioning, while lesions that are made later do not; why thalamic or sensory cortical lesions degrade trace conditioning more than delay conditioning; why hippocampal lesions during trace conditioning experiments degrade recent but not temporally remote learning; why orbitofrontal cortical lesions degrade temporally remote but not recent or post-lesion learning; why temporally graded amnesia is caused by ablation of prefrontal cortex after memory consolidation; and how the neurotrophin BDNF influences memory formation and consolidation.

Paradoxical memory consolidation data follow from three obvious behavioral facts. I will explain one of these cases here; namely, why hippocampal lesions during trace conditioning experiments degrade recent but not temporally remote learning. The interested reader can find the other explanations in my Open Access article with Dan: https://link.springer.com/article/10.3758%2Fs13415-016-0463-y. Before explaining this case, I want to emphasize that nSTART can explain all these data as emergent properties of three behavioral competences that many would find intuitively obvious, even though, when their mechanistic embodiments interact together, their emergent properties explain the above highly non-intuitive symptoms.

What are these three behavioral competences? They are just the three main behavioral competences that the START model realizes:

(1) fast motivated attention to focus on salient events (Figure 13.2);

(2) adaptively timed responding to prevent premature responses from occurring (Figure 15.20); and

(3) adaptively timed duration of both motivated attention and inhibition of orienting responses (Figure 15.19), to prevent distractions from aborting the adaptively timed response before it can occur.

These are behavioral competences that every successful terrestrial animal needs to have. They are also properties that everyone can understand and agree upon, just based upon our day-to-day experiences. The fact that such a paradoxical array of data properties about failures in memory consolidation after early or late lesions follow from such obvious hypotheses shows once again the power of models that correctly embody key brain designs. The current model hereby embodies a solution to a "multiple constraint satisfaction problem" that evolution has discovered in order to facilitate our species' survival. I have increasingly come to call such explanations examples of The Gift That Keeps On Giving. They exemplify why it pays to take the time and effort needed to correctly identify the design principles that evolution has discovered with which to shape our brains.

Why do early hippocampal lesions interfere with memory consolidation but late ones do not? I will now summarize data about the different effects of early vs. later ablations of hippocampus after some previous conditioning trials end, and how the nSTART model explains these data. The role of the hippocampus has been studied by many labs during the acquisition of trace eye blink conditioning (Figure 15.1), and the adaptive timing of conditioned responses (Figure 15.4; Berger, Laham, and Thompson, 1980; Mauk and Ruiz, 1992; Schmaltz and Theios, 1972; Sears and Steinmetz, 1990; Woodruff-Pak, 1993; Woodruff-Pak and Disterhoft, 2007). If a hippocampal lesion or other system disruption occurs before trace conditioning acquisition (Ivkovich and Stanton, 2001; Kaneko and Thompson, 1997; Weiss and Thompson, 1991a, 1991b; Woodruff-Pak, 2001), or shortly thereafter (Kim et al., 1995; Moyer, Deyo, and Disterhoft, 1990; Takehara et al., 2003), the conditioned response, or CR, is not obtained or retained. Trace conditioning is impaired by pre-acquisition hippocampal lesions that are created during laboratory experimentation on animals (Anagnostaras, Maren, and Fanselow, 1999; Berry and Thompson, 1979; Garrud et al., 1984; James, Hardiman, and Yeo, 1987; Kim et al., 1995; Orr and Berger, 1985; Schmajuk, Lam, and Christiansen, 1994; Schmaltz and Theios, 1972; Solomon and Moore, 1975), and in humans with amnesia (Clark and Squire, 1998; Gabrieli et al., 1995; McGlinchey-Berroth et al., 1997), Alzheimer's disease, or age-related deficits

(Little, Lipsitt, and Rovee-Collier, 1984; Solomon et al., 1990; Weiss and Thompson, 1991a; Woodruff-Pak, 2001).

The data show that, during trace conditioning, there is successful post-acquisition performance of the CR only if the hippocampal lesion occurs after a critical period of hippocampal support of memory consolidation within the neocortex (Kim et al., 1995; Takashima et al., 2009; Takehara et al., 2003). Data from *in vitro* cell preparations also support the time-limited role of the hippocampus in new learning. In particular, activity in hippocampal CA1 and CA3 pyramidal neurons peaks 24 hours after conditioning is completed and decays back to baseline within 14 days (Thompson, Moyer, and Disterhoft, 1996). The effect of early versus late hippocampal lesions is challenging to explain because, after conditioning, no overt training occurs during the period before hippocampal ablation. There must be an active, but time-limited, process going on within the brain after conditioning ends that supports this kind of memory consolidation.

After consolidation due to hippocampal involvement is accomplished, thalamocortical signals in conjunction with the cerebellum determine the timed execution of the CR during performance (Gabreil, Sparenborg, and Stolar, 1987; Sosina, 1992). Indeed, " . . . there are two memory circuitries for trace conditioning. One involves the hippocampus and the cerebellum and mediates recently acquired memory; the other involves the mPFC (medial prefrontal cortex) and the cerebellum and mediates remotely acquired memory" (Takehara et al., 2003, p. 9904; see also Berger, Weikart, Basset, and Orr, 1986; O'Reilly et al., 2010).

Based on the extent and timing of hippocampal damage, learning impairments range from needing more training trials than normal in order to learn successfully, through persistent response timing difficulties, to the inability to learn and form new memories. The nSTART model explains the need for the hippocampus during trace conditioning in terms of how the hippocampus supports strengthening of partially conditioned thalamocortical and corticocortical category learning connections during memory consolidation (Figure 15.2).

The hippocampus has this ability because it includes circuits that can bridge the temporal gap between CS and US during trace conditioning, unlike the amygdala, and can learn to adaptively time these temporal gaps in its responses, as originally simulated in the START model (Grossberg and Merrill, 1992, 1996; Grossberg and Schmajuk, 1989). The nSTART model extends this analysis by explaining how endogenous hippocampal activation and BDNF modulation after conditioning ends explain the time-limited role of the hippocampus in terms of its support of the consolidation of thalamocortical and corticocortical category learning into enduring long-term memories.

BDNF in learning and memory consolidation. How memory consolidation supports an enduring memory of new learning has been extensively studied at least since HM had his operation (McGaugh, 2000, 2002; Mehta, 2007; Nadel and Bohbot, 2001; Takehara, Kawahara, and Krino, 2003; Squire and Alverez, 1995; Takashima et al., 2009; Thompson, Moyer, and Disterhoft, 1996; Tyler et al. 2002). These data show time-limited involvement of the limbic system, which includes the hippocampus, amygdala, and hypothalamus, and long-term involvement of neocortex. This consolidation process has also been linked to the action of neurotrophins (Zang et al., 2007), especially Brain Derived Neurotrophic Factor, or BDNF, a complex class of proteins that have important effects on learning and memory (Heldt et al., 2007; Hu and Russek, 2008; Monteggia et al., 2004; Purves, 1988; Rattiner, Davis, and Ressler, 2005; Schuman, 1999; Thoenen, 1995; Tyler et al., 2002). Postsynaptically, neurotrophins enhance responsiveness of target synapses (Kang and Schuman, 1995; Kohara et al., 2001) and allow for quicker processing (Knipper et al., 1993; Lessman, 1998). Presynaptically, they act as retrograde messenger signals (Davis and Murphy, 1994; Ganguly, Kiss, and Poo, 2000) that arise within a target cell population and flow back to excitatory source cells, where they increase the flow of transmitter from the source cell population, thereby generating a positive feedback loop between the source and the target cells (Schinder, Berninger, and Poo, 2000). Such a positive feedback loop has also been posited in some neural models of learning and memory search, notably the ART 3 model that I published with Gail Carpenter in 1990 (Carpenter and Grossberg, 1990).

BDNF has also been interpreted as an essential component of long-term potentiation (LTP) in normal cell processing (Chen et al., 1995; Phillips et al., 1990). The functional involvement of existing BDNF receptors is critical in early LTP (up to 1 hour) during the acquisition phase of learning the CR, whereas continued activation of the slowly decaying late phase LTP signal (3+ hours) requires new protein synthesis and gene expression. It has also been shown that hippocampal dopamine and the ventral tegmental area provide a temporally sensitive trigger for the expression of BDNF that is essential for long-term consolidation of memory related to reinforcement learning (Rossato et al., 2009).

The BDNF response to a particular stimulus event may vary from milliseconds (initial acquisition) to several days or weeks (long-term memory consolidation). Neurotrophins thus play a role whether the phase of learning is one of initial synaptic enhancement, or of long-term memory consolidation (Kang et al., 1999; Singer, 1999). Furthermore, blockade of BDNF shows that it is essential for memory development at different phases of memory formation (Kang et al., 1997), and during all ages of an individual (Cabelli, Hohn, and Shatz, 1995; Tokuoka et al., 2000). Correspondingly, nSTART qualitatively simulates a role for neurotrophins during both the initial acquisition of a memory, as well as during its ongoing maintenance and memory consolidation.

BDNF is heavily expressed in the hippocampus as well as in the neocortex (cf. Figure 15.2), where neurotrophins figure largely in activity-dependent development and plasticity, not only to build new bridges as needed, but also to inhibit and dismantle old synaptic bridges. A process of competition among axons for BDNF during the development of nerve connections (Bonhoffer, 1996; Tucker, Meyer, and Barde, 2001; Tyler et al., 2002; Van Ooyen and Willshaw, 1999) exists both in young and mature animals (Phillips et al, 1990). BDNF also maintains cortical circuitry for long-term memory that may be shaped by various BDNF-independent factors during and after consolidation (Gorski et al., 2003).

BDNF started to play a role in the models that I developed with my PhD students with the article that Aaron Seitz and I published in 2003 on the development of visual cortex (Grossberg and Seitz, 2003). Here, we modeled in a simple way data about how BDNF may amplify the amounts of both the excitatory transmitter, glutamate, and the inhibitory transmitter, GABA, that regulate cortical development (Berardi and Maffei, 1999). Either too much or two little BDNF interferes with the development of the ocular dominance columns where inputs from the left eye and the right eye are segregated in the visual cortex (Cabelli et al., 1995, 1997). This is thus another Inverted-U property; cf. Figure 1.18.

The nSTART model went considerably beyond this simple beginning to simulate how BDNF may amplify and temporally extend activity-based signals within the hippocampus and the neocortex that facilitate endogenous strengthening of memory without further explicit learning. In particular, memory consolidation may be mechanistically achieved by means of a sustained cascade of BDNF expression beginning in the hippocampus and spreading to the cortex (Buzsáki and Chrobak, 2005; Cousens and Otto, 1998; Hobson and Pace-Schott, 2002; Monteggia et al., 2004; Nádasdy et al., 1999; Smythe, Colom, and Bland, 1992; Staubli and Lynch, 1987; Vertes, Hoover, and Di Prisco, 2004), which is modeled in nSTART by endogenous bursting activity of the hippocampus, abetted by BDNF, after conditioning trials end.

Hippocampal bursting activity is not the only bursting activity that drives consolidation. Long-term activity-dependent consolidation of new learning is also supported by the synchronization of thalamocortical interactions in response to thalamic or cortical inputs (Llinas et al., 1994; Steriade, 1999). This synchronization is a form of adaptive resonance (Figures 2.2 and 5.19). Thalamic bursting neurons may lead to synaptic modifications in cortex, and cortex can in turn influence thalamic oscillations (Sherman and Guillery, 2003; Steriade, 1999).

Thalamocortical resonance has been described as a basis for temporal binding and consciousness in increasingly specific models over the years. These models simulate how specific and nonspecific thalamic nuclei interact with the reticular nucleus and multiple stages of laminar cortical circuitry (Buzsáki et al., 2012; Engel, Fries, and Singer, 2001; Grossberg, 1980, 1999, 2003; Grossberg and Versace, 2008; Pollen, 1999). nSTART qualitatively explains consolidation without including individual bursts, although oscillatory dynamics of this kind arise naturally in finer spiking versions of rate-based cortical models such as SMART (Grossberg and Versace, 2008; Palma, Grossberg, and Versace, 2012; Palma, Versace, and Grossberg, 2012).

The nSTART model focuses on amygdala and hippocampal interactions with thalamus and neocortex during conditioning (Figure 15.2). As noted above, the model simulates how the hippocampus supports thalamocortical and corticocortical category learning that becomes well established during memory consolidation through its endogenous activity (Siapas, Lubenov, and Wilson, 2005; Sosina, 1992) that is supported by neurotrophin mediators (Destexhe, Contreras, and Steriade, 1998). nSTART proposes that thalamocortical sustained activity is maintained through the combination of two mechanisms: the level of cortical BDNF activity, and the learned thalamocortical adaptive weights, or long-term memory (LTM) traces, that are strengthened by the memory consolidation process. This proposal is consistent with trace conditioning data showing that, after consolidation, when the hippocampus is no longer required for performance of CRs, the orbitofrontal cortex is critical for CR performance when it is activated by a thalamic sensory input. The kind of retrograde amnesia that HM experienced is hereby understood as a failure to retain memory, rather than by a failure of adaptive timing (Takehara, Kawahara, and Krino, 2003).

Two kinds of hippocampally-mediated memory consolidation

The previous paragraphs indicate how the nSTART model helps to explain one way in which the hippocampus supports memory consolidation, especially for learned associations between stimuli that are separated by a time interval, as occurs during trace conditioning (Figure 15.1). It does this by maintaining adaptively timed incentive motivation from the hippocampus that supports the memory consolidation process after learning trials end (Figure 15.2).

Chapter 5 discussed a second hippocampally-mediated process that supports a different kind of memory consolidation. Here, corticohippocampal interactions between the attentional and orienting systems in an ART category learning system discover new recognition categories with which to recognize novel objects and events in the world (Figure 5.19). As these objects and events become familiar, the orienting system is automatically disengaged, so that presentation of a familiar object or event can directly activate the learned category that best matches it.

It is important to distinguish these two different kinds of mechanisms when trying to explain failures of memory consolidation. One of them depends on hippocampal adaptive timing and endogenous activation after conditioning trials end. The other depends upon hippocampal sensitivity to mismatch, or novel, events, and how it responds to these events to discover and learn predictive recognition categories.

Failure of adaptive timing in autistic individuals

The failure of adaptive timing in individuals with autism is one of the problems that they can experience. In particular, when learning a conditioned eye blink response, such individuals often perform short-latency, high-amplitude responses, rather than the adaptively timed response that a normal learning subject would generate. I reviewed abundant experimental evidence in my 2006 article with Don Seidman that there can be major cerebellar dysfunction in individuals with autism (Grossberg and Seidman, 2006).

The same kind of premature responses are generated after eye blink conditioning is carried out in normal rabbits, if their cerebellar cortex is then ablated. Figure 15.24a summarizes data showing two different normally timed responses (solid curves), along with the premature responses (dashed curves) that occur after the cerebellar cortex is ablated (Perrett, Ruiz, and Mauk, 1993). When the cerebellar cortex is ablated in the model cerebellum that is summarized in Figure 15.20, premature responses again occur. The model response after ablation in Figure 15.24b was generated after conditioning occurred with an ISI of 500 msec. Figure 15.25a shows the adaptively timed long-term depression (LTD) that was learned at the model Purkinje cells during normal conditioning, and Figure 15.25b shows the disinhibition of the timed response in the cerebellar nuclei that was caused by this timed reduction in cerebellar inhibition.

Because the conditioned eye blink paradigm involves the kind of cerebellar circuitry that is used to adaptively time many kinds of actions, it provides a relatively simple way to test a cerebellar adaptive timing deficit that may also express itself in more complex and socially important behaviors. Indeed, individuals with autism also have difficulty in controlling the timing of their responses in

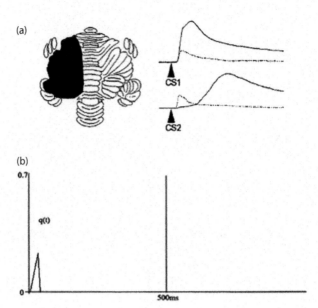

FIGURE 15.24. (a) Data showing normally timed responding (solid curve) and short latency responses after lesioning cerebellar cortex (dashed curve). (b) computer simulation of short latency response after ablation of model cerebellar cortex.

a temporal reproduction paradigm (Szelag et al., 2004). They are unable to match their responses to varying auditory and visual stimulus durations, and consistently reproduced the same response duration independent of stimulus duration. Here again, the adaptive timing function that is controlled by the cerebellum was missing. Don Seidman and I have reviewed other data showing timing problems of such cognitively important abilities as the orienting of visual attention, as well as in the eye movements, arm movements, and jaw movements that are important to carry out properly timed responses in social settings.

Interactions of multiple imbalanced brain regions during autism. A failure of spectrally timed learning in the cerebellum leading to premature responding is just one of the problems that individuals with autism may experience. If the spectral timing circuit in the hippocampus is also affected, then motivated attention may not be maintained on salient goal objects for the necessary amount of time to carry out socially important actions. The exposition of Adaptive Resonance Theory in Chapter 5 additionally noted that autistic individuals may have their vigilance stuck at abnormally high values, leading to hyperspecific category learning and a narrow focus of attention in the neocortex. Chapter 13 showed how underaroused emotional depression of drive and value representations in the hypothalamus and amygdala may lead to a paradoxical combination of flat affect to some situations, combined with intense emotional responses to others. Figure 15.26 summarizes various regions of the brain that may contribute to autistic symptoms due to imbalances, or failures,

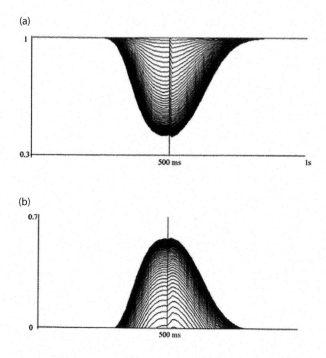

FIGURE 15.25. Computer simulations of (a) adaptively timed long term depression at Purkinje cells, and (b) adaptively timed activation of cerebellar nuclear cells.

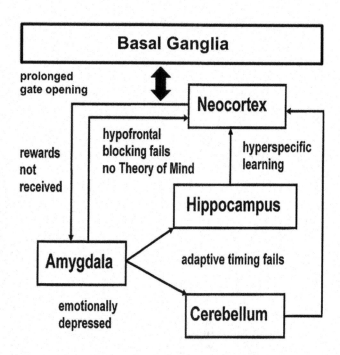

FIGURE 15.26. Brain regions and processes that contribute to autistic behavioral symptoms when they become imbalanced in prescribed ways.

of several different kinds of processes, consistent with the fact that autism may be influenced by multiple genes. Figure 15.26 also includes the basal ganglia. I will propose later in this chapter how particular imbalances in the basal ganglia may cause the types of repetitive behaviors that are found in many individuals with autism.

In general, the core symptoms of autism spectrum disorder have been defined clinically to include deficits in social communication with regards to social reciprocity, communication towards social interaction and skills required to develop, maintain and understand relationships. Along with the insufficiencies in social communication, the presence of restricted and repetitive patterns of behavior is required for a diagnosis of autism spectrum disorder (*Diagnostic and Statistical Manual of Mental Disorders, Fifth Edition*; American Psychiatric Association, 2013). The imbalanced Spectrally Timed Adaptive Resonance Theory, or iSTART, model that I mentioned in Chapter 5 already discussed how abnormally high vigilance can cause a narrow focus of attention and hyperspecific category learning in some autistic individuals. When supplemented, as in Figure 15.26, by the explanation below of how repetitive behaviors due to basal ganglia abnormalities cause repetitive movements, iSTART proposes mechanistic explanations of how all the autistic symptoms listed in Figure 15.26 may be caused, and how they interact together either directly within the brain, or indirectly via environmental feedback.

The effects of indirect environmental feedback should not be ignored, if only because they may intensify and perpetuate autistic symptoms. For example, drive satisfaction often depends upon behaviors that are elicited in response to valued events that have been previously experienced. In order for drive satisfaction to be forthcoming, these behaviors often need to be properly timed to avoid socially disruptive consequences. When drive satisfaction is chronically prevented from occurring as a result of either hyperspecific learning or poorly timed responding, then the corresponding drive representations may become depressed due to disuse. Thus, either hyperspecific learning in neocortical circuits, or failures in adaptive timing in cerebellar or hippocampal circuits, can contribute *indirectly* to underaroused emotional depression in hypothalamic and amygdala circuits, in addition to the *direct* effects on emotional depression of an improper calibration of the tonic arousal that inputs to drive representations and calibrates their sensitivity to external and internal stimuli.

How to break an environmentally-mediated vicious circle that perpetuates symptoms? A "vicious circle" of environmentally mediated feedback can result in which depressed drive representations, say as measured by a hypoactive amygdala, fail to support learning of adaptively timed behaviors in hippocampus and cerebellum, whose absence enables the orienting system in hippocampus to spuriously reset cognitive representations in the neocortex during times when attention should be sustained upon a particular task, which then leads to hyperspecific learning of neocortical recognition categories, which then makes it easier to generate mismatch events with sensory cues, which then prevents the normal frequency of behaviorally-appropriate rewarding signals from being received from the amygdala and other reward centers, which then contributes to the maintenance of depressed drives at these centers.

Understanding of how such a vicious circle may work raises the issue: How can it be broken by various kinds of intervention?

Outstanding questions for further experimentation and theorizing include the following: Can underaroused emotional depression and hypervigilant cognitive learning both sometimes have a similar underlying cause? This is a reasonable question to ask, because both underaroused depression and hypervigilant learning are problems due to incorrectly calibrated gains. In the case of underaroused depression, it is the gain of the excitatory signals that tonically arouse the drive representations, say in the hypothalamus and amygdala. In the case of hypervigilant learning, it is the gain of the excitatory signals that activate, or are activated by, the orienting system, say in the nonspecific thalamus and hippocampal system.

By clarifying that several different routes to autism may exist, and the mechanistic interactions that help to perpetuate autistic symptoms, the iSTART model may help to differentiate individuals with autism early in life in terms of which route they may be on. Such a clinical differentiation may help to discover more individualized treatments in the future.

Fragile X syndrome: Adaptive timing, trace conditioning, and mGluR. Let us now return to a discussion of Fragile X syndrome (FXS) which exhibits just the kind of linkage between adaptively timed learning, trace conditioning, and mGluR that is also found in autism. To get started, what is FXS? As noted by Mark Bear, Kimberly Huber, and Stephen Warren in 2004, FXS is the most common inherited form of mental retardation (Bear, Huber, and Warren, 2004). These authors further posit what they call "the mGluR theory of Fragile X mental retardation". In support of this hypothesis, Matthew Belmonte and Thomas Bourgeron wrote in 2006 that, unlike autism, which may involve symptoms related to multiple genes, "FXS, in contrast, is caused by the silencing of a single gene (FMR1) that codes for the Fragile X mental retardation protein (FMRP), an RNA-binding protein normally produced in response to activation of group-1 metabotropic glutamate receptors" (Belmonte and Bourgeron, 2006). Belmonte and Bourgeron also noted that, while "most cases of autism are not associated with FXS (prevalence 4% or less), the converse is not necessarily true: estimates of the prevalence of autism in FXS have ranged from 5% to as much as 60% . . . Recent studies . . . have yielded prevalence estimates for autism in the FX population between 18% and 33% . . . and

most of the variance between autistic and non-autistic FXS subgroups seems to be within autism's social and communicative dimensions, rather than the dimension of repetitive behaviors and restricted interest."

Ming-Gao Zhao, Hiroki Toyoda, Shanelle Ko, Hoi-Ki Ding, Long-Jun Wu, and Min Zhuo additionally wrote in 2005 (Zhao et al., 2005) that "Children with Fragile X exhibit behavioral problems of severe inattention (Fryns et al., 1984; Baumgardner et al., 1995) and many are diagnosed with ADHD (Cornish et al., 2004)." These authors also performed experiments that support the predicted role of mGluR in the control of adaptively timed learning. They used a mouse model for Fragile X syndrome where the FMR1 gene is silenced, and the action of mGluR thereby disrupted. These mice were trained in trace conditioning experiments wherein a temporal gap between a conditioned stimulus (CS) and a shock unconditioned stimulus (US) needs to be bridged, as in Figure 15.1. Trace conditioning was severely impaired, as would be expected without mGluR to support spectral timing dynamics.

Additional experiments have shown that deletion of FMR1 in cerebellar Purkinje cells causes abnormalities in delay eyeblink conditioning, thereby clarifying how mGluR abnormalities in the adaptively timed learning processes of both the hippocampus and cerebellum may contribute to cognitive and motor deficits in Fragile X individuals (Guo et al., 2012; Huber et al., 2002; Koekkoek et al., 2005; Nosyreva and Huber, 2006; Vinueze Veloz et al., 2012).

Adaptive timing of reward expectation by the basal ganglia substantia nigra pars compacta. So far, I have shown that both the hippocampus and the cerebellum use spectral timing to achieve adaptively timed conditioning. Another part of the brain, the *basal ganglia*, also uses spectral timing, as well as a very similar circuit to compute it. The basal ganglia is a group of subcortical nuclei with multiple connections to other brain regions, and a complex internal structure. In this book, I will focus on two of its main functions: adaptively timed reinforcement learning, and selective gate opening and closing of perceptual, cognitive, emotional, and motor processes that determines whether and when each of these processes may be carried out. The basal ganglia spectral timing circuit includes the *substantia nigra pars compacta*, or SNc. The basal ganglia gating function includes the *substantia nigra pars reticulata*, or SNr.

The SNc adaptively timed circuit is activated by unexpected rewards or punishments. That is why this circuit is sometimes called a *reward expectation filter*, as I noted in Chapter 14. When rewards or punishments unexpectedly occur or do not occur, animals need to learn new ways to acquire or avoid them. These events can be unexpected either in terms of their timing or their amplitude. For example, either delaying food or altering the amount

MODEL OF SPECTRALLY TIMED SNc LEARNING

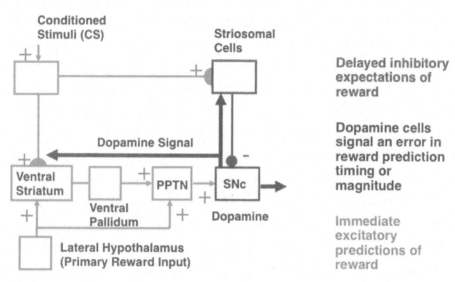

Delayed inhibitory expectations of reward

Dopamine cells signal an error in reward prediction timing or magnitude

Immediate excitatory predictions of reward

Brown, Bullock, and Grossberg (1999)

FIGURE 15.27. Brain regions and processes that contribute to the release of dopaminergic Now Print signals by the substantia nigra parts compacta, or SNc, in response to unexpected reinforcing events. See the text for details.

of available food can trigger new learning to cope with the change.

When an unexpected reward or punishment occurs, activated SNc cells broadcast learning signals to many parts of the brain, including the basal ganglia themselves. These signals are sometimes called Now Print signals because they support the learning of new associations that enable a human or animal to better cope with the unexpected event. After the brain learns to predict the new reinforcer timing and amplitude, the valued event is no longer unexpected, so SNc is no longer activated. This is thus a self-terminating learning process.

In 1999, my PhD student Joshua Brown and I, along with my colleague Daniel Bullock, published a model of how the basal ganglia reward expectation filter works, and used it to explain and simulate many of the neurophysiological data that had recently been recorded from the SNc in response to unexpected and expected reinforcers (Brown, Bullock, and Grossberg, 1999). Figure 15.27 summarizes the model circuit that we proposed. This circuit is also shown in Figure 14.4a.

It is repeated in Figure 15.27 with additional notations to emphasize points made in the text. Figure 15.28 summarizes some of the most important neurophysiological data from the SNc of monkeys that were recorded by Wolfram Schultz and his colleagues (Schultz et al., 1993), and a computer simulation of these data. This is just a small subset of the data that the model circuit in Figure 15.27 has explained and simulated, but it makes the main points. I will summarize how the model works before using it to explain the data in Figure 15.28.

As in the spectral timing circuit within the cerebellum (Figure 15.20), the basal ganglia circuit is controlled by two parallel pathways in which conditioning occurs: an excitatory pathway (in green) and an adaptively timed inhibitory pathway (in red) that converge on the SNc (Figure 15.27). Again as in the cerebellum, both of these adaptive pathways are activated by a CS. In the model circuit in Figure 15.27, one site of learning is in the ventral striatum S, and the other in the striosomes. Learning in the ventral striatum enables a CS to activate the SNc all by itself, and thus trigger a Now Print learning signal. Learning in the striosomes adaptively times an inhibitory

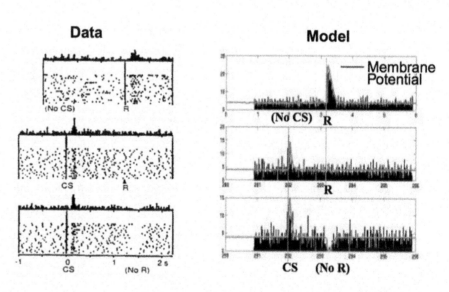

FIGURE 15.28. Neurophysiological data (left column) and model simulations (right column) of SNc responses. See the text for details.

EXCITATORY PATHWAY

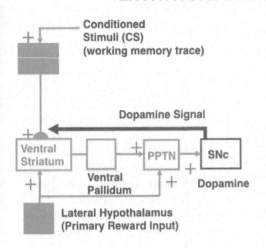

FIGURE 15.29. Excitatory pathways that support activation of the SNc by a US and the conditioning of a CS to the US.

signal from the striosomes to the SNc. Green arrowheads at the ends of pathways denote excitatory pathways, red circles denote inhibitory pathways, and green hemidisks denote excitatory synapses at which learning occurs. Thick purple pathways denote dopaminergic signals. Figures 15.29-15.32 break down the dynamics of this circuit into its component pathways.

Even before a CS can activate the SNc due to conditioning, a US can do so. I will use information in both Figure 14.4a and 15.27 to explain this process. These figures show that a US activates an input I_R from the lateral hypothalamus. This input excites the SNc via the pedunculo-pontine tegmental nucleus, or PPTN, with strength W_{RP}. The PPTN, in turn, activates the SNc with strength W_{PD}. The net effect is that a sufficiently strong US can activate the SNc and thereby trigger a Now Print signal, without requiring any new learning. This figure shows only the Now Print pathway to the ventral striatum and striosomal cells. In reality, the Now Print signal reaches many more brain regions. For example, Chapter 14 summarized its importance in regulating learning in the PFC.

This Now Print signal releases the transmitter dopamine, which modulates the course of learning. Here I will focus on the role of Now Print signals in regulating the two kinds of learning that control SNc Now Print outputs. In addition to activating the SNc, the US also acts as a teaching signal in the ventral striatum S. It reaches S via a pathway with strength W_{RS}. Multiple CSs also input to

S. In particular, the ith CS, CS_i, activates an input I_i that is multiplied by an adaptive weight W_{iS} on its way to S. The gated signal from CS_i to S is $I_i W_{iS}$. Pairing CS_i with the US strengthens the weight W_{iS} until CS_i can activate S all by itself, and thereby also trigger a Now Print output signal. It should be noted that this excitatory pathway gets conditioned to CS_i if it overlaps with a US because the US supplies both a teaching signal to S *and* a dopaminergic Now Print burst to S via the SNc.

Figure 15.30 summarizes the inhibitory conditioning pathway. Each CS_i also sends an input I_i to the striosomes along this pathway with adaptive weight Z_{ij}. Just one such weight is labeled in Figure 14.4a, for simplicity, but the diagram is intended to depict that there is a different weight for each cell site in a spectral timing circuit whose activities x_{ij} respond to I_i at different rates r_j, just as in Figure 15.19. The activity x_{ij} triggers an output signal G_{ij} that is multiplied, or gated, by a habituative transmitter Y_{ij} before it is gated again by the adaptive weight Z_{ij}, just as in Figures 15.3 and 15.11-15.13. When a doubly-gated signal $G_{ij}Y_{ij}Z_{ij}$ is received at the striosomes at the same time as a US-activated dopaminergic burst, the corresponding adaptive weight Z_{ij} is strengthened.

In this way, each CS_i activates a *spectral timing* circuit at the striosomal cells (Figure 15.31). Adaptively timed learning in the inhibitory pathway occurs if one or more of the spectral timing cells has been activated by the CS_i

INHIBITORY PATHWAY

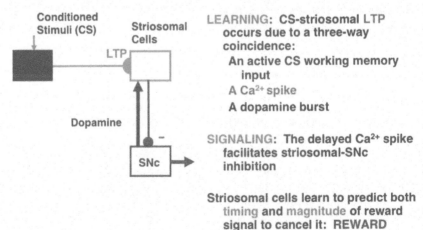

FIGURE 15.30. The inhibitory pathway from striosomal cells to the SNc is able to inhibit the SNc when a reward occurs with expected timing and magnitude.

EXPECTATION TIMING
HOW DO CELLS BRIDGE HUNDREDS OF MILLISECONDS?

Timing Spectrum

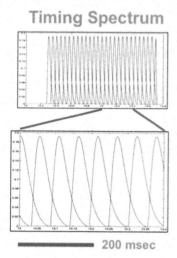

200 msec

CS activates a population of cells with delayed transient signals mGluR

Fiala, Grossberg and Bullock (1996)
Grossberg and Merrill (1992, 1996)
Grossberg and Schmajuk (1989)

Each has a different delay, so that the range of delays covers the entire interval

Delayed transients gate both learning **and** read-out **of expectations**

FIGURE 15.31. The CS activates a population of striosomal cells that respond with different delays in order to enable adaptively timed inhibition of the SNc.

signal at the same time that a US-activated dopamine burst occurs from the SNc. The population sum of such doubly-gated adaptive signals causes adaptively timed inhibition of SNc to peak at that time, just as in Figures 15.3c and 15.3d.

As in the hippocampus and cerebellum, it is assumed that the different activation rates r_j in the spectrum are due to a calcium gradient that interacts with mGluR; hence the phrase "Ca^{2+} spike" in Figure 15.30. Inhibition from this adaptively timed CS-activated pathway inhibits activation of the SNc when a US reward has the expected timing and magnitude. In other words, if a US inputs to the SNc with the expected magnitude and timing after a CS, then the adaptively timed inhibition from the striosomes will cancel it, thereby preventing the SNc from activating Now Print signals when nothing unexpected is happening.

Figure 15.32 clarifies how this adaptively timed learning matches both the expected US timing *and* magnitude. If reward intensity is greater than expected, then a dopamine *burst* causes the striosomal connection strength to increase, so that the striosomal inhibition is big enough to cancel it. However, if reward intensity is less than expected, then a dopamine *dip* causes striosomal connection strength to decrease, so that the striosomal inhibition is again

matched to the expected US intensity. These properties embody a negative feedback loop that terminates SNc Now Print learning signals when the learned inhibitory expectation signals from the striosomal cells match the timing *and* amplitude of the excitatory US signals to the SNc.

The data in Figure 15.28 can now easily be explained. Before conditioning, the monkey does not know that the CS (in this case, a light) predicts reward. Thus the US can activate SNc without any effect of the CS. Figure 15.28 (top row) shows the SNc activity burst when the US reward (R) occurs. After conditioning occurs, the monkey learns to expect the reward amplitude and timing. Presentation of the CS followed by the US in the same way as during conditioning trials now leads to a different result: Figure 15.28 (middle row) shows that the US excitatory input to SNc is cancelled by the spectrally timed inhibitory input to SNc, so no SNc burst occurs at R. However, because the CS has been conditioned to activate SNc via the striatal-pallidal-PPTN-SNc route, an SNc burst does occur right after the CS is presented. Finally, suppose that the CS is presented after conditioning, but the US is not. Then, as shown in Figure 15.28 (bottom row), the CS again causes a burst. In addition, the adaptively timed inhibition causes a dip in SNc firing at the time when the US was expected to occur. Due to the absence of the US, there is no excitatory input to cancel the inhibition.

The data and simulations in Figure 15.28 are repeated in Figure 14.4b. While I am at it, let me note that

INHIBITORY PATHWAY: EXPECTATION *MAGNITUDE*

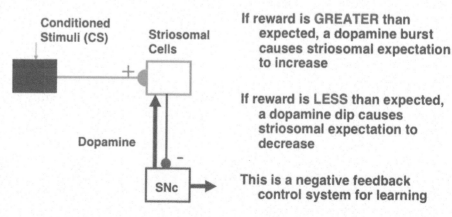

If reward is GREATER than expected, a dopamine burst causes striosomal expectation to increase

If reward is LESS than expected, a dopamine dip causes striosomal expectation to decrease

This is a negative feedback control system for learning

FIGURE 15.32. The SNc can generate both dopamine bursts and dips in response to rewards whose amplitude is unexpectedly large or small.

the model also explains the data in the five conditions (A–E) of Figure 14.4c, among others. In A, the dopamine cells learn to fire in response to the earliest consistent predictor of reward. In particular, when a CS_2 (instruction) consistently precedes the original CS (trigger) by a fixed interval, the dopamine cells learn to fire only in response to CS_2 (Schultz et al., 1993). In B, during training, the cell fires weakly in response to both the CS and reward (Ljungberg et al., 1992). Condition C illustrates what happens when there is temporal variability in reward occurrence: When reward is received later than predicted, a depression occurs at the time of predicted reward, followed by a phasic burst at the time of actual reward. In D, if reward occurs earlier than predicted, a phasic burst occurs at the time of actual reward. No depression follows because the CS is released from working memory (Hollerman and Schultz, 1998). In E, when there is random variability in the timing of primary reward across trials (e.g., when the reward depends on an operant response to the CS), the striosomal cells produce a Mexican Hat depression on either side of the dopamine spike (Schultz et al., 1993).

A calcium spectrum in HeLa cancer cells, Xenopus oocytes, and cardiac myocytes. Spectral timing seems to be an ancient discovery that reappears in various forms in many living systems. Even in non-neural tissues, these timed spectra are due to quantal release of Ca^{2+} gradients from inositol 1,4,5-trisphosphate (IP_3)-sensitive intracellular stores (cf. Figure 15.23). Such a timed spectrum has, for example, been reported in HeLa cancer cells. A HeLa cell is a cell type in an immortal cell line that was derived from cervical cancer cells taken on February 8, 1951 from Henrietta Lacks. A spectrum in the form of an "intracellular Ca^{2+} pool in HeLa cells is composed of functionally discrete units. Upon stimulation by histamine, these units produce localized Ca^{2+} signals. The sequential activation and summation of these units results in Ca^{2+} wave propagation and, furthermore, the differential recruitment of these units may underlie the graded amplitude of the intracellular Ca2+ signals" (Bootman and Berridge, 1996, p. 855). In other words, a gradient of Ca^{2+} concentrations seems to be responsible for the spectrum in HeLa cells, just as it is in the spectra in cerebellum, hippocampus, and basal ganglia.

Variations of these dynamics can be found in many kinds of cells, including the "puffs" in *Xenopus* oocytes (Yao, Choi, and Parker, 1995) and the "sparks" in cardiac myocytes (Cannell, Cheng, and Lederer, 1995; López-López et al., 1995). The evolution of spectral timing from an ancient and widespread process governing Ca^{2+} signalling to a process that can be modulated by associative learning to carry out adaptively timed brain functions is a fascinating topic that merits much more experimentation and theorizing.

Basal ganglia gating of all behaviors. In addition to the role of the SNc in generating widespread dopaminergic Now Print signals to support new associative learning (Figure 15.27), Chapter 12 also noted that the basal ganglia also control the opening and closing of gates in the substantia nigra pars reticulata (SNr) to activate and terminate cognitive, emotional, and motor processes. I will now describe several kinds of timed behaviors that this gating function controls in both typical individuals and clinical patients, notably individuals with autism.

Figures 6.13 and 15.33 illustrate that the basal ganglia are organized into multiple feedback loops to selectively accomplish this gating function. The orbitofrontal dynamics of the MOTIVATOR model (Figure 14.3a) are, for example, gated in one of these loops (see the blue arrow in Figure 15.33). The DLPFC and FEF that I discussed in Chapter 14 are gated by two other basal ganglia loops. Moreover, distinct zones in the basal ganglia are devoted to each of these loops (Figure 15.34) to enable their selective action.

The SNr and SNc carry out complementary functions, for the same reason that CogEM and the reward expectation filter do. An SNr gate opens to enable a behavior to occur. Then the SNc is activated if the behavior leads to an unexpected reward. This cycle repeats itself until the reward is expected. Then, CogEM incentive motivation and the corresponding SNr gate together enable the orbitofrontal cortex to continue reading out its action until the next unexpected reward occurs.

Basal ganglia gating during normal and autistic repetitive behaviors. The SNr gating function is vividly illustrated by its effects on motor control, both in normal individuals and in clinical patients. Perhaps Parkinson's disease is the most familiar clinical example of how abnormal basal ganglia gating can cause both motor and cognitive disabilities. In the next few sections, I will summarize how opening an SNr gate can release an action whose properties are controlled by downstream circuits. Normally, such gating events are under volitional control. Sometimes the gate is open for a brief time, so that one action can be performed. Other times it is kept open for such a long time that repetitive behaviors, such as walking or running, can occur. These repetitive behaviors are typically controlled by recurrent shunting on-center off-surround networks that are downstream from the gates. Chapters 1 and 4 have already discussed some of the valuable properties of this class of recurrent networks. In the present examples, the recurrent network responds to gate opening by generating sustained oscillations in downstream networks that cause the same behavior to occur over and over again.

You might naturally ask: Why were oscillations not generated in the recurrent shunting on-center off-surround networks that were previously mentioned? One main reason can be summarized in a single word: Parameters!

MOTIVATOR MODELS ONE OF SEVERAL
THALAMOCORTICAL LOOPS THROUGH BASAL GANGLIA

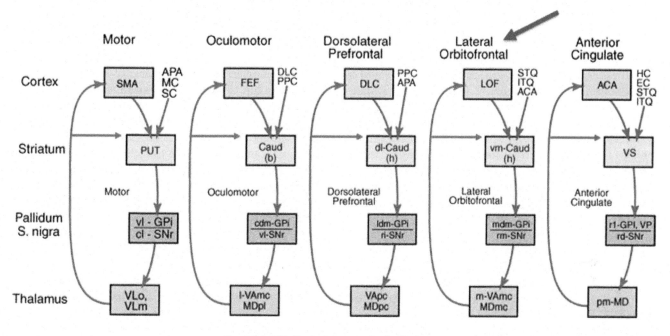

Adapted from *Fundamental Neuroscience*. Copyright Elsevier.

FIGURE 15.33. The basal ganglia gate neural processing in many parts of the brain. The feedback loop through the lateral orbitofrontal cortex (blue arrow) is the one that MOTIVATOR models.

DISTINCT BASAL GANGLIA ZONES FOR EACH LOOP

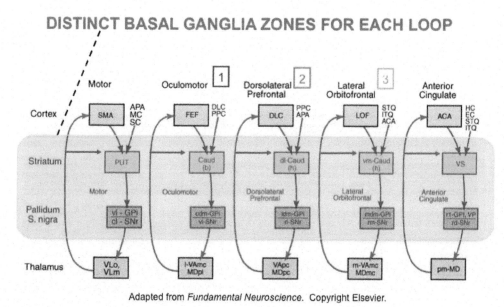

Adapted from *Fundamental Neuroscience*. Copyright Elsevier.

FIGURE 15.34. The colored regions are distinct parts of the basal ganglia in the loops depicted in Figure 15.33.

I published an article in 1975 with my PhD student Samuel Ellias (Ellias and Grossberg, 1975) that begin a systematic mathematical analysis of conditions under which such a recurrent network does, or does not, oscillate. One factor that facilitates oscillations is to slow down the rate with which its recurrent inhibitory interneurons respond to their inputs. Then a network that cannot oscillate can bifurcate into one that can. Another factor, even in a network whose inhibitory interneurons are "slow", is how aroused the network is; in other words, how open the gate is. The fact that the same network can exist in both a steady state and an oscillatory mode clarifies how we can, for example, sit or stand quite happily for awhile, yet also get up to walk or even run when we want to do that instead.

The next sections summarize how the basal ganglia can cause repetitive behaviors in normal individuals by keeping gates open for a long time, under volitional control. These examples illustrate the machinery for repetitive behaviors that exists in all brains. After that, I will propose how repetitive behaviors in autistic individuals, such as repetitive hand clapping or rocking behaviors (Bodfish et al., 2000; McBride, 2015; Militerni et al., 2002; Turner, 1999), may be generated by imbalances in basal ganglia circuitry that keep gates for a long time, even without volitional control. These results were published in 2018 with my graduate student Devika Kishnan (Grossberg and Kishnan, 2018).

The results raise the basic question: How does "volition" open a basal ganglia gate? What part of the brain generates the signals to the basal ganglia that opens these gates? A proposed answer to this question was given in Chapter 12 when I described how gating works within the TELOS and lisTELOS models, including how planned behaviors can be learned using the prefrontal cortex, and how these prefrontal representations can learn to selectively open the basal ganglia gates that enable expression of these behaviors.

Repetitive behaviors in normal individuals: Motor gaits and saccade staircases. Normal repetitive behaviors include repetitive motor gaits, such as walking or running (Brown, 1911), and saccade staircases, which are series of stereotyped saccadic eye movements that are caused by sustained electrical stimulation of the superior colliculus (Schiller and Stryker, 1972). Neither of these behaviors is always repetitive: Sustained postures such as standing or sitting typically alternate with walking or running, and individual saccades to visual targets are the norm, not saccade staircases.

Both of these repetitive behaviors may be traced to

prolonged opening of an appropriate SNr gate, or equivalent event, throughout the repetitive performance. During gaits, opening an appropriate gate has the effect of disinhibiting a GO signal that drives a central pattern generator, or CPG, in the spinal cord. I published in 1997 with my PhD student Christopher Pribe, and my colleague Michael Cohen, a neural model of CPG dynamics that we used to simulate well-known gates, such as a walk, trot, pace, or gallop (Figure 15.35b), and the observed transitions between them (Pribe, Grossberg, and Cohen, 1997). This CPG is a specialized recurrent shunting on-center off-surround network (Figure 15.35a). Increasing the model's GO signal causes the CPG to transition from one gait pattern to the next. We simulated gaits and their transitions that are familiar in cats (walk-trot-pace-gallop), humans (walk-run), and elephants (amble-walk) using variants of this CPG circuit. Increasing the GO signal corresponds to the desire to go faster.

The basal ganglia also control the release of ballistic eye movements called saccades, whereby humans and many other animals rapidly move their eyes to point their foveal regions directly at objects of interest (Handel and Glimcher, 1999, 2000; Hikosaka and Wurtz, 1983; Kori et al., 1995; Shaikh et al, 2011). As I discussed in Chapter

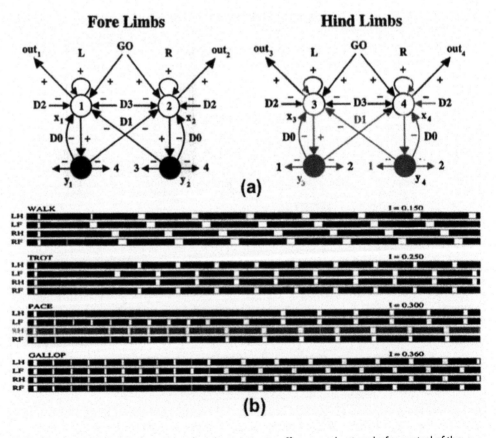

FIGURE 15.35. (a) A pair of recurrent shunting on-center off-surround networks for control of the fore limbs and hind limbs. (b) Varying the GO signal to these networks can trigger changes in movement gaits. See the text for details.

3 and Figure 3.4, the fovea is the region of highest acuity in retinas that have them. In a normal brain, the SNr tonically inhibits the deeper layers of superior colliculus, or SC. I noted in Chapter 6, during my discussion of blindsight, that the SC contains a map of visual space. Activation of any position in this map can command saccades in both eyes that point the eyes at the corresponding position in space. Such activation can be caused by disinhibiting the tonic SNr inhibition of that position in the SC map. The SC output signal is then converted, by a downstream recurrent network, into a saccade with the correct direction and distance to foveate the desired position in space. This kind of circuit is called a *saccade generator*, or SG. The SG occurs in the peripontine reticular formation, or PPRF (Keller, 1974; Raybourn and Keller, 1977; Robinson, 1981).

To explain how the saccade generator works, along with lots of behavioral, anatomical, and neurophysiological data about saccadic eye movement properties, I published in 1998 with my PhD student Gregory Gancarz (Gancarz and Grossberg, 1998) a model of the PPRF SG that we called the FOVEATE, or Feedback Opponent VEctor ArchiTEcture, model. Figure 15.36a summarizes this network. The Right and Left inputs to the network come from the model SC. They activate the SG's long lead burst neurons (LLBN). The LLBN then send excitatory signals to the excitatory burst neurons (EBN). The EBN excite inhibitory burst neurons (IBN), which inhibit the LLBN that led to their excitation. This negative feedback loop is responsible for eliciting saccade staircases when it is allowed to oscillate through time.

FOVEATE also models how omnipause neurons (OPN) maintain tonically active inhibition of the EBN that keeps these cells inhibited until a saccade is desired. When the OPN are active, the EBN cannot fire. Since the EBN activate the tonic neurons (TN), which in turn activate the motor neurons (MN) that move the eyes, no saccade occurs until the OPN shuts off.

Figure 15.37 describes the cyclic dynamics whereby the OPN shut off and the LLBN-EBN-IBN-LLBN feedback loop generates one or more saccades. During fixation, the model is in the rest phase. As shown in Fig. 15.37A, the OPNs are then active, thereby inhibiting the EBNs and suppressing saccades. When the Right or Left inputs to the SG are turned on, the LLBN activity begins to build. This is known as the *charge phase* (Figure 15.37B). The LLBN then inhibits the OPN. Once the LLBN has successfully turned the OPN off, the EBN is free to burst due to excitation from the LLBN, and the model enters the *burst phase* (Figure 15.37C). During the burst phase, negative feedback from the EBN to the LLBN, through the IBN, causes the LLBN activity to decay. The EBN activity then also decays, because the excitatory input from the LLBN to the EBN is decreasing. Once the EBN burst has turned off the LLBN through the negative feedback loop, the model enters the *shutdown phase* (Figure 15.37D).

With the LLBN off, inhibition of the OPN is removed, and the OPN begins to fire again. The OPN activity strongly inhibits the EBN, in effect 'resetting' it. The model is now once again at the rest phase, and the reset cycle is complete.

If the input to the model SG is left on, say by direct and sustained electrical stimulation of a LLBN, then the LLBN again begins to charge in response to the sustained input, and the saccadic cycle continues. Sustained electrical stimulation to the deeper layers of the SC has an effect equivalent to keeping a basal ganglia gate open for an unusually long time, and also results in a saccade staircase (McIlwain, 1986; Schiller and Stryker, 1972). As shown in Figure 15.36b, a saccade staircase is also generated by the FOVEATE model when the SC gate remains open for a long enough time. This figure depicts a simulated saccade staircase of three saccades. Eye position was sampled during each saccade at regular time intervals. The dots in the image show the simulated eye position at these times.

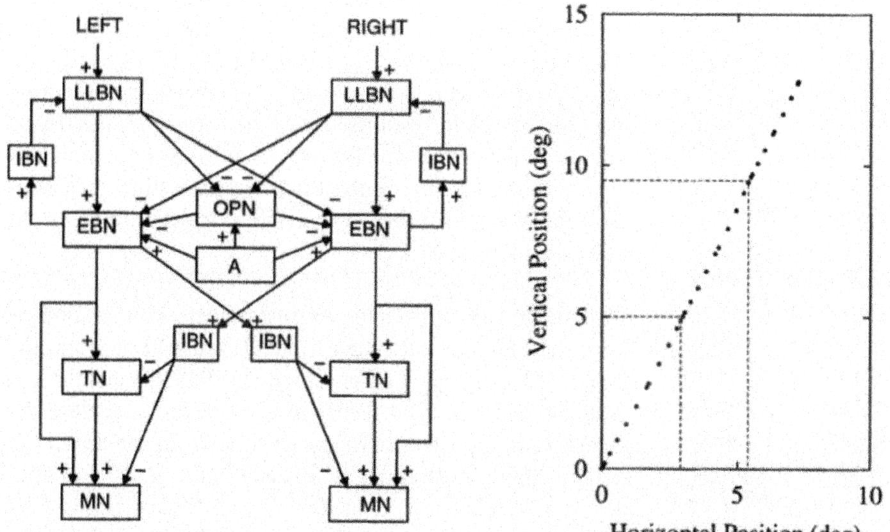

(a)

(b)

FIGURE 15.36. (a) The FOVEATE model circuit for the control of saccadic eye movements within the peri-pontine reticular formation. (b) A simulated saccade staircase. See the text for details.

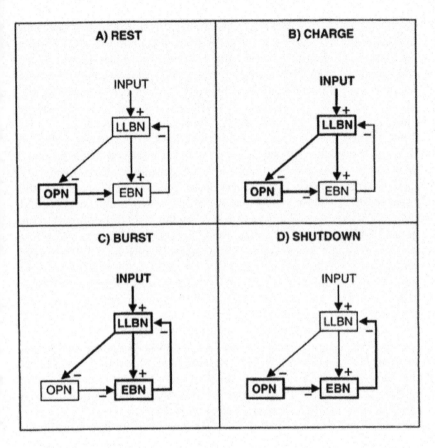

FIGURE 15.37. Steps in the FOVEATE model's generation of a saccade. See the text for details.

The above examples show how, in normal individuals, sustained opening of an SNr gate can trigger repetitive behaviors that are controlled by recurrent neural circuits that are downstream from the open gate.

Repetitive behaviors in restricted environments: Tonic motor drive. Repetitive behaviors also occur in normal animals who are housed in restricted environments, such as in a zoo, farm, and laboratory (Mason, 1991; Wurbel, 2001), or who experience early social deprivation (Harlow, Dodsworth, and Harlow, 1965). Unlike repetitive behaviors that are caused when a phasically active basal ganglia gate stays open for too long, these repetitive behaviors may be energized by tonically active GO signals. These long-acting GO signals typically energize exploratory behaviors that may go on for hours during a terrestrial animal's waking hours, and enable them to find food and other necessities, This kind of exploration is, however, prevented in restricted environments. The tonically active GO signals may nonetheless still remain ON, because they are energized by output signals of a circadian pacemaker in the suprachiasmatic nuclei (SCN) of the hypothalamus (Stephan and Nunez, 1977). During waking hours, these circadian signals provide a critical component of the arousal that

energizes the gated dipoles within the amygdalar/hypothalamic value categories of the CogEM and MOTIVATOR models (Figures 1.14, 1.15, 13.1, and 14.3a).

Hypothalamic circadian oscillator arouses appetitive drive representations. The next section will briefly summarize a model of the SCN circadian pacemaker, called the Gated Pacemaker model, to provide a clearer picture of how it may arouse hypothalamic gated dipole drive representations. This summary will show that, remarkably, the appetitive hypothalamic networks in CogEM and MOTIVATOR and the circadian hypothalamic networks in the Gated Pacemaker both seem to be variations of the same network design; namely, a recurrent gated dipole network. The appetitive networks are not, however, endogenously active oscillators, whereas the circadian network is. This comparison will thus provide yet another example wherein one variant of a brain design reacts phasically to its inputs, whereas another sustains endogenous oscillations.

Recall that we saw the same kind of comparison when I discussed how variants of recurrent shunting on-center off-surround networks can support synchronous oscillations in Chapter 5. The mechanisms that account for the phasic vs. oscillatory dichotomy in both examples are also mathematically similar. In a gated pacemaker oscillator, habituative transmitter gates are a key factor in maintaining oscillations in response to a tonic arousal level. These transmitter gates are the "slow variable" in this circuit. In the on-center off-surround networks, inhibitory interneurons play the role of the slow variable, again in response to a tonic arousal level.

Circadian and appetitive hypothalamic circuit homologs. The Gated Pacemaker model (Figure 15.38a) was introduced by Gail Carpenter and me in 1983 (Carpenter and Grossberg (1983, 1984, 1985) to explain and simulate the plentiful quantitative behavioral data about circadian activity cycles in both diurnal animals (left circuit) and nocturnal animals (right circuit) that are controlled by SCN dynamics (e.g., Figure 15.38b). See also Butler et al. (2012). Our hypothesis was that the SCN pacemaker arouses goal-oriented operant behaviors that can fill an animal's waking hours with specific behaviors that are appropriate to different environmental conditions. Given sufficient arousal from the SCN circadian oscillator, different behaviors were proposed to be energized at appetitive value

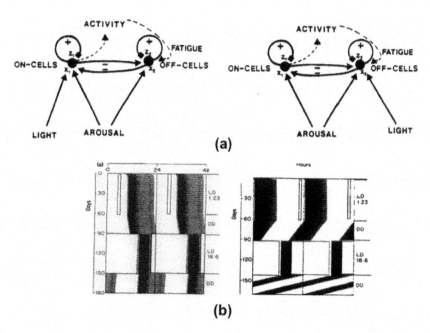

(a)

(b)

FIGURE 15.38. (a) The Gated Pacemaker model for the control of circadian rhythms is a recurrent shunting on-center off-surround network whose excitatory feedback signals are gated by habituative transmitters. Tonic arousal signals energize the pacemaker. Diurnal (left) and nocturnal (right) pacemakers are determined by whether phasic light signals turn the pacemaker on or off. An activity-dependent fatigue signal prevents the pacemaker from becoming overly active for too long. (b) Two simulations of circadian activity cycles during different schedules of light (L) and dark (D). See the text for details.

categories by the usual sensory-drive heterarchical constraints on how reinforcing and drive cues interact, as in the CogEM model (Figures 1.17 and 13.1). Data supporting the hypothesis that such a behavioral arousing function of the SCN exists have been reported by several groups (e.g., Abrahamson, Leak, and Moore, 2001; Deurveilher and Semba, 2005; Saper et al, 2005).

As I will now summarize, key circuit elements in the SCN gated pacemaker and the appetitive value categories are homologous. Both types of circuits also occur close to each other in the hypothalamus. It is therefore tempting to believe that they are variations of a shared circuit design. For starters, both are opponent processes with ON and OFF cells. The gates in the gated pacemaker model are habituative transmitters (Figure 15.38), just as in a gated dipole hypothalamic drive representation, as can be better seen by the more explicit model circuits in Figure 15.39 that show the gated dipole hypothalamic drive representations in the MOTIVATOR model (in the lower left dashed box). In the circadian clock circuit, the opponent process is a recurrent on-center off-surround network whose circadian oscillation is energized by a tonically active arousal level, just as in a gated dipole drive representation. Habituative gating in a hypothalamic eating circuit can modulate the time course of eating and other appetitive behaviors, just as habituative gating in the SCN circadian

circuit can determine the period of the circadian clock in the dark. Just as an external food cue can energize the ON channel of a hypothalamic gated dipole eating circuit to trigger eating behavior, a light cue can energize an SCN diurnal gated dipole circuit to trigger operant exploratory behavior (Figure 15.38a, left circuit). Just as a satiety signal to the OFF channel of a hypothalamic gated dipole eating circuit can inhibit eating behavior, a fatigue signal to the OFF channel of an SCN gated dipole can inhibit operant behavior (Figure 15.38a). The hypothalamic SCN circadian clock design is thus strikingly similar to that of the nearby hypothalamic gated dipole drive circuits of the CogEM model that it arouses.

Transfer from one operant activity to another in restricted environments. In a restricted environment, the persistently active GO signal from the SCN cannot be fully expressed and fatigued by the exploratory behaviors that they normally support. How, then, is all this unused GO "energy" expressed? Instead, of getting utilized by exploratory behaviors, the GO signal can energize the kinds of behaviors that *are* possible in a restrictive environment, much as "generalized drives" can transfer from one operant activity to another under certain conditions (Amsel and Maltzman, 1950; Miller, 1948). Due to the tonic nature of the GO signal, and the slow time scale of the drive inputs, the gates that control the possible behaviors can remain open for longer than is normally the case, thereby enabling persistent repetitions of them. In particular, the GO-derived arousal inputs vary on a circadian time scale, or time scale of around a day, and the internal drive inputs vary on an ultradian time scale, or time scale of several hours. When these sustained internal inputs combine with more rapidly varying conditioned reinforcer cue inputs at a value category such as the amygdala/hypothalamus (Figure 13.1), they can activate incentive motivational signals to object-value categories in the orbitofrontal cortex, and thereby trigger the corresponding operant behaviors, for as long as the internal inputs support the polyvalent constraints on cell firing. At the same time, the amygdala value category helps to activate the basal ganglia GO signal gates that allow the behavior to be expressed (Friedman, Aggleton, and Saunders, 2002; Groenewegen, 2003; Voorn et al., 2004). The above explanations of gate control and saccade staircases illustrate how keeping basal ganglia gates open for a longer time can generate repetitive behaviors, even if the environments are not restricted.

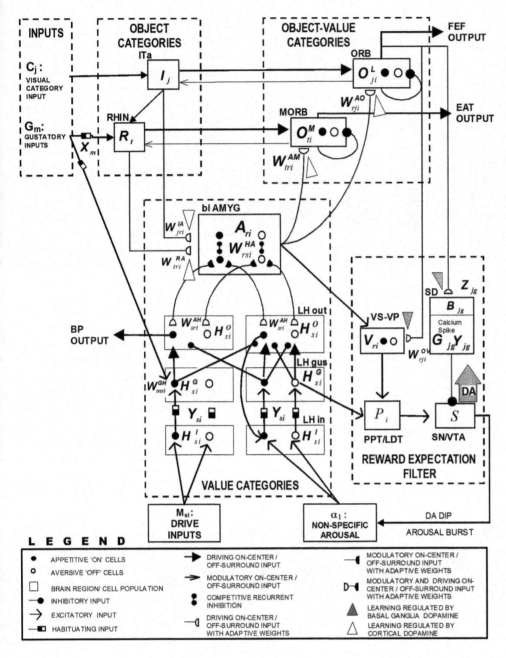

FIGURE 15.39. Circuits of the MOTIVATOR model that show hypothalamic gated dipoles.

architecture that is capable of learning and performing multiple sensory-motor tasks. I already summarized in Chapter 12 how TELOS can balance the demands of reactive and planned movements, and how it "knows before it knows" that it is in the process of selecting a movement plan, and keeps movement gates closed to prevent an unappropriate reactive movement from being triggered during the selection process. A movement plan is chosen by a frontal-parietal resonance that enables the movement gate of the contextually-correct planned movement to open and release the movement (Figure 12.59).

As illustrated in Figure 15.40, the direct pathway carries out a GO function, while the indirect pathway carries out a STOP function (Gerfen and Bolam, 2010; Haynes and Haber, 2013; Jin et al, 2014). The direct pathway can open a gate by activating an inhibitory projection—that uses the inhibitory transmitter GABA—from the dorsal striatum to the globus pallidus (GPi) of the SNr, which in turn sends inhibitory GABAergic neurons to the thalamus. Activating the GO signal hereby disinhibits target thalamic cells, thereby enabling their thalamocortical loop in Figures 15.33 and 15.34 to fire. In contrast, the indirect pathway carries out a STOP function because it contains inhibitory GABAergic projections to the external globus pallidus (GPe), which further inhibits the GPi (Gerfen and Bolam, 2010; Graybiel, 2000).

In all, activation of the striatum in the GO pathway at the initiation of an action inhibits the GPi, thereby disinhibiting the thalamus and permitting the release of action sequences. Activating the STOP pathways at the end of the action sequence inhibits the GPe, which disinhibits

Prolonged gate opening and involuntary repetitive movements in autism. The examples of gait control and saccade staircases show how sustained opening of an SNr gate can elicit a repetitive behavior even in normal individuals, when the open gate energizes oscillations of a recurrent circuit downstream. I will now summarize how sustained gate opening can occur in autistic individuals as a result of enhanced activation of the basal ganglia direct pathway or suppression of its indirect pathway (Figure 15.40), or a combination of the two. Figure 12.58 shows how the direct and indirect pathways are included in the larger TELOS

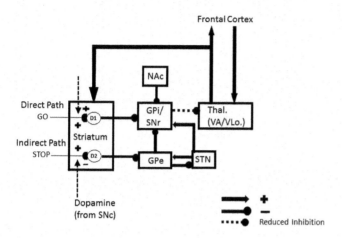

FIGURE 15.40. The direct and indirect basal ganglia circuits that control GO and STOP movement signals. See the text for details.

the GPi, thus counteracting the action of the GO signal. The non-execution of a plan or action has been attributed in TELOS modeling studies to either the inability to activate a sufficiently strong GO signal, or an overactive STOP signal that blocks plan implementation, or some combination of these GO and STOP signals acting together (Brown, Bullock and Grossberg, 2004).

My 2018 article on Fragile X syndrome and repetitive behaviors in autistic individuals with Devika Kishnan (Grossberg and Kishnan, 2018) summarizes experiments that illustrate how sustained gate opening due to an imbalance in the direct and indirect pathways can cause prolonged gate opening that releases repetitive behaviors from recurrent networks further downstream.

D1 and D2 receptors and nucleus accumbens for direct and indirect pathway control. Here I will summarize one important additional fact that is reviewed in greater detail in my article with Devi. As noted in Figure 15.40, the D1 dopamine receptor has been found to be expressed mainly by neurons in the direct pathway, while the D2 dopamine receptor is expressed mostly by neurons of the indirect pathway (Gerfen and Bolam, 2010; Graybiel et. al, 2000). D1 receptors have been suggested to excite the direct pathway, while D2 receptors have an inhibitory effect on the indirect pathway (Wichmann and DeLong, 1996).

Another important region is the nucleus accumbens (NAc), which is a part of the ventral striatum of the basal ganglia that is significant for reward processing (Figure 15.40; Kelley, Smith-Roe, and Holahan, 1997; Knutson et al., 2001). The NAc is also known to have GABAergic projections to the globus pallidus (Mogenson, Jones, and Yim, 1980; Newman and Winan, 1980; Swanson and Cowan, 1975), which could be significant for regulating behaviors. One possibility is that an increase in the inhibitory activity from the NAc to the GPi could contribute in reducing the

effect of the STOP signal, leading to perseverative behavior through the action of downstream recurrent circuits. In other words, an increase in inhibition of the GPi by the NAc could be one of the causes for an imbalance between direct and indirect pathways that can support perseverative behaviors by enabling a basal ganglia gate to remain open longer than is necessary for eliciting an individual behavioral response.

The following experimental data are consistent with this working hypothesis: An imaging study using fMRI and other imaging techniques studied the shape of the basal ganglia in boys with autism, comparing them to a control group. In the group of autistic boys, they observed an overgrowth of the nucleus accumbens in the form of an outward deformation. The volume of this overgrowth was positively correlated with greater social and communication deficits (Qiu et al. 2010).

A model for initiation of locomotor action has been proposed that includes the caudate nucleus, ventral tegmental area, NAc, and the GP (Mogenson, Jones, and Yim, 1980). The NAc region in mice has been shown to receive inputs from both the hippocampus and the prefrontal cortex. The hippocampus mediates transmission through D1 medium spiny neurons (MSNs), while the PFC mediates transmission occurs through D2 MSNs. An abnormality in one or both of these pathways could shift the balance of activation in the NAc. For example, a hypoactive prefrontal cortex (Figure 15.26) might not generate sufficient input to the indirect pathway to shut a gate in a timely way with a STOP signal.

Autistic repetitive behaviors can also help to perpetuate a vicious cycle. For example, although a repetitive behavior may help to satisfy the need of an autistic individual for sameness by focusing attention on the repeated behavior, and staying away from events that could cause aversive hypersensitive emotional reactions, by the same token, such a repetitive behavior can prevent attention from being focused on reinforcing or socially important sensory cues, and can thereby prevent the kind of recognition learning and social cognitive learning that might help to overcome some of the social isolation that the repetitive behavior perpetuates (Figure 15.26).

Imitation learning and social cognition

We have now reached a point in the book where I have discussed many of the processes that are engaged when we learn skills by observing teachers who are performing them. This kind of learning is called *imitation learning*. Imitation learning is one of the many skills that are needed to achieve *social cognition*, which includes all the many ways that we learn and apply information about other people appropriately in social situations. Social cognition is accordingly a vast subject without which civilization as we know it would not be possible. Here I will only comment upon a few of the core neural mechanisms and behaviors that enable us to achieve predictive success in a social world.

Many of the processes that I have already discussed depend upon explicit teachers, or the great implicit teacher, the world itself. Explicit teachers include people who reward or punish us. The world also rewards or punishes us in myriad ways, as when it supplies ripe wild blueberries on a bush, along with the sharp thorns on which we may tear our skin when picking them. Learning to imitate a skill by observing a teacher performing it in space requires a more sophisticated coordination of multiple perceptual, cognitive, affective, spatial, motor, and timing processes, as I will now discuss.

The critical importance of joint attention in imitation learning. The spatial and motor processes that are needed include the ability to make motor-equivalent reaches that I explained in Chapter 12, and the spatial affordance for tool use that this ability implies (Figures 12.13 and 12.14). Because of the spatial affordance for tool use, a monkey who picks up a stick could direct its endpoint to desired positions in space. If during exploratory movements using the stick, the monkey happened to put the end of the stick into an anthill, and then removed the stick with ants attached, the monkey could then learn this skill as a way to efficiently eat ants. Indeed, as I noted in Chapter 12, reaching (with or without a tool) and eating are part of a primordial sensory-motor system whose chewing component evolved into the capability for motor-equivalent coarticulation during speaking (Figure 12.15).

This skill could not, however, efficiently be learned by other monkeys by imitating the first monkey's behavior until social cognitive abilities like *joint attention* developed. Joint attention includes the ability of a learner to follow the gaze of a teacher during the demonstration of a motor skill. Without joint attention, and the ability to learn how to imitate actions that are performed by a teacher in different spatial coordinates, social cognition can be seriously impaired, as it is in various individuals with autism.

Chapter 5 already discussed how abnormally high vigilance can cause a narrow focus of attention and hyperspecific category learning in some autistic individuals, as my colleague Don Seidman and I proposed in our 2006 article about the imbalanced Spectrally Timed Adaptive Resonance Theory, or iSTART, model (Grossberg and Seidman, 2006). High vigilance can hereby also cause problems with learning joint attention. Chapters 13 and the current chapter have discussed how problems with learning the affective meaning of events, and adaptively timing appropriate responses to these events, can cause

additional behavioral problems in social situations. Indeed, if an individual cannot recognize the affective meaning of a smile or a frown, or cannot delay responses to another individual's acts until they can be well-received, then myriad problems with social interactions can occur. However, even beyond these problems are the ones that arise when learning to imitate a teacher's actions simply because a learner and teacher always experience the world from different vantage points.

From intrapersonal circular reactions to interpersonal circular reactions: Mirror neurons. I proposed in 2010, in an article with my postdoctoral fellow Tony Vladusich (Grossberg and Vladusich, 2010), how imitation learning utilizes what I call *inter*personal circular reactions that take place between teacher and learner, and distinguish them from the classical *intra*personal circular reactions of Piaget that take place within a single learner, such as the one that I discussed in Chapter 12 that enables reaching behaviors to be learned (Figure 12.13). To emphasize this point, I called the model the Circular Reactions for Imitative Behavior, or CRIB, model. The CRIB model proposes how interpersonal circular reactions can build upon intrapersonal circular reactions to explain how joint attention and imitation learning can develop, notably how a learner can follow a teacher's gaze to fixate a valued goal object. Thus, after a child can volitionally reach objects on its own, it can also learn, using an interpersonal circular reaction, to reach an object at which a teacher is looking, such as a stick with which to retrieve ants from an anthill. By building upon intrapersonal circular reactions that are capable of learning motor-equivalent reaches, the CRIB model hereby clarifies how a pupil can learn from a teacher to manipulate a tool in space.

In order to achieve joint attention and imitation learning, the learner needs to be able to bridge the gap between the teacher's coordinates and its own. In the neurobiological literature, this capability is often attributed to *mirror neurons* that fire either if an individual is carrying out an action or just watching someone else perform the same action (Rizzolatti, 2005; Rizzolatti and Craighero, 2004). This attribution does not, however, mechanistically explain how the properties of mirror neurons arise. The CRIB model proposes that the "glue" that binds these two coordinate systems, or perspectives, together is a surface-shroud resonance (Figure 6.2). Here is a summary of how this works:

First, the student needs to be able to recognize a teacher's face when it is seen in any pose, and thus learns an *invariant* object category of the teacher's face, among other body parts. Chapter 6 explains how this happens using a surface-shroud resonance to maintain activity of an emerging invariant object category, at the same time that it controls the eye movements to salient features on the object surface, so that multiple object views can be associated with the emerging invariant category (Figures 6.14-6.16).

Second, the student needs to be able to recognize a particular pose of a teacher's face relative to the position of the student. In particular, the student needs to be able to recognize how the teacher's eyes look when her face is staring at a particular position in space.

Thus, the student needs to learn both invariant categories *and* position-view categories. The ARTSCAN and pARTSCAN models propose that these kinds of categories are learned in ITa and ITp, respectively using ART feature-category resonances.

Third, the invariant object category of the teacher's face can be associated with the positive emotions that the teacher elicits, much as a baby looks at its mother's face when it is experiencing the positive feelings that occur as the mother feeds and cares for it. This association occurs via a cognitive-emotional resonance (Figure 13.1 and 13.4).

After both kinds of learning occur, when the student scans a scene with spontaneous attention shifts and saccades, an attentional spotlight that happens to fall on the teacher's face can generate a surface-shroud resonance (Figures 6.2 and 6.7) that, in turn, can synchronize with the feature-category resonances that support recognition of the teacher's face (Figure 6.27). As the invariant category of the teacher's face starts to resonate, it can trigger a cognitive-emotional resonance that amplifies this category using motivated attention (Figure 13.4). The teacher's face can hereby win the competition among other objects in the scene that are bidding for spatial and object attention. As a result, the student can look at the teacher's face by using these winning synchronous categories to solve the Where's Waldo problem, in the manner that I discussed in Chapters 6 and 14.

Now suppose that the teacher turns her face to look where she wants to put an object down, or pick it up while looking at it. When the teacher turns her face, it activates transient cells in the Where cortical stream of the student that rapidly attract spatial attention to that part of her body (Figure 6.8). The teacher's head turn will often precede the arm movement that it guides, which also creates transient motion signals, albeit a little later in time. A wave of spatial attention can thus flow from the teacher's face to the teacher's hand, much as a G-wave flows during long-range apparent motion (Figures 8.12-8.16), ending in a surface-shroud resonance that surrounds the teacher's hand.

The transient G-wave and the surface-shroud resonance attract the student's eyes to look at the terminal position of the teacher's hand.

An association can then be learned between the teacher's facial pose and the position in space where she is looking, much as association are learned in the TELOS model from ITp to FEF (Figure 12.58), or in the pART model from VPA to FEF (Figure 14.2), both of them gated on and off by the substantia nigra pars reticulata, or SNr, as I explained earlier in this chapter (Figure 15.40). On subsequent trials, the student can look at the teacher's facial pose and use this association to immediately look at the position in space where the teacher will be moving her hand. Joint attention has hereby been achieved.

In addition, once the student looks at this terminal position, an intrapersonal circular reaction can be activated that moves the student's hand to the position in space where the teacher will move her hand. An interpersonal circular reaction has hereby been achieved. Moreover, on future trials, the student can move her hand to a position that the teacher merely looks at, even if the teacher does not carry out an arm movement herself.

This kind of behavior can also be adaptively timed to imitate the timing of the movements that the teacher demonstrates (Figure 15.20).

This brief overview illustrates how many of the processes that I have explained throughout the book come together to enable simple kinds of imitation learning in space. The field of social cognition will, I believe, grow explosively during the next few decades, both to understand how social behaviors are carried out in societies of humans and other primates, and to inspire new designs for autonomous adaptive mobile robots.

16

Learning Maps to Navigate Space

From grid, place, and time cells to autonomous mobile agents

How do we know where we are in space?

Humans have sought to represent where they are in space throughout history. Making maps of a spatial region is an ancient way to satisfy this pressing need. *Wikipedia* notes that the word "cartography" comes from the Greek words χάρτης khartēs, "papyrus, sheet of paper, map" and γράφειν graphein, "write". Cartography is thus the study and practice of making maps. Maps are invaluable in every human activity, ranging from depicting the locations and layouts of farms, houses, and cities, to navigating on land or sea. Early humans drew maps as part of wall paintings and rock carvings for thousands of years before they were ever drawn on papyrus or paper.

Mathematicians have sought to formalize our understanding of space by developing geometrical concepts such as points, lines, angles, surfaces, and solids. Such concepts brought much greater precision to measuring properties of maps. Many of us have learned in elementary school how to represent space using the classical Euclidean geometry that was developed by Euclid of Alexandria in his classical book *Elements* around 300 BC. For many years it was thought that only Euclidean geometry described spatial facts about the world. This faith was shattered by the discovery of non-Euclidean geometries in 1813 by the great German mathematician, Carl Friedrich Gauss, and shortly thereafter by the Hungarian mathematician, Janos Bolyai, and the Russian mathematician, Nilolai Lobachevsky. These geometries all tried, in one way or another, to generalize ideas about whether and how parallel lines could intersect. In 1854, the great German mathematician, Bernhard Riemann, introduced a different non-Euclidean geometry, today called Riemannian geometry, to explain properties that were shown to be much more than a mathematical curiosity when Albert Einstein used it in 1916 to describe curved relativistic space-time in his epochal General Theory of Relativity.

For present purposes, the diversity of ways to draw maps and to represent geometry raises the intriguing question: How have the brains of humans and other terrestrial animals figured out how to represent space for many thousands of years before any maps or geometries were ever discovered by the most brilliant cartographers and

Conscious MIND Resonant BRAIN. Stephen Grossberg, Oxford University Press. © Oxford University Press 2021.
DOI: 10.1093/oso/9780190070557.003.0016

mathematicians? Do we all, in fact, have some sort of map of the world in our brains, or do we navigate using quite different resources? If we do use some type of map, then what sort of geometry does it embody? In my discussions of boundary completion and surface filling-in in Chapters 3-6, I already showed that our brains use very different geometrical representations to see the world than those taught in Euclidean or non-Euclidean geometry. That still leaves open the question: What sort of maps do our brains construct? And how do these maps enable humans and other terrestrial animals to navigate our world even if we do not know any geometry?

Place cells and the hippocampus as a cognitive map

Perhaps the modern area in studying spatial navigation scientifically can be dated to the classical 1948 article of the great American psychologist Edward Tolman (Tolman, 1948) called "Cognitive Maps in Mice and Men". Tolman described experiments on how rats learn to navigate in spatial mazes using information about the position of a goal object *in space*, rather than just by learning a particular *route* to the goal. The epochal report in 1971 by John O'Keefe and Jonathan Dostrovsky (O'Keefe and Dostrovsky, 1971) of *place cells* in the hippocampus of rats began the modern era of neurophysiological studies of spatial navigation. A place cell derived its name from the fact that it fires whenever a rat is located at the position that the place cell represents. Figure 16.1 summarizes a figure from their article in which the place cell from which the recording was done fires selectively when the rat is in position A.

As the authors noted in their article: "These findings suggest that the hippocampus provides the rest of the brain with a spatial reference map. Deprived of this map . . . it could not learn to go from where it happened to be in the environment to a particular place independently of any particular route (as in Tolman's experiments) . . ." (pp. 174-175). John O'Keefe won the Nobel Prize in Physiology or Medicine in 2014 for this and subsequent work on how spatial navigation works. A video and PowerPoint lecture of his Nobel Lecture called Spatial Cells in the Hippocampal Formation can be found at https://www.nobelprize.org/nobel_prizes/medicine/laureates/2014/okeefe-lecture.html.

Figure 16.2 summarizes neurophysiological data of Matthew Wilson and Bruce McNaughton (Wilson and McNaughton, 1993) showing spatial receptive fields of 18 different place cells as a rat navigates its environment. In this color-coded representation, red designates positions

where a cell fires most vigorously, then yellow for somewhat less vigorous firing, even less for green, and finally blue for baseline or no firing. Many experiments such as these confirm the hypothesis that the set of all place cells compute an *ensemble code for space*. The 1978 book of O'Keefe and Lynn Nadel called *The Hippocampus as a Cognitive Map* (O'Keefe and Nadel, 1978) is a classic exposition of the data and heuristic concepts that support this hypothesis.

Some remaining unanswered questions: What was missing? Although these experiments suggested how space may be represented in the hippocampus, they also raised fundamental questions: Is there a mechanistic, not just a descriptive, sense in which the hippocampus computes a "map"? Is there a mechanistic sense in which this map is "cognitive", as Tolman suggested? And finally, how do place cells arise? Even the experiments that recorded the data in Figure 16.2 suggested that place cells were somehow learned as an animal navigates a novel environment. Given that that place cells might be learned from

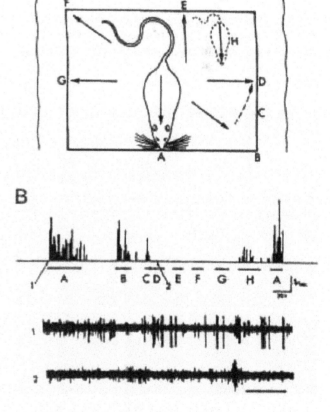

FIGURE 16.1. The experimental chamber (A) and neurophysiological recordings from a rat hippocampus (B) that led to the discovery of place cells. See the text for details.

properties of the spaces that an animal navigates, how did they manage to represent spaces that can be many meters in size? I like to recast this question as: How do little nerve cells learn to represent big spaces?

For many years after these seminal discoveries were made, even though the above questions were not answered, neurophysiologists and modelers managed to do productive work using facts about place cells to derive an increasingly clear picture of how spatial navigation might work. It was not atypical for models to begin with simulations of Gaussian receptive fields of place cells that mimicked the appearance of the data in Figure 16.2. These place cells were centered at different positions in a space whose coordinates were defined by two-dimensional Cartesian (x,y) coordinates. Such models were then used to draw conclusions about spatial navigation that were based upon how these place cells could interact in this representation of space.

I did not participate in these developments because I could not see how to answer the above questions. For me, it was unsatisfying to assume Cartesian coordinates and to assume Gaussian place cell receptive fields in them. I wanted to understand *how* place cells learn their receptive fields and, in so doing, learn to create the spatial representations, including the coordinates, in which these receptive fields occur. Only then could one provide a linking hypothesis between these self-organized receptive fields and how they control spatial navigation in a Cartesian world.

I had already done a lot of modeling work that involved the hippocampus in at least two ways, so my inability to move forward was not due to a lack of interest in how the hippocampus works. One contribution to understanding

hippocampus was described by Adaptive Resonance Theory, or ART, starting in 1976, in its analysis of how the temporal cortex interacts with the hippocampus to drive a mismatch-activated search for a better category with which to represent incoming sensory data (e.g., Figure 5.19). Another way was described by the Spectrally Timed ART, or START, model starting in 1989, in its analysis of how adaptively timed hippocampal circuits support cognitive-emotional learning in which a CS shuts off before the US to which it is associated turns on, as happens during trace conditioning, delayed non-match to sample, and related conditioning paradigms (e.g., Figure 15.2).

Something basic seemed to be missing that I could not see as a theorist, even given all my theoretical tools and empirical knowledge. What was missing was supplied in a remarkable 2005 *Nature* article that summarized one of the most exciting neuroscience discoveries in several decades. This was the discovery of *grid cells* in the entorhinal cortex that inputs to the hippocampus. Grid cells were discovered in the Norwegian laboratory of the husband and wife team of May-Britt and Edvard Moser (Hafting et al., 2005). The Mosers then went on to publish with their colleagues a series of important articles that characterized a wide range of fascinating facts about these grid cells. The Mosers shared the 2014 Nobel Prize in Physiology or Medicine with John O'Keefe for this epochal work, which triggered a flood of additional studies by investigators all over the world. The Nobel lectures of each of the Mosers can be found at https://www.nobelprize.org/nobel_prizes/medicine/laureates/2014/may-britt-moser-lecture.html and https://www.nobelprize.org/nobel_prizes/medicine/laureates/2014/edvard-moser-lecture.html.

Why are grid cells so remarkable? One reason is that they exhibit one of the most extraordinary receptive field structures in any part of the brain. A *single* grid cell can fire selectively at the vertices of a regular hexagonal grid of spatial positions when a rat navigates in an open field. Figure 16.3 reproduces a figure from a 2008 article by Edvard and May-Britt Moser with their colleague Emilio Kropff (Moser, Kropff, and Moser, 2008) showing (a) a recording of a place cell in the hippocampus and (b) of a grid cell in the medial entorhinal cortex. Positions where each cell emitted spikes are shown in red. They are superimposed on the animal's trajectory in the recording enclosure, which is shown in black. Most place cells have a single preferred firing position, but can also exhibit multiple firing fields in large spaces. Different place cells respond when an animal is in different positions (Figures 16.2 and 16.3a), so that

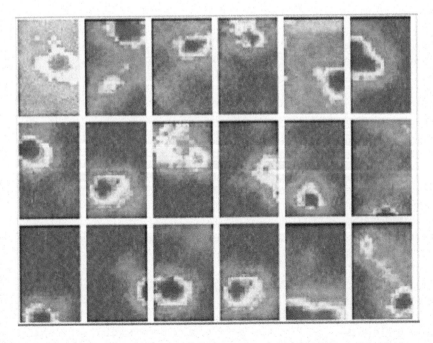

FIGURE 16.2. Neurophysiological recordings of 18 different place cell receptive fields. See the text for details.

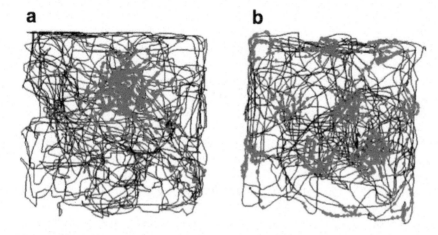

FIGURE 16.3. As a rat navigates in its experimental chamber (black curves), neurophysiological recordings disclose the firing patterns (in red) of (a) a hippocampal place cell and (b) an entorhinal grid cell.

all the place cells, as an ensemble, enable the animal to localize itself in an environment. In contrast to the firing field of a typical place cell, a *single* grid cell can fire at periodic hexagonally-organized positions across an entire open space in which the animal navigates (Figure 16.3b). Neighboring grid cells fire with different spatial phases, but share the same spatial scale. Different grid cells also fire at multiple spatial scales, with the scale size increasing as one progresses along a dorsoventral axis within the medial entorhinal cortex, where most of the grid cells are found.

An emerging unified theory of how grid cells and place cells are learned

For me and many others, the discovery of grid cells provided a crucial missing link. Suddenly many things seemed clear that were mysterious before. In response to this missing link, I and several gifted collaborators published a series of articles that together offered satisfying, indeed elegant and parsimonious, answers to all of the above questions. Each article brought us closer to a unified theory of how grid cells and place cells are learned, along with predictions about when grid cells are important for the learning of place cell receptive fields, and when they are not. To me it was at least as exciting that we were able to offer a satisfying explanation of why spatial *and* temporal representations both exist in the entorhinal-hippocampal system. For reasons that I will explain below, I like to say, perhaps too enthusiastically, that "space and time are one" and summarize this belief with the provocative phrase *neural relativity.*

In my summary below, I will necessarily omit a lot of excellent work by other investigators. But I will also compare and contrast our own models with those of several leading labs, including the Moser lab, after introducing you to our own conclusions. This is a very hot field with a lot of excellent work being done, so the state of the art is a rapidly moving target. I will nonetheless try to convince you that the hypotheses that led to our results are so elementary that they would seem to be a lasting part of this evolving story.

Both visual and path integration cues are used to navigate in the world. Since the work of O'Keefe and Dostrovsky in 1971, research on place cells has shown that they receive two kinds of inputs: one conveys information about the sensory, notably visual, context that is experienced from a given place, whereas the other comes from a navigational, or *path integration*, system that tracks relative position in the world by integrating angular and linear velocity estimates that are activated by the individual's own rotational and translational movements. respectively. An important open problem is to explain how visual and path integration information are combined in the control of navigation (Chen et al., 2013; Etienne, Maurer, and Seguinot, 1996; Gothard, Skaggs, and McNaughton, 1996).

This chapter focuses upon a model of how path integration information is represented by entorhinal cortical grid cells and hippocampal place cells. The previous chapter summarized modeling results about how visual tracking and optic flow help to control navigational movements in response to visual cues. A complete theory needs to characterize how these different kinds of information, which are received by our brains in different coordinates (e.g., retinotopic for vision, and body-centered for path integration) can be rendered dimensionally consistent through adaptive coordinate changes, whereby they can learn consistent control parameters in response to either, or both, types of information.

SOVEREIGN: Balancing reactive and planned behaviors during spatial navigation

One step forward in this direction was taken with my PhD student, William Gnadt. In 2008, we published a model called SOVEREIGN because this acronym memorably summarized the main processes that it synthesizes in order to control navigation: Self-Organizing, Vision, Expectation, Recognition, Emotion, Intelligent, Goal-oriented Navigation (Gnadt and Grossberg, 2008). SOVEREIGN contributes to answering a basic question that was analyzed from a different perspective by the TELOS and lisTELOS models in Chapter 12: How do reactive and planned behaviors interact in real time? How are sequences of such behaviors released at appropriate times during autonomous navigation to realize valued goals?

In Chapter 12, the question of how our brains balance between reactive and planned behaviors was used to address the problem of how our eyes know where to look next. This analysis focused on orienting in a stationary or moving world, rather than navigating through that world. Balancing between reactive and planned movement during navigation occurs during the transition between exploratory behaviors in novel environments and planned behaviors that are learned as a result of previous exploration. During initial exploration of a novel environment, many reactive movements may occur in response to unexpected and unfamiliar environmental cues (Leonard and McNaughton, 1990). These movements may initially appear to be locally random, as an animal orients toward and approaches many stimuli. As an animal becomes familiar with its surroundings, it learns to discriminate between objects likely to yield a reward and those that lead to punishment.

Such approach-avoidance behavior is often learned via a perception-cognition-emotion-action cycle during which an action and its consequences elicit sensory cues that are associated with them. Rewards and punishments affect the likelihood that the same actions will be repeated in the future. When objects are not visible when navigation begins, multiple reactive exploratory movements may be needed to reach them. Eventually, these reactive exploratory behaviors are replaced by more efficient planned sequential trajectories within a familiar environment. One of the main accomplishments of SOVEREIGN is to explain how erratic reactive exploratory behaviors lead to learning of the most efficient routes whereby to acquire a valued goal, without losing the ability to balance reactive and planned behaviors so that planned behaviors can be carried out where appropriate, without losing the ability to respond quickly to novel reactive challenges.

From locally ignorant components and circuits to emergence of intelligent adaptive functions. Many of the design principles and circuits within SOVEREIGN shed light on data about the interactions of the hippocampus with the prefrontal cortex and related brain areas that regulate the learning, planning, and execution of thought and action sequences that are aimed at acquiring valued goals (e.g., Buzsáki, 2015; Jones and Wilson, 2005, Ôlafsdóttir,

Bush, and Barry, 2017; Zielinski, Tang, and Jadhav, 2020). The explanations in Chapter 14 about how the prefrontal cortex works provide a lot of information about this issue. Much further work remains to be done to analyze and refine these architectures to the point where they can explain the kinds of coordinated rhythms, such as the hippocampal theta oscillations (6-12 Hz; Hz = cycles per second) and high frequency ripple oscillations (150-250 Hz), also called sharp wave ripples, that can co-occur with cortical spindles (12-18 HZ), delta waves (104 Hz), and slow oscillations (0.1-4 Hz) during corticohippocampal interactions (English et al., 2014; Fernández-Ruiz et al., 2019; Siapas, Lubenov, and Wilson, 2005; Siapas and Wilson, 1998, Sirota et al., 2003; Wikenheiser and Redish, 2013; Zielinski et al., 2020).

Throughout this book, I have provided many examples of how the brain deviates from classical ideas about space and time. Buzsáki and Tingley (2018) make the following observations that are consistent with this perspective when studying how the hippocampus contributes to spatial navigation:

"The current conceptual framework in neuroscience is based on the space and time ideas of classical physics. However, in contemporary physics "there is no longer space which 'contains' the world, and there is no time 'in which' events occur" . . . We suggest neuroscience requires a similar update in paradigm. When the concepts of space and time are scrutinized, they turn out to be mere human-invented terms conveniently classifying events of the world, rather than independent entities. At the experimental level, we consider that conceptualizing the hippocampal system as a device that computes space and time fails to account for many experimental observations . . . because the hippocampus may be 'blind' regarding the modality of its inputs. Whatever information is presented to it, from whichever parts of the neocortex, it activates the same computational algorithms. Thus, the specific terms that we tend to assign to generic hippocampal computation may reflect largely the experimental conditions and the engaged neocortical inputs rather than an internal computation of space or time".

The SOVEREIGN architecture that I will outline below continues in this vein by showing how navigational learning, planning, and action can emerge from a symphony of coordinated interactions among locally computed quantities that have no knowledge about their function or their macroscopic properties. Much future work remains to be done to more completely explain how evolution chose the particular constraints on brain organization—such as complementary computing, hierarchical resolution of uncertainty, and laminar computing—that have led to such a remarkable degree of behavioral success.

The text below will provide a detailed explanation of how entorhinal grid cells and hippocampal place cells are learned during development and sustained with sufficient stability to support successful spatial navigation. It will also propose how the theta rhythm can naturally arise in the circuits that embody these cells.

The remaining exposition of SOVEREIGN will qualitatively summarize several additional design principles and architectures that are needed to autonomously learn, plan, and execute cognitive, emotional, and behavioral sequences that are aimed at acquiring valued goals. The key circuits within these architectures are explained in greater detail throughout the book. The exposition is thus one of synthesis. I hope that this synthesis may be useful, not only towards understanding how our brains make our minds, but also in the design of future autonomous adaptive mobile agents for engineering and technological applications.

Homologous circuits for looking/reaching and spatial navigation. Our eyes and arms coordinate their responses to incoming visual information with our navigational movements through the world, such as when we move our body with respect to a goal object with the intention of grasping or otherwise manipulating it. This coordination is facilitated by the fact that there are computational homologs between how commands are made for navigating in the world, and for looking at and reaching objects in the world. Movements of the body and of the hand/arms are hereby controlled by circuits that share many properties. Recall that, for a similar reason, there are homologs between the circuits that control motor-equivalent reaching and speaking, as explained by the DIRECT and DIVA models, respectively (Figure 12.15).

Chapter 12 has already discussed key aspects of how arm movements are controlled using models such as VITE, VAM, FLETE, and DIRECT to explain how different movement control problems are solved and used to explain increasing amounts of movement data (e.g., Figures 12.2-12.14). To generate an arm movement, VITE computes a representation of where the arm wants to move (i.e., a *target position vector T* in Figure 12.2) and subtracts from the target position an outflow representation of where the arm is now (i.e., a *present position vector P* in Figure 12.2). This difference provides an estimate of the direction and distance that the arm must move to reach the target (i.e., a *difference vector D* in Figure 12.2). Basal ganglia volitional signals of various kinds (e.g., the volitional GO signal G in Figure 12.2), transform the difference vector into a representation of desired speed by multiplying D with G, before this product is integrated by P to create motor trajectory whose speed increases with G, other things being equal. As P approaches T, D approaches zero, so the movement terminates at the desired target position.

Because the arm is attached to the body, present position of the arm can be directly computed using outflow, or corollary discharge, movement commands that explicitly code the commanded arm position. In contrast, when a body moves with respect to the world, no such immediately available present position command is available. The ability to compute a difference vector between a target position and the present position of the body, to determine the direction and distance that the body needs to navigate to acquire the target, requires more elaborate brain machinery. Hippocampal place cells provide such information. Once our brains can compute a difference vector between present and desired bodily position, a volitional GO signal can move the body towards the desired goal object, just as in the case of an arm movement, and can even do so with different gaits, such as walk or run in bipeds, and walk, trot, pace, and gallop in quadrupeds, as the GO signal size increases (e.g., Figure 15.35). In summary, both navigational movement in the world and movement of limbs with respect to the body use a difference vector computational strategy.

As I noted above, a considerable amount of additional machinery is needed to successfully navigate in the world. For the moment, I will just note that "social" place cells in the hippocampus can fire in a bat as it observes another bat navigating a maze to reach a reward. The observer bat was motivated to do this so that it could subsequently navigate the same route to get the same reward. In this situation, a social place cell can fire in the brain of the observing bat that corresponds to the position of the observed bat (Omer et al., 2018; Schafer and Schiller, 2018, 2020).

These observations support a role for hippocampus, as part of its interactions with many other brain regions, in computing both present position vectors P and target position vectors T during spatial navigation, as well as difference vectors D from them that can control navigational directions.

Learning a labeled graph of angles and distances during route navigation. The SOVEREIGN model explains how this difference vector strategy may be computationally realized, including how arbitrary navigational trajectories can be decomposed into sequences of turns and linear movements until the next turn. In other words, the model explains how route-based navigation can be learned as a *labeled graph* of *angles* turned and *distances* that are traveled between turns. The angular and linear velocity signals that are experienced at such times are used in the model to learn the angles that a navigator turns, and the distances that are traveled in a straight path before the next turn.

This proposal that a labeled graph is learned during route navigation has recently received experimental support in Warren et al. (2017) who show how, when humans navigate in a virtual reality environment, such a labeled graph controls their navigational choices during route finding, novel detours, and shortcuts.

SOVEREIGN also explains how the angles and distances that constitute each route can trigger learning of cognitive plans whose activation can generate commands to execute these routes in the future. This central theme of the model is described in the subtitle of the article: "An Autonomous Neural System for Incrementally Learning Planned Action Sequences to Navigate Towards a Rewarded Goal". The central role of angular and linear velocity signals in spatial navigation will become clearer when I discuss below how head direction cells and stripe cells contribute to the learning of grid cells and place cells (see Figure 16.10 below), after which I will return to a more complete description of how the complete SOVEREIGN architecture learns sequential movement plans by exploring its environments at variable speeds.

Grid cells and place cells are spatial categories in a hierarchy of self-organizing maps

With this movement homology in mind, I will now offer an explanation of how place cells are learned, and of the important role of grid cells in supporting this learning process.

As noted above, grid cells in superficial layers of medial entorhinal cortex, or MEC, fire in multiple places that may form a regular hexagonal grid across the navigable environment (Hafting et al., 2005). The primary determinants of grid cell firing are path integration inputs (McNaughton et al., 2006). The path integration signals that are sensed at each of the hexagonally-distributed spatial firing positions of a single grid cell are different, as they are at different grid cells. The ensemble of all the entorhinal grid cells selectively respond to these varying patterns of path integration inputs before inputting to hippocampal place cells that are one synapse away (Figure 16.4).

The spatial fields of grid cells recorded from a given dorsoventral location in rat MEC exhibit different phases; that is, they are offset from each other (Hafting et al., 2005). In addition, the spacing between neighboring fields and the field sizes of grid cells increase, on average, from the dorsal to the ventral end of the MEC (Brun et al., 2008; Sargolini et al., 2006; Stensola et al., 2012). These properties have led to the suggestion that a place cell with spatial selectivity for a given position may be derived by selectively combining grid cells with multiple spatial phases and scales that are coactive at that position (McNaughton et al., 2006; O'Keefe and Burgess, 2005; Gorchetchnikov

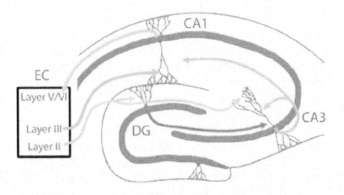

FIGURE 16.4. Cross-section of the hippocampal regions and the inputs to them. See the text for details.

and Grossberg, 2007). In other words, the maximal size of the environment in which a place cell exhibits only a single firing field can be much larger than the individual scales of grid cells that are combined to fire the place cell. Models have been proposed in which place fields in one-dimensional and two-dimensional spaces are learned based on inputs from hard-wired grid cells of multiple spatial scales and phases (Gorchetchnikov and Grossberg, 2007; Molter and Yamaguchi, 2008; Rolls, Stringer, and Elliot, 2006; Savelli and Knierim, 2010).

Each of the sections below summarizes an accomplishment of the GridPlaceCell neural model that I published with my postdoctoral fellow, Praveen Pilly, in a series of articles between 2012 and 2014 (Grossberg and Pilly, 2012, 2014; Pilly and Grossberg, 2012, 2013a, 2013b, 2014). A large body of navigational and neurophysiological data about spatial navigation and adaptively timed conditioning was explained and predicted using this model. In addition to its explanatory capabilities, the GridPlaceCell model exhibits parsimonious, and even beautiful, design properties that are worth summarizing right away, before I explain them more thoroughly in subsequent sections.

For starters, the GridPlaceCell model explains how grid cells and place cells may arise during development through a learning process that uses the *same* Self-Organizing Map, or SOM, laws for learning both types of cells, despite their strikingly different receptive field properties! As I explained in Chapter 5 (cf. Figures 5.10-5.18) and elsewhere in the book, variants of circuits that combine associative learning and contrast-enhancing competition to learn different kinds of recognition categories using a SOM—whether it is an invariant object category, value category, object-value category, or list category—have been used to explain many data about vision, audition, and cognition. Now we will see how a SOM can learn the basic cell properties that are used in spatial navigation.

These model properties are, moreover, obtained using either rate-based or spiking neurons, but additional properties, such as theta band modulation of cell firing, also arise in the spiking neuron version of the model.

The model will next be used to explain how the observed gradient of grid cell spatial scales, from smaller to larger, is learned along the dorsoventral axis of the MEC, and explains anatomical and neurophysiological data about how distinct grid cell modules and different frequencies of subthreshold membrane potential oscillations may arise through this developmental process.

Then I can explain the exciting "neural relativity" proposal that the gradient of spatial scales that arises through the MEC and its hippocampal projections to place cells, may use neural mechanisms that are homologous to those that create the observed gradient of temporal scales through the lateral entorhinal cortex, or LEC, and its hippocampal projections. In both cases, a *spectrum* of small cell sizes, or scales, whether spatial or temporal, gives rise to larger scales that can represent spatial or temporal properties of observable behaviors. Because both spatial and temporal information of this kind is incorporated into episodic memories, this mechanistic homolog may help to clarify how episodic learning occurs.

Another parsimonious property of the GridPlaceMap model concerns how the path integration inputs that activate and drive the learning of grid cells are represented. These inputs compute linear velocity—which is the speed of travel straight ahead—and angular velocity—which is the speed of rotation to change direction. Every movement can be decomposed into linear and angular velocity components, as my remarks above about the learning of labeled graphs by the SOVEREIGN model have already noted. Our model shows how both linear velocity and angular velocity can be represented by the same kind of circuit, which is called a *ring attractor* circuit for reasons that I will explain below.

Spatial navigation uses a self-stabilizing ART spatial category learning system

Another major problem has a parsimonious solution in the model, and one that is used in various forms throughout our brains. *Every* learning process needs to deal with the stability-plasticity dilemma that I discussed in Chapters 5, 6, and 10. The same is true for the process that learns grid cells and place cells. Without appropriate mechanisms, the learned receptive fields of these cells could become unstable in response to ever-changing series of path integration inputs through time. In particular, these receptive fields could drift and become spatially non-specific, thereby destabilizing all navigational skills based upon them. The model explains how Adaptive Resonance Theory, or ART, top-down attentional matching mechanisms from the hippocampal cortex (area CA1) to the entorhinal cortex (MEC)

may dynamically stabilize the learned grid and place cells, and explains anatomical and neurophysiological data that have been reported about this process. In other words, the entorhinal-hippocampal spatial navigation system is an *ART spatial category learning system*!

This model extension makes possible the explanation of how, during the learning of new place cells in a novel environment, top-down attentive matches that obey the ART Matching Rule (Figure 1.25) may cause fast gamma oscillations during a good match, and slower beta oscillations during a sufficiently bad mismatch. This is the mechanism that I discussed in Chapter 5 to explain the Inverted-U in beta power through time that Joshua Berke and his colleagues observed in 2008 when new hippocampal place cells were being learned during navigation of a novel environment.

With this background in hand, the model can explain how inactivating either the medial septum, or top-down inputs from the hippocampus to the MEC, may cause adverse effects on grid cell firing. I can then also explain what I believe are serious conceptual and explanatory problems of alternative *oscillatory interference* and *continuous attractor* models of grid cells, and how they fail to explain core data about spatial navigation.

How do grid cells and place cells arise through development and learning?

The GridPlaceMap neural model proposes how grid cells and place cells may develop in a hierarchy of SOMs, as illustrated by Figure 16.5. Recall that, in a SOM, input patterns are processed by an adaptive filter (Figure 5.10). The filtered inputs activate a recurrent competitive network whose lateral inhibitory interactions choose the maximally activated cell (population), or a small number of the most highly activated cells. The winning cells trigger learning in the adaptive weights that exist at the synapses of the adaptive filter pathways which end at the winning cells. The adaptive weights learn a normalized time-average of the inputs that they receive during the time intervals when their target cell wins the competition. As a result, the total synaptic weight to each map cell tends to be conserved, or normalized, due to competitive interactions among incoming axons, as has also been reported in experiments (Royer and Pare, 2003). In this way, the vector of adaptive weights to each cell in the map becomes tuned to the statistics of the inputs that enabled it to win the competition. The SOM can hereby more strongly activate each winning cell in response to these and similar inputs in the future. Each such cell becomes a *category*, or compressed representation, of the inputs that are able to activate it. In the

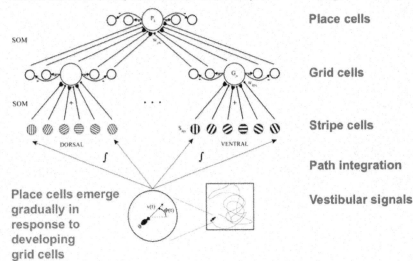

GridPlaceMap MODEL: RATE-BASE AND SPIKING
Pre-wired 1D stripe cells, learns both 2D grid and place cells!
Pilly and Grossberg, 2012
Same laws for both; both select most frequent and energetic inputs

Place cells

Grid cells

Stripe cells

Path integration

Vestibular signals

Place cells emerge gradually in response to developing grid cells

FIGURE 16.5. Macrocircuit of the GridPlaceMap model, which can learn both 2D grid cells and place cells in response to realistic trajectories of navigating rats using a hierarchy of SOMs with identical equations.

case of grid cells and place cells, they are *spatial* categories that help to represent an animal's position in space.

In the GridPlaceMap model, two successive SOMs exist. The first SOM, which represents medial entorhinal cortex, is activated by linear and angular velocity path integration inputs. The second SOM, which represents hippocampal cortex, is activated by output signals from the grid cells that are being learned within the first SOM (Figure 16.5). The grid cell and place cell receptive fields are both learned as spatial categories in their respective SOMs. The model converts realistic rat navigational trajectories into the path integration inputs that trigger learning of grid cells with hexagonal grid firing fields of multiple spatial scales, and place cells with one or more firing fields. Place cells can represent positions in much larger spaces than grid cells, which enable them to support useful navigational behaviors. I will say more about how this happens in a moment.

Why are there hexagonal grid cell receptive fields? The trigonometry of spatial navigation

The current model builds on a general observation about the trigonometry of two-dimensional space that

was published with my PhD student Himanshu Mhatre and postdoctoral fellow Anatoli Gorchetchnikov in 2012 (Mhatre, Grossberg, and Gorchetchnikov, 2012). Our brains learn to embody these trigonometrical properties into representations of our current positions as we navigate in such a space. Remarkably, these representations naturally take the form of a hexagonal firing pattern as an animal navigates in a sufficiently large open field.

Because this result builds on such a basic, and to my mind unassailable, foundation, even if the current model needs to be refined, as every model eventually does, these basic facts about trigonometry and SOMs would, I think, need to be a part of any future, more mature, model.

The new insight about the trigonometry of spatial navigation is most easily understood in terms of path integration cells each of which fires periodically whenever an animal moves a fixed distance in the cell's favored direction (Figure 16.6). We call these cells *stripe cells* for reasons that I will explain in a moment. The basic trigonometric insight holds independently of how such cells may be constructed, just so long as the cell firing patterns can be used to drive learning within a SOM.

You might immediately wonder: What does a SOM have to do with this? Remember that the winning category cells in a SOM get the *biggest total inputs*, and that these cells are designed to fire vigorously only if *all* their inputs are big enough. Each SOM cell fires selectively due to the fact that the total strength of adaptive weights that converge on it tends to be normalized, just as in the case of a Masking Field (Figures 12.46 and 12.47). Keep this in mind as I explain how multiple stripe cells send inputs to each grid cell, even while at a higher SOM level, multiple grid cells send inputs to each place cell. Himanshu, Anatoli, and I predicted the existence of stripe cells as being the cells that respond to combinations of linear and angular velocity path integration inputs. Why we did this, and subsequent data supporting our prediction, will be described as I go along.

Because the main ideas can be stated using only high-school trigonometry, I will describe them mathematically, so that readers can fully understand this basic fact about how we can navigate our world. Figure 16.6 depicts two directions of movement, one along the x-axis, which is defined as direction 0, and the other at a tilt of θ degrees. I assume that a stripe cell fires in the direction 0 whenever the animal moves a distance l in that direction. I also assume that a different stripe cell fires in the direction θ when the animal moves a distance l in that direction. Each stripe cell fires again when the animal moves another l

THE TRIGONOMETRY OF SPATIAL NAVIGATION
COACTIVATION OF STRIPE CELLS

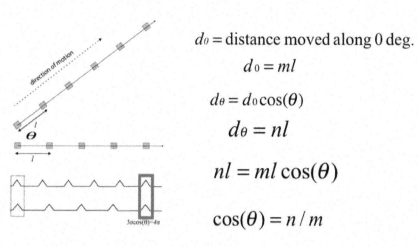

d_0 = distance moved along 0 deg.

$$d_0 = ml$$

$$d_\theta = d_0 \cos(\theta)$$

$$d_\theta = nl$$

$$nl = ml \cos(\theta)$$

$$\cos(\theta) = n/m$$

FIGURE 16.6. The learning of hexagonal grid cell receptive fields as an animal navigates an open field is a natural consequence of simple trigonometric properties of the positions at which the firing of stripe cells that are tuned to different directions will co-occur.

units in its preferred direction. Thus, stripe cells are tuned to different movement directions and each has a preferred firing period. Not only the two directions 0 and θ are coded by stripe cells. I will say more momentarily about how these directions are chosen. For the moment, let me just say that the cells of the first SOM in Figure 16.6 fire at positions where *all* the stripe cells fire simultaneously, and thus maximally activate a winning category cell in the SOM. The positions where this happens occur within the hexagonal grid that characterizes a grid cell's receptive field (Figure 16.3b)!

You might then ask: What about all the other positions where fewer inputs to different SOM cells may simultaneously be active? Why don't they cause trouble? The answer is that the competition between SOM cells allows only the maximally activated cells to get chosen, and only these cells will cause learning in the adaptive weights from the stripe cells to the grid cells, as in Figures 5.16 and 5.17.

To understand why these positions sweep out a hexagonal grid, let d_θ represent the distance travelled by the animal along the direction θ and let l be the firing period of the stripe cells, as in Figure 16.6. Then the stripe cell oriented along direction θ will get periodically activated whenever $d_\theta = nl$, with n equal to any integer 1, 2, 3, . . . Consider the coactivation of the stripe cell oriented at 0 degrees with stripe cells oriented at other angles. The stripe cell oriented along 0 degrees will be activated whenever $d_0 = ml$, with m equal to any integer 1, 2, 3, . . . If the animal traverses distance d_0 along 0 degrees, then its relative displacement along direction θ is just given by the trigonometry of right triangles; namely,

$$d_\theta = d_0 \cdot \cos(\theta) \tag{1}$$

Coactivation of these two stripe cells will happen whenever both have covered multiples of length l; that is, when $d_\theta = nl$ and $d_0 = ml$. Substituting this constraint into equation (1) gives

$$nl = ml \cdot \cos(\theta), \tag{2}$$

which reduces to

$$\cos(\theta) = n/m. \tag{3}$$

An example of this is shown at the positions enclosed by the red rectangle in Figure 16.6 with $n = 4$ and $m = 5$. As the integers n and m increase, the distance needed to be traversed to reach the next position where coactivation occurs also increases. The larger this distance, the less frequent the coactivations of these stripe cells will be while the animal runs in the environment. Thus, if we exclude the case of $n = m$, the most frequent coactivations will occur for the smallest possible values of n and m; namely, the values $n = \pm 1$ and $m = \pm 2$, which leads to

$$\cos(\theta) = \pm\tfrac{1}{2}, \text{ or } \theta = \pm 60° \pm 180° \tag{4}$$

A *180°* difference leads to the exact same angle, so it is sufficient to set $\theta = \pm 60°$. Hence, the most frequent coactivations will occur for angle differences between stripe cell orientations that are ±60° apart. These positions lie on a hexagonal grid, and cells in a SOM will maximally fire when these positions are attained. This is how the trigonometry of 2D space translates into the hexagonal firing fields of individual grid cells when an animal navigates in an open field!

Converting angular and linear velocity into a representation of position: Stripe cells

The model hereby predicts that grid cells learn to form their regular hexagonal firing pattern through a process of SOM learning based on input from *stripe cells* that code directional displacements. Stripe cells are predicted to occur in layer III of entorhinal cortex, from which they input to the grid cells in layer II. The displacement along a direction that is coded by a stripe cell is a measure of the relative distance covered by a navigating animal along that direction during a free movement in the environment.

STRIPE CELLS

Stripe cells are predicted to exist in (or no later than) EC layer (III, V/VI)

Linear path integrators: **represent** distance **traveled using**
linear velocity **modulated with** head direction **signal**

Ring attractor circuit: **the activity bump represents distance traveled**
stripe cells with same spatial period and directional preference
fire with different spatial phases at different ring positions

Distance is computed directly
It does not require decoding by oscillatory interference

Periodic **stripe cell activation due to ring anatomy: periodic boundary conditions**

Stripe firing fields with multiple orientations, phases and scales

FIGURE 16.7. Stripe cells were predicted in Mhatre, Gorchetchnikov, and Grossberg (2012) to convert linear velocity signals into the distances traveled in particular directions. They are modeled by directionally-selective ring attractors, which help to explain their periodic activation as an animal continues to move in a given direction. See the text for details.

moves in the direction of the red arrows along the ring attractor as the animal moves in the corresponding direction in space. Movement of the activity bump is driven by an input that is proportional to the component of an animal's linear velocity in the preferred direction of the attractor circuit, just as in Figure 16.6. When this velocity is zero, the activity bump remains stationary, so that the same cells remain active during this time interval, thereby helping to represent the animal's current position. Because the ring has a finite length and closes upon itself, each stripe cells thus has a spatial period l, as in Figure 16.6. There are multiple ring attractors, each with its own preferred direction and spatial period. The *population* of all these stripe cells hereby computes a distributed representation of an animal's positions and movements through an environment.

It can now be seen why we called these cells stripe cells: The positions where each cell in the ring fires resembles parallel stripes oriented perpendicular to the cell's

I just showed, using cosines, how this relative distance is formally computed at each stripe cell when the animal is moving in a different direction than the stripe cell's preferred direction. But how do the individual stripe cells know in what direction the animal is moving? This conversion is carried using a head direction signal that computes the direction in which the animal is moving (Figure 16.7). Since the integration of velocity cannot continue indefinitely due to limited resources, at some point it has to reset back to zero and start counting distance traveled again, in effect creating a periodicity in the output of the cells that are responsible for performing the integration operation.

Figure 16.7 shows a circuit that can generate the desired stripe cell periodicity and reset. It is a one-dimensional *ring attractor*. Such a ring of cells is depicted by the green circle in Figure 16.7, along which stripe cells (purple dots) with the same directional preference and spatial period are arranged. These stripe cells are activated sequentially when the animal moves in the ring's preferred direction. In such an attractor, a peak of activity, or activity bump,

EVIDENCE FOR STRIPE-LIKE CELLS

Entorhinal cortex data

Sargolini , Fyhn, Hafting, McNaughton, Witter, Moser, and Moser, 2006

Krupic, Burgess, and O'Keefe, 2012

Similar hypothetical construct used by Interference model but position is decoded by grid cell oscillatory interference

Band Cells
Burgess, 2008

FIGURE 16.8. Some experimental evidence for stripe-like cell receptive fields has been reported. The band cells posited by Neil Burgess also exhibit the one-dimensional firing symmetry of stripe cells, but are modeled by oscillatory interference. See the text for details.

GRIDSmap

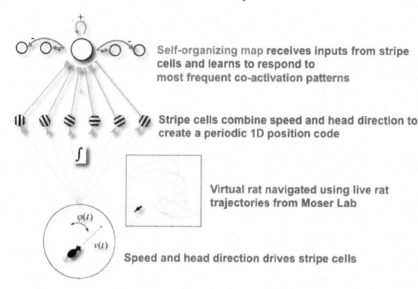

Self-organizing map **receives inputs from stripe cells and learns to respond to most frequent co-activation patterns**

Stripe cells combine speed and head direction to create a periodic 1D position code

Virtual rat navigated using live rat trajectories from Moser Lab

Speed and head direction drives stripe cells

FIGURE 16.9. The GRIDSmap model used algorithmically defined stripe cells to process realistic rat trajectories. The stripe cell outputs then formed inputs to the adaptive filter of a self-organizing map which learned hexagonal grid cell receptive fields.

preferred direction. The firing patterns of three stripe cells with different directional preferences are shown at the bottom of Figure 16.7. The top half of Figure 16.8 summarizes some of the experimental evidence for stripe cells, and two of the labs that reported it. The bottom half of Figure 16.8 notes that Neil Burgess of University College London proposed a cell type in 2008 that also generates stripes (Burgess, 2008). His proposal, called a *band cell*, is part of a very different kind of grid cell model, called the *oscillatory interference* model. Despite its ingenuity, this model seems to have conceptual and explanatory problems that make it implausible, as I will explain shortly.

GRIDSmap: From stripe cells to grid cells

As with most biological neural models, our understanding of how grid cells and place cells are learned emerged in stages. One stage was the GRIDSmap (Grid Regularity from Integrated Distance through Self-Organizing map) model that I developed with Himanshu and Anatoli. The circuit for this model is shown in Figure 16.9. A larger model circuit is also provided in Figure 16.10. I will return to this expanded model right after I explain how GRIDSmap learns grid cell receptive fields.

The model receives inputs from movement trajectories that were recorded from live rats as they navigated in the

Moser lab. The trajectories were converted into activations of angular and linear velocities, which were in turn converted, using a simple algorithm, into activations of stripe cells. Then the output signals from the stripe cells activated a SOM. Because the winning SOM cells are the ones to receive the biggest total inputs, they are the ones where a maximal number of stripe cells is simultaneously coactivated, and thus tend to occur at hexagonal positions across the space that is being navigated. The winning SOM cells hereby learn to be selectively activated when the model animal, or *animat*, is at these hexagonal positions, while learning by cells that are activated at other positions is inhibited by the recurrent competition that chooses the SOM winning cells.

Does this SOM learning scheme work? The affirmative answer is illustrated by the simulations in Figures 16.11-16.13. Figure 16.11 shows that grid cells with the same spatial scale, but different spatial phases of their hexagonal firing fields can develop. Other simulations show how grid cells with different spatial scales can develop in the same way.

Figure 16.12 illustrates how the grid fields develop on successive navigational experiences, with some grid regularity emerging, at least in the model, by the third learning

GRIDSmap
Pre-wired 2D stripe cells, learns 2D grid cells

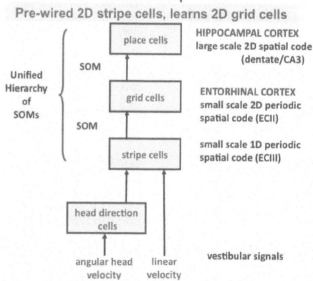

FIGURE 16.10. The GRIDSmap model is embedded into a more complete representation of the processing stages from receipt of angular head velocity and linear velocity signals to the learning of place cells.

SIMULATION RESULTS

Multiple phases per scale

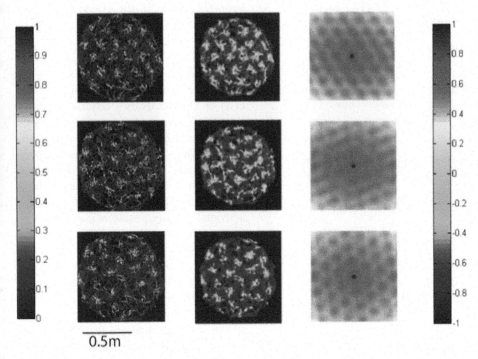

0.5m

FIGURE 16.11. GRIDSmap simulation of the learning of hexagonal grid fields. See the text for details.

TEMPORAL DEVELOPMENT OF GRID FIELDS

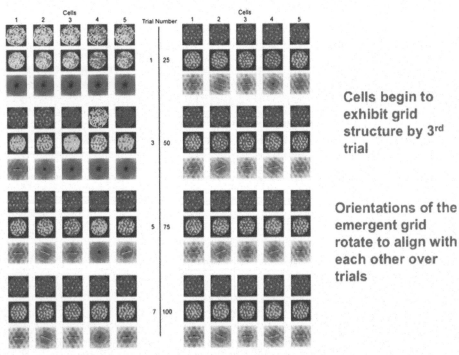

Cells begin to exhibit grid structure by 3rd trial

Orientations of the emergent grid rotate to align with each other over trials

FIGURE 16.12. Temporal development of grid cell receptive fields on successive learning trials (1, 3, 5, 7, 25, 50, 75, 100).

trial. These grid fields also tend to align their orientations in space as learning proceeds.

How many oriented stripe cells are needed to learn hexagonal grids? Figure 16.13 shows a conceptually very important simulation. It responds to the critical design question: How precisely do the orientations of stripe cells need to be determined for grid cells to learn? And how many different orientations are needed for this to happen?

Figures 16.14 and 16.15 illustrate this issue. Figure 16.14 illustrates how three stripe cell ring attractors whose orientations differ by 60 degrees can generate a hexagonal grid by superimposing their firing fields. They all intersect in a hexagonal grid, and those are the positions that SOM category cells will learn.

One might therefore want to assume that stripe cells have preferred orientations that differ by 60 degrees. But how do stripe cells know how to do this?! This is non-local knowledge that cannot be assumed without trepidation. Moreover, what if the stripe cell orientations differ by 45 degrees, not 60 degrees, as in Figure 16.15. Then the intersections of these stripe cell firing fields would generate a rectangular grid, not a hexagonal grid. But hexagonal grids do not develop when an animal navigates in an open field. As I will explain below, an oscillatory interference model must have three, and only three, stripe, or band, cells oriented by precisely 60 degrees to generate a hexagonal grid. If not, other grids that are not found in the data, including a rectangular grid, would be generated just as easily. That is one reason why the oscillatory interference model fails to explain how grid fields are learned.

Figure 16.13 shows that the GRIDSmap model, and its

DEVELOPMENT OF GRID CELLS USING VARIOUS ANGULAR SEPARATIONS OF STRIPE CELLS

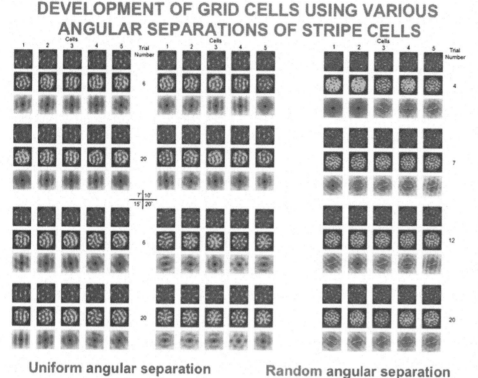

Uniform angular separation   **Random angular separation**

FIGURE 16.13. Hexagonal grid cell receptive fields develop if their stripe cell directional preferences are separated by 7, 10, 15, 20, or random numbers degrees. The number and directional selectivities of stripe cells can thus be chosen within broad limits without undermining grid cell development.

generalization by the GridPlaceMap model, does not have this problem. This simulation summarizes how five different combinations of stripe cells all lead to learning of a hexagonal grid pattern. The four simulations on the left side of the figure use stripe cells whose orientations differ by 7, 10, 15, and 20 degrees. None of these cases have stripe directions that differ only by 60 degrees, and they all use more than three different preferred stripe directions. The simulation on the right chooses a *random* angular separation of the stripe cells, and shows how a hexagonal grid even develops in this case. Learning trials 4, 7, 12, and 20 are shown to illustrate how the grids develop with experience.

Why do all these cases work? It is because of the same SOM learning property that I already mentioned: Only the *maximally* activated SOM cells can win the competition, and they learn the hexagonal constraint that is imposed by the trigonometry of two-dimensional space, even if the stripe cells do not optimally represent this trigonometry.

How do hippocampal place cells learn to represent much larger spaces than grid cells can? Because of the small spatial period of stripe cells, they cannot represent large spaces. As illustrated in Figure 16.9, stripe cells together represent a distributed one-dimensional (1D) periodic spatial code on a scale of tens of centimeters. This length scale is much smaller than the spatial scale of place cells, which can represent distances at least as large as the sizes of the environments that animals typically navigate. SOM models of spatial navigation show how to represent larger spaces in stages. For example, the expanded GRIDSmap model in Figure 16.10 depicts a second SOM which learns to convert grid cells with multiple spatial scales into a still larger-scale 2D map of place cells.

This second SOM was not simulated as part of the original GRIDSmap model in Figure 16.9. A SOM from grid cells to place cells had earlier been simulated in an article that I published in 2007 with Anatoli Gorchetchnikov (Gorchetchnikov and Grossberg, 2007).

GRIDSmap: FROM STRIPE CELLS TO GRID CELLS

Grid-cell Regularity from Integrated Distance through Self-organizing map

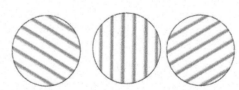

Superimposing firing of stripe cells oriented at intervals of 60 degrees

Hexagonal grid!

FIGURE 16.14. Superimposing firing of stripe cells whose directional preferences differ by 60 degrees supports learning hexagonal grid cell receptive fields in GRIDSmap.

WHY IS A HEXAGONAL GRID FAVORED?

Superimposing firing of stripe cells oriented at intervals of 45 degrees

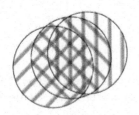

Rectangular grid

This and many other possibilities do not happen **in vivo**

They do happen in the oscillatory interference model

How are they prevented in GRIDSmap?

FIGURE 16.15. Superimposing stripe cells oriented by 45 degrees does not lead to learning of rectangular grids in GRIDSmap, but it does in an oscillatory interference model.

This article used pre-wired 1D grid cells, each with a different spatial scale, as inputs to a SOM that learns place cells (Figure 16.16). This SOM also chooses cells that are activated simultaneously by the maximum number of grid cells.

Learning place cells that can represent large spaces requires that *each* of them receives inputs from an array of grid cells that have multiple spatial scales. As always, a winning SOM cell fires when all of its grid cell inputs are active. When grid cells with multiple scales are the inputs, then the SOM can learn place cells with a spatial scale that is equal to the *least common multiple* of all these grid cell spatial scales, since these are the positions where all the grid cells are active. Figure 16.16 illustrates how two or three grid cell scales whose spatial periodicity is in the centimeter range can drive learning of place cells that can represent spaces that span many meters, even kilometers (!), if the grid cell scales have that large a least common multiple, as in the case where the grid cells scales happen to be 41, 53, and 59 centimeters.

In summary, I had shown via the two articles with Himanshu and Anatoli how pre-wired 2D stripe cells can learn 2D hexagonal grid fields, and how pre-wired 1D grid cells can learn place cells with a spatial scale equal to the least common

multiple of the grid cells that input to them. What still remained to be done was to simulate a SOM hierarchy in which pre-wired stripe cells input to two successive SOMs wherein the first SOM learns 2D grid fields of multiple spatial scales, and the second SOM learns large-scale 2D place cells in response to these emerging multiple-scale grid fields in real time. This is what the GridPlaceMap model that I started publishing in 2012 with Praveen Pilly finally achieved (Figure 16.5).

The trigonometry of space revisited: Coding the most frequent and energetic coactivations

Before explaining how grid and place cells can be learned in a coordinated way, let me describe one refinement in

GRID-TO-PLACE SELF-ORGANIZING MAP
Formation of place cell fields via grid-to-place cell learning
Gorchetchnikov and Grossberg, 2007, Neural Networks

Least Common Multiple

Grid scales	Place scales
40, 50, 60cm	6m
50, 60, 70cm	21m
41, 53, 59cm	1.282km
Our simulations	
40, 50cm	2m
44, 52cm	5.72m

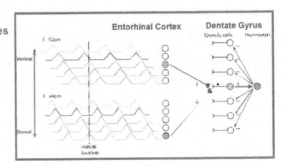

Our SOM:

Spiking Hodgkin-Huxley membrane equations
Nonlinear choice by contrast-enhancing recurrent on-center off-surround net

Choice triggers back-propagating action potentials that induce STDP-modulated learning on cell dendrites

FIGURE 16.16. In the place cell learning model of Gorchetchnikov and Grossberg (2007), three populations of five cells each of entorhinal grid cells (only two are shown) with different spatial periods input to the model's dentate gyrus. The grid cells are one-dimensional and defined algorithmically. A model dentate gyrus granule cell that receives strong projections from all three grid cell scales fires (green cell) and activates a recurrent inhibitory interneuron that inhibits other granule cells. It also generates back-propagating action potentials that trigger learning in the adaptive weights of the projections from the grid cells, thereby causing learning of place cell receptive fields.

our understanding of the trigonometry of space that leads to learning of a hexagonal grid during spatial navigation. This refinement was discovered when I began my work with Praveen Pilly, who had become my postdoctoral fellow after having done his PhD research with me to explain the kinds of probabilistic motion decision-making data that I summarized in Chapter 8 (Figures 8.57-8.62).

Figures 16.17a and 16.17b depict what happens when an animal moves along the horizontal axis from the origin. The average length of piecewise linear segments in the real rat trajectory in Figures 16.5 and 16.9 is 0.88 centimeters, which is much less than the smallest stripe spacing of 20 centimeters in the simulations. Consideration of such an extended linear trajectory does, however, help to clarify this new insight.

First consider the situation in Figure 16.17a. Here, a stripe cell that is tuned to *0* degrees will become active periodically as the animat moves forward. While this is happening, a stripe cell tuned to the perpendicular direction of 90 degrees whose firing field coincides with the horizontal trajectory will be continually active. This is true because the zero velocity projected along its direction does not move the activity bump around in its ring attractor. So, if *s* is the stripe spacing, then the set of stripe cells whose directions differ by 90 degrees will be coactive every *s* units. However, as illustrated in Figure 16.17b, the set of stripe cells whose directions differ by 60 degrees will be coactive every 2*s* units. As shown in Figure 16.17c, sets of two stripe cells with the same spatial period whose preferred directions differ by 90 degrees have the maximal coactivation

frequency. However, as shown in Figure 16.17d, sets of three stripe cells whose directions differ from each other by 60 degrees exhibit only near-to-maximal coactivation frequency, but they also provide the maximally energetic input patterns to the SOM map cells, because three stripe cell inputs converge on SOM grid cells in the 60 degree case, whereas only two stripe cell inputs converge on SOM grid cells in the case of 90 degrees.

For example, in a 100 × 100 centimeter environment, with a stripe spacing of 20 centimeters, pairs of stripe cells differing in their preferred directions by 90 degrees have 25 coactivation points each, but summate inputs from only two cells to their corresponding SOM map cells. In contrast, triplets of stripe cells differing in their preferred directions by 60 degrees have 23 coactivation points each, but summate inputs from three stripe cells to their corresponding SOM map cells. Since $(25 \times 2) < (23 \times 3)$, self-organized learning favors hexagonal grids as opposed to rectangular grids because the largest inputs—due to a combination of most frequent *and* energetic inputs—converge on SOM grid cells from the positions of a hexagonal grid.

A hierarchy of identical SOMs for coordinated learning of grid cells and place cells. Remarkably, many anatomical and neurophysiological properties of grid cells and place cells can be explained by a hierarchy of SOMs wherein each SOM in the hierarchy uses the *same laws* to learn either grid cell or place cell receptive fields. Moreover, each SOM amplifies and learns to categorize the most frequent and energetic co-occurrences of its inputs, while suppressing the representations of less frequent and energetic input patterns using its recurrent inhibitory interactions (Figure 16.5). The different grid cell and place cell receptive field properties emerge because they experience different inputs. Figure 16.18 shows a simulation of the beautiful hexagonal grid fields and unimodal place cells that are learned by this SOM hierarchy. The left column in this figure represents in blue the movement trajectory, and in red the positions where the cells fire. The first row summarizes stripe cell firing, the second row summarizes grid cell firing, and the third row summarizes place cell firing.

Place cell learning without grid cells: Why are grid cells needed? In the GridPlaceMap model, place cells learn only by receiving inputs from grid cells. However, it has also been reported that some place cells may occur before vigorous grid cell development is initiated during

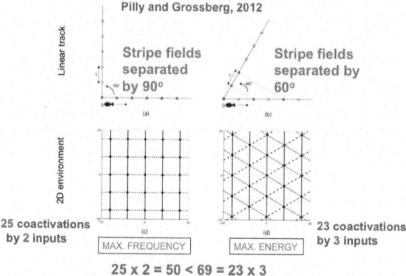

FIGURE 16.17. A finer analysis of the 2D trigonometry of spatial navigation showed that both the frequency and amplitude of coactivations by stripe cells determine the learning of hexagonal grid fields.

SPIKES ON TRAJECTORY   UNSMOOTHED RATE MAP   SMOOTHED RATE MAP

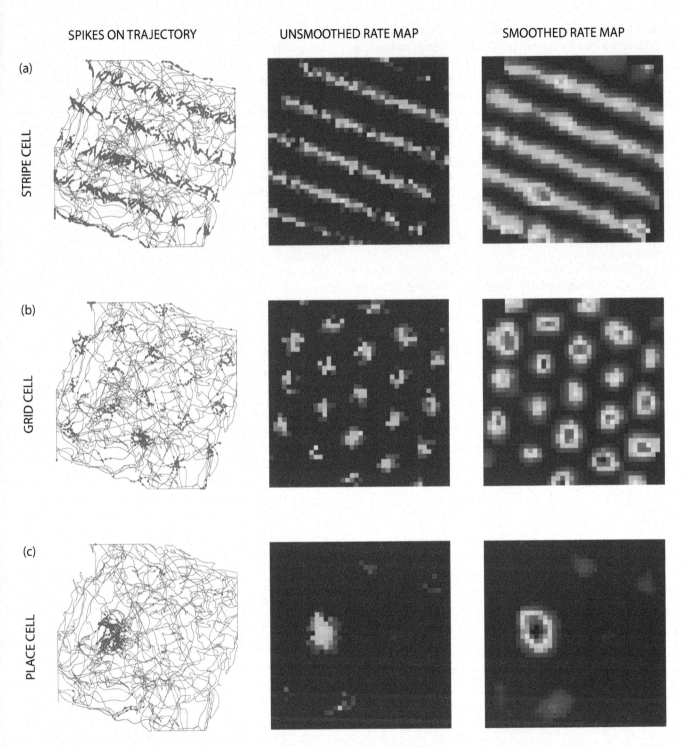

FIGURE 16.18. Simulations of coordinated learning of grid cell receptive fields (second row) and unimodal place cell receptive fields (third row) by the hierarchy of SOMs in the GridPlaceMap model. Note the exquisite regularity of the hexagonal grid cell firing fields.

development (Langston et al., 2010; Wills et al., 2010). If place cells can develop without grid cells, then why are grid cells needed at all? Indeed, from a purely technical viewpoint, place cells could be learned directly from stripe cells, say via a direct pathway from entorhinal cortex to the hippocampal CA1 region that is known to exist.

There are several possible reasons for place cell development to occur before grid cells themselves vigorously develop, including the fact that place cells can respond to both visual and path integration inputs (Chen et al., 2013), which enables them to use visual landmarks as well as proprioceptive information about current position in order to navigate. However, our model proposes a more basic role for grid cells in place cell development, and one that is consistent with facts about navigation in very young rat pups; namely, grid cells enable place cell spatial scales to represent spaces that are as large as the least common multiple of the grid cell scales which drive them. Grid cells hereby enable spatial navigation on the scale that adult rats and other terrestrial animals experience. Before such large-scale navigation emerges, which happens when rats are around two-and-one-half weeks old, rat pups tend to stay in, or very near, their nests. They do not need to represent large spaces at this time. Exploration of larger spaces tends to occur at around the same time when grid cells tend to rapidly develop (Langston et al., 2010; Muessig et al., 2015; Wills, Barry, and Cacucci, 2012; Wills et al., 2010), and to drive the learning of place cells capable of representing positions in these larger spaces.

Learning a dorsoventral gradient of grids and oscillation frequencies: Neural relativity

In order to learn place cells whose spatial scale is the least common multiple of the several grid cell scales that input to them, the grid cells themselves need to develop with multiple spatial scales. It is known that both spatial and temporal properties of grid cells vary along the dorsoventral axis of medial entorhinal cortex, or MEC (e.g., Brun et al., 2008; Giocomo et al., 2007). The GridPlaceMap model demonstrates that the observed anatomical gradient of increasing grid spatial scales can be learned by cells that respond more slowly along the dorsoventral axis to their inputs from stripe cells of multiple scales. Remarkably, the rate gradient that leads to learning of multiple grid cell spatial scales is computationally homologous to the rate gradient that I already described in Chapter 15 whereby Spectral Timing is achieved. That is why I like to call the grid cell gradient mechanisms Spectral Spacing. As I noted above, the phrase "space and time are one" is a catchy way to summarize the fact that spatial and temporal representations in the entorhinal-hippocampal system may both arise from homologous mechanisms. The term *neural relativity* is an even more daring way to say this.

Praveen and I did not just arbitrarily decide to use a rate gradient to learn grid cells. We were forced into this assumption by the data. Indeed, properties of these learned representations quantitatively simulate neurophysiological data about the dorsoventral gradient of oscillation frequencies, among several other neurophysiological properties for which we knew no other compelling explanation. The following properties were simulated, among others: *In vitro* recordings of medial entorhinal layer II stellate cells, where the grid cells mostly occur, have revealed subthreshold membrane potential oscillations (MPOs) whose temporal periods, and time constants of excitatory postsynaptic potentials (EPSPs), both tend to increase along the dorsoventral axis (Garden et al., 2008; Giocomo and Hasselmo, 2008; Giocomo et al., 2007; Yoshida et al., 2011). Slower subthreshold MPOs and slower EPSPs correlate with larger grid spacings and field widths as one progresses down the dorsoventral axis. Figure 16.19 summarizes data showing the increasing grid cell spatial scale along the MEC dorsoventral axis. Figure 16.20 does the same for the dorsoventral gradient in the rate of synaptic integration of MEC layer II stellate cells. Figure 16.21 shows the dorsoventral gradient in the frequency of membrane potential oscillations in these cells. Finally, Figure 16.22 shows the dorsoventral gradient in afterhyperpolarization (AHP) kinetics of these cells.

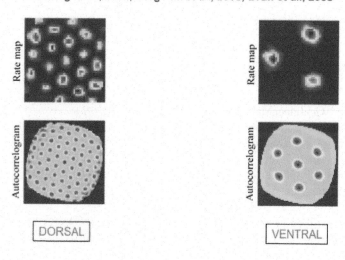

Spatial scale of grid cells increase along the MEC dorsoventral axis
Hafting et al., 2005; Sargolini et al., 2006; Brun et al., 2008

How does the spatial scale increase along the MEC dorsoventral axis?

FIGURE 16.19. Neurophysiological data showing the smaller dorsal grid cell scales and the larger ventral grid cell scales.

Dorsoventral gradient in the rate of synaptic integration of MEC layer II stellate cells

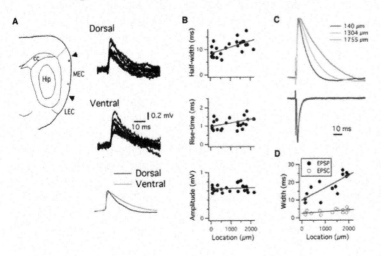

Both rise and fall times of EPSPs increase from dorsal to ventral end of MEC (slower rates)   Garden et al., 2008

FIGURE 16.20. Integration rate of grid cells decreases along the dorsoventral gradient of the medial entorhinal cortex, or MEC.

dorsoventral gradient (Figure 16.23). Due to the way that cells integrate their inputs through time, a faster response rate in a cell also leads to a larger peak firing rate, followed by faster habituation and subsequent recovery of the neurotransmitter that gates the cell activity. This habituative gating process has properties similar to those of afterhyperpolarization currents.

As in the case of Spectral Timing, the gated signals of cells with variable response rates are active during different time intervals and the widths of these intervals increases as the cell activity responds more slowly (Figure 15.3a). In the Spectral Spacing model, due to the above properties, the duration of gated cell activity increases as cells respond more slowly along the dorsoventral axis. These variable durations of activity define the sampling times when spectrally spaced learning occurs, just as they are the sampling times when spectrally timed learning occurs. In the case of Spectral Timing, the longer durations of activity

From Spectral Timing to Spectral Spacing: Solving the scale selection problem

The GridPlaceMap model provides a unified mechanistic explanation of all these spatial and temporal gradient properties, and simulates all of them. The intuitive idea that enables this unified explanation is simple to understand once one also understands how Spectral Timing works. In the Spectral Spacing model, stripe cells of multiple scales send converging inputs to the SOM cells that will learn how to select these scales along the

Dorsoventral gradient in the frequency of membrane potential oscillations of MEC layer II stellate cells

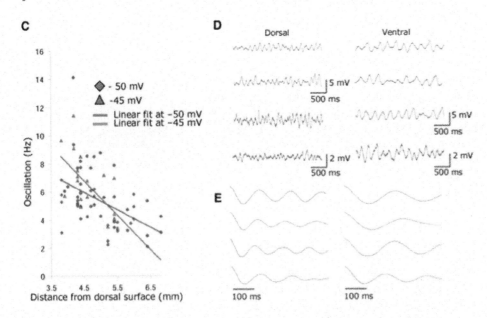

Both membrane potential oscillation frequency and resonance frequency decrease from the dorsal to ventral end of MEC   Giocomo et al., 2007

FIGURE 16.21. Frequency of membrane potential oscillations in grid cells decreases along the dorsoventral gradient of the MEC.

Dorsoventral gradient in afterhyperpolarization (AHP) kinetics of MEC layer II stellate cells

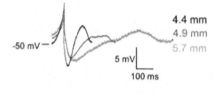

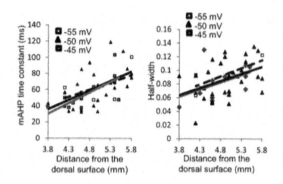

Time constants and duration of AHP increase from the dorsal to the ventral end of MEC layer II

Effectively, the relative refractory period is longer for ventral stellate cells in MEC layer II

Navratilova et al., 2012

FIGURE 16.22. Time constants and duration of afterhyperpolarization currents of grid cells increase along the dorsoventral gradient of the MEC.

conditioned stimuli lead to learned response curves with broader variances. Hippocampal "time cells" with all the properties that I predicted in 1989 to achieve spectral timing, including the Weber law, were reported in 2011 by McDonald et al. (2011). These authors wrote that ". . . the mean peak firing rate for each time cell occurred at sequential moments, and the overlap among firing periods from even these small ensembles of time cells bridges the entire delay. Notably, the spread of the firing period for each neuron increased with the peak firing time . . . ".

It remains to be directly tested whether the spectrum of time cells arises from a gradient in a single rate

along the gradient embody the famous Weber law that is a hallmark of Spectral Timing (e.g., Figure 15.3d). In the case of Spectral Spacing, because they are active for longer durations, cells further along the dorsoventral axis can effectively sample larger scales, and thereby learn grid cells with larger spatial scales.

Does a calcium gradient enable mGluR to generate all rate spectra? In Chapter 15, the Spectral Timing model was used to explain and simulate data about the role of hippocampus in learning behaviors that bridge temporal gaps, such as occurs during trace conditioning and delayed matching-to-sample, in both normal individuals and amnesic patients. As noted above, spectrally timed learning has Weber law properties such that larger inter-stimulus intervals between unconditioned and

SPECTRAL SPACING MODEL
Map cells responding to stripe cell inputs of multiple scales

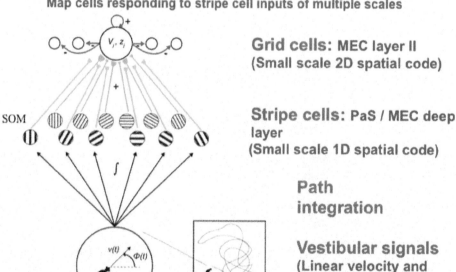

Grid cells: MEC layer II (Small scale 2D spatial code)

Stripe cells: PaS / MEC deep layer (Small scale 1D spatial code)

Path integration

Vestibular signals (Linear velocity and angular head velocity)

How do entorhinal cells solve the scale selection problem?

FIGURE 16.23. The Spectral Spacing Model uses a rate gradient to learn a spatial gradient of grid cell receptive field sizes along the dorsoventral gradient of the MEC.

parameter, as is predicted by the Spectral Timing model. A biophysical interpretation of this rate parameter has been given in terms of calcium dynamics in the metabotropic glutamate receptor, or mGluR, system for the case of spectral timing in the cerebellum (Fiala, Grossberg, and Bullock, 1996). The most parsimonious prediction is that a similar mGluR mechanism holds in all cases of spectral timing throughout the brain, as well as in the case of spectral spacing. As noted in Chapter 15, to the present, spectral timing has been modeled in the hippocampus, cerebellum, and basal ganglia, as well as in non-neural tissues, such as HeLa cancer cells. It remains to be seen if other neural and non-neural systems embody variants of Spectral Spacing.

In summary, dorsoventral gradients in single rate parameters within the entorhinal-hippocampal system may create multiple spatial and temporal scales in the entorhinal cortices that can be fused into larger spatial and temporal scales in the hippocampal cortex, indeed scales that are large enough to control adaptive behaviors in space and time. The mechanistic homology between these spatial and temporal mechanisms suggests why they may occur side-by-side in the medial and lateral streams through entorhinal cortex into the hippocampus. Spatial representations in the *Where* cortical stream go through postrhinal cortex and medial entorhinal cortex on their way to hippocampal cortex, and object representations in the *What* cortical stream go through perirhinal cortex and lateral entorhinal cortex on their way to hippocampal cortex (Aminoff, Gronau, and Bar, 2007; Eichenbaum and Lipton, 2008; Hargreaves et al., 2005; Keene et al., 2016; Kerr et al., 2007; van Strien, Cappaert, and Witter, 2009). The existence of computationally homologous spatial and temporal representations in the hippocampus may help to clarify its role in mediating episodic learning and memory, which has been studied since Tulving (1972; see also Tulving and Thomson, 1973) proposed that each episode in memory consists of a specific spatio-temporal combination of stimuli and behavior.

Data and model simulations of grid cell properties along the dorsoventral axis of MEC

What kind of model choices enabled it to generate simulations of so many challenging neurophysiological data? Figure 16.24 summarizes the parameters that were used to simulate the Spectral Spacing model, including the number of stripe cell directions (9), spatial phases per direction (4), and number of spatial scales (2). Ten different cell response rates were implemented along the model's dorsoventral axis, with the same habituation rate used at all these cells, just as in the case of Spectral Timing (Figure 15.10).

For completeness, Figure 16.25 summarizes the Spectral Spacing equations to show how standard STM, MTM, and LTM laws can trigger learning of the grid cell spatial gradient when the activation rates are chosen to be slower along the dorsoventral axis.

Figures 16.26-16.29 summarize data and simulations by the Spectral Spacing model of the main spatial and temporal gradients that are found along the dorsoventral axis.

SIMULATION SETTINGS

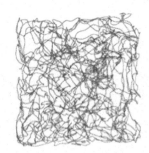

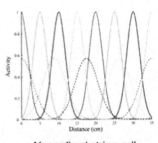

Normalized stripe cell
receptive fields

| Learning trials: **40** |
| Input |
| **Real rat trajectory of ~10 min** |
| **100 cm x 100 cm environment** |
| **Sargolini et al. (2006)** |
| Stripe cells (*assumed*) |
| **9 directions in steps of 20°** |
| **4 spatial phases per direction** |
| **2 spatial scales (20 cm, 35 cm)** |
| Response rate gradient along DV axis of MEC |
| **1, 0.9, 0.8, 0.7, 0.6, 0.5, 0.4, 0.3, 0.2, 0.1** |
| **Garden et al. (2008)** |
| Habituation rate fixed along DV axis of MEC |
| Grid cells (*potential*) |
| **25 per response rate** |

FIGURE 16.24. Parameter settings in the Spectral Spacing Model that were used in simulations.

SPECTRAL SPACING MODEL EQUATIONS

STM $\quad \dfrac{dV_j^m}{dt} = \mu_m\left[-AV_j^m + \left(B - V_j^m\right)\left(\sum_{dps} w_{dpsj}^m x_{dps} + f\left(V_j^m\right)z_j^m\right) - \left(C + V_j^m\right)\sum_{k \neq j} g\left(V_k^m\right)\right]$

Rate spectrum

MTM $\qquad\qquad \dfrac{dz_j^m}{dt} = \eta_m\left[\left(1 - z_j^m\right) - \gamma z_j^m \left(f\left(V_j^m\right)\right)^2\right]$

LTM $\qquad\qquad \dfrac{dw_{dpsj}^m}{dt} = \lambda g\left(V_j^m\right)\left[\left(1 - w_{dpsj}^m\right)x_{dps} - w_{dpsj}^m \sum_{\{p,q,r\}\neq(d,p,s)} x_{pqr}\right]$

FIGURE 16.25. Spectral Spacing Model STM, MTM, and LTM equations. The rate spectrum that determines the dorsoventral gradient of multiple grid cell properties is defined by μ_m.

mapping from stripe cells to grid cells of individual scales is not consistent with data about grid cell modules. My article with Praveen in 2012 showed that some key module properties develop naturally in the model, as illustrated in Figures 16.35b-16.35g. These simulations are also consistent with experiments showing spreads in intrinsic properties of MEC layer II stellate cells at the same dorsoventral locations (e.g., Giocomo et al., 2007; Garden et al., 2008; Boehlen, Heinemann, and Erchova, 2010; Navratilova et al., 2012). Further work is to be desired on this fascinating topic.

Figures 16.30-16.34 summarize additional data and simulations about both grid and place cell properties that emerge from the SOM learning dynamics of the GridPlaceMap model.

Homologous processing of angular and linear velocity path integration inputs

Now is a good time to say more about another beautiful computational homology that exists in the model, since

Development of grid cell modules

Additional properties of considerable importance also emerge from the Spectral Spacing dynamics. Grid cells along the dorsoventral axis "cluster into a small number of layer-spanning anatomically overlapping modules with distinct scale, orientation, asymmetry and theta-frequency modulation" (Stensola et al., 2012, p. 72). These grid cell modules are distributed across wide regions along the dorsoventral axis with substantial overlaps among the different clusters (Figure 16.35a).

If indeed grid cells develop from path integration inputs that are mediated by stripe cells, then these data imply that the problem of selecting from multiple scales of stripe cells during development is a real one, since a simple topographic

Gradient of grid spacings along dorsoventral axis of MEC

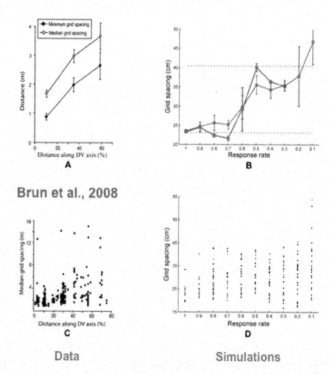

Brun et al., 2008

Data   Simulations

FIGURE 16.26. Data (left column) and simulations (right column) of the gradient of increasing grid cell spacing along the dorsoventral axis of MEC.

Gradient of field width along dorsoventral axis of MEC

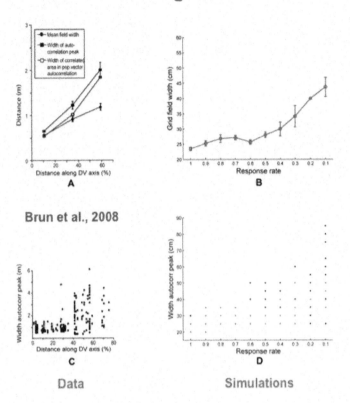

Brun et al., 2008

Data   Simulations

FIGURE 16.27. Data (left column) and simulations (right column) of the gradient of increasing grid cell field width along the dorsoventral axis of MEC.

of the difference between the current heading direction of movement and the ring attractor's directional preference. Each stripe cell ring attractor also has its own spatial scale, which determines how long a linear motion it can encode. Stripe cells occur at different positions within each ring attractor circuit so that they are activated at different spatial phases as an activity bump moves across their own position. Stripe cells hereby code linear displacements in a given direction, and are activated periodically as the activity bump moves around the ring more than once in response to the animal's navigational movements, leading to the spatially periodic responses that are summarized in Figures 16.7 and 16.18.

The model's assumption that both HD cells and stripe cells are computed by ring attractors that drive grid and place cell development is consistent with data showing that adultlike HD cells already exist in parahippocampal regions of rat pups when they actively move out of their nests for the first time at around two weeks of age (Langston et al., 2010; Wills et al., 2010). They are thus then ready to support the rapid learning of grid cells and place cells with which to represent the larger spaces that young rats will then experience for the first time. As I noted in Figure 6.8, the predicted existence of stripe cells has received some experimental support from a report of cells with similar spatial firing properties in dorsal parasubiculum Krupic, Burgess, and O'Keefe, 2012), which projects directly to layer II of MEC where the grid cells are found (Caballero-Bleda and Witter, 1993, 1994).

it has important implications for how grid cells may develop. As noted in Figures 16.5 and 16.10, the inputs that drive the initial development of grid cells and place cells are vestibular angular velocity and linear velocity signals that are activated by an animal's navigational movements. The model proposes that both angular and linear velocity signals are processed by ring attractor neural circuits. Angular velocity signals are integrated by head direction (HD) cells (Ranck, 1984; Taube, Muller, and Ranck, 1990) that fire selectively when an animal's head points in different directions. HD cells are often modeled as part of ring attractor circuits (Blair and Sharp, 1995, 1996; Boucheny, Brunel, and Arleo, 2005; Fortenberry, Gorchetchnikov, and Grossberg, 2012; Skaggs et al., 1995; Redish, Elga, and Touretzky, 1996; Goodridge and Touretzky, 2000; Song and Wang, 2005). The position of an activity bump in a HD ring attractor maximally activates cells that code the current head direction. Similarly, as summarized in Figure 16.7, linear velocity signals are proposed to be integrated by ring attractors that are composed of stripe cells.

Output signals from HD cells are assumed to modulate linear velocity signals to create multiple stripe cell ring attractor circuits with different preferred directions of linear motion. This modulation is sensitive to the cosine

Stable place cell learning, memory, and attention

Place cell selectivity can develop within seconds to minutes, and can remain stable for months (Wilson and

Peak and mean rates at different locations along DV axis of MEC

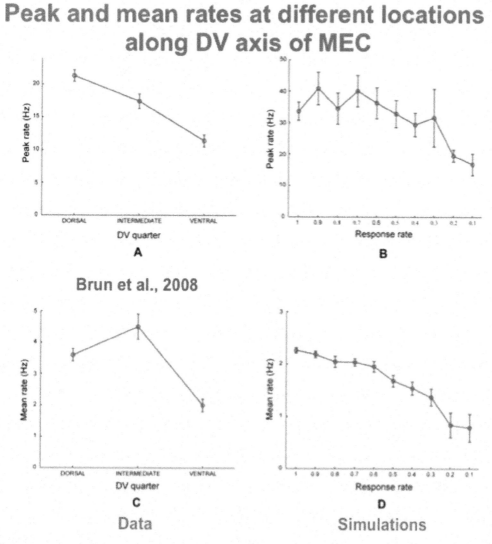

Brun et al., 2008

Data

Simulations

FIGURE 16.28. Data (left column) and simulations (right column) about peak and mean grid cell response rates along the dorsoventral axis of MEC.

McNaughton, 1993; Muller, 1996; Frank, Stanley, and Brown, 2004). The hippocampus needs additional mechanisms to ensure this long-term stability. This combination of fast learning and stable memory is yet another example of how the brain solves the *stability-plasticity dilemma*, which I already discussed in Chapters 5, 6, and 10. As I explained in Chapter 5, SOMs are themselves insufficient to solve the stability-plasticity dilemma in environments whose input patterns are dense and are non-stationary through time (e.g., Figure 5.18), as occurs regularly during real-world navigation. These chapters also explained how Adaptive Resonance Theory, or ART, circuits can dynamically stabilize the learned categorical memories of SOMs (e.g., Figure 5.19). ART shows how SOMs may be augmented by learned top-down expectations that are

matched against bottom-up signals using the ART Matching Rule (Figure 1.25). ART proposes that top-down expectations focus attention on salient combinations of features, while suppressing unmatched features, and how such top-down attentive matching helps to solve the stability-plasticity dilemma. In particular, when a good enough match occurs, a synchronous resonant state emerges that embodies an attentional focus and is capable of driving fast learning by the adaptive weights that control activation of bottom-up recognition categories and top-down expectations; hence the name *adaptive resonance*.

Neurophysiological data about the hippocampus from several labs are compatible with ART predictions about the role of top-down expectations and attentional matching in stabilizing learned grid cells and place cells. For example, a beautiful 1998 article from the laboratory of the Nobel Prize winner Eric Kandel reported that "conditions that maximize place field stability greatly increase orientation to novel cues. This suggests that storage and retrieval of place cells is modulated by a top-down cognitive process resembling attention and that place cells are neural correlates of spatial memory" (Kentros et al., 2004). The Kandel lab had earlier reported that NMDA receptors, which are implicated in many learning processes in the brain, also mediate long-lasting hippocampal place field memory in novel environments (Kentros et al., 1998). The laboratory of Richard Morris had even earlier proposed in 1997 that hippocampal plasticity reflects an "automatic recording of attended experience." (Morris and Frey, 1997). It was furthermore shown by the Moser lab in 2013 that hippocampal inactivation causes grid cells to lose their spatial firing patterns (Bonnevie et al., 2013). These hippocampal inactivation data will be explained and simulated below.

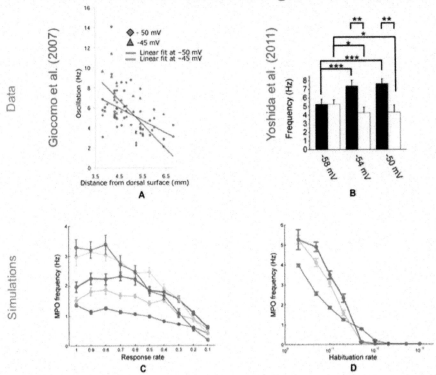

FIGURE 16.29. Data (top row) and simulations (bottom row) showing decreasing frequency of subthreshold membrane potential oscillations along the DV axis of MEC.

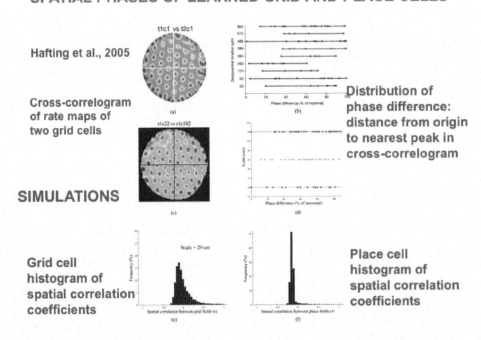

FIGURE 16.30. Data (top row) and simulations (bottom two rows) of spatial phases of learned grid and place cells.

MULTIMODAL PLACE CELL FIRING IN LARGE SPACES
Fenton et al., 2008; Henriksen et al., 2010; Park et al., 2011

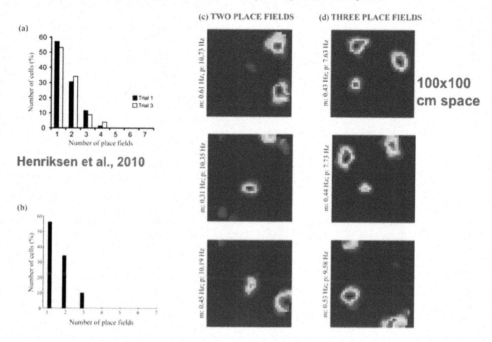

100x100 cm space

FIGURE 16.31. Data (a) and simulations (b-d) about multimodal place cell receptive fields in large spaces. The simulations are the result of learned place fields.

MODEL FITS DATA ABOUT GRID CELL DEVELOPMENT

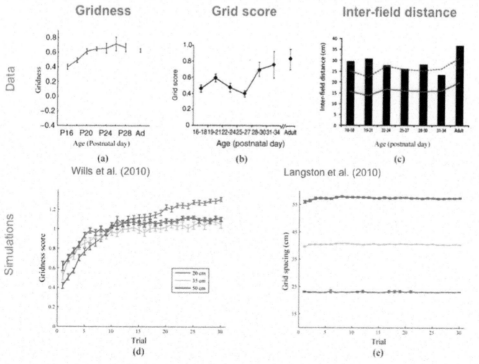

FIGURE 16.32. Data (top row) and simulations (bottom row) about grid cell development in juvenile rats. Grid score increases (a-b and d), whereas grid spacing remains fairly flat (c and e).

MODEL FITS DATA ABOUT PLACE CELL DEVELOPMENT

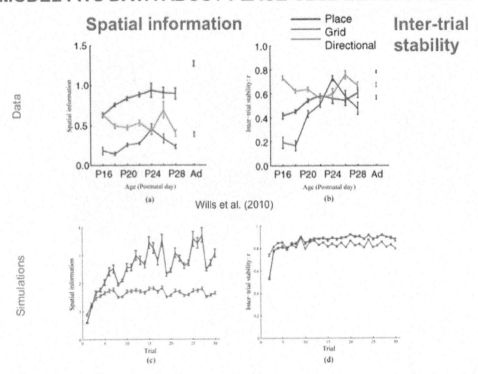

FIGURE 16.33. Data (top row) and simulations (bottom row) of changes in place cell properties in juvenile rats, notably about spatial information (a, c) and inter-trial stability (b, d).

THETA-MODULATED CELLS IN SPIKING MODEL

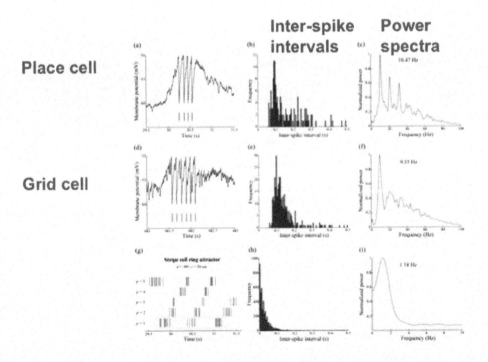

FIGURE 16.34. The spiking GridPlaceMap model generates theta-modulated place and grid cell firing, unlike the rate-based model.

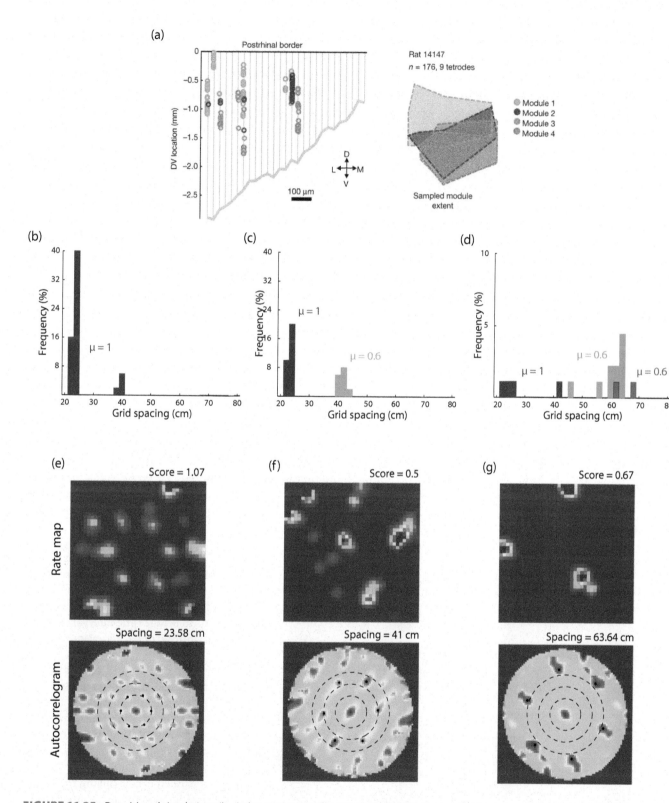

FIGURE 16.35. Data (a) and simulations (b, c) about anatomically overlapping grid cell modules. (a) shows the anatomical distribution of grid cells belonging to different modules in one animal. (b) shows the simulated distribution of learned grid cell spacings from two stripe cell scales. (c) shows what happens when half the cells respond with one rate and half another rate. (d) shows the same with three rates. (e-g) show spatial maps and autocorrelograms of grid cells that arise from the different rates in (d).

An ART spatial category learning system: The hippocampus IS a cognitive map!

Taken together, these experiments provide accumulating evidence for how cognitive processes like top-down attentional matching from the hippocampal cortex to the entorhinal cortex may play a role in ensuring the stability of entorhinal-hippocampal spatial learning and memory. Taken together, they all support the hypothesis that grid cell and place cell learning in the entorhinal-hippocampal system is an ART spatial category learning system (Figure 16.36). Said in another way, this ART system provides a computational verification and major elaboration of the main hypothesis that John O'Keefe and Lynn Nadel proposed in their classical 1978 book, *The Hippocampus as a Cognitive Map*. Indeed, the entorhinal-hippocampal spatial navigation learning system as a whole is used to learn and dynamically stabilize the memory of this cognitive map.

The hippocampus is MORE than a cognitive map: Three interacting learning processes

As I have explained in Chapters 5 and 15, the hippocampus is also more than a cognitive map. It supports at least three interacting learning processes that I will now summarize all in one place.

Mismatch mediated learning and memory consolidation during recognition learning. The first process was explained in Chapter 5. It uses the ART memory search and category learning cycle to learn new recognition categories (Figure 5.19). During this process, the hippocampus, as part of the brain's orienting system, responds to a sufficiently novel object or event by resetting the currently active recognition category, while driving a memory search and hypothesis testing to discover a new recognition category with which to better represent it. After this object or event becomes familiar, it can directly access the recognition category without requiring a memory search that engages the hippocampus. This is the first kind of memory consolidation that the hippocampus regulates. This matching process also resets currently active recognition categories when inputs are received that mismatch them sufficiently, whether or not these inputs represent familiar or unfamiliar events.

Adaptively timed learning and memory consolidation during reinforcement learning. The second kind of memory consolidation uses the ability of the hippocampus to bridge time intervals of hundreds of milliseconds, or even seconds, between offset of a conditioned cue and onset of an unconditioned cue, as occurs during trace conditioning, among other reinforcement learning paradigms (Figure 15.2). Hippocampal "time cells" have the predicted properties that are needed to bridge such a temporal gap. They enable associative learning to occur between temporally separated events during reinforcement learning, support the consolidation of these learned memories after learning trials end by using endogenous hippocampal bursting, and support adaptively timed motivated attention with which to carry out timed actions towards valued goals after learning ends.

ENTORHINAL-HIPPOCAMPAL INTERACTIONS AS AN ART SYSTEM
HIPPOCAMPAL PLACE CELLS AS SPATIAL CATEGORIES

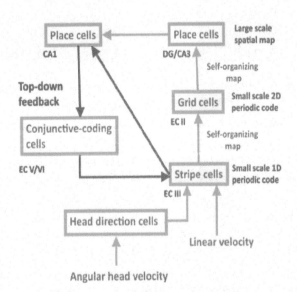

FIGURE 16.36. The entorhinal-hippocampal system has properties of an ART spatial category learning system, with hippocampal place cells as the spatial categories. See the text for details.

There is a beautiful mechanistic homolog between the ART circuits that support the learning of recognition categories and the nSTART circuits that support adaptively timed reinforcement learning and performance. Figures 15.16 and 15.19 summarize, in particular, how adaptively timed motivated attention can support the release of adaptively timed actions, even as it inhibits orienting responses that would otherwise have forced a premature shift of attention, a motivational rebound, and the activation of exploratory behaviors that could have led to relentless seeking of immediate gratifications.

Spatial navigation, neural relativity, and episodic learning and memory. The third kind of learning and memory develops grid cells and place cells for spatial navigation, and uses ART top-down attentive matching from CA1 to the entorhinal cortex to dynamically stabilize this kind of learning and memory. The Spectral Spacing and GridPlaceMap models for this kind of spatial learning are, moreover, computationally homologous to the Spectral Timing model for adaptively timed reinforcement learning, thereby clarifying, from a rigorous mechanistic viewpoint, why these spatial and temporal processes occur side-by-side in the entorhinal-hippocampal system.

Beta and gamma oscillations in hippocampus and cortical areas V1, V2, and V4

Properties of hippocampal oscillations provide further support for the hypothesis that the entorhinal-hippocampal system is an ART spatial category learning system. Here is a good place to recall my explanation in Chapter 5 of how the Synchronous Matching ART, or SMART, laminar cortical model (Figure 5.38; Grossberg and Versace, 2008) generates fast gamma oscillations that enable spike-timing dependent plasticity to occur when there is a sufficiently good top-down match with bottom-up signal patterns, whereas a big enough mismatch can trigger slow beta oscillations and a shift of attention while inhibiting learning (Figure 5.40). I used these properties to explain there how an Inverted-U in beta power through time occurs in the hippocampus during the learning of place fields in novel environments (Berke et al., 2008; Grossberg, 2009a), and have the beta oscillation properties that are expected when mismatches occur and category refinements are learned. Such an Inverted-U in beta power through time is thus a signature of ART category learning in any novel learning situation.

Chapter 5 also reviewed experiments that support the match/mismatch gamma/beta prediction in V1, V2, and V4, notably data from the lab of Bob Desimone showing that mismatch reset, and thus beta oscillations, are initiated as

predicted in the deeper layers of the visual cortex (Figure 5.42), and data from the lab of Earl Miller about the frontal eye fields and extrastriate cortical area V4 during shifts in spatial attention. Thus, the predicted match/mismatch dynamics leading to gamma/beta oscillations seem to occur in multiple brain systems, and thereby support the proposed role of ART category learning processes in all of these systems.

Many finer questions are worthy of additional experimental and theoretical analysis. For example, there is a direct entorhinal-to-CA1 pathway and an indirect entorhinal-to-CA3-to-CA1 pathway that also includes grid cells (Figure 16.36). The direct pathway has been shown to support a faster gamma oscillation, whereas the indirect pathway supports a slower gamma oscillation (Colgin et al., 2009; Colgin and Moser, 2010). As I noted earlier, gamma oscillations emerge in the SMART model during good enough matches between bottom-up inputs and learned top-down expectations (Figure 5.40). Because of the possibility that the direct entorhinal-to-CA1 pathway may become active before a rat pup begins to explore its environment extensively beyond its nest, it is of interest to ask: Does fast gamma support early development of place cells that can selectively represent positions in or near the nest? Do the slower gamma oscillations of the indirect pathway support later development of grid cells and place cells that can represent the large spaces within which adult rats navigate? In particular, do the slower gamma frequencies of the indirect pathway begin to emerge later than the faster gamma frequencies of the direct pathway? This is an area rich with unexplored possibilities.

Grid cell realignment and place cell remapping

Several other kinds of data support the hypothesis that grid and place cell learning are carried out by an ART spatial category learning system. They all consider how grid and place cells are altered when one or another problem occurs with hippocampal-to-entorhinal feedback. One such kind of data concern conditions when realignment of grid cells and remapping of place cells occurs, including loss of the tight distributions of grid orientations across similar grid cell scales.

Coordinated grid realignment and place cell remapping were reported in a 2007 article from the Moser lab (Fyhn et al., 2007). In their study, global remapping was induced by two different procedures. In one, rats were tested in the same location in either a square or circular enclosure. In the other, the rats alternated between similar square boxes in two different rooms. As global place cell remapping in the hippocampus occurred, the grid cell map in the medial entorhinal cortex also realigned, but without losing its intrinsic spatial phase structure. This tight correlation between the grid and place cell representations supports the hypothesis, that is mechanistically explained herein, "that the grid network is a universal metric for path-integration-based navigation" (p. 193).

Remapping could occur, for example, when the path integration inputs activate one combination of grid and place cells via bottom-up pathways from medial entorhinal cortex to hippocampus, but visual inputs activate a different combination by top-down pathways from hippocampus to medial entorhinal cortex (Figure 16.36). In any ART system, a big enough mismatch can cause a global reset event. In this way, top-down attentive matching may underlie the phenomena of global remapping in the hippocampus and grid realignment in the medial entorhinal cortex

Top-down matching from place cells to grid cells can also help to align grid orientations. Such global alignment by top-down matching has also been simulated in other brain systems. For example, as part of a proposed solution of the global aperture problem (Figures 8.31 and 8.36), top-down matching from area MST to area MT in the motion system may align perceived motion directions across spatial locations to conform to a higher-level choice of object motion direction in cortical area MT of winning motion directions in cortical area MST (Figures 8.36-8.39). The coordinated properties of remapping and realignment of grid and place cells could benefit from a similar detailed modeling study of the specific effects of changing the size and shape of enclosures.

been demonstrated by temporarily inactivating the hippocampus, and thus its feedback signals to entorhinal cortex. A 2013 article from the Moser lab (Bonnevie et al., 2013) reported two major kinds of effects after the hippocampus was inactivated in rats by local infusion of the $GABA_A$ receptor agonist 5-aminomethyl-3-hydroxy-isoxazole, or muscimol, through cannulae implanted in the dorsal pole of each rat's hippocampus. This manipulation abolished nearly all firing in place cells of the dorsal hippocampus. This was followed by a substantial reduction in the average rate and spatial periodicity of grid cell firing. Instead, the grid cells that lost their grid fields became tuned to the direction of the rat's head. Figure 16.37 shows how grid cell properties deteriorate after hippocampus is silenced, and then recover after hippocampal firing is restored.

Bonnevie et al. (2013) also proposed a model to simulate their data. I will explain below why their model is incompatible with other data that I have described above, and thus seems to be incorrect in its present form. The ART circuit that is summarized in Figure 16.36 also provides an explanation of their data, and this explanation is consistent with the data of other experiments that the proposal of Bonnevie et al. (2013) did not explain.

Before mentioning details, let us acknowledge immediately from basic properties of ART that removing top-down hippocampal-to-entorhinal attentive feedback in

When hippocampal feedback fails: Grid cell spatial periodicity and firing rate collapse

The importance of hippocampal feedback for grid and place cell stability has also

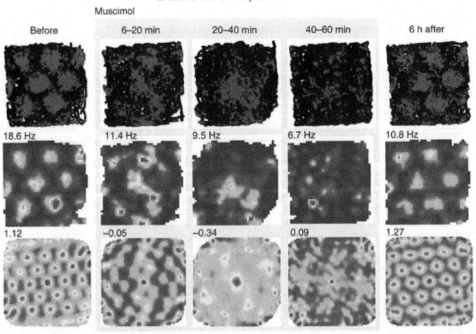

HIPPOCAMPAL INACTIVATION DISRUPTS GRID CELLS
Bonnevie et al., 2013

FIGURE 16.37. Data showing the effect of hippocampal inactivation by muscimol on grid cell firing before before, during, and six hours after the muscimol, reading from left to right.

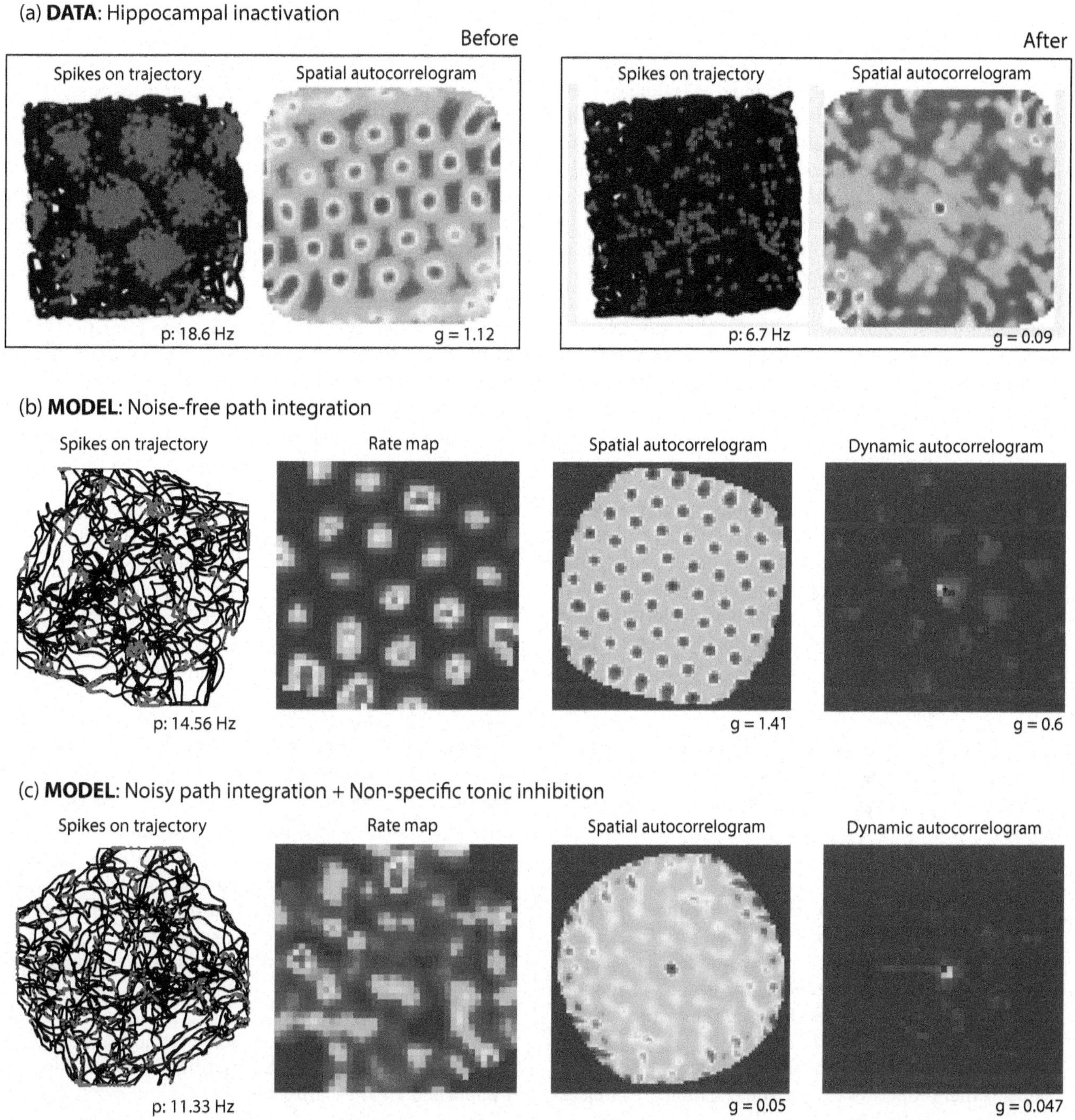

(a) **DATA**: Hippocampal inactivation

Before

After

(b) **MODEL**: Noise-free path integration

(c) **MODEL**: Noisy path integration + Non-specific tonic inhibition

FIGURE 16.38. Role of hippocampal feedback in maintaining grid fields. (a) Data showing the effect of hippocampal inactivation before and during muscimol inhibition of hippocampal cells, as in Figure 16.37. (b) Model simulation with normal grid fields. (c) Model simulation that emulates the effect of hippocampal inhibition on grid fields.

Figure 16.36 would destabilize grid fields as an animal navigates its environment. Figure 16.38 summarizes simulations of how this happens in our model. To carry out this simulation without having to simulate the entire circuit in Figure 16.36, the following approximations were made that embody the rate-limiting computations:

First, to emulate the destabilizing effect of removing hippocampal feedback, noise was added to the bottom-up path integration inputs during navigation.

Second, removal of hippocampal top-down, modulatory on-center, off-surround feedback would shift the balance of excitation and inhibition across the entorhinal cortex.

In particular, if only some hippocampal cells (e.g., in the dorsal hippocampus) were silenced, this could disinhibit nearby hippocampal cells by releasing them from recurrent inhibition from other hippocampal cells (Figure 16.5), thereby possibly strengthening their driving inhibitory off-surround inputs to the grid cells that lost their excitatory hippocampal modulation. In addition, attentionally-modulated grid cells could inhibit their unmodulated neighbors more than conversely. The net effect could be to significantly increase the inhibition of the unmodulated grid cells. This effect was approximated in the simulations by delivering an extra uniform inhibitory signal to the affected grid cells. Figure 16.38b shows the grid field that develops during noise-free path integration. Figure 16.38c simulates how the grid field collapses in response to noisy inputs and nonspecific tonic inhibition.

Another relevant factor in the firing of grid cells is the ability of cells in a normal SOM network to respond more strongly to the most frequent and energetic combinations of inputs. If upsetting the excitatory-inhibitory balance could shift the response threshold to lower values, then the effects of individual stripe cells could be more evident in grid cell responses, thereby helping to explain the head directional influence on grid cell firing after hippocampal inactivation.

Effects on grid cells of inactivating medial septum and the theta rhythm

Another kind of experimental data also support the current model. Although at least one laboratory that carried out this experiment were motivated by a desire to support the oscillatory interference model, it turned out that our alternative explanation seems to be a more correct one, not one based upon oscillatory interference.

A major fact that motivated the oscillatory interference model is that properties of spatial navigation are often associated with a rhythm that oscillates in the theta range, which is typically 6-10 Hz, when a rat in engaged in active motor behaviors such as walking or exploratory sniffing. A lower frequency range, around 6-7 Hz, may occur when a rat is not moving, but is nonetheless alert. When a rat eats, sleeps, or grooms, hippocampal EEG usually exhibits large irregular activity, or LIA.

The hippocampal theta rhythm depends critically on projections from the medial septal (MS) area in the basal forebrain, which itself receives inputs from the hypothalamus, among other brain regions, while generating and maintaining network theta rhythm in the hippocampal and parahippocampal areas (Vertes and Kocsis, 1997) via

reciprocal interactions among GABAergic interneurons (Toth, Borhegyi, and Freund, 1993; Wang, 2002a). It is also known that theta oscillations may be influenced by mechanisms that are both extrinsic and intrinsic to the hippocampus (Bland and Colom, 1993; Smythe, Colom, and Bland, 1992; Vanderwolf, 1988), with the influence of MS on theta being one of the extrinsic influences.

One strong point of the oscillatory interference model is that it assumes a theta rhythm, and then uses oscillatory interference of its waxing and waning signals to try to explain how it can be used to form grid cell firing patterns. This assumption is, however, a double-edged sword, since by assuming a theta rhythm, one loses the ability to explain it as an emergent property of network interactions, including when it does not occur. My own belief is that a modeler should mechanistically explain how and when theta arises and changes with an animal's behavior in order to really understand it, just as I believe that one should not just assume a spatial representation within which spatial navigation occurs, but should rather try to explain how such an spatial representation develops due to experience, as in the GridPlaceMap proposal.

Experiments that reduced the theta rhythm by inactivating the MS demonstrated a correlated reduction in the hexagonal spatial firing patterns of grid cells (Brandon et al. 2011; Koenig et al., 2011). Figure 16.39 shows the effects of MS inactivation on the collapse of grid fields, and their recovery after MS inactivation wears off. During MS inactivation, affected grid cells tended to code the rat's head direction (see the middle curve in the fifth row on Figure 16.39A). Because MS inactivation interfered with the theta rhythm, Brandon et al. concluded that "spatial coding by grid cells requires theta oscillations" and that their data "support a role of neuronal oscillations in the coding of spatial information". In other words, these authors proposed that their data support a mechanism of oscillatory interference in the creation of hexagonal grid fields.

Acetylcholine modulates vigilance control of cognitive, motor, and spatial category learning. Praveen Pilly and I published an alternative explanation and simulations of these data in a 2013 article (Pilly and Grossberg, 2013a). We focused upon the fact that the signals from the MS to entorhinal grid cells typically release acetylcholine, or ACh. As I will explain more completely below, this is a kind of vigilance control that modulates the learning of hippocampal *spatial* categories.

I have already described to you, again in the context of vigilance control (Figure 5.43), how important it is to control ACh levels for purposes of normal *cognitive* category learning and memory. Indeed, Chapter 5 describes how breakdowns in vigilance-modulating ACh release from the nucleus basalis of Meynert, for any of several reasons, can lead to symptoms of autism, Alzheimer's

DISRUPTIVE EFFECTS OF MEDIAL SEPTUM INACTIVATION IN MEDIAL ENTORHINAL CORTEX

Brandon et al., 2011; Koenig et al., 2011

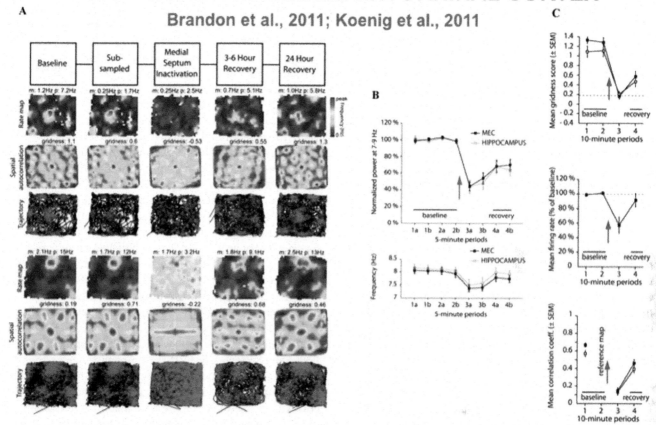

FIGURE 16.39. Data showing effects of medial septum (MS) inactivation on grid cells and network theta oscillations in medial entorhinal cortex (MEC). (A) Examples of disruption in the spatial expression of the hexagonal grid structure for two grid cells (Brandon et al., 2011). (B) Temporal reduction in the power and frequency of network theta oscillations (Koenig et al., 2011). (C) Temporary reduction in the gridness score, mean firing rate, and spatial stability of grid cells (Koenig et al., 2011).

disease, and disrupted slow wave sleep as a result of how tonic and/or phasic vigilance control is impaired in each case.

Another brain system where ACh-modulated vigilance control plays an important role is in the learning of the movement map within the deeper layers of the superior colliculus (SC) that controls the position to which the next saccadic eye movement will move. In this multimodal movement map, inputs from vision, audition, and planning circuits all come together to cooperate and compete in the superior colliculus to determine whether we will look reactively at a current visual or auditory cue, or at a planned target position, such as a position in space that we believe will soon register a valued goal object.

The SACCART model proposes how this SC movement map is learned as part of a *motor* category learning process, and how this learning is dynamically stabilized by a top-down attentional feedback circuit that

obeys the ART Matching Rule (Grossberg et al., 1997). The SACCART model was supported by its explanations of challenging neurophysiological and anatomical data about cell types in the SC that are called burst cells and buildup cells, among other data. After SACCART was published, the role of ACh in this kind of category learning process was studied by Eric Knudsen in the optic tectum of the pigeon, which is a homolog of the mammalian superior colliculus (Hyde and Knudsen, 2002; Knudsen, 2002, 2011). I was able to explain the newer optic tectum data in a 2016 article by describing how ACh-modulated inputs to the SC from the nucleus isthmi pars parvocellularis (Ipc) may regulate vigilance during multimodal motor category learning (Grossberg, Palma, and Versace, 2016).

In all, the learning of spatial, cognitive, and motor categories seem to depend in similar ways upon ACh-modulated vigilance control.

In the entorhinal-hippocampal system, ACh modulates the learning of place cell spatial categories. Here, MS inactivation eliminates, or at least greatly reduces, the ACh input to grid cells (Mitchell et al., 1982). This collapse of ACh increases the conductances of leak potassium and slow and medium after-hyperpolarization channels (Klink and Alonso, 1997; Lape and Nistri, 2000; Madison et al., 1987; Müller, Misgeld, and Heinemann, 1988). As a result, the rate of membrane depolarization is slowed, and there is greater spike frequency adaptation and longer refractory periods. Recall that control of the duration of grid cell sampling of stripe cell inputs is needed within the Spectral Spacing model to learn grid cells with any given spatial scale, let alone with multiple spatial scales (Figure 16.23). The deleterious effects of MS inactivation on normal ACh release would therefore be expected to dramatically impair grid cell firing and spatial periodicity.

And in fact, it does. Model simulations show spatial disorganization of grid fields in addition to reductions in firing rate and spatial stability (Figure 16.40c) when MS inactivation is invoked by either a temporary reduction in cell response rates (Figure 16.40d) or a temporary increase in leak conductances (Figure 16.40e). The fact that a head direction bias remains after the duration of path integration sampling is disorganized follows directly from the head-directionally-selective path integration inputs from stripe cells to grid cells in our model (Figure 16.36).

Grid cells without oscillatory interference. Koenig et al. (2011) examined the effects of inactivating MS on hippocampal place cells, and found that they largely maintain their place fields, but show reductions in firing rate and theta band modulation. This provides additional support to our model's prediction that the theta rhythm is not *necessary* for medial entorhinal-hippocampal cells to encode spatial information. Longer refractory periods that result from reduced cholinergic action do not adversely affect place cells because place cells do not have the multiple periodic spatial fields of grid cells and, in addition to grid cell inputs, they also receive reliable sensory, notably visual, inputs in a familiar environment.

At the time that Praveen and I published our results, we also summarized other data that we believe supported our view. In particular, knockout of the HCN1 gene in mice flattens the frequency of membrane potential oscillations along the dorsoventral axis, but does not undermine the development of multiple grid cell spatial scales in a dorsoventral gradient (Giocomo and Hasselmo, 2009; Giocomo et al., 2011). Grid firing fields can, in fact, develop without any theta band modulation, as they do in bats (Yartsev et al., 2011). Neither of these results is obviously consistent with an oscillatory interference model of grid cell development.

If grid cells can exist without theta oscillations, then the foundational hypothesis of oscillatory interference models would not be supported. Two other labs used *in vivo* whole-cell recordings during virtual reality navigation to conclude that the spatially selective firing of grid cells is better explained by membrane potential ramps caused by integration of synaptic inputs on a slower, sub-theta time scale, and not by constructive interference among intrinsic membrane potential oscillations in the theta band (Domnisoru, Kinkhabwala, and Tank, 2013; Schmidt-Heiber and Hausser, 2013). Such temporal integration occurs naturally in the SOM model, and is the mechanism whereby different grid spatial scales may be learned.

Direct support for our prediction about how MS inactivation could prevent ACh modulation of grid cell learning was not long in coming. While our own article was in press, the laboratory of my Boston University colleague Michael Hasselmo, that published the original 2011 Brandon et al. (2011) article about the effects of MS inactivation, published supportive data. For example, in 2012, Caswell Barry and James Heys published an article with Hasselmo (Barry, Heys, and Hasselmo, 2012) with the title "Possible Role of Acetylcholine in Regulating Spatial Novelty Effects on Theta Rhythm and Grid Cells". In 2014, Ehren Newman and Jason Climer published a follow-up article with Hasselmo (Newman, Climer, and Hasselmo, 2014) with the title "Grid Cell Spatial Tuning Reduced Following Systematic Muscarinic Receptor Blockade".

A large-scale modeling study of how variations in the timing and amplitude of ACh signalling to entrorhinal cortex is much to be desired, as is a comparative analysis of how ACh signalling modulates category learning across multiple brain systems.

Three types of grid cell models

SOM models. The text above illustrates why I believe a SOM-based model like the GridPlaceMap model provides a correct foundation for understanding how grid cells and place cells develop. Not surprisingly, given the intense interest in the neuroscience community in this topic, ours is not the only kind of model. Models of grid cells can be divided into three classes: SOM models; oscillatory interference models (e.g., Burgess, 2008; Burgess, Barry, and O'Keefe, 2007; Hasselmo, Giocomo, and Zilli, 2007); and continuous attractor models (e.g., McNaughton et al., 2006; Burak and Fiete, 2006; Fuhs and Touretzky, 2006; Guanella, Kiper, and Verschure, 2007). Eric Zilli provided a review in 2012 of some basic properties of the models that were published between 2005-2011 (Zilli, 2012). Below I will briefly summarizes some of the problematic properties of oscillatory interference and continuous attractor models that I believe have been overcome by SOM models.

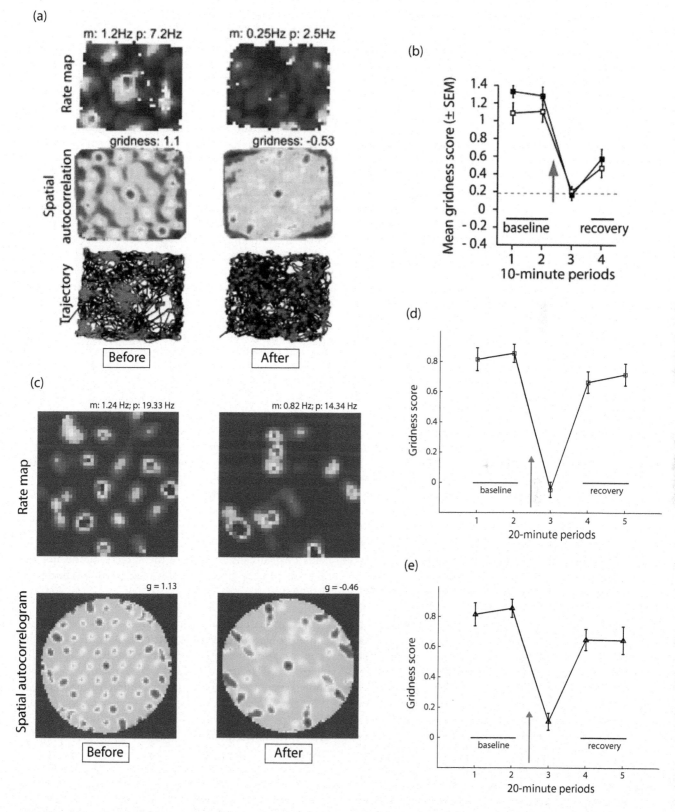

FIGURE 16.40. Effects of medial septum (MS) inactivation on grid cells. (a) Each row shows data and different data-derived measures of grid cell responsiveness, starting from the left with the baseline response to the middle column with maximal inhibition. (b) Data showing the temporary reduction in the gridness scores during MS inactivation, followed by recovery. (c) Simulation of the collapse in gridness, achieved by reduction in cell response rates to mimic reduced cholinergic transmission. (d, e) Simulations of the reduction in gridness scores in (d) by reduction of cell response rates, in (e) by changing the leak conductance. See the text for details.

Only SOM models have thus far demonstrated how both grid cell and place cell receptive fields may be learned using local interaction laws as an animal navigates realistic trajectories. Another model that can learn its grid cells was published in 2008 by Emilio Kropff and Alessandro Treves (Kropff and Treves, 2008). This model is not, however, based on path integration, but on adaptive inputs from place cells. This developmental hypothesis may be challenged from the perspective of the experiments that I have already summarized. Another concern is that grid cells can show spatial responses in any environment, unlike place cells (Fyhn et al., 2007). Finally, the Knopff-Treves model uses an algorithmic iterative normalization of cell activities and adaptive weights—hence is not a real-time model—and simulates less data than the GridPlaceMap model.

Oscillatory interference models. Oscillatory interference models propose that the grid pattern arises due to interference among, typically, three oscillators of fixed frequency whose directional preferences differ by 60 degrees. As noted above, various data that were originally collected to support this hypothesis have more complete explanations using a SOM model, and oscillatory interference in incompatible with data from a number of experiments that were done to test it.

The most challenging problems for oscillatory interference are conceptual and foundational. The model leads to the wrong answers when there are more than three oscillators and/or their preferred directions do not differ by 60 degrees; e.g., Figure 16.15. These errors occur because the oscillatory interference model has no mechanisms whereby less favored combinations of inputs from stripe cells, or band cells, can be suppressed. The recurrent competition at the spatial category learning stage of a SOM model has this function, as it does in all applications of SOM models in many parts of the brain (Figures 16.9, 16.16, and 16.23).

Despite these differences, oscillatory interference and SOM models share a basic design constraint that contrasts with continuous attractor models: They both assume that two-dimensional hexagonal grids arise from input combinations of one-dimensional band cells or stripe cells, respectively. *Band cells* were proposed in the initial presentation of the interference model by Neil Burgess, Colin Barry, and John O'Keefe in 2007 (Burgess, Barry, and O'Keefe, 2007) and were used as the generators of the directional oscillations whose interference gives the model its name. The stripe cells proposed here are based on a different mechanism that does not rely on oscillatory interference.

A parsimonious property of the SOM model is that it uses homologous ring attractors to code both types of path integration inputs to the model: angular velocity, via head direction cells, and linear velocity, via stripe cells (Figures 16.5 and 16.10). I earlier noted that several investigators have used ring attractors to model the head direction cells

that respond to vestibular angular velocity signals. Some oscillatory interference models also include ring attractors for linear velocity path integration (e.g., Blair, Gupta, and Zhang, 2008), but their ring attractors for computing angular and linear velocity are not homologous.

That is because the ring attractor for linear velocity path integration "is produced by subcortical ring attractor networks that function as frequency-modulated oscillators, and that these networks provide the neural substrate for storing and updating the phase-coded position signal . . . In accordance with the principles of oscillatory interference, we show that outputs from theta cells residing in different (but not the same) ring attractors can be combined to form spatially periodic oscillations, which are similar to the observed firing patterns of grid cells." In contrast, the SOM stripe cell ring attractor is phasically driven by linear velocity signals created by movements through an environment, and its head direction ring attractor is phasically driven by angular velocity signals when the head moves.

Continuous attractor models. These models propose that grid cell firing may arise *directly* from recurrent interactions in a two-dimensional network of grid cells in response to path integration inputs. One problem with these models is that their network connections need to be finely tuned and have spatially *anisotropic* weights, notably asymmetric two-dimensional recurrent inhibitory interactions. These asymmetric connection weights are not yet supported by experimental evidence or computer simulations showing how this weight structure can be learned in real time during navigation. Such simulations would be challenging for a continuous attractor model because anatomically nearby grid cells can belong to different scale-specific modules (Figure 16.35a), and spatial fields of grid cells that share the same scale do not exhibit any noticeable topographic organization (Hafting et al., 2005).

In contrast, the SOM model can develop grid and place cells using spatially *isotropic* recurrent inhibitory connections. The SOM model has directional asymmetries in the various one-dimensional stripe cell ring attractors for path integration (Figure 16.7), rather than directly in a two-dimensional field of grid cells. One might legitimately ask: Why are asymmetric connections in a one-dimensional ring attractor more plausible than directionally asymmetric connections across a two-dimensional attractor network?

Actually, it is easy to imagine how a developmental gradient among the cells in a one-dimensional network like a ring attractor can cause the strengths of inhibitory connections to be greater in one direction than the opposite direction, for the same reason that long-range filter cells for motion integration can develop directionally-anisotropic receptive fields in response to the statistics of directional motion through time (e.g., Figures 8.25 to 8.31).

In a one-dimensional head direction ring attractor, asymmetric inhibitory interactions suffice to move an activity bump across the network's head direction cells in response to angular velocity inputs. Given such an asymmetric gradient, the key problem is then how head direction cells can be calibrated to represent prescribed head directions. Aspects of how this may happen have been explained and simulated using the HeadMoVVes model that I published in 2012 with my PhD student Bret Fortenberry and postdoc Anatoli Gorchetchnikov (Fortenberry, Gorchetchnikov, and Grossberg, 2012). This model simulates how path integration angular velocity inputs, motor outflow movement commands, and visual feedback to a ring attractor of head direction cells may be calibrated by learning. The resultant learned cell properties simulate data about the anatomy and neurophysiology of head direction cells in the multiple brain regions that are used by the brain to calibrate head direction. This model provides a proof of principle that learned calibration of one-dimensional ring attractors is possible.

Continuous attractor with top-down uniform positive hippocampal-to-entorhinal feedback. A continuous attractor model from the Moser lab (e.g., Bonnevie et al., 2013) was used to propose an explanation of why grid cell firing is disorganized when hippocampal feedback is silenced. The main hypothesis of this model is that there is a spatially uniform, driving, excitatory top-down input from the hippocampus to the entorhinal cortex, as well as recurrent inhibition governed by two-dimensional spatially anisotropic connections. In addition, the bottom-up input is assumed to be a directionally-modulated velocity input. When the uniform excitatory top-down feedback is shut off, then the grid cells exhibit properties that are qualitatively similar to those found in the data.

Both the excitatory and inhibitory interactions that are posited in their model raise concerns. The assumption that the top-down feedback signal from hippocampal place cells to grid cells is a spatially uniform and driving input seems to be incompatible with properties of place cell firing. First, place cells are selective to specific places of an environment (Figures 16.3 and 16.18). In order for a uniform excitatory feedback signal to occur, each place cell would need to deliver a spatially uniform excitatory input to all grid cells. This hypothesis is, however, incompatible with data that I summarized above from several labs which suggest that top-down attentional connections underlie dynamic stabilization of hippocampal spatial memory. Such an attentional matching input would be expected to be spatially selective, not uniform. It would also not be a driving excitatory input, because attention is known to have a modulatory on-center in all other modalities where it has been studied (Figure 1.25). Finally, top-down uniform excitatory feedback could not dynamically stabilize learning of grid cells and place cells, as the ART

Matching Rule provably does, despite the known fact that this system solves the *stability-plasticity dilemma*.

The Bonnevie et al. (2013) model also assumes that the two-dimensional asymmetric recurrent inhibitory connections of each cell are sensitive to its preferred direction. As noted above, there seems to be no experimental data to support this assumption. It is also not clear how the dependence on a single directional preference in both bottom-up and recurrent interaction kernels would develop.

Intrinsic theta rhythm from a dissociation between associative read-out and read-in

The discussion above clarifies how an extrinsic source of the theta rhythm, with signals from the medial septum, provides cholinergic modulation of the learning of grid cells and place cells. There is also an intrinsic source of theta within the hippocampus itself. How might that arise?

A lot of data, theoretical concepts, and mathematical models of how theta rhythms may be generated have been reported in a vibrant literature. György Buzsáki at New York University is a leader in all aspects of work on the theta rhythm (e.g., Buzsáki, 2002; Buzsáki and Moser, 2013). Here I just want to summarize, in a non-technical way, a basic design problem that is faced by all brain systems, and how it seems to be solved. This resolution can then be used to explain key qualitative properties of the relationship that has been reported between the theta rhythm and learning as manifestations of this design. This explanation will also clarify how the grid cell and place cell learning processes that I have already discussed emerge naturally in circuits that exhibit oscillatory dynamics.

As I noted in Chapter 2, the functional units of STM and LTM are spatial patterns of activation that are distributed across networks of neurons and their synapses, respectively (Figures 2.9-2.11). My explanation of theta rhythm concerns how STM and LTM are coordinated to achieve effective learning and prediction, in particular within SOM models. As with so many explanations in this book, the basic design constraint concerns how to coordinate the contrast-enhancing competition that occurs in STM, leading to choices of most salient feature combinations at any given time, with associative learning and LTM of these chosen combinations.

Competitive choices in STM. Both non-recurrent and recurrent on-center off-surround networks whose cells obey the membrane equations of neurophysiology (viz. shunting dynamics) can represent distributed spatial patterns of activation, or STM, across feature detectors of any kind (e.g., Figures 1.6-1.9) without being contaminated by either noise or saturation, thereby solving the fundamental *noise-saturation dilemma* that I described in Chapter 1 (Figure 1.5).

From READ circuits to SOM theta rhythm: Dissociating associative read-out from read-in. The problem that is faced during learning of grid cells and place cells is the same problem that is faced by reinforcement learning using affective opponent processes that are modeled by gated dipoles. Recall from Chapter 13 how our brains seem to solve the problem of maintaining the plasticity throughout life of synapses that learn cognitive-emotional associations from object categories to value categories (Figure 13.1). This problem concerns: If adaptive synapses between an object category and its value category get reinforced time and time again, then what prevents these synapses from hitting their maximal values and becoming unable to learn new reinforcement contingencies in the future? A REcurrent Associative Dipole, or READ, circuit proposes a solution of this problem that has many attractive properties, including the ability to learn changing reinforcement contingencies without saturation throughout the life span (Figure 13.37–13.39). The READ circuit does this by carrying out a process that I called *dissociation of associative read-out from read-in* when I discovered it in 1975 (Grossberg, 1975a). Many subsequent data, in several different brain systems, have confirmed this basic insight.

The basic problem is that read-*out* of a previously learned adaptive weight to a target cell should *not* always trigger new learning—that is, read-*in*—by that adaptive weight, even if it succeeds in activating its target cell. Correlation learning *per se* is not sufficient. To understand why automatic read-in would cause a serious problem, consider the total activity *pattern* across all the cells of a network, not just the activity of a single cell. There can be multiple inputs converging on each cell across such a network. Each input can be active at different times and to different degrees to the various cells in the network. What if all the inputs across the network summed up to create approximately equal inputs to, and thus activities of, all the cells in the network for a significant duration of time? This uniform pattern of activities would be uninformative because it does not prefer any particular feature combination that is represented by a subset of these cells to any other. A uniform activity pattern represents functional "noise". It should thus emphatically *not* drive new learning, because if it did, then previous learning could quickly be washed away by new learning of "noise". The *stability-plasticity dilemma* would fail in a dramatic way if associative read-out always forced new associative read-in.

Instead, as in a READ circuit, contrast-enhancing competition across the entire network occurs in response to each input pattern, before the activity that wins the competitive choice is used to create a teaching signal that drives new learning. If all the inputs are approximately equal, then the uniform activity pattern that they cause will be suppressed by the competition, no teaching signal will be emitted, and no new learning will occur. If some of the inputs are sufficiently bigger than others, then they will be contrast-enhanced, normalized, and stored by the recurrent on-center off-surround network. A teaching signal will be emitted only by the cell populations that win the competition. Only the winning cells will therefore be able to drive learning of the incoming input pattern. As a result, the "noise learning catastrophe" will not occur.

How do contrast-enhanced activities trigger a teaching signal? In the READ circuit, they activate dendrites via back-propagating action potentials (Figure 13.38). These back-propagating action potentials are the teaching signals that are associated with simultaneously active CS input signals to the chosen dendrites.

How does a theta rhythm enter this story? A rhythm is needed because the following kind of cycle needs to occur again and again through time:

1. read-*out* of cue-activated LTM-gated signals, as from the conditionable signals $S_k z_{ki}$ with adaptive weights z_{ki} in the READ circuit in Figure 1.15;

2. contrast-enhancing competition via the on-center off-surround feedback loops in Figure 1.15;

3. read-*in* of the new pattern of contrast-enhanced and normalized activities into the adaptive weights z_{ki} in Figure 1.15; and

4. repeat.

SOM theta rhythm dissociates read-out from read-in with back-propagating teaching signals. How does such a recurring read-out/choice/read-in cycle play out in a SOM and lead to a theta rhythm? Figure 16.41 depicts my proposed answer. Figure 16.41 shows two competing SOM category cells that each receive multiple inputs via their dendritic trees, which are drawn above the cell bodies. These inputs arrive from the feature detectors of the SOM spatial category learning cells, whether from stripe cells to developing grid cells, or from developing grid cells to developing place cells (Figure 16.5). In Figure 16.41a, the left cell receives a bigger total input than the right cell (thick vs. thin green arrows). The left cell can therefore inhibit the right cell more than conversely (thick vs. thin red arrows; Figure 16.41b) while its activity is contrast-enhanced by its recurrent on-center (curved green arrow; Figure 1.7). It thereby wins the competition with the right cell, shutting it off. As this happens, it also generates a back-propagating action potential through its dendritic tree (upward green arrow; Figure 16.41c), which acts as a teaching signal that supports associative learning in the dendrites that are currently receiving inputs. This cycle continues to repeat itself through time as different input patterns choose different winning category cells. Such a back-propagating action potential was also used as a teaching signal during reinforcement learning in the amygdala (Figures 13.38 and 1.15). I will now explain how learning that uses this kind of read-out/choice/read-in cycle is supported by a rhythm.

Why a rhythm at all? The cyclic nature of this process is, on the face of it, "rhythmic". But we can now also begin to understand basic mechanistic and functional reasons for this cycle. The first reason is that an electrical signal cannot go both down a dendrite (Figure 16.41a) and up it (Figure 16.41b) at the same time. This functional property requires a rhythmic alternation between the down-state of read-out, and the up-state of read-in. But how is this functional property achieved mechanistically?

One can discuss this property on multiple levels of sophistication, but here is a simple primary reason for it: When recurrent on-center off-surround networks are designed with inhibitory off-surround interneurons that react more slowly than their on-center cells, and they are driven by external inputs, then they tend to oscillate. This kind of result was first mathematically proved and simulated in an article that I published in 1975 with my PhD student Samuel Ellias (Ellias and Grossberg, 1975). It has been modeled in scores of articles since by many authors.

As a result, when inputs drive the activation of some category cells, they also initiate the rhythm that will cause their own suppression in the next phase of the oscillation, but not before the back-propagating teaching signals of each cycle can be generated.

Articles like the classical review in 2002 by Buzsáki about theta oscillations in the hippocampus (Buzsáki, 2002) describe many important facts about the theta rhythm that are consistent with my explanation. Buzsáki notes, in particular, that "theta oscillation may provide a mechanism for bringing together in time afferent-induced depolarization of pyramidal cell dendrites and dendritic invasion of fast spikes, the key elements for the induction of synaptic plasticity" (p. 325). His discussion describes many useful biophysical facts about this kind of learning, but not in terms of the basic design problem of how it prevents the catastrophic forgetting that would have occurred without dissociation of associative read-out from read-in.

Why phase precession of the theta rhythm? Using back-propagating action potentials as teaching signals also helps to explain intriguing parametric properties of the theta rhythm, such as its famous *phase precession* whereby action potentials occur on progressively earlier phases of the theta cycle as the rat traverses the place field of the recorded unit (O'Keefe and Recce, 1993; Skaggs et al., 1996)). Phase precision in the GridPlaceMap model follows from two interacting properties:

First, each SOM category cell is activated through time via a receptive field whose input connections increase in strength as an animal navigates closer to the center of the receptive field. A Gaussian receptive field is a classical example. This key property is needed to solve the scale selection problem (Figure 16.19, 16.23, 16.25, and 16.27).

Second, the category cells interact via shunting dynamics (Figure 16.25). As a result, larger inputs are integrated more quickly through time, thus leading to their activation earlier in each theta cycle at the center of the cell's receptive field is approached.

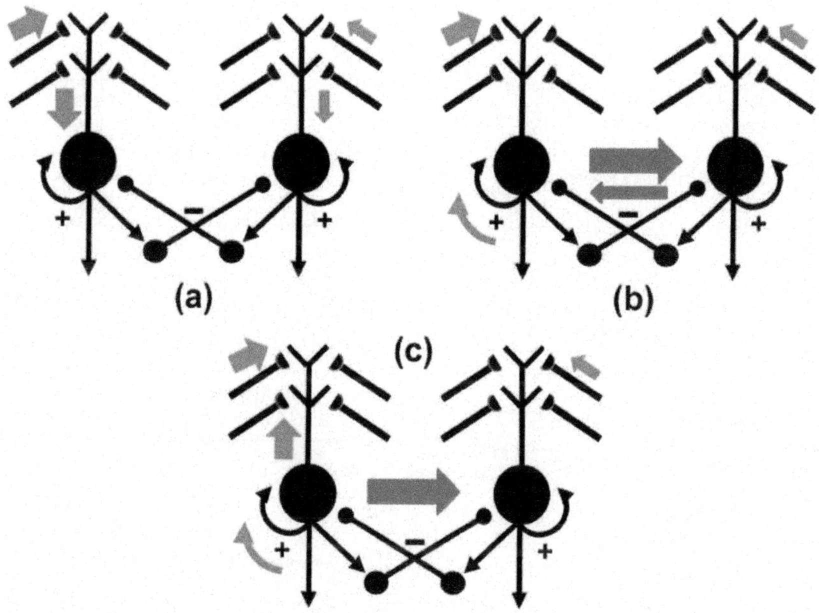

In summary, phase precision occurs in the GridPlaceMap model because its category cells interact via shunting recurrent on-center off-surround networks whose cells receive inputs from receptive fields whose connections grow as the animal approaches the cell's preferred position. Cholinergic inputs from the medial

FIGURE 16.41. How back-propagating action potentials, supplemented by recurrent inhibitory interneurons, control both learning within the synapses on the apical dendrites of winning pyramidal cells, and regulate a rhythm by which associative read-out is dissociated from read-in. See the text for details.

septum can extrinsically modulate this intrinsic theta rhythm, but do not create it.

In addition to grid cells and place cells, several other types of cells have been reported that help to create a representation of space that animals use while they navigate. One particularly interesting type of cell is called a *border cell* because it fires when an animal is at or near the border of an enclosure. Solstad et al. (2008, p. 1865) reported that border cells are found throughout the medial entorhinal cortex, as well as the parasubiculum, and "may be instrumental in planning trajectories and anchoring grid fields and place fields to a geometric reference frame". I will defer a discussion and analysis of how border cells may form and work to another place and time.

SOVEREIGN's cognitive-emotional architecture for reactive and planned navigation

With the above explanation of how our brains learn grid cells and place cells by navigating through space, we can now see how representations of both the present positions and target positions of our body can be learned in response to visual and path integration information. We can also see how the brain represents the angular velocity and linear velocity signals at head direction and stripe cells (Figure 16.10) on which to build representations of the sequences of turns and linear excursions that can represent an arbitrary navigational trajectory. The control architecture of SOVEREIGN uses such ingredients to compute difference vectors with which to determine the next movement direction and distance, along with cognitive working memory and list chunking circuits, such as LIST PARSE and Masking Field circuits (Figures 12.42, 12.43, 12.46, and 12.47), modulated by reinforcement learning circuits, such as READ circuits (Figure 1.15), in order to carry out reactive navigation, while also incrementally learning cognitive plans against which to balance reactive movements, so that sequential navigational plans can, where appropriate, be used instead to reach valued goal objects in space. Moreover, SOVEREIGN explains and simulates how these reactive and planned trajectories can be carried out under the

volitionally-controlled variable movement speed conditions that are a basic fact of daily life.

The following circuit diagrams illustrate the SOVEREIGN architecture on several levels of detail. For example, Figure 16.42 illustrates how the general flow of information is organized, including visual and proprioceptive inputs as they interact with cognitive, emotional, and motor processes.

Parallel What and Where streams for visual categorization and directional movement. One of the most important and remarkable syntheses that our brains accomplish to overcome complementary computational limitations occurs between the What ventral cortical stream and the Where dorsal cortical stream (Figure 1.19; Table 1.2). Figure 16.43 shows how visual inputs activate the parvocellular visual form system in parallel with the magnocellular visual motion system (cf. Figures 0.1 and 3.1). The former drives the learning and recognition of invariant visual object categories, while the latter helps to compute the directions in which movement will occur.

Figure 16.44 illustrates some of the interactions whereby both reactive and planned difference vectors (DV) are adaptively calibrated, computed, and interact to determine whether a reactive or planned DV will be executed next. A stored Visual Reactive Target Position Vector, or TPV, is used to compute a Reactive DV by subtracting a

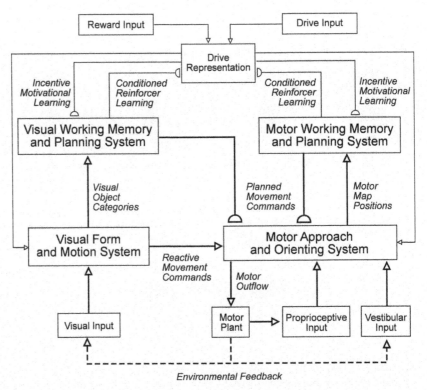

FIGURE 16.42. Macrocircuit of the main SOVEREIGN subsystems.

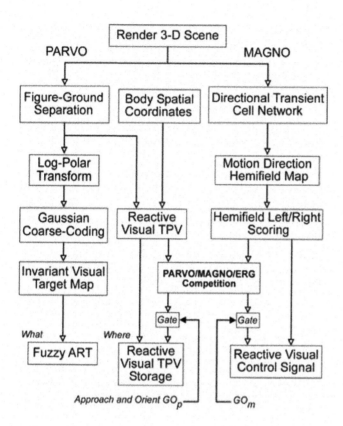

FIGURE 16.43. The main visual form and motion processing stream mechanisms of SOVEREIGN, many of them described at length in previous chapters.

NET vector from it. NET plays the role during navigation that a Present Position Vector plays during the control of an arm movement. NET vectors during spatial navigation are derived from combinations of visual, proprioceptive, and vestibular inputs, leading to representations of present position such as place cells. A learned coordinate transformation enables a NET signal, that is derived from path integration signals, to be subtracted from a TPV, that is derived from visually looking at a target. The result is a DV that can move the animal's navigational movements towards the TPV. These interactions also provide information that is transferred to the planned movement control system.

Decomposing navigational movements into sequences of angles turned and linear distances. Figure 16.45 summarizes some of the transformations of (distance, angle), or (d, a), movements. Each (d, a) vector represents an elementary navigational movement; namely, a linear movement for a distance d, followed by

a turn by angle a. Here, visual, vestibular, and motor coordinate information again need to be fused by adaptive coordinate transformations to support the best movement decisions based upon currently available information from multiple modalities.

Parallel What and Where streams for working memory, planning, and voting. After early What and Where processing computes basic properties of object and movements, these complementary streams store sequences of the objects and movements that have been experienced. Sequences are first stored in working memories, which support the learning of sequential plans, or list chunks, whose read-out predicts the next behaviors (see Chapter 14). Such object and spatial working memories and list chunks operate in parallel before their active list chunks combine their best predictions by voting to overcome complementary kinds of ignorance.

To illustrate the kinds of ignorance that I have in mind, imagine that an animal or animat learns to navigate several different mazes to either approach a valued outcome, or to avoid an aversive one. Restricting this example to mazes is not a serious limitation, if only because in many situations, choices are made in response to sequences of previously seen visual cues and previously executed movements. Suppose that in two mazes the sequences of visual cues at the end of each linear track in the maze are the same, but that the sequences of turns are different. In one maze, after experiencing these sequences, a right turn will lead to a reward, and a left turn will lead to a punishment. In the other maze, a right turn will lead to a punishment, and a left turn will lead to a reward. In these mazes, the sequence of visual cues is not predictive. Only the sequence

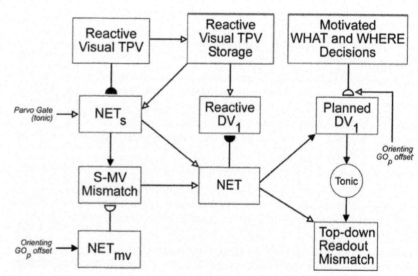

FIGURE 16.44. The main target position vector (TPV), difference vector (DV), and volitional GO computations in SOVEREIGN that bring together reactive and planned signals to control decision-making and action. See the text for details.

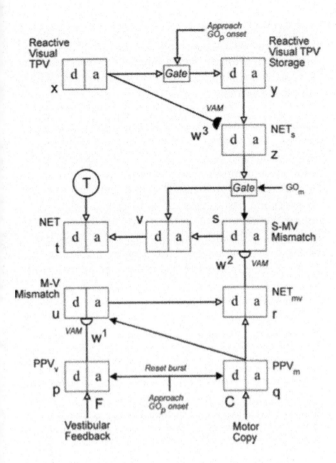

FIGURE 16.45. The main distance (d) and angle (a) computations that bring together and learn dimensionally-consistent visual and motor information whereby to make the currently best decisions and actions. See the text for details.

of movements is. By using both kinds of information to vote for a decision, the right answer can be made. The same is true if one considers mazes where the same sequences of turns occur, but different sequences of visual cues predict different outcomes.

Figures 16.46a and 16.46b show that, despite the fact that the What and Where streams compute complementary kinds of information, subsequent processing stages can be realized by homologous circuits, notably working memory and list chunk (e.g., Masking Field) circuits. In particular, these parallel cortical streams can be used to store sequences of experienced objects and sequences of experienced movements in working memory, respectively. The contents of these parallel streams can then use homologous circuits for unitizing them in object and movement list chunks, respectively. These list chunks, in turn, can be motivationally amplified or suppressed via reinforcement learning, based on reinforcement success or failure while experiencing these object and movement sequences. The winning list chunks are then used to release planned movements towards valued goal objects based on the previously experienced sequential context.

Parallel READ circuits for reward, motivation, and cognitive-emotional interactions. Figure 16.47 summarizes how multiple READ circuits that process inputs in parallel from multiple internal drive sources can be coordinated to realize a sensory-drive heterarchy (Figure 1.17) in response to changing sources and levels of reward and punishment that can maximally amplify the motivationally currently favored option, other things being equal.

Simulating exploration and learned navigation in a virtual reality environment. The SOVEREIGN architecture was used to simulate how a model rat, or animat, could learn the most efficient navigational pathway at which a rewarded goal object could be found. Learning was simulated in a cross maze (Figure 16.48a) that was seen by the animat as a virtual reality 3D rendering of the maze as it navigated it through time. At the end of each corridor in the maze, a different visual cue was displayed (triangle, star, cross, and square). Sequences of virtual reality views on two navigational routes, shown in color for vividness, are summarized in Figures 16.48b and 16.49c, where the floor is green, the walls are blue, the ceiling is black, and the interior corners where pairs of maze corridors meet are in red. Figure 16.48b illustrates how the views change as the animat navigates straight down one corridor, and Figure 16.48c illustrates how the views change as the animal makes a turn from facing one corridor to facing a perpendicular one.

Figure 16.49 shows a typical task for an animat; namely, to learn how to transform an inefficient and meandering reactive pathway through the maze (Figure 16.49a) into an efficient direct goal-oriented pathway to the rewarded object (Figure 16.49b). All the visual, motor, vestibular, spatial, cognitive, emotional, and motor circuits of SOVEREIGN autonomously interact with each other to achieve this result.

It is important to realize that most of these model circuits were developed to explain databases that did not involve spatial navigation. SOVEREIGN shows that these processes nonetheless have just the properties that were needed to also explain navigational data. This was thus, once again, an example of The Gift That Keeps On Giving.

Towards a synthesis of declarative and episodic learning and memory

The working memory and list chunking properties that are summarized in Figure 16.46 can be understand as part of a larger brain design in the light of pART prefrontal cortical circuits for object and spatial working memory and list chunking (Figure 14.2). When this is done, one can

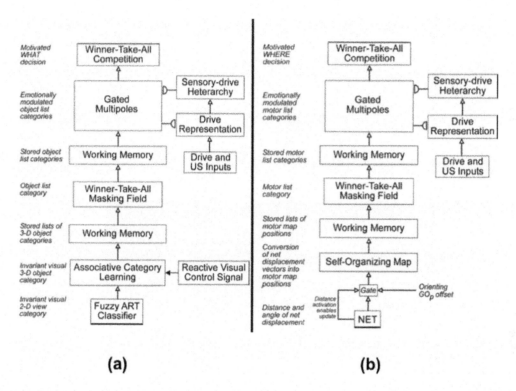

FIGURE 16.46. SOVEREIGN uses homologous processing stages to model the (a) What cortical stream and the (b) Where cortical stream, including their cognitive working memories and chunking networks, and their modulation by motivational mechanisms. See the text for details.

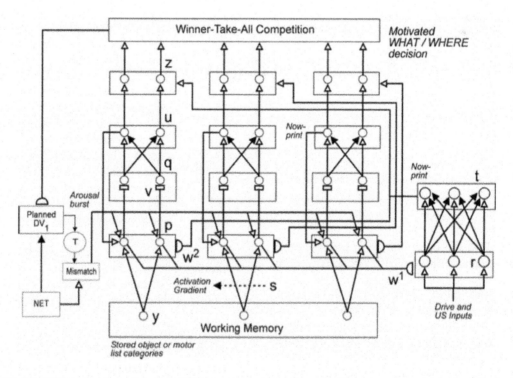

FIGURE 16.47. SOVEREIGN models how multiple READ circuits, operating in parallel in response to multiple internal drive sources, can be coordinated to realize a sensory-drive heterarchy that can maximally amplify the motivationally most currently favored option.

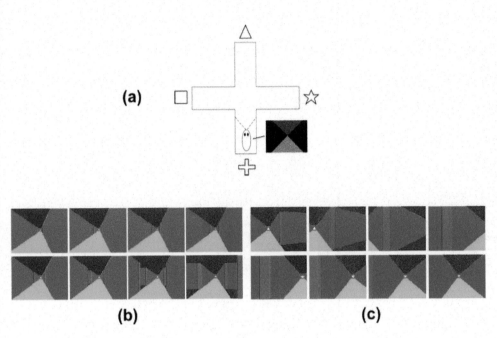

(a)

(b)   **(c)**

FIGURE 16.48. SOVEREIGN was tested using a virtual reality 3D rendering of a cross maze (a) with different visual cues at the end of each corridor.

can support more successful predictions and actions towards valued goals. The perirhinal and parahippocampal projections to the hippocampal cortex support adaptively timed reinforcement learning and spatial navigational processes, respectively, that are modeled by the Spectral Timing and Spectral Spacing models (Figure 16.50). Taken together, these sequence-sensitive processes support and coordinate both declarative learning and memory that includes the prefrontal cortex, and episodic learning and memory that includes the hippocampal cortex.

From SOVEREIGN to true autonomous adaptive mobile intelligence: SOVEREIGN2. With SOVEREIGN as a foundation, I have described how many of the models in the current book can be unified in a more powerful autonomous adaptive intelligent controller for a mobile agent that I have, rather undramatically, called SOVEREIGN2 (Grossberg, 2019). SOVEREIGN2 will embody resonant dynamics, including states that in humans support consciousness, because of the deep computational connection that has been modeled between conscious states and the choice of effective task-relevant actions (Table 1.3). ART hereby provides explanations of *what* goes on in each of our brains when we consciously see, hear, feel, or know something; *where* it is going on; and *why* evolution may have been driven to discover conscious states of mind.

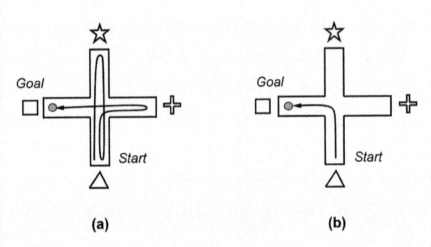

Goal   *Goal*

Start   *Start*

(a)   **(b)**

FIGURE 16.49. The animat learned to convert (a) inefficient exploration of the maze into (b) an efficient direct learned path to the goal.

see more clearly how the perirhinal and parahippocampal cortices contribute with parallel projections to both prefrontal cortex and hippocampal cortex. In both cases, sequences of stored object and spatial representations are used. The perirhinal and parahippocampal projections to the prefrontal cortex input to cognitive working memory in the ventrolateral prefrontal cortex (VLPFC) and motor working memory in the dorsolateral prefrontal cortex (DLPFC), respectively. These projections provide object and spatial contextual information that can modulate working memory storage of object and spatial sequences, thereby facilitating learning of list chunks that

Additional processes to be incorporated in SOVEREIGN2 include circuits that I have described throughout the book. They include circuits for:

target tracking with smooth pursuit and saccadic eye or camera movements;

visual form and motion perception in response to noisy and incomplete sensor signals;

incremental unsupervised view-, size-, and position-specific object category learning and

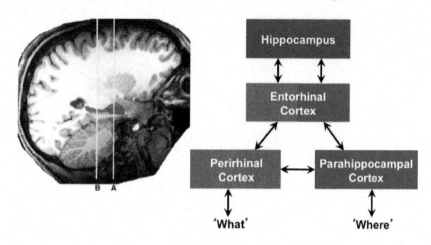

WHAT AND WHERE INPUTS TO HIPPOCAMPUS
Adaptively Timed Conditioning and Spatial Navigation

Diana, Yonelinas, and Ranganath (2007)

FIGURE 16.50. The perirhinal and parahippocampal cortices enable adaptively timed reinforcement learning and spatial navigational processes that are modeled by Spectral Timing and Spectral Spacing models in the What and Where cortical streams, respectively, to be fused in the hippocampus.

hypothesis testing in real time in response to arbitrarily large nonstationary databases that may include unexpected events;

incremental unsupervised learning of view-, size-, and position-invariant object categories during free scanning of a scene with eye or camera movements;

temporary selective storage in working memory of task-relevant object, spatial, or motor event sequences; unsupervised learning of cognitive and motor plans based upon working memory storage of event sequences in real time, and Where's Waldo search for currently valued goal objects;

unsupervised learning of reaching behaviors that automatically supports accurate tool manipulation in space;

unsupervised learning of present position in space using path integration during spatial navigation; platform-independent navigational control using either leg or wheel movements;

unsupervised learning of adaptively timed actions and maintenance of motivated attention while these actions are executed; and

social cognitive capabilities like joint attention and imitation learning whereby a classroom of mobile robots can learn spatial skills by each observing a teacher from its own unique spatial perspective.

SOVEREIGN, and its descendants like SOVEREIGN2, illustrate how all of the principles, equations, modules, and architectures that the book has described come together in the design of an autonomous adaptive mobile animal or animat control system. Although a great deal more work needs to be, and will be, done by many researchers for many years to further develop such autonomous adaptive intelligent systems, I hope you agree that the book provides a useful foundation for this kind of work, and more importantly for a better understanding of biological intelligence.

A Universal Developmental Code

Mental measurements embody universal laws of cell biology and physics

In this final chapter, I will take the liberty of discussing, in an often speculative way, some of the far-ranging implications of the discoveries that this book has described of how our brains give rise to our minds. These reflections range from lessons about how to live more fulfilling lives, how many of the most perplexing and difficult aspects of the human condition derive from breakdowns of one or another kind of mental balance, and how to scientifically understand deep human cravings for ethical value systems and religious experiences. I will also discuss implications of our brains' self-organizing universal measurement process that generalize to all cellular biological systems, and beyond to the physical world with which our minds are in constant communication and adaptation.

Resonant conscious experiences of perceiving, feeling, and knowing

These wide-ranging comments are possible because all the concepts that I have summarized in the book have multiple implications that generalize beyond our minds *per se*. Before turning to this discussion, let me set the stage by first recalling that one of the most important themes in the book is how and *why* our brains have become conscious.

A universal computational code for mental life: Life's moments cohere in a sense of self. The claim that "all conscious events are resonant events" emphasizes that all of our conscious experiences of perceiving, feeling, and knowing use similar design principles and mechanisms. This is thus a *universal* type of computation that embraces all of our mental faculties. Variations on shared designs in different parts of the brain generate resonances that support conscious perceptual awareness and cognitive knowledge about external sensory inputs, leading to conscious percepts of sights and sounds, or about internal sensory

Conscious MIND Resonant BRAIN. Stephen Grossberg, Oxford University Press. © Oxford University Press 2021.
DOI: 10.1093/med/9780190070557.003.0017

inputs, leading to consciously felt emotions. Each resonance supports an attentional focus upon the perceptual or affective representations that becomes conscious, and synchronizes with related resonances that enable conscious recognition, or knowing, about the perceptual or affective event (e.g., Figures 6.27 and 13.1). Spatial, object, and motivated attention all play a role in these resonant events, and are embodied in a similar type of circuit that obeys the ART Matching Rule (Figure 1.25). By sharing a universal computational substrate, conscious perceptual, cognitive, and affective representations can all resonate together, so that individuals can experience coherent conscious moments that unify all these kinds of awareness.

Because such resonances are adaptive (Figure 2.2), and support fast learning about attended data without experiencing catastrophic forgetting, our minds can shape themselves for successful adaptation, and even transcendence, in response to a changing world that is filled with unexpected events. By solving the *stability-plasticity dilemma* using a universal computational code whose percepts, feelings, and knowledge can all resonate together in unified moments of conscious awareness, we can build an ever-expanding sense of self from a lifetime of learned experiences.

Why we become conscious: Hierarchical resolution of complementarity and uncertainty. Knowing how we become conscious is a deep thing to contemplate. But knowing *why* evolution was driven to discover conscious awareness somehow feels even deeper, and is relevant to why lessons about mind generalize to many parts of biology and physics.

One basic reason is that our brains are organized into computationally *complementary* cortical processing streams (Table 1.1 and Figure 3.1). Each stream can compute one combination of essential properties well, but not the complementary properties that would also be needed to achieve effective adaptation to a changing world. Interactions between streams are needed to overcome their complementary computational deficiencies. These interactions are organized in multiple processing stages via a *hierarchical resolution of uncertainty* (e.g., Figures 0.1, 3.1, and 14.2). I noted in Chapter 6 that such a hierarchical resolution of uncertainty can require multiple processing stages, including both interactions across complementary cortical streams, and within each stream, to overcome the computational uncertainties that are present in all sensory data (e.g., Figures 3.4 and 3.5).

Established physical theories also have complementarity and uncertainty principles at their foundations, and why this may be so is one of the topics that I will discuss below. The following basic fact about why we are conscious points to one reason why our brains have also embodied complementarity and uncertainty principles at their own foundations.

Consciousness and the brain-environment loops that drive brain self-organization. A classical example of such a hierarchical resolution of uncertainty is the computation of visual boundaries and surfaces (Figures 1.21, 3.7, 3.15, 4.4-4.6, 4.15-4.17, 4.21-4.25, 4.54-4.56). Such a distributed and hierarchical mode of computation raises the grave risk that an insufficiently informative perceptual representation that is computed at an early processing stage could trigger maladaptive behaviors that could kill the actor. Instead, evolution seems to have introduced conscious resonance as an "extra degree of freedom" that is triggered at processing stages that compute sufficiently complete, context-sensitive, and stable perceptual or affective representations with which to control successful behaviors. It is in this sense that we consciously see in order to look and reach; consciously hear in order to make communication sounds, including speaking; and consciously feel in order to direct our actions to realize valued goals (Table 1.3). This book has summarized six of the resonances that support different kinds of conscious awareness (Table 1.4) and has explained in some detail their functional roles and mechanistic substrates in different parts of our brains.

This fundamental computational link from conscious perceiving, feeling, and knowing to the control of adaptive actions provides a general theoretical perspective from which to understand how our brains are organized into brain-environment cyclic interactions using perception-cognition-emotion-action loops. The fact that these brain-environment loops drive the self-organization of our brains' universal measurement code highlights why our brains have embodied designs over the millennia that reflect the physical laws of the external world with which they ceaselessly interact.

Complementarity of the laws for perception/cognition/ emotion and action

Complementary computing plays a fundamental role in enabling us to ceaselessly interact with the external world, since perception, cognition, and emotion obey computationally complementary laws to those that control action. The complementary processes of perception and cognition typically occur in the ventral What cortical stream, whereas those for action occur in the dorsal Where cortical stream, respectively (Figure 1.19). Moreover, perceptual and cognitive processes themselves embody complementary properties, such as the complementarity of visual boundaries and surfaces (Figure 3.7) and of the attentional and orienting systems that support stable category learning (Figure 5.20).

I explained in Chapter 5 how perceptual and cognitive processes in the What ventral processing stream use ART excitatory matching and match-based learning (Table 1.2) to learn attentive representations of objects and events in the world (Figure 5.19). Match-based learning solves the *stability–plasticity dilemma* and can occur quickly without causing catastrophic forgetting, much as new faces can be learned quickly without forcing unselective forgetting of familiar faces. Excitatory matching can also support sustained resonance, and thus sometimes conscious awareness, when a good enough match with object information occurs.

Such match-based learning supports the creation of category representations at higher cortical levels that are increasingly invariant under changes in an object's views, positions, and sizes when it is registered on our retinas. I explained in Chapter 6 how such match-based learning can support *invariant* category learning, which enables us to categorize the world without experiencing a combinatorial explosion of individual object exemplars. These invariant recognition properties can easily draw motivated attention to themselves when they are emotionally salient (Figures 13.1 and 13.2). They are not, however, sufficient for a brain to accomplish autonomous adaptation to a changing world, if only because positionally-invariant object category representations cannot, by themselves, be used to manipulate objects at particular positions in space.

Computationally complementary spatial and motor processes in the Where/How dorsal cortical processing stream can be used to trigger actions for manipulating objects in space. To do so, they often use VAM-like inhibitory matching and mismatch learning (Table 1.2; Figures 12.2 and 12.9) to continually update spatial maps and sensorymotor movement gains as bodily parameters change through time, whether for reaching or for speech production (Figure 12.15). These circuits cannot support an adaptive resonance under any conditions, and thus do not support conscious awareness.

Although each type of matching and learning in Table 1.2 is insufficient on its own to learn about the world and to effectively act upon it, together they can. Perceptual and cognitive processes use excitatory matching and match-based learning to create self-stabilizing representations of objects and events that embody increasing expertise about the world, and conscious awareness of it. Complementary spatial and motor processes use inhibitory matching and mismatch learning to continually update spatial maps and sensory-motor gains to compensate for bodily changes throughout life. Our brains have discovered how to bridge the ventral What stream and dorsal Where stream divide in order to carry out the brain-environment interactions that enable us to adapt in real time to an ever-changing world (e.g., Figure 14.2). Taken together, they provide a self-stabilizing perceptual and cognitive front end for conscious awareness and knowledge acquisition, which can

intelligently manipulate more labile spatial and motor processes that enable our changing bodies to act effectively upon a changing world.

Learning causes and realizing valued goals through action and error. It is because our percepts, concepts, and emotions are tested in the world through ceaseless action that we can learn what situations may be expected to cause particular consequences. We can thereby gradually get better at learning what we value, and at carrying out the kinds of actions that realize these values. My discussions of blocking and unblocking (Figures 1.10 and 13.10-13.12) illustrated how we can gradually learn to pay attention to combinations of cues that cause valued consequences, while ignoring cues that are predictively irrelevant. Unblocking, and with it the discovery of unexpected causes, cannot happen, however, unless we are willing to act in uncertain environments, and to make mistakes along the way. Part of the art of living is to be willing to take moderate risks in novel environments, while doing our best to avoid the kinds of errors that can lead to grave, or even fatal, consequences. By focusing on the most complete, context-sensitive, and stable representations that our modalities can construct as a basis for action, conscious awareness helps to restrict the kinds of action-based errors that we make to ones that are less likely to be fatal (Table 1.3).

"Use your head!" to predict the most valued outcomes. The cognitive-emotional interactions that enable blocking and unblocking to occur are, however, only part of the brain machinery that enables us to achieve some degree of mastery over our lives. Chapter 14 described the key role that purely cognitive processes also play, notably how our prefrontal cortices interact with each other and with many other brain regions (Figure 14.2) to focus attention on the sequences of events that may be expected to cause the best outcomes in given situations, and to carry out appropriate actions to achieve these outcomes. These cognitive processes include temporary storage of recently experienced event sequences in working memory, the learning of list chunks, or plans, that are selectively activated by different event sequences, and the choice of the most predictive list chunks in a given environment with which to understand the current situation and act upon it. Such a choice is based on a combination of cognitive and cognitive-emotional factors, including both how many previous events are used to select each plan (Figures 12.46 and 12.47), and how well particular sequences predicted successful outcomes in the past.

Thus, we have to "use our head" with all the cognitive apparatus at our disposal, as well as our current feelings and knowledge about which choices have been successful in the past, to select the most likely actions for achieving valued goals in the present and the future. Both cognition and emotion hereby work together ceaselessly to gradually build a satisfying life. As I noted in Chapter 13, either underaroused or overaroused emotional depression (Figure 1.18) can break this cognitive-emotional loop, and thereby prevent effective thought and decision-making in individuals with mental disorders such as autism or schizophrenia.

Are all values relative? Wherefore morality? So, where does that leave us when it comes to evaluating moral decisions about what is good and what is evil? Is "all that there is" an amazing functional system, as illustrated by the pART architecture in Figure 14.2, that can be equally well used to achieve *any* desired goal, whether for good or evil, and whose ultimate criterion of success is that it predicted what we want, and got it for us? Are no actions morally better than others?

But if this is so, then why is the striving to define what is good, and what constitutes a good and well-lived life, such a deeply felt and universal part of individual and social action? Why is religion such a basic need of societies across the globe if all values are completely relative? And even without organized religion as a guide, why is it so broadly believed that a spiritually rich life is a more fulfilling one than a life that is lived for only short-term gain, without higher goals?

Symmetry-breaking of positive and negative in cognition and emotion: A reason for hope. As with all predictive behaviors, there are cognitive and emotional reasons for morality that are built into the most basic properties of our brains. In both cognition and emotion, there is, I will argue, a *broken symmetry* between positive and negative processes, with the positive emphasized. Because it is *just* a broken symmetry, much as every source of light can cast a shadow, both good and evil deeds are possible, although I would claim that there is a built in bias towards the good, so that values are not purely relative.

I believe that this asymmetry helps to drive the evolution of individual brains, no less than the evolution of societies, to realize ever more complex organizational possibilities, albeit perhaps not without detours along the way. The broken symmetry enables learned behaviors to be flexible and adaptive, two properties that are essential for surviving a wide range of changing environmental challenges. However, it is this very same flexibility and adaptivity that enables both good and evil acts to be carried out, even while supporting increasingly complex cognitive and cognitive-emotional processing in individual minds, and increasingly complex societies wherein these minds can survive and even thrive.

Symmetry-breaking between approach and avoidance in emotion and action. How does this broken symmetry manifest itself in our emotional circuitry? As I have shown in several parts of the book, our emotions are organized into opponent processes with opposite affective valences, such as fear vs. relief (Figures 1.13-1.15, 13.24, 13.31, 13.41, and 13.43). Due to the asymmetry in how these emotions work, negative emotional experiences, such as a shock that causes pain and fear, can suppress ongoing consummatory behaviors (Figure 13.32). Shock cannot easily be used to *directly* learn and motivate new consummatory behaviors, except for behaviors aimed at escaping the shock. Such avoidance learning can occur when *offset* of a shock during escape causes a relief rebound that can be used to motivate future shock avoidance behaviors.

Learned avoidance behaviors can persist for a long time (Figure 13.41) without having to re-experience the fearful situations that they were learned to avoid. In fact, such avoidance behaviors are often described as nonchalant (Solomon, Kamin, and Wynne, 1953), which makes sense if their continued occurrence is motivated by relief, rather than fear. Similarly, after learned avoidance responses enable soldiers who have been treated for PTSD to reduce their fear or anxiety, they "appear to be very relaxed and nonchalant in performance of their avoidance response . . . reduction of fear or anxiety is the mechanism that maintains avoidance behavior . . . " (Chemtob, Roitblat, and Hamada, 1988). As I explained in Chapter 1, when escape behaviors just lead to continued shock, learned helplessness may result whereby an individual passively accepts the shock without trying to escape.

In contrast to successful learned avoidance behaviors, which do not rapidly extinguish, cues that predict learned fear do extinguish if they are not punished later on. This is just the familiar example from Chapter 13 that conditioned excitors extinguish, whereas conditioned inhibitors do not (Figures 13.40 and 13.41). Chapter 13 also noted how these fearful memories could be replaced by memories that do not cause fear during a *reconsolidation* time interval after the fear-triggering cue is presented.

Unlike responses to negative emotions like fear, positive appetitive drives, such as hunger, *can* trigger innate approach and eating of food. Conditioned reinforcers can also be learned during these feeding experiences. These conditioned reinforcers can range from the sight of food being paired with the taste of food, to advertisements that print the menu choices for a new restaurant that has gotten rave reviews. When food as an unconditioned reinforcer is replaced by thirst or sexual desire, similar conclusions may be drawn, including how the multibillion-dollar advertisement industry sells just about any product by using conditioned reinforcers to "turn on" its potential customers.

Positive emotions facilitate positive sustainable motivations and empathy. Thus, there is a major approach-avoidance dichotomy built into our brains for dealing with events that cause positive vs. negative emotions. Behaviors that cause positive emotions can directly support new learned behaviors, whereas negative emotions tend to suppress ongoing behaviors, or cause efforts to escape from their source.

This dichotomy illustrates the broken symmetry between positive and negative emotions upon which moral and legal systems can build. Moral and legal systems can build upon this foundation because many of the acts that are considered immoral cause negative consequences like pain and fear, and well-conceived laws often encourage behaviors that reduce or eliminate such consequences, and thus, like all good escape and avoidance responses, may hope to persist by building on positive emotions that may be amplified and additionally sustained by social acceptance.

Social factors are supported by brain processes that can create empathically felt emotions when watching the faces of others who are exhibiting those emotions. These processes are part of our capacity for social cognition. They are also sometimes described as being due to *mirror neurons* (Gallese, 2001, 2003; Rizzolatti, Fogassi, and Gallese, 2001; Schulte-Rüther et al., 2007). It is sufficient, for example, for a smiling face that we see to activate a learned object category, and from there the same amygdala/hypothalamic value category (Figure 13.1) that is activated when we ourselves smile and feel a similar emotion (Burgdorf and Panksepp, 2006).

Relief can motivate many sustained positive behaviors: Relaxation response and creativity. Relief can be used to motivate many positive and sustained behaviors. Some of these behaviors may be specific, such as learning how to avoid getting burned on the stove, or to avoid cutting yourself while slicing bread. In these situations, rebounds from fear to relief often occur. Relief may also have nonspecific uses. This can occur when an individual learns to harness relief as a motivation for a wide range of constructive activities, without having to first experience avoidance of fear. One such activity is the *relaxation response* (Benson, Beary, and Carol, 1974; Benson and Klipper, 1975), with its many benefits for stress reduction and the improvement of autonomic functions and general health. Individuals can learn to more efficiently and strongly activate the relaxation response using a wide range of approaches to meditation and yoga.

An even broader range of uses occurs when relief is harnessed to motivate creative activities that may require months or years of hard work before any specific rewards may be experienced, such as writing a book or developing a new scientific theory. This kind of motivation is often described using phrases like "a labor of love" or an "intrinsically motivated state". Mark Lepper, David Greene, and Richard Nisbett showed that children's intrinsic interest in drawing could actually be decreased by giving them a specific reward for this activity (Lepper, Greene, and Nisbett, 1973). One can think of this result in terms of how the specific motivation that was activated by the reward competed with relief as a nonspecific source of sustained positive emotion.

This kind of result raises many questions, not the least of which is: Is it better to seek fame and fortune when doing creative work, or to stay in tune with the intrinsic motivations that drove your creative work when you first started it? Many Hollywood movies have milked this theme to death, but that does not make it any less serious and interesting.

In my own life, although I was always first in my class and considered a "brilliant" student, which gave me many positive specific rewards, including the scholarships that enabled me to continue my education, many people started to ask "What happened to Grossberg?" when I took a lonely and independent path to make my first scientific discoveries. If I continued to depend upon specific extrinsic rewards to motivate my creative work, it would never have gotten done, since I was often "far ahead of my time". Instead, I have always felt motivated by a deep-seated need to get closer to the beauty of the world during the short time that we are given to experience it. At the risk of sounding too pious, I might summarize this need as a passionate desire to get "a little closer to God" before I die. Although I am very grateful and happy when my colleagues do acknowledge my work, when I do finally see a little more of this beauty after working hard to make my next discovery, I feel a high, a kind of rapture, that I like to joke is better than sex. This feeling is, I think, relief on steroids.

The Dark Side: Learned helplessness, self-punitive behaviors, and fetishes. There is also a Dark Side, however, to this broken symmetry, and the flexibility and adaptivity that it affords. Because the broken symmetry is so important for successful adaptation to changing environmental demands, it has been selected and maintained by Darwinian selection, with the Dark Side riding its coattails.

The Turkey-Lover Fiasco that I described in Chapter 13 provides a glimpse into what can go wrong: Cues can sometimes get conditioned to disastrous consequences if attention is not properly regulated by attentive feedback interactions, such as those that occur in the CogEM model (Figure 13.2). These feedback interactions solve the Persistence Problem of associating the right cues with the right motivations and actions in situations where multiple motivationally-incompatible cues occur at the same time. For this to happen properly, attention needs to switch correctly between different sensory cues and the drive states, or value categories, that can adaptively support the behaviors that they elicit.

Another example of the Dark Side is the learned helplessness that I discussed in Chapter 1 and earlier in this chapter. The two-way shuttle box illustrates how this emotional disaster may occur, albeit in a stripped down environment. Here, an animal who experiences the pain and fear elicited by a shock that electrifies the floor in one half of the shuttle box escapes to the other half, where shock is momentarily not on. Normally, a wave of relief would provide motivation for the animal to learn how to avoid the shock in the first half of the box by quickly running to the second half of the box. After the animal learns this behavior, it may nonchalantly avoid the shock by jumping into the second half of the box. However, in the two-way shuttle box, when the animal runs into the second half of the box, its floor is also then electrified, driving the animal to escape back to the first half of the box. By repeating this cycle of punishment, each half of the box becomes a source of both conditioned fear and relief, which tend to cancel each other out by opponent extinction (Figure 13.39), which is usually an adaptive mechanism that helps to ensure life-long affective learning. All motivation for action is hereby inhibited, as are expectations of any no-shock place to which to escape. The animal may then passively remain in one position, accepting the shock throughout its duration, without even trying to escape.

As I noted in Chapter 1, humans can also experience learned helplessness, such as poor people living in ghettos where an occasional opportunity for positive reward may be more than cancelled by negative economic or social conditions. The hallmark of learned helplessness is, as Maier and Seligman (1976, p. 3) write, "that exposure to uncontrollable events interferes with the organism's tendency to perceive contingent relationships between its behavior and outcomes." These "uncontrollable events" are often created by economic and social conditions that poor people may have experienced from birth through no fault of their own. In order to break this cycle of learned helplessness and dependence, external agents need to create new opportunities whereby positive behaviors and expectations may be learned and persistently practiced that will not be inexorably undermined. Such opportunities can have benefits that ramify far beyond the affected individuals, by creating productive members of society who are not driven in desperation to lives of crime or drugs as the only behaviors available to realize rewarding outcomes.

Classical reports of *self-punitive behavior* in rats have a similar interpretation (Brown, Martin, and Morrow, 1964; Renner and Tinsley, 1976). I will not review details of the well-designed experimental manipulations that were carried out to study this phenomenon. Let me just note the following: Rats were first trained to escape a shocked start box by running down a runway to a goal box that was not shocked. After they had acquired this behavior, extinction trials were carried out during which no shock occurred in the start box, but the runway between the start and goal boxes was either not shocked at all, shocked in the last part of the runway before the goal box, or shocked throughout the runway before the goal box. The results indicated that

rats who were shocked in the runway did not stop running sooner than those given no shock there, and even resisted extinction significantly longer than unpunished rats.

Some experimentalists have called this a form of *experimental masochism* (e.g., Masserman, 1946; Masserman and Jacques, 1948). Studies on humans have led to an alternative to the masochism interpretation by distinguishing "instrumental learning about response-contingent outcomes (expectancy) and motivational states (preference)" (Dreyer and Renner, 1971). In my mechanistic neural explanation, a distinction between expectancy and motivation is also paramount, although how these concepts are understood may be quite different from the ones offered in the experimental articles. In my proposed explanation, a relief rebound in the goal box in response to a prior fearful cue motivates avoidance behavior. Additional shocks in the runway do not disconfirm the learned expectation of non-occurrence of shock in the goal box. Instead, they may actually cause larger relief rebounds when the goal box is reached, because offset of fear is then more immediate. A larger relief rebound may hereby be caused, thus strengthening the learned motivation, and thereby the persistence, of the learned avoidance behavior. It would be interesting to redo these experiments without discriminative cues of a goal box, so that only a runway existed after the start box was escaped.

There are many different types of self-punitive behavior, including *self-inflicted wounding*. The explanation above calls attention to the need to combine the effects of direct and rebounded reinforcing events, learned cognitive expectations, and how they are timed throughout the behaviors. In cases of self-inflicted wounding, these processes may also interact with changing internal states of autonomic arousal and cognitive control to determine the net reinforcing effects of these actions (e.g., Novak, 2003).

Various properties of *fetishism* also emerge naturally from cognitive-emotional mechanisms that I have described in Chapters 1, 13, and elsewhere in the book. Even defining what a fetish is can be a challenging task because this concept may be used in different ways in studies of anthropology, sexuality, and psychoanalysis. For example, *Wikipedia* defines fetishism from an anthropological perspective as "the attribution of religious or mystical qualities to inanimate objects". It goes on to say that sexual fetishism is "a sexual attraction to objects or body parts of lesser sexual importance (or none at all) such as feet or certain types of clothing". In general, fetishism concerns how an individual may attribute animate, emotional, or spiritual properties to any object.

Sigmund Freud wrote in his 1927 analysis of fetishism (Freud, 1927) that "When now I announce that the fetish is a substitute for the penis, I shall certainly create disappointment; so I hasten to add that it is not a substitute for any chance penis, but for a particular and quite special penis that had been extremely important in early childhood but had later been lost. That is to say, it should normally have been given up, but the fetish is precisely designed to preserve it from extinction. To put it more plainly: the fetish is a substitute for the woman's (the mother's) penis that the little boy once believed in and—for reasons familiar to us—does not want to give up . . . In conclusion we may say that the normal prototype of fetishes is a man's penis, just as the normal prototype of inferior organs is a woman's real small penis, the clitoris."

From the perspective of this book, how any object, not just a penis, can acquire fetishistic properties may be explained by abnormal properties of learning due to alterations in brain processing, or by normal properties of learning in environments that may make the resulting associations more focused and rigid than would usually be the case.

The Turkey-Lover Fiasco provides one example of how a fetish may be learned due to an abnormality in brain learning. Any mechanism that prevents top-down motivated attention from selecting only motivationally compatible representations at each time could, in this situation, let us learn to have sexual feelings towards turkeys, or indeed any other object with which a source of sexual gratification was associated. For example, if there is a hypofrontal condition (see Chapter 14) that weakens top-down attention from orbitofrontal cortex to sensory cortex (Figure 13.2), or weakens the competition between orbitofrontal object-value representations (Figure 13.12 (right column)), then such a fetish could more easily be learned.

A fetish can also be learned using processes that do not require a failure of selective attention. Even just persistent pairing of a sexually arousing individual, or pictures of such an individual, with a particular object until it becomes predictive of that individual's identity, can attach sexual feelings to that object using either primary or secondary classical conditioning (Figure 13.7). This normal conditioning process may, more generally, be used to attach to objects any form of emotion, including fear. A key issue is whether the object learns to become *and remain* a conditioned reinforcer that elicits sexual arousal, and is not just extinguished as a predictively irrelevant distractor (Figure 1.10). Maintaining the fetish does not require that the reinforcer occur on every appearance of the object, as I explained in Chapter 1 when I discussed the partial reinforcement acquisition effect and superstitious behaviors. All that is required to maintain such learning is that the association is rewarded sufficiently often to overcome the counter-conditioning that would otherwise cause extinction during unreinforced trials.

How do occasional rewards significantly retard, or even reverse, the extinguishing effects of more frequent non-rewarded trials? Imagine that an expectation starts to be learned that the next experience will not be rewarded by a sexual cue, but is then unexpectedly rewarded. This direct reinforcing effect can summate with the rebound caused by the unexpected disconfirmation to make this experience even more sexually rewarding. The added potency of occasional rewards on a partial reward schedule can hereby sustain fetishes and beliefs that are not really causal.

Living and planning for A Rush? The fact that an unexpected reward may be amplified by its very unexpectedness has sobering implications when one realizes that some people may learn to live for such A Rush. This may especially be true when the variety of possible rewards that are available to many of us are not available to them. They may then try to manipulate their environments to increase the probability of experiencing such an intense positive emotional event. For example, creating a fearful situation that will terminate with a sexual experience may be one strategy. If this is done only to oneself, it can be bad enough. But when it involves another person, it can lead to tragedy. I will leave to the reader to contemplate the variety of possibilities here, and also to think about how they may, in their own small way, try to improve others' lives to make such options unappealing.

In summary, our brain designs include a bias towards positivity, and with it the capacity to learn behaviors that can achieve and maintain constructive goals. My discussion in Chapter 14 of how the prefrontal cortex works clarifies how positive emotions can amply cognitive plans that can choose and trigger context-appropriate behaviors with which to achieve positive goals. On the other hand, negative emotions are also needed, if only to help us to escape dangerous experiences, whether they are imposed by the world itself, or by other individuals. Our ability to use these positive and negative emotions to flexibly adapt to a changing world will always burden discussions of morality with disturbing and even tragic counterexamples to the idea that people are basically good.

Symmetry breaking, adaptive resonance, and believing in God. The above kinds of considerations have helped me personally to cope with the existence of evil in the world without losing hope for the future of humanity. Just a broken symmetry towards positivity is not, however, sufficient to explain why so many of us want to believe in a higher power or understanding than our own, and how this need may lead us to religion. Many wise, and some not so wise, people have written about religion. I do not presume to encapsulate this enormous literature here. Nor will I describe any personal beliefs that I may have about whether or not particular religious beliefs are factually true.

I do, however, want to add some observations that I have found to be personally helpful in thinking about religion. First, there is the role of adaptive resonance in enabling us to keep learning about the world in a stable way, leading incrementally over a lifetime to a unified sense of self. This drive towards unification and coherence is, I think, an important contributor to religious belief. Second, there is the fact that adaptive resonance is the "common coin" in which all of our conscious experiences are unified, including all religious beliefs (Table 1.4). Third, there is the fact that conscious resonances bind us to the world around us, if only because consciousness makes it possible for us to act effectively on the world in multiple ways that help us to survive and even to flourish (Table 1.3). These links between brain and environmental action confront us inexorably with the need to predict and control our world.

Fourth, when we do learn new things about our own experiences, we tend to learn the most general categories that can be used to understand them. Learning general categories also has the benefit of conserving memory resources, as occurs during the process of *match tracking* (Figures 5.30 and 5.31). Said in another way, we tend to overgeneralize. As I noted in Chapter 5, overgeneralization is seen even in young children until further learning leads to category refinement (Chapman et al., 1986; Clark, 1973; Smith et al., 1985; Smith and Kemler, 1978; Ward, 1983). Category refinement is often driven by a predictive disconfirmation that is elicited by actions triggered by our current learned categories.

In earlier times when human scientific understanding was poor at best, very general categories could be learned and sustained in our attempts to explain natural events, even if they had little or no merit in predicting events causally, because there were few good theories to disconfirm them. This is a problem that can burden all beliefs about nature, whether they are about the efficacy of the spells of a medicine man, or about the existence of a volcano god. The beliefs that are embodied by these categories would typically be named, as essentially all important concepts are (Figures 5.1 - 5.3). Moreover, when individual or group behaviors seemed to reduce a fearful consequence, at least some of the time, affective support for the belief could be strengthened, making it quite resistant to extinction, for the reasons that I summarized above. Organized social events, including religious ceremonies, can provide even more affective support, just like meditation or yoga practiced in a group with a master can. But so can any method that an individual uses to generate regular positive motivation with which to maintain this belief structure, without generating too many predictive disconfirmations of it.

A universal developmental code for biology: Computing with cellular patterns

The facts that our minds are part of the physical world, and that fundamental mechanistic links exist between consciousness and action in the world, help to explain why our mental designs may have incorporated variants of basic physical designs, such as complementarity and uncertainty principles. There are two different, but related, paths to describing these connections, one focused on the biological world of living things, and the other on the rest of the physical world that does not include living things. I will first discuss some universal themes that we share with other living creatures in the biological world.

Cooperation and competition among species and among cells. Charles Darwin revolutionized science and society by demonstrating that all species have descended from common ancestors. As many people well know, the idea that we are descended from apes, and even simpler organisms before them, was not universally well received, despite its compelling factual support. With Alfred Russel Wallace, Darwin also described natural selection, or survival of the fittest, as a basic mechanism whereby species evolved. Darwin's book, *On The Origin of Species*, or more completely, *On the Origin of Species by Means of Natural Selection, or the Preservation of Favoured Races in the Struggle for Life*, was published in 1859, and still stands as one of the great scientific classics of all time (Darwin, 1859).

This scientific breakthrough highlighted the importance of competition, or more accurately competition interacting with cooperation, as a mechanism for driving the evolution of *species*. My book describes, in addition, the critical role of cooperation and competition on the level of *cells* in order to solve the fundamental *noise-saturation dilemma* (Figure 1.5). The mechanisms of cooperation and competition on the species level translate into on-center off-surround networks on the cellular level (Figure 1.6).

Self-organizing pattern transformations within and between cells: STM, MTM, and LTM. The cell activations that are transformed by on-center off-surround networks to solve the noise-saturation dilemma are a form of short-term memory, or STM. More generally, essentially all brain computations that are used to represent and learn about the world are done using some combination of distributed *spatial patterns* of cell activation (STM), activity-dependent habituation (MTM), and synaptic modification through learning (LTM); see Figures 2.9-2.11. Spatial pattern processing provides contextual constraints that can help to overcome the informational ambiguities that occur when only individual components are processed, much as the individual pixels in a picture are meaningless out of context. Choosing the wrong functional unit has led to serious mistakes in thinking about how our brains work. For example, because Donald Hebb used a too local computational unit for learning—namely, a single LTM trace at the end of a single axon, instead of a spatial pattern of LTM traces across multiple axons to a network of cells (Figure 5.12)—he posited an incorrect learning rule (Hebb, 1949).

The fact that these pattern transformations occur *within* cells, not only between them, is of fundamental importance. Indeed, brain dynamics embody a *calculus of self-organizing pattern transformations within and between cells*. I would further claim that these processes are part of a *universal developmental code* whose basic design principles are exploited in all cellular organisms, and not just within their nervous systems.

Some historical background about the discovery of this universal developmental code might be worth summarizing here. Because of the connections that I perceived between neural and non-neural development and learning, I wrote two foundational articles in 1978 that have proved to have enduring value. One of them, devoted to achieving a better understanding of mind and brain, was called "A Theory of Human Memory: Self-Organization and Performance of Sensory-Motor Codes, Maps, and Plans" (Grossberg, 1978a). The other, devoted to demonstrate striking homologs between neural STM and LTM, and non-neural developmental processes in multiple organisms, was called "Communication, Memory, and Development" (Grossberg, 1978c). It was the latter article that proposed a universal developmental code for both neural and non-neural cellular systems.

I had originally conceived of these articles as being part of a book, but was inexperienced in getting a book published, due to a combination of shyness and youth. As things turned out, Robert Rosen, who was a leader in mathematical biology at that time, and a supportive follower of my work, asked to publish both of the articles back-to-back in the 1978 annual volume of *Progress in Theoretical Biology* that he edited with Fred Snell. The articles hereby appeared together, but did not have the visibility that they would have had as a stand-alone book.

STM, MTM, and LTM may seem to be a peculiar place to start a study of development. First, these processes have been used throughout the book to mostly explain adult behaviors. Second, they involve only the brain. What do these adult processes how to do with development, and in what sense are they universal? The link is provided by the following crucial facts. STM, MTM, and LTM involve the parallel processing of continuously fluctuating patterned information in the presence of noise. This is a very general problem, and one that must be solved by any system that tries to deal with fluctuating patterns—in particular, by developing systems. In effect, the geometrical and statistical rules that must be satisfied to solve the problem are very much the same no matter how they are implemented in special cases.

Brain as a universal self-organizing measurement system. There is another reason why problems involving the nervous system can have solutions that apply to other systems. Our nervous systems enjoys a property of *universality*. All the data from our senses—both exteroceptive and interoceptive—are translated into a common neural language that ultimately supports a unitary personality. Our brains are a kind of universal measuring device, and they are so sensitive that they can measure even a few quanta of light. Indeed, the problem of pattern processing can be restated as a problem of measurement, or of communication, between interacting cells.

I noted in Chapter 2 that many of the most fundamental discoveries in physics can be understood as advances in our understanding of physical measurements, including the discoveries of scientists like Newton, Einstein, and Heisenberg. I also noted that, in all of these theories, the measurer who initiates and records the measurements remained outside the measurement process.

In studies of how our brains work, this is no longer possible. As I noted in Chapter 2, the brain *is* the measurement device, and the process of understanding mind and brain is the study of how our brains measure the world, including how other brains carry out their own measurements. As a result of these measurements, brains can alter their structure, through development and learning, in response to the signals that they are measuring, and do so at a remarkably rapid rate. Brains can also unify into coherent moments of conscious experience measurements taken from multiple physical sources—light, sound, pressure, temperature, bodily biochemical processes, and the like. The brain is thus a *universal self-organizing measurement system* of the world, and in the world. Hence, it should not be too surprising that mechanisms which help a brain to process patterns in its universal language should also be relevant to the systems, both inside and outside the body, with which brains interact.

In order to illustrate what I mean by a universal developmental code, I will discuss examples of morphogenesis in primitive organisms that I originally brought together in my 1978 "Communication, Memory, and Development" article. These examples include how *Hydra* regenerates a missing head (Gierer and Meinhardt, 1972); how slime molds aggregate in their search for food (Bonner, 1974; Meinhardt and Gierer, 1974); how the folds in the cuticle of *Rhodnius*, a genus of assassin bugs, are determined (Lawrence, Crick, and Munro, 1972); how a sea urchin blastula becomes a gastrula (Gustafson and Wolpert, 1967); how the French Flag Problem is solved, namely how an organ's shape can be maintained even as its size increases during the development of animals and their body parts; and how early neural development can be refined by adult learning because the laws for prenatal growth of cell connections during morphogenesis are formally similar to the STM and LTM laws that control postnatal synaptic learning in response to external inputs.

These examples may be complemented by the discussion in Chapter 15 of how spectral coding in non-neural HeLa cervical cancer cells are a variant of neural spectrally-timed learning in humans and many other animals.

Chapter 15 explained how spectrally-timed learning may, in turn, be viewed as a specialized kind of interaction between STM, MTM, and LTM (Figures 15.7-15.13). Both of these examples illustrate how activity amplitude is traded against activity timing in many biological systems.

All of these examples, taken together, suggest that general properties of pattern regulation and self-organization in both neural and non-neural developing systems have formal properties that are shared with neural STM, MTM, and LTM laws. The examples also clarify how it is possible for neurons to regulate the functions of cells in many non-neural tissues, since they all develop using variants and specializations of similar laws.

In these descriptions, as throughout biology, the devil is in the details. I will not try to explain how specific genes, or the complex temporal unfolding of other structural specializations, respond to these universally shared mechanisms; e.g., Bode and Müller (2003). Once one realizes that they are shared, however, that raises questions about whether the constraints that the details obey are also variations on a design theme, so that the universally shared STM and LTM mechanisms may be properly expressed during morphogenesis. This book will not attempt to address that question.

Reaction-diffusion models in development: The great Alan Turing.   Alan Turing wrote a classic paper on morphogenesis in 1952 (Turing, 1952) that has had an immense impact on future research in this field. Many readers may better know Turing's great work on inventing the Turing Machine (Turing, 1937), a truly epochal discovery that formalized computational laws for a general purpose computer that led, in stages, to the modern digital computer. It is also broadly known that Turing played a critical role in helping the Allies win World War II by breaking German coded transmissions.

Despite his incredibly important work in science and society, Turing was prosecuted by the British government in 1952 for his homosexuality. To avoid imprisonment, he accepted chemical castration, and also lost his security clearance, among other indignities. Instead of being able to bask in the reverence that his enormous contributions warranted, he committed suicide in 1954 by taking cyanide, at the age of 42 (Hodges, 2014). This great injustice and huge lose of one of the most creative geniuses of the past century reminds us that evil is here to stay.

In his article on morphogenesis, Turing showed how a combination of chemical reactions and diffusion can generate and sustain spatially inhomogeneous activity patterns such, as stripes, spots, and spirals, in response to a spatially homogeneous initial state. Reaction-diffusion theories of morphogenesis have served as a basic model in theoretical biology since that time.

A striking parallel exists between the dynamics of the reaction-diffusion systems that have been used to describe development and of the kinds of recurrent neural systems that I have described in this book (Table 17.1). However, there are also differences between reaction-diffusion systems and biological neural networks. Most notably, the reaction-diffusion systems typically do not describe key properties of *cells*. In particular, their variables are typically not bounded, unlike cells that have only a finite number of excitable sites. Many reaction-diffusion models, in contrast, discuss interactions between chemicals in a non-cellular medium that allows variables to become arbitrarily large or small. Because the shunting dynamics that bound cell activations are missing in these reaction-diffusion systems, so too are the automatic gain control properties that arise when these shunting terms interact with all kinds of signals. As I will discuss below, these are not minor differences. I would argue that biological models of the development of cellular organisms should use a formalism that describes cells.

Regeneration of Hydra's heads.   A class of reaction-diffusion systems of particular interest was introduced by Alfred Gierer and Hans Meinhardt beginning in 1972 (Gierer and Meinhardt, 1972; Meinhardt and Gierer, 1974). This model discusses both asymptotic steady states and traveling waves of chemical activity. The former option was applied to model the regeneration of *Hydra*'s heads.

TABLE 17.1.   Homologs between reaction-diffusion and recurrent shunting cellular network models of development.

REACTION-DIFFUSION	RECURRENT SHUNTING NET
Activator	Excitatory activity
Inhibitor	Inhibitory activity
Morphogen source density	Inputs
Firing of morphogen gradient	Contrast enhancement
Maintenance of morphogen gradient	Short-term memory
Power or sigmoid signal functions	Power or sigmoid signal functions
On-center off-surround interactions via diffusion	On-center off-surround interactions via signals
Self-stabilizing distributions of morphogens if inhibitors equilibrate rapidly	Short-term memory pattern if inhibitors equilibrate rapidly
Periodic pulses if inhibitors equilibrate slowly	Periodic pulses if inhibitors equilibrate slowly
Regulation	Adaptation

Hydra is a small freshwater hydrozoan polyp (Figure 17.1) that has a remarkable ability to regenerate amputated parts of its body. As noted in *Wikipedia*, "biologists are especially interested in *Hydra* because of their regenerative ability—they do not appear to die of old age, or indeed to age at all". Figure 17.2 summarizes a series of experiments that illustrate this ability (Wilby and Webster, 1970a, 1970b; Wolpert, Hicklin, and Hornbruck, 1971). A key conclusion of these experiments is how excitatory and inhibitory morphogens spread across the *Hydra* to activate or inhibit head growth. One of their main conclusions was that excitation spreads less than inhibition, much as happens in an on-center off-surround neural network (Figures 2.10, 2.34, and 2.35). Another conclusion was that local self-excitation causes contrast enhancement that converts small initial differences into larger differences.

To describe these experiments, the *Hydra*'s body is represented as a head followed by four sections (H1234), as in Figure 17.2a. If the head if cut off (Figure 17.2b), then another head regenerates. The new head is designated by an asterisk (*) in Figure 17.2b. If section 1 of a second *Hydra* is grafted onto a decapitated 1234, then one head grows (Figure 17.2c). If sections 12 of a second *Hydra* are grafted onto a decapitated 1234, then two heads grow (Figure 17.2d). In effect, mutual inhibition between the two 1 sections prevents growth of a second head in Figure 17.2c. This inhibition cannot, however, traverse the space between the two 1 segments in Figure 17.2d with sufficient strength to prevent two heads from growing. In Figure 17.2e, an H12 section is grafted onto a 1234 section. No head grows at 1 in 1234. Somehow the H region in H12 can inhibit 1 in 1234 more vigorously than 1 could in 12 of Figure 17.2d. Nonetheless, if H123 is grafted into 1234, the inhibition from H is too weak to prevent head growth at 1 in 1234 (Figure 17.2f).

Transplantation of a head from the distal to the proximal end (1234H) gives rise to a head at 1 (Figure 17.2g), but this does not happen if a head is transplanted to the 4 end sufficiently before the original head is removed from the 1 end (Figure 17.2h). Figures 17.2g and 17.2h suggest that inhibition can spread from the transplanted head to the 1 area to inhibit formation of a second head, much as the extra head in Figure 17.2d can inhibit second head growth better than section 1 can in 12 of Figure 17.2c. In other words, inhibition spreads over a wider region than excitation, and both excitation and inhibition can build up in prescribed regions through time.

Gierer-Meinhardt reaction-diffusion model of development. To explain these effects, Gierer and Meinhardt

FIGURE 17.1. A *Hydra*.

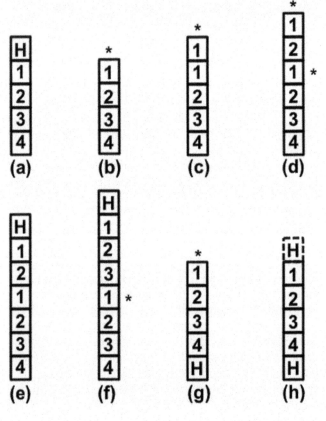

FIGURE 17.2. Schematics of how different cuts and grafts of the normal *Hydra* in (a) may (*) or may not lead to the growth of a new head. See the text for details.

introduced a class of reaction-diffusion systems in which the concentration of activators $x(w, t)$ and inhibitors $y(w, t)$ at positions w control development through time t. One such system describes the time rates of change of x, denoted by $\partial x / \partial t$, and the time rate of change of y, denoted by $\partial y / \partial t$, by the equations:

$$\frac{\partial x}{\partial t} = -A_x x + B_x(w) y^{-1} f(x) + D_x \frac{\partial^2 x}{\partial w^2} + I(w)$$

and

$$\frac{\partial y}{\partial t} = -A_y x + B_y(w) g(x) + D_y \frac{\partial^2 y}{\partial w^2} + I(w).$$

The first equation says that the activity of the activator x at each position w is inhibited by y (term y^{-1}). The activator x also amplifies its own activity via the faster-than-linear positive feedback signal $f(x)$ (cf., Figure 1.7) in response to the morphogen input $I(w)$. As this is going on, x diffuses across space (term $\frac{\partial^2 x}{\partial w^2}$) but with a smaller diffusion constant D_x than the diffusion constant D_y that occurs in the equation for y. That is why the "on-center" is narrower than the "off-surround" in this reaction-diffusion model. The equation for the inhibitor y is similar to that of the excitor, but it is activated both by the morphogen input $I(w)$ and by positive feedback $f(x)$ from the activator at each position w.

Gierer and Meinhardt considered conditions under which a slight peak of initial activator concentration (for example, near section 1 in 1234) leads to further increases of activation at that position. They wanted these small initial concentration differences to generate large final concentration differences, which are thereupon self-maintaining. At a region of peak activator concentration, a new developmental stage is triggered (Figure 17.3); for example, head formation in the *Hydra* at the 1 position in 1234. The other developmental outcomes in Figure

17.2 can all be explained by how these core properties are expressed in different *Hydra* transplants. Meinhardt and Gierer reiterated their modeling approach in a 2000 article that was called "Pattern Formation by Local Self-Activation and Lateral Inhibition" (Meinhardt and Gierer, 2000), but again in a non-cellular reaction-diffusion framework.

Comparing reaction-diffusion and recurrent shunting network models of development. The properties of the Gierer and Meinhardt reaction-diffusion model are strikingly similar to properties of contrast-enhancement and short-term memory storage in recurrent shunting on-center off-surround neural networks (Figures 1.6-1.9). These neural network *cellular* properties have been used to explain how various neural systems develop since the 1970s. In particular, my own 1975 model of geniculocortical development (Grossberg, 1975b) was discovered right after I mathematically proved key properties of recurrent shunting on-center off-surround networks—notably, contrast enhancement, noise suppression, normalization, and STM storage—in 1973 (Grossberg, 1973). The title of my 1975 article reflects my realization that reaction-diffusion systems shared key properties with the recurrent neural networks that I had published at around the same time: "On the Development of Feature Detectors in the Visual Cortext with Applications to Learning and Reaction-Diffusion Systems". My article also noted that the reaction-diffusion models lacked critical cellular properties, such as boundedness and automatic gain control, that I could use to explain more data, such as data that exhibited total activity normalization and contrast normalization properties.

My 1975 article about development also set the stage for me to propose laws for the modern theory of competitive learning and self-organizing maps in 1976 (Grossberg, 1976a, 1976b, 1978a), and to hereby unify models for early development and life-long learning. I could also introduce Adaptive Resonance Theory in these articles (e.g., Grossberg, 1976b), because I had earlier proved how competitive learning and self-organizing maps experienced catastrophic forgetting. I was able to correct this problem by further developing insights from my earlier work on reinforcement learning, where I used top-down attentional mechanisms to explain attentional blocking and unblocking (Figure 13.2; Grossberg, 1975a).

As in the model of Gierer and Meinhardt, my 1975 model of development showed how small differences in bottom-up inputs within the adaptive filter in a competitive learning or self-organizing map model cause small initial differences in the resultant activities of category learning cells. These small category activity differences were then contrast enhanced using the recurrent on-center off-surround network into large activity differences. Only one, or possibly a small number, of large cell activities

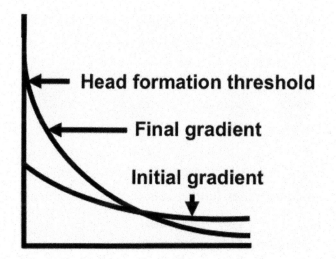

FIGURE 17.3. How an initial morphogenetic gradient may be contrast enhanced to exceed the threshold for head formation in its most active region.

survived this competition, and were then stored in STM. Then the large stored STM activities triggered the next developmental stage, in this case learning by the adaptive filter weights and their storage in LTM (e.g., Figures 5.16 and 5.17).

In order to eliminate any remaining ambiguity, I will compare the reaction-diffusion and recurrent shunting network models of development term-by-term (Table 17.1). Just as Gierer and Meinhardt make a distinction between the density $I(w)$ of morphogen sources and morphogen concentration of activator $x(w)$ and inhibitor $y(w)$ at each position w, I distinguish between input intensity I_i and excitatory and inhibitory activities at each cell i (Figure 2.10). They introduce activators and inhibitors, whereas I introduce excitatory and inhibitory neurons. They call the mechanism whereby small differences become large differences "firing" of a gradient, whereas I call it contrast enhancement. The conditions under which firing and contrast enhancement occur are similar. A faster-than-linear positive feedback signal accomplishes this in both cases (Figure 1.7). In neural networks, sigmoid signals are also used in order to ensure that this signal remains bounded as it causes contrast enhancement and noise suppression (Figure 1.9). In both kinds of systems, exponential decay of concentration of activities occurs. In both systems, activators or excitatory potentials can excite both themselves and inhibitors, whereas inhibitors can inhibit activators and possibly, but not necessarily, themselves. In both systems narrower spread of excitation and broader spread of inhibition occurs. In reaction-diffusion systems, this is due to passive diffusion. In neural networks, it is often due to signals that are transmitted via spikes through axonal pathways (Figure 2.3), but may also occur electrotonically from cell to cell. The diffused inhibitor in a reaction-diffusion system contributes to inhibiting activators at its new positions, just as inhibitory signals do in neural networks.

Both kinds of systems can approach steady states in response to constant inputs, or can oscillate in response to them. In both cases, if the effects of inhibition equilibrate sufficiently rapidly, then steady states are typically approached, whereas if inhibition equilibrates slowly relative to the rate of excitatory equilibration, then oscillatory dynamics, including traveling waves, can occur (e.g., Ellias and Grossberg, 1975).

The analogy between regulation and adaptation: Form invariance when size changes. There is also a striking analogy between the property of network adaptation and one of the most sought-after properties in reaction-diffusion systems. This is the property of *regulation,* which can be described in several ways. One way is to note that a living thing can increase in size dramatically while maintaining a remarkably constant form; for example, a growing leaf, or a teenager. A more abstract way to frame

this property is to ask: How can the same developmental pattern be created in two regions of different size, such as in Figure 17.4? In Figure 17.4, the problem for both of the cells that are represented by red dots is to generate a white color because they both lie in the middle third of their field. But how can the *cells* know this using only local information at their particular positions? This is the famous French Flag Problem that Lewis Wolpert introduced into the developmental literature (Wolpert, 1969). Said in another way, how does each cell acquire *positional information* so that the same developmental pattern can be generated independent of the total field size. This is a *normalization* property of an organ or whole organism that makes each cell aware of its *relative position.* The Gierer and Meinhardt equations have approximately this property if the positive feedback signal $f(x)$ is a suitable sigmoid function of w, although the analysis of Gierer and Meinhardt does not explain why this happens.

In shunting networks, *regulation* is replaced by the kind of *adaptation* whereby recurrent shunting networks use automatic gain control to *normalize* their total activity. This normalization property preserves a record of the relative magnitude of activation at each position, and hereby achieves sensitivity to the relative positions in a morphogenetic gradient as the tissue in which it occurs grows. In addition, the sigmoid signal in such networks is the simplest positive feedback signal that can suppress noise and remain bounded at large values (Figures 1.7-1.9). Being able to process distributed input patterns in the presence of noise is also a basic problem in all developing and adult biological systems.

MORPHOGENESIS: MORE RATIOS
Shape preserved as size increases
French flag problem
Wolpert (1969)

Use cellular models! Grossberg (1976, 1978)

vs. chemical or fluid reaction-diffusion models

Turing (1952)

Gierer and Meinhardt (1972)

FIGURE 17.4. The French Flag Problem of Wolpert (1969) asks how form is preserved during development as size changes. See the text for details.

In other words, the French Flag Problem can be solved in recurrent shunting on-center off-surround networks as a consequence of their ability to solve the much more basic noise-saturation dilemma. It is quite delightful to be able to say that solving the noise-saturation dilemma—and thus being able to process distributed patterns in noisy systems of whatever kind—created the foundation for letting all living things "grow up" and become much larger in the process without becoming unrecognizable. Because the reaction-diffusion equations of Gierer and Meinhardt do not embody cellular dynamics, they do not provide the kind of elegant solution of this problem that a shunting recurrent on-center off-surround network does.

Blastula to gastrula in the sea urchin. Not all forms during development remain unchanged except for increasing their size. After a certain point, previous developmental stages trigger the formation of later stages, leading to the progressive differentiation of cellular tissues into increasingly complex organs and organisms. One interesting classical example of how a previous developmental stage triggers the next one was studied by Wolpert with Tryggve Gustafson in 1967 (Gustafson and Wolpert, 1967). Their experiments used time-lapse cinematography to clarify a small number of mechanisms that operate at early developmental stages of the sea urchin. They also summarized data concerning development in other organisms in which similar mechanisms were reported. Here I will take the further step of noting that the morphogenetic mechanisms that were reported for sea urchin development are formally strikingly similar to the mechanisms in the competitive learning and self-organizing map models of cortical development (e.g., Grossberg,

1975b, 1976a; Grossberg and Seitz, 2003; Grossberg and Williamson, 2001). To make my main point, I will just summarize highlights of one stage of development. Once the formal connection is made, the rest of the data can be similarly analyzed.

Consider the dramatic step whereby the almost spherical blastula is deformed to produce a primitive gut in the gastrula (Figure 17.5). To explain this transformation, Gustafson and Wolpert (1967) identified the following mechanisms:

(1) Cells can form pseudopods that are capable of growing and stretching over considerable intraembryonic distances.

(2) Cells can become adhesive, or sticky, to other cells that contact them.

(3) Pseudopods can contract and thereby generate forces that are strong enough to cause cells that they connect to be pulled closer together.

Gustafson and Wolpert describe how these properties can create a gastrula if they occur in the proper order among blastula cells. Figure 17.5 shows that a subset of mesenchymal cells start to send out pseudopods within a given time interval. These pseudopods randomly explore the blastula cavity. During an overlapping time interval, a subset of ectodermal cells becomes relatively adhesive. Consequently, with higher probability, the pseudopods will adhere to these ectodermal cells. Gustafson and Wolpert argued, in addition, that pseudopods eventually aggregate in the direction of greatest adhesiveness. They show that individual pseudopods are continually making and breaking their cell contacts, but that there is a progressive

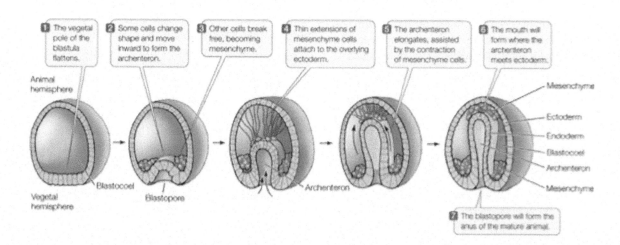

Concept 38.3, www.macmillanhighered.com

FIGURE 17.5. How a blastula develops into a gastrula. See the text for details.

fusion of the pseudopods into a *syncytium*, or mass of cytoplasm that is not separated into individual cells. This syncytium statistically determines a strong connection between the mesenchymal cells and the ectodermal cells. Once their aggregate connection is established, pseudopodal contractions generate enough force to bring these cells closer together, and eventually to form a primitive gut.

How gastrula initiation uses STM and LTM laws. In order to describe the formal similarity between how a gastrula forms and how cortical learning occurs, I will introduce some mathematical notation. Readers who are not interested in this level of detail can skip this section without missing the big picture.

To start, divide the blastula into two classes of cells, mesenchymal cells v_1 and ectodermal cells v_2. Let v_1 contain n cells v_{1i}, i = 1, 2, . . . , n, and v_2 contain m cells v_{2j}, j = 1, 2, . . . , m. Suppose that v_{1i} generates $p_{1i}(t)$ pseudopods in the time interval [t, t + Δt]. Each pseudopod tends to randomly explore the blastula cavity from its vantage point. The number of pseudopods that contact v_{2j} from v_{1i} is $S_{ij}(t) = p_{1i}(t)c_{ij}(t)$, where $c_{ij}(t)$ is a slowly varying function that describes structural factors such as how close v_{1i} is to v_{2j}. Let $p_{2j}(t)$ be the adhesiveness of cell v_{2j} in the time interval [t, t + Δt]. If we suppose that pseudopodal connections from v_{1i} to v_{2j} are formed when a pseudopod from v_{1i} sticks to v_{2j}, then the rate of forming such pseudopods is proportional to $S_{ij}(t)p_{2j}(t)$. Choose the proportionality constant equal to one for simplicity. If we suppose that connections continue to form at this rate, then the total number $w_{ij}(t)$ of connections from v_{1i} to v_{2j} at time t increases at the following rate at every time:

$$\frac{dw_{ij}}{dt} = S_{ij}p_{2j},$$

which implies that $w_{ij}(t)$ equals the continuous sum, or integral, of all these rates from the start time 0 to the present time t, assuming that there are no connections at time t = 0:

$$w_{ij}(t) = \int_0^t S_{ij}(v)p_{2j}(v)dv.$$

If, however, connections also break at a spontaneous rate, then:

$$\frac{dw_{ij}}{dt} = -b_{ij}w_{ij} + S_{ij}p_{2j},$$

where b_{ij} is the rate of breakage of pseudopods between v_{1i} and v_{2j}. Using the definition of $S_{ij}(t) = p_{1i}(t)c_{ij}(t)$, this equation may be rewritten as:

$$\frac{dw_{ij}}{dt} = -b_{ij}w_{ij} + c_{ij}p_{1i}p_{2j}.$$

We can now see that this last equation is formally identical to an associative learning equation for an LTM trace $w_{ij}(t)$

with a passive rate b_{ij} of memory decay, plus a learning term that correlates the STM traces $p_{1i}(t)$ and $p_{2j}(t)$ at a rate that depends on the structural factors $c_{ij}(t)$ through time. In other words, the pseudopodal activity of mesenchymal cells could be compared with STM activity of, say, neurons in the lateral geniculate nucleus, or LGN, and the adhesiveness of ectodermal cells could be compared with the STM activity of cells in cortical area V1 (Figure 1.21). These "fast" STM variables influence "slow" LTM changes in intercellular connection strengths in both the sea urchin and the geniculocortical example. In the sea urchin, LTM leads to the formation of a blastula. In the geniculocortical example, it leads to the development of simple cell receptive fields in V1 (Figures 4.15 and 4.16).

Invoking cellular STM and LTM dynamics to explain syncytium formation. Suppose for the sake of argument that the two systems are attempting to describe formally identical, albeit mechanistically different, processes. What would adding *cells* to the STM and LTM model of sea urchin development achieve? In a cellular model, mesenchymal cells v_1 and ectodermal cells v_2 would be separately capable of normalizing, or adapting, their activities to produce positional information. They would accomplish this by using signals within themselves that switch on and off cellular mechanisms by mass action laws. These signals would be organized in an on-center off-surround configuration of excitatory and inhibitory morphogens that together would solve the noise-saturation dilemma, with normalization supporting the computation of positional information as a result. In particular, excitatory morphogens could switch on cellular mechanisms, while inhibitory morphogens switch them off, in a positionally sensitive manner.

If this cellular analogy is consistently developed, it leads to some unexpected issues and results. For example, in the cortical model, the LTM traces help to determine the postsynaptic STM traces in v_2 by multiplicatively gating the signals that they receive from v_1 (Figure 2.10). The net signal from v_{1i} to v_{2j} is thus $S_{ij}w_{ij}$. In the sea urchin setting, this process would imply that, at each time t, pseudopodal contacts carry *signals* from the mesenchymal cells v_{1i} to the ectodermal cells v_{2j} with which they connect. In the geniculocortical model, these signals are contrast-enhanced in the cortex, and thereby help to focus, sharpen, and strengthen the adaptive tuning of the correct geniculocortical connections (Figure 5.17). In a sea urchin example, such a "contrast enhancement" process would, in a similar way, focus, sharpen, and strengthen the spatial distribution of pseudopodal contacts to create a syncytium. Such a positive feedback signal would also function as a self-corrective mechanism for growing a correctly positioned syncytium should a small genetic or morphogenetic error occur.

What does it mean, physically speaking, for a pseudopodal contact to function as a signal? For one, it means that pseudopodal contacts can increase the adhesiveness of ectodermal cells that they contact, and the total signal to each ectodermal cells, from all the mesenchymal cells which contact it, will help to determine how adhesive it will become. This hypothesis is consistent with the conclusion of Gustafson and Wolpert (1967, pp. 471-472) that "The adhesiveness . . . is thus non-specific in the sense that it serves in the mutual contact of ectodermal cells as well as the contact between mesenchymal pseudopods and the ectoderm." The idea that pseudopods act as signals then reduces to the property that stickiness can increase cell contact, and conversely.

As in the cortical model, the initial signals can be similar in size because the various pseudopods are randomly exploring the blastula cavity. When, however, certain ectodermal cells get a larger signal, the autocatalytic contrast-enhancing process can accelerate the formation of the syncytium. As to why certain ectodermal cells get bigger signals, this is because of their position in the blastula relative to the pseudopod-generating mesenchymal cells, and also because of the morphogenetic gradient within the ectodermal cells that causes some cells to be more sticky initially.

The functioning of a pseudopodal contact as a signal also implies that, as some ectodermal cells get increasingly sticky due to contrast enhancement, these ectodermal cells will start inhibiting the stickiness of ectodermal cells that receive fewer pseudopods via their off-surround signals. Consequently, even more pseudopods will stick to the preferred ectodermal cells, thereby making them even more sticky. This process eventually equilibrates because the total amount of adhesiveness across the ectodermal cells is normalized by its shunting on-center off-surround interactions. In summary, the analogy with cortical tuning suggests a self-correction procedure for synchronizing mesenchymal and ectodermal interactions, and a mechanism of syncytium formation due to positive feedback between pseudopodal aggregation and the adhesiveness of ectodermal cells, supplemented by contrast enhancement, normalization, and STM of the pattern of adhesiveness.

An LTM cascade of directed growth followed by learned synaptic tuning. The formal similarity of the STM and LTM laws for directed growth of connections and of learned tuning of already established connections has important implications for the proper functioning of thalamocortical and corticocortical connections. For example, consider the connections that form from the LGN to V1 before learned tuning of these connections can take place in response to environmental inputs. There is an active modeling literature about how thalamocortical and corticocortical development is controlled, including studies with my PhD students Aaron Seitz and James Williamson about how this happens in the laminar circuits of neocortex (e.g., Grossberg and Seitz, 2003; Grossberg and Williamson, 2001). Independent of these details, the formal homologs of STM and LTM laws between directed growth of

connections during development, and refinement of these connections during later learning, implies that *learning can build upon the foundation that was laid by development* in a computationally consistent way. Indeed, this formal homolog is what enables me to talk about "refinement" of connections with some confidence in the first place.

Biochemical memory and the folds of Rhodnius. The development of the insect *Rhodnius*, also called the South American kissing bug, has been studied since the path-breaking studies of Sir Vincent Brian Wigglesworth, who established the field of insect biology in his classic textbook, *Insect Physiology*, that was first published in 1934 (Wigglesworth, 1934). Later scientists became interested in how the folds in the adult epicuticle of *Rhodnius* develop. The epicuticle is the outer layer of the cuticle, and exhibits characteristic folds. Michael Locke (Locke, 1959, 1960, 1967) described a segmental gradient that controls the polarity of epidermal cells and carries positional information. Polarity is expressed by the orientation of folds in the adult epicuticle, which are parallel to the contours of the gradient.

Reaction-diffusion models were later proposed to test whether one of them could match the cuticle pattern in adult insects after rotation of square pieces of epidermis in insect larvae, for example the model introduced by Peter A. Lawrence and his colleagues (Lawrence et al., 1972). They ruled out a model in which the gradient depends only on the activities of a line of source cells at one end of the segment and a line of sink cells at the other end. Instead, a model in which each cell is a homeostatic unit in the gradient was found to fit the data well. In such a model, each cell participates in establishing and maintaining the gradient, as in a reverberating network. They also found that a given cell attempts to maintain its original, or "set", concentration when it is transplanted to a new position in the segment. In other words, each cell remembers its positional information. Once moved to a new position, the cell's activity is gradually influenced by contiguous activities to produce an intermediate activity level.

The existence of an intracellular memory of position requires recurrent, or feedback, intracellular interactions that can preserve a record of the relative position of the cell in the tissue. Each cell needs to be sensitive to both excitor and inhibitor morphogenetic gradients across the tissue in order to establish its representation of relative position within it. These excitor and inhibitor processes should be able to maintain their relative values via recurrent STM interactions when the cell is moved. After the cell is moved, the excitor and inhibitor morphogens can interact with the excitor and inhibitor morphogenetic values of neighboring cells in its new position within the tissue, just as they did in their original location to compute their initial representation of relative position.

A position-sensitive intracellular memory can be realized by a recurrent gated dipole circuit (Figure 1.15) because it can maintain its relative ON cell and OFF cell activities using its recurrent shunting *intra*cellular on-center off-surround interactions. These ON cell and OFF cell activities become the relative excitor and inhibitor morphogenetic values when embedded within a developing *Rhodnius*. When such a recurrent gated dipole is embedded in a network of such dipoles, the result is a *gated dipole field*. In a gated dipole field, each recurrent gated dipole attempts to retain its relative activity using its *intra*cellular interactions, even while *inter*cellular interactions, notably of the more broadly spreading inhibitor morphogens, gradually influence the relative activity of the cell that has been moved to achieve an intermediate activity level, while also renormalizing all the relative activities to accommodate their new cellular configuration. I have already discussed a variant of such a gated dipole field in Chapter 4. This gated dipole field models a double opponent network of cells in a chromatic Filling-In-DOmain, or FIDO, that controls when and how boundary-gated feature contour signals fill in a region with surface color or brightness (Figure 4.47).

Lawrence et al. (1972, pp. 826-827) also find that "the homeostatic level of each cell is reset at some stage in the cell cycle to the ambient concentration at that time". Such a reset operation is characteristic of STM, and reminds us that STM is distinguished from LTM not just by its possible duration, but by how rapidly it can be erased by a reset signal or competing events.

Slime mold aggregation and slug motion. A slime mold can live freely as multiple individual amoeboid cells, or these cells can aggregate together to form a multicellular organism that is capable of reproducing itself. The name slime mold reflects the fact that, during part of this life cycle, the slime mold can appear as a gelatinous "slime". When food is abundant, a slime mold may exist as single cell amoebas that individually move around seeking food. When food is not abundant, these amoebas may aggregate into a multicellular form that can be carried much further by water currents, potentially to new locales where food is more abundant once more. As Evelyn Keller and Lee Segel (Keller and Segel, 1970) have reviewed, both attractive and repulsive interactions occur in slime molds. Right after germination, the cells disperse as if they are mutually repulsed. When a source of food, such as bacteria, is present, the cells are attracted to it. After exhausting the food supply, the amoebae first distribute themselves uniformly over the space that they inhabit, but later aggregate into a number of centers at which multicellular forms emerge.

John Tyler Bonner (Bonner, 1967, 1969, 1974) elegantly summarized the various stages whereby hungry amoebas aggregate into a slug, which thereupon is capable of organized movement until it forms a fruiting body. Bonner (1969) also described experiments that implicate cyclic adenosine monophosphate, or cAMP, as the intercellularly diffusing agent that causes amoebas to stream together to form a slug. Both Gierer and Meinhardt (1972) and Keller and Segel (1970) described such aggregation as an instability in a reaction-diffusion system. This instability becomes the property of contrast enhancement in the analogous cellular network, which in this case does use diffusion to carry morphogenetic influences between individual amoebas swimming in water. In particular, after food is removed, each amoeba begins to produce more cAMP. By chance, some amoebas produce more cAMP initially. Contrast enhancement amplifies these small differences in initial cAMP production until they become large differences. As in a neural network, contrast enhancement will occur if the cAMP signals $f(w)$ that are emitted by individual amoebas are sigmoid, or S-shaped, functions of an intracellular activity level w (Figures 1.8 and 1.9).

Such a sigmoid signal function can be generated in the following way. Suppose that, as an amoeba's activity level increases, more cAMP production sites can be recruited because their production thresholds are Gaussianly distributed around some mean value, as in Figure 17.6 (left image). Then the total population output signal is a sigmoid function of the input, as in Figure 17.6 (right image). In the classical literature, this activity level was assumed to be mediated by a chemical that was called *acrasin*, which is degraded by an extracellular enzyme that was

HOW BINARY CELLS WITH A GAUSSIAN DISTRIBUTION OF OUTPUT THRESHOLDS GENERATES A SIGMOID POPULATION SIGNAL

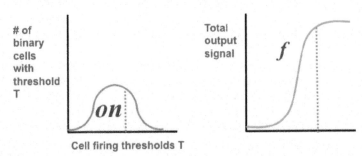

Cell population with firing thresholds Gaussianly distributed around a mean value
As input increases (dashed line), more cells in population fire with binary signals
Total population output obeys a sigmoid signal function f

FIGURE 17.6. Summing over a population of cells with binary output signals whose firing thresholds are Gaussianly distributed (left image) generates a total output signal that grows in a sigmoid fashion with increasing input size (dashed vertical line).

called *acrasinase*, with acrasin later identified to be cAMP (Bonner, 1969; Keller and Segel, 1970). Acrasin, or cAMP, and acrasinase are assumed to control the recurrent on-center and off-surround interactions, respectively, that occur among the amoebae. Acrasinase acts by converting cAMP, which may also be written as 3',5'-cyclic AMP, to chemotactically inactive 5'-AMP (Chang, 1968; Keller and Segel, 1970). Acrasinase has been identified as the enzyme 2-amino-4-hydroxypteridine aminohydrolase (Jayaraman et al., 2016; Levenberg and Hayaishi, 1959).

A baseline level of activity can occur without causing contrast enhancement, just so long is it is smaller than the *quenching threshold* of the interacting cells (Figure 1.9). As food becomes less available, activity increases until it exceeds the quenching threshold and contrast enhancement begins. My analysis in Grossberg (1978c) discusses how cells that are a focus of relatively fast contrast enhancement attract less active cells more than conversely, and that cells that are drawn within the on-center of such an enhanced focus form clumps that stick together. These interactions hereby lead to the formation of one or more multicellular slugs, with the number of slugs depending upon such factors as how far apart the amoebae may initially be relative to the spatial scale of acrasinase influence. Either a steady, monotonic, formation of slugs is possible in such a network, or a more pulsatile, rhythmic, motion of amoebae towards one another. In recurrent shunting on-center off-surround networks, the latter kind of dynamics is expected if the inhibitory morphogen reacts more slowly than the excitatory morphogen. It is known that, during cell aggregation, cAMP is released in a pulsatile manner by an aggregation center (Van Haastert, 1983). This property is consistent with the fact that acrasin diffuses relatively quickly compared to acrasinase (Bonner et al., 1969; Keller and Segel, 1970).

In summary, the above examples sketch how formal STM and LTM laws may be realized during the development of both neural and non-neural cellular structures. They hereby illustrate how these laws may form an important part of the foundation for a universal developmental code.

A universal measurement device of the world and in the world: Brains adapt to physics

Brain as a universal self-organizing measurement device of and in the physical world. I explained in Chapter 1 how the progress of physical theory during the past few centuries has led to an increasingly deep understanding of the measurement processes whereby we learn about the world. There I noted that breakthroughs of great physicists like Isaac Newton, Albert Einstein, and Werner Heisenberg refined our understanding of these measurement processes and their limitations. I also noted, however, that in all of these theories, the physicists who initiated and recorded the measurements remained outside the theoretical explanations of the measurement process itself.

Such a physicist uses his or her own brain to carry out and interpret these measurements, and does so without causing an infinite regress in which someone else is needed to measure the brain of the physicist to complete the physical measurement. When we study our brains, as this book has done, the brain *is* the measurement device, and the process of understanding mind and brain is the study of how our own brains measure the world, whether during a physics experiment or daily life. The measurement process itself is hereby brought into physical theory to an unprecedented degree.

As a result of their measurement processes, brains can alter their structure, through development and learning, in response to the signals that they are measuring, and do so at a remarkably rapid rate. These structural changes can include the growth of new connections, or the adaptive tuning of connections that already exist, in the manner that I sketched in this and earlier chapters. We often think of established connections as being structural. However, they are really just dynamical states that can persist for an unusually long time if they remain in equilibrium with the processes with which they interact. This dynamism becomes apparent when the equilibrium is disrupted, either through injury or death. Then relatively rapid changes can occur in the connections, including their total decomposition. It is profitable to think of the connections and their adaptations as a cascade of coexisting dynamical states that operate at different time scales. Even after the connections are established, multiple time scales need to be considered, as my explanations of STM, MTM, and LTM throughout the book have illustrated.

As I explained in Chapter 5, using the resonant dynamics that are organized by, and that energetically support, these structures, brains can also bind into coherent moments of conscious experience, within a unified self, measurements taken from multiple physical sources—light, sound, pressure, temperature, bodily biochemical processes, and the like. The brain is thus a *universal self-organizing measurement system* of the world, and in the world. Chapter 1 explained that, due to this universal measurement process, brains play a role that may be compared with the role played in physics by Max Planck's law of black-body radiation. By describing a radiation spectrum that is universal across all matter, Planck's law ushered in Quantum Mechanics whereby to explain all subatomic phenomena. The brain's universal measurement process can be expected to have a comparable impact on future science, once its implications are more broadly understood. Brain dynamics operate, however, above the quantum level, although they do so with remarkable efficiency, responding to just a few photons of light in the dark, and to faint sounds whose amplitude is just above the level of thermal noise in otherwise quiet spaces. Knowing more about how this exquisite tuning arose during evolution could provide important new information about the design of perceptual systems, no less than about how quantum processes interface with processes whose main interactions seem to be macroscopic.

Chapter 1 also asked, given that brains are universal measurement devices, how do they differ from classical physical theories about measurement? I proposed there that it is the brain's ability to rapidly *self-organize*, through development and life-long learning, that sets it apart from discoveries in previous physical theories. Brain theory may thus be viewed as a new frontier in measurement theory for the physical sciences, no less than the biological sciences. It remains to be seen whether and how future physical theories of non-neural processes will incorporate concepts about the self-organization of matter, and how these theories will compare with the special case of brain self-organization.

Complementarity, uncertainty, and resonance in brains and the world. I reviewed in Chapter 1 that complementarity and uncertainty principles are foundations of quantum mechanics, notably the complementarity principle introduced by Niels Bohr, and the uncertainty principle introduced by Werner Heisenberg. These physical principles help to explain why complementary properties of objects, such as position and momentum, or wave and particle, cannot be observed or measured with equal precision at the same time. Both classical and quantum mechanics also use resonant states to help explain the stability of matter. For example, in Bohr's theory, observed atomic orbits are resonances of an electron's wavelength. Our brains also use principles of complementarity, uncertainty, and resonance. A major question for future research is to clarify how the ceaseless interactions of brains with their physical environments throughout evolution may have shaped these neural principles, and whether there are deeper mechanistic analogs of physical principles of complementarity, uncertainty, and resonance in their neural counterparts than have to the present been understood.

From the perspective of how our brains work, various physical experiments seem "unnatural" in the sense that the perturbed systems are not designed to operate that way in nature. For example, accelerating a large number of particles to extremely high energies near the speed of light and allowing them to smash together, as is done in CERN's Large Hadron Collider, is not the way that these particles typically interact in nature, even though it may lead to spectacular discoveries, such as confirmation in 2012 of the Glashow-Weinberg-Salam Standard Model prediction

that Higgs Bosons exist (Aad et al., 2012). Doing the analog of a collider experiment on a brain might be compared to violently perturbing the boundary formation process in the cortical interblob stream and testing how it reorganizes the surface-filling in process in the complementary cortical blob stream (Figure 3.7).

Unlike such an experiment, sensory inputs to these complementary cortical streams typically input to *both* of them at once, and only then do the streams interact in a balanced way. The same holds for all complementary pairs of brain processes (Table 1.1). Fortunately, due to the macroscopic nature of brain measurements, it is possible for brain scientists to measure both the inputs to these processes and their responses to them, without causing disruptively large perturbations of the processes. This gives brain scientists a great advantage, and one that is needed because of the sheer complexity of our brains. Because human observers are macroscopic, it seems unlikely that we can carry out this kind of balanced experiment in the quantum realm. But then even more imagination is required of theoretical physicists to be able to infer from these violent collisions the kind of balanced physical interactions that may normally occur. The remarkable explanatory and predictive successes of the Standard Model illustrate that humans can do this, at least to a certain level of refinement.

The book has explained how brain interactions transform complementary and uncertain computations into effective perceptual, cognitive, emotional, and motor representations whereby to predict and control our world (e.g., Table 1.1 and Figure 3.1). As noted above, one important example of complementary computing is how our brains use balanced interactions between complementary properties of visual boundaries and surfaces to see and recognize objects and events in the world (Figure 3.7). Visual perception also provides several examples of hierarchical resolution of uncertainty, such as how *end cuts* at hypercomplex cells overcome positional uncertainties due to the orientational tuning of simple cells. By completing boundaries at line ends and other high curvature contours, end cuts allow better control of surface filling-in (Figures 4.15 and 4.21-4.27). Another general theme in the book, discussed in Chapter 5, is the role of resonant states that are stable and energetic enough through time to drive adaptive changes in brain structure in response to environmental challenges (Figures 2.2 and 5.19). As I explained in Chapters 1, 4, and 6, the combined effects of complementary computing and hierarchical resolution of uncertainty are, I believe, among the evolutionary pressures that led to the discovery of conscious awareness using resonant states of the brain. In particular, a *surface-shroud resonance* between cortical areas V4 and PPC is proposed to "light up" the surface representations in V4 and to thereby enable our brains to use them to direct predictive looking and reaching behaviors (Tables 1.3 and 1.4).

Microscopic reversibility, macroscopic irreversibility, and arrow in time: Serial learning. Many physical processes obey a property of *microscopic reversibility*, whereby individual reactions at equilibrium occur with equal forward and backward rates. Despite this fact, such processes often exhibit a property of *macroscopic irreversibility*, which is related to the entropy of a system and how it evolves through time. Irreversibility is conceptually important because it has been used to explain how, despite the fact of microscopic reversibility, there is an "arrow in time" from past to future in physical processes. As recently as 2016, articles have been written stating that "The relation between macroscopic irreversibility and microscopic reversibility is a present unsolved problem" (Lucia, 2016).

An analog of these concepts exists in how our brains discover an arrow in time. Recall my discussion in Chapter 2 of serial verbal learning, whose properties also hold during the serial learning of other kinds of event sequences. The underlying neural networks that model serial learning obey microscopic reversibility in two different senses. First, there is the sense that the parameters that define the cells and their interactions may be identical in both the temporally forward and backward directions. Second, there is the phenomenon of backward learning; namely, when learning the short list AB, one also automatically begins to learn the reverse list BA (Figure 2.8). It is instructive to interpret this result by saying that, even as one is learning the forward direction in time (AB), one is also learning the backward direction in time (BA). In contrast, when learning longer lists, such as ABC, even though the backward BA may start to be learned before C occurs, the forward association BC eventually wins over BA, thereby learning a macroscopically irreversible "arrow in time" from A to B to C. The entire literature on serial verbal learning, along with its famous bowed serial position curve (Figure 2.5), may be viewed from this perspective as data about how the recurrent STM and LTM interactions in brain networks convert microscopic reversibility into macroscopic irreversibility and the learning of a global arrow in time from past to future.

Dimensions of space and time? A perceived global arrow in time is thus an emergent property of associative and competitive interactions in a recurrent network. Even though a global arrow in time can often be constructed, there are many other examples, in different cortical streams and at different processing levels, where future events can influence percepts of past events, ranging from delta motion (Figure 8.8) and long-range formotion interactions (Figure 8.11) to the auditory continuity illusion (Figure 12.17) and phonemic restoration (Figure 1.22).

Many people accept as a given that we live in a three-dimensional, or 3D, world that obeys the axioms of Euclidean geometry, including the idea that a straight line is a collinear succession of points in space. In physics,

however, this idea has been challenged several times. One famous example is how Einstein's theory of general relativity replaces 3D Euclidean space by 4D Riemannian space-time to describe events at cosmological spatial and temporal scales that are much larger than the ones that we experience in our daily lives. The more recent, and less widely accepted, string theory, with its superstring and M-theory variants (e.g., Witten, 1995), bridges very small and very large scales with an 11-dimensional space that tries to unify particle physics with gravity.

How we perceive the dimensions of space in our daily lives is, just as in the case of our perceptions of a global arrow in time, an emergent property of a complex neural system whose complementary computations are integrated using hierarchical resolutions of uncertainty (Figure 3.1). Even the widely shared belief that we live in a 3D world that obeys Euclidean axioms is a perceptual and cognitive construct that has developed as a result of multiple mathematical discoveries about geometry that have tried to summarize our experiences of how we see and manipulate the visual world using the circular reactions that I described in Chapter 15.

The fact that our percepts of lines in space do not obey Euclidean axioms about collinear series of points is strikingly demonstrated by properties of boundary completion using bipole grouping cells (e.g., Figures 1.4, 4.29, 11.13, 11.25, 11.33, and 11.40). The fact that we do not perceive surfaces based on normal lines that are perpendicular to local surface elements is dramatically shown via properties of surface filling-in (e.g., Figures 1.4, 4.1, 4.4-4.6, 11.13, and 11.25).

The following two examples from visual form and motion perception exemplify how differently our minds perceive spatial dimensions than the way they are described in Euclidean geometry: First, for an example of perceiving visual form, recall the 2D image in Figure 1.3 in which the two rectangles above and below the horizontal rectangle are perceived as a partially occluded vertical rectangle that is completed "behind" its occluder. How is anything perceived "behind" anything else in a 2D picture? Second, for an example of perceiving visual motion, recall the percept of element motion in response to a Ternus display, during which the flanking disks in apparent motion are perceived to jump over the intervening two stationary disks (Figure 8.23). How can an object "jump over" the positions of other objects in a 2D picture? Many examples of 3D percepts that I described in Chapter 11 allow us to draw the same conclusions about 3D Euclidean geometry.

Given that visual percepts are derived from high dimensional dynamical systems, how do our minds ever come up with an idea, albeit only an approximation, that space can be represented by three dimensions? How seeing and movement are correlated using circular reactions provides one important way that we can intuitively understand spatial dimensions. For example, during reaching movements, we can carry out the three S's of movement control: Synergy, Synchrony, and Speed (Figure 12.2). By binding reaching movements into synergies, approximately straight movements in space can be composed using multiple muscle groups, and thereby sweep out a single "dimension" in space. The same thing is true about the synergies that control the directions of our saccadic eye movements to desired target positions in space (Figures 6.14-6.16). Using this kind of heuristic motor understanding of visual space, mathematicians could intuitively understand how many "dimensions" were needed to describe every position in space, and could formalize these intuitions into geometrical axioms, albeit axioms that do not illuminate the visuomotor brain representations whereby we come to understand these dimensions.

Another motoric way to understand space was described in Chapter 16, where I summarized models of how we can learn about space by navigating it. Our navigational movements trigger path integration signals that activate entorhinal grid cell and hippocampal place cell representations with which to represent the space around us. Here too, the way in which our brains decompose the directions in which navigational movements can occur provides insight into the number of "dimensions" of control that are needed to navigate in any direction; e.g., Figures 16.17 and 16.18. In summary, our representations of physical space, whether derived from vision, visually-based movements like looking or reaching, or path integration signals when we walk or run, need to be understood as emergent invariants of the dynamics of large recurrent neural networks. In all these cases, correlations between seeing and movement provide evidence for the minimal number of "dimensions" that are needed to represent any position in space.

Wave-particle duality vs. resonant choice and synchronous oscillations. Brain dynamics also exhibit a kind of *wave-particle duality*, which is one of the properties that complementarity and uncertainty principles in physics were introduced to explain. Einstein was led to the concept of wave-particle duality in order to explain the photoelectric effect, for which he won the Nobel Prize in 1921. The photoelectric effect is said to occur when shining a light on certain metals leads to an electric current. Einstein explained this by positing the existence of photons, or light quanta, and proposed how the energy of ejected electrons increased with the frequency of the light, but not its amplitude, which only influenced how many electrons of a given energy are ejected. This explanation thus used properties of light as both a particle and a wave. As Einstein wrote in his 1938 book with Leopold Infeld called *The Evolution of Physics* (Einstein and Infeld, 1938, pp. 262-263): "But what is light really? Is it a wave or a shower of photons? There seems no likelihood for forming a consistent description of the phenomena of light by a choice of only one of the

two languages. It seems as though we must use sometimes the one theory and sometimes the other, while at times we may use either. We are faced with a new kind of difficulty, We have two contradictory pictures of reality, separately neither of them fully explains the phenomena of light, but together they do". Since Einstein wrote this, scientists have suggested many variations of this theme, including the both-particle-and-wave, wave-only, particle-only, and neither-wave-nor-particle views (Wave-particle duality, *Wikipedia*).

The "waves" that occur in our brain are due to the fan-out, or divergence, of signals that are emitted by individual neurons (e.g., Figure 1.11). A single source hereby sends a "wave" of signals to multiple target neurons. The basic brain learning circuits like outstars and instars illustrate the kind of simultaneous divergence and convergence of signals that occur ubiquitously in our brains (Figures 5.11-5.15). Various brain mechanisms also exist to ensure, in many cases, that all the signals arrive at their target cells at approximately the same times, or synchronously, even if the axons that carry them may differ in length. By one such mechanism, longer axons are wider, and wider axons transmit spikes faster, thereby compensating for the extra distance that they need to travel (Gasser and Grundfest, 1939). Even when the relationship between axon diameter and spike speed is not exactly proportional, the resonance integration time of recipient cells can re-synchronize arriving impulses that are slightly asynchronous via a process that is called *perceptual framing* (Grossberg and Grunewald, 1997). This compensatory mechanism allows us to understand how brains can grow and change their shape during development without necessarily undermining the synchronous action of such diverging "wave-like" signals.

What then would be an analog of a "particle" in this interpretation? Here, *competition* across neurons is essential to choose the cells that will fire in response to a wave of diverging and converging signals. Competitive choice in brains is an appealing analog of the *collapse* of a quantum field into an absorbing atom, just as if it were a particle. An early example of such a collapse is how a "wave" of initial possible boundary groupings collapses into a final choice of a single sharp boundary grouping due to cooperative-competitive feedback (Figure 3.15). This kind of choice, or localization of the wave of signals, typically occurs as part of an adaptive resonance (Figures 2.2 and 12.47). Then, the chosen cell, or cells, absorbs all the network activity, and maintains it coherently, often as a synchronous oscillation with a characteristic frequency, long enough for adaptive changes to occur in the weights that will carry the wave in the future. In this comparison, why does a human measurement tend to trigger such a collapse? The neural analog here is an external input, even just a priming input, that changes the balance of the competition and can thereby force a choice to be made.

Are physical constants like mass emergent properties of bound states in recurrent networks? In ending this section, I will indulge myself with a thought that I had as a graduate student who was deciding whether to study brains or theoretical physics. One of the issues that disturbed me a lot in the early 1960s was how the fundamental constants of physics maintain their stability over time. In the physics that I learned, properties like the mass or charge of a particle were described as nothing more than scalar numbers. I found this to be both disappointing and mysterious, since it did not explain the process whereby mass maintains its stability over time, or how that process determines the numerical value of the mass. I thought that some sort of positive feedback within a suitable network of interactions, suitably balanced by negative feedback, would be needed to explain mass as a bound state of the network, just as a resonance is a bound state of a brain network.

I mention mass in particular because the discovery of the Higgs Boson has been described as necessary to explain mass. Perhaps because I am no longer an avid student of high energy physics, I could not see in the descriptions of the Higgs Boson an answer to my question in terms of such a bound state. On the other hand, superstring theory attempts to explain properties such as mass and charge in terms of the vibrational state of the string. Perhaps this kind of theory can eventually explain all physical properties using network interactions whose bound states explain parameters like mass, charge, and spin. When this happens, perhaps it will bring physics closer to explaining the self-organization of matter, and from that derive from physical principles a deeper understanding of our brains' own self-organizing measurement process.

A final thought: Rebalancing what we know about ourselves and about the external world

The following quote has been attributed to Albert Einstein: "It has become appallingly obvious that our technology has exceeded our humanity." In my own experience as a professor, scientist, and citizen, it has become clear that what we learn in school is predominantly about the external world and its many artifacts in our lives. One of these artifacts was the atomic bomb, which led Einstein to make his statement.

Our knowledge of the external world is often used to develop new technologies without much consideration or knowledge about the minds that make these advances, or about the minds that will be influenced by them, sometimes with tragic consequences. One has only to consider the kinds of examples that are used to teach elementary mathematics in public and high school to realize the extent of this imbalance. Information about our own minds is typically taught only at higher levels of education, often in elective courses, and often with little or no understanding of how our brains give rise to our minds, or how this linkage can illuminate the human condition. Yet what could be more interesting to students than learning about their own minds and how they see, hear, feel, and know things about their world? Because how we learn underlies all these experiences, one can perhaps think of this project as one about Learning About Learning.

I believe that this imbalance needs to be corrected very soon before it leads to tragedies that may dwarf the atomic bomb. To this end, our educational and political systems could profitably incorporate much more understanding of how human minds work. On the educational side, such knowledge could enrich several kinds of curricula.

Web-based curricula to reach millions of students and adults around the world. For example, I organized in 2004, and led as its Director for five years, a Science of Learning Center that was funded by the National Science Foundation. This center was called CELEST, for Center of Excellence for Learning in Education, Science, and Technology. One of the many activities that my colleagues and I carried out with CELEST funding was to begin to develop web-based curricula that could teach millions of students and adults around the world. Indeed, we made plans for such dissemination to occur with established on-line platforms as our curricula were incrementally developed.

We believed that self-contained and accessible web-based curricula that were made freely available to all who wanted to learn from them could begin to overcome otherwise formidable problems in helping to redress the grave imbalance in how little we know about ourselves when compared with our knowledge of science and technology. One such problem was how to get this kind of knowledge taught without having to first formally train a whole generation of teachers in their content. By making the materials freely available and self-contained, teachers who were ready and able to use them could do so, wherever they might be.

Another problem was to help teachers to motivate students to learn basic mathematics and science. All too often, mathematics and science curricula use old examples from the physical sciences that may be hard to get most students excited about. However, all students are interested in themselves, their place in the world, and how their own minds work. Teachers with whom we worked were extremely excited to get their hands on such intrinsically motivating curriculum materials.

Finally, there was the problem that there are typically so many required courses that adding an "elective" would preclude the use of the curricula by many schools. Our goal was thus to use the new curricula to teach mathematics content that was already required in existing curricula, but to do so in a much more exciting way.

To accomplish these goals, our idea was to create multiple web-based modules which would start out with vivid and exciting examples of how we see, hear, feel, know, and act upon the world. The modules would then develop explanations, in easy steps, of how these competences are enabled by brain designs that enable us to adapt autonomously to our own unique and changing experiences. These steps would gradually be used to teach elementary concepts in mathematics that could be used to model these brain processes. The steps in each module would continue to get richer and richer until they included material that would be of interest to both students and adults, no less than to practitioners of the mind and brain sciences who may wish to understand the leading theories that mechanistically explain how brains make minds.

While teaching students and adults the basics about how they see, hear, feel, know, and act, as a way to make standard curricula more exciting, the curricula could also help them, through growing self-understanding, to better cope with a rapidly changing world that is filled with unexpected, and sometimes scary, events. On the political side, such curricula could provide a moderating influence against factually unfounded prejudices about other people that are all too often used to justify evil acts.

After an exciting start, our curriculum development goals stalled because of the short-term nature of the scientific grants that we were able to use to get them off the ground. This kind of urgent literacy development requires long-range funding—possibly through a combination of philanthropy, educational/technology company long-range research and development, and long-range government commitment to improving mathematics and science literacy—that is relatively immune to political pressures and leadership changes.

Whether or not such large-scale efforts are realized, I very much hope that books like the current one will make knowledge about how brains give rise to minds more broadly accessible. I also hope that they will encourage a process of knowledge diffusion though society until the imbalance between our knowledge of technology and of humanity is corrected, so that our technological advances can take full account of who we are, and our mental lives, as well as our physical lives, can thereby be enriched.

Credits

Preface

Figure 0.1 - Reprinted from Figure 4 in: Felleman, D. J., and Van Essen, D. C. (1991). Distributed hierarchical processing in the primate cerebral cortex. *Cerebral Cortex*, 1, 1–47.

Chapter 1

Figure 1.1 – author created

Figure 1.2 – no discernable source, no credit

Figure 1.3 - no discernable source, no credit

Figure 1.4 - Top row (left column): "Nuove Ricerche Sperimentali Sulla Totalizzazione Percettiva," by G. Petter, 1956, Rivista di Psicologia. 50. Copyright 1956 by Giunti: Gruppo Editoriale.

Top row (right column): "Seeing and Thinking," by G. Kanizsa, 1985, Acta Psycologia, 59. Copyright 1985 by Elsevier Science.

Bottom row is adapted from: Grossberg, S., and Yazdanbaksh, A. (2005). Laminar cortical dynamics of 3D surface perception: Stratification, transparency, and neon color spreading. *Vision Research*, **45**, 1725–1743.

Figure 1.5 – author created

Figure 1.6 - Adapted from Figure 8 in: Grossberg, S. (2018). Desirability, availability, credit assignment, category learning, and attention: Cognitive-emotional and working memory dynamics of orbitofrontal, ventrolateral, and dorsolateral prefrontal cortices. *Brain and Neuroscience Advances*, May 8, 2018.

Figure 1.7 - Reprinted from Figure 8 in: Grossberg, S. (2013). Recurrent neural networks, *Scholarpedia*, http://www.scholarpedia.org/article/Recurrent_neural_networks

Figure 1.8 - Reprinted from Figure 9 in: Grossberg, S. (2013). Recurrent neural networks, *Scholarpedia*, http://www.scholarpedia.org/article/Recurrent_neural_networks

Figure 1.9 – author created

Figure 1.10 – author created

Figure 1.11 – author created

Figure 1.12 - Adapted from Figure 17 in: Grossberg, S. (1975). A neural model of attention, reinforcement, and discrimination learning. *International Review of Neurobiology*, 18, 263–327.

Figure 1.13 – author created

Figure 1.14 - Adapted from Figure 4 in: Grossberg, S. (1984). Some normal and abnormal behavioral syndromes due to transmitter gating of opponent processes. *Biological Psychiatry*, 19, 1075–1118.

Figure 1.15 - Adapted from Figure 3 in: Grossberg, S. and Schmajuk, N.A. (1987). Neural dynamics of attentionally-modulated Pavlovian conditioning: Conditioned reinforcement, inhibition, and opponent processing. *Psychobiology*, 15, 195–240.

Figure 1.16 - (left panel) Adapted from Figure 14 in: Grossberg, S. (1975). A neural model of attention, reinforcement, and discrimination learning. *International Review of Neurobiology*, 18, 263–327, and from Figure 4c in: Chang, H.-C., Grossberg, S., and Cao, Y. (2014) Where's Waldo? How perceptual cognitive, and emotional brain processes cooperate during learning to categorize and find desired objects in a cluttered scene. *Frontiers in Integrative Neuroscience*, doi: 10.3389/fnint.2014.0043.

(right panel) Adapted from: Barbas, H. (1995). Anatomic basis of cognitive-emotional interactions in the primate prefrontal cortex. *Neuroscience and Biobehavioral Reviews, 19*, 499–510.

Figure 1.17 - Adapted from Figure 8 in: Grossberg, S. (1975). A neural model of attention, reinforcement, and discrimination learning. *International Review of Neurobiology*, 18, 263–327.

Figure 1.18 - Adapted from Figure 1 in: Grossberg, S. (2000). The imbalanced Brain: From normal behavior to schizophrenia. *Biological Psychiatry*, 48, 81–98.

Figure 1.19 - Adapted from Figure 1 in: Two-streams hypothesis, *Wikipedia*, https://en.wikipedia.org/wiki/Two-streams_hypothesis

Table 1.1 - Adapted from Table 1 in: Grossberg, S. (2000). The complementary brain: Unifying brain dynamics and modularity. *Trends in Cognitive Sciences*, **4**, 233–246, and Table 3 in: Grossberg, S. (2017). Towards solving the Hard Problem of Consciousness: The varieties of brain resonances and the conscious experiences that they support. *Neural Networks*, 87, 38–95.

Table 1.2 - Reprinted from Table 4 in: Grossberg, S. (2017). Towards solving the Hard Problem of Consciousness: The varieties of brain resonances and the conscious experiences that they support. *Neural Networks*, 87, 38–95.

Figure 1.20 - Reprinted from Chapter 6, Figure 32, in: J. C. Lynch, *The Cerebral Cortex*, Published on 6-13-15 by admin, Filed under Basic Science

Figure 1.21 - Adapted from Figure 1 in: DeYoe, E. A., and van Essen, D. C. (1988). Concurrent processing streams in monkey visual cortex. *Trends in Neurosciences*, 11, 219–226.

Figure 1.22 - Adapted from: Warren, R. M., and Warren, R. P. (1970). Auditory illusions and confusions. *Scientific American*, 223, 30–36.

Figure 1.23 - Adapted from Figures 4 and 5 in: Grossberg, S., and Myers, C. W. (2000). The resonant dynamics of speech perception: Interword integration and duration-dependent backward effects. *Psychological Review*, 107, 735–767.

Figure 1.24 - Reprinted from Figure 31 (left panel) in: Grossberg, S. (2017). Towards solving the Hard Problem of Consciousness: The varieties of brain resonances and the conscious experiences that they support. *Neural Networks*, 87, 38–95.

Figure 1.25 - Adapted from Figure 12 in: Grossberg, S. (2017). Towards solving the Hard Problem of Consciousness: The varieties of brain resonances and the conscious experiences that they support. *Neural Networks*, 87, 38–95.

Table 1.3 - Reprinted from Table 1 in: Grossberg, S. (2017). Towards solving the Hard Problem of Consciousness: The varieties of brain resonances and the conscious experiences that they support. *Neural Networks*, 87, 38–95.

Table 1.4 - Reprinted from Table 2 in: Grossberg, S. (2017). Towards solving the Hard Problem of Consciousness: The varieties of brain resonances and the conscious experiences that they support. *Neural Networks*, 87, 38–95.

Chapter 2

Figure 2.1 – no discernable source, no credit

Figure 2.2 - Reprinted from Figure 13 in: Grossberg, S., and Zajak, L. (2017). How humans consciously see paintings and paintings illuminate how humans see. *Art & Perception*, 5, 1–95.

Figure 2.3 – author created

Figure 2.4 – author created

Figure 2.5 – author created

Figure 2.6 – author created

Figure 2.7 – author created

Figure 2.8 – author created

Figure 2.9 – author created

Figure 2.10 – author created

Figure 2.11 – author created

Figure 2.12 – author created

Figure 2.13 – author created

Figure 2.14 – author created

Figure 2.15 – author created

Figure 2.16 – author created

Figure 2.17 – author created

Figure 2.18 – author created

Figure 2.19 – author created

Figure 2.20 – author created

Figure 2.21 – author created

Figure 2.22 – author created

Figure 2.23 – author created

Figure 2.24 – author created

Figure 2.25 – author created

Figure 2.26 – author created

Figure 2.27 – author created

Figure 2.28 – author created

Figure 2.29 – author created

Figure 2.30 – author created

Figure 2.31 – author created

Figure 2.32 – author created

Figure 2.33 – author created

Figure 2.34 – author created

Figure 2.35 – author created

Figure 2.36 – author created

Figure 2.37 - Reprinted from Figure 1 in: Grossberg, S. (2018). A half century of progress towards a unified neural theory of mind and brain with applications to autonomous adaptive agents and mental disorders. In R. Kozma, C. Alippi, Y. Choe, and F. C. Morabito (Eds.). *Artificial Intelligence in the Age of Neural Networks and Brain Computing*. Cambridge, MA: Academic Press.

Figure 2.38 - Adapted from Figure 1 in: Grossberg, S. (2018). A half century of progress towards a unified neural theory of mind and brain with applications to autonomous adaptive agents and mental disorders. In R. Kozma, C. Alippi, Y. Choe, and F. C. Morabito (Eds.). *Artificial Intelligence in the Age of Neural Networks and Brain Computing*. Cambridge, MA: Academic Press.

Chapter 3

Figure 3.1 - Reprinted from Figure 3 in: Grossberg, S. (2018). A half century of progress towards a unified neural theory of mind and brain with applications to autonomous adaptive agents and mental disorders.

In R. Kozma, C. Alippi, Y. Choe, and F. C. Morabito (Eds.). *Artificial Intelligence in the Age of Neural Networks and Brain Computing*. Cambridge, MA: Academic Press.

Figure 3.2 - Reprinted from figure on p. 97 in: Kanizsa, G. (1979). *Organization of vision: Essays on Gestalt perception*. New York: Praeger. Copyright 1979 by Greenwood Publishing Group, Westport, CT.

Figure 3.3 - Figure in (a) reprinted from Kanizsa, G. (1976). Subjective contours. *Scientific American*, 234, p. 51. The figures in (b)-(d) are variations of figures found in this archival article.

Figure 3.4 - Part 1, Figure 1, in: Kolb, H. Webvision: The Organization of the Retina and Visual System: http://webvision.med.utah.edu/book/part-i-foundations/simple-anatomy-of-the-retina/

Figure 3.5 - Reprinted from Figure 1 in: Saidha, S. et. Al. (2011), Primary retinal pathology in multiple sclerosis as detected by optical coherence tomography. *Brain*, 134, 518–533.

Figure 3.6 – author created

Figure 3.7 - Reprinted from Figure 3 in: Grossberg, S. (2014). How visual illusions illuminate complementary brain processes: illusory depth from brightness and apparent motion of illusory contours. *Frontiers in Human Neuroscience*, doi: 10.3389/fnhum.2014.00854

Figure 3.8 - Reprinted from Figure 6 in: Grossberg, S., and Zajac, L. (2017). How humans consciously see paintings and paintings illuminate how humans see. *Art & Perception*, 5, 1–95.

Figure 3.9 - Reprinted from Figure 7 in: Grossberg, S., and Zajac, L. (2017). How humans consciously see paintings and paintings illuminate how humans see. *Art & Perception*, 5, 1–95.

Figure 3.10 - This illusion was discovered by D. Varin and described in: Varin, D. (1971). Fenomeni di contrasto e diffusione cromatica nell'organizzazione spaziale del campo percettivo. *Rivista di Psicologia*, 65, 101–128.

Figure 3.11 - This version of the illusion was discovered by H. F. J. M van Tuijl and described in: Van Tuijl, H. F. J. M. (1975). A new visual illusion: Neonlike color spreading and complementary color induction between subjective contours" *Acta Psychologica*, 39, 441–445.

Figure 3.12 - bpk Bildagentur / Photograph. Inv. FM-2012/200.248./ Art Resource, NY

Figure 3.13 - Ehrenstein, W. (1954). *Probleme der ganzheitspsychologischen Wahrnehmungslehre*. Leipzig: Barth.

Figure 3.14 - Kennedy, J. (1979). Subjective contours, contrast, and assimilation. In C. F. Nodine and D. F. Fisher (Eds.), *Perception and Pictorial Representation*, pp. 167–195. New York: Praeger.

Figure 3.15 - Reprinted from Figure 27 in: Grossberg, S., and Zajac, L. (2017). How humans consciously see paintings and paintings illuminate how humans see. *Art & Perception*, 5, 1–95.

Figure 3.16 - Reprinted from Figure 1a in: Beck, J. (1966). Effect of orientation and of shape similarity on perceptual grouping. *Perception & Psychophysics*, 1, 300–302.

Figure 3.17 - Reprinted from Figure 2 in: Beck, J., and Stevens, K. A. (1988). Visual representation of texture. Final report AFOSR Grant 85-0359.

Figure 3.18 - Reprinted from Figure 12 in: Grossberg, S. and Mingolla, E. (1987). Neural dynamics of surface perception: Boundary webs, illuminants, and shape-from-shading. *Computer Vision, Graphics, and Image Processing*, 37, 116–165.

Figure 3.19 - Adapted from Figure I.7-13 in: Grossberg, S. (2017). The visual world as illusion: The ones we know and the ones we don't. In A. Shapiro and D. Todorovic (Eds.), *Oxford Compendium of Visual Illusions*. Oxford, United Kingdom: Oxford University Press, Chapter 7, pp. 90–118.

Figure 3.20 – Seam Williams

Figure 3.21 - (c) Adapted from: Todd, J., and Akerstrom, R. (1987). Perception of three-dimensional form from patterns of optical texture. *Journal of Experimental Psychology: Human Perception and Performance*, 13, 242–255. (no source information provided for a,b, or d)

Figure 3.22 - Reprinted from Figure 12 in: Grossberg, S., and Zajac, L. (2017). How humans consciously see paintings and paintings illuminate how humans see. *Art & Perception*, 5, 1–95.

Figure 3.23 - Art Institute of Chicago, Chicago, Illinois.

Figure 3.24 - Simulation reprinted from Figure 1 in: Mingolla, E., Ross, W., and Grossberg, S. (1999). A neural network for enhancing boundaries and surfaces in synthetic aperture radar images. Neural Networks, 12, 499–511.

Figure 3.25 - Photograph © The State Hermitage Museum. Photo by Vladimir Terebenin. © 2020 Succession H. Matisse / Artists Rights Society (ARS), New York.

Figure 3.26 - Adapted from Figure 2 in: Grossberg, S., and Hong, S. (2006). A neural model of surface perception: Lightness, anchoring, and filling-in. *Spatial Vision*, 19, 263–321.

Figure 3.27 - Collection of Mr. and Mrs. John Hay Whitney, National Gallery of Art © 2020 Succession H. Matisse / Artists Rights Society (ARS), New York.

Figure 3.28 - Pinna, B. (1987). Un effetto di colorazione. In Il laboratorio e la città. XXI Congresso degli Psicologi Italiani, V. Majer, M. Maeran, and M. Santinello (Eds.). Edizioni SIPs, Societá Italiana di Psiocologia, Milano, 1987, p. 158.

Figure 3.29 - (left image) Rembrandt van Rijn, Self-portrait as a Young Man, 1628, Rijksmuseum, Amsterdam. (right image). Graham Rust (2019). http://grahamrust.squarespace.com/home/

Figure 3.30 - Digital Image © The Museum of Modern Art/Licensed by SCALA / Art Resource, NY. By permission of Jo Baer.

Figure 3.31 – Henry Hensche, The Bather, oil on board, 24" x 20", c. 1970s, collection of Lois Griffel

Figure 3.32 – Claude Monet, Poppies Near Argenteuil

Figure 3.33 - Upper left figure in: Zavagno, D. (1999). Some new luminance-gradient effects. *Perception*, 28, 835–838.

Lower left figure in: Beck, J., and Prazdny, S. (1981). Highlights and the perception of glossiness. *Perception and Psychophysics*, 30, 407–410.

Upper right figure in: Bressan, P. (2001). Explaining lightness illusions. *Perception*, 30, 1031–1046.

Lower left figures from Figure 17 in: Grossberg, S., and Hong, S. (2006). A neural model of surface perception: Lightness, anchoring, and filling-in. *Spatial Vision*, 19, 263–321.

Figure 3.34 - (Left image) Ross Bleckner, Galaxy painting, 1993. Linda Pace Foundation Collection, San Antonio, Texas. Courtesy of the artist and Petzel, New York.

(Right image) Ross Bleckner, Galaxy with Birds painting, 1993. Courtesy of the artist and Petzel, New York.

Figure 3.35 - Adapted from Figure 2 in: Grossberg, S., and Hong, S. (2006). A neural model of surface perception: Lightness, anchoring, and filling-in. *Spatial Vision*, 19, 263–321.

Figure 3.36 - Adapted from Figure 2 in: Grossberg, S., and Hong, S. (2006). A neural model of surface perception: Lightness, anchoring, and filling-in. *Spatial Vision*, 19, 263–321.

Figure 3.37 - Reprinted from Figure 3 in: Grossberg, S., and Hong, S. (2006). A neural model of surface perception: Lightness, anchoring, and filling-in. *Spatial Vision*, 19, 263–321.

Figure 3.38 - (Top left image) This painting is in the Museum of Fine Arts, Boston, Massachusetts. © 2020 Estate of Jules Olitski / Licensed by VAGA at Artists Rights Society (ARS), NY

(Bottom left image) This painting is in the Tate Museum, London, Great Britain. © 2020 Estate of Jules Olitski / Licensed by VAGA at Artists Rights Society (ARS), NY

(Top right image) This painting is in the Guggenheim Museum, New York, New York. © 2020 Estate of Jules Olitski / Licensed by VAGA at Artists Rights Society (ARS), NY

(Bottom right image) Comprehensive Dream, 1965. © 2020 Estate of Jules Olitski / Licensed by VAGA at Artists Rights Society (ARS), NY

Figure 3.39 - (Left image) This painting is in the Smithsonian American Art Museum, Washington, D. C. © 2020 Estate of Gene Davis / Artists Rights Society (ARS), New York

(Right image) Flamingo, 1965. Photo by Joshua Nefsky. © 2020 Estate of Gene Davis / Artists Rights Society (ARS), New York

Figure 3.40 – no credit

Figure 3.41 – author created

Figure 3.42 - © 2020 Frank Stella / Artists Rights Society (ARS), New York

Figure 3.43 – Claude Monet, Rouen Cathedral, Musée d'Orsay, Paris, France

Figure 3.44 - Claude Monet, Rouen Cathedral, Setting Sun (Symphony in Pink and Grey), National Museum, Cardiff, Wales.

Figure 3.45 - Claude Monet, Rouen Cathedral, Full Sunlight, Musée d'Orsay, Paris, France.

Figure 3.46 - Adapted from Claude Monet, Rouen Cathedral, Full Sunlight, Musée d'Orsay, Paris, France.

Chapter 4

Figure 4.1 – author created

Figure 4.2 - Adapted from Plates 1 and 2 in: Grossberg, S. and Todorovic, D. (1988). Neural dynamics of 1-D and 2-D brightness perception: A unified model of classical and recent phenomena. *Perception and Psychophysics*, 43, 241–277.

Figure 4.3 – author created

Figure 4.4 – author created

Figure 4.5 – author created

Figure 4.6 – author created

Figure 4.7 - Adapted from Figure 10a in: Grossberg, S. and Todorovic, D. (1988). Neural dynamics of 1-D and 2-D brightness perception: A unified model of classical and recent phenomena. *Perception and Psychophysics*, 43, 241–277.

Figure 4.8 - Adapted from Figure 10b in: Grossberg, S. and Todorovic, D. (1988). Neural dynamics of 1-D and 2-D brightness perception: A unified model of classical and recent phenomena. *Perception and Psychophysics*, 43, 241–277.

Figure 4.9 - Adapted from Figure 12c in: Grossberg, S. and Todorovic, D. (1988). Neural dynamics of 1-D and 2-D brightness perception: A unified model of classical and recent phenomena. *Perception and Psychophysics*, 43, 241–277.

Figure 4.10 - Adapted from Figure 13a in: Grossberg, S. and Todorovic, D. (1988). Neural dynamics of 1-D and 2-D brightness perception: A unified model of classical and recent phenomena. *Perception and Psychophysics*, 43, 241–277.

Figure 4.11 - Adapted from Figure 14 in: Grossberg, S. and Todorovic, D. (1988). Neural dynamics of 1-D and 2-D brightness perception: A unified model of classical and recent phenomena. *Perception and Psychophysics*, 43, 241–277.

Figure 4.12 - Adapted from Figure 18 in: Grossberg, S. and Todorovic, D. (1988). Neural dynamics of 1-D and 2-D brightness perception: A unified model of classical and recent phenomena. *Perception and Psychophysics*, 43, 241–277.

Figure 4.13 - Adapted from Figure 24 in: Grossberg, S. and Todorovic, D. (1988). Neural dynamics of 1-D and 2-D brightness perception: A unified model of classical and recent phenomena. *Perception and Psychophysics*, 43, 241–277.

Figure 4.14 - Adapted from Figure 2 in: Arrington, K. F. (1994). The temporal dynamics of brightness filling-in. *Vision Research*, 34, 3371–3387.

Figure 4.15 - Reprinted from Figure 22 in: Grossberg, S., and Zajac, L. (2017). How humans consciously see paintings and paintings illuminate how humans see. *Art & Perception*, 5, 1–95.

Figure 4.16 – author created

Figure 4.17 – author created

Figure 4.18 - Reprinted from Figure 8a in: Grossberg, S. (2007). Form Perception. *Encyclopedia of Neuroscience*, Windhorst, U., Binder, M. D., and Hirokawa, N. (Eds.) Heidelberg: Springer-Verlag.

Figure 4.19 – author created

Figure 4.20 - This figure was adapted from Figures 13 and 14 in: Gove, A., Grossberg, S., and Mingolla, E. (1995). Brightness perception, illusory contours, and corticogeniculate feedback. *Visual Neuroscience*, 12, 1027–1052.

Figure 4.21 – author created

Figure 4.22 - Adapted from Figure 5 in: Grossberg, S., and Mingolla, E. (1985). Neural dynamics of perceptual grouping: Textures, boundaries, and emergent segmentations. *Perception and Psychophysics*, 38, 141–171.

Figure 4.23 – author created

Figure 4.24 – author created

Figure 4.25 - Reprinted from Figure 4a in: Grossberg, S. (2017). Towards solving the Hard Problem of Consciousness: The varieties of brain resonances and the conscious experiences that they support. *Neural Networks*, 87, 38–95.

Figure 4.26 – author created

Figure 4.27 – author created

Figure 4.28 – author created

Figure 4.29 – author created

Figure 4.30 - Adapted from Figure 12 in: Bosking, W. H., Zhang, Y., Schofield, B., and Fitzpatrick, D. (1997). Orientation selectivity and the arrangement of horizontal connections in tree shrew striate cortex. *The Journal of Neuroscience*, 17, 2112–2127.

Figure 4.31 - This figure was adapted from lecture notes on neural models of visual perception created by S. Grossberg and E. Mingolla.

Figure 4.32 - Adapted from Figure 3 in: Grossberg, S., and Pessoa, L. (1998). Texture segregation, surface representation, and figure-ground separation. *Vision Research*, 38, 2657–2684.

Figure 4.33 - (Top figure) Reprinted from Figure 13a, and (Bottom figures) Reprinted from Figures 12 and 14b in: Beck, J., Prazdny, K., and Rosenfeld, A. (1983). A theory of textural segmentation. In Beck, J., Hope, B., and Rosenfeld, A. (Eds.). *Human and Machine Vision*. New York: Academic Press.

Figure 4.34 - In Cruthirds, D. R., Gove, A., Grossberg, S., and Mingolla, A. (1991). Preattentive texture segmentation and grouping by the boundary contour system. In *Proceedings of the International Joint Conference on Neural Networks*, Vol. 1, pp. 655-660. N. J.: IEEE Service Center. Also: Cruthirds, D. R., Grossberg, S., and Mingolla, A. (1993). Emergent groupings and texture segregation. *Investigative Ophalmology and Visual Science*, 34, 1237.

Figure 4.35 - Reprinted from Figure 2 in: Ramachandran, V. S., Ruskin, D., Cobb, S., Rogers-Ramachandran, D., and Tyler, C.W. (1994). On the perception of illusory contours, *Vision Research*, 34, 3145–3152.

Figure 4.36 - (Left image) Photo of a graffiti painting by Banksy.

(Middle image) Reprinted from Face #13 in: Mooney, C. M. (1957). Age in the development of closure ability in children. *Canadian Journal of Psychology*, 11, 219–226.

(Right image) Mooney Face #13 with brick pattern added. Entire figure reprinted from p. 2 in:

Rubin, N. (2015). Banksy's graffiti art reveals insights about perceptual surface completion, *Art & Perception*, 3, 1–17.

Figure 4.37 - Adapted from Figure 2 in: Grossberg, S., Mingolla, E., and Ross, W.D. (1997). Visual brain and visual perception: How does the cortex do perceptual grouping? *Trends in Neurosciences, 20,* 106–111.

Figure 4.38 - This figure was adapted from lecture notes on neural models of visual perception created by S. Grossberg and E. Mingolla.

Figure 4.39 - Adapted from Figure 5 in: Grossberg, S. (1999). How does the cerebral cortex work? Learning, attention and grouping by the laminar circuits of visual cortex. *Spatial Vision, 12,* 163–186.

Figure 4.40 - Adapted from: Koffka, K. (1935). *Principles of Gestalt Psychology.* New York: Harcourt & Brace

Figure 4.41 - Adapted from: Kanizsa, G., and Minguzzi, G. F. (1986). An anomalous brightness differentiation. *Perception,* 15, 223–226.

Figure 4.42 - Reprinted from Figure 23 in: Grossberg, S., and Todorovic, D. (1988). Neural dynamics of 1-D and 2-D brightness perception: A unified model of classical and recent phenomena. *Perception and Psychophysics,* 43, 241–277.

Figure 4.43 - (a) reprinted from Figure 6 in: Kelly, F. J., and Grossberg, S. (2000). Neural dynamics of 3-D surface perception: Figure-ground separation and lightness perception. *Perception and Psychophysics,* 62, 1596–1619.

(b) adapted from: Necker, L. A. (1832). LXI. Observations on some remarkable optical phaenomena seen in Switzerland; and on an optical phaenomenon which occurs on viewing a figure of a crystal or geometrical solid. *The London and Edinburgh Philosophical Magazine and Journal of Science,* 329–337.

(c) reprinted from Figure 1a in: Tse, P. U. (2005). Voluntary attention modulates the brightness of overlapping transparent surfaces. *Vision Research,* 45, 1095–1098

Figure 4.44 - Reprinted from Figure 2 in: Grossberg, S., Yazdanbakhsh, A., Cao, Y., and Swaminathan, G. (2008). How does binocular rivalry emerge from cortical mechanisms of 3-D vision? *Vision Research,* 48, 2232–2250.

Figure 4.45 - Reprinted from Figure 49 in: Grossberg, S. (1994). 3-D vision and figure-ground separation by visual cortex. *Perception and Psychophysics,* 55, 48–120.

Figure 4.46 - Adapted from Figure 48 in: Grossberg, S. (1994). 3-D vision and figure-ground separation by visual cortex. *Perception and Psychophysics,* 55, 48–120.

Figure 4.47 - Adapted from Figure 46 in: Grossberg, S. (1994). 3-D vision and figure-ground separation by visual cortex. *Perception and Psychophysics,* 55, 48–120.

Figure 4.48 - Adapted from Figure 4 in: Cao, Y., and Grossberg, S. (2005). A laminar cortical model of stereopsis and 3D surface perception: Closure and da Vinci stereopsis. *Spatial Vision,* 18, 515–578. (This journal no longer exists.) Reprinted from Figure 9 in: Grossberg, S. (2014). How visual illusions illuminate complementary brain processes: illusory depth from brightness and apparent motion of illusory contours. *Frontiers in Human Neuroscience*

Figure 4.49 - Adapted from Figure 1 in: Grossberg, S., and McLoughlin, N. (1997). Cortical dynamics of 3-D surface perception: Binocular and half-occluded scenic images. *Neural Networks,* 1997, 10, 1583–1605.

Figure 4.50 – author created

Figure 4.51 - Reprinted from Figure 10 in Grossberg, S. (2014). How visual illusions illuminate complementary brain processes: Illusory depth from brightness and apparent motion of illusory contours. *Frontiers in Human Neuroscience*

Figure 4.52 - Adapted from Figure 1 in: Fang, L. and Grossberg, S. (2009) From stereogram to surface: How the brain sees the world in depth. *Spatial Vision,* 22, 45–82.

Figure 4.53 - Reprinted from Figure 11 in: Grossberg, S. (2014). How visual illusions illuminate complementary brain processes: Illusory depth from brightness and apparent motion of illusory contours. *Frontiers in Human Neuroscience*

Figure 4.54 – author created

Figure 4.55 – author created

Figure 4.56 – author created

Figure 4.57 - Reprinted from Figure 2 in: Grossberg, S., and Yazdanbakhsh, A. (2005). Laminar cortical dynamics of 3D surface perception: Stratification, transparency, and neon color spreading. *Vision Research,* 45, 1725–1743.

Figure 4.58 - Reprinted from Figure 1 in: Grossberg, S., and Yazdanbakhsh, A. (2005). Laminar cortical dynamics of 3D surface perception: Stratification, transparency, and neon color spreading. *Vision Research,* 45, 1725–1743.

Chapter 5

Figure 5.1 – author created

Figure 5.2 – author created

Figure 5.3 – author created

Figure 5.4 - Image reprinted from: YAS Psych Txtbk, 2 Neuroscience, 2.2 NeuroMacro, 2.2b Limbic System

Figure 5.5 - Reprinted from Figure 2 in: Gove, A., Grossberg, S., and Mingolla, E. (1995). Brightness perception, illusory contours, and corticogeniculate feedback. *Visual Neuroscience, 12,* 1027–1052.

Figure 5.6 - Reprinted from Figure 5 in: Gove, A., Grossberg, S., and Mingolla, E. (1995). Brightness perception, illusory contours, and corticogeniculate feedback. *Visual Neuroscience, 12,* 1027–1052.

Figure 5.7 - Reprinted from Figure 6 in: Gove, A., Grossberg, S., and Mingolla, E. (1995). Brightness perception, illusory contours, and corticogeniculate feedback. *Visual Neuroscience, 12,* 1027–1052.

Figure 5.8 - Reprinted from Figure 4 in: Gove, A., Grossberg, S., and Mingolla, E. (1995). Brightness perception, illusory contours, and corticogeniculate feedback. *Visual Neuroscience, 12,* 1027–1052.

Figure 5.9 - Reprinted from Figure 9 in: Gove, A., Grossberg, S., and Mingolla, E. (1995). Brightness perception, illusory contours, and corticogeniculate feedback. *Visual Neuroscience, 12,* 1027–1052.

Figure 5.10 – author created

Figure 5.11 - Reprinted from Figure 3 in: Grossberg, S. (2013). Recurrent neural networks, *Scholarpedia,* http://www.scholarpedia.org/article/Recurrent_neural_networks

Figure 5.12 - Reprinted from Figure 5 in: Grossberg, S. (2013). Recurrent neural networks, *Scholarpedia,* http://www.scholarpedia.org/article/Recurrent_neural_networks

Figure 5.13 – author created

Figure 5.14 - Reprinted from Figure 1 in: Grossberg, S. (2013). Recurrent neural networks, *Scholarpedia,* http://www.scholarpedia.org/article/Recurrent_neural_networks

Figure 5.15 - Reprinted from Figure 2 in: Grossberg, S. (2013). Recurrent neural networks, *Scholarpedia,* http://www.scholarpedia.org/article/Recurrent_neural_networks

Figure 5.16 – author created

Figure 5.17 – author created

Table 5.1 - Adapted from Table 1 in: Grossberg, S. (1999). The link between brain learning, attention, and consciousness. *Consciousness and Cognition, 8,* 1–44.

Figure 5.18 – author created

Figure 5.19 - Reprinted from Figure 13 in: Grossberg, S. (2017). Towards solving the Hard Problem of Consciousness: The varieties of brain resonances and the conscious experiences that they support. *Neural Networks, 87,* 38–95.

Figure 5.20 - Adapted from Figure 11 in: Grossberg, S. (2017). Towards solving the Hard Problem of Consciousness: The varieties of brain resonances and the conscious experiences that they support. *Neural Networks, 87,* 38–95.

Figure 5.21 – author created

Figure 5.22 – author created

Figure 5.23 – author created

Figure 5.24 – author created

Figure 5.25 – author created

Figure 5.26 – author created

Figure 5.27 – author created

Figure 5.28 – author created

Figure 5.29 – author created

Figure 5.30 – author created

Figure 5.31 – author created

Figure 5.32 - Reprinted from Figure 9 in: Carpenter, G.A., and Grossberg, S. (1987). A massively parallel architecture for a self-organizing neural pattern recognition machine. *Computer Vision, Graphics, and Image Processing, 37,* 54–115.

Figure 5.33 – author created

Figure 5.34 - Adapted from Figures 9c and 9d in: Carpenter, G. A., Gopal, S., Macomber, S., Macomber, S., Woodcock, C. E., and Franklin, J. (1999). A neural network method for efficient vegetation mapping. *Remote Sensing of Environment, 70,* 326–338.

Figure 5.35 – author created

Figure 5.36 - Adapted from Figure 6 in: Carpenter, G.A., and Grossberg, S. (1987). A massively parallel architecture for a self-organizing neural pattern recognition machine. *Computer Vision, Graphics, and Image Processing, 37,* 54–115.

Figure 5.37 - Reprinted from Figure 2 in: Franklin, D. J., and Grossberg, S. (2017). A neural model of normal and abnormal learning and memory consolidation: Adaptively timed conditioning, hippocampus, amnesia, neurotrophins, and consciousness. *Cognitive, Affective, and Behavioral Neuroscience, 17,* 24–76.

Figure 5.38 - Reprinted from Figure 3c in: Grossberg, S., and Versace, M. (2008). Spikes, synchrony, and attentive learning by laminar thalamocortical circuits. *Brain Research, 1218,* 278–312.

Figure 5.39 - Reprinted from Figure 5 in: Grossberg, S., and Versace, M. (2008). Spikes, synchrony, and attentive learning by laminar thalamocortical circuits. *Brain Research, 1218,* 278–312.

Figure 5.40 - Adapted from Figure 14 and 15 in: Grossberg, S., and Versace, M. (2008). Spikes, synchrony, and attentive learning by laminar thalamocortical circuits. *Brain Research*, 1218, 278–312.

Figure 5.41 - Reprinted from Figure 10 in: Grossberg, S., and Versace, M. (2008). Spikes, synchrony, and attentive learning by laminar thalamocortical circuits. *Brain Research*, 1218, 278–312.

Figure 5.42 - Adapted from Figure 1 in: Buffalo, E. A., Fries, P., Landman, R., Buschman, T. J., and Desimone, R. (2011). Laminar differences in gamma and alpha coherence in the ventral stream. *Proceedings of the National Acadmy of Sciences*, 108, 11262–11267.

Figure 5.43 - Adapted from Figure 12c in: Grossberg, S., and Versace, M. (2008). Spikes, synchrony, and attentive learning by laminar thalamocortical circuits. *Brain Research*, 1218, 278–312.

Figure 5.44 – author created

Figure 5.45 – author created

Figure 5.46 - Adapted from Figure 4 in: Amis, G. P., Carpenter, G. A., Ersoy, B., and Grossberg, S. (2009). Cortical learning of recognition categories: A resolution of the exemplar vs. prototype debate.

Figure 5.47 - Reprinted from Figure 5 in: Grossberg, S., and Raizada, R. (2000). Contrast-sensitive perceptual grouping and object-based attention in the laminar circuits of primary visual cortex. *Vision Research*, 40, 1413–1432.

Figure 5.48 - Reprinted from Figure 6 in: Grossberg, S., and Raizada, R. (2000). Contrast-sensitive perceptual grouping and object-based attention in the laminar circuits of primary visual cortex. *Vision Research*, 40, 1413–1432.

Figure 5.49 - Reprinted from Figure 9 in: Grossberg, S. (2017). Acetylcholine neuromodulation in normal and abnormal learning and memory: Vigilance control in waking, sleep, autism, amnesia, and Alzheimer's disease. *Frontiers in Neural Circuits*, November 2, 2017

Chapter 6

Figure 6.1 – author created

Figure 6.2 - Reprinted from Figure 14 in: Grossberg, S. (2017). Towards solving the Hard Problem of Consciousness: The varieties of brain resonances and the conscious experiences that they support. *Neural Networks*, 87, 38–95.

Figure 6.3 - Reprinted from Figure 15 in: Grossberg, S., and Zajac, L. (2017). How humans consciously see paintings and paintings illuminate how humans see. *Art & Perception*, 5, 1–95.

Figure 6.4 - Reprinted from Figure 16 in: Grossberg, S., and Zajac, L. (2017). How humans consciously see paintings and paintings illuminate how humans see. *Art & Perception*, 5, 1–95.

Figure 6.5 - Adapted from: Roelfsema, P. R., Lamme, V. A. F., and Spekreijse, H. (1998). Object-based attention in the primary visual cortex of the macaque monkey. *Nature*, 395, 376–381.

Figure 6.6 - Adapted from Figure 3 in: Grossberg, S., and Raizada, R. (2000). Contrast-sensitive perceptual grouping and object-based attention in the laminar circuits of primary visual cortex. *Vision Research*, 40, 1413–1432.

Figure 6.7 – author created

Figure 6.8 - Adapted from Figure 2 in: Foley, N.C., Grossberg, S. and Mingolla, E. (2012). Neural dynamics of object-based multifocal visual spatial attention and priming: Object cueing, useful-field-of-view, and crowding. *Cognitive Psychology*, 65, 77–117.

Figure 6.9 - Adapted from Figure 8a in: Foley, N.C., Grossberg, S. and Mingolla, E. (2012). Neural dynamics of object-based multifocal visual spatial attention and priming: Object cueing, useful-field-of-view, and crowding. *Cognitive Psychology*, 65, 77–117.

Figure 6.10 - Reprinted from Figures 5A and 5B in: Schira, M. M., Wade, A. R., and Tyler, C. W. (2007). Two-dimensional mapping of the central and parafoveal visual field to human visual cortex. *Journal of Neurophysiology*, 97, 4284–4295.

Figure 6.11 - Adapted from Figure 8b in: Foley, N.C., Grossberg, S. and Mingolla, E. (2012). Neural dynamics of object-based multifocal visual spatial attention and priming: Object cueing, useful-field-of-view, and crowding. *Cognitive Psychology*, 65, 77–117.

Figure 6.12 – author created

Figure 6.13 - Reprinted from Figure 1 in: Grahn, J. A., Parkinson, J. A., and Owen, A. M. (2009). *Behavioural Brain Research*, 199, 53-60. Adapted from Figure 3 in: Alexander, G. E., DeLong, M. R., and Strick, P. L. (1986). Parallel organization of functionally segregated circuits linking basal ganglia and cortex. *Annual Review of Neuroscience*, 9, 357–381.

Figure 6.14 - Adapted from Figure 19 in: Grossberg, S. (2017). Towards solving the Hard Problem of Consciousness: The varieties of brain resonances and the conscious experiences that they support. *Neural Networks*, 87, 38–95.

Figure 6.15 - Adapted from Figure 21 in: Grossberg, S. (2017). Towards solving the Hard Problem of Consciousness: The varieties of brain resonances and the conscious experiences that they support. *Neural Networks*, 87, 38–95.

Figure 6.16 - Adapted from Figure 22 in: Grossberg, S. (2017). Towards solving the Hard Problem of Consciousness: The varieties of brain resonances and the conscious experiences that they support. *Neural Networks*, 87, 38–95.

Figure 6.17 - Adapted from Figure 4b in: Tomita, H., Ohbayashi, M., Nakahara, K., Hasegawa, I., and Miyashita, Y. (1999). Top-down signal from prefrontal cortex in executive control of memory retrieval. Nature, 401, 699–703.

Figure 6.18 - Adapted from Figure 2 in: Cao, Y., Grossberg, S., and Markowitz, J. (2011). How does the brain rapidly learn and reorganize view- and positionally-invariant object representations in inferior temporal cortex? *Neural Networks*, 24, 1050–1061.

Figure 6.19 - Reprinted from Figure 4 in: Cao, Y., Grossberg, S., and Markowitz, J. (2011). How does the brain rapidly learn and reorganize view- and positionally-invariant object representations in inferior temporal cortex? *Neural Networks*, 24, 1050–1061.

Figure 6.20 - Adapted from Figure 1 in: Cao, Y., Grossberg, S., and Markowitz, J. (2011). How does the brain rapidly learn and reorganize view- and positionally-invariant object representations in inferior temporal cortex? *Neural Networks*, 24, 1050–1061.

Figure 6.21 - Adapted from Figure 1 in: Grossberg, S., Markowitz, J., and Cao, Y. (2011). On the road to invariant recognition: Explaining tradeoff and morph properties of cells in inferotemporal cortex using multiple-scale task-sensitive attentive learning. *Neural Networks*, 24, 1036–1049.

Figure 6.22 - Experimental stimulus images adapted from: Akrami, A., Liu, Y., Treves, A., and Jagadeesh, B. (2009). Converging neuronal activity in inferior temporal cortex during the classification of morphed stimuli. *Cerebral Cortex*, 19, 760–776.

Figure 6.23 - Data images adapted from Akrami, A., Liu, Y., Treves, A., and Jagadeesh, B. (2009). Converging neuronal activity in inferior temporal cortex during the classification of morphed stimuli. *Cerebral Cortex*, 19, 760–776. Model simulation reprinted from Figure 1d in:

Grossberg, S., Markowitz, J., and Cao, Y. (2011). On the road to invariant recognition: Explaining tradeoff and morph properties of cells in inferotemporal cortex using multiple-scale task-sensitive attentive learning. *Neural Networks*, 24, 1036–1049.

Figure 6.24 - Adapted from Figure 1 in: Fang, L. and Grossberg, S. (2009) From stereogram to surface: How the brain sees the world in depth. *Spatial Vision*, 22, 45–82

Figure 6.25 - Reprinted from Figure 24 in: Grossberg, S. (2017). Towards solving the Hard Problem of Consciousness: The varieties of brain resonances and the conscious experiences that they support. *Neural Networks*, 87, 38–95. Adapted from Figure 4 in: Grossberg, S., Srinivasan, K., and Yazdanbakhsh, A. (2014). Binocular fusion and invariant category learning due to predictive remapping during scanning of a depthful scene with eye movements. *Frontiers in Psychology: Perception Science*

Figure 6.26 - Adapted from Figure 3 in: Grossberg, S., Srinivasan, K., and Yazdanbakhsh, A. (2014). Binocular fusion and invariant category learning due to predictive remapping during scanning of a depthful scene with eye movements. *Frontiers in Psychology: Perception Science*

Figure 6.27 - Adapted from Figure 25 in: Grossberg, S. (2017). Towards solving the Hard Problem of Consciousness: The varieties of brain resonances and the conscious experiences that they support. *Neural Networks*, 87, 38–95.

Figure 6.28 – author created

Chapter 7

Figure 7.1 - Adapted from Figure 5 in: Francis, G., Grossberg, S., Mingolla, E. (1994). Cortical dynamics of feature binding and reset: Control of visual persistence. *Vision Research*, 34, 1089–1104.

Figure 7.2 - Adapted from Figure 1 in: Francis, G., Grossberg, S., Mingolla, E. (1994). Cortical dynamics of feature binding and reset: Control of visual persistence. *Vision Research*, 34, 1089–1104.

Figure 7.3 - Adapted from Figure 10 in: Francis, G., Grossberg, S., Mingolla, E. (1994). Cortical dynamics of feature binding and reset: Control of visual persistence. *Vision Research*, 34, 1089–1104.

Figure 7.4 - Adapted from Figure 2 in: Francis, G., Grossberg, S., Mingolla, E. (1994). Cortical dynamics of feature binding and reset: Control of visual persistence. *Vision Research*, 34, 1089–1104.

Figure 7.5 - Adapted from Figure 8 in: Francis, G., Grossberg, S., Mingolla, E. (1994). Cortical dynamics of feature binding and reset: Control of visual persistence. *Vision Research*, 34, 1089–1104.

Figure 7.6 - Adapted from Figure 3 in: Francis, G., Grossberg, S., Mingolla, E. (1994). Cortical dynamics of feature binding and reset: Control of visual persistence. *Vision Research*, 34, 1089–1104.

Figure 7.7 - Adapted from Figure 4 in: Francis, G., Grossberg, S., Mingolla, E. (1994). Cortical dynamics of feature binding and reset: Control of visual persistence. *Vision Research*, 34, 1089–1104.

Chapter 8

Figure 8.1 - Reprinted from Figure 13 in: Grossberg, S. (2014). How visual illusions illuminate complementary brain processes: illusory depth from brightness and apparent motion of illusory contours. *Frontiers in Human Neuroscience*

Figure 8.2 - Reprinted from Figures 1D and 1E in: Foster, K. H., Gaska, J. P., Nagler, M., and Pollen, D. A. (1985). Spatial and temporal frequency selectivity of neurons in visual cortical areas V1 and V2 of the macaque monkey. *Journal of Physiology*, 365, 331–363.

Figure 8.3 – author created

Figure 8.4 – author created

Figure 8.5 – author created

Figure 8.6 – author created

Figure 8.7 – author created

Figure 8.8 - Adapted from Figure 39 in: Grossberg, S., and Rudd, M.E. (1992). Cortical dynamics of visual motion perception: Short-range and long-range apparent motion. *Psychological Review*, 99, 78–121.

Figure 8.9 - Adapted from Figure 32 in: Grossberg, S., and Rudd, M.E. (1992). Cortical dynamics of visual motion perception: Short-range and long-range apparent motion. *Psychological Review*, 99, 78–121.

Figure 8.10 - Adapted from Figure 31 in: Grossberg, S., and Rudd, M.E. (1992). Cortical dynamics of visual motion perception: Short-range and long-range apparent motion. *Psychological Review*, 99, 78–121.

Figure 8.11 - Adapted from: Ramachandran, V. S. (1985). Apparent motion of subjective surfaces. *Perception*, 14, 127–134.

Figure 8.12 - Adapted from Figure 5 in: Grossberg, S., and Rudd, M. E. (1989). A neural architecture for visual motion perception: Group and element apparent motion, *Neural Networks*, 2, 421–450.

Figure 8.13 - Adapted from Figure 6 in: Grossberg, S., and Rudd, M. E. (1989). A neural architecture for visual motion perception: Group and element apparent motion, *Neural Networks*, 2, 421–450.

Figure 8.14 - Reprinted from Figure 6 in: Anstis, S., and Ramachandran, V. S. (1987). Visual inertia in apparent motion. *Vision Research*, 27, 755–764.

Figure 8.15 - Adapted from Figure 7 in: Grossberg, S., and Rudd, M. E. (1989). A neural architecture for visual motion perception: Group and element apparent motion, *Neural Networks*, 2, 421–450.

Figure 8.16 - Adapted from Figure 8 in: Grossberg, S., and Rudd, M. E. (1989). A neural architecture for visual motion perception: Group and element apparent motion, *Neural Networks*, 2, 421–450.

Figure 8.17 - Adapted from Figure 9 in: Grossberg, S., and Rudd, M. E. (1989). A neural architecture for visual motion perception: Group and element apparent motion, *Neural Networks*, 2, 421–450.

Figure 8.18 – author created

Figure 8.19 - Adapted from Figure 10 in: Grossberg, S., and Rudd, M. E. (1989). A neural architecture for visual motion perception: Group and element apparent motion, *Neural Networks*, 2, 421–450.

Figure 8.20 – author created

Figure 8.21 - Adapted from Figure 11 in: Grossberg, S., and Rudd, M. E. (1989). A neural architecture for visual motion perception: Group and element apparent motion, *Neural Networks*, 2, 421–450.

Figure 8.22 - Data from: Korte, A. (1915). Kinematoskopische Untersuchungen. *Zeitschriftfur Psychologies*, 194–296. Simulation from Figure 2 in: Francis, G., and Grossberg, S. (1996). Cortical dynamics of form and motion integration: Persistence, apparent motion, and illusory contours. *Vision Research*, 36, 149–173.

Figure 8.23 - Adapted from Figure 3b in: Grossberg, S., and Rudd, M. E. (1989). A neural architecture for visual motion perception: Group and element apparent motion, *Neural Networks*, 2, 421–450.

Figure 8.24 - Adapted from Figure 15b in: Grossberg, S., and Rudd, M.E. (1992). Cortical dynamics of visual motion perception: Short-range and long-range apparent motion. *Psychological Review*, 99, 78–121.

Figure 8.25 - Adapted from Figure 21 in: Grossberg, S., and Rudd, M.E. (1992). Cortical dynamics of visual motion perception: Short-range and long-range apparent motion. *Psychological Review*, 99, 78–121.

Figure 8.26 - Adapted from Figure 6 in: Berzhanskaya, J., Grossberg, S. and Mingolla, E. (2007). Laminar cortical dynamics of visual form and motion interactions during coherent object motion perception. *Spatial Vision*, 20, 337–395.

Figure 8.27 - Adapted from Figure 18 in: Grossberg, S., and Rudd, M. E. (1989). A neural architecture for visual motion perception: Group and element apparent motion, *Neural Networks*, 2, 421–450.

Figure 8.28 - Adapted from Figures 13 and 14 in: Grossberg, S., and Rudd, M. E. (1989). A neural architecture for visual motion perception: Group and element apparent motion, *Neural Networks*, 2, 421–450.

Figure 8.29 - Reprinted from Figure 5A, 5B, and 5C in: Tinsley, C. J., Webb, B. S., Barraclough, N., Vincent, C. J., Parker, A., and Derrington, A. M. (2003). The nature of V1 neural reponses to 2D moving patterns depends on receptive-field structure in the marmoset monkey. *Journal of Neurophysiology*, 90, 930–937.

Figure 8.30 - Data from Figure 3 in: Castet, E., Lorenceau, J., Shiffrar, M., and Bonnet, C. (1993). Perceived speed of moving lines depends on orientation, length, speed and luminance. *Vision Research*, 33, 1921–1936. Simulation from Figure 2b in: Chey, J., Grossberg, S., and Mingolla, M. (1997). Neural dynamics of motion grouping: From aperture ambiguity to object speed and direction. *Journal of the Optical Society of America*, 14, 2570–2594.

Figure 8.31 – author created

Figure 8.32 - Reprinted from Figure 1 in: Chey, J., Grossberg, S., and Mingolla, E. (1998). Neural dynamics of motion processing and speed discrimination. *Vision Research*, 38, 2769–2786.

Figure 8.33 - Reprinted from Figure 3 in: Chey, J., Grossberg, S., and Mingolla, E. (1998). Neural dynamics of motion processing and speed discrimination. *Vision Research*, 38, 2769–2786.

Figure 8.34 - Adapted from Figure 1 in: Browning, A., Grossberg, S., and Mingolla, M. (2009). Cortical dynamics of navigation and steering in natural scenes: Motion-based object segmentation, heading, and obstacle avoidance. *Neural Networks*, 22, 1383–1398.

Figure 8.35 – author created

Figure 8.36 - This figure was adapted by S. Grossberg for this book from his lecture notes, combined with Figure 4 in: Grossberg, S., Mingolla, E., and Viswanathan, L. (2001). Neural dynamics of motion integration and segmentation within and across apertures. *Vision Research*, 41, 2521–2553.

Figure 8.37 - Adapted from Figures 6 and 9 in: Chey, J., Grossberg, S., and Mingolla, M. (1997). Neural dynamics of motion grouping: From aperture ambiguity to object speed and direction. *Journal of the Optical Society of America*, 14, 2570–2594.

Figure 8.38 - Data adapted from Figure 2c in: Pack, C. C., and Born, R. T. (2001). Temporal dynamics of a neural solution to the aperture problem in visual area MT of macaque brain. *Nature*, 409, 1040-1042. Simulation adapted from Figure 10 in: Chey, J., Grossberg, S., and Mingolla, M. (1997). Neural dynamics of motion grouping: From aperture ambiguity to object speed and direction. *Journal of the Optical Society of America*, 14, 2570–2594.

Figure 8.39 - Figure adapted from Figure 11 in: Chey, J., Grossberg, S., and Mingolla, M. (1997). Neural dynamics of motion grouping: From aperture ambiguity to object speed and direction. *Journal of the Optical Society of America*, 14, 2570–2594.

Figure 8.40 - Adapted from Figure 1a in: Lorenceau, J., and Alais, D. (2001). Form constraints in motion binding. *Nature Neuroscience*, 4, 745–751.

Figure 8.41 - Adapted from Figure 20 in: Grossberg, S., Mingolla, E., and Viswanathan, L. (2001). Neural dynamics of motion integration and segmentation within and across apertures. *Vision Research*, 41, 2521–2553.

Figure 8.42 - Adapted from Figure 3 in: Berzhanskaya, J., Grossberg, S. and Mingolla, E. (2007). Laminar cortical dynamics of visual form and motion interactions during coherent object motion perception. *Spatial Vision*, 20, 337–395.

Figure 8.43 – author created

Figure 8.44 – author created

Figure 8.45 – author created

Figure 8.46 – author created

Figure 8.47 – author created

Figure 8.48 - Adapted from Figure 3 in: Grossberg, S., Leveille, J., and Versace, M. (2011). How do object reference frames and motion vector decomposition emerge in laminar cortical circuits? *Attention, Perception, and Psychophysics*, 73, 1147–1170.

Figure 8.49 – author created

Figure 8.50 – author created

Figure 8.51 - Adapted from Figure 7 in: Grossberg, S., Leveille, J., and Versace, M. (2011). How do object reference frames and motion vector decomposition emerge in laminar cortical circuits? *Attention, Perception, and Psychophysics*, 73, 1147–1170.

Figure 8.52 - Adapted from Figure 8 in: Grossberg, S., Leveille, J., and Versace, M. (2011). How do object reference frames and motion vector decomposition emerge in laminar cortical circuits? *Attention, Perception, and Psychophysics*, 73, 1147–1170.

Figure 8.53 – author created

Figure 8.54 - Adapted from Figure 12 in: Grossberg, S., Leveille, J., and Versace, M. (2011). How do object reference frames and motion vector decomposition emerge in laminar cortical circuits? *Attention, Perception, and Psychophysics*, 73, 1147–1170.

Figure 8.55 – author created

Figure 8.56 - This figure was adapted by S. Grossberg for this book from his lecture notes, and from Figure 14 in: Grossberg, S., Leveille, J., and Versace, M. (2011). How do object reference frames and motion vector decomposition emerge in laminar cortical circuits? *Attention, Perception, and Psychophysics*, 73, 1147–1170.

Figure 8.57 - Adapted from Figure 8.34 and Figure 1 in: Grossberg, S., and Pilly, P. (2008). Temporal dynamics of decision-making during motion perception in the visual cortex. *Vision Research*, 48, 1345–1373.

Figure 8.58 - Adapted from Figures 5a and 5b in: Grossberg, S., and Pilly, P. (2008). Temporal dynamics of decision-making during motion perception in the visual cortex. *Vision Research*, 48, 1345–1373.

Figure 8.59 - Adapted from Figure 9 in: Grossberg, S., and Pilly, P. (2008). Temporal dynamics of decision-making during motion perception in the visual cortex. *Vision Research*, 48, 1345–1373.

Figure 8.60 - Adapted from Figures 6a and 6b in: Grossberg, S., and Pilly, P. (2008). Temporal dynamics of decision-making during motion perception in the visual cortex. *Vision Research*, 48, 1345–1373

Figure 8.61 - Adapted from Figures 6c and 6d in: Grossberg, S., and Pilly, P. (2008). Temporal dynamics of decision-making during motion perception in the visual cortex. *Vision Research*, 48, 1345–1373.

Figure 8.62 - Adapted from Figure 10 in: Grossberg, S., and Pilly, P. (2008). Temporal dynamics of decision-making during motion perception in the visual cortex. *Vision Research*, 48, 1345–1373.

Chapter 9

Figure 9.1 – author created

Figure 9.2 - This figure was adapted by S. Grossberg for this book from his lecture notes based upon a figure on p. 125 in: Gibson, J. J. (1950). *The Perception of the Visual World*. Oxford, England: Houghton Mifflin Company.

Figure 9.3 - This figure was adapted by S. Grossberg for this book from his lecture notes based upon Figures 1-3 in: Warren, W. H., and Hannon, D. J. (1990). Eye movements and optical flow. *Optical Society of America, Journal, A: Optics and Image Science*, 7, 160–169.

Figure 9.4 - This figure was adapted by S. Grossberg for this book from his lecture notes based upon Figures 1–3 in: Warren, W. H., and Hannon, D. J. (1990). Eye movements and optical flow. *Optical Society of America, Journal, A: Optics and Image Science*, 7, 160–169.

Figure 9.5 - This figure was adapted by S. Grossberg for this book from his lecture notes based upon Figures 1–3 in: Warren, W. H., and Hannon, D. J. (1990). Eye movements and optical flow. *Optical Society of America, Journal, A: Optics and Image Science*, 7, 160–169.

Figure 9.6 – author created

Figure 9.7 – author created

Figure 9.8 - Adapted from Figure 3 in: Grossberg, S., Mingolla, E., and Pack, C. (1999). A neural model of motion processing and visual navigation by cortical area MST. *Cerebral Cortex*, 9, 878–895.

Figure 9.9 - Adapted from Figures 7b and 9 in: Graziano, M. S. A., Andersen, R. A., and Snowden, R. (1994). Tuning of MST neurons to spiral motions. *The Journal of Neuroscience*, 14, 54–67

Figure 9.10 - Adapted from Figure 12 in: Grossberg, S., Mingolla, E., and Pack, C. (1999). A neural model of motion processing and visual navigation by cortical area MST. *Cerebral Cortex*, 9, 878–895.

Figure 9.11 - (Left image) Adapted from Figure 10 in: Warren, W. H., and Hannon, D. J. (1990). Eye movements and optical flow. *Optical Society of America, Journal, A: Optics and Image Science*, 7, 160–169.

(Right image) Adapted from Figure 16b in: Grossberg, S., Mingolla, E., and Pack, C. (1999). A neural model of motion processing and visual navigation by cortical area MST. *Cerebral Cortex*, 9, 878–895.

Figure 9.12 – author created

Figure 9.13 – author created

Figure 9.14 - (top row, left column) By fitting MT tuning curves with Gaussian receptive fields, a tuning width of 38^0 is estimated, and leads to the observed standard spiral tuning of 61^0 in MSTd. Reprinted from Figure 6 in: Grossberg, S., Mingolla, E., and Pack, C. (1999). A neural model of motion processing and visual navigation by cortical area MST. *Cerebral Cortex*, 9, 878–895. (bottom row, left column) The spiral tuning estimate in Figure 9.16 maximizes the position invariant of MSTd receptive fields. Reprinted from Figure 8 in Grossberg, S., Mingolla, E., and Pack, C. (1999). A neural model of motion processing and visual navigation by cortical area MST. *Cerebral Cortex*, 9, 878–895. (top row, right column) Heading sensitivity is not impaired by these parameter choices. Reprinted from Figure 17 in Grossberg, S., Mingolla, E., and Pack, C. (1999). A neural model of motion processing and visual navigation by cortical area MST. *Cerebral Cortex*, 9, 878–895.

Figure 9.15 – author created

Figure 9.16 - Adapted from Figure 1a in: Srihasam, K., Bullock, D., and Grossberg, S. (2009). Target selection by frontal cortex during coordinated saccadic and smooth pursuit eye movements. *Journal of Cognitive Neuroscience*, 21, 1611–1627.

Figure 9.17 - Reprinted from Figure 1 in: Pack, C., Grossberg, S., and Mingolla, E. (2001). A neural model of smooth pursuit control and motion perception by cortical area MST. *Journal of Cognitive Neuroscience*, 13, 102–120.

Figure 9.18 - Reprinted from Figure 3 in: Pack, C., Grossberg, S., and Mingolla, E. (2001). A neural model of smooth pursuit control and motion perception by cortical area MST. *Journal of Cognitive Neuroscience*, 13, 102–120.

Figure 9.19 - Reprinted from Figure 2 in: Pack, C., Grossberg, S., and Mingolla, E. (2001). A neural model of smooth pursuit control and motion perception by cortical area MST. *Journal of Cognitive Neuroscience*, 13, 102–120.

Figure 9.20 - Adapted from Figures 3 and 10 in: Reprinted from Figure 1 in: Fajen, B. R., and Warren, W. H. (2003). Behavioral dynamics of steering, obstacle avoidance, and route selection. *Journal of Experimental Psychology: Human Perception and Performance*, 29, 343–362.

Figure 9.21 – author created

Figure 9.22 – author created

Figure 9.23 - Adapted from Figure 1.2 in: Browning, A., Grossberg, S., and Mingolla, M. (2009). A neural model of how the brain computes heading from optic flow in realistic scenes. *Cognitive Psychology*, 59, 320–356.

Figure 9.24 - Adapted from Figure 1.3 in: Browning, A., Grossberg, S., and Mingolla, M. (2009). A neural model of how the brain computes heading from optic flow in realistic scenes. *Cognitive Psychology*, 59, 320–356.

Figure 9.25 - Adapted from Figure 1.5 in: Browning, A., Grossberg, S., and Mingolla, M. (2009). A neural model of how the brain computes heading from optic flow in realistic scenes. *Cognitive Psychology*, 59, 320–356.

Figure 9.26 - Adapted from: Browning, A., Grossberg, S., and Mingolla, M. (2009). A neural model of how the brain computes heading from optic flow in realistic scenes. *Cognitive Psychology*, 59, 320–356.

Chapter 10

Figure 10.1 – author created

Figure 10.2 – author created

Figure 10.3 – author created

Figure 10.4 – author created

Figure 10.5 – author created

Figure 10.6 - Adapted from Figure 6a in: Grossberg, S., and Raizada, R. (2000). Contrast-sensitive perceptual grouping and object-based attention in the laminar circuits of primary visual cortex. *Vision Research*, 40, 1413–1432.

Figure 10.7 - Adapted from Figure 6a in: Grossberg, S., and Raizada, R. (2000). Contrast-sensitive perceptual grouping and object-based attention in the laminar circuits of primary visual cortex. *Vision Research*, 40, 1413–1432.

Figure 10.8 - Adapted from Figure 6a in: Grossberg, S., and Raizada, R. (2000). Contrast-sensitive perceptual grouping and object-based attention in the laminar circuits of primary visual cortex. *Vision Research*, 40, 1413–1432.

Figure 10.9 - Adapted from Figures 6a and 6c in: Grossberg, S., and Raizada, R. (2000). Contrast-sensitive perceptual grouping and object-based attention in the laminar circuits of primary visual cortex. *Vision Research*, 40, 1413–1432.

Figure 10.10 – author created

Figure 10.11 - Adapted from Figures 6a and 6c in: Grossberg, S., and Raizada, R. (2000). Contrast-sensitive perceptual grouping and object-based attention in the laminar circuits of primary visual cortex. *Vision Research*, 40, 1413–1432.

Figure 10.12 - Adapted from Figure 6e in: Grossberg, S., and Raizada, R. (2000). Contrast-sensitive perceptual grouping and object-based attention in the laminar circuits of primary visual cortex. *Vision Research*, 40, 1413–1432.

Figure 10.13 - Adapted from Figures 6a and 6c in: Grossberg, S., and Raizada, R. (2000). Contrast-sensitive perceptual grouping and object-based attention in the laminar circuits of primary visual cortex. *Vision Research*, 40, 1413–1432.

Figure 10.14 - Adapted from Figures 6b and 6c in: Grossberg, S., and Raizada, R. (2000). Contrast-sensitive perceptual grouping and object-based attention in the laminar circuits of primary visual cortex. *Vision Research*, 40, 1413–1432.

Figure 10.15 - The data from Reynolds et al. (1999) and the simulation from Grossberg and Raizada (2000) are adapted with permission.] (Left column) Data adapted from Figure 6 in: Reynolds, J., Chelazzi, L., and Desimone, R. (1999). Competitive mechanisms subserve attention in macaque areas V2 and V4. *The Journal of Neuroscience*, 19, 1736–53.

(Right column) Simulation adapted from Figure 2e in: Grossberg, S., and Raizada, R. (2000). Contrast-sensitive perceptual grouping and object-based attention in the laminar circuits of primary visual cortex. *Vision Research*, 40, 1413–1432.

Figure 10.16 - (Left image) Data adapted from: Polat, U., Mizobe, K., Pettet, M. W., Kasamatsu, T., and Norcia, A. M. (1998). Collinear stimuli regulate visual responses depending on cell's contrast threshold. *Nature*, 391, 580–584.

(Right image) Simulation adapted from Figure 1c in: Grossberg, S., and Raizada, R. (2000). Contrast-sensitive perceptual grouping and object-based attention in the laminar circuits of primary visual cortex. *Vision Research*, 40, 1413–1432.

Figure 10.17 - (Left image) Data adapted from Figure 3b in: DeWeerd, P., Peralta, M. R., Desimone, R., and Ungerleider, L. G. (1999). Loss of attentional stimulus selection after extrastriate cortical lesions in macaques. *Nature Neuroscience*, 2, 753–758.

(Right image) Simulation adapted from Figure 2d in: Raizada, R., and Grossberg, S. (2001). Context-sensitive bindings by the laminar circuits of V1 and V2: A unified model of perceptual grouping, attention, and orientation contrast. *Visual Cognition*, 8, 431–466.

Figure 10.18 - (Left image) Data adapted from Figure 10 in: Knierim, J. J., and Van Essen, D. C. (1992). Neuronal responses to static texture patterns in area V1 of the alert macaque monkey. *Journal of Neurophysiology*, 67, 961–980.

(Right image) Simulation adapted from Figure 2d in: Raizada, R., and Grossberg, S. (2001). Context-sensitive bindings by the laminar circuits of V1 and V2: A unified model of perceptual grouping, attention, and orientation contrast. *Visual Cognition*, 8, 431–466.

Figure 10.19 - Reprinted from Figure 2b in: Watanabe, T., Nanez, J. E., and Sasaki, Y. (2001). Perceptual learning without perception. *Nature*, 413, 844–848.

Chapter 11

Figure 11.1 – author created

Figure 11.2 – author created

Figure 11.3 – author created

Figure 11.4 – no source cited

Figure 11.5 – author created

Figure 11.6 – author created

Figure 11.7 - Figure adapted from Figure 5a in: Cao, Y., and Grossberg, S. (2005). A laminar cortical model of stereopsis and 3D surface perception: Closure and da Vinci stereopsis. *Spatial Vision*, 18, 515–578.

Figure 11.8 – author created

Figure 11.9 – author created

Figure 11.10 - Adapted from Figure 5a in: Cao, Y., and Grossberg, S. (2005). A laminar cortical model of

stereopsis and 3D surface perception: Closure and da Vinci stereopsis. *Spatial Vision*, 18, 515–578.

Figure 11.11 - author created

Figure 11.12 – author created

Figure 11.13 - Adapted from Figure 1 in: Grossberg, S., and Howe, P. D. L. (2003). A laminar cortical model of stereopsis and three-dimensional surface perception. *Vision Research*, 43, 801–829.

Figure 11.14 - Simulation adapted from Figure 14a in: Grossberg, S., and Howe, P. D. L. (2003). A laminar cortical model of stereopsis and three-dimensional surface perception. *Vision Research*, 43, 801–829.

Figure 11.15 - Simulation adapted from Figure 14b in: Grossberg, S., and Howe, P. D. L. (2003). A laminar cortical model of stereopsis and three-dimensional surface perception. *Vision Research*, 43, 801–829.

Figure 11.16 - Simulation adapted from Figure 15a in: Grossberg, S., and Howe, P. D. L. (2003). A laminar cortical model of stereopsis and three-dimensional surface perception. *Vision Research*, 43, 801–829.

Figure 11.17 - Simulation adapted from Figure 15b in: Grossberg, S., and Howe, P. D. L. (2003). A laminar cortical model of stereopsis and three-dimensional surface perception. *Vision Research*, 43, 801–829.

Figure 11.18 - Simulation adapted from Figure 20a in: Cao, Y., and Grossberg, S. (2005). A laminar cortical model of stereopsis and 3D surface perception: Closure and da Vinci stereopsis. *Spatial Vision*, 18, 515–578.

Figure 11.19 - Simulation adapted from Figure 20b in: Cao, Y., and Grossberg, S. (2005). A laminar cortical model of stereopsis and 3D surface perception: Closure and da Vinci stereopsis. *Spatial Vision*, 18, 515–578.

Figure 11.20 - Simulation adapted from Figure 5 in: Grossberg, S., and Howe, P. D. L. (2003). A laminar cortical model of stereopsis and three-dimensional surface perception. *Vision Research*, 43, 801–829.

Figure 11.21 - Simulation adapted from Figure 7b in: Grossberg, S., and Howe, P. D. L. (2003). A laminar cortical model of stereopsis and three-dimensional surface perception. *Vision Research*, 43, 801–829.

Figure 11.22 - Simulation adapted from Figure 16 in: Grossberg, S., and Howe, P. D. L. (2003). A laminar cortical model of stereopsis and three-dimensional surface perception. *Vision Research*, 43, 801–829.

Figure 11.23 - Simulation adapted from Figures 1b, 1c, and 1d in: Fang, L. and Grossberg, S. (2009) From stereogram to surface: How the brain sees the world in depth. *Spatial Vision*, 22, 45–82.

Figure 11.24 - Simulation adapted from Figures 1a and 1c in: Fang, L. and Grossberg, S. (2009) From stereogram to surface: How the brain sees the world in depth. *Spatial Vision*, 22, 45–82.

Figure 11.25 - Simulation adapted from Figures 1b and 1d in: Fang, L. and Grossberg, S. (2009) From stereogram to surface: How the brain sees the world in depth. *Spatial Vision*, 22, 45–82.

Figure 11.26 – author created

Figure 11.27 - (Left image) Adapted from Figure 4 in: Grossberg, S. (1994). 3-D vision and figure-ground separation by visual cortex. *Perception and Psychophysics*, 55, 48–120.

(Right image) Adapted from Figure 1 in: Brown, J. M., and Weisstein, N. (l988). A spatial frequency effect on perceived depth. Perception and Psychaphysics, 44, 157–166.

Figure 11.28 - Adapted from Figure 41 in: Grossberg, S. (1994). 3-D vision and figure-ground separation by visual cortex. *Perception and Psychophysics*, 55, 48–120.

Figure 11.29 - (Left image) Reprinted from Figure 24a in: Hubel, D. H., and Wiesel, T. N. (1977). Functional architecture of macaque monkey visual cortex, *Proceedings of the Royal Society of London B*, 198, 1–59.

(Right image) Reprinted from Figure 14 in: Schmolesky, M. The primary visual cortex, Webvision

Figure 11.30 – author created

Figure 11.30(2) - Adapted from Figure 6a in: Grossberg, S., Kuhlmann, L., and Mingolla, E. (2007). A neural model of 3D shape-from-texture: Multiple-scale filtering, boundary grouping, and surface filling-in. *Vision Research*, 47, 634–672.

Figure 11.31 - (Upper image) Simulation reprinted from Figure 2a in: Grossberg, S., Kuhlmann, L., and Mingolla, E. (2007). A neural model of 3D shape-from-texture: Multiple-scale filtering, boundary grouping, and surface filling-in. *Vision Research*, 47, 634–672.

(Lower image) Data adapted from several figures in: Todd, J. T., and Akerstrom, R. A. (1987). Perception of three-dimensional form from patterns of optical texture. *Journal of Experimental Psychology: Human Perception and Performance*, 13, 242–255.

Figure 11.32 - Adapted from: Kulikowski, J. J. (1978). Limit of single vision in stereopsis depends on contour sharpness. *Nature*, 275. 126–127.

Figure 11.33 - Adapted from: Kaufman, L. (1974). *Sight and Mind: An Introduction to Visual Perception*. New York: Oxford University Press.

Figure 11.34 - Adapted from Table 1 in: Grossberg, S., Yazdanbakhsh, A., Cao, Y., and Swaminathan, G. (2008). How does binocular rivalry emerge from cortical mechanisms of 3-D vision? *Vision Research*, 48, 2232–2250.

Figure 11.35 - Adapted from Figure 1 in: Grossberg, S., Yazdanbakhsh, A., Cao, Y., and Swaminathan, G. (2008). How does binocular rivalry emerge from cortical mechanisms of 3-D vision? *Vision Research*, 48, 2232–2250.

Figure 11.36 - Adapted from Figure 6 in: Grossberg, S., Yazdanbakhsh, A., Cao, Y., and Swaminathan, G. (2008). How does binocular rivalry emerge from cortical mechanisms of 3-D vision? *Vision Research*, 48, 2232–2250.

Figure 11.37 - Reprinted from Figure 8 in: Grossberg, S., Yazdanbakhsh, A., Cao, Y., and Swaminathan, G. (2008). How does binocular rivalry emerge from cortical mechanisms of 3-D vision? *Vision Research*, 48, 2232–2250.

Figure 11.38 - Reprinted from Figure 9 in: Grossberg, S., Yazdanbakhsh, A., Cao, Y., and Swaminathan, G. (2008). How does binocular rivalry emerge from cortical mechanisms of 3-D vision? *Vision Research*, 48, 2232–2250.

Figure 11.39 - Reprinted from Figure 10 in: Grossberg, S., Yazdanbakhsh, A., Cao, Y., and Swaminathan, G. (2008). How does binocular rivalry emerge from cortical mechanisms of 3-D vision? *Vision Research*, 48, 2232–2250.

Figure 11.40 - Adapted from Figure 1a in: Grossberg, S., and Swaminathan, G. (2004). A laminar cortical model for 3D perception of slanted and curved surfaces and of 2D images: development, attention and bistability. *Vision Research*, 44, 1147–1187.

Figure 11.41 - Adapted from Figure 2a in: Grossberg, S., and Swaminathan, G. (2004). A laminar cortical model for 3D perception of slanted and curved surfaces and of 2D images: development, attention and bistability. *Vision Research*, 44, 1147–1187.

Figure 11.42 - Adapted from Figure 6b in: Grossberg, S., and Swaminathan, G. (2004). A laminar cortical model for 3D perception of slanted and curved surfaces and of 2D images: development, attention and bistability. *Vision Research*, 44, 1147–1187.

Figure 11.43 - Reprinted with permission.

Figure 11.44 - Reprinted from Figure 8 in: Cao, Y., and Grossberg, S. (2019). A laminar cortical model for 3D boundary and surface representations of complex natural scenes. In *From Parallel to Emergent Computing*, Chapter 24. Adamatzky, A., Akl, S., and Sirakoulis, G. (Eds.). Boca Raton, FL: CRC Press, Taylor & Francis Group.

Figure 11.45 - Adapted from Figure 6 in: Mingolla, E., Ross, W., and Grossberg, S. (1999). A neural network for enhancing boundaries and surfaces in synthetic aperture radar images. *Neural Networks*, 12, 499–511.

Chapter 12

Figure 12.1 - Reprinted from Figure 1 in: Rauschecker, J. P., and Scott, S. K. (2009). Maps and streams in the auditory cortex: Nonhuman primates illuminate human speech processing. *Nature Neuroscience*, 12, 718–724.

Figure 12.2 - Adapted from Figure 17 in: Bullock, D., and Grossberg, S. (1988). Neural dynamics of planned arm movements: Emergent invariants and speed-accuracy properties during trajectory formation. *Psychological Review*, 95, 49–90.

Figure 12.3 - (Left image) Adapted from Figure 4 in: Georgopoulos, A. P., Kalaska, J. F., Caminiti, R., and Massey, J. T. (1982). On the relations between the direction of two-dimensional arm movements and cell discharge in primate motor cortex. *The Journal of Neuroscience*, 2, 1527–1537.

(Right image) Adapted from: Georgopoulos, A. P., Schwarz, A. B., and Kettner, R. E. (1986). Neuronal population coding of movement direction. *Science*, 233, 1416–1419.

Figure 12.4 - (Top image) Reprinted from Figure 2 in: Georgopoulos, A. P., Kalaska, J. F., Caminiti, R., and Massey, J. T. (1982). On the relations between the direction of two-dimensional arm movements and cell discharge in primate motor cortex. *The Journal of Neuroscience*, 2, 1527–1537.

(Bottom image) Adapted from Figure 18 in: Bullock, D., and Grossberg, S. (1988). Neural dynamics of planned arm movements: Emergent invariants and speed-accuracy properties during trajectory formation. *Psychological Review*, 95, 49–90.

Figure 12.5 - Reprinted from Figure 19 in: Bullock, D., and Grossberg, S. (1988). Neural dynamics of planned arm movements: Emergent invariants and speed-accuracy properties during trajectory formation. *Psychological Review*, 95, 49–90.

Figure 12.6 - Reprinted from Figure 9 in: Georgopoulos. A. P. Kalaska. J. F. and Massey. J. T. (1981). Spatial trajectories and reaction times of aimed movements: Effects of practice, uncertainty. and change in target location. *Journal of Neurophysiology*, 46. 725–743.

Figure 12.7 - Simulation adapted from Figure 23 in: Bullock, D., and Grossberg, S. (1988). Neural dynamics of planned arm movements: Emergent invariants and speed-accuracy properties during trajectory formation. *Psychological Review*, 95, 49–90.

Figure 12.8 - Reprinted from Figure 16 in: Bullock, D., and Grossberg, S. (1988). Neural dynamics of planned arm movements: Emergent invariants and

speed-accuracy properties during trajectory formation. *Psychological Review*, 95, 49–90.

Figure 12.9 - Adapted from Figure 4 in: Gaudiano P., and Grossberg S. (1991). Vector associative maps: Unsupervised real-time error-based learning and control of movement trajectories. *Neural Networks*, 4, 147–183.

Figure 12.10 - Reprinted from Figure 1 in: Bullock, D., Cisek, P., and Grossberg, S. (1998). Cortical networks for control of voluntary arm movements under variable force conditions. *Cerebral Cortex*, 8, 48–62.

Figure 12.11 - Reprinted from Figure 3 in: Bullock, D., Cisek, P., and Grossberg, S. (1998). Cortical networks for control of voluntary arm movements under variable force conditions. *Cerebral Cortex*, 8, 48–62.

Figure 12.12 - Reprinted from Figure 2 in: Contreras-Vidal, J.L., Grossberg, S., and Bullock, D. (1997). A neural model of cerebellar learning for arm movement control: Cortico-spino-cerebellar dynamics. *Learning and Memory*, 3, 475–502.

Figure 12.13 - Adapted from Figure 4 in: Bullock, D., Grossberg, S., and Guenther, F.H. (1993). A self-organizing neural model of motor equivalent reaching and tool use by a multijoint arm. *Journal of Cognitive Neuroscience*, 5, 408–435.

Figure 12.14 - Adapted from Figure 8 in: Bullock, D., Grossberg, S., and Guenther, F.H. (1993). A self-organizing neural model of motor equivalent reaching and tool use by a multijoint arm. *Journal of Cognitive Neuroscience*, 5, 408–435.

Figure 12.15 - (Left image) Adapted from Figure 8 in: Bullock, D., Grossberg, S., and Guenther, F.H. (1993). A self-organizing neural model of motor equivalent reaching and tool use by a multijoint arm. *Journal of Cognitive Neuroscience*, 5, 408–435.

(Right image) Adapted from Figure 2 in: Guenther, F. (1995). Speech sound acquisition, coarticulation, and rate effects in a neural network model of speech production. *Psychological Review*, 102, 594–621.

Figure 12.16 - Reprinted from Figure 1 in: Guenther, F. H., Ghosh, S. S., and Tourville, J. A. (2006). Neural modeling and imaging of the cortical interactions underlying syllable production. *Brain and Language*, 96, 280–301.

Figure 12.17 – author created

Figure 12.18 - Adapted from Figure 8a in: Grossberg , S., Govindarajan, K.K., Wyse, L.L., and Cohen, M.A. (2004). ARTSTREAM: A neural network model of auditory scene analysis and source segregation. *Neural Networks*, 17, 511–536.

Figure 12.19 - Reprinted from Figure 33 in: Grossberg , S., Govindarajan, K.K., Wyse, L.L. , and Cohen, M.A.

(2004). ARTSTREAM: A neural network model of auditory scene analysis and source segregation. *Neural Networks*, 17, 511–536.

Figure 12.20 - Adapted from Figure 1 in: Cohen, M.A., Grossberg, S., and Wyse, L.L. (1995). A spectral network model of pitch perception. *Journal of the Acoustical Society of America*, 98, 862–879.

Figure 12.21 - Adapted from Figure 6 in: Cohen, M.A., Grossberg, S., and Wyse, L.L. (1995). A spectral network model of pitch perception. *Journal of the Acoustical Society of America*, 98, 862–879.

Figure 12.22 – By permission of George Gibson

Figure 12.23 - (left column, top row) Adapted from Figure 16 in Grossberg, S., Govindarajan, K.K., Wyse, L.L. , and Cohen, M.A. (2004). ARTSTREAM: A neural network model of auditory scene analysis and source segregation. *Neural Networks*, 17, 511–536.

(left column, bottom row) Adapted from Figures 17 and 18 in Grossberg , S., Govindarajan, K.K., Wyse, L.L. , and Cohen, M.A. (2004). ARTSTREAM: A neural network model of auditory scene analysis and source segregation. *Neural Networks*, 17, 511–536.

(right column) Reprinted from Figure 11 in Grossberg , S., Govindarajan, K.K., Wyse, L.L. , and Cohen, M.A. (2004). ARTSTREAM: A neural network model of auditory scene analysis and source segregation. *Neural Networks*, 17, 511–536.

Figure 12.24 - Reprinted from Figure 2 in http://www.indiana.edu/~p1013447/dictionary/vot.htm

Figure 12.25 - (Left image) Reprinted from Figure 15 in: Cohen, M.A., Grossberg, S., Stork, D.G. (1988). Speech perception and production by a self-organizing neural network. In Lee. Y. C. (Ed.), *Evolution, learning, cognition, and advanced architectures*. Hong Kong : World Scientific Publishers, pp.217–231.

(Right image) Reprinted from Figure 1 in: Ames, H., and Grossberg, S. (2008). Speaker normalization using cortical strip maps: A neural model for steady state vowel categorization. *Journal of the Acoustical Society of America*, 124, 3918–3936.

Figure 12.26 - Reprinted from Figures 4 and 5 in: Ames, H., and Grossberg, S. (2008). Speaker normalization using cortical strip maps: A neural model for steady state vowel categorization. *Journal of the Acoustical Society of America*, 124, 3918–3936.

Figure 12.27 - Adapted from http://www.weizmann.ac.il/brain/images/cubes.html.

Figure 12.28 - Reprinted from Figures 4 and 6 in: Grossberg, S., and Repin, D. (2003) A neural model of how the brain represents and compares multi-digit numbers: spatial and categorical processes. *Neural Networks*, 16, 1107–1140.

Figure 12.29 - Reprinted from Figures 15 and 16 in: Grossberg, S., and Repin, D. (2003) A neural model of how the brain represents and compares multi-digit numbers: spatial and categorical processes. *Neural Networks*, 16, 1107–1140.

Figure 12.30 - Adapted from Figure 1 in: Grossberg, S., and Kazerounian, S. (2011). Laminar cortical dynamics of conscious speech perception: A neural model of phonemic restoration using subsequent context in noise. *Journal of the Acoustical Society of America*, 130, 440–460.

Figure 12.31 – author created

Figure 12.32 - Adapted from Figure 1 in: Murdock, B. B. Jr. (1962). The serial position effect of free recall. *Journal of Experimental Psychology*, 64, 482–488

Figure 12.33 – author created

Figure 12.34 – author created

Figure 12.35 – author created

Figure 12.36 – author created

Figure 12.37 - Simulations adapted from Figures 12b and 12c in: Grossberg, S., and Pearson, L. (2008). Laminar cortical dynamics of cognitive and motor working memory, sequence learning and performance: Toward a unified theory of how the cerebral cortex works. *Psychological Review*, 115, 677–732.

Figure 12.38 – author created

Figure 12.39 – author created

Figure 12.40 – author created

Figure 12.41- Adapted from Figure 2 in: Averbeck, B. B., Chafee, M. V., Crowe, D. A., and Georgopoulos, A. P. (2002). Parallel processing of serial movements in prefrontal cortex, *Proceedings of the National Academy of Sciences*, 99, 13172–13177. Copyright (2002) National Academy of Sciences, U.S.A

Figure 12.42 - Adapted from Figure 1 in: Grossberg, S., and Pearson, L. (2008). Laminar cortical dynamics of cognitive and motor working memory, sequence learning and performance: Toward a unified theory of how the cerebral cortex works. *Psychological Review*, 115, 677–732.

Figure 12.43 - Adapted from Figure 2 in: Grossberg, S., and Pearson, L. (2008). Laminar cortical dynamics of cognitive and motor working memory, sequence learning and performance: Toward a unified theory of how the cerebral cortex works. *Psychological Review*, 115, 677–732.

Figure 12.44 - (left column, top row) Data adapted from Henson, R. N. A., Norris, D. G., Page, M. P. A., and Baddeley, A. D. (1996). Unchained memory: error patterns rule out chaining models of immediate serial recall. *Quarterly Journal of Experimental Psychology*,

49A, 80–115. Simulation adapted from Figure 7 in Grossberg, S., and Pearson, L. (2008). Laminar cortical dynamics of cognitive and motor working memory, sequence learning and performance: Toward a unified theory of how the cerebral cortex works. *Psychological Review*, 115, 677–732.

(right column, top row) Simulation reprinted from Figure 6 in Grossberg, S., and Pearson, L. (2008). Laminar cortical dynamics of cognitive and motor working memory, sequence learning and performance: Toward a unified theory of how the cerebral cortex works. *Psychological Review*, 115, 677–732. Data reprinted from Cowan, N., Nugent, L. D., Elliott, E. M., Ponomarev, I., and Saults, J. S. (1999). The role of attention in the development of short-term memory: Age differences in the verbal span of apprehension. *Child Development*, 70, 1082–1097.

(left column, bottom row) Data adapted from Baddeley, A. D., and Hitch, G. J. (1974). Working memory. In Bower, G. H. (Ed.), *Recent Advances in Learning and Motivation* (Vol. 8), New York: Academic Press, and from Crannell, C. W., and Parrish, J. M. (1957). A comparison of immediate memory span for digits, letters and words. *The Journal of Psychology*, 44, 319–327. Simulation adapted from Figure 8a in Grossberg, S., and Pearson, L. (2008). Laminar cortical dynamics of cognitive and motor working memory, sequence learning and performance: Toward a unified theory of how the cerebral cortex works. *Psychological Review*, 115, 677–732.

(right column, bottom row) Data adapted from Murdock, B. B. (1961). The retention of individual items. *Journal of Experimental Psychology*, 62, 618–625. Simulation adapted from Figure 8c in Grossberg, S., and Pearson, L. (2008). Laminar cortical dynamics of cognitive and motor working memory, sequence learning and performance: Toward a unified theory of how the cerebral cortex works. *Psychological Review*, 115, 677–732.

Figure 12.45 - (left column) Simulationa adapted from Figure 17 in Grossberg, S., and Pearson, L. (2008). Laminar cortical dynamics of cognitive and motor working memory, sequence learning and performance: Toward a unified theory of how the cerebral cortex works. *Psychological Review*, 115, 677–732.

(right column) Data adapted from Tan, L., and Ward, J. A. (2000). A recency-based account of the primacy effect in free recall. *Journal of Experimental Psychology: Learning, Memory, and Cognition*, 26, 1589–1625. Simulation adapted from Figure 9 in Grossberg, S., and Pearson, L. (2008). Laminar cortical dynamics of cognitive and motor working memory, sequence learning and performance: Toward a unified theory of how the cerebral cortex works. *Psychological Review*, 115, 677–732.

Figure 12.46 - Adapted from Figure 2 in: Cohen, M.A., and Grossberg, S. (1986). Neural dynamics of speech and language coding: Developmental programs, perceptual grouping, and competition for short-term memory. *Human Neurobiology*, 5, 1–22.

Figure 12.47 - Reprinted from Figure 7 in: Grossberg, S. (2018). Desirability, availability, credit assignment, category learning, and attention: Cognitive-emotional and working memory dynamics of orbitofrontal, ventrolateral, and dorsolateral prefrontal cortices. *Brain and Neuroscience Advances*, May 8, 2018.

Figure 12.48 - Adapted from Figure 1 in Grossberg, S., and Myers, C.W. (2000) The resonant dynamics of speech perception: Interword integration and duration-dependent backward effects. *Psychological Review*, 107, 735–767.

Figure 12.49 - Adapted from Figure 3 in: Grossberg, S., and Myers, C.W. (2000) The resonant dynamics of speech perception: Interword integration and duration-dependent backward effects. *Psychological Review*, 107, 735–767.

Figure 12.50 - Adapted from Figure 4 in: Grossberg, S., and Myers, C.W. (2000) The resonant dynamics of speech perception: Interword integration and duration-dependent backward effects. *Psychological Review*, 107, 735–767.

Figure 12.51 - (left column) author created

(right column) Adapted from Figure 11 in Grossberg, S., and Myers, C.W. (2000) The resonant dynamics of speech perception: Interword integration and duration-dependent backward effects. *Psychological Review*, 107, 735–767.

Figure 12.52 - Adapted from Figure 3 in: Grossberg, S., and Kazerounian, S. (2011). Laminar cortical dynamics of conscious speech perception: A neural model of phonemic restoration using subsequent context in noise. *Journal of the Acoustical Society of America*, 130, 440–460.

Figure 12.53 - Adapted from Figure 5 in: Grossberg, S., and Kazerounian, S. (2011). Laminar cortical dynamics of conscious speech perception: A neural model of phonemic restoration using subsequent context in noise. *Journal of the Acoustical Society of America*, 130, 440–460.

Figure 12.54 - Adapted from Figure 6 in: Grossberg, S., and Kazerounian, S. (2011). Laminar cortical dynamics of conscious speech perception: A neural model of phonemic restoration using subsequent context in noise. *Journal of the Acoustical Society of America*, 130, 440–460.

Figure 12.55 - Adapted from Figure 7 in: Grossberg, S., and Kazerounian, S. (2011). Laminar cortical dynamics of conscious speech perception: A neural model of phonemic restoration using subsequent context in noise. *Journal of the Acoustical Society of America*, 130, 440–460.

Figure 12.56 - Adapted from Figure 18 in: Grossberg, S., and Pearson, L. (2008). Laminar cortical dynamics of cognitive and motor working memory, sequence learning and performance: Toward a unified theory of how the cerebral cortex works. *Psychological Review*, 115, 677–732.

Figure 12.57 - Adapted from Figure 1 in: Silver, M.R., Grossberg, S., Bullock, D., Histed, M.H., and Miller, E.K. (2011). A neural model of sequential movement planning and control of eye movements: Item-order-rank working memory and saccade selection by the supplementary eye fields. *Neural Networks*, 26, 29–58.

Figure 12.58 - Adapted from Figure 2 in: Brown, J.W., Bullock, D., and Grossberg, S. (2004). How laminar frontal cortex and basal ganglia circuits interact to control planned and reactive saccades. *Neural Networks*, 17, 471–510.

Figure 12.59 - Adapted from Figures 1 and 3 in: Brown, J.W., Bullock, D., and Grossberg, S. (2004). How laminar frontal cortex and basal ganglia circuits interact to control planned and reactive saccades. *Neural Networks*, 17, 471–510.

Figure 12.60 - Data adapted from: Averbeck, B. B., Chafee, M. V., Crowe, D. A., and Georopoulos, A. P. (2003). Neural activity in prefrontal cortex during copying geometrical shapes: I. Single cells encode shape, sequence, and metric parameters. *Experimental Brain Research*, 150, 127–141;

and Figure 3a in: Isoda, M., and Tanji, J. (2002). Cellular activity in the supplementary eye field during sequential performance of multiple saccades. *Journal of Neurophysiology*, 88, 3541–3545.-

Figure 12.61 – author created

Figure 12.62 - Adapted from Figure 14c in: Silver, M.R., Grossberg, S., Bullock, D., Histed, M.H., and Miller, E.K. (2011). A neural model of sequential movement planning and control of eye movements: Item-order-rank working memory and saccade selection by the supplementary eye fields. *Neural Networks*, 26, 29–58.

Figure 12.63 - Adapted from Figures 14a and 14b in: Silver, M.R., Grossberg, S., Bullock, D., Histed, M.H., and Miller, E.K. (2011). A neural model of sequential movement planning and control of eye movements: Item-order-rank working memory and saccade selection by the supplementary eye fields. *Neural Networks*, 26, 29–58.

Figure 12.64 - Reprinted from Figure 2a in: Munoz-Lopez, M. M., Mohedano-Moriano, A., and Insausti, R. (2010) Anatomical pathways for auditory memory in primates. *Frontiers in Neuroanatomy*, October 8, 2010.

Figure 12.65 – (Left column top image) Adapted from Figure 1a in: Boardman, I., Grossberg, S., Myers, C., and Cohen, M. (1999). Neural dynamics of perceptual order and context effects for variable-rate speech syllables. *Perception and Psychophysics*, 6, 1477–1500.

(Left column bottom image) Adapted from Figure 9 in: Grossberg, S., Boardman, I., and Cohen, C. (1997). Neural dynamics of variable-rate speech categorization. *Journal of Experimental Psychology: Human Perception and Performance*, 23, 418–503.

(Right column image) Data reprinted from Repp, B. H. (1980). A range-frequency effect on perception of silence in speech. Status Report on Speech Research SR-6, pp. 151–165. New Haven, CT: Haskins Laboratories.

Figure 12.66 - (left column) author created

(right column) Adapted from Figure 1 in Schwab, E. C., Sawusch, J. R., and Nusbaum, H. C. (1981). The role of second formant transitions in the stop-semivowel distinction. *Perception and Psychophysics*, 21, 121–128.

Figure 12.67 – author created

Figure 12.68 - Adapted from Figures 5 and 6 in: Grossberg, S., Boardman, I., and Cohen, C. (1997). Neural dynamics of variable-rate speech categorization. *Journal of Experimental Psychology: Human Perception and Performance*, 23, 418–503.

Figure 12.69 - Data in (a) adapted from Figure 2A and in (b) adapted from Figure 1A in: Schvaneveldt, R. W., and McDonald, J. E. (1981). Semantic context and the encoding of words: Evidence for two modes of stimulus analysis. *Journal of Experimental Psychology: Human Perception and Performance*, 7, 673–687.

Figure 12.70 - Reprinted from Figure 5 in: Grossberg, S., and Stone, G.O. (1986). Neural dynamics of word recognition and recall: Attentional priming, learning, and resonance. *Psychological Review*, 93, 46–74.

Figure 12.71 - Reprinted from: Underwood. B. J., and Freund, J. S. (1970). Word frequency and short term recognition memory. *American Journal of Psychology*, 83, 343–35.

Chapter 13

Figure 13.1 - Reprinted from Figure 36 in: Grossberg, S. (2017). Towards solving the Hard Problem of Consciousness: The varieties of brain resonances and the conscious experiences that they support. *Neural Networks*, 87, 38–95.

Figure 13.2 – author created

Figure 13.3 - Adapted from Figure 4 in: Barbas, H. (1995). Anatomic basis of cognitive-emotional interactions in the primate prefrontal cortex. *Neuroscience and Biobehavioral Reviews*, 19, 499–510.

Figure 13.4 – author created

Figure 13.5 – author created

Figure 13.6 - (left column) The data in the figure were derived from: Smith, M. C., Coleman, S. R., and Gormezano, I. (1969). Classical Conditioning of the rabbit's nictitating membrane response at backward, simultaneous, and forward CS-US intervals. *Journal of Comparative and Physiological Psychology*, 69, 226–231, and Schneiderman, N., and Gormezano, I. (1964). Conditioning of the nictitating membrane response of the rabbit as a function of the CS-US interval. *Journal of Comparative and Physiological Psychology*, 57, 188–195.

(right column) Adapted from Figure 2 in: Grossberg, S., and Levine, D.S. (1987). Neural dynamics of attentionally modulated Pavlovian conditioning: Blocking, inter-stimulus interval, and secondary reinforcement. *Applied Optics*, 26, 5015–5030.

Figure 13.7 – author created

Figure 13.8 – author created

Figure 13.9 – author created

Figure 13.10 – author created

Figure 13.11 - Adapted from Figure 5 in: Grossberg, S., and Levine, D.S. (1987). Neural dynamics of attentionally modulated Pavlovian conditioning: Blocking, inter-stimulus interval, and secondary reinforcement. *Applied Optics*, 26, 5015–5030.

Figure 13.12 - (left column) Adapted from Figure 6 in: Grossberg, S., and Levine, D.S. (1987). Neural dynamics of attentionally modulated Pavlovian conditioning: Blocking, inter-stimulus interval, and secondary reinforcement. *Applied Optics*, 26, 5015–5030.

(right column) Adapted from Figure 9 in: Grossberg, S., and Levine, D.S. (1987). Neural dynamics of attentionally modulated Pavlovian conditioning: Blocking, inter-stimulus interval, and secondary reinforcement. *Applied Optics*, 26, 5015–5030.

Figure 13.13 - (top row) Adapted from Figure 10 in Grossberg, S., and Levine, D.S. (1987). Neural dynamics of attentionally modulated Pavlovian conditioning: Blocking, inter-stimulus interval, and secondary reinforcement. *Applied Optics*, 26, 5015–5030.

(bottom row) Adapted from Figure 12 in Grossberg, S., and Levine, D.S. (1987). Neural dynamics of attentionally modulated Pavlovian conditioning: Blocking, inter-stimulus interval, and secondary reinforcement. *Applied Optics*, 26, 5015–5030.

Figure 13.14 – author created

Figure 13.15 - Neural network image adapted from Figure 11 in: Buonomano, D. V., Baxter, D. A., and Byrne, J. H. (1990). Small networks of empirically derived adaptive elements simulate some higher-order features of classical conditioning. *Neural Networks*, 3, 507–523.

Figure 13.16 - (left column) Adapted from Figure 3 in Grossberg, S. (1982). A psychophysiological theory of reinforcement, drive, motivation, and attention. *Journal of Theoretical Neurobiology*, 1, 286–369.

(right column) Adapted from Figure 4 in Grossberg, S. (1982). A psychophysiological theory of reinforcement, drive, motivation, and attention. *Journal of Theoretical Neurobiology*, 1, 286–369.

Figure 13.17 - Both images are adapted from Figure 5 in Grossberg, S. (1982). A psychophysiological theory of reinforcement, drive, motivation, and attention. *Journal of Theoretical Neurobiology*, 1, 286–369.

Figure 13.18 - Circuits (a), (b), and(d) adapted from Figure 6 in Grossberg, S. (1982). A psychophysiological theory of reinforcement, drive, motivation, and attention. *Journal of Theoretical Neurobiology*, 1, 286–369.

Circuit (e), adapted from Figure 7 in Grossberg, S. (1982). A psychophysiological theory of reinforcement, drive, motivation, and attention. *Journal of Theoretical Neurobiology*, 1, 286–369.

Figure 13.19 - (left column, top row) Adapted from Figure 8 in Grossberg, S. (1982). A psychophysiological theory of reinforcement, drive, motivation, and attention. *Journal of Theoretical Neurobiology*, 1, 286–369.

(bottom row) Adapted from Figurs 9 and 11 in Grossberg, S. (1982). A psychophysiological theory of reinforcement, drive, motivation, and attention. *Journal of Theoretical Neurobiology*, 1, 286–369.

(right column, top row) Redrawn from Figure 11 in Grossberg, S. (1982). A psychophysiological theory of reinforcement, drive, motivation, and attention. *Journal of Theoretical Neurobiology*, 1, 286–369.

Figure 13.20 - (top image) Adapted from Figure 5 in Grossberg, S. (1969). Some networks that can learn, remember, and reproduce any number of complicated space-time patterns, I. *Journal of Mathematics and Mechanics*, 19, 53–91.

(bottom image) Adapted from Figure 13 in Grossberg, S. (1974). Classical and instrumental learning by neural networks. In Rosen, R. and F. Snell, F. (Eds.) *Progress in Theoretical Biology*. New York: Academic Press, pp. 51–141.

Figure 13.21 - (left column) Data on which the figure is based are in Stein, P. S. (1971). Intersegmental coordination of swimmeret motoneuron activity in crayfish. *Journal of Neurophysiology*, 34, 310–318.

(right column) Reprinted from http://www.scholarpedia.org/article/File:Rnn-songbird-pattern-generator.png. Figure based upon data in Hahnloser, R. H. R., Kozhevnikov, A. A., and Fee, M. S. (2002). An ultra-sparse code underlies the generation of neural sequences in a songbird. *Nature*, 419, 65–70.

Figure 13.22 – author created

Figure 13.23 - (left column) Adapted from Figure 24 in Grossberg, S. (2013). Recurrent neural networks, *Scholarpedia,* http://www.scholarpedia.org/article/Recurrent_neural_networks

(right column) Adapted from Figure 25 in Grossberg, S. (2013). Recurrent neural networks, *Scholarpedia,*

http://www.scholarpedia.org/article/Recurrent_neural_networks

Figure 13.24 – author created

Figure 13.25 – author created

Figure 13.26 – author created

Figure 13.27 – author created

Figure 13.28 – author created

Figure 13.29 – author created

Figure 13.30 – author created

Figure 13.31 – author created

Figure 13.32 - Data adapted from Reynolds, G. S. (1968). *A Primer of Operant Conditioning.* Glenview, Ill.: Scott, Foresman and Co.

Figure 13.33 – author created

Figure 13.34 – author created

Figure 13.35 – author created

Figure 13.36 – author created

Figure 13.37 – author created

Figure 13.38 – author created

Figure 13.39 – author created

Figure 13.40 – author created

Figure 13.41 – author created

Figure 13.42 – author created

Figure 13.43 – author created

Figure 13.44 - Reprinted from Figure 6.1 in: Damasio, A. (1999). *The Feeling of What Happens: Body and Emotion in the Making of Consciousness.* New York: Houghton Mifflin Harcourt.

Chapter 14

Figure 14.1 - Roelf J Cruz-Rizzolo, Miguel AX De Lima, Edilson Ervolino, José A de Oliveira and Claudio A

Casatti (2011) Cyto-, myelo- and chemoarchitecture of the prefrontal cortex of the Cebus monkey BMC Neuroscience 2011.

Figure 14.2 - Reprinted from Figure 1 in: Grossberg, S. (2018). Desirability, availability, credit assignment, category learning, and attention: Cognitive-emotional and working memory dynamics of orbitofrontal, ventrolateral, and dorsolateral prefrontal cortices. *Brain and Neuroscience Advances*, May 8, 2018.

Figure 14.3 - Reprinted from Figures 1 and 7c in: Dranias, M., Grossberg, S., and Bullock, D. (2008). Dopaminergic and non-dopaminergic value systems in conditioning and outcome-specific revaluation. *Brain Research*, 1238, 239–287.

Figure 14.4 - Reprinted from Figures 4, 1, and 2, respectively, in: Brown, J., Bullock, D., and Grossberg, S. (1999). How the basal ganglia use parallel excitatory and inhibitory learning pathways to selectively respond to unexpected rewarding cues. *Journal of Neuroscience*, 19, 10502–10511.

Figure 14.5 - Reprinted from Figure 1a in: Buschman, T. J., and Miller, E. K. (2007). Top-down versus bottom-up control of attention in the prefrontal and posterior parietal cortices. *Science*, 315, 1860–1862.

Figure 14.6 - Reprinted from Figure 1a in: Grossberg, S., and Huang, T.-R. (2009). ARTSCENE: A neural system for natural scene classification. *Journal of Vision*, 9, 1–19.

Figure 14.7 - Reprinted from Figure 1b in: Grossberg, S., and Huang, T.-R. (2009). ARTSCENE: A neural system for natural scene classification. *Journal of Vision*, 9, 1–19.

Figure 14.8 - Reprinted from Figure 4 in: Huang, T.-R., and Grossberg, S. (2010). Cortical dynamics of contextually cued attentive visual learning and search: Spatial and object evidence accumulation. *Psychological Review*, 117, 1080–1112.

Figure 14.9 - Reprinted from Figure 16 in: Grossberg, S. (2018). Desirability, availability, credit assignment, category learning, and attention: Cognitive-emotional and working memory dynamics of orbitofrontal, ventrolateral, and dorsolateral prefrontal cortices. *Brain and Neuroscience Advances*, May 8, 2018.

Chapter 15

Figure 15.1 - Adapted from Figure 1 in: Franklin, D. J., and Grossberg, S. (2017). A neural model of normal and abnormal learning and memory consolidation: Adaptively timed conditioning, hippocampus, amnesia, neurotrophins, and consciousness. *Cognitive, Affective, and Behavioral Neuroscience*, 17, 24–76.

Figure 15.2 - Adapted from Figure 2 in: Franklin, D. J., and Grossberg, S. (2017). A neural model of normal and abnormal learning and memory consolidation: Adaptively timed conditioning, hippocampus, amnesia, neurotrophins, and consciousness. *Cognitive, Affective, and Behavioral Neuroscience*, 17, 24–76.

Figure 15.3 - Adapted from Figures 7, 5b, 5c, and 5d in that order in: Grossberg, S. and Schmajuk, N.A. (1987). Neural dynamics of attentionally-modulated Pavlovian conditioning: Conditioned reinforcement, inhibition, and opponent processing. *Psychobiology*, **15**, 195–240.

Figure 15.4 - Left and right images from:

Smith, M. C. (1968). CS-US interval and US intensity in classical conditioning of the rabbit's nictitating membrane response. *Journal of Comparative and Physiological Psychology*, 3, 679–687, and

Millenson, J. R., Kehoe, E. J., and Gormenzano, 1. (1977). Classical conditioning of the rabbit's nictitating membrane response under fixed and mixed CS-US intervals. *Learning and Motivation*, 8, 351–366

Figure 15.5 - Adapted from Figure 11 in: Grossberg, S. and Schmajuk, N.A. (1987). Neural dynamics of attentionally-modulated Pavlovian conditioning: Conditioned reinforcement, inhibition, and opponent processing. *Psychobiology*, **15**, 195–240.

Figure 15.6 - Adapted from Figure 26 in: Grossberg, S., and Merrill, J.W.L. (1992). A neural network model of adaptively timed reinforcement learning and hippocampal dynamics. *Cognitive Brain Research*, 1, 3–38.

Figure 15.7 – author created

Figure 15.8 – author created

Figure 15.9 – author created

Figure 15.10 - Adapted from Figure 3 in: Grossberg, S. and Schmajuk, N.A. (1987). Neural dynamics of attentionally-modulated Pavlovian conditioning: Conditioned reinforcement, inhibition, and opponent processing. *Psychobiology*, **15**, 195–240.

Figure 15.11 – author created

Figure 15.12 - Adapted from Figure 4 in: Grossberg, S. and Schmajuk, N.A. (1987). Neural dynamics of attentionally-modulated Pavlovian conditioning: Conditioned reinforcement, inhibition, and opponent processing. *Psychobiology*, **15**, 195–240.

Figure 15.13 – author created

Figure 15.14 – author created

Figure 15.15 – author created

Figure 15.16 - Adapted from Figure 33 in: Grossberg, S., and Merrill, J.W.L. (1992). A neural network model of adaptively timed reinforcement learning and hippocampal dynamics. *Cognitive Brain Research*, 1, 3–38.

Figure 15.17 – author created

Figure 15.18 – author created

Figure 15.19 - Adapted from Figure 30 in: Grossberg, S., and Merrill, J.W.L. (1992). A neural network model of adaptively timed reinforcement learning and hippocampal dynamics. *Cognitive Brain Research*, 1, 3–38.

Figure 15.20 - Reprinted from Figure 6 in: Grossberg, S., and Merrill, J. W. L. (1996). The hippocampus and cerebellum in adaptively timed learning, recognition, and movement. *Journal of Cognitive Neuroscience*, 8, 257–277.

Figure 15.21 - Reprinted from: Becker, E. B. E., and Stoodley, C. J. (2013). Autism spectrum disorder and the cerebellum. *International Review of Neurobiology*, 113, 1–34.td

Figure 15.22 - Adapted from Figure 3 in: Baylor, D. A., and Hodgkin, A. L. (1974). Changes in time scale and sensitivity in turtle photoreceptors. *The Journal of Physiology*, 242, 729–758.

Figure 15.23 - Reprinted from Figure 6 in: Fiala, J.C., Grossberg, S., and Bullock, D. (1996). Metabotropic glutamate receptor activation in cerebellar Purkinje cells as substrate for adaptive timing of the classically conditioned eye blink response. *Journal of Neuroscience*, 16, 3760–3774.

Figure 15.24 - (a) is reprinted from Figure 1B in: Perrett, S. P., Ruiz, B. P., Mauk, M. D., (1993). Cerebellar cortex lesions disrupt learning-dependent timing of conditioned eyelid responses. *The Journal of Neuroscience*, 13, 1708–1718.

(b) is reprinted from Figure 12 in: Bullock, D., Fiala, J. C., and Grossberg, S. (1994). A neural model of timed response learning in the cerebellum. *Neural Networks*, 7, 1101–1114.

Figure 15.25 - (a) and (b) reprinted from Figures 8 and 9, respectively, in: Bullock, D., Fiala, J. C., and Grossberg, S. (1994). A neural model of timed response learning in the cerebellum. *Neural Networks*, 7, 1101–1114.

Figure 15.26 - Expanded adaptation of Figure 1 in: Grossberg, S., and Kishnan, D. (2018). Neural dynamics of autistic repetitive behaviors and Fragile X syndrome: Basal ganglia movement gating and mGluR-modulated adaptively timed learning. *Frontiers in Psychology, Psychopathology*.

Figure 15.27 - Adapted from Figure 4 in: Brown, J., Bullock, D., and Grossberg, S. (1999). How the basal ganglia use parallel excitatory and inhibitory learning pathways to selectively respond to unexpected rewarding cues. *Journal of Neuroscience,* 19, 10502–10511.

Figure 15.28 - Data reprinted from Figure 2 in: Schultz, W. (1998). Predictive reward signal of dopamine neurons. *Journal of Neurophysiology,* 80, 1-27. Simulation reprinted from Figure 1 in: Brown, J., Bullock, D., and Grossberg, S. (1999). How the basal ganglia use parallel excitatory and inhibitory learning pathways to selectively respond to unexpected rewarding cues. *Journal of Neuroscience,* 19, 10502–10511.

Figure 15.29 - Adapted from Figure 4 in: Brown, J., Bullock, D., and Grossberg, S. (1999). How the basal ganglia use parallel excitatory and inhibitory learning pathways to selectively respond to unexpected rewarding cues. *Journal of Neuroscience,* 19, 10502–10511.

Figure 15.30 - Adapted from Figure 4 in: Brown, J., Bullock, D., and Grossberg, S. (1999). How the basal ganglia use parallel excitatory and inhibitory learning pathways to selectively respond to unexpected rewarding cues. *Journal of Neuroscience,* 19, 10502–10511.

Figure 15.31 - Adapted from Figure 5 in: Brown, J., Bullock, D., and Grossberg, S. (1999). How the basal ganglia use parallel excitatory and inhibitory learning pathways to selectively respond to unexpected rewarding cues. *Journal of Neuroscience,* 19, 10502–10511.

Figure 15.32 - Adapted from Figure 4 in: Brown, J., Bullock, D., and Grossberg, S. (1999). How the basal ganglia use parallel excitatory and inhibitory learning pathways to selectively respond to unexpected rewarding cues. *Journal of Neuroscience,* 19, 10502–10511.

Figure 15.33 - Adapted from Figure 31.5 in: Squire, L. R., Berb, D., Bloom, F., Du Lac, S., Ghosh, A., and Spitzer, N. (Eds). *Fundamental Neuroscience,* Third Edition. Amsterdam: Elsevier.

Figure 15.34 - Adapted from Figure 31.5 in: Squire, L. R., Berb, D., Bloom, F., Du Lac, S., Ghosh, A., and Spitzer, N. (Eds). *Fundamental Neuroscience,* Third Edition. Amsterdam: Elsevier.

Figure 15.35 - Reprinted from Figures 2 and 7, respectively, in: Pribe, C., Grossberg, S., and Cohen, M.A. (1997). Neural control of interlimb oscillations, II: Biped and quadruped gaits and bifurcations. *Biological Cybernetics,* 77, 141–152.

Figure 15.36 - Reprinted from Figures 2a and 7, respectively, in: Gancarz, G., and Grossberg, G. (1998). A neural model of the saccade generator in the reticular formation. *Neural Networks,* 11, 1159–1174.

Figure 15.37 - Reprinted from Figure 4 in: Gancarz, G., and Grossberg, G. (1998). A neural model of the saccade generator in the reticular formation. *Neural Networks,* 11, 1159–1174.

Figure 15.38 - Reprinted from Figures 4 and 1, respectively, in: Carpenter, G.A., and Grossberg, S. (1985). A neural theory of circadian rhythms: Split rhythms, after-effects, and motivational interactions. *Journal of Theoretical Biology,* 113, 163–223.

Figure 15.39 - Reprinted from Figure 8 in: Dranias, M., Grossberg, S., and Bullock, D. (2008). Dopaminergic and non-dopaminergic value systems in conditioning and outcome-specific revaluation. *Brain Research,* 1238, 239–287.

Figure 15.40 - Reprinted from Figure 4 in: Brown, J.W., Bullock, D., and Grossberg, S. (2004). How laminar frontal cortex and basal ganglia circuits interact to control planned and reactive saccades. *Neural Networks,* 17, 471–510.

Chapter 16

Figure 16.1 - O'Keefe, J., and Dostrovsky, J. (1971). The hippocampus as a spatial map. Preliminary evidence from unit activity in the freely-moving rat. *Brain Research,* 34, 171–175.

Figure 16.2 - Reprinted from: Wilson, M. A., and McNaughton, B. L. (1993). Dynamics of the hippocampal ensemble code for space. *Science,* 261, 1055–1058.

Figure 16.3 - Reprinted from Figure 1 in: Moser, E. L., Kropff, E., and Moser, M. B. (2008). Place cells, grid cells, and the brain's spatial representation system. *Annual Review of Neuroscience,* 31, 69–89.

Figure 16.4 - Figure 4, from: Petrantonakis PC and Poirazi P (2014) A compressed sensing perspective of hippocampal function. *Front. Syst. Neurosci.* 8:141

Figure 16.5 - Adapted from Figure 1 in: Grossberg, S., and Pilly, P. K. (2014). Coordinated learning of grid cell and place cell spatial and temporal properties: multiple scales, attention, and oscillations. *Philosophical Transactions of the Royal Society B.,* 369, 20120524.

Figure 16.6 - Adapted from Figure 2 in: Mhatre, H., Gorchetchnikov, A., and Grossberg, S. (2012). Grid cell hexagonal patterns formed by fast self-organized learning within entorhinal cortex. *Hippocampus,* 22, 320–334.

Figure 16.7 – author created

Figure 16.8 - Rerpinted from Figure 2c in: Sargolini, F., Fyhn, M., Hafting, T., McNaughton, B. L., Witter, M. P., Moser, M-B., and Moser, E. I. (2006). Conjunctive representation of position, direction, and velocity in entorhinal cortex. *Science*, 312, 758–762.

Figure 16.9 - Adapted from Figure 4 in: Mhatre, H., Gorchetchnikov, A., and Grossberg, S. (2012). Grid cell hexagonal patterns formed by fast self-organized learning within entorhinal cortex. *Hippocampus*, 22, 320–334.

Figure 16.10 - Adapted from Figure 1 in: Mhatre, H., Gorchetchnikov, A., and Grossberg, S. (2012). Grid cell hexagonal patterns formed by fast self-organized learning within entorhinal cortex. *Hippocampus*, 22, 320–334.

Figure 16.11 – author created

Figure 16.12 - Reprinted from Figure 5 in: Mhatre, H., Gorchetchnikov, A., and Grossberg, S. (2012). Grid cell hexagonal patterns formed by fast self-organized learning within entorhinal cortex. *Hippocampus*, 22, 320–334.

Figure 16.13 - Reprinted from Figures 8 and 7, respectively, in: Mhatre, H., Gorchetchnikov, A., and Grossberg, S. (2012). Grid cell hexagonal patterns formed by fast self-organized learning within entorhinal cortex. *Hippocampus*, 22, 320–334.

Figure 16.14 – author created

Figure 16.15 – author created

Figure 16.16 - Adapted from Figure 2 in: Gorchetchnikov, A., and Grossberg, S. (2007). Space, time, and learning in the hippocampus: How fine spatial and temporal scales are expanded into population codes for behavioral control. *Neural Networks*, 20, 182–193.

Figure 16.17 - Adapted from Figure 4 in: Pilly, P. K., and Grossberg, S. (2012). How do spatial learning and memory occur in the brain? Coordinated learning of entorhinal grid cells and hippocampal place cells. *Journal of Cognitive Neuroscience*, 24, 1031–1054.

Figure 16.18 - Reprinted from Figure 2 in: Pilly, P. K., and Grossberg, S. (2013). Spiking neurons in a hierarchical self-organizing map model can learn to develop spatial and temporal properties of entorhinal grid cells and hippocampal place cells. *PLoS. One*, 8, e0060599.

Figure 16.19 - Adapted from: Hafting, T., Fyhn, M., Molden, S., Moser, M. B., and Moser, E. I. (2005). Microstructure of a spatial map in the entorhinal cortex. *Nature*, 436, 801–806.

Figure 16.20 - Adapted from Figure 1 in: Garden, D. L. F., Dodson, P. D., O'Donnell, C., White, M. D., and Nolan, M. F. (2008). Tuning of synaptic integration in the medial entorhinal cortex to the organization of grid cell firing fields. *Neuron*, 60, 875–889.

Figure 16.21 - Adapted from Figure 1 in: Giocomo, L. M., Zilli, E., Fransen, E., Hasselmo, and M. E. (2007). Temporal frequency of subthreshold oscillations scales with entorhinal grid cell field spacing. *Science*, 315, 1719–1722.

Figure 16.22 - Adapted from Figure 8 in: Navratilova, Z., Giocomo, L. M., Fellous, J. M., Hasselmo, M. E., and McNaughton, B. L. (2012). Phase precession and variable spatial scaling in a periodic attractor map model of medial entorhinal grid cells with realistic afterspike dynamics. *Hippocampus*, 22, 772–789.

Figure 16.23 - Adapted from Figure 2 in: Grossberg, S., and Pilly, P.K. (2012). How entorhinal grid cells may learn multiple spatial scales from a dorsoventral gradient of cell response rates in a self-organizing map. *PLoS Computational Biology* 8(10): e1002648.

Figure 16.24 - Images adapted from Figures 1b and 1c in: Grossberg, S., and Pilly, P.K. (2012). How entorhinal grid cells may learn multiple spatial scales from a dorsoventral gradient of cell response rates in a self-organizing map. PLoS Computational Biology 8(10): e1002648.

Figure 16.25 – author created

Figure 16.26 - Adapted from Figure 4 in: Grossberg, S., and Pilly, P.K. (2012). How entorhinal grid cells may learn multiple spatial scales from a dorsoventral gradient of cell response rates in a self-organizing map. *PLoS Computational Biology* 8(10): e1002648.

Figure 16.27 - Adapted from Figure 5 in: Grossberg, S., and Pilly, P.K. (2012). How entorhinal grid cells may learn multiple spatial scales from a dorsoventral gradient of cell response rates in a self-organizing map. *PLoS Computational Biology* 8(10): e1002648.

Figure 16.28 - Adapted from Figure 6 in: Grossberg, S., and Pilly, P.K. (2012). How entorhinal grid cells may learn multiple spatial scales from a dorsoventral gradient of cell response rates in a self-organizing map. *PLoS Computational Biology* 8(10): e1002648.

Figure 16.29 - Adapted from Figure 15 in: Grossberg, S., and Pilly, P.K. (2012). How entorhinal grid cells may learn multiple spatial scales from a dorsoventral gradient of cell response rates in a self-organizing map. *PLoS Computational Biology* 8(10): e1002648.

Figure 16.30 - Data in (a) and (b) adapted from Figure 3b and 3c in: Hafting, T., Fyhn, M., Molden, S., Moser, M. B., and Moser, E. I. (2005). Microstructure of a spatial map in the entorhinal cortex. *Nature*, 436, 801–806. Simulations adapted from Figures 5c-5f in: Pilly, P. K., and Grossberg, S. (2012). How do spatial learning and memory occur in the brain? Coordinated learning of entorhinal grid cells and hippocampal place cells. *Journal of Cognitive Neuroscience,* 24, 1031–1054.

Figure 16.31 - Data in (a) adapted from Figures 4 and 5a in: Henriksen, E. J., Colgin, L. L., Barnes, C. A., Witter, M. P., Moser, M.-B., and Moser, E. I. (2010). Spatial representation along the proximodistal axis of CA1. *Neuron,* 68, 127-137. Simulations adapted from Figures 5a – 5d in: Pilly, P. K., and Grossberg, S. (2013). Spiking neurons in a hierarchical self-organizing map model can learn to develop spatial and temporal properties of entorhinal grid cells and hippocampal place cells. *PLoS. One,* 8, e0060599.

Figure 16.32 - Data in (a) from Figure 3 in: Wills, T. J., Cacucci, F., Burgess, N., O'Keefe, J. (2010). Development of the hippocampal cognitive map in preweanling rats. *Science,* 328, 1573–1576.

Data from (b) and (c) in Figures 2 and 3 in: Langston, R. F., Ainge, J. A., Couey, J. J., Canto, C. B., Bjerknes, T. L., and Witter, M. P. (2010). Development of the spatial representation system in the rat. *Science,* 328, 1576-1580. Simulations adapted from Figures 13d and 13e in: Pilly, P. K., and Grossberg, S. (2013). Spiking neurons in a hierarchical self-organizing map model can learn to develop spatial and temporal properties of entorhinal grid cells and hippocampal place cells. *PLoS. One,* 8, e0060599.

Figure 16.33 - Data in (a) from Figure 3A in: Wills, T. J., Cacucci, F., Burgess, N., O'Keefe, J. (2010). Development of the hippocampal cognitive map in preweanling rats. *Science,* 328, 1573–1576. Simulations adapted from Figures 14c and 114d in: Pilly, P. K., and Grossberg, S. (2013). Spiking neurons in a hierarchical self-organizing map model can learn to develop spatial and temporal properties of entorhinal grid cells and hippocampal place cells. *PLoS. One,* 8, e0060599.

Figure 16.34 - Simulations adapted from Figure 15 in: Pilly, P. K., and Grossberg, S. (2013). Spiking neurons in a hierarchical self-organizing map model can learn to develop spatial and temporal properties of entorhinal grid cells and hippocampal place cells. *PLoS. One,* 8, e0060599.

Figure 16.35 - Data adapted from: Stensola, H., Stensola, T., Solstad, T., Frøland, K., Moser, M.-B., and Moser, E. I. (2012). The entorhinal grid map is discretized. *Nature,* 492, 72–78. Simulations adapted from Figures 4B-4G in: Pilly, P.K., and Grossberg, S. (2014). How does the modular organization of entorhinal grid cells develop? *Frontiers in Human Neuroscience,* doi:10.3389/fnhum.2014.0037,

Figure 16.36 - Adapted from Figure 1 in: Mhatre, H., Gorchetchnikov, A., and Grossberg, S. (2012). Grid cell hexagonal patterns formed by fast self-organized learning within entorhinal cortex. *Hippocampus,* 22, 320–334.

Figure 16.37 - Data adapted from Figure 2a in: Bonnevie, T., Dunn, B., Fyhn, M., Hafting, T., Derdikman, D., Kubie, J. L., Roudi, Y., Moser, E. I., and Moser, M.-B. (2013). Grid cells require excitatory drive from the hippocampus. *Nature Neuroscience,* 16, 309–319.

Figure 16.38 - Data adapted from Figure 2a in: Bonnevie, T., Dunn, B., Fyhn, M., Hafting, T., Derdikman, D., Kubie, J. L., Roudi, Y., Moser, E. I., and Moser, M.-B. (2013). Grid cells require excitatory drive from the hippocampus. *Nature Neuroscience,* 16, 309–319.

Figure 16.39 - Data in (A) adapted from Figure 1C in: Brandon, M. P., Bogaard, A. R., Libby, C. P., Connerney, M. A., Gupta, K., Hasselmo, and M. E. (2011). Reduction of theta rhythm dissociates grid cell spatial periodicity from directional tuning. *Science,* 332, 595–599. Data in (B) and (C) adapted from Figures 1C, 1D, and 2B-2D in: Koenig, J., Linder, A. N., Leutgeb, J. K., and Leutgeb, S. (2011). The spatial periodicity of grid cells is not sustained during reduced theta oscillations. *Science,* 332, 592–595.

Figure 16.40 - Data in (a) adapted from Figure 1C in: Brandon, M. P., Bogaard, A. R., Libby, C. P., Connerney, M. A., Gupta, K., Hasselmo, and M. E. (2011). Reduction of theta rhythm dissociates grid cell spatial periodicity from directional tuning. *Science,* 332, 595–599.

Data in (b) adapted from Figure 2B in: Koenig, J., Linder, A. N., Leutgeb, J. K., and Leutgeb, S. (2011). The spatial periodicity of grid cells is not sustained during reduced theta oscillations. *Science,* 332, 592–595. Simulations in (c) - (e) adapted from Figures 7 (c) - (e) in: Grossberg, S., and Pilly, P. K. (2014). Coordinated learning of grid cell and place cell spatial and temporal properties: multiple scales, attention, and oscillations. *Philosophical Transactions of the Royal Society B.,* 369, 20120524.

Figure 16.41 – author created

Figure 16.42 - Reprinted from Figure 2 in: Gnadt, W., and Grossberg, S. (2008) SOVEREIGN: An autonomous neural system for incrementally learning planned action sequences to navigate towards a rewarded goal. *Neural Networks,* 21, 699–758.

Figure 16.43 - Reprinted from Figure 5 in: Gnadt, W., and Grossberg, S. (2008) SOVEREIGN: An autonomous neural system for incrementally learning planned action sequences to navigate towards a rewarded goal. *Neural Networks,* 21, 699–758.

Figure 16.44 - Reprinted from Figure 10 in: Gnadt, W., and Grossberg, S. (2008) SOVEREIGN: An autonomous neural system for incrementally learning planned action sequences to navigate towards a rewarded goal. *Neural Networks*, 21, 699–758.

Figure 16.45 - Reprinted from Figure 12 in: Gnadt, W., and Grossberg, S. (2008) SOVEREIGN: An autonomous neural system for incrementally learning planned action sequences to navigate towards a rewarded goal. *Neural Networks*, 21, 699–758.

Figure 16.46 - Reprinted from Figures 17 and 18 in: Gnadt, W., and Grossberg, S. (2008) SOVEREIGN: An autonomous neural system for incrementally learning planned action sequences to navigate towards a rewarded goal. *Neural Networks*, 21, 699–758.

Figure 16.47 - Reprinted from Figure 20b in: Gnadt, W., and Grossberg, S. (2008) SOVEREIGN: An autonomous neural system for incrementally learning planned action sequences to navigate towards a rewarded goal. *Neural Networks*, 21, 699–758.

Figure 16.48 - Reprinted from Figure 1 in: Gnadt, W., and Grossberg, S. (2008) SOVEREIGN: An autonomous neural system for incrementally learning planned action sequences to navigate towards a rewarded goal. *Neural Networks*, 21, 699–758.

Figure 16.49 - Reprinted from Figure 16 in: Gnadt, W., and Grossberg, S. (2008) SOVEREIGN: An autonomous neural system for incrementally learning planned action sequences to navigate towards a rewarded goal. *Neural Networks*, 21, 699–758.

Figure 16.50 - Adapted from Figure 3 in: Diana, R. A., Yonelinas, A. P., and Ranganath, C. (2007). Imaging recollection and familiarity in the medial temporal lobe: A three-component model. *Trends in Cognitive Sciences*, 11. 379–386.

Chapter 17

Table 17.1 – no source cited

Figure 17.1 – Wikipedia

Figure 17.2 - Reprinted from Figure 16 in:

Grossberg, S. (1978). Communication, memory, and development. In Rosen, R. and Snell, F. (Eds.), *Progress in Theoretical Biology*, Volume 5. New York: Academic Press, pp. 183–232.

Adapted from data in: Wilby, O. K., and Webster, L. (1970a). Experimental studies on axial polarity in Hydra. *Journal of Embryology and Experimental Morphology*, 24, 595–613, and

Wilby, O. K., and Webster, L. (1970b). Studies on the transmission of hypostome inhibition in hydra. *Journal of Embryology and Experimental Morphology*, 24, 583–593, and

Wolpert, L., Hicklin, J., and Hornbruck, A. (1971). Positional information and pattern regulation in regeneration of hydra. *Symposia of the Society of Experimental Biology*, 25, 391–416 (1971).

Figure 17.3 - Redrawn from Figure 17 in: Grossberg, S. (1978). Communication, memory, and development. In Rosen, R. and Snell, F. (Eds.), *Progress in Theoretical Biology*, Volume 5. New York: Academic Press, pp. 183–232. Adapted from simulations in: Meinhardt, H., and Gierer, A. (1974). Applications of a theory of biological pattern formation based on lateral inhibition. *Journal of Cell Science*, 15, 321–346.

Figure 17.4 – author created

Figure 17.5 - *Principles of Life 2e* by David Hillis (9781464156410), concept 38.3

Figure 17.6 – author created

References

Aad, G. et al. (2012). Observation of a new particle in the search for the Standard Model Higgs boson with the ATLAS detector at the LHC. *Physics Letters B*, 716, 1–29.

Abbott, L. F., Varela, K., Sen, K., and Nelson, S. B. (1997). Synaptic depression and cortical gain control. *Science*, 275, 220–223.

Abrahamson, E. E., Leak, R. K., and Moore, R. Y. (2001). The suprachiasmatic nucleus projects to posterior hypothalamic arousal systems. *NeuroReport*, 12, 435–440.

Achtman, R. L., Green, C. S., and Bavelier, D. (2008). Video games as a tool to train visual skills. *Restorative Neurology and Neuroscience*, 26, 435–446.

Ackermann, J. (2008). Cerebellar contributions to speech production and speech perception: Psycholinguistic and neurobiological perspectives. *Trends in Neurosciences*, 31, 265–272.

Ackley, D. H., Hinton, G. E., and Sejnowski, T. J. (1985). A learning algorithm for Boltzmann machines. *Cognitive Science*, 9, 147–169.

Adelson, E. H., and Movshon, J. A. (1982). Phenomenal coherence of moving visual patterns. *Nature*, 300, 523–525.

Agam, Y., Bullock, D., and Sekuler, R. (2005). Imitating unfamiliar sequences of connected linear motions. *Journal of Neurophysiology*, 94, 2832–2843.

Agam, Y., Galperin, H., Gold, B. J., and Sekuler, R. (2007). Learning to imitate novel motion sequences. *Journal of Vision*, 7, doi: 10.1167/7.5.1.

Aggleton, J. P. (1993) The contribution of the amygdala to normal and abnormal emotional states. *Trends in Neurosciences*, 16, 328–333.

Aggleton, J. P., and Passingham, R. E. (1981). Syndrome produced by lesions of the amygdala in monkeys (Macaca mulatta). *Journal of Comparative and Physiological Psychology*, 95, 961–977.

Aggleton, J. P., and Saunders. J. P. (2000). The amygdala—what's happened in the last decade? In J. P. Aggleton (Ed.). *The Amygdala: A Functional Analysis, Second Edition*. Oxford: Oxford University Press, pp. 1–30.

Ahissar, M., and Hochstein, S. (1997). Task difficulty and the specificity of perceptual learning. *Nature*, 387, 401–406.

Ahmed, B., Anderson, J. C., Martin, K. A. C., and Nelson, J. C. (1997). Map of the synapses onto layer 4 basket cells of the primary visual cortex of the cat. *Journal of Comparative Neurology*, 380, 230–242.

Akhbardeh, A., Junnila, S., Koivistoinen, T., and Varri, A. (2007). An intelligent ballistocardiographic chair using a novel SF-ART neural network and biorthogonal wavelets. *Journal of Medical Systems*, 31, 69–77.

Akrami, A., Liu, Y., Treves, A., and Jagadeesh, B. (2009). Converging neuronal activity in inferior temporal cortex during the classification of morphed stimuli. *Cerebral Cortex*, 19, 760–766.

Albright, T. D. (1984). Direction and orientation selectivity of neurons in visual area MT of the macaque. *Journal of Neurophysiology*, 52, 1106–1130.

Albright, T. D. (1995). My most true mind thus makes mine eye untrue. *Trends in Neurosciences*, 18, 331–333.

Albert, A. (1972). *Regression and the Moore-Penrose Pseudoinverse*. Burlington, MA: Elsevier.

Alexander, G. E., and Crutcher, M. D. (1990). Functional architecture of basal ganglia circuits: Neural substrates of parallel processing. *Trends in Neurosciences*, 1, 266–271.

Alexander, G. E., DeLong, M., and Strick, P. L. (1986). Parallel organization of functionally segregated circuits linking basal ganglia and cortex. *Annual Review of Neuroscience*, 9, 357–381.

Aloimonos, J., Weiss, I., and Bandyopadhyay, A. (1988). Active vision. *International Journal of Computer Vision*, 1, 333–356.

Amari, S.-I. (1972). Learning patterns and pattern sequences by self-organizing nets of threshold elements. *IEEE Transactions on Computers*, 11, 1197–1206.

American Psychiatric Association. *Diagnostic and Statistical Manual of Mental Disorders, Fifth Edition* (2013). Arlington, VA: Author.

Ames, H., and Grossberg, S. (2008). Speaker normalization using cortical strip maps: A neural model for steady state vowel categorization. *Journal of the Acoustical Society of America*, 124, 3918–3936.

Aminoff, E., Gronau, N., and Bar, M. (2007). The parahippocampal cortex mediates spatial and nonspatial associations. *Cerebral Cortex*, 17, 1493–1503.

Amis, G., and Carpenter, G. (2007). Default ARTMAP 2. *Proceedings of the International Joint Conference on Neural Networks (IJCNN'07)*, 777–782. Orlando, Florida, IEEE Press.

Amis, G. P., and Carpenter, G. A. (2010). Self-supervised ARTMAP. *Neural Networks*, 23, 265–282.

Amis, G., Carpenter, G. A., Ersoy, B., and Grossberg, S. (2009). Cortical learning of recognition categories: A resolution of the exemplar vs. prototype debate (unpublished manuscript).

Amsel, A. (1962). Frustrative nonreward in partial reinforcement and discriminative learning: Some recent history and a theoretical extension. *Psychological Review*, 69, 306–328.

Amsel, A. (1992). *Frustration theory: An analysis of dispositional learning and memory*. Cambridge, UK: Cambridge University Press.

Amsel, A., and Maltzman, I. (1950). The effect upon generalized drive strength of emotionality as inferred from the level of consummatory responses. *Journal of Experimental Psychology*, 40, 563–569.

Anagnostopoulos, G. C., and Georgiopoulos, M. (2000). Hypersphere ART and ARTMAP for unsupervised and supervised incremental learning. In *Neural Networks,*

Proceedings of the IEEE-INNS-ENNS International Joint Conference on Neural Networks, Vol. 6, pp. 59–64.

Anagnostaras, S. G., Maren, S., and Fanselow, M. S. (1999). Temporally graded retrograde amnesia of contextual fear after hippocampal damage in rats: Within-subjects examination. *Journal of Neuroscience,* 19, 1106–1114.

Anderson, J. A., Silverstein, J. W., Ritz, S. R., and Jones, R. S. (1977). Distinctive features, categorical perception, and probability learning: Some applications of a neural model. *Psychological Review,* 84, 413–451.

Andersen, R. A., Essick, G. K., and Siegel, R. M. (1985). Encoding of spatial location by posterior parietal neurons. *Science,* 230, 456–458.

Andersen, R., Essick, G., and Siegel, R. (1987). Neurons of area 7 activated by both visual stimuli and oculomotor behavior. *Experimental Brain Research,* 67, 316–322.

Andersen, R. A., and Mountcastle, V. B. (1983). The influence of the angle of gaze upon the excitability of the light-sensitive neurons of the posterior parietal cortex. *The Journal of Neuroscience,* 3, 532–548.

Anstis, S. M. (1990). Imperceptible intersections: The chopstick illusion. In *AI and the Eye.* A. Blake, and T. Troscianko (Eds.), pp. 105–117. New York: John Wiley and Sons.

Anstis, S. M., and Ramachandran, V. S. (1987). Visual inertia in apparent motion. *Vision Research,* 27, 755–764.

Antonini, A., and Stryker, M. P. (1993). Functional mapping of horizontal connections in developing ferret visual cortex: Experiments and modeling. *The Journal of Neuroscience,* 14, 7291–7305.

Anton-Rodriguez, M., Diaz-Pernas, F. J., Diez-Higuera, J. F., Martinez-Zarzuela, M., Gonzalez-Ortega, D., and Boto-Giralda, D. (2009). Recognition of coloured and textured images through a multi-scale neural architecture with orientational filtering and chromatic diffusion. *Neurocomputing,* 72, 3713–3725.

Arana, F. S., Parkinson, J. A., Hinton, E., Holland, A. J., Owen, A. M., and Roberts, A. C. (2003). Dissociable contributions of the human amygdala and orbitofrontal cortex to incentive motivation and goal selection. *Journal of Neuroscience,* 2003, 23, 9632–9638.

Armony, J. L., Aube, W., Angulo-Perkins, A., Peretz, I., and Concha, L. (2015). The specificity of neural responses to music and their relation to voice processing: An fMRI study. *Neuroscience Letters,* 593, 35–39.

Arnold, S. E., Hyman, B. T., Flory, J., Damasio, A. R., and Van Hoesen, G. W. (1991). The topological and neuroanatomical distribution of neurofibrillary tangles and neuritic plaques in the cerebral cortex of patients with Alzheimer's disease. *Cerebral Cortex,* 1, 103–116.

Arrington, K. F. (1993). *Neural Network Models for Color and Brightness Perception and Binocular Rivalry.* PhD Dissertation, Boston University. University Microfilms International, Ann Arbor, Michigan.

Arrington, K. F. (1994). The temporal dynamics of brightness filling-in. *Vision Research,* 34, 3371–3387.

Ashley, M. L. (1898). Concerning the significance of intensity of light in visual estimates of depth. *Psychological Review,* 5, 595–615.

Assad, J. A., and Maunsell, J. H. R. (1995). Neural correlates of inferred motion in primate posterior parietal cortex. *Nature,* 373, 518–521.

Assad, W. F., Lauro, P. M., Perge, J. A., and Eskandar, E. N. (2017). Prefrontal neurons encode a solution to the credit-assignment problem. *The Journal of Neuroscience,* 37, 6995–7007.

Atkeson, C. G., and Hollerbach, J. M. (1985). Kinematic features of unrestrained vertical arm movements. *The Journal of Neuroscience,* 5, 2318–2330.

Atzori, M., Lei, S., Evans, D. I. P., Kanold, P. O., Phillips-Tansey, E., McIntyre, O., and McBain, C. J. (2001). Differential synaptic processing separates stationary from transient inputs to the auditory cortex. *Nature Neuroscience,* 4, 1230–1237.

Aubert, H. (1886). Die Bewegungsempfinung. *Pfluggers Archive,* 39, 347–370.

Auer, E. T. Jr., and Luce, P. A. (2008). Probabilistic phonotactics in spoken word recognition. In D. B. Pisoni and R. E. Remez (Eds.). *The Handbook of Speech Perception.* Wiley Online Library, DOI 10.1002/9780470757024.ch25.

Averbeck, B. B., Chafee, M. V., Crowe, D. A., and Georgopoulos, A. P. (2002). Parallel processing of serial movements in prefrontal cortex. *Proceedings of the National Academy of Sciences,* 99, 13172–13177.

Averbeck, B. B., Crowe, D. A., Chafee, M. V., and Georgopoulos, A. P. (2003a). Neural activity in prefrontal cortex during copying geometrical shapes. I. Single cells encode shape, sequence, and metric parameters. *Experimental Brain Research,* 150, 127–141.

Averbeck, B. B., Crowe, D. A., Chafee, M. V., and Georgopoulos, A. P. (2003b). Neural activity in prefrontal cortex during copying geometrical shapes. II. Decoding shape segments from neural ensembles. *Experimental Brain Research,* 150, 142–153.

Awh, E. Jonides, J., Smith, E. E., Schumacher, E. H., Koeppe, R. A., and Katz, S. (1996). Dissociation of storage and rehearsal in verbal working memory. *Psychological Science,* 7, 25–31.

Awh, E., and Vogel, E. K. (2008). The bouncer in the brain. *Nature Neuroscience* 11, 5–6.

Backhaus, A., Heinke, D., and Humphreys, G. W. (2005). Contextual learning in the selective attention for identification model (CL-SAIM): Modeling contextual cueing in visual search tasks. *Proceedings of the 2005 IEEE Computer Society Conference on Computer Vision and Pattern Recognition-Workshops,* 3, 87–87.

Badcock, D. R., and Westheimer, G. (1985a). Spatial location and hyperacuity: The centre/surround localization contribution function has two substrates. *Vision Research,* 25, 1259–1267.

Badcock, D. R., and Westheimer, G. (1985b). Spatial location and hyperacuity: Flank position within the centre and surround zones. *Spatial Vision,* 1, 3–11.

Baddeley, A. (1986). *Working memory.* Oxford, UK: Clarendon Press.

Ball, G. J., Gloor, P., and Schaal, N. (1977). The cortical electromicrophysiology of pathological delta waves in the electroencephalogram of cats. *Electroencephalography and Clinical Neurophysiology,* 43, 346–361.

Baars, B. (2005). Global workspace theory of consciousness: Towards a cognitive neuroscience of human experience? *Progress in Brain Research,* 150, 45–53.

Baker, J. K., Fenning, R. M., Erath, S. A., Baucom, B. R., Moffitt, J., and Howland, M. A. (2017). Sympathetic underarousal and externalizing behavior problems in children with autism spectrum disorder. *Journal of Abnormal Child Psychology,* July 24. Doi:10.1007/s10802-0332-3.

Baldauf, D., and Desimone, R. (2014). Neural mechanisms of object-based attention. *Science,* 344, 424–427.

Baloch, A. A., and Grossberg, S. (1997). A neural model of high-level motion processing: Line motion and formotion dynamics. *Vision Research,* 37, 3037–3059.

Baloch, A. A., Grossberg, S., Mingolla, E., and Nogueira, C. A. M. (1999). A neural model of first-order and second-order motion perception and magnocellular dynamics. *Journal of the Optical Society of America A,* 16, 953–978.

Baloch, A. A., and Waxman, A. M. (1991). Visual learning, adaptive expectations, and behavioral conditioning of the mobile robot MAVIN. *Neural Networks,* 4, 271–302.

Ban, T. A. (1973). *Recent advances in the biology of schizophrenia.* Springfield, IL: C. C. Thomas.

Banks, M. S., Ehrlich, S. M., Backus, B. T., and Crowell, J. A. (1996). Estimating heading during real and simulated eye movements. *Vision Research,* 36, 431–443.

Banksy (2005). *Wall and Piece.* London, UK: Random House.

Banquet, J. P., and Grossberg, S. (1987). Probing cognitive processes through the structure of event-related potentials during learning: An experimental and theoretical analysis. *Applied Optics,* 26, 4931–4946.

Bar, M., Tootell, R. B. H., Schacter, D. L., Greve, D. N., Fischl, B., Mendola, J. D., Rosen, B. R., and Dale, A. M. (2001). Cortical mechanisms specific to explicit object recognition. *Neuron,* 29, 529–535.

Barbas, H. (1995). Anatomic basis of cognitive-emotional interactions in the primate prefrontal cortex. *Neuroscience and Biobehavioral Reviews,* 19, 499–510.

Barbas, H. (2007). Flow of information for emotions through temporal and orbitofrontal pathways. *Journal of Anatomy,* 211, 237–249.

Barbas, H., and Pandya, D. (1987). Architecture and frontal cortical connections of the premotor cortex (area 6) in the rhesus monkey. *The Journal of Comparative Neurology,* 256, 211–228.

Baron-Cohen, S. (1989). The autistic child's theory of the mind: A case of specific developmental delay. *Journal of Child Psychology and Psychiatry, and Allied Disciplines,* 30, 285–297.

Barry, C., Heys, J. G., and Hasselmo, M. E. (2012). Possible role of acetylcholine in regulating spatial novelty effects on theta rhythm and grid cells. Frontiers in Neural Circuits, 20 February https://doi.org/10.3389/fncir.2012.00005.

Bartley, S. H. (1941). *Vision, a Study of its Basis.* New York: Von Nostrand Reinhold.

Bastos, A. M., Loonis, R., Kornblith, S., Lundqvist, M., and Miller, E. K. (2018). Laminar recordings in frontal cortex suggest distinct layers for maintenance and control of working memory. *Proceedings of the National Academy of Sciences,* 115, 1117–1122.

Baumgardner, T. L., Reiss, A. L., Freund, L. S., and Abrams, M. T. (1995). Specification of the neurobehavioral phenotype in males with fragile X syndrome. *Pediatrics,* 95, 744–752.

Baxter, M. G., Parker, A., Lindner, C. C. C., Izquierdo, A. D., and Murray, E. A. (2000). Control of response selection by reinforcer value requires interaction of amygdala and orbital prefrontal cortex. *The Journal of Neuroscience,* 20, 4311–4319.

Baylor, D. A., and Hodgkin, A. L. (1974). Changes in time scale and sensitivity in turtle photoreceptors. *Journal of Physiology,* 242, 729–758.

Bazhenov, M., Timofeev, I., Steriade, M., and Sejnowski, T. J. (2002). Model of thalamocortical slow-wave sleep oscillations and transitions to activated states. *The Journal of Neuroscience,* 22, 8691–8704.

Bear, M. F., Huber, K. M., and Warren, S. T. (2004). The mGluR theory of fragile X mental retardation. *Trends in Neurosciences,* 27, 370–377.

Beardsley, S. A., and Vaina, L. M. (2001). A laterally interconnected neural architecture in MST accounts for psychophysical discrimination of complex motion patterns. *Journal of Computational Neuroscience,* 10, 255–280.

Bechara, A., Damasio, H., Damasio, A. R., and Lee, G. P. (1999). Different contributions of the human amygdala and ventromedial prefrontal cortex to decision-making. *The Journal of Neuroscience,* 19, 5473–5481.

Beck, J. (1966). Effect of orientation and of shape similarity on perceptual grouping. *Perception & Psychophysics,* 1, 300–302.

Beck, J., and Prazdny, S. (1981). Highlights and the perception of glossiness. *Perception & Psychophysics,* 30, 407–410.

Beck, J., Prazdny, K., and Rosenfeld, A. (1983). A theory of textural segmentation. In J. Beck, B. Hope, and A. Rosenfeld (Eds.). *Human and Machine Vision: Notes and Reports in Computer Science and Applied Mathematics,* pp. 1–38. New York: Academic Press.

Beck, J., and Stevens, K. A. (1986). Visual representations subserving texture perception. Defense Technical Information Center, Accession Number ADA168613, pp. 1–105.

Beck, J., Sutter, A., and Ivry, R. (1987). Spatial frequency channels and perceptual grouping in texture segregation. *Computer Vision, Graphics, and Image Processing,* 37, 299–325.

Beggs, W. D. A., and Howarth, C. I. (1972). The movement of the hand towards a target. *Quarterly Journal of Experimental Psychology,* 14, 448–453.

Behrmann, M., Geng, J. J., and Shomstein, S. (2004). Parietal cortex and attention. *Current Opinion in Neurobiology,* 14, 212–217.

Belin, P., Zatorre, R. J., Lafaille, P., Ahad, P, and Pike, B. (2000). Voice-selective areas in human auditory cortex. *Nature,* 403, 309–312.

Bellmann, A., Meuli, R., and Clarke, S. (2001). Two types of auditory neglect. *Brain,* 124, 676–687.

Belmonte, M. K., and Bourgeron, T. (2006). Fragile X syndrome and autism at the intersection of genetic and neural networks. *Nature Neuroscience,* 9, 1221–1225.

Belova, M. A., Paton, J. J., Morrison, S. E., and Salzman, D. (2007). Expectation modulates neural responses to pleasant and aversive stimuli in primate amygdala. *Neuron,* 55, 970–984.

Belova, M. A., Paton, J. J., and Salzman, D. (2008). Moment-to-moment tracking of state value in the amygdala. *The Journal of Neuroscience,* 28, 10023–10030.

Bengio, Y., and LeCun, Y. (2007). Scaling learning algorithms towards AI. In L. Bottou, O. Chapelle, D. DeCoste, and J.

Weston (Eds.). *Large Scale Kernel Machines*, pp. 321–360. Cambridge, MA: MIT Press.

Ben-Shahar, O., and Zucker, S. (2004). Sensitivity to curvatures in orientation-based texture segmentation. *Vision Research*, 44, 257–277.

Benson, H., Beary, J. R., and Carol, M. P. (1974). The relaxation response. *Psychiatry*, 37, 37–46.

Benson, H., and Klipper, M. Z. (1975). *The Relaxation Response*: New York: William Morrow and Co.

Berdyyeva, T., and Olson, C. (2009). Monkey supplementary eye field neurons signal the ordinal position of both actions and objects. *The Journal of Neuroscience*, 29, 591–599.

Berger, T. W., Berry, S. D., and Thompson, R. F. (1986). Role of the hippocampus in classical conditioning of aversive and appetitive behaviors. In R. L. Isaacson and K. H. Pribram (Eds.). *The Hippocampus, Volume 4*. New York: Plenum Press, pp. 203–239.

Berger, T. W., Laham, R. I., and Thompson, R. F. (1980). Hippocampal unit-behavior correlations during classical conditioning. *Brain Research*, 193, 229–248.

Berger, T. W., and Thompson, R. F. (1978). Neuronal plasticity in the limbic system during classical conditioning of the rabbit nictitating membrane response, I: The hippocampus. *Brain Research*, 145, 323–346.

Berger, T. W., Weikart, C. L., Basset, J. L., and Orr, W. B. (1986). Lesions of the retrosplenial cortex produce deficits in reversal learning of the rabbit nictitating membrane response: implications for potential interactions between hippocampal and cerebellar brain systems. *Behavioral Neuroscience*, 100, 802–809.

Berke, J. D., Hetrick, V., Breck, J., and Green, R. W. (2008). Transient 23–30-Hz oscillations in mouse hippocampus during exploration of novel environments. *Hippocampus*, 18, 519–529.

Berman, P. W., and Leibowitz, H. W. (1965). Some effects of contour on simultaneous brightness contrast. *Journal of Experimental Psychology*, 69, 251–256.

Berardi, N., and Maffei, L. (1999). From visual experience to visual function: Roles of neurotrophins. *Journal of Neurobiology*, 41, 119–126.

Berzhanskaya, J., Grossberg, S., and Mingolla, E. (2007). Laminar cortical dynamics of visual form and motion interactions during coherent object motion perception. *Spatial Vision*, 20, 337–395.

Besson, M., Faita, F., Peretz, I., Bennel, A.-M., and Requin, J. H. (1998). Singing in the brain: Independence of lyrics and tunes. *Psychological Science*, 9, 494–498.

Bhatt, R., Carpenter, G., and Grossberg, S. (2007). Texture segregation by visual cortex: perceptual grouping, attention, and learning. *Vision Research*, 47, 3173–3211.

Bi, G. Q., and Poo, M. (2001). Synaptic modification by correlated activity: Hebb's postulate revisited. *Annual Review of Neuroscience*, 24, 139–166.

Bichot, N. P., Heard, M. T., DeGennaro, E. M., and Desimone, R. (2015). A source for feature-based attention in the prefrontal cortex. *Neuron*, 88, 832–844.

Bisley, J. W., Krishna, B. S., and Goldberg, M. E. (2004). A rapid and precise on-response in posterior parietal cortex. *The Journal of Neuroscience*, 24, 1833–1838.

Blair, H. T., Gupta, K., and Zhang, K. (2008). Conversion of a phase- to a rate-coded position signal by a three-stage model of theta cells, grid cells, and place cells. *Hippocampus*, 18, 1239–1255.

Blair, H., and Sharp, P. (1995). Anticipatory head direction signals in anterior thalamus: evidence for a thalamocortical circuit that integrates angular head motion to compute head direction. *The Journal of Neuroscience*, 15, 6260–6270.

Blair, H., and Sharp, P. (1996). Visual and vestibular influences on head direction cells in the anterior thalamus of the rat. *Behavioral Neuroscience*, 10, 643–660.

Blake, R. (1989). A neural theory of binocular rivalry. *Psychological Review*, 96, 145–167.

Blake, R., and Fox, R. (1974). Binocular rivalry suppression: Insensitive to spatial frequency and orientation change. *Vision Research*, 14, 687–692.

Blake, R., and Logothetis, N. (2002). Visual competition. *Nature Reviews Neuroscience*, 3, 13–23.

Blake, R., Westendorf, D. H., and Overton, R. (1980). What is suppressed during binocular rivalry. *Perception*, 9, 223–231.

Blake, R., Yu, K., Lokey, M., and Norman, H. (1998). Binocular rivalry and motion perception. *Journal of Cognitive Neuroscience*, 10, 46–60.

Bland, B. H., and Colom, L. V. (1993). Extrinsic and intrinsic properties underlying oscillation and synchrony in limbic cortex. *Progress in Neurobiology*, 41, 157–208.

Blasdel, G. G., and Lund, J. S. (1983). Termination of afferent axons in macaque striate cortex. *The Journal of Neuroscience*, 3, 1389–1413.

Blasdel, G. G., Lund, J. S., and Fitzpatrick, D. (1985). Intrinsic connections of macaque striate cortex: axonal projections of cells outside lamina 4C. *The Journal of Neuroscience*, 5, 3350–3369.

Boardman, I., Grossberg, S., Myers, C., and Cohen, M. (1999). Neural dynamics of perceptual order and context effects for variable-rate speech syllables. *Perception & Psychophysics*, 6, 1477–1500.

Bode, H. B., and Müller, R. (2003). Possibility of bacterial recruitment of plant genes associated with the biosynthesis of secondary metabolites. *Plant Physiology*, 132, 1153–1161.

Bodfish, J. W., Symons, F. J., Parker, D. E., and Lewis, M. H. (2000). Varieties of repetitive behavior in autism: Comparisons to mental retardation. *Journal of Autism and Developmental Disorders*, 30, 237–243.

Boehlen, A., Heinemann, U., and Erchova, I. (2010). The range of intrinsic frequencies represented by medial entorhinal cortex stellate cells extends with age. *The Journal of Neuroscience*, 30, 4585–4589.

Bohland, J. W., Bullock, D., and Guenther, F. H. (2010) Neural representations and mechanisms for the performance of simple speech sequences. *Journal of Cognitive Neuroscience*, 22, 1504–1529.

Bonhoffer, T. (1996). Neurotrophins and activity-dependent development of the neocortex. *Current Opinion in Neurobiology*, 6, 119–126.

Bonneh, Y. S., Cooperman, A., and Sagi, D. (2001). Motion-induced blindness in normal observers. *Nature*, 411, 798–801.

Bonneh, Y., and Sagi, D. (1999). Configuration saliency revealed in short duration binocular rivalry. *Vision Research*, 39, 271–291.

Bonneh, Y., Sagi, D., and Karni, A. (2001). A transition between eye and object rivalry determined by stimulus coherence. *Vision Research*, 41, 981–989.

Bonnel, A.-M., Faita, F., Peretz, I., and Besson, M. (2001) Divided attention between lyrics and tunes of operatic songs: Evidence for independent processing. *Perception and Psychophysics*, 63, 1201–1213.

Bonner, J. T. (1967). *The Cellular Slime Molds*, 2nd edition. Princeton, NJ: Princeton University Press.

Bonner, J. T. (1969). Hormones in social amoebae and mammals. *Scientific American*, 220, 78–91.

Bonner, J. T., Barkley, D. S., Hall, E. M., Konijn, T. M., Mason, J. W., O'Keefe III, G., and Wolfe, P. B. (1969). Acrasin, Acrasinase, and the sensitivity to acrasin in *Dictyostelium discoideum*, *Developmental Biology*, 20, 72–87.

Bonner, J. T. (1974). *On Development: The Biology of Form*. Cambridge, MA: Harvard University Press.

Bonnevie, T., Dunn, B., Fyhn, M., Hafting, T., Derdikman, D., Kubie, J. L., Roudi, Y., Moser, E. I., and Moser, M.-B. (2013). Grid cells require excitatory drive from the hippocampus. *Nature Neuroscience*, 16, 309–319.

Bootman, M. D., and Berridge, M. J. (1996). Subcellular Ca2+ signals underlying waves and graded responses in HeLa cells. *Current Biology*, 6, 855–865.

Boring, E. G. (1950). *A History of Experimental Psychology*. Englewood Cliffs, NJ: Prentice-Hall.

Born, R., and Tootell, R. (1992). Segregation of global and local motion processing in macaque middle temporal cortex. *Nature*, 357, 497–499.

Bosking, W. H., Zhang, Y., Schofield, B., and Fitzpatrick, D. (1997). Orientation selectivity and the arrangement of horizontal connections in tree shrew striate cortex. *The Journal of Neuroscience*, 17, 2112–2127.

Boucheny, C., Brunel, N., and Arleo, A. (2005). A continuous attractor network model without recurrent excitation: Maintenance and integration in the head direction cell system. *Journal of Computational Neuroscience*, 18, 205–227.

Bouma, H. (1970). Interaction effects in parafoveal letter recognition. *Nature*, 226, 177–178.

Bouma, H. (1973). Visual interference in the parafoveal recognition of initial and final letters of words. *Vision Research*, 13, 767–782.

Bowen, R., Pola, J., and Matin, L. (1974), Visual persistence: Effects of flash luminance, duration and energy. *Vision Research*, 14, 295–303.

Bower, G. H. (1981). Mood and memory. *American Psychologist*, 36, 129–148.

Bowns, L. (1996). Evidence for a feature tracking explanation of why Type II plaids move in the vector sum direction at short durations. *Vision Research*, 36, 135–147.

Braddick, O. (1974). A short range process in apparent motion. *Vision Research*, 14, 519–527.

Braddick, O. (1980). Low-level and high-level processes in apparent motion. *Philosophical Transactions of the Royal Society. Series B. Biological Sciences*, 290, 137–151.

Braddick, O., and Adlard, A. (1978). Apparent motion and the motion detector. In *Visual Psychophysics and Psychology*. J. C. Armington, J. Krauskopf, and B. R. Wooten (Eds.). San Diego, CA: Academic Press.

Bradley, D. C., Qian, N., and Andersen, R. A. (1995). Integration of motion and stereopsis in middle temporal cortical area of macaques. *Nature*, 373, 609–611.

Bradley, D. R., and Dumais, S. T. (1984). The effects of illumination level and retinal size on the depth stratification of subjective contour figures. *Perception*, 13, 155–164.

Bradski, G., Carpenter, G., and Grossberg, S. (1992). Working memory networks for learning temporal order with application to 3-D visual object recognition. *Neural Computation*, 4, 270–286.

Bradski, G., Carpenter, G. A., and Grossberg, S. (1994). STORE working memory networks for storage and recall of arbitrary temporal sequences. *Biological Cybernetics*, 71, 469–480.

Bradski, G., and Grossberg, S. (1995). Fast learning VIEWNET architectures for recognizing 3-D objects from multiple 2-D views. *Neural Networks*, 8, 1053–1080.

Brady, T. F., and Chun, M. M. (2007). Spatial constraints on learning in visual search: Modeling contextual cueing. *Journal of Experimental Psychology: Human Perception & Performance*, 33, 798–815.

Brandon, M. P., Bogaard, A. R., Libby, C. P., Connerney, M. A., Gupta, K., and Hasselmo, M. E. (2011). Reduction of theta rhythm dissociates grid cell spatial periodicity from directional tuning. *Science*, 332, 595–599.

Brannon, N. G., Seiffertt, J. E., Draelos, T. J., and Wunsch, D. C. II (2009). Coordinated machine learning and decision support for situation awareness. *Neural Networks*, 22, 316–325.

Bregman, A. S. (1990). *Auditory scene analysis: The perceptual organization of sound*. Cambridge, MA: MIT Press.

Breitmeyer, B. G., and Ritter, A. (1986a). The role of visual pattern persistence in bistable stroboscopic motion. *Vision Research*, 26, 1801–1806.

Breitmeyer, B. G., and Ritter, A. (1986b). Visual persistence and the effect of eccentric viewing, element size, and frame duration of bistable stroboscopic motion percepts. *Perception & Psychophysics*, 39, 275–280.

Bressan, P. (2001). Explaining lightness illusions. *Perception*, 30, 1031–1046.

Brincat, S. L., and Miller, E. H. (2015). Frequency-specific hippocampal-prefrontal interactions during associative learning. *Nature Neuroscience*, 18, 576–581.

Britt, R., and Starr, A. (1976). Synaptic events and discharge patterns of cochlear nucleus cells: Frequency modulated tones. *Journal of Neurophysiology*, 39, 179–194.

Brockmole, J. R., and Henderson, J. M. (2006). Using real-world scenes as contextual cues for search. *Visual Cognition*, 13, 99–108.

Brockmole, J. R., Castelhano, M. S., and Henderson, J. M. (2006). Contextual cueing in naturalistic scenes: Global and local contexts. *Journal of Experimental Psychology: Learning, Memory, and Cognition*, 32, 699–706.

Brodmann, K. (1909). *Vergleichende Lokalisationslehre der Grosshirnrinde in Ihren Prinzipien Dargestellt auf Grund des Zellenbaues*. Leipzig: Barth.

Bronkhorst, A. W., and Plomp, R. (1988). The effect of head-induced interaural time and level differences on speech intelligibility in noise. *The Journal of the Acoustical Society of America*, 83, 1508.

Brown, G. T. (1911). The intrinsic factors in the act of progression in the mammal. *Proceedings of the Royal Society, London B*, 84, 302–319.

Brown, J. M., and Denney, H. I. (2007). Shifting attention into and out of objects: Evaluating the processes underlying the object advantage. *Perception and Psychophysics*, 69, 606–618.

Brown, J. M., and Weisstein, N. (1988). A spatial frequency effect on perceived depth. *Perception & Psychophysics*, 44, 157–166.

Brown, J. S., Martin, R. C., and Morrow, M. W. (1964). Self-punitive behavior in the rat: Facilitative effects of punishment on resistance to extinction. *Journal of Comparative and Physiological Psychology*, 57, 127–133.

Brown, J. W., Bullock, D., and Grossberg, S. (1999). How the basal ganglia use parallel excitatory and inhibitory learning pathways to selectively respond to unexpected rewarding cues. *Journal of Neuroscience*, 19, 10502–10511.

Brown, J. W., Bullock, D., and Grossberg, S. (2004). How laminar frontal cortex and basal ganglia circuits interact to control planned and reactive saccades. *Neural Networks*, 17, 471–510.

Browning, A., Grossberg, S., and Mingolla, M. (2009a). A neural model of how the brain computes heading from optic flow in realistic scenes. *Cognitive Psychology*, 59, 320–356.

Browning, A., Grossberg, S., and Mingolla, M. (2009b). Cortical dynamics of navigation and steering in natural scenes: Motion-based object segmentation, heading, and obstacle avoidance. *Neural Networks*, 22, 1383–1398.

Brun, V. H., Solstad, T., Kjelstrup, K. B., Fyhn, M., Witter, M. P., Moster, E. I., and Moser, M.-B. (2008). Progressive increase in grid scale from dorsal to ventral medial entorhinal cortex. *Hippocampus*, 18, 1200–1212.

Brunel, N. (2003). Dynamics and plasticity of stimulus selective persistent activity in cortical network models. *Cerebral Cortex*, 13, 1151–1161.

Bruner, J. S. (1975). The ontogenesis of speech acts. *Journal of Child Language*, 2, 1–19.

Buckner, R. (2013). The brain is a bag of tricks. Lecture given as part of the symposium on *Models of the mind: How neuroscience, psychology, and the law collide*. Sponsored by the Center for Law, Brain, and Behavior and the Affective Sciences Institute, Harvard Medical School.

Buffalo, E. A., Fries, P., Landman, R., Buschman, T. J., and Desimone, R. (2011). Laminar differences in gamma and alpha coherence in the ventral stream. *Proceedings of the National Academy of Sciences*, 108, 11262–11267.

Bujnakova, I., Ondrejka, I., Mestanik, M., Visnovcova, Z., Mestanikova, A., Hrtanek, I., Fleskova, D., Calkovska, A, and Tonhajzerova, I. (2016). Autism spectrum disorder is associated with autonomic underarousal. *Physiological Research*, 65 (Suppl. 5), S673–S682.

Bullier, J., Hupé, J. M., James, A., and Girard, P. (1996). Functional interactions between areas V1 and V2 in the monkey. *Journal of Physiology (Paris)*, 90, 217–220.

Bullock, D., Cisek, P., and Grossberg, S. (1998). Cortical networks for control of voluntary arm movements under variable force conditions. *Cerebral Cortex*, 8, 48–62.

Bullock, D., and Grossberg, S. (1988). Neural dynamics of planned arm movements: Emergent invariants and speed-accuracy properties during trajectory formation. *Psychological Review*, 95, 49–90.

Bullock, D., and Grossberg, S. (1989). VITE and FLETE: Neural modules for trajectory formation and postural control. In W. Hershberger (Ed.), *Volitional Action*. Amsterdam: North-Holland, pp. 253–297.

Bullock, D. and Grossberg, S. (1991). Adaptive neural networks for control of movement trajectories invariant under speed and force rescaling. *Human Movement Science*, 10, 3–53.

Bullock, D., Grossberg, S., and Guenther, F. H. (1993). A self-organizing neural model of motor equivalent reaching and tool use by a multijoint arm. *Journal of Cognitive Neuroscience*, 5, 408–435.

Buonomano, D. V., Baxter, D. A., and Byrne, J. H. (1990). Small networks of empirically derived adaptive elements simulate some higher-order features of classical conditioning. *Neural Networks*, 3, 507–523.

Burak, Y., and Fiete, I. R. (2009). Accurate path integration in continuous attractor network models of grid cells. *PLoS Comput. Biol.* 5:e1000291. doi: 10.1371/journal.pcbi.1000291.

Burgdorf, J., and Panksepp, J. (2006). The neurobiology of positive emotions. *Neuroscience & Biobehavioral Reviews*, 30, 173–187.

Burgess, N. (1995). A solvable connectionist model of immediate recall of ordered lists. In Tesauro, G., Touretzky, D. S., and Leen, T. K. (Eds.). *Advances in Neural Information Processing Systems*, 7, Cambridge, MA: MIT Press, pp. 51–58.

Burgess, N. (2008). Grid cells and theta as oscillatory interference. Theory and predictions. *Hippocampus*, 18, 1157–1174.

Burgess, N., Barry, C., and O'Keefe, J. (2007). An oscillatory interference model of grid cell firing. *Hippocampus*, 17, 801–812.

Burgess, N., and Hitch, G. J. (1992). Toward a network model of the articulatory loop. *Journal of Memory and Language*, 31, 429–460.

Burr, D. C., and Morrone, M. C. (2011). Spatiotopic coding and remapping in humans. *Philosophical Transactions of the Royal Society of London B Biological Sciences*, 365, 504–515.

Buschman, T. J., and Miller, E. K. (2007). Top–down versus bottom–up control of attention in the prefrontal and posterior parietal cortices. *Science*, 315, 1860–1862.

Bushnell, M. C., Goldberg, M. E., and Robinson, D. L. (1981). Behavioral enhancement of visual responses in monkey cerebral cortex. I. Modulation in posterior parietal cortex related to selective visual attention. *Journal of Neurophysiology*, 46, 755–772.

Butler, M. P., Rainbow, M. N., Rodriguez, E., Lyon, S. M., and Silver, R. (2012). Twelve-hour days in the brain and behavior of split hamsters. *European Journal of Neuroscience*, 36, 2556–2566.

Buzsáki, G. (2002). Theta oscillations in the hippocampus. *Neuron*, 33, 325–340.

Buzsáki, G. (2015). Hippocampal sharp wave-ripple: A cognitive biomarker for episodic memory and planning. *Hippocampus*, 25, 1073–1188.

Buzsáki, G., Bickford, R. G., Ponomareff, G., Thal, L. J., Mandel, R., and Gage, F. H. (1988). Nucleus basalis and thalamic control of neocortical activity in the freely moving rat. *The Journal of Neuroscience*, 8, 4007–4026.

Buzsáki, G., and Chrobak, J. J. (2005). Synaptic plasticity and self-organization in the hippocampus. *Nature Neuroscience*, 8, 1418–1420.

Buzsáki, G., Llinás, R., Singer, W., Berthoz, A., and Christen, Y. (2012). *Temporal Coding in the Brain*. Berlin: Springer Science & Business Media.

Buzsáki, G., and Moser, E. I. (2013). Memory, navigation and theta rhythm in the hippocampal entorhinal system. *Nature Neuroscience*, 16, 130–138.

Buzsáki, G., and Tingley, D. (2018). Space and time: The hippocampus as a sequence generator. *Trends in Cognitive Sciences*, 22, 853–869.

Caballero-Bleda, M., and Witter, M. P. (1993). Regional and laminar organization of projections from the presubiculum and parasubiculum to the entorhinal cortex: An anterograde tracing study in the rat. *The Journal of Comparative Neurology*, 328, 115–129.

Caballero-Bleda, M., and Witter, M. P. (1994). Projections from the presubiculum and the parasubiculum to morphologically characterized entorhinal-hippocampal projection neurons in the rat. *Experimental Brain Research*, 101, 93–108.

Cabelli, R. J., Hohn, A., and Shatz, C. J. (1995). Inhibition of ocular dominance column formation by infusion of NT-4/5 or BDNF. *Science*, 267, 1662–1666.

Cabelli, R. J., Shelton, D. L., Segal, R. A., and Shatz, C. J. (1997). Blockade of endogenous ligands of trkB inhibits formation of ocular dominance columns. *Neuron*, 19, 63–76.

Cai, Y., Wang, J.-Z., Tang, Y., and Yang, Y.-C. (2011). An efficient approach for electric load forecasting using distributed ART (adaptive resonance theory) and HS-ARTMAP (Hyper-spherical ARTMAP network) neural network. *Energy*, 36, 1340–1350.

Caianiello, E. R. (1961). Outline of a theory of thought-processes and thinking machines. *Journal of Theoretical Biology*, 1, 204–235.

Callaway, E. M. (1998). Local circuits in primary visual cortex of the macaque monkey. *Annual Review of Neuroscience*, 21, 47–74.

Calloway, E. M., and Katz, L. C. (1990). Emergence and refinement of clustered horizontal connections in cat striate cortex. *The Journal of Neuroscience*, 10, 1134–1153.

Callaway, E. M., and Wiser, A. K. (1996). Contributions of individual layer 2-5 spiny neurons to local circuits in macaque primary visual cortex. *Visual Neuroscience*, 13, 907–922.

Calvet, J., Fourment, A., and Thieffry, M. (1973). Electrical activity in neocortical projection and association areas during slow wave sleep. *Brain Research*, 52, 173–187.

Cameron, S., Grossberg, S., and Guenther, F. H. (1998). A self-organizing neural network architecture for navigation using optic flow. *Neural Computation*, 10, 313–352.

Cannell, M. B., Cheng, H., and Lederer, W. J. (1995). The control of calcium release in heart muscle. *Science*, 268, 1045–1049.

Cano-Izquierdo, J.-M., Almonacid, M., Pinzolas, M., and Ibarrola, J. (2009). dFasArt: dynamic neural processing in FasArt model. *Neural Networks*, 22, 479–487.

Cant, B. R., and Bickford, R. G. (1967). The effect of motivation on the contingent negative variation (CNV). *Electroencephalography and Clinical Neurophysiology*, 23, 594.

Cao, Y., and Grossberg, S. (2005). A laminar cortical model of stereopsis and 3D surface perception: Closure and da Vinci stereopsis. *Spatial Vision*, 18, 515–578.

Cao, Y., and Grossberg, S. (2012). Stereopsis and 3D surface perception by spiking neurons in laminar cortical circuits: A method of converting neural rate models into spiking models. *Neural Networks*, 26, 75–98.

Cao, Y., and Grossberg, S. (2019). A laminar cortical model for 3D boundary and surface representations of complex natural scenes. In A. Adamatzky, S. G. Akl, and G. Ch. Sirakoulis (Eds.), *From Parallel to Emergent Computing*. Taylor & Francis/CRC, pp. 509–545.

Cao, Y., Grossberg, S., and Markowitz, J. (2011). How does the brain rapidly learn and reorganize view- and positionally-invariant object representations in inferior temporal cortex? *Neural Networks*, 24, 1050–1061.

Caplovitz, G. P., and Tse, P. U. (2007). V3A processes contour curvature as a trackable feature for the perception of rotational motion. *Cerebral Cortex*, 17, 1179–1189.

Caputo, G., and Guerra, S. (1998). Attentional selection by distractor suppression. *Vision Research*, 38, 669–689.

Carandini, M., and Heeger, D. J. (2012). Normalization as a canonical neural computation. *Nature Reviews Neuroscience*, 13, 51–62.

Cardinal, R. N., Parkinson, J. A., Hall, J., and Everitt, B. J. (2002). Emotion and motivation: The role of the amygdala, ventral striatum, and prefrontal cortex. *Neuroscience and Biobehavioral Reviews*, 26, 321–352.

Carpenter, G. A. (1976). Nerve impulse equations. In P. Hilton (Ed.). *Structural Stability, the Theory of Catastrophes, and Applications to the Sciences, Springer Series: Lecture Notes in Mathematics*, 525, 58–76.

Carpenter, G. A. (1977a). A geometric approach to singular perturbation problems with applications to nerve impulse equations. *Journal of Differential Equations*, 23, 335–367.

Carpenter, G. A. (1977b). Periodic solutions of nerve impulse equations. *Journal of Mathematical Analysis and Applications*, 58, 152–173.

Carpenter, G. A. (1979). Bursting phenomena in excitable membranes. *SIAM Journal on Applied Mathematics*, 36, 334–372.

Carpenter, G. A. (1981). Normal and abnormal signal patterns in nerve cells. In S. Grossberg (Ed.), *Mathematical psychology and psychophysiology* (pp. 49–90). Providence, RI: American Mathematical Society.

Carpenter G. A. (1997). Distributed learning, recognition, and prediction by ART and ARTMAP neural networks. *Neural Networks*, 10, 1473–1494.

Carpenter, G. A. (2003). Default ARTMAP. Proceedings of the International Joint Conference on Neural Networks (IJCNN'03), 1396–1401.

Carpenter, G. A., and Gaddam, S. C. (2010). Biased ART: A neural architecture that shifts attention toward previously disregarded features following an incorrect prediction. *Neural Networks*, 23, 435–451.

Carpenter, G. A., Gjaja, M. N., Gopal, S., and Woodcock, C. A. (1996). ART neural networks for remote sensing: Vegetation classification from Landsat TM and terrain data.

International Geoscience and Remote Sensing Symposium, 1996, 1. Piscataway, NJ: IEEE Press, 529–531.

Carpenter, G. A., and Grossberg, S. (1981). Adaptation and transmitter gating in vertebrate photoreceptors. *Journal of Theoretical Neurobiology*, 1, 1–42.

Carpenter, G. A., and Grossberg, S. (1983). A neural theory of circadian rhythms: The gated pacemaker. *Biological Cybernetics*, 48, 35–59.

Carpenter, G. A., and Grossberg, S. (1984). A neural theory of circadian rhythms: Aschoff's rule in diurnal and nocturnal mammals. *American Journal of Physiology (Regulatory, Integrative, and Comparative Physiology)*, 24, R1067–R1082.

Carpenter, G. A., and Grossberg, S. (1985). A neural theory of circadian rhythms: Split rhythms, after-effects, and motivational interactions. *Journal of Theoretical Biology*, 113, 163–223.

Carpenter, G. A., and Grossberg, S. (1987a). A massively parallel architecture for a self-organizing neural pattern recognition machine. *Computer Vision, Graphics, and Image Processing*, 37, 54–115.

Carpenter, G. A., and Grossberg, S. (1987b). ART 2: Stable self-organization of pattern recognition codes for analog input patterns. *Applied Optics*, 26, 4919–4930.

Carpenter, G. A., and Grossberg, S. (1990). *Pattern Recognition by Self-organizing Neural Networks*. Cambridge, MA: MIT Press.

Carpenter, G. A., and Grossberg, S. (1993). Normal and amnesic learning, recognition, and memory by a neural model of cortico-hippocampal interactions. *Trends in Neurosciences*, 16, 131–137.

Carpenter, G. A., Grossberg, S., Markuzon, N., Reynolds, J. H., and Rosen, D. B. (1992). Fuzzy ARTMAP: a neural network architecture for incremental supervised learning of analog multidimensional maps. *IEEE Transactions on Neural Networks*, 3, 698–713.

Carpenter, G. A., Grossberg, S., and Reynolds, J. H. (1991). ARTMAP: supervised realtime learning and classification of nonstationary data by a self-organizing neural network. *Neural Networks*, 4, 565–588.

Carpenter, G. A., Grossberg, S., and Rosen, D. B. (1991). Fuzzy ART: Fast stable learning and categorization of analog patterns by an adaptive resonance system. *Neural Networks*, 4, 759–771.

Carpenter, G. A., Martens, S., and Ogas, O. J. (2005). Self-organizing information fusion and hierarchical knowledge discovery: a new framework using ARTMAP neural networks. *Neural Networks*, 18, 287–295.

Carpenter, G. A., Milenova, B. L., and Noeske, B. W. (1998). Distributed ARTMAP: a neural network for fast distributed supervised learning. *Neural Networks*, 11, 793–813.

Carpenter, G. A., and Ravindran, A. (2008). Unifying multiple knowledge domains using the ARTMAP information fusion system. *Proceedings of the 11th International Conference on Information Fusion*, Cologne, Germany, June 30–July 3, 2008.

Carpenter, G. A., Rubin, M. A., and Streilein, W. W. (1997). ARTMAP-FD: Familiarity discrimination applied to radar target recognition. *Proceedings of the International Conference on Neural Networks (ICNN'97)*, 3, Piscataway, NJ: IEEE Press, 1459–1464.

Carrasco, M., Penpeci-Talgar, C., and Eckstein, M. (2000). Spatial covert attention increases contrast sensitivity across the CSF: support for signal enhancement. *Vision Research*, 40, 1203–1215.

Castet, E., Lorenceau, J., Shiffrar, M., and Bonnet, C. (1993). Perceived speed of moving lines depends on orientation, length, speed, and luminance. *Vision Research*, 33, 1921–1936.

Caudell, T., Smith, S., Johnson, C. Wunsch, D. C. II., and Escobedo, R. (1990). A data compressed ART1 neural network algorithms. *Proceedings of the SPIE Conference on Aerospace Sensing*, April.

Caudell, T., Smith, S., Johnson, C. Wunsch, D. C. II., and Escobedo, R. (1991). An industrial application of neural networks to reusable design. *Proceedings of the International Joint Conference on Neural Networks*, Vol. 2. Seattle, WA, p. 919.

Caudell, T. P. (1992). Hybrid optoelectronic adaptive resonance theory neural processor, ART 1. *Applied Optics*, 31, 6220–6229.

Caudell, T. P., Smith, S. D. G., Escobedo, R., and Anderson, M. (1994). NIRS: Large scale ART-1 neural architectures for engineering design retrieval. *Neural Networks*, 7, 1339–1350.

Caudell, T. P., Smith, S. D. G., Johnson, G. C., Wunsch, D. C. II, and Escobedo, R. (1991). An industrial application to neural networks to reusable design. *Neural Networks, International Joint Conference on Neural Networks*, 2, 919.

Cavanagh, P. (1992). Attention-based motion perception. *Science*, 257, 1563–1565.

Cavanagh, P., Hunt, A. R., Afraz, A., and Rolfs, M. (2010). Visual stability based on remapping of attention pointers. *Trends in Cognitive Sciences*, 14, 147–153.

Cavanagh, P., Labianca, A. T., & Thornton, I. M. (2001). Attention-based visual routines: sprites. *Cognition*, 80, 47–60.

Chagnac-Amitai, Y., and Connors, B. W. (1989). Synchronized excitation and inhibition driven by intrinsically bursting neurons in neocortex. *Journal of Neurophysiology*, 62, 1149–1162.

Chalmers, D. G. (1995). Facing up to the problem of consciousness. *Journal of Consciousness Studies*, 2, 200–219.

Chandler, B., and Grossberg, S. (2012). Joining distributed pattern processing and homeostatic plasticity in recurrent on-center off-surround shunting networks: Noise, saturation, short-term memory, synaptic scaling, and BDNF. *Neural Networks*, 25, 21–29.

Chang, H.-C., Grossberg, S., and Cao, Y. (2014) Where's Waldo? How perceptual cognitive, and emotional brain processes cooperate during learning to categorize and find desired objects in a cluttered scene. *Frontiers in Integrative Neuroscience*, doi: 10.3389/fnint.2014.0043.

Chang, Y. Y. (1968). 3', 5'-adenosine monophosphate phosphodiesterase produced by the slime mold Dictyostelium discoideum. *Science*, 160, 57–59.

Chao, H.-C., Hsiao, C.-M., Su, W.-S., Hsu, C.-C., and Wu, C.-Y. (2011). Modified adaptive resonance theory for alarm correlation based on distance hierarchy in mobile networks. 13th *AsiaPacific Network Operations and Management Symposium*, pp. 1–4.

Chapman, K. L., Leonard, L. B., and Mervis, C. G. (1986). The effect of feedback on young children's inappropriate word usage. *Journal of Child Language*, 13, 101–107.

Chau, B. K. H., Sallet, J., Papageorgiou, G. K., Noonan, M. P., Bell, A. H., Walton, M. E., and Rushworth, M. F. S. (2015). Contrasting roles for orbitofrontal cortex and amygdala in credit assignment and learning in Macaques. *Neuron, 87,* 1106–1118.

Chelazzi, L., Miller, E. K., Duncan, J., and Desimone, R. (2001). Responses of neurons in macaque area V4 during memory-guided visual search. *Cerebral Cortex, 11,* 761–774.

Chemtob, C., Roitblat, H. L., and Hamada, R. S. (1988). A cognitive action theory of post-traumatic stress disorder. *Journal of Anxiety Disorders, 2,* 253–275.

Chen, C., Kano, M., Abeliovich, A., Chen, L., Bao, S., Kim, J. J., Hashimoto, K., Thompson, R. F., and Tonegawa, S. (1995). Impaired motor coordination correlates with persistent multiple climbing fiber innervation in PKC-gamma mutant mice. *Cell, 83,* 1233–1242.

Chen, C., King, J. A., Burgess, N., and O'Keefe, J. (2013). How vision and movement combine in the hippocampal place code. *Proceedings of the National Academy of Sciences, 110,* 378–383.

Cherng, S., Fang, C.-Y., Chen, C.-P., and Chen, S.-W. (2009). Critical motion detection of nearby moving vehicles in a vision-based driver-assistance system. *IEEE Transactions on Intelligent Transportation Systems, 10,* 70–82.

Chey, J., Grossberg, S., and Mingolla, M. (1997). Neural dynamics of motion grouping: From aperture ambiguity to object speed and direction. *Journal of the Optical Society of America, 14,* 2570–2594.

Chey, J., Grossberg, S., and Mingolla, E. (1998). Neural dynamics of motion processing and speed discrimination. *Vision Research, 38,* 2769–2786.

Chiu, Y. C., and Yantis, S. (2009). A domain-independent source of cognitive control for task sets: shifting spatial attention and switching categorization rules. *The Journal of Neuroscience, 29,* 3930–3938.

Chomsky, N. (1957). *The Structure of Language.* The Hague: Mouton.

Chomsky, N. (1959). A review of B. F. Skinner's *Verbal Behavior. Language, 35,* 26–58.

Chouinard, S., Poulin, J., Stip, E., and Godbout, R. (2004). Sleep in untreated patients with schizophrenia: A meta-analysis. *Schizophrenia Bulletin, 30,* 957–967.

Chun, M. M. (2000). Contextual cueing of visual attention. *Trends in Cognitive Sciences, 4,* 170–178.

Chun, M. M., and Jiang, Y. (1998). Contextual cueing: implicit learning and memory of visual context guides spatial attention. *Cognitive Psychology, 36,* 28–71.

Chun, M. M., and Jiang, Y. (1999). Top-down attentional guidance based on implicit learning of visual covariation. *Psychological Science, 10,* 360–365.

Church, B. A., Krauss, M. S., Lopata, C., Toomey, J. A., Thomeer, M. L., Coutinho, M. V., Volker, M. A., and Mercado, E. (2010). Atypical categorization in children with high-functioning autism spectrum disorder. *Psychonomic Bulletin & Review, 17,* 862–868.

Cisek, P., Grossberg, S., and Bullock, D. (1998). A cortico-spinal model of reaching and proprioception under multiple task constraints. *Journal of Cognitive Neuroscience, 10,* 425–444.

Clark, E. V. (1973). What's in a word? On the child's acquisition of semantics in his first language. In *Cognitive development and the acquisition of language,* T. E. Morre (Ed.), 65–110. New York: Academic Press.

Clark, R. E., Manns, J. R., and Squire, L. R. (2001). Trace and delay eyeblink conditioning: contrasting phenomena of declarative and nondeclarative memory. *Psychological Science, 12,* 304–308.

Clark, R. E., and Squire, L. R. (1998). Classical conditioning and brain systems: The role of awareness. *Science, 280,* 77–81.

Clarke, S., and At, A. (2013). Sound localization disorders and auditory neglect. In G. G. Celesia (Ed.). *Handbook of Clinical Neurophysiology, 10,* 423–434. Amsterdam: Elsevier.

Cohen, M. A., and Grossberg, S. (1984). Neural dynamics of brightness perception: Features, boundaries, diffusion, and resonance. *Perception and Psychophysics, 36,* 428–456.

Cohen, M. A., and Grossberg, S. (1986). Neural dynamics of speech and language coding: Developmental programs, perceptual grouping, and competition for short-term memory. *Human Neurobiology, 5,* 1–22.

Cohen, M. A., and Grossberg, S. (1987). Masking fields: A massively parallel neural architecture for learning, recognizing, and predicting multiple groupings of patterned data. *Applied Optics, 26,* 1866–1891.

Cohen, M. A., and Grossberg, S. (1997). Parallel auditory filtering by sustained and transient channels separates co-articulated vowels and consonants. *IEEE Transactions on Speech and Audio Processing, 5,* 301–318.

Cohen, M. A., Grossberg, S., Stork, D. G. (1988). Speech perception and production by a self-organizing neural network. In Y. C. Lee (Ed.), *Evolution, Learning, Cognition, and Advanced Architectures.* Hong Kong: World Scientific Publishers, pp. 217–231.

Cohen, M. A., Grossberg, S., and Wyse, L. L. (1995). A spectral network model of pitch perception. *Journal of the Acoustical Society of America, 98,* 862–879.

Cohen, N. J. (1984). Preserved learning capacity in amnesia: Evidence for multiple memory systems. In *The Neuropsychology of Memory,* L. Squire and N. Butters (Eds.). New York: Guilford Press, pp. 83–103.

Cohen, N. J., and Squire, L. R. (1980). Preserved learning and retention of a pattern-analyzing skill in amnesia: Dissociation of knowing how and knowing that. *Science, 210,* 207–210.

Colburn, H. S. (1973). Theory of binaural interaction based on auditory nerve data. I. General strategy and preliminary results on interaural discrimination. *The Journal of the Acoustical Society of America, 54,* 1458–1470.

Colburn, H. S. (1977). Theory of binaural interaction based on auditory-nerve data. II. Detection of tones in noise. *The Journal of the Acoustical Society of America, 61,* 525–533.

Colby, C. L., and Goldberg, M. E. (1999). Space and attention in parietal cortex. *Annual Review of Neuroscience, 22,* 319–359.

Colgin, L. L., and Moser, E. I. (2010). Gamma oscillations in the hippocampus. *Physiology, 25,* 319–329.

Colgin, L. L., Denninger, T., Fyhn, M., Hafting, T., Bonnevie, T., Jensen, O, Moser, M.-B., and Moser, E. I. (2009). Frequency of gamma oscillations routes flow of information in the hippocampus. *Nature, 462,* 353–357.

Collection: MOCA's First 30 Years, Museum of Contemporary Art, Los Angeles, 2010 November 15, 2009–May 3, 2010.

Comon, P. (1994). Independent component analysis, a new concept? *Signal Processing*, 36, 287–314.

Connors, B. W. (1984). Initiation of synchronized neuronal bursting in neocortex. *Nature*, 310, 685–687.

Contreras-Vidal, J. L., Grossberg, S., and Bullock, D. (1997). A neural model of cerebellar learning for arm movement control: Cortico-spino-cerebellar dynamics. *Learning and Memory*, 3, 475–502.

Conway, C. M., and Christiansen, M. H. (2001). Sequential learning in non-human primates. *Trends in Cognitive Sciences*, 5, 539–546.

Corbetta, M., and Shulman, G. L. (2002). Control of goal-directed and stimulus-driven attention in the brain. *Nature Reviews Neuroscience*, 3, 201–215.

Corkin, S. (2002). What's new with the amnesic patient HM? *Nature Reviews Neuroscience*, 3, 153–160.

Cornish, K., Sudhalter, V., and Turk, J. (2004). Attention and language in fragile X. *Mental Retardation and Developmental Disabilities Research Reviews*, 10, 11–16.

Cousens, G., and Otto, T. (1998). Long-term potentiation and its transient suppression in the rhinal cortices induced by theta-related stimulation of hippocampal field CA1. *Brain Research*. 780, 95–101.

Cowan, N. (2001). The magical number 4 in short-term memory: A reconsideration of mental storage capacity. *Behavioral and Brain Sciences*, 24, 87–185.

Coyle, J. T., Price, D. L., and DeLong, M. R. (1983). Alzheimer's disease: a disorder of cortical cholinergic innervation. *Science*, 219, 1184–1190.

Crick, F. (1994). *The Astonishing Hypothesis: The Scientific Search for the Soul*. New York: Scribner Book Company.

Crick, F., and Koch, C. (1990). Towards a neurobiological theory of consciousness. *Seminars in the Neurosciences*, 2, 263–275.

Crick, F., and Koch, C. (1995). Are we aware of neural activity in primary visual cortex? *Nature*, 375, 121–123.

Cromer, J. A., Roy, J. E., and Miller, E. K. (2010). Representation of multiple, independent categories in the primate prefrontal cortex. *Neuron*, 66, 796–807.

Cruthirds, D. R., Grossberg, S., and Mingolla, E. (1993). Emergent groupings and texture segregation. *Investigative Ophthalmology & Visual Science*, 34, 1237.

Cutting, J. E., Springer, K., Braren, P. A., and Johnson, S. H. (1992). Wayfinding on foot from information in retinal, not optical, flow. *Journal of Experimental Psychology: General*, 121, 41–72.

Daffner, K. R., Mesulam, M.-M., Cohen, L. G., and Scinto, L. F. (1999). Mechanisms underlying diminished novelty-seeking behavior in patients with probable Alzheimer's disease. *Neuropsychiatry, Neuropsychology, & Behavioral Neurology*, 12, 58–66.

Damasio, A. R. (1999). *The Feeling of What Happens: Body and Emotion in the Making of Consciousness*. New York: Harcourt Brace & Company.

Daniel, P. M., and Whitteridge, D. (1961). The representation of the visual field on the cerebral cortex in monkeys. *Journal of Physiology*, 159, 203–221.

Darwin, C. (1859). *On the Origin of Species by Means of Natural Selection*. London: John Murray.

Darwin, C. J., and Hukin, R. W. (1999). Auditory objects of attention: The role of interaural time differences. *Journal of Experimental Psychology: Human Perception and Performance*, 25, 617–629.

Das, A., and Gilbert, C. D. (1995). Long-range horizontal connections and their role in cortical reorganization revealed by optical recording of cat primary visual cortex. *Nature*, 375, 780–784.

Da Silva, L. E. B., Elnabarawy, I., and Wunsch, D. C. II. (2019). A survey of Adaptive Resonance Theory neural network models for engineering applications. *Neural Networks*, 120, 167–210.

Da Silva, L. E. B., Elnabarawy, I., and Wunsch, D. C. II. (2020). Distributed dual vigilance fuzzy adaptive resonance theory learns online, retrieves arbitrarily-shaped clusters, and mitigates order dependence. *Neural Networks*, 121, 208–228.

Davidson, T. L., Altizer, A. M., Benoit, S. C., Walls, E. K., and Powley, T. L. (1997). Encoding and selective activation of "metabolic memories" in the rat. *Behavioral Neuroscience*, 111, 1014–1030.

Davis, C. J. (2010). The spatial coding model of visual word identification. *Psychological Review*, 117, 713–758.

Davis, G. W., and Murphy, R. K. (1994). Long-term regulation of short-term transmitter release properties: retrograde signaling and synaptic development. *Trends in Neurosciences*, 17, 9–13.

Davis, H. P., and Squire, L. R. (1984). Protein synthesis and memory: A review. *Psychological Bulletin*, 96, 518–559.

Davis, M. (1994). The role of the amygdala in emotional learning. *International Review of Neurobiology*, 36, 225–265.

Deadwyler, S. A., West, M. O., and Lynch, G. (1979). Activity of dentate granule cells during learning: Differentiation of perforant path inputs. *Brain Research*, 169, 29–43.

Deadwyler, S. A., West, M. O., and Robinson, J. H. (1981). Entorhinal and septal inputs differentially control sensory-evoked responses in the rat dentate gyrus. *Science*, 211, 1181–1183.

DeAngelis, G. C., Cumming, B. G., and Newsome, W. R. (1998). Cortical area MT and the perception of stereoscopic depth. *Nature*, 394, 677–680.

Dehaene, S. (1992). Varieties of numerical abilities. *Cognition*, 44, 1–42.

Dehaene, S. (1997). The number sense: How the mind creates mathematics. New York, NY: Oxford University Press.

Dehaene, S. (2014). *Consciousness and the brain*. New York, NY: Viking Press.

Delgutte, B., and Kiang, N. Y. S. (1984a). Speech coding in the auditory nerve I: Processing schemes for vowel-like sounds. *Journal of the Acoustical Society of America*, 75, 866–878.

Delgutte, B., and Kiang, N. Y. S. (1984b). Speech coding in the auditory nerve II: Vowel-like sounds. *Journal of the Acoustical Society of America*, 75, 879–886.

Delgutte, B., and Kiang, N. Y. S. (1984c). Speech coding in the auditory nerve III: Voiceless fricative consonants. *Journal of the Acoustical Society of America*, 75, 887–896.

Demetgul, M., Tansel, I. N., and Taskin, S. (2009). Fault diagnosis of pneumatic systems with artificial neural network architectures. *Expert Systems with Applications*, 36, 10512–10519.

Deneve, S., and Pouget, A. (2003). Basis functions for object-centered representations. *Neuron*, 37, 347–359.

Dennett, D. (1991). *Consciousness explained.* Boston, MA: Little, Brown.

Denny, M. R. (1971). Relaxation theory and experiments. In F. R. Brush (Ed.). *Aversive Conditioning and Learning.* New York: Academic Press.

Depue, R. A. (1974). The specificity of response interference in schizophrenia. *Journal of Abnormal Psychology,* 83, 529–532.

Desimone, R. (1998). Visual attention mediated by biased competition in extrastriate visual cortex. *Philosophical Transactions of the Royal Society of London,* 353, 1245–1255.

Desimone, R., and Duncan, J. (1995). Neural mechanisms of selective visual attention. *Annual Review of Neuroscience,* 18, 193–222.

DeSilva, H. R. (1926). An experimental investigation of the determinants of apparent visual movement. *American Journal of Psychology,* 37, 469–501.

Desimone, R., Albright, T. D., Gross, C. G., and Bruce, C. (1984). Visual properties of neurons in a polysensory area in superior temporal sulcus of the macaque. *Journal of Neurophysiology,* 46, 369–384.

Desimone, R., and Schein, S. J. (1987). Visual properties of neurons in area V4 of the macaque: Sensitivity to stimulus form. *Journal of Neurophysiology,* 57, 835–868.

Destexhe, A., Contreras, D., and Steriade, M. (1998). Mechanisms underlying the synchronizing action of corticothalamic feedback through inhibition of thalamic relay cells. *Journal of Neurophysiology,* 79, 999–1016.

Deurveilher, S., and Semba, K. (2005). Indirect projections from the suprachiasmatic nucleus to major arousal-promoting cell groups in rat: Implications for the circadian control of behavioural state. *Neuroscience,* 130, 165–183.

Deutsch, D. (1975). Two-channel listening to musical scales. *Journal of the Acoustical Society of America,* 57, 1156–1160.

Deutsch, D. (Ed.) (2013). *The Psychology of Music. Third edition.* Amsterdam: Elsevier.

DeWeerd, P., Peralta, M. R., Desimone, R., and Ungerleider, L. G. (1999). Loss of attentional stimulus selection after extrastriate cortical lesions in macaques. *Nature Neuroscience,* 2, 753–758.

DeYoe, E. A., and Van Essen, D. C. (1988). Concurrent processing streams in monkey visual cortex. *Trends in Neurosciences,* 11, 219–226.

Diana, R. A., Yonelinas, A. P., and Ranganath, C. (2007). Imaging recollection and familiarity in the medial temporal lobe: A three-component model. *Trends in Cognitive Sciences,* 11, 379–386.

Diaz-Caneja, E. (1928). Sur l'alternance binoculaire. *Ann Ocul (Paris),*165, 721–731.

Ditterich, J. (2006a). Stochastic models of decisions about motion direction: Behavior and physiology. *Neural Networks,* 19, 981–1012.

Ditterich, J. (2006b). Evidence for time-variant decision making. *European Journal of Neuroscience,* 24, 3628–3641.

Domnisoru, C., Kinkhabwala, A. A., and Tank, D. W. (2013). Membrane potential dynamics of grid cells. *Nature,* 495, 199–204.

Dorrn, A. L., Yuan, K., Barker, A. J., Schreiner, C. E., and Froemke, R. C. (2010). Developmental sensory experience balances cortical excitation and inhibition. *Nature,* 465, 932–936.

Dosher, B. A., Sperling, G., and Wurst, S. A. (1986). Tradeoffs between stereopsis and proximity luminance covariance as determinants of perceived 3D structure. *Vision Research,* 6, 973–990.

Downing, C. J. (1988). Expectancy and visual-spatial attention: effects on perceptual quality. *Journal of Experimental Psychology: Human Perception and Performance,* 14, 188–202.

Douglas, R. J., Koch, C., Mahowald, M., Martin, K. A. C., and Suarez, H. H. (1995). Recurrent excitation in neocortical circuits. *Science,* 269, 981–985.

Dranias, M., Grossberg, S., and Bullock, D. (2008). Dopaminergic and non-dopaminergic value systems in conditioning and outcome-specific revaluation. *Brain Research,* 1238, 239–287.

Drevets, W., Burton, H., Videen, T., Snyder, A., Simpson, J., Jr., and Raichle, M. (1995). Blood flow changes in human somatosensory cortex during anticipated stimulation, *Nature,* 373, 249–252.

Dreyer, P., and Renner, K. E. (1971). Self-punitive behavior: Masochism or confusion? *Psychological Review,* 78, 333–337.

Driver, J., and Mattingley, J. B. (1998). Parietal neglect and visual awareness. *Nature Neuroscience,* 1, 17–22.

Dubin, M. W., and Cleland, B. G. (1977). Organization of visual inputs to interneurons of lateral geniculate nucleus of the cat. *Journal of Neurophysiology,* 40, 410–427.

Dubois, B., Burn, D., Goetz, C., Aarsland, D., Brown, R. G., Broe, G. A., Dickson, D., Duyckaerts, C., et al. (2007). Diagnostic procedures for Parkinson's disease dementia: Recommendations from the Movement Disorder Society Task Force. *Movement Disorders,* 22, 2314–2324.

Dudai, Y. (1996). Consolidation: Fragility on the road to the engram. *Neuron,* 17, 367–370.

Dudai, Y. (2004). The neurobiology of consolidations, or, how stable is the engram? *Annual Review of Psychology,* 55, 51–86.

Duffy, C. J. (1998). MST neurons respond to optic flow and translational movement. *Journal of Neurophysiology,* 80, 1816–1827.

Duffy, C. J., and Wurtz, R. H. (1995). Response of monkey MST neurons to optic flow stimuli with shifted centers of motion. *Journal of Neuroscience,* 15, 5192–5208.

Duhamel, J. R., Colby, C. L., and Goldberg, M. E. (1992). The updating of the representation of visual space in parietal cortex by intended eye movements. *Science,* 255, 90–92.

Dukelow, S. P., DeSouza, J. F., Culham, J. C., van den Berg, A. V., Menon, R. S., and Vilis, T. (2001). Distinguishing subregions of the human MT+ complex using visual fields and pursuit eye movements. *Journal of Neurophysiology,* 86, 1991–2000.

Dunbar, G. (2012). Adaptive resonance theory as a model of polysemy and vagueness in the cognitive lexicon. *Cognitive Linguistics,* 23, 507–537.

Duncan, J. (1984). Selective attention and the organization of visual information. *Journal of Experimental Psychology: General,* 113, 501–517.

Duncan, J., and Humphreys, G. W. (1989). Visual search and stimulus similarity. *Psychological Review,* 96, 433–458.

Duncan-Johnson, C. C., and Donchin, E. (1977). On quantifying surprise: The variation in event-related potentials with subjective probability. *Psychophysiology,* 14, 456–467.

Duncker, K. (1938). Induced motion. In *A Sourcebook of Gestalt Psychology*. W. D. Ellis (Ed.). London: Routledge & Kegan Paul, 1938. (Originally published in German, 1929).

Dursteler, M. R., Wurtz, R. H., and Newsome, W. T. (1987). Directional pursuit deficits following lesions of the foveal representation within the superior temporal sulcus of the macaque monkey. *Journal of Neurophysiology*, 57, 1262–1287.

Dursteler, M. R., and Wurtz, R. H. (1988). Pursuit and optokinetic deficits following chemical lesions of cortical areas MT and MST. *Journal of Neurophysiology*, 60, 940–965.

Eckhorn, R., Bauer, R., Jordan, W., Brosch, M., Kruse, W., Munk, M., and Reitboeck, H. J. (1988). Coherent oscillations: A mechanism of feature linking in the visual cortex? *Biological Cybernetics*, 60, 121–130.

Edelman, G. M., and Tononi, G. (2000). *A Universe of Consciousness: How Matter Becomes Imagination*. New York: Basic Books.

Egeth, H., Virzi, R. A., and Garbart, H. (1984). Searching for conjunctively defined targets. *Journal of Experimental Psychology: Human Perception and Performance*, 10, 32–39.

Egly, R., Driver, J., and Rafal, R. D. (1994). Shifting visual attention between objects and locations: Evidence from normal and parietal lesion subjects. *Journal of Experimental Psychology: General*, 123, 161–177.

Egusa. H. (1983). Effects of brightness, hue, and saturation on perceived depth between adjacent regions in the visual field. *Perception*, 12, 167–175.

Eichenbaum, H., and Lipton, P. A. (2008). Towards a functional organization of the medial temporal lobe memory system: role of the parahippocampal and medial entorhinal cortical areas. *Hippocampus*, 18, 1314–1324.

Eifuku, S., and Wurtz, R. H. (1998). Response to motion in extrastriate area MSTl: Center-surround interactions. *Journal of Neurophysiology*, 80, 282–296.

Einstein, A. (1905). On the electrodynamics of moving bodies. *Annals of Physics*, 322, 891–921.

Einstein, A. (1915). The field equations of gravitation. *Königlich Preussische Akademie der Wissenschaften*, 844–847.

Einstein, A., and Infeld, L. (1938). *The Evolution of Physics*. New York: Simon & Schuster.

Elder, D., Grossberg, S., and Mingolla, E. (2009). A neural model of visually guided steering, obstacle avoidance, and route selection. *Journal of Experimental Psychology: Human Perception & Performance*, 35, 1501–1531.

Ellias, S. A., and Grossberg, S. (1975). Pattern formation, contrast control, and oscillations in the short-term memory of shunting on-center off-surround networks. *Biological Cybernetics*, 20, 69–98.

Elliott, R., Dolan, R. J., and Frith, C. D. (2000). Dissociable functions in the medial and lateral orbitofrontal cortex: Evidence from human neuroimaging studies. *Cerebral Cortex*, 10, 308–317.

Engel, A. K., Fries, P., and Singer, W. (2001). Dynamic predictions: Oscillations and synchrony in top-down processing. *Nature Reviews Neuroscience*, 2, 704–716.

English, D. R., Peyrache, A., Stark, E., Roux, L., Vallentin, D., Long, M. A., and Buzsáki, G. (2014). Excitation and inhibition compete to control spiking during hippocampal ripples: Intracellular study in behaving mice. *The Journal of Neuroscience*, 34, 16509–16517.

Erhan, D., Bengio, Y., Courville, A., Manzagol, P.-A., and Vincenter, P. (2010). Why does unsupervised pre-training help deep learning? *Journal of Machine Learning Research*, 11, 625–660.

Escobedo, R., Smith, S. D. G., and Caudell, T. P. (1993). A neural information retrieval system. *The International Journal of Advanced Manufacturing Technology*, 8, 269–273.

Esser, S. K., Hill, S., and Tononi, G. (2009). Breakdown of effective connectivity during slow wave sleep: Investigating the mechanism underlying a cortical gate using large-scale modeling. *Journal of Neurophysiology*, 102, 2096–2111.

Estes, W. K. (1950). Toward a statistical theory of learning. *Psychological Review*, 57, 94–107.

Etienne, A. S., Maurer, R., and Seguinot, V. (1996). Path integration in mammals and its integration with visual landmarks. *Journal of Experimental Biology*, 199, 201–209.

Evarts, E. V. (1973). Motor cortex reflexes associated with learned movement. *Science*, 179, 501–503.

Exner, S. (1875). Ueber das Sehen von Bewegungen und die Theorie des zusammengesetzen Auges. *Sitzungsberichte Akademie Wissenschaft Wien*, 72, 156–190.

Fajen, B. R., and Warren, W. H. (2003). Behavioral dynamics of steering, obstacle avoidance, and route selection. *Journal of Experimental Psychology: Human Perception and Performance*, 29, 343–362.

Fang, L., and Grossberg, S. (2009). From stereogram to surface: How the brain sees the world in depth. *Spatial Vision*, 22, 45–82.

Farrell, J., Pavel, M., and Sperling, G. (1990). The visible persistence of stimuli in stroboscopic motion. *Vision Research*, 30, 921–936.

Farrell, S., and Lewandowsky, S. (2004). Modeling transposition latencies: Constraints for theories of serial order memory. *Journal of Memory and Language*, 51, 115–135.

Faubert, J., and von Grünau, M. (1992). The extent of split attention and attribute priming in motion induction. *Perception*, 21, 195b.

Faubert, J., and von Grünau, M. (1995). The influence of two spatially distinct primers and attribute priming on motion induction. *Vision Research*, 35, 3119–3130.

Fazl, A., Grossberg, S., and Mingolla, E. (2009). View-invariant object category learning, recognition, and search: How spatial and object attention are coordinated using surface-based attentional shrouds. *Cognitive Psychology*, 58, 1–48.

Fecteau, S., Armony, J. L., Joanette, Y., and Belin, P. (2004). Is voice processing species-specific in human auditory cortex? An fMRI study. *NeuroImage*, 23, 840–848.

Felleman, D. J., and Van Essen, D. C. (1991). Distributed hierarchical processing in the primate cerebral cortex. *Cerebral Cortex*, 1, 1–47.

Fellows, L. K., and Farah, M. J. (2003). Ventromedial frontal cortex mediates affective shifting in humans: evidence from a reversal learning paradigm. *Brain*, 126, 1830–1837.

Fernández-Ruiz, A., Oliva, A., de Oliveira, E. F., Rocha-Almeida, F., Tingly, D., and Buzaki, G. (2019). Long-duration hippocampal sharp wave ripples improve memory. *Science*, 364, 1082–1086.

Ferrera, V. P., and Wilson, H. R. (1990). Perceived direction of moving two-dimensional patterns. *Vision Research*, 30, 273–287.

Ferrera, V. P., and Wilson, H. R. (1991). Perceived speed of moving two-dimensional patterns. *Vision Research*, 31, 877–893.

Ferster, D., Chung, S., and Wheat, H. (1996). Orientation selectivity of thalamic input to simple cells of cat visual cortex. *Nature*, 380, 249–252.

Fiala, J. C., Grossberg, S., and Bullock, D. (1996). Metabotropic glutamate receptor activation in cerebellar Purkinje cells as substrate for adaptive timing of the classically conditioned eye blink response. *The Journal of Neuroscience*, 16, 3760–3774.

Field, D. J., Hayes, A., and Hess, R. F. (1993). Contour integration by the human visual system: Evidence for a local "association field". *Vision Research*, 33, 173–193.

Filehne, W. (1922). Uber das optische Wahrnehmen von Bewegunggen. Zeitschrift fur Sinnephysiologie, 53, 134–145.

Finch, E. A., and Augustine, G. J. (1998). Local calcium signalling by inositol-1,4,5-triphosphate in Purkinje cell dendrites. *Nature*, 396, 753–756.

Fischer, B. (1973). Overlap of receptive field centers and representation of the visual field in the cat's optic tract. *Vision Research*, 13, 2113–2120.

Fitzpatrick, D. (1996). The functional organization of local circuits in visual cortex: Insights from the study of tree shrew striate cortex. *Cerebral Cortex*, 6, 329–341.

Fitzpatrick, D., Lund, J. S., and Blasdel, G. G. (1985). Intrinsic connections of macaque striate cortex: afferent and efferent connections of lamina 4C. *The Journal of Neuroscience*, 5, 3329–3349.

Fleischl, E. V. (1882). Physiologisch-optische Notizen, 2 Mitteilung. *Sitzung Winer Bereich der Akademie der Wissenschaften*, 3, 7–25.

Foa, E. B., Keane, T. M., Friedman, M. J., and Cohen, J. A. (2009). *Effective treatments for PTSD: Practice guidelines from the International Society for Traumatic Stress Studies, Second Edition.* New York: Guilford Press.

Foley, N. C., Grossberg, S., and Mingolla, E. (2012). Neural dynamics of object-based multifocal visual spatial attention and priming: Object cueing, useful-field-of-view, and crowding. *Cognitive Psychology*, 65, 77–117.

Fortenberry, B., Gorchetchnikov, A., and Grossberg, S. (2012). Learned integration of visual, vestibular, and motor cues in multiple brain regions computes head direction during visually-guided navigation. *Hippocampus*, 22, 2219–2237.

Foster, K. H., Gaska, J. P., Nagler, M., and Pollen, D. A. (1985). Spatial and temporal frequency selectivity of neurons in visual cortical areas V1 and V2 of the macaque monkey. *The Journal of Physiology*, 365, 331–363.

Fox, R. (1991). Binocular rivalry. In D. M. Regan (Ed.). *Binocular Vision and Psychophysics*. London: MacMillan Press, pp. 93–110.

Fraisse, P. (1982). Rhythm and tempo. In D. Deutsch (Ed.). *The psychology of music*, pp. 149–180. New York: Academic Press.

Franchak, J. M., Kretch, K. S., Soska, K. C., and Adolph, K. E. (2011). Head-mounted eye tracking: A new method to describe infant looking. *Child Development*, 82, 1738–1750.

Francis, G. (1996). Cortical dynamics of visual persistence and temporal integration. *Vision Research*, 58, 1204–1212.

Francis, G. (1997). Cortical dynamics of lateral inhibition: Metacontrast masking. *Psychological Review*, 104, 572–594.

Francis, G. (2000). Quantitative theories of metacontrast masking. *Psychological Review*, 107, 768–785.

Francis, G., and Grossberg, S. (1996). Cortical dynamics of boundary segmentation and reset: Persistence, afterimages, and residual traces. *Perception*, 35, 543–567.

Francis, G., Grossberg, S., Mingolla, E. (1994). Cortical dynamics of feature binding and reset: Control of visual persistence. *Vision Research*, 34, 1089–1104.

Francis, P. T., Palmer, A. M., Snape, M., and Wilcock, G. K. (1999). The cholinergic hypothesis of Alzheimer disease: a review of progress. *Journal of Neurology, Neurosurgery, & Psychiatry*, 66, 137–147.

Frank, L. M., Stanley, G. B., and Brown, E. N. (2004). Hippocampal plasticity across multiple days of exposure to novel environments. *The Journal of Neuroscience*, 24, 7681–7689.

Frank, M. J., (2005). Dynamic dopamine modulation in the basal ganglia: A neurocomputational account of cognitive deficits in medicated and non-medicated Parkinsonism. *Journal of Cognitive Neuroscience*, 17, 51–72.

Frank, M. J., Loughry, B., and O'Reilly, R. C. (2001). Interactions between the frontal cortex and basal ganglia in working memory: A computational model. *Cognitive, Affective, and Behavioral Neuroscience*, 1, 137–160.

Franklin, D. J., and Grossberg, S. (2017). A neural model of normal and abnormal learning and memory consolidation: Adaptively timed conditioning, hippocampus, amnesia, neurotrophins, and consciousness. *Cognitive, Affective, and Behavioral Neuroscience*, 17, 24–76.

Freedman, D. J., Riesenhuber, M., Poggio, T., and Miller, E. K. (2001). Categorical representation of visual stimuli and the primate prefrontal cortex. *Science*, 291, 312–316.

Freedman, D. J., Riesenhuber, M., Poggio, T., and Miller, E. K. (2003). A comparison of primate prefrontal and inferior temporal cortices during visual categorization. *The Journal of Neuroscience*, 23, 5235–5246.

Freeman, A. W. (2005). Multistage model for binocular rivalry. *Journal of Neurophysiology*, 94, 4412–4420.

Freud, S. (1927). Fetishism. *The Standard Edition of the Complete Psychological Works of Sigmund Freud, Volume XXI*. Psychoanalytic Electronic Publishing, ISSN 2472–6982.

Friedman, D. P., Aggleton, J. P., and Saunders, R. C. (2002). Comparison of hippocampal, amygdala, and perirhinal projections to the nucleus accumbens: Combined anterograde and retrograde tracing study in the Macaque brain. *Journal of Comparative Neurology*, 450, 345–365.

Friedman, E., Lerer, B., and Kuster, J. (1983). Loss of cholinergic neurons in the rat neocortex produces deficits in passive avoidance learning. *Pharmacology, Biochemistry, and Behavior*, 19, 309–312.

Fries, P. (2009). Neuronal gamma-band synchronization as a fundamental process in cortical computation. *Annual Review of Neuroscience*, 32, 209–224.

Fries, P., Reynolds, J. H., Rorie, A. E., and Desimone, R. (2001). Modulation of oscillatory neuronal synchronization by selective visual attention *Science*, 291, 1560–1563.

Frith, C. D. (1998). The role of the prefrontal cortex in self-consciousness: the case of auditory hallucinations. In A. C. Roberts, T. W. Robbins, and L. Weiskrantz (Eds.), *The Prefrontal Cortex: Executive and Cognitive Functions*, pp. 181–194. Oxford: Oxford University Press.

Frith, C. D., and Dolan, R. J. (1997). Brain mechanisms associated with top-down processes in perception. *Philosophical Transactions of the Royal Society of London B*, 352, 1221–1230.

Fritsch, T., Smyth, K. A., Debanne, S. M., Petot, G. J., and Friedland, R. P. (2005). Participation in novelty-seeking leisure activities and Alzheimer's disease. *Journal of Geriatric Psychiatry and Neurology*, 28, 134–141.

Fryns, J. P., Jacobs, J., Kleczkowska, A., and Van den Berghe, H. (1984). The psychological profile of the fragile X syndrome. *Clinical Genetics*, 25, 131–134.

Fuhs, M. C., and Touretzky, D. S. (2006). A spin glass model of path integration in rat medial entorhinal cortex. *The Journal of Neuroscience*, 26, 4266–4276.

Funahashi, S., Inoue, M., and Kubota, K. (1997). Delay-period activity in the primate prefrontal cortex encoding multiple spatial positions and their order of presentation. *Behavioral Brain Research*, 84, 203–223.

Fuster, J. M. (1973). Unit activity in prefrontal cortex during delayed-response performance: neuronal correlates of transient memory. *Journal of Neurophysiology*, 36, 61–78.

Fuster, J. M. (2015). *The Prefrontal Cortex, Fifth Edition*. London, UK: Academic Press.

Fuster J. M., and Jervey, J. P. (1981). Inferotemporal neurons distinguish and retain behaviorally relevant features of visual stimuli. *Science*, 212, 952–955.

Fyhn, M., Hafting, T., Treves, A., Moser, M.-B., and Moser, E. I. (2007). Hippocampal remapping and grid realignment in entorhinal cortex. *Nature*, 446, 190–194.

Gabreil, M., Sparenborg, S. P., and Stolar, N. (1987). Hippocampal control of cingulate cortical and anterior thalamic information processing during learning in rabbits. *Experimental Brain Research*, 67, 131–52.

Gabrieli, J. D., McGlinchey-Berroth, R., Carrillo, M. C., Gluck, M. A., Cermak, L. S., and Disterhoft, J. F. (1995). Intact delay-eyeblink classical conditioning in amnesia. *Behavioral Neuroscience*, 109, 819–827.

Gaffan, D. (1974). Recognition impaired and association intact in the memory of monkeys after transection of the fornix. *Journal of Comparative and Physiological Psychology*, 86, 1100–1109.

Gaffan, D. (1985). Hippocampus: Memory, habit, and voluntary movement. *Philosophical Transactions of the Royal Society of London, B.* 308, 87–99.

Galantucci, B., Fowley, C. A., and Turvey, M. T. (2006). The motor theory of speech perception reviewed. *Psychonomic Bulletin and Review*, 13, 361–377.

Gallagher, M., McMahan, R. W., and Schoenbaum, G. (1999). Orbitofrontal cortex and representation of incentive value in associative learning. *The Journal of Neuroscience*, 19, 6610–6614.

Gallese, V. (2001). The "shared manifold" hypothesis. From mirror neurons to empathy. *Journal of Consciousness Studies*, 8, 33–50.

Gallese, V. (2003). The roots of empathy: The shared manifold hypothesis and the neural basis of intersubjectivity. *Psychopathology*, 36, 171–180.

Galton, F. (1881). Visualised numerals. *The Journal of the Anthropological Institute of Great Britain and Ireland*, 10, 85–102.

Galuske, R. A. W., and Singer, W. (1996). The origin and topography of the long-range intrinsic projections in cat visual cortex: A developmental study. *Cerebral Cortex*, 6, 417–430.

Gancarz, G., and Grossberg, G. (1998). A neural model of the saccade generator in the reticular formation. *Neural Networks*, 11, 1159–1174.

Gancarz, G., and Grossberg, G. (1999). A neural model of the saccadic eye movement control explains task-specific adaptation. *Vision Research*, 39, 3123–3143.

Ganguly, K., Kiss, L., and Poo, M.-M. (2000). Enhancement of presynaptic neural excitability by correlated presynaptic and postsynaptic spiking. *Nature Neuroscience*, 3, 1018–1026.

Ganz, L., and Day, R. H. (1965). An analysis of the satiation-fatigue mechanism in figural aftereffects. *American Journal of Psychology*, 78, 345–361.

Gao, E., and Suga, N. (1998). Experience-dependent corticofugal adjustment of midbrain frequency map in bat auditory system. *Proceedings of the National Academy of Sciences*, 95, 12663–12670.

Garden, D. L. F., Dodson, P. D., O'Donnell, C., White, M. D., and Nolan, M. F. (2008). Tuning of synaptic integration in the medial entorhinal cortex to the organization of grid cell firing fields. *Neuron*, 60, 875–889.

Garrud, P., Rawlins, J. N. P., Mackintosh, N. J., Godall, G., Cotton, M. M., and Feldon, J. (1984). Successful overshadowing and blocking in hippocampectomized rats. *Behavioural Brain Research*, 12, 39–53.

Gasser, H. S., and Grundfest, H. (1939). Axon diameters in relation to the spike dimensions and the conduction velocity in mammalian A fibers. *American Journal of Physiology*, 127, 393–414.

Gaudiano P., and Grossberg S. (1991). Vector associative maps: Unsupervised real-time error-based learning and control of movement trajectories. *Neural Networks*, 4, 147–183.

Gaudiano, P., and Grossberg, S. (1992). Adaptive vector integration to endpoint: Self-organizing neural circuits for control of planned movement trajectories. *Human Movement Science*, 11, 141–155.

Gauss, C. F. (1814). Methodus nova integralium valores per approximationem inveniendi. *Commentationes Societatis Regiae Scientiarium Gottingensis*, 39–76.

Gaymard, B., Pierrot-Deseilligny, C., and Rivaud, S. (1990). Impairment of sequences of memory-guided saccades after supplementary motor area lesions. *Annals of Neurology*, 28, 622–626.

Gaymard, B., Ploner, C., Rivaud-Pechoux, S., and Pierrot-Deseilligny, C. (1999). The frontal eye field is involved in spatial short-term memory but not in reflexive saccade inhibition. *Experimental Brain Research*, 129, 288–301.

Gazzaniga, M. S. (1967). The split brain in man. *Scientific American*, 217, 24–29.

Gelfand, J. R., and Bookheimer, S. Y. (2003). Dissociating neural mechanisms of temporal sequencing and processing phonemes. *Neuron*, 38, 831–842.

Gengerelli, J. A. (1948). Apparent movement in relation to homonymous and heteronymous stimulation of the cerebral hemispheres. *Journal of Experimental Psychology*, 38, 592–599.

Georgopoulos, A. P., Kalaska, J. F., Caminiti. R., and Massey, J. T. (1982). On the relations between the direction of two-dimensional arm movements and cell discharge in primate motor cortex. *Journal of Neuroscience, 2*, 1527–1537.

Georgopoulos, A. P., Kalaska, J. F., and Massey, J. T. (1981). Spatial trajectories and reaction times of aimed movements: Effects of practice, uncertainty, and change in target location. *Journal of Neurophysiology, 46*, 725–743.

Georgopoulos, A. P., Schwartz, A. B., and Kettner, R. E. (1986). Neuronal population coding of movement direction. *Science, 233*, 1416–1419.

Gerfen, C. R., and Bolam, J. P. (2010). The Neuroanatomical Organization of the Basal Ganglia. In *Handbook of Behavioral Neuroscience, Volume 20*, Chapter 1, pp. 3–28.

Giaschi, D., and Anstis, S. (1989). The less you see it, the faster it moves: Shortening the "on-time" speeds up apparent motion. *Vision Research, 29*, 335–347.

Gibbon, J. (1977). Scalar expectancy theory and Weber's law in animal timing. *Psychological Review, 84*, 279–325.

Gibbon, J. (1991). The origins of scalar timing. *Learning and Motivation, 22*, 3–38.

Gibson, J. J. (1950). *The Perception of the Visual World*. Oxford, England: Houghton Mifflin.

Gibson, J. J., and Radner, M. (1937). Adaptation, after-effect and contrast in the perception of tilted lines. I. Quantitative studies. *Journal of Experimental Psychology, 20*, 453–467.

Gierer, A., and Meinhardt, H. (1972). A theory of biological pattern formation. *Kybernetik, 12*, 30–39.

Gilbert, C. D., and Wiesel, T. N. (1979). Morphology and intracortical projections of functionally characterised neurones in the cat visual cortex. *Nature, 280*, 120–125.

Gilbert, C. D., and Wiesel, T. N. (1992). Receptive field dynamics in adult primary visual cortex. *Nature, 356*, 150–152.

Gilchrist, A. L., Kossyfidis, C., Bonato, F., Agostini, T., Cataliotti, J., Li, X., Spehar, B., Annan, V., and Economou, E. (1999). An anchoring theory of lightness perception. *Psychological Review, 106*, 795–834.

Gillam, B., Blackburn, S., and Nakayama, K. (1999). Stereopsis based on monocular gaps: Metrical encoding of depth and slant without matching contours. *Vision Research, 39*, 493–502.

Giocomo, L. M., and Hasselmo, M. E. (2008). Time constants of h current in layer II stellate cells differ along the dorsal to ventral axis of medial entorhinal cortex. *The Journal of Neuroscience, 28*, 9414–9425.

Giocomo, L. M., and Hasselmo, M. E. (2009). Knockout of HCN1 subunit flattens dorsal-ventral frequency gradient of medial entorhinal neurons in adult mice. *The Journal of Neuroscience, 29*, 7625–7630.

Giocomo, L. M., Hussaini, S. A., Zheng, F., Kandel, E. R., Moser, M. B., and Moser, E. I. (2011). Increased spatial scale in grid cells of HCN1 knockout mice. *Cell, 147*, 1159–1170.

Giocomo, L. M., Zilli, E., Fransen, E., Hasselmo, and M. E. (2007). Temporal frequency of subthreshold oscillations scales with entorhinal grid cell field spacing. *Science, 315*, 1719–1722.

Glass, L. (1969). Moire effect from random dots. *Nature, 223*, 578–580.

Gloor, P., Olivier, A., and Quesney, L. F. (1982). The role of the limbic system in experiential phenomena of temporal lobe epilepsy. *Annals of Neurology, 12*, 129–144.

Glotin, H., Warnier, P., Dandurand, F. Dufau, S., Lété, B., Touzet, C., Ziegler, J. C., and Grainger, J. (2010). An adaptive resonance theory account of the implicit learning of orthographic word forms. *Journal of Physiology-Paris, 104*, 19–26.

Gnadt, J. W., and Andersen, R. A. (1988). Memory related motor planning activity in posterior parietal cortex of macaque. *Experimental Brain Research, 70*, 216–220.

Gnadt, W., and Grossberg, S. (2008). SOVEREIGN: An autonomous neural system for incrementally learning planned action sequences to navigate towards a rewarded goal. *Neural Networks, 21*, 699–758.

Gochin, P. M., Miller, E. K., Gross, C. G., and Gerstein, G. L. (1991). Functional interactions among neurons in inferior temporal cortex of the awake macaque. *Experimental Brain Research, 84*, 505–516.

Goebel, R., Khorram-Sefat, D., Muckli, L., Hacker, H., and Singer, W. (1998). The constructive nature of vision: Direct evidence from functional magnetic resonance imaging studies of apparent motion and motion imagery. *European Journal of Neuroscience, 10*, 1563–1573.

Gold, J. I., and Shadlen, M. N. (2001). Neural computations that underlie decisions about sensory stimuli. *Trends in Cognitive Sciences, 5*, 10–16.

Gold, J. I., and Shadlen, M. N. (2007). The neural basis of decision-making. *Annual Review of Neuroscience, 30*, 535–574.

Goldinger, S. D. (1996). Words and voices: Episodic traces in spoken word identification and recognition memory. *Journal of Experimental Psychology: Learning, Memory, and Cognition, 22*, 1166–1183.

Goldinger, S. D., and Azuma, T. (2003). Puzzle-solving science: The quixotic quest for units in speech perception. *Journal of Phonetics, 31*, 305–320.

Goldman-Rakic, P. S. (1987). Circuitry of primate prefrontal cortex and regulation of behavior by representational memory. In *Handbook of Physiology*, Volume 5, Part 1. Mountcastle, V. B., and Plum, G. (Eds.), pp. 373–417. Bethesda, MD: American Physiological Society.

Goldman-Rakic, P. S. (1988). Topography of cognition: Parallel distributed networks in primate association cortex. *Annual Review of Neuroscience, 11*, 137–156.

Goodale, M. A., and Milner, A. D. (1992) Separate visual pathways for perception and action. *Trends in Neurosciences, 15*, 20–25.

Goodale, M. A., Milner, A. D., Jakobson, L. S., and Carey, D. P. (1991). A neurological dissociation between perceiving objects and grasping them. *Nature, 349*, 154–156.

Goodridge, J. P., and Touretzky, D. S. (2000). Modeling attractor deformation in the rodent head-direction system. *Journal of Neurophysiology, 83*, 3402–3410.

Gorchetchnikov, A., and Grossberg, S. (2007). Space, time, and learning in the hippocampus: How fine spatial and temporal scales are expanded into population codes for behavioral control. *Neural Networks, 20*, 182–193.

Gore, F., Schwartz, E. C., Brangers, B. C., Aladi, S., Stujenske, J. M., Likhtik, E., Russo, M. J., Gordon, J. A., Salzman, C.

D., and Axel, R. (2015). Neural representations of unconditioned stimuli in basolateral amygdala mediate innate and learned responses. *Cell*, 162, 134–145.

Gorski, J. A., Zeiler, S. R., Tamowski, S, and Jones, K. R. (2003). Brain-derived neurotrophic factor is required for the maintenance of cortical dendrites. *The Journal of Neuroscience*, 23, 6856–6865.

Gothard, K. M., Skaggs, W. E., and McNaughton, B. L. (1996). Dynamics of mismatch correction in the hippocampal ensemble code for space: interaction between path integration and environmental cues. *The Journal of Neuroscience*, 16, 8027–8040.

Gottlieb, J., Kusunoki, M., and Goldberg, M. E. (1998). The representation of visual salience in monkey parietal cortex. *Nature*, 391, 481–484.

Gottfried, J. A., O'Doherty, J., and Dolan, R. J. (2003). Encoding predictive reward value in human amygdala and orbitofrontal cortex. *Science*, 301, 1104–1107.

Gould, L. N. (1949). Auditory hallucinations and subvocal speech. *Journal of Nervous and Mental Disorders*, 109, 418–427.

Gove, A., Grossberg, S., and Mingolla, E. (1995). Brightness perception, illusory contours, and corticogeniculate feedback. *Visual Neuroscience*, 12, 1027–1052.

Graf, P., Squire, L. R., and Mandler, G. (1984). The information that amnesic patients do not forget. *Journal of Experimental Psychology: Learning, Memory, and Cognition*, 10, 164–178.

Graham, N., Beck, J., and Sutter, A. (1992). Nonlinear processes in spatial-frequency channel models of perceived texture. *Vision Research*, 32, 719–743.

Grahn, J. A., Parkinson, J. A., and Owen, A. M. (2009). The role of the basal ganglia in learning and memory: Neuropsychological studies. *Behavioural Brain Research*, 199, 53–60.

Grant, D. A. (1973). Cognitive factors in eyelid conditioning. *Psychophysiology*, 10, 75–81.

Gray, C. M., and Singer, W. (1989). Stimulus-specific neuronal oscillations in orientation columns of cat visual cortex. *Proceedings of the National Academy of Sciences*, 86, 1698–1702.

Graybiel, A. M. (2000). The basal ganglia. *Current Biology*. 10, R509–R511.

Graybiel, A. M., Canales, J. J., and Capper-Loup, C. (2000). Levodopa-induced dyskinesias and dopamine-dependent stereotypies: a new hypothesis. *Trends in Neurosciences*, 23, S71–S77.

Graziano, M. S., Andersen, R. A., and Snowden, R. J. (1994). Tuning of MST neurons to spiral motions. *The Journal of Neuroscience*, 14, 54–67.

Green, C. S., and Bavelier, D. (2003). Action video game modifies visual selective attention. *Nature*, 423, 534–537.

Green, C. S., and Bavelier, D. (2007). Action-video-game experience alters the spatial resolution of vision. *Psychological Science*, 18, 88–94.

Gregoriou, G. G., Gotts, S. J., Zhou, H., and Desimone, R,. (2009). High-frequency, long-range coupling between prefrontal and visual cortex during attention. *Science*, 324, 1207–1210.

Gregorious, G. G., Rossi, A. F., Ungerleider, L. G., and Desimone, R. (2014). Lesions of prefrontal cortex reduce attentional modulation of neuronal responses and synchrony in V4. *Nature Neuroscience*, 17, 1003–1011.

Gregory, R. L. (1972). Cognitive contours. *Nature*, 238, 51–52.

Grey, J. M. (1977). Multidimensional perceptual scaling of musical timbres. *Journal of the Acoustical Society of America*, 61, 1270–1277.

Grimson, W. E. (1981). A computer implementation of a theory of human stereo vision. *Philosophical Transactions of the Royal Society (B)*, 292, 217–253.

Grindley, G. C., and Townsend, V. (1965). Binocular masking induced by a moving object. *Quarterly Journal of Experimental Psychology*, 17, 97–109.

Grinvald, A., Lieke, E. E., Frostig, R. D., and Hildesheim, R. (1994). Cortical point-spread function and long-range lateral interactions revealed by real-time optical imaging of macaque monkey primary visual cortex. *The Journal of Neuroscience*, 14, 2545–2568.

Groenewegen, H. J. (2003). The basal ganglia and motor control. *Neural Plasticity*, 10, 107–120.

Groner, R., Hofer, D. and Groner, M. (1986). The role of anticipation in the encoding of motion signals—sensitization or bias. In *Human Memory and Cognitive Capabilities*. F. Klix and H. Hagendorf (Eds.). Amsterdam, Elsevier.

Grosof, D. H., Shapley, R. M., and Hawken, M. J. (1993). Macaque V1 neurons can signal 'illusory' contours. *Nature*, 365, 550–552.

Grossberg, S. (1964). *The Theory of Embedding Fields with Applications to Psychology and Neurophysiology*. New York: Rockefeller Institute for Medical Research. http://sites.bu.edu/steveg/files/2016/06/Gro1964EmbeddingFields.pdf

Grossberg, S. (1967). Nonlinear difference-differential equations in prediction and learning theory. *Proceedings of the National Academy of Sciences*, 58, 1329–1334.

Grossberg, S. (1968a). A prediction theory for some nonlinear functional–differential equations, II: learning of patterns. *Journal of Mathematical Analysis and Applications*, 22, 490–522.

Grossberg, S. (1968b). Global ratio limit theorems for some nonlinear functional differential equations, II. *Bulletin of the American Mathematical Society*, 74, 101–105.

Grossberg, S. (1968c). Some nonlinear networks capable of learning a spatial pattern of arbitrary complexity. *Proceedings of the National Academy of Sciences*, 59, 368–372.

Grossberg, S. (1968d). Some physiological and biochemical consequences of psychological postulates. *Proceedings of the National Academy of Sciences*, 60, 758–765.

Grossberg, S. (1969a). On learning and energy-entropy dependence in recurrent and nonrecurrent signed networks. *Journal of Statistical Physics*, 1, 319–350.

Grossberg, S. (1969b). On the production and release of chemical transmitters and related topics in cellular control. *Journal of Theoretical Biology*, 22, 325–364.

Grossberg, S. (1969c). On the serial learning of lists. *Mathematical Biosciences*, 4, 201–253.

Grossberg, S. (1970). Some networks that can learn, remember, and reproduce any number of complicated space-time patterns, II. *Studies in Applied Mathematics*, 49, 135–166.

Grossberg, S. (1971a). On the dynamics of operant conditioning. *Journal of Theoretical Biology*, 33, 225–255.

Grossberg, S. (1971b). Pavlovian pattern learning by nonlinear neural networks. *Proceedings of the National Academy of Sciences*, 68, 828–831.

Grossberg, S. (1972a). A neural theory of punishment and avoidance, I: Qualitative theory. *Mathematical Biosciences*, 15, 39–67.

Grossberg, S. (1972b). A neural theory of punishment and avoidance, II: Quantitative theory. *Mathematical Biosciences*, 15, 253–285.

Grossberg, S. (1972c). Neural expectation: Cerebellar and retinal analogs of cells fired by learnable or unlearned pattern classes. *Kybernetik*, 10, 49–57.

Grossberg, S. (1973). Contour enhancement, short-term memory, and constancies in reverberating neural networks. *Studies in Applied Mathematics*, 52, 213–257.

Grossberg, S. (1974). Classical and instrumental learning by neural networks. In R. Rosen, & F. Snell (Eds.), *Progress in Theoretical Biology*, pp. 51–141. New York: Academic Press.

Grossberg, S. (1975a). A neural model of attention, reinforcement, and discrimination learning. *International Review of Neurobiology*, 18, 263–327.

Grossberg, S. (1975b). On the development of feature detectors in the visual cortex with applications to learning and reaction-diffusion systems. *Biological Cybernetics*, 21, 145–159.

Grossberg, S. (1976a). Adaptive pattern classification and universal recoding, I: Parallel development and coding of neural feature detectors. *Biological Cybernetics*, 23, 121–134.

Grossberg, S. (1976b). Adaptive pattern classification and universal recoding, II: Feedback, expectation, olfaction, and illusions. *Biological Cybernetics*, 23, 187–202.

Grossberg, S. (1978a). A theory of human memory: Self-organization and performance of sensory-motor codes, maps, and plans. In R. Rosen and F. Snell (Eds.). *Progress in Theoretical Biology*, Volume 5. New York: Academic Press, pp. 233–374.

Grossberg, S. (1978b). Behavioral contrast in short-term memory: Serial binary memory models or parallel continuous memory models? *Journal of Mathematical Psychology*, 3, 199–219.

Grossberg, S. (1978c). Communication, memory, and development. In R. Rosen and F. Snell (Eds.), *Progress in Theoretical Biology*, Volume 5. New York: Academic Press, pp. 183–232.

Grossberg, S. (1978d). Competition, decision, and consensus. *Journal of Mathematical Analysis and Applications*, 66, 470–493.

Grossberg, S. (1978e). Decisions, patterns, and oscillations in nonlinear competitive systems with applications to Volterra-Lotka systems. *Journal of Theoretical Biology*, 73, 101–130.

Grossberg, S. (1980). How does a brain build a cognitive code? *Psychological Review*, 87, 1–51.

Grossberg, S, (1982). Processing of expected and unexpected events during conditioning and attention: A psychophysiological theory. *Psychological Review*, 89, 529–572.

Grossberg, S. (1984a). Outline of a theory of brightness, color, and form perception. In E. Degreef and J. van Buggenhaut (Eds.), *Trends in Mathematical Psychology*. Amsterdam: North-Holland, pp. 59–85.

Grossberg, S. (1984b). Some normal and abnormal behavioral syndromes due to transmitter gating of opponent processes. *Biological Psychiatry*, 19, 1075–1118.

Grossberg, S. (1984c). Some psychophysiological and pharmacological correlates of a developmental, cognitive, and motivational theory. In Karrer, R., Cohen, J., and Tueting, P. (Eds.). *Brain and Information: Event Related Potentials*. New York: New York Academy of Sciences, pp. 58–142.

Grossberg, S. (1984d). Unitization, automaticity, temporal order, and word recognition. *Cognition and Brain Theory*, 7, 263–283.

Grossberg, S. (1986). The adaptive self-organization of serial order in behavior: Speech, language, and motor control. In E. C. Schwab and H. C. Nusbaum (Eds.), *Pattern Recognition by Humans and Machines, Vol. 1: Speech Perception*. New York: Academic Press, pp. 187–294.

Grossberg, S. (1987a). Cortical dynamics of three-dimensional form, color, and brightness perception, I: Monocular theory. *Perception and Psychophysics*, 41, 87–116.

Grossberg, S. (1987b). Cortical dynamics of three-dimensional form, color, and brightness perception, II: Binocular theory. *Perception and Psychophysics*, 41, 117–158.

Grossberg, S. (1988). Nonlinear neural networks: Principles, mechanisms, and architectures. *Neural Networks*, 1, 17–61.

Grossberg, S. (1991). Why do parallel cortical systems exist for the perception of static form and moving form? *Perception & Psychophysics*, 49, 117–141.

Grossberg, S. (1994). 3-D vision and figure-ground separation by visual cortex. *Perception and Psychophysics*, 55, 48–120.

Grossberg, S. (1997). Cortical dynamics of three-dimensional figure-ground perception of two-dimensional figures. *Psychological Review*, 104, 618–658.

Grossberg, S. (1998). How is a moving target continuously tracked behind occluding cover? In *High Level Motion Processing: Computational, Neurobiological, and Psychophysical perspectives*. T. Watanabe (Ed.). Cambridge, MA: MIT Press, pp. 3–52.

Grossberg, S. (1999). How does the cerebral cortex work? Learning, attention and grouping by the laminar circuits of visual cortex. *Spatial Vision*, 12, 163–186.

Grossberg, S. (2000a). How hallucinations may arise from brain mechanisms of learning, attention, and volition. *Journal of the International Neuropsychological Society*, 6, 579–588.

Grossberg, S. (2000b). The complementary brain: Unifying brain dynamics and modularity. *Trends in Cognitive Sciences*, 4, 233–246.

Grossberg, S. (2000c). The imbalanced Brain: From normal behavior to schizophrenia. *Biological Psychiatry*, 48, 81–98.

Grossberg, S. (2003). How does the cerebral cortex work? Development, learning, attention, and 3D vision by laminar circuits of visual cortex. *Behavioral and Cognitive Neuroscience Reviews*, 2, 47–76.

Grossberg, S. (2007a). Towards a unified theory of neocortex: Laminar cortical circuits for vision and cognition. For *Computational Neuroscience: From Neurons to Theory and Back Again*, eds: Paul Cisek, Trevor Drew, John Kalaska; Elsevier, Amsterdam, pp. 79–104.

Grossberg, S. (2007b). Consciousness CLEARS the mind. *Neural Networks*, 20, 1040–1053.

Grossberg, S. (2008). The art of seeing and painting. *Spatial Vision*, 21, 463–486.

Grossberg, S. (2009a). Beta oscillations and hippocampal place cell learning during exploration of novel environments. *Hippocampus*, 19, 881–885.

Grossberg, S. (2009b). Cortical and subcortical predictive dynamics and learning during perception, cognition, emotion, and action. *Philosophical Transactions of the Royal Society of London*, special issue "Predictions in the brain: Using our past to generate a future", 364, 1223–1234.

Grossberg, S. (2010). Towards building a neural networks community. *Neural Networks*, 23, 1135–1138.

Grossberg, S. (2013a). Adaptive Resonance Theory: How a brain learns to consciously attend, learn, and recognize a changing world. *Neural Networks*, 37, 1–47.

Grossberg, S. (2013b). Recurrent neural networks. *Scholarpedia*, 8(2):1888. (http://www.scholarpedia.org/article/Recurrent_neural_networks).

Grossberg, S. (2016a). Cortical dynamics of figure-ground separation in response to 2D pictures and 3D scenes: How V2 combines border ownership, stereoscopic cues, and gestalt grouping rules. *Frontiers in Psychology*. 26 January 2016. http://journal.frontiersin.org/article/10.3389/fpsyg.2015.02054/full.

Grossberg, S. (2016b). Neural dynamics of the basal ganglia during perceptual, cognitive, and motor learning and gating. In *The basal ganglia: Novel perspectives on motor and cognitive functions*. J.-J. Soghomonian (Ed.). Berlin: Springer, 457–512.

Grossberg, S. (2017a). Acetylcholine neuromodulation in normal and abnormal learning and memory: Vigilance control in waking, sleep, autism, amnesia, and Alzheimer's disease. *Frontiers in Neural Circuits*, November 2, 2017, https://doi.org/10.3389/fncir.2017.00082.

Grossberg, S. (2017b). Towards solving the Hard Problem of Consciousness: The varieties of brain resonances and the conscious experiences that they support. *Neural Networks*, 87, 38–95.

Grossberg, S. (2018). Desirability, availability, credit assignment, category learning, and attention: Cognitive-emotional and working memory dynamics of orbitofrontal, ventrolateral, and dorsolateral prefrontal cortices. *Brain and Neuroscience Advances*, May 8, 2018. http://journals.sagepub.com/doi/full/10.1177/2398212818772179.

Grossberg, S. (2019). The embodied brain of SOVEREIGN2: From space-variant conscious percepts during visual search and navigation to learning invariant object categories and cognitive-emotional plans for acquiring valued goals. *Frontiers in Computational Neuroscience*. Published online: June 25, 2019. In the Research Topic: *The embodied brain: Computational mechanisms of integrated sensorimotor interactions with a dynamic environment*. M. Senden, J. Peters, F. V. Rohrbein, R. Goebel, and G. Deco (Eds.).https://www.frontiersin.org/articles/10.3389/fncom.2019.00036/full

Grossberg, S. (2020a). A path towards Explainable AI and autonomous adaptive intelligence: Adaptive Resonance Theory and biological neural networks. *Frontiers in Neurorobotics*. In the research topic: *Explainable Artificial Intelligence*, J. L. Olds, J. L. Krichmar, H. Tang, and J. V. Sanchez-Andres (Eds.).

Grossberg, S. (2020b). Developmental designs and adult functions of cortical maps in multiple modalities: Perception, attention, navigation, numbers, streaming, speech, and cognition. *Frontiers in Neuroinformatics*. In the Research Topic: *Cortical maps: Data and models*, N. Swindale and G. Goodhill (Eds.).

Grossberg, S. (2021). Towards understanding the brain dynamics of music: Learning and performance of lyrics and melodies with different beats. Submitted for publication.

Grossberg, S., Boardman, I., and Cohen, C. (1997). Neural dynamics of variable-rate speech categorization. *Journal of Experimental Psychology: Human Perception and Performance*, 23, 418–503.

Grossberg, S., Bullock, D., and Dranias, M. (2008). Neural dynamics underlying impaired autonomic and conditioned responses following amygdala and orbitofrontal lesions. *Behavioral Neuroscience*, 122, 1100–1125.

Grossberg, S., Govindarajan, K. K., Wyse, L. L., and Cohen, M. A. (2004). ARTSTREAM: A neural network model of auditory scene analysis and source segregation. *Neural Networks*, 17, 511–536.

Grossberg, S., and Grunewald, A. (1997). Cortical synchronization and perceptual framing. *Journal of Cognitive Neuroscience, 9*, 117–132.

Grossberg, S. and Gutowski, W. E. (1987). Neural dynamics of decision making under risk: Affective balance and cognitive-emotional interactions. *Psychological Review*, 94, 300–318.

Grossberg, S., and Hong, S. (2006). A neural model of surface perception: Lightness, anchoring, and filling-in. *Spatial Vision*, 19, 263–321.

Grossberg, S., and Howe, P. D. L. (2003). A laminar cortical model of stereopsis and three-dimensional surface perception. *Vision Research*, 43, 801–829.

Grossberg, S., and Huang, T.-R. (2009). ARTSCENE: A neural system for natural scene classification. *Journal of Vision*, 9, 6, 1–19.

Grossberg, S., Hwang, S., and Mingolla, E. (2002). Thalamocortical dynamics of the McCollough effect: Boundary-surface alignment through perceptual learning. *Vision Research*, 42, 1259–1286.

Grossberg, S., and Kuperstein, M. (1986). *Neural Dynamics of Adaptive Sensory-Motor Control: Ballistic Eye Movements*. Amsterdam; New York; North-Holland; (1989). *Neural Dynamics of Adaptive Sensory-Motor Control: Expanded Edition*. Elmsford, NY: Pergamon Press.

Grossberg, S., and Kazerounian, S. (2011). Laminar cortical dynamics of conscious speech perception: A neural model of phonemic restoration using subsequent context in noise. *Journal of the Acoustical Society of America*, 130, 440–460.

Grossberg, S., and Kazerounian, S. (2016). Phoneme restoration and empirical coverage of Interactive Activation and Adaptive Resonance models of human speech processing, *Journal of the Acoustical Society of America*, 140, 1130; https://doi.org/10.1121/1.4946760.

Grossberg, S., and Kelly, F. J. (1999). Neural dynamics of binocular brightness perception. *Vision Research*, 39, 3796–3816.

Grossberg, S., and Kishnan, D. (2018). Neural dynamics of autistic repetitive behaviors and Fragile X syndrome: Basal ganglia movement gating and mGluR-modulated adaptively timed learning. *Frontiers in Psychology, Psychopathology*. https://doi.org/10.3389/fpsyg.2018.00269.

Grossberg, S., Kuhlmann, L., and Mingolla, E. (2007). A neural model of 3D shape-from-texture: Multiple-scale filtering, boundary grouping, and surface filling-in. *Vision Research*, 47, 634–672.

Grossberg, S., and Kuperstein, M. (1986). *Neural Dynamics of Adaptive Sensory-Motor Control: Ballistic Eye Movements*. Amsterdam, New York; North-Holland.

Grossberg, S., Leveille, J., and Versace, M. (2011). How do object reference frames and motion vector decomposition emerge in laminar cortical circuits? *Attention, Perception, & Psychophysics*, 73, 1147–1170.

Grossberg, S. and Levine, D. (1976). On visual illusions in neural networks: Line neutralization, tilt aftereffect, and angle expansion. *Journal of Theoretical Biology*, 61, 477–504.

Grossberg, S., and Levine, D. S. (1987). Neural dynamics of attentionally modulated Pavlovian conditioning: Blocking, inter-stimulus interval, and secondary reinforcement. *Applied Optics*, 26, 5015–5030.

Grossberg, S., Markowitz, J., and Cao, Y. (2011). On the road to invariant recognition: Explaining tradeoff and morph properties of cells in inferotemporal cortex using multiple-scale task-sensitive attentive learning. *Neural Networks*, 24, 1036–1049.

Grossberg, S., and Marshall, J. (1989). Stereo boundary fusion by cortical complex cells: A system of maps, filters, and feedback networks for multiplexing distributed data. *Neural Networks*, 2, 29–51.

Grossberg, S., and McLoughlin, N. (1997). Cortical dynamics of 3-D surface perception: Binocular and half-occluded scenic images. *Neural Networks*, 10, 1583–1605.

Grossberg, S., and Merrill, J. W. L. (1992). A neural network model of adaptively timed reinforcement learning and hippocampal dynamics. *Cognitive Brain Research*, 1, 3–38.

Grossberg, S., and Merrill, J. W. L. (1996). The hippocampus and cerebellum in adaptively timed learning, recognition, and movement. *Journal of Cognitive Neuroscience*, 8, 257–277.

Grossberg, S., and Mingolla, E. (1985a). Neural dynamics of form perception: Boundary completion, illusory figures, and neon color spreading. *Psychological Review*, 92, 173–211.

Grossberg, S., and Mingolla, E. (1985b). Neural dynamics of perceptual grouping: Textures, boundaries, and emergent segmentations. *Perception and Psychophysics*, 38, 141–171.

Grossberg, S., and Mingolla, E. (1987). Neural dynamics of surface perception: Boundary webs, illuminants, and shape-from-shading. *Computer Vision, Graphics, and Image Processing*, 37, 116–165.

Grossberg, S., Mingolla, E., and Pack, C. C. (1999). A neural model of motion processing and visual navigation by cortical area MST. *Cerebral Cortex*, 9, 878–895.

Grossberg, S., Mingolla, E., and Ross (1994). A neural theory of attentive visual search: Interactions of boundary, surface, spatial, and object representations. *Psychological Review*, 101, 470–489.

Grossberg, S., Mingolla, E., and Ross, W. D. (1997). Visual brain and visual perception: How does the cortex do perceptual grouping? *Trends in Neurosciences*, 20, 106–111.

Grossberg, S., Mingolla, E., and Viswanathan, L. (2001). Neural dynamics of motion integration and segmentation within and across apertures. *Vision Research*, 41, 2521–2553.

Grossberg, S., and Myers, C. W. (2000) The resonant dynamics of speech perception: Interword integration and duration-dependent backward effects. *Psychological Review*, 107, 735–767.

Grossberg, S., Palma, J., and Versace, M. (2016). Resonant cholinergic dynamics in cognitive and motor decision-making: Attention, category learning, and choice in neocortex, superior colliculus, and optic tectum. *Frontiers in Neuroscience: Decision Neuroscience*, http://journal.frontiersin.org/article/10.3389/fnins.2015.00501/full

Grossberg, S., and Pearson, L. (2008). Laminar cortical dynamics of cognitive and motor working memory, sequence learning and performance: Toward a unified theory of how the cerebral cortex works. *Psychological Review*, 115, 677–732.

Grossberg, S., and Pepe, J. (1970). Schizophrenia: Possible dependence of associational span, bowing, and primacy vs. recency on spiking threshold. *Behavioral Science*, 15, 359–362.

Grossberg, S., and Pepe, J. (1971). Spiking threshold and overarousal effects in serial learning. *Journal of Statistical Physics*, 3, 95–125.

Grossberg, S., and Pessoa, L. (1998). Texture segregation, surface representation, and figure-ground separation. *Vision Research*, 38, 2657–2684.

Grossberg, S., and Pilly, P. (2008). Temporal dynamics of decision-making during motion perception in the visual cortex. *Vision Research*, 48, 1345–1373.

Grossberg, S., and Pilly, P.K. (2012). How entorhinal grid cells may learn multiple spatial scales from a dorsoventral gradient of cell response rates in a self-organizing map. *PLoS Computational Biology* 8(10): e1002648. doi:10.1371/journal.pcbi.1002648.

Grossberg, S., and Pilly, P. K. (2014). Coordinated learning of grid cell and place cell spatial and temporal properties: multiple scales, attention, and oscillations. *Philosophical Transactions of the Royal Society B*, 369, 20120524.

Grossberg, S., and Raizada, R. (2000). Contrast-sensitive perceptual grouping and object-based attention in the laminar circuits of primary visual cortex. *Vision Research*, 40, 1413–1432.

Grossberg, S., and Repin, D. (2003) A neural model of how the brain represents and compares multi-digit numbers: Spatial and categorical processes. *Neural Networks*, 16, 1107–1140.

Grossberg, S., Roberts, K., Aguilar, M., and Bullock, D. (1997). A neural model of multimodal adaptive saccadic eye movement control by superior colliculus. *The Journal of Neuroscience*, 17, 9706–9725.

Grossberg, S., and Rudd, M. (1989). A neural architecture for visual motion perception: Group and element apparent motion. *Neural Networks*, 2, 421–450.

Grossberg, S., and Rudd, M. E. (1992). Cortical dynamics of visual motion perception: Short-range and long-range apparent motion. *Psychological Review*, 99, 78–121.

Grossberg, S., and Schmajuk, N. A. (1987). Neural dynamics of attentionally-modulated Pavlovian conditioning: Conditioned reinforcement, inhibition, and opponent processing. *Psychobiology*, 15, 195–240.

Grossberg, S., and Schmajuk, N. A. (1989). Neural dynamics of adaptive timing and temporal discrimination during associative learning. *Neural Networks*, 2, 79–102.

Grossberg, S., and Seidman, D. (2006). Neural dynamics of autistic behaviors: Cognitive, emotional, and timing substrates. *Psychological Review*, 113, 483–525.

Grossberg, S., and Seitz, A. (2003). Laminar development of receptive fields, maps, and columns in visual cortex: The coordinating role of the subplate. *Cerebral Cortex*, 13, 852–863.

Grossberg, S., Srihasam, K., and Bullock, D. (2012). Neural dynamics of saccadic and smooth pursuit eye movement coordination during visual tracking of unpredictably moving targets. *Neural Networks*, 27, 1–20.

Grossberg, S., Srinivasan, K., and Yazdanbakhsh, A. (2014). Binocular fusion and invariant category learning due to predictive remapping during scanning of a depthful scene with eye movements. *Frontiers in Psychology: Perception Science*, doi: 10.3389/fpsyg.2014.01457 http://journal.frontiersin.org/Journal/10.3389/fpsyg.2014.01457/full.

Grossberg, S., and Stone, G. O (1986a). Neural dynamics of attention switching and temporal order information in short-term memory. *Memory and Cognition*, 14, 451–468.

Grossberg, S., and Stone, G. O. (1986b). Neural dynamics of word recognition and recall: Attentional priming, learning, and resonance. *Psychological Review*, 93, 46–74.

Grossberg, S., and Swaminathan, G. (2004). A laminar cortical model for 3D perception of slanted and curved surfaces and of 2D images: development, attention and bistability. *Vision Research*, 44, 1147–1187.

Grossberg, S., and Todorovic, D. (1988). Neural dynamics of 1-D and 2-D brightness perception: A unified model of classical and recent phenomena. *Perception and Psychophysics*, 43, 241–277.

Grossberg, S., and Versace, M. (2008). Spikes, synchrony, and attentive learning by laminar thalamocortical circuits. *Brain Research*, 1218, 278–312.

Grossberg, S., and Vladusich, T. (2010). How do children learn to follow gaze, share joint attention, imitate their teachers, and use tools during social interactions? *Neural Networks*, 23, 940–965.

Grossberg, S., and Williamson, J. R. (2001). A neural model of how horizontal and interlaminar connections of visual cortex develop into adult circuits that carry out perceptual grouping and learning. *Cerebral Cortex*, 11, 37–58.

Grossberg, S., and Yazdanbakhsh, A. (2005). Laminar cortical dynamics of 3D surface perception: Stratification, transparency, and neon color spreading. *Vision Research*, 45, 1725–1743.

Grossberg, S., Yazdanbakhsh, A., Cao, Y., and Swaminathan, G. (2008). How does binocular rivalry emerge from cortical mechanisms of 3-D vision? *Vision Research*, 48, 2232–2250.

Grossberg, S., and Zajac, L. (2017). How humans consciously see paintings and paintings illuminate how humans see. *Art & Perception*, 5, 1–95.

Grossman, E. D., and Blake, R. (2002). Brain areas active during visual perception of biological motion. *Neuron*, 35, 1167–1175.

Guenther, F. H. (1995). Speech sound acquisition, coarticulation, and rate effects in a neural network model of speech production. *Psychological Review*, 102, 594–621.

Guanella, A., Kiper, D., and Verschure, P. (2007). A model of grid cells based on a twisted torus topology. *International Journal of Neural Systems*, 17, 231–240.

Guenther, F. H., Ghosh, S. S., and Tourville, J. A. (2006). Neural modeling and imaging of the cortical interactions underlying syllable production. *Brain and Language*, 96, 280–301.

Guenther, F. H., Hampson, M., and Johnson, D. (1998). A theoretical investigation of reference frames for the planning of speech movements. *Psychological Review*, 105, 611–633.

Guilford, J. P. (1929). Illusory movement from a rotating barber pole. *American Journal of Psychology*, 41, 686.

Guo, W., Murthy, A. C., Zhang, L., Johnson, E. B., Schaller, E. G., Allan, A. M., and Zhao, X. (2012). Inhibition of GSK3β improves hippocampus-dependent learning and rescues neurogenesis in a mouse model of fragile X syndrome. *Human Molecular Genetics*, 21, 681–691.

Gustafson, T., and Wolpert, L. (1967). Cellular movement and contract in sea urchin morphogenesis. *Biological Reviews*, 42, 442–498.

Gutschalk, A., and Dykstra, A. (2015). Auditory neglect and related disorders. *Handbook of Clinical Neurology*, 129, 557–571.

Gutschalk, A., Rupp, A., and Dykstra, A. R. (2015). Interaction of streaming and attention in human auditory cortex. PLOS ONE, March 18, 10(3): e0118962. https://doi.org/10.1371/journal.pone.0118962

Haarmeier, T., Their, P., Repnow, M., and Petersen, D. (1997). False perception of motion in a patient who cannot compensate for eye movements. *Nature*, 389, 849–852.

Hafting, T., Fyhn, M., Molden, S., Moser, M. B., and Moser, E. I. (2005). Microstructure of a spatial map in the entorhinal cortex. *Nature*, 436, 801–806.

Hahnloser, R. H. R., Kozhevnikov, A. A., and Fee, M. S. (2002). An ultra-sparse code underlies the generation of neural sequences in a songbird. *Nature*, 419, 65–70.

Halgren, E., Walter, R. D., and Cherlow, D. G. (1978). Mental phenomena evoked by electrical stimulation of the human hippocampal formation and amygdala. *Brain*, 101, 83–117.

Handel, A., and Glimcher, P. W. (1999). Quantitative analysis of substantia nigra pars reticulate activity during a visually guided saccade task. *Journal of Neurophysiology*, 82, 3458–3475.

Handel, A., and Glimcher, P. W. (2000). Contextual modulation of substantia nigra pars reticulata neurons. *Journal of Neurophysiology* 83, 3042–3048.

Hanson, H. M., and Chuang, E. S. (1999). Glottal characteristics of male speakers: Acoustic correlates and comparison with female data. *The Journal of the Acoustical Society of America*, 105, 1064–1077.

Haralanova, E., Haralanov, S., Veraldi, A., Möller, H.-J., and Hennig-Fast, K. (2011). Subjective emotional over-arousal to neutral social scenes in paranoic schizophrenia. *European Archives of Psychiatry and Clinical Neuroscience*, 262, 59–68.

Hargreaves, E. L., Rao, G., Lee, I., and Knierim, J. J. (2005). Major dissociation between medial and lateral entorhinal input to dorsal hippocampus. *Science*, 308, 1792–1794.

Harlow, H. F., Dodsworth, R. O., and Harlow, M. K. (1965). Total social isolation in monkeys. *Proceedings of the National Academy of Sciences*, 54, 90–97.

Harman, P. M. (1990). *The Scientific Letters and Papers of James Clerk Maxwell, Volume I, 1846-1862*. Cambridge, England: Cambridge University Press.

Harnad, S. (1990). The symbol grounding problem. *Physica B*, 42, 335–346.

Harries, M. H., and Perrett, D. I. (1991). Visual processing of faces in temporal cortex: Physiological evidence for a modular organization and possible anatomical correlates. *Journal of Cognitive Neuroscience*, 3, 9–24.

Hartley, T., and Houghton, G. (1996). A linguistically constrained model of short-term memory for nonwords. *Journal of Memory and Language*, 35, 1–31.

Hartline, H. K., and Ratliff, F. (1957). Inhibitory interaction of receptor units in the eye of Limulus. *The Journal of General Physiology*, 40, 357–376.

Hasselmo, M. E., Giocomo, L. M., and Zilli, E. A. (2007). Grid cell firing may arise from interference of theta frequency membrane potential oscillations in single neurons. *Hippocampus*, 17, 1252–1271.

Hasselmo, M. E., Rolls, E. T., and Baylis, G. C. (1989). The role of expression and identity in the face-selective responses of neurons in the temporal visual cortex of the monkey. *Behavioural Brain Research*, 32, 203–218.

Hatfield, T., Han, J.-S., Conley, M., Gallagher, M., and Holland, P. C. (1996). Neurotoxic lesions of basolateral, but not central, amygdala interfere with Pavlovian second-order conditioning and reinforcer-devaluation effects. *The Journal of Neuroscience*, 16, 5256–5265.

Hawthorne, C. W. (1938/1960). *Hawthorne on Painting*. Mineola, NY: Dover.

Haynes, W. I. A., and Haber, S. N. (2013). The organization of prefrontal-subthalamic inputs in primates provides an anatomical substrate for both functional specificity and integration: Implications for basal ganglia models and deep brain stimulation. *The Journal of Neuroscience*, 33, 4804–4814.

He, H., Caudell, T. P., Menicucci, D. F., and Mammoli, A. A. (2012). Application of adaptive resonance theory neural networks to monitor solar hot water systems and detect existing or developing faults. *Solar Energy*, 86, 2318–2333.

He, J., Tan, A.-H., and Tan, C.-L. (2000). A comparative study on Chinese text categorization methods. In *Proceedings of PRICAI'2000*.

He, S., Cavanagh, P., and Intriligator, J. (1996). Attentional resolution and the locus of visual awareness. *Nature*, 383, 334–337.

He, Z. J., and Nakayama, K. (1992). Surface features in visual search. *Nature*, 359, 231–233.

Healy, M. J., Caudell, T. P., and Smith, S. D. G. (1993). A neural architecture for pattern sequence verification through inferencing. *IEEE Transactions on Neural Networks*, 4, 9–20.

Hebb, D. O. (1949). *The Organization of Behavior: A Neuropsychological Theory*. New York: John Wiley and Sons, Inc.

Hebb, D. O. (1955). Drives and the CNS (conceptual nervous system). *Psychological Review*, 1955, 62, 243–254.

Hecht-Nielsen, R. (1987). Counterpropagation networks. *Applied Optics*, 26, 4979–4983.

Heeger, D. J. (1992). Normalization of cell responses in cat striate cortex. *Visual Neuroscience*, 9, 181–197.

Heekeren, H. R., Marrett, S., and Ungerleider, L. G. (2008). The neural systems that mediate human perceptual decision making. *Nature Reviews Neuroscience*, 9, 467–479.

Heide, W., Binkofski, F., Seitz, R., Posse, S., Nitschke, M., Freund, H., and Kömpf, D. (2001). Activation of frontoparietal cortices during memorized triple-step sequences of saccadic eye movements: an fMRI study. *European Journal of Neuroscience*, 13, 1177–1189.

Heilman, K. M., Bowers, D., Coslett, H. B., Whelan, H., and Watson, R. T. (1985). Directional hypokinesia. *Neurology*, 35, 855–859.

Heisenberg, W. (1927). Uber den anschaulichen Inhalt der quantentheoretischen Kinematik und Mechanik, *Zeitschrift für Physik*, 43, 172–198.

Heldt, S. A., Stanek, L., Chhatwal, J. P., and Ressler, K. J. (2007). Hippocampus-specific deletion of BDNF in adult mice impairs spatial memory and extinction of aversive memories. *Molecular Psychiatry*, 12, 655–670.

Helmholtz, H. von (1866). *Handbuch der Physiologischen Optik*. Leipzig: Leopold Voss.

Helmholtz, H. von (1875). *On the Sensations of Tone as a Physiological Basis for the Theory of Music*. London, England: Longmans, Green, and Co.

Helmholtz, H. von (1924). In J. P. C. Southall (Ed.), *Helmholtz's Treatise on Physiological Optics* (translated from the Third German Edition, 3 v. ill. 28 cm).

Helmholtz, H. von. (1962). *Treatise on Physiological Optics*. J. P. C. Southall (Trans.). New York: Dover.

Henle, M. (1971). *The selected papers of Wolfgang Köhler*. New York: Liveright.

Hensche, H. (1988). *The Art of Seeing and Painting*. Portier Gorman, Thibodaux, LA, USA.

Henson, R. N. A. (1998a). Item repetition in short-term memory: Ranschburg repeated. *Journal of Experimental Psychology: Learning, Memory, and Cognition*, 24, 1162–1181.

Henson, R. N. A. (1998b). Short-term memory for serial order: The start-end model of serial recall. *Cognitive Psychology*, 36, 73–137.

Herzog, M. H., Sayim, B., Chicherov, V., and Manassi, M. (2015). Crowding, grouping, and object recognition: A matter of appearance. *Journal of Vision*, Vol. 15, 5. Doi:10.1.1167/15.6.5.

Hickok, G., and Poeppel, D. (2007). The cortical organization of speech processing. *Nature Reviews Neuroscience, 8*, 393–402.

Hikosaka, O., Miyauchi, S., and Shimojo, S. (1993a). Focal visual attention produces illusory temporal order and motion sensation. *Vision Research*, 33, 1219–1240.

Hikosaka, O., Miyauchi, S., and Shimojo, S. (1993b). Voluntary and stimulus induced attention detected as motion sensation. *Perception*, 22, 517–526.

Hikosaka, K., and Watanabe, M. (2000). Delay activity of orbital and lateral prefrontal neurons of the monkey varying with different rewards. *Cerebral Cortex*, 10, 263–271.

Hikosaka, O., and Wurtz, R. H. (1983). Visual and oculomotor functions of monkey substantia nigra pars reticulata. IV.

Relation of substantia nigra to superior colliculus. *Journal of Neurophysiology*, 49, 1285–1301.

Hikosaka, O., and Wurtz, R. H. (1989). The basal ganglia. In R. Wurtz, and M. Goldberg (Eds.). The neurobiology of saccadic eye movements, pp. 257–281. Amsterdam: Elsevier.

Hildreth, E. (1984). *The Measurement of Visual Motion*. Cambridge, MA: MIT Press.

Hilgard, E. R., and Bower, G. H. (1975). *Theories of Learning*. Englewood Cliffs, NJ: Prentice Hall Inc.

Hilgard, E. R., Campbell, A. A., and Sears, W. N. (1937). Conditioned discrimination: Development with and without verbal report. *American Journal of Psychology*, 49, 564–580.

Hinton, G., Deng, L., Yu, D., Dahl, G. E., Mohamed, A-r., Jaitly, N., Senior, A., Vanhoucke, V., Nguyen, P., Sainath, T. N., and Kingsbury, B. (2012). Deep neural networks for acoustic modeling in speech recognition: The shared views of four research groups. *IEEE Signal Processing Magazine*, 29, 82–97.

Hirsch, M. W. (1982). Systems of differential equations which are competitive or cooperative, I: Limit sets. *SIAM Journal of Mathematical Analysis*, 13, 167–179.

Hirsch, M. W., Smale, S., and Devaney, R. L. (2012), *Differential Equations, Dynamical Systems, and an Introduction to Chaos*. Waltham, MA: Academic Press.

Histed, M. H., and Miller, E. K. (2006). Microstimulation of frontal cortex can reorder a remembered spatial sequence. *Public Library of Science: Biology*, 4(5):e134.

Ho, C. S., Liou, J. J., Georgiopoulos, M., Heileman, G. L., and Christodoulou, C. (1994). Analogue circuit design and implementation of an adaptive resonance theory (ART) network architecture. *International Journal of Electronics*, 76, 271–291.

Hobson, J. A., and Pace-Schott, E. F. (2002). The cognitive neuroscience of sleep: neuronal systems, consciousness and learning. *Nature Reviews Neuroscience*, 3, 679–693.

Hochstein, S., and Ahissar, M. (2002). View from the top: Hierarchies and reverse hierarchies in the visual system. *Neuron*, 36, 791–804.

Hodges, A. (2014). *Alan Turing: The Enigma*. Princeton, NJ: Princeton University Press.

Hodgkin, A. L., and Huxley, A. F. (1952). A quantitative description of membrane current and its application to conduction and excitation in nerve. *Journal of Psychology*, 117, 500–544.

Hogan, N, (1984). An organizing principle for a class of voluntary movements. *The Journal of Neuroscience*, 4. 2745–2754.

Holland, P. C., and Straub, J. J. (1979). Differential effects of two ways of devaluing the unconditioned stimulus. *Journal of Experimental Psychology*, 5, 65–78.

Hollerman, J. R., and Schultz, W. (1998). Dopamine neurons report an error in the temporal prediction of reward during learning. *Nature Neuroscience*, 1, 304–309.

Hong, S., and Grossberg, S. (2004). A neuromorphic model for achromatic and chromatic surface representation of natural images. *Neural Networks*, 2004, 17, 787–808.

Houghton, G. (1990). The problem of serial order: A neural network model of sequence learning and recall. In R. Dale, C. Mellish, C, and M. Zock (Eds.) *Current Research in Natural Language Generation*. London: Academic Press, pp. 287–319.

Hovland, C. (1938a). Experimental studies in rote-learning theory. I. Reminiscence following learning by massed and by distributed practice. *Journal of Experimental Psychology*, 22, 201–224.

Hovland, C. (1938b). Experimental studies in rote-learning theory. II. Reminiscence with varying speeds of syllable presentation. *Journal of Experimental Psychology*, 22, 201–224.

Hovland, C. (1938c). Experimental studies in rote-learning theory. III. Distribution of practice with varying speeds of syllable presentation. *Journal of Experimental Psychology*, 23, 172–190.

Howard, I. P., and Rogers, B. J. (1995). *Binocular Vision and Stereopsis*. New York: Oxford University Press.

Hsieh, K.-L. (2008). The application of clustering analysis for the critical areas on TFT-LCD panel. *Expert Systems with Applications*, 34, 952–957.

Hsieh, K.-L., and Yang, I.-Ch. (2008). Incorporating PCA and fuzzy-ART techniques into achieve organism classification based on codon usage consideration. *Computers in Biology and Medicine*, 38, 886–893.

Hsu, S.-C., and Chien, C.-F. (2007). Hybrid data mining approach for pattern extraction from wafer bin map to improve yield in semiconductor manufacturing. *International Journal of Production Economics*, 107, 88–103.

Hu, Y., and Russek, S. J. (2008). BDNF and the diseased nervous system: a delicate balance between adaptive and pathological processes of gene regulation. *Journal of Neurochemistry*, 105, 1–17.

Humphreys, G. W., Quinlan, P. T., and Riddoch, M. J. (1989). Grouping processes in visual search: Effects with single- and combined-feature targets. *Journal of Experimental Psychology: General*, 118, 258–279.

Huang, T.-R., and Grossberg, S. (2010). Cortical dynamics of contextually cued attentive visual learning and search: Spatial and object evidence accumulation. *Psychological Review*, 117, 1080–1112.

Hubbard, E. M., and Ramachandran, V. S. (2005). Neurocognitive mechanisms of synesthesia. *Neuron*, 48, 509–520.

Hubel, D. H., and Wiesel, T. N. (1962). Receptive fields, binocular interaction and functional architecture in the cat's visual cortex. *Journal of Physiology*, 160, 106–154.

Hubel, D. H., and Wiesel, T. N. (1968). Receptive fields and functional architectures of monkey striate cortex. *Journal of Physiology*, 195, 215–243.

Hubel, D. H., and Wiesel, T. N. (1977). Functional architecture of macaque monkey visual cortex. *Proceedings of the Royal Society of London (B)*, 198, 1–59.

Huber, K. M., Gallagher, S. M., Warren, S. T., and Bear, M. F. (2002). Altered synaptic plasticity in a mouse model of fragile X mental retardation. *Proceedings of the National Academy of Sciences*, 99, 7746–7750.

Huerta, M., and Kaas, J. (1990). Supplementary eye field as defined by intracortical microstimulation: Connections in macaques. *The Journal of Comparative Neurology*, 293, 299–330.

Huk, A. C., Dougherty, R. F., and Heeger, D. J. (2002). Retinotopy and functional subdivision of human areas MT and MST. *The Journal of Neuroscience*, 22, 7195–7205.

Hull, C. L. (1943). *Principles of Behavior: An Introduction to Behavior Theory.* Oxford, England: Appleton-Century.

Hunt, R. R., and Lamb, C. A. (2001). What causes the isolation effect? *Journal of Experimental Psychology: Learning, Memory and Cognition,* 27, 1359–66.

Hupé, J. M., James, A. C., Girard, D. C., and Bullier, J. (1997). Feedback connections from V2 modulate intrinsic connectivity within V1. *Society for Neuroscience Abstracts,* 406, 1031.

Hupé, J. M., James, A. C., Payne, B. R., Lomber, S. G., Girard, P., and Bullier, J. (1998). Cortical feedback improves discrimination between figure and background by V1, V2 and V3 neurons. *Nature,* 394, 784–787.

Husain, M., and Nachev, P. (2007). Space and the parietal cortex. *Trends in Cognitive Sciences,* 11, 30–36.

Hyde, P. S., and Knudsen, E. I. (2002). The optic tectum controls visually guided adaptive plasticity in the owl's auditory space map. *Nature,* 415, 73–76.

Hyvärinen, A., and and Oja, E. (2000). Independent component analysis: Algorithms and applications. *Neural Networks,* 13, 411–430.

Ichise, T., Kano, M., Hashimoto, K., Yangihara, D., Nakao, K., Shigemoto, R., Katsuki, M., and Aiba, A. (2000). mGluR1 in cerebellar Purkinje cells essential for long-term depression, synapse elimination, and motor coordination. *Science,* 288, 1832–1835.

Ingvar, D. H. (1985). Memory of the future. An essay on the temporal organisation of conscious awareness. *Human Neurobiology,* 4, 127–136.

Inoue, M., and Mikami, A. (2006). Prefrontal activity during serial probe reproduction task: encoding, mnemonic and retrieval processes. *Journal of Neurophysiology,* 95, 1008–1041.

Intriligator, J., and Cavanagh, P. (2001). The spatial resolution of visual attention. *Cognitive Psychology,* 43, 171–216.

Iqbal, K., and Grundke-Iqbal, I. (2008). Alzheimer neurofibrillary degeneration: significance, etiopathogenesis, therapeutics and prevention. *Journal of Cellular and Molecular Medicine,* 12, 38–55.

Irwin, D. A., Rebert, C. S., McAdam, D. W., and Knott, J. R. (1966). Slow potential change (CNV) in the human EEG as a function of motivational variables. *Electroencephalography and Clinical Neurophysiology,* 21, 412–413.

Irwin, D. E. (1991). Information integration across saccadic eye movements. *Cognitive Psychology,* 23, 420–456.

Isoda, M., and Tanji, J. (2002). Cellular activity in the supplementary eye field during sequential performance of multiple saccades. *Journal of Neurophysiology,* 88, 3541–3545.

Isoda, M., and Tanji, J. (2003). Contrasting neuronal activity in the supplementary and frontal eye fields during temporal organization of multiple saccades. *Journal of Neurophysiology,* 90, 3054–3065.

Ito, M. (1984). *The Cerebellum and Neural Control.* New York: Raven Press.

Ito, M., Westheimer, G., and Gilbert, C. D. (1998). Attention and perceptual learning modulate contextual influences on visual perception. *Neuron,* 20, 1191–1197.

Itti, L., and Koch, C. (2000). A saliency-based search mechanism for overt and covert shifts of visual attention. *Vision Research,* 40, 1489–1506.

Ivkovich, D., and Stanton, M. E. (2001). Effects of early hippocampal lesions on trace, delay, and long-delay eyeblink conditioning in developing rats. *Neurobiology of Learning and Memory,* 76, 426–446.

Izquierdo, A., and Murray, E. A. (2007). Selective bilateral amygdala lesions in rhesus monkeys fail to disrupt object reversal learning. *Journal of Neuroscience,* 24, 7540–7548.

Jackson, J. H. (1874). On the nature of the duality of the brain. *Medical Press and Circular,* Vol. i, 80–86.

James, W. (1907). *Pragmatism: A New Name for Some Old Ways of Thinking.* New York: Longmans, Green, and Co.

James, G. O., Hardiman, M. J., and Yeo, C. H. (1987). Hippocampal lesions and trace conditioning in the rabbit. *Behavioural Brain Research,* 23, 109–116.

Janeczek, M., Gefen, T., Samimi, M., Kim, G., Weintraub, S., Bigio, E., Rogalski, E., Mesulam, M.-M., and Geula, C. (2017). Variations in acetylcholinesterase activity within human cortical pyramidal neurons across age and cognitive trajectories. *Cerebral Cortex,* 28, 1329–1337.

Janik, A., and Toulmin, S. (1973). *Wittgenstein's Vienna.* New York: Simon & Schuster.

Jayaraman, A., Thandeeswaran, M., Priyadarsini, U., Sabarathinam, S., Nawaz, K. A. A., and Palaniswamy, M. (2016). Characterization of unexplored amidohydrolase enzyme—pterin deaminase. *Applied Microbiology and Biotechnology,* 100, 4779–4789.

Jiang, Y., and Wagner, L. C. (2004). What is learned in spatial contextual cueing: Configuration or individual locations? *Perception & Psychophysics,* 66, 454–463.

Jin, X., Tecuapetla, F., and Costa, R. M. (2014). Basal ganglia subcircuits distinctively encode the parsing and concatenation of action sequences. *Nature Neuroscience,* 17, 423–430. doi: 10.1038/nn.3632

Johansson, G. (1950). *Configurations in Event Perception.* Uppsala: Almqvist and Wiksell.

Jones, B., and Mishkin, M. (1972). Limbic lesions and the problem of stimulus-reinforcement associations. *Experimental Neurology,* 36, 362–377.

Jones, D., Farrand, P., Stuart, G., and Morris, N. (1995). The functional equivalence of verbal and spatial memory in serial short-term memory. *Journal of Experimental Psychology: Learning Memory and Cognition,* 21, 1008–1018.

Jones, M. W., and Wilson, M. A. (2005). Theta rhythms coordinate hippocampal-prefrontal interactions in a spatial memory task. *PLoS Biology,* 3, 2187–2199.

Jonides, J., Irwin, D. E., and Yantis, S. (1982). Integrating visual information from successive fixations. *Science,* 215, 192–194.

Ju, Y.-E. S., Lucey, B. P., and Holtzman, D. M. (2014). Sleep and Alzheimer disease pathology—a bidirectional relationship. *Nature Reviews Neurology,* 10, 115–119.

Julesz, B. (1971). *Foundations of Cyclopean Perception.* Chicago: University of Chicago Press.

Julesz, B., and Schumer, R. A. (1981). Early visual perception. *Annual Review of Psychology,* 32, 572–627.

Juola, J. F., Fischler, I., Wood, C. T., and Atkinson, R. C. (1971). Recognition time for information stored in long-term memory. *Perception & Psychophysics,* 10, 8–14.

Kahneman, D., and Beatty, J. (1966). Pupil diameter and load on memory. *Science,* 154, 1583–1585.

Kalaska, J. F., Cohen, D. A. D., Hyde, M. L., and Prud'homme, M. J. (1989). A comparison of movement direction-related versus load direction-related activity in primate motor cortex using a two-dimensional reaching task. *The Journal of Neuroscience*, 9, 2080–2102.

Kamin, L. J. (1968). Attention-like processes in classical conditioning. *Miami symposium on the prediction of behavior: Aversive stimulation*. M. R. Jones (Ed.). Miami: University of Miami Press.

Kamin, L. J. (1969). Predictability, surprise, attention, and conditioning. *Punishment and aversive behavior*. B. A. Campbell and R. M. Church (Eds.). New York: Appleton-Century-Crofts.

Kamin, L. J., Brimer, C. J., and Black, A. H. (1963). Conditioned suppression as a monitor of fear in the course of avoidance training. *Journal of Comparative and Physiological Psychology*, 56, 497–501.

Kandel, E. R., and O'Dell, T. J. (1992). Are adult learning mechanisms also used for development? *Science*, 258, 243–245.

Kaneko, T., and Thompson, R. F. (1997). Disruption of trace conditioning of the nictitating membrane response in rabbits by central cholinergic blockade. *Psychopharmacology*, 131, 161–166.

Kaneoke, Y., Bundou, M., Koyama, S., Suzuki, H., and Kakigi, R. (1997). Human cortical area responding to stimuli in apparent motion. *NeuroReport*, 8, 677–682.

Kang, H., and Schuman, E. M. (1995). Long-lasting neurotrophin-induced enhancement of synaptic transmission in the adult hippocampus, *Science*, 267, 1658–1662.

Kang, H, Welcher, A. A., Shelton, D., and Schuman, E. M. (1997). Neurotrophins and time: different roles for TrkB signaling in hippocampal long-term potentiation. *Neuron*, 19, 653–664.

Kanizsa, G. (1955). Margini quasi-percettivi in campi con stimulazione omogenea, *Revista di Psicologia*, 49, 7–30.

Kanizsa, G. (1974). Contours without gradients or cognitive contours. *Italian Journal of Psychology*, 9, 93–113.

Kanizsa, G. (1976). Subjective contours. *Scientific American*, 234, 48–53.

Kanizsa, G., and Minguzzi, G. F. (1986). An anomalous brightness differentiation. *Perception*, 15, 223–226.

Kapadia, M. K., Ito, M., Gilbert, C. D., and Westheimer, G. (1995). Improvement in visual sensitivity by changes in local context: Parallel studies in human observers and in VI of alert monkeys. *Neuron*, 15, 843–856.

Kar, S., Seto, D., Gaudreau, P., and Quirion, R. (1996). β-amyloid-related peptides inhibit potassium-evoked acetylcholine release from rat hippocampal slices. *The Journal of Neuroscience*, 16, 1034–1040.

Karadi, Z., Oomura, Y., Nishino, H., Scott, T. R., Lenard, L., and Aou, S. (1992). Responses of lateral hypothalamic glucose-sensitive and glucose-insensitive neurons to chemical stimuli in behaving rhesus monkeys. *Journal of Neurophysiology*, 67, 389–400.

Karnath, H.-O., Ferber, S., and Himmelbach, M. (2001). Spatial awareness is a function of the temporal not the posterior parietal lobe. *Nature*, 411, 950–953.

Karnath, H.-O., and Rorden, C. (2012). The anatomy of spatial neglect. *Neuropsychologia*, 50, 1010–1017.

Kashino, M. (2006). Phonemic restoration: The brain creates missing speech sounds. *Acoustical Science and Technology*, 6, 318–321.

Kastner, S., and Ungerleider, L. G. (2001). The neural basis of biased competition in human visual cortex. *Neuropsychologia*, 39, 1263–1276.

Kaufman, L. (1974). *Sight and Mind: An Introduction to Visual Perception*. New York: Oxford University Press.

Kawamura, T., Takahashi, H., and Honda, H. (2008). Proposal of new gene filtering method, BagPART, for gene expression analysis with small sample. *Journal of Bioscience and Bioengineering*, 105, 81–84.

Kaylani, A., Georgiopoulos, M., Mollaghasemi, M., and Anagnostopoulos, G. C. (2009). AG-ART: an adaptive approach to evolving ART architectures. *Neurocomputing*, 72, 2079–2092.

Kazerounian, S., and Grossberg, S. (2014). Real-time learning of predictive recognition categories that chunk sequences of items stored in working memory. *Frontiers in Psychology: Language Sciences*, doi:10.3389/fpsyg.2014.01053. http://www.ncbi.nlm.nih.gov/pmc/articles/PMC418634

Keizer, A. W., Hommel, B., and Lamme, V. A. F. (2015). Consciousness is not necessary for visual feature binding. *Psychonomic Bulletin and Review*, 22, 453–460.

Keller, E. F., and Segal, L. A. (1970). Initiation of slime mold aggregation viewed as an instability. *Journal of Theoretical Biology*, 26, 399–415.

Keller, E. L. (1974). Participation of the medial pontine reticular formation in eye movement generation in monkey. *Journal of Neurophysiology*, 37, 316–332.

Kelley, A. E., Smith-Roe, S. L., and Holahan, M. R. (1997). Response-reinforcement learning is dependent on N-methyl-d-aspartate receptor activation in the nucleus accumbens core. *Proceedings of the National Academy of Sciences*, 94, 12174–12179.

Kellman, P. J., and Shipley, T. F. (1991). A theory of visual interpolation in object perception. *Cognitive Psychology*, 23, 141–221.

Kelly, F. J., and Grossberg, S. (2000). Neural dynamics of 3-D surface perception: Figure-ground separation and lightness perception. *Perception & Psychophysics*, 62, 1596–1619.

Keene, C. S., Bladon, J., McKenzie, S., Liu, C. D., O'Keefe, J., and Eichenbaum, H. (2016). Complementary functional organization of neuronal activity patterns in the perirhinal, lateral entorhinal, and medial entorhinal cortices. *The Journal of Neuroscience*, 36, 3660–3675.

Kennedy, 1. M. (1979). Subjective contours, contrast, and assimilation. In *Perception and Pictorial Representation*. C.F. Nodine and D.F. Fisher (Eds.). New York: Praeger.

Kennedy, 1. M. (1988). Line endings and subjective contours. *Spatial Vision*, 3, 151–158.

Kentros, C. G., Agniotri, N. T., Streater, S., Hawkins, R. D., and Kandel, E. R. (2004). Increased attention to spatial context increases both place field stability and spatial memory. *Neuron*, 42, 283–295.

Kentros, C. G, Hargreaves, E., Hawkins, R. D., Kandel, E. R., Shapiro, M., and Muller, R. V. (1998). Abolition of long-term stability of new hippocampal place cell maps by NMDA receptor blockade. *Science*, 280, 2121–2126.

Kerr, K. M., Agster, K. L., Furtak, S. C., and Burwell, R. D. (2007) Functional neuroanatomy of the parahippocampal region:

the lateral and medial entorhinal areas. *Hippocampus*, 17, 697–708.

Kersten, D., Mamassian, P., and Yuille, A. (2004). Object perception as bayesian inference. *Annual Review of Psychology*, 55, 271–304.

Kersten, D., and Yuille, A. (2003). Bayesian models of object perception. *Current Opinion in Neurobiology*, 13, 1–9.

Keskin, G. A., and Ozkan, C. (2009). An alternative evaluation of FMEA: fuzzy ART algorithm. *Quality and Reliability Engineering International*, 25, 647–661.

Kilgard, M. P., and Merzenich, M. M. (1998). Cortical map reorganization enabled by nucleus basalis activity. *Science*, 279, 1714–1718.

Kim, J. J., Clark, R. E., and Thompson, R. F. (1995). Hippocampectomy impairs the memory of recently, but not remotely, acquired trace eyeblink conditioned responses. *Behavioral Neuroscience*, 109, 195–203.

Kim, J., and Wilson, H. R. (1993). Dependence of plaid motion coherence on component grating directions. *Vision Research*, 33, 1479–1489.

Kimble, G. A, (1962). Classical conditioning and the problem of awareness. *Journal of Personality*, 30, 27–45.

Kintsch, W. (1967). Memory and decision aspects of recognition learning. *Psychological Review*, 74, 496–504.

Kisvarday, Z. F., Cowey, A., Smith, A. D., and Somogyi, P. (1989). Interlaminar and lateral excitatory amino acid connections in the striate cortex of monkey. *The Journal of Neuroscience*, 9, 667–682.

Klink, R., and Alonso, A. (1997). Muscarinic modulation of the oscillatory and repetitive firing properties of entorhinal cortex layer II neurons. *Journal of Neurophysiology*, 77, 1813–1828.

Knierim, J. J., and Van Essen, D. C. (1992). Neuronal responses to static texture patterns in area V1 of the alert macaque monkey. *Journal of Neurophysiology*, 67, 961–80.

Knill, D., and Pouget, A. (2004). The bayesian brain: the role of uncertainty in neural coding and computation. *Trends in Neuroscience*, 27, 712–719.

Knipper, M., de Pehna Berzaghi, M., Blochl, A., Breer, H., Thoenen, H., and Lindholm, D. (1993). Positive feedback between acetylcholine and the neurotrophins nerve growth factor and brain-derived neurotrophic factor in rat hippocampus. *European Journal of Neuroscience*, 6, 668–671.

Knoedler, A. J., Hellwig, K. A., and Neath, I. (1999). The shift from recency to primacy with increasing delay. *Journal of Experimental Psychology: Learning, Memory and Cognition*, 25, 474–487.

Knowlton, B. J., and Squire, L. R. (1993). The learning of categories: Parallel brain systems for item memory and category knowledge. *Science*, 262, 1747–1749.

Knudsen, E. I. (2002). Instructed learning in the auditory localization pathway of the barn owl. *Nature*, 417, 322–328.

Knudsen, E. I. (2011). Control from below: The role of a midbrain network in spatial attention. *European Journal of Neuroscience*, 33, 1961–1972.

Knutson, B., Adams, C. M., Fong, G. W, and Hommer, D. (2001). Anticipation of increasing monetary reward selectively recruits nucleus accumbens. *The Journal of Neuroscience*, 21 RC159, 1–5.

Koch, C., Massimini, M., Boly, M., and Tononi, G. (2016). Neural correlates of consciousness: Progress and problems. *Nature Reviews Neuroscience*, 17, 307–321.

Koch, C., and Tsuchiya, N. (2007). Attention and consciousness: two distinct brain processes. *Trends in Cognitive Sciences*, 11, 16–22.

Koekkoek, S. K. E., Yamaguchi, K., Milojkovic, B. A., Dortland, B. R., Ruigrok, T. J. H., Maex, R., DeGraaf, W., Smit, A. E., VanderWerf, F., Bakker, C. E., Willemsen, R., Ikeda, T., Kakizawa, S., Onodera, K., Nelson, D. L., Mientjes, E., Joosten, M., DeSchutter, E., Oostra, B. A., Ito, M., and DeZeeuw, C. I. (2005). Deletion of FMR1 in Purkinje cells enhances parallel fiber LTD, enlarges spines, and attenuates cerebellar eyelid conditioning in Fragile X synchrome. *Neuron*, 47, 339–352.

Koenig, J., Linder, A. N., Leutgeb, J. K., and Leutgeb, S. (2011). The spatial periodicity of grid cells is not sustained during reduced theta oscillations. *Science*, 332, 592–595.

Koffka, K. (1935). *Principles of Gestalt Psychology*. New York: Harcourt & Brace.

Kohara, K., Kitamura, A., Morishima, M., and Tsumoto, T. (2001). Activity-dependent transfer of brain-derived neurotrophins to postsynaptic neurons. *Science*, 291, 2419–2423.

Köhler, W., and Wallach, H. (1944). Figural after-effects. An investigation of visual processes. *Proceedings of the American Philosophical Society*, 88, 269–357.

Kohonen, T. (1984). *Self-organization and Associative Memory*. New York: Springer Verlag.

Kojima, S., and Goldman-Rakic, P. S. (1984). Functional analysis of spatially discriminative neurons in prefrontal cortex of rhesus monkey. *Brain Research*, 291, 229–240.

Kolers, P. (1972). *Aspects of Motion Perception*. Oxford, UK: Pergamon Press.

Kolers, P. A., and von Grünau, M. (1975). Visual construction of color is digital. *Science*, 189, 757–759.

Komatsu, H., and Wurtz, R. H. (1989). Modulation of pursuit eye movements by stimulation of cortical areas MT and MST. *Journal of Neurophysiology*, 62, 31–47.

Kondoh, T., Mori, M., Ono, T., and Torii, K. (2000). Mechanisms of umami taste preference and aversion in rats. *Journal of Nutrition*, 130, 966S–970S.

Kong, L., Michalka, S. W., Rosen, M. L., Sheremata, S. L., Swisher, J. D., Shinn-Cunningham, B. G., and Somers, D. C. (2012). Auditory spatial attention representations in the human cerebral cortex. *Cerebral Cortex*, 24, 773–784.

Kooistra, C. A., and Heilman, K. M. (1989). Hemispatial visual inattention masquerading as hemianopia. *Neurology*, 20, 303–330.

Kori, A., Miyashita, N., Kato, M., Hikosaka, O., Usui, S., and Matsumura, M. (1995). Eye movements in monkeys with local dopamine depletion in the caudate nucleus. II. Deficits in voluntary saccades. *The Journal of Neuroscience*, 15, 28–941.

Korte, A. (1915). Kinematoskopische Untersuchungen. *Zeitschrift für Psychologie*, 72, 194–296.

Kosslyn, S. M., Pascual-Leone, A., Felician, O., Camposano, S., Keenan, J. P., Thompson, W. L., Ganis, G., Sukel, K. E., and Albert, N. M. (1999). The role of area 17 in visual imagery: Convergent evidence from PET and rTMS. *Science*, 284, 167–170.

Kraus, N., McGee, T., Littman, T., Nicol, T., and King, C. (1994). Nonprimary auditory thalamic representation of acoustic change. *Journal of Neurophysiology*, 72, 1270–1277.

Krauskopf, I. (1963). Effect of retinal image stabilization on the appearance of heterochromatic targets. *Journal of the Optical Society of America*, 53, 741–744.

Kropff, E., and Treves, A. (2008). The emergence of grid cells: Intelligent design or just adaptation. *Hippocampus*, 18, 1256–1269.

Krumhansl, C. L. (2000). Rhythm and pitch in music cognition. *Psychological Bulletin*, 126, 159–179.

Krupa, D. J., Ghazanfar, A. A., and Nicolelis, M. A. L. (1999). Immediate thalamic sensory plasticity depends on cortico-thalamic feedback. *Proceedings of the National Academy of Sciences*, 96, 8200–8205.

Krupic, J., Burgess, N., O'Keefe, and J. (2012). Neural representations of location composed of spatially periodic bands. *Science*, 337, 853–857.

Kulikowski, J. J. (1978). Limit of single vision in stereopsis depends on contour sharpness. *Nature*, 275, 126–127.

Kunisaki, O., and Fujisaki, H. (1977). On the influence of context upon perception of voiceless fricative consonants. *Annual Bulletin, Research Institute of Logopedics and Phoniatrics*, 85–91.

Kwak, H.-W., Dagenbach, D., and Egeth, H. (1991). Further evidence for a time-independent shift of the focus of attention. *Perception & Psychophysics*, 49, 473–480.

Ladefoged, P., and Disner, S. F. (2012). *Vowels and consonants, Third edition*. Chichester, West Sussex, UK: Wiley-Blackwell.

Laing, C. R., and Chow, C. C. (2002). A spiking neuron model for binocular rivalry. *Journal of Computational Neuroscience*, 12, 39–53.

Lamme, V. A. F. (1996). Contextual modulation in primary visual cortex.

Lamme, V. A. F. (2006). Towards a true neural stance on consciousness. *Trends in Cognitive Sciences*, 10, 494–501.

Lamme, V. A. F., Rodriguez-Rodriguez, V., and Spekreijse, H. (1999). Separate processing dynamics for texture elements, boundaries and surfaces in primary visual cortex of the macaque monkey. *Cerebral Cortex*, 9, 406–413.

Lamme, V. A. F., Supèr, H., and Spekreijse, H. (1998). Feedforward, horizontal and feedback processing in the visual cortex. *Current Opinion in Neurobiology*, 8, 529–35.

Land, E. H. (1977). The retinex theory of color vision. *Scientific American*, 237, 108–128.

Land, E. H. (1983). Color vision and the natural image: III. Recent advances in retinex theory and some implications for cortical computations. *Proceedings of the National Academy of Sciences*, 80, 5163–5169.

Land, E. H., and McCann, J. J. (1971). Lightness and retinex theory. *Journal of the Optical Society of America*, 61, 1–11.

Langston, R. F., Ainge, J. A., Couey, J. J., Canto, C. B., Bjerknes, T. L., and Witter, M. P. (2010). Development of the spatial representation system in the rat. *Science*, 328, 1576–1580.

Lankheet, M. J. (2006). Unraveling adaptation and mutual inhibition in perceptual rivalry. *Journal of Vision*, 6, 304–310.

Lape, R., and Nistri, A. (2000). Current and voltage clamp studies of the spike medium afterhyperpolarization of hypoglossal motoneurons in a rat brain stem slice preparation. *Journal of Neurophysiology*, 83, 2987–2995.

Lappe, M., Bremmer, F., Pekel, M., Thiele, A., and Hoffmann, K.-P. (1996). Optic flow processing in monkey STS: A theoretical and experimental approach. *The Journal of Neuroscience*, 16, 6265–6285.

Lappe, M., Bremmer, F., and van den Berg, A. V. (1999). Perception of self-motion from visual flow. *Trends in Cognitive Sciences*, 3, 329–336.

Lawrence, P. A., Crick, F. H. C., and Munro, M. (1972). A gradient of positional information in an insect, Rhodnius. *Journal of Cell Science*, 112, 815–853.

LeCun, Y., Bengio, Y., and Hinton, G., (2015). Deep learning. *Nature*, 521, 436–444.

LeDoux, J. E. (1993). Emotional memory systems in the brain. *Behavioral Brain Research*, 58, 69–79.

LeDoux, J. E. (1996). *The Emotional Brain: The Mysterious Underpinnings of Emotional Life*. New York: Simon and Schuster.

LeDoux, J. E. (2012). Rethinking the emotional brain. *Neuron*, 73, 653–676.

Lee, S. H., and Blake, R. (1999). Rival ideas about binocular rivalry. *Vision Research*, 39, 1447–1454.

Lee, S. H., and Blake, R. (2002). V1 activity is reduced during binocular rivalry. *Journal of Vision*, 2, 618–626.

Lenck-Santini, P.-P. (2017). Stereotypical activation of hippocampal ensembles during seizures. *Brain*, 140, 2254–2264.

Leonard, B., and McNaughton, B. L. (1990). Spatial representation in the rat: Conceptual, behavioral, and neurophysiological perspectives. In R. P. Kesner and D. S. Olton (Eds.). *Neurobiology of Comparative Cognition*, Chapter 13, pages 363–422. Hillsdale, NJ: Lawrence Erlbaum Associates.

Leopold, D. A., and Logothetis, N. K. (1996). Activity changes in early visual cortex reflect monkeys' percepts during binocular rivalry. *Nature*, 379, 549–553.

Lepper, M. R., Greene, D., and Nisbett, R. E. (1973). Undermining children's intrinsic interest with extrinsic reward: A test of the "overjustification" hypothesis. *Journal of Personality and Social Psychology*, 28, 129–137.

Lesher, G. W., and Mingolla, E. (1993) The role of edges and line ends in illusory contour formation. *Vision Research*, 33, 2253–2270.

Lessmann, V. (1998). Neurotrophin-dependent modulation of glutamatergic synaptic transmission in the mammalian CNS. *General Pharmacology*, 31, 667–674.

Levenberg, B., and Hayaishi, O. (1959). A bacterial pterin deaminase. *Journal of Biological Chemistry*, 234, 955–961.

Leveille, J., Versace, M., and Grossberg, S. (2010). Running as fast as it can: How spiking dynamics form object groupings in the laminar circuits of visual cortex. *Journal of Computational Neuroscience*, 28, 323–346.

Levi, D. M. (2008). Crowding—An essential bottleneck for object recognition: A mini-review. *Vision Research*, 48, 635–654.

Levine, D. (2018). *Introduction to Neural and Cognitive Modeling: Third Edition*. Milton Park, Oxfordshire UK: Taylor & Francis.

LeVine, S. (2017). Artificial intelligence pioneer says we need to start over. *Axios*, September 15.

Levy, W. B., Brassel, S. E., and Moore, S. D. (1983). Partial quantification of the associative synaptic learning rule of the dentate gyrus. *Neuroscience*, 8, 799–808.

Levy, W. B., and Desmond, N. L. (1985). The rules of elemental synaptic plasticity. In *Synaptic Modification, Neuron Selectivity, and Nervous System Organization*. W. B. Levy, J. A. Anderson, and S. Lehmkuhle (Eds.). Hillsdale, NJ: Lawrence Erlbaum Associates, pp. 105–121.

Levy, W. B., and Steward, O. (1983). Temporal contiguity requirements for long term associative potentiation/depression in the hippocampus. *Neuroscience*, 8, 791–797.

Li, L., Sweet, B. T., and Stone, L. S. (2006). Humans can perceive heading without visual path information. *Journal of Vision*, 6, 874–881.

Li, N., and DiCarlo, J. J. (2008). Unsupervised natural experience rapidly alters invariant object representation in visual cortex. *Science*, 321, 1502–1507.

Li, N., and DiCarlo, J. J. (2010). Unsupervised natural visual experience rapidly reshapes size invariant object represent in inferior temporal cortex. *Neuron*, 67, 1062–1075.

Liberman, A. M., and Mattingly, I. G. (1985). The motor theory of speech perception revised. *Cognition*, 21, 1–36.

Libet, B., Gleason, C. A., Wright, E. W., and Pearl, D. K. (1983). Time of conscious intention to act in relation to onset of cerebral activity (readiness-potential). *Brain*, 106, 623–642.

Libby, L. A., Hannula, D. E., and Ranganath, C. (2014). Medial temporal lobe coding of item and spatial information during relational binding in working memory. *Journal of Neuroscience*, 34, 14233–14242.

Lindsey, D. T., and Todd, J. T. (1996). On the relative contributions of motion energy and transparency to the perception of moving plaids. *Vision Research*, 36, 207–222.

Lisberger, S. G., Morris, E. J., and Tychsen, L. (1987). Visual motion processing and sensory-motor integration for smooth pursuit eye movements. *Annual Review of Neuroscience*, 10, 97–129.

Little, A. H., Lipsitt, L. P., and Rovee-Collier, C. (1984). Classical conditioning and retention of the infant's eyelid response: Effects of age and interstimulus interval. *Journal of Experimental Child Psychology*, 37, 512–524.

Liu, L., Huang, L., Lai, M., and Ma, C. (2009). Projective ART with buffers for the high dimensional space clustering and an application to discover stock associations. *Neurocomputing*, 72, 1283–1295.

Liu, D., Pang, Z., and Lloyd, S. R. (2008). A neural network method for detection of obstructive sleep apnea and narcolepsy based on pupil size and EEG. *IEEE Transactions on Neural Networks*, 19, 308–318.

Livingstone, M. S., and Hubel, S. H. (1987). Psychophysical evidence for separate channels for the perception of form, color, movement, and depth. *The Journal of Neuroscience*, 7, 3416–3468.

Livingstone, M. S., and Hubel, S. H. (1988). Segregation of form, color, movement, and depth: Anatomy, physiology, and perception. *Science*, 240, 740–749.

Ljungberg, T., Apicella, P., and Schultz, W. (1992). Responses of monkey dopamine neurons during learning of behavioral reactions. *Journal of Neurophysiology*, 67, 145–163.

Lleras, A., and von Mühlenen, A. (2004). Spatial context and top-down strategies in visual search. *Spatial Vision*, 17, 465–482.

Llinas, R., Ribary, U., Contreras, D., and Pedroarena, C. (1998). The neuronal basis for consciousness. *Philosophical Transactions of the Royal Society of London B*, 353, 1841–1849.

Llinas, R., Ribary, U., Joliot, M., and Wang, X. T. (1994). Content and context in temporal thalamocortical binding. In G. Buzsáki, R. Llinas, W. Singer, A. Berthoz, and Y. Christen (Eds.), *Temporal Coding in the Brain*. Berlin: Springer-Verlag, pp. 251–272.

Locke, M. (1959). The cuticular pattern in an insect, *Rhodnius prolixux Stål. Journal of Experimental Biology*, 36, 459–477.

Locke, M. (1960). The cuticular pattern in an insect—the intersegmental membranes. *Journal of Experimental Biology*, 37, 398–406.

Locke, M. (1967). The development of patterns in the integument of insects. In M. Abercrombie and J. Brachet (Eds.). *Advances in Morphogenesis, Volume 6*, New York: Academic Press, pp. 33–87.

LoConte, G., Bartolini, L., Casamenti, F., Marconcini-Pepeu, I., and Pepeu, G. (1982). Lesions of cholinergic forebrain nuclei: changes in avoidance behavior and scopolamine actions. *Pharmacology, Biochemistry, and Behavior*, 17, 933–937.

Logothetis, N. K. (1998). Single units and conscious vision. *Philosophical Transactions of the Royal Society of London, B, Biological Sciences*, 353, 1801–1818.

Logothetis, N. K., Leopold, D. A., and Sheinberg, D. L. (1996). What is rivaling during binocular rivalry? *Nature*, 380, 621–624.

Lopes, M. L. M., Minussi, C. R., and Lotufo, A. D. P. (2005). Electric load forecasting using a fuzzy ART & ARTMAP neural network. *Applied Soft Computing*, 5, 235–244.

López-López, J. R., Shacklock, P. S., Balke, C. W., and Wier, W. G. (1995). Local calcium transients triggered by single L-type calcium channel currents in cardiac cells. *Science*, 268, 1042–1045.

Lowel, S., and Singer, W. (1992). Selection of intrinsic horizontal connections in the visual cortex by correlated neuronal activity. *Science*, 255, 209–212.

Lorenceau, J., and Alais, D. (2001). Form constraints in motion binding. *Nature Neuroscience*, 4, 745–751.

Lorenceau, J., and Shiffrar, M. (1992). The influence of terminators on motion integration across space. *Vision Research*, 32, 263–273.

Lu, Z.-L., and Dosher, B. A. (2004). Perceptual learning retunes the perceptual template in foveal orientation identification. *Journal of Vision*, Vol. 4, 5. Doi:10.1167/4.1.5.

Lubenov, E. V., and Siapas, A. G. (2009). Hippocampal theta oscillations are travelling waves. *Nature*, 459, 534–539.

Luce, R. D. (1986). *Response Times: Their Role in Inferring Elementary Mental Organization*. New York, NY: Oxford University Press.

Luce, P. A., and McLennan, C. T. (2008). Spoken Word Recognition: The challenge of variation. In D. B. Pisoni and R. E. Remez (Eds.). *The Handbook of Speech Perception*. Wiley Online Library DOI 10.1002/9780470757024.ch24.

Lucia, U. (2016). Macroscopic irreversibility and microscopic paradox: A Constructal law analysis of atoms as open systems, *Scientific Reports*, 6, Article number: 35796.

Luck, S. J., Chelazzi, L., Hillyard, S. A., and Desimone, R. (1997). Neural mechanisms of spatial selective attention in areas V1, V2, and V4 of macaque visual cortex. *Journal of Neurophysiology, 77*, 24–42.

Lueck, C. J., Zeki, S., Friston, K. J., Deiber, M.-P., Cope, P., Cunningham, V. J., Lammertsma, A. A., Kennard, C., and Frackowiak, R. S. J. (1989). The colour centre in the cerebral cortex of man. *Nature, 340*, 386–389.

Lumer, E. D. (1998). A neural model of binocular integration and rivalry based on the coordination of action-potential timing in primary visual cortex. *Cerebral Cortex, 8*, 553–561.

Lund, J. S., and Boothe, R. G. (1975). Interlaminar connections and pyramidal neuron organisation in the visual cortex, area 17, of the macaque monkey. *Journal of Comparative Neurology, 159*, 305–334.

Lundqvist, M., Rose, J., Herman, P., Brincat, S. L., Buschman, T. J., and Miller, E. K. (2016). Gamma and beta bursts underlie working memory. *Neuron, 90*, 152–164.

Lundqvist, M., Herman, P., Warden, M. R., Brincat, S. L., and Miller, E. K. (2018). Gamma and beta bursts during working memory readout suggest roles in its volitional control. *Nature Communications, 9*, 394.

Luria, A. R. (1966). *Higher cortical functions in man.* New York: Basic Books.

Lysle, D. T., and Fowler, H. (1985). Inhibition as a "slave" process: Deactivation of conditioned inhibition through extinction of conditioned excitation. *Journal of Experimental Psychology: Animal Behavior Processes, 11*, 71–94.

Lynch, G., McGaugh, J. L., and Weinberger, N. M. (Eds.) (1984). *Neurobiology of Learning and Memory.* New York: Guilford Press.

MacDonald, C. J., Lepage, K. Q., Eden, U. T., and Eichenbaum, H. (2011). Hippocampal "time cells" bridge the gap in memory for discontiguous events. *Neuron, 71*, 737–749.

Mach, E. (1914). *The Analysis of Sensations and the Relation of the Physical to the Psychical* (translated by C. M. Williams, revised by Sidney Waterlow). Chicago and London: The Open Court Publishing Company.

MacNeilage, P. R. (1998). The frame/content theory of evolution of speech. *Behavioral and Brain Sciences, 21*, 499–546.

Madison, D. V., Lancaster, B., and Nicoll, R. A. (1987). Voltage clamp analysis of cholinergic action in the hippocampus. *Journal of Neuroscience, 7*, 733–741.

Magee, J. C., and Johnston, D. (1997). A synaptically controlled, associative signal for Hebbian plasticity in hippocampal neurons. *Science, 275*, 209–213.

Magezi, D. A., and Krumbholz, K. (2010). Evidence for opponent-channel coding of interaural time differences in human auditory cortex. *Journal of Neurophysiology, 104*, 1997–2007.

Maier, S. F., and Seligman, M. E. P. (1976). Learned helplessness: Theory and evidence. *Journal of Experimental Psychology: General, 105*, 3–46.

Maier, S. F., Seligman, M. E. P., and Solomon, R. L. (1969). Pavlovian fear conditioning and learned helplessness effects on escape and avoidance behavior of (a) the CS-US contingency and (b) the independent of the US and voluntary responding. In *Punishment and Aversive Behavior.* B. A. Campbell and R. M. Church (Eds.). New York: Appleton.

Málková, L., Gaffan, D., and Murray, E. A. (1997). Excitotoxic lesions of the amygdala fail to produce impairment in visual learning for auditory secondary reinforcement but interfere with reinforcer devaluation effects in rhesus monkeys. *The Journal of Neuroscience, 17*, 6011–6020.

Malpeli, J. G., Schiller, P. H., and Colby, C. L. (1981). Response properties of single cells in monkey striate cortex during reversible inactivation of individual lateral geniculate laminae. *Journal of Neurophysiology, 46*, 1102–1119.

Malsburg, C. von der (1973). Self-organization of orientation sensitive cells in the striate cortex. *Kybernetik, 14*, 85–100.

Manassi, M., Lonchampt, S., Clarke, A., and Herzog, M. H. (2016). What crowding can tell us about object representations. *Journal of Vision*, Vol. 16, 35. Doiu:10.1167/16.3.35.

Mandler, G. (1980). Recognizing: The judgment of previous occurrence. *Psychological Review, 87*, 252–271.

Mann, V. A., and Repp, B. H. (1980). The influence of vocalic context on perception of the [ʃ]-[s] context. *Perception and Psychophysics, 28*, 213–228.

Mannion, A., and Leader, G. (2014). Sleep problems in autism spectrum disorder: A literature review. *Review Journal of Autism and Developmental Disorders, 1*, 101–109

Manns, J. R., Clark, R. E., and Squire, L. R. (2000). Parallel acquisition of awareness and trace eyeblink classical conditioning. *Learning & Memory, 7*, 267–272.

Marchiori, S. C., da Silveira, M. do C., Lotufo, A. D. P., Minussi, C. R., and Lopes, M. L. M. (2011). Neural network based on adaptive resonance theory with continuous training for multi-configuration transient stability analysis of electric power systems. *Applied Soft Computing, 11*, 706–715.

Margo, A., Hemsley, D. R. and Slade, P.D. (1981). The effects of varying auditory input on schizophrenic hallucinations. *British Journal of Psychiatry, 39*, 101–107.

Markram, H., Helm, P. J., and Sakmann, B. (1995). Dendritic calcium transients evoked by single back-propagating action potentials in rat neocortical pyramidal neurons. *Journal of Physiology, 485*, 1–20.

Markram, H., Lubke, J., Frotscher, M., and Sakmann, B. (1997). Regulation of synaptic efficacy by coincidence of postsynaptic APs and EPSPs. *Science, 275*, 213–215.

Marr, D., and Poggio, T. (1976). Cooperative computation of stereo disparity. *Science, 194*, 283–287.

Marr, D., and Ullman, S. (1981). Directional selectivity and its use in early visual processing. *Proceedings of the Royal Society, London, B, 211*, 151–180.

Marshall, J. C. (2001). Auditory neglect and right parietal cortex. *Brain, 124*, 645–646.

Marshall, L., Helgadóttir, H., Mölle, M., and Born, J. (2006). Boosting slow oscillations during sleep potentiates memory. *Nature, 444*, 610–613.

Martin, J. H. (1989). *Neuroanatomy: Text and Atlas.* Norwalk, CT: Appleton and Lange.

Martin-Guerrero, J. D., Lisboa, P. J. G., Soria-Olivas, E., Palomares, A., and Balaguer, E. (2007). An approach based on the adaptive resonance theory for analyzing the viability of recommender systems in a citizen web portal. *Expert Systems with Applications, 33*, 743–753.

Mason, G. J. (1991). Stereotypies: a critical review. *Animal Behavior, 41*, 1015–1037.

Masserman, J. H. (1946). *Principles of Dynamic Psychiatry, including an Integrative Approach to Abnormal and Clinical Psychology.* Oxford, England: W. B. Saunders.

Masserman, J. H., and Jacques, M. G. (1948). Experimental masochism. *Archives of Neurology & Psychiatry*, 60, 402–404.

Massimini, M., Huber, R., Ferrarelli, F., Hill, S., and Tononi, G. (2004). The sleep slow oscillation as a traveling wave. *The Journal of Neuroscience*, 24, 6862–6870.

Massey, L. (2009). Discovery of hierarchical thematic structure in text collections with adaptive resonance theory. *Neural Computation & Applications*, 18, 261–273.

Masterson, F. A. (1970). Is termination of a warning signal an effective reward for the rat? *Journal of Comparative and Physiological Psychology*, 72, 471–475.

Mathot, S., and Theeuwes, J. (2010). Gradual remapping results in early retinotopic and late spatiotopic inhibition of return. *Psychological Science*, 21, 1793–1798.

Matisse, H. (1947/1992). *Jazz*. George Braziller, Scranton, PA, USA.

Matsuoka, K. (1984). The dynamic model of binocular rivalry. *Biological Cybernetics*, 49, 201–208.

Mattingley, J. B., Bradshaw, J. L., and Bradshaw, J. A. (1995). The effects of unilateral visuospatial neglect on perception of Muller-Lyer illusory figures. *Perception*, 24, 415–433.

Mattingley, J. B., Davis, G., and Driver, J. (1997). Preattentive filling-in of visual surfaces in parietal extinction. *Science*, 275, 671–674.

Mattingley, J. B., Husain, M., Rorden, C., Kennard, C., and Driver, J. (1998). Motor role of human inferior parietal lobe revealed in unilateral neglect patients. *Nature*, 392, 179–182.

Mauk, M. D., and Ruiz, B. P. (1992). Learning-dependent timing of Pavolian eyelid responses: Differential conditioning using multiple interstimulus intervals. *Behavioral Neuroscience*, 106, 666–681.

Maunsell, J. H. R., and Van Essen, D. (1983). Response properties of single units in middle temporal visual area of the macaque. *Journal of Neurophysiology*, 49, 1127–1147.

Mayer, K., Wyckoff, S. N., and Stehl, U. (2016). Underarousal in adult ADHD: How are peripheral and cortical arousal related? *Clinical EEG and Neuroscience*, 47, 171–179.

Mazurek, M. E., Hanks, T., Yang, T., and Shadlen, M. N. (2005). Prior probability changes the rate of evidence accumulation in a motion discrimination task: Behavior and LIP physiology. *Society of Neuroscience Abstracts*, 621.3.

McAdams, S. (2013). Musical timbre perception. In D. Deutsch (Ed.). *The Psychology of Music. Third Edition*, pp. 35–68. Amsterdam: Elsevier.

McAllister, W. R., and McAllister, D. E. (1958). Effect of knowledge of conditioning upon eyelid conditioning. *Journal of Experimental Psychology*, 25, 579–583.

McBride, P. (2015). The disrupted basal ganglia and behavioural control: an integrative cross-domain perspective of spontaneous stereotypy. *Behavioural Brain Research*, 276, 45–58. doi: 10.1016/j.bbr.2014.05.057

McClelland, J. L., and Elman, J. L. (1986). The TRACE model of speech perception. *Cognitive Psychology*, 18, 1–86.

McClelland, J. L., and Rumelhart, D. E. (1981). An interactive activation model of context effects in letter perception: Part I. An account of basic findings. *Psychological Review*, 88, 375–407.

McClelland, J. L., and Rumelhart, D. E. (1982). An interactive activation model of context effects in letter perception: Part II. The contextual enhancement effect and some tests and extensions of the model. *Psychological Review*, 89, 60–94.

McCollough, C. (1965). Color adaptation of edge-detectors in the human visual system. *Science*, 149, 1115–1116.

McCulloch, W. S., and Pitts, W. (1943). A logical calculus of the ideas immanent in nervous activity. *The Bulletin of Mathematical Biophysics*, 5, 115–133.

McDonald, C. J., Lepage, K. Q., Eden, U. T., and Eichenbaum, H. (2011). Hippocampal "time cells" bridge the gap in memory for discontiguous events. *Neuron*, 71, 737–749.

McGaugh, J. L. (2000). Memory—a century of consolidation. *Science*, 287, 248–251.

McGaugh, J. L. (2002). Memory consolidation and the amygdala: A systems perspective. *Trends in Neurosciences*, 25, 456–461.

McGlinchey-Berroth, R., Brawn, C., and Disterhoft J. F. (1999). Temporal discrimination learning in severe amnesic patients reveals an alteration in the timing of eyeblink conditioned responses. *Behavioral Neuroscience*, 113, 10–18.

McGlinchey-Berroth, R., Carrillo, M. C., Gabrieli, J. D., Brawn, C. M., and Disterhoft, J. F. (1997). Impaired trace eyeblink conditioning in bilateral, medial-temporal lobe amnesia. *Behavioral Neuroscience*, 111, 873–882.

McGlinchey-Berroth, R., Milberg, W. P., Verfaellie, M., Alexander, M., and Kilduff, P. T. (1993). Semantic processing in the neglected visual field: Evidence from a lexical decision task. *Cognitive Neuropsychology*, 10, 79–108.

McGuire, B. A., Hornung, J. P., Gilbert, C. D., and Wiesel, T. N. (1984). Patterns of synaptic input to layer 4 of cat striate cortex. *The Journal of Neuroscience*, 4, 3021–3033.

McIlwain, J. T. (1986). Effects of eye position on saccades evoked electrically from superior colliculus of alert cats. *Journal of Neurophysiology*, 55, 97–112.

McKee, S. P., Bravo, M. J., Smallman, H. S. and Legge, G. E. (1995). The 'uniqueness constraint' and binocular masking. *Perception*, 24, 49–65.

McKee, S. P., Bravo, M. J., Taylor, D. G., and Legge, G. E. (1994). Stereo matching precedes dichoptic masking. *Vision Research*, 34, 1047–1060.

McLennan, C. T., Conor, T., and Luce, P. A. (2005). Examining the time course of indexical specificity effects in spoken word recognition. *Journal of Experimental Psychology: Learning, Memory, and Cognition*, 31, 306–321.

McLennan, C. T., Luce, P. A., and Charles-Luce, J. (2003). Representation of lexical form. *Journal of Experimental Psychology: Learning, Memory, and Cognition*, 29, 539–553.

McLoughlin, N. P. and Grossberg, S. (1998). Cortical computation of stereo disparity. *Vision Research*, 38, 91–99.

McNab, F., and Klingberg, T. (2008). Prefrontal cortex and basal ganglia control access to working memory. *Nature Neuroscience*, 11, 103–107.

McNaughton, B. L., Battaglia, F. P., Jensen, O., Moser, E. I., and Moser, M. B. (2006). Path integration and the neural basis of the 'cognitive map'. *Nature Reviews Neuroscience*, 7, 663–678.

Medin, D. L., Dewey, G. I., and Murphy, T. D. (1983). Relationships between item and category learning: Evidence that abstraction is not automatic. *Journal of Experimental Psychology: Learning and Memory*, 9, 607–625.

Medin, D. L., and Schaffer, M. M. (1978). Context theory of classification learning. *Psychological Review*, 85, 207–238.

Medin, D. L., and Smith, E. E. (1981). Strategies and classification learning. *Journal of Experimental Psychology: Human Learning and Memory*, 7, 241–253.

Mehta, M. R. (2007). Cortico-hippocampal interaction during up-down states and memory consolidation. *Nature Neuroscience*, 10, 13–15.

Meinhardt, H., and Gierer, A. (1974). Applications of a theory of biological pattern formation based on lateral inhibition. *Journal of Cell Science*, 15, 321–346.

Meinhardt, H., and Gierer, A. (2000). Pattern formation by local self-activation and lateral inhibition. *Bioessays*, 22, 753–760.

Melcher, D. (2007). Predictive remapping of visual features precedes saccadic eye movements. *Nature Neuroscience*, 10, 903–907.

Melcher, D. (2008). Dynamic, object-based remapping of visual features in trans-saccadic perception. *Journal of Vision*, 8, 1–17.

Melcher, D. (2009). Selective attention and the active remapping of object features in trans-saccadic perception. *Vision Research*, 49, 1249–1255.

Mendelson, J., Schreiner, C., Sutter, M, and Grasse, K. (1993). Functional topography of cat primary auditory cortex: responses to frequency-modulated sweeps. *Experimental Brain Research*, 94, 65–87.

Mesulam, M.-M. (1999). Spatial attention and neglect: parietal, frontal and cingulate contributions to the mental representation and attentional targeting of salient extrapersonal events. *Philosophical Transactions of the Royal Society B*, 354, 1325–1346.

Meyer, G., Lawson, R. and Cohen, W. (1975). The effects of orientation specific adaptation on the duration of short-term visual storage. *Vision Research*, 15, 569–572.

Meyer, G, and Ming, C. (1988). The visible persistence of illusory contours. *Canadian Journal of Psychology*, 42, 479–488.

Mhatre, H., Gorchetchnikov, A., and Grossberg, S. (2012). Grid cell hexagonal patterns formed by fast self-organized learning within entorhinal cortex. *Hippocampus*, 22, 320–334.

Micheyl, C., Carlyon, R. P., Gutschalk, A., Melcher, J. R., Oxenham, A. J., Rauschecker, J., Tian, B., and Wilson, E. C. (2007). The role of auditory cortex in the formation of auditory streams. *Hearing Research*, 229, 116–131.

Middleton, F., and Strick, P. (2000). Basal ganglia and cerebellar loops: Motor and cognitive circuits. *Brain Research Reviews*, 31, 236–250.

Mikami, A. (1991). Direction selective neurons respond to short-range and long-range apparent motion stimuli in macaque visual area MT. *International Journal of Neuroscience*, 61, 101–112.

Militerni, R., Bravaccio, C., Falco, C., Fico, C., and Palermo, M. T. (2002). Repetitive behaviors in autistic disorder. *European Child & Adolescent Psychiatry*, 11, 210–218.

Millenson, J. R., Kehoe, E. J., and Gormenzano, 1. (1977). Classical conditioning of the rabbit's nictitating membrane response under fixed and mixed CS-US intervals. *Learning and Motivation*, 8, 351–366.

Miller, E. K., Li, L., and Desimone, R. (1991). A neural mechanism for working and recognition memory in inferior temporal cortex. *Science*, 254, 1377–1379.

Miller, E. K., and Cohen, J. D. (2001). An integrative theory of prefrontal cortex function. *Annual Review of Neuroscience*, 24, 167–202.

Miller, G. A. (1956). The magical number seven, plus or minus two: some limits on our capacity for processing information. *Psychological Review*, 63, 81–97.

Miller, J. L. (1980). Contextual effects in the discrimination of stop consonants and semivowels. *Perception & Psychophysics*, 25, 457–465.

Miller, J. L., and Liberman, A. M. (1979). Some effects of later-occurring information on the perception of stop consonant and semivowel. *Perception & Psychophysics*, 25, 457–465.

Miller, N. E. (1948). Theory and experiment relating psychoanalytic displacement to stimulus-response generalization. *The Journal of Abnormal and Social Psychology*, 43, 155–178.

Miller, R. R., and Schachtman, T. R. (1985). Conditioning context as an associative baseline: Implications for response generation and the nature of conditioned inhibition. In R. R. Miller and N. E. Spear (Eds.). *Information Processing in Animals: Conditioned Inhibition*. Hillsdale, NJ: Erlbaum.

Miller, S., Yasuda, M., Coats, J. K., Jones, Y., Martone, M. E., and Mayford, M. (2002). Disruption of dendritic translation of CaMKIIa impairs stabilization of synaptic plasticity and memory consolidation. *Neuron*, 36, 507–519.

Mingolla, E., Ross, W., and Grossberg, S. (1999). A neural network for enhancing boundaries and surfaces in synthetic aperture radar images. *Neural Networks*, 12, 499–511.

Mink, J. (1996). The basal ganglia: focused selection and inhibition of competing motor programs. *Progress in Neurobiology*, 50, 381–425.

Mishkin, M. (1982). A memory system in the monkey. *Philosophical Transactions of the Royal Society of London. B: Biological Sciences*, 298, 85–95.

Mishkin, M., and Delacour, J. (1975). An analysis of short-term visual memory in the monkey. *Journal of Experimental Psychology: Animal Behavior Processes*, 1, 326–334.

Mishkin, M. Ungerleider, L. G., and Macko, K. A. (1983). Object vision and spatial vision: Two cortical pathways. *Trends in Neurosciences*, 6, 414–417.

Mitchell, S. J., Rawlins, J. N., Steward, O., and Olton, D. S. (1982). Medial septal area lesions disrupt theta rhythm and cholinergic staining in medial entorhinal cortex and produce impaired radial arm maze behavior in rats. *The Journal of Neuroscience*, 2, 292–302.

Mitroff, S. R., and Scholl, B. J. (2005). Forming and updating object representations without awareness: Evidence from motion-induced blindness. *Vision Research*, 45, 961–967.

Miyashita, Y., and Chang, H. S. (1988). Neuronal correlate of pictorial short-term memory in the primate temporal cortex. *Nature*, 331, 68–70.

Miyata, M., Finch, E. A., Khiroug, L., Hashimoto, K., Hayasaka, S., Oda, S.-I., Inouye, M., Takagishi, Y., Augustine, G. J., and Kano, M. (2000). Local Calcium release in dendritic spines required for long-term synaptic depression. *Neuron*, 28, 233–244.

Mogenson, G. J., Jones, D. L., and Yim, C. Y. (1980). From motivation to action: functional interface between the limbic system and the motor system. *Progress in Neurobiology,* 14, 69–97.

Møller, A. R. (1983). *Auditory Physiology.* New York: Academic Press.

Molter, C., and Yamaguchi, Y. (2008). Entorhinal theta phase precession sculpts dentate gyrus place fields. *Hippocampus,* 18, 919–930.

Monteggia, L. M., Barrett, M., Powell, C. M., Berton, O., Galanis, V., Gemelli, T., Meuth, S., Nagy, A., Greene, R. W., and Nestler, E. J. (2004). Essential role of brain-derived neurotrophic factor in adult hippocampal function. *Proceedings of the National Academy of Sciences USA,* 101, 10827–10832.

Mooney, C. M. (1957). Age in the development of closure ability in children. *Canadian Journal of Psychology,* 11, 219–226.

Moore, C. M., and Egeth, H. (1997). Perception without attention: evidence of grouping under conditions of inattention. *Journal of Experimental Psychology: Human Perception and Performance,* 23, 339–352.

Moore, C. M., Yantis, S., and Vaughan, B. (1998). Object-based visual selection: Evidence from perceptual completion. *Psychological Science,* 9, 104–110.

Morris, R. G. M. (1981). Spatial localisation does not depend on the presence of local cues. *Learning and Motivation,* 12, 239–260.

Morris, R. G. M., and Frey, U. (1997). Hippocampal synaptic plasticity: role in spatial learning or the automatic recording of attended experience? *Proceedings of the Royal Society B.,* 1360, 1469–1503.

Morrison, S. E., Saez, A., Lau, B., and Salzman, C. D. (2011). Different time courses for learning-related changes in amygdala and orbitofrontal cortex. *Neuron,* 71, 1127–1140.

Morrison, S. E., and Salzman, C. D. (2010). Re-valuing the amygdala. *Current Opinion in Neurobiology,* 20, 221–230.

Mort, D. J., Malhotra, P., Mannan, S. K., Rorden, C., Pambakian, A., Kennard, C., and Husain, M. (2003). The anatomy of visual neglect. *Brain,* 126, 1966–1997.

Moruzzi, G., and Magoun, H. W. (1949). Brain stem reticular formation and activation of the EEG. *Electroencephalography and Clinical Neurophysiology,* k1, 455–473.

Moser, E. L., Kropff, E., and Moser, M. B. (2008). Place cells, grid cells, and the brain's spatial representation system. *Annual Review of Neuroscience,* 31, 69–89.

Mountcastle, V. B. (1957). Modality and topographic properties of single neurons of cat somatic sensory cortex. *Journal of Neurophysiology,* 20, 408–434.

Mounts, J. R. W. (2000). Evidence for suppressive mechanisms in attentional selection: feature singletons produce inhibitory surrounds. *Perception & Psychophysics,* 62, 969–983.

Moyer, J. R., Jr., Deyo, R. A., and Disterhoft, J. F. (1990). Hippocampectomy disrupts trace eye-blink conditioning in rabbits. *Behavioral Neuroscience,* 104, 243–252.

Mueller, T. J. (1990). A physiological model of binocular rivalry. *Visual Neuroscience,* 4, 63–73.

Mueller, T. J., and Blake, R. (1989). A fresh look at the temporal dynamics of binocular rivalry. *Biological Cybernetics,* 61, 223–232.

Muessig, L., Hauser, J., Wills, T. J., and Cacucci, F. (2015). A developmental switch in place cell accuracy coincides with grid cell maturation. *Neuron,* 86, 1167–1173.

Mukherjee, P. K., Kumar, V., Mal, M., and Houghton, P. J. (2007). Acetylcholinesterase inhibitors from plants. *Phytomedicine,* 14, 289–300.

Mulder, S. A., and Wunsch, D. C. II. (2003). Million city traveling salesman problem solution by divide and conquer clustering with adaptive resonance neural networks. *Neural Networks,* 16, 827–832.

Muller, R. A. (1996). A quarter of a century of place cells. *Neuron,* 17, 813–822.

Müller, W., Misgeld, U., and Heinemann, U. (1988). Carbachol effects on hippocampal neurons *in vitro*: dependence on the rate of rise of carbachol tissue concentration. *Experimental Brain Research,* 72, 287–298.

Mumford, D. (1992). On the computational architecture of the neocortex, II, the role of corticocortical loops. *Biological Cybernetics,* 66, 241–251.

Muramoto, K., Ono, T., Nishijo, H., and Fukuda, M. (1993). Rat amygdaloid neuron responses during auditory discrimination. *Neuroscience,* 52, 621–636.

Murdock, B. B. Jr. (1962). The serial position effect of free recall. *Journal of Experimental Psychology,* 64, 482–488.

Murphy, P. C., Duckett, S. G., and Sillito, A. M. (1999). Feedback connections to the lateral geniculate nucleus and cortical response properties. *Science,* 286, 1552–1554.

Murphy, P. C., and Sillito, A.M. (1987). Corticofugal influences on the generation of length tuning in the visual pathway. *Nature,* 329, 727–729.

Näätänen, R. (1982). Processing negativity: An evoked-potential reflection. *Psychological Bulletin,* 92, 605–640.

Näätänen, R., Simpson, M., and Loveless, N. E. (1982). Stimulus deviance and evoked potentials. *Biological Psychiatry,* 14, 53–98.

Nachev, P., and Husain, M. (2006). Disorders of visual attention and the posterior parietal cortex. *Cortex,* 42, 766–773.

Nádasdy, Z., Hirase, H., Czurkó, A., Csicsvari, J., and Buzsáki, G. (1999). Replay and time compression of recurring spike sequences in the hippocampus. *The Journal of Neuroscience,* 19, 9497–9507.

Nadel, L., and Bohbot, V. (2001). Consolidation of memory. *Hippocampus,* 11, 56–60.

Nader, K., Schafe, G. E., and LeDoux, J. E. (2000). Fear memories require protein synthesis in the amygdala for reconsolidation after retrieval. *Nature,* 406, 722–726.

Nagel, T. (1974). What is it like to be a bat? *The Philosophical Review,* 83, 435–450.

Nagele, R. G., D'Andrea, M. R., Anderson, W. J., and Wang, H.-Y. (2002). Intracellular accumulation of β-amyloid$_{1-42}$ in neurons is facilitated by the α7 nicotinic acetylcholine receptor in Alzheimer's disease. *Neuroscience,* 110, 199–211.

Nakamura, K., and Ono, T. (1986). Lateral hypothalamus neuron involvement in integration of natural and artificial rewards and cue signals. *Journal of Neurophysiology,* 55, 163–181.

Nakamura, K., Ono, T., and Tamura, R. (1987). Central sites involved in lateral hypothalamus conditioned neural responses to acoustic cues in the rat. *Journal of Neurophysiology,* 58, 1123–1148.

Nakayama, K., and Shimojo, S. (1990). Da Vinci stereopsis: Depth and subjective occluding contours from unpaired image points *Vision Research,* 30, 1811–1825.

Nakayama, K., and Silverman, G. H. (1986). Serial and parallel processing of visual feature conjunctions. *Nature, 320,* 264–265.

Nakayama, K., and Silverman, G. H. (1988a). The aperture problem. I: Perception of nonrigidity and motion direction in translating sinusoidal lines. *Vision Research, 28,* 739–746.

Nakayama, K., and Silverman, G. H. (1988b). The aperture problem. II: Spatial integration of velocity information along contours. *Vision Research, 28,* 747–753.

Navon, D. (1977). Forest before trees: The precedence of global features in visual perception. *Cognitive Psychology, 9,* 353–383.

Navratilova, Z., Giocomo, L. M., Fellous, J. M., Hasselmo, M. E., and McNaughton, B. L. (2012). Phase precession and variable spatial scaling in a periodic attractor map model of medial entorhinal grid cells with realistic after-spike dynamics. *Hippocampus, 22,* 772–789.

Necker, L. A. (1832). LXI. Observations on some remarkable optical phaenomena seen in Switzerland; and on an optical phaenomenon which occurs on viewing a figure of a crystal or geometrical solid. *The London and Edinburgh Philosophical Magazine and Journal of Science,* 329–337.

Neumann, A., Raedt, R., Steenland, H., Sprengers, M., Bzymek, K., Navratilova, Z., Mesina, L., Xie, J., Lapointe, V., Kloosterman, F., Vonck, K., Boon, P. A. J. M., Soltesz, I., McNaughton, B. L., and Luczak, A. (2017). Involvement of fast-spiking cells into ictal sequences during spontaneous seizures in rats with chronic temporal lobe epilepsy. *Brain, 140,* 2355–2369.

Newman, A. J., Bavelier, D., Corina, D., Jazzard, P., and Neville, H. J. (2002). A critical period for right hemisphere recruitment in American Sign Language processing. *Nature Neuroscience, 5,* 76–80.

Newman, E. L., Climer, J. R., and Hasselmo, M. E. (2014). Grid cell spatial tuning reduced following systemic muscarinic receptor blockade. *Hippocampus, 24,* 643–655.

Newman, R., and Winan, S. S. (1980). An experimental study of the ventral striatum of the golden hamster. II. Neuronal connections of the olfactory tubercle. *Journal of Comparative Neurology, 191,* 193–212.

Newsome, W., Mikami, A., and Wurtz, R. (1986). Motion selectivity in macaque visual cortex. III. Psychophysics and physiology of apparent motion. *Journal of Neurophysiology, 55,* 1340–1351.

Newsome, W. T., Wurtz, R. H., and Komatsu, H. (1988). Relation of cortical areas MT and MST to pursuit eye movements. II. Differentiation of retinal from extraretinal inputs. *Journal of Neurophysiology, 60,* 604–620.

Newton, I. (1704). *Opticks: or, a Treatise of the Reflexions, Refractions, Inflexions, and Colours of Light.* London, England: Royal Society of London.

Nieder, A., and Miller, E. K. (2003). Coding of cognitive magnitude: Compressed scaling of numerical information in the primate prefrontal cortex. *Neuron, 37,* 149–157.

Nieder, A., and Miller, E. K. (2004). A parieto-frontal network for visual numerical information in the monkey. *Proceedings of the National Academy of Sciences, 101,* 7457–7462.

Nishijo, H., Ono, T., and Nishino, H. (1988a). Single neuron responses in amygdala of alert monkey during complex sensory stimulation with affective significance. *Journal of Neuroscience, 8,* 3570–3583.

Nishijo, H., Ono, T., and Nishino, H. (1988b). Topographic distribution of modality-specific amygdalar neurons in alert monkey. *The Journal of Neuroscience, 8,* 3556–3569.

Norman-Haignere, S., Kanwisher, N. G., and McDermott, J. H. (2015). Distinct cortical pathways for music and speech revealed by hypothesis-free voxel decomposition. *Neuron, 88,* 1281–1296.

Nosofsky, R. M. (1984). Choice, similarity, and the identification-categorization relationship. *Journal of Experimental Psychology: Learning, Memory, and Cognition, 10,* 104–114.

Nosofsky, R. M. (1987). Attention and learning processes in the identification-categorization of integral stimuli. *Journal of Experimental Psychology: Learning, Memory, and Cognition, 13,* 87–108.

Nosofsky, R. M., Kruschke, J. K., and McKinley, S. C. (1992). Combining exemplar-based category representation and connectionist learning rules. *Journal of Experimental Psychology: Learning, Memory, and Cognition, 18,* 211–233.

Nosyreva, E. D., and Huber, K. M. (2006). Metabotropic receptor-dependent long-term depression persists in the absence of protein synthesis in the mouse model of Fragile X syndrome. *Journal of Neurophysiology, 95,* 3291–3295.

Novak, M. A. (2003). Self-injurious behavior in rhesus monkeys: New insights into its etiology, physiology, and treatment. *American Journal of Primatology, 59,* 3–19.

Nowak, A. J., and Berger, T. (1992). *Society for Neuroscience Annual Meeting, Vol. 18,* p. 321.

Nozari, N., Mirman, D., and Thompson-Schill, S. L. (2016). The ventrolateral prefrontal cortex familiates processing of sentential context to locate references. *Brain and Language, 157,* 1–13.

O'Craven, K. M., Rosen, B. R., Kwong, K. K., Treisman, A., and Savoy, R. L. (1997). Voluntary attention modulates fMRI activity in human MT-MST. *Neuron, 18,* 591–598.

Ogawa, T., and Komatsu, H. (2004). Target selection in area V4 during a multidimensional visual search task. *The Journal of Neuroscience, 24,* 6371–6382.

O'Herron, P., and von der Heydt, R. (2009). Short-term memory for figure-ground organization in the visual cortex. *Neuron, 61,* 801–809.

O'Keefe, J., and Burgess, N. (2005). Dual phase and rate coding in hippocampal place cells: theoretical significance and relationship to entorhinal grid cells. *Hippocampus, 15,* 853–866.

O'Keefe, J., and Dostrovsky, J. (1971). The hippocampus as a spatial map. Preliminary evidence from unit activity in the freely-moving rat. *Brain Research, 34,* 171–175.

O'Keefe, J., and Nadel, L. (1978). *The Hippocampus as a Cognitive Map.* Oxford, UK: Clarendon Press.

O'Keefe, J., and Recce, M. L. (1993). Phase relationship between hippocampal place units and the EEG theta rhythm. *Hippocampus, 3,* 317–330.

Ólafsdóttir, H. F., Bush, D., and Barry, C. (2017). The role of hippocampal replay in memory and planning. *Current Biology, 28,* R37–R50.

Olitski, J. (1994). Clement Greenberg in my studio, *American Art, 8,* 125–129.

Oliva, A., and Torralba, A. (2001). Modeling the shape of the scene: A holistic representation of the spatial envelope. *International Journal of Computer Vision*, 42, 145–175.

Olson, I. R., and Chun, M. M. (2002). Perceptual constraints on implicit learning of spatial context. *Visual Cognition*, 9, 273–302.

Omer, D. B., Maimon, S. R., Las, L., and Ulanovsky, N. (2018). Social place-cells in the bat hippocampus. *Science*, 359, 218–224.

Öngür, D., An, X., and Price, J. L. (1998). Prefrontal cortical projection to the hypothalamus in Macaque monkeys. *Journal of Comparative Neurology*, 401, 480–505.

Öngür, D., and Price, J. L. (2000). The organization of networks within the orbital and medial prefrontal cortex of rats, monkeys and humans. *Cerebral Cortex*, 10, 206–219.

Ono, T., Nakamura, K., Nishijo, H., and Fukuda, M. (1986). Hypothalamic neuron involvement in integration of reward, aversion, and cue signals. *Journal of Neurophysiology*, 56, 63–79.

O'Reilly, J. X., Beckmann, C. F., Tomassini, V., Ramnani, N., Johansen-Berg, H. (2010). Distinct and overlapping functional zones in the cerebellum defined by resting state functional connectivity. *Cerebral Cortex*, 20, 953–965.

Orhan, I., Sener, B., Choudhary, M. I., and Khalid, A. (2004). Acetylcholinesterase and butyrylcholinesterase inhibitory activity of some Turkish medicinal plants. *Journal of Ethnopharmacology*, 91, 57–60.

Orr, W. B., and Berger, T. W. (1985). Hippocampectomy disrupts the topography of conditioned nictitating membrane responses during reversal learning. *Behavioral Neuroscience*, 99, 35–45.

Ostroff, L. E., Cain, C. K., Bedont, J., Monfils, M. H., and LeDoux, J. E. (2010). Fear and safety learning differentially affect synapse size and dendritic translation in the lateral amygdala. *Proceedings of the National Academy of Sciences*, 107, 9418–9423.

Otto, T., and Eichenbaum, H. (1992). Neuronal activity in the hippocampus during delayed non-match to sample performance in rats: Evidence for hippocampal processing in recognition memory. *Hippocampus*, 2, 323–334.

Owega, S., Khan, B.-U.-Z., Evans, G. J., Jervis, R. E., and Fila, M. (2006). Identification of long-range aerosol transport patterns to Toronto via classification of back trajectories by cluster analysis and neural network techniques. *Chemometrics and Intelligent Laboratory Systems*, 83, 26–33.

Owren, M. J., and Kaplan, P. S. (1981, April). On the failure to extinguish Pavlovian conditioned inhibition: A test of a reinstatement hypothesis. Paper presented to the meeting of the Midwestern Psychological Association, Detroit.

Pack, C. C., and Born, R. T. (2001). Temporal dynamics of a neural solution to the aperture problem in visual area MT of macaque brain. *Nature*, 409, 1040–1042.

Pack, C., Grossberg, S. and Mingolla, E. (2001). A neural model of smooth pursuit control and motion perception by cortical area MST. *Journal of Cognitive Neuroscience*, 13, 102–120.

Packard, V. O. (1957). *The Hidden Persuaders*. Philadelphia, PA: David McKay Publications. Published in Great Britain by Longmans, Green & Co.

Page, M. P. A., and Norris, D. (1998). The primacy model: A new model of immediate serial recall. *Psychological Review*, 105, 761–781.

Page, W. K., and Duffy, C. J. (1999). MST neuronal responses to heading direction during pursuit eye movements. *Journal of Neurophysiology*, 81, 596–610.

Palma, J., Grossberg, S., and Versace, M. (2012). Persistence and storage of activity patterns in spiking recurrent cortical networks: Modulation of sigmoid signals by after-hyperpolarization currents and acetylcholine. *Frontiers in Computational Neuroscience*, 6:42. Doi: 10.3389. fncom.2012.00042.

Palma, J., Versace, M., and Grossberg, S. (2012). After-hyperpolarization currents and acetylcholine control sigmoid transfer functions in a spiking cortical model. *Journal of Computational Neuroscience*, 32, 253–280.

Palmer, J., Huk, A., and Shadlen, M. N. (2005). The effect of stimulus strength on the speed and accuracy of a perceptual decision. *Journal of Vision*, 5, 376–404.

Palmeri, T. J., Goldinger, S. D., and Pisoni, D. B. (1993). Episodic encoding of voice attributes and recognition memory for spoken words. *Journal of Experimental Psychology: Learning, Memory, and Cognition*, 19, 309–328.

Palmeri, T. J., and Nosofsky, R. M. (1995). Recognition memory for exceptions to the category rule. *Journal of Experimental Psychology: Learning, Memory, and Cognition*, 21, 548–568.

Pantle, A. J., and Petersik, J. T. (1980). Effects of spatial parameters on the perceptual organization of a bistable motion display. *Perception & Psychophysics*, 27, 307–312.

Pantle, A. J., and Picciano, L. (1976). A multistable movement display: Evidence for two separate motion systems in human vision. *Science*, 193, 500–502.

Panum, P. L. (1858). Physiologische Untersuchungen ueber das Sehen mit zwei Augen. Kiel: Schwerssche Buchhandlung), translated by C Hubscher 1940 (Hanover, NH: Dartmouth Eye Institute).

Papka, M., Ivry, R., and Woodruff-Pak, D. S. (1997). Eyeblink classical conditioning and awareness revisited. *American Psychological Society*, 8, 404–408.

Paradiso, M. A., and Hahn, S. (1996). Filling-in percepts produced by luminance modulation. *Vision Research*, 36, 2657–2663.

Paradiso, M. A., and Nakayama, K. (1991). Brightness perception and filling-in. *Vision Research*, 31, 1221–1236.

Parker, D. B. (1982). Learning logic: Invention report S81-64, File 1, Office of Technology Licensing. Stanford University.

Parker, D. B. (1985). Learning-Logic. Technical Report TR-47, Center for Computational Research in Economics and Management Science, MIT.

Parker, D. B. (1986). A comparison of algorithms for neuron-like cells. In J. Denker (Ed.). *Proceedings of the Second Annual Conference on Neural Networks for Computing*. Proceedings Vol. 151, pp. 327–332. New York: American Institute of Physics.

Parker, D. B. (1987). Optimal algorithms for adaptive networks: Second order back propagation, second order direct propagation, and second order Hebbian learning. *Proceedings of the 1987 IEEE International Conference on Neural Networks*, II, pp. 593–600. New York: IEEE Press.

Parker, J. L., and Dostrovsky, J. O., (1999). Cortical involvement in the induction, but not expression, of thalamic plasticity. *The Journal of Neuroscience*, 19, 8623–8629.

Parsons, O., and Carpenter, G. A. (2003). ARTMAP neural networks for information fusion and data mining: map production and target recognition methodologies. *Neural Networks*, 16, 1075–1089.

Pascual-Leone, A., and Walsh, V. (2001). Fast backprojections from the motion to the primary visual area necessary for visual awareness. *Science*, 292, 510–512.

Pashler. H. (1988). Familiarity and visual change detection. *Perception & Psychophysics*, 44, 369–378.

Pasupathy, A., and Miller, E. K. (2004). Different time courses of learning-related activity in the prefrontal cortex and striatum. *Nature*, 433, 873–876.

Paton, J. J., Belova, M. A., Morrison, S. E., and Salzman, C. D. (2006). The primate amygdala represents the positive and negative value of visual stimuli during learning. *Nature*, 439, 865–870.

Patterson, R., Holdsworth, J., Nimmo-Smith, I., and Rice, P. (1987). An efficient auditory filterbank based on the gammatone function. Annex B of the SVOS Final Report (Part A: The Auditory Filterbank). APU Report No. 2341.

Pavlov, I. P. (1927). *Conditional reflexes: An investigation of the physiological activity of the cerebral cortex*. Oxford, England: Oxford University Press.

Perner, J., Frith, U., Leslie, A. M., and Leekam, S. R. (1989). Exploration of the autistic child's theory of the mind: Knowledge, belief, and communication. *Child Development*, 60, 688–700.

Perrett, S. P., Ruiz, B. P., and Mauk, M. D. (1993). Cerebellar cortex lesions disrupt learning-dependent timing of conditioned eyelid responses. *The Journal of Neuroscience*, 13, 1708–1718.

Perry, E. K., Court, J. A., Johnson, M., Piggott, M. A., and Perry, R. H. (1992). Autoradiographic distribution of [³H] nicotine binding in human cortex: relative abundance in subicular complex. *Journal of Chemical Neuroanatomy*, 5, 399–405.

Perry, E. K., Lee, M. L. W., Martin-Ruiz, C. M., Court, J. A., Volsen, S. G., Merrit, J., Folly, E., Iversen, P. E., Bauman, M. L., Perry, R. H., and Wenk, G. L. (2001). Cholinergic activity in autism: abnormalities in the cerebral cortex and basal forebrain. *The American Journal of Psychiatry*, 158, 1058–1066.

Perry, L. C. (1927). Reminiscences of Claude Monet from 1889 to 1909. *The American Magazine of Art*, 18, 119–126.

Pessoa, L. (2008). On the relation between emotion and cognition. *Nature*, 9, 148–158.

Pessoa, L. (2009). How do emotion and motivation direct executive control? *Trends in Cognitive Sciences*, 13, 160–166.

Pessoa, L., and Adolphs, R. (2010). Emotion processing and the amygdala: from a "low road" to "many roads" of evaluating biological significance. *Nature Reviews Neuroscience*, 11, 773–782.

Peterhans, E., and von der Heydt, R. (1989). Mechanisms of contour perception in monkey visual cortex. II. Contours bridging gaps. *The Journal of Neuroscience*, 9, 1749–1763.

Peterson, G. E., and Barney, H. L. (1952). Control methods used in a study of the vowels. *Journal of the Acoustical Society of America*, 24, 175–184.

Petit, L., Orssaud, C., Tzourio, N., Crivello, F., Berthoz, A., and Mazoyer, B. (1996). Functional anatomy of a prelearned sequence of horizontal saccades in humans. *The Journal of Neuroscience*, 16, 3714–3726.

Petrides, M., Alivisatos, V., and Frey, S. (2002). Differential activation of the human orbital, mid-ventrolateral, and mid-dorsolateral prefrontal cortex during the processing of visual stimuli. *Proceedings of the National Academy of Sciences*, 99, 5649–5654.

Petrides, M., and Pandya, D. N. (2002). Comparative cytoarchitectonic analysis of the human and the macaque ventrolateral prefrontal cortex and corticocortical connection patterns in the monkey. *European Journal of Neuroscience*, 16, 291–310.

Peuskens, H., Sunaert, S., Dupont, P., Van Hecke, P., Orban, G. A. (2001). Human brain regions involved in heading estimation. *The Journal of Neuroscience*, 21, 2451–2461.

Phillips, D. P. (1993). Representation of acoustic events in the primary auditory cortex. *Journal of Experimental Psychology: Human Perception and Performance*, 19, 203–216.

Phillips, H. S., Hains, J. M., Laramee, G. R., Rosenthal, A., and Winslow, J. W. (1990). Widespread expression of BDNF but not NT3 by target areas of basal forebrain cholinergic neurons. *Science*, 250, 290–294.

Phillips, W. A. (1974). On the distinction between sensory storage and short-term visual memory. *Perception & Psychophysics*, 16, 283–290.

Piaget, J. (1945). *La Formation du Symbole Chez L'enfant*. Paris: Delachaux Niestle, S.A.

Piaget, J. (1951). *Play, Dreams and Imitation in Childhood*. C. Gattegno and C. F. M. Hodgson (Trans.). London: Routledge and Kegan Paul.

Piaget, J. (1952). *The Origins of Intelligence in Children*. New York: International Universities Press.

Picard, R. W. (1997) *Affective Computing*. Cambridge, MA: MIT Press.

Pickles, J. O. (1988). *An Introduction to the Physiology of Hearing, Second Edition*. New York: Academic Press.

Picton, W. T. (1992). The P300 wave of the human event-related potential. *Journal of Clinical Neurophysiology*, 456–479.

Pilly, P. K., and Grossberg, S. (2012). How do spatial learning and memory occur in the brain? Coordinated learning of entorhinal grid cells and hippocampal place cells. *Journal of Cognitive Neuroscience*, 24, 1031–1054.

Pilly, P. K., and Grossberg, S. (2013a). How reduction of theta rhythm by medium septum inactivation may disrupt periodic spatial responses of entorhinal grid cells by reduced cholinergic transmission. *Frontiers in Neural Circuits*, doi: 10.3389/fncir.2013.00173, http://www.frontiersin.org/Journal/10.3389/fncir.2013.00173/full?utm_source=newsletter&utm_medium=email&utm_campaign=Neuroscience-w46-2013.

Pilly, P. K., Grossberg, S. (2013b). Spiking neurons in a hierarchical self-organizing map model can learn to develop spatial and temporal properties of entorhinal grid cells and hippocampal place cells. *PLoS. One*, 8, e0060599. http://dx.plos.org/10.1371/journal.pone.0060599.

Pilly, P. K., and Grossberg, S. (2014). How does the modular organization of entorhinal grid cells develop? *Frontiers in Human Neuroscience*, doi:10.3389/fnhum.2014.0037, http://journal.frontiersin.org/Journal/10.3389/fnhum.2014.00337/full.

Pimplikar, S. W. (2009). Reassessing the amyloid cascade hypothesis of Alzheimer's disease. *The International Journal of Biochemistry and Cell Biology*, 41, 1261–1268.

Pinna, B. (1987). Un effetto di colorazione. In V. Majer, M. Maeran, and M. Santinello, *Il laboratorio e la città. XXI Congresso degli Psicologi Italiani*, 158.

Pinna, B., and Grossberg, S. (2005). The watercolor illusion and neon color spreading: A unified analysis of new cases and neural mechanisms. *Journal of the Optical Society of America A*, 22, 2207–2221.

Poggio, G. F. (1991). Physiological basis of stereoscopic vision. In *Vision and Visual Dysfunction. Binocular Vision*, pp. 224–238. Boston, MA: CRC Press.

Polat, U., Mizobe, K., Pettet, M. W., Kasamatsu, T., and Norcia, A. M. (1998). Collinear stimuli regulate visual responses depending on cell's contrast threshold. *Nature*, 391, 580–584.

Polat, U., and Sagi, D. (1993). Lateral interactions between spatial channels: Suppression and facilitation revealed by lateral masking experiments. *Visual Research*, 33, 993–999.

Polimeni, J. R., Balasubramanian, M., and Schwartz, E. L. (2006). Multi-area visuotopic map complexes in macaque striate and extra-striate cortex. *Vision Research*, 46, 3336–3359.

Pollen, D. A. (1999). On the neural correlates of visual perception. *Cerebral Cortex*, 9, 4–19.

Polonsky, A., Blake, R., Braun, J., and Heeger, D. J. (2000). Neuronal activity in human primary visual cortex correlates with perception during binocular rivalry. *Nature Neuroscience*, 3, 1153–1159.

Ponce, C. R., Lomber, S. G., and Born, R. T. (2008). Integrating motion and depth via parallel pathways. *Nature Neuroscience*, 11, 216–223.

Port, R. F., and Dalby, J. (1982). Consonant/vowel ratio as a cue for voicing in English. *Perception & Psychophysics*, 32, 315–322.

Posner, M. I. (1980). Orienting of attention. *Quarterly Journal of Experimental Psychology*, 32, 3–25.

Posner, M. I., and Keele, S. W. (1970). Retention of abstract ideas. *Journal of Experimental Psychology*, 83, 304–308.

Posner, M. I., Rafal, R. D., Choate, L. S., and Vaughan, J. (1985). Inhibition of return: Neural basis and function. *Cognitive Neuropsychology*, 2, 211–228.

Posner, M. I., Walker, J. A., Friedrich, R. J., and Rafal, R. D. (1984). Effects of parietal injury on covert orienting of attention. *The Journal of Neuroscience*, 4, 1863–1874.

Pouget, A., Dayan, P., and Zemel, R. S. (2003). Inference and computation with population codes. *Annual Review of Neuroscience*, 26, 381–410.

Prasad, V. S. S., and Gupta, S. D. (2008). Photometric clustering of regenerated plants of gladiolus by neural networks and its biological validation. *Computers and Electronics in Agriculture*, 60, 8–17.

Prescott, T. J., Gurney, K., and Redgrave, P. (2003). Basal ganglia. In M. A. Arbib (Ed.). *The Handbook of Brain Theory and Neural Networks* (2nd Edition). Cambridge, MA: MIT Press.

Pribe, C., Grossberg, S., and Cohen, M. A. (1997). Neural control of interlimb oscillations, II: Biped and quadruped gaits and bifurcations. *Biological Cybernetics*, 77, 141–152.

Price, J. L. (1999). Prefrontal cortical networks related to visceral function and mood. *Annals of the New York Academy of Sciences*, 877, 383–396.

Pribram, K. H. (1986). The hippocampal system and recombinant processing. In *The Hippocampus*, Volume 4. In R. L. Isaacson and K. H. Pribram (Eds.). New York: Plenum Press, pp. 329–370.

Purghé, F., and Coren, S. (1992). Amodal completion, depth stratification, and illusory figures: A test of Kanizsa's explanation. *Perception*, 21, 325–335.

Purves, D. (1988). *Body and brain: A trophic theory of neural connections*. Cambridge, MA: Harvard University Press.

Pylyshyn, Z. (1989). The role of location indexes in spatial perception: A sketch of the FINST spatial-index model. *Cognition*, 32, 65–97.

Qian, N., and Andersen, R. A. (1994). Transparent motion perception as detection of unbalanced motion signals. II. Physiology. *The Journal of Neuroscience*, 14, 7367–7380.

Qian, N., Andersen, R. A., and Adelson, E. H. (1994). Transparent motion perception as detection of unbalanced motion signals. III. Modeling. *The Journal of Neuroscience*, 14, 7381–7392.

Qiu, A., Adler, M., Crocetti, D., Miller, M. I., and Mostofsky, S. H. (2010). Basal ganglia shapes predict social, communication, and motor dysfunctions in boys with autism spectrum disorder. *Journal of the American Academy of Child Adolescent Psychiatry*, 49, 539–551.

Qiu, F. T., Sugihara, T., and von der Heydt, R. (2007). Figure-ground mechanisms provide structure for selective attention. *Nature Neuroscience*, 10, 1492–1499.

Qiu, F. T., and von der Heydt, R. (2005). Figure and ground in the visual cortex: V2 combines stereoscopic cues and Gestalt rules. *Neuron*, 47, 155–166.

Rabiei, Z., Rafieian-kopaei, M., Heidarian, E., Saghaei, E., and Modhtari, S. (2014). Effects of *Zizyphus jujube* extra on memory and learning impairment induced by bilateral electric lesions of the nucleus basalis of Meynert in rat. *Neurochemical Research*, 39, 353–360.

Raizada, R., and Grossberg, S. (2001). Context-sensitive bindings by the laminar circuits of V1 and V2: A unified model of perceptual grouping, attention, and orientation contrast. *Visual Cognition*, 8, 431–466.

Raizada, R., and Grossberg, S. (2003). Towards a theory of the laminar architecture of cerebral cortex: Computational clues from the visual system. *Cerebral Cortex*, 13, 100–113.

Ramachandran, V. S. (1985). Apparent motion of subjective surfaces. *Perception*, 14, 127–134.

Ramachandran, V. S., and Gregory, R. L. (1991). Perceptual filling-in of artificially induced scotomas in human vision. *Nature*, 350, 699–702.

Ramachandran, V. S., and Inada, V. (1985). Spatial phase and frequency in motion capture of random-dot patterns. *Spatial Vision*, 1, 57–67.

Ramachandran, V. S., and Nelson, J. I. (1976). Global grouping overrides point-to-point disparities. *Perception*, 5, 125–128.

Ramachandran, V. S., Rao, V. M., and Vidyasagar, T. R. (1973). Apparent motion with subjective contours. *Vision Research*, 13, 1399–1401.

Ranck, J. B., Jr. (1984). *Head-direction cells in the deep cell layers of dorsal presubiculum in freely moving rats*. Proceedings of the Annual Conference of the Society for Neuroscience, Anaheim, CA. 10, 599.

Rankin, A. (1987). Ross Bleckner. BOMB Magazine, 19, Spring.

Rao, R. P. N., and Ballard, D. H. (1999). Predictive coding in the visual cortex: a functional interpretation of some extra-classical receptive field effects. *Nature Neuroscience*, 2, 79–87.

Rappelsberger, P., Pockberger, H., and Petsche, H. (1982). The contribution of the cortical layers in the generation of the EEG: field potential and current source density analyses in the rabbit's visual cortex. *Electroencephalography and Clinical Neurophysiology*, 53, 254–269.

Ratliff, F., Hartline, H. K., and Miller, W. H. (1963). Spatial and temporal aspects of retinal inhibitory interaction. *Journal of the Optical Society of America*, 53, 110–120.

Ratliff, F., and Sirovich, L. (1978). Equivalence classes of visual stimuli. *Vision Research*, 18, 845–851.

Rattiner, L. M., Davis, M., and Ressler, K. J. (2005), Brain-derived neurotrophic factor in amygdala-dependent learning. *The Neuroscientist*, 11, 323–333.

Rauschecker, J. P. (1998). Cortical processing of complex sounds. *Current Opinion in Neurobiology*, 8, 516–521.

Rauschecker, J. P., and Scott, S. K. (2009). Maps and streams in the auditory cortex: nonhuman primates illuminate human speech processing. *Nature Neuroscience*, 12, 718–724.

Rauschecker, J. P., and Singer, W. (1979). Changes in the circuitry of the kitten visual cortex are gated by postsynaptic activity. *Nature*, 280, 58–60.

Rauschecker, J. P., and Tian, B. (2000). Mechanisms and streams for processing of "what" and "where" in auditory cortex. *Proceedings of the National Academy of Sciences*, 97, 11800–11806.

Raybourn, M. S., and Keller, E. L. (1977). Colliculoreticular organization in primate oculomotor system. *Journal of Neurophysiology*, 40, 861–878.

Rayleigh, L. (1907). On our perception of sound direction. *Philosophical Magazine*, 13, 2–4-232.

Recanzone, G. H., Wurtz, R. H., and Schwarz, U. (1997). Responses of MT and MST neurons to one and two moving objects in the receptive field. *Journal of Neurophysiology*, 78, 2904–2915.

Redies, C., Crook, J. M., and Creutzfeldt, O. D. (1986). Neuronal responses to borders with and without luminance gradients in cat visual cortex and dLGN. *Experimental Brian Research*, 61, 469–481.

Redies, C., and Spillmann, L. (1981). The neon color effect in the Ehrenstein illusion. *Perception*, 10, 667–681.

Redish, A. D., Elga, A. N., and Touretzky, D. S. (1996). A coupled attractor model of the rodent head direction system. *Network: Computation in Neural Systems*, 7, 671–685.

Reiner, A. (2016). Teaching men to be emotionally honest. *The New York Times*, April 4, 2016, https://www.nytimes.com/2016/04/10/education/edlife/teaching-men-to-be-emotionally-honest.html.

Remez, R. E. (2003). Establishing and maintaining perceptual coherence: Unimodal and multimodal evidence. *Journal of Phonetics*, 31, 293–304.

Remez, R. E., Pardo, J. S., Piorkowski, R. L., and Rubin, P. E. (2001). On the bistability of sine wave analogues of speech. *Psychological Science*, 12, 24–29.

Remez, R. E., Rubin, P. E., Berns, S. M., Pardo, J. S., and Lang, J. M. (1994). On the perceptual organization of speech. *Psychological Review*, 101, 129–156.

Remington, R. J. (1969). Analysis of sequential effects in choice reaction times. *Journal of Experimental Psychology*, 2, 250–257.

Remington, R., and Pierce, L. (1984). Moving attention: Evidence for time-invariant shifts of visual selective attention. *Perception & Psychophysics*, 35, 393–399.

Renner, K. E., and Tinsley, J. B. (1976). Self-punitive behavior. *Psychology of Learning and Motivation*, 10, 155–198.

Rensink, R. A., O'Regan, J. K., and Clark, J. J. (1997). To see or not to see: The need for attention to perceive changes in scenes. *Psychological Science*, 8, 368–373.

Repp, B. H. (1978). Perceptual integration and differentiation of spectral cues for intervocalic stop consonants. *Perception & Psychophysics*, 24, 471–485.

Repp, B. H. (1980). A range-frequency effect on perception of silence in speech. *Status Report on Speech Research SR-61*, pp. 151–165. New Haven, CT: Haskins Laboratories.

Repp, B. H., Liberman, A. M., Eccardt, T., and Pesetsky, D. (1978). Perceptual integration of acoustic cues for stop, fricative, and affricate manner. *Journal of Experimental Psychology: Human Perception and Performance*, 4, 621–637.

Reynierse, J. H., and Rizley, R. C. (1970). Relaxation and fear as determinants of maintained avoidance in rats. *Journal of Comparative and Physiological Psychology*, 72, 223–232.

Reynolds, G. S. (1968). *Primer of Operant Conditioning*. Glenview, IL: Scott, Foresman.

Reynolds, J., Chelazzi, L., and Desimone, R. (1999). Competitive mechanisms subserve attention in macaque areas V2 and V4. *The Journal of Neuroscience*, 19, 1736–1753.

Reynolds, J. H., and Desimone, R. (2003). Interacting roles of attention and visual salience in V4. *Neuron*, 37, 853–863.

Reynolds, J. H., and Heeger, D. J. (2009). The normalization model of attention. *Neuron*, 61, 168–185.

Reynolds, J. H., Pasternak. T., and Desimone, R. (2000). Attention increases sensitivity of V4 neurons. *Neuron*, 26, 703–714.

Rhode, W. S., and Smith, P. H. (1986a). Encoding timing and intensity in the ventral cochlear nucleus of the cat. *Journal of Neurophysiology*, 56, 261–287.

Rhode, W. S., and Smith, P. H. (1986b). Physiological studies on neurons in the dorsal cochlear nucleus of the cat. *Journal of Neurophysiology*, 56, 287–307.

Rich, A. N., and Mattingley, J. B. (2002). Anomalous perception in synaesthesia: A cognitive neuroscience perspective. *Nature Reviews Neuroscience*, 3, 43–52.

Richards, W. A., and Kaye, M. G. (1974). Local versus global stereopsis Two mechanisms. *Vision Research*, 14, 1345–1347.

Riggs, T. (1997). Instant Loveland, 1968. Retrieved from http://www.tate.org.uk/art/artworks/olitski-instant-loveland-t07244/text-summary. Accessed December 26, 2016.

Ringach, D. L., and Shapley, R. (1996). Spatial and temporal properties of illusory contours and amodal boundary completion. *Vision Research*, 36, 3037–3050.

Rizzolatti, G. (2005). The mirror neuron system and its function in humans. *Anatomy and Embryology*, 210, 419–421.

Rizzolatti, G., and Craighero, I. (2004). The mirror-neuron system. *Annual Review of Neuroscience*, 27, 169–192.

Rizzolatti, G., Fogassi, L., and Gallese, V. (2001). Neurophysiological mechanisms underlying the understanding and imitation of action. *Nature Review Neuroscience*, 2, 661–670.

Roberts, A. C. (2006). Primate orbitofrontal cortex and adaptive behavior. *Trends in Cognitive Sciences*, 10, 83–90.

Robertson, I. H., Manly, T., Beschin, N., Daini, R., Haeske-Dewick, H., Homberg, V., Jehkonen, M., Pizzamiglio, G., Shiel, A., and Weber, E. (1997). Auditory sustained attention is a marker of unilateral spatial neglect. *Neuropsychologia*, 35, 1527–1532.

Robichaux, J. W. (1997). *Hensche on Painting*. Dover, Mineola, NY.

Robinson, D. A. (1981). Models of the mechanics of eye movements. In B. L. Zuber (Ed.). *Models of Oculomotor Behavior and Control*. Boca Raton, FL: CRC Press.

Rockland, K. S., and Virga, A. (1989). Terminal arbors of individual "feedback" axons projecting from area V2 to V1 in the macaque monkey: a study using immunohistochemistry of anterogradely transported phaseolus vulgaris-leucoagglutinin. *Journal of Comparative Neurology*, 285, 54–72.

Rodman, H. R., and Albright, T. D. (1987). Coding of visual stimulus velocity in area MT of the macaque. *Vision Research*, 27, 2035–2048.

Roelfsema, P. R., Lamme, V. A. F., and Spekreijse, H. (1998). Object-based attention in the primary visual cortex of the macaque monkey. *Nature*, 395, 376–381.

Roesch, M. R., and Olson, C. R. (2004). Neuronal activity related to reward value and motivation in primate frontal cortex. *Science*, 304, 307–310.

Roggeveen, A., Pilz, K., Bennett, P., and Sekuler, A. (2009). Individual differences in object based attention. *Journal of Vision*, 9, 143.

Roitman, J. D., and Shadlen, M. N. (2002). Response of neurons in the lateral intraparietal area during a combined visual discrimination reaction time task. *The Journal of Neuroscience*, 22, 9475–9489

Rolls, E. T. (1999). *The Brain and Emotion*. Oxford: Oxford University Press.

Rolls, E. T. (2000). The orbitofrontal cortex and reward. *Cerebral Cortex*, 10, 284–294.

Rolls, E. T., Critchley, H. D., Browning, A. S., Hernadi, I., and Lenard, L. (1999). Responses to the sensory properties of fat of neurons in the primate orbitofrontal cortex. *Journal of Neuroscience*, 19, 1532–1540.

Rolls, E. T., Hornak, J., Wade, D., and McGrath, J. (1994). Emotion-related learning in patients with social and emotional changes associated with frontal lobe damage. *Journal of Neurology, Neurosurgery, and Psychiatry*, 57, 1518–1524.

Rolls, E. T., Stringer, S. M., and Elliot, T. (2006). Entorhinal cortex grid cells can map to hippocampal place cells by competitive learning. *Network*, 17, 447–465.

Roozendaal, B., McReynolds, J. R., Van der Zee, E. A., Lee, S., McGaugh, J. L., and McIntyre, C. K. (2009). Glucocorticoid effects on memory consolidation depend on functional interactions between the medial prefrontal cortex and basolateral amygdala. *The Journal of Neuroscience*, 29, 14299–14308.

Rosenblatt, F. (1958). The perceptron: A probabilistic model for information storage and organization in the brain. *Psychological Review*, 65, 386–408.

Rosenblatt, F. (1962). *Principles of Neurodynamics: Perceptrons and the Theory of Brain Mechanisms*. Washington DC: Spartan Books.

Ross, W., Grossberg, S. and Mingolla, E. (2000). Visual cortical mechanisms of perceptual grouping: Interacting layers, networks, columns, and maps. *Neural Networks*, 13, 571–588.

Rossato, J. I., Bevilaqua, L. R. M., Izquierdo, I, Medina, J. H. and Cammarota, M. (2009). Dopamine controls persistence of long-term memory storage. *Science*, 325, 1017–1020.

Royden, C. S., Banks, M. S., and Crowell, J. A. (1992). The perception of heading during eye movements. *Nature*, 360, 583–585.

Royden, C. S., Crowell, J. A., and Banks, M. S. (1994). Estimating heading during eye movements. *Vision Research*, 34, 3197–3214.

Royden, C. S., and Vaina, L. M. (2004). Is precise discrimination of low level motion needed for heading discrimination. *Neuroreport*, 15, 1013–1017.

Royer, S., and Pare, D. (2003). Conservation of total synaptic weight through balanced synaptic depression and potentiation. *Nature*, 422, 518–522.

Rubin, N. (2015). Banksy's graffiti art reveals insights about perceptual surface completion. *Art & Perception*, 3, 1–17.

Rudebeck, P. H., Saunders, R. C., Prescott, A. T., Chau, L. S., and Murray, E. A. (2013). Prefrontal mechanisms of behavioral flexibility, emotion regulation, and value updating. *Nature Neuroscience*, 16, 1140–1145.

Rudebeck, P. H., Saunders, R. C., Lundgren, D. A., and Murray, E. A. (2017). Specialized representations of value in the orbital and ventrolateral prefrontal cortex: Desirability versus availability of outcomes. *Neuron*, 95, 1208–1220.

Rueckert, L., and Grafman, J. (1988). Sustained attention deficits in patients with lesions of parietal cortex. *Neuropsychologia*, 36, 653–660.

Rumelhart, D. E., Hinton, G. E., and Williams, R. J. (1986). Learning representations by back-propagating errors. *Nature*, 323, 533–536.

Rushton, S. K., Harris, J. M., Lloyd, M. R., and Wann, J. P. (1998). Guidance of locomotion on foot uses perceived target location rather than optic flow. *Current Biology*, 8, 1191–1194.

Rust, G. (1988). *The Painted House*. New York City, NY: Alfred A. Knopf.

Ruthazer, E. S., and Stryker, M. P. (1996). The role of activity in the development of long-range horizontal connections in area 17 of the ferret. *The Journal of Neuroscience*, 15, 7253–7269.

Saar, D., Grossman, Y., and Barkai, E. (2001). Long-lasting cholinergic modulation underlies rule learning in rats. *The Journal of Neuroscience*, 21, 1385–1392.

Sachs, M. B., and Young, E. D. (1979). Encoding of steady state vowels in the auditory nerve: Representations in terms of discharge rate. *Journal of the Acoustical Society of America*, 66, 470–479.

Saito, H., Yukie, M., Tanaka, K., Hikosaka, K., Fukada, Y., and Iwai, E. (1986). Integration of direction signals of image motion in the superior temporal sulcus of the macaque monkey. *The Journal of Neuroscience*, 6, 145–157.

Sammler, D., Baird, A., Valabregue, R., Clement, S., Dupont, S., Belin, P., and Samson, S. (2010). Processing of unfamiliar songs: A functional magnetic resonance adaptation study. *The Journal of Neuroscience*, 30, 3572–3578.

Sams, M., Paavilainen, P., Alho, K., and Näätänen, R. (1985). Auditory frequency discrimination and event-related potentials. *Electroencephalography and Clinical Neurophysiology/Evoked Potentials Section*, 62, 437–448.

Samuel, A. G. (1981a). The role of bottom-up confirmation in the phonemic restoration illusion. *Journal of Experimental Psychology: Human Perception and Performance*, 7, 1124–1131.

Samuel, A. G. (1981b). Phonemic restoration: Insights from a new methodology. *Journal of Experimental Psychology: General*, 110, 474–494.

Samuel, A. G., van Santen, J. P. H, and Johnston, J. C. (1982). Length effects in word perception: We is better than I but worse than you or them. *Journal of Experimental Psychology*, 9, 321–322.

Samuel, A. G., van Santen, J. P. H, and Johnston, J. C. (1983). Reply to Mattei: We really is worse than you or them, and so are ma and pa. *Journal of Experimental Psychology*, 8, 91–105.

Sanchez-Vives, M. V., and Mattia, M. (2014). Slow wave activity as the default mode of the cerebral cortex. *Archives Italiennes de Biologie*, 152, 147–155.

Sanchez-Vives, M. V., and McCormick, D. A. (2000). Cellular and network mechanisms of rhythmic recurrent activity in neocortex. *Nature Neuroscience*, 3, 1027–1034.

Saper, D. B., Lu, J., Chou, T. C., and Gooley, J. (2005). The hypothalamic integrator for circadian rhythms. *Trends in Neurosciences*, 28, 152–157.

Sargolini, F., Fyhn, M., Hafting, T., McNaughton, B. L., Witter, M. P., Moser, M-B., and Moser, E. I. (2006). Conjunctive representation of position, direction, and velocity in entorhinal cortex. *Science*, 312, 758–762.

Sarter, M., Givens, B., and Bruno, J. P. (2001). The cognitive neuroscience of sustained attention: Where top-down meets bottom-up. *Brain Research Reviews*, 35, 146–160.

Savelli, F., and Knierim, J. J. (2010). Hebbian analysis of the transformation of medial entorhinal grid-cell inputs to hippocampal place fields. *Journal of Neurophysiology*, 103, 3167–3183.

Saygin, A. P., and Sereno, M. I. (2008). Retinotopy and attention in human occipital, temporal, parietal, and frontal cortex. *Cerebral Cortex*, 18, 2158–2168.

Schafer, M., and Schiller, D. (2018). Navigating social space. *Neuron*, 100, 476–489.

Schafer, M., and Schiller, D. (2020). The brain's social road maps. *Scientific American*, February, pp. 31–35.

Schiller, D., Monfils, M. H., Raio, C. M., Johnson, D. C., LeDoux, H. E., and Phelps, E. A. (2010). Preventing the return of fear in humans using reconsolidation update mechanisms. *Nature*, 463, 49–53.

Schiller, P. H., and Lee, K. (1991). The role of the primate extrastriate area V4 in vision. *Science*, 251, 1251–1253.

Schiller, P. H., and Stryker, M. (1972). Single-unit recording and stimulation in superior colliculus of the alert rhesus monkey. *Journal of Neurophysiology*, 35, 915–924.

Schinder, A. F., Berninger, B., and Poo, M-m. (2000). Postsynaptic specificity of neurotrophin-induced presynaptic potentiation. *Neuron*, 25, 151–163.

Schlag, J., and Schlag-Rey, M. (1987). Evidence for a supplementary eye field. *Journal of Neurophysiology*, 57, 179–200.

Schmajuk, N. A., Lam, P., and Christiansen, B. A. (1994). Hippocampectomy disrupts latent inhibition of the rat eyeblink conditioning. *Physiology and Behavior*, 55, 597–601.

Schmaltz, L. W., and Theios, J. (1972). Acquisition and extinction of a classically conditioned response in hippocampectomized rabbits. *Journal of Comparative Physiological Psychology*, 79, 328–333.

Schmidt-Heiber, C., and Hausser, M. (2013). Cellular mechanisms of spatial navigation in the medial entorhinal cortex. *Nature Neuroscience*, 16, 325–331.

Schoenbaum, G., Chiba, A. A., and Gallagher, M. (1998). Orbirofrontal cortex and basolateral amygdala encode expected outcomes during learning. *Nature Neuroscience*, 1, 155–159.

Schoenbaum, G., Setlow, B., Saddoris, M. P., and Gallagher, M. (2003). Encoding predicted outcome and acquired value in orbitofrontal cortex during cue sampling depends upon input from basolateral amygdala. *Neuron*, 39, 855–867.

Schor, C. M., and Tyler, C. W (1981). Spatio-temporal properties of Panum's fusional area. *Vision Research*, 21, 683–692.

Schor, C. M., and Wood, I. (1983). Disparity range for local stereopsis as a function of luminance spatial frequency. *Vision Research*, 23, 1649–1654.

Schor, C. M., Wood, I., and Ogawa, J. (1984). Binocular sensory fusion is limited by spatial resolution. *Vision Research*, 24, 651–665.

Schulte-Rüther, M., Markowitsch, H. J., Fink, G. R., and Piefke, M. (2007). Mirror neuron and theory of mind mechanisms involved in face-to-face interactions: A functional magnetic resonance imaging approach to empathy. *Journal of Cognitive Neuroscience*, 19, 1354–1372.

Schultz, W. (1998). Predictive reward signal of dopamine neurons. *Journal of Neurophysiology*, 8, 1–27.

Schultz, W., Dayan, P., and Montague, P. (1997). A neural substrate of prediction and reward. *Science*, 275, 1593–1598.

Schultz, W., Apicella, P., Scarnati, E., and Ljungberg, T. (1992). Neuronal activity in monkey ventral striatum related to the expectation of reward. *Journal of Neuroscience*, 12, 4595–4610.

Schultz, W., Apicella, P., and Ljungberg, T. (1993). Responses of monkey dopamine neurons to reward and conditioned stimuli during successive steps of learning a delayed response task. *Journal of Neuroscience*, 13, 900–913.

Schultz, W., Apicella, P., Ljungberg, T., Romo, R., and Scmati, E. (1993). Chapter 15: Reward-related activity in the monkey striatum and substantia nigra. *Progress in Brain Research*, 99, 227–235.

Schultz, W., Romo, R., Ljungberg, T., Mirenowicz, J., Hollerman, J., and Dickinson, A. (1995). Reward related signals carried by dopamine neurons. In *Models of Information Processing in the Basal Ganglia*. J. Houk, J. Davis, and D. Beiser (Eds.), pp. 11–27. Cambridge: MIT Press.

Schulz, K. (2010). *Being Wrong: Adventures in the Margin of Error*. Portobello Books.

Schumacher, E. J., Lauber, E., Awh, E., Jonides, J., Smith, E. E., and Koeppe, R. A. (1996). PET evidence for an amodal verbal working memory system. *Neuroimage*, 3, 79–88.

Schuman, E. M. (1999). Neurotrophin regulation of synaptic transmission. *Current Opinion in Neurobiology*, 9, 105–109.

Schvaneveldt, R. W., and McDonald, J. E. (1981). Semantic context and the encoding of words: Evidence for two modes of stimulus analysis. *Journal of Experimental Psychology: Human Perception and Performance*, 7, 673–687.

Schwab, E. C., Sawusch, J. R., and Nusbaum, H. C. (1981). The role of second formant transitions in the stop-semivowel distinction. *Perception & Psychophysics*, 21, 121–128.

Schwartz, B. J., and Sperling, G. (1983). Luminance controls the perceived 3D structure of dynamic 2D displays. *Bulletin of the Psychonomic Society*, 21, 456–458.

Schwartz, E. L. (1984). Spatial mapping and spatial vision in primate striate and mferotemporai cortex. In *Sensory Experience, Adaptation and Perception*. L. Spillmann and B. R. Woolen (Eds.), pp. 73–104. Hillsdale, NJ: Erlbaum.

Schyns, P. G., and Oliva, A. (1994). From blobs to boundary edges: Evidence for time-and-spatial-scale-dependent scene recognition. *Psychological Science*, 5, 195–200.

Scoville, W. B., and Milner, B. (1957). Loss of recent memory after bilateral hippocampal lesions. *Journal of Neurology, Neurosurgery, and Psychiatry*, 20, 11–21.

Searle, J. R. (1998). How to study consciousness scientifically. *Philosophical Transactions of the Royal Society of London, Biological Sciences*, 353, 1935–1942.

Sears, L. L., Finn, P. R., and Steinmetz, J. E. (1994). Abnormal classical eye-blink conditioning in autism. *Journal of Autism and Developmental Disorders*, 24, 737–751.

Sears, L. L., and Steinmetz, J. E. (1990). Acquisition of classically conditioned-related activity in the hippocampus is affected by lesions of the cerebellar interpositus nucleus. *Behavioral Neuroscience*, 104, 681–92.

Seger, C. A., and Miller, E. K. (2010). Category learning in the brain. *Annual Review of Neuroscience*, 33, 203–219.

Sekuler, R., and Ball, K. (1977). Mental set alters visibility of moving targets. *Science*, 198, 60–62.

Seligman, M. E. P., and Csikszentmihalyi, M. (2000). Positive psychology: An introduction. *American Psychologist*, 55, 5–14.

Seligman, M. E. P., and Maier, S. F. (1967). Failure to escape traumatic shock. *Journal of Experimental Psychology*, 74, 1–9.

Shadlen, M. N., and Newsome, W. T. (2001). Neural basis of a perceptual decision in the parietal cortex (area LIP) of the rhesus monkey. *Journal of Neurophysiology*, 86, 1916–1936.

Shaikh, A. G., Xu-Wilson, M., Grill, S., and Zee, D. S. (2011). 'Staircase' square-wave jerks in early Parkinson's disease. *British Journal of Ophthalmology*, 95, 705–709.

Shallice, T. (1988). *From Neuropsychology to Mental Structure*. Cambridge, UK: Cambridge University Press.

Shannon, C. E. (1948). A mathematical theory of communication. *Bell System Technical Journal*, 27, 379–423.

Sherman, S. M., and Guillery, R. W. (2003). The role of thalamus in the flow of information to cortex. *Philosophical Transactions of the Royal Society of London. B: Biological Sciences*, 357, 1695–1708.

Shieh, M.-D., Yan, W., and Chen, C.-H. (2008). Soliciting customer requirements for product redesign based on picture sorts and ART2 neural network. *Expert Systems with Applications*, 34, 194–204.

Shimizu, N., Oomura, Y., and Sakata, T. (1984). Modulation of feeding by endogenous sugar acids acting as hunger or satiety factors. *American Journal of Physiology: Regulatory, Integrative, and Comparative Physiology*, 246, 542–550.

Shimojo, S., Silverman, G. H., and Nakayama, K. (1989). Occlusion and the solution to the aperture problem for motion. *Vision Research*, 29, 619–626.

Shipley, T. F., and Kellman, P. J. (1992). Strength of visual interpolation. *Perception & Psychophysics*, 52, 97–106.

Siapas, A. G., Lubenov E. V., and Wilson, M. A. (2005). Prefrontal phase locking to hippocampal theta oscillations. *Neuron*, 46, 141–151.

Siapas, A. G., and Wilson, M. A. (1998). Coordinated interactions between hippocampal ripples and cortical spindles during slow-wave sleep. *Neuron*, 21, 1123–1128.

Sigala, N., and Logothetis, N. K. (2002). Visual categorization shapes feature selectivity in the primate temporal cortex. *Nature*, 415, 318–320.

Sikström, S., and Söderlund, G. (2007). Stimulus-dependent dopamine release in attention deficit hyperactivity disorder. *Psychological Review*, 114, 1047–1075.

Sillito, A. M., Jones, H. E., Gerstein, G. L. and West, D. C. (1994). Feature-linked synchronization of thalamic relay cell firing induced by feedback from the visual cortex. *Nature*, 369, 479–482.

Silva, L. S., Amitai, Y., and Connors, B. W. (1991). Intrinsic oscillations of neocortex generated by layer 5 pyramidal neurons. *Science*, 251, 432–435.

Silver, M. A., and Kastner, S. (2009). Topographic maps in human frontal and parietal cortex. *Trends in Cognitive Sciences*, 13, 488–495.

Silver, M. R., Grossberg, S., Bullock, D., Histed, M. H., and Miller, E. K. (2011). A neural model of sequential movement planning and control of eye movements: Item-order-rank working memory and saccade selection by the supplementary eye fields. *Neural Networks*, 26, 29–58.

Simons, D. J., and Chabris, C. F. (1999). Gorillas in our midst: Sustained inattentional blindness for dynamic events. *Perception*, 28, 1059–1074.

Simons, D. J., and Levin, D. T. (1998). Failure to detect changes to people during a real-world interaction. *Psychological Bulletin & Review*, 5, 644–659.

Simons, D. J., and Rensink, R. A. (2005). Change blindness: Past, present, and future. *Trends in Cognitive Sciences*, 9, 16–20.

Singer, W. (1983). Neuronal activity as a shaping factor in the self-organization of neuron assemblies. *Synergetics of the Brain*, Volume 23 in *Springer Series in Synergetics*, pp. 89–101.

Singer, W. (1998). Consciousness and the structure of neuronal representations. *Philosophical Transactions of the Royal Society B*, 353, 1829–1840.

Singer, W. (1999). Time as coding space. *Current Opinion in Neurobiology*, 9,189–194.

Sirota, A., Csicsvari, J., Buhl, D, and Buzsáki, G. (2003). Communication between neocortex and hippocampus during sleep in rodents. *Proceedings of the National Academy of Sciences USA*, 100, 2065–2069.

Skaggs, W. E., Knierim, J., Kudrimoti, H. S., and McNaughton, B. L. (1995). A model of the neural basis of the rat's sense of direction. *Advances in Neural Information Processing Systems*, 7, 173–180.

Skaggs, W. E., McNaughton, B. L., and Wilson, M. A., and Barnes, C. A. (1996). Theta phase precession in hippocampal neuronal populations and the compression of temporal sequences, *Hippocampus*, 6. 149–172.

Skinner, B. F. (1938). *The Behavior of Organisms: An experimental analysis.* New York: Appleton-Century-Crofts.

Sleve, L. R., and Okada, B. M. (2015). Processing structure in language and music: a case for shared reliance on cognitive control. *Psychological Bulletin and Review*, 22, 637–652.

Smale, S. (1976). On the differential equations of species in competition. *Journal of Mathematical Biology*, 3, 5–7.

Smallman, H. S., and McKee, S. P. (1995). A contrast ratio constraint on stereo matching. *Proceedings of the Royal Society of London B*, 260, 265–271.

Smith, A. (1776). *The Wealth of Nations.* London: W. Strahan and T. Cadell.

Smith, C., Carey, S., and Wiser, M. (1985). On differentiation: A case study of the development of the concept of size, weight, and density. *Cognition*, 21, 177–237.

Smith, L. B., and Kemler, D. G. (1978). Levels of experienced dimensionality in children and adults. *Cognitive Psychology*, 10, 502–532.

Smith, J. D., and Minda, J. P. (1998). Prototypes in the mist: the early epochs of category learning. *Journal of Experimental Psychology: Learning, Memory, and Cognition*, 24, 1411–1430.

Smith, J. D., and Minda, J. P. (2000). Thirty categorization results in search of a model. *Journal of Experimental Psychology: Learning, Memory, and Cognition*, 26, 3–27.

Smith, J. D., Murray, M. J., and Minda, J. P. (1997). Straight talk about linear separability. *Journal of Experimental Psychology: Learning, Memory, and Cognition*, 23, 659–680.

Smith, L. B., Yu, C., Yoshida, H., and Fausey, C. M. (2015). Contributions of head-mounted cameras to studying the visual environments of infants and young children. *Journal of Cognition and Development*, 16, 407–419.

Smith, M. C. (1968). CS-US interval and US intensity in classical conditioning of the rabbit's nictitating membrane response. *Journal of Comparative and Physiological Psychology*, 3, 679–687.

Smythe, J. W., Colom, L. V., and Bland, B. H. (1992). The extrinsic modulation of hippocampal theta depends on the coactivation of cholinergic and GABA-ergic medial septal inputs. *Neuroscience & Biobehavioral Reviews*, 16, 289–308.

Snowden, R. J., Treue, S., Erickson R. G., and Andersen R. A. (1991). The response of area MT and V1 neurons to transparent motion. *The Journal of Neuroscience*, 11, 2768–2785.

Snyder, L. H., Batista, A. P., and Andersen, R. A. (1997). Coding of intention in the posterior parietal cortex. *Nature*, 386, 167–170.

Snyder, L. H., Batista, A. P., and Andersen, R. A. (1998). Change in motor plan, without a change in the spatial locus of attention, modulates activity in posterior parietal cortex. *Journal of Neurophysiology*, 79, 2814–2819.

Sokolov, E. N. (1968). *Mechanisms of Memory.* Moscow: Moscow University Press.

Solomon, P. R., Groccia-Ellison, M., Levine, E., Blanchard, S., and Pendlebury, W. W. (1990). Do temporal relationships in conditioning change across the life span? Perspectives from eyeblink conditioning in humans and rabbits. *Annals of the New York Academy of Science*, 608, 212–238.

Solomon, R. L., Kamin, L. J., and Wynne, L. C. (1953). Traumatic avoidance learning: The outcome of several extinction procedures with dogs. *Journal of Abnormal Social Psychology*, 48, 291–302.

Solomon, P. R., and Moore, J. W. (1975). Latent inhibition and stimulus generalization of the classically conditioned membrane response in rabbits (*Oryctolagus cuniculus*) following dorsal hippocampal ablation. *Journal of Comparative Physiological Psychology*, 89, 1192–1203.

Solstad, T., Boccara, C. N., Kropff, E., Moser, M.-B., and Moser, E. I. (2008). Representation of geometric borders in the entorhinal cortex, *Science*, 322, 1865–1868.

Somers, D. C., Dale, A. M., Seiffert, A. E., & Tootell, R. B. (1999). Functional MRI reveals spatially specific attentional modulation in human primary visual cortex. *Proceedings of the National Academy of Sciences USA*, 96, 1663–1668.

Sommer, M. A., and Wurtz, R. H. (2006). Influence of the thalamus on spatial vision processing in frontal cortex. *Nature*, 444, 374–377.

Song, P., and Wang, X. J. (2005). Angular path integration by moving "hill of activity": A spiking neuron model without recurrent excitation of the head-direction system. *The Journal of Neuroscience*, 25, 1002–1014.

Soriano, M., Spillman, L., and Bach, M. (1996). The abutting grating illusion. *Vision Research*, 36, 109–116.

Sosina, V. D. (1992). The EEG analysis of the interrelationships of structures of the thalamofrontal system during the recovery of conditioned reflex behavior of amygdalectomized rats. Institute of Higher Nervous Activity and Neurophysiology, Russian Academy of Sciences, Moscow. Translated by I. P. Pavlova from *Zhurnal Vysshei Nervnoi Deyatel'nosti imeni*, 42, 672–678. Plenum Publishing Corporation, 0097-0549/93/2305-0398, pp. 398–403.

Sperry, R. W. (1950). Neural basis of the spontaneous optokinetic response produced by visual inversion. *Journal of Comparative and Physiological Psychology*, 43, 482–489.

Sperry, R. W. (1964). The great cerebral commissure. *Scientific American*, 210, 42–53.

Spiegler, B. J., and Mishkin, M. (1981). Evidence for the sequential participation of inferior temporal cortex and amygdala in the acquisition of stimulus-reward associations. *Behavioral Brain Research*, 3, 303–317.

Spigel, I. M. (1968). *Problems in the Study of Visually Perceived Movement: An Introduction.* New York: Holt, Rinehart & Winston.

Spitzer, H., Desimone, R., and Moran, J. (1988). Increased attention enhances both behavioral and neuronal performance. *Science*, 240, 338–340.

Squire, L. R., and Alverez, P. (1995). Retrograde amnesia and memory consolidation: a neurobiological perspective. *Current Opinion in Neurobiology*, 5, 178–183.

Squire, L. R., and Butters, N. (Eds.) (1984). *Neuropsychology of Memory.* New York: Guilford Press.

Squire, L. R., and Cohen, N. J. (1984). Human memory and amnesia. In *Neurobiology of Learning and Memory.* G. Lynch, J. McGaugh, and N.M. Weinberger (Eds.). New York: Guilford Press, pp. 3–64.

Squires, K. C., Wickens, C., Squires, N. K., and Donchin, E. (1976). The effect of stimulus sequence on the waveform of the cortical event-related potential. *Science*, 193, 1142–1146.

Squires, N. K., Donchin, E., Squires, K. C., and Grossberg, S. (1977). Bisensory stimulation: Inferring decision-related processes from the P300 component. *Journal of Experimental Psychology*, 3, 299–315.

Squires, N. K., Squires, K. C., and Hillyard, S. A. (1975). Two varieties of long-latency positive waves evoked by unpredictable auditory stimuli in man. *Electroencephalography and Clinical Neurophysiology*, 38, 387–401.

Squires, P. C. (1931). The influence of hue on apparent visual movement. *American Journal of Psychology*, 43, 49–64.

Srihasam, K., Bullock, D., and Grossberg, S. (2009). Target selection by frontal cortex during coordinated saccadic and smooth pursuit eye movements. *Journal of Cognitive Neuroscience*, 21, 1611–1627.

Staddon, J. E. R. (1983). *Adaptive Learning and Behavior.* Cambridge, UK: Cambridge University Press.

Staubli, U., and Lynch, G. (1987). Stable hippocampal long-term potentiation elicited by theta pattern stimulation. *Brain Research*, 435, 227–234.

Steiger, H. (1980). Some informal observations concerning the perceptual organization of patterns containing frequency glides. Technical report, McGill University, Montreal.

Steiger, H., and Bregman, A. S. (1981). Capturing frequency components of glided tones: frequency separation, orientation, and alignment. *Perception and Psychophysics*, 30, 425–435.

Stein, P. S. (1971). Intersegmental coordination of swimmeret motoneuron activity in crayfish. *Journal of Neurophysiology*, 34, 310–318.

Steinbuch, J. G. (1811). *Beytrag zur Physiologie der Sinne.* Nürnberg: Schrag.

Steinman, B. A., Steinman, S. B., and Lehmkuhle, S. (1995). Visual attention mechanisms show a center-surround organization. *Vision Research*, 35, 1859–1869.

Stelmach, L. B., and Herdman, C. M. (1991). Directed attention and perception of temporal order. *Journal of Experimental Psychology: Human Perception and Performance*, 17, 549–550.

Stelmach, L. B., Herdman, C. M., and McNeil, R. (1994). Attentional modulation of visual processes in motion perception. *Journal of Experimental Psychology*, 20, 108–121.

Stensola, H., Stensola, T., Solstad, T., Frøland, K., Moser, M.-B., and Moser, E. I. (2012). The entorhinal grid map is discretized. *Nature*, 492, 72–78.

Stephan, F. K., and Nunez, A. A. (1977). Elimination of circadian rhythms in drinking, activity, sleep, and temperature by isolation of the suprachiasmatic nuclei. *Behavioral Biology*, 20, 1–16.

Steriade, M. (1999). Coherent oscillations and short-term plasticity in corticothalamic networks. *Trends in Neurosciences*, 22, 337–345.

Steriade, M. (2004). Acetylcholine systems and rhythmic activities during the waking-sleep cycle. *Progress in Brain Research*, 145, 179–196.

Steriade, M. (2006). Grouping of brain rhythms in corticothalamic systems. *Neuroscience*, 137, 1087–1106.

Steriade, M., Contreras, D., Dossi, R. C., and Nunez, A. (1993). The slow (<1Hz) oscillation in reticular thalamic and thalamo-cortical neurons: scenario of sleep rhythm generation in interacting thalamic and neocortical networks. *The Journal of Neuroscience*, 13, 3284–3299.

Steriade, M., Nuñez, A., and Amzica, F. (1993a). A novel slow (<1 Hz) oscillation of neocortical neurons *in vivo*: depolarizing and hyperpolarizing components. *The Journal of Neuroscience*, 13, 3252–3265.

Steriade, M., Nuñez, A., and Amzica, F. (1993b). Intracellular analysis of relations between the slow (<1 Hz) neocortical oscillation and other sleep rhythms of the electroencephalogram. *The Journal of Neuroscience*, 13, 3266–3283.

Steriade, M., and Timofeev, I. (2003). Neuronal plasticity in thalamocortical networks during sleep and waking oscillations. *Neuron*, 37, 563–576.

Stigler, R. (1910). Chronophotische studien über den umgebungskontrast. *Pflüger's Archiv für die Gesamte Physiologie des Menschen und der Tiere (European Journal of Physiology)*, 134, 365–435.

Stocker, A. A., and Simoncelli, E. P. (2006). Noise characteristics and prior expectations in human visual speed perception. *Nature Neuroscience*, 9, 578–585.

Stollenwerk, L., and Bode, M. (2003). Lateral neural model of binocular rivalry. *Neural Computation*, 15, 2863–2882.

Stone, L. S., and Perrone, J. A. (1994). A role for MST neurons in heading estimation. In *RECON no. 20010116589. Society for Neuroscience, Miami Beach, FL, United States, 13–18 November.*

Stone, L. S., Watson, A. B., and Mulligan, J. B. (1990). Effect of contrast on the perceived direction of a moving plaid. *Vision Research*, 30, 1049–1067,

Stratford, K. J., Tarczy-Hornoch, K., Martin, K. A. C., Bannister, N. J., and Jack, J. J. B. (1996). Excitatory synaptic inputs to spiny stellate cells in cat visual cortex. *Nature*, 382, 258–261.

Sudhakara Pandian, R., and Mahapatra, S. S. (2009). Manufacturing cell formation with production data using neural networks. *Computers & Industrial Engineering*, 56, 1340–1347.

Sundberg, J. (1977). The acoustics of the singing voice. *Scientific American*, 236, 82–91.

Sutter, A., Beck, J., and Graham, N. (1989). Contrast and spatial variables in texture segregation: Testing a simple spatial-frequency channels model. *Perception & Psychophysics*, 46, 312–332.

Sutton, S., Braren, M., Zubin, J., and John, E. R. (1965). Evoked-potential correlates of stimulus uncertainty. *Science*, 150, 1187–1188.

Suzuki, M., and Gottlieb, J. (2013). Distinct neural mechanisms of distractor suppression in the frontal and parietal lobe. *Nature Neuroscience*, 16, 98–104.

Swanson, L. W., and Cowan, W. M. (1975). Hippocampo-hypothalamic connections: origin in subicular cortex, not ammon's horn. *Science*, 189, 303–304.

Swisher, J. D., Halko, M. A., Merabet, L. B., McMains, S. A., and Somers, D. C. (2007). Visual topography of human intraparietal sulcus. *Journal of Neurophysiology*, 27, 5326–5337.

Szelag, E., Kowalska, J., Galkowski, T., and Poppel, E. (2004). Temporal processing deficits in high-functioning children with autism. *British Journal of Psychiatry.* 95, 269–282.

Takahashi, H., Murase, Y., Kobayashi, T., and Honda, H. (2007). New cancer diagnosis modeling using boosting and projective adaptive resonance theory with improved reliable index. *Biochemical Engineering Journal*, 33, 100–109.

Takashima, A., Nieuwenhuis, I. L. C., Jensen, O., Talamini, L. M., Rijpkema, M., and Guillén Fernández, G. (2009). Shift from hippocampal to neocortical centered retrieval network with consolidation. *The Journal of Neuroscience*, 29, 10087–10093.

Takechi, H., Eilers, J., and Konnerth, A. (1998). A new class of synaptic response involving calcium release in dendritic spines. *Nature*, 396, 757–760.

Takehara, K., Kawahara, S., and Krino, Y. (2003). Time-dependent reorganization of the brain components underlying memory retention in trace eyeblink conditioning. *The Journal of Neuroscience*, 23, 9897–9905.

Takeichi, H., Shimojo, S., and Watanabe, T. (1992). Neon flank and illusory contour: Interaction between the two processes leads to color filling-in. *Perception*, 21, 313–324.

Tamietto, M., and De Gelder, B. (2010). Neural bases of the non-conscious perception of emotional signals. *Nature Reviews Neuroscience*, 11, 697–709.

Tan, A.-H. (1997). Cascade ARTMAP: integrating neural computation and symbolic knowledge processing. *IEEE Transactions on Neural Networks*, 8, 237–250.

Tan, T. Z., Quek, C., Ng, G. S., and Razvi, K. (2008). Ovarian cancer diagnosis with complementary learning fuzzy neural network. *Artificial Intelligence in Medicine*, 43, 207–222.

Tan, A.-H., and Teo, C. (1998). Learning user profiles for personalized information dissemination. *IEEE World Congress on Computational Intelligence*, 1, 183–188.

Tanaka, K. (1996). Inferotemporal cortex and object vision. *Annual Review of Neuroscience*, 19, 109–139.

Tanaka, K., Saito, H., Fukada, Y., and Moriya, M. (1991). Coding visual images of objects in the inferotemporal cortex of the macaque monkey. *Journal of Neurophysiology*, 66, 170–189.

Tanaka, K., Sugita, Y., Moriya, M., and Saito, H. (1993). Analysis of object motion in the ventral part of the medial superior temporal area of the macaque visual cortex. *Journal of Neurophysiology*, 69, 128–142.

Taube, J. S., Muller, R. U., and Ranck Jr, J. B. (1990). Head-direction cells recorded from the postsubiculum in freely moving rats. I. Description and quantitative analysis. *The Journal of Neuroscience*, 10, 420–435.

Tausch, R. (1953). Die beidaugige Raumwahrnehmung-ein Prozess auf Grund der Korrespondenz und Disparation von Gestalten anstelle der Korrespondenz oder Disparation einzelner Netzhautelemente. *Zeitschrift für Experimentelle und Angewandte Psychologie*, 1, 394–421.

Tecce, J. J. (1972). Contingent negative variation (CNV) and psychological processes in man. *Psychological Review*, 77, 73–108.

Temereanca, S., Brown, E. N., and Simons, D. J. (2008). Rapid changes in thalamic firing synchrony during repetitive whisker stimulation. *The Journal of Neuroscience*, 28, 11153–11164.

Temereanca, S., and Simons, D. J. (2001). Topographic specificity in the functional effects of corticofugal feedback in the whisker/barrel system. *Society for Neuroscience Abstracts*, 393, 6.

Ternus, J. (1926/1950). Experimentelle Untersuchungen über phänomenale Identität. *Psychologische Forschung*, 7, 81–136. Also in *A Source Book of Gestalt Psychology* (1950). W. D. Ellis (Ed. And Trans.). New York: Humanities Press.

Ternus, J. (1938). The problem of phenomenal identity. In W. D. Ellis (Ed.). *A Source Book of Gestalt Psychology* (1950). New York: Humanities Press, pp. 149–160. London, England: Kegan Paul, Trench, Trubner & Company.

Terrace, H. S. (1963). Discrimination learning with and without "errors". *Journal of the Experimental Analysis of Behavior*, 6, 1–27.

Theeuwes, J., Mathot, S., and Kingstone, A. (2010). Object-based eye movements: the eyes prefer to stay within the same object. *Attention, Perception, and Psychophysics*, 72, 597–601.

Thoenen, H. (1995). Neurotrophins and neural plasticity. *Science*, 270, 593–598.

Thom, R. (1977). What is catastrophe theory about? *Synergetics*, 2, 26–32, from the *Springer Series in Synergetics*, H. Haken (Ed.). Berlin: Springer-Verlag.

Thompson, L. T., and Best, P. J. (1990). Long-term stability of the place-field activity of single units recorded from the dorsal hippocampus of freely behaving rats. *Brain Research*, 509, 299–308.

Thompson, L. T., Moyer Jr, J. R., and Disterhoft, J. F. (1996). Transient changes in excitability of rabbit CA3 neurons with a time course appropriate to support memory consolidation. *Journal of Neurophysiology*, 76, 1836–1849.

Thompson, R. F. (1988). The neural basis of basic associative learning of discrete behavioral responses. *Trends in Neurosciences*, 11, 152–155.

Thompson, R. F., Clark, G. A., Donegan, N. H., Lavond, G. A., Lincoln, D. G., Maddon, J. IV., Mamounas, L. A., Mauk, M. D., and McCormick, D. A. (1987). Neuronal substrates of discrete, defensive conditioned reflexes. conditioned fear states, and their interactions in the rabbit. In I. Gormezano, W. F. Prokasy, and R. F. Thompson (Eds.), *Classical Conditioning, Third Edition*. Hillsdale, NJ: Erlbaum Associates, pp. 371–399.

Thorell, L. G., DeValois, R. L., and Albrecht, D. G. (1984). Spatial mapping of monkey V1 cells with pure color and luminance stimuli. *Vision Research*, 24, 751–769.

Thorndike, E. L. (1927). The law of effect. *The American Journal of Psychology*, 39, 212–222.

Thornton, T. L., and Gilden, D. L. (2007). Parallel and serial processes in visual search. *Psychological Review*, 114, 71–103.

Thorpe, S. J., Fize, D., and Marlot, C. (1996). Speed of processing in the human visual system. *Nature*, 381, 520–522.

Thorpe, S. J., Rolls, E. T., and Maddison, S. (1983). The orbit-ofrontal cortex: Neuronal activity in the behaving monkey. *Experimental Brain Research*, 49, 93–115.

Tian, B., and Raushecker, J. (1994). Processing of frequency-modulated sounds in the cat's anterior auditory field. *Journal of Neurophysiology*, 71, 1959–1975.

Timofeev, I., and Steriade, M. (1996). Low-frequency rhythms in the thalamus of intact-cortex and decorticated cats. *Journal of Neurophysiology*, 76, 4152–4168.

Todd, J. T., and Akerstrom, R. A. (1987). Perception of three-dimensional form from patterns of optical texture. *Journal of Experimental Psychology: Human Perception and Performance*, 13, 242–255.

Todorovic, D. (1987). The Craik-O'Brien-Cornsweet effect: New varieties and their theoretical implications. *Perception & Psychophysics*, 42, 545–560.

Toet, A., and Levi, D. M. (1992). The two-dimensional shape of spatial interaction zones in the parafovea. *Vision Research*, 32, 1349–1357.

Tokuoka, H., Saito, T., Yorifugi, H., Kishimoto, T., and Hisanaga, S. (2000). Brain-derived neurotrophic factor-induced phosphorylation of neurofilament-H subunit in primary cultures of embryo rat cortical neurons. *Journal of Cell Science*, 113, 1059–1068.

Tolias, A. S., Moore, T., Smirnakis, S. M., Tehovnik, E. J., Siapas, A. G., and Schiller, P. H. (2001). Eye movements modulate visual receptive fields of V4 neurons. *Neuron*, 29, 757–767.

Tolman, E. C. (1948). Cognitive maps in rats and men. *Psychological Review*, 55, 189–208.

Tomita, H., Ohbayashi, M., Nakahara, K., Hasegawa, I., and Miyashita, Y. (1999). Top-down signal from prefrontal cortex in executive control of memory retrieval. *Nature* 401, 699–703.

Tomlinson, B. E., Blessed, G., and Roth, M. (1968). Observations on the brains of non-demented old people. *Journal of the Neurological Sciences*, 7, 331–356.

Tomlinson, B. E., Blessed, G., and Roth, M. (1970). Observations on the brains of demented old people. *Journal of the Neurological Sciences*, 11, 205–242.

Tononi, G. (2004). An information integration theory of consciousness. *BMC Neuroscience*, doi:10.1186/1471-2202-5-42.

Tononi, G. (2012). Integrated information theory of consciousness: An updated account. *Archives Italiennes de Biologie*, 150, 290–326.

Tononi, G. (2015). Integrated information theory. *Scholarpedia*, 10(1):4164.

Tootell, R. B. H., Silverman, M. S., Switkes, E., and DeValois, R. L. (1982). Deoxyglucose analysis of retinotopic organization in primate striate cortex. *Science*, 218, 902–904.

Torralba, A., Oliva, A., Castelhano, M., and Henderson, J. (2006). Contextual guidance of eye movements and attention in real-world scenes: The role of global features in object search. *Psychological Review*, 113, 766–786.

Toth, K., Borhegyi, Z., and Freund, T. F. (1993). Postsynaptic targets of GABAergic hippocampal neurons in the medial septum-diagonal band of broca complex. *The Journal of Neuroscience*, 13, 3712–3724.

Townsend, J. T. (1972). Some results concerning the identifiability of parallel and serial processes. *British Journal of Mathematical and Statistical Psychology*, 25, 168–199.

Toyomitsu, Y., Nishijo, H., Uwano, T., Kuratsu, J., and Ono, T. (2002). Neuronal responses of the rat amygdala during extinction and reassociation learning in elementary and configural associative tasks. *European Journal of Neuroscience*, 15, 753–768.

Traub, R. D., Spruston, N., Soltesz, I., Konnerth, A., Whittington, M. A., and Jefferys, G. R. (1998). Gamma-frequency oscillations: a neuronal population phenomenon, regulated by synaptic and intrinsic cellular processes, and inducing synaptic plasticity. *Progress in Neurobiology*, 55, 563–575.

Treisman, A. M., and Gelade, G. (1980). A feature-integration theory of attention. *Cognitive Psychology*, 12, 97–136.

Treisman, A. M., and Gormican, S. (1988). Feature analysis in early vision: Evidence from search asymmetries. *Psychological Review*, 95, 15–48.

Tremblay, L, and Schultz, W. (1999). Relative reward preference in primate orbitofrontal cortex. *Nature*, 398, 704–708.

Treue, S., and Martinez Trujillo, J. C. (1999). Feature-based attention influences motion processing gain in macaque visual cortex. *Nature*, 399, 575–579.

Treue, S., and Maunsell, J. H. (1996). Attentional modulation of visual motion processing in cortical areas MT and MST. *Nature (London)*, 382, 539–541.

Treue, S., and Maunsell, J. H. (1999). Effects of attention on the processing of motion in macaque middle temporal and medial superior temporal visual cortical areas. *The Journal of Neuroscience*, 19, 7591–7602.

Tse, P. U. (2005). Voluntary attention modulates the brightness of overlapping transparent surfaces. *Vision Research*, 45, 1095–1098.

Tse, P., and Cavanagh, P. (1995). Line motion occurs after surface parsing. *Investigative Ophthalmology and Visual Science*, 36, S417.

Tse, P., Cavanagh, P., and Nakayama, K. (1996). The role of parsing in high level motion processing. In *High Level Motion Processing: Computational, Neurobiological, and Psychophysical Perspectives*. T. Watanabe (Ed.). Cambridge, MA: MIT Press, pp. 249–266.

Tsodyks, M. V., and Markram, H. (1997). The neural code between neocortical pyramidal neurons depends on neurotransmitter release probability. *Proceedings of the National Academy of Sciences*, 94, 719–723.

Tsuchiya, N., Wilke, M., Frassle, S., and Lamme, V. A. F. (201). No-report paradigms: Extracting the true neural correlates of consciousness. *Trends in Cognitive Sciences*, 19, 757–770.

Tsushima, Y., Seitz, A. R., and Watanabe, T. (2008). Task-irrelevant learning occurs only when the irrelevant feature is weak. *Current Biology*, 18, R516–R517.

Tucker, K. L., Meyer. M., and Barde, Y. A. (2001). Neurotrophins are required for nerve growth during development. *Nature Neuroscience*, 4, 29–37.

Tueting, P., Sutton, S., and Zubin, J. (1970). Quantitative evoked potential correlates of the probability of events. *Psychophysiology*, 7, 385–394.

Tulving, E. (1972). Episodic and semantic memory. In E. Tulving and W. Donaldson (Eds.). *Organization of Memory*. New York, NY: Academic Press.

Tulving, E. (1976). Ecphoric processes in recall and recognition. In J. Brown (Ed.). *Recall and Recognition.* Oxford, England: John Wiley & Sons.

Tulving, E., and Thomson, D. M. (1973). Encoding specificity and retrieval processes in episodic memory. *Psychological Review,* 80. 352–373.

Turing, A. (1937). On computable numbers, with an application to the Entscheidungsproblem. *Proceedings of the London Mathematical Society,* Series 2, 42. https://doi.org/10.1112/plms/s2-42.1.230.

Turing, A. (1952). The chemical theory of morphogenesis. *Philosophical Transactions of the Royal Society B,* 237, 37–72.

Turner, M. (1999). Repetitive behavior in autism: A review of psychological research. *The Journal of Child Psychology and Psychiatry and Allied Disciplines,* 40, 839–849.

Turrigiano, G. G. (1999). Homeostatic plasticity in neuronal networks: The more things change, the more they stay the same. *Trends in Neurosciences,* 5, 221–227.

Tyler, C. W. (1975). Spatial organization of binocular disparity sensitivity. *Vision Research,* 15, 583–590.

Tyler, C. W. (1983). Sensory processing of binocular disparity. In C. M. Schor and K. J. Cuffreda (Eds.), *Vergence Eye Movements,* pp. 199–295. Boston: Butterworths.

Tyler, C. W., and Kontsevich, L. L. (1995). Mechanisms of stereoscopic processing: stereoattention and surface perception in depth reconstruction. *Perception,* 24, 127–153.

Tyler, W. J., Alonso, M., Bramham, C. R., and Pozzo-Miller, L. D. (2002). From acquisition to consolidation: On the role of brain-derived neurotrophic factor signaling in hippocampal-dependent learning. *Learning & Memory,* 9, 224–237.

Umeno, M. M., and Goldberg, M. E. (1997). Spatial processing in the monkey frontal eye fields, I: predictive visual responses. *Journal of Neurophysiology,* 78, 1373–1383.

Underwood. B. J., and Freund, J. S. (1970). Word frequency and short term recognition memory. *American Journal of Psychology,* 83, 343–351.

Ungerleider, L. G., and Mishkin, M. (1982). Two cortical visual systems: Separation of appearance and location of objects. In D. L. Ingle, M. A. Goodale and R. J. W. Mansfield (Eds.) *Analysis of Visual Behavior,* Cambridge: MIT Press, 549–586.

Unsworth, N., and Robison, M. K. (2015). Individual differences in the allocation of attention to items in working memory: Evidence from pupillometry. *Psychological Bulletin and Review,* 22, 757–765.

van den Berg, A. V. (1993). Perception of heading. *Nature,* 365, 497–498.

van den Berg, A. V., and Brenner, E. (1994). Humans combine the optic flow with static depth cues for robust perception of heading. *Vision Research,* 34, 2153–2167.

van der Waals, H. G., and Roelofs, C. O. (193). Optische scheinbewegung [visual illusion]. *Zeitschrift für Psychologie und Physiologie des Zinnesorgane,* 115, 91–190.

van der Waals, H. G., and Roelofs, C. O. (193). Optische scheinbewegung [visual illusion]. *Zeitschrift für Psychologie und Physiologie des Zinnesorgane,* 114, 241–288.

van der Werf, Y. D., Witter, M. P., and Groenewegen, H. J. (2002). The intralaminar and midline nuclei of the thalamus. Anatomical and functional evidence for participation

in processes of arousal and awareness. *Brain Research Reviews,* 39, 107–40.

Vanderwolf, C. H. (1988). Cerebral activity and behavior: Control by central cholinergic and serotonergic systems. *International Review of Neurobiology,* 30, 225–340.

Vanduffel, W., Tootell, R. B., and Orban, G. A. (2000). Attention-dependent suppression of metabolic activity in the early stages of the macaque visual system. *Cerebral Cortex,* 10, 109–126.

Van Essen, D. C., and DeYoe, E. A. (1995). Concurrent processing in the primate visual cortex. In *The Cognitive Neurosciences,* Chapter 24. M. S. Gazzaniga (Ed.), pp. 383–400.

Van Essen, D. C., and Maunsell, J. H. R. (1983). Hierarchical organization and functional streams in the visual cortex. *Trends in Neurosciences,* 6, 370–375.

Van Haastert, P. J. M. (1983). Sensory adaptation of Dictyostelium discoideum cells to chemotactic signals. *The Journal of Cell Biology,* 96, 1559–1565.

Van Ooyen, A., and Willshaw, D. J. (1999). Competition for neurotrophic factor in the development of nerve connections. *Proceedings of the Royal Society of London. B: Biological Sciences,* 266, 883–892.

van Strien, N. M., Cappaert, N. L. M., and Witter, M. P. (2009). The anatomy of memory: an interactive overview of the parahippocampal-hippocampal network. *Nature Reviews Neuroscience,* 10, 272–282.

Van Tuijl, H. F. J. M. (1975). A new visual illusion: Neonlike color spreading and complementary color induction between subjective contours. *Acta Psychologica,* 39, 441–445.

Van Tuijl, H. F. J. M., and de Weert, C. M. M. (1979). Sensory conditions for the occurrence of the neon spreading illusion. *Perception,* 8, 211–215.

Varin, D. (1971). Fenomini di contrasto e diffusione chromatica nell organizzazone spaziale del campo percettivo. *Rivista di Psicologia,* 65, 101–128.

Vertes, R. P., Hoover, W. B., and Di Prisco, G. V. (2004). Theta rhythm of the hippocampus: Subcortical control and functional significance. *Behavioral and Cognitive Neuroscience Reviews,* 3, 173–200.

Vertes, R. P., and Kocsis, B. (1997). Brainstem-diencephalo-septohippocampal systems controlling the theta rhythm of the hippocampus. *Neuroscience,* 81, 893–926.

Vinogradova, O. S. (1975). Functional organization of the limbic system in the process of registration of information: Facts and hypotheses. In *The hippocampus, Volume 2* R. L. Isaacson, and K. H. Pribram (Eds.), pp. 3–69. New York: Plenum Press.

Vinueze Veloz, M. F., Buijsen, R. A. M., Willemsen, R., Cupido, A., Bosman, L. W. J., Koekkkoek, S. K. E., Potters, J. W., Oostra, B. A., and DeZeeuw, C. I. (2012). The effect of mGluR5 inhibitor on procedural memory and avoidance discrimination impairments in Fmr1 KO mice. *Genes, Brain, and Behavior,* 11, 325–331.

Vitevitch, M. S., and Donoso, A. (2011). Processing of indexical information requires time: Evidence from change deafness. *The Quarterly Journal of Experimental Psychology,* 64, 1484–1493.

Vitevitch, M. S., and Luce, P. A. (1999). Probabilistic phonotactics and neighborhood activation in spoken word recognition. *Journal of Memory and Language,* 40, 374–408.

Vladusich, T., Lafe, F., Kim, D.-S., Tager-Flusberg, H., and Grossberg, S. (2010). Prototypical category learning in high-functioning autism. *Autism Research*, 3, 226–236.

Vogels, T. P., Sprekeler, H., Zenke, F., Clopath, C., and Gerstner, W. (2011). Inhibitory plasticity balances excitation and inhibition in sensory pathways and memory networks. *Science*, 334, 1569–1573.

Volgushev, M., Chauvette, S., Mukovski, M., and Timofeev, I. (2006). Precise long-range synchronization of activity and silence in neocortical neurons during slow-wave sleep. *The Journal of Neuroscience*, 26, 5665–5672.

von der Heydt, R., and Peterhans, E. (1989). Mechanisms of contour perception in monkey visual cortex. I. Lines of pattern discontinuity. *The Journal of Neuroscience*, 9, 1731–1748.

von der Heydt, R., Peterhans, E., and Baumgartner, G. (1984). Illusory contours and cortical neuron responses. *Science*, 224, 1260–1262.

von der Heydt, R., Zhou, H., and Friedman, H. S. (2000). Representation of stereoscopic edges in monkey visual cortex. *Vision Research*, 40, 1955–1967.

von der Malsburg, C. (1973). Self-organization of orientation sensitive cells in the striate cortex. *Biological Cybernetics*, 14, 85–100.

von Grünau, M., and Faubert, J. (1994). Intraattribute and interattribute motion induction. *Perception*, 23, 913–928.

von Grünau, M., Racette, L., and Kwas, M. (1996). Measuring the attentional speed-up in the motion induction effect. *Vision Research*, 36, 2433–2446.

Von Holst, E. (1954). Relations between the central nervous system and the peripheral organs. *British Journal of Animal Behaviour*, 2, 89–94.

Von Neumann, J. (1958). *The Computer and the Brain*. New Haven: Yale University Press.

Von Restorff, H. (1933). Über die Wirkung von Bereichsbildungen im Spurenfeld (The effects of field formation in the trace field). *Psychologie Forschung*, 18, 242–299.

von Tschermak-Seysenegg, A. (1952). *Introduction to physiological Optics*. P. Boeder (Trans.) Springfield, IL: Thomas

Voorn, P., Vanderschuren, L. J. M. J., Groenewegen, H. J., Robbins, T. W., and Pennartz, C. M. A. (2004). Putting a spin on the dorsal-ventral divide of the striatum. *Trends in Neurosciences*, 27, 468–474.

Wallach, H. (1976). *On perception*. Quadrangle/The New York Times Book Co., New York, NY.

Wallis, T. S. A., and Arnold, D. H. (2009). Motion-induced blindness and motion streak suppression. *Current Biology*, 19, 325–329.

Walter, W. G. (1964). Contingent negative variation: An electric sign of sensori-motor association and expectancy in the human brain. *Nature*, 230, 380–384.

Wang, H.-Y., Lee, D. H. S., D'Andrea, M. R., Peterson, P. A., Shank, R. P., and Reitz, A. B. (2000a). β-amyloid$_{1–42}$ binds to α7 nicotinic acetylcholine receptor with high affinity: implications for Alzheimer's disease pathology. *Journal of Biological Chemistry*, 275, 5626–5632.

Wang, H.-Y., Lee, D. H. S., Davis, C. B., and Shank, R. P. (2000b). Amyloid peptide Aβ$_{1–42}$ binds selectively and with picomolar affinity to α7 nicotinic acetylcholine receptors. *Journal of Neurochemistry*, 75, 1155–1161.

Wang, W.-J., (2002a). Pacemaker neurons for the theta rhythm and their synchronization in the septohippocampal reciprocal loop. *Journal of Neurophysiology*, 87, 889–900.

Wang, X.-J. (2002b). Probabilistic decision making by slow reverberation in cortical circuits. *Neuron*, 36, 955–968.

Wang, Z., and McCormick, D. A. (1993). Control of firing mode of corticotectal and cortiopontine Layer V burst-generating neurons by norepinephrine, acetylcholine and 1S,3R-ACPD. *The Journal of Neuroscience,* 13, 2199–2216.

Wanning, A., Stanisor, L., and Roelfsema, P. R. (2011). Automatic spread of attentional response modulation along Gestalt criteria in primary visual cortex. *Nature Neuroscience*, 14, 1243–1244.

Ward, T. B. (1983). Response tempo and separable-integral responding: Evidence for an integral-to-separable processing sequencing in visual perception. *Journal of Experimental Psychology: Human Perception and Performance*, 9, 1029–1051.

Warden, M. R., and Miller, E. K. (2010). Task-dependent changes in short-term memory in the prefrontal cortex. *The Journal of Neuroscience*, 30, 15801–15810.

Warmflash, D. (2016). Santiago Ramon y Cajal and Camillo Golgi: The two fathers of neuroscience. *Visionlearning Vol. SCIRE-2(8)*: https://www.visionlearning.com/en/library/Inside-Science/58/Santiago-Ram%C3%B3n-y-Cajal-and-Camillo-Golgi/233.

Warren, W. H., and Hannon, D. J. (1988). Direction of self-motion is perceived from optical flow. *Nature*, 336, 162–163.

Warren, W. H., and Hannon, D. J. (1990). Eye movements and optical flow. *Optical Society of America, Journal, A: Optics and Image Science*, 7, 160–169.

Warren, W. H., Rothman, D. B., Schnapp, B. H., and Ericson, J. D. (2017). Wormholes in virtual space: From cognitive maps to cognitive graphs. *Cognition*, 166, 152–163.

Warren, W. H., Kay, B. A., Zosh, W. D., Duchon, A. P., and Sahuc, S. (2001). Optic flow is used to control human walking. *Nature Neuroscience*, 4, 213–216.

Warren, R. M., and Sherman, G. L. (1974). Phonemic restorations based on subsequent context. *Perception & Psychophysics*, 16, 150–156.

Warren, R. M., and Warren, R. P. (1970). Auditory illusions and confusions. *Scientific American*, 223, 30–37.

Warrington, E. K., and Weiskrantz, L. (1974). The effect of prior learning on subsequent retention in amnesic patients. *Neuropsychology*, 12, 419–428.

Washburn, D. A. and Rumbaugh, D. M. (1991). Ordinal judgments of numerical symbols by macaques (Macaca mulatta). *Psychological Science*, 2, 190–193.

Watanabe, T., Náñez, J. E., and Sasaki, Y. (2001). Perceptual learning without perception. *Nature,* 413, 844–848.

Watson, L. M., Wong, M. M. K., and Becker, E. B. E. (2015). Induced pluripotent stem cell technology for modeling and therapy of cerebellar ataxia. *Open Biology*, 1: 150056; http://dx.doi.org/10.1098/rsob.150056.

Weyandt, L. L., Oster, D. R., Marraccini, M. E., Gudmundsdottir, B. G., Munro, B. A., Zavras, B. M., and Kuhar, B. (2014). Pharmacological interventions for adolescents and adults with ADHD: Stimulant and non-stimulant medications and misuse of prescription stimulants. *Psychology Research and Behavior Management*, 7, 223–249.

Weber, A. J., Kalil, R. E., and Behan, M. (1989). Synaptic connections between corticogeniculate axons and interneurons in the dorsal lateral geniculate nucleus of the cat. *Journal of Comparative Neurology*, 289, 156–164.

Webster, M. J., Bachevalier, J., and Ungerleider, L. G. (1994). Connections of inferior temporal areas TEO and TE with parietal and frontal cortex in macaque monkeys. *Cerebral Cortex*, 4, 470–483.

Weiss, C., and Thompson, R. F. (1991a). The effects of age on eyeblink conditioning in the freely moving rat: Optimizing the conditioning parameters. *Behavioral Neuroscience*, 113, 1100–1105.

Weiss, C., and Thompson, R. F. (1991b). Trace eyeblink conditioning in the freely moving Fischer-344 rat. *Neurobiology of Aging*, 12, 249–254.

Weiss, Y., Simoncelli, E. P., and Adelson, E. H. (2002). Motion illusions as optimal percepts. *Nature Neuroscience*, 5, 598–604.

Werblin, F. S. (1971). Adaptation in a vertebrate retina: Intracellular recordings in Necturus. *Journal of Neurophysiology*, 34, 228–241.

Werbos, P. (1974). *Beyond Regression: New Tools for Prediction and Analysis in the Behavioral Sciences*. Unpublished Doctoral Dissertation, Harvard University.

Werbos, P. (1994). *The roots of backpropagation: From ordered derivatives to neural networks and political forecasting*. New York: John Wiley & Sons, Inc.

Werner, H. (1937). Dynamics in binocular depth perception. *Psychological Monograph* (Whole No. 218).

Wertheimer, M. (1961). Experimentelle studien uber das sehen von bewegung. In *Classics in Psychology*. T. Shipley (Ed. And Trans.). New York: Philosophical Library (Original work published 1912).

Wespatat, V., Tennigkeit, F., and Singer, W. (2004). Phase sensitivity of synaptic modifications in oscillating cells of rat visual cortex. *The Journal of Neuroscience*, 24, 9067–9075.

Wheeler, D. D. (1970). Processes in word recognition. *Cognitive Psychology*, 1, 45–65.

Whitehouse, P. J., Price, D. L., Struble, R. G., Clark, A. W., Coyle, J. T., and Delon, M. R. (1982). Alzheimer's disease and senile dementia: Loss of neurons in the basal forebrain. *Science*, 215, 1237–1239.

Wichmann, T., and DeLong, M. R. (1996). Functional and pathophysiological models of the basal ganglia. *Current Opinion in Neurobiology*, 6, 751–758.

Widrow, B. (1962). Generalization and information storage in networks of Adaline neurons. In M. C. Yovits, G. T. Jacobi, and G. D. Goldstein (Eds.), *Self-Organizing Systems*. Washington DC: Spartan Books.

Wienke, D., and Buydens, L. (1995). Adaptive resonance theory based neural networks—the "ART" of real-time pattern recognition in chemical process monitoring. *Trends in Analytical Chemistry*, 14, 398–406.

Wigglesworth, V. B. (1934). *Insect Physiology*. London: Methuen.

Wikenheiser, A. M., and Redish, A. D. (2013). The balance of forward and backward hippocampal sequences shifts across behavioral states. *Hippocampus*, 23, 22–29.

Wilby, O. K., and Webster, L. (1970a). Experimental studies on axial polarity in Hydra. *Journal of Embryology and Experimental Morphology*, 24, 595–613.

Wilby, O. K., and Webster, L. (1970b). Studies on the transmission of hypostome inhibition in hydra. *Journal of Embryology and Experimental Morphology*, 24, 583–593.

Wilde, K. (1950). Der Punktreiheneffekt und die Rolle der binocularen Querdisparation beim Tienfenshen. *Psychologische Forschung*, 23, 223–262.

Wilkie, R. M., and Wann, J. P. (2003). Controlling steering and judging heading: Retinal flow, visual direction and extraretinal information. *Journal of Experimental Psychology*, 29, 363–378.

Wilkie, R. M., and Wann, J. P. (2006). Judgments of path, not heading, guide locomotion. *Journal of Experimental Psychology: Human Perception and Performance*, 32, 88–96.

Williams, D. W., and Sekuler, R. (1984). Coherent global motion percepts from stochastic local motions. *ACM SIGGRAPH Computer Graphics*, 18, 24.

Wills, T. J., Barry, C., and Cacucci, F. (2012). The abrupt development of adult-like grid cell firing in the medial entorhinal cortex. *Frontiers in Neural Circuits*, 27 April 2012 https://www.frontiersin.org/articles/10.3389/fncir.2012.00021/full.

Wills, T. J., Cacucci, F., Burgess, N., and O'Keefe, J. (2010). Development of the hippocampal cognitive map in preweanling rats. *Science*, 328, 1573–1576.

Willshaw, D. J., and Malsburg, C. von der (1976). How patterned neural connections can be set up by self-organization. *Proceedings of the Royal Society of London*, 194, 431–445.

Wilson, H. R. (2003). Computational evidence for a rivalry hierarchy in vision. *Proceedings of the National Academy of Sciences USA*, 100, 14499–14503.

Wilson, H. R. (2005). Rivalry and perceptual oscillations: A dynamical synthesis. In *Binocular Rivalry*, D. Alais and R. Blake (Eds.) Cambridge: MIT Press, pp. 317–335.

Wilson, H. R., Ferrera, V. P., and Yo, C. (1992). A psychophysically motivated model for two-dimensional motion perception. *Visual Neuroscience*, 9, 79–97.

Wilson, M. A., and McNaughton, B. L. (1993). Dynamics of the hippocampal ensemble code for space. *Science*, 261, 1055–1058.

Wise, S. P. (2008). Forward frontal fields: Phylogeny and fundamental function. *Trends in Neurosciences*, 31, 599–608.

Witcher, E. S. (1978). *Extinction of Pavlovian Conditioned Inhibition*. Unpublished doctoral dissertation, University of Massachusetts, Amherst.

Witten, E. (1995). String theory dynamics in various dimensions. *Nuclear Physics B*, 443, 85–126,

Wolfe, J. M. (1994). Guided search 2. A revised model of visual search. *Psychonomic Bulletin and Review*, 1, 202–238.

Wolfe, J. M. (1998). What do 1,000,000 trials tell us about visual search? *Psychological Science*, 57, 33–39.

Wolfe, J. M., Cave, K. R., and Franzel, S. L. (1989). Guided search: An alternative to the feature integration model for visual search. *Journal of Experimental Psychology: Human Perception and Performance*, 15, 419–433.

Wolpert, L. (1969). Positional information and the spatial pattern of cellular differentiation. *Journal of Theoretical Biology*, 25, 1–47.

Wolpert, L., Hicklin, J., and Hornbruck, A. (1971). Positional information and pattern regulation in regeneration of hydra. *Symposia of the Society of Experimental Biology*, 25, 391–416 (1971).

Wong-Riley, M. (1979). Changes in the visual system of monocularly sutured or enucleated cats demonstrable with cytochrome oxidase histochemistry. *Brain Research*, 171, 11–28.

Woodruff-Pak, D. S. (1993). Classical eye-blink conditioning in H.M.: Delay and trace paradigms. *Behavioral Neuroscience*, 107, 911–925.

Woodruff-Pak, D. S. (2001). Eyeblink classical conditioning differentiates normal aging from Alzheimer's disease. *Integrative Physiological and Behavioral Science*, 36, 87–108.

Woodruff-Pak, D. S., and Disterhoft, J. F. (2007). Where is the trace in trace conditioning? *Trends in Neurosciences*, 31, 105–112.

Wuerger, S., Shapley, R., and Rubin, N. (1996). 'On the visually perceived direction of motion' by Hans Wallach: 60 years later. *Perception*, 25, 1317–1367.

Wunsch, D. C. II. (2019). Admiring the Great Mountain: A celebration special issue in honor of Stephen Grossberg's 80th birthday. Neural Networks special issue dedicated to the 80th birthday of Stephen Grossberg, Vol. 120, December.

Wunsch, D. C. II, Caudell, T. P., Capps, C. D., Marks, R. J. II, and Falk, R. A. (1993). An optoelectronic implementation of the adaptive resonance neural network. *IEEE Transactions on Neural Networks*, 4, 673–684.

Wurbel, H. (2001). Ideal homes? Housing effects on rodent brain and behaviour. *Trends in Neurosciences*, 24, 207–211.

Wutz, A., Loonis, R., Roy, J. E., Donoghue, J. A., and Miller, E. K. (2018). Different levels of category abstraction by different dynamics in different prefrontal areas. *Neuron*, 97, 1–11.

Xie, L., Kang, H., Xu, Q., Chen, M. J., Liao, Y., Thiyagarajan, M., O'Donnell, J., Christensen, D. J., Nicholson, C., Iliff, J. J., Takano, T., Deane, R., and Nedergaard, M. (2013). Sleep drives metabolite clearance from the adult brain. *Science*, 342, 373–377.

Xu, Z., Shi, X., Wang, L., Luo, J., Zhong, C.-J., and Lu, S. (2009). Pattern recognition for sensor array signals using fuzzy ARTMAP. *Sensors and Acuators B: Chemical*, 141, 458–464.

Yan, J., and Scott, T. R. (1996). The effect of satiety on responses of gustatory neurons in the amygdala of alert cynomolgus macaques. *Brain Research*, 740, 193–200.

Yang, S., Heinen, S., and Missal, M. (2008). The effects of microstimulation of the dorsomedial frontal cortex on saccade latency. *Journal of Neurophysiology*, 99, 1857–1870.

Yang, G., Pan, F., and Gan, W. B. (2009). Stably maintained dendritic spines are associated with lifelong memories. *Nature*, 462, 920–924.

Yantis, S., and Jonides, J. (1990). Abrupt visual onsets and selective attention: Voluntary versus automatic allocation. *Journal of Experimental Psychology: Human Perception and Performance*, 16, 121–134.

Yao, Y., Choi, J., and Parker, I. (1995). Quantal putts of intracellular Ca^{2+} evoked by inositol trisphosphate in Xenopus oocytes. *Journal of Physiology*, 482, 533–553.

Yarbus, A. L. (1967). *Eye Movements and Vision*. New York: Plenum Press.

Yartsev, M. M., Witter, M. P., and Ulanovsky, N. (2011). Grid cells without theta oscillations in the entorhinal cortex of bats. *Nature*, 479, 103–107.

Yazdanbakhsh, A., and Grossberg, S. (2004). Fast synchronization of perceptual grouping in laminar visual cortical circuits. *Neural Networks*, 17, 707–718.

Yazdanbakhsh, A., and Watanabe, T. (2004). Asymmetry between horizontal and vertical illusory lines in determining the depth of their embedded surface. *Vision Research*, 44, 2621–2627.

Yo, C., and Wilson, H. R. (1992). Perceived direction of moving two-dimensional patterns depends on duration, contrast, and eccentricity. *Vision Research*, 32, 79–97.

Yoshida, H., and Smith, L. B. (2008). What's in view for toddlers? Using a head camera to study visual experience. *Infancy*, 13, 229–248.

Yoshida, M., Giocomo, L. M., Boardman, I., Hasselmo, and M. E. (2011). Frequency of subthreshold oscillations at different membrane potential voltages in neurons at different anatomical positions on the dorsoventral axis in the rat medial entorhinal cortex. *The Journal of Neuroscience*, 31, 12683–12694.

Young, E. D., and Sachs, M. B. (1979). Representation of steady-state vowels in the temporal aspects of the discharge patterns of populations of auditory nerve fibers. *Journal of the Acoustical Society of America*, 66, 1381–1403.

Young, L. R., Forster, J. D., and van Houtte, N. (1968). A revised stochastic sampled model for eye tracking movements. *4th Annual NASA-University Conference on Manual Control*, University of Michigan, Ann Arbor.

Zaki, S. R., Nosofsky, R. M., Jessup, N. M., and Unversagt, F. W. (2003). Categorization and recognition performance of a memory impaired group: evidence for single-system models. *Journal of the International Neuropsychological Society*, 9, 394–406.

Zang, H. T., Li, L. Y, Zou, X. L., Song, X. B., Hu, Y. L., Feng, Z. T., and Wang, T. T. H. (2007). Immunohistological distribution of NGF, BDNF, NT-3, and NT-4 in adult rhesus monkey brains. *Journal of Histochemistry and Cytochemistry*, 55, 1–19.

Zavagno, D. (1999). Some new luminance-gradient effects, *Perception*, 28, 835–838.

Zeki, S. M. (1974). Functional organization of a visual area in the posterior bank of the superior temporal sulcus of the rhesus monkey. *The Journal of Physiology*, 236, 549–573.

Zelaznik, H., Schmidt, R. A., and Gielen, S. C. (1986). Kinematic properties of rapid aimed hand movements. *Journal of Motor Behavior*, 18, 353–372.

Zeki, S. (1983). Colour coding in the cerebral cortex: The reaction of cells in monkey visual cortex to wavelengths and colours. *Neuroscience*, 9, 741–765.

Zeki, S., and Shipp, S. (1988). The functional logic of cortical connections. *Nature*, 335, 311–317.

Zhang, N., and Kezunovic, M. (2007). A real time fault analysis tool for monitoring operation of transmission line protective relay. *Electric Power Systems Research*, 77, 361–370.

Zhang, N. R., and von der Heydt, R. (2010). Analysis of the context integration mechanisms underlying figure-ground organization in the visual cortex. *The Journal of Neuroscience*, 30, 6482–6496.

Zhang, Y., Suga, N., and Yan, J. (1997). Corticofugal modulation of frequency processing in bat auditory system. *Nature*, 387, 900–903.

Zhao, M.-G., Toyoda, H., Ko, S. W., Ding, H.-K., Wu, L.-J., and Zhuo, M. (2005). Deficits in trace fear memory and long-term potentiation in a mouse model for fragile X syndrome. *The Journal of Neuroscience*, 25, 7385–7392.

Zhou, H., Friedman, H. S., and von der Heydt, R. (2000). Coding of border ownership in monkey visual cortex. *The Journal of Neuroscience*, 20, 6594–6611.

Zielinski, M. C., Tang, W., and Jadhav, S. P. (2020). The role of replay and theta sequences in mediating hippocampal-prefrontal interactions for memory and cognition. *Hippocampus*, 30, 60–72.

Zilli, E. A. (2012). Models of grid cell spatial firing published 2005-2011. *Frontiers in Neural Circuits*, 18 April 2012 https://doi.org/10.3389/fncir.2012.00016.

Zimmer-Hart, C. L., and Rescorla, R. A. (1974). Extinction of Pavlovian conditioned inhibition. *Journal of Comparative and Physiological Psychology*, 86, 837–845.

Zitnick, C. L., and Kanada, T. (2000). A cooperative algorithm for stereo matching and occlusion detection. *IEEE Transactions on Pattern Analysis and Machine Intelligence*, 22, 675–684.

Zoccolan, D., Kouh, M., Poggio, T., and DiCarlo, J. J. (2007). Trade-off between object selectivity and tolerance in monkey inferotemporal cortex. *The Journal of Neuroscience*, 27, 12292–12307.

Zola-Morgan, S. M., and Squire, L. R. (1990). The primate hippocampal formation: Evidence for a time-limited role in memory storage. *Science*, 250, 288–290.

Index

References to figures and tables are denoted by an italicized *f* and *t*, respectively.